THE MEANINGS OF DRESS

THE MEANINGS OF DRESS

THIRD EDITION

Kimberly A. Miller-Spillman
UNIVERSITY OF KENTUCKY

Andrew Reilly
UNIVERSITY OF HAWAI'I, MĀNOA

Patricia Hunt-Hurst
UNIVERSITY OF GEORGIA

FAIRCHILD BOOKS, INC.

NEW YORK

Fairchild Books

An imprint of Bloomsbury Publishing Inc

175 Fifth Avenue	50 Bedford Square
New York	London
NY 10010	WC1B 3DP
USA	UK

www.fairchildbooks.com

First edition published 1999
Second edition published 2004
This edition first published 2012

© Bloomsbury Publishing Inc, 2012

Library of Congress Cataloging-in-Publication Data

A catalog record for this book is available from the Library of Congress.

2012936309

ISBN: 978-1-60901-278-6

Typeset by Susan Ramundo
Cover Design by Erin Fitzsimmons
Cover Art: Yasmin Le Bon; JasonSchmidt/trunkarchive.com
Printed and bound in the United States of America

CONTENTS

PREFACE

Since 2005 we have made several changes for the third edition of *The Meanings of Dress*. Kimberly A. Miller-Spillman returns as an editor of the third edition, while Andrew Reilly and Patricia Hunt-Hurst have been added as editors. We have added several new chapters and revised and updated others. Six new chapters along with 85 new readings have been added (with nine readings retained from the second edition). Also, Chapters 1 and 14 now include readings, unlike previous editions. In addition to dress and culture we have increased information on theory, choosing readings that make the link between theory and dress.

Emphasis on Culture and Theory

Cultural perspectives are key to the third edition. We worked to include as many perspectives as possible. For example there are readings on Japanese whiteness, the Tanzania *kanga*, Puerto Rican peasants' clothing, *kente* cloth from Ghana, fashion and politics in Sweden in the 1960s, Muslim Americans in the U.S., men's fashion in 1960s London, the Norwegian *bunad*, Spanish Catholic dress, Asante women, anime costumes, and video dress attire. The authors of these readings vary in gender, ethnicity, cultural backgrounds, age, and work roles. We hear from academics, journalists, business professionals, novelists, and students. They demonstrate how dress is a central factor in most areas of everyday life, such as work, school, sports, rituals and celebrations, fantasy and play, and aging and development throughout a person's lifespan.

 The Meanings of Dress also takes an interdisciplinary approach. Articles relate to psychology, sociology, anthropology, material culture, history, communications, semiotics, aesthetics, consumer behavior, marketing, business management, consumer economics, popular culture, gender studies, feminist scholarship, minority studies, and more. Dress is a multifaceted phenomenon; therefore, one viewpoint is just not enough.

Plan of the Book

We reorganized the text for easy flow of concepts and topics. Chapter 1 is new and introduces the book while Chapter 2 discusses the theoretical underpinnings of fashion. Chapter 3 discusses the nonverbal aspects of fashion and dress, and Chapter 4 discusses the body in different cultures. Chapters 5 through 8 examine dress and demographics such as gender, sexuality, ethnicity, race, religion, the lifespan, and death. Chapter 9 discusses how dress is used to demonstrate inequality and status among people while Chapter 10 looks at work-related issues connected to dress and Chapter 11 looks at media-related issues connected to dress. Along with Chapters 9 and 11, Chapter 12 is a new one—and a fun one—that examines how fashion is fanciful and is used for costumes and hidden identities. Chapter 13 examines new technologies in dress. And Chapter 14—another new chapter—examines ethics in the fashion industry. More detail about each chapter follows.

Chapter 1: Introduction to Dress, Culture, and Theory is a new chapter that provides definitions of terms and explanations of theories that are fundamental to the text. Connecting theory to dress is another goal of this chapter, allowing the reader to make these connections throughout the text. One objective of this chapter is to challenge students to think about their own culture from another's cultural perspective.

Chapter 2: Fashion as a Dynamic Process illustrates how fashion can be explained through theory. It includes a historic perspective of how the mechanics of fashion have changed over time, commentary about working in luxury sales, and an analysis of fashion styles in Tokyo.

Chapter 3: Dress as Nonverbal Communication considers how messages are conveyed through the dress of Muslim women, *kente* cloth from Ghana, the Hawaiian shirt, and a Japanese kimono. A model of clothing in context is illustrated along with the effect of postmodernism on dress.

Chapter 4: The Body has been updated and examines different cultural views of the body and what is valued and prized by a group of people—from size to color to decoration. Topics include men's body image, skin bleaching, and body image of Caucasian and African American women.

Chapter 5: Appearance for Gender and Sexual Identity has been updated with articles on androgyny, the connection between gay men and the Mods of the 1960s, and an issue of cross-dressing in Afghanistan where girls dress like boys in order to attend school.

Chapter 6: Race and Ethnicity examines how racial and ethnic identity are manifested in dress and then—controversially—adopted into fashion. An article on the Norwegian *Bunad* examines authenticity in manufacturing this folk costume while an editorial piece condemns the fashion industry for adopting cultural symbols for fashion purposes.

Chapter 7: Dress and Religion considers the ideology of several religions and how ideology affects religious dress. New readings on Buddhism and Hinduism expand the Third Edition's scope beyond Judaism, Islam, and Christianity.

Chapter 8: Dressing for Life and Death combines Chapters 8 and 9 from the Second Edition. This chapter continues to address issues related to childhood, late adolescence, and adulthood; however, it adds a new section on dressing for death with historic, cultural, and contemporary examples.

Chapter 9: Fashion, Status, and Inequality in Dress is new and examines how status and inequality are represented by dress. Fashion is discussed as a reflection of status. Readings in this chapter focus on the use of dress and textiles to reflect fashion, status, and inequality in such places as Puerto Rico, Tanzania, and Spain.

Chapter 10: Dress in the Workplace is updated with a couple of new readings. This chapter examines some of the ways that dressing for work has changed and how it has remained the same. It also looks at some recent controversies related to dress in the workplace and how specific dress in the workplace may identify a person's status or rank, as in the case with military personnel.

Chapter 11: Dress and Media is a new chapter for this edition. This chapter focuses on some of the controversies related to appearance and clothing as discussed in articles from popular magazines, research journals, and newspapers.

Chapter 12: Fashion and Fantasy is another new chapter for this edition. This chapter focuses on the many ways that fashion and fantasy are intertwined through the lens of the public, private, and secret self model. Readings cover fantasy in runway shows, shopping behavior, advertising, and design.

Chapter 13: Dress and Technology focuses on the relationship between technology, fashion, and culture. There are a variety of technological advances in the apparel industry at any given time, which can be an indicator of status. Some consumers are slower to accept new technologies than others. The apparel industry in the U.S. is considered in this chapter, especially regarding how slow the industry has been in adopting methods that promote sustainability.

Chapter 14: Ethics in Fashion is new. We recognize and introduce some of the issues students will face in the fashion industry and include ongoing issues such as sweatshops and child labor, counterfeiting, animal by-products used as fashion (e.g., fur, feathers), and the little-discussed topic of circumcision.

ACKNOWLEDGMENTS

The third edition of readings and activities is the result of the combined efforts of many individuals. We thank all who helped for their time, effort, and support.

We thank the writers who eagerly allowed us to include their work. They have added critical perspectives to the book. We especially thank the contributors of original manuscripts for their interest in the book and their willingness to comply with our editorial suggestions.

We commend our editor, Jaclyn Bergeron, for her patience and understanding in dealing with our already full schedules. She was encouraging throughout the process and she took on the tedious task of tracking permissions for articles and art. Olga Kontzias, the first edition editor, has kept the momentum going through all three editions and we thank her for her support.

Kimberly Miller-Spillman would like to acknowledge and thank her co-editors. Andy and Patti made the experience of revising the third edition a revitalizing and affirming one. I thank Ann Vail and my colleagues in the School of Human Environmental Sciences for financial and collegial support. I thank my family for support during this process. My husband, Charles L. Spillman, and our children, Charles Lee and Audrey, provided a supportive environment that made working on the book possible. Lastly, I thank all of the students I have worked with over the years, who continue to challenge my thinking.

Andrew Reilly acknowledges his co-editors and thanks Kimberly Miller-Spillman for including him on this volume. He also thanks Marcia Morgado for her willingness to always review and proof manuscripts; the authors who agreed to write new articles for this edition; and his family and friends for their continued suppport.

Patricia Hunt-Hurst would like to thank Kim and Andy for being a wonderful team to work with through the entire process of putting this textbook together. Also, she thanks the authors who contributed their work; the original and reprinted readings add an important component to the cultural and contemporary aspects of this book. Her thanks also go to faculty, staff, and students in the Department of Textiles, Merchandising and Interiors who often found her door closed (rather than open) so that she had blocks of time to research, think, and write. Their support was immeasurable. She would also like to thank her husband, Tom Hurst, their daughter, Caitlin, and her mom for their love, support, and encouragement.

March 2012
Kimberly A. Miller-Spillman
Andrew Reilly
Patricia Hunt-Hurst

CHAPTER 1

INTRODUCTION TO DRESS, CULTURE, AND THEORY

Kimberly A. Miller–Spillman

After reading this chapter you will understand:

- The definition of basic terms used in the scholarly study of dress
- The importance of cultural diversity to our world
- How scientific theories can be used to study dress
- How global awareness is created through a study of dress

Dress is often considered simultaneously important and unimportant, resulting in a complex field of study. Dress is a tool that tells individuals how to behave in social situations; it helps us to define gender, age, profession, and interests. All people wear clothes or adorn their bodies and learn from an early age how to "read" the dress of others. From this perspective dressing is unique to humans. However, some people take dress for granted and believe it is not a valid field of scientific inquiry. The goal of this book is to illuminate the vast amount of cultural information communicated through dress every day. For instance, we will examine the daily assumptions and stereotypes that people subconsciously make within seconds of encountering another individual based on his or her appearance.

Another goal of this book is to foster the reader's global awareness through a study of dress and appearance. We will study culture: what it means, how it works, and what we can learn about our own culture while studying the culture of others. Our hope is that this book will develop readers' critical thinking skills related to culture instead of teaching the specific dress details of any one particular culture.

Theory is another topic that is central to this text. We have purposefully chosen readings that illustrate the connection between theory and dress. Each chapter includes examples of readings from experts in the field of dress and culture.

Defining Basic Concepts

Dress

Dress is defined as any intentional modifications of the body and/or supplements added to the body (Roach-Higgins and Eicher, 1992). This includes garments worn on the body but also includes spray-on suntans, color contact lenses, makeup, earrings, shoes, tattoos, and diet and exercise that change one's body shape. Other terms used to refer to dress are "fashion," "costume," "clothing," "apparel," and "adornment." For the purposes of this book, we will use the term "dress" to encompass each of these terms and more.

There is evidence that dress has powerful effects in situations of human interaction such as job interviews, first impressions, and experiments. Research confirms that initial impressions are made within the first five seconds of encountering a stranger; we also know that first impressions affect the outcome of job interviews. First impressions have also been studied when asking a stranger for change or to complete a survey. A few studies have also demonstrated the power of clothing on perceptions, such as in legal cases when the clothing of a rape victim is introduced as evidence in court (Lennon, Lennon, and Johnson, 1992–1993). Dress is powerful because it communicates who one is and who one is not.

One early experiment that revealed the power of dress was a study—not about dress but about prison life (Haney, Banks, and Zimbardo, 1973). Psychologist Zimbardo and his graduate students at Stanford University used dress and environment to create roles for college men who volunteered for the study. The research study was about the dehumanizing effects of prisons. Men were randomly assigned to one of two groups, either prison guard or prisoner. A makeshift prison was constructed in the basement of the psychology building for the study. "Guards" were given khaki shirts and pants, a whistle, a police nightstick, and reflecting sunglasses. "Prisoners" were given a loose-fitting muslin smock with an identification number on the front and back, rubber sandals, and a cap made from a nylon stocking. These clothing items were intended to aid the study volunteers in their respective roles. According to Haney et al. (1973):

> The outfitting of both prisoners and guards in this manner served to enhance group identity and reduce individual uniqueness within the two groups. The khaki uniforms were intended to convey a military attitude while the whistle and night-stick were carried as symbols of control and power. The prisoners' uniforms were designed not only to deindividuate the prisoners but to be humiliating and serve as symbols of their dependence and subservience. (p. 8)

Given the extent to which the college men embraced their assigned roles, the study had to be discontinued prematurely. Although the physical surroundings reinforced the prison atmosphere, dress certainly added to the interactions between guards and prisoners.

A more recent dress experiment, also carried out at a university, took place in 2010. An individual student, rather than a team of researchers, decided to conduct a post-9/11 experiment that resulted in unanticipated reactions from those around her. In the reading "'Undercover' in Hijab: Unveiling One Month Later," Cassidy Herrington, a reporter for her college newspaper, wore a hijab (head scarf) for one month while continuing her normal routine as a University of Kentucky student. She wore the hijab to use her "affiliation with 'white,' non-Muslims to build rapport with the Islamic community and at the same time show non-Muslims the truth from an unheard voice" (p. 6). One month after completing the experiment, Herrington spoke to a general education diversity class and reported that her newspaper column resulted in 30,000 e-mails from 122 nations, which represented the largest number of responses to any article in the paper's history (Herrington, personal communication, November 17, 2010). Although Herrington's article and class talk did not divulge details about the range of responses she received (she does plan to write a book, however), this project undoubtedly required personal courage and fortitude. These experiments illustrate how much dress—such as a simple square of fabric worn on the head—can affect interactions in daily life (see Figure 1.1).

Given the above examples, it is clear that dress is far from inconsequential.

Culture

Another concept that is instrumental to this book is that of culture. **Culture** is utilized by many disciplines such as anthropology, psychology, business, and family and consumer sciences. There is no one universally agreed-upon definition of culture. We will use the following definition:

Figure 1.1 American Caucasian, African American, and Muslim American college students interact on campus.

> Culture is defined as a set of human-made objective and subjective elements that in the past have increased the probability of survival and resulted in satisfaction of the participants in an ecological niche, and thus became shared among those who could communicate with each other because they had a common language and lived in the same time and place (Triandis, 1994, p. 22).

This definition distinguishes objective elements of culture (which include tools, buildings, dress, media outlets, etc.) from subjective aspects of culture (which include categorization, associations, norms, roles, and values). The objective elements refer to a culture's artifacts or objects that have been made by humans. Dress is an artifact that throughout history reveals (among other things) different levels of technology used to make fabric and garments. For example, a simple back-strap loom compared to a computerized loom illustrates the range of technology used to make clothing (see Figures 1.2a and 1.2b).

The subjective elements of each culture are organized into unique patterns of beliefs, attitudes, norms (shared expectations of behavior), and values. Social stratification is an example of a subjective element of culture in which humans create categories for people according to age, race, and income level. This also includes social norms, stereotypes, and prejudices.

In addition to defining culture, Triandis identifies four cultural syndromes that apply to all cultures: cultural complexity, cultural tightness, individualism, and collectivism.

Cultural complexity In complex cultures, people make large numbers of distinctions among objects and events in their environment. This means that generally societies that subsist

Figure 1.2 Cultural tools to create fabric for dress can range from a simple back-strap loom (a) to a computerized loom (b).

on hunting and gathering tend to be simple; agricultural societies tend to be somewhat complex; industrial societies are more complex; and information societies are the most complex. The contrast between simple and complex cultures is considered the most important factor of cultural variations in social behavior (Chanchani and Theivanathampillai, 2002). In an information society such as the United States, dress is varied. For example, Silicon Valley employees may dress in casual T-shirts, jeans, and tennis shoes since they work on computers and seldom interact face-to-face with customers. Another example would be CEOs of large corporations, who may choose to dress in expensive business suits. Generally speaking, dress choices of complex cultures are far greater than those of simple cultures.

Tight and loose cultures Tight cultures have clear norms and deviations are met with sanctions. In tight cultures, if a person does what everyone else is doing, he or she is protected from criticism. Tightness is more likely when norms are clear; this requires a relatively homogenous culture. Loose cultures have unclear norms or tolerate deviance from norms. Cultural heterogeneity, strong influences from other cultures, and crowded conditions can lead to looseness. Urban environments are usually looser than rural ones. Tight cultures would likely frown upon those who do not strictly adhere to dress norms (see "Toyko-A-Go-Go" in Chapter 2). If you grew up in a small town in the United States, you can probably relate to the tighter constraints on rural dress compared to urban dress.

Individualism and collectivism Individualists place high value on self-reliance, independence, pleasure, affluence, and the pursuit of happiness. The behavior of individualists tends to be friendly but non-intimate (i.e., emotionally detached) toward a wide range of people outside the family. Individualists thrive on individual expression through dress and can be found among those wearing subcultural styles such as piercings, tattoos, Goth, punk, etc. Adolescent dress in the United States is a good example of individualist dress. Generally, adolescents are permitted to experiment with dress and "try on" different identities without penalty.

Characteristics of collectivists often (but not always) include organization in a hierarchical manner with a tendency to be concerned about the results of their actions on members within their close-knit groups, sharing of resources with group members, feeling interdependent with group members, and feeling involved in the lives of group members (Hui and Triandis, 1986). Collectivists also feel strongly about the integrity of their groups. Amish dress is a good example of a collectivist culture in the United States where all members are supported by the group and held to certain standards of behavior, including dress (Boynton-Arthur, 1993).

In addition to the above information about culture, there are two theoretical concepts that directly connect dress and culture and were developed or adapted by dress scholars. First, dress is a part of the material culture of the society in which it is worn. **Material culture** consists of the artifacts created or utilized in a society or community. Through the material culture of a society, it is possible to explore the nonmaterial aspects of the culture: the values, ideas, attitudes, and assumptions present in that society. A material culture process has been developed by dress scholars specifically to study clothing as material culture (Severa and Horswill, 1989). Within this method are three stages. These stages are: (1) determining modal type; (2) analyzing material, design and construction, and workmanship; and (3) examining identification, evaluation, cultural analysis, and interpretation.

Elements of the material culture, such as dress, are often related to the nonmaterial culture of a society in complex ways (Tortora, 2010). For example, in some cultures wedding dresses are preserved and only worn once (i.e., sentiment is valued over recycling and saving space), but other cultures may wear the dress many times after the wedding.

When conducting a material culture analysis, one must critically examine the styling details of a wedding dress to determine whether or not they match the fashion of the period. If the styling details do not match the fashions for the date of the wedding, it is possible that the dress was repurposed for a later occasion. For instance, consider a gown from 1892 that is embellished with silver-lined beads around the neckline, on the bodice front, and around the hem of the bodice. These details are quite elaborate compared to wedding gowns of that period. Also, the sleeves are short and puffed compared to the more conservative long, fitted sleeves on wedding dresses from that time. Both the bodice embellishment and the sleeve style indicate that the wearer repurposed the gown at a later date—perhaps for a ball gown (Blackwell, 2012). The simple addition of adding beads to the bodice would make the gown more appropriate for a ball. In addition, the interior construction of the sleeves adds further support for the theory of repurposing. Even though the owner of the dress married into a wealthy family, she chose to repurpose her dress for another occasion several years after her wedding. This tells us something about how the family valued conservation despite their economic standing and their ability to buy a new gown.

Secondly, **cultural authentication** in dress is a process of assimilation through which a garment or an accessory external to a culture is adopted and changed. With this change, over time, the artifact becomes a vital, valued part of the adopting culture's dress (Vollmer, 2010). The steps of cultural authentication are: (1) selection, (2) characterization, (3) incorporation, and (4) transformation. Cases of cultural authentication have been documented. One study connects Indian madras plaid to the Kalabari in Nigeria (Eicher and Erekosima, 1995); another is a case study of the Hawaiian holoku (Arthur, 1997). The holoku is a loose-fitting dress with no defined waistline. It was fashioned after a muumuu-style dress worn by Western missionaries to Hawaii in 1820. The indigenous Hawaiians adapted the muumuu-style dress into what they now refer to as the holoku. Look for other examples of material culture and cultural authentication throughout this text.

Why Does Culture Matter?

Many universities have created diversity requirements for their students. Although the effort is not always perfect (there is evidence that stand-alone diversity courses actually reinforce negative stereotypes rather than erase them; see Miller-Spillman, Michelman, and Huffman in Chapter 14), the general consensus is that American college students will need skills in order to navigate a world that is increasingly diverse. Unless you plan to inherit a family-owned business that operates among a narrow, select clientele, chances are you will need interpersonal skills while working with a range of diverse individuals. In addition, many faculty of the 21st century would likely argue that being a global citizen is part of being an educated person.

Wade Davis, author of the reading "On Native Ground," provides a compelling argument regarding the preservation of cultures on earth. Davis relates that all cultures make choices and choices have consequences, "and [American] choices have, by any definition, ridden rough-shod over the planet" (p. 108). In other words, America may be seen as economically and technologically successful, but that success has come at a price to the planet. Davis compares our concern for the loss of biodiversity to our lack of concern for the loss of culture. He states that of the six thousand languages on earth, only half of those are being taught to children. A staggering loss of humanity is occurring with the loss of these languages, which is comparable to old-growth forest loss. Davis ends his article with advice for the world traveler.

When traveling to other countries, which do you think the locals would prefer: an American tourist who is only superficially aware of the country she is visiting, or an American tourist who has taken the time to educate herself about the country she is visiting? Culture is important to everyone, and Americans who have chosen to arrive in another country uninformed about the culture they are visiting shouldn't be surprised to be dismissed or ignored by the locals. It is a matter of respecting the culture of another.

Being culturally sensitive when you travel will be appreciated by the people with whom you interact. Cultural sensitivity means learning some basic words in their language, knowing something about their country's history and the current political issues, and knowing how to dress to fit in. Conversely, arriving at your destination with no preparation or consideration of the culture may be viewed as disrespectful even if you believe you are contributing to the local economy. One way to stand out is to dress as an American with no attempt to fit in; others include making demands that your expectations are met such as refusing to try local foods, refusing to try a few words in their language, and rejecting other customs.

Being an informed traveler means doing research before you leave home so you will have an accurate frame of reference for your experience. Travel guidebooks are available for most destinations from public libraries. But what should you wear? See the reading "Etiquette 101: Dress Codes." Review and consider the dress advice for different countries. Some might surprise you.

Theory

Theories are helpful to scholars and individuals who wish to explain a particular phenomenon. Dress scholars, for example, may wish to formally explain the emphasis on individual expression through dress in Western cultures, versus the emphasis on traditional dress in some non-Western cultures. In addition, an individual encountering a barista at a coffee bar may speculate (or theorize) why a young person would want several face piercings. See Figure 1.3.

A variety of scientific theories helps us understand the effect of dress on interpersonal relationships. One theory that is particularly useful is **symbolic interaction theory**. The theory contains a broad set of premises about how an individual defines her- or himself through inter-actions and relationships with others (Mead, 1934). We will focus on only a small portion of the theory. Symbolic interaction theorists contend that to develop a sense of self as a human being, one must interact with other people. Other people respond to an individual (both verbally and nonverbally) about how he or she is doing, what he or she is supposed to be doing, what the value or worth of that individual is, and how the individual is identified (Stone, 1965). Continuous presentation of **programs** of dress (programs could include other types of behavior) and reflection upon others' **reviews** or reactions to dress allow an individual to gain a sense of how others see and assign meaning to him or her (Stone, 1965).

Because dress is a part of our interactions with others, we learn some things about ourselves through the responses others give to our appearance. This is the process of discourse involving the presentation of appearance programs and receiving reviews. In addition, we interact with others on the basis of what their appearances mean to us (Shilling, 1993; Stone, 1965). For example, consider this in light of your own behavior with classmates versus authority figures.

Cooley (1902) compared the process of development of self to looking in a mirror. He outlined the general process as:

1. Individuals attempt to perceive themselves by imagining how others perceive them or by reflecting on reviews by others.
2. Individuals may reject or accept other people's reflections of the self, but these reflections nevertheless have an impact.

This process of using other people as mirrors to tell us who we are is the **"looking glass self"** process. So, who we are depends very much on the people with whom we interact, their reactions to us and evaluations of us, and our reflections on these reactions as guides to future

behavior, including how to dress. We continually try out new presentations of self through dress or stick to old ways of dressing that we feel are successful or safe. We learn the self, or who we are, through continued reflection and action. This constant experimentation and exploration is, in a sense, a **self-indication process** (Blumer, 1969). Our reflections on others' responses or how we interpret what other people mean is as crucial to self as is our own behavior and the responses of others. Our interpretations may not always be accurate; we develop skills throughout life at placing the self in another person's position in order to understand the other or to understand the self from the other's point of view (Mead, 1934). Taking other people's perspectives to understand their responses is called *taking on the role of the other*. Seeing the self and the world from another person's perspective is crucial to the looking glass self.

An integral part of the self is the roles we take on. **Role theory** helps us to understand the roles we play and how dress is a part of our roles. **Roles** are positions that people occupy in a group or society (Biddle and Thomas, 1966). These positions are defined by social relationships; people take on roles in relation to other persons. Performance of a

Figure 1.3 Multiple piercings on a young person's body may cause the viewer to theorize about why a person would do that.

role is guided by social expectations for the role-player's behavior (including dress), knowledge, and attitudes.

Adults tend to have multiple roles that define parts of the self. At any one time, a man may be 42 years old (age role), male (gender role), Puerto Rican (ethnic role), a chef and a boss to junior chefs (employment roles), a father, a husband, a brother, a son (family roles), a best friend of another man (social role), and a coach for a girls' soccer team (community leadership role). He may express some of these roles through dress, but not all of these roles in any one appearance. These roles are parts of the puzzle that makes up the man's **identity.** Other aspects of identity include unique personal traits and interests that are not necessarily role related. The Puerto Rican man might run five miles alone every morning and think of himself as defined in part by running. He, in a sense, has many identities that make up his total self. We would need to examine his total wardrobe to begin to grasp the multiple identities of this man, but some of his identity might never be expressed through dress.

Lastly, one sociologist used a **dramaturgical approach** to study dress and appearances. Goffman (1959) introduced the idea that life is played out on a stage and is similar to the theater in that actors can appear on the front or back stage. Goffman pointed out that individuals behave differently depending on the audience. Front stage behavior includes dress that is planned and controlled, whereas backstage dress is casual and impulsive. An example in retail would be the dress and behavior that sales associates display while on the sales floor with customers. That may include professional dress or dress items from the retail store along with friendly, helpful behavior such as helping the customer pick out clothes for an upcoming event. Once the sales associate steps backstage into an area labeled "Employees Only," where she is no longer seen by the customer, she may grab a bite to eat, smoke a cigarette, chew gum, complain about customers' demands, and take off a jacket or untuck a shirttail. The dramaturgical approach also has common features to dress and the public, private, and secret self, as described in Chapter 12.

How Theories Help Us to Study and Understand Dress Meanings

Meanings of dress are central to this area of study. Stone (1965) proposed that meaning can vary from boring (so mundane that no one even notices it) to nonsense (mixing many styles together, making their meaning unintelligible). Typically, individuals use those around them at home and work to gain ideas about dress. More formal avenues are fashion magazines, newspapers, television shows, and movies. More recently, social media (e.g., Facebook and YouTube) are adding to the influences on how we interpret dress (see the reading "The Campus as Runway" in Chapter 9).

Dress scholar Marcia Morgado provides readers with a process for discovering the meanings of dress in the reading "How Dress Means: Abductive Inference and the Structure of Meanings." Morgado uses the field of **semiotics**, the study of signs, to describe how dress items carry meanings. Three semiotic principles are needed to understand how to use the theory. Those principles are:

1. Nothing has meaning in and of itself.
2. Meaning results from relationships drawn between things and what those things represent.
3. Cultures are structured on systems of rules.

From observations of funeral dress to a screen-printed pattern on the backside of a short skirt, Morgado examines the process of abductive inference.

Collective Selection Theory

Often the term "fashion" is used mistakenly for "dress." Many products, if not all, are affected by fashion, from vehicles to home decor to "fashionable" places to eat and drink. Fashion has a specific meaning and is related to time. New ideas for fashion may first be introduced by designers or innovative individuals. Fashion magazines, advertising, retail displays, and celebrities may promote a style as fashionable, the latest thing, and attractive. If a significant number of consumers decide to adopt the style, it actually becomes a fashion, though only certain segments of consumers may wear the style. The style may take on added meaning of representing the lifestyles of people who adopt the new look.

Collective selection is a theory related to fashion (Blumer, 1969). We often believe in America that we are individuals acting upon impulses that are uniquely our own; to some extent that is true. We are less likely to acknowledge the collective forces that shape our impulses such as our clothing choices. Blumer called this collective selection because many individuals' choices are needed to make a dress item a fashion. And our choices are created by similar forces (e.g., what we see in the media and hear on the radio and in conversation with others). See more on collective selection in Chapter 12.

The Chanel suit is one dress item that has been collectively selected over time to represent a classic style. In the reading "Shades of Chanel. Design Award: Effective Use of Historical Influences, 2005," designer and faculty member Tracy Jennings used Gabrielle Chanel as inspiration to create a modern version of the classic suit. Jennings' inspiration included Chanel's construction techniques and suits on display at the Metropolitan Museum of Art in 2005. Compare the images of a classic Chanel suit (1960s) with the *Shades of Chanel* suit (2005; see Figures 1.4a and 1.4b). Can you identify the commonalities between the images? Fashionable dress has a long history beginning in the Middle Ages and informs the future when new designs emanate from historic inspiration.

Figure 1.4 A classic Chanel suit from the 1960s (a) and an updated version from 2005 (b) by designer Tracy Jennings.

What's the Benefit of Being a Global Citizen?

In this book, the authors combine dress and culture while discussing ideas beyond simply what is fashionable. However, people use dress as a vehicle to learn more about our culture as well as other cultures. Fashion is certainly a global phenomenon thanks to the Internet. Knowing how to comfortably interact with those from other cultures is a life skill worth cultivating. In this section we will consider why it is important to become a global citizen.

What's so great about being a global citizen? Does being a global citizen mean that you can no longer appreciate where you grew up? The reading "On Native Ground" provides examples of why being an American is not necessarily better than being from another country. In addition, the reading "Body Ritual among the Nacirema" is an examination of a unique culture.

Americans are often accused of believing that they are the center of the universe and everyone else is looking at Americans for ideas on how to dress, live, and enjoy life—a very ethnocentric view. But how does the rest of the world view the United States? The reading "Etiquette 101: What the World Thinks about Us" features a list of 10 common misperceptions about American culture (see Figure 1.5). Compare these stereotypes of Americans to stereotypes that Americans have of people from other cultures.

Ethnocentrism is judging people from other cultures and backgrounds by one's own cultural standards and beliefs. **Pluralism** is the acceptance of differences in others while not necessarily wanting to adopt those differences for the self. In other words, you do not have to turn your back on your upbringing and cultural roots in order to become more pluralistic. However, becoming more pluralistic may help you to succeed in business or any public arena (such as local government). Moving from an ethnocentric view to a pluralistic one is a goal of this course. Since we see another's dress before we speak to that person, assumptions are made based on dress and appearance alone. We see skin color, hair texture, and items of clothing and—without talking to this person—make assumptions based on stereotypes. In a fast-paced world we cannot speak to everyone; our judgments of others are made quickly.

Figure 1.5 The rest of the world may perceive Americans as fast-food junkies.

Summary

Dress is a complex topic because meanings are based on personal experience as well as cultural rules. This chapter serves as an introduction to basic concepts needed to study dress and culture. In this text we will explore the intersections of dress and culture; theory will be used to explain dress meanings. Dress, culture, and theory are recurring themes throughout the text that will enable the reader to expand his or her knowledge of dress meanings and interpretations. Global awareness, pluralism, and critical thinking about dress and culture are skills necessary to be successful in a world of increasing complexity. Several theories were introduced in this chapter and will be described in greater detail in the following chapters. Theories include symbolic interaction theory, role theory, semiotics, and collective selection theory. Other valuable concepts include material culture, cultural authentication, dramaturgical approach, global citizenship, ethnocentrism, and pluralism.

Suggested Readings

"Cross-cultural/International communication." 2012. From the *Encyclopedia of Business* (2nd ed.) Retrieved from: http://www.referenceforbusiness.com/encyclopedia/Cos-Des/Cross-Cultural-International-Communication.html

Kawamura, Y. 2011. *Doing Research in Fashion and Dress: An Introduction to Qualitative Methods* (Google eBook). Oxford: Berg.

Kotkin, J. and T. Tseng, 2003. (July 13). American youth moving beyond ethnicity: Change blooming in the streets, marketplace. *Lexington Herald-Leader*, Sunday, July 13, 2003, D1 and D6. (reprinted from *The Washington Post*).

Trayte, D. J. 1995. Nineteenth Century Missionary Views of the Hygiene and Dress of the Eastern Dakota. In M. E. Roach-Higgins, J. B. Eicher, and K. P. Johnson (Eds.) *Dress and Identity*. New York: Fairchild.

Winge, T. M. 2003. Constructing "Neo-Tribal" Identities Through Dress: Modern Primitives and Body Modifications. In D. Muggleton and R. Weinzierl (Eds.) *The Post Subcultures Reader*. Oxford: Berg.

Learning Activity 1.1: Body Space Difference Between Cultures

Pair off in the classroom with the person sitting either directly in front or in back of you. While standing, face the other person with your toes touching and talk to each other for 60 seconds. After you are seated, share with the class how it felt to participate in this exercise. Most comments will relate how uncomfortable it was to be that close while talking. This can lead to a discussion about body space across cultures. Americans tend to stand an arm's length apart when speaking and have issues with closeness such as bad breath, food in teeth, and body odor. Some cultures have a closer body space. Conversations between two people from different cultures can sometimes result in a humorous "dance" in which one partner is advancing and the other partner is backing up.

Learning Activity 1.2: Resolving a Cross-Cultural Misunderstanding—Jogging Alone

Objectives

- To understand that cross-cultural misunderstandings are common occurrences.
- To identify a solution to a cross-cultural misunderstanding.

Procedures

1. Read about the way in which individuals in the Dominican Republic misunderstood an American Peace Corps volunteer who was doing something that in the United States is perfectly normal.

2. Read the Peace Corps volunteer's account below titled "Jogging Alone." Think about how you might solve the dilemma as you read. Work in pairs with your classmates to respond to the questions below.

3. Offer responses to each question during a class discussion. Allow for differing responses to be considered.

Jogging Alone: An Account of a Peace Corps Volunteer Serving in the Dominican Republic

When I first arrived in my village in the Dominican Republic, I began to have a problem with my morning jogging routine. I used to jog every day when I was at home in the United States, so when I arrived in my village in the Dominican Republic, I set myself a goal to continue jogging two miles every morning. I really liked the peaceful feeling of jogging alone as the sun came up. But this did not last for long. The people in my village simply couldn't understand why someone would want to run alone. Soon people began to appear at their doorways offering me a cup of coffee; others would invite me to stop in for a visit. Sometimes this would happen four or five times as I tried to continue jogging. They even began sending their children to run behind me so I wouldn't be lonely. They were unable to understand the American custom of exercising alone. I was faced with a dilemma. I really enjoyed my early morning runs. However, I soon realized that it's considered impolite in Dominican villages not to accept a cup of coffee, or stop and chat, when you pass people who are sitting on their front steps. I didn't want to give up jogging. But, at the same time, I wanted to show respect for the customs of the Dominican Republic—and not be viewed as odd or strange.[1]

Endnote

1. This and other classroom activities can be accessed from Building Bridges: A Peace Corps Classroom Guide to Cross-Cultural Understanding Coverdell World Wise Schools, http://www.peacecorps.gov/wws/publications/bridges/. Peace Corps. (2002). *Building bridges: A Peace Corps classroom guide to cross-cultural understanding*. Washington, DC: Peace Corps Paul D. Coverdell World Wise Schools.

Discussion Questions

1. What was the American's point of view here?
2. What American cultural norm, or custom, did the American think would be viewed as perfectly normal in the Dominican Republic?
3. Describe a way you think that the American could respect the Dominican need to show hospitality to a stranger and, at the same time, not have to give up jogging.
4. What was the Dominicans' point of view here?
5. What was the reason for the Dominicans' point of view? What cultural norm did the Dominicans have that made them view the American's behavior as strange?
6. How might the Dominicans begin to understand and respect American cultural norms and, at the same time, satisfy their own need to show hospitality to strangers?

References

Arthur, L. (1997). Cultural authentication refined: The case of the Hawaiian Holoku. *Clothing and Textiles Research Journal*, 15 (3): 125–139.

Biddle, B. J., and E. J. Thomas. (1966). *Role Theory: Concepts and Research*. New York: Wiley.

Boynton-Arthur, L. (1993). Clothing, Control, and Women's Agency: The Mitigation of Patriarchal Power. In S. Fisher and K. Davis (Eds.), *Negotiating at the Margins*, 66–84. New Brunswick, NJ: Rutgers University Press.

Blackwell, C. R. (2012). A Family Affair: An Analysis of the Means-Seaton Family Wedding Gowns from 1885–1892. Unpublished master's thesis, University of Kentucky.

Blumer, H. (1969). *Symbolic Interactionism: Perspective and Method*. Englewood Cliffs, NJ: Prentice Hall.

Cooley, C. H. (1902). *Human Nature and the Social Order*. New York: Charles Scribner's Sons.

Chanchani, S. and P. Theivanathampillai. (2002). "Typologies of culture," University of Otago, Department of Accountancy and Business Law Working Papers Series, 04: 10/02. Dunedin: University of Otago.

Eicher, J. B. and T. V. Erekosima. (1995). Why do they call it Kalabari?: Cultural authentication and the demarcation of ethnic identity. In J. B. Eicher (Ed.), *Dress and ethnicity* (139–164). Oxford: Berg.

Goffman, E. (1959). *The presentation of self in everyday life*. New York: Doubleday.

Haney, C., C. Banks and P. G. Zimbardo. (1973). A study of prisoners and guards in a simulated prison. *Naval Research Reviews*, Office of Naval Research, Washington, D.C., 1–17.

Hui, C. H. and H. C. Triandis. (1986). Individualism and collectivism: A study of cross-cultural researchers. *Journal of Cross-Cultural Psychology*, 17:225–248.

Lennon, T. L., S. J. Lennon and K. K. P. Johnson. (1992–1993). Is clothing probative of attitude or intent? Implication for rape and sexual harassment cases. *Law & Inequality: A Journal of Theory and Practice*, 11(2), 391–415.

Mead, G. H. (1934). *Mind, Self, and Society* (Charles W. Morris, Ed.). Chicago: University of Chicago Press.

Roach-Higgins, M. E., and J. B. Eicher. (1992). Dress and identity. *Clothing and Textiles Research Journal*, 10(4): 1–8.

Severa, J. and M. Horswill. (1989). Costume as material culture. *Dress*, 15:51–64.

Shilling, C. (1993). *The Body and Social Theory*. Newbury Park, CA: Sage.

Sproles, G. B., and L. D. Burns. (1994). *Changing Appearances*. New York: Fairchild Publications.

Stone, G. P. (1965). Appearance and the self. In M. E. Roach and J. B. Eicher (Eds.), *Dress, Adornment and the Social Order* (216–245). New York: John Wiley.

Tortora, P. (2010). Introduction to Cultural Groups. In *Berg Encyclopedia of World Dress and Fashion: Volume 3—The United States and Canada*. Retrieved 6 June 2011, from www.bergfashionlibrary.com/view/bewdf/BEWDF-v3/EDch3062a.xml.

Triandis, H. C. (1994). *Culture and Social Behavior*. New York: McGraw-Hill.

Vollmer, J. (2010). Cultural Authentication in Dress. In *Berg Encyclopedia of World Dress and Fashion: Volume 10—Global Perspectives*. Retrieved 6 June 2011, from www.bergfashionlibrary.com/view/bewdf/BEWDF-v10/EDch10009.xml.

"UNDERCOVER" IN HIJAB: UNVEILING ONE MONTH LATER

Cassidy Herrington

Hilton Als, an African American writer, says our worldview and sense of "otherness" is created in our mother's lap.

Mother's lap is protective and familiar. Leaving this worldview can be uncomfortable, but I can assure you, the rewards are much greater.

Figure 1.6 Student journalist Cassidy Herrington (a) wore a hijab (b) for one month to better understand the Muslim-American community.

Hijab

Last month, I climbed out of my "lap" and wore a hijab, the Muslim head scarf. I thought this temporary modification of my appearance would bring me closer to an understanding of the Muslim community, but in retrospect, I learned more about my place in the world.

Simplified, one piece of fabric is all it takes to turn perspectives upside-down.

The hijab is a contested, sacred, and sometimes controversial symbol, but it is just a symbol. It is a symbol of Islam, a misconstrued, misunderstood religion that represents the most diverse population of people in the world—a population of more than one billion people.

I realized the best way to identify with Muslims was to take a walk in their shoes. On Oct. 1, I covered my head with a gauze scarf and grappled with the perceptions of strangers, peers, and even my own family.

Because of perceptions, I even struggled to write this column. My experience with the hijab was personal, but I hope sharing what I saw will open a critical conversation.

My hijab silenced, but simultaneously, my hijab brought unforgettable words.

Idea

In the first column I wrote this semester, I compared college to an alarm clock saying, "we see the face of a clock, but rarely do we see what operates behind it." At the time, I did not realize how seriously I needed to act on my own words—as a journalist, a woman and a human.

A few weeks after I wrote that piece, a guest columnist addressed Islamophobic sentiments regarding the proposed "ground zero" mosque. The writer was Muslim, and she received a flurry of feedback.

The comments online accumulated like a swarm of mindless pests. The collective opinion equated Islam to violence and terrorism.

In response to her column, one comment said, "[The writer] asks us to trust Islam. Given our collective experience, and given Islam's history I have to wonder what planet she thinks we are on."

Although I did not know the voices behind these anonymous posts, I felt involuntarily linked to them—because I am not Muslim. I wanted to connect people, and almost instinctively, I decided that a hijab was necessary. A hijab could help me use my affiliation with "white," non-Muslims

This article originally appeared in *The Kentucky Kernel*, student newspaper of the University of Kentucky. Reprinted with permission.

to build rapport with the Islamic community and at the same time, show non-Muslims the truth from an unheard voice. Above all, I wanted to see and feel the standard lifestyle for so many women around the world—because I'm curious, and that's why I'm a journalist.

Before I took this step, I decided to propose my idea to the women who wear head scarves every day. Little did I know, a room full of strangers would quickly become my greatest source of encouragement and would make this project more attainable.

The Handshake

Initially, I worried about how the Muslim community would perceive a non-Muslim in a hijab, so I needed its approval before I would start trying on scarves. On Sept. 16, I went to a Muslim Student Association meeting to introduce myself.

When I opened the door to the meeting room, I was incredibly nervous. To erase any sign of uncertainty, I interjected to a girl seated across the room, "meeting starts at 7, right?" The girl, it turns out, was Heba Suleiman, the MSA president. After I explained my plan, her face lit up.

"That is an amazing idea," she said.

I felt my tension and built-up anxiety melt away. In the minutes following, I introduced myself to the whole group with an "asalaam ane aylaykum," and although I was half-prepared for it, I was alarmed to hear dozens of "wa asalaam ane aylaykum" in response.

Before I left, several girls approached me. I will not forget what one girl said, "this gives me hope." Another girl said, "I'm Muslim, and I couldn't even do that." It did not hit me until then, that this project would be more than covering my hair. I would be representing a community and a faith, and consequentially, I needed to be fully conscious of my actions while in hijab.

First Steps "Undercover"

Two weeks later, I met Heba and her friend Leanna for coffee, and they showed me how to wrap a hijab. The girls were incredibly helpful, more than

they probably realized. Although this project was my personal undertaking, I knew I wouldn't be alone—this thought helped me later when I felt like ripping off the hijab and quitting.

Responses to my hijab were subtle or nonexistent. I noticed passing glances diverted to the ground, but overall, everything felt the same. Near the end of the month, a classmate pointed out that a boy had been staring at me, much to my oblivion. The hijab became a part of me, and until I turned my head and felt a gentle tug, I forgot it was there.

For the most part, I carried out life as usual while in hijab. I rode my bike and felt the sensation of wind whipping under my head scarf. I walked past storefront windows, caught a glimpse of a foreign reflection and had to frequently remind myself that the girl was me. Hijab became part of my morning routine, and on one morning I biked to class and turned around because I realized I left without it. At the end of the day, I laughed at my "hijab hair" pressed flat against my scalp.

The hijab sometimes made me uneasy. I went to the grocery store and felt people dodge me in the aisles—or was that just my imagination?

I recognize every exchange I had and every occurrence I report may be an assumption or over-analysis because few of my encounters were transparent. The truth is, however, very few of my peers said anything about the hijab. My classmates I've sat next to for more than a year, my professors, and my friends from high school—no one addressed the obvious, and it hurt. I felt separated from the people who know me best—or so I thought.

A gap in the conversation exists, and it's not just surrounding my situation.

Just over a week ago, I turned on the news to see Juan Williams, a former NPR news analyst fired for commentary about Islam. Williams said, "If I see people who are in Muslim garb and I think, you know, they are identifying themselves first and foremost as Muslims, I get worried. I get nervous."

His statement revealed an internalized fear. And I saw this fear when my colleagues dodged the topic. When I went back to ask "why?," several said it was too "touchy" or insensitive to bring up.

A hijab [is] a symbol, like a cross, a star or an American flag. I am still the same Cassidy Herrington—I didn't change my identity, but I was treated like a separate entity.

Talk Is Not Cheap

When someone mentioned my hijab without my provocation, I immediately felt at ease. A barista at my usual coffee stop politely asked, "Are you veiling?" A friend in the newsroom asked, "Are your ears cold?"

My favorite account involves a back-story.

I love Mediterranean and Middle Eastern cuisine, and I garnered an appetite when I was young. My childhood home neighbored my "third grandmother," the most loving second-generation Lebanese woman and exceptional cook (not an exaggeration, she could get me to eat leafy vegetables when I was a child zealot of noodles and cheese). I remember knocking on her back door when I was five, asking for Tupperware brimming with tabouleh.

When King Tut's opened on Limestone, my school year swiftly improved to a fabulously garlicky degree. At least once a week, I stopped by to pick up the tabouleh, hummus or falafel to medicate my case of the newsroom munchies.

On Oct. 21, the owner, Ashraf Yousef, stopped me before I went inside.

"I heard about your project, and I like it," he said. "And you look beautiful in your hijab." This encounter was by far the best. And it made my shawarma sandwich taste particularly delicious. I went back on my last day to thank him, and Yousef said, "I'm just giving my honest opinion, with the hijab, you look beautiful. It makes your face look better."

Yousef asked if I would wear the hijab to his restaurant when the project was over. I nodded, smiled and took a crunchy mouthful of fattoush.

False Patriotism

I did not receive intentional, flagrant anti-Muslim responses. I did, however, receive an e-mail allegedly "intended" for another reader. The e-mail was titled "My new ringtone." When I opened the audio file, the Muslim prayer to Mecca was abruptly silenced by three gunshots and the U.S. national anthem.

I spoke to the sender of the e-mail, and he said, "It was just a joke." Here lies a problem with phobias and intolerance—joking about it doesn't make it less of an issue. When was it ever okay to joke about hatred and persecution? Was it acceptable when Jews were grotesquely drawn in Nazi cartoons? Or when Emmet Till was brutally murdered?

The e-mail is unfortunate evidence that many people inaccurately perceive Islam as violent or as "the other." A Gallup poll taken last November found 43 percent of Americans feel at least a "little" prejudice against Muslims. And if you need further confirmation that Islamophobia exists, consult Ann Coulter or Newt Gingrich.

Hijab-less

I've been asked, "Will you wear the hijab when it's over?" and initially, I didn't think I would—because I'm not Muslim, I don't personally believe in hijab. Now that I see it hanging on my wall and I am able to reflect on the strength it gave me, I think, yes, when I need the head scarf, I might wear it.

Ashraf said, "A non-Muslim woman who wears a hijab is just wearing a head scarf" (and apparently, my face "looks better"). Appearances aside, when I wore the hijab, I felt confident and focused. I wore the hijab to a news conference for Rand Paul, and although an event coordinator stopped me (just me, except for one elusive blogger) to check my credentials, I felt I accurately represented myself as an intelligent, determined journalist—I was not concerned with how I looked, but rather, I was focused on gathering the story.

So now, I return to my first column of the year. I've asked the questions, and I've reached across the circles. Now, it's your turn. You don't have to wear a hijab for a month to change someone's life or yours. The Masjid Bilial Islamic Center will host a "get to know your neighbors" on November 7, and UK's Muslim Student Association is having "The Hajj" on November 8. These are opportunities for non-Muslims to be better informed and make meaningful connections.

I want to thank Heba for being a friend and a resource for help. Thank you to Ashraf Yousef and King Tut for the delicious food and the inspiration. Finally, I apologize to the individuals who feel I have "lied" to them about my identity or who do not agree with this project. I hope this page clears things up—you have the truth now, and I hope you find use for it.

Why are we so afraid to talk about this? We are not at war with Islam. In fact, Muslim soldiers are defending this country. Making jokes about terrorism is not going to make the situation less serious. Simply "tolerating" someone's presence is not enough.

If you turn on the news, you will inevitably hear the prefix, "extremist," when describing Islam. What you see and hear from the media is fallible—if you want the truth, talk to a Muslim.

Discussion Questions

1. What do you think caused Herrington to make the decision to wear a hijab for a month, and why do you think she stuck to it?
2. Would you take on a Muslim dress code for a month? Why or why not?
3. How instructive do you think this exercise was on a personal level for Herrington, on a university level, and internationally?

1.2

ON NATIVE GROUND

Wade Davis

Halepotra, Pemón, Akha, Makuleke . . . the names of these ancient peoples are unfamiliar to our ears, but their remarkable lives and cultures help us to grasp humanity's full potential. Renowned anthropologist Wade Davis spoke with *Condé Nast Traveler* about the riches embodied in even the most remote societies—and how many of them are putting out the welcome mat.

Some people have asked, "Why does it matter to me in Chicago if some tribe in Africa disappears?" My answer is that it probably doesn't matter to you at all in Chicago if a tribe in Africa disappears. And what does it matter to a tribe in Africa if Chicago disappears? Again, not at all. But wouldn't the world be a weaker, more impoverished place were either of those to occur? Diversity is not just a foundation of stability; it is an article of faith, and it is a fundamental indicator of the way the world is supposed to be.

The dominant culture—whether it is Aztec or Greek or, today, American—always believes that it exists outside of culture, outside of history. It doesn't perceive itself as a culture; it is just the real world.

We don't see our development paradigm of globalization as being what it is—simply one form of economic activity emanating from one part of the world that happens to have been very successful. We see it as the wave of history. If you don't get on that wave, you are going to miss out. The truth is, our economy is but a reflection of our culture, and our culture is but one of several thousand options.

The choices that cultures make have consequences, and our choices have, by any definition, ridden roughshod over the planet.

Davis, Wade. (2008, December). *On Native Ground. Condé Nast Traveler*, pp. 106–109, 188. Reprinted by permission of Condé Nast Publications.

We have this conceit in the West that while we've been busy with technological innovation, the other peoples of the world have somehow been intellectually idle. Nothing could be further from the truth. What is science but the pursuit of the truth? What is Buddhism but 2,500 years of empirical observation as to the nature of mind? The Buddhists would say that the proof of the efficacy of their science is the serenity achieved by those who pursue the path. A Tibetan monk once told me, "We don't believe that you went to the moon, but you did. You may not believe that we achieve enlightenment in one lifetime, but we do."

Other cultures are not failed attempts at being us. They are unique manifestations of the human imagination and the human heart. When asked the meaning of being human, they respond with six thousand distinct voices, and those voices collectively become the human repertoire for dealing with the challenges that will confront us as a species. The modern industrial society as we know it is three hundred years old. That shallow history shouldn't suggest that we have all the answers for the ensuing millennia.

Yet in the same way that biologists are concerned with a loss of biodiversity, so too in the realm of culture we are seeing a collapse of diversity that is truly astonishing. The most apocalyptic scenario in the realm of biological diversity scarcely approaches what we know to be the most optimistic scenario in the realm of cultural diversity—and a great indicator of that is language loss. A language is not just a grammar and a vocabulary. It is a flash of the human spirit, the soul of a culture, the old-growth forest of the mind. Of the six thousand languages living on the earth, half are not being taught to children. That means we are living through a time when fully half of humanity's social, spiritual, and ecological knowledge is being lost in a generation. This is the hidden backdrop of our age.

But why is the loss of culture so important? What does it mean that every culture is a unique facet of the human imagination? Biologists have finally proven what philosophers have always dreamed to be true: We are all relatives. If you accept that we are all cut from the same genetic cloth, then all human populations share the same potential, the same raw intellectual genius. Whether a culture realizes this potential through technological wizardry, as has been the great success of the West, or through unraveling the complex threads of memory inherent in a myth is simply a matter of choice and cultural orientation. There is no trajectory of progress in human affairs. The old Victorian idea that there was a social Darwinian ladder to success that invariably placed us at the apex of the pyramid is now seen as ethnocentric myopia.

We have this notion that indigenous people, quaint and colorful though they may be, are nevertheless frail and fragile, somehow destined to fade away as if by natural law—the implication being that they are failed attempts at being modern, at keeping up. The truth is that these are dynamic, living peoples being driven out of existence by identifiable forces: disease pathogens, egregious industrial decisions or well-intentioned but ill-conceived development schemes, or ideological conflicts. But the bottom line is that in every case we can identify a concrete and specific cause of the humanitarian crisis. This is an optimistic observation, for it suggests that if human beings are the agents of cultural destruction, we can also be the facilitators of cultural survival.

Ecotourism can be corrosive, to be sure, but it can also be profoundly empowering. If one approaches another culture with a reflexive air of superiority, overt or implicit, the impact is invariably detrimental. But if you encounter another people on their terms, open to the reality that their knowledge is as deep as your own, their insights as precise, their hopes and prayers as profound, then magic happens. I learned this as a young student of plants in the Amazon. Though trained at one of the finest universities, I went to the forest as an acolyte, knowing full well that the shamans were the masters of the botanical realm and that nothing I had learned at Harvard could compare with what they had learned in the forest.

The suggestion that none of these other peoples have meaningful contributions to make, that they are only there to entertain us or to bemuse us or to be collected, as we would collect a postcard or an experience, is just wrong. You can go to Hawaii, into the most remote part of that ar-chipelago, and still embrace it as some post-Don Ho fantasy. Or you can do some reading and try to understand what Polynesia was—the greatest cul-ture sphere ever brought into being by the human imagination, tens of thousands of islands flung like jewels across the southern seas.

For years, the genius of the Polynesians was denied by Western academics. That they had in-habited ten million square miles of the planet—from Hawaii to New Zealand, Samoa to Easter Island, and beyond—was a historical fact. But academics maintained that the diaspora had been accidental, a consequence of serendipitous diffu-sion, as if fishermen went out looking for tuna and caught islands instead. In truth, these were the greatest navigators in human history. James Cook wrote of Polynesian vessels that could do three leagues for every two leagues he could do in his mother ship. He spoke with navigators who could place pebbles in the sand accurately representing every island group in the Pacific. He found men in Tahiti who could understand the people from the Marquesas.

Even today, the navigators of Polynesia can name 250 stars in the night sky. These are sail-ors who can sense the presence of a distant group of islands beyond the horizon simply by watch-ing the reverberation of waves across the hull of their vessels. These are men and women who, in the hulls of their sacred canoes, can identify a dozen distinct wave patterns, distinguishing waves caused by local weather systems from the great currents that pulsate across the ocean and can be followed with the same ease that a terrestrial ex-plorer can follow a river to the sea. Indeed, if you took all the genius that allowed us to put a man on the moon and applied it to understanding the ocean, what you get is Polynesia.

Culture is not trivial. It is not decorative, it is not feathers and bells. It is not even the songs we sing or the prayers we utter, all of which are sym-bols of our culture. Culture is a body of ethical and moral values wrapped around each individual that keeps at bay the barbaric heart which history teaches us lies just beneath the surface of every human being. It is culture that allows us to make sense out of sensation, to find order and meaning in a universe which has none. It is culture that al-lows us as individuals to reach always, as Lincoln said, for the better angels of our nature.

As cultural roots wither, individuals often remain shadows of their former selves, caught in time, unable to return to the past yet denied any real possibility of securing a place in the world whose values they may seek to emulate and whose wealth they long to acquire. The fate of the vast majority who sever their ties with their traditions will not be to attain the prosperity of the West but to join the legions of urban poor, trapped in squa-lor, struggling to survive. This is a very dangerous and explosive situation. Anthropology teaches that when people and cultures are squeezed, extreme ideologies sometimes emerge, inspired by strange and unexpected beliefs. Al Qaeda, the Maoists in Nepal, the Shining Path in Peru, the Khmer Rouge of Pol Pot—all these malevolent groups emerged out of chaotic conditions of cultural disintegration and disenfranchisement. So the plight of indige-nous peoples' cultural survival is not only a matter of human rights but also of geo-political stability.

This is not to suggest that cultures should be reduced to zoological specimens in a rain forest park of the mind. Change is the one constant. All peoples are always dancing with new possibilities for life. Neither change nor technology is a threat to culture. The Lakota Sioux didn't stop being Sioux when they gave up the bow and arrow for the rifle any more than American farmers stopped being farmers when they gave up the horse and plow for the tractor.

No one should be denied the brilliance of modernity. If I rip my arm off in a car accident, I don't want to be taken to an herbalist, and nor does anyone else. Our goal should not be to freeze cultures in time but to find ways to allow all peoples to engage in the brilliance of modernity without that engagement demanding the death of their ethnicity.

The question is to figure out how free peo-ple can choose the components of their lives in a truly multicultural, pluralistic world. I recently visited the polar Eskimo in northern Greenland. They live in wonderful houses imported from Denmark. They have DVDs, TVs, cell phones, a fine health clinic, a fully stocked co-op store, and a community hall where elders gather. What they don't have are snowmobiles. They continue to hunt and travel by dog team, with at least ten dogs for every person. They saw what happened when the Inuit of the Canadian Arctic became dependent on machines, and they recognized that maintaining their dogs was a cultural pivot. Even though you can get to your hunting area faster on a snowmobile, once you're there, you're severely limited by the need for oil, gasoline, and so on; and the whole idea of free-form movement over sacred geography, over the landscape of your tradition, is impossible. On a deeper level, the very act of keeping the dogs alive and trained demands skills that root people in their tradition in a very powerful way. The people have their language, which is taught in school; they have their dogs; the men are still hunters. The culture has changed, but it hasn't been transformed.

Tourism, one of the largest sectors of the global economy, can be a tremendous force for good, and if done with respect it sends a strong message. Because visitors are prepared to pay, they are essentially saying, This stuff matters, this counts. People in whatever culture measure the legitimacy of an institution at some level by economic values. A technique that doesn't produce food in the forest will be dropped; a technique that does will be picked up. Compared with the threats implied by, for instance, the unconstrained extraction of oil or egregious industrial logging, ecotourism is benign. One example is the Cofán, an extraordinarily isolated tribe that had the misfortune to live on top of what became Ecuador's oil supply. When I was there in 1974, Lago Agrio looked pretty dreary—an exploding whorehouse town, oil pipelines, roads across the Andes, colonists pouring in, a government not just insensitive but completely dismissive of anything indigenous. Traditionally, the chief in the Cofán community was a shaman, because the only threat was from forces of the metaphysical realm. When oil was found, suddenly the forces were very real, very concrete. So the Cofán selected Randy Borman as their chief. The son of missionaries, Randy grew up Cofán, spoke the language as his mother tongue, and lived in the community. He was not only thought of as a brother but was equipped to go up to Quito, to speak English, to speak Spanish. He began a political process to secure Cofán land and started an ecotourism operation that the Cofán controlled one hundred percent. People would fly in to learn about Cofán culture: How do the people make curare? What is the nature of their medicinal botany? What are their stories and myths? What is the nature of their social relations?

When you visit another culture, try to reach beyond the mere exoticism. If you sit and talk with a child in Peru, for example, who believes that the mountain is a deity, an Apu spirit that will direct his destiny, consider for a moment what he is really saying. Think about what that really means, and how different that is from being raised in America and believing that a mountain is just a pile of rocks.

Now, forget who's right. After all, who is to say? The interesting observation is how the belief system changes with the relationship to the land.

I was raised in British Columbia to believe that the vast temperate rain forests existed to be cut. That was the foundation of the ideology of scientific forestry that I was taught in school and that I practiced as a logger in the woods. It made me totally different from my friends among the Kwakiutl, who believed that those same forests were the abode of the Crooked Beak of Heaven and the cannibal spirits who dwell at the north end of the world, spirits that young men had to confront during the Hamatsa initiation. Was that forest mere cellulose or was it the domain of the spirits? Those who believed the latter had lived with a very light ecological footprint for several thousand years. My worldview had laid waste to the landscape in less than two generations.

In Australia, people frequently travel to Uluru, or Ayers Rock. They have heard that it is sacred and invariably are impressed by its scale and beauty. Perhaps they buy some Aboriginal art or music, spend a little time with an Aboriginal tour guide. They've had a cultural experience of a sort. But if they had a chance to go to a deeper reality, they might understand what the Aboriginal worldview teaches us about the very nature of existence.

When the British first arrived on the shores of Australia, they encountered a people with a rudimentary material culture, with no knowledge of ceramics or agriculture—an entire island continent where nobody had ever attempted, or so it appeared, to improve upon their lot. The British, by contrast, had made a cult of progress. Everything about the Aboriginal people offended them.

The British, of course, had no way of appreciating the subtlety of the Aboriginal mind, which exists in two parallel universes—the phenomenalist realm and the world of the Dreaming. These were and remain a people with no notion of linear time. Theirs is one of the great experiments in human thought.

Whereas the entire ethos of the British was the pursuit of change, the essence of the Aboriginal civilization was the notion that the world exists as a perfect whole, and that the singular duty of humanity is to maintain the land, through ritual activity, precisely as it existed when the Rainbow Serpent embarked on the journey of creation. The Logos of the Dreaming was constancy, balance, symmetry. In the moment, there is deductive reasoning—on a hunt, for instance, when the men pay attention to signs with a perspicacity that would put Sherlock Holmes to shame. But in life there is only the Dreaming, in which every thought, every plant and animal, is inextricably linked as a single impulse, the inspiration of the first dawning. Had humanity followed this track in the human imagination, it is true that we would never have put a man on the moon. But we would certainly not be speaking of our capacity to compromise the life supports of the planet. I have never in all my travels been so moved by a vision of another possibility, born 55,000 years ago.

Being a responsible traveler implies being informed, and this requires effort. If you are joining a tour group, find out the operator's history, who works for them, what kind of efforts they've made to pay back the communities in which they are active, what kind of partnerships they have with those communities. How is the local community engaged, how many benefit, and how is revenue shared?

How do they choose their guides and other employees? Hospitality is a universal cultural impulse. In almost every case, indigenous societies throughout the world already have structures in place to welcome visitors. There's really no excuse anymore for not dealing directly with the leadership of these communities and facilitating the economic exchange with them.

And stay away from ecotourism operations that flaunt their ability to bring you to the most remote, least contacted of tribal societies. Those who make such promises are most likely distorting the truth or—if the people truly are isolated—acting irresponsibly. A trip based on such a premise is ethnographic voyeurism. Moral and ethical issues aside, assume for a moment that an operator could deliver such an encounter. What possible dialogue could ensue in the moment? None at all. All a traveler could do is gawk, and in this there is something obscene. The more valid and rewarding experience is to go where the balance between your authority and economic charisma is matched by the authority and charisma of the other. Then a real dialogue is possible.

It's exciting to go to places where, in spite of all the ravages of the twentieth century, cultures are still vibrant and alive. You can visit remote parts of Tibet, Nepal, the Andes in Peru. One of my favorite places is Cuzco, the ancient capital of the Inca and the center today of a remarkable pan-Andean culture, informed by both Spanish and pre-Columbian roots. The Quechua language is respected and maintained, spoken by millions; agricultural systems are intact; old forms of labor exchange are thriving; traditional rituals are not only still practiced but are honored by the highest levels of the Peruvian government.

It may sound naive, but when you enter a cross-cultural situation, you are by definition an ambassador for your culture. Decency and pride dictate that we present ourselves well, with respect and integrity. Think of every such cultural encounter as a reciprocal obligation. If you make a promise to return to a village, to send a photograph, keep it. Always leave behind more than you bring away, give more than you take. Whether we travel as tourists, journalists, or academic anthropologists, it is our comparative wealth that allows us to be in these places, to have these life-affirming interactions. This is always a privilege but never a right. The goal of travel is to return transformed. And that's the gift of engagement with another cultural reality.

1. What do you think of Davis's comparison between the loss of biodiversity and the loss of cultures? Do you think they are equally important? Explain why or why not.
2. What do you think of Davis's argument that even though America is the leading culture in terms of money and technology, the United States hasn't taken very good care of the planet, yet other cultures have?
3. What could you do to prepare for a trip to Africa? What resources could you use to help prepare for your trip? Why is it important to know as much as possible before arriving at your destination?

1.3

ETIQUETTE 101: DRESS CODES
Condé Nast Traveler

Rule 1: Leave the Fanny Pack

What makes an Ugly American ugly? Is it the timbre of our voices? Or the way we travel in herds? Or is it (as we suspect) our love of sweatpants, baseball caps, and yes, fanny packs, no matter the occasion or place? While it can sometimes seem that the world has fallen victim to a sort of sartorial globalization, where jeans are welcome anytime, anywhere, the truth is—of course—more nuanced. What works in surprisingly laid-back Singapore will be greeted with looks of horror on the streets (or in the boardrooms) of Paris. And ladies, while you can (and should) pile on the gold and jewels in Greece, quirky and stripped-down is the way to go in Germany. So here are the rules on looking not just appropriate but actually stylish around the globe, whether you're in a meeting, at a party, or just walking outdoors. Plus: Tips on how to wear a head scarf, what to pack for safari, and how to play European for a day. Ugly American? Fuhgeddaboudit.

Africa/The Middle East

In general, coverage is key. But while merely clothing your collarbone is enough in Jordan, just an inch of shoulder skin could get you arrested in Iran; over in Dubai, you'll need a brand or two to make it big. Men are usually fine in long pants, and women carry shawls for a quick conservative fix, but consider yourself forewarned: Style is a sensitive subject here.

Dubai

At a meeting: Women's pantsuits should be sheeny and glam; men's duds are buffed, black, and paired with slim ties.

On the street: The mall, not the street, is the social arena. Here, girls in T-shirts (their shoulders covered out of respect and as a remedy against the freezing AC blasts) tote the latest Louis Vuittons. Carry a pashmina to cover up in case you find yourself in a traditional souk—although you'll see miniskirts and shorts, they're for people who know the city well enough to avoid ultra-conservative quarters. On men, reflective aviators abound, as do Gucci sandals.

At a party: Go glam to the gills: No Swarovski is too shiny and no Giuseppe Zanotti is too high. Men wear Y3 trainers and tailored blazers over graphic tees.

This article originally appeared in the October 2009 issue of *Condé Nast Traveler*. Reprinted by permission of Condé Nast Publications.

P.S. Put on clean socks if you're going to a local's house—you'll leave your shoes at the door.

Iran

At a meeting: Men wear crisp Italian suits and shined shoes. A chador (hooded floor-length cloak) is needed for a woman meeting a clerical group, but for most gatherings, she should slip on a black manteau (a loose coatlike garment), low closed-toe pumps, and an Iranian hijab. Locally bought products drape best and look contextually refined.

On the street: Special police enforce the Islamic dress code, which requires women (non-Muslims included) to be covered from head to toe. The working classes wear full-length black chadors, but a manteau over jeans is an acceptable alternative. Hijabs are often patterned or pinned with pretty brooches. Makeup should be minimal, and while bright lipstick isn't allowed, flawless eyebrows are an absolute must.

At a party: Wear whatever you want under your outer cloak; the young remove their voluminous robes to show off tight jeans and strappy stilettos at friends' informal gatherings. Older intellectuals conceal elegant suits under their cloaks.

P.S. They're credited with creating the first perfume, so it's no surprise that the Iranians are scent savvy: Although women might be cloaked, they're often doused in glam, sexy fragrances like Azzaro's vetiver and pimento tonics.

Jordan

At a meeting: Suits and shoes should be simple, and dresses work for women provided they're shin-length and sleeved. Big hair is not for the Jordanian boardroom: Tie long locks into chignons and keep short dos neat. The "Hillary Clinton look" is a woman's best bet, according to John Shoup, author of *Culture and Customs of Jordan*.

On the street: Rich red embroidery is popular, so Western women can don detailed tunics over loose trousers (many local women wear pants) or black cotton dresses embellished with traditional needlework. Men wear khakis and collared shirts.

At a party: King Abdullah II is a sartorial guide; he's almost always dressed in navy suits for nighttime (gray for daytime) and a light-colored silk tie. Queen Rania set a haute new tone by sporting Lanvin, Dior, and Elie Saab to evening affairs, but the first lady covers her shoulders and legs (with couture) when she's out in Amman.

P.S. The veil's a release of sorts for trendy young women, who can show a little more skin as long as the head is covered.

What to Wear on Safari

Conjure "safari style" and you'll likely envision a smart pocketed Proenza Schouler ensemble or Cavalli's sheeniest leopard-print dress—but show up wearing either in an actual African wildlife reserve and you'll spend the week banished to the back of your camp's SUV. The safari-bound have plenty of things to avoid: The color red spells danger to lions; military fatigues look fraudulent; perfumes, hair gels, and aftershaves bother the animals; and shiny baubles might catch a leopard's roving eye. In the bush, form usually takes a backseat to function.

These issues notwithstanding, weight is your biggest concern. Hippo Creek Safaris, for example, limits baggage to 35 pounds, and Premier Tours' camping safaris allow you only 26. For successful stalking style, pack a Kelty duffle (which measures 30 inches but weighs only one pound) with basic pieces that are both snappy and sound: a Polartec fleece and long pants for chilly morning game drives, a pair of khaki pants or shorts (or pants that zip into shorts—though these we won't sartorially condone), and for women, a tank top to layer under a muted Ralph Lauren linen button-down. "I roll it to the elbow in the morning, unbutton it all the way if I'm really hot, and wear it at night with a nice piece of jewelry," says Nina Wennersten, a travel specialist with Hippo Creek Safaris. Teva sandals will work for every stroll through the African bush, so leave the heavy hiking boots at home.

Come evening, "nobody wants to sit down to dinner and feel schleppy next to the perfect Italian tourists at camp," Wennersten says. Channel Romans on holiday in black slacks (no skirts, since malaria-ridden mosquitoes come out after dark), driving shoes, your trusty linen button-down, and a silver necklace or silk scarf. Don't worry about re-wearing: Laundry's taken away in the morning and returned by sundown every day.

How to Wear a Hijab

A head scarf is a head scarf is a head scarf—right? Not really. You can actually tell a lot about a woman by the way she wears her scarf. Here, we show you how to wear your hijab no matter the occasion—and, of course, what not to do as well.

Start by pinning your hair back securely, then tie it in a bun at the nape of your neck. A high bun whose outline can be clearly seen through the hijab is viewed as provocative.

At a Gathering

Although women are traditionally expected to wear a black scarf tightly secured so as to show only the oval of the face, today's young Iranian women push the envelope by pulling a printed colored scarf loosely around the head and leaving an inch or two of the hairline daringly exposed.

At a Bazaar

In the throng of a crowded market, a loosely tossed scarf isn't fashionable; it's troublesome. Women tired of worrying about crooked head coverings instead float a large scarf over the crown and clip it below the chin (special clasps are made for this particular purpose, but safety pins work too), then throw each of the long ends over the opposite shoulder.

At an Informal Meeting

Large kerchiefs worn babushka-style work for informal meetings with nonsecular colleagues. To get the look, fold a square scarf into a triangle and rest the base of the triangle at the top of the forehead, then tie the ends below the chin. Make sure the back tip of the triangle covers the nape of your neck.

At Official Places

The most classic hijab, and the most universally acceptable, is the Al-Amira style—essentially a hood that reaches past the bust, with a hole for the oval of the face. It comes in cotton, silk, rayon, and a myriad of prints, from florals to fleur-de-lis.

At Religious Places

Forget the hijab; it's time to break out the big guns: the chador. A mark of piety and the easiest way to go unnoticed in the most religious areas of Kuwait and Iran, the full-length, cloak-like chador is thrown over the hair and held closed in the front.

At a Young, Liberal Party

Flashing a hint of hair in Iran is like showing a little leg in the United States, so girls keep their bangs pinned back and their scarves opaque unless they're headed somewhere young and free. At such parties and private gatherings, it's coquettish to have bangs peeking out from under a sheer scarf.

Headbands = Nerdy

Layering a stretchy headband under a tight-fitting hijab screams "dork" to trendy young Iranians. The same hijab sans headband is socially acceptable.

Asia

You'll need a myriad of outfit options for a transcontinental Asian trek. Miniskirts and monochrome black are safe bets from Jakarta to Japan, but women in India and Pakistan cover their legs and sport vibrant, rich hues. In fact, very few styles would work in every country: Flip-flops, for instance, are trendy in Singapore, verboten in China, and, in Indonesia, acceptable only for shower wear. Here's how to prep before you pack.

Japan

At a meeting: "The Japanese word for dress shirt, *wai shatsu*, comes from the English for 'white shirt,' which gives you an idea of the range of colors worn at work," says Dan Rosen, professor at Tokyo's Chuo Law School, who recommends basic black suits. In 2005, the government launched a Cool Biz initiative meant to lower AC costs by encouraging lighter work attire; it's been met with fierce resistance by the jacket-and-tie-loving Japanese working class.

On the street: For Tokyo youth, nothing's too studied or over-the-top, so the laissez-faire American norm is seen as slovenly. Women should wear heels, makeup, and a dose of frills, and men must be clean shaven and must spend time on their hair.

At a party: Agnès B. and Louis Vuitton are the easiest icebreakers, since the Japanese love labels—along with the stylish shapes by local designers like Yohji Yamamoto. No sweatsuits, please!

P.S. Planning to shop here? Note that Japanese sizes run significantly smaller than those in the States. If you wear a medium in the United States, a Japanese XL might be a squeeze.

Singapore

At a meeting: You wouldn't think so, given Singapore's rules-happy reputation, but business meetings are actually super casual here (well, dresswise at least). Jackets aren't required, ties are rare, and both sexes wear oxfords and slacks. For women, trendy peg-leg pants are often permissible.

On the street: Those in their 20s and 30s strut in tank tops, hot pants (board shorts for boys), and flip-flops. A polo shirt by Fred Perry or Ralph Lauren is a popular option, as well as anything from casual mass-market stores.

At a party: "A Marni dress with Giuseppe Zanotti sandals for house parties," says Aun Koh, director of Singapore-based Ate Consulting. Brands are important to upper-class dames, who competitively collect Hermès bags. Men wear designer jeans from the likes of G-Star Raw and Dr. Denim.

P.S. Hems are worn high at every age—get your gams ready.

Europe

If there's one hard and fast sartorial rule in Europe, it's this: Shabby is never chic. And no one, whether in London or Leipzig, likes the American travel-comfort gear of clunky sneakers and shapeless skirts. That having been said, style varies wildly from country to country. The mullets that will make you a star in Moscow won't fly in peg-leg-trousers-crazed London or sleek Paris. So how should you dress? Just stay simple, look to the locals, and follow a few basic rules.

France

At a meeting: Dark, tailored, unflashy suits by Dior Homme or Jil Sander for both women and men (who need not wear ties).

On the street: Avoid bright colors—even kids' clothes come mainly in cream, navy, gray, and brown—and take care to shun the plethora of other offenses: pleated chinos, walking shorts, sport sandals, baseball caps, golf attire, loud logos, sneakers, T-shirts, and sexy clothes. "In France, it's always best to keep things simple, neutral, and classic rather than too trendy," says Miles Socha, European editor for *Women's Wear Daily*.

At a party: On a normal night out, overdressing's okay, but if it's black-tie, underdress: Men should wear business suits sans ties, women should slip on cocktail dresses, and for a normal night out, *femmes* should keep it simple, silky, and black.

P.S. "One's shoes and belt should always match," advises François Delahaye, former general manager at Paris's legendary Plaza Athénée. But, he adds, a man's tie should never mirror his silk pocket square.

Turkey

At a meeting: Neither men nor women should go without manicures, since Turks are known for being perfectly groomed. Hair should be trimmed, suits fitted (jackets and pants need not match), button-downs left open and worn without undershirts peeking through. Tailoring is a primary indicator of class, so no matter how cheap the suit, it should fit well.

On the street: "I once heard that a woman had trouble getting a tea-man to serve her because she dressed like a frumpy housewife," says White. So dressing down is not an option. Men and women cultivate a studied casual look in designer jeans, Tod's loafers, and ironed high-end T-shirts (like James Perse)—never shorts.

At a party: Visible brand names are seen as cheap and low-class. Truly chic women wear Matthew Williamson florals rather than triangle-stamped Prada, and accessorize with one large statement bauble, like a giant cocktail ring by Turkish-born Sevan Biçakçi. Hair is tightly pulled back. Men wear open shirts under light jackets with dark pants (or vice versa).

P.S. "Never wear a long raincoat," White says. "Even when it's pouring, a secular Turk will wear a short coat so as not to be mistaken for a conservative Islamist."

United Kingdom

At a meeting: The downtown banking-and-newspaper bustle calls for a suit and tie (no tie on Fridays), but you'll be laughed out of Soho or Kensington ad agencies in the same getup: There, cool execs don a uniform of the newest Nikes and skinny jeans.

On the street: Quirky Kate Moss–inspired London girls throw on a high-low mix of Top Shop and Temperley; they're freer and less polished than other city style-setters. Men wear peg-leg trousers in primary colors with plaid shirts or tees. Don't opt for chinos and polos—the preppy look won't fly in London. At a party: Skinny jeans take a girl or boy from meetings to a cutesy mews (switch from heels to Chuck Taylors) to a Shoreditch pub crawl (back to heels).

P.S. Wellies might be as British as it gets, but they're really country wear. Do take them off if you're lounging indoors.

A Tale of Two Cities

Can anyone really not call Paris and Milan the fashion capitals of the world? After all, one is home to Chanel and Dior, the other to Prada and Armani. But how can you tell your Milanese hipster from your Parisian sylph? We asked Scott Schuman, the mastermind behind the popular fashion blog The Sartorialist, for some clues (his book, *The Sartorialist*, was released in August).

Milan

Hair should be up.

"The Milanese girl wears whatever's on trend in a sexy, overt way. She doesn't do anything vintage or sporty."

Must be a colorful print.

"The overall effect is resilient and formal. She's not one to mess around."

"Milanese girls' style is set: all Italian, all big brands, all off the runway. She loves D&G. Prada's too intellectual, Marni's too quirky."

Skin should be tanned.

"Shoes must be high to show off her legs."

Paris

Hair must be mussed.

"Unlike the Milanese girl, she's not brand obsessed: The Parisian will mix vintage with French brands like Isabel Marant and Vanessa Bruno, and throw in some cheap stuff from A.P.C."

Oversized white tee falling off her shoulder.

"There's a come-hither kind of sexiness to a Parisian girl: She's covered up but seems somehow barer, more fragile. She's more precious than your Milanese young thing: The Parisian girl is like a gift, with a sultry quality that's underlying but never plain."

These are her boyfriend's.

Her shoes are Balmain.

Discussion Questions

1. Which countries' dress code surprised you the most? Why?
2. Where do your assumptions about dress come from?
3. Were you aware how most non-Americans view the American habit of wearing a fanny pack?

HOW DRESS MEANS: ABDUCTIVE INFERENCE AND THE STRUCTURE OF MEANINGS

Marcia A. Morgado

One of the most popular subjects in the study of clothing and appearance concerns dress as a symbolic system that conveys an array of personal, social, and cultural meanings. In works on this subject writers variously deal with the context and person-dependent nature of communication through dress; they examine the ambiguous nature of clothing and appearance messages; and they describe changes in the meanings of dress as these occur over time. I offer an alternative approach to thinking about questions of meaning in dress. Rather than deal with the conditions, consequences, or meanings of dress per se, my interest is in how the meanings of dress are generated and how interpretations of meaning are formed. Familiarity with theories about the meaning-making process can provide insights into how our personal meanings of dress are constructed, can guide us in examining our assumptions about the meanings that others attribute to clothing and appearance-related phenomena, and can enable us to generate hypotheses about the bases on which the meanings of dress rely.

Abductive inference is a theory about how meanings are generated and how interpretations of meaning are formed. The theory is proposed in the work of Charles S. Peirce (1931/1958), an American philosopher and a major figure in the field of semiotics. Semiotics is concerned with the study of signs. The word "sign" is a semiotic concept that is defined as: anything that is taken to mean something other than itself. When meanings are attributed to clothing and appearance-related phenomena, those phenomena are functioning as signs. Any object, idea, or expression can serve as a sign, but meanings are not the property of the sign vehicle (i.e., the object, idea, etc.). Meaning is construed in an observer's or an interpreter's mind. Peirce's theory deals with the cognitive process through which signification (i.e., meaning-making) occurs.

To appreciate the usefulness of the theory for the study of dress, one must be familiar with three semiotic principles. The first principle is that nothing has meaning in and of itself. Things have meaning only when those things are interpreted as signs. Thus, the interpretive process is fundamental to meaning. The second principle is that meaning results from relationships that are drawn between things and what those things represent (i.e., what they mean). These relationships are theorized as sociocultural principles or rules. Conventional dress derives its meanings from conventionalized rules, i.e., rules that are generally accepted as truths. For example, a generally accepted convention of dress is that the clothing worn to a funeral should be somber in nature.

The third principle is that cultures are structured on systems of rules. These rules guide the beliefs, principles, thoughts, and behaviors of a culture's members. The rules provide instructions for how situations are interpreted; they function as guidelines for determining what things "mean." Communications scholar A. A. Berger explains that "to be socialized" and to participate in a culture "means, in essence, to be taught a number of [rules], most of which are quite specific to a person's social class, geographic location, [and] ethnic group" (1982, p. 34). Although people are generally "not consciously aware of the rules . . . and cannot articulate them," they necessarily use and respond to them (p. 22). People who share social and/or cultural backgrounds generally draw from a common storehouse of rules. However, they may draw on different rules in common circumstances, and their individual experiences may shape the rules on which they rely. Consider this example:

Original for this text.

Recently, I attended a funeral with my friend Chelsea. Chelsea and I walk our dogs together, enjoy outings with our families, and sometimes meet for lunch at Macy's. But we don't shop together. Chelsea has no interest in fashion and her taste in dress is conservative and traditional, while I'm fascinated by fashion and my taste often runs to glitz and kitsch.

At the funeral someone points out the deceased's grandson who sits in the front row, quietly sobbing, as a girlfriend gently pats his back. The young man appears to be in his early 20s. He is of Asian-Caucasian heritage with a golden brown complexion, a handsome face, a beautifully toned body, and professionally styled hair. He is wearing dress pants with a fabulous Ed Hardy T-shirt—black, with a large, silver graphic design that integrates a human skull with elegant loops and swirls (Figure 1.7). The shirt is to die for; it must have set him back at least a hundred bucks. And the kid is drop-dead gorgeous. He looks like he just walked off the cover of *Details*.

I look at the young man and Death's head reminds me to reflect upon my own death, which now appears more imminent than I'd prefer. I think: *memento mori*. I too will die.

Figure 1.7 This image, which appeared on a T-shirt worn to a funeral, prompted one observer to draw on the fact that all of us will die, and the symbol is an expression of grief. Another viewer found the image inappropriate for a funeral, and thus concluded that the wearer was improperly dressed.

"Did you see the grandson?" Chelsea asks. "Did you see what he's wearing? Uh-uh," she says, shaking her head back and forth. "That is very, very wrong." The irony of Chelsea's comment does not escape me: The definitive image of Death is not appropriate at a funeral.

To interpret the embellishment on the young man's shirt as a sign of his grief and attachment to his grandfather, I read the motif as *memento mori*—a Latin phrase and classical pictorial tradition wherein Death's head serves to remind people of their own mortality. The interpretation took this form: Observation: A sorrowful young man in a shirt embellished with a classic representation of Death. Rule: *Memento mori*. Remember that you too will die. Meaning: The young man's attire symbolizes his awareness of his own mortality and his recognition that all of us will share in his grandfather's fate.

But this association was not spontaneous for my friend. And, because the situation is not conducive to interrogation, I make an educated guess about the semiotic process that leads Chelsea to say: "That is very, very wrong." I assume she has pointed out that the young man is inappropriately dressed. Observation: That [embellishment] is very, very wrong. Possible rule: Discretion prohibits the display of obvious symbols of death at a funeral. Meaning: The young man mocks conventional values regarding the funeral ritual (probably).

Of course, other interpretations are possible. The imagery might have led me to assume that the grandson is insensitive to decorum; that the graphic is simply a fashion statement. Ed Hardy's skull imagery is the icon du jour on Christian Audigier's high-end clothing line, and perhaps the young man is simply a cool dude who donned hot duds for this special dress-up event. Or I might have concluded that he intends the embellishment as a symbol of his identification with a Goth subculture, a group whose appearance style revolves around dark, glamorized images of death. And Chelsea's "uh-uh" comment might not be a response to the graphic design at all. The T-shirt itself could disturb her—a casual garment worn in an inappropriate context. These interpretations are also the result of conventional rules that link appearance expressions with meanings: shallow people keep up with fads and fashions; dress communicates group identification and affiliation; casual dress is inappropriate to the solemnity of a funeral.

On the other hand, there are no conventions linking highly novel dress forms with particular meanings. For example, there are no conventions linking the visual expressions "necktie worn with T-shirt" or "necktie worn bare-chested" with specific meanings. But a lack of convention does not suggest that novel expressions lack meaning. To make sense of unusual forms, interpreters unconsciously draw from their own cognitive data banks—their unique mental storehouses of rules. From these rules interpreters generate their own varied and idiosyncratic meanings. Abductive inference is theorized as the process through which this occurs. Abduction involves the intuitive generation of rules that connect an object or expression with some meaning.

Inferential Reasoning Based on Abduction

Peirce postulates abduction as a natural, instinctive mode of reasoning that is hard-wired into human cognition and expressed through "spontaneous conjectures" (1931/1958, 6:475) that provisionally explain unusual or unfamiliar observations. It is the process that results in what we sometimes describe as having an "aha!" experience, a moment of insight, or a creative leap of mind. Abduction is theorized as an inferential leap in which something is explained on the basis of assumptions and hypotheses about a probable law.

Peirce was a logician. He described abductive inference as a formal propositional argument that he compared with formal arguments based on deductive and inductive inference. Each argument consists of three statements: two premises and a conclusion. The purpose of the deductive argument is to test truth claims, and each statement in the argument is either true or false. If the premises are true they guarantee the truth of the conclusion (Gregory, 2004):

Rule: All cats can climb. **Case:** Mizzi is a cat. **Conclusion:** Mizzi can climb (Moser, 1999, p. 13).

The inductive argument also tests truth claims. But in the argument based on inductive inference, the truth of the premises suggests that the conclusion is probably or plausibly true:

Observation: Mizzi climbs up a tree. **Case:** Mizzi is a cat. **Rule:** All cats can (possibly) climb (p. 13).

The argument based on abductive inference has a different objective. It is not an attempt to make a truth claim or to predict a likely truth. Rather, abductive inference is an attempt to find a conclusion which, if true, would show the premises to be probable (Gregory, 2004, p. 7):

Observation: A black creature (possibly Mizzi) is climbing up a tree. **Possible rule:** All cats can climb. **Case:** The black creature is (possibly) a cat (Moser, 1999, p. 13).

Thus, abductive reasoning results in a possible explanation (The black creature is possibly a cat) that indicates that a rule (All cats can climb) is also possibly true.

The value of the abductive reasoning argument is that it theorizes how the mind generates intuitive conclusions. The argument parallels two semiotic principles: (1) that meaning results from relationships drawn between things and what those things represent, and that (2) the relationship is a sociocultural principle or rule. In actual practice, our conscious mind bypasses the possible rule, bringing us directly to an "aha!" conclusion: We see an appearance form and we infer a meaning. But to connect the observation with a conclusion, we must intuit a rule. Reminder: People are generally "not consciously aware of the rules . . . and cannot articulate them," but they necessarily use and respond to them (Berger, 1982, p. 22). We can use the abductive inference argument as a model for thinking about and attempting to reconstruct our own inferences regarding the meanings of dress. We can also use the model for conceptualizing how we interpret others' meanings related to clothing and appearance. And we can use it to hypothesize the rules and principles on which the meanings of dress are structured.

Example 1: Abductive Inference to a Sociocultural Principle of Dress

Some time ago, an unusual style was introduced that involved a screen-printed pattern on the backside of a short skirt. The print made it appear as though the skirt was transparent and that the wearer's legs and bikini panties were visible through the fabric. I found the garment clever and amusing, but others who commented on the skirt found it tasteless or insulting.

I used the model of the abductive argument as a frame of reference against which to reconstruct the instinctive inference that connected my observation of an unusual garment with my conclusion regarding the garment's meaning. I begin with conscious knowledge: I've observed a skirt that is printed to appear as though the wearer's legs and panties are visible. I also have some understanding of what the garment means to me: It is amusing and clever. I know that the observation and the meaning are connected through a possible rule or principle. What rule can I imagine that would plausibly connect the observation with the meaning? And why would that result in my thinking that the garment is amusing and clever? After some thought, I come up with the following:

Observation: A skirt printed to appear as though the wearer's legs and panties are visible. **Possible Rule:** Underwear is meant to be worn, but not to be seen (a likely principle). **Case:** The skirt (or wearer) makes an ironic comment on a principle governing appropriate dress (probably). The same rule also applies when I try to reconstruct the bases on which others interpret the garment as tasteless: **Observation:** A skirt printed to appear as though the wearer's legs and panties are visible. **Possible Rule:** Underwear is meant to be worn, but not to be seen (a likely principle). **Case:** The skirt (or wearer) ridicules conventional standards of dress (probably).

And the rule also applies when I consider how it is that others conclude that the garment is insulting: **Observation:** A skirt printed to appear as though the wearer's legs and panties are visible. **Possible Rule:** Underwear is meant to be worn, but not to be seen (a likely principle).

Case: The skirt (or wearer) insults women by displaying female garments and body parts that should be concealed (probably). Because the rule appears applicable across multiple conclusions, I suspect my analysis reveals what is probably a commonly held sociocultural principle of dress.

Example 2: Abductive Inference to Common Knowledge in My Professional Field

A female student in my introductory aesthetics course comes to class wearing cute flannel pajamas and fluffy, pink bedroom slippers. These familiar garments appear bizarre in the context of my classroom, and I'm unable to draw on the convention that links their meaning with bedtime. But I want to understand what I see. To make sense of the observation I generate a principle based on my knowledge as a textiles and apparel scholar, and I hypothesize a plausible conclusion based on that principle: **Observation:** A student wears pajamas and bedroom slippers to class. **Possible Rule:** Pajamas and slippers are intended for wear at home and in private. **Case:** This is an intentional violation of a rule governing the situational appropriateness of particular clothing styles. Active learning assignments are common at the university, and the student is carrying out an assignment on situational incongruity for one of her textiles and apparel classes (probably). The reconstructed abduction rests on the storehouse of knowledge I've acquired as a result of my education and profession.

Example 3: Abductive Reasoning to a Principle Unique to Individual Circumstance

On a visit to an urban shopping mall with my 80-year-old mother, I see an African-American youngster in sagging jeans that expose his undershorts and a portion of his buttocks. My observation triggers an immediate response: The kid is into hip-hop. But my mother's flash of insight is very different: "Zat iss a gengster!" she declares, *sotto voce*, in her heavy Eastern European accent.

And her body shudders as she moves to redirect our path to the other side of the mall. Our flash-of-insight responses are derived from different knowledge bases. I'm familiar with pop culture, youth styles, and social-psychological principles of dress. But my mother is not. I imagine that if I ask her to explain, she will tell me that neighbors in her ultraconservative community have warned her about people who wear transgressive fashions. To interpret my mother's response I consider her statement, her behavior, and her situation, and I hypothesize a new rule to account for the connection she has drawn between the clothing style and the wearer: **Observation:** A young man in oversized trousers that expose his underwear and highlight his buttocks. **Possible Rule:** People who violate dress norms also violate other norms, including those formalized as law (probably). **Case:** The man is dangerous (probably).

Peirce suggests that abductive inference occurs in situations wherein the observer is faced with an unusual situation. But contemporary scholars suggest that virtually all inferential and interpretive reasoning occurs through abductive inference, and that it is the principle mechanism through which we comprehend much of everyday life. Abduction is postulated as the primary means through which we process visual information (Moriarty, 1996), use and interpret non-literal or metaphoric language (Arrighi & Ferrario, 2008); understand movies and make sense of television commercials (Langrehr, 2003), and navigate the Internet (Shank & Cunningham, 1996, p. 5). It is proposed as the primary interpretive device on which students rely (Langrehr, 2003), as the kind of thinking that is central to aesthetic and design creativity (e.g., Martin, 2005), and as a technique through which we can uncover the cultural principles that underlie consumption symbolism (Mick, 1986, p. 202). Peirce's theory of abductive inference provides a model for thinking about the principles that guide our intuitive understandings in everyday life.

It is likely that many of our interpretations of the meanings of clothing and appearance phenomena occur automatically, with little thought given to how those interpretations are derived or to the nature of the assumptions that underlie the meanings we attribute to dress. Abductive inference provides a model for thinking about the interpretive process. It is a model for thinking about thinking. Like learning any new skill, learning to think about how we think requires patience and practice. The potential benefit is that it offers an alternative lens through which to contemplate the meanings of dress. It suggests that, in addition to answering the question "What do you think are the meanings of dress?" we can also draw hypotheses on the question "How do you think about the meanings of dress?"

References

Arrighi, C. & Ferrario, R. (2008, March). Abductive reasoning, interpretation and collaborative processes. Foundations of Science, 35(1), 75–87. Retrieved from http://www.loa-chr.it/files/MBR04 ArrighiFerrario.pdf.

Berger, A. A. (1982). Media analysis techniques. Newbury Park, CA: Sage.

Gregory, P. (2004). A brief introduction to logic. Retrieved from http://classes.colgate.edu/pgregory/ BriefLogic.html.

Langrehr, D. (2003, May). From a semiotic perspective: Inference formation and the critical comprehension of television advertising. Reading Online. Retrieved from http://www.readingon line.org/articles/langrehr/.

Martin, R. L. (2005, Aug. 3). Creativity that goes deep. *Business Week.* Retrieved from http://www. businessweek.com/innovate/content/aug2005/ di2005083_823317.htm.

Mick, D. G. (1986). Consumer research and semiotics: Exploring the morphology of signs, symbols, and significance. *Journal of Consumer Research,* 13, 196–213.

Moriarty, S. (1996, May). Abduction and a theory of visual interpretation [Electronic Version, 1–18]. *Communication Theory,* 6(2), 167–187. Retrieved from http://spot.colorado.edu/~moriarts/ abduction.html.

Moser, H. (1999). Thick description and abduction: Paradigm change in social research.

Praxisforschung. Retrieved from http://www.schulnetz. ch/unterrichten/fachbereiche/medienseminar/ paradigms.htm.

Peirce, C. S. (1931/1958). Collected papers of Charles Sanders Peirce, edited by C. Hartshorne and P. Weiss. Cambridge, MA: Harvard University Press.

Shank, G. & Cunningham, D. J. (1996). Modeling the six modes of Peircean abduction for educational purposes. Retrieved from http://www.cs.indiana. edu/event/maics96/Proceedings/shank.html.

Contemporary semioticians have altered the terminology and the order of elements in the abductive argument (e.g., Mick, 1986; Moser, 1999). Because these revisions more closely approximate the description of the abductive process than does Peirce's own model of the argument, the revised model is presented here.

Discussion Questions

1. What meanings do you associate with (a) an illustration or other depiction (such as a charm or pendant) of a human skull? (b) an actual human skull? (c) T-shirts? (d) T-shirts printed with skull-like imagery? (e) funerals? (f) clothing appropriate for attending funerals?
2. Work in groups to compare your answers to Question 1. Record similarities and differences in the meanings that group members attributed to each element, and suggest how similarities and/or differences in your backgrounds (such as home environments, upbringing, geographic location, and ethnicity) may have contributed to your interpretations of the meanings of each element.
3. Abductive inference is theorized as a cognitive process in which a rule is instinctively generated that connects an observation or idea with a meaning. You used abductive inference to answer each of the parts of Question 1. Try to reconstruct your abductions by identifying the rules you may have generated in order to attribute meaning to each of the elements in Question 1.
4. Work in groups to discuss your answers to Question 3 and to generate additional rules that might be used to link those signs with meanings. Share the results of your discussion with the class.

1.5

SHADES OF CHANEL

DESIGN AWARD: EFFECTIVE USE OF HISTORICAL INFLUENCES, 2005

Tracy Jennings, Dominican University

Shades of Chanel is a two-piece tweed suit influenced by the many design touches pioneered by Coco Chanel, including frayed edges, ribbon accents, decorative shirring, uneven hemlines, texture mixing, and gilt trim (Figures 1.8a and b). Examples of her designs were observed in a 2005 Metropolitan Museum of Art exhibition. The exhibition demonstrated how Chanel influenced dress and style during much of the 20th century. The suit features Chanel's trademark couture construction techniques in its bound buttonholes, matched plaids, and chain-weighted hemline.

Design Inspiration

Shades of Chanel was inspired by the designs of Gabrielle "Coco" Chanel (1883–1971) and the Metropolitan Museum of Art exhibition showcasing the designer that ran from May 5 through August 7, 2005. The exhibition demonstrated how the Chanel style came to embody the spirit of the independent, modern woman of the 20th century. Chanel streamlined designs by favoring body-skimming silhouettes over padded shoulders and confining corsets. She pioneered many innovative design touches, including the deconstructionist technique of fraying. The wool two-piece *Day Suit* shown in the exhibit exemplified fraying hems and edges. Chanel also questioned conventional tailoring by blurring the distinction between the inside and outside of the garment.

Tracy Jennings, *Clothing and Textiles Research Journal*, 26 pp. 91–93, © 2008 by (SAGE Publications) Reprinted by permission of SAGE Publications.

She often brought the lining fabric to outer collars and lapels and exposed seams and the inner workings of garments.

Chanel can be credited for defining the modern suit. Although she borrowed many details from menswear, she softened traditional styling with construction techniques used in day wear and fabrics that naturally follow body contours. Fabrications displayed in the museum exhibition include lace, tulle, chiffon, boucle, and loosely woven tweed. Ribbons, gilt trimming, and uneven hemlines were also featured prominently. Chanel often combined different materials to achieve unusual textural effects.

Coco Chanel was also known for fine tailoring and couture finishing. Koda (2005), in the exhibition catalog that accompanied the exhibit, is quoted as saying, "For Chanel, elegance emanated from barely perceptible but labor-intensive finishes" (p. 11). Chanel frequently used quilted linings, hand stitching, and bound buttonholes. The hemlines of her jackets were often balanced with a chain weight. In the museum exhibit, many garment hemlines were finished with fine picot edging.

Description of Design

Shades of Chanel is not a reproduction of any single style or technique. Rather, it attempts to embody the essence of Chanel. It interprets and combines the concepts of fraying, mixing textures, blending the inner and outer, ribbon trimming, shirring, gilt finishes, and even the notable Chanel red color. It juxtaposes a loosely woven signature wool-and-rayon plaid with a watercolor chiffon. Just as Chanel combined tailoring and dressmaking techniques in a single garment, the draped and graduated godets soften the harshness of the structured plaid. The textured suit's hems, godets, and center front are unfinished and frayed.

Chanel's hallmark blending of the inner and outer garment is interpreted into sporadic double-shirred medallions. The delicate chiffon circles break through the textured suiting, leaving frayed edges. The medallions are drawn

closed with satin ribbons that leave just a peek of flesh in the center. The ribbons are finished with gold beads and twists of chiffon. Chanel's penchant for U-shaped décolletages, intentional seaming, gold-trimmed buttons, and shirred sheers is also reflected in the garment (see Figures 1.8a and b).

a   b

Figure 1.8 Front (a) and back (b) views of the *Shades of Chanel* suit design by Tracy Jennings.

Techniques Used

Although the design of *Shades of Chanel* is interpretive, Chanel's couture construction techniques are intentionally emulated. The suit features a quilted jacket lining, bound buttonholes, and machine-picot edging. The plaids of the jacket and skirt are matched horizontally and vertically. Also, so the jacket hangs smoothly over the body, the hemline is weighted with a chain weight that begins at the jacket facing and continues around the jacket hem.

Flat pattern and draping techniques were used to create *Shades of Chanel*. The suit was completed in May 2005.

Reference

Koda, H. (2005). Introduction. In H. Koda and A. Bolton (Eds.), *Chanel*. [Exhibition catalog] New York: Metropolitan Museum of Art.

1. How were details of the classic Chanel suit reinterpreted into the 2005 suit?
2. Learning about a designer's approach to dress can expand understanding of the clothing he or she designed. What did you learn from this article about Chanel that you did not previously know?
3. On a scale of 1–10 (where 1= lowest rating and 10= highest rating), rate the 2005 suit as to how well it used historical inspiration to create a new suit. Would you buy this 2005 suit? Why or why not?

1.6

BODY RITUAL AMONG THE NACIREMA

Horace Miner, University of Michigan

The anthropologist has become so familiar with the diversity of ways in which different peoples behave in similar situations that he is not apt to be surprised by even the most exotic customs. In fact, if all of the logically possible combinations of behavior have not been found somewhere in the world, he is apt to suspect that they must be present in some yet undescribed tribe. This point has, in fact, been expressed with respect to clan organization by Murdock (1949: 71). In this light, the magical beliefs and practices of the Nacirema present such unusual aspects that it seems desirable to describe them as an example of the extremes to which human behavior can go.

Professor Linton first brought the ritual of the Nacirema to the attention of anthropologists twenty years ago (1936: 326), but the culture of this people is still very poorly understood. They are a North American group living in the territory between the Canadian Cree, the Yaqui and Tarahumare of Mexico, and the Carib and Arawak of the Antilles. Little is known of their origin, although tradition states that they came from the east. According to Nacirema mythology, their nation was originated by a culture hero, Notgnihsaw, who is otherwise known for two great feats of strength—the throwing of a piece of wampum across the river to Pa-To-Mac and the chopping down of a cherry tree in which the Spirit of Truth resided.

Nacirema culture is characterized by a highly developed market economy which has evolved in a rich natural habitat. While much of the people's time is devoted to economic pursuits, a large part of the fruits of these labors and a considerable portion of the day are spent in ritual activity. The focus of this activity is the human body, the appearance and health of which loom as a dominant concern in the ethos of the people. While such a concern is certainly not unusual, its ceremonial aspects and associated philosophy are unique.

The fundamental belief underlying the whole system appears to be that the human body is ugly and that its natural tendency is to debility and disease. Incarcerated in such a body, man's only hope is to avert these characteristics through the use of the powerful influences of ritual and ceremony. Every household has one or more shrines devoted to this purpose. The more powerful individuals in the society have several shrines in their houses and, in fact, the opulence of a house is often referred to in terms of the number of such ritual centers it possesses. Most houses are of wattle and daub construction, but the shrine rooms of the more wealthy are walled with stone.

American Anthropologist, New Series, Vol. 58, No. 3 (Jan., 1956) pp. 503–507.

Poorer families imitate the rich by applying pottery plaques to their shrine walls.

While each family has at least one such shrine, the rituals associated with it are not family ceremonies but are private and secret. The rites are normally only discussed with children, and then only during the period when they are being initiated into these mysteries. I was able, however, to establish sufficient rapport with the natives to examine these shrines and have the rituals described to me.

The focal point of the shrine is a box or chest which is built into the wall. In this chest are kept the many charms and magical potions without which no native believes he could live. These preparations are secured from a variety of specialized practitioners. The most powerful of these are the medicine men, whose assistance must be rewarded with substantial gifts. However, the medicine men do not provide the curative potions for their clients, but decide what the ingredients should be and then write them down in an ancient and secret language. This writing is understood only by the medicine men and by the herbalists who, for another gift, provide the required charm.

The charm is not disposed of after it has served its purpose, but is placed in the charm-box of the household shrine. As these magical packets are specific for certain ills, and the real or imagined maladies of the people are many, the charm-box is usually full to overflowing. The magical packets are so numerous that people forget what their purposes were and fear to use them again. While the natives are very vague on this point, we can only assume that the idea in retaining all the old magical materials is that their presence in the charm-box, before which the body rituals are conducted, will in some way protect the worshipper.

Beneath the charm-box is a small font. Each day every member of the family, in succession, enters the shrine room, bows his head before the charm-box, mingles different sorts of holy water in the font, and proceeds with a brief rite of ablution. The holy waters are secured from the Water Temple of the community, where the priests conduct elaborate ceremonies to make the liquid ritually pure.

In the hierarchy of magical practitioners, and below the medicine men in prestige, are specialists whose designation is best translated "holy-mouth-men." The Nacirema have an almost pathological horror of and fascination with the mouth, the condition of which is believed to have a supernatural influence on all social relationships. Were it not for the rituals of the mouth, they believe that their teeth would fall out, their gums bleed, their jaws shrink, their friends desert them, and their lovers reject them. They also believe that a strong relationship exists between oral and moral characteristics. For example, there is a ritual ablution of the mouth for children which is supposed to improve their moral fiber.

The daily body ritual performed by everyone includes a mouth-rite. Despite the fact that these people are so punctilious about care of the mouth, this rite involves a practice which strikes the uninitiated stranger as revolting. It was reported to me that the ritual consists of inserting a small bundle of hog hairs into the mouth, along with certain magical powders, and then moving the bundle in a highly formalized series of gestures.

In addition to the private mouth-rite, the people seek out a holy-mouth-man once or twice a year. These practitioners have an impressive set of paraphernalia, consisting of a variety of augers, awls, probes, and prods. The use of these objects in the exorcism of the evils of the mouth involves almost unbelievable ritual torture of the client. The holy-mouth-man opens the client's mouth and, using the above mentioned tools, enlarges any holes which decay may have created in the teeth. Magical materials are put into these holes. If there are no naturally occurring holes in the teeth, large sections of one or more teeth are gouged out so that the supernatural substance can be applied. In the client's view, the purpose of these ministrations is to arrest decay and to draw friends. The extremely sacred and traditional character of the rite is evident in the fact that the natives return to the holy-mouth-men year after year, despite the fact that their teeth continue to decay.

It is hoped that, when a thorough study of the Nacirema is made, there will be careful inquiry into the personality structure of these people. One has but to watch the gleam in the eye of a holy-mouth-man, as he jabs an awl into an exposed nerve, to suspect that a certain amount of sadism is involved. If this can be established, a very interesting pattern emerges, for most of the population show definite masochistic tendencies. It was to these that Professor Linton referred in discussing a distinctive part of the daily body ritual which is performed only by men. This part of the rite involves scraping and lacerating the surface of the face with a sharp instrument. Special women's rites are performed only four times during each lunar month, but what they lack in frequency is made up in barbarity. As part of this ceremony, women bake their heads in small ovens for about an hour. The theoretically interesting point is that what seems to be a preponderantly masochistic people have developed sadistic specialists.

The medicine men have an imposing temple, or *latipso*, in every community of any size. The more elaborate ceremonies required to treat very sick patients can only be performed at this temple. These ceremonies involve not only the thaumaturge but a permanent group of vestal maidens who move sedately about the temple chambers in distinctive costume and headdress.

The *latipso* ceremonies are so harsh that it is phenomenal that a fair proportion of the really sick natives who enter the temple ever recover. Small children whose indoctrination is still incomplete have been known to resist attempts to take them to the temple because "that is where you go to die." Despite this fact, sick adults are not only willing but eager to undergo the protracted ritual purification, if they can afford to do so. No matter how ill the supplicant or how grave the emergency, the guardians of many temples will not admit a client if he cannot give a rich gift to the custodian. Even after one has gained admission and survived the ceremonies, the guardians will not permit the neophyte to leave until he makes still another gift.

The supplicant entering the temple is first stripped of all his or her clothes. In everyday life the Nacirema avoids exposure of his body and its natural functions. Bathing and excretory acts are performed only in the secrecy of the household shrine, where they are ritualized as part of the body-rites. Psychological shock results from the fact that body secrecy is suddenly lost upon entry into the latipso. A man, whose own wife has never seen him in an excretory act, suddenly finds himself naked and assisted by a vestal maiden while he performs his natural functions into a sacred vessel. This sort of ceremonial treatment is necessitated by the fact that the excreta are used by a diviner to ascertain the course and nature of the client's sickness. Female clients, on the other hand, find their naked bodies are subjected to the scrutiny, manipulation, and prodding of the medicine men.

Few supplicants in the temple are well enough to do anything but lie on their hard beds. The daily ceremonies, like the rites of the holy-mouth-men, involve discomfort and torture. With ritual precision, the vestals awaken their miserable charges each dawn and roll them about on their beds of pain while performing ablutions, in the formal movements of which the maidens are highly trained. At other times they insert magic wands in the supplicant's mouth or force him to eat substances which are supposed to be healing. From time to time the medicine men come to their clients and jab magically treated needles into their flesh. The fact that these temple ceremonies may not cure and may even kill the neophyte in no way decreases the people's faith in the medicine men.

There remains one other kind of practitioner, known as a "listener." This witch-doctor has the power to exorcise the devils that lodge in the heads of people who have been bewitched. The Nacirema believe that parents bewitch their own children. Mothers are particularly suspected of putting a curse on children while teaching them the secret body rituals. The counter-magic of the witch-doctor is unusual in its lack of ritual. The patient simply tells the "listener" all his troubles and fears, beginning with the earliest difficulties he can remember. The memory displayed by the Nacirema in these exorcism sessions is truly remarkable. It is not uncommon for the patient to bemoan the rejection he felt upon being weaned as a babe, and a few individuals even see their troubles going back to the traumatic effects of their own birth.

In conclusion, mention must be made of certain practices which have their base in native esthetics but which depend upon the pervasive aversion to the natural body and its functions. There are ritual fasts to make fat people thin and ceremonial feasts to make thin people fat. Still other rites are used to make women's breasts larger if they are small, and smaller if they are large. General dissatisfaction with breast shape is symbolized in the fact that the ideal form is virtually outside the range of human variation. A few women afflicted with almost inhuman hyper-mammary development are so idolized that they make a handsome living by simply going from village to village and permitting the natives to stare at them for a fee.

Reference has already been made to the fact that excretory functions are ritualized, routinized, and relegated to secrecy. Natural reproductive functions are similarly distorted. Intercourse is taboo as a topic and scheduled as an act. Efforts are made to avoid pregnancy by the use of magical materials or by limiting intercourse to certain phases of the moon. Conception is actually very infrequent. When pregnant, women dress so as to hide their condition. Parturition takes place in secret, without friends or relatives to assist, and the majority of women do not nurse their infants.

Our review of the ritual life of the Nacirema has certainly shown them to be a magic-ridden people. It is hard to understand how they have managed to exist so long under the burdens which they have imposed upon themselves. But even such exotic customs as these take on real meaning when they are viewed with the insight provided by Malinowski when he wrote (1948:70):

Looking from far and above, from our high places of safety in the developed civilization, it is easy to see all the crudity and irrelevance of magic. But without its power and guidance early man could not have mastered his practical difficulties as he has done, nor could man have advanced to the higher stages of civilization.

References

Linton, Ralph. 1936. *The Study of Man*. New York, D. Appleton-Century Co.

Malinowski, Bronislaw. 1948. *Magic, Science, and Religion*. Glencoe, The Free Press.

Murdock, George P. 1949. *Social Structure*. New York, The Macmillan Co.

Discussion Questions

1. Do you know what culture Miner is describing? What were the clues? At what point in the reading did you recognize the culture that was being described?
2. How does it feel to be described in this way?
3. Do you think that an ethnocentric view from outside one's culture can be a healthy exercise? Why or why not?

1.7

ETIQUETTE 101: WHAT THE WORLD THINKS ABOUT US

Boris Kachka

They love our movies. They hate our politicians (well, most of them). But what about our manners? We found out what everyone thinks of our behavior—be it good, bad, or just plain perplexing.

There have been better times to be an American, at least in terms of world opinion, yet tourists and immigrants continue to flock to the United States. And when they do, they find that

Kachka, Boris. (2008, November). "Etiquette 101: What the World Thinks About Us." *Condé Nast Traveler*. Reprinted by permission of Condé Nast Publications.

our mores are a lot more complicated than what pop culture, or the chance encounter with fanny-packing tourists, has led them to believe. For all our vastness and diversity, we do have a culture of etiquette—one that can be just as confusing for the visitor to navigate as Japan's, or Egypt's, or France's is for the American tourist. Which is why this edition of Etiquette 101 is an inside-out affair, an introspective examination of the U.S.A. in the eyes of the rest of the world.

1. They Think We're a "Look, but Don't Touch" Culture . . .

The smile: One of the qualities that sets us most apart is how often we smile—even at strangers. "It really is peculiar to Americans," says Gary Weaver, a professor of international communications at American University, who's trained many a foreigner. Visitors often take a smile very seriously, "and then when they realize that it extends to everybody, [they assume] it's because Americans are phony." But it's just a basic signal of politeness—mixed with perhaps a preoccupation with first impressions. "We're a very mobile society," says James L. Bullock, a diplomat at the American embassy in Paris. "We're always trying to fit in—that's why other people think we're always smiling."

Eye contact: Whereas in other cultures avoiding eye contact—particularly with an elder—can be a sign of respect, here eye contact is mandatory, even if you're just making small talk about the weather.

Personal distance: Weaver warns visitors that Americans are not to be touched beyond the forearm, and estimates personal space here at nearly two feet—twice what it is in the Arab world and in Mediterranean countries. The author Aleksandar Hemon, who emigrated to the United States from Bosnia in his late twenties, noticed that people here flinched at his touch. It's not that Americans are cold or that Eastern Europeans are pushy, he says. It's just a cultural difference related to notions of personal space and privacy. (See Learning Activity 1.1 on p. 11.)

2. . . . And That Our Women Are Teases

In most countries, a scantily clad woman smiling at a stranger is an invitation. "We've had major issues," says Pamela Eyring, director of the Protocol School in Washington, D.C., "especially with the Russians and Serbians." Some men have even given female colleagues the keys to their hotel rooms. Eyring is currently preparing a course on dressing conservatively. "That's an area we're having trouble with in the United States." Weaver finds himself having to emphasize that "when an American woman says no, she means no. It doesn't mean ask me again," as it often does in other cultures.

3. They Think We Make Meaningless Small Talk

Small talk—which Hemon calls "the verbal equivalent of smiling"—is a staple worldwide, but it seems that we Americans do it the most. Take the phrase "How are you?" "In many countries where people say 'How are you,' they really mean 'How are you?'" says Weaver. "We just want people to say 'fine.' It's not an invitation to a health report." Sherry Mueller, head of the National Council for International Visitors, gives detailed workshops on small talk. "I recommend that they read a local newspaper or a magazine. That gives them topics and conversation skills." It's a way to avoid just discussing the weather, or topics you'd rather not hear about, because . . .

4. We Do Have Our Sore Spots

Religion and politics are two topics that often get passionately discussed at European dinner parties but are studiously avoided here. Part of this, of course, has to do with our astonishing diversity: You just don't know what your acquaintance believes, or how strongly he or she believes it. "People who are spiritual tend to share it," Mueller says. "But they usually share it with people they know are of the same religion." The same could be said for politics.

5. They Think We're All Business, No Ceremony

Time management: Compared with the rest of the world, Americans do business at a furious pace. Weaver tries to explain to visitors that "because we measure productivity based on time, when people come to meetings late, we get upset, we feel that you stole our money. Whereas in other countries, time stretches."

Business on the first meeting: "Things that would normally take a lot of time and massaging to get done in your home country, you don't require that here," says Karim Haggag, a press attaché at the Egyptian embassy in Washington, D.C. This means more efficiency but also leads to a feeling of having to strike early to develop sources. "It's always finding the right hook with whomever you're dealing with to take you beyond the initial phone call," he says. "If you don't find that hook—the issue at hand, whether he feels it is a benefit to him—the relationship can be halted very abruptly."

A business lunch is a business lunch: Americans don't always talk business at dinner, but there is no real break in the workday. "Something people are startled by is that we have working lunches," says Mueller. "We are determined to use every possible part of the workday to get something done."

Cards and titles are no big deal: Whether we're throwing them around the room—the "shotgun" approach—or unceremoniously stuffing them in our pockets, we just don't give business cards the attention other cultures do. "The verbal introduction is the most important part, not the business card," says Eyring. It's much more important to remember someone's first name than his title.

Our first question is "What do you do?": "Our identity as Americans has a lot to do with the work we do," says Bullock, "whereas others identify themselves in terms of who they are, their tra-ditions, and where they're from." So naturally, our first question of others is about their jobs—even in social settings.

But we may not talk as much about money as you'd think: Visitors can be forgiven for asking impolite questions about money in a country where making it and spending it seems to be of unusual importance. They're shocked to discover that "how much do you make" is a rude question. In many places, it isn't.

6. They Think We Eat Funny

One of the common misconceptions about our eating habits (aside from the assumption that we eat only junk food) is that we're basically Europeans. So even European visitors or those from other countries who were educated in the "Continental" style may find subtle contrasts:

- We often keep our hands in our laps at the dinner table, which the French consider rude.
- We generally put our knives down after cutting, switch our fork hand, and pierce our food, rather than use the knife in conjunction with the fork to cut our food and scoop it onto our fork.
- We eat much more quietly than people from some cultures: no slurping, loud sipping, or open-mouthed chewing. This seems normal to us but unnecessarily uptight to many others.
- We almost never use a fork to eat a burger or a pizza—or at least that's what their guidebooks warn them about. In truth, we do, but mostly in formal restaurants or situations.
- We don't know how to throw a dinner party—at least not by the highly choreographed, festive, and communal standards of many other cultures. The idea of just getting one serving, on a paper plate—of being told to "help yourself" to something from the fridge—leaves many visitors perplexed. Weaver tries to explain that visits to people's homes are a less planned-out

affair than they are elsewhere. "'Grab a beer, make yourself at home'—we interpret that as meaning you're one of us," says Weaver. "But it comes across in exactly the opposite way."

- We don't cook nearly as often, and we go out or order in a lot more. There's a much broader variety of price points and ordering options here than pretty much anywhere else in the world.

- For Americans, eating on the go may literally involve going while eating. That's one of the reasons so much of our fast food is handheld. In most countries, eating and walking are (sensibly) mutually exclusive activities.

- Whether we're inhaling takeout or drinking green shakes, to many visitors we just don't seem to savor our food. "You eat to lose weight or to keep yourself healthy, not to enjoy food," says Hemon. To be sure, he's talking about a rather upscale demographic, but the other extreme—grabbing a Croissandwich for breakfast, a taco to eat in front of the computer at work, and a Domino's pizza for a late dinner after soccer—is just as strange compared with the practices of many cultures where family meals dominate the day.

. . . And What Is It with Those Doggie Bags?

The takeaway bag for the balance of our dinner is an American phenomenon. Ask a French waiter if you can have the rest of your cake to go and you might find him scooping up scraps from everyone's dessert plates, assuming it's actually meant for your dog. Taking food home is tacky to people in many other countries, who don't go out as often and generally eat smaller portions than we do. The forerunner of the doggie bag actually evolved in the Old World—in ancient Rome, to be precise: Many guests at a banquet would bring their own oversized napkins and, at the end of the night, fill them with leftovers.

7. They Think We Know Less about Them Than They Do about Us

It's true that Americans can't find a good number of countries—or even our own states—on a map. Yes, most of us don't have passports. So that part of the equation is, regrettably, largely correct. But how well do they really know us? "They'll say, 'We know all about you because we watched your movies and we watch CNN,'" says Weaver. "But what they see are sensational stories. They just don't realize until they get to the United States that it's really a distortion, an entertainment." This is why so many visitors are astonished that all Americans don't have guns and that the chances of getting mugged are higher in London than in New York.

8. They Think We Treat Our Pets like Kids, and Our Kids like Princes

Pets are not coddled in many cultures—much less given elective surgery and organic treats or blessed with a master who dutifully carries around their droppings in a bag. And in many places, children aren't dealt with in the same way ours are, either. Bullock is married to a Frenchwoman, and his French relatives and friends like to say that American children "aren't badly brought up, they're not brought up at all." The American idea that "a child is a seed, and you're supposed to water it and tend to it" conflicts with the concept behind the strict French school system: "The child is a wild creature, and you have to tame it." It comes down to: "Are you being broken, or are you being nurtured? My children go to an American school, by the way. I don't want them broken."

9. They Think We Don't Dress Well Enough

When Hemon was attending graduate school in the United States, he often wore a suit to class.

It was, after all, a public space "where you meet people, where relationships are established." But most other people were wearing sweatpants and "would not dress up in an attractive way." Eventually he met them halfway. But his observation wasn't unusual. The contrast is even more striking for, say, the French, who wear makeup to the grocery store.

10. They Think We Don't Respect Our Elders

We don't address them properly: Part of this perception comes from our penchant for first names. It's an extension of our general informality, but it isn't easy for a businessman in his sixties from a culture where people use different verbs depending on their age to get used to a 22-year-old calling him Bob.

We throw them out of the house: Weaver often has to deal with the perception that we put elders away in nursing homes because we don't respect them. And while there might be a grain of truth to that, he sees it differently—more as a by-product of our independent streak. "Most people who are old want to be independent. If you want to kill older people, make them live with their children." He remembers a group of Russians taking offense upon being guided through a cathedral by a senior citizen. "They said, 'Why do you make your old people work?' But they're not working. They're being valuable. They enjoy it. It's a very different world."

Discussion Questions

1. Out of the ten categories listed, is there one or more that offends you the most? Why?
2. Do you think that Americans traveling in other cultures are equally as affected by media stereotypes prior to their travel? Why or why not?
3. How does a person truly open themselves up to genuine interaction with someone from another culture? Brainstorm ideas with a small group to add to a class discussion.

CHAPTER 2

FASHION AS A DYNAMIC PROCESS

Andrew Reilly

After you have read this chapter, you will understand:

- Why fashion is a social process requiring human interaction
- The complex interaction of cultural, industrial, group, and individual factors that fuels fashion change
- That many theories are useful for explaining the fashion change process
- How fashion change has continual impact on meanings of styles
- That not all styles are fashion and that some cultures, groups, and individuals opt not to participate in the larger fashion system

Fashion Lifecycle

Fashion is a social process which encompasses many different groups of people who meet at different junctures, each with their own particular function. Fashion is created and influenced by one's culture, one's social organization, and one's psyche. Though each is necessary for the dissemination of fashion they are not mutually exclusive for they support and interact with each other. And interlaced through culture, society, and one's psyche is the fashion system, which strives to serve the needs of each.

It is virtually impossible to trace the origin of a fashion trend. Fashion, by definition, is what is popular, and popularity is required for something to be observed and documented as a trend. Who was the first to wear or invent a style before it became a trend is often unknown, though historians and fashion critics do have good arguments for some notable apparel items, such as the little black dress (Chanel) or the miniskirt (Courrèges or Mary Quant, depending on your source).

What can be traced and understood with more certainty is the lifecycle of a fashion trend, which mimics a bell curve (see Figure 2.1). A lifecycle can last for a few months or even years.

The process of fashion diffusion begins when fashion innovators wear a new article of clothing or devise a new way of wearing an existing piece. **Fashion innovators** are people who create a new style; they can be fashion designers or individuals with an artistic, unique sense of style. **Fashion leaders** are people who are seen as authorities on clothing matters and are sought out for their opinions. Fashion leaders pick up on the new style and adopt it, increasing the number of people who see the trend. By virtue of them wearing a new style it is exposed to **early adopters**, who increase the visibility of the style. By this point the trend has reached maximum exposure and starts to decline. **Late adopters** are the next category of consumers to adopt the style. They are people who do not feel comfortable wearing a new style until it has been established as a trend. Finally, **fashion followers** adopt the trend during the tail-end when the style is nearing obsolescence. Some people argue that late adopters and fashion followers are people who cannot afford to wear the latest styles; this position may be accurate in some cases, but with the proliferation of fashion styles reaching all price points and markets nearly simultaneously, it is not an absolute.

The life of a fashion trend, however, is different from a fashion classic or fashion fad. A **classic** rarely changes drastically (a few stylish details might be altered); the overall concept remains recognizable from season to season. Blue blazers and white cotton shirts are often considered fashion classics. Their lives are long and strong, remaining fairly constant over time. The flipside of a classic is a **fad**, which has a short, energetic life. It appears on the fashion scene quickly, is adopted by many, and then dies soon after. Fads are easily forgotten and are remembered with horror (and laughter) when reviewing old photographs or yearbooks. Slatted sunglasses were a fashion fad in the 1980s and have made sporadic faddish returns for short periods since then.

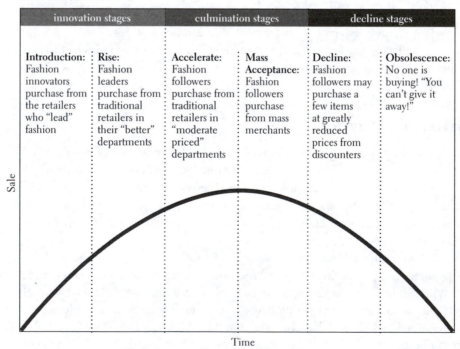

THE FASHION CYCLE

innovation stages		culmination stages		decline stages	
Introduction: Fashion innovators purchase from the retailers who "lead" fashion	**Rise:** Fashion leaders purchase from traditional retailers in their "better" departments	**Accelerate:** Fashion followers purchase from traditional retailers in "moderate priced" departments	**Mass Acceptance:** Fashion followers purchase from mass merchants	**Decline:** Fashion followers may purchase a few items at greatly reduced prices from discounters	**Obsolescence:** No one is buying! "You can't give it away!"

Figure 2.1 The fashion curve illustrates the lifecycle of a fashion, from inception to obsolescence.

A fashion classic can sometimes have trendy or faddish styling. For example, Converse shoes are considered a classic—their shape does not change from season to season, but their color can change to match the latest trend (see Figures 2.2 a–c). The little black dress is considered a classic but its particular rendering—the length of the hemline, the silhouette, the neckline, the fabric—can all change.

Fashion is a complex process that cannot be explained by a single theory. Different theories examine different phases and sections of the fashion process. In order to understand the process, we will use a continuum developed by Jean Hamilton (1997), who organizes fashion from the macro (or group) level to the micro (or individual) level. Hamilton's con-

Figure 2.2 Converse sneakers are considered a classic (a), but the specific styling of them can be fashionable (b and c).

tinuum, as seen in Table 2.1, argues that the cultural system influences the fashion system, which influences social groups, which influences individual choices. Further, these four levels of the continuum are interconnected and work together simultaneously.

Cultural System

The culture of a society will determine whether a fashion system exists. Style change is found most frequently in cultures that value technological progress, individual expression, and capitalistic free-market exchange (Sporles and Burns, 1994; Kaiser, Nagasawa, and Hutton, 1995).

TABLE 2.1

Hamilton's Micro–Macro Continuum

Level		Influencing Factors
Macro-level		
M	Cultural system	• Cultural values and ideology
A		• Tradition versus change
C		• Media, arts, economy, religion, politics
R		• Generation and population trends
O		
•	Fashion system	• Retail buyers, fashion designers
		• Fashion media and promotions
•		• Global production system
•	Negotiation with others	• Conformity
		• Fashion leaders and innovators
•		• Trickle-down theory
		• Trickle-across diffusion
M		• Trickle-up theory
I		
C	Negotiation with self	• Individual choice, tastes
R		• Aesthetic learning
O		• Ambivalence
Micro-level		

Table expanded from Hamilton (1997).

Cultures that allow youthful experimentation and search for identity are also conducive to rapid changes in styles. An economic situation in which a significant portion of the population has discretionary income to spend on nonessentials is also necessary, as fashion change requires expenditure on new styles before clothing is completely worn out. Fashion has a difficult time existing—or must exist underground—in cultures where there is reverence for tradition or there is little freedom of individual expression. Native American and Japanese cultures value tradition and their traditional styles of clothing have remained relatively unchanged for generations. Cultures such as Communist China value the state over the individual, and fashion shows or fashion expression were often risky undertakings that could be met with punishment.

A new style is likely to be adopted when it fits with the zeitgeist (Blumer, 1969). *Zeitgeist* is a German word meaning "time" (*zeit*) and "ghost" (*geist*), translated as "spirit of the times," and fashion is a material reflection of the times. Nystrom (1928) identified five areas that comprise the zeitgeist: dominating events, dominating ideals, dominating social groups, dominating attitudes, and dominating technology. By examining these areas, one can see how they influence and affect fashion choices. The New Look exemplifies the relationship between fashion and the zeitgeist.

The New Look. When WWII ended, a young man named Christian Dior wanted to open his own fashion house. He had worked for other designers and had the knowledge and talent to design, but he did not have the financial capital. He asked a man named Marcel Boussac to fund his business. Boussac was an entrepreneur who owned many textile companies and agreed to finance Christian Dior's business, providing he use lots of fabric and purchase the fabric from Boussac's companies. Dior agreed. He then had to figure out how to design beautiful clothes using lots of fabric. Fortunately, an exhibition of the Belle Epoch was held in Paris at the time; Dior used this era of excess in fashion as his inspiration. And although Dior could design beautiful clothing, he could not be certain that women would wear his clothes. By the time WWII ended women had been dressing in masculine, tubular, close-fitting dresses for nearly a decade due to shortages of fabric and they were ready for a change. When Dior unveiled his first collection for the House of Dior in 1947—full of voluminous skirts, wide collars, pleats, and a definite feminine flair—women were excited. Carmel Snow, then editor-in-chief of *Harper's Bazaar*, called it a "new look" for women. The New Look is an example of the zeitgeist because it combines economics, business, history, aesthetics, and the general attitudes of the day (see Figure 2.3).

Today's zeitgeist is affecting fashion in different ways and is influenced by what Teri Agins (1999) calls "megatrends." In her article "What Happened to Fashion?" Agins presents four megatrends in U.S. culture that

Figure 2.3 Dior's "new look" revolutionized fashion in 1947 and embodied the zeitgeist of the era.

phenomenally changed the fashion system at the end of the 20th century. A complex shift of a variety of cultural patterns changed consumer lifestyles and employment situations, and restructured consumer values and consequent clothing purchases. Within the postmodern climate of questioning authority, consumers stopped looking to top designers to dictate what was fashionable. Tradition-oriented retailers and design firms have lost strong impact, and new influences in fashion leadership are emerging, such as bloggers and virtual stores on the Internet.

Fashion System

The fashion system works simultaneously with the cultural system. It is a globally based set of business establishments, small entrepreneurs, industry and government institutions, trade unions, and other agencies that have an impact on what products the consumer has to choose from in the marketplace. Economic interests drive most fashion system decisions, though government interests such as a trade agreement with, or boycott of, a nation, can also affect choices. George Sproles (1985) refers to this as the Market-Infrastructure Theory. Not everything is available at any given time; rather, the fashion system has pared down from the untold thousands of options and variations what its leaders believe the consumer wants. Rita Kean discusses this further in her article "The Role of the Fashion System in Fashion Change: A Response to the Kaiser, Nagasawa, and Hutton Model" to argue that consumer choice is dramatically limited by the industry because the industry makes many fashion and style decisions based on such matters as cost, production feasibility, government import quotas, and gut-level guesses about what will sell to the mass market, market segments, and niche markets.

Gatekeepers are people who make choices for consumers. In the late 19th and early 20th centuries, at the height of couture, fashion was a top-down business, meaning decisions made by designers such as Charles Worth and Cristobal Balenciaga were deemed infallible; they set the trends in fashion. However, fashion is a different sort of business today, with trends coming from a number of other sources such as cultural niches, political movements, or celebrities. These numerous, varied potential fashion influences make it difficult for one person to predict the next big trend. Fashion forecasters are a type of gatekeeper who help designers, marketers, and buyers make decisions about what will sell in the future. Fashion forecasting services help other fashion businesses by researching the current influences on fashion and organizing the material in books that provide guidance. The books offer "styles" and "looks" that are predicted to become popular. Fashion forecasting services can be very lucrative—providing, of course, that their predictions are accurate.

Designers, marketers, and buyers use the above-mentioned style guides offered by forecasters when making their decisions. This creates an interesting theoretical conundrum: those who use forecasting services know their competition does too and know their competition are looking at the same or similar guides. Therefore, they have a good idea of what their competition will offer and know they need to offer similar products so they do not lose their own consumers. This is one reason why a trend, such as the military trend in the early 2000s, will appear simultaneously in many designers' collections and retail stores—everyone is looking at the same sources of information. Of course, not all businesses can afford forecasting services and some must rely on their own instinct, observation, and skill at assessing the society's current and future climate.

Other gatekeepers include marketers, merchandisers, and buyers. People in these positions looks for opportunities to sell merchandise to consumers. They review designers' lines, edit down what they can sell to their customers, and make suggestions to designers about how to change a product to suit their customers' tastes. Farnaz Fassihi discusses another type of gatekeeper, the salesperson, in the article "In Tehran, Boutiques Stock Hot Outerwear under the Counter." Due to the conservative nature of the Iranian government many fashion items are prohibited, but a relationship with a salesperson can help consumers clandestinely acquire the latest trends. For an additional view about the importance of the client/salesperson relationship, see Patric Richardson's "Tips for Working in Luxury Sales."

Social System

Regardless of how much power gatekeepers have and what they decide to offer consumers, it is ultimately the consumers who make a style fashionable. A number of theories have been proposed and studied in an attempt to understand why styles are adopted and discarded. These theories come from disciplines such as psychology, economics, sociology, marketing, politics, and art.

One of the earliest theories of fashion change is known as the **trickle-down theory** (Simmel, 1904; Veblen, 1912). This theory is based on the idea of social class emulation. High society introduces new styles, which are seen and copied by the middle class. Once the middle class has adopted the style, the lower class adopts it. When the upper class sees their style adopted by the lower classes, they discard that particular style in favor of a new one, and the cycle begins again. This theory is relevant in cultures that have distinct social strata, such as Edwardian England, but today it is difficult to find styles that begin in the upper class. Each social class in the United States may have its own aesthetic and may not necessarily want to look like their social "superiors." A variation of this theory is known as the **trickle-across theory** (King, 1963). King argues that a style can appear simultaneously in all class strata, just at different price points. This is due to designers and merchandisers with a keen understanding of fashion forecasting and with multiple lines for different markets (e.g., Giorgio Armani, Armani Collezioni, Armani Emporio, Armani Exchange; or Polo, Polo Purple Label, Polo Black Label, Polo Blue Label, Chaps, Polo Sport, RLX, and Lauren) and retail giants offering similar trends at different price points in order to capture a larger market share. Another social-class theory is the **trickle-up theory** (Hedbidge, 1979; Sproles, 1985), where fashion begins in the lower classes and is copied by a society's higher classes. An example of this theory is denim jeans. Originally intended as work wear for miners during the California gold rush of 1849, denim jeans were eventually worn by artists, rebellious teenagers, and the mass population.

Sociologist and researcher Herbert Blumer (1969), however, had other ideas about fashion change. He argued that it was not class imitation and differentiation that drove fashion, but rather any group that captures the zeitgeist. As long as their dress reflected the attitudes and desires of the time, they were likely to inspire fashion trends as people outside the group found those attitudes and desires relatable. In the 1970s hippies had an impact on driving fashion, in the 1980s yuppies (Figure 2.4) and punks, and in the 1990s grunge and rap musicians all influenced the fashion scene to some degree.

Blumer called his theory **collective selection**. Sometimes it is referred to as the **subcultural leadership model** (Sproles, 1985). Beth Hughes documents this phenomenon in her article on Japanese Harajuku fashion, "Tokyo A-Go-Go: Cool Teens in Harajuku Make a Fashion Assault from Their Imaginations." Harajuku—a district in Tokyo—became a hot spot beginning in the late 1960s for young people to express their individuality in a culture that prizes conformity and harmony. The irreverent styles found in Harajuku have become a phenomenon that today is influencing worldwide fashion.

Closely related to this is **Social Identity Theory** (Tajfel and Turner, 1986). According to this theory, people strive to either align with or distance themselves from specific categories of people. One way to achieve this is through clothing. As people dress to align themselves with their race or sexual orientation or political views or economic aspirations, etc., the group's style might become noticed by fashion innovators as something unique. Goths, punks, gamers, gay men, and lesbians are just some examples of groups whose distinct style illustrates these concepts. Douglas Haddow writes about hipsters as both a social group and a consumer group in "Hipster: The Dead End of Western Civilization." He argues that this is the first subcultural group created by corporate advertising. Nonetheless, hipster style has become a major force in the fashion industry affecting design, marketing, and merchandising.

Figure 2.4 Young urban professionals, or yuppies, were a source of fashion inspiration in the 1980s due to their unique style that incorporated an upwardly mobile lifestyle.

The Individual

The theories discussed so far examine fashion at the macro (group) level. Now we will examine fashion at the micro level. Whereas the macro level is about negotiations with culture or society or the fashion system, the micro level is about negotiations with the self. The macro level will offer and guide fashion selections, but the individual's unique tastes will also shape the adoption of new styles. Economic, political, sexual, and psychological circumstances can largely determine what consumers can afford and are willing to use. Each individual has his or her own speed at becoming accustomed to and accepting (or rejecting) new aesthetic combinations and forms (Sproles, 1985).

Symbolic Interaction (Kaiser, Nagasawa, and Hutton, 1995) is a theory that strives to explain the relationship between the macro level and the micro level. Contrary to other theories that argue that fashion starts at the social or cultural level, this theory argues that fashion starts at the individual level. In short, the theory proposes the idea that people experience ambivalence when they feel conflicted or pulled in different directions. The marketplace is simultaneously offering new, appearance-modifying commodities to express such ambivalence; appearances created using these products will also convey ambivalence. The meaning of these ambivalent creations will be negotiated in social settings; styles that prove meaningful will be adopted. If the style does not resolve ambivalence then it will be continually modified until it does. For example, a new shirt can be worn different ways—tucked in, untucked, partially tucked, collar up, collar down, sleeves cuffed, etc.—until it is deemed "right" or "appropriate" or "cool."

One could also argue that fashion at the macro level is about conformity and the desire to look like others. Fashion at the micro level can support this desire by adopting what is currently in fashion or it can disrupt the progress by not conforming (Figure 2.5). The desire to be different is addressed by **Uniqueness Theory**, which argues that fashion trends begin when people adopt

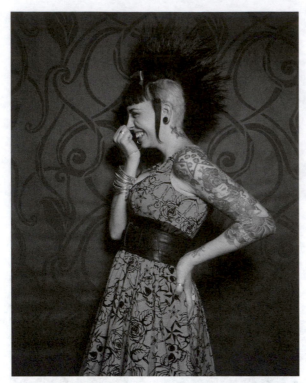

Figure 2.5 Uniqueness is one of the driving forces that prompts a new style and causes an old one to end.

a style that is exclusive or distinctive to current modes. Interestingly—and ironically—is that once the unique style is adopted by enough people to be considered "fashion," it loses its impact as something innovative, and people striving to be different must find something new to wear that expresses their individuality. At this point we can see the relationship between uniqueness and fashion innovators, for fashion innovators are usually people willing to take a risk to look unique or different from others. Thus, the fashion cycle begins anew.

Summary

Macro-level and micro-level factors and influences help shape individual choices about dress. We look to others, to industry offerings, and to cultural themes and trends to help in deciding what to wear. Fashion systems require social interaction. Individuals who are innovative, as well as consumers who are conforming, are both necessary for the process of fashion diffusion. Industry marketers or famous designers alone cannot make fashion trends happen without consumer acceptance and adoption of styles.

The process of fashion change and individual adoption or rejection is complex and involves all levels of society. Characteristics of culture are reflected in the fashion trends of a society. Trends in the arts, technology, and popular culture shape style trends. Large population groups sometimes shape fashion trends because of their vast market potential. Smaller groups— such as segments of the upper class, punk rockers, or rappers—may inspire fashion trends if they capture the zeitgeist. But rejection of the status quo can also inspire fashion change.

Suggested Readings

Balasescu, A. (2003). Tehran Chic: Islamic Headscarves, Fashion Designers, and New Geographies of Modernity. *Fashion Theory* 7 (1): 39–56.

Bikhchandani, S., D. Hirshleifer, and I. Welch. (1992). A Theory of Fads, Fashion, Custom, and Cultural Change as Information Cascades. *Journal of Political Economy* 100 (5): 992–1026.

King, C. W., and L. J. Ring. (1980). The Dynamics of Style and Taste Adoption and Diffusion: Contributions from Fashion Theory. *Advances in Consumer Research* 7:13–16.

Sproles, G. B. (1985). Behavioral Science Theories of Fashion. In M. R. Solomon (Ed.), *The Psychology of Fashion*, pp. 55–70. Lexington, MA: Lexington Books.

Welters, L., and P. A. Cunningham. (2005). *Twentieth-century American Fashion*. Oxford: Berg.

Learning Activity 2.1: The Little Black Dress

Find images of the little black dress throughout the 20th century. What elements of this garment make it a classic? What were some trend influences of the time that were incorporated into it? Illustrate or draw how you would reinterpret the little black dress for the next fashion season. What classic elements would you keep? What trendy elements would you incorporate?

Learning Activity 2.2: Brand Markets

Find images of a trend that appear in all lines of a brand (e.g., Giorgio Armani, Armani Collezioni, Armani Emporio, Armani Exchange; or Polo, Polo Purple Label, Polo Black Label, Polo Blue Label, Chaps, Polo Sport, RLX, and Lauren). List how the trend is reinterpreted for the different markets and discuss your list with your classmates.

References

Blumer, H. (1969). Fashion: From Class Differentiation to Collective Selection. *Sociology Quarterly* 10:275–291.

Hamilton, J. A. (1997). The Macro-Micro Interface in the Construction of Individual Fashion Forms and Meanings. *Clothing and Textiles Research Journal* 15 (3): 164–171.

Hebdige, D. (1979). *Subculture: The Meaning of Style*. London: Methuen.

Horn, M. J., and L. M. Gurel. (1981). *The Second Skin* (3rd ed.). Boston: Houghton Mifflin.

Kaiser, S. B., R. Nagasawa, and S. Hutton. (1995). Construction of an SI Theory of Fashion Part 1: Ambivalence and Change. *Clothing and Textiles Research Journal* 13 (3): 172–183.

King, C. W. (1963). Fashion Adoption: A Rebuttal to the "Trickle-Down" Theory. In S. A. Greyser (Ed.), *Toward Scientific Marketing*, pp. 108–125. Chicago: American Marketing Association.

Nystrom, P. H. (1928). *Economics of Fashion*. New York: The Ronald Press Co.

Simmel, G. (1904). Fashion. *International Quarterly* 10:130–155.

Sproles, G. B. (1985). Behavioral Science Theories of Fashion. In M. R. Solomon (Ed.), *The Psychology of Fashion*, pp. 55–70. Lexington, MA: Lexington Books.

Sproles, G. B., and L. D. Burns. (1994). *Changing Appearances*. New York: Fairchild Publications.

Tajfel, H. and J. C. Turner. (1986). The Social Identity Theory of Inter-Group Behavior. In S. Worchel and L.W. Austin (Eds), *Psychology of Intergroup Relations*, pp. 33–47. Chicago: Nelson-Hall.

Veblen, T. (1912). *The Theory of the Leisure Class*. New York: Macmillan.

WHAT HAPPENED TO FASHION?

Teri Agins

Supermodel Naomi Campbell has a killer body, a sassy strut, and a $10,000-a-day attitude. Famous for being fashionably late for work, she has left more than a few designers in the lurch right before a big show, wondering when—or if—she would appear. But the supermodel wasn't quite so cavalier when it came to Isaac Mizrahi, her buddy and the darling of America's designers. Nobody lit up a runway the way Isaac did during the 1990s. His witty, high-energy fashion shows were always the highlight of the New York collections.

On the evening of April 10, 1997, Mizrahi's fashion spectacle took place near Madison Square Garden, at the Manhattan Center on West 34th Street. At a quarter to six, with more than an hour to spare, the diva of the catwalks made her entrance, in sunglasses, $500 Manolo Blahnik stilettos, and a stunning spotted coat. On cue, bounding down the stage steps, emerged the man in black, Isaac Mizrahi, brandishing a Camel Light like a conductor's baton.

"There she is! *Na-o-mi!*" he exclaimed, swooping in to buss her on both cheeks. "Fab-u-lous." Mizrahi ooohed and ahhed, checking out her genuine leopard wrap. Evidently, the anti-fur era was over and out. Campbell was sporting the most politically incorrect of furs; leopards had been an endangered species since before she was born.

Naomi did a little pirouette, then swung open her vintage coat. The bronze satin lining was embroidered with the name of its famous original owner: Ann-Margret. "I got it in Los Angeles from this dealer," she explained in her girlish-British lilt. Suddenly, André Leon Talley, *Vogue*'s main man-about-Paris, stormed in to boom: "Girl, that coat is *major!*" The trio huddled for a dishy chat, then Mizrahi scooted her off backstage to get made up with the rest of the "girls," models like Kristen McMenamy and Shalom Harlow. As Campbell slipped away, her Hermès tote let out

a "brrring," from her cellular phone. A cigarette ash fell to the floor as Mizrahi spun around, his arms flying as he jabbered some directions to his backstage crew. "I just *love* this," he muttered to no one in particular.

This drive-by vignette from fashion's fast lane harked back to *Unzipped*, the lively 1995 documentary that followed Mizrahi through the exhilarating fits and starts during the months when he prepared his 1994 fall collection. *Unzipped*, which won the audience award at the Sundance Film Festival, captured all the hyperbole, razzle-dazzle, and parody of high fashion, juiced up by the ebullient Mizrahi, a showman so delicious you couldn't make him up.

Straight out of Brooklyn's well-to-do Jewish enclave, Mizrahi got fixed on fashion early in life. His elegant mother decked herself out in Norman Norell and Yves Saint Laurent, while his father, a children's-wear manufacturer, bought Isaac his first sewing machine when he was still in grade school.

By the time Mizrahi was fifteen, he was stitching up a storm, designing a collection called "IS New York" which he sold to friends and a few neighborhood boutiques. He was also an imp and a cutup who in the 1970s starred onstage at the High School of Performing Arts and as an extra in the movie *Fame*. After studying fashion at New York's Parsons School of Design, he moved on to Seventh Avenue, where he became an assistant to designers Perry Ellis, Jeffrey Banks, and Calvin Klein.

Ambitious and fast-tracking, Mizrahi was ready to do his own thing by the time he reached twenty-five. He invested the $50,000 trust fund his late father had left him to launch his eponymous fashion house in a brick-walled loft in downtown

SoHo. His March 1988 debut runway show was one of those rare and unforgettable moments that left fashion editors agog. They knew they had just witnessed the start of something big.

That spring, Bloomingdale's rushed to put Mizrahi's debut collection in its windows on Fifty-ninth Street and Lexington Avenue, where Mizrahi showed up in person to greet shoppers. The most enthusiastic fashionistas swallowed the hype and splurged on their first Mizrahis. Kal Rutenstein, Bloomie's fashion director, remembered: "We sold Isaac to the customer who was aware of what he was doing."

What Mizrahi was doing was cool and high-concept. He had a sophisticated take on American sportswear, inspired by fashion's modern masters Claire McCardell and Geoffrey Beene, with a nod to Mary Tyler Moore, Mizrahi's favorite TV muse. But he also pulled a few tricks from up his own sleeve.

Throughout the 1990s, Mizrahi stood out as America's most prolific idea man, turning out one innovation after another, in a splash of Technicolor delight: paper-bag-waist pants, a tartan kilt strapless dress, fur-trimmed parkas, and boxy jackets. He spiked his fashion-show programs with puns to describe fabrics and colors: "Burlapse," "Fantasy Eyelet," "Lorne Green," and "James Brown." The fashion editors lapped it up, with page after page of pictures and kudos. But among retail buyers, there was decidedly less of a consensus. Barneys New York and Ultimo in Chicago were among the handful of stores whose fashion-forward clientele craved the labels with the most buzz. Accordingly, such retailers could move a few racks of Mizrahi's $800 jackets and $350 pants most every season. But Mizrahi barely caused a blip at chains like Neiman Marcus and Saks Fifth Avenue, where his spirited fashions got buried in the broad mix of up-and-coming designer brands.

Gilding the Mizrahi mystique was his colorful, megawatt persona. With a bandanna headband taming his frizzy black hair, he was an adorable cartoon. Isaac was fashion's funniest Quotron, who chirped frothy declarations with the push of a button, just like Diana Vreeland, the legendary *Vogue* editor of the 1970s whose snappy sound bites ("Pink is the navy blue of India") have

entered fashion's lexicon. "Le Miz"—as *WWD* dubbed fashion's wonder boy—once exclaimed about a chubby fake fur jacket: "It looks *divine* in beast." He held forth to *WWD* about his 1992 spring collection: "It will be all about irresistible clothes. The *only* kind that will sell."

But what merchandise actually sold was of little concern to the members of the Council of Fashion Designers of America and other fashion industry groups, who showered Isaac with a number of "best designer" awards during his first years. All Mizrahi needed now was solid capital backing to take his business to the next stage. "All my life, I dreamed of a design house like that of Calvin Klein, Armani or Yves Saint Laurent," Mizrahi once wrote in a pitch letter to potential financiers. His dream seemed like a foregone conclusion by 1992 when the venerable house of Chanel in Paris stepped in to help, signing on to become Mizrahi's financial partner. Chanel certainly had the expertise, having successfully staged its own renaissance in the 1980s, with management's deft handling of Chanel's perfumes and accessories, bolstered by the ingenious Karl Lagerfeld, who had become Chanel's couturier in 1982. Chanel was poised to parlay Mizrahi's marquee image into profits with the 1994 introduction of "Isaac," a bread-and-butter department store collection of $150 dresses and $300 jackets.

Meanwhile, Le Miz continued to reign as Mr. Fabulous on the high-fashion runways, as he mined his bottomless pit of creativity. And after his wacky performance in *Unzipped*, a star was born. Among his TV and movie credits, playing a fashion designer, naturally, was his bit part in the Michael J. Fox comedy *For Love or Money*. He was also a jovial guest on the TV game show *Celebrity Jeopardy!*, where he was the winner.

But while Isaac, the stylish personality, was in high demand, his clothes weren't. By 1996, Mizrahi's runway collections weren't wowing the fashionistas anymore, as Gucci and Prada were now the favorite flavors of the moment. Meanwhile, the Isaac collection on which Mizrahi banked his future just didn't click with shoppers, who were far too savvy to fork over $150 for a cotton shift designer dress when chains like Bebe and The Limited were turning out similar styles for as little as $49.99. As reality bit harder, Mizrahi had no choice but to close his Isaac division at the end of 1997, leaving his struggling fashion house hanging by a thread.

That's fashion. And that's the curious way success plays out in the fashion world. A designer can be deemed hot by buzz alone—as Mizrahi was from the start—even though the sales of his collections were barely tepid. But people outside the fashion loop would never be the wiser, because fashion coverage in newspapers and magazines was all about style, not substance.

The fact that Mizrahi's sportswear was thoroughly modern should have worked to his advantage, but his business habits were pretty old-fashioned. He saw himself as a latter-day couturier who designed for supermodels and the coolest fashionistas—but not ordinary women. Mizrahi couldn't connect with the critical masses because he didn't relate to them. For example, when retail buyers once begged him to repeat one of his few best-sellers—paper-bag-waist pants—Mizrahi couldn't bring himself to do a rerun. "I just got *bored* with them," he later recollected.

Flashing back to the final scene in *Unzipped*, Mizrahi showed what really mattered to him. There was Mizrahi, in post-fashion-show anxiety at a Manhattan newsstand, hovering over a copy of *WWD*, which applauded his latest collection, proclaiming "the man has a hit on his hands." The camera zoomed in on a giddy Mizrahi, who was bouncing down the street. But what was missing from this happy ending was the only review that counted in the real world: sales in stores.

Mizrahi, aloft in a cloud of chiffon, had yet to get serious about the bottom line. He was an artiste who refused to become another Seventh Avenue garmento. "Look, it is all I can do to make fabulous collections and fabulous clothes," he explained in July 1997. "That is *all* I can do. You know I can't imagine after all these years, *I can't imagine* how it will translate at retail."

On October 1, 1998, the curtain finally came down on Mizrahi's fashion show. Ten years of terrific reviews added up to little; the House of Mizrahi chalked up no more than an estimated $15 million at its peak in 1996—and zero in the profit column. The money men at Chanel, realizing that Mizrahi's moment had passed, slammed the door on America's most beloved Little Fashion House That Could. "Mizrahi unzipped" played like an obituary across the bottom of the front page of *The New York Times*. Out of fashion and headed toward a career in Hollywood, Mizrahi was sanguine—leaving the door open for his possible comeback. "I will always have a great love of fashion. I'll always be a fashion designer," he told *WWD*. [See Discussion Question 3 for an update.]

There's no better example than Mizrahi to show what has been happening lately in the real world of fashion. It's not only the end of the millennium, but the end of fashion as we once knew it.

Mizrahi is a direct descendant of the trickledown school of fashion, the aspirational system in which high-fashion designers, their affluent clients buoyed by scads of publicity in *WWD* and *Vogue*, dictated the way everyone dressed. The old order was starting to unravel when Mizrahi first went into business in 1987. But failing to read the shifts in the marketplace, Mizrahi became the quintessential fashion victim; he arrived on the scene just when fashion was changing. By the early 1990s, a confluence of phenomena arising from retailing, marketing, and feminism began transforming the ways of fashion forever.

For all of its glamour and frivolity, fashion happens to be a relevant and powerful force in our lives. At every level of society, people care greatly about the way they look, which affects both their self-esteem and the way other people interact with them. And it has been true since the beginning of time that people from all walks of life make the effort to dress in style.

Yet fashion, by definition, is ephemeral and elusive, a target that keeps moving. A clothing style becomes fashionable when enough people accept it at any given time. And conversely, fashions go out of style when people quit wearing them. Traditionally, the fashion system has revolved around the imperative of planned obsolescence—the most familiar examples being the rise and fall in skirt lengths, and for men the widening and narrowing of trousers and neckties. Every few years, when the silhouettes change, women and men have been compelled to go shopping and to rebuild their wardrobes to stay in style.

In America's consumer society, which burgeoned after World War II, apparel makers, designers, retailers, and their symbiotic agents, the fashion press, were the omnipotent forces pushing fashion's revolving door. They have been responsible for creating new fashion trends and inducing people to shop until they dropped, to scoop up the novelties the industry promoted. This order was a mighty mandate that prevailed throughout the 1980s, a system which established a consensus that kept millions of consumers moving in lockstep. Perhaps that's what William Shakespeare foresaw when he wrote: "Fashion wears out more apparel than the man."

But in recent years, a number of circumstances caused a revolutionary shift that upset the old order and wrested control away from the forces in the fashion industry. In 1987, designers missed the boat when they failed to sell women on short skirts. They misfired again, a few seasons later, with the somber "monastic" look and other fads, resulting in millions of dollars of losses to the industry. By the mid-1990s the forces of fashion had lost their ability to dictate trends. Increasingly, the roles have reversed. The power now belongs to us, the consumers, who decide what we want to wear, when we buy it, and how much we pay for it. And nowadays, consumers are a lot savvier and more skeptical when it comes to fashion.

Four megatrends sent fashion rolling in a new direction:

1. *Women let go of fashion.* By the 1980s, millions of baby-boomer career women were moving up in the workplace and the impact of their professional mobility was monumental. As bank vice presidents, members of corporate boards, and partners at law firms, professional women became secure enough to ignore the foolish runway frippery that bore no connection to their lives. Women began to behave more like men in adopting their own uniform: skirts and blazers and pantsuits that gave them an authoritative, polished, power look.

    Fashion's frothy propaganda no longer rallied the troops. The press beat the drums

for a decade, but the name Isaac Mizrahi still drew a blank with millions of American women who hadn't bothered to notice.

A defining moment in high fashion occurred in 1992 with the closing of Martha, the venerable dress salon on Park Avenue. Starting in the 1930s, Martha Phillips, a feisty entrepreneur with impeccable taste, began her reign as one of America's leading standard-bearers for snob appeal and Paris originals. And for nearly six decades, elegant women beat a path to the pink-walled emporium on shopping trips that took hours as Phillips and her attentive staffers put their clients together in head-to-toe perfection. Such was the drill during an era when rich women derived much of their self-worth from wearing the best couture labels.

Martha's demise was the latest casualty in a rash of salon deaths, coming just months after the closing of such salons as Loretta Blum in Dallas, Amen Wardy in Beverly Hills, and Sara Fredericks in Boston. Martha Phillips and her exquisite counterparts couldn't hack it anymore because the pace-setting socialites who once spent a fortune on their wardrobes no longer devoted so much time and money to getting dressed up. Park Avenue style maven and decorator Chessy Rayner, who used to be a front-row regular at the Paris fashion shows, was among those who had made the conversion from clothes horse to fashion renegade. In 1992, she recalled: "Today my style is totally pared-down and non-glitz."

As such salons folded, many of their suppliers, namely the couture houses in Paris, faced a precarious future. For most of the twentieth century, Paris designers had set the standard, introducing the full-skirted "New Look" after World War II, the "sack" silhouette of the fifties, the "space age" sleek of the sixties, and the "pouf" party dress in the eighties. Such were the trends that Seventh Avenue manufacturers slavishly copied and adapted for the mass market. But by the 1990s, most Paris designers couldn't set the world's fashion agenda anymore. Styles were no longer trickling down from the couture to the masses. Instead, trends were bubbling up from the streets, from urban teenagers and the forces in pop music and counterculture with a new vital ingenuity that was infectious. The powers in Paris were taken aback when their captivated clients awoke from the spell of couture and defected in droves. And thus, the fortress of French fashion came tumbling down.

2. *People stopped dressing up.* By the end of the 1980s, most Americans were wedded to jeans, loose knit tops, and Nike shoes, which became the acceptable standard of everyday dress even in offices. Leading the charge for informality were men, in their rejection of the business suit, which since the start of the industrial age had been the symbol of masculine authority and the uniform of the corporate workplace.

Starting in the 1980s, the bespectacled computer nerds at the helms of America's buoyant high-tech industries broke the pattern of stuffed-shirt formality in business. Microsoft Corp. founder Bill Gates emerged as the world's wealthiest man—and the personification of the Internet-set look, dressed for success in chinos and sports shirts.

In America's more traditional corporations, the men's fashion revolt first erupted in Pittsburgh, of all places. In the fall of 1991, Pittsburgh-based Alcoa, the giant aluminum concern, became the first major corporation to sanction casual office attire. The move came about after Alcoa had allowed employees who contributed to the United Way to dress casually during a two-week fund drive. The perk proved so popular that Alcoa decided to give its employees the option of never having to dress up again. Even Alcoa's top honchos stopped suiting up. One typical weekday morning in March 1992, Ronald Hoffman, an Alcoa executive vice president, was working in his suite on the thirty-seventh floor wearing a yellow V-neck sweater, an open-neck shirt, and slacks. "There used to be a time when a white shirt went with your intelligence," Hoffman told *The Wall Street Journal*. "But now there's no reason to do this anymore."

Before long, the rest of corporate America had shifted into khakis and knit shirts at least one day of the week, which became known as "casual Friday." Computer giant IBM went so far as to go casual every day, starting in 1995. Levi Strauss & Co., the world's biggest apparel maker, caught the wave in the early 1990s with its loose-fitting Dockers casual pants, which quickly became a popular wardrobe staple for men. It took less than five years for Dockers to explode into a $1 billion-a-year business.

Without enough suit buyers to go around, many of America's fine haberdasheries and boutiques suffered the fate of Martha. Charivari, a flashy New York chain known for its dressy and expensive European designer imports for men and women during the 1980s, planned to ride out the dress-down trend. In 1991, Charivari plastered on billboards: "Ripped Jeans, Pocket Tees, Back to Basics. Wake us when it's over. Charivari." Instead, seven years later, it was Charivari that was over—and out of business.

Indeed, it seemed as though not only dress-up clothes, but good taste, had fallen by the wayside as millions of Americans sank into sloppiness, wedded to their fanny packs, T-shirts, jeans, and clunky athletic shoes. "Have We Become a Nation of Slobs?" blared the cover headline of *Newsweek*, February 20, 1995. The accompanying article provided a mountain of evidence that people were no longer dressing to impress, including a Boston funeral director who said that some families were now asking for their loved ones to be buried without a coat and tie.

3. *People's values changed with regard to fashion.* Most people used to put "fashion" on a pedestal. There was a sharp delineation between ordinary clothes from Casual Corner and Sears and true "fashion" from Paris couturiers and boutiques like Charivari and Martha. But such a divide existed

before so many options for fashion became widely available at every price level. Stores like Ann Taylor, The Limited, Gap, Banana Republic, and J. Crew turned out good-looking clothes that deflated the notion that fashion belonged exclusively to the elite. In effect, designer labels started to seem like a rip-off. Increasingly, it became a badge of honor to be a bargain hunter, even among the well-to-do. Discounter Target Stores struck the right chord with this tagline in its ads: "It's fashionable to pay less."

Many people like Deirdre Shaffer, a thirty-one-year-old part-time psychotherapist from a New Jersey suburb, learned this lesson quite by accident. In 1994, Shaffer and her husband attended a cocktail party at their local country club to which she wore a black dress from Ann Taylor and $12.99 black suede sandals that she had just purchased from Kmart. Earlier that day, Shaffer didn't have enough time to comb the upscale malls where she usually bought her clothes. So, while she was shopping in Kmart for paper towels and toothpaste, she wandered over to the shoe racks, where she found the sandals. That evening, Shaffer was feeling quite satisfied with her budget find. "I got more compliments on the shoes than my dress," she recalled, noting that her friends were "impressed when I told them they came from Kmart."

Indeed, seeing was believing for Shaffer and millions of folks who wised up. It was akin to a Wizard-of-Oz discovery: Behind the labels of many famous name brands was some pretty ordinary merchandise. Increasingly, the savviest shoppers started paying closer attention to details like fabric, workmanship, and value—and thus became less impressed with designer labels. *Consumer Reports*, which is best known for its evaluations of kitchen appliances and cars, helped millions of shoppers see the light when the magazine began testing different brands of clothes for durability, fiber content, and wear. The truism "You get what you pay for" was proven false. In a 1994 test of che-

nille sweaters, *Consumer Reports* concluded that a $340 rayon chenille sweater from the upscale Barneys New York "was only a bit higher in quality" than a $25 acrylic chenille sweater from Kmart. In another trial in 1997, the magazine gave its highest ranking for men's polo knit shirts to Honors, a store brand that sold for only $7 at Target, but whose quality scored well above those versions by Polo Ralph Lauren at $49, Tommy Hilfiger at $44, Nautica at $42, and Gap at $24.

Marketing analysts describe consumers' new embrace of the most functional and affordable clothes as the "commoditization" of fashion. Beginning in the 1980s, more apparel makers shifted most of their manufacturing from the United States to low-cost factories in the Far East, where they were able to provide more quality at an attractive price: good-looking polo shirts and other apparel that were perfectly acceptable to most people—with no sustainable difference between one brand or another. As more people had no reason or burning desire to dress up anymore, they had no qualms about buying their clothes wherever they could get the best deal—just as Deirdre Shaffer did at Kmart.

The commoditization of clothes coincided with the most popular clothing trends of the 1990s: the "classics," "simple chic," and "minimalism." This comes as no surprise. Such mainstream styles are far easier for designers to execute on a commercial scale, in that they are cheaper and safer to produce, with less margin for error in the far-flung factories in China, Hong Kong, Korea, and Mexico, where much of today's apparel is made.

Furthermore, there's a whole generation of people under forty who don't know how to discern quality in clothes. Generation X-ers born in the 1970s didn't grow up wearing dresses and panty hose in high school, nor did they own much in the way of "Sunday clothes." These young people are largely ignorant of the hallmarks of fine tailoring and fit. Jeans, T-shirts, stretch fabrics, and clothes sized in small, medium, large, and extra-large are what this blow-dry, wash-and-wear generation have worn virtually all of their lives. While their mothers and grandmothers donned slips and girdles—and pulled out the ironing board before they got dressed—these young people had already formed the habit of wearing comfortable, carefree clothes.

4. *Top designers stopped gambling on fashion.* Isaac Mizrahi mistakenly believed that there were enough fashion mavens still willing to put their trust in his taste level. But the best-selling designers nowadays know better. Liz Claiborne, Polo Ralph Lauren, and Tommy Hilfiger are among the fashion houses that grew into billion-dollar empires of apparel, handbags, cosmetics, and home furnishings. Such fashion houses just also happen to be publicly traded companies, which must maintain steady, predictable growth for their shareholders. The upshot: The big guns can't afford to gamble on fashion whims. Fashion as we have known it requires a certain degree of risk-taking and creativity that is impossible to explain to Wall Street. Even though the leading designers tart up their runways with outlandish, crowd-pleasing costumes, they are grounded in reality. The bulk of the actual merchandise that hits the sales floor is always palatable enough for millions of consumers around the world, thus generating the bottom line that Wall Street expects.

With so much consumer rejection of fanciful fashions, will the world turn into a sea of khakis and T-shirts? Will Paris couture and the likes of Mizrahi and Charivari ever rise again? And moreover, will fashion ever matter as it used to?

"The fact is that women are interested in clothes, but the average consumer isn't interested in the 'fashion world,'" observes Martha Nelson, the editor of *In Style* magazine. Women want attractive clothes that function in the real world, "not something that is impossible to walk and drive in. You know, clothes that fit into your life."

So, that's why we've come to the end of fashion. Today, a designer's creativity expresses itself more than ever in the marketing rather than in the actual clothes. Such marketing is complicated, full of nuance and innovation, requiring far more planning than what it takes to create a fabulous ball gown, as well as millions of dollars in advertising. In a sense, fashion has returned to its roots: selling image. Image is the form and marketing is the function.

Nowadays, a fashion house has to establish an image that resonates with enough people—an image so arresting that consumers will be compelled to buy whatever that designer has to offer. The top designers use their images to turn themselves into mighty brands that stand for an attitude and a lifestyle that cuts across many cultures. Today's "branding" of fashion has taken on a critical role in an era when there's not much in the way of new styling going on—just about every store in the mall is peddling the same styles of clothes. That's why designer logos have become so popular; logos are the easiest way for each designer to impart a distinguishing characteristic on what amounts to some pretty ordinary apparel.

Having burnished his image through millions of dollars of advertising, Calvin Klein towers as a potent brand name and leverages his CK logo across a breadth of categories—$6.50 cotton briefs, $1,000 blazers, and $40 bath towels—even though there are plenty of cheaper options widely available.

Image, of course, works in conjunction with the intrinsics—the style, quality, and price of each actual item—and image comes from everywhere: the ambiance of the location where the clothes are sold, the advertising, the celebrities who wear the clothes, and so forth. Image is how the Gap sells a $12.50 pocket T-shirt, how Ralph Lauren pushes a $40 gallon of wall paint, and how Giorgio Armani moves $1,500 blazers.

These designers assault the American public with their ubiquitous advertising, most typically seen in the fashion press. But the roles have reversed there as well. Fashion publications like *WWD*, *Vogue*, *Harper's Bazaar*, *GQ*, and the rest have lost their power in their editorial pages to make or break fashion trends—the same power designers have lost to the consumer. Nowadays, the mightiest fashion brands, by virtue of their heavy-duty advertising, take their message directly to the public—unfiltered by the subjectivity of the editors: Ralph Lauren's ten-page advertising inserts in the front of *Vogue* and *Vanity Fair* are more arresting than any fashion spread featuring his clothes in the editorial pages of the magazine.

It was always confounding, this business of selling fashion. And now the industry has become fragmented into so many niches in which scores of companies churn out more and more merchandise at every price range, season after season. The fashion-industry powers at the head of the class prevail because they swear by retailing's golden rule: The consumer is king.

The following chapters (in *The End of Fashion*) capture some of the industry's best-known players in recent years, as they've succeeded—and sputtered—in their quest to make fashion for profit, as well as for glory. Fashion, which began in the hallowed ateliers of Parisian couture, now emanates from designers and retailers from around the world, reaching the masses at every level. In today's high-strung, competitive marketplace, those who will survive the end of fashion will reinvent themselves enough times and with enough flexibility and resources to anticipate, not manipulate, the twenty-first-century customer. There's just no other way.

Reference

Agins, T. (1999). *The End of Fashion*. New York: Quill

Discussion Questions

1. Has fashion died, or has it become something other than it was during the 1950s? Look at our definition of fashion. Think of how that definition fits with the four megatrends that Agins outlines. Is fashion still alive and relevant? If so, what is it?
2. Is "casual" the opposite of "fashion"? Explain.
3. For an update on designer Isaac Mizrahi, see "Movin' On Up" in *Vogue*, March 2003, pp. 554–561 and 593. Mizrahi now designs a line for Target while also reviving his upscale line. How might designing for Target help Mizrahi fit more successfully into today's fashion system?

2.2

THE ROLE OF THE FASHION SYSTEM IN FASHION CHANGE: A RESPONSE TO THE KAISER, NAGASAWA AND HUTTON MODEL

Rita C. Kean

The public is told that each season's fashions are new, different. But they are not really new. All the filling in is done on the same basic patterns . . . It is the proud boast of some wholesalers that they make up a whole line with only three dress patterns. The newness, so loudly called for, is new trimming, new collars and cuffs, new glass buttons, new flowers, and all of this, not too new, please . . .

Elizabeth Hawes, 1938
(as quoted in Gregory, 1948)

Introduction and Premise

Kaiser, Nagasawa and Hutton (1995) have presented an extremely thoughtful and comprehensive

Rita Kean, *Clothing and Textiles Research Journal*, 15 (3) pp. 172–177, copyright © 1997 by (SAGE Publications). Reprinted by Permission of SAGE Publications.

model of fashion change. The major premise of the Kaiser, Nagasawa and Hutton model is that the global nature of capitalist society facilitates a heterogenous range of products. The postmodern condition contributes to cultural ambiguity, which in turn leads to use of appearance modifying commodities to symbolize self meaning. Kaiser, Nagasawa and Hutton believe that there is an assortment of differentiated products available to the consumer in the marketplace. Furthermore, consumers individualize their selections and intensify the symbolic ambiguity through negotiation and manipulation of the selected items. The Kaiser, Nagasawa and Hutton model accounts for the consumer's role in fashion change with minor attention directed toward the role of production and distribution systems in fashion change.

This paper is a response to the Kaiser, Nagasawa and Hutton model. It is not an attempt to reconstruct their theoretical model, but to offer another perspective on fashion change. Kaiser, Nagasawa and Hutton (1995) and others (Guisinger & Blatt, 1994; Triandis, 1989) believe that modern Western culture promotes individualism. According to Triandis (1989), an individualistic culture is characterized by complexity, affluence and to a lesser degree, mobility (within and among social classes). The more complex and affluent the culture, the more emphasis there is on individualism, self-reliance, independence and creative self-expression. Self-identity is often reflected through manipulation of possessions such as appearance and dress.

I agree that the individual differentiates him/herself through manipulation of his/her appearance and dress. I do not agree with Kaiser, Nagasawa and Hutton that the consumer chooses articles of appearance and dress from a heterogenous assortment of products in the marketplace, but, rather, that the consumer selects products from a homogeneous assortment of like items at varying price points. The ideas presented in this paper reflect my belief that industry, rather than the consumer, is the more powerful change agent in the fashion system.

Due to technology and globalization of world markets, there is increased homogeneity of goods produced by the fashion system.[1] The premise for my statement is as follows: Appearance modifying commodities or goods produced by the fashion system are homogenous. Increased homogeneity is the result of access to new technologies by the more powerful and influential actors in the fashion system. Goods are generally edited at each level of the fashion system by the prior actor(s) in the sequence, or by more powerful or influential actors at the same level. The combination of technology and the degree of industry's influence in the fashion system contributes to product homogeneity. Technology simplifies the complexity of production and distribution in the fashion system. Products in the marketplace, that is, appearance modifying commodities, are only slightly different from each other. Therefore, lack of product differentiation intensifies the need for individual expression on the consumer level.

This paper is divided into three sections. Section one focuses briefly on competition in the fashion system, followed by a discussion of technology in the fashion system in section two. To illustrate the dynamics of the association between the role of technology in distribution and fashion change in the third section, a conceptual model is presented. Summary statements are offered to tie together the ideas presented in the paper.

Competition in the Fashion System

How much actual differentiation is there in the apparel market? Although a broad range of apparel goods is available, there exists in the range a common theme that categorizes apparel as either fashion (perceived newness) or nonfashion (staple items). From the consumer perspective, there may be heterogeneous assortments of useful products; however, industry already has sorted goods for the consumer. We live in a world of mass-produced, substitute goods that are available at many price levels. From the perspective of actors in the fashion system, mass-produced goods are categorical and distributed in bulk. Triandis (1989) lends support to this argument. He states that in an individualistic culture when "complexity reaches very high levels, moves toward simplification emerge as reactions to too much complexity" (p. 512). His statement is applicable to the fashion system. With few exceptions, such as the [declining] haute couture, production is based on projected demand in relationship to economies of scale. In the modern fashion system, advanced technology, pressure from substitute goods, economies of scale and the balance in bargaining power between suppliers and buyers (Porter, 1985) drive industry competition. Although consumers perceive choice at the point of purchase, choice has been manipulated by industry.

White (1959) suggests that the role of merchants in society is to consolidate and streamline the functions of marketplace exchange by offering bulk assortments of goods to the members of society. Acquiring and selling these assortments of goods fosters competition among the merchant group, eliminating those merchants whose offerings do not meet needs and wants of society. White contends that as stronger merchants emerge, marketplace power becomes concentrated among a few merchants, leading to a monopoly of the market by a few. Gregory (1948) describes the fashion industry as an example of (modified) monopolistic competition. He believes fashion is a device to stimulate obsolescence and premature replacement of differentiated products and services. Those outside the fashion system see replacement as indicative of social and/or cultural change, but for those inside the system, the primary motive is profit. Competition in the fashion industry is not based solely on price changes, but also on societal interpretation of changes in the environment.

The more powerful the merchant, the more forceful its presence will be in the marketplace. Because of channel dominance by large manufacturing and retailing firms in the fashion system, fashion is determined before it reaches the consumers' level. This phenomenon was reported by Blumer (1969), who observed the Paris fashion industry and was astonished that managerial staff could identify which 30 out of 100 models apparel buyers would select as their core group for final edit. Fashion, according to Blumer, is a collective synthesis of historical and modern forms which bring order to an evolving society. The forms are edited as they pass through the fashion system to consumers.

The same principle holds true today as sophisticated technology and management systems replace intuitive "mavens" of the past. Apparel lines are computer-modeled and edited, and runs are projected before the retail buyer's selection of items. Retailers, in turn, present segments of "like" merchandise to predetermined groups of consumers. Success in the fashion industry is heightened by ability to anticipate change (Robinson, 1961). The ultimate goal of entrepreneurs in the fashion system is to offer a timely, profitable product that generates meaning for, and ultimate acceptance by, the masses, that is, fashion.

Technology and the Fashion System

A major contributor to globalization of the fashion system is technology. Technology is no longer culture bound, particularly in textile, apparel and retail industries (Ostroff & Emert, June 15, 1995). Levitt (1989) argues that technology forces homogeneity in the consumer goods' market. Low price goods at the highest available quality contribute to consumers' preference for standardized products on a worldwide basis. There may be minor product changes to suit national tastes, but the most successful marketers are those who sell essentially the same product abroad as they do domestically.

Consumers are attracted to technology in easing everyday tasks, contributing to more discretionary time and purchasing power. As the world becomes "smaller" consumers become more aware and desire "like" products. Over time, blending of tastes and traditions tends to standardize products, manufacturing and trade practices. Levitt (1989) states:

> Different cultural preferences, national tastes and standards, and business institutions are vestiges of the past. Some inheritances die gradually; others prosper and expand into mainstream global preference. So-called ethnic markets are a good example . . . They are market segments that exist in worldwide proportions. They don't deny or contradict global homogenization but confirm it. (p. 7)

Levitt cites Levi Jeans®, McDonald's®, Coke® and pizza as prime examples of global products that have been mass produced and distributed at relatively low cost. In other words, those with influence, power and greater resource base will have an impact on the types of goods and services available to global consumers.

One role of retailers is to serve as a cultural broker, to clarify cultural ambiguity through visual and verbal cues. Successful retailers have done this through defining a niche for themselves and not trying to be all things to all people. For example, the product assortments of The Gap® and The Limited® follow a market segmentation strategy. Their target markets are clearly defined, and their focus is on private label, narrow and deep assortments, moderate price points, a "safe" degree of fashion innovation and sophisticated management information systems (Salmon & Cmar, 1987). In both cases, merchandise sales must generate sufficient revenue to offset production costs. Economies of scale enter into decisions as to what goods are produced and disseminated.

Achabal and McIntyre (1992) contend that to gain a sustainable competitive advantage firms need to embrace technology.

> Massive data storage capacity along with data compression techniques and advanced data servers will support real-time access to huge databases. (p. 110)

The goal of technology is not just to supply data, but to generate usable information in the form of simulations and models. Achabal and McIntyre (1992) identify three emergent trends in the information relationship between vendors and retailers that have significance for the fashion system. These are:

1. From Electronic Data Interchange to Quick Response. Reduction of time needed in the "merchandising pipeline" (production and distribution cycle) is projected to improve inventory turns and markdown performance. Use of third party networks, that is, central mainframes that receive, process and dispense information from both retail stores and vendors is expected to increase, thus providing cost reductions and time effective procedures for ordering, producing and shipping merchandise.

2. From Slow to Rapid Product Development Cycles. The major factor in competition will be time. Through use of sophisticated electronic communications and computer driven machinery, merchandisers will be able to access goods and services worldwide. Computer manufacturing technology will be able to provide more goods in smaller and smaller lots. It will not be as necessary to place large orders for better price. More retailers will be able to access goods more quickly and more cheaply.

3. From Vendor Push to Retailer Pull. On large orders of goods, buyers often let vendors fill in distribution. With electronic information and capacity for simulation and model building, retailers can decide their own breakdowns, thus having more control in purchase decisions.

If the scenario offered by Achabal & McIntyre is valid, vendors and retailers have to move to relationship marketing using electronic tracking systems to monitor not only goods that have sold, but also individual customer's lifestyles. Schultz (1992) predicts that manufacturers will form strategic alliances to protect them from retail giants to develop market equilibrium, or become expert at using direct marketing methods to reach end-use customers. At a meeting of the International Apparel Federation, the CEO of V.F. Corporation, Mackay McDonald, stressed the need for U.S. apparel manufacturers and retailers to ally with each other to serve the domestic and global markets (Ostroff & Emert, June 15, 1995). A report by Arthur Anderson & Co. (1994) suggested that small retailers protect themselves from larger competitors by seeking alliances with key vendors to share information about markets, customers and trends. These alliances may require capital investment in appropriate technology by small retailers. Retailers' long range dividends of having up-to-date information would exceed the initial outlay for equipment.

Positioning of key actors in the fashion system raises some thoughts about who has access to fashion goods. The assumption made by Kaiser, Nagasawa and Hutton is that all consumers have access to the same goods at the same time. A significant question to raise is, how much of the ability to access fashion goods and to affect fashion change is a function of dynamics of the distribution channel, rather than acceptance or rejection by the consumer?

It is important to examine those levels of the marketing channel that process products and deliver these to consumers. Acceptance in the consumer marketplace is the ultimate test for an item to become fashion. Consumer acceptance is not serendipitous, but rather it is a result of conscious efforts of those in the production and distribution system to provide consumers with what they think they want to properly present the self. This is not a conspiracy, but rather a result of natural dominance of manufacturing and retail companies due to technological advancement and largess.

Gronmo Typology of Strategic Positioning in an Information Society

The Gronmo (1987) typology of strategic positions within the distribution system is used to sort out possible congruities and conflicts among various actors in the fashion system that affect fashion change. This typology can be useful in illustrating the dominance of firms in the fashion system and their influence on fashion change.

Gronmo (1987) proposed a conceptual framework for studying the position of consumers in a society in which technology drives production and distribution of goods. He asserts that technology and society have an interdependent relationship.

The structural changes related to the use of computer technology in various economies and social processes may alter the general conditions for human activity and social interaction, including activities and interaction involved in shopping and consumption. (p. 44)

Gronmo conceptualized the impact of technology on the distribution process, and in turn, the effect on consumers and the other actors in the chain based on theories of group interests and power relations. He defined the strategic position of a group as its ability to advance its own interests in relation to other groups in society. Interest is defined as whatever is profitable to a group or whatever helps the group get what it wants or will eventually find valuable.

Specific interests are determined by roles of buyers of goods and services and by the relationship between buyers and sellers of goods and services in the marketing channel. Stem & El-Ansary (1982) describe marketing channels as social systems in which the behavior of one member affects the actions of other channel members. Channel member satisfaction with the relationship(s) between and among members is a function of the strength of each member's power base and level of dependency on the other channel member(s). Satisfaction with relationships is measured by the degree of conflict or cooperation between channel members.

The greater the dependency of one channel member on others, the more the dependent channel member will strive for a cooperative relationship with the more powerful channel member, thereby avoiding conflict (Frazier, Gill & Kale, 1989).

Gronmo (1987) believes that conflict characterizes the natural state of channel relationships where the strategic position of the group and the group's interests are at stake. When channel members' interests are congruent, the level of conflict diminishes. Gronmo theorizes that "the more common the interests and greater collectivity among effected parties, the better the strategic position" (p. 47). He states that relationships change over time and are dependent on a number of different factors, such as politics, technology, economies of scale and degree of social change.

Strategic position depends on the pattern of common and conflicting interests with respect to both sets of relationships. To support his thesis, Gronmo depicts channel relationships between consumers and other actors in his typology of strategic positions (Figure 2.6). The four strategic positions are Potentially Influential, Potentially Powerful, Protected and Powerless. He believes that potentially influential and potentially powerful relationships are strengthened by commonalities that advance the group's interest through organized action. The strength of Gronmo's model is that it highlights the impact of technology on the polarization between the powerful and the less powerful. As I reflected on Gronmo's model, it occurred to me that his typology of consumers and their strategic position in the market channel can help explain the strategic position of retailers to other actors in the fashion system. The dynamics of relationships between retailers and members of the fashion system can be examined, as well as relationships among retailers themselves in affecting fashion change. Thus, consumer choice in the marketplace is affected by the results of the interplay among the actors in the fashion system. In the next section, each of the typologies in Gronmo's model is briefly explained, and then examples are given of how these typologies apply to the relationships in the fashion system.

Potentially Influential Retailers have potential influence when their interests are congruent. A collaborative relationship is formed which influences market offerings. An example would be membership in a buying group, particularly where a major function is to develop private label programs. Generally, items chosen for private label development are fashion items. Dependent on the level of retail (for example, specialty versus mass merchandising), items are already accepted by consumers or there exist firm indications that they will be accepted by consumers. Private label goods are generally produced in narrow and deep assortments. Thus, the influence of the retailer is dependent on the degree to which other actors or channel members in the system, such as manufacturers, wholesalers, importers and government agencies, are dependent on the retailer's relative economic position in the marketplace. Obviously, large retail organizations, such as Federated Stores or WalMart, have greater influence in market direction than the small independent retailer.

Potentially Powerful Retailers can be united as a group and yet have conflicting interests with other channel members. They are then considered as potentially powerful in advancing their group's interests. Gronmo contends that real power lies with those who are dominant forces within the channel, particularly those in collaboration with authorities. The more power an organization has, the more influence it has to determine inter- and intra-exchange relationships (Emerson, 1962). Retailer power is manifested in the ability to advance group interests through organized action. The import/export situation is an example of a conflicting interest between retailers and other channel members, such as apparel manufacturers. This is evidenced in lobbying efforts of organized coalitions such as The Fiber, Fabric and

		Relationships Among Retailers	
		Common Interests	Conflicting Interests
Relationships Between Retailers and Other Channel Members in the Fashion System	Common Interests	POTENTIALLY INFLUENTIAL membership in buying groups	PROTECTED Robinson-Patman Act 1936
	Conflicting Interests	POTENTIALLY POWERFUL Retail Industry Trade Action Coalition	POWERLESS vertical integration by manufacturers/ retailers

Figure 2.6 Gronmo's typology of strategic positions for groups (group interests vs. power relations) in the information society as applied to retailers in the fashion system.

Apparel Coalition for Trade (FFACT), a manufacturing led group formed to support the Textile and Apparel Trade Enforcement Act of 1985 that would have placed more control and restrictions on imported goods. The Retail Industry Trade Action Coalition (RITAC), composed of retailers and importers, was constructed to counteract FFACT's lobbying efforts (Dickerson, 1995).

Protection Retailers may have diverse interests within their group on particular issues that conflict results. Conflicting interests among retailers may occur in combination with common interests between retailers and other channel members. As a group, retailers may hold differing positions on legislative policy. Unless there is some protection for small independent retailers, the more dominant retailers would receive an unbalanced share of benefits. For example, legislative protection exists for smaller retailers who might be denied access to their fair share of advertising dollars. Under the Robinson-Patman Act of 1936, manufacturers must distribute advertising dollars on an equally proportionate basis to all retail clientele (Kotler & Armstrong, 1987).

Powerless When there are conflicting interests among retailers and between retailers and other channel members, independent retailers may find themselves powerless. As a single unit, the small independent retailer has no power in the market and is subject to decisions already made by more powerful retailers and manufacturers. A recent trend among large manufacturers and retailers is to vertical integration of operations. Once channel partners, manufacturers and retailers are now competing for control of brand name, image and customer contact (Reda, 1995). How does a local retailer who has enjoyed a good track record with a particular brand name compete with the retail division of the same brand name's company that produces and distributes the same or similar goods? How does the same retailer compete with the larger retailer who has the technology and resources to identify and quickly respond to consumer wants with private label goods at a value price? If large manufacturers and/or retailers are setting direction for production and dis-

tribution of apparel, then can a small retailer truly find product uniqueness and differentiation in the wholesale market? Finally, how much choice do consumers have among products in the marketplace? There may be many retailers, but the styles of dress they carry are very similar as a result of market leaders setting direction and consumer response to the direction.

Conclusion

The major point of the previous discussion is that the ability to influence and advance the agenda of a group is dependent on the degree to which the group's interests are in common with the more powerful group in the fashion system. In our complex society, market leaders are those more highly sophisticated firms with technological resources and flexibility to efficiently anticipate, create and/or respond to consumers' wants. These firms have greater influence in the marketplace than firms that are dependent on market leaders to pave the way for their later entry into the market. Given economies of scale, there is more incentive for larger firms to simplify the manufacturing process through mass production of goods. This, in turn, leads to standardization and homogenization of marketplace offerings.

Those who have access to information, production efficiency and distribution will naturally evolve as dominant forces in the fashion system. The outcome of technology innovation is, and will increasingly be, more standardized products distributed on a global level to defined market segments.

The intent of this paper was to respond to the Kaiser, Nagasawa and Hutton model of fashion change from the viewpoint that industry is the more powerful change agent for fashion, not consumers. Technology and globalization of markets are two factors that affect the ability of firms in the fashion system to obtain powerful market position through rapid production and distribution of "like" goods to sell to consumers on a worldwide basis. Consumers' selection of fashion goods in the marketplace is limited to what is being mass produced and distributed. The true differentiation of the product is reached through manipulation by consumers seeking individuality.

References

Achabal, D., & McIntyre, S. (1992). Emerging technology in retailing: Challenges and opportunities for the 1990s. In R. A. Peterson (Ed.), *The future of U.S. retailing: An agenda for the 21st century.* New York: Bantam Books.

Arthur Anderson & Co. (1994). *Small store survival.* Chicago: Illinois Retail Merchants Association.

Blumer, H. (1969). Fashion: From class differentiation to collective selection. *The Sociological Quarterly,* 10, 275–291.

Dickerson, Kitty. (1995). *Textiles and apparel in the global economy* (2nd Ed.). Englewood Cliffs, NJ: Prentice-Hall.

Emerson, R. (1962). Power-dependence relations. *American Sociological Review,* 27, 31–41.

Frazier, G. L., Gill, J. D., & Kale, S. H.. (1989). Dealer dependence levels and reciprocal actions in a channel of distribution in a developing country. *Journal of Marketing,* 53, 50–69.

Gregory, P. (1948). Fashion and monopolistic competition. In G. B. Sproles (Ed.), *Perspectives of Fashion.* Minneapolis, MN: Burgess.

Gronmo, S. (1987). The strategic position of consumers in the information society. *Journal of Consumer Policy,* 10, 43–67.

Guisinger, S. & Blatt, S. J. (1994). Individuality and relatedness: Evolution of a fundamental dialectic. *American Psychologist,* (42)9, 104–111.

Kaiser, S. Nagasawa, R., & Hutton, S. (1995). Construction of an SI theory of fashion: Part 1 ambivalence and change. *Clothing and Textiles Research Journal,* (13)3, 172–183.

Kotler, P., & Armstrong, G. (1987). *Marketing: An introduction.* Englewood Cliffs, NJ: Prentice-Hall.

Levitt, R. (1989). In J. Sheth & A. Eshghi, (Eds.), *Global marketing perspectives.* Cincinnati: South-Western.

Ostroff J., & Emert, C. (1995, June 15). More consolidation around the comer, IAF parley is warned. *Women's Wear Daily,* pp. 1, 8.

Porter, M. (1985). *Competitive strategy.* New York: Free Press.

Reda, S. (1995, June). When vendors become retailers. Stores. Washington, D.C.: NRF Enterprises, pp. 18–21.

Robinson, D. E. (1961). The economics of fashion demand. *The Quarterly Journal of Economics,* 75, 367–398.

Salmon, W. J. & Cmar, K. A. (1987, May–June). Private labels are back in fashion. *Harvard Business Review,* (3), 99–106.

Schultz, Don (1992). The direct/database marketing challenge to fixed-location retailers. In R. A. Peterson (Ed.), *The future of U.S. retailing: An agenda for the 21st century.* New York: Bantam.

Stem, L.W. & El-Ansary, A. I. (1982). *Marketing channels.* Englewood Cliffs, NJ: Prentice-Hall.

Triandis, H. C. (1989). The self and social behavior in differing cultural contexts. *Psychological Review,* (936), 506–520.

White, L. (1959). *The evolution of culture.* New York: McGraw-Hill.

Endnote

1. Fashion system refers to the channel structure in the textile and apparel industry. A channel structure is "a set of agencies, institutions, and establishments through which the product must move" (Stern and El-Ansary, 1982, p. 3) to reach the consumer.

Discussion Questions

1. What are the significant differences between Kaiser et al.'s view of fashion change and Kean's view of fashion change? With whom do you agree?

2. What role does technology play in fashion change? Provide examples of how technology has changed fashion styles.

IN TEHRAN, BOUTIQUES STOCK HOT OUTERWEAR UNDER THE COUNTER

Farnaz Fassihi

Katayoun Alf, a designer of Islamic outerwear in one of the world's strictest Islamic states, knows her customers. They are women such as Sepideh Karimi, a 28-year-old with golden highlights in her hair who strolled into a boutique here recently. The racks in this store in a suburban mall were crammed with women's clothing that would shock the founding fathers of Iran's Islamic revolution. Traditional Islamic women's wear is a long, loose and shapeless black or brown *hijab* that reaches the ankles. The garb's main purpose is to hide curves and smother all sexuality. But Ms. Karimi, like more and more young women in Iran's urban centers, wants something different.

"This is too loose," said Ms. Karimi as she modeled a blue coat, known as a "manteau," that hangs just below her hips, hugging her figure. "The sleeves are too long. I'm looking for something more sexy and see-through."

Women's wear has long been an Iranian social and political battleground, especially among the country's educated and relatively well-off urban elite. Millions of religious Iranian women still willingly wear hijab every day as part of their devotion to Islam. But for women who chafe at government-dictated religious rules, stretching the dress code has become a passion. And, try as it has, the conservative government hasn't been able to put a stop to it.

Hijab, a word that means "veil," is an outgrowth of Islamic Sharia law, which requires all females over the age of 10 to conceal their hair under a scarf and wear a long, loose cloak that extends to the ankles. Reza Shah, founder of the Pahlavi dynasty in Iran and father of the Shah whom the Iranian revolution ousted in 1979, was keen on making Iran a secular, modern society. Headscarves, to him, were a sign of backwardness, and he ordered soldiers to rip them off women's heads. But when religious leader Ayatollah Khomeini came to power, Islamic revolutionary forces reversed the edict.

The hijab law written into Iran's constitution after the Islamic Republic's victory in 1979 made many Iranian women even more determined to bend the rules, an inch at a time, starting with the hemlines. The government pushed back. At first, stores and restaurants shunned women who weren't properly dressed, and a now-defunct police unit, known as "moral police," set up checkpoints to stop, fine and even arrest women who violated the rules. That didn't work, restrictions were eased, and women went wild.

"Everyone wants tight, tight, tight," said the salesman at the mall. "Let me show you Ms. Alf's most popular style," he told Ms. Karimi. "It's flying off the shelves."

With that, he pulled a definite no-no off the rack: a paper-thin beige tunic made of stretchy material with two slits on each side. It comes with a matching tank-top to wear underneath and sleeves decorated with brown Indian motifs. Ms. Karimi's eyes lit up. She quickly tried it on, then paid $35 to make the outfit her own.

Ms. Alf, a 46-year-old former computer engineer, is one of a handful of Iranian designers determined to transform hijab from shapeless to chic. These designers have a lot to do with the surprising, and to the conservative Iranian government, appalling, fashion display in the streets of Tehran and other big cities.

"The trend began two years ago when the government eased social restrictions. Suddenly we looked around us and said 'wow!'" said Ms. Alf, a tall, Iranian-born woman with layered brown hair and a round face, clad in one of her own designs: a black linen, knee-length coat with matching slacks. "Women are fed up," she continued. "They come to the shops and say, 'the sexier the better,' and we meet their demands or we won't sell a single item."

Soaring demand prompted the government, in late May, to attempt another of its periodic crackdowns on what it considers risqué women's outerwear. Its focus this time is on shop owners. For the first time, the government issued a written warning to stores and designers against making or selling "un-Islamic" manteaux and threatening heavy fines for shops that disobey.

A poster in the suburban mall where Ms. Karimi bought her Alf creation warns stores not to sell tight-fitting manteaux with slits longer than six inches and hemlines above the knee. Bright colors, such as red and pink, are also banned.

So shopkeepers are now keeping daring designs such as Ms. Alf's in out-of-the-way places and bringing them out only when customers ask for them. The crackdown has merely increased demand among young Iranians tired of religious intrusions into their lives.

In the days after the 1979 revolution, Ms. Alf and others were already resisting. They let their hair stick out from under their scarves, wore red lipstick when they went shopping and decorated their loose outfits with gold appliqué and diamond studs. Ms. Alf was fired from her computer job in part, she says, because the way she dressed was deemed un-Islamic. She decided to put her sewing skills and love of design to work making Islamic dress fashionable.

"I looked around me and saw that no one, including myself, enjoyed looking like a head-to-toe black blob. We all wanted to maintain our individuality while observing this hijab law. Plus, it's really boring to wear the same thing day after day," said Ms. Alf, sitting in her studio while a dozen workers cut cloth and sewed her summer collection.

Each season she designs and produces a collection of manteaux with the styles and colors derived from the latest European fashions. Her collection is sold at the well-known Malakouti boutique chain, which specializes in Islamic outerwear and has branches in Tehran and other major Iranian cities.

Ms. Alf, who is divorced and has a 21-year-old son, watches the Fashion Channel on satellite television religiously. She makes regular trips to Istanbul and Dubai in search of the latest trends. Last winter, all her coats were made of suede and trimmed in fur. This summer, she is pushing a figure-hugging linen tunic that hangs just below the hip and has long slits on the sides. Wide belts—and thin ones with beads hanging from the side—have been popular, as well. Light colors, including powder blue, beige and white, are selling well.

Given the new restrictions, Ms. Alf is thinking about next year. More clever than confrontational, she is planning a safari line: long, loose cloak manteaux that are stylish but technically within the restrictions. They will have zippered slits from hemline to waist, allowing women to adjust them at a moment's notice, and long sleeves that can be buttoned up to the shoulder.

Crackdowns just help business, Ms. Alf insists. She has been through them before. "The more they tighten the leash, the more resolve women get. It's one fight the clerics will never win."

Discussion Questions

1. Why, when they are required to dress very modestly, are many Iranian women interested in fashion?
2. Are the fashions Iranian women are buying the same as the ones people in the United States are buying? Why or why not?
3. Women in Iran are at great risk of punishment for wearing clothing that is too short, tight, or revealing in some way. Why would they risk violating the rules just to wear new styles? Is fashion somehow subversive in a political system like Iran?
4. Why are Iranian salespeople men?

TIPS FOR WORKING IN LUXURY SALES

Patric Richardson

Getting ready for work this morning, I put on a navy pinstripe suit, a navy-and-white striped shirt, but what else? The Hermès knit tie with the saddle stitching down the middle, or the Lanvin ascot? It wouldn't matter so much, but today I have a very important client coming in and she is not only a friend, but one of my best customers.

Decisions like that, while seemingly minor, have helped shape my career in luxury retail for more than a dozen years. Similar to custom-painted buttons on a jacket or a hand-rolled lapel, this is an industry where small details matter. My job, while challenging, led to a career far beyond my expectations, and has taken me more places than I thought possible. However, I would have gotten there a lot faster if I had known these five tips:

1. Dress the part: When I started the first day of my career in fine apparel, I had forgotten to pack socks. I had moved halfway across the United States and my belongings were coming eight days later. So for the first few days, it was hotel living. I bought a new suit, which I was certain would impress, had my favorite blue shirt and a paisley tie and a pair of black cap toe shoes, but I forgot to pack socks! I decided that since I was going to work at a very fine retailer I could pick some up at the store and it would be a funny first-day story. I explained to the human resources person what happened, and he took me up onto the floor to pick up a pair of socks. I got some charcoal grey ones and had someone ring them up for me. They were $45! That was nearly what I was paying each night for my hotel, and now I was paying more for socks than I had paid for my shirt or tie. I bit the bullet and handed over the cash, but remembered to never make that mistake again.

    Although that first-day experience was a necessity to get through the day, consumers of fine apparel do not expect the salespeople to dress the way they do. Consumers who shop for beautiful things also do not expect their salesperson to have the same lifestyle, so no one wishing to work in luxury should feel that they need every single thing on page 143 of *Vogue* or *GQ*. Their salesperson should, however, look like they are current and understand the need for fine things. I would recommend wearing a small piece that works within your budget to indicate to the customer that you understand the value of luxury. Beyond that, one needs to always look in style but understated, because you never want to upstage the customer.

2. Know your stuff: This is a job where being well-rounded is crucial. Make it a goal to be fluent in all interests of the customer. My single biggest sale ever was to a basketball star. I know NOTHING about basketball. In fact, I didn't know who he was. But I knew about Prada shoes. We started talking while I was assisting him with shoes and he mentioned he drove a Bentley. We had a terrific conversation about cars and shoes and the best place to get a cheeseburger, and all the while he was buying clothes. At the end of the conversation, it took two rolling racks to hold all his purchases. My co-workers were all talking to him about his celebrity, but because he and I were able to carry on an actual conversation, he enjoyed our time together as much as I did. I don't own a Bentley, but because I knew enough, I could start the conversation. I just had to listen and be curious and, as a result, now I know much more than I did.

    Anyone interested in luxury sales should read their local daily newspaper, a national

Original for this text.

newspaper, and a few magazines to stay current and be able to make interesting conversations with clients. Think of a newsstand as your source for continuing education. It helps me not only to read fashion magazines but to read popular culture magazines as well since many people want to buy the same jeans their favorite singer wore to check into rehab, or someone will want the same dress their favorite movie star wore to her opening. I also devour the *New York Times* because it's a perfect source for information about cars and travel and food and culture—all topics that are great conversation starters with clients.

3. Zsa Zsa Gabor is not your typical client: In movies and TV, the wealthy are sometimes portrayed as feeling superior to the help, but unless you're dealing with the Queen of England, chances are, your good clients are going to be grateful for your assistance. Some of my most cherished friends started out as customers and our relationships naturally developed over time. Many clients have art collections that rival those in museums and houses that could easily appear in magazines, and because we have become friends I have gotten to experience them firsthand. I live vicariously through my clients because they do incredible things and share their experiences firsthand. If you are good at your job, after a while you become friends with those you assist. You may even have the opportunity to go to a charity event and experience how your clients live.

    Offer your customers advice on what to buy and how to wear it. Talking with the customer about clothes is why they come in. Customers want to hear opinions and suggestions about what to wear and where to wear it. Here is where your research comes in handy. Feel free to suggest to your customers where to go and where to stay. You can think of yourself as a type of concierge.

    One key way that luxury differs from regular sales is that you are not only selling the jacket, you are selling the lifestyle of the jacket. One of my best friends started

as a customer; I helped plan her wedding from the bridal party's attire to the color of the flowers to the design of the cake. As she continued to shop with me, we realized how much we have in common and we became close friends. We were able to become friends and have a close relationship once we both stopped focusing on how much money she has and that she enjoys spending it with me.

4. Try it, you'll like it—and if you don't, at least you'll know: I always have my tuxedo ready to go! It isn't unusual for the store management to have tickets to VIP events or charity functions hosted by our customers. Whether I was personally asked to attend, or I was the only sales guy who showed up in a tuxedo, I always said yes to the opportunity. My employer over time has identified me as a go-to party guest because I am not shy or easily intimidated. My employer can count on me to make a great impression with the client. These are crucial skills to have when working in luxury sales.

    At my first tuxedoed event for work, I went to a major charity gala with my store manager and several seasoned employees. I knew which fork to use and other basic manners (if you are doubtful on this, read Emily Post) but some things made me a little nervous, like how a silent auction works (or how a live auction works, for that matter)! I watched what other people did and learned to play along. I didn't win anything at the auction, but I still came out a winner because I was no longer afraid to interact with the guests at the gala who are our customers. At my second gala, I actually ran into a customer wearing a dress she bought from me and she introduced me to her five friends who had all admired her outfit—and they all wanted to come see me! These introductions are crucial, and they can make you very successful. Referrals are always best because the client already has an idea of how the process of luxury sales works.

    One night after staying late at work to assist a great customer, he offered to take me to dinner at one of the chicest restaurants in the city. Of course I said yes. While there, I found that I love foie gras! I was intimidated at first, but I couldn't pass up the opportunity to go to an impossible-to-get-into restaurant with a worldly guide. This gave me a great chance to try something new and expand my knowledge. I have found that any time I jump at an invitation it works, because most people who shop luxury and live that lifestyle want to share their experiences.

5. Never forget the sale is bigger than the purchase: When you sell something to your client, they aren't only buying the sweater or the suit or the necklace, they are buying esteem and worth. No one really needs a $10,000 jacket, a $40 jacket will work, but it doesn't have the same sense of luxury and exclusivity. My customers want the best, they want to project a certain image and allure. I once had a customer tell me that she couldn't fit into designer clothes and so she didn't buy them. I showed her a Gucci dress that would be perfect for her and into the fitting room she went. When she opened the door, she glowed! She told me she had never felt sexier or better about herself. That day she did buy an expensive dress, but more than that she bought a new way of looking at herself. For me, that was the day that customer became a client.

Always look for a way to make your clients happy—maybe just by sending them a handwritten thank-you note, or perhaps convincing them to buy something outside their comfort zone. Explaining the story of vicuna to a customer makes him stand a little taller in the $2,000 scarf. When customers love what they buy, it makes them feel proud to wear the clothes, or makes them feel like they are giving the ultimate gift, and that value can't be measured by the price tag. It can be measured, however, on your commission statement, because when customers feel great about what they buy, they always come back.

Conclusion

So, back to my neckwear dilemma. I decided to wear a yellow bow tie, because yellow is the customer's favorite color. She came in this afternoon; we looked all over the floor to find her the very best clothes, shoes, and jewelry that fashion had to offer. We then had someone help us with some new cosmetics and a new perfume for spring. A quick trip for a hostess gift and a little something for her husband and we wrapped it all up. We caught up on her daughter in college and her son's school trip to Africa. By this time, we both had worked up quite an appetite. We had a great lunch where we discussed our favorite TV show and laughed and laughed. Finally, back at the store, I grabbed all of her bags and walked her to her car, gave her a hug, and she left.

Every day the trick is to go to work and enjoy every part of the process. Love steaming out the clothes because that is the best way to learn all the details. Enjoy putting things carefully on the hanger because that is how the customer is going to see them for the first time. Smile when someone walks onto the floor because she might become your next good friend. Laugh while you talk and sell, remember that the process is so much more enjoyable that way. As you wrap up their purchase and carry it to the car, remember that everyone is happy because they gained something. Finally, when spending your hard-earned paycheck, enjoy, because there is no way better to earn a living.

Discussion Questions

1. What would you change about the list of tips for someone working in a budget-priced store? Mid-priced store?
2. What role does the salesperson play in disseminating fashion? How much power does the salesperson have? How does the salesperson fit into the overall process of fashion?

TOKYO A-GO-GO: COOL TEENS IN HARAJUKU MAKE A FASHION ASSAULT FROM THEIR IMAGINATIONS

Beth Hughes

To the list of site-specific fashion archetypes such as Parisian, Sloan Ranger, cowboy and California, it's now time to add Harajuku, an area of Tokyo that is dominated by cool teens and those who want to be just like them (Figure 2.7). Or at least that's what pop diva Gwen Stefani would have us believe. Her song "Harajuku Girls" praises the blindingly vibrant pedestrian street scene and the pedestrians' ability to accessorize; lists bleeding-edge Japanese labels Super Lovers, Bathing Ape and Hysteric Glamour for the hipness impaired; mentions designers Yoji Yamamoto, Vivienne Westwood and John Galliano, who've been cutting the edge for years; and sticks in a plug for her own clothing line, L.A.M.B. The only thing she doesn't mention is the burning sweet smell of cooking crepes, Harajuku's signature snack.

Is Stefani big in Japan? Humongous in the subculture of Harajuku? "I get that question quite often," said Shoichi Aoki, the Japanese photographer whose second book tracking Tokyo street fashion, "Fresh Fruits" (Phaidon Press), has just been released. She's not, he suggested in an e-mail interview, but the looks she describes explode any remaining stereotype anybody may have about Japanese fashion. And Aoki's work, which hovers somewhere in the artistic space bordered by anthropology, fashion, documentary and portraiture, is to Stefani as Jennie Livingston's documentary "Paris Is Burning" was to Madonna's song "Vogue"—it's the real deal.

"While Madonna culled her style tips from fringe communities in the United States, Stefani borrows heavily from Japanese youth culture," said Rachel Weingarten, a onetime celebrity stylist who is now a New York beauty guru.

Stefani's homage is not surprising considering that Japanese culture heavily influences our modern tastes, ranging from sushi being sold in

Figure 2.7 The Harajuku district of Tokyo, Japan, is home to people with a unique style, which has inspired fashion designers to adopt and interpret.

supermarkets to Quentin Tarantino's celebrating Japanese film styles with his "Kill Bill" movies.

Aoki began recording street fashions in the mid-'80s, after teaching himself photography while living in London. By 1987, he began publishing a magazine called *Street* in Tokyo, which featured his photographs and emphasized his philosophy about the importance of what people wear in real life versus the runways. "I think the real fashion is what people wear on the streets, the clothes that they wear, the way that they wear them," he said in an Australian radio interview that coincided with a 2003 show of his photographs in Sydney. "What you see in fashion magazines, on models, has been styled, and it is more commercial, and that's the reason I began *Street*."

Street, which is published monthly and sold in hip Bay Area shops, features Japanese, American and European designer fashion alongside Tokyo residents dressed to the nines in a city that prides itself on being well turned out. By the mid-'90s, Aoki noticed another strain emerging in street fashion, particularly in Harajuku, where the streets were closed to traffic on Sunday, and there had been a long-running, almost carnival-like scene in nearby Yoyogi Park, with live bands attracting dancers, some dressed in Elvis-era styles, others sporting the filmy balloon pants of "Arabian Nights" fantasies.

He spotted young fashionistas who no longer followed Western trends. Instead, they adapted secondhand clothes, local alternative fashions and customized obi, kimono and geta—traditional Japanese clothing—to create styles that are something irreverent, otherworldly and jubilant. Harajuku became a fashion incubator. Aoki began photographing the sometimes outrageous looks, asking the people he selected to explain themselves and their clothes briefly by answering a questionnaire that includes musical and fashion influences, age and job.

In a country with a short history of wearing Western clothing, Aoki found it revolutionary that some no longer needed or wanted designers to suggest what was proper to wear. "In Japan, having a different style is a kind of risk," he said. In 1997, he launched another magazine, *Fruits*, which in 2000 resulted in Aoki's first book of photographs, *Fruits*.

Aoki recorded punks. He photographed looks that sprang from manga and anime, or comic books and cartoons. He tracked the emergence of decora, which is clothing hyper-decorated with tiny toys and plastic jewelry to create a constantly shifting garment usually in the bright colors found in crayon boxes and children's clothing.

Gothic Lolitas? Aoki captured them in their glory, where 19th-century ladies' maids meet the 21st century wearing pale makeup with dramatic eyes and lips, lacy white baby-doll dresses, black lace crinolines, corsets, bat-shaped bags and all the variations the basics can generate.

Wamono, the deconstruction and reinterpretation of traditional Japanese clothing, also intrigued him. What makes him notice a particular look? "It is hard to describe, like music and pictures," he said. It's an ineffable combination of "beauty, class, style."

He records cogals, short for "cosmopolitan girls," with their artistically decorated nails, short skirts and overall perfection, and ganguro, who wear dark makeup and hip-hop styles to copy African Americans. With the exceptions of Lolitas, which Aoki says are "not real fashion," and cogals, the looks defied gender and inspired their own designers and brands: Baby the stars shine bright, Takuya Angel, 20471120 and Ohya received international notice in the magazine and in the "Fruits" books.

"I realized the meaning of art in fashion, which does not come from the designer or the clothes themselves," said Aoki. "I was inspired by the entire shape of the full-length figure when they are dressed. These have to be recorded, or they will volumize in time."

Indeed, Aoki sees his work as "partly anthropology, and partly a record of art." With the art comes a keen sense of fun, which is tinged with just a little bit of desperation, just like high school.

"The idea is that you're a conformist six days of the week," said Peter Macias, co-author with Tomohiro Machiyama of *Cruising the Anime City, an Otaku Guide to Neo Tokyo*. "On Sunday, you're allowed the space to show off and be seen. That's for you, to hang out with your friends and eat crepes."

The looks emerge seemingly from nowhere. "It's spontaneous," said Gerry Poulos, a writer for the U.S. edition of *New Type*, a Japanese magazine on cosplay, or dressing as anime, video game or manga characters in the way some fans dress as their favorite "Star Wars" characters. The author of the forthcoming book *How to Cosplay*, the first in an eight-part series on getting the costumes exactly right, Poulos says that spontaneity then solidifies into the precise way to create a look.

"There are magazines of instructions on how to cut your T-shirt just right, how to do your makeup," said Josephine Yun, a 25-year-old Belmont native now living in Baltimore who tracked Japanese youth culture for her book, *JRock, Ink.* "In the U.S., people reject what is immediately past. In Japan, there's more respect for what's happened in fashion or music. Whether it happened last year or 30 years ago, they're bent on upholding a fashion style or a music style they admire. They take pleasure in it."

Yun, a fan of Aoki's work, suggests that Americans are trying so hard to be individuals, "they're all the same. In Japan, everyone is just like you, you're on the same page of the same book at the same time" in schools nationwide, "so to express yourself, you have to try harder, and there will be at least three people with you."

Highly individualized fashion morphing into a mini-group-think "is bizarre when you try to equate it with something in the U.S.," said Yun. "But what I see is people enjoying themselves. It's obvious they're having fun being with each other, being in the company of friends. I don't think that's bizarre at all."

Discussion Questions

1. Do you agree with Aoki's assessment that fashion is what is worn on the streets rather than what is worn on the runway? How does this relate to the definition of fashion as a social process?
2. How does Harajuku fashion fit into the topic of postmodern fashion?
3. When have other Japanese groups inspired global fashion trends?
4. What other influence—besides Gwen Stefani—do you think inspired the adoption of Harajuku style into fashion?

2.6

HIPSTER: THE DEAD END OF WESTERN CIVILIZATION

Douglas Haddow

We've reached a point in our civilization where counterculture has mutated into a self-obsessed aesthetic vacuum. So while hipsterdom is the end product of all prior countercultures, it's been stripped of its subversion and originality.

I'm sipping a scummy pint of cloudy beer in the back of a trendy dive bar turned nightclub in the heart of the city's heroin district. In front of me stand a gang of hippiesh grunge-punk types, who crowd around each other and collectively scoff at the smoking laws by sneaking puffs of "f*ck-you," reveling in their perceived rebellion as the haggard, staggering staff look on without the slightest concern.

The "DJ" is keystroking a selection of MP3s off his MacBook, making a mix that sounds like

he took a hatchet to a collection of yesteryear billboard hits, from DMX to Dolly Parton, but mashed up with a jittery techno backbeat.

"So . . . this is a hipster party?" I ask the girl sitting next to me. She's wearing big dangling earrings, an American Apparel V-neck tee, non-prescription eyeglasses and an inappropriately warm wool coat.

"Yeah, just look around you, 99 percent of the people here are total hipsters!"

"Are you a hipster?"

"F*ck no," she says, laughing back the last of her glass before she hops off to the dance floor.

Reprinted by permission of the author.

Ever since the Allies bombed the Axis into submission, Western civilization has had a succession of counterculture movements that have energetically challenged the status quo. Each successive decade of the post-war era has seen it smash social standards, riot and fight to revolutionize every aspect of music, art, government and civil society.

But after punk was plasticized and hip-hop lost its impetus for social change, all of the formerly dominant streams of "counterculture" have merged together. Now, one mutating, trans-Atlantic melting pot of styles, tastes and behavior has come to define the generally indefinable idea of the "hipster."

An artificial appropriation of different styles from different eras, the hipster represents the end of Western civilization—a culture lost in the superficiality of its past and unable to create any new meaning. Not only is it unsustainable, it is suicidal. While previous youth movements have challenged the dysfunction and decadence of their elders, today we have the hipster—a youth subculture that mirrors the doomed shallowness of mainstream society.

Take a stroll down the street in any major North American or European city and you'll be sure to see a speckle of fashion-conscious twenty-somethings hanging about and sporting a number of predictable stylistic trademarks: skinny jeans, cotton spandex leggings, fixed-gear bikes, vintage flannel, fake eyeglasses and a keffiyeh—initially sported by Jewish students and Western protesters to express solidarity with Palestinians, the keffiyeh has become a completely meaningless hipster cliché fashion accessory.

The American Apparel V-neck shirt, Pabst Blue Ribbon beer and Parliament cigarettes are symbols and icons of working or revolutionary classes that have been appropriated by hipsterdom and drained of meaning. Ten years ago, a man wearing a plain V-neck tee and drinking a Pabst would never be accused of being a trend-follower. But in 2008, such things have become shameless clichés of a class of individuals that seek to escape their own wealth and privilege by immersing themselves in the aesthetic of the working class.

This obsession with "street-cred" reaches its apex of absurdity as hipsters have recently and wholeheartedly adopted the fixed-gear bike as the only acceptable form of transportation—only to have brakes installed on a piece of machinery that is defined by its lack thereof.

Lovers of apathy and irony, hipsters are connected through a global network of blogs and shops that push forth a global vision of fashion-informed aesthetics. Loosely associated with some form of creative output, they attend art parties, take lo-fi pictures with analog cameras, ride their bikes to night clubs and sweat it up at nouveau disco-coke parties. The hipster tends to religiously blog about their daily exploits, usually while leafing through generation-defining magazines like *Vice, Another Magazine* and *Wallpaper.* This cursory and stylized lifestyle has made the hipster almost universally loathed.

"These hipster zombies . . . are the idols of the style pages, the darlings of viral marketers and the marks of predatory real-estate agents," wrote Christian Lorentzen in a *Time Out New York* article entitled "Why the Hipster Must Die." And they must be buried for cool to be reborn."

With nothing to defend, uphold or even embrace, the idea of "hipsterdom" is left wide open for attack. And yet, it is this ironic lack of authenticity that has allowed hipsterdom to grow into a global phenomenon that is set to consume the very core of Western counterculture. Most critics make a point of attacking the hipster's lack of individuality, but it is this stubborn obfuscation that distinguishes them from their predecessors, while allowing hipsterdom to easily blend in and mutate other social movements, subcultures and lifestyles.

* * *

Standing outside an art party next to a neat row of locked-up fixed-gear bikes, I come across a couple of girls who exemplify hipster homogeneity. I ask one of the girls if her being at an art party and wearing fake eyeglasses, leggings and a flannel shirt makes her a hipster.

"I'm not comfortable with that term," she replies.

Her friend adds, with just a flicker of menace in her eyes, "Yeah, I don't know, you shouldn't use that word, it's just . . ."

"Offensive?"

"No . . . it's just, well . . . if you don't know why then you just shouldn't even use it."

"Ok, so what are you girls doing tonight after this party?"

"Ummm . . . We're going to the after-party."

* * *

Gavin McInnes, one of the founders of *Vice*, who recently left the magazine, is considered to be one of hipsterdom's primary architects. But, in contrast to the majority of concerned media-types, McInnes, whose "Dos and Don'ts" commentary defined the rules of hipster fashion for over a decade, is more critical of those doing the criticizing.

"I've always found that word ['hipster'] is used with such disdain, like it's always used by chubby bloggers who aren't getting laid anymore and are bored, and they're just so mad at these young kids for going out and getting wasted and having fun and being fashionable," he says. "I'm dubious of these hypotheses because they always smell of an agenda."

Punks wear their tattered threads and studded leather jackets with honor, priding themselves on their innovative and cheap methods of self-expression and rebellion. B-boys and B-girls announce themselves to anyone within earshot with baggy gear and boomboxes. But it is rare, if not impossible, to find an individual who will proclaim themself a proud hipster. It's an odd dance of self-identity—adamantly denying your existence while wearing clearly defined symbols that proclaim it.

* * *

"He's 17 and he lives for the scene!" a girl whispers in my ear as I sneak a photo of a young kid dancing up against a wall in a dimly lit corner of the after-party. He's got a flipped-out, do-it-yourself haircut, skin-tight jeans, leather jacket, a vintage punk tee and some popping high-tops.

"Shoot me," he demands, walking up, cigarette in mouth, striking a pose and exhaling. He hits a few different angles with a firmly unimpressed expression and then gets a bit giddy when I show him the results.

"Rad, thanks," he says, re-focusing on the music and submerging himself back into the sweaty funk of the crowd where he resumes a jittery head bobble with a little bit of a twitch.

The dance floor at a hipster party looks like it should be surrounded by quotation marks. While punk, disco and hip-hop all had immersive, intimate and energetic dance styles that liberated the dancer from his/her mental states—be it the head-spinning B-boy or violent thrashings of a live punk show—the hipster has more of a joke dance. A faux shrug shuffle that mocks the very idea of dancing or, at its best, illustrates a non-committal fear of expression typified in a weird twitch/ironic twist. The dancers are too self-aware to let themselves feel any form of liberation; they shuffle along, shrugging themselves into oblivion.

Perhaps the true motivation behind this deliberate nonchalance is an attempt to attract the attention of the ever-present party photographers, who swim through the crowd like neon sharks, flashing little blasts of phosphorescent ecstasy whenever they spot someone worth momentarily immortalizing.

Noticing a few flickers of light splash out from the club bathroom, I peep in only to find one such photographer taking part in an impromptu soft-core porno shoot. Two girls and a guy are taking off their clothes and striking poses for a set of grimy glamour shots. It's all grins and smirks until another girl pokes her head inside and screeches, "You're not some club kid in New York in the nineties. This shit is so hipster!"—which sparks a bit of a catfight, causing me to beat a hasty retreat.

In many ways, the lifestyle promoted by hipsterdom is highly ritualized. Many of the partygoers who are subject to the photoblogger's snapshots no doubt crawl out of bed the next afternoon and immediately reexperience the previous night's debauchery. Red-eyed and bleary, they sit hunched over their laptops, wading through a sea of similarity to find their own (momentarily) thrilling instant of perfected hipster-ness.

What they may or may not know is that "cool-hunters" will also be skulking the same sites, taking note of how they dress and what they consume. These marketers and party promoters get paid to co-opt youth culture and then re-sell it back at a profit. In the end, hipsters are sold what they think they invent and are spoon-fed their prepackaged cultural livelihood.

Hipsterdom is the first "counterculture" to be born under the advertising industry's microscope, leaving it open to constant manipulation but also forcing its participants to continually shift their interests and affiliations. Less a subculture, the hipster is a consumer group—using their capital to purchase empty authenticity and rebellion. But the moment a trend, band, sound, style or feeling gains too much exposure, it is suddenly looked upon with disdain. Hipsters cannot afford to maintain any cultural loyalties or affiliations for fear they will lose relevance.

An amalgamation of its own history, the youth of the West are left with consuming cool rather that creating it. The cultural zeitgeists of the past have always been sparked by furious indignation and are reactionary movements. But the hipster's self-involved and isolated maintenance does nothing to feed cultural evolution. Western civilization's well has run dry. The only way to avoid hitting the colossus of societal failure that looms over the horizon is for the kids to abandon this vain existence and start over.

"If you don't give a damn, we don't give a f*ck!" chants an emcee before his incitements are abruptly cut short when the power plug is pulled and the lights snapped on.

Dawn breaks and the last of the after-after-parties begin to spill into the streets. The hipsters are falling out, rubbing their eyes and scanning the surrounding landscape for the way back from which they came. Some hop on their fixed-gear bikes, some call for cabs, while a few of us hop a fence and cut through the industrial wasteland of a nearby condo development.

The half-built condos tower above us like foreboding monoliths of our yuppie futures. I take a look at one of the girls wearing a bright pink kef-fiyeh and carrying a Polaroid camera and think, "If only we carried rocks instead of cameras, we'd look like revolutionaries." But instead we ignore the weapons that lie at our feet—oblivious to our own impending demise.

We are a lost generation, desperately clinging to anything that feels real, but too afraid to become it ourselves. We are a defeated generation, resigned to the hypocrisy of those before us, who once sang songs of rebellion and now sell them back to us. We are the last generation, a culmination of all previous things, destroyed by the vapidity that surrounds us. The hipster represents the end of Western civilization—a culture so detached and disconnected that it has stopped giving birth to anything new.

Discussion Questions

1. How do hipsters challenge the status quo?
2. What does the author mean when he writes that hipsters are not authentic?
3. How does the hipster culture fit into the postmodern era?

CHAPTER 3

DRESS AS NONVERBAL COMMUNICATION

Kimberly A. Miller-Spillman

After you have read this chapter, you will understand:

- The substantial complexity underlying communication through dress
- The basic components of the structure of dress communication systems
- How people put together appearance according to "rules" or guidelines for dress shaped by cultural, historical, and group factors as well as personal tastes and preferences
- The characteristics of the present era that influence the way consumers "produce" appearances

We express much through dress, including our personal identities, our relationships with others, and the types of situations in which we are involved. A phenomenal amount of information is transmitted in one's appearance, and human beings have an amazing capacity to make sense of a substantial amount of detail in a very short time. In this chapter we will consider both the complexity of communicating through appearance and factors that influence messages sent through appearance. We will look closely at the process of creating meanings about the self and society through dress.

What Is Nonverbal Communication?

Dress is one of several modes of nonverbal communication that does not necessarily involve verbal expression through speaking or writing.[1] Other types of nonverbal communication include facial expressions, physical movement and actions (kinetics), the physical distances people maintain from one another (proxemics), touch (haptics), the sound of the voice while delivering verbal communications (paralinguistics), and hand gestures. All of these types of nonverbal communication involve behaviors that are informative and meaningful.

Dress serves as a backdrop while other forms of communication—verbal and nonverbal—occur. Unlike many other modes of communication, dress often tends to be stable or unchanging for many hours of the day. Dress, then, is usually **nondiscursive**—or fixed—behavior (McCracken, 1988). (See Chapter 13 for an update on how technology can change some clothing while it is being worn.) Two different definitions of communication are useful in understanding dress. One definition, mapped out by Burgoon and Ruffner (1974), contains a number of premises about sending and receiving messages:

1. *Communication is an interactive process between two or more people.* Millions of people can be involved when television and other media send messages to a vast audience. The performer may never interact directly with most viewers, but an interaction nonetheless occurs. For example, when presidential candidates run for office, their dress is often scrutinized and critiqued as an indicator of what type of leader that person will be. People discuss with friends, on blogs, and in newspaper pieces the color, size, and fabrications, and styles each candidate was wearing. In response, friends reply, people respond on blogs, and newspapers have letters to the editors for a continued discourse.

2. *Communication involves the sending of messages to at least one receiver who, for a complete act of communication, sends a feedback message to the original sender.* Feedback messages sent about dress are not always obvious and overt. Occasionally, one may receive a direct compliment or insult about dress. A long stare or whistle might constitute the feedback. In many instances, lack of comments serves as feedback that nothing was terribly wrong with one's appearance. Getting a job or a date may indicate that one's dress was appropriate or approved.

3. *Communication is a process that is ongoing and dynamic. Meanings are negotiated and created to reach common understanding.* According to the three-part definition of communication, sender and receiver must come to a minimal level of agreement about the meanings of dress for a complete communication interaction to occur. This may happen to some extent in purposeful efforts at impression management, such as a suit worn to a job interview, a wedding dress, or a uniform for a job role. But for most, dress wearer and observer never converse specifically about dress and often do not completely agree on what each other's dress means (Tseèlon, 1992). Since dress is very **polysemic** (i.e., it sends a great amount of messages all at one time), it is difficult to find agreement on all of the meanings packed into one appearance.

A second, broader definition of communication emphasizes that dress is "the production and exchange of meanings" (Fiske, 1990, p. 2). A wearer puts clothing, hairdo, accessories, and grooming together to produce an appearance and may assign meanings to that assembled appearance. Each observer of that appearance may agree on some meanings but may also have a unique interpretation of the appearance. According to the second definition, disagreement does not mean that communication stops or fails. It is the sum of how the wearer and observers interact (or not) on the basis of appearance that produces meanings for the wearer and the observers.

Throughout much of the world during the early 21st century, dress meanings tend to be vague and hard to verbalize. A picture, such as an appearance, tells a thousand words, but those thousand words are difficult to pin down precisely. In addition, changing fashion trends continually modify meanings of dress, adding further to the lack of clarity of meanings. Umberto Eco (1976) refers to this vagueness of meanings as **undercoding**. Meanings of dress in U.S. society today are coded only generally and imprecisely, leaving much to the imagination of the perceiver.

In contrast to "modern" attire worn throughout the world today, dress in traditional cultures tends to change slowly over time and may incorporate long-used symbols that are steeped with meanings. One example of this can be seen in Kente cloth. As Professor Docea Fianu writes in the "Historical Background of Kente," the cloth has been in production in Ghana since the 17th century and has an established system of color meanings (e.g., blue portrays love) and status meanings (e.g., originally meant for royalty and wealthy). The exact origin of Kente is not known but Fianu traces the many stories of origin and states that Ghana had contact with cultures in the Mediterranean, Asia, and Europe for a period of 3,000 years, indicating a mixture of influences. See images of Kente cloth in Figure 3.5 (pages 91–92).

The Structure of Dress Communication Systems

Channels of Transmission

Dress as a communication system is extremely complex. In any one appearance, messages may be sent simultaneously through a variety of channels. Berlo (1960) defined **channels of communication** as the five physiological senses. We often study how dress is used to communicate via the visual channel. However, we might also send messages via the hearing channel (e.g., the clanging of bangle bracelets, the clickety-clack of high heels on an uncarpeted hallway, the rustle of taffeta) or via the sense of smell (e.g., perfumes, deodorants to mask body odor, new leather). The sense of touch is inherent in perceiving clothing, as textiles have a tactile component. However, we can also look at a fabric sometimes and guess that it is soft (e.g., velvet) or slick (e.g., vinyl). These sensory transmissions may have meanings for observers. For example, many business dress advisors suggest that clanging jewelry and obvious perfumes convey an image that is less than professional in the office environment (Fashion Workshop, 1989; Fiore and Kimle, 1997; Roscho, 1988). The sense of taste is not strongly related to appearance. There are flavored lipsticks, balms, mouthwashes, toothpastes, and other grooming products, but because they are not easily seen their relationship to fashion is rarely used, other than a few amusing and/ or erotic novelty dress products that are flavored. (For more information on dress and sense, see suggested reading Breu [2007]).

An array of elements may be compiled on the body to complete a dressed appearance. When hairdo, facial grooming or makeup, clothing, scent, jewelry, shoes, and accessories are all combined, a tremendous amount of organization has taken place. The rules we use to put all of these components together on the body are loosely held guidelines for what is appropriate, fashionable, and attractive. The rules are a sort of grammar of dress. We learn the grammar of dress through the media and through groups and families to which we belong.

Any dress grammar rule can be broken; however, some rules are held seriously in some societies. For instance, in most communities in the United States today, it is illegal for women to go topless and for men to display their genitals in public. These laws stem from moral taboos related to a sense of modesty and sexual behavior. In France, a presidential commission proposed a law that would prohibit students from wearing veils or head scarves to school for religious reasons (Ganley, 2003). Banning other forms of religious dress in schools was under consideration. Government authorities contended that religious expression through dress might be undermining the constitutional guarantee of secular control. Some government officials feared that communities with high levels of immigration of fundamentalist Muslims could be threatening preservation of France's secular identity. (For an update, see "France Enforces Ban on Full-Face Veils in Public" in Chapter 7.)

Banning students from wearing certain forms of dress is not always an easy means of controlling their behavior in the United States. In 2011 nine students in Michigan were suspended from high school for wearing apparel items printed with images of the Confederate flag. The courts have supported the rights of students to wear the flag symbols in some cases, leaving schools with no options other than mandatory school uniform policies.

Miller-Spillman and Hunt (2005) report data from a study of sorority women attending the University of Kentucky. In contrast to common stereotypes about conformity within college sororities, the members interviewed did not feel that their houses required strict adherence to particular ideals of dress. Instead, sorority members felt that rules for dress were very tolerant and general; they needed to attend to basic elements of hygiene and cleanliness, but had no particular style requirements.

Elements of Dress Signs

Elementary components of clothing that may convey messages are listed in Figure 3.1 within the inner oval of the diagram. These are "perceptual elements" that are the integral units of fabric and apparel that can be perceived by humans. Many of these elements are the basic elements of design (Davis, 1980; Fiore and Kimle, 1997). Some of the elements have multiple subcomponents that influence meaning; for example, color has hue (the color family), value (lightness versus darkness), and intensity (brightness versus dullness). Fiber names can be meaningful (e.g., silk is a luxury fiber) as are fabrics such as denim (i.e., the fabric denotes America's casual lifestyle; Berger, 1984). These elementary units are relevant for clothing, but other aspects of dress such as hair, tattoos, and shoes have different sets of elementary perceptual units.

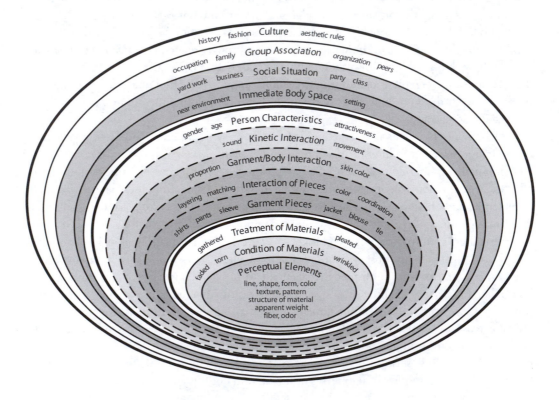

Figure 3.1 Model of clothing in context.

During the 20th century in North America, rounded design lines and flowing and delicate, translucent fabrics (such as voile) could be worn by women but were not traditionally seen in men's dress. Men tended to wear angular lines and sturdy, smooth, "hard" woven fabrics (McCracken, 1985). These differences in lines and fabrics reflected differences in traditional concepts of what is male (e.g., active, sturdy, strong) and female (e.g., soft, fragile). Today, women borrow masculine fabrics and design lines freely, as they take on roles and behaviors traditionally reserved for men. The increasing incorporation of menswear symbols into women's wear is helping (along with other societal changes) to obscure the traditional gender meanings of design lines and fabrics. See Chapter 5 for more on this topic.

Context of Use

In any appearance, a great number of perceptual elements are combined according to or in violation of some rules of grammar. How elements are combined and placed on the body, who wears them, and in what situation they are worn shapes meanings of perceptual elements. Combinations of elements and surrounding situations make up **context** (cf. Bateson, 1979). Figure 3.1 maps components of context that may shape meanings of clothing (Damhorst, 1984–1985). In the reading "Manja Weinstein's Halloween Kimono," Marcia Morgado and her co-authors examine how a kimono may have been interpreted in the context of traditional Japanese society and an American costume party. In this reading, a Japanese woman gives a kimono to her Jewish American employer in 1950 and begins three different interpretations of the kimono. First, the original kimono is seen as a ritual garment in Japanese culture. Secondly, the kimono becomes a symbol of friendship and gratitude when given as a gift to her employer. Third, in 1952, when worn as a Halloween costume in the pseudodisguise as a geisha, the kimono is a simple icon of Japan's national costume.

The inner ovals of Figure 3.1 that surround the core perceptual elements pertain to "clothing materials" and how they influence meanings. For example, observers do not only see the clothing of another but they take notice of the condition of the clothing such as how new/fresh it looks or how old/worn it looks. The condition of materials, such as stains or tears, could lower the impression given by a job applicant. The meaning of fading and tears can vary with the whims of fashion, however; distressed and stonewashed jeans have been popular for casual clothing. "Treatment of materials," another oval surrounding the core perceptual elements, includes gathers that may add fullness and softness to clothing, whereas pressed pleats may appear precise and sharp.

The next several layers of the clothing context model relate clothing to the body of the wearer. Garment pieces become familiar objects in a culture and are usually associated with coverage of one area of the body. Certain arrangements of elements (i.e., lines, shapes, fabrics, patterns) within a garment piece may then add meanings. For instance, denim jeans are a highly familiar garment symbol worldwide expressing the casual lifestyle of Americans.

The wearer's shape fills out a garment, and skin and hair coloring interact with garment elements. Body size also influences meanings of clothing. Clayton, Lennon, and Larkin (1987) found that garments worn by larger-size female models tended to be evaluated as less fashionable. This could pose a problem in marketing to larger-size women via catalogs and magazine ads. Do larger-size women see plus-size garments as less fashionable than garments worn by slim models? To approach the size issue cautiously, many mail-order firms feature plus-size models who are actually only a size 12 or 14, larger than average fashion models (size 0 to 4) but not in the size ranges offered in women's larger sizes (16W and

Figure 3.2 Johnny Cash was known as "The Man in Black."

up). Numerous characteristics of the wearer can also influence interpretation of clothing meanings. For example, an ice-cream stain on the shirt of a toddler may be perceived as cute or amusing, but might not be so cute on a 42-year-old.

The "interaction of pieces" section of Figure 3.1 refers to matching, color, and co-ordination. Within a particular occupation, some individuals adopt dress that becomes their signature style. Johnny Cash (Figure 3.2), the famous country music singer and songwriter, expressed his unconventional performance persona through the color of his clothing. Long before the 1990s when black became a conforming fashion color, Cash symbolized his uniqueness from mainstream country and western performers (who were often seen wearing brightly colored clothing with sequins) through his characteristic color choice. He was known as "The Man in Black."

The outer layers of the model in Figure 3.1 relate to the situation surrounding the wearer. Let's leap to the outer rim and examine the all-encompassing context of culture (Firth, 1957). Elements and grammar of clothing take on meaning in cultural context. Consider the color red, for example. Red is an appropriate color for traditional Chinese bridal dresses, but what would the meaning of red convey in an American bride's dress? Similarly, bright red is the traditional color for funerals in Ghana, Africa, but is not usually an appropriate color to wear to funerals in the United States. In Chapter 9 the reading "Female Tradition in a New Context: The Case of the *Khanga*" discusses the varied meanings of the Tanzanian *khanga*, including politics, economic status, gender equality, and sexual intimacy.

Moving to the "group association" level of the clothing in context model, groups and organizations vary with each culture and over time, and the role of dress varies across groups. In North America, the medical doctor's white coat is associated with laboratory science, cleanliness, purity, godlike control over life, and impartial treatment of all—concepts relevant to modern medicine (Blumhagen, 1979). But by the end of the 20th century, as doctors took on a more egalitarian role with patients and emphasized preventive medicine, many physicians abandoned the white coat for clothing that was more similar to patients' attire. Similarity and casualness were expected to reduce barriers to effective communication, essential to fully assessing the patient's health status. However, some patients still feel more comforted by the white coat, a familiar symbol of medical authority and expertise (see Figure 3.3).

Dress helps us define social situations. Some social critics fear that the invasion of casual dress into business organizations will diminish the seriousness and professionalism of business interactions, while many workers enjoy the relaxed tone set on "casual days." Similarly, a party to which everyone wears tuxedos and formal gowns might have a different atmosphere or definition than a party to which everyone wears T-shirts and jeans.

Immediate surroundings of space and people can also influence interpretations of dress. The interaction between people and the immediate surroundings gives meaning and substance to dress. One particular item can be interpreted differently based on altering the "stage." For example a man in a wig at Mardi Gras in New Orleans provides a different interpretation than a man wearing a wig in a circus, an office, or an art gallery. To further illustrate the relationship between context and interpretation of dress, Marcia Morgado and Andrew Reilly explore inferred meanings of the Hawaiian shirt in "Funny Kine Clothes." They examine how the Hawaiian shirt is portrayed in comic strips and find three themes: the shirt as source of ridicule, as source of lax attitudes, and as symbol of reverence—all depending on the "staging" of the shirt.

To summarize the model of clothing in context, it is not individual colors or garment pieces that dominate an appearance to create meanings. How all elements are combined on the body within cultural context is crucial for meanings. As Roach-Higgins and Eicher (1992) emphasized, dress is an assemblage. How the wearer uses clothing and other components of dress in context makes dress meaningful.

Figure 3.3 The white coat of a physician conveys authority, expertise, and respect. The length of the coat, however, conveys whether the wearer is a resident (beginning physician) or established doctor.

Meanings of Dress Messages

In "How Dress Means" (Chapter 1 reading), recall that semiotics is a field in which dress items carry meanings beyond the clothing object itself. Dress refers to meanings more abstract than the actual physical objects of dress. For example, dress makes visual proclamations such as "this person is male," "the wearer is competent at her job," "this person is fashionable," "this person is Nigerian," "I'm attending a black-tie affair," "I completed the 2002 10 K Fox Valley Run," or "I wanna be like Lady Gaga." Many dress messages are such that we might feel a bit silly having to verbally announce them during first meetings with others.

McCracken (1988) contended that, because dress remains fixed or unchanged during most interactions, it tends to communicate stable characteristics of the wearer. Keep in mind, however, that many of us change our clothing and sometimes other aspects of grooming every day or more than once a day. The "stable" characteristics we communicate may be stable only for a few hours. One morning, a student might throw on a sloppy sweatsuit to go to class because he's having a bad day and doesn't want to pay much attention to dress. Usually, however, that same student rarely wears sweats to class, preferring jeans and sweaters. Another student might dress in sweats every day; his attire might indicate personal attitudes about school, self, and dress. The meanings of his dress may be far more complex than not caring about his appearance, however. In the student's mind, and to the group he belongs to on campus, sloppy may be "cool." Surface-level interpretations do not always accurately reveal the meanings of dress.

In 2011, Saudi Arabia was considering banning "sexy eyes" as noted by Didymus in the reading "Saudi Women with 'Sexy Eyes' Will Have to Cover Them Up in Public." In Saudi Arabia, women are required to remain covered from head to toe when in public. They wear a veil that has a slit for their eyes (so they can see where they are going), but now men are claiming that some women have tempting eyes and are advocating for a law to require women with sexy eyes to keep them covered in public.

The fact that dress can be misinterpreted was acutely demonstrated in rape and sexual assault trials at the end of the 20th century. Many men accused of rape claimed that the survivor's attire was a sign of consent. Many trials admitted as evidence the clothing the survivor was wearing, such as leopard-print underwear, a blouse with a plunging neckline that revealed a bra, or short and tight skirts. Lennon, Johnson, and Schulz's (1999) research found that women's motives for wearing "sexy" clothing were different from how it was perceived by men; women viewed their clothing as stylish or fashionable, while men viewed it as a sign the woman was interested in a sexual encounter. Today, in the United States, many states ban the admission of clothing into evidence as a sign of sexual consent, though it may be admitted as evidence of attack (e.g., torn fabric, blood stains). However, there are still disturbing cases where clothing is said to be a sign of consent.

Former South Africa President Jacob Zuma was accused of rape and during his trial he said the fact that his victim was wearing a skirt signaled to him that she was interested in sex. In Canada, the Chief Constable of Police told women that they could avoid rape and assault if they didn't dress like a slut. One response to the social culture where rape is blamed on clothing are demonstrations called "Slut Walks" as noted by Gillian Schutte (2011) in "South Africa: Semantics of the Slut Walk." After a young girl was brutally assaulted by taxi drivers for wearing a short denim skirt, women in many countries donned their skimpy dress to participate in organized events carrying slogans such as "Don't tell us what to wear—Tell men not to rape." Women, by way of these demonstrations, are reclaiming the right to wear sexy dress without fear of being raped. For another clothing example of fighting violence against women, see suggested reading by Hipple (2000).

The Present-Day Cultural "Moment"

The present situation in U.S. culture very much shapes how consumers assemble appearances and send messages through dress. The characteristics of U.S. culture, as well as many cultures around the world, at the end of the 20th century and the beginning of the 21st century were sometimes referred to as "**postmodern**" (Gitlin, 1989). This term is useful in summarizing some present-day trends in consumer life. Morgado (1996) thoroughly analyzes postmodern influences on dress. We focus on four characteristics of consumer culture—eclecticism, nostalgia, questioning of rules, and simulation—that are reflected in how we currently purchase and present our appearances.

Postmodern appearances are **eclectic** in that consumers often mix and match a diverse array of styles and influences in any one appearance or throughout a wardrobe. For example, African-inspired fabrics (e.g., Kente cloth) are sewn into American styles; a Peruvian-knitted alpaca sweater might be worn with jeans. Consumers and designers borrow fabrics, hairstyles, jewelry, and diverse symbols across cultures, making the market for clothing very globally inspired (even though many consumers do not know the origin and meaning of their borrowings). Postmodern consumers are prone to mix diverse brands and designers in one appearance and buy parts and pieces of an ensemble at an array of price levels. Mixing Target and Gucci can be cool (Agins, 1999). Buying separates and mixing them with diverse accessories is quite common. Consumers mix and match not just to save money, but also to have more freedom in putting together unique combinations. Nostalgia is another component of postmodernism. Nostalgia is a longing for another time that is viewed with reverence and longing. Nostalgia may explain the recurrence of past period styles into contemporary fashions. For example, flared pant legs popular in the 1960s and 1970s were common in the early and mid-2000s; likewise, aesthetics of the 1980s (big shoulders, neon colors, and pegged pants) are popular again in the 2010s.

Questioning of traditions and rules seems to be a given during the postmodern era (Featherstone, 1991). We see fashionable combinations of masculine and feminine symbols, casual combined with formal, and interesting mixes of fabrics that challenge old rules about not mixing patterns in one look (see Figure 3.4). During a time when many traditional aspects of culture, such as gender roles, sexuality, bases of economic power dis-

Figure 3.4 The ensemble worn by this model includes combinations of patterns not usually seen together. Is this postmodern chic or fashion faux pas?

tribution, and ethnic hegemony, are questioned, it is no wonder that questioning of traditional rules for dress should also occur. By the early 1990s, rap artists (certainly not mainstream power leaders) became a major source of fashion inspiration for young men in the United States (Spiegler, 1996). And tattoos and piercings became both fashionable and a statement of defiance against mainstream norms of body modification (Peace, in press). Rap artists and piercings and tattoos questioned established traditions by challenging commonly accepted standards, values, and aesthetics. People began to accept different viewpoints and in doing so changed fashion.

Finally, Baudrillard (1983) suggested that during the postmodern era, **simulations** are becoming as valuable as what is real and rare. For example, since the late 1980s, animal prints and fake furs have been featured in top designer lines, perhaps to save endangered species while affording enjoyment of natural forms, even if they look fake. We also live in an era when cosmetic surgery is more accepted, when one can modify the natural body and acquire a "simulated" perfect figure or face. Simulations in general probably are increasing because of technological innovations that allow us to simulate materials (and bodies) effectively. Refer to Chapter 4 for more on this topic.

The issues surrounding postmodernism are numerous and complex; the issues they subsequently raise are not easy to solve. Susan Kaiser discusses postmodernism more in "Identity,

Postmodernism, and the Global Apparel Marketplace." What is interesting is that some scholars are arguing that postmodernism is dead and a new era is upon us, though what that new era is—or even what to name it—is still up for debate.

Summary

The vast complexity of communicating through dress has become heightened during the postmodern era. Old rules of dress are questioned, symbols are borrowed and used out of historical and cultural context, and what is real can be simulated. Communicating through dress may less often involve clearly shared meanings. The perceiver may have to work hard at making sense of a postmodern appearance. Nevertheless, dress is still significant human behavior that takes on a rich array of meanings within the surrounding context of individual wearer, social interactions, family, organizations, and culture.

Endnote

1. Verbal communications may be transmitted via dress, as when a brand logo is emblazoned on a garment or a saying or message is printed on a T-shirt.

Suggested Readings

Barnard, M. (1996). *Fashion as Communication*. London: Routledge.
Breu, M. R. (2007). The Role of Scents and the Body in Turkey. In Donald Clay Johnson and Helen Bradley Foster (Eds.), *Dress and Sense: Emotional and Sensory Experiences of the Body and Clothes*. Oxford: Berg.
Gitlin, T. (1989, July/August). Postmodernism Defined, At Last! *Utne Reader*, 52–61.
Hipple, P. C. (2000). Clothing their Resistance in Hegemonic Dress: The Clothesline Project's Response to Violence Against Women. *Clothing and Textiles Research Journal* 18(3):163–177.
McCracken, G. (1988). *Culture and Consumption*. Bloomington: Indiana University Press.
Morgado, M. A. (1996). Coming to Terms with Postmodern: Theories and Concepts of Contemporary Culture and Their Implications for Apparel Scholars. *Clothing and Textiles Research Journal* 14(1): 41–53.

Learning Activity 3.1: Dressing out of Context

Objective

The experience of how others respond when your dress does not match with the social context in which you appear will demonstrate how context affects meanings of dress. Using systematic observation techniques, record others' reactions to your dress and your own reactions to their feedback.

Procedures

Select one of the levels of context from the model in Figure 3.1. Plan to wear dress that is incongruent with that component of context during one day of the week when you will interact with others for several hours. For example:

Level of Context	Incongruent Dress Possibility
Culture	Wear dress that is normative to a culture other than the one in which you live or are from (e.g., wear a sari or a Scottish kilt to classes in the United States).
Social Situation	Wear a formal gown or a tuxedo to classes.
Person Characteristics	Wear an outfit that is appropriate for a person much younger or older than yourself.
Garment/Body Interaction	Wear an outfit that is too small for you or extremely large.
Interaction of Pieces	Wear unmatched plaids and prints together in one ensemble.
Garment Pieces	Wear a pair of jeans on your head all day.
Condition of Materials	Wear to class a garment that is notably stained or ripped.

Wear your out-of-context dress for at least six hours in one day. Try to wear it on a day when you will be seen by and interact with a variety of people you know, as well as people you know very little or not at all. Pretend you think nothing is odd about your appearance. Let others react to you before explaining that you are doing an experiment.

Recording Your Experience

Carry a notebook to record your reactions and the reactions of others as the experiment progresses. Record:

- Positive and negative responses
- Responses from males and females
- Verbal and nonverbal responses
- Responses from acquaintances, friends, and strangers
- Your feelings and thoughts about yourself before you venture out wearing the costume and as the experiment progresses
- Comparisons of yourself with others' appearances

Also, describe the places you went, situations you were involved in, types of people with whom you interacted, types of people you were seen by but with whom you did not specifically interact, date and times of day for each entry in your recordings, and weather conditions you experienced.

Questions to Ponder

1. Did you learn anything about how people respond to others on the basis of appearance? What types of meanings did various others seem to assign to your dress?
2. Was there more than one aspect of context affecting how your dress was interpreted?
3. What factors may have affected your accuracy in interpreting responses from others?
4. Will you ever dress this way again? Why or why not?

References

Agins, T. (1999, June 11). Fashion: Cheapskate Chic. *Wall Street Journal*, W1.

Bateson, G. (1979). *Mind and Nature*. New York: E. P. Dutton.

Baudrillard, J. (1983). *Simulations* (P. Foss, P. Patton, and P. Beitchman, trans.). New York: Semiotext(e), Inc.

Berger, A. A. (1984). *Signs in Contemporary Culture*. New York: Longman.

Berlo, D. K. (1960). *The Process of Communication*. New York: Holt, Rinehart and Winston.

Blumhagen, D. W. (1979). The Doctor's White Coat: The Image of the Physician in Modern America. *Annals of Internal Medicine* 91:111–116.

Burgoon, M., and M Ruffner. (1974). *Human Communication*. New York: Holt, Rinehart and Winston.

Clayton, R., S. J. Lennon, and J. Larkin. (1987). Perceived Fashionability of a Garment as Inferred from the Age and Body Type of the Wearer. *Home Economics Research Journal* 15:237–246.

Damhorst, M. L. (1984–1985). Meanings of Clothing Cues in Social Context. *Clothing and Textiles Research Journal* 3 (2): 39–48.

Davis, M. L. (1980). *Visual Design in Dress*. Englewood Cliffs, NJ: Prentice Hall.

Eco, U. (1976). *A Theory of Semiotics*. Bloomington: Indiana University Press.

Fashion Workshop: Real Life Cues to Clothes for Your Job. (1989, October). *Glamour*, 203–206.

Featherstone, M. (1991). *Consumer Culture and Postmodernism*. London: Sage.

Fiore, A. M., and P. A. Kimle. (1997). *Understanding Aesthetics: For Merchandising and Design Professionals*. New York: Fairchild Publications.

Firth, J. R. (1957). *Papers in Linguistics, 1934–1951*. London: Oxford University Press.

Fiske, J. (1990). *Introduction to Communication Studies*. London: Routledge.

Ganley, E. (2003, December 12). French Group Backs Ban on Head Scarves. *The Des Moines Register*, 3A.

Gitlin, T. (1989, July/August). Postmodernism Defined, At Last! *Utne Reader*, 52–61.

Lennon, S. J., K. K. P. Johnson, and T. L. Schulz. (1999). Forging Linkages between Dress and Law in the U. S., Part II: Rape and Sexual Harassment. *Clothing and Textiles Research Journal* 17: 144–156.

McCracken, G. (1985). The Trickle-Down Theory Rehabilitated. In M. R. Solomon (Ed.), *The Psychology of Fashion*, 39–54. Lexington, MA: Lexington Books.

McCracken, G. (1988). *Culture and Consumption*. Bloomington: Indiana University Press.

Miller(-Spillman), K. A. and S. A. Hunt. (2005). It's All Greek to Me: Sorority Members and Identity Talk. In M. L. Damhorst, K. A. Miller, and S. O. Michelman (Eds.), *The Meanings of Dress* (2nd ed., pp. 83–87). New York: Fairchild Publications.

Morgado, M. A. (1996). Coming to Terms with Postmodern: Theories and Concepts of Contemporary Culture and Their Implications for Apparel Scholars. *Clothing and Textiles Research Journal* 14 (1): 41–53.

Peace, W. J. (in press). The Artful Stigma. *Disability Studies Quarterly*. Journal available at www.afb.org/dsq/.

Roach-Higgins, M. E., and J. B. Eicher. (1992). Dress and Identity. *Clothing and Textiles Research Journal* 10 (4): 1–8.

Roscho, L. (1988, October). The Professional Image Report. *Working Woman*, 109–113, 148.

Spiegler, M. (1996, November). Marketing Street Culture: Bringing Hip-Hop Style to the Mainstream. *American Demographics* 18 (11): 29–34.

Tseëlon, E. (1992). Self Presentation through Appearance: A Manipulative vs. a Dramaturgical Approach. *Symbolic Interaction* 15 (4): 501–513.

HISTORICAL BACKGROUND OF KENTE

Docea A. G. Fianu

Kente is a cloth that is hand woven. It is a century-old tradition of strip weaving which was inspired by the demands of royalty, ceremony and the aesthetic taste of the wealthy (Adler and Barnard, 1995). To meet this requirement, Ashanti and Ewe weavers produced, and still produce, Kente cloths using different colours, fibers and intricate motifs. Ewe weaving, in contrast to that of Ashanti, however, has no connection with a court or with royalty (Cole and Ross, 1977). Originally, Ewe weavers used mainly cotton yarns while Ashantis used silk and cotton yarns. Since colours

on cotton tend to mature over time, Ewe Kente looked dull while Ashanti ones looked, and still look, vividly bright (Glover, 1997). It must be noted, however, that Ewe weavers now use silk yarns in addition to cotton and rayon yarns. They, thus, produce Kente cloths with bright colours, intricate motifs and texture similar to those of the Ashantis (see Figure 3.5a).

There are other strip-woven fabrics that are produced by Ashantis, Ewes and inhabitants of Northern Ghana. Ashantis call the cloth "Ahwepan" named after the type of weave and the sounds that comes from the loom when the cloth is being woven. Some Ewes call the cloth "Shan-Shan" (shine-shine) due to the shiny metallic yarns that are used in combination with other yarns (see Figure 3.5b). Even though the production process is the same and similar yarns are used for these fabrics, the "Ahwepani/Shan-Shan" do not have unique and intricate motifs. They do not carry messages associated with indigenous Kente but they are known as Kente.

Figure 3.5b Kente cloth that incorporates shiny metallic yarns.

Excerpted from *Ghana's Kente & Adinkra: History and Socio-Cultural Significance in a Contemporary Global Economy*. Accra, Ghana: Black Mask Ltd., 2007. Reprinted by permission of the author.

Figure 3.5a Traditional Kente—woven strips sewn together with bright colours and intricate designs.

"Printex" (formerly Spintex), a textile manufacturing company in Ghana, produces fabrics with Kente motifs. These fabrics look exactly like Kente from a distance. However, since "Printex" fabrics are produced on power looms, they are without the strips of fabric found in typical and traditional hand-woven Kente cloths. These Kente-like fabrics can correctly be labeled "Imitation" or "Factory-Produced" Kente cloths (Figure 3.5c). Any class of consumers can afford their use and possess as many different ones as possible because, unlike indigenous Kente, especially those with motifs, they are relatively less expensive.

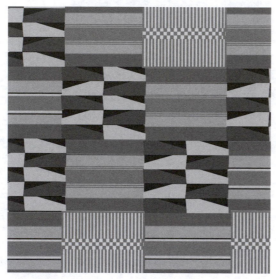

Figure 3.5c Factory-produced or factory-printed Kente cloth.

The term "Kente" is reported to be associated with the Fanti (an ethnic Ghanaian group) word "Kenten," meaning basket (Adler and Barnard, 1995; Ofori-Ansa, 1993). The first weavers of Kente were believed to have used raffia to weave Kente cloths that looked like a "Kenten" (basket). The cloths were, therefore, referred to as "Kenten ntoma" (basket cloth). The letter "n" on "Kenten," as time went on, was overlooked (dropped). The cloth was thus labelled "Kente Ntoma" or "Kente" for short. Ofori-Ansa (1993) also reported that the original name of the cloth was "Nsaduaso" or "Nwontoma" (a cloth that is hand woven on a loom). Ashanti weavers and elders still use this name but Kente is the universal name used in Ghana (Ofori-Ansa, 1993).

Kente is also believed to have been developed in Ghana in the 17th century during the reign of Oti Akenten, an early Ashanti Chief (Rattray, 1969). How the weaving technique was established and refined to the current high level represented by the various types of Kente, however, is not precisely known (Adler and Barnard, 1995). Nevertheless, it is told that a chief of Bonwire in Ashanti, Nana Okai Ababio, reported that "Ananse" (the spider) taught two farmers, Krugu Amoanya and Watah Kraban, how to weave.

Rattray (1969) indicated that probably the farmers observed how the spider produced its web and then tried to duplicate it on the loom. They were successful and came up with the process of weaving Kente. The first cloth was woven in white colour for presentation to the Asantehene, Nana Osei Tutu. Later, black and white yarns were used for Kente until the reign of Asantehene, Nana Agyeman Prempeh I, in the 20th century, when coloured yarns were used.

The first cloth produced in Ashanti with coloured yarns was labelled "Oyokoman," a tribute to the "Oyoko" clan and Nana Agyeman Prempeh 1 (Rattray, 1969). The weavers were probably from the Oyoko clan. Rattray (1969) reported that any time Nana Ababio narrated the genius of his ancestors, he insisted on pouring libation in memory of them. The origin of Kente weaving, therefore, can be labelled as a legend and one with a religious beginning.

The beginnings of Kente weaving can also be explained with a historical account. In a different report, Rattray (1969) indicated that one Ota Kraban brought the first loom from Gyaman (now Cote d' Ivoire) and later set up the industry in Bonwire near Kumasi. It must be noted that the name Kraban was mentioned in the legend about the spider already narrated. In another context, Rattray (1969) reported that he strongly believed the art of weaving Kente was introduced into Ashanti from the North of Africa and not by sea route from Europe. He was almost certain that the agent of introduction and inspiration was trade. The Phoenician Arabs and Romans might have brought the technique during their trips down the Sahara to the ancient Ghana Empire. The luxury of the Phoenician textiles possibly fascinated the inhabitants of the empire (Adler and Barnard, 1995). The art was probably carried with them when they migrated to settle at the present day Ashanti Region in Ghana.

Ofori-Ansa (1993) also reported that Kente weaving could be traced to the early weaving traditions in Ancient West African Kingdom that flourished between AD 300 and 1600. Examples of such woven fabrics have been found in the caves of Bandiagara Cliffs of Mali. These cloths were possibly used for burial in medieval Ghana (Ofori-Ansa, 1993). This is also a probable report since there was the Ghana Empire. Ewes from Agotime Kpetoe in Ghana also believe that Ashantis learned the art of weaving from them. According to oral history, Ewes migrated from the area of the Ghana Mali Empire and brought that art with them. In 1869, there was a war between Ewes and Ashantis. Ewes were defeated and the art of Kente weaving was one of the booties taken from Eweland to Ashanti. It was emphasized that the term Kente came from two Ewe words which are "Ke" (open it) and "Te" (press it). When an apprentice is being taught how to weave, these words are used to direct him. Ashanti warriors learned these words and called the cloth "Kete." How the letter "N" was added to "Kete" to become "Kente" is, however, not known.

The type and scale of indigenous Kente cloth production in the early days is difficult to be known precisely. The fact that the region was in contact with the Mediterranean, Asian and European "civilizations" for a period of 3,000 years, however, points to a textile history of mixed origin (Adler and Barnard, 1995). Whatever the origins of Kente weaving might be, Bonwire, near Kumasi and Agotime Kpetoe in the Volta Region, are two main centers for Kente weaving in the Republic of Ghana since the 17th century.

Colours and Colour Symbolism in Kente Cloths

Colour means a lot to the Ghanaian. It is used, among others, to portray mood, the occasion, the sex of an individual and aesthetic taste (Ofori-Ansa, 1993). Ofori-Ansa further reported that there are gender-colour preferences directed by tradition, individual taste and by the spirit of the occasion. Women appear to prefer pink, purple, light blue, light yellow, light green, white and turquoise, while men prefer the shades of blue, green, maroon, yellow, orange and red.

In Silk-Kente, white is associated with ivory, white glass and eggshell, and this colour represents purity, virtue, innocence, joy and victory. The colour is worn by brides, girls in the first stage of puberty initiation, patients cured of a long illness or relations at the end of mourning for a deceased person. Black Kente cloth is worn during the initial stages of funeral ceremonies.

Gold is associated with a controlled fire, and it portrays royalty, continuous life and warmth. Chiefs used to wear this colour. Yellow is similar to fowl fat and stands for royalty, prosperity, glory, maturity and the prime of life. Yellow Kente was mostly worn by chiefs. Green is identified with new leaves and stands for newness, vitality and primeness of growth. It is usually worn by teenagers during puberty rites. Red is associated with blood and represents vice, deep melancholy such as death, war, anger, calamity or dissatisfaction and worn during funerals and political rallies.

Blue is likened to silver and early dawn and portrays love, female tenderness and frequently, the rule of a queen mother; while gray is likened to ashes and represents degradation and shamefulness. Kente cloth with white is an indication of a bountiful harvest.

It must be added here that due to social change and modern mode of living, these traditional norms in the use of colours are scarcely considered. Colour choice may be based mostly on individual taste. Colours such as bottle green, pink, mustard and some shades and tints of purple which were earlier on not seen in Ghana Kente are blended with "traditional" colours to produce beautiful Kente cloths.

References

Adler, P. & Barnard, N. (1995). "The African Majesty: The Textile Art of the Ashanti and Ewe." Thames and Hudson Ltd. London.

Cole, M. & Ross, D. H. (1977). "The Arts of Ghana." University of California (Museum of Cultural History), pp. 38–47.

Glover, A. (1997). Personal Communication. Nungua, Ghana.

Ofori-Ansa, K. (1993). "History and Significance of Ghana's Kente." (A Poster) Sankofa Publications. 2211 Amherst Rd, Hyattsville, MD 20783.

Rattray, R. S. (1969). "Religion and Art in Ashanti." Oxford University Press. pp. 220–268.

Discussion Questions

1. Can you think of colors that have a specific meaning in the United States? List as many examples as you can of a color and its meaning in America. Compare lists with your classmates, then compare your list to the color meanings in Fianu's reading.
2. How are the strip-woven and factory-produced Kente cloths perceived differently? What aesthetics contribute to these differences?
3. In addition to the two Ghanaian cultures mentioned in the reading (Ewe and Ashanti), what other cultures may have influenced Kente cloth beginning 3,000 years ago? How did each culture contribute to what is known as Kente cloth today?

3.2

MANJA WEINSTEIN'S HALLOWEEN KIMONO

Marcia Morgado, Alexandra Shields, Sophie Sun, and Cindy Urbane

How do context and circumstance influence the meanings associated with dress? This is the question my students and I asked when we took on the study of a vintage Japanese kimono that I inherited from my mother, Manja Weinstein. The kimono was a gift from Toshiko Arikawa,[1] a young Japanese woman who lived in our home in Salt Lake City, Utah, in the early 1940s. Mother kept the garment carefully preserved in its original wrappings and wore it only once. The occasion was a Halloween party sponsored by the Sisterhood of the B'nai Israel Synagogue in the early 1950s.

Manja was not Japanese, and she knew little of Japanese customs or costume. Neither was she entirely American, for she was nearly 24 years old when she immigrated to the United States from Libau, a Baltic seaport town in the Russian state of Latvia. A self-described fashion plate, Manja loved dressing up and going out and was delighted that the Halloween gala provided an opportunity to wear the unusual garment. It is not likely that she gave thought to what the kimono might have meant in its original context, nor is it likely that she gave conscious thought to what it meant in the context of either Toshi's life or her own. But we saw the kimono as a curious cultural artifact—one that had been transported across time, and place, and people. We challenged ourselves to see what we could learn about the garment in its traditional context and how the contexts in which the kimono was worn might have influenced its meanings.

Manja Weinstein's Kimono in Traditional Context

The word *kimono* literally means "clothing" or "thing to wear," and in its basic T-shaped form and standard size dimensions the garment appears to be as simple as the definition. All kimono are constructed from a single bolt of cloth, and the entire

Original for this text.

bolt is used for a single garment. The basic pattern consists of four pieces, two of which cover the front and back of the body. The other two pieces form the sleeves. While Western garments characteristically involve cutting, shaping, sewing, and molding the textile to the body shape through darts, yokes, and seams, the kimono is flat, two-dimensional, and not at all representative of the natural body shape. But the simplicity of the form disguises a highly detailed and complex garment, for every element of the kimono's structure and design resonates with meaning. (See Figure 3.6.)

Unlike Western garments, each kimono is a one-of-a-kind creation in which a textile artist manipulates the woven structure and the surface designs to create an original work of art. In traditional Japanese culture, the garment that results is not only a unique artistic creation, it is also understood as an expression of the individuality of the wearer, an expression of Japanese society, and a reflection of the Japanese aesthetic tradition (Yang & Narasin, 1989, p. 6). The simplicity of the form directs the focus of attention to the surface designs—the prints and patterns, the colors, and the textures. A layering of pattern-on-pattern technique produces a multilayered illusion that requires contemplation and is appreciated for its complexity. Additionally, the design elements in the layered patterns are highly symbolic. While the symbolism is evident in its native context, an outsider must learn the interpretations.

All kimono are similarly constructed, but subtle variations produce multiple kimono styles. Manja Weinstein's kimono is a *furisode*, a richly colored, heavily patterned ceremonial garment. The *furisode* is the only kimono to have long sleeves, and it is worn only by unmarried girls. The garment is made specifically to honor a young woman's coming-of-age celebration, which occurs during the year she turns 20. Once she has married, the *furisode* is laid to rest.

Manja's *furisode* is fabricated in a silk textile that is constructed in *rinzu*—a self-patterned satin weave with satin floats on a satin background. The woven motifs are numerous and complex, and these are overlaid with equally complex sur-

Figure 3.6 Manja Weinstein's Kimono—Rear View. Note elements of the woven pattern that are especially visible in the lighter, cloud-like areas of the painted pattern. Also note the lack of symmetry between the patterns on the sleeves.

Figure 3.7 Detail of the Layered Kimono Patterns. The painted pattern superimposed on the woven pattern produces a dizzying array of shapes.

face designs and colors. The surface designs are painted through a resist method called *yuzen*, characterized by fine lines of natural colored silk

Figure 3.9 Detail of Yuzen Painted Pattern. Pictured in this detail of the painted pattern is a peony flower, leaves, a diaper patterned treasure boat, and stylized clouds.

Figure 3.8 Detail of Rinzu Woven Pattern. Pictured in this detail of the woven pattern are stylized clouds, a royal carriage with bamboo screens, a partially submerged cartwheel, running water, and multiple decorative diaper patterns.

that delineate the borders of individual pattern elements. Additionally, in isolated areas, the pattern is overlaid with decorative silk embroidery-work in satin and seed stitches. And gold foil-covered threads are couched onto the fabric to emphasize pattern outlines.

We were not accustomed to looking at flat, patterned textiles as three-dimensional structures. But considering the decorative elements in terms of multilayered structures helped us to visually separate between the surface designs and the woven pattern so as to visually isolate and identify the various motifs. We found 8 discrete motifs in varying sizes in the woven pattern, 10 motifs in multiple versions of the painted designs, and 15 color variations.

We identified the traditional symbolism of each of the decorative elements, and drew connections from the symbolism to traditional Japanese cultural ideals regarding balance and harmony, the integration of human life with na-

ture, the spirits of natural elements as sources of protection, and the natural, timeless flow of life. We also identified elements that signify strength, dignity, courage, celebration, prosperity, good relationships, love, joy, affection, grace, and serenity. (See Figures 3.7–3.9.)

Manja Weinstein's Kimono in Altered Contexts

Historians trace the origins of the kimono to a wrapped garment that appeared in ancient China during the early Han dynasty (200 BC to 200 AD). But the history of Manja Weinstein's kimono begins in the much more recent past, in the context of events and circumstances that prevailed at the time of the Second World War.

In her comprehensive study of kimono, Dalby (2001) reminds us that "dress can never be analyzed separately from the universe of possibilities that shape its particular historical meaning. The relevance of an item of dress may lie in a single attribute or in a web of intricate detail. The challenge is to reconstruct the social and aesthetic meanings attached to the clothes as and when they were worn" (p.4). We hypothesized alternative meanings of Manja Weinstein's kimono by considering it in the context of the historic circumstances and social histories of the two women who shared the garment.

Context: A World on the Brink of War

It is spring of 1936. Manja Weinstein, age 24, is boarding a train that will take her from the lovely Latvian Baltic seaport town of Libau across the European continent. She will traverse the English Channel by ferry, board the *Queen Mary* for its maiden voyage from Southampton-Cherbourg to New York, and from New York she will travel by train to the Mormon state of Utah on the edge of the Mojave Desert.

Manja is engaged to David Alder, a young American who has spent the past two years wandering about Eastern Europe while waiting for the U.S. economy to pull out of the depression that followed in the aftermath of the First World War. In Libau, David finds that Jews are nervous. The state's political regime—a national dictatorship—is unstable, anti-Semitism is rising, and tensions are mounting across the continent. Adolf Hitler, chancellor of Germany, is advocating a new world order based on racial supremacy and has begun to remilitarize the Rhineland. "Every Jew I knew in Libau," David said, "wanted to get out."

There are very few ways to get out, and all require entry permission from another country. The U.S. National Origins Quota of 1924 severely restricts the number of Eastern European Jews who may enter the United States. However, the U.S. Married Woman's Act of 1922 allows naturalization benefits to women married to U.S. citizens, and Manja's engagement to David secures a visa that will allow her entry into the United States. Manja tells her family that, when she is established in America, she will find a way to get them out. But her attempts to rescue family members are stymied by the U.S. quota, and her escape from Libau occurs on the brink of World War II.

On June 12 of 1940, Manja's only child is born. Two days later, the Soviet Union invades the Balkan countries, liquidates the Latvian government, and initiates arrests, executions, and deportations against the resident population. Within a year, the Soviet occupation of Libau is displaced by the Nazi invasion of Latvia, and a strategy for "quick implementation of the Jewish problem" (Ezergailis, 1996) begins immediately. Between July and December of 1941, 5,000 of Libau's remaining 5,700 Jews, along with an assortment of Gypsies, communists, the mentally ill, and other hostages, are rounded up and herded to the parks and beaches, where they are put to work digging trenches. When the trenches are complete, Nazi troops fire on the undesirables, *en masse*. By December of 1941, all of Manja's family members have been exterminated by Soviet bullets, annihilated in Nazi massacres, dispatched to penal colonies in Soviet Siberia, or transported to the German concentration camp at Kaiserwald.

On December 7, 1941, Japan sends warplanes to bomb American naval forces stationed at Pearl Harbor, and the U.S. declares war on Japan.

The bombing of Pearl Harbor leads the U.S. to suspect that Japan is "preparing for a full-scale attack on the West Coast of the United States" (Japanese American, n.d., p. 3). Fear and hysteria lead the country to imagine that all ethnic Japanese, including American-born citizens with as little as one-sixteenth Japanese blood, pose a serious threat to national security. Two months after the attack on Pearl Harbor, President Franklin D. Roosevelt signs Executive Order 9066 excluding all people of Japanese ancestry from the Pacific coast. Those living in coastal areas will be forcibly relocated to hastily constructed War Relocation Camps. Approximately 120,000 of the 127,000 Japanese Americans living in the continental United States are removed to the camps (p. 11). Over two-thirds of the internees are American citizens and have been so from birth (*Minidoka*, n.d., p. 4).

Context: A Country Riddled by Fear

It is May of 1942. Toshiko (Toshi) Arakawa, age 19, is at a transport terminal in downtown Seattle waiting for the bus that will take her to the Puyallup Civilian Assembly Center located on the Western Washington Fairgrounds. Puyallup is one of 18 temporary holding facilities for Japanese awaiting incarceration in U.S. internment camps (*Camp Harmony*, n.d.). For the next three years the five Arakawas, including the three American-born children, will be identified as Family #37810 (Roundup, n.d.). The Arakawa family, along with 7,400 other American Japanese West Coast residents, will spend the next four months in the Puyallup Center, awaiting relocation (Japanese American, n.d.). Named after an indigenous American Indian tribe, the word *Puyallup* translates as "generous people." In a double twist of irony, the location is temporarily renamed Camp Harmony. Barbed-wire fencing surrounds the camp, and armed guards patrol the grounds.

In August of 1942, the 7,400 residents of Camp Harmony begin transport by train to the Minidoka Relocation Center in south-central Idaho. Another 5,600 internees from Oregon and Alaska will join them for a total Minidoka population of 13,000. The location is a barren wasteland of sagebrush and dust, and the camp is still under construction. There is no hot water, and there is no sewage system. The barracks are wooden frames covered with tar paper; they are not insulated. Each barrack is divided into six one-room apartments containing only army cots and pot-bellied stoves. There is a communal dining room, a communal shower, and a communal toilet. Winter temperatures fall to minus 21 degrees Fahrenheit. In spring there are ferocious dust storms. And when the dust storms cease, the driving rain leaves mud that is ankle deep. In summer temperatures climb to 104 (*Minidoka*, n.d., pp. 2–3).

Among the articles of dress in Toshi's suitcase is a richly patterned kimono—a *furisode* that her mother wore for her own coming-of-age celebration in Japan in 1907. This is the year that Toshi turns 20, and it is now her turn to wear the *furisode*. The family will honor Toshi's coming-of-age celebration in the United States, surrounded by armed guards and barbed-wire fences. The kimono—rich in symbols of balance, harmony, prosperity, peaceful life, and good relationships—has acquired a new meaning: It is certainly a reminder of the past. It may offer hope for the future. But its original meanings are now entirely eclipsed, for they are the antithesis of life in the camp.

Meanwhile, the Remington Arms Plant has opened a facility in Salt Lake City for the manufacture of munitions. Manja Weinstein takes a job as a supervisor on a bullet production line. Every bullet that comes off her assembly line must be perfect, because one of them will kill Adolf Hitler. Manja contacts the internment camp and asks that a young woman be released to her custody to care for the baby while she works. Toshiko is released from camp and granted permission to live and work in Manja's home. When the exclusion order is rescinded in 1945, the U.S. government gives Toshiko $25 and a train ticket back to Seattle (Japanese American, n.d., p. 15).

Context: The Kimono as Expression of Interwoven Lives

In 1950 Toshiko marries a Nisei (American-born Japanese) veteran of the U.S. Army 442nd regiment. The 442nd, composed entirely of Japanese-American infantrymen who fought on the European front during World War II, will be recognized as the most decorated unit in the history of American warfare. As a married woman, Toshiko can no longer wear the *furisode*. She carefully wraps and sends the garment to Manja. The kimono is still an icon of Japanese culture, and the woven motifs, painted patterns, and exotic colors remain intact. But its original meanings, overlaid by the irony of those meanings in the context of the internment camp, are now eclipsed by new meanings: The kimono has become a token of gratitude and an expression of affection and kinship between the women.

In 1952, the opportunity for Manja to wear the kimono arises. Temple B'nai Israel Sisterhood is having a Halloween party, and all are invited to attend in costume. Manja arrives dressed as a geisha. Her hair is styled in a Japanese knot, and through the knot Manja inserts ivory chopsticks from China—a gift from a Jewish refugee who fled Nazi Germany to the United States by way of Shanghai. The kimono has once again acquired new meaning: It is now a pseudodisguise, a lovely party outfit, and a confirmation of Manja's self-perception as a fashion plate.

Manja Weinstein's Halloween kimono originated as a ceremonial garment. Woven into every aspect of the garment—its cut and shape, its fabrication, its surface embellishments, and its intended purpose—are the values of traditional Japanese culture. While the garment remains the same, its meaning undergoes significant change. In the coming-of-age celebration for which it was intended, the kimono's meaning is derived from the interwoven threads of its intended symbolism and the harsh realities of life in the Minidoka internment facility. In its passage as a gift between women whose lives were entangled by the fabric of World War II, the kimono becomes a symbol of friendship and gratitude. And as a Halloween costume, the kimono is both a simple icon of Japan, expressed in a widely recognized national costume, and a statement reflecting the personality of the garment's wearer. (See Figure 3.10.)

Although Manja Weinstein's kimono resonates with the aesthetic and cultural values of traditional Japan, the meanings associated with those traditions are largely abstract meanings, removed from the realities of the lives of the women who shared the garment. We suggest that more concrete meanings may be derived from the contexts and circumstances in which the garment was worn. Interwoven with the silken threads of

Figure 3.10 Manja Weinstein in her Halloween kimono, 1952.

Manja Weinstein's Halloween kimono are the lives of an Eastern European Jewish immigrant who came to America to escape persecution and an American-born citizen who suffered prejudice at home and spent much of World War II in an American concentration camp.[2]

References

Camp Harmony [aka Puyallup Assembly Center–1942]. (n.d.). Retrieved from http://www.historylink.org/index.cfm?DisplayPage=output.cfm&file_id=8748.

Dalby, L. C. (2001). *Kimono. Fashioning culture.* New Haven, CT: Yale University Press.

Ezergailis, A. (1996). *The Holocaust in Latvia, 1941–1944: The missing center.* Riga, Latvia: The Historical Institute of Latvia.

Japanese American internment (n.d.). *Wikipedia.* Retrieved from http://en.wikipedia.org/wiki/Japanese_American_internment.

Minidoka Internment (n.d.). U.S. Department of the Interior National Park Service. Retrieved from http://www.nps.gov/miin/index.htm.

Roundup to the camp (n.d.). *Camp Harmony exhibit.* Retrieved from http://www.lib.washington.edu/exhibits/harmony/exhibit/transport.html.

Yang, S. & Narasin, R. M. (1989). *Textile art of Japan.* Tokyo, Japan: Shufunotomo Co., Ltd.

Endnotes

1. We used a pseudonym for the family name and altered the family's identification number.
2. Debate over the phrase "concentration camp" in reference to U.S. Japanese-American internment camps is ongoing. While most sources we accessed avoided making a direct comparison with the Nazi camps, we found common use of the phrase "concentration camp" in the *Neise Veteran's Newsletter* and related sources.

1.   What is the difference between casual perception and analytical perception?
2.   What were the varied meanings of the kimono? How did they change over time?
3.   How can a garment be imbued with meaning or symbolism?
4.   Do you have any garments that have multiple meanings? What are the garments, and what are the multiple meanings?

3.3

FUNNY KINE CLOTHES: THE HAWAIIAN SHIRT AS POPULAR CULTURE

Marcia Morgado and Andrew Reilly, University of Hawai`i at Manoa

In the Land of Aloha *funny kine clothes* is a pidgin expression that refers to a peculiar dress form. The Hawaiian shirt is funny kine clothes. At its inception it was highly peculiar in terms of characteristics of its design and fabrication. Its contemporary status as an indigenous regional dress form is peculiar as well, for its origins are not with the indigenous people of the Islands, nor did it develop from the folk dress of any of the Islands' multicultural populations. But the Hawaiian shirt is funny kine clothes in other ways, as well. Few elements of dress have such strong iconic value in popular culture. No other dress form is approached with the reverence accorded the Hawaiian shirt in local Hawai`i[1] culture. And no other form has as long a history as an object of humor and ridicule. In this paper we examine these highly divergent and highly charged meanings.

Theoretical Frame

Existing studies of the Hawaiian shirt are plentiful. These variously address the garment as an aspect in the development of a garment manufacturing industry in the Hawaiian Islands (e.g., Fundaburk, 1965); in the context of the ethnic cultures, social circumstances, and historic events that contributed to the shirt's significance in Island life (e.g., Arthur, 2000; Brown & Arthur, 2002); in terms of the social history of designers, manufacturers, and promoters who figured significantly in its creation (e.g., Hope, 2000); as a tool in marketing a fantasy vision of Hawai`i as a romantic visitor designation (e.g., Brown, 1982); as a unique form of folk art (e.g., Steele, 1984); as an example of shifts in the aesthetic value of fashion apparel (e.g., Morgado, 2003); and in terms of its commercial value as a vintage collectible (e.g., Blackburn, 2001; Schiffer, 1989; 1997; 2005). We address the shirt as a curious popular culture artifact and ask what might be learned from an examination of its varied meanings.

The examination is framed on a premise derived from Structuralism. Structuralism is an approach to semiotic analysis that is concerned with the conditions and processes that enable the production of meaning, rather than with meaning *per se*. A principle derived from this approach is that binary opposition (i.e., a positive term paired with its negation) or paired contrasts that function as oppositions are fundamental to the production of meaning (e.g., Jakobson & Halle, 1956; Saussure, 1916/1966). An underlying assumption is that binary thought is basic to the operation of the human mind and/or that it is acquired through cultural practice. A consequence is that in all cultural products "there must be some kind of a systematic and interrelated set of oppositions that can be elicited" (Berger, 1982, p. 30). The pattern of oppositions is referred to as the *paradigmatic structure* of meaning.

The paradigmatic structure is also called the *deep structure* (Chomsky, 1965) of meaning. As this phrase suggests, the conditions that give rise to and support meanings are suppressed; the binary oppositions are not readily apparent. What appear transparent are surface or superficial meanings—meanings that seem to be natural, uncontestable truths.[2] But those meanings are neither natural nor uncontestable. Rather, they represent the ideology of dominant social groups. And their seeming naturalness is an illusion that serves a tactical purpose: It perpetuates the dominant social group's preferred meanings. The objective of *paradigmatic analysis* is to identify the paradigmatic structures on which the seemingly natural meanings are framed. A result of such analyses is that one gains insight into the assumptions that shape dominant groups' intentions with regard to preferred meanings.

Review of Literature

A number of scholars have generated paradigmatic analyses relative to aspects of fashion and dress and/or have based appearance-related studies on the principle that meaning is derived from relations of difference and opposition. Barthes based his analysis of the fashion system (1983) on a dichotomy drawn between a vestimentary (clothing) code and a rhetorical (written/spoken) system. Berger (1984) constructed bipolar oppositions between elements associated with denim work clothes and contrasting elements associated with high fashion apparel. Davis (1985) constructed a similar argument in which he proposed fashion as an oppositional expression relative to clothing. Fiske (1989) analyzed generic and designer blue jeans and uncovered a paradigmatic structure based on binary oppositions such as classless/upscale, country/city, communal/socially distinctive, unchanging/transient, and traditional/contemporary. Morgado (2007) described the semiotic system of hip-hop dress in terms of binary oppositions such as size/

fit, private/public, and derogatory/laudatory. Polhemus (1988) generated paradigmatic structures for each of nineteen different appearance styles (e.g., Beats, Mods, Punks, Hippies, Preppies, Executives) based on expressive characteristics he associated with each of the styles. Polhemus and Proctor (1978) analyzed a dichotomy between classic styles of dress, which they referred to as antifashion, and a fashion code. Sahlins (1976) argued that socio-cultural categories are encoded in binary structures associated with the design elements of dress. And Simmel (1957) characterized behaviors associated with fashion in terms of tensions between a bipolar system based on individuality and conformity.

Method

We identified three salient conditions wherein the Hawaiian shirt plays an iconic role as a marker of meaning: (1) humorous depictions in which the shirt is a central element of the stereotype of the tourist as sartorial clod; (2) humorous depictions of the Hawaiian shirt as preeminent symbol of casual dress or a leisurely lifestyle; and (3) serious depictions of the Hawaiian shirt as a revered icon of the spirit of local Island culture. In the fall of 2010 we conducted paradigmatic analyses of these iconic forms following examination of an extensive body of existing written and visual materials. We read descriptions of the shirt as recorded in social and economic histories, news reports, and journal and magazine articles; in advice columns and other texts concerned with dress and appearance standards; and on websites advertising Hawaiians shirts for sale. We examined hundreds of visual images in books about the shirt, in commercial photographs available online from Getty Images and Google Images, and in cartoons on Hawaiian shirts published in *The New Yorker* magazine. We considered descriptive terminology, physical characteristics of wearers, other aspects of the contexts in which the shirts signified, and rhetorical and visual techniques on which meanings relied. We extrapolated from the texts, photographs, and cartoon images to propose terminology that captured the essence of the shirt as depicted in these works. And we generated oppositional or contrasting terminology to indicate expressions that were absent from the materials but structurally necessary to the meanings of the shirt in its various iconic forms.

Funny Kine Clothes: A Peculiar Shirt

The association of the Hawaiian shirt with souvenir products and tourist culture is a more-or-less natural consequence of both commerce and circumstance. The peculiar shirt originated in small dry goods and custom tailor shops operated by Chinese and Japanese immigrants who arrived in the Islands in the late 19th and early 20th centuries in response to a need for plantation labor (Fundaburk, 1965). Prototypes of the shirt were available in the early 1920s. These were wide and boxy, rather than tailored to the body, and sported unusual one-piece collars that were larger and floppier than those on ordinary men's shirts. The garments had straight hemlines, rather than shirt-tails, and the shirts were worn outside of, rather than tucked into, the trousers. At the outset, these features signaled a comparative difference from typical men's wear of the time, to the extent that in the Islands, even conservative, solid-colored shirts with these style characteristics were prohibited from the workplace (Morgado, 2003, p. 79). But the printed patterns and colors that came to typify the Hawaiian shirt were even more curious.

The first print goods with motifs drawn from the local environment were tropical floral patterns. These appeared in 1935 on textiles intended as upholstery fabrics (Fundaburk, 1965, pp. 58, 71). The idea was immediately translated into textiles suitable for apparel products and, within a year, dozens of print designs featuring indigenous elements of the natural and social environments were evident. The time was not only coincident with a growing tourist trade in the Islands, but also with significant increases in the numbers of U.S. Naval personnel in Hawai`i, and the demand for Hawaiian souvenirs was substantial. By 1936, shirts in bright, radiant colors and advertised as "Specials for Tourists!" were widely available in a plethora of unique Island print designs (pp. 64–65).

By 1939 sales of the peculiar shirt—made up in equally remarkable fabrics that sported cartoon-like images of grass shacks, hula dancers, Hawaiian words, flower leis, and scantily clad natives—had propelled the Island's garment industry into a big business (Arlen, 1940, p. 77). Most of that business was derived from overseas retail orders and local sales to tourists and military personnel. Among the resident population there was little interest in the shirt other than as a boost to the tourist trade. Furthermore, the shirt was banned for employees of City, State and Federal offices and from banks and corporate offices on grounds that its appearance would induce sloppy work habits. And businesses outside the tourist-dense Waikiki area prohibited employees from wearing the shirt, as well. Nearly a decade would pass before the Hawaiian shirt made any significant inroads into the dress of local islanders, and almost 25 years passed before it became a staple item of local Island dress (Morgado, 2003, p. 79).

We determined that from the outset, the meaning of the Hawaiian shirt revolves around its difference relative to *customary dress*, its *peculiarity*, rather than *familiarity*, in terms of design features, its *bright*, colorful nature relative to *subdued* conventional dress, and the interpretation of the garment as conducive to *sloppiness* as contrasted with *neatness*:

> Hawaiian Shirt/Customary dress
> Peculiar/Familiar
> Bright/Subdued
> Sloppy/Neat

A Shirt That Makes Us Laugh (at tourists)

By the mid-1950s tourism was rampant, and an inexorable link was established between the tourist and the Hawaiian shirt. Features associated with the shirt—its peculiarity relative to customary dress, the unusually bright colors, the curious prints, and the unconventional styling details—became associated with the tourist. And characteristics typically attributed to the tourist, such as being fat, badly dressed, and unattractive (e.g., Pearce,

2005, p. 19) became associated with the shirt (Morgado, 2003). We found multiple examples of this in both photographs and written works. For example, visual images of the Hawaiian shirted tourist as an overweight clod and/or buffoon are common in commercial photographs. Figure 3.11a provides a classic illustration: An overweight young man attired in badly mismatched Hawaiian shirt and shorts is pictured in a ridiculous pose and a silly grin, waving to viewers as he leans against a palm tree on a sunny beach (Herholdt, n.d.[a]).[3] In Figure 3.11b an obese, bare-chested sunbather wears Hawaiian printed swim shorts; his female companion sports a Hawaiian shirt (McClymont, n.d.).

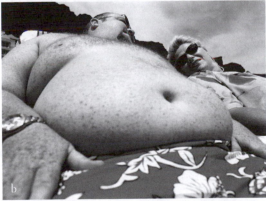

Figure 3.11a and b By the 1950s, the Hawaiian shirt was commonly associated with overweight and sloppy American tourists.

In written works, instances wherein journalists address the Hawaiian-shirted tourist with jests, jibes, and name-calling are abundant. This version of the tourist is variously referred to as the "universal geek," the "universal clod," the "yokel," and the "hayseed" (Berendt, 1987, p. 24; Cocks, 1985, p. 88; Fujii, 1977, p. 45; 1999, p. 85; Shindler, 1979, p. 48). The garment itself is described as "flashy-trashy tourist stuff" (Cheever, 1983, p. 33), "the most obvious souvenir of Hawaii that anyone ever took home" (Brown, 1982, p. 106), and as "one of the world's kitschiest garments" (Barchfield, 2010). Several commercial websites offer custom and ready-made shirts marketed as "kitsch," or "tacky," or "really bad," and one such site lets consumers know that "You don't have to be crazy to wear [a Hawaiian-style shirt], but it helps!" (Tropically Yours, n.d.). In the *Encyclopedia of Bad Taste*, Stern and Stern (1991) describe Hawaiian shirts as "masterworks" of bad taste (p. 8) that "engender shrieks, belly laughs, or exasperated anger because they are so awfully inappropriate" (p. 9), and offer that "a Hawaiian shirt worn anywhere other than near a beach or swimming pool is the classic way a vulgarian announces that he is unbounded by the livery constraints of polite society" (p. 147).

A number of sources variously admonish tourists for looking "like they are going to a Hawaiian luau" (Nine ways . . . , n.d.), for wearing Hawaiian shirts "except in Hawaii" (How to identify tourists, n.d.), and simply for looking like tourists (How to avoid . . . , n.d.). They advise tourists against dress code infractions that include: wearing Hawaiian shirts, wearing shirts worn hanging outside the trousers; appearing in bright Hawaiian printed garb; wearing bright colors; wearing white stockings with shorts; wearing black stockings with sandals; wearing message-printed T-shirts; wearing baseball caps; wearing hats; and carrying bags, water bottles, and cameras (e.g., Duvauchelle, n.d.; Fujii, 1999; Heckathorn, 1988; Nine ways . . . , n.d.; How to avoid . . . , n.d.). The humor in Shanahan's cartoon (2002) (Figure 3.12) is largely derived from the multiplicity of tourist dress code violations: the garish Hawaiian printed shirt; the shirt worn outside the trousers; the stockings with sandals, the baseball cap, camera, water bottle, large bag, and message T-shirt—all inappropriate garb for visitors. These American tourists are perfectly disguised as American tourists.[4,5]

We summarized these expressions regarding the aesthetics of the Hawaiian shirt with the terms *bizarre* as compared with *ordinary*; *vulgar* as contrasted with *sophisticated*; *tawdry* rather than *fashionable*; and indicative of *bad taste* as compared with *good taste*:

> Bizarre/Ordinary
> Vulgar/Sophisticated
> Tawdry/Fashionable
> Bad taste/Good taste

A particularly egregious dress code infraction involves a male/female couple dressed in a Hawaiian shirt and matching mu`umu`u[6] (e.g., Fujii, 1999). One humorist recorded a musical number on this theme. The lyrics read:

They wore a matching shirt and muumuu, so you knew their love was true.

With a matching shirt and muumuu, you know who belongs to who.

It's a wild and a passionate attraction. Like a flickering flame to a moth.

When they wear the very same fashion, you know they're cut from the very same cloth

Dana, ca. 1960

Figure 3.13 shows a middle-aged tourist couple dressed in a matching Hawaiian shirt and mu`umu`u (Smith, n.d.). The garments are rendered in a highly iconic print that carries additional meaning relative to the tourist stereotype: Some Hawaiian prints are considered more typical than others, and thus more indicative of a tourist, an outsider, and an unsophisticated aesthetic. The large scale *pareau* (i.e., stylized floral) motif

Figure 3.12 This cartoon from *The New Yorker* depicts a variety of typical tourist dress code violations.

executed in bright, primary colors is an example. Thus, while the print-matching aesthetic itself is subject to sneers (on the part of those who presume to have more sophisticated taste), particular characteristics of the textile prints in which the shirt and accompanying mu`umu`u are fabricated are also important in estimations of the tourist value or kitsch value of the garment. We summarized these expressions with the phrase *down market* as contrasted with *upscale* and *déclassé* compared with *refined*:

> Down market/Upscale
> Déclassé/Refined

Additionally, we identified *tourist* as essential to the meaning of the shirt, and paired this with the term *traveler*—a much more sophisticated tourist. And we added the contrast between *outside* and *inside* to address the idea that tourists are outside of a local context and culture:

> Tourist/Traveler
> Outsider/Insider

Figure 3.13 A particularly egregious dress code infraction involves a male-female couple dressed in a Hawaiian shirt and matching mu`umu`u.

In the Museum of International Folk Art in Santa Fe is a three-dimensional installation that features a larger-than-life caricature of a mule arranged in a deck chair in a laconic, human-like pose. The animal is outfitted in sunglasses, walking shorts, and a vibrantly colorful Hawaiian printed shirt. The humor is self-evident: Only a jackass on vacation would dress like this. We found that humor relative to the Hawaiian-shirted tourist was generated on techniques such as caricature, burlesque, and exaggeration, but that it also drew on ridicule, insults, over-literalness, facetiousness, and sarcasm. For example, among other techniques, the *New Yorker* cartoon illustrated in Figure 3.12 employs absurdity, facetiousness, and ridicule to accomplish the humor. And all of the written works that point to the tourist as hayseed, nerd, loudmouth, and vulgarian generate humor as a consequence of insults and ridicule.

Virtually all of the humorous visual images involving tourists in Hawaiian shirts rest on presentations of the tourist as foolish, dense, or obese, and in many cases, all characteristics are employed. Figure 3.14a shows the plump young man in garishly mismatched Hawaiian printed shirt and shorts. It also features tourist-related dress code violations that include sandals worn with stockings and a baseball cap worn back to front (Herholdt, n.d.[b]). The presentation is accessorized with bright pink childrens' beach toys and a very foolish facial expression. Figure 3.14b (Durfee, n.d.) pictures a silly couple in Hawaiian shirts camping it up for the camera by engaging in juvenile antics. In Figure 3.14c (DKAR, n.d.) a vacationing couple in Hawaiian shirts sport silly sunglasses and equally silly facial expressions. And Figure 3.14d (Comstock, n.d.) pictures a young man in a Hawaiian shirt who appears to be dumbfounded by the map he is holding, as well as badly dressed.

We identified three oppositions that synthesize these ideas about physical and mental characteristics of the tourist in the Hawaiian shirt: *fat* as contrasted with *fit*, *foolish* compared with *sensible*, and *inferior* as opposed to *superior*:

> Fat/Fit
> Foolish/Sensible
> Inferior/Superior

Figure 3.14a–d These photographs play on the stereotype that tourists in Hawaiian shirts are foolish, dense, or obese.

A Shirt That Says "Relax" (under some conditions)

The second iconic form concerns the Hawaiian shirt as an emblem of leisure or a laid-back life-style and as the definitive symbol of casual dress. We collapse two ideas under this heading: the icon of casual dress and the icon of leisure. In their account of the history of the Hawaiian shirt, Brown and Arthur (2002) suggest that the con-temporary business practice of designating Friday as casual dress day originated in Hawai`i in the mid-1960s (pp. 78–79). Ironically, prior to that time, even solid-colored shirts with a single, tiny

Hawaiian emblem embroidered on the pocket were considered inappropriate to Hawai`i business environments. A petition to the State Legislature generated by the local garment industry (along with a gift of two Hawaiian shirts to each legislator) ultimately resulted in a Legislative resolution that promoted Hawaiian shirts as appropriate business wear on the last day of the workweek. In the Islands wearing Hawaiian shirts on Fridays was institutionalized in a Legislative mandate that recognized every Friday as "Aloha Friday." Elsewhere, a permissible dress-down day at the end of the workweek is known as "Casual Friday" (pp. 78–79).

The Hawaiian shirt is typically employed as a symbol of Casual Friday. One cartoon from Getty Images depicts five outfits on hangers, each identified by a day of the week on which the outfit presumably is worn. The Monday through Thursday garb is portrayed as identical business suits; the image for Friday is a brilliantly colored and wildly patterned Hawaiian shirt and a pair of blue jeans (Karas, n.d.). In a *New Yorker* cartoon (Cullum, 1998), a penguin arrives for the day's activities wearing a Hawaiian shirt and finds the rest of the flock outfitted in their typical formal attire. The surprised bird says "You're kidding. I thought it was Friday." *New Yorker* cartoons can be accessed at cartoonbank.com.[6] Serious work requires serious clothes: In another *New Yorker* cartoon (Leighton, 2007), one of a group of astronauts boarding a rocket ship wears a Hawaiian shirt; the others are dressed in space suits. The gag line comes from the Hawaiian-shirted crew member who has forgotten when the scheduled takeoff is to occur. He remarks: "Oh. Is that today?" And in another *New Yorker* cartoon (Stevens, 2006), captioned "Casual Sunday," a priest outfitted in a Hawaiian shirt addresses his congregation with a recitation that begins "And on the seventh day. . . ."

We determined that the terms *leisure* as contrasted with *work* and *inappropriate* as opposed to *appropriate* aptly summarized these characteristics attributed to the Hawaiian shirt:

Leisure/Work
Inappropriate/Appropriate

There is also another meaning attributed to the shirt relative to the workplace. The shirt represents not only casual dress; it is also a sign of a creative approach to the business of doing business. In one *New Yorker* cartoon (Diffee, 2009) a group of businessmen, appropriately dressed in suits and ties, surround a conference table. They have apparently reached consensus on a course of action. The chairman concludes the meeting with the comment: "Sounds good. Well just have to run it by the Hawaiian shirts." We understand that the reference is to the more creative professionals in the firm, and can likely assume that the "Hawaiian shirts" are members of either the creative marketing team or the information technology group. The term *creative* identifies this attribution to the Hawaiian shirt, and we paired it with the term *conforming*:

Creative/Conforming

A noticeable difference occurs in the methods through which humor is generated relative to the lifestyle icon as compared with the icon wherein the shirt functions as a characteristic of the tourist. Humor in the tourist-related cartoons and commercial photos is characteristically predicated on ridicule and insults. But humor in cartoons wherein the Hawaiian shirt is indicative of a leisurely, laid-back lifestyle is generated through gentler techniques such as exaggeration and absurdity. An example is Mankoff's cartoon (1996) for *The New Yorker*, illustrated in Figure 3.15. A gentleman opens his door to find that the Grim Reaper has come to call attired in a floral printed shirt and matching beach shorts. It's awfully hard to take Death seriously when he arrives in a Hawaiian shirt. The gentleman comments: "You call this 'death with dignity'?"

Similarly, Cotham (2004) employs absurdity as a humorous device in his *New Yorker* cartoon wherein a businessman turns away a Hawaiian shirted, cocktail carrying beggar with the line: "You don't look like a hurricane victim to me." In Wilson's (2000) *New Yorker* cartoon a doctor addresses the wife of a patient who is lying in a hospital bed wearing a Hawaiian shirt and holding a tropical drink. The doctor says: "As you can

"You call this 'death with dignity'?"

Figure 3.15 This cartoon from *The New Yorker* relies on the leisurely and laid-back connotations that the Hawaiian shirt implies.

see, we've transferred your husband from intensive to casual care." Zeigler's (2004) *New Yorker* cartoon illustrates an ordinary looking guy in Hawaiian shirt and shorts, suspended in the air over a tropical beach. Through the caption we are able to identify the flying figure as Superman, now outfitted for relaxation. The caption reads: "The Man of Steel (in retirement) hovering over the ladies' bath-house at the Sand 'N' Surf Club in Boca Raton." In Maslin's (1996) comic sketch, mourners pass by an open coffin wherein rests a corpse dressed in a Hawaiian shirt and *lauhala* (woven fiber) hat. One passerby remarks, "Wherever he's going, I just hope they have frozen banana daiquiris." The word *play* in contrast to the word *work* expresses the fundamental idea expressed in these cartoons:

Play/Work

A Shirt That Is Revered (and romanticized)

There is a context wherein death in a Hawaiian shirt is an entirely serious matter. In the Islands the Hawaiian shirt is, in fact, the definitive ritual burial garment. It is a statement of reverence—not just for the shirt, but for all that the shirt signifies. This is the third iconic form: the Hawaiian shirt as an icon of local culture.

In the Islands, the Hawaiian shirt is more commonly known as the Aloha shirt. Many people are familiar with the word *aloha* as a greeting—an equivalent for hello or goodbye. But the meaning of aloha is much deeper and more profound than the simple salutation. The word has a spiritual quality or spiritual essence. It is described as akin to the idea of "the breath of life" (To-Hawaii.com). The word also connotes love and self-respect. And it speaks to a psychic sense of positive energy and to life lived in harmony with others and with the environment. Aloha is a powerful word. And in its local context, the Aloha shirt is said to embody the powerful spirit of aloha. But the shirt embodies more: The shirt is closely tied to a romanticized image of old Hawai`i as a tropical paradise.

Descriptions of the garment as an icon of old Hawai`i are drawn from books and magazine articles authored by local writers and others who feel closely connected to the Islands. Their statements have a poetic quality. Consider these examples:

> Hawaii, awash in romance, marbled by different cultures, saturated with beauty, and compelling in contrasts gave birth . . . to the renowned Aloha shirt. Like a lei, the . . . shirt is worn as a statement of one's love for, and connection to, a most special place.
>
> T. Holmes, in Hope, 2000, p. v.

> . . . a marvelous cultural icon, so evocative of the spirit of its home, is woven with the mystery and allure of Hawaii and the stories of those who have lived there.
>
> Hope, 2000, p. xiii.

> The Aloha shirt is "the history and culture of Hawaii on fabric . . . [it] is art . . . and it's laughter . . . [it's] entertainment, education, aesthetics, and nostalgia. It's hard to expect more out of a single garment."
>
> Fujii, 1999, p. 80.

> . . . the essence of the "warmth, friendliness, and pride of the Hawaiian people."
>
> Steele, 1984, p. 8.

> It's comfortable, casual and bright as all the colors of the rainbow—and sometimes as subtle as early dawn at the beach.
>
> Heckathorn & Black, 1988, p. 60.

> a garment that "celebrate(s) a joy for life."
>
> C. Shelton, in Tominaga, 2000, p. 28.

> I once theorized a workable plan for world peace . . . you just issue every soldier on both sides a beautiful Hawaiian shirt . . .
>
> Vintage Hawaiian, 2003.

> When people go to a rack of shirts, they'll pick out the [Aloha shirt] that satisfies their soul.
>
> D. Hope, in Simon, 2000, p. 34.

> the warmth of the sun . . . trade winds caressing your skin . . . sand between your toes . . . [and] the fragrance of a plumeria lei . . . come together to inspire the canvas that is the [Aloha] shirt.
>
> Hope, 2000, p. xiii.

Comparable pictorial images (e.g., Arthur, 2000; Brown, 1982; Brown & Arthur, 2002; Hope, 2000; Steele, 1985) depict the shirt in old Hollywood movie settings, replicate vintage textile prints based on old Matson ocean liner menu covers, or depict the shirt in the context of other icons and in the style of 1950s picture postcards of the Islands. These coexist alongside descriptions and depictions of the Hawaiian shirt as a central element in the image of the tourist as sartorial clod and the shirt as an emblem of leisure. Figure 3.16 shows a Hawaiian shirt fabricated in a classic vintage print of hibiscus blossoms on vintage rayon fabric and accompanied by a straw hat. This photograph exemplifies visual images that depict the Hawaiian shirt as a romanticized icon of old Hawai`i.

Key elements of the shirt in this iconic form involved a sense of *history* (the *past*), as contrasted with the *present*, the shirt as a unique *art form*, rather than a *commodity*, a strong sense of place (i.e., the *Hawaiian Islands*), as contrasted with *elsewhere*; and the *authenticity* of the shirt as a *cultural artifact*, rather than an *inauthentic tourist souvenir*:

> History (past)/Present
> Art form/Commodity
> Hawaiian Islands/Elsewhere
> Authentic/Inauthentic
> Cultural artifact/Tourist souvenir

Figure 3.16 Some images of the Hawaiian shirt present it as a romanticized icon of old Hawaii.

Conclusion: Paradigmatic Structure and Implications of the Study

The analysis resulted in three meaning clusters. But the paired opposition did not necessarily cluster as we anticipated, and the themes around which the paired terms coalesced required alternative titles. One cluster is governed by the opposition Them/Us. Oppositions in this cluster include Tourist/Traveler; Vulgar/Sophisticated; Tawdry/Fashionable; Bad taste/Good taste; Outsiders/Insiders; Down market/Upscale; Déclassé/Refined, Fat/Fit; Foolish/Sensible; and Inferior/Superior. A second cluster of meanings referenced the Hawaiian shirt and its difference as compared to ordinary or customary dress. This thematic cluster is designated Different/Same. Included in this theme are the oppositions Hawaiian shirt/Customary dress; Peculiar/Familiar; Bright/Subdued;

Sloppy/Neat; Leisure/Business; Inappropriate/Appropriate; Creative/Conforming; and Play/Work. A third thematic cluster is designated Culture/Commerce. This theme speaks exclusively to the shirt as a revered icon of local culture. It includes the oppositions History (past)/Present; Art/Commodity; Hawaiian Islands/Elsewhere; Authentic/Inauthentic, and Artifact/Souvenir. The paradigmatic structure of meanings associated with iconic forms of the Hawaiian shirt is illustrated in Table 3.1.

Our interest in examining the Hawaiian shirt was motivated by the peculiar nature of the garment: its uniqueness in terms of design and fabrication, the frequency with which it appears in humorous images and commentary about the American tourist, its function as key icon of leisure dress and a casual lifestyle, and the reverence it is accorded in local Island culture. A semiotic framework that recast the subject of our study from an examination of surface meanings to a paradigmatic analysis of the framework on which those meanings rely enabled us to move beyond the humor and the romanticism associated with the shirt and to concentrate on the deep structure that supports the meaning attributions. Three meaning clusters emerged from the analysis, each representing a thematic paradigm: Them/Us, Different/Same, and Culture/Commerce.

The Them/Us theme is commonly revealed in paradigmatic analyses of cultural phenomena, and this distinction is generally understood as a natural condition of social life (e.g., Chandler. 2002, pp. 101–105). But the theme does not appear to have been directly addressed in existing analyses of fashion and appearance. It is an intuitively obvious feature of dress, and its absence suggests that the absence itself may be an interesting subject for investigation. But the most significant aspect of the theme is that the contrasting elements of the paradigm address a central issue of our theoretical frame: In this case, the surface meanings of the popular culture product are cast as good-humored jokes about aesthetics and taste, while the deep structure reveals power relationships and social group tensions. The privileged elements in the Them/Us paradigm address a social group that defines itself as

TABLE 3.1
Paradigmatic Structure of Iconic Meanings Attributed to the Hawaiian Shirt

Theme #1		Theme #2		Theme #3	
THEM	US	DIFFERENT	SAME	CULTURE	COMMERCE
Tourist	Traveler	Hawaiian	Customary	History (past)	Present
Vulgar	Sophisticated	shirt	dress	Art form	Commodity
Tawdry	Fashionable	Peculiar	Familiar	Hawaiian Islands	Elsewhere
Bad taste	Good taste	Bright	Subdued	Authentic	Inauthentic
Outsiders	Insiders	Sloppy	Neat	Artifact	Souvenir
Down market	Upscale	Bizarre	Ordinary		
Déclassé	Refined	Leisure	Business		
Fat	Fit	Inappropriate	Appropriate		
Foolish	Sensible	Creative	Conforming		
Inferior	Superior	Play	Work		

sophisticated, sensible, and superior, while those outside the group are identified as vulgar, foolish, and inferior. Berger (1984) points to theories in the works of Hobbs and Freud that suggest that humor is based on feelings of superiority that arise when one openly diminishes the status of others (p. 72). Although we tend to read humorous ridicule and insults as good-natured jests, the search for the deep structure of meanings attributed to popular phenomena suggests that we look beyond our surface interpretations in order to examine the foundations on which those meanings are structured.

The Different/Same theme has not been identified as such in other paradigmatic analyses of dress and appearance, although the opposition is akin to the dichotomy Davis (1985) identified between fashion and clothing, Polhemus and Proctor (1978) identified between fashion and anti-fashion, and that Morgado (2007) proposed between extraordinary and ordinary dress. The repetition of this theme in dress and appearance studies suggests it warrants further examination, especially in the postmodern context, when fashion trends that encourage expressions of uniqueness and individuality in appearance may be erasing both the distinctive and the oppositional character of unusual appearance forms.

The Culture/Commerce theme is also not apparent in other works on dress and may be unique to the contexts and circumstances surrounding the Hawaiian shirt. However other work

has addressed binary oppositions that support distinctions between culturally authentic experiences and synthetic events manufactured for tourist consumption, and between legitimate cultural objects and inauthentic tourist souvenirs (e.g., Culler, 1988; MacCannell, 1976). Examinations of other apparel and appearance related souvenir products would provide additional insights on this phenomenon.

Several limitations of our analysis need to be addressed. One is that some readers may challenge the notion that meaning is constructed on the basis of binary oppositions and/or paired contrasts; that the meanings of social and cultural (or any) phenomena are better addressed as continua than as oppositions. There is, however, strong scholarly support for the idea that binary thinking is—if not an integral component of the human mind—an integral component of our language system. Furthermore, the question that must be addressed is: Have we learned anything of value from the paradigmatic analysis? If we have come to new or different understandings about the nature of meaning as a result of the analysis, there is value in the assumptions that underlie the study.

A second limitation concerns the particular binary oppositions and paired contrasts that emerged in the study. Some readers may argue that the oppositions we elicited are not properties of the structural framework that supports meanings attributed to the shirt. Rather, the oppositions are products of the authors' minds. With this, we concur. Meaning is always predicated on interpretation and interpretation was central to our discoveries. However, the results of the analysis appear to be intuitively reasonable, and other interpreters may elicit additional components of the thematic clusters we identified or may suggest alternative terminology.

It is likely that few garments are as rich in iconic value as is the funny kine clothes that originated in the commercial culture of an exotic locale. However, it is very likely that other dress forms exhibit peculiar meanings that warrant examination. The present study offers insights into the dress form that was examined. It also offers insights into the role of dress as a popular culture artifact. It suggests that eliciting the contradictory meaning clusters that surround dress forms can also provide insights into the cultures that invest those forms with meaning. And it models a form of inquiry that can be fruitful in examinations of other forms of funny kine clothes.

References

Arlen, L. (1940, January–March). Pins and needles in Hawaii. *Pan Pacific* 1(4), No. 1. 77–79. (Reprinted from *The Honolulu Advertiser*, 1939, February 19, Magazine section).

Arthur, L. B. (2000). *Aloha attire. Hawaiian dress in the twentieth century*. Atglen, PA: Schiffer Publishing.

Barchfield, J. (2010, Oct. 7). Ode to the aloha shirt. *Honolulu Star Advertiser*. Retrieved from http://www.staradvertiser.com/features/20101007_Ode_to_the_aloha_shirt.html

Barthes, R. (1983). *The fashion system* (M. Ward & R. Howard, Trans.). London: Cape. (Original work published 1967).

Berendt, J. (1987, August). The Hawaiian shirt. *Esquire*, 24.

Berger, A. A. (1982). *Media Analysis Techniques*. Newbury Park, CA: Sage Publications.

Berger, A. A. (1984). *Signs in contemporary culture*. Salem, WI: Sheffield Publishing Company.

Blackburn, M. (2001). *Hawaiiana. The best of Hawaiian design* (2nd ed., revised). Atglen, PA: Schiffer Publishing.

Brown, D. (1982). *Hawaii recalls. Selling romance to America*. Honolulu: Editions Limited.

Brown, D. & Arthur, L. B. (2002). *The art of the aloha shirt*. Waipahu, HI: Island Heritage Publishing.

Chandler, D. (2002). *Semiotics: The basics*. London: Routledge.

Cheever, D. (1983). *Hawaiian Fashion Guild strategic marketing plan*. Unpublished internal trade document available from the association.

Chomsky, N. (1965). *Aspects of the theory of syntax*. Cambridge, MA: MIT Press.

Cocks, J. (1985, June). High, wide and Hawaiian. *Time* 12(22), 88.

Comstock. (n.d.). Comical portrait of tourist [Photograph]. #78494729 retrieved from http://www.gettyimages.com.

Cotham, F. (2004, October 4). You don't look like a hurricane victim to me [Cartoon]. *The New Yorker*, 54. SKU:128113 retrieved from newyorkercartoonbank.com.

Culler, J. (1988). *Framing the sign: Criticism and its institutions*. Oxford, England: Basil Blackwell.

Cullum, L. (1998). You're kidding. I thought it was Friday [Cartoon]. SKU:117305 retrieved from http://www.cartoonbank.com (Originally published in *The New Yorker*, May 18, 1998, p. 50.

DAJ. (n.d.). Vintage silky shirt with straw hat [Photograph]. #79310422 retrieved from gettyimages.com.

Dana, B. (ca. 1960). Matching Shirt and Muumuu. In *Bill Dana's brand new old traditional Hawaiian album* [Record]. Honolulu, HI: Bill Dana's Brand New Old Traditional Record Company.

Davis, F. (1985). Clothing and fashion as communication. In M. R. Solomon (Ed.), *The Psychology of Fashion* (pp. 15–27). Lexington, MA: D. C. Heath.

Diffee, M. (2009, March 16). Sounds good. We'll just have to run it by the Hawaiian shirts [Cartoon]. *The New Yorker*, 80. SKU:132619 retrieved from newyorkercartoonbank.com.

DKAR Images (n.d.). Couple in comic sunglasses #a0261-000009 [Photograph]. Retrieved from gettyimages.com.

Durfee, D. (n.d.). Couple in Hawaiian shirts BC7089-001 [Photograph]. Retrieved from gettyimages.com.

Duvauchelle, J. (n.d.). How to dress in Hawaii and not look like a tourist. *Travel tips by demand media*. Retrieved from http://traveltips.usatoday.com/dress-hawaii-not-look-like-tourist-4533.html.

Fiske, J. (1989). *Understanding popular culture*. London: Routledge.

Fujii, J. (1977, October). It's twilight time for aloha wear. *Honolulu*, 45–47.

Fujii, J. (1999, March/April). It's a shirt thing. *Westways*, 80–85.

Fundaburk, E. L. (1965). Contemporary accounts of the development of the garment manufacturing industry of Hawaii (Part 1, Vol. 2). *The garment manufacturing industry of Hawaii*. HI: Economic Research Center, University of Hawaii.

Heckathorn, J. & Black, T. J. (1988, March). 100 years of Island fashion. *Honolulu*, 60; 66–67; 70–72; 74–76.

Herholdt, F. (n.d. [a]). Overweight tourist in Hawaiian shirt BC8630-001 [Photograph]. Retrieved from gettyimages.com.

Herholdt, F. (n.d.[b]). Tourist in mismatched Hawaiian garb and beach toys BC8630-002 [Photograph]. Retrieved from gettyimages.com.

THE MEANINGS OF DRESS

Hope, D. (2000). *The aloha shirt. Spirit of the Islands.* Hillsboro, OR: Beyond Words Publishing.

How to avoid looking like an American tourist (n.d.). *wikiHow*. Retrieved from http://www.wikihow.com/Avoid-Looking-Like-an-American-Tourist.

How to identify tourists (n.d.). *Uncyclopedia*. Retrieved from http://uncyclopedia.wikia.com/wiki/War_on_Tourism.

Jakobson, R & Halle, M. (1956). *Fundamentals of language.* The Hague: Mouton.

Karas, B. (n.d.). Monday, Tuesday, Wednesday, Thursday, Friday. *#bsl038* [Photograph]. Retrieved from gettyimages.com.

Leighton, R. (2007, April 16). Oh. Is that today? [Cartoon]. *The New Yorker*, 98. SKU:130840 retrieved from newyorkercartoonbank.com.

MacCannell, D. (1976). *The tourist.* NY: Oxford University Press.

Maslin, M. (1996, December 16). Wherever he's going I just hope they have frozen banana daiquiris [Cartoon]. *The New Yorker*, 54. SKU:113051 retrieved from newyorkercartoonbank.com.

Mankoff, R. (1996, November 25). You call this "death with dignity"? [Cartoon]. *The New Yorker*, 81.

McClymont, S. (n.d.). Overweight sunbather *#BD7173-002* [Photograph]. Retrieved from gettyimages.com.

Morgado, M. A. (2003). From kitsch to chic: The transformation of Hawaiian shirt aesthetics. *Clothing and Textiles Research Journal 21*(2), 75–88.

Morgado, M. A. (2007). The semiotics of extraordinary dress. A structural analysis and interpretation of hip-hop style. *Clothing & Textiles Research Journal 25* (2), 131–155.

Nine (9) ways not to look like a tourist (n.d.). *HowNottoDo*. Retrieved from http://www.hownottodo.com/not-look-like-a-tourist/.

Pearce, P. L. (2005). *Tourist behavior. Themes and conceptual schemes.* Clevedon, UK: Channel View Publications.

Polhemus, T. (1988). *Body style.* Beds, UK: Lennard.

Polhemus, T. & Proctor, L. (1978). *Fashion and antifashion.* London: Thames & Hudson.

Sahlins, M. D. (1976). *Culture and practical reason.* Chicago: University of Chicago Press.

Saussure, F. de (1916/1966). *Course in general linguistics* (W. Baskin, Trans.). NY: McGraw-Hill.

Schiffer, N. (1989). *Tropical shirts and clothing.* Atglen, PA: Schiffer Publishing.

Schiffer, N. (1997). *Hawaiian shirt designs.* Atglen, PA: Schiffer Publishing.

Schiffer, N. (2005). *Hawaiian shirts. Dress right for paradise.* Atglen, PA: Schiffer Publishing.

Shanahan, D. (2002, November 4). *The Great Satan* [Cartoon]. *The New Yorker*, 81.

Shindler, M. (1979, July 2). Aloha shirts. *New West*, 48–50, 53.

Simmel, G. (1957). Fashion. *American Journal of Sociology*, 62, 541–558. (Original work published 1904.)

Simon, L. (2000, August/September). Fashion statements. A manifesto of island style. *Hana Hou!*, 31–41 [also called *Hawaiian Airlines Magazine*].

Smith, S. (n.d.). Tourists in matching shirt and mu`umu`u *#200452491-001* [Photograph]. Retrieved from gettyimages.com.

Steele, T. J. (1984). *The Hawaiian shirt. Its art and history.* NY: Abbeville Press.

Stern, J. & Stern, M. (1991). *The encyclopedia of bad taste.* NY: HarperCollins Publishers (Originally published 1990).

Stevens, M. (2006, November 13). Casual Sunday [Cartoon]. *The New Yorker*, 75. SKU: 130246 retrieved from newyorkercartoonbank.com.

To-Hawaii.com. Travel Guide (n.d.). http://www.to-hawaii.com/aloha.php.

Tominaga, L. (2000, June). Dressing up with aloha. *Spirit of aloha*, 26–29; 34.

Tropically Yours. (n.d.). *Home of the tacky shirt.* Retrieved: http://www.tropicallyyours.com/.

Vintage Hawaiian Shirt: An Artistic Retrospective, The (2003). Anachronistic Productions. Retrieved from http://www.vintagehawaiianshirt.net/aboutmeT2.htm.

Wilson, G. (2000, September 25). As you can see, we've transferred your husband from intensive to casual care [Photograph]. *The New Yorker*. 46. SKU:119950 retrieved from newyorkercartoonbank.com.

Ziegler, J. (2004, July). The Man of Steel (in retirement) hovering over the ladies' bath-house at the Sand "N" Surf Club in Boca Raton. *The New Yorker*. 89. SKU:127593 available at newyorkercartoonbank.com.

Endnotes

1. The current practice is to write the name of the state with a diacritical mark between the first and second letter "i": Hawai`i. In older materials the name appears without the diacritical mark, and some writers continue the practice of writing without the mark: Hawaii. We use the diacritical mark, but preserve the older form when it appears in others' texts. The word "Hawaiian" never takes the diacritical mark.

2. We asked students in an introductory fashion class at the University of Hawai`i to explain why Island locals appear to believe that tourists have bad taste in their selection of Hawaiian shirts. The students' overwhelming response was "Because tourists do have bad taste in Hawaiian shirts!" The response suggests that the association between tourists and bad taste in dress is a good example of a seemingly natural, uncontestable truth.

3. Color versions of the photographs from Getty Images can be accessed online at http://www.gettyimages.com.

4. Cartoons from *The New Yorker* described in this paper can be accessed online by entering the cartoon's reference number in the search box at the website http://www.cartoonbank.com.

5. The tourists in this cartoon are obviously traveling in a Middle Eastern country that is likely Iran. The humor is based on the idea that "The Great Satan" is a derogatory epithet for the USA that appears in Iranian foreign policy statements.

6. The contemporary practice is to use the diacritical marks in writing the word *mu`umu`u*. In earlier works the word is written without the pronunciation marks: *muumuu*.

Discussion Questions

1. What makes the Hawaiian shirt "funny kine" dress?
2. What other garments could be classified as "funny kine"?
3. What are the ways in which the Hawaiian shirt is perceived?

3.4

SAUDI WOMEN WITH "SEXY EYES" WILL HAVE TO COVER THEM UP IN PUBLIC

John Thomas Didymus

Saudi women with "sexy eyes" will soon have to cover them up in public. The government of Saudi Arabia has decided that its men would do better without the "tempting eyes" of attractive Saudi women in public places.

A representative of Saudi Arabia's "Orwellian" Committee for the Promotion of Virtue and Prevention of Vice, Sheikh Motlab al Nabet, has announced that a proposal to make it law that women with "sexy eyes" must cover them in public is being considered. *The Daily Beast* reports that Nabet said:

> The men of the committee will interfere to force women to cover their eyes, especially the tempting ones . . . [We] have the right to do so.

Already, women in Saudi Arabia are required by law to wear a long black robe called "abaya." The abaya covers up practically every part of a woman's body from feet to hair. A little slit-like space is left at the eyes to allow the woman to see when she goes in public. Saudi women who dare appear in public without the abaya may be punished with fines and public flogging.

But it seems now that even this little necessary allowance for vision is offensive to the pious men of the Kingdom of Saudi Arabia. According to *Daily Mail*, the suggestion that women should cover their eyes too in public came after a pious member of the Committee for the Promotion of Virtue and Prevention of Vice fell to the wiles of a woman with "sexy eyes" as he walked innocently down a street. According to the story, when the man's eyes strayed in the direction of alluring female eyes, the husband took offense. A fight followed in which the man with straying eyes was stabbed twice in the hand.

The Saudi Arabian Committee for the Promotion of Virtue and Prevention of Vice, founded in 1940, is the morals watchdog of Saudi Arabian

Figure 3.17 "Sexy" eyes of Saudi Arabian women are considered too provocative despite their otherwise conservative dress.

society. Its job is to ensure that society keeps to the strict rules of morality according to Koranic laws. According to NDTV, the committee, in its zeal for Islamic morality, refused to allow evacuation of girls from a school that was on fire because it was the holy month of Ramadan. The sight of "immodestly" dressed girls in the holy month could cause the men to sin by eyeing the girls' uncovered bodies lustfully. It was alleged that 15 of the girls died in the fire after their evacuation from the building was delayed while the Committee considered the best method to move them without tempting the men.

The Committee, according to NDTV, was also responsible for the ban on women driving. A woman in Saudi Arabia is not allowed to travel without approval of a male guardian or husband. A woman was sentenced to 10 lashes for violating the ban on women driving in September, but was spared when King Abdullah graciously intervened.

According to *The Daily Beast,* even though the Committee for the Promotion of Virtue and Prevention of Vice has not provided a legal definition of "sexy eyes," a Saudi journalist bravely attempted a guess:

> uncovered eyes with a nice shape and makeup. Or even without makeup, if they are beautiful, the woman will be in trouble.

But after taking the trouble to provide a legal definition of "sexy eyes," the Saudi journalist concluded:

> It's so stupid . . . I don't know what to say. They have to stop this. Many people will oppose this in the country. They won't be silent."

Stupid? The Saudi state evidently does not think so. The Committee for the Promotion of Virtue and Prevention of Vice, according to *The Daily Beast,* has full support of the state. Recently, heir to the Saudi throne, Prince Naif, extolled the virtues of the Committee and pledged state support:

> The committee is supported by all sides. . . . It should be supported because it is a pillar from Islam. If you are a Muslim, you should support the committee.

King Abdullah, pleased with the work of the committee, recently gave it an extra 200 million riyals ($53 million) to allow it to perform better its duty of promoting virtue and preventing vice.

Discussion Questions

1. What are the characteristics of "sexy eyes" and eyes that aren't sexy?
2. How does this issue reflect gender issues in Saudi?
3. Does this issue compare to comments that women should avoid "sexy clothes" if they want to remain safe?

SOUTH AFRICA: SEMANTICS OF THE SLUT WALK

Gillian Schutte

In 2008 hundreds of South African women donned their miniskirts and protested at the taxi rank where a young girl was brutally accosted by taxi drivers and hawkers for wearing a short denim skirt. The men who accosted her stuck their fingers into her vagina and called her a "slut."

Women were outraged. The angry protestors wore mini skirts and T-Shirts saying, "Pissed-Off Women." They stormed the ranks and told the perpetrators in no uncertain terms to lay off women and girls who wore jeans and short skirts. Their message was clear. Don't tell us what to wear and don't think that our short skirts are an invitation either.

This past weekend about 2,000 women and men gathered in Cape Town for South Africa's first of a series of Slut Walk initiatives, which are also set to take place in Johannesburg and Durban in September. Everyone dressed up in clothing that would typically be considered "slutty" and placards sporting messages such as "Patriarchs se poes!" and "Proud Slut" abounded (Figure 3.18). The atmosphere was electric with ribaldry, revolution and a celebratory freedom of sexual expression most often linked to Gay Pride. What this tells us is that South African women from different social classes and cultures have collectively had enough of sexual assault, rape and the patriarchal controlling attitudes toward them. They have joined the global Slut Walk movement to add their voices to the powerful message that enough is enough.

The Slut Walk phenomenon began in Toronto in April this year when a policeman offered advice to students on how to avoid sexual assault in a crime safety forum at the Toronto University this year. His comment to them: "You know, I think we're beating around the bush here. I've been told I'm not supposed to say this. However, women should avoid dressing like sluts in order not to be victimized."

Figure 3.18 After the first Slut Walk in Toronto, Canada, similar protests spread to cities worldwide. Here, a woman holds a banner at a Slut Walk in Amsterdam, Netherlands.

Little did he realize that his utterances would spark a worldwide feminine movement which deconstructs the patriarchal view that it is what women wear that causes the perpetrator to rape. Nor did he realize that the very word he used in a derogatory sense would be the very word that would be adopted as the signifier for this rebellion.

The organizers of the first march in Toronto seized the word "slut" and reclaimed their right to wear what they want and express their sexuality freely. The message was loud and clear: "Don't

Reprinted by permission of the author.

tell us what to wear—Tell men not to rape." After this first Slut Walk in Toronto, it became a phenomenon that rapidly spread to London, Orlando, Mexico City, Melbourne and Delhi and more recently to Cape Town. Facebook also boasts close to 100 Slut Walk pages from countries around the world including Helenski, Mumbai, Morocco and Singapore.

This Slut Walk phenomenon shows no signs of abating any time soon. It is a movement that refuses to be shamed and the messages from every country are similar. "This is what I was wearing when I got raped & I still did not ask for it," states a purple placard carried by a voluptuous woman wearing a low cut black lace top and leggings. "I was wearing jeans and a button-up collar shirt when I got raped," states another. "I was 10 when my father raped me and he did not care what I was wearing," shouts another. "I wear heels to be tall. Not raped!" says a placard carried by a short woman in heels and tight mini skirt. "Control yourselves—not women!" states a placard carried by a longhaired young man holding hands with his girlfriend.

Whether the messages on these placards are raunchy, poignant, witty or angry, the memorandum is unambiguous. Women have had enough of being told that they are the ones to blame—of being taught to police themselves instead of men being taught not to rape—of being labelled as sluts as if this label justifies their mistreatment. And uncannily it is this very label that fuels the movement. It seems that in the reclamation of the slut label, the word has been alchemically transformed into an elixir for change.

Few would have guessed that this little word contains so much power. It has been used against women for centuries—to denigrate working women, persecute women with libido and even burn women at the stake. It has been used to hypersexualize and objectify women and to turn women into repressed joyless vessels and sexual victims. It has been a tool of control utilized to maximum effect by misogynists, witch hunters, and rapists throughout the centuries.

But now that women have seized and reclaimed this word it is being wielded as a revolutionary tool to rebel against this ongoing patri-archal hold on the feminine. This four-lettered word has proved its potency in a short space of time and has catapulted the issue of sexual abuse and rape right into a global public arena with an effectiveness never witnessed before.

While there are some feminists who dismiss the use of a word that has such negative connotations to make a point about sexual assault and women's empowerment, the Slut Walk has become a global phenomenon that has been endorsed by feminists such as Germaine Greer, while Eve Ensler, famous for the Vagina Monologues, is quoted in numerous slogans carried by Slut Walkers.

Poet and feminist Alice Walker has also recently sanctioned it in an interview with *Guernica Magazine*. She succinctly encapsulates the essence of the movement in her interpretation of the use of the controversial word when she says: "I've always understood the word 'slut' to mean a woman who freely enjoys her own sexuality in any way she wants to; undisturbed by other people's wishes for her behavior. Sexual desire originates in her and is directed by her. In that sense it is a word well worth retaining. As a poet, I find it has a rich, raunchy, elemental, down to earth sound, that connects us to something primal, moist, and free.

In my view the word slut is a signifier for the resurgence of the primal sexual nature of women that has been pushed underground and controlled by a misogynistic order for centuries. It seems to me that women are responding to a collective archetypal call to seize back the freedom to be themselves. It is also about rebelling against the social and public discourse that has been controlled by a patriarchal hold over language, a phenomenon that continues in the neoliberal discourse of today. It is about the power of the word slut—a power that resides within its etymology.

In short, a slut has historically been defined as a woman who is at once hyper-sexual (having "too much" sex, "dirty" sex, or sex with too many partners) but also a woman who is filthy, incompetent, or in some way distasteful. The sexual definition is the one that persists to this day—women are constantly called sluts in an attempt to shame and denigrate them. Slut-shaming has become a form of controlling women and a means of pushing the libidinous wild woman underground and silencing her. It is a word that perpetuates the patriarchal agenda in multifarious ways.

For me the adoption of this word as the signifier to this global feminine rebellion is directly rooted in language similar to the poststructuralist feminist movement of the 1970s. This movement was born out of a common need for all women to create a language that escapes the clutches of the panoptical patriarch that has established himself as a jailor in our collective feminine consciousness.

In opposition to Western phallogocentrism, these feminists identified language as a means by which "man objectifies the world, reduces it to his own terms, speaks in place of everything and everyone else—including women." The movement called on women to find a language that spoke to their sex and existed outside of the patriarchal hold over discourse.

The Slut Walkers are seen to subvert this patriarchal institution of language through the reclamation of the word slut—and have thus redirected a celebratory sexuality back to womankind. And women all over the world have responded in a joyful but revolutionary spirit and joined the Slut Walk. The use of the word slut and the carnivalesque, celebratory protest that accompanies the movement then becomes the expression of female sexuality and pleasure that manifests outside the male libidinal economy.

Women are building up their revolutionary linguistic arsenal having already reclaimed the words "vagina," "cunt," and "slut." With the ongoing reclamation of these feminine words, the public discourse will inevitably find its way back into the feminine arena. This is why we need the Slut Walk.

It is a manifestation of our collective desire to no longer be obedient. It speaks of necessary subversiveness. It also tells men that their sexual abuses of women will no longer be tolerated. It unites women in a common sisterhood and it raises our voices in a collective feminine language such that we will no longer be spoken for.

Discussion Questions

1. How will movements or parades like the "Slut Walk" have an impact on society or culture?
2. Do you think people are responsible for their own safety, even if it means restricting their dress? Articulate how you would balance safety with freedom of expression.

3.6

IDENTITY, POSTMODERNITY, AND THE GLOBAL APPAREL MARKETPLACE

Susan B. Kaiser, University of California, Davis

Today, a visit to another country—or even to another city or state in our own country—often yields surprises when observing what is available for purchase, what people are actually wearing, and—in some cases, most significantly—how people are wearing what they are wearing. For example, one might see the same basic products everywhere, but worn in a variety of ways. Jeans, baseball caps, T-shirts, or other fairly basic items may be worn in many different ways: tight or baggy; shaped in a variety of ways; tucked or loose; and the like. So,

Original for this text.

it is not only what we buy, but also how we wear what we buy that expresses our identities: that is, who we are and how we see ourselves at any point in time. We can shape these ideas in relation to ourselves as individuals, as well as the groups and communities to which we belong, and even the nations or societies in which we live.

The idea that appearance styles, or "looks," are negotiated as people influence each other on what to wear and how to wear it is fundamental in understanding social processes of fashion (Kaiser, Nagasawa, & Hutton, 1991; Kaiser, 1997). Places and communities have identities, too. The latter, in fact, is no longer restricted to geographic location. Global technologies, the worldwide production and distribution of apparel, and the circulation of images of style across national and cultural boundaries all contribute to what might be characterized as a larger, complicated negotiation of global style, or international dress (Eicher, 1995).

It is possible to be influenced not only by immediate, local culture(s) but also by globally circulating images and commodities. Constructing and reconstructing appearance and, in part, identity, becomes a process of figuring out how we "fit" in and "depart" from a vast array of possible looks. The contemporary social and economic conditions that shape the global apparel marketplace and our multiple possibilities for shaping identity within it are often referred to as "postmodernity" (Lyon, 1994). The commodities and images that were once only available through travel or other cross-cultural contact are now globally and quickly produced, distributed, and consumed.

In the process, more and more global locations are touched by "global style" in some way, as apparel manufacturers search around the world for (1) new sources of labor that are less expensive, more timely in response, and higher in quality, and (2) new consuming markets. A nation's level of economic development influences whether it will be regarded as a source of labor or a consuming market, or both. Yet the picture is even more complicated than that: Pockets of poverty exist within relatively wealthy nations, and pockets of wealth exist within relatively impoverished nations.

The issue of who can afford to buy which goods in the global marketplace becomes one that is ethical, as well as economic.

What is for sale in the postmodern, global marketplace? Objects, images, and the marketers' constructions of reality. On a daily basis, consumers around the world are bombarded with new ideas and possibilities, whether they can afford to buy them or not. If one can afford to participate, it is possible to be part of larger (even global) communities ranging from the business world to leisure interest groups (e.g., rap or reggae or country western music; skateboarding or biking or golfing) and more fundamental identity-based communities (e.g., gay and lesbian; African diasporas; youth) to the more local hometown community where someone lives. Magazines, catalogs, and television and Internet shopping help to bring a world of possibilities for consuming and shaping identity to the fingertips of global consumers.

How do we make sense of who we are and who we are not in the context of postmodernity: a time characterized by media and commodity saturation, in a marketplace that may seem more global than personal? And how does fashion influence individual and collective searches for identity? The term *fashion* implies change; it also implies processes of imitation and differentiation.

To some extent, we want to express our inclination and ability to belong to certain groups and communities. Yet somehow we balance this desire with assertions of individual uniqueness. A hundred years ago, sociologist Georg Simmel, who has been described by some as one of the earliest postmodern thinkers, noticed this interplay between imitation and differentiation in fashion change (Simmel, 1904). Even more generally, he indicated that in times of intense societal change or transition, we (collectively) become more concerned about representing who we are by how we consume: by what we buy and how we use and display it in our expressions of identity to others (Lyon, 1994).

Identity politics are involved in processes of imitation and differentiation. The word *fashion* is related to the Latin word *factio*, which implies faction or political distinctions (Barnard, 1996).

Issues of gender, race and ethnicity, sexuality, nationality, social class, age, and leisure-time preferences all enter into the creation of the groups in which we see and do not see ourselves. These issues have always been factors in how we consume fashion. Since the late 1960s and early 1970s, however, we have become more aware of these issues due to social movements and related academic areas of study (i.e., feminist, ethnic, and cultural studies). The media have also played a huge role in shaping a larger cultural awareness of identity politics. In 1997, when Ellen "came out" as a lesbian on her television situation comedy, the whole media discourse (on talk shows, in magazines, and on the Internet) emerged to learn more and express views about diverse sexualities.

In addition to promoting awareness of differences through a complex expression and discovery of identity politics, postmodern culture seems to thrive on the juxtaposition of component parts from different social, cultural, and historical contexts.

Traditional categories and boundaries collapse, or at least budge, as they are stretched by a bending, blending, and blurring of ideas and images (e.g., gender blending, retro looks, subcultural fusions). It is not so much that this idea of mixing and blending is completely new. The history of clothing and appearance styles has probably always relied on blending to some extent. But now there are technological and economic conditions that bring all of these possibilities into our televisions and computers. And there is a lot of profit to be made. Consider the following:

Gender and sexual blending is evident in media that highlights drag or cross-dressing. A "lesbian chic" look (short hair, black pantsuits, masculine black shoes) becomes widely popularized in films, television, and in the workplace.

The growth of casual businesswear creates a need to mix and match separates, potentially blurring a number of boundaries: formality, status, gender, age, and the like.

Junior high girls wear dresses to dances and parties that would once be reserved for women who are adults: very long dresses (with slits) or very short, sexy black evening dresses worn with high-heeled, strappy black sandals.

Appearance styles ("looks") tend to be eclectic, visually stimulating, and confusing when consciously contemplated. How can we explain this complexity of style in the contemporary marketplace, and what is the impact on our perceptions of identity? On a cultural level, through talk shows or other interactions with media, as well as through "global style" per se, we seem to be collectively working through ideas or conducting "cultural conversations" about what appearances say about individual, community, national, and global identities. We are also interested in how and why we rely on style to work through ideas. These self-examining tendencies are often characterized as indicating a kind of postmodern reflexivity. This reflexivity refers, for example, to the media analysis of media coverage (e.g., "Are we paying too much attention to political scandals, showing the same images over and over until they become imprinted in viewers' minds?"), to the self-conscious and critical examination of fashion and beauty issues by fashion and beauty magazines whose pages depict thin models, at least some of whom have undergone breast augmentation surgery (e.g., "Is plastic surgery really necessary?"), and to public discussions of dress codes in the context of concerns regarding gang symbolism (e.g., "Will school uniforms really eliminate violence?").

Are we losing ourselves in a sea of surface-level judgments? In some ways, images are almost amazingly important for politicians and celebrities, as well as for the public in general. Consider the number of times and the variety of ways in which Madonna has "remade" herself. A whole page on the World Wide Web—"Hillary's Hair"—is devoted to Hillary Clinton's changing hairstyles.

And, consider the popularity of "makeovers" on daily talk shows. Witness the increase in elective cosmetic surgery, the explosion of the fitness market, incidences of eating disorders, and the importance of designer or status labels in more and more contexts (including the football field).

Or, are we reaching new heights of understanding about ourselves and developing new, integrated ways of relating to one another? In a recent (1998) visit of the Pope to Cuba, communist leader Fidel Castro greeted him in a business suit: a symbol of Western, masculine capitalism.

The international media reported on the political significance of this stylistic choice and its global, economic consequences. Did this signal the fall or decline of communism in Cuba? Or is it possible that new models of government could emerge, combining some of the most humane, equitable, and freedom-inspired qualities of communism and democracy with capitalism? Although the media did not comment on it, Castro's trademark beard remained intact. Consistent with his speeches, he seemed to be conveying the idea that this country was moving in new directions and creating new syntheses or collages of political ideas, rather than portraying a mere capitulation to Western, capitalist democracy.

In the everyday context, style affords an outlet for experimenting with a whole host of changing boundaries and collages of ideas and identities. Most likely, those who experiment the most with style have the most to gain from new aesthetic and status boundaries—namely, women, ethnic minorities, and working-class youth. Those whose physical appearances coincide with traditional notions of power (i.e., northern European white male heritage) seem to have the most to lose from changing aesthetic and status boundaries (for example, any move away from the century-old, and remarkably stable, male business suit).[1] Yet there are signs that these boundaries are indeed changing, as evident in the "casualization" of businesswear (that is, the move away from suits toward a mixing and matching of separates, for at least some days of the week). And those who seemingly have the most to lose are participating in the shift to "casual Fridays" or even "casual weeks." Women and ethnic minorities have probably had some visual influence on this trend, because their relative tendency to be "more into style" has added variety and complexity into the visual culture of the workplace. On the other hand, some women and ethnic minorities in midmanagement positions worry that the casual businesswear trend may serve to "keep them in their places," with the glass ceiling intact (Janus, 1998).

So style, in many ways, seems to be a "mixed bag." Signs of progressive change, whether anticipated or reflected through style, coincide with the suggestion—so embedded in modern, Western thought—that playing with appearances is shallow or superficial. About 100 years ago, Oscar Wilde (gay author and leader in the "aesthetics movement" who espoused "art for art's sake") said, "It is only shallow people who do not judge by appearances." In other words, the true mystery of our realities may reside in the visible, tangible, and taken-for-granted realm of appearances. We may be able to express something about ourselves and our cultures through the medium of personal appearance that we are unable to get across through other means.

In the postmodern cultural context, it seems as though a lot of the pieces of the puzzle that compose our realities are "up for grabs" or dislodged from their usual locations and juxtaposed with one another in a way that does not seem to fit. Shared yearnings lead us to search for new ways of understanding our identities and communities (hooks, 1990). Simultaneously, advanced-stage or global capitalism compels us to want and "need" more than ever. The promise of improving ourselves (for a price) is alluring and intoxicating, as evident in slogans such as "Shop 'til you drop," "When the going gets tough, the tough go shopping," and "Truth, knowledge, new clothes."

Are we in the process of shaping new realities or merely serving as pawns in the marketplace? Let's consider this question by exploring three topics close to the heart of postmodernity: choice, confusion, and creativity.

Choice

Eclecticism is the degree zero of contemporary general culture: one listens to reggae, watches a Western, eats McDonald's food for lunch and local cuisine for dinner, wears Paris perfume in Tokyo and "retro" clothes in Hong Kong. (Lyotard, 1988)

Choice is often regarded as the mainstay of freedom. In the global context, the desire for and availability of consumer goods is equated with progress. To a great extent, freedom and democracy are associated with an unlimited range of options in the consumer marketplace. And in the capitalist apparel marketplace, the range of choice is tremendous because goods are produced and distributed worldwide. (Often, textiles and apparel are the first items produced in nations taking the first steps toward becoming more industrialized.) The assortment of styles, colors, and textures is enormous, if not overwhelming. In the apparel marketplace, at least in the industrialized nations, the world is at our fingertips. Yet another trend seems to contradict this idea of increased variety in the marketplace.

In some ways, there is a globalization of style, with some looks (often those associated with Western capitalism, modernity, and democracy) having the most global potency. At the same time, the choice within a given store or community seems to have increased, drawing from (and often appropriating) all kinds of cultural and subcultural traditions and innovations.[2] This tendency toward both increased variety within geographic locations and a homogenizing effect across locations represents a global paradox. Still, catalogs stuffing the mailboxes of middle-class consumers defy any problems with geographic access. The concept of choice itself becomes more complicated and harder to interpret.

Perhaps it is easiest to comprehend choice by examining its limits. The limits to choice are primarily economic. Not everyone can afford the latest, most popular brand of shorts for their children. Not everyone can afford to travel and be inspired by diverse cultural expressions of style.

Not everyone can afford to diversify his or her wardrobe to engage in a daily, pleasurable, and postmodern play with style. And often those who actually make our clothes (i.e., apparel workers around the world, including those who live in immigrant communities in postmodern cities such as Los Angeles) are least likely to be able to afford to purchase the clothes for which their labor is responsible.

Yet in many modernized societies, even within very basic categories of commodities, including those at lower price points (e.g., disposable diapers, coffee, pantyhose), there can be a confusing array of choices. Buying even seemingly generic or standard items (e.g., Nike shoes, Levi jeans) requires complicated thought processes as one contemplates the range of features

from which to select, the statement he or she will be making, and the contexts in which the item is likely to be worn:

A woman in her thirties goes to a discount outlet shopping mall to buy a pair of athletic shoes and is confronted with a large store filled with thousands of boxes. What she thought would be a generic item actually presents a vast array of options. She must make numerous choices. Which brand should she choose? Should she go with high-tops or the standard models? What color does she want? Will she be using the shoes for aerobics, step class, walking, running, playing tennis or basketball, or some combination thereof? Does she really need the $200 shoes with the air pumps? Can she wear the shoes for multiple functions even though they are intended for specific functions? Should she select leather, vinyl, or canvas? How do the shoes compare in terms of how they fit and feel? And what can she wear with them?

The same woman stops at a convenience store on her way home to buy pantyhose for the next day. She wants a quick and easy decision, after the multiple choices she has confronted in her purchase of athletic shoes. She walks over to a display of pantyhose in egg-shaped containers. What size is she: A, B, or Queen? She briefly checks the height and weight table to confirm her size and then begins to address the other choices she must make: color, sheer versus reinforced toe, control top versus sheer-to-the-waist versus regular top, and so forth. As she makes her choice, she must: (1) consider what garments she will wear with the pantyhose, (2) analyze her figure and examine how she feels about it, and (3) debate whether the sheer styles will be less durable.

A 9-year-old boy goes to the department store with his father to buy some jeans for school. The two of them are confronted with rows and rows of jeans, folded neatly in shelves built into the wall. Once they find what they think is his size, they unfold the jeans to examine the stylistic variations.

Does he want basic indigo blue or some fashionable color? Faded (and if so, how faded)? Preshrunk or shrink-to-fit? Zipper or button fly? Standard five-pocket or extra pockets on the legs, and if so, how low can they be without suggesting gang membership? Flared, straight leg, or "pipe" style? Then, when beginning to try on some of the options to arrive at the best "fit," questions surface regarding how long, how baggy, and how low the jeans should be worn. And what are the current features and ways of wearing jeans that are associated with gang involvement? Does the school have a dress code—implicit or explicit?

Thus, even in the realm of standard or basic items, the range of choice is evident in today's marketplace. Choice can also be subtle but still require a great deal of thought and attention. In some ways, choices that are not obvious or readily visible when entering a store may be even more complicated. On the surface, one is making a "basic" purchase. So why does so much thought need to go into the decision making? Why are there so many issues to be weighed?

Perhaps we need new ways of thinking about choice in a global economy. For example, how do we perceive choice, and how do these perceptions compare with what apparel producers and marketers are trying to achieve? Whose cultural traditions and innovations become a part of the package of choice, and who receives credit for these traditions and innovations? Who profits? What are the effects of the complexities of choice? One possibility is that too much choice may create a feeling of overload that contributes to a preference for simplicity. Hence, the now "classic" popularity of black and (more recently) dark brown or gray, after every conceivable color combination has been seen on the body and head; the return of basic jeans after the heyday of designer jeans in the 1970s; the return to unisex disposable diapers by one manufacturer, after a decade of gender-coded diapers (for example, blue or male-patterned and "functionally altered" diapers for males). Yet even these "simpler" styles reflect a diversity of choices; the choices are merely more subtle.

Hence, choice can lead to confusion, ambiguity, and a desire for relief. At the same time, diversity in the marketplace can contribute to a celebration of style. The postmodern marketplace allows for a creative search for and expression of identity. In some ways, it is easier to figure out who we are not than it is to affirm a positive identity.

In the retail setting, one can survey the options visually, scanning and eliminating the more obvious expressions of "not me," or "identity not" (Freitas et al., 1997). Then comes the even more complex process of gauging, mixing and matching, and the fine-tuning of possible, positive identity expressions ("me" or, more accurately, multiple "me's"). Even if one is not inclined to revel in the play of appearances, a certain amount of energy, in addition to money, is required to put together an appearance. Hence, choice contributes to confusion on the one hand and creativity on the other.

Confusion

"Culture is in a process of recycling: everything is juxtaposable to everything else because nothing matters" (Gitlin, 1989).

"Schizophrenic . . . an experience of isolated, disconnected, discontinuous material signifiers which fail to link up into a coherent sequence" (Jameson, 1983).

Postmodern eclecticism can foster ambiguity. U.S. culture, for example, is not sending straightforward messages about what is fashionable. We are bombarded with a diverse array of everyday looks of the people around us (intensified in an urban context), commodities in stores, images advertised and promoted in fashion magazines, and appearance styles we see in films and television sitcoms, mail catalogs, and music videos.

There is likely to be a confusion about issues of time (e.g., are we looking forward or backward?), place (e.g., is there a local look anymore?), and existence (e.g., why are we so caught up in image?). Image and style seem to be in a constant state of flux:

- Apparel manufacturers traditionally produced only a few lines of garments per year, and retailers could reorder successful styles. Today, some produce as many as 12 lines per year and do not accept reorders.
- One can observe a vast range of styles in media such as music videos. Moreover, characters in the videos frequently change their looks numerous times in the space of a few

minutes, suggesting that identity is changeable in the flick of a second. A somewhat similar pattern is found in Hindi films produced in Bombay, India.

- Youth subcultures seem to multiply overnight, and they stylistically blend into one another. The visual images that identify them precede verbal labels (e.g., punk or postpunk, new age, gothic, motorhead, boardhead, skater, or surfer).

Part of our confusion about culture and fashion probably stems from ambivalence, which has always been with us but is probably intensified in the postmodern context. In fact, we seem to be ambivalent about capitalism itself: We both love and hate what capitalism represents and promotes (Wilson, 1985). We also seem to be ambivalent about our identities, and fashion can give aesthetic form to unconscious tensions linked to gender, age, and status (Davis, 1992). And we are probably ambivalent about our own absorption in issues of style, appearance, and image; they seem both trivial and practical, superficial and complex, personal and global. At any rate, the stage is set for experimentation. Fashion seems to provide a way of articulating individual and cultural ambivalences that are not easily expressed otherwise (Kaiser, Nagasawa, & Hutton, 1991; Kaiser, Nagasawa, & Hutton, 1995). In any case, ambivalence and confusion provide creative fuel for aesthetic exploration.

Creativity

According to the French sociologist Jean Baudrillard (1975), it is not so much a matter of being the self as it is producing the self. To consume is to produce again. Part of what we produce as consumers are our appearance styles. In addition to its relation to the word *factio*, the term *fashion* also derives from the Latin *facere*, which means "to make or to do." Using fashion as a verb or a process in this way, we can consider how fashioning appearance style is one way—a visual and creative way—of producing identity. In African American culture, the term "style" is often used similarly as a verb or process, in a way that implies

that styling is a way of producing not only identity but also a sense of community with others (Hall, 1993). That is, it becomes a process of creating a cultural bond with others.

We could argue about whether or not we are more likely to experiment with our appearance styles, and hence, our identities, in the postmodern context. Is our current level of "producing identity" at a record high, historically speaking?

Clothing historian Rachel Pannabecker (1997) suggests that although there do seem to be some unique aspects of contemporary appearance styles, they need to be examined in the context of larger, historical trends.

What we do know is that today, more than one look can simultaneously be regarded as fashionable. As clothing scholar Jean Hamilton (1990) comments, it becomes an issue of looks for spring, rather than a single look for spring. So there are many ways that we can create our appearance styles and still be considered fashionable. This seems to represent a shift toward a greater plurality of popular styles, perhaps to parallel an increasing awareness of what it means to live in a multicultural society. Yet we also live in a global society, as noted earlier, and our clothes are being produced in a larger array of places around the world, as apparel and retail companies search for or "source" new locations with lower labor costs for sewing clothes. And, perhaps in part as a result, there is a stronger emphasis on mixing and matching separates, because the pieces that are produced and worn together are produced, and often purchased, in different locations. These pieces come together, somehow, in our wardrobes and our appearances.

So, on a daily basis, we engage in the process of managing our appearances, almost unconsciously using our creative abilities. I recently asked a close friend, Carol, and my son, Nathan, to describe where and when they obtained the different pieces comprising their ensembles. Carol, who is 30 years old and from Louisiana, is now living in California and is dressed for a Sunday afternoon play we are attending together. Nathan, who is 20 years old and a student, has come home for Sunday dinner. Both are dressed casually and comfortably, and the total looks they have created are understated and well coordinated. Yet a discussion about each article comprising the look reveals a more complex state of affairs:

- Carol, who is 30 years old, is wearing black straight jeans (relaxed fit) bought at the Gap and made in the United States. She has on a black leather belt (made in Italy) with antiqued brush silver (scroll design) hardware; her sister bought it for her as a birthday gift while they were shopping together at The Limited a few years ago. Her long-sleeved brown knit top buttons up the front and has a V-neck. It was made in Taiwan, but she bought it at Lerner New York in Baton Rouge, Louisiana. She is wearing a black "pleather" vest over it, made of 100% polyurethane. It was made in China, and she bought it for seven dollars at a discount store in Baton Rouge (where all separates are seven dollars) a few years ago, when she was on a tighter budget. She has only worn it once before, but really likes the way it fits. And this is the first time she feels as though she has really worn it. She is wearing dark brown boots with heels; she bought them at Mervyn's in Woodland, California, and they were made in China. She's also wearing knee-high black socks purchased at Sears in Sacramento, California; she actually had meant to buy trouser socks. She is also wearing a scarf of 100% polyester that was made in Italy. It is square, with a black border and different shades of beige in an abstract design. She "borrowed" it from her sister. She's also wearing a silver ring with a swirl design; she bought it in San Francisco from an Asian street vendor for five dollars. She is also wearing a sterling silver ring with a V-shaped design; she got it at Rich's department store in Atlanta, in one of her favorite neighborhoods (and stores). She is also wearing silver antiqued drop earrings from The Limited; they were a Christmas gift from her sister. There is another, identical pair that is currently circulating between her and her sisters. Her watch, which she wears every day, is a silver chained style; it was made in Japan, and she bought it at a time that she was consciously moving toward wearing silver. She bought the watch in Marietta, north of Atlanta, at Sears in the Galleria shopping center. She is also carrying a black leather Etienne Aigner purse; it has a drawstring style with gold hardware and a detachable shoulder strap with a fixed shorter strap that can be worn over the wrist, "lady style." It has a matching wallet. She bought it at an outlet mall in Gonzales, Louisiana. She is also wearing a new fragrance (Clinique Wrappings), made in the United States. Overall, she realizes that her outfit is the result of six years of acquisition of goods, although she has never worn all of these pieces together before. She put the overall look together (especially her boots) to go with her recent, short-cropped haircut. She calls the whole outfit a typical "sister style" outfit. The term has a double meaning. She associates the look and some of the component parts with her sisters; they would all "fit" together with a look like this. In a larger sense, the outfit also represents "sistuh style"; it is a "constructed" and "achieved" look that she associated with the process and outcome of African American female styling.

- Nathan, who is 20 years old, begins by describing his gray-and-black baseball cap with "Oakley" embroidered into it. The cap was made in Bangladesh. He purchased the cap for five dollars from a street vendor in Mexico during spring break about a year ago. After purchasing the cap, he began to compare it with other caps with the same brand name, and he's noticed that the "a" on his cap is shaped differently. He is wearing a T-shirt that says "Glacier Point: Coolest Apartments in Davis." The T-shirt was given to him by his apartment complex about six months ago to celebrate its grand opening. The T-shirt was made in Jamaica. Over the T-shirt, he's wearing a gray, long-sleeved pullover top with a collar and cuffs and a small white stripe as a trim. He bought it at the Gap in Sacramento, California, a few months ago, but it was made in the northern Mariana Islands. He's also wearing Gap jeans, worn loose but not too baggy, and just long enough to "scrunch" over his shoes. The jeans were made in the United States. He's also wearing black Nike high-tops, with a "swoosh" trademark symbol. He bought them in Texas on a family trip to visit relatives almost a year ago. They were made in Indonesia. He doesn't remember where he got his white socks; he pulls them straight up, but not quite all the way. His Guess watch was a Christmas present from his parents. He realizes that he has only worn this complete outfit a couple of times, but it is a fairly typical "student" outfit for him.

Whether or not we are conscious of it, a lot of effort and eclecticism goes into our created selves. On a routine basis, we assemble elements from different times and places in our lives. The objects themselves are produced in an even wider range of locations throughout the world. The net result of our coordinating efforts may be subtle, or it may reveal a mood celebrating the possibilities of color, texture, and form. In any case, we are participating in a process of producing identity when we construct our looks. Perusing the labels indicating the country of origin also reminds us of the labor "behind the scenes," although this labor, in many ways, remains invisible in a global economy.

Some appearances may seem more postmodern than others, but the point is not one of classifying appearances or styles as traditional, modern, or postmodern. Instead, what seems to capture the idea of postmodern best lies in minding, managing, and perceiving appearance styles and component parts from a perspective that is perhaps more tolerant of diversity and ambiguity, more exploratory, and more "constructed" of elements from various places around the world. We are fashion consumers in a larger, global marketplace that is profit-motivated, often exploitative of developing societies, and endangering to a sense of place. The upshot of the contradictions that seem to be part and parcel of postmodernity is

as follows: There is a promise of a new way of seeing the world as at once pluralistic and democratic, expressive and creative. But there are also cultural and personal costs associated with this new insight—namely, the possible threat of further exploitation on a global scale, a blurring of cultural traditions into a vast uniform global context, and a confusion between who we are and how we look.

These may be the ultimate choices to which fashion in the postmodern context refers. Perhaps we will be able to arrive at some form of synthesis through new imagery, new social arrangements, and new ways of viewing ourselves.

Hopefully, such a solution will be kinder and gentler to women, ethnic minorities, and people of developing nations. We are at a critical juncture in our global society, and fashion plays a part in shaping and defining this juncture. Consciously or unconsciously, we are both commodity consumers and identity producers as we manage our appearances and continue to create ourselves and our communities. With increased awareness of identity politics, global inequities, and industry and media influences, perhaps we can create new, more complex understandings as well.

References

Barnard, M. (1996). *Fashion As Communication*. New York: Routledge.

Baudrillard, J. (1975). *The Mirror of Production* (M. Poster, trans.). St. Louis, MO: Telos Press.

Davis, F. (1992). *Fashion, Culture, and Identity*. Chicago: University of Chicago Press.

Eicher, J. B. (1995). Cosmopolitan and international dress. In M. E. Roach-Higgins, J. B. Eicher, & K. K. P. Johnson (Eds.), *Dress and Identity*. New York: Fairchild.

Freitas, A. J., Kaiser, S. B., Chandler, J., Hall, C., Kim, J-W., & Hammidi, T. (1997). Appearance management as border construction: Least favorite clothing, group distancing, and identity . . . not! *Sociological Inquiry*, 67(3):323–335.

Gitlin, T. (1989, July/August). Postmodernism defined, at last! *Utne Reader*, 52–61.

Hall, C. (1993). Toward a gender-relational understanding of appearance style in African-American culture. Master's thesis, University of California, Davis.

Hamilton, J. (1990). "The silkworms of the East must be pillaged": The cultural foundations of mass fashion. *Clothing and Textiles Research Journal*, 8(4):40–48.

Hooks, B. (1990). *Yearning: Race, Gender, and Cultural Politics*. Boston: South End Press.

Jameson, F. (1983). Postmodernism and consumer society. In H. Foster (Ed.), *The Anti-Aesthetic: Essays on Postmodern Culture*, pp. 111–125. Port Townsend, WA: Bay Press.

Janus, T. (1998). Negotiations @ work: Analysis of the casual businesswear trend. Master's thesis, University of California, Davis.

Kaiser, S. B. (1997). *The Social Psychology of Clothing: Symbolic Appearances in Context* (2nd ed. rev.). New York: Fairchild.

Kaiser, S. B., Nagasawa, R. H., & Hutton, S. S. (1991). Fashion, postmodernity and personal appearance: A symbolic interactionist formulation. *Symbolic Interaction*, 14(2):165–185.

Kaiser, S. B., Nagasawa, R. H., & Hutton, S. S. (1995). Construction of an SI theory of fashion: Part 1. Ambivalence and change. *Clothing and Textiles Research Journal*, 13(3):172–183.

Kaiser, S. B., Nagasawa, R. H., & Hutton, S. S. (1997). Truth, knowledge, new clothes: Responses to Hamilton, Kean, and Pannabecker. *Clothing and Textiles Research Journal*, 15(3):184–191.

Kean, R. (1997). The role of the fashion system in fashion change: A response to the Kaiser, Nagasawa and Hutton model. *Clothing and Textiles Research Journal*, 15(3):172–177.

Lyon, D. (1994). *Postmodernity*. Minneapolis: University of Minnesota Press.

Lyotard, J. F. (1988). *The Postmodern Condition: A Report on Knowledge* (G. Bennington & B. Messumi, trans.). Minneapolis: University of Minnesota Press.

Pannabecker, R. (1997). Fashioning theory: A critical discussion of the symbolic interactionist theory of fashion. *Clothing and Textiles Research Journal*, 15(3):178–183.

Paoletti, J. B. (1985). Ridicule and role models as factors in American men's fashion change, 1880–1910. *Costume*, 19:121–134.

Simmel, G. (1904). Fashion. *International Quarterly*. Reprinted in *American Journal of Sociology*, 62(1957, May):541–558.

Wilson, E. (1985). *Adorned in Dreams: Fashion and Modernity*. London: Virago Press.

Endnotes

1. The "sack suit" emerged from a longer process of a masculine move away from anything feminine, frivolous, or fussy (see Paoletti, 1985).
2. There is an ongoing debate in the textiles and apparel field on whether the range of choice increases or decreases in the context of global capitalism (see Kaiser, Nagasawa, & Hutton, 1995; Kean, 1997; Kaiser, Nagasawa, & Hutton, 1997; Kaiser, 1997).

Discussion Questions

1. How is fashion currently a part of identity politics?
2. If fashion is global how can "Made in the USA" campaigns or "buy local" campaigns be successful?
3. How does postmodern emphasis on choice and creativity cause confusion? Is confusion an essential part of postmodern dress? What does it accomplish?

CHAPTER 4

THE BODY

Andrew Reilly

After you have read this chapter, you will understand:

- Frameworks for viewing the body and dress
- How to critically analyze media images of the body
- Potentially negative consequences of appearance-management behaviors
- Cultural alternatives to the American ideal of thinness

The human body has many possibilities for adornment; it can be considered a canvas for self-expression. Not only is it the foundation for the garments people wear, but it is also manipulated and decorated. For example, the body can be pierced, tattooed, injected with chemicals to remove wrinkles, have the fat sucked out, have its shape changed with undergarments, and have its texture altered with moisturizers or depilatories, among other possibilities. It changes with food intake, exercise, and age, and varies by gender and ethnicity. In this chapter you will read about different attitudes toward the body and how the body has been altered and changed to create different forms of beauty.

Frameworks for Viewing the Body

Several scholars have devised ways to view the clothed body, and their work provides a basis not only for viewing the body but also for performing research studies on dress. Eicher and Roach-Higgins (1992) created a classification system for types and properties of dress. Body modifications and supplements can be classified according to their respective properties. For example, skin can be transformed by tattooing (modification), which alters its color (property) and surface design (property). Body piercing not only modifies the body's skin, but allows for a ring to be attached to the body (supplement).

Susan Kaiser (1997) proposed a contextual perspective when viewing the body and dress. Awareness of the social, cultural, and historical influences at any given time is essential to understanding dress and its meaning, according to Kaiser. The contextual perspective draws from the fields of sociology, psychology, and anthropology, allowing researchers to understand meanings below the surface. Mary Lynn Damhorst created a model that considers the context of a person's dress and appearance (see Figure 3.1 on page 82). Underlying the contextual model are two premises: (1) in real life, we seldom see clothes divorced from social context, and (2) it has been demonstrated that interpretations of clothing vary along contextual lines (Damhorst, 1985).

Still, other scholars consider and study dress with an emphasis on visual perception. Marilyn DeLong (1998) presents a method for analyzing appearance that includes a sensitivity to visual aesthetic dimensions of perception. Robert Hillestad (1980) uses a structural approach to explore interactions between the body and clothing. Whether we approach the study of the body from a social, psychological, cultural, historical, or aesthetic perspective (or a combination of perspectives), one overarching concept remains clear: The body and all its attachments communicate volumes about an individual, a society, a culture, and a time.

Critical Thinking about the Body

To begin the process of critically thinking about the body, it is instructive to examine one's own cultural ideals. A cultural ideal is the type of person a culture identifies as highly desirable or attractive. Angelina Jolie and Brad Pitt are two examples of ideals in American culture in 2012; you can probably think of many others. When we examine a cultural ideal, we begin by asking questions:

- Where did these ideals come from? (Informs us of our ethnic heritage.)
- When did these ideals develop? (Provides a historical context.)
- Who do these ideals benefit? (Gives us information about the cultural rewards for ascribing to an ideal.)
- Who do they hurt? (Tells us the negative consequences for not ascribing to an ideal.)
- After the reader has examined his or her cultural ideals, it is especially informative to compare ideals from several cultures because these demonstrate different viewpoints and practices. This chapter is intended to generate critical questions about cultural body ideals.

Analyzing American Ideals

Before embarking on an examination of dress and appearance across many cultures, it is helpful to create a list of culturally ideal characteristics for American women and men. What are the ideal characteristics for women? What are the ideal characteristics for men? Men are typically thought to be ideal if they are muscular or lean, tan, with blond or dark hair. Women are typically thought to be ideal if they are thin or toned, blond, and petite. General ideals such as good hygiene, nice eyes, and a bright smile apply to both genders. Consider where these gender-specific ideals originated. You may want to refer to Chapter 11, "Dress and Media," when devising your list.

Once you have created your list, critically analyze it. Seriously consider if these ideals are actually worthy to you. Do you fit the ideal? Do your parents? Your siblings? Your (potential) partner? How many people match the ideals? How realistic are these ideals to the average man and woman in the United States? Why would they (or you) pursue these ideals? What are the payoffs for approximating the ideal? What are the risks for not being anywhere near the ideal or intentionally challenging the ideal? The readings in this chapter should help you arrive at some answers to these questions.

Body Image and Appearance Management

Body image is the mental construct people have about their bodies and includes "a person's perceptions, thoughts, and feelings about his or her body" (Grogan, 2008, p. 3). How a person views their body (body perception) affects not only how they present their physical selves to the public but also what they are willing to do in order to attain their ideal body. Several researchers have looked for a connection between body perception and self-esteem. Self-esteem involves individual feelings of self-worth (Rosenberg, 1985). Not surprisingly, when we feel better about our bodies, we feel better about ourselves. However, many people feel poorly about their bodies or experience body dissatisfaction.

Body dissatisfaction is common among the U.S. population and it is believed that very few people are perfectly satisfied with their bodies. Body dissatisfaction can lead to excessive exercise and dieting, self-induced vomiting, and plastic surgery. The extent of body dissatisfaction is not surprising, especially when one considers that comparing one's body to others and striving for a "better" body begins before becoming a teenager (Pope, Jr., Phillips, and Olivardia, 2000).

Body dissatisfaction was long thought to be only a woman's problem, but within the last few decades there has been an increase in men's concerns about the body. Men have likely been concerned about their bodies for longer than the last few decades, but two explanations can offer reasons why this focus has recently come to light. First, as women became more independent during the last several decades and did not need a man to support them, men had to compete with each other for female attention in ways other than economically; a desirable male body therefore became a commodity. Second, concerns about appearance had long been viewed as vain and feminine, and men likely thought it was unmanly to talk about their issues with weight, body shape, and muscle tone. Whereas women always have had a venue to discuss their anxieties, men have had to suffer in silence, until recently when diagnoses for body disorders became more frequent and support groups for men with body issues became more prevalent. Hannah Frith and Kate Gleeson further examine the issue of men and concern about appearance in "Clothing and Embodiment: Men Managing Body Image and Appearance." They reach the conclusion that there are four areas that concern men: practicality of clothing, lack of interest in appearance, how clothing can be used to make the body attractive, and conforming to a cultural ideal.

All people participate in appearance-management behaviors (AMBs): activities that create a desired aesthetic and generally relate to one or more of the five senses. For example, combing hair relates to the visual appearance, ironing clothing relates to the sense of touch, perfume to the sense of smell, the jingle of dangling bracelets or the sounds of taffeta to the sense of hearing, and flavored lip gloss to the sense of taste. More often, one AMB can overlap into multiple senses, such as mouthwash helping with both taste and smell or fabric selection addressing sight, sound, and touch.

AMBs can be divided into two categories, routine and non-routine. Routine AMBs are commonplace and tend to be non-painful, such as brushing teeth, shaving, moisturizing, trimming nails, painting nails, applying makeup, etc. Non-routine AMBs are engaged in less frequently and tend to carry a degree of pain, discomfort, or health risk because of their invasive nature, such as liposuction, tattooing, branding (burning the skin with hot metal), and using anabolic steroids (Figure 4.1). Reilly and Rudd (2009) found the use of non-routine AMBs to be related to social anxiety, such that the more concerned or stressed someone is about being viewed in public situations, the more likely that person will consider a non-routine AMB activity. It appears that the non-routine AMBs offer some people a quick solution to their appearance worries.

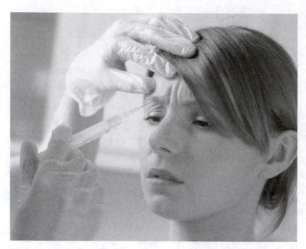

Figure 4.1 Botox injections are an example of non-routine appearance management behaviors. Such behaviors tend to be invasive or painful.

The concern over the body and how to alter it for aesthetic reasons is found throughout history. Among varied cultures, people have sought to change almost every part of their body, including head shape, feet, nails, waist, teeth, legs, buttocks, and skin texture. In the late 19th century, a beautiful ear was an important physical asset (see "Beauty and Hygiene, XV—Concerning the Ear"). *Harper's Bazaar* published this helpful beauty and hygiene note in 1896.

Cosmetic surgery has become big business, and many people are turning to surgeons to change their appearance. From 2009 to 2010 there was a 9% increase in cosmetic procedures (155% since 1997). In 2010, breast augmentations are the most popular for women, while the most popular cosmetic procedure for men was liposuction. In total, over $10.7 billion was spent on cosmetic procedures in 2010. (American Society for Aesthetic Plastic Sugery, n.d.). Joel Stein writes in "Boytox: Botox for Men" of the growing use of cosmetic surgery among men. Whereas women were once the major consumers of cosmetic surgery, he finds that men are seeking it as a means to feel better about themselves as well.

Altering skin tone is another common AMB related to body image. People believe a tanned person to be more attractive than an untanned person (Keesling and Friedman, 1987; Broadstock, Borland, and Gason, 1992; Garvin and Wilson, 1999); however, this was not always the case. Pale skin was once fashionable because it signified social and economic status. When European and American societies were based on agrarian manual labor, a tan indicated that one was a field worker, whereas pale skin indicated a life of leisure and indoor activities. In pre-Revolutionary France, members of the aristocracy would even paint blue veins on their skin to emphasize their paleness. However, with the increased ratio of indoor work due to the Industrial Revolution, the perceptions of a tan changed. A pale pallor now meant that one worked indoors, while a tan indicated leisure activities outside.

Many people believe tanning can reduce or clear up acne (e.g., dry the oil glands), accelerate dieting (e.g., sweat out water retention), or aid in musculature (e.g., a tan helps define muscular curvature). However, tanning has its risks, including premature aging (ironic, considering the obsession with youthful beauty) and cancer. In one of the largest studies of its type, Geller et al. (2002) surveyed 10,000 children and adolescents on their tanning and sunscreen use and found they do not use recommended sun protection, found a notable difference between boys and girls, and found an increase in tanning bed use as age increases. At the opposite end of the spectrum are people who desire to lighten their skin tones and engage in skin-bleaching processes. Reasons appear to be similar to tanning (e.g., self-esteem, peer pressure, aesthetics), as Christopher Charles writes in "Skin Bleaching: The Complexion of Identity, Beauty, and Fashion." His research finds that this AMB is not necessarily due to race but to perceptions of beauty.

In addition to tanning and bleaching of the skin, a more permanent change to the body's color and texture is tattooing. Tattoos were once the domain of specific non-Western tribes and peoples (such as Pacific and African cultures), outlaws, sailors, and artists, but in recent decades they have become not only acceptable but fashionable. The desire to permanently mark the body can be attributed to personal identity, group affiliation, or aesthetic expression. However, until very recently, tattoos were rarely seen in public and were often hidden by clothing, likely due to perceptions of professionalism. Yet, as Guy Trebay writes in "Even More Visible Ink," that boundary is being stretched as neck and arm tattoos are becoming more frequent in the mainstream world.

Critical Analysis of Media Images

How much impact does a cultural ideal have on an individual? Ideals are pervasive throughout the media (refer to Chapter 11: Fashion and Media for an extended discussion). Airbrushed photographs of fashion models (Figure 4.2) and the use of body doubles in popular movies are two ways that unrealistic ideals are perpetuated.

All humans are adversely affected by these fake images (Bordo, 2004). One study of Americans found that 15% of women and 11% of men surveyed would trade more than five years of their lives to be at their ideal body weight (Garner, 1997). This finding is a strong indication that media ideals do affect us on an individual level. Another result of the same study found that men and women name the stomach as the most problematic area of the body. Is the desire for a slim waistline a 20th-century phenomenon carried into the 21st century? Just when did this fixation with the stomach begin? There is archaeological evidence that today's desire for a slim waistline began with the ancient Greeks. Minoan (ancient Greek) artifacts, dating from 2900 to 1150 B.C., illustrate both men and women with extremely tiny waists (Tortora and Eubank, 1998, p. 48). Whether these artifacts reflect actual practices of young children wearing tight belts to shape the waist, or the artist's imagination, one thing is clear: the desire for a small waist was valued by both men and women.

Researchers and health professionals typically blame media images of thinness for incidents of anorexia and bulimia among adolescents. To measure exactly how women have been portrayed in magazines, Paff and Lakner (1997) conducted a study of advertisements in *Vogue* and *Good Housekeeping* from 1950 to 1994. The researchers found that the way women were portrayed (dress and body position) in 1994 did not differ much from the way women were portrayed in 1950. This is an indication that even though women's roles changed considerably between 1950 and 1994, the way women were portrayed in popular magazines did not. One reason may be that advertisers had yet to understand or value women's changing roles. Additional research has been conducted to extend Paff and Lakner's analysis to 2002 (Sprigler and Miller-Spillman, 2004). Preliminary indications are that women's portrayals in *Vogue* and *Good Housekeeping* advertisements between 1994 and 2002 are creeping, slowly, toward a less stereotypical (e.g., corporate career women, independent) feminine presentation. Although these researchers did not set out to make a direct link between media images and eating disorders, stereotypical images of women in magazine advertisements is one of the many ways that the thin ideal is promoted in the Western world (Bordo, 2004).

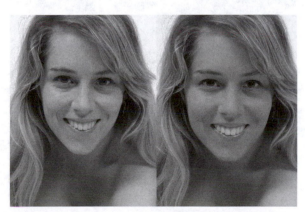

Figure 4.2 Media images are often airbrushed in order to remove any flaws and present a perfect appearance.

The fashion industry is also blamed for the obsession with body ideals, especially thinness for women and muscularity for men. These expectations are placed on fashion models; not meeting the expectations results in not being hired. Unfortunately, a number of models have died due to eating disorders in an effort to be or remain thin, including American model Margaux Hemingway in 1996; Brazilian model Ana Carolina Reston died in 2006; Uruguayan sisters and models Luisel Ramos in 2006 and Eliana Ramos in 2007; and French model Isabel Caro in 2010. Their deaths highlighted a growing concern about body image and led to some changes, such as Madrid Fashion Week instituting a minimum body mass index (weight to height ration) and Italian fashion designers banning size 0 models, both in 2006. Dove, the soap company, instituted the "Dove Campaign for Real Beauty" in 2004 in hopes of changing perceptions of what is a "beautiful" body by using marketing with normal-sized women in ad campaigns and videos.

The way men are portrayed in the media has also changed in recent decades. When reviewing male models in advertisements from the 1950s–1980s, the men had underdeveloped bodies, compared to today's muscular, buff models. Their bodies were not particularly lean and they had minimum musculature. However, in the early 1990s, designer Calvin Klein helped launch a craze for muscular models when he hired the muscular actor/singer Mark Wahlberg for an advertising campaign (see Figure 4.3). Since then, the bodies of men shown in the media have become more muscular, toned, and taut. The fashion of muscular bodies even affected children's action figures. Toys such as GI Joe, Batman, and Star Wars characters have evolved from having an average body to having a hyper-muscular body, with biceps as large as or larger than their head (Pope, Phillips, and Olivardia, 2000).

Figure 4.3 Calvin Klein's use of muscular Mark Wahlberg started a desire for images of muscular men.

One way to combat pervasive idealized images is to become a critical viewer of media. Rather than zoning out in front of the TV and passively ingesting idealized images, begin by actively critiquing what you see. Is it healthy (or even attractive, for that matter) for collarbones and ribs to protrude from the body? This became commonplace on sitcoms, reality television shows, and daytime soap operas. Can feet and lower backs survive a constant regimen of 4-inch stilettos, as routinely seen on *Gossip Girl* or *The Young and the Restless*? By 2010 there had been numerous reality television shows with the goal of changing the body into an ideal. On *The Swan* and *Extreme Makeover*, contestants vied for plastic surgery makeovers. On *Bridalplasty*, which offered a similar competition for brides-to-be, contestants who were cut from the show each week were dismissed with a curt phrase that their wedding would not be perfect, implying that the lack of a perfect body equates to a less-than-perfect wedding.

There is evidence that being a critical viewer of media images can help a person resist unrealistic images and the effect they have. Research indicates that African American adolescent females are less likely to be affected by media images than white adolescent females (Parker et al., 1995). Remember, being thin is not idealized everywhere. Peck (2005) found that in Africa, thinness is stigmatized. Those afraid of contracting HIV avoid thin individuals. This was also common among gay communities in the 1980s when thinness was equated with AIDS, regardless of one's HIV status. Among the Kalabari, also in Africa, fatness for women indicates a woman's fertility and therefore her value. In Jamaica, a thin person is viewed as someone who has low status and is not loved or cared for by others (Sobo, 1994). In Africa, a beauty pageant is held to celebrate a woman's plumpness (Knickmeyer, 2001). The suggested reading by Knickmeyer (2001) includes the interesting cross-cultural observation that Americans focus on the size of a woman's bust line (as illustrated by Barbie, originally a German invention), while Africans focus on the size of a woman's derrière. An examination of many cultures and their approaches to dress and body size can be enlightening (Eicher, 1995). The reading "A Quantitative Study of Females: Ethnicity and Its Influence on Body Image, Thin Internalization, and Social Comparison" by Brantley, Jackson, and Lee further explores the cross-ethnic issue of body image and how white and black women differ in their internalization of the thin ideal.

Many of the Euro-American ideals for women are attributed to a patriarchal society, that is, a society that traces descendants through the father and makes men the center of power. In patriarchal societies, women are supposed to be less powerful than, and even subordinate to, men. This passive ideal is expressed through a thin, childlike body and a high-pitched voice—in other words, a dependent who needs a strong man to take care of her. However, the growing Hispanic and African American segments of the American population are challenging this hegemonic power. In addition female bodybuilders (Schulze, 1990) and gay men further challenge traditional patriarchy by daring to thrive without dependence on heterosexual men for money, power, or sexual pleasure.

Cultural Standards of Beauty

One way to protect oneself from unrealistic ideals and gain some perspective is to look at other cultures' definitions of beauty. One connecting factor among all cultures is that we are all human beings, and many of us simply are not satisfied with what nature has given us. It seems to be human nature to want to "improve" upon the characteristics with which we were born. Because all cultures define ideals for their members, most individuals will spend time and energy trying to attain that ideal. As social beings, we also want acceptance from others. One way to demonstrate that need for acceptance is the effort put into some approximation of one's cultural ideal.

Ethnocentrism is the belief that one's own culture has the "right" way to do things. But when we make comparisons cross-culturally, can one honestly say that there is a difference between wearing high-heeled shoes and the bound lily foot (bound Chinese foot)? Is scarification (cutting or branding the body) different from having a facelift or a nose job? Euro-American ideals often seem harsh when compared with those of other cultures.

In Africa, the Suri and Mursi women use a labret or disk made of clay or wood to stretch their lips; the Shuwa, Dinka, and Yorba scarify their face; while the Bororo, Kambathi, and Kikuru paint their faces for beauty and status (See Figures 4.4a–c). How different is this from cutting holes in one's body to wear earrings, brow rings, or lip rings? Or adding silicone implants to one's breasts? Or using makeup to "enhance one's natural beauty"? Or lying in the sun to change the color of one's skin? Other cultures may view these practices as extreme, unnecessary, and unflattering.

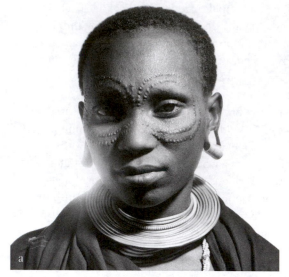

Figure 4.4 Different cultures such as the Yorba (a), Kikuru (b), and Euro-Americans (c) hold different opinions of beauty.

Summary

This chapter reviewed different ways that the body is considered beautiful and how people have altered the body—both good and bad—to achieve a cultural ideal. Some people focus on changing the entire body (e.g., silhouette), while others focus on smaller details (e.g., the ear). Beauty is not something that is easily attained—perhaps that is why everyone wants it so desperately—and the examples of what is beautiful change from age to age and culture to culture.

Newman, in "The Enigma of Beauty," points out just how elusive a definition of beauty can be. How do you describe beauty? How do you know it when you see it? Is beauty found only in physical characteristics? Or does "personality" factor into the equation? See the suggested readings by Teilhet-Fisk (1995) for a Polynesian definition of beauty—that includes personality—and Knickmeyer (2001) for beauty pageants that celebrate a woman's (large) size. One way scientists have tried to quantify beauty is through symmetrical facial features. Newman's article includes an array of cultural and historical examples of beauty.

Suggested Readings

Freson, T. S., and L. B. Arthur. (2008). Fashioning men's bodies: Masculinity and Muscularity. In A. Reilly and S. Cosbey (Eds.), *The Men's Fashion Reader* (pp. 337–354). New York: Fairchild Books.

Grogan, S. (2007). *Body Image: Understanding Body Dissatisfaction in Men, Women, and Children.* New York: Routledge.

Johnson, J., and J. Taylor. (2008). Feminist Consumerism and Fat Activist: A Comparative Study of Grassroots Activism and the Dove Real Beauty Campaign. *Journal of Women in Culture and Society* 33 (4): 941–966.

Knickmeyer, E. (2001, August 7). African Beauty Pageant a Celebration of Size. *The Toronto Star*. Accessed February 19, 2004, at seattlepi.nwsource.com/national/34191_pageant07 .shtml.

Ogle, J. P., and E. Thornburg. (2003). An Alternate Voice amid Teen 'Zines: An Analysis of Body-Related Content in *Girl Zone*. *Journal of Family and Consumer Sciences* 95 (1): 47–56.

Pitts, V. (2003). *In the Flesh: The Cultural Politics of Body Modification*. New York: Palgrave Macmillan.

Sanders, C., with D. A. Vail. (2008). *Customizing the Body: The Art and Culture of Tattooing*. Philadelphia, PA: Temple University Press.

Teilhet-Fisk, J. (1995). The Miss Heilala Beauty Pageant: Where Beauty Is More Than Skin Deep. In C. Cohen, R. Wilk, and B. Stoeltje (Eds.), *Beauty Queens on the Global Stage*. New York: Routledge.

Wolf, N. (1991). *The Beauty Myth: How Images of Beauty Are Used Against Women*. New York: Doubleday.

Learning Activity 4.1: Selected Images of Pregnancy through Time

Pregnancy is an interesting stage of a woman's body that is associated with cultural expectations. For example, in the *Arnolfini Wedding Portrait* from 1434 (see Figure 4.5), the bride appears to be pregnant when in reality she is not. Her appearance is fulfilling a social expectation. In Europe at that time, great emphasis was placed on replenishing society because of losses from wars and plagues.

Most Americans reacted similarly after World War II by replenishing society, resulting in the baby boom generation. Postwar fashions for women are often noted for emphasizing a woman's reproductive capacities (Storm, 1987). A common example of this is Dior's New Look in 1947.

Moving ahead to the early 1970s, we see women exposing their pregnant bellies unapologetically (see Figure 4.6). One might assume that these women are hippies or those who adopted the philosophy of "let it all hang out" quite literally. No bashful pretenses here!

In the 1980s, Princess Diana (see Figure 4.7) took a very conservative approach to her dress for impending motherhood. Note

Figure 4.5 In Jan van Eyck's *Arnolfini Wedding Portrait* (1434), the bride is conforming to the 15th-century body ideal for European women.

Figure 4.6 Exposing their abdomens, these women from the early 1970s are visually challenging cultural expectations of pregnant women.

Figure 4.7 Princess Diana conservatively dressed in maternity attire.

the details of Princess Diana's dress: ruffles around the neck and wrists, white hose, and black patent leather shoes with bows. It appears as if she is dressed as the child she is about to give birth to! Certainly, cultural expectations of Diana greatly affected her choice of dress while pregnant with the future king of England. This is quite a shift from the previous 1970s illustration.

Also during the 1980s, there was a need for more professional dress than what Princess Diana was wearing (Miller, 1985). Many women in the 1980s were working to establish a career before having a family. You can imagine how difficult it might be for an attorney or physician to instill confidence in her professional abilities while wearing ruffles and bows to her law or medical office (see Belleau, Miller, and Church, 1988). Several companies during the 1980s developed a line of maternity clothing especially for professional women (see Figure 4.8).

Now let's turn our attention to the 1990s. Actress Demi Moore was pictured on the cover of *Vanity Fair*, pregnant and nude, in 1992—quite a bold step that resulted in an interesting reaction to this issue. Some cities in the United States required that the magazine be wrapped in brown paper (much like pornographic magazines); other cities banned the sale of that issue completely. These reactions raise questions. Why was the cover of *Vanity Fair* so disturbing to some people that it had to be covered or banned? Why are Americans so uncomfortable with the sight of a pregnant woman (a natural state of the body)?

It would appear as though Demi Moore was making a brave and somewhat risky career move by posing nude for the magazine cover. It would also seem likely that she was interested in challenging cultural norms about the expectations of pregnant women. During the Victorian era in America, women were expected to stay at home and out of view when they were "in the

Figure 4.8 Career maternity apparel worn by professional women in the 1980s.

Figure 4.9 Supermodel Heidi Klum proudly displays her pregnant figure on the red carpet.

family way." Demi very visibly challenged that old notion. Demi seems to have started a trend. After her daring cover other celebrity moms-to-be took similar turns posing nude on magazine covers: Britney Spears on *Harper's Bazaar* (2006), Cindy Crawford on *W* (2010), and Jessica Simpson on *Elle* (2012).

Today, showing off one's expanding body is a source of pride and seems to have returned to the sentiment of the 1970s. Not only is casual attire made for pregnant women, but so too are formal clothes. Heidi Klum's numerous walks down red carpets have represented another shift in attitudes towards pregnancy. Her sleek gowns are fitted, tailored, and revealing. With dresses exposing the leg thorough a high slit or strapless tops baring the décolleté, and feet in high heels, Heidi seems to be saying, "Yes I'm pregnant and I'm sexy." (See Figure 4.9.)

Writing Activity

Write a paragraph or two expressing your thoughts on why the Demi Moore photograph was covered in brown paper or banned. Also include any ideas that came to mind while you looked at the images of pregnant women (real or imagined). How have ideas about pregnancy changed over time? How have those changes been reflected in dress? In the 1990s, concern for body weight affected some women's decisions regarding childbirth. More women were deciding not to have children because of the potential weight gain and difficulty in losing pregnancy weight (Garner, 1997). What implications does the decision not to have children have for American society? Also, consider the social class and status of the women illustrated. How might Princess

Diana's status affect her dress as compared with the women from the early 1970s? How does today's emphasis on extreme thinness compare to Heidi's glamorous, figure-fitting gowns? How will this change perceptions about the pregnant body?

Group Activity

After writing down your thoughts, divide into small groups and share your ideas with your classmates.

References

American Society for Aesthetic Plastic Surgery. (n.d.). Quick Facts: Highlights of the ASPAS 2010 Statistics on Cosmetic Surgery. http://www.surgery.org/sites/default/files/2010-quickfacts_0.pdf. Downloaded February 20, 2012.

Belleau, B. D., K. A. Miller, and G. E. Church. (1988). Maternity Career Apparel and Perceived Job Effectiveness. *Clothing and Textiles Research Journal* 6 (2): 30–36.

Bordo, S. (2004). *Unbearable Weight: Feminism, Western Culture, and the Body*. Berkeley: University of California Press.

Broadstock, M., R. Borland, and R. Gason. (1992). Effects of Suntan on Judgments of Healthiness and Attractiveness by Adolescents. *Journal of Applied Social Psychology* 22:157–172.

Damhorst, M. L. (1985). Meanings of Clothing Cues in Social Context. *Clothing and Textiles Research Journal* 3:39–48.

DeLong, M. R. (1998). *The Way We Look: Dress and Aesthetics* (2nd ed.). New York: Fairchild Publications.

Eicher, J. B. (1995). *Dress and Ethnicity*. Oxford: Berg Press.

Eicher, J. B., and M. E. Roach-Higgins. (1992). Definition and Classification of Dress. In R. Barnes and J. B. Eicher (Eds.), *Dress and Gender: Making and Meaning*, pp. 8–28. Oxford: Berg Press.

Garner, D. M. (1997, January/February). The 1997 Body Image Survey Results. *Psychology Today* 30 (1): 30–44, 75–76, 78, 80, 84.

Garvin, T., and K. Wilson. (1999). The Use of Storytelling for Understanding Women's Desire to Tan: Lessons from the Field. *Professional Geographer* 51 (2): 269–306.

Geller, A. C., G. Colditz, S. Oliveria, K. Emmons, C. Jorgensen, G. N. Aweh, and A. L. Frazier. (2002). Use of Sunscreen, Sunburning Rates, and Tanning Bed Use among More Than 10,000 U.S. Children and Adolescents. *Pediatrics* 109 (6): 1009–1014.

Grogan, S. (2008). *Body Image: Understanding Body Dissatisfaction in Men, Women and Children* (2nd ed.) London: Routledge.

Hillestad, R. (1980). The Underlying Structure of Appearance. *Dress* 5:117–125.

Kaiser, S. B. (1997). *The Social Psychology of Clothing* (2nd ed. rev.). New York: Fairchild Publications.

Keesling, B., and H. S. Friedman. (1987). Psychosocial Factors in Sunbathing and Sunscreen Use. *Health Psychology* 6:477–493.

Knickmeyer, E. (2001, August 7). African Beauty Pageant a Celebration of Size. *The Toronto Star*. Accessed February 19, 2004, at seattlepi.nwsource.com/national/34191_pageant07.shtml.

Miller, K. A. (1985). Clothing Preferences for Maternity Career Apparel and Its Relationship to Perceived Job Effectiveness. Unpublished master's thesis, Louisiana State University, Baton Rouge.

Paff, J. L., and H. B. Lakner. (1997). Dress and the Female Gender Role in Magazine Advertisements of 1950–1994: A Content Analysis. *Family and Consumer Sciences Research Journal* 26:29–58.

Parker, S., M. Nichter, M., N. Vuckovic, C. Sims, and C. Ritenbaugh. (1995). Body Image and Weight Concerns among African American and White Adolescent Females: Differences That Make a Difference. *Human Organization* 54 (2): 103–114.

Peck, D. (2005). The weight of the world. In M. L. Damhorst, K. A. Miller-Spillman, S. O. Michelman (Eds). *The Meanings of Dress* (2nd ed.), pp. 42–43. Fairchild Publications.

Pope, Jr., H. G., K. A. Phillips, and R. Olivardia. (2000). *The Adonis Complex: The Secret Crisis of Male Body Obsession*. New York: Free Press.

Reilly, A., and N. A. Rudd. (2009). Social Anxiety as Predictor of Personal Aesthetic for Women.

Clothing and Textiles Research Journal 27 (3): 227–239.

Rosenberg, M. (1985). Self-Concept and Psychological Well-Being. In R. L. Leahy (Ed.), *The Development of the Self.* Orlando, FL: Academic Press.

Schulze, L. (1990). On the Muscle. In J. Gaines and C. Herzog (Eds.), *Fabrications, Costume and the Female Body,* pp. 59–65 (excerpt). New York: Routledge.

Sobo, E. J. (1994). The Sweetness of Fat: Health, Procreation, and Sociability in Rural Jamaica. In N. Sault (Ed.), *Many Mirrors: Body Image and Social Relations.* New Brunswick, NJ: Rutgers University Press.

Sprigler, M. J., and K. A. Miller-Spillman. (2004). *A Postmodern Portrayal of Women: A Content Analysis of* Vogue *and* Good Housekeeping, *1994–2002.* Manuscript in preparation, University of Kentucky.

Storm, P. (1987). *Functions of Dress.* Englewood Cliffs, NJ: Prentice Hall.

Teilhet-Fisk, J. (1995). The Miss Heilala Beauty Pageant: Where Beauty Is More Than Skin Deep. In C. Cohen, R. Wilk, and B. Stoeltje (Eds.), *Beauty Queens on the Global Stage.* New York: Routledge.

Tortora, P., and K. Eubank. (1998). *Survey of Historic Costume* (3rd ed.). New York: Fairchild.

CLOTHING AND EMBODIMENT: MEN MANAGING BODY IMAGE AND APPEARANCE

Hannah Frith and Kate Gleeson
University of the West of England

Research suggests that cultural shifts in the ways men's bodies are represented lead men to feel increasingly dissatisfied with their appearance. Clothing is an ideal but underresearched mechanism for appearance management; however, little is known about men's presentation of their bodies through clothed displays. This article explores the ways in which men's subjective feelings about their bodies influence their clothing practices. Thematic analysis revealed four key themes: practicality of clothing choices, lack of concern about appearance, use of clothing to conceal or reveal the body, and use of clothing to fit cultural ideals. This article demonstrates the pervasive and mundane role of clothing in men's self-surveillance and self-presentation and the range and complexity of the processes involved in clothing the body.

Although not typically addressed by psychologists, we argue that men's embodied clothing practices is an interesting and important topic for several reasons. First, research suggests that changing representations of the male body make men increasingly aware of and dissatisfied with bodies that do not meet this cultural ideal. Although psychologists have looked to extreme forms of body modification (e.g., plastic surgery, excessive exercise, bodybuilding) as evidence of men's attempts to mold their bodies to fit the ideal, more mundane self-presentation strategies have been overlooked. We propose that men's clothing practices are an important and pervasive form of appearance management that reflects the continued monitoring of their visual selves.

Second, it is often assumed that men are uninterested in fashion and clothing, and most research focuses exclusively on women. However, analyses in sociology and cultural studies suggest that changes in the advertising of men's clothing lead them to develop new, more narcissistic relationships to their clothed selves. Little empirical research exploring the possible impact of these trends on men's clothing practices exists. We aim to contribute to the existing literature in these two disparate areas (clothing practices and body image) and to develop an analysis of clothing as an embodied and situated practice (cf. Entwistle, 2001).

Clothing Practices

Clothing and fashion are typically seen as frivolous, trivial, and inconsequential and have been dismissed as unworthy of serious academic analysis. Within psychology, clothing is marginalized within the narrowly focused field of person perception, which addresses how clothing is perceived by others rather than how the wearer uses clothing to construct a particular image (see Damhorst, 1990, for an overview). This approach is limited because it uses artificial clothing stimuli (e.g., uniformed or ritualized dress), ignores people's everyday clothing practices, and overlooks the context-specific meaning of clothing (Tsëlon, 2001). It also treats clothing as the expression of preexisting essentialized identities.

Only a handful of studies have investigated the possible connections between body image and clothing practices, and all focus on women. These suggest that women use clothing to manage their appearance and camouflage their size and shape (Rudd & Lennon, 2000). Typically, these studies attempt to establish the existence of individual differences in clothing practices and are underpinned by the assumption of a causal

Frith, Hannah and Gleeson, Kate. (2004). Clothing and Embodiment: Men Managing Body Image and Appearance. *Psychology of Men and Masculinity*, 5, 40–48. Reprinted by permission of the authors.

relationship between body satisfaction and clothing practices. Women who are less satisfied with their body apparently choose clothing to conceal the body, whereas those who are more satisfied choose clothing to accentuate the body (Harden, Butler, & Scheetz, 1998). When women "feel fat," they use clothes for comfort and camouflage; when they "feel slim" they use clothes to express their individuality, to gain confidence, and to look fashionable (Kwon & Parham, 1994). However, women with different body builds are equally interested in, and concerned about, clothing (Davis, 1985), and women's generally high interest in clothing makes it difficult to distinguish between different groups of women on the basis of clothing practices (Kwon, 1992). These contradictory findings suggest that our understanding of the links between body image and clothing practices is far from complete.

Psychological research on dress and clothing practices is concerned almost exclusively with women. One rationale for this is that men are less interested in clothing (Kwon, 1997; Minshall, Winakor, & Swinney, 1982; Solomon & Schloper, 1982), spend less money on clothing (Crane, 2000; Nelson, 1989), and are less involved in shopping for clothes (Peters, 1989). It is often assumed that

> Men dress for fit and comfort rather than style; that women dress and buy clothes for men; that men who dress up are peculiar (one way or another); that men do not notice clothes; and that most men have not been duped into the endless pursuit of seasonal fads. (Craik, 1994, p. 176)

However, the rapid expansion of menswear since the 1980s (Edwards, 1997; Nixon, 1996; Spencer, 1992) and the development of specialist style magazines (such as *Gentlemen's Quarterly* and *Arena*) enable men to relate to their clothed bodies in new ways.

The fusion of consumption and identity apparent in market segmentation places a greater emphasis on narcissistic aspects of self previously unavailable to men and evokes a greater emphasis on appearance and display. Despite these trends, we could find no studies that explore the interconnection of body image and clothing practices for men.

Appearance and Body Image

Most psychological research on body image focuses on women because it is assumed that they face greater pressures than men to be a particular size and shape. Such research adopts a causal model in which cultural standards of beauty define unrealistic body shapes as "ideal." Consequently, women become dissatisfied with less than ideal bodies and adopt (more or less) harmful practices to modify their bodies. However, over the last 15 years, men have come under increasing pressure to conform to the cultural ideal of a lean, well-toned, muscular build, which is reflected in cultural representations (Mishkind, Rodin, Silberstein, & Striegel-Moore, 1986; Mort, 1988; Weinke, 1998). Male action toys (Pope, Olivardia, Gruber, & Borowiecki, 1999) and male centerfolds (Leit, Pope, & Grey, 2001) have become more muscular, and the naked male body has featured more frequently in women's magazines (Pope, Olivardia, Borowiecki, & Cohane, 2001). A substantial and growing proportion of men are dissatisfied with their bodies (Mishkind et al., 1986), and the gap between men's and women's dissatisfaction is decreasing (McCaulay, Mintz, & Glenn, 1988). Men express particular dissatisfaction with their biceps, shoulders, chest, and muscle tone (Cash, Winstead, & Janda, 1986; Furnham & Greaves, 1994). Men's ideal chest size is often significantly larger than their actual chest size (Thompson & Tantleff, 1992), and many say they want a larger chest (Tantleff-Dunn & Thompson, 2000). Men and boys do not necessarily view thinness as an advantage and are as likely to want to be bigger or heavier as they are to want to be thinner (Davis & Cowles, 1991).

Many of the recognized psychometric scales may misrepresent men's dissatisfaction because they are oriented toward concerns about being overweight when men are equally concerned about being underweight (Grogan, 1999). In addition, more extreme forms of body dissatisfaction and distortion are a growing but underrecognized problem. Pope, Gruber, Choi, Olivardia, and Phillips (1997) coined the term *muscle dysmorphia* to describe a pathological preoccupation with muscularity and the perception of being small despite having a very muscular physique (see also Olivardia, 2001). Others have proposed that machismo nervosa, a psychological disorder manifested by excessive weight training, abnormal eating habits, and cognitive abnormalities, may be connected to the hypermesomorphic ideal body image (Connan, 1998).

Men engage in various practices to alter the shape of their bodies and conform to the muscular ideal. They exercise to gain weight, develop muscles, and change their shape (Davis & Cowles, 1991); have plastic surgery to swell their pectoral muscles (Thompson, Heinberg, Altabe, & Tantleff-Dunn, 1999); and use anabolic steroids to develop muscle more quickly than is possible by weight training alone (Rickert, Pawlak-Morello, Sheppard, & Jay, 1992; Wroblewska, 1997). These appearance-management techniques, ranging from the mundane (e.g., daily grooming) to the extreme (e.g., cosmetic surgery, self-starvation), provide further evidence of men's dissatisfaction. Although most psychological research has, understandably, focused on those forms of appearance management that directly impact health, this has been at the expense of theorizing the links among body image, subjectivity, and everyday practices. As Weinke (1998) noted,

> The implication of existing research is that there are great social-psychological costs for not fitting the cultural ideal. Yet this research does not consider the ways men engage with, and actually respond to, the muscular ideal within the context of their everyday lives; nor does it give attention to the strategies men use to make sense of their own bodies in relation to the cultural ideal. (p. 259)

We focus on mundane methods of appearance management, such as clothing practices, because this form of body management is currently underrepresented in empirical research and may be more pervasive than other, more extreme forms of body modification. Specifically, we explore men's subjective understanding of the importance of their feelings about their body in guiding their clothing practices and whether men use clothing to alter their appearance by concealing or revealing particular aspects of their body.

Method

Participants

Using an opportunity, snowball-sampling strategy, undergraduate psychology students recruited two participants for a study on clothing and the body. A total of 75 men participated. They ranged in age from 17 to 67 ($M = 25.79$ years, $SD = 11.01$ years), although the majority (74%) were in the 17- to 26-year age group. Volunteers received no remuneration for their participation. Most participants were White (93.4%); 3.9% described themselves as Pakistani, Black, and mixed race. Participants described the main breadwinner in their household as an employer or manager (28%), a higher professional (20%), an intermediate professional (13%), or a lower professional (13%). Clearly, volunteer bias means that this sample is not representative of the male population in the United Kingdom, and the specificity of the sample is acknowledged.

Procedure

Participants received a pack containing an information sheet, consent form, demographic form, and The Clothing and the Body Questionnaire to complete. The information sheet outlined the purpose of the research, the nature of their participation, how data might be used, how to withdraw data, and, because body image is a sensitive topic, details about relevant counseling services. The Clothing and the Body Questionnaire contained four questions: How much does the way you feel about your body influence the kinds of clothing you buy or wear? Do you dress in a way that hides aspects of your body? Do you dress in a way that emphasizes aspects of your body? Is there anything else you think we should know, or are there any questions we should have asked but didn't? Respondents were instructed to answer questions fully, giving specific examples and spending some time thinking about their answers before they started to write. Spaces for written responses were provided, and once completed the forms were returned in sealed envelopes.

Analysis

Responses were analyzed using the inductive thematic analysis procedure described by Hayes (2000). First, the data were read carefully to identify meaningful units of text relevant to the research topic.

Second, units of text dealing with the same issue were grouped together in analytic categories and given provisional definitions. The same unit of text could be included in more than one category. Third, the data were systematically reviewed to ensure that a name, definition, and exhaustive set of data to support each category were identified. The inductive thematic analysis resulted in 50 categories, which were grouped into five key themes (see the Appendix for a full list of themes). The analysis was exhaustive in that 86.6% of the data were allocated to at least one category. The coherence and replicability of the themes were established by a second researcher who recoded the first question (61.5% of the data) with a high level of interrater reliability ($K = 0.9089$, $SD = 0.1382$). Levels of agreement for individual categories are shown on Table 4.1.

TABLE 4.1

The Level of Agreement between Two Analysts in Coding the Themes

Theme	Agreement	Quality
1. Comfort is my priority.	0.913	Very good
2. I like to stand out.	1	Very good
3. I like to blend in.	0.765	Good
4. I like to look masculine.	1	Very good
5. I want to look heterosexual.	1	Very good
6. I want to look muscled.	0.871	Very good
7. Continuity in appearance is valued.	1	Very good
8. Age affects choice.	0.600	Good
9. Emphasis on functionality/practicality/purpose.	0.859	Very good
10. Clothes are used to communicate about roles.	0.600	Good
11. I respond to fashion.	0.818	Very good
12. I am not a fashion victim.	1	Very good
13. I don't want to appear vain.	1	Very good
14. We shouldn't care too much about appearance.	1	Very good
15. I like labels.	0.846	Very good
16. I hate labels.	1	Very good
17. I like my clothes to fit well.	0.789	Good
18. I use clothing to motivate weight loss.	0.429	Moderate
19. I want clothes to flatter my body.	1	Very good
20. I want to make my body attractive to women.	1	Very good
21. I want to look taller.	0.875	Very good
22. I want to appear slim.	1	Very good
23. I don't want to appear too slim.	1	Very good
24. I want to hide my body.	0.945	Very good
25. My physical size limits what I can wear.	0.882	Very good
26. The shape of my body is irrelevant.	0.956	Very good
27. Using clothes to look attractive is not an issue for men.	1	Very good
28. My style is important.	0.692	Good
29. I like to look tidy.	1	Very good
30. Clothing choices are linked to confidence.	1	Very good
31. There is pressure from others about appearance.	1	Very good
32. Look good.	0.840	Very good
33. Cost is an issue.	1	Very good
34. Not being smart.	1	Very good
35. Clothes affect people's judgments.	1	Very good
36. I use clothes to communicate.	1	Very good
37. Acceptance!	0.857	Very good
38. It matters!	1	Very good

Results

Although some men wrote at length about how their use of clothing relates to their feelings about their body, others wrote very little. The most verbose responses were given to the first question, in which men wrote an average of 68 words (SD = 41.48, range = 3–206). In response to Questions 2 and 3, which asked about whether clothing was used to hide or emphasize the body, men wrote an average of 17.96 (SD = 13.35, range = 1–67) and 18.08 (SD = 18.49, range = 1–78) words, respectively. Analysis of these responses revealed four key themes[1]: (a) Men value practicality, (b) men should not care about how they look, (c) clothes are used to conceal or reveal, and (d) clothes fit a cultural ideal.

Men Value Practicality

Perhaps unsurprisingly, men emphasized the importance of practical rather than aesthetic aspects of clothing. Clothes should be functional [14]; they should be fit for purpose, practical, and necessary for everyday living: "The clothes I buy tend to have a specific purpose and function." The prioritization of comfort [34] suggests that, although other factors do affect clothing choice, for many men "comfort and practicability comes first." To look good and feel comfortable clothes must fit well [13]: "I think I spend most effort on finding the best fitting/most comfortable clothes at a particular occasion." There are constraints on finding clothing to meet their needs, which relate to the cost of clothes [5] and the fact that physical size imposes limitations on finding suitable clothes [12]. The frustration of trying to fit into average-sized clothing was tangible for unusually tall, broad-shouldered, or short men: "I'm not short but I find trousers are often too long, making me fairly paranoid in the length of my legs."

This approach might have been predicted by marketing research literature and by gender stereotypes.

Although women see shopping as an opportunity to "try on" new identities (and, therefore, try on a number of different outfits), men regard shopping simply as a process of acquiring new clothes; if a garment fits correctly, then they are likely to buy it (Underhill, 1999). The look of the garment is apparently irrelevant.

Men Should Not Care How They Look

A second theme depicts a lack of concern with, or rejection of, the importance of appearance. Few men argued that body shape does matter [9]; many more argued that the shape of their body is irrelevant [30], that it does not influence their choice of clothing, and that they are not unduly concerned about their appearance.

A typical response was: "I don't tend to be concerned about the way I look when I shop for clothes." Some men insisted that we should not care too much about appearance [7] (e.g., "you should not be overly concerned with your appearance as it is not the most important thing in life"). Such responses map onto male gender stereotypes, which suggest that men are not supposed to be interested in shopping, adornment, and appearance.

Despite this apparent lack of concern, many participants described in detail how their clothing practices were influenced by their feelings about their body:

> I don't really choose clothing in relation to my body. But I guess when I try them on then I am taking into account how they look on me and my body.

> I am not very fussed about my body or the way it looks to extremes. I am aware that clothing is able to make the body look better and sometimes I will use this to improve my appearance.

Men talked about wanting to look good [12] and wanting clothes that flatter the body [16]. They demonstrate expertise in self-presentation and knowledge about which styles complement their particular body shape. They use vertical stripes, the "shirt over the T-shirt" trick, and dark colors to streamline their shape and enhance their appearance. As one said, "I do not have a complex about my body, but I do know what type of clothing makes the most of my build."

Men's purported lack of interest in the body is undermined by their careful attention to their clothed appearance.

Clothes Are Used to Conceal or Reveal

Men's concerns about their appearance were highlighted when they wrote about using clothing to hide the body [64], often to conceal being overweight.

> If I am feeling fat or unappealing, then the clothes I buy will be thicker, darker, or less revealing.

> I tend to wear baggy tops to hide my stomach depending on how I am feeling about myself on the day.

Clothing practices were linked to confidence with the body [9]. As one participant noted, "I am not very confident about my body as I am very thin and don't have much muscle tone. So, I tend to wear loose fitting clothes to give the impression that I appear to be larger than I actually am."

Some men felt they had nothing to hide [18] and wrote about wanting to display their bodies [15] and to emphasize particular parts of the body [29]. One wrote, "My bum is my best feature and it is important to me that my trousers, including jeans, fit nicely."

Some clearly had mixed feelings about displaying the body [17], wanting to both display and conceal different aspects. Men are engaged in an ongoing negotiation body display, which takes into account their changing perceptions of their physical shape.

> If I'm thinking I'm a fat git, I'll have a tendency to wear loose clothes and adhere to various methods employed to make a person look thinner (e.g., a shirt over a T-shirt). However, on a day when I'm feeling good, I'll be thinking under that fat is a reasonable-sized pair of pecs and I'll wear something accordingly.

Shifts in attitudes to the body and its display occur on a daily basis, and clothing becomes involved in an ongoing negotiation of the body as men try literally to get it into shape.

> My wardrobe is full of a variety of different styles that satisfy how I feel about my body at the time.

> I often buy clothing that I don't intend to wear until I broaden (arms and upper body) like vests and tank tops.

These men are clearly concerned with appearance and the deliberate "performance" of appearance involving revealing, concealing, and displaying the body. Decisions about revealing and concealing the body are not simple, one-time event choices; men monitor a range of factors in making such decisions. Ideas about self-presentation shift depending on whether one is having a "fat day" or a "thin day," suggesting that body image is not a fixed essence for our participants but rather a matter of negotiation.

Clothes Are Used to Fit a Cultural Ideal

The final theme highlights the pressure to conform to an idealized male body that is tall, muscular, and slim. Some men show an awareness of this ideal but do not find it particularly problematic. Instead, they express an acceptance of their body [22]: "Although I don't have a particularly good body (i.e., muscles) it has never bothered me." For others, the cultural ideal presents problems as they aspire to a muscular, tall, and slim body. Men wrote about wanting to appear taller [9] and focused on wearing clothes that increase the appearance of height (e.g., "Buying shoes that increase my height gives me a more confident feeling"). They also wrote about wanting to look muscular [19] and focused on the importance of having muscular arms, a toned upper body, and an athletic-looking body.

> I have started to bulk out and put on weight and gain more confidence about my body shape and have started buying more tight-fitting clothing.

When I was doing weights, I felt confident enough to buy a tank top; however, since I've stopped I feel more reluctant to show off my arms in public.

A muscular body is clearly one to show off to others, whereas a less developed physique is something to be ashamed of.

I am not one to work out and, therefore, would not consider wearing tight T-shirts that cling to upper arm muscles and chest as they would make my body look inadequate.

Finally, these men wrote about wanting to appear slim [28] but not too thin [20] and used clothing to manage this.

I tend to wear a great deal of black, which gives the impression of slimness along with baggy clothing (i.e., jumpers, jeans).

Very rarely do I wear short-sleeved shirts as I am uncomfortable with my arms, which I believe to be too thin.

These men use clothing to modify and manage the appearance of their bodies depending on how well it currently fits with the ideal. Our data suggest that muscularity and not being over- or underweight play an important role in men's decisions about clothing. Men's clothing practices reflect their concerns and anxieties about their appearance and how others will evaluate their body.

APPENDIX 4.1
Complete Set of Themes Identified

Men are very practical in choosing their clothes.	Real men shouldn't care about how they look.	Clothes are used to conceal or reveal.	Clothes are used to fit a cultural ideal.	Miscellaneous
Comfort is a priority. Clothes must fit well. Clothes must be functional. Cost of clothes is important. Physical size imposes limitations. Clothes are used to communicate about roles.	**Body shape does matter.** **We shouldn't care too much about appearance.** **The shape of my body is irrelevant.** **I want to look good.** **I want clothes that flatter the body.** I respond to fashion. I am not a fashion victim. I don't want to appear vain. Using clothes to look attractive is not an issue for men. My personal style is important. I want to look tidy. Clothes affect people's judgments. I want my clothes to reflect my images.	**Clothing is used to hide the body.** **Men have nothing to hide.** **I have mixed feelings about displaying the body.** **I use clothes to emphasize particular features of the body.** **Clothing choices are linked to confidence.** **Age affects clothing choice.** Clothing is used to reflect a desire to blend in. Clothing can reflect shyness.	**Clothing reflects acceptance of the body.** **I want to appear taller.** **I want to appear muscular.** **I want to appear slim.** **I am concerned with not appearing too thin.** I want to look masculine. I want to appear heterosexual. Continuity in appearance is valued. I like labels. I hate labels. I use smaller clothes to motivate weight loss. I want to be attractive to others. Clothing can reflect not being smart. There is pressure from others about appearance.	Overlapping and specificity of the questions. Shoes and accessories. Style and color. Cross-dressing. Cultural aspects of clothing. Is it the body or the clothes that make the difference? Male image as holistic.

Note: The themes are grouped according to order in which they appear in text. Themes that were associated with a large number of text units are shown in bold. Themes that received few mentions are shown in plain type.

Discussion

Challenging the idea that men have little invested in their appearance, our participants deliberately and strategically use clothing to manipulate their appearance to meet cultural ideals of masculinity. They vary the color, texture, pattern, fit, and size of garments to appear slimmer, taller, bigger, or more muscular than they believe their actual body shape to be. Clothing is an everyday body-modification practice that may not be as dramatic or permanent as plastic surgery and exercise but requires knowledge, attention, and financial resources. Further research is needed to map these processes in more detail. We know little about the time and energy men spend shopping for, selecting, and maintaining clothes. How do men acquire the knowledge to be able to skillfully alter their appearance using different styles of clothing, and what role do style magazines and significant others play in socializing men into appearance regimes? Although our data suggest that men's practices are flexible and varied, we know little about how they make decisions about how to present their bodies in different contexts and in relation to different audiences.

In addition, although some men express acceptance and admiration of their bodies, for many there is a battle being fought with a less than acceptable body in which clothing is a necessary armor. Our data raise questions for psychologists interested in body image. Body image is typically conceptualized as an internal and enduring "essence," but our data suggest that it is fluid, contradictory, and constantly renegotiated. Men's subjective experience of their body image shifts constantly between, for example, "fat days" and "thin days" and when different aspects of the body may become salient. Men might emphasize parts of the body of which they feel proud and hide aspects of the body of which they feel ashamed. Global measures of body satisfaction may not adequately capture men's lived experience of their bodies.

Our data reveal gaps in current understandings of body image and clothing practices, but it has not allowed us to explore these in detail. We know little about how these processes operate or how they might operate differently for diverse groups of men. For example, do pressures to conform to an ideal masculine body have more impact on some groups than others? Our sample was skewed toward young men and our findings may not apply equally to all ages, although research on age differences in body image is currently inconclusive (e.g., Pliner, Chaiken, & Flett, 1990; Lamb, Jackson, Cassiday, & Priest, 1993). We have also been unable to explore the ways in which these practices might intersect with other aspects of identity such as race, class, or sexual orientation.

However, previous work suggests that gay men, for example, value aspects of physical appearance highly (Sergios & Cody, 1985–1986) and spend more money on clothing than do heterosexual men (Rudd, 1996). We also do not know whether those who are diagnosed as having pathological relationships to their bodies (the anorexic, the compulsive exerciser) share the same knowledge, expertise, and clothing practices as average men. Clearly, there is scope for further research exploring the appearance-management strategies of those with and without pathological relationships to their bodies.

Finally, it is clear from our data that men feel they should express uninterest in their appearance. Relying on a volunteer sample might have meant that we accessed only those men who have a specific interest in clothing; however, when asked directly, the men in our study often denied the importance of the body in their clothing practices. Men's reluctance to be too interested in appearance and fashion may reflect attempts to distance themselves from stereotypes that position women as fashion dupes who squeeze themselves into ill-fitting or ridiculously uncomfortable clothing and men who are interested in fashion as effeminate. If "appearances have an added importance for the gay community" (cf. Edwards, 2000, p. 139), then men may need to signal not only their masculinity but also their heterosexuality in a way that women do not. The men in our study are aware of the appraising audience that observes and evaluates their appearance, but do men dress for a potential sexual partner (only two units of our data referred to dressing to be attractive to women) or the appraising look of other men? In view of the increasing objectification and sexualization of the male body, further research is needed to explore the ways in which men negotiate the competing demands placed on them to be both mindful and unconcerned about their appearance.

Furthermore, such research should consider the ways in which these demands might intersect with other aspects of identity (i.e., race, class, sexual orientation) and different audiences (e.g., work colleagues, sexual partners, friends).

Researchers who focus on clothing practices rarely explore embodiment, and those studying body image rarely look at clothing practices. However, our data demonstrate that dressing is an embodied practice; men are aware of and concerned about how their body will appear to others, and they strategically use clothing to alter and manipulate their appearance. Clothing as an appearance-management technique for men has been underresearched, and our study demonstrates that it is an area worthy of more attention.

However, men's ambivalence about their clothing practices suggests that quantitative measures may fail to capture their interest in and concerns about clothing practices, and that qualitative methods may enable the researcher to explore these contradictions more fully. We hope that this article goes some way toward demonstrating the pervasive yet mundane nature of men's self-surveillance and self-presentation and the range and complexity of the processes involved in clothing the body and displaying the visual self.

References

Cash, T., Winstead, B., & Janda, L. (1986). The great American shape-up: Body image survey report. *Psychology Today, 20,* 30–37.

Connan, F. (1998). Machismo nervosa: An ominous variant of bulimia nervosa. *European Eating Disorders Review, 6,* 154–159.

Craik, I. (1994). *The face of fashion: Cultural studies in fashion.* New York: Routledge.

Crane, D. (2000). *Fashion and its social agendas: Class gender and identity in clothing.* Chicago: University of Chicago Press.

Damhorst, M. L. (1990). In search of a common thread: Classification of information communicated through dress. *Clothing and Textiles Research Journal, 8,* 1–12.

Davis, C., & Cowles, M. P. (1991). Body image and exercise: A study of relationships and comparisons between physically active men and women. *Sex Roles, 25,* 33–44.

Davis, L. L. (1985). Perceived somotype, body cathexis, and attitudes towards clothing among college females. *Perceptual and Motor Skills, 61,* 119–125.

Edwards, T. (1997). *Men in the mirror: Men's fashion, masculinity and consumer society.* London: Cassell.

Edwards, T. (2000). *Contradictions of consumption: Concepts, practices and politics in consumer society.* Buckingham, England: Open University Press.

Entwistle, J. (2001). The dressed body. In J. Entwistle & E. Wilson (Eds.), *Body dressing* (pp. 33–58). Oxford, England: Berg.

Furnham, A., & Greaves, N. (1994). Gender and locus of control correlates of body image dissatisfaction. *European Journal of Personality, 8,* 183–200.

Grogan, S. (1999). *Body image: Understanding body dissatisfaction in men, women, and children.* London: Routledge.

Harden, A. J., Butler, S., & Scheetz, M. (1998). Body perceptions of bulimic and nonbulimic groups. *Perceptual and Motor Skills, 87,* 108–110.

Hayes, N. (2000). *Doing psychological research.* Buckingham, England: Open University Press.

Kwon, Y. H. (1992). Body consciousness: Self-consciousness and women's attitudes toward clothing practices. *Social Behavior and Personality, 20,* 295–307.

Kwon, Y. H. (1997). Sex, sex-role, facial attractiveness, social self-esteem and interest in clothing. *Perceptual and Motor Skills, 84,* 899–907.

Kwon, Y. H., & Parham, E. S. (1994). Effects of state of fatness perception on weight conscious women's clothing practices. *Clothing and Textiles Research Journal, 12,* 16–21.

Lamb, S., Jackson, L., Cassiday, P., & Priest, D. (1993). Body figure preferences of men and women: A comparison of two generations. *Sex Roles, 28,* 345–358.

Leit, R. A., Pope, H. G., & Grey, J. J. (2001). Cultural expectations of muscularity in men: The evolution of the *Playgirl* centerfolds. *International Journal of Eating Disorders, 22,* 90–93.

McCaulay, M., Mintz, L., & Glenn, A. A. (1988). Body image, self-esteem, and depression proneness: Closing the gender gap. *Sex Roles, 18,* 381–391.

Minshall, B., Winakor, G., & Swinney, J. L. (1982). Fashion preferences of males and females, risks perceived, and temporal quality of styles. *Home Economics Research Journal, 10,* 369–380.

Mishkind, M. E., Rodin, J., Silberstein, L. R., & Striegel-Moore, R. H. (1986). The embodiment of masculinity: Cultural, psychological and behavioral dimensions. *American Behavioral Scientist, 29,* 545–562.

Mort, F. (1988). Boy's own? Masculinity, style and popular culture. In R. Chapman & J. Rutherford (Eds.), *Male order: Unwrapping masculinity* (pp. 193–224). London: Lawrence and Wishhart.

Nelson, I. A. (1989). Individual consumption within the household: A study of expenditures on clothing. *Journal of Consumer Affairs, 23,* 21–24.

Nixon, S. (1996). *Hard looks: Masculinities, spectatorship and contemporary consumption.* London: UCL Press.

Olivardia, R. (2001). Mirror, mirror on the wall, who is the largest of them all? The features and phenomenology of muscle dysmorphia. *Harvard Review of Psychiatry, 9,* 254–259.

Peters, J. F. (1989). Youth clothes shopping behavior: An analysis by gender. *Adolescence, 95,* 575–580.

Pliner, P., Chaiken, S., & Flett, G. (1990). Gender differences in concern with body weight and physical appearance over the life span. *Personality and Social Psychology Bulletin, 16,* 263–273.

Pope, H. G., Gruber, A. J., Choi, P., Olivardia, R., & Phillips, K. A. (1997). "Muscle dysphoria": An underrecognized form of body dysmorphic disorder. *Psychosomatics, 38,* 548–557.

Pope, H. G., Olivardia, R., Borowiecki, I. I., & Cohane, G. H. (2001). The growing commercial value of the male body: A longitudinal survey of advertising in women's magazines. *Psychotherapy and Psychosomatics, 70,* 189–192.

Pope, H. G., Olivardia, R., Gruber, A., & Borowiecki, J. (1999). Evolving ideals of male body image as seen through action toys. *International Journal of Eating Disorders, 26,* 65–72.

Rickert, V., Pawlak-Morello, C., Sheppard, V., & Jay, S. (1992). Human growth hormone: A new substance abuse among adolescents? *Clinical Pediatrics, 31,* 723–726.

Rudd, N. A. (1996). Appearance and self-presentation research in gay consumer cultures: Issues and impacts. *Journal of Homosexuality, 31,* 109, 134.

Rudd, N. A., & Lennon, S. J. (2000). Body image and appearance-management behaviors in college women. *Clothing and Textiles Research Journal, 18,* 152–162.

Sergios, P., & Cody, J. (1985–1986). Importance of physical attractiveness and social assertiveness in male homosexual dating behavior and partner selection. *Journal of Homosexuality, 12,* 71–84.

Solomon, M. R., & Schloper, J. (1982). Self-consciousness and clothing. *Personality and Social Psychology Bulletin, 8,* 508–514.

Spencer, N. (1992). Menswear in the 1980s: Revolt into conformity. In J. Ash & E. Wilson (Eds.), *Chic thrills: A fashion reader* (pp. 40–48). London: Pandora Press.

Tantleff-Dunn, S., & Thompson, J. K. (2000). Breast and chest size satisfaction: Relation to overall body image and self-esteem. *Eating Disorders, 8,* 241–246.

Thompson, J. K., Heinberg, L. J., Altabe, M., & Tantleff-Dunn, S. (1999). *Exacting beauty: Theory, assessment and treatment of body image disturbance.* Washington, DC: American Psychological Association.

Thompson, J. K., & Tantleff, S. (1992). Female and male ratings of upper torso: Actual, ideal and stereotypical conceptions. *Journal of Social Behavior and Personality, 7,* 345–354.

Tseëlon, E. (2001). Fashion research and its discontents. *Fashion Theory, 5,* 435–452.

Underhill, P. (1999). *Why we buy: The science of shopping.* London: Orion Business Books. Weinke, C. (1998). Negotiating the male body: Men, masculinity, and cultural ideals. *Journal of Men's Studies, 6,* 255–282.

Wroblewska, A. M. (1997). Androgenic-anabolic steroids and body dysmorphia in young men. *Journal of Psychosomatic Research, 42,* 225–234.

Endnote

1. To aid readability, categories of each theme are presented followed by the number of units relating to each category in brackets.

Discussion Questions

1. How do you reconcile the finding that men said they were not concerned about appearance (theme 1) but then said they use clothing to hide flaws (theme 2)? What do you think is the reason for this contradiction?
2. How similar or different do you think the themes found are in relation to women?
3. Do you recognize any of yourself, your friends, or your family in these themes?

BEAUTY AND HYGIENE, XV—CONCERNING THE EAR

Harper's Bazaar

A beautiful ear may be best defined by negatives. It must be neither too large nor too small, too fleshy nor too thin, too broad nor too narrow, too red nor too pale; it must be set neither too high nor too low on the head, and must neither stand out unduly from it nor lie too close against it. Where these defects exist, however, they may be remedied in some degree, if not altogether corrected.

For the lobe which is too large there is but one remedy, excision of the superfluous part by the surgeon's scissors, an operation which, although it is said to be almost painless and to be attended by no bad results, one would hesitate a little about submitting to. But a lobe which is too thin or too short may be easily stimulated to growth in the desired direction by pinching and pulling it persistently, using at the same time the aromatic tincture for promoting the growth of the muscular tissues, for which a receipt has been given in a previous paper. In the same way the vessels of nutrition may be stimulated to increased action in any other part of the ear, which has not developed in harmony with the line of beauty.

When the ear is set too close against the head a wedge-shaped fold of linen worn for a time at night between the ear and the head will generally suffice to separate them somewhat. When the fashion of wearing the hair will admit of it, this result may be hastened by letting a lock of hair take the place of the wedge of linen during the daytime.

Where the opposite defect exists, that is to say, where the ear stands out too far from the head, an opposite course of treatment is to be pursued. The ear is to be bound to the head at night and, as far as may be possible, during the daytime, by a band of linen, or a ribbon, or by the hair. Only time and perseverance are needed to correct both of these defects.

Where the ear is deformed beyond all hope of remedy, a judicious arrangement of the hair will do much to disguise the deformity, the present fashion of drawing the hair down over the ears is advantageous in such cases.

Beauty and Hygiene, XV—Concerning the Ear. (1896, August 29). *Harper's Bazaar*, 29(35): 724.

Discussion Questions

1. Why do you think the ear was important in the late 19th century?
2. What other body parts are people concerned about today? In 50 years do you think people will still be concerned about these parts?

BOYTOX: BOTOX FOR MEN

Joel Stein

Botox is now being used by men, some of whom did not even run for President. The number of men in the U.S. who paid to get a series of tiny injections in their face nearly tripled from 2001 to 2007—to 300,000, or about 7% of the total Botoxed population. And despite the recession, those numbers aren't going down yet; one of the many things the laid-off cannot afford is to look their age.

Men usually get Botox to remove those two vertical lines between their eyebrows that make them look angry and confused and thus, one could argue, masculine. They also use the product to smooth out the horizontal creases in their foreheads, though, unlike women, they don't tend to worry about crow's feet. Men do, however, fret a lot more about the pain. "They get so jacked up worrying that it will hurt," says Botox enthusiast and nine-time Olympic gold medalist Mark Spitz. "Maybe that's why women have babies and we don't."

When 1970s Olympic heroes—and mustachioed ones at that—get work done, it would seem to mark social acceptability among guys. Spitz, though, is a spokesman for Allergan, the company that makes Botox and has started to market directly to men via its website. Sure, Spitz first considered getting the world's most common cosmetic procedure after a friend, former Olympic gymnast Nadia Comaneci, told him that the wrinkles between his eyes made him look old and overly serious, but he got a whole lot more interested when Allergan started paying him.

Who, then, are the other 299,999 dudes getting Botox? And are any of them not famous or not gay? I searched among my friends for a straight male Botox user and quickly found out that Bill Torres, a heterosexual fifth-grade teacher, had done it. Yes, the 42-year-old lives in Los Angeles, and yes, his wife is Jackie Guerra—the actress who wrote *Under Construction*, about losing 170 lb. (75 kg) and rebuilding herself with plastic surgery—but he is straight. So I went to his house with Dr. William Murphy to see Torres get Botoxed up.

If you were very sick and could barely move, you wouldn't be able to find a doctor to make a home visit, but lots of M.D.s will happily travel to your house to temporarily paralyze your facial muscles. Murphy, who wears a bow tie, cuff links and monogrammed sleeves, is an ophthalmologist, but he spends almost no time working on eyes and almost all of it driving from Palm Springs to

L.A., youthanizing people for $500 to $600 a session. (Prices could start to come down nationwide if the FDA approves the first Botox rival, Reloxin, possibly as early as April.) He has given out offers for free procedures in gift bags at the Emmys and Latin Grammys and says three-quarters of the recipients—including the men—cashed them in.

The vast majority of Murphy's male clients are indeed gay, though he has several straight actors and even a hetero sportscaster among his regular stops. Compared with his female clients, the men—in addition to being far more nervous about the pain—are extra-cautious about making sure they don't overdo it. "Five years ago, everybody wanted that frozen look," he says. "Now they tell me, 'Make me look refreshed. As few lines as possible, but I still need to have expression.'"

It isn't long into Murphy's visit before Torres' reason for getting Botox becomes obvious: his wife stands inches away, urging him to get as many injections as possible. And she gets so excited when the doctor suggests erasing the furrowed brow lines in addition to the "11s" between her husband's eyebrows that she throws up her hands in victory. "Thank God!" she yells. "They drive me insane. It's like when somebody has a big zit on the side of their face and they don't pop it. Just pop it!" She had already persuaded Torres to dye his hair, go for massages, shave his chest and get regular manicures and pedicures, but Botox took a little longer, in part because it meant scheduling appointments every four months.

While Torres breathes his way through some painful-looking injections right over his eye as part of his "lunchtime lift," i.e., a mini-face-lift so speedy and subtle you can go back to work that day, the good doctor asks me if I'm ready for my shots. At 37, and complimented more on my skin than on any of my other stunning physical attributes, I didn't expect to be told I needed Botox. "I would suggest just lightly across your forehead," he says. As I ponder this, he keeps going. "You have a very thick brow and deep-set eyes. It would be nice to do just a little brow lift so you have a more serene, refreshed, younger look." And then: "And a little bit around the eyes." When I demur, Murphy tells me that if I wait, the wrinkles will set deeper and require a bigger dose of expression-limiting

Botox. "Honestly, with you I would start now," he says. "It would make such a difference."

Though Torres and his wife are cheering me on and the thrill of expensing Botox during a recession is compelling, I wimp out. It's not that I don't believe it would make me look better or that I'd be glad I did it. Shallow as it is, I just don't want to think of myself as a guy who gets cosmetic surgery. Plus, those needles really did look like they hurt.

Discussion Questions

1. What are some reasons why it is now more acceptable for men to receive cosmetic enhancements?
2. Do you think Botox injections is just currently fashionable or will it become a staple of creating one's appearance?

4.4

SKIN BLEACHING: THE COMPLEXION OF IDENTITY, BEAUTY, AND FASHION

Christopher A. D. Charles, Ph.D.
University of the West Indies, Mona

Introduction

On the TNT cable channel, basketball star Charles Barkley derisively jeered baseball star Sammy Sosa because Sosa was bleaching his skin. Barkley, who wore white makeup, said, in part, "I know you want to get in the Hall of Fame, but going white ain't the way to go. . . . Stop it, stop it, Sammy Sosa!"(*Huffington Post*, 2009). Skin bleaching (also called skin lightening and skin whitening) is a very old practice that is now global in scope (Al-Saleh & Al-Doush, 1997; Blay, 2007; Mire, 2009). The expensive and formal skin bleaching procedure offered by dermatologists is beyond the scope of this chapter. This work explains the non-medical bleaching of the skin, without making an evaluative judgment of the practice. Although there are many reasons for this controversial practice in the contemporary era (Blay, 2007; Charles, 2003, 2006, 2009a, 2010b; Hope 2009), the present discussion focuses on the reasons of identity, beauty, and fashion among non-Whites (Blacks, Arabs, and Asians, etc.) and Whites (Caucasians). The chapter commences with the conceptual framework of colorism.

Next is a discussion of skin bleaching followed by colorism-driven explanations of skin bleaching through identity negotiation, the perceived beauty of light skin, and the construction of the modified complexion as fashion.

Colorism

Hunter (2007, p. 237) defines colorism as "the process of discrimination that privileges light-skinned people of color over their dark skin counterparts." This definition of colorism places the phenomenon solely among non-Whites, but colorism also occurs among Whites. The values of contemporary colorism have their roots in the European colonization of Africa, Asia-Pacific, the Middle East, and the Americas (Charles, 2010a). European colonial exploitation was informed by racism, which posited that the Caucasian race is superior to other races. Although racism is the source of colorism, it is different from colorism to the extent that racism discriminates based on race, and colorism does so based on complexion

Original for this text.

(Hunter, 2007). The complexion consensus empowers light-skinned people with more opportunities, status, and prestige in nearly all societies, but this process is mediated by talent, social class, social networks, and educational attainment. The values and norms of the complexion consensus influence some people to bleach their skin (Charles, 2010a).

Skin Bleaching

Skin bleaching is the lightening of the skin through the use of homemade products, cosmetic products, and dermatological products. Some people bleach only their faces, while others bleach their faces and bodies. Some also bleach for a specific social occasion. People of all ages, races, complexions, and social class participate in this global practice; the practice also stands regardless of gender or level of education. The lightening of the skin occurs in contemporary Africa (Blay, 2007, 2009; de Souza, 2008), Asia (Ashikari, 2005; Karan, 2008; Prasetyaningsih, 2007), the Caribbean (Charles, 2003a, 2010b; Hope, 2009), Latin America (Winders, Jones III & Higgins, 2005), the Middle East (Al-saleh & Al-Doush, 1997; Hamed, Tayyem, Nimer & AlKhatib, 2010), Europe (Mire, 2009; Petit, Cohen-Ludmann, Cleverbergh, Bergmann & Dubertret, 2006), and North America (Hall, 1995). The societal preoccupation with skin color is not new. The ancient Egyptians used white lead on their skins (Jablonski, 2006), as did those in ancient Greece, and, in more recent history, the Japanese Geishas. Skin bleaching products were popular in medieval Europe (Da Soller, 2005; Jablonski, 2006). Some captive Africans on sugar plantations in the colonial Caribbean used cashew oil to lighten their skins (Charles, 2010a; Coleman, 2003), and skin bleaching was also popular in colonial Africa. The sale of skin bleaching products to African-Americans has been popular in the United States since the early 20th century, if not before (Porter, 2006; Williams, 2006).

There are many reasons for contemporary skin bleaching. These include the fashionableness of skin bleaching; the popularity of the prac-tice; the support the practice receives from family and friends; the belief that light skin attracts intimate partners; spousal desire; the belief that one's skin is too dark; the belief that light skin is beautiful; an attempt to remove facial pimples and blemishes; an effort to tone the skin; the belief that light complexion facilitates social mobility; the desire for identity negotiation; as a result of miseducation; and self-hatred, which is the commonest reason purported (Al Ghamdi, 2010; Blay, 2007; Charles, 2003a, 2003b, 2006, 2009a; Hope, 2009; Kpanake, Sastre &Mullet, 2010; Mahe, Ly & Gounongbe, 2004). The self-hate argument is problematic because it is an erroneously universalizing explanation. It is mistakenly assumed that skin bleaching Blacks, Arabs, Asians, and Whites all over the world bleach for the same reasons, despite their different values, personalities, and motivations, and the varying contexts, histories, and cultures they experience (Charles, 2009b, 2010b). While some skin bleachers have low self-esteem (a form of self-hate), others clearly do not (Charles, 2003a, 2006, 2010b). The latter skin bleachers demonstrate complex personhood and live well-adjusted lives. Since some skin bleachers have high self-esteem, this chapter examines the influence of the colorized culture on their behavior (Charles, 2009a, 2009b, 2010a, 2010b, 2010c, 2010d).

The international cosmetic companies tap into the racial and complexion norms and values in various countries in the global marketing of skin bleaching products, especially on the Internet (Mire, 2009). Some popular skin bleaching products are Maxi White, Sure White, Clear Fast, Nadinola Skin Fade Cream, African Queen Beauty Cream, Symba Cream, Neoprozone Gel, Topiclear, Madre Perla, Michael Jackson, Immediate Clear, and Body Clear. There are also products (for specific areas) such as Facial Fade Lightening Cream, Hand and Body Lightening Cream, Knee and Elbow Lightening Stick, and Leg Fade Cream. The brands sell their skin bleaching products in various forms such as creams, gels, lotions, cleansers, soaps, sticks, and serums (Charles, 2006, 2010a).

Because many of the skin bleaching products contain mercury and hydroquinone, they are regulated in Europe, Japan, the United States, and in some developing countries (Al-saleh & Al-Doush, 1997; Charles, 2006; de Souza, 2008). The use of the unsafe skin bleaching products has led to ophthalmologic problems (e.g., cataracts and glaucoma), neurological problems (e.g., memory loss, irritability, insomnia, and neuropathies), dermatological problems (e.g., pitch-black pigmentation, scabies, colloid milium ochronosis, and fragile skin), and a host of other medical problems (e.g., immunosuppression, Cushing's syndrome, renal damage, hypertension, vulval warts, and adrenal insufficiency) among users especially in the developing world (Dadze & Petit, 2009; Kpanake, Sastre & Mullet, 2010; Mahe, Ly & Perret, 2005; Petit, Cohen-Ludmann, Clevenbergh, Bergmann & Dubertret, 2006). Not all the skin bleaching products on the market are unsafe. Through trial and error and interaction with other skin bleachers and vendors of bleaching products, some skin bleachers have developed a skin bleaching technology. This know-how does less damage to skin, especially if the skin bleachers engage in "light bleaching" compared to "heavy bleaching" (Charles, 2010a). The motivations for skin bleaching are strong, despite the health dangers associated with the practice. One such powerful motivation is the culture-driven need to create a colorized self (Charles, 2009a, 2010b).

Identity

Social identity is people's attachment to social groups through social relations, and a sense of belonging based on commonly shared attributes (Tajfel & Turner, 1986). People negotiate several context-dependent social identities based on ethnicity, social class, skin color, gender, occupation, religion, nationality, sexual orientation, and race, all of which are integrated or ordered in terms of salience (Deaux, 2000). Some people reinforce their identity by managing their appearance as they transact their identity with others. Identity transactions or "doing identity" is a universal psychological process. There are several modes of identity transactions such as buffering, bonding, bridging, and code switching. People buffer discrimination with their identity to protect the self. Bonding oc-

curs with people one knows and for whom one has an affinity. People also use their identity to bridge with strangers by using their interpersonal skills in new social interactions to find common ground. In code switching, a person downplays one identity and highlights another identity because the situation requires it. The colorized societal values influence identity negotiations and transactions (Cross & Straus, 1998; Cross, 2010).

Colorism influences some southern Europeans who have darker skin than Northern Europeans to bleach their complexion to reach the Northern European skin ideal. These southern Europeans alter their complexion to reinforce their identities as Europeans and to be biologically further from non-Whites (Mire, 2009). They negotiate their European social identity by managing their biological appearance. The fact that some Europeans bleach their skin may be surprising, but skin bleaching is more complex and nuanced than many people realize (Charles, 2003b, 2009b, 2010a). Colorism also influences the sense of self for some non-Whites. These skin bleachers are aware of the societal values that stigmatize dark skin. Light skin brings perceived social benefits. The skin bleachers use the colorized values about complexion to define who they are by creating a new meaning of the self (Ashikari, 2005; Blay, 2007; Winders, Jones III & Higgins, 2005; Prasetyaningsih, 2007). The skin bleachers' alteration of their physicality relocates them in the social identity category of the people with light skin in the society, including friends (Hall, 1995; Mahe, Ly & Gounongbe, 2004). It does not matter to these skin bleachers whether or not they are accepted by the light-skinned people in the society. What matters to the skin bleachers is that they had a desire to relocate their social and biological meanings of self, and this was achieved (Blay, 2009; Charles, 2009a).

Some non-White skin bleachers transact or express their identity with others by buffering themselves against people who hurl insults at them for bleaching their skin. In a study conducted by Charles (2009b, p.36) some female skin bleachers stated "I curse them" and "I ignore them." These skin bleachers protect themselves by cursing those who disrespect them, while others ignore the criticisms they receive. The female skin bleachers also bridge with strangers who compliment them on their bleached skin. They stated "I talked to them" and "I said thank you" (Charles, 2009b, p.36). The skin bleachers who bridged found common ground with these strangers. These skin bleachers also bonded with people who complimented them about their lovely complexion. According to Charles (2009b, p.36), some stated, "I treated them good" and "I treated them like friends." The skin bleachers transacted the bleached self with these people by treating them in a warm and friendly way because these people said the skin bleachers were beautiful.

Beauty

Beauty is "a combination of qualities, such as shape, color, or form, that pleases the aesthetic senses, especially the sight" (Oxford Dictionary, 2010). Beautiful people are perceived to have good qualities, greater employment suitability, higher income, and greater popularity. Beauty is also equated with youth, and some people experience intra-psychic conflicts driven by the societal norms of beauty. Plastic surgery is used by people to bring their bodies in line with the dominant beauty ideal, thereby resolving the inner conflict (Lijtmaer, 2010). Across cultures, the personal evaluation of the aesthetic physicality of others influences the evaluator's psychic development of beauty, which is also influenced by interpersonal, cultural, and political factors (Olarte, 2010). Cosmetic companies advertise "beauty" that women use to perform the aesthetic self in transaction with others (Millard, 2009). There are more favorable attitudes toward a product that is relevant for physical attractiveness when the product is advertised by a beautiful model, than a product that is less relevant for attractiveness that is advertised by a beautiful model (Trampe, Stapel, Siero & Mulder, 2010). White beauty is portrayed as the ideal in many advertisements, and some people believe light skin, unlike dark skin, is beautiful (Hunter, 2007). This socially approved light complexion aesthetic is seen by skin bleachers as beautiful,

sexy, and fashionable, all of which collectively attracts intimate partners (Charles, 2009a).

Colorism also influences some White women to bleach their skin not only to become whiter but also to acquire beauty. Some White women in Europe and elsewhere bleach the age spots and the wrinkles on their skin, because in the West many people equate beauty with a White youthful appearance of Northern Europe (Lijtmaer, 2010; Mire, 2009). Bleaching to acquire beauty is driven by the same desires that influence some women to undergo plastic surgery to meet the dominant beauty ideal in society (Charles, 2003a; Lijtmaer, 2010). Some skin bleaching products are advertised using beautiful and youthful-looking White female models to make the cosmetic products more attractive to women (see Figure 4.10) (Mire, 2009). There are nuances to colorism among Whites because some tan their skin and braid their hair. Tans and braided hair are status symbols and fashion statements, especially if they were

Figure 4.10 Cosmetic companies often feature White models in advertisements for skin-lightening products even though they aren't their target market.

acquired on holiday at a tropical vacation resort. However, a tan and braided hair are temporary fashion-driven physical modifications, and Whites who tan and braid do not reject Whiteness, which they police by determining who is White.

Some non-White skin bleachers also argue that skin bleaching makes the skin beautiful. As one female skin bleacher noted, "I like to bleach because it makes me look pretty" (Charles, 2010a, p. 174). The prevailing belief system driven by colorized values is that the beautiful and socially elevated light skin in society should be acquired through skin bleaching (Hamed, Tayyem, Nimer & AlKhatib, 2010; Prasetyaningsih, 2007). Beautiful light skin is also sexy and attractive to potential intimate partners who like this skin color (Blay, 2007, 2009; Charles, 2010d; Jablonski, 2006; Karan, 2008; Mire, 2009; Pierre, 2008). One male skin bleacher reported in a study that he bleached "to get more girls" (Charles, 2009a, p.164). Some people also bleach their skin to satisfy the complexion desire of their partner because light skin is very important in some intimate-partner relationships (Blay, 2007, 2009; Fokuo, 2009; Mahe, Ly & Gounongbe, 2004).

Despite the prominence of colorized values in many societies, many non-Whites in these societies do not bleach their skin and they find non-White skin attractive. Non-Whiteness in general is not viewed the same way by all non-Whites, because they do not experience non-Whiteness the same way (Charles, 2003b). There are also several very popular African supermodels in international fashion. These models are perceived to be prestigious and beautiful fashion icons because of the commercialized exotic Blackness of the fashion industry. However, the average non-White woman is not necessarily viewed the same way as the African supermodels because of selective colorism and racism. Non-White women in general do not have the fashion prowess of the African supermodels, but some construct their own fashion by modifying their complexion.

Fashion

Fashion consumers engage with ads to transport (get a good story), to identify, to immerse, to feel

the ads, and to act (Phillips & McQuarrie, 2010). Fashion ads grab the visual attention of young women because their eyes are fixated on the model; and the internalization of the thin ideal influences the length of time they looked at the model (Ju & Johnson, 2010). Men and women who were exposed to ads with average-sized fashion models had a more positive body image compared to those who viewed no models. Average-sized models can be used to appeal to consumers and promote a positive body image (Diedrichs & Lee, 2010). Women and fashion change agents reflected a fashion problem recognition style influenced by their wants. There was a difference among male fashion followers whose problem recognition style was driven by their needs. Therefore, group membership and gender influence fashion consumers' problem recognition style (Workman & Studak, 2006). Styles of fashion designs are related to consumers' sensibilities and emotions (Na, 2009). Sometimes stigmatized social practices become fashionable over time (Sandick & Ger, 2010). The various popular music genres that are international have their associated fashion styles (Baxter & Marina, 2008), and celebrities also create fashion (Barron, 2007). People in many cultures use their skin to make fashion statements (Jablonski, 2006), including some skin bleachers who view their altered complexion as fashionable and popular as body aesthetics (Hope, 2009; Mahe, Ly & Gounongbe, 2004).

"It's all about the flavor fashion" (Charles, 2010a, p.174). This quote from a female skin bleacher captures, in essence, the views of the skin bleachers who construct their modified complexion as fashion (Al-saleh & Al-Doush, 1997; Karan, 2008). The bleached body is interpreted as aesthetically appealing. The altered body is not just fashion but it is fashion with a nice flavor. Hope (2009) also finds the same fashion theme among some hard-core fans of dancehall music. Skin bleaching is glorified and celebrated in some dancehall songs. Some fans of dancehall music view skin bleaching as "fashion and style" and an appropriate and beautiful way of being similar to how dancehall clothing and accessories are experienced. Mahe, Ly, and Gounongbe (2004) also find that among some skin bleachers the altered complexion is a fashion phenomenon undergirded by femininity, urbanity, and modernization. Skin bleaching as body fashion should not only be understood from the point of view of the critics of the skin bleachers, but also from the subjective interpretations of the skin bleachers and their social spaces and social networks that validate their sense of fashion. Skin bleaching was a stigmatized social practice that became fashionable over time because it provides some skin bleachers a positive body image.

Conclusion

This chapter focused on skin bleaching to create a colorized identity because bleaching provides the socially accepted complexion, which is perceived to be beautiful and fashionable. Skin bleaching is another body modification procedure like tattooing, cosmetic surgery, body piercing, and decorative scarring. This chapter did not focus on the skin bleachers who hate themselves. Self-hate is just one of the many reasons for skin bleaching. Whites who tan are not viewed as self-haters, so we should not assume that all non-Whites who bleach hate themselves. Also, non-Whites who bleach their skin do not expect to get White skin, and they cannot become Whites because non-White albinos and other non-Whites who lose the melanin in their skin because of vitiligo are not socially accepted as Whites. Whiteness is socially constructed and policed by Caucasians who are the gatekeepers of Whiteness and White racial identity. Therefore, focusing on the cultural norms and values about skin color in various countries provides the best analytical framework to understand the complex practice of skin bleaching.

References

Al Ghamdi, K. M. (2010). The use of topical bleaching agents among women: A cross sectional study of knowledge, attitudes and practices. *Journal of the European Academy of Dermatology and Venereology, 24,* 1214–1219.

Al-Saleh, I. & Al-Doush, I. (1997). Mercury content in skin lightening creams and potential hazards to the health of Saudi Women. *Journal of Toxicology and Environmental Health, 51,* 123–130.

Ashikari, M. (2005). Cultivating Japanese whiteness—the whitening cosmetics boom and the Japanese identity. *Journal of Material Culture, 10,* 73–91.

Barron, L. (2007). The habitus of Elizabeth Hurley: celebrity, fashion, and identity branding. *Fashion Theory, 11,* 443–462.

Baxter, V. K. & Marina, P. (2008). Cultural meaning and hip-hop fashion in the African-American male youth subculture of New Orleans. *Journal of Youth Studies, 11,* 93–113.

Blay, Y. A. (2007). Yellow fever: Skin bleaching and the politics of skin color in Ghana. Ph.D. Dissertation. Temple University.

Blay, Y. A. (2009). Ahoofe Kasa!: Skin Bleaching and the function of beauty among Ghanaian women. *Jenda: A Journal of Culture and African Women Studies, 14,* 51–85.

Charles, C.A.D. (2003a). Skin bleaching, self-hate and Black identity in Jamaica. *Journal of Black Studies, 33,* 711–728.

Charles, C.A.D. (2003b). Skin bleaching and the deconstruction of blackness. *Ideaz, 2,* 42–54.

Charles, C.A.D. (2006) The Crowning of the Browning: Skin Bleaching and the Representation of Black Identity in the Context of Dancehall Music. MA thesis. Hunter College.

Charles, C.A.D. (2009a). Skin bleachers' representations of skin color in Jamaica. *Journal of Black Studies, 40,* 153–170. doi: 10.1177/0021934707307852.

Charles, C.A.D. (2009b). Liberating skin bleachers: From mental pathology to complex personhood. *Jenda: A Journal of Culture and African Women Studies, 14,* 86–100.

Charles, C.A.D. (2010a). Representations of colorism in the Jamaican culture and the practice of skin bleaching. Ph.D. Dissertation. City University of New York.

Charles, C.A.D. (2010b). Skin bleaching in Jamaica: Self esteem, racial self esteem, and black identity transactions. *Caribbean Journal of Psychology, 3,* 25–39.

Charles, C.A.D. (2010c). The complex lives of the skin bleachers and the self hate myth. Unpublished paper.

Charles, C.A.D. (2010d). Colorism, skin bleaching and sexual attraction. Unpublished paper.

Coleman, D. (2003). Janet Schaw and the complexion of empire. *Eighteenth Century Studies, 36,* 169–193.

Cross, W. E. Jr. & Strauss, L. (1998). The everyday functions of African American identity. In J. Swim & C. Stangor (Eds.), *Prejudice: The Target's Perspective* (pp. 267–279), San Diego: Academic Press.

Cross, W. E. Jr. (2010). The enactment of race and other social identities during everyday transactions. Unpublished paper.

Da Soller, C. (2005). The beautiful woman in medieval Iberia: Rhetoric, cosmetics, and evolution. Ph.D. Dissertation. University of Missouri-Columbia.

Deaux, K. (2000). Identity. In Alan E. Kazdin (Ed.), *Encyclopedia of psychology* (Vol. 4, pp. 222–225). Washington: American Psychological Association.

de Souza, M. M. (2008). The concept of skin bleaching in Africa and its devastating health implications. *Clinics in Dermatology, 26,* 27–29.

Diedrichs, P. C. & Lee, C. (2010). GI Joe or Average Joe? The impact of average-size and muscular male fashion models on men's and women's body image and advertisement effectiveness. *Body Image, 7,* 218–226.

Fokuo, J. K. (2009). The lighter side of marriage: Skin bleaching in post-colonial Ghana. *African and Asian Studies 8,* 125–146.

Hall, R. E. (1995). The bleaching syndrome: African Americans' response to cultural domination vis-à-vis skin color. *Journal of Black Studies, 26,* 172–184.

Hamed, S. H., Tayyem, R., Nimer, N. & AlKhatib, H. S. (2010). The skin lightening practice among women living in Jordan: Prevalence, determinance, and user's awareness. *International Journal of Dermatology, 49,* 414–420.

Hope, D. P. (2009). Fashion ova style: Contemporary notions of skin bleaching in Jamaican dancehall culture. *Jenda: A Journal of Culture and African Woman Studies, 14,* 101–26.

Huffington Post. (2009). Charles Barkley, in white makeup, mocks Sammy Sosa. 12 November. http://www.huffingtonpost.com/2009/11/12/charles-barkley-in-white_n_356338.html.

Hunter, M. L. (2007). The persistent problem of colorism: Skin tone, status, and inequality. *Sociology Compass, 1,* 237–254.

Jablonski, N.G. (2006). Skin: A natural history. Los Angeles: University of California Press.

Ju, H. W. & Johnson. K.K.P. (2010). Fashion advertisements and young women: Determining visual attention using eye tracking. *Clothing and Textiles Research Journal, 28,* 159–173.

Karan, K. (2008). Obsessions with fair skin: Color discourses in Indian advertising. *Advertising Society & Review, 9,* 1–13.

Kpanake, L., Sastre, M.T.M. & Mullet, E. (2010). Skin bleaching among Togolese: An inventory of motives. *Journal of Black Psychology, 36,* 350–368.

Lijtmaer, R. (2010). The beauty and the beast inside: The American beauty—Does cosmetic surgery help? *Journal of the American Academy of Psychoanalysis & Dynamic Psychiatry, 38,* 203–218.

Mahe, A., Ly, F. & Guonongbe, A. (2004). The cosmetic use of bleaching products in Dakar, Senegal: Socio-factors and claimed motivations. *Sciences Sociales et Sante, 22,* 5–33.

Mahe, A., Ly, F.& Perret, J. (2005). Systematic complications of the use of skin-bleaching products. *International Journal of Dermatology, 44,* 37–38.

Millard, J. (2009). Performing beauty: Dove's "Real Beauty" campaign. *Symbolic Interaction, 32,* 146–168.

Mire, A. A. (2009). "Soaping the cells": Science, beauty, and the practice of skin-whitening biotechnology. PhD. Dissertation. University of Toronto, Canada.

Na, Y. (2009). Fashion design styles recommended by consumers' sensibility and emotion. *Human Factors and Ergonomics in Manufacturing, 19,* 158–167.

Olarte, S. W. (2010). Cross-cultural aspects of beauty. *Journal of the American Academy of Psychoanalysis & Dynamic Psychiatry, 38,*199–202.

Oxford Dictionary. (2010). http://www.oxforddictionaries.com/definition/beauty?view=uk.

Petit, A., Cohen-Ludmann,C., Clevenbergh, P., Bergmann, J. F. & Dubertret, L. (2006). Skin lightening and its complications among African people living in Paris. *Journal of American Academy of Dermatology, 55,* 873–878.

Phillips, B. J. & McQuarrie, E. F. (2010). Narrative and persuasion in fashion advertising. *Journal of Consumer Research, 37,* 368–392.

Pierre, J. (2008). "I like your color!" Skin bleaching and geographies of race in urban Ghana. *Feminist Review, 90,* 9–29. doi:10.1057/fr.2008.36.

Porter, E. (2006). Black no more?: Walter White, hydroquinone, and the "Negro problem." *American Studies, 47,* 5–30.

Prasetyaningsih, L. A. S. (2007). The maze of gaze: The color of beauty in transnational Indonesia. Ph.D. Dissertation. University of Maryland, College Park.

Sandick, O. & Ger, G. (2010). Veiling in style: How does a stigmatized practice become fashionable? *Journal of Consumer Research, 37,* 15–36.

Tajfel, H. & Turner, J. C. (1986). The social identity theory of intergroup conflict. In S. Worchel & W. Austin (Eds.), *Psychology of intergroup relations* (pp. 2–24). Chicago: Nelson Hall.

Trampe. D., Stapel, D. A., Siero, F. W. & Mulder, H. (2010). Beauty as a tool: The effect of model attractiveness, product relevance, and elaboration likelihood on advertising effectiveness. *Psychology & Marketing, 27,* 1101–1121.

Williams, M. E. (2006). The crisis cover girl: Lena Horne, the NAACP, and representations of African American femininity. *American Periodicals, 16,* 200–218.

Winders, J., Jones III, J. P. & Higgins, M. J. (2005). Making gueras: Selling white identities on late-night Mexican television. *Gender, Place and Culture, 12,* 71–93.

Workman, J. E. & Studak, C. M. (2006). Fashion consumers and fashion problem recognition style. *International Journal of Consumer Studies, 30,* 75–84.

Discussion Questions

1. How is colorism different from racism?
2. What are the arguments for and against skin bleaching?
3. Have you engaged in colorism? What were the circumstances?
4. What methods have you used to change the color of your skin? Why did you want to change the color of your skin? Did you get the benefits you thought you would from changing your skin color?

4.5

EVEN MORE VISIBLE INK

Guy Trebay

Who in the world gets a neck tattoo? A couple of years back you could have narrowed the answer to gang members, prison inmates, members of the Russian mob and the rapper Lil Wayne. Then something occurred.

In a mysterious and inexorable process that seems to transform all that is low culture into something high, permanent ink markings began creeping toward the traditional no-go zones for all kinds of people, past collar and cuffs, those twin lines of clothed demarcation that even now some tattoo artists are reluctant to cross (Figure 4.11).

Not entirely surprisingly, facial piercing followed suit.

Suddenly it is not just retro punks and hardcore rappers who look as if they've tossed over any intention of ever working a straight job.

Artists with prominent Chelsea galleries and thriving careers, practicing physicians, funeral directors, fashion models and stylists are turning up with more holes in their faces than nature provided, and all manner of marks on their throats and hands.

A year ago, Jenny Dembrow, an associate executive director of the Lower Eastside Girls Club, a Manhattan social service agency, decided to add to her collection of body modifications, which already included a Greek key necklace inked below her clavicle and draped across her shoulders, holes pierced in her cheeks, and earlobe perforations that have been stretched an inch wide over time.

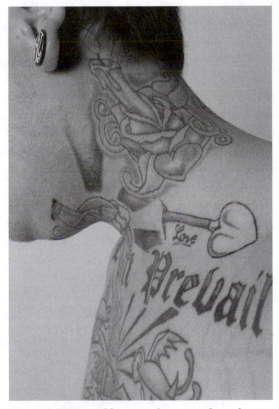

Figure 4.11 Are visible tattoos becoming less taboo?

"I've always been drawn to tattoos and counterculture," Ms. Dembrow said one afternoon last week, as she presided over a tea party held for the girls and young women served by her agency. "At this point, though, it almost seems as if you're more outside the mainstream if you don't have a tattoo."

The design Ms. Dembrow chose was a fanciful vine with no real botanical basis; its burgundy colored tendrils twine around her face and down her neck. "For me it's just very decorative, like a permanent necklace," she explained.

The effect of the neck tattoo is lovely, if startling. "I have definitely had parents that were taken aback or freaked out about what I look like," Ms. Dembrow said. "And I have had conversations with the girls where I tell them that it absolutely limits your options and that I'm lucky to have a job where it isn't an issue."

Who can say, she added, what would happen if she were thrust back into the work force? "Would I be forced to sell punk rock T-shirts in some horrible shop on St. Marks Place?" she said.

She might. While there is ample evidence of tattooing's migration from the backwaters of alternative culture into the mainstream (or at least onto some part of David Beckham's body), we are still a long way from seeing facial tattoos on the selling floor at Bloomingdale's or the trading floor of the stock exchange.

In case after case, the courts have found on-the-job appearance requirements—including policies forbidding tattoos and body modifications—to be nondiscriminatory.

Among the better publicized cases was that of Kimberly Cloutier, a Massachusetts woman who sued for the right to wear her 11 earrings and eyebrow piercings while at work as a Costco cashier. Claiming membership in the Church of Body Modifications, Ms. Cloutier argued her piercings were a form of religious expression. Although she ultimately lost, her case was soon followed by others in Massachusetts and in Washington State.

"There is a lot of employee activism," said Laurel A. Van Buskirk, a New Hampshire lawyer who has written extensively about body modification and the law. "And because the cost of defending these cases is quite big, it makes employers a little uncomfortable when they start delving into that sphere."

One result of "employee pushback," Ms. Van Buskirk said, is that the shape of that sphere has begun to shift. Defining what the courts in the Cloutier case called a "neat, clean and professional" workplace image becomes more challenging when you consider that in 2006, a Pew Research Center survey found that 36 percent of people age 18 to 25, and 40 percent of those age 26 to 40, have at least one tattoo.

"Popular culture has had a huge effect" on acceptance of tattoos in the workplace, said Alexis Handelman, the owner of Alexis Baking Company, a cafe in Napa, Calif., whose clientele ranges from "banker people to hipster people to gazillionaire people."

"Watching a show like 'Project Runway,' where the guy who won Season 3 had his son's name tattooed on his neck," Ms. Handelman added, referring to Jeffrey Sebelia, "I was, like, 'Whoa.' It wasn't a prison tattoo. It wasn't sailors or criminals. It was this real-life person that you saw being creative and successful, and it really affected your perception about who gets tattooed."

Ms. Handelman found those perceptions tested last summer when Jay Sizemore applied for a job. "He's all tatted up," Ms. Handelman said of the 18-year-old artist. "He had these two cheek piercings, tattooed elbows, a tattoo on the inside of his mouth and nickel-sized rings in his ears."

Leery that customers would find Mr. Sizemore's appearance "hostile or too in-your-face," she hired him nevertheless and found that the reaction "has been a big nothing," she said.

Likewise in the case of the fashion model Freja Beha, who recently had the word "float" inscribed in cursive on her neck, a visible tattoo had little affect on her ability to earn a living, said Ivan Bart, the senior vice president of IMG Models, which represents her.

Nor do the rings she has tattooed on one of her hands. In great demand as a catwalk model for American and European runway shows this season, Ms. Beha is also featured in advertising campaigns for Emporio Armani, Gucci and Gap.

"I myself don't really care for tattoos," Mr. Bart said. "I prefer the human body in its unadorned state." But, in business terms, Ms. Beha's tattoo is irrelevant, he said. "I don't think I've had anybody say, no, we won't use her. And anybody doing a print campaign, they just airbrush it out."

A gig as a barista or a model is not a job at Morgan Stanley (although neither is a job at Morgan Stanley, anymore). The day when most businesses are blasé about visible tattoos on employees seems a ways off. But then, it is only relatively recently that tattoo artists were comfortable inking neck and hands.

"In the old days tattooists wouldn't do it," said Bob Baxter, the editor of the tattoo journal *Skin & Ink*. "There are 528 shops in New York and maybe 10 won't do it now."

Necks and hands, said Joshua Lord, an owner of East Side Ink on Manhattan's Lower East Side, were the last taboo. Now it is common for customers to seek them, he said. "Before it was people in industries that are forgiving," he said, meaning principally music or art. "But recently I've done them for doctors and funeral directors and teachers, and a lot of hairdressers," who use hand tattoos as conversation starters, he said.

In earlier times, the only people who wore neck and hand tattoos—besides folks seeking to advertise outlaw affiliation—were those who had run out of space elsewhere on their bodies.

In fact, Mr. Baxter said, "There is resentment" among old-timers of the recent trend to get hands and necks done before having experienced the cost and discomfort of inking the rest of the body. And there is also a sense, familiar to those in subcultures that get drafted into the mainstream, that it is becoming harder to set oneself apart.

"The tattoo community sees them as posers," Mr. Baxter said of the newly inked people. "It's like going out in the 1960s to buy a Beatles wig."

But Beatles wigs came off easily and tattoos do not. "It's 20 times more painful to get it removed than to get it," Mr. Baxter said. Part of that pain must surely be the mortification of having stamped oneself with an outdated motif.

"There's no question" that more people have begun to tattoo themselves in more visible areas in the last two years, said Dr. Roy G. Geronemus, the director of the Laser & Skin Surgery Center of New York. "We've also seen an increase in the number of people coming in to have the cosmetic and decorative tattoos removed," he added, and for reasons that will come as no surprise.

"A certain number of people, when they become new parents, find they underestimated the image they want to project. The tattoo no longer fits the image of the establishment."

It is possible, though, that the establishment is also easing up somewhat on its image requirements. "I have a doctorate, but I also have dreadlocks and visible tattoos on both arms," said Robin Turnbow, a pediatric physical therapist in Manhattan. "Sometimes, when I go to do an evaluation of a kid on Park Avenue, I get stopped by the doorman and the concierge before they'll even call up. But then a lot of times they see me and they say, 'Wow, I can't believe it! How great! You're the PT!'"

Discussion Questions

1. Are there certain geographic areas of the world where tattoos would not hinder employment opportunities? Why do you think this is?
2. Should employers be allowed to discriminate against tattoos if it protects their brand image?

A QUANTITATIVE STUDY OF FEMALES: ETHNICITY AND ITS INFLUENCE ON BODY IMAGE, THIN-INTERNALIZATION, AND SOCIAL COMPARISON

Aquiashala S. Brantley, Vanessa Jackson, and Min-Young Lee
University of Kentucky

Introduction

Caucasian American (CA) women have been reported to have extremely low body image in comparison to African American (AA) women, but questions remain about whether this finding still has its validity. This study examined if one's ethnicity was a predictor of their body image, thin-internalization, and social comparison. In advanced Western democracies, there have been dramatic changes in what is considered to be attractive in a female (Furnham, Hester, & Weir, 1990). America has seen everything from a full-figured voluptuous woman to a thin-framed physique being admired. However, the petite physique has been known as the dominant standard of beauty (Mazur, 1986). This prominent norm is known as the ideal thin-figured woman. Unfortunately, research has found that these perceived pressures to be thin have stemmed from family, friends, and even the media, and are leading to strong amounts of body dissatisfaction in women (Stice & Thompson, 2001). The fashion industry is noted as being one of the highest endorsers for reflecting the social message of the importance of a thin body (Tate & Shafer, 1982). A majority of fashion industries use mannequins that have ideal body proportions—tall and thin—to display clothing in stores. The same body ideal requirements are used for hiring fashion models (Tate & Shafer, 1982). The issue that exists is that the media frenzy thin ideal is vanishing; therefore advertisers and marketers should try to incorporate more realistic-sized models in the media because of the increased appeal it could have with the consumer. The research published on body image, women, and their acceptance of the thin ideal has been extensive. However, it has historically represented a Caucasian perspective, which sees "thin as in" (Chetty, 2008). A majority of past studies have concluded that African American women are more satisfied with their bodies, on average, than Caucasian women (Altabe, 1998; Parker et al., 1995).

Molloy and Herzberger (1998) stated that African American women's cultural loyalty and strong ethnic identity protect them from the thin ideal standards of American culture. Are African Americans less likely to accept this thin-internalization because of their ethnicity and culture? Could it be that they are less likely to engage in comparing themselves to others to form an opinion about what should be deemed "attractive"? This exploratory study will examine whether or not ethnicity is influential on women's body image, acceptance of thin-internalization, and involvement in social comparison. The purpose of this study is to determine if there is a discrepancy in the acceptance of the dominant standard of beauty and if it is influenced by ethnicity. The study examined body image, thin-internalization, and social comparison as predictors of the acceptance of the dominant standard of beauty. The research questions developed for this study included: 1) does ethnicity influence the importance of body image among women; 2) does ethnicity influence thin-internalization among women; 3) does ethnicity influence social comparison among women; and 4) does social comparison influence body image and thin-internalization among women?

Original for this text.

Review of Related Literature

Body Image and Ethnicity. Body image is defined as the mental picture we have of our bodies that affects the perception of our physical appearance and even how others perceive us (Cash & Pruzinsky, 2002; Sloan, 2000; Witmer, 2009). From childhood into adulthood, experiences occur that help form perceptions of individuals' self. Body image is often based on perceptions, not reality, therefore it can change because it reflects individuals' mood swings, physical environments, and even experiences (Main, 2009; Witmer, 2009). Research shows that African American and Caucasian women embrace significantly different definitions of beauty and perceptions of themselves (Huber, Fuccella, Kohn, & Cox, 1995; Molloy & Herzberger, 1998; Parker et al., 1995). Many research studies have stated that African American females' perception of beauty is more flexible than Caucasian women's, whereas African Americans report being less preoccupied with weight and dieting concerns (Altabe, 1998; Parker et al., 1995). In a 1993 study conducted by Abrams & colleagues, it was found that 64% of the African American women surveyed concluded that they would rather be a "little overweight" than "a little underweight." One of the reasons these differences occur is because women of all ethnic groups try to obtain the look they feel is most appealing or desirable to the men of their race (Abrams et al., 1993).

Thin-Internalization and Ethnicity. The average woman in the United States is 5 ft 4 in and weighs 140 pounds (Lacey, 2009). Unlike the average woman's measurements, the "ideal" woman perceived in the media averages out to be 5 ft 7 in and weighs 100 pounds (Lacey, 2009; Centers for Disease and Control Prevention, 2008). Thin-internalization has been defined as referring to the "extent to which an individual cognitively 'buys into' socially defined ideas of attractiveness and engages in behaviors designed to produce an approximation of these ideals" (Stice & Thompson, 2001) and "uses these ideals as specific values to the point that they become guiding principles" (Thompson et al., 1996). Researchers revealed media has not targeted African American women with their messages, and Caucasian women have more role models who depict thinness as a successful image (Bissell, 2002). From the media outlets that were studied, television measured alone reported having 5.6% of its characters that are African American women (Mastro & Greenberg, 2000; Schooler et al., 2004), and only 2–3% appear in mainstream magazine advertisements (Bowen & Schmid, 1997). Even though there are a handful of African American women who are presented as beauty ideals in the media (e.g., Halle Berry, Tyra Banks), these are exceptions rather than the norm (Schooler et al., 2004). Schooler et al. (2004) reported that Caucasian women are more likely than African American women to have more negative thoughts about their body after viewing the television shows. Allan, Mayo, & Michel (1993) suggested it could be because African Americans have been said to have different notions of what beauty actually does represent.

Social Comparison and Ethnicity. Generally people do not evaluate themselves against others who are too different from themselves. In fact, if given a range of people they will choose someone most like themselves for comparison (Festinger, 1954). Unfortunately, the comparisons that people make are usually made with individuals who are often found within the media. Few studies have been conducted that relate social comparison and ethnicity. Blanton et al. (2000) reported that African American women only compare themselves in a social environment when it involves an individual from their own race.

Conceptual Framework

The proposed conceptual framework states that social comparison and ethnicity could influence the variance in body image. An important quality of human interaction is that we relate our own features to others (Krones, 2008). We as human beings engage in social comparisons to others in order to make conclusions about our own feelings, traits, and abilities (Festinger, 1954). Buunk and Mussweiler (2001) assert that individual differences determine the extent to which people compare themselves with others, and those comparisons are then interpreted. Generally, findings have suggested that those who report social comparisons based upon physical attributes were more likely to have negative body image (Stormer & Thompson, 1996). Frisby (2004) reported that African American women have less body dissatisfaction and are not affected by images of Caucasian women. But other investigators have tried to determine if results measuring African American women changed if they were exposed to idealized images of beautiful African American women (Blanton et al., 2000). Krones (2008) reported that individuals who are known for having low self-esteem tend to feel better about themselves when they are compared with similar individuals. Furthermore, when social comparisons are made with role models, a feeling of inspiration occurs, yet low self-esteem is revisited when that same success as the role model seems unobtainable.

Method

Participants. Two hundred and sixty-seven survey questionnaires were collected. The participants ranged in ages 18 and older, with 87 participants being between the ages of 18 and 21 and 37 participants between the ages of 41 and 50. One hundred and twenty-two participants (45.7%) were CA, and one hundred and seventeen participants (43.8%) were AA. The majority of participants (n = 129, 48.3%) had some form of college education. When asked to estimate yearly income, the mode response was less than $10,000 (n = 104, 39.0%), and 178 respondents (66.7%) reported they were single, not yet married.

Sample Selection and Data Collection. The participants for this study were a convenience sample of university students and members of a sorority located in a Southeastern community who were adults 18 and older. Students in merchandising, apparel, and textiles classes were administered the questionnaire at a time identified by the instructors. Collection of data was also conducted using an online survey tool. Local community members of a prominent AA sorority were recruited to participate in the

online survey. These members were approached at a monthly chapter meeting and had the survey explained to them and why their participation was important. From there they were provided with an e-mail link to insert into an Internet browser window that would allow them to complete a questionnaire for the study. Snowball sampling was used to increase the number of participants completing the questionnaire online. Snowball sampling relies on referrals from initial recruited subjects in order to generate additional subjects (Stat Pac, 2009). The members of the organization were asked to ask any of their fellow family, friends, and peers for their participation as well.

Instrumentation

Social Comparison. Social comparison is defined as when individuals seek to compare themselves with someone against whom they believe should have reasonable similarity (Wagner, 2009). A revised version of The Comparison to Models Survey (CMS) (Strowman, 1996) was used to measure the extent of social comparison. The 8-item scale evaluated the degree to which individuals compare themselves to media models. The scale measured the amount of comparisons but also related them in terms of attributes similar to cultural stereotypes. These attributes included physical appearance, exercise habits, popularity, happiness, career success, and eating habits. The 5-point scale ranges from 1 (*never*) to 5 (*always*). Sample items include "In reference to your peers, how often do you compare yourself to them" . . . in terms of career success? In terms of intelligence? In terms of happiness? The Comparison to Models Survey reported previously reliability coefficients for men (.84) and women (.86) (Strowman, 1996).

Body Image. A revised version of the Body Image Ideals Questionnaire (BIQ; Cash & Szymanski, 1995) was used in order to measure body image. The questionnaire is a 22-item assessment that was developed to measure self-perceived discrepancies and importance of idealized ideals for a number of physical attributes (Cash & Szymanski, 1995; Szymanski & Cash, 1995). The questionnaire asked participants to evaluate how well their bodies matched their physical ideals based on 10 attributes: height, facial features, chest size, weight, physical strength, physical coordination, muscle tone & definition, hair texture & thickness, skin complexion, body proportions, and overall physical appearance. The two dimensions found using the BIQ were discrepancy and importance (Cash & Szymanski, 1995). The BIQ used a Likert scale to measure discrepancy in order to rate the extent to which participants believed they look like or match their ideal. Discrepancy was rated on a 4-point Likert scale that anchored as: 1 (*exactly as I am*); 2 (*almost as I am*); 3 (*fairly unlike me*); and 4 (*very unlike me*). Importance was measured by asking participants to rate their personal importance of each characteristic previously measured using a 4-point Likert scale: 1(*not important*); 2 (*somewhat important*); 3 (*moderately important*); and 4 (*very important*). Some sample items included "My ideal hair texture & thickness are . . . ," "How important to you is your ideal muscle tone and definition," and "How important to you is your ideal weight." The internal consistencies for the two dimensions of the BIQ were estimated using Cronbach efficient alpha. Alphas for discrepancy and importance are .75 and .82, respectively (Thompson et al., 1996; Cash & Szymanski, 1995; Szymanski & Cash, 1995).

Thin Internalization. The Sociocultural Attitudes Toward Appearance Scale (SATAQ) is a scale that assessed internalization of media messages in reference to the thin ideal and was used in this study to measure thin-internalization among the participants (Cusumano & Thompson, 1997; Thompson et al., 1996). In order to organize the scale in a more efficient way, some questions were omitted and rearranged by category and topic. The scale consisted of 21 items with 4 factors that include: Internalization-Information, Internalization-Pressures, Internalization-General, and Internalization-Athlete. The SATAQ-3 has internalization subscales with excellent reliability: Internalization-Information (Cronbach alpha = .96), Internalization-Pressure (Cronbach alpha = .92), Internalization-General (Cronbach alpha = .96), and Internalization-

Athlete (Cronbach alpha = .95) (Thompson, et al., 2003). Response options on this scale anchored as: 1 (*never*); 2 (*once in a while*); 3 (*about half of the time*); 4 (*most of the time*); and 5 (*always*). Some sample items included: "TV programs are an important source of information about fashion and being attractive," "Attractiveness is very important if you want to get ahead in our culture," and "I would like my body to look like women who appear in TV shows and movies."

Results

Body Image. Differences in body image for CA and AA women were first examined by comparing the mean scores using an independent sample t-test. The results from the independent t-test revealed there is not a significant difference between CA and AA women with regard to body image $p < .000$.

Thin-Internalization. An independent t-test was computed to compare thin internalization for CA and AA women. The t-test indicated a significant difference between CA and AA women with regard to thin-internalization. Mean comparisons indicated that CA women place more emphasis on thin-internalization than AA women ($t = 4.566$, $p = .000$). Principal Component Factor Analysis with varimax rotation was conducted on the SATAQ scale and revealed three Internalization factors: pressures, social stereotypes, and self-confidence. The Cronbach Alpha coefficients were pressures ($\alpha = .862$), social stereotypes ($\alpha = .773$), and self-confidence ($\alpha = .407$). The third factor (self-confidence) reported a low reliability ($\alpha = .407$). An independent sample t-test was conducted to determine the differences between CA and AA women with regard to pressures and social stereotypes. Based on the results, there was a significant difference between CA and AA women for pressures ($p = .000$) and social stereotypes ($p = .000$). In addition, the mean comparisons indicated that CA women were affected by pressures and social stereotypes more so than AA women.

Social Comparison. An Independent Sample t-test was conducted in order to compare the mean scores of CA and AA women for social comparison. The t-test reported that there was a significant difference between CA and AA women with regard to social comparison ($t = 8.049$, $p < .001$). According to the findings, CA women seek to compare themselves to others more so than AA women.

Relationship of Social Comparison to Body Image and Thin-Internalization. Social comparison was predicted to influence the body image and thin-internalization of CA and AA women. Linear regression was computed to test the amount of change in body image and thin-internalization by social comparison. The reported r-square was .125 ($\beta = .614$, $t = .409$, $p < .001$). The findings suggest that social comparison only accounts for a 12.5 percent change in body image. Thin-internalization factors (pressures and stereotypes) were examined as predictors of social comparison. The linear regression reported the r-square to be .362 ($\beta = .393$, $t = 11.528$, $p < .001$) for pressures and .202 ($\beta = .225$, $t = 7.810$, $p < .001$) for social stereotypes.

Discussion

While many past studies have concluded that CA and AA women differ in the acceptance of the dominant standard of beauty (Garner et al., 1980), previous research has not examined the assumption based on various factors other than body image. The purpose of this study was to determine if there is a discrepancy in the acceptance of the dominant standard of beauty and if it is influenced by social comparison and ethnicity. This study examined these factors based on obtained responses from CA and AA participants.

In general, social comparison was predicted to have an influence on body image among CA and AA women. Although significance was found between the two factors, the findings revealed that social comparison accounted for a low percent change in body image. This implies that perhaps other underlying variables might account for the change in body image besides social comparison.

Similarly, there was significance found connecting thin-internalization and social comparison. However, the percent of change for the two factors (pressures and social stereotypes) was low as well. This too indicates that perhaps other underlying factors may need to be identified that influence pressures and social stereotypes.

This study predicted that ethnicity may influence body image differently among CA and AA women. However, the results confirmed that there was not a significant difference between CA and AA women in terms of body image importance. This finding does not support previous research that states there is a significant variation in body image importance among these groups and that AA women are more satisfied with their bodies, on average, than CA women (Abrams et al., 1993; Altabe, 1998; Parker et al., 1995). Although the results were not significant, there was still a slight difference in the attitude among the ethnicity groups toward body image. CA women's attitude toward their body image was more important than AA women. These findings are congruent with a study conducted by Roberts, Cash, Feingold and Johnson (2006). Although the difference was limited, perhaps other underlying factors may differ as to how body image is measured between the sample groups.

This study also predicted that ethnicity may influence thin-internalization differently among CA and AA women. The findings clearly indicate a variation in how the sample groups internalized a thin ideal. CA women placed more emphasis on thin-internalization than AA women. This conclusion supports previous research that AA women do not internalize the idea of thin-internalization as much as CA women do (Bissell, 2002). As discussed in the literature, thin ideals have been epitomized in Western culture for years (Lamb et al., 1993). These standards have continued to exist consistently throughout the media. But research has revealed that AA women, although one of the highest media consumers, are not affected by messages that endorse the thin ideal (Schooler et al., 2004). It could be possible that AA women tend to dismiss the appearance standards in the media because they see few representations of themselves there (Bowen & Schmid, 1997; Bissell, 2002; Jefferson & Stake, 2009). Further, AA women could define their beauty ideals not through thinness but through characteristic traits such as style, personality, etc. (Schooler et al., 2004). Thus, maybe researchers are correct in their findings that a strong cultural loyalty shields AA women from the ideal standards of thinness that are popular in Western society (Perez & Joiner, 2002).

To date, not as much research has been conducted on whether ethnicity plays a role in how social comparison affects an individual. But Festinger (1954) argued that if social comparisons were made with other individuals, then it would provide valuable information in the research of self-evaluations. It appears from this study that social comparison is different between Caucasian American and African American women. The results suggest that, similarly, both ethnicities are said to compare themselves with someone against whom they feel should have reasonable similarity. Although statistical significance was reached, Caucasian American women were still reported to compare themselves with others more so than African American women do, which supports previous research that has reported the same (Blanton et al., 2000). Furthermore, maybe African American women are less likely to make upward or downward comparisons because the African American women that are represented in the media embody a wider range of body sizes (Tirodkar & Jain, 2003). Thus, the ideals that Caucasian American women internalize are more than likely emphasizing a thinner shape, making it possible to believe that Caucasian American women tend to make social comparisons with others in order to form opinions of themselves more so than African American women.

References

Abrams, K., Allen, L., & Gray, J. (1993). Disordered eating attitudes and behaviors, psychological adjustments, and ethnic identity: A comparison of black and white female college students. *International Journal of Eating Disorders, 14,* 49–57.

Allan, J., Mayo, K., & Michel, Y. (1993). Body Size Values of White and Black Women. *Research in Nursing and Health, 16,* 323–333.

Altabe, M. (1998). Ethnicity and Body Image: Quantitative and Qualitative Analysis. *International Journal of Eating Disorders, 23,* 153–159.

Bissell, K. (2002). I want to be thin, like you: Gender and race as predictors of cultural expectations for thinness and attractiveness in women. *News Photographer, 57,* 4–12.

Blanton, H., Crocker, J., & Miller, D. (2000). The Effects of In-Group versus Out-Group Social Comparison on Self-Esteem in the Context of a Negative Stereotype. *Journal of Experimental Social Psychology, 36,* 519–530.

Bowen, L., & Schmid, J. (1997). Minority presence and portrayal in mainstream magazine advertising: An update. *Journalism and Mass Communication Quarterly, 74*(1), 134–146.

Buunk, B., & Mussweiler, T. (2001). New directions in social comparison research. *European Journal of Social Psychology, 31,* 467–475.

Cash, T., & Pruzinsky, T. (Eds.). (2002). *Body Image: A handbook on theory, research and clinical practice.* New York: Guilford Press.

Cash, T., & Szymanski, M. (1995). The development and validation of the body-image ideals questionnaire. *Journal of Personality Assessment, 64,* 466–477.

Centers for Disease Control and Prevention (2008). National Health and Nutrition Examination Survey Data. Retrieved November 17, 2009, from http://www.cdc.gov/nchs/about/major/nhancs/datablelink.htm.

Chetty, V. (2008). A Study of Stereotypical Ideal Body Images for African American and Caucasian Women. Retrieved September 5, 2008, from http://www.clearinghouse.missouriwestern.edu/manuscripts.asp.

Cusumano, D., & Thompson, J. (1997). Body image and body shape ideals in magazines: exposure, awareness & internalization. *Sex Roles, 37,* 701–721.

Festinger, L. (1954). A theory of social comparison processes. *Human Relations, 7,* 117–140.

Frisby, C. (2004). Does Race Matter? Effects of Idealized Images on African American Women's Perception of Body Esteem. *Journal of Black Studies, 34,* 323.

Furnham, A., Hester, C., & Weir, C. (1990). Sex Differences in the Preferences for Specific Female Body Shapes. *Sex Roles: A Journal of Research, 22,* 743–754.

Garner, D., Garfinkel, P., Schwartz, D., & Thompson, M. (1980). Cultural expectations of thinness in women. *Psychological Reports, 47,* 483–491.

Grabe, S., & Hyde, J. (2006). Ethnicity and body dissatisfaction among women in the United States: A meta-analysis. *Psychological Bulletin, 134,* 460–476.

Huber, J., Fuccella, J., Kohn, A., & Cox, M. (1995). *Cross Cultural Examination of Women's Body Image Perception.* Paper presented at the Annual Meeting of the North American Society of Alderian Psychology.

Jefferson, D., & Stake, J. (2009). Appearance self-attitudes of African American and European American women: Media comparisons and internalization of beauty ideals. *Psychology of Women Quarterly, 33,* 396–409.

Krones, P. (2008). *Believing the Thin-Ideal Is the Norm Promotes Body Image Concerns: Beauty Is "Thin Deep?"* (Doctoral dissertation, University of Texas at Austin, 2008) Pro-Quest LLC, 3320904.

Lacey, L. (2009). What Size Is the Average Woman? Retrieved from http://www.fullandfabulous.org/articles_view.asp?articleid=17064.

Lamb, C., Jackson, L., Cassiday, P., & Priest, D. (1993). Body figure references of men and women: A comparison of two generations. *Sex Roles, 28,* 345–358.

Main, A. (2009). Gender impact assessment: Body image Retrieved April 9, 2009, from http://www.whv.org.

Mastro, D., & Greenberg, B. (2000). Portrayals of racial minorities on prime time television. *Journal of Broadcasting & Electronic Media, 44,* 699–703.

Mazur, A. (1986). U.S. trends in feminine beauty overadaptation. *Journal of Sex Research, 22,* 281–303.

Molloy, B., & Herzberger, S. (1998). Body image and self esteem: A comparison of African American and Caucasian American women. *Sex Role: A Journal of Research, 38,* 631–643.

Montepare, J. (1996). Actual and subjective age-related differences in women's attitudes toward their bodies across life span. *Journal of Adult Development, 3*(3), 171–182.

National Eating Disorders Association (2008). Body Image. Retrieved February 17, 2009, from http://www.nationaleatingdisorders.org/nedaDir/files/documents/handouts/BodyImag.pdf.

Nunnally, J., & Bernstein, I. (1994). *Psychometric Theory* (3rd ed.). New York: McGraw-Hill, Inc.

Parker, S., Nichter, M., Nichter, M., Vuckovic, N., Sims, C., & Ritenbaugh, C. (1995). Body image and weight concerns among African American and White adolescent females: Differences that make a difference. *Human Organization, 54,* 103–114.

Perez, M., & Joiner., T. (2002). Body image dissatisfaction & disordered eating in black and white women. *International Journal of Eating Disorders, 33,* 342–350.

Roberts, A., Cash, T., Feingold, A., & Johnson, B. (2006). Are Black-White differences in females' body dissatisfaction decreasing? A meta-analytic review. *Journal of Consulting and Clinical Psychology, 74,* 1121–1131.

Schooler, D., Ward, M., Merriweather, A., & Caruthers, A. (2004). Who's that girl: Television's roles in the body image development of young White and Black women. *Psychology of Women's Quarterly, 28,* 38–47.

Sloan, B. (2000). Ohio State University Factsheet: Body Image. Retrieved November 14, 2008, from http://www.ohioline.edu/hyg-fact/5000/5238.html.

Stat Pac (2009). Sampling methods. Retrieved April 21, 2009, from http://www.statpac.comsurveys/sampling.htm.

Stice, E., & Thompson, J. (2001). Thin-ideal internalization: Mounting evidence for a new risk factor for body-image disturbance and eating pathology. *Current Directions in Psychological Science, 10,* 181–183.

Stice, E., Presnell, K., & Spangler, D. (2002). Risk factors for binge eating onset: A prospective investigation. *Health Psychology, 21,* 131–138.

Stormer, S., & Thompson, J. (1996). Explanations of body image disturbance: A test of maturational status, negative verbal commentary, social comparison & sociocultural hypotheses. *International Journal of Eating Disorders, 19,* 193–202.

Strowman, S. (1996). *The relation between media exposure and body satisfaction: An examination of moderating variables derived from social comparison theory.* Unpublished doctoral dissertation, University of New Hampshire, Durham.

Szymanski, M., & Cash, T. (1995). Body-image disturbances and self discrepancy theory: Expansion of the Body-Image Ideal Questionnaire. *Journal of Social and Clinical Psychology, 14,* 134–136.

Tate, S., & Shafer, M. (1982). *The complete book of fashion illustration.* New York: Harper & Row.

Thompson, S., Sargent, R., & Kemper, K. (1996). Black and white adolescent males' perceptions of ideal body size. *Sex Roles, 34,* 341–406.

Tirodkar, M., & Jain, A. (2003). Food messages on African American television shows. *American Journal of Public Health, 93,* 439–441.

Witmer, D. (2009). What is body image? Retrieved April 9, 2009, from http://www.parentingteens.about.com/cs/bodyimage/a/bodyimage.htm.

Discussion Questions

1. As a man or woman, what is your opinion of the importance of the body image of the opposite sex? How do you think it should influence media advertising?

2. Why do you think media should consider body image in their development of advertisements?

3. Watch various examples of television shows that are directly targeting specific ethnic groups. What factors can you identify that may lead you to believe that the importance of body image may vary by ethnic group?

4. Interview two to three people from two different ethnic groups about the importance of body image and how it is reflected in their selection of clothing. What information surprised you?

THE ENIGMA OF BEAUTY

Cathy Newman

Sheli Jeffry is searching for beauty. As a scout for Ford, one of the world's top model agencies, Jeffry scans up to 200 young women every Thursday afternoon. Inside agency headquarters in New York, exquisite faces stare down from the covers of *Vogue*, *Glamour*, and *Harper's Bazaar*. Outside, young hopefuls wait for their big chance.

Jeffry is looking for height: at least five feet nine. She's looking for youth: 13 to 19 years old. She's looking for the right body type.

What is the right body type?

"Thin," she says. "You know, the skinny girls in school who ate all the cheeseburgers and milkshakes they wanted and didn't gain an ounce. Basically, they're hangers for clothes."

In a year, Jeffry will evaluate several thousand faces. Of those, five or six will be tested. Beauty pays well. A beginning model makes $1,500 a day; those in the top tier, $25,000; stratospheric supermodels, such as Naomi Campbell, four times that.

Jeffry invites the first candidate in.

"Do you like the camera?" she asks Jessica from New Jersey.

"I love it. I've always wanted to be a model," Jessica says, beaming like a klieg light.

Others seem less certain. Marsha from California wants to check out the East Coast vibes, while Andrea from Manhattan works on Wall Street and wants to know if she has what it takes to be a runway star. (Don't give up a sure thing like a well-paying Wall Street job for this roll of the dice, Jeffry advises.)

The line diminishes. Faces fall and tears well as the refrain "You're not what we're looking for right now" extinguishes the conversation—and hope.

You're not what we're looking for. . . .

Confronted with this, Rebecca from Providence tosses her dark hair and asks: "What are you looking for? Can you tell me exactly?"

Jeffry meets the edgy, almost belligerent, tone with a composed murmur. "It's hard to say. I know it when I see it."

What is beauty? We grope around the edges of the question as if trying to get a toehold on a cloud.

"I'm doing a story on beauty," I tell a prospective interview. "By whose definition?" he snaps.

Define beauty? One may as well dissect a soap bubble. We know it when we see it—or so we think. Philosophers frame it as a moral equation. What is beautiful is good, said Plato. Poets reach for the lofty. "Beauty is truth, truth beauty," wrote John Keats, although Anatole France thought beauty "more profound than truth itself."

Others are more concrete. "People come to me and say: 'Doctor, make me beautiful,'" a plastic surgeon reveals. "What they are asking for is high cheekbones and a stronger jaw."

Science examines beauty and pronounces it a strategy. "Beauty is health," a psychologist tells me. "It's a billboard saying 'I'm healthy and fertile. I can pass on your genes.'"

At its best, beauty celebrates. From the Txikão warrior in Brazil painted in jaguar-like spots to Madonna in her metal bra, humanity revels in the chance to shed its everyday skin and masquerade as a more powerful, romantic, or sexy being.

At its worst, beauty discriminates. Studies suggest attractive people make more money, get called on more often in class, receive lighter court sentences, and are perceived as friendlier. We do judge a book by its cover.

We soothe ourselves with clichés. It's only skin-deep, we cluck. It's only in the eye of the beholder. Pretty is as pretty does.

Reprinted by permission of The National Geographic Society.

In an era of feminist and politically correct values, not to mention the closely held belief that all men and women are created equal, the fact that all men and women are not—and that some are more beautiful than others—disturbs, confuses, even angers.

For better or worse, beauty matters. How much it matters can test our values. With luck, the more we live and embrace the wide sweep of the world, the more generous our definition becomes.

Henry James met the English novelist George Eliot when she was 49 years old. *Silas Marner, Adam Bede,* and *The Mill on the Floss* were behind her. *Middlemarch* was yet to come.

"She is magnificently ugly," he wrote his father. "She has a low forehead, a dull grey eye, a vast pendulous nose, a huge mouth, full of uneven teeth. . . . Now in this vast ugliness resides a most powerful beauty which, in a very few minutes, steals forth and charms the mind, so that you end as I ended, in falling in love with her."

In fairy tales, only the pure of heart could discern the handsome prince in the ugly frog. Perhaps we are truly human when we come to believe that beauty is not so much in the eye, as in the heart, of the beholder.

The search for beauty spans centuries and continents. A relief in the tomb of the Egyptian nobleman Ptahhotep, who lived around 2400 B.C., shows him getting a pedicure. Cleopatra wore kohl, an eyeliner made from ground-up minerals.

Love of appearance was preeminent among the aristocracy of the 18th century. Montesquieu, the French essayist, wrote: "There is nothing more serious than the goings-on in the morning when Madam is about her toilet." But monsieur, in his wig of cascading curls, scented gloves, and rouge, was equally narcissistic. "They have their color, toilet, powder puffs, pomades, perfumes," noted one lady socialite, "and it occupies them just as much as or even more than us."

The search for beauty could be macabre. To emphasize their noble blood, women of the court of Louis XVI drew blue veins on their necks and shoulders.

The search for beauty could be deadly. Vermilion rouge used in the 18th century was made of a sulfur and mercury compound. Men and women used it at the peril of lost teeth and inflamed gums. They sickened, sometimes died, from lead in the white powder they dusted on their faces. In the 19th century women wore whalebone and steel corsets that made it difficult to breathe, a precursor of the stomach-smooshing Playtex Living Girdle.

The search for beauty is costly. In the United States last year people spent six billion dollars on fragrance and another six billion on makeup. Hair- and skin-care products drew eight billion dollars each, while fingernail items alone accounted for a billion. In the mania to lose weight 20 billion was spent on diet products and services—in addition to the billions that were paid out for health club memberships and cosmetic surgery.

Despite the costs, the quest for beauty prevails, an obsession once exemplified by the taste of Copper Eskimo women for a style of boot that let in snow but was attractive to men because of the waddle it inflicted on the wearer—a fashion statement not unlike the ancient Chinese custom of foot binding (see Figure 4.12) or the 20th-century high heel shoe.

I am standing behind a one-way mirror watching a six-month-old baby make a choice.

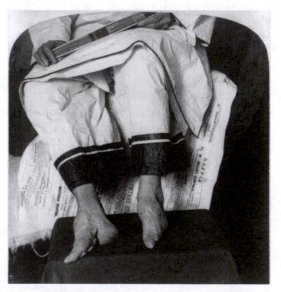

Figure 4.12 The tiny, narrow feet that resulted from the practice of foot binding were once considered beautiful by the Chinese.

The baby is shown a series of photographs of faces that have been rated for attractiveness by a panel of college students. A slide is flashed; a clock ticks as the baby stares at the picture. The baby looks away; the clock stops. Then it's on to the next slide.

After more than a decade of studies like these, Judith Langlois, professor of psychology at the University of Texas in Austin, is convinced that this baby, like others she has tested, will spend more time looking at the attractive faces than the unattractive ones.

What's an attractive face? It's a symmetrical face. Most important, it's an averaged face, says Langlois. Averaged, that is, in terms of position and size of all the facial features. As the slides flash in front of the baby, I see what she means. Some faces are more pleasing to look at than others. It's a question of harmony and the placement of features. The picture of the young girl with wide-set eyes and a small nose is easier on the eye than the one of the young girl with close-set eyes and a broad nose. Extremes are off-putting and generally not attractive, Langlois says.

The idea that even babies can judge appearance makes perfect sense to Don Symons, an anthropologist at the University of California at Santa Barbara.

"Beauty is not whimsical. Beauty has meaning. Beauty is functional," he says. Beauty, his argument goes, is not so much in the eye as in the brain circuitry of the beholder.

In studies by psychologists such as Victor Johnston at New Mexico State University and David Perrett at St. Andrews University in Scotland, men consistently showed a preference for women with larger eyes, fuller lips, and a smaller nose and chin. Studies by psychologist Devendra Singh at the University of Texas show a preference for the classic hourglass-shaped body with a waist-hip ratio of seven to ten.

"That men prefer women with smooth skin, big eyes, curvaceous bodies, and full lips is anything but random," Symons insists. All these traits are reliable cues to youth, good health, and fertility. Take lips, which, plumped up by estrogen, reach their fullness at 14 to 16 when women enter the fertile stage of their life. With menopause and the loss of fertility, lips lose their fullness. Likewise lesions or sores on the skin signal the presence of infectious disease or parasites. Clear, smooth skin speaks of youth and good health.

In the scenario envisioned by Symons and other evolutionary scientists, the mind unconsciously tells men that full lips and clear skin equal health, fertility, and genetic soundness. It's an instinct honed over a hundred thousand years of selection, Symons believes. Because we are mortgaged to our evolutionary history, the instinct persists.

Not everyone agrees. "Our hardwiredness can be altered by all sorts of expectations—predominantly cultural," says C. Loring Brace, an anthropologist at the University of Michigan. "The idea that there is a standard desirable female type tells you more about the libidinous fantasies of aging male anthropologists than anything else."

Douglas Yu, a biologist from Great Britain, and Glenn Shepard, an anthropologist at the University of California at Berkeley, found that indigenous peoples in southeast Peru preferred shapes regarded as overweight in Western cultures: "A fuller evolutionary theory of human beauty must embrace variation," Yu says.

To think you've found a cultural universal is thrilling, says Elaine Hatfield, professor of psychology at the University of Hawaii, "but you don't want to deceive yourself into thinking that biology accounts for everything. The sociobiologists say we're trapped in our Pleistocene brains. The idea can be slightly bullying, as well as chauvinistic."

What about those who are not so symmetrical or well formed? Is anyone immune to feelings of inadequacy? Eleanor Roosevelt was once asked if she had any regrets. Only one, she said. She wished she had been prettier.

I knew I was an ugly baby when my parents gave me an electric toaster as a bathtub toy. . . . The joke is told by Joan Rivers, so I call her up—she lives in New York these days—to ask if the humor isn't just a little too dark.

"I always wonder what my life would have been if I had had that wonderful ingredient called beauty," the unmistakable raspy voice responds.

"Marilyn Monroe said to a friend of mine, 'I knew I had power when I was eight. I climbed a tree and four boys helped me down.'"

"On the other hand, not being pretty gave me my life. You find other ways. It made me funny. It made me smarter. I wasn't going to get into college as Miss Cheerleader."

There's a hint of wistful in the voice. "Beauty is based on youth and on a certain look. When you're old, you're invisible. No matter how they lie to us and tell us Barbra Streisand is beautiful, if you woke up without her enormous talent would you rather look like her or Michelle Pfeiffer?"

In the world of beauty there are many variations on a theme, but one thing seems clear. Every culture has its bad hair day. In central Australia balding Aranda Aborigines once wore wigs made of emu feathers. Likewise, the Azande in Sudan wore wigs made of sponge. To grow long hair among the Ashanti in Nigeria made one suspect of contemplating murder, while in Brazil the Bororo cut hair as a sign of mourning.

Hair has other shades of meaning. Although the archetypal male hero in Western civilization is tall, dark, and handsome like Cary Grant, blond women have sometimes been imagined as having more fun.

Blond is the color of fairy-tale princesses like Cinderella and Rapunzel, not to mention the siren in *Farewell, My Lovely*, of whom Raymond Chandler wrote: "It was a blonde. A blonde to make a bishop kick a hole in a stained glass window."

Jean Harlow was a blonde. So were Carole Lombard and Marilyn Monroe (only their hairdressers knew for sure), who said she liked to "feel blond all over." A dark-haired colleague admits to "blonde anxiety," adding her observation that in California blondes have blonde insecurity. "They don't feel they're blond enough."

Hair-care product companies estimate that in the U.S. 40 percent of women who color their hair choose blond, a choice women also made in ancient Greece. From a biological perspective some researchers say blondness suggests a childlike appearance. Many newborns are blond and darken with time.

What other signals does hair send? In most societies, short hair means restraint and discipline: Think West Point, Buddhist monks, and prison. Long hair means freedom and unconventional behavior: Think Lady Godiva and Abbie Hoffman. Hair says I'm grown-up, and let's get that first haircut. It's the stages of life, from pigtails to ponytail to gray hair.

"This is what I looked like at age five," Noliwe Rooks, a visiting assistant professor of history and African-American studies at Princeton, tells me.

We're at her dining table drinking tea and talking about hair—specifically African-American hair—and how it defines culture, politics, and the tension between generations. The photograph she shows me is of a little girl with a big puff ball of an Afro staring up at the camera.

"My mother was a political activist, and so I wore my hair like this until I was 13," Rooks says, smiling.

"My grandmother had this huge issue with it. I was her only grandchild, and she couldn't stand it. It wasn't cute. It wasn't feminine. You couldn't put little bows in it. Every summer my mother would take me down to Florida to stay with her. As soon as my mother left, my grandmother would take me to Miss Ruby's beauty parlor and straighten my hair. Issues between my mother, my grandmother, and me got worked out around my hair."

While in college Rooks decided to let her hair "lock," or grow into a mass of pencil-thin dreadlocks.

"Before I was able to tell my grandmother, she had a stroke. I found myself on a plane flying to her bedside, rehearsing how I was going to explain the locks. The doctors didn't know the extent of the damage. She hadn't spoken. All she could make were garbled sounds. I couldn't wear a hat to hide my hair. It was Florida. It was 80 degrees. I walked into her hospital room, expecting the worst, when all of a sudden she opened her eyes and looked at me.

"'What did you do to your hair?' she said, suddenly regaining the power of speech."

After her grandmother died, Rooks found herself in front of the mirror cutting her hair in a gesture of mourning.

"When my grandmother was in the hospital, I'd brushed her hair. I pulled the gray hairs out of the brush, put them in a plastic bag, and

THE MEANINGS OF DRESS

put it in front of her picture. That was hair for me. There was so much about it that defined our relationship. It meant closeness, and then, finally, acceptance."

Gravity takes its toll on us all. That, along with time, genetics, and environment, is what beauty's archenemy, aging, is about. "The bones stay upright until you go permanently horizontal," says Dr. Linton Whitaker, chief of plastic surgery at the University of Pennsylvania Medical Center. "As the soft tissue begins to sag off the bones, the rosy cheeks of childhood become the sallow jowls of the elderly. What was once jawline becomes a wattle."

Blame the vulnerability of flesh on collagen and elastin—materials found in the second layer of our skin that give it elasticity.

"Collagen under a microscope is like a knit sweater," Whitaker explains. "After the 10,000th wearing and stretching, it becomes baggy, and the same with skin. When the knit of collagen and elastin begins to fragment, skin loses its elasticity." Then gravity steps in.

"If aging is a natural process, isn't there something unnatural about all this surgical snipping and stitching to delay the inevitable?" I ask.

"I guess it's not natural, but what is?" Whitaker sighs. "It's the world we live in. Right or wrong, it's a judgment. But it's doable and makes people happy."

It makes many people happy. According to the American Society for Aesthetic Plastic Surgery, almost three million cosmetic procedures were performed in the United States in 1998. Baby boomers (35 to 50) accounted for 42 percent.

The quest for the perfect look is global. In Russia cut-price plastic surgery lures patients from as far away as London and Sydney. In Australia, where a short-lived magazine called *Gloss* trumpeted the glories of cosmetic surgery, penile enlargements are among the six cosmetic procedures most popular with males, along with nose jobs, eyelid lifts, liposuction, face-lifts, and ear corrections.

In China plastic-surgery hospitals are sprouting up faster than bamboo shoots in spring. Patients can check into a 12,000-square-foot palace of plastic surgery called the Dreaming Girl's Fantasy on Hainan Island.

In Brazil, says Dr. Ivo Pitanguy, a world-famous plastic surgeon, "women get liposuction at 18 and breast reduction at between 16 and 22. They prefer small breasts and big derrieres, whereas Americans want big chests. In the 1970s only 8 percent of my patients were men. Now it's 25 percent. Today society accepts the idea of improving one's image."

The line between self-improvement and neurosis can blur. I hear about a town in Texas where breast augmentations are given as graduation gifts. And how to make sense of singer Michael Jackson with his reported inventory of four nose jobs, a chin implant, eyelid surgery, a facelift, lip reduction, skin bleaching, and assorted touch-ups?

("Michael designed the way he wants to look," said a source close to the star. "It's no different from choosing your jewelry, your clothing, or your hairstyle.")

"Suppose I'm not so cute when I grow up as I am now?" Shirley Temple is said to have asked with some prescience when she was eight. Fret not. What goes down, comes up. For falling hair, Rogaine. For the drooping face, Retin-A. Prozac for the sagging soul and Viagra for the sagging penis.

"Old age is not for sissies," I say to a friend, quoting one of Bette Davis's favorite lines.

"No, no," she corrects. "Old age is not for narcissists. If you are wrapped up in yourself, you have nothing but the potential for loss."

Even non-sissies have trouble with aging. Martha Graham, a powerful woman and possibly the most influential force in modern dance, grew bitter as she grew old. She would call Bertram Ross, one of her dancers, in the middle of the night. "Die while you're young and still beautiful," she would hiss into the phone, then hang up.

At 48, gravity has taken its toll on me. I look at the mirror and note the delta of wrinkles starting to branch from the corners of my eyes. My chin has begun to blur into my neck. There is a suggestion of jowliness.

Of course I could consult a plastic surgeon like Dr. Sherwood Baxt. On the day I visit his office in Paramus, New Jersey, Baxt, a tall man with a sweep of graying hair, is dressed in a well-cut charcoal double-breasted suit with a pinstripe shirt, yellow silk tie affixed by a gold safety pin, and a pair of black tasseled calf loafers.

You might say that Baxt, who has not one but three different lasers for sculpting, peeling, and taming the bumps and wrinkles of imperfect flesh, offers one-stop shopping for cosmetic surgery. The centerpiece of his office complex is an operating suite that would be the envy of a small community hospital.

"Plastic surgery is exciting," Baxt tells me in calm, reassuring tones. "We're lifting, tightening, firming. We change people's lives."

"How and why?" I want to know.

"Most of my patients work," he says. "I see a lot of high-power women who can't fit into a suit anymore because of hormonal changes and pregnancies. They're in a competitive world. Liposuction is the most common procedure. The face is the next order of business—the eyes, double chins. All of that says to the workforce, 'You look a bit tired. You're a bit over the hill. You're having trouble keeping up.'"

Wondering how I'd fare with nip and tuck of my own, I've asked for a consultation. Thanks to computer imaging, I can get a preview. An assistant takes front and side views of my face with a Polaroid camera and scans them into a computer. As I watch, my face pops up on the screen and then morphs as Baxt manipulates the image. The softness under my chin retracts into firmness; the circles under my eyes disappear; wrinkles smooth out. I'm looking younger—not the hard, stiff, pulled-tight mask-look that screams "face-lift! face-lift!"—but more subtly younger.

"First I did your upper eyelids," Baxt explains, pointing at the screen. "I removed a bit of fatty tissue. I also took off some of the fat pockets over the lower lid, then lasered the skin smooth and tight. Next I did some liposuction on the wad of fat under the chin and brought the chin forward with an implant. You've got two things going for you: good skin and a full face. You age better if you have a full face. You don't need to be lifted and pulled at this point. Maybe in ten years."

The tab? About nine or ten thousand dollars. Of course my insurance would never pay this bill. It's strictly out-of-pocket. No problem. Baxt offers an installment plan.

Back home, I stare at myself in the mirror. I've always scoffed at plastic surgery. Then 50 loomed into view. Now I'm more tolerant. We are living longer. We are healthier. Today the average life expectancy is 76 years. Fifty years ago it was 68. One hundred years ago it was 48. The face in the mirror doesn't always reflect how old or young we feel.

The sad, sometimes ugly, side of beauty: In a 1997 magazine survey, 15 percent of women and 11 percent of men sampled said they'd sacrifice more than five years of their life to be at their ideal weight. Others were prepared to make other sacrifices. One 25-year-old Maryland woman said: "I love children and would love to have one more—but only if I didn't have to gain the weight."

Is life not worth living unless you're thin? "Girls are literally weighing their self-esteem," says Catherine Steiner Adair, a psychologist at the Harvard Eating Disorders Center in Boston. "We live in a culture that is completely bonkers. We're obsessed with sylphlike slimness, yet heading toward obesity. According to one study, 80 percent of women are dissatisfied with their bodies. Just think about how we talk about food: 'Let's be really bad today and have dessert.' Or: 'I was good. I didn't eat lunch.'"

In one of its worst manifestations, discontent with one's body can wind up as an eating disorder, such as anorexia, a self-starvation syndrome, or bulimia, a binge-and-purge cycle in which people gorge and then vomit or use laxatives. Both can be fatal.

Today eating disorders, once mostly limited to wealthy Western cultures, occur around the world. "I was in Fiji the year television was introduced," says Dr. Anne Becker, director of research at the Harvard center. "Eating disorders were virtually unknown in Fiji at that time." When she returned three years later, 15 percent of the girls she was studying had tried vomiting to lose weight.

In Japan anorexia was first documented in the 1960s. It now affects an estimated one in one hundred Japanese women and has spread to other parts of Asia, including Korea, Singapore, and Hong Kong. In the U.S., according to the Menninger Clinic in Topeka, Kansas, the proportion of females affected by eating disorders is around 5 to 10 percent.

To say that all women with eating disorders want to look like runway models is to gloss over a complex picture that weaves biology and family dynamics in with cultural influences. One thing can be said: Eating disorders are primarily a disease of women.

"It's easy to be oversimplistic in defining causes," says Emily Kravinsky, medical director at the Renfrew Center in Philadelphia, a treatment center for women with eating disorders. "Some of these women don't know how to cope or soothe themselves. They have low self-esteem. Also, there's increasing evidence that biology and genetics play a role. Finally, the distance between the cultural ideal of what we would like to look like and the reality of what we actually look like is becoming wider. If Marilyn Monroe walked into Weight Watchers today, no one would bat an eye. They'd sign her up."

Late one winter afternoon at Renfrew I sat in what once was the drawing room of an elegant mansion—it is now a space used for group therapy—and had a conversation with two young women who are patients. The subject was beauty and self-image and how that sometimes goes uncontrollably awry. The two sat next to each other on a sofa, occasionally turning to tease or reassure the other, in the easy, bantering way that friends do. One, a former gymnast, was short and compact and very overweight. The other, a former dancer, was tall, and very, very thin.

"My family moved here so I could attend the gymnastics academy," said the former gymnast we'll call Sarah. "I was three years old. Every week they would put us on the scale and call out our weight so everyone could hear. By 13, I was anorexic. And then I started eating and couldn't stop. I became bulimic."

"For me it was the mirrors and being in leotards and tights," said the former dancer we'll call Leah. "It was seeing the parts go to the prettier girls. I thought: 'If only I were thinner.'"

It has been a long struggle and will continue to be so, both said. There are no shortcuts in the search for equilibrium of the soul.

"I want a relationship," Leah said wistfully. "I say to myself: You don't have to be thin. Then I open a magazine and see these gorgeously thin women, and they all have a handsome guy next to them. I tell myself, oh, so you do have to be thin."

And yet, despite setbacks and constant self-vigilance, both could finally begin to see the glimmer of another possibility. There are other ideas of beauty, the two agreed.

"Beauty is all the wonderful creative things that a person is, how they handle themselves and treat other people," Sarah said. "My brother has Down's syndrome, and I judge people by how they treat him. It doesn't matter if you weigh 600 pounds. If you treat him well, you are beautiful."

There is a pause, then a quiet moment of insight offered in a very small voice: "Of course it's a lot easier for me to see beauty in others than in myself." She takes a breath and goes on. "Still, I know more than ever before that there are things about me other than my body. Things that—I can almost say—are beautiful."

The preoccupation with beauty can be a neurosis, and yet there is something therapeutic about paying attention to how we look and feel.

One day in early spring, I went to Bliss, a spa in New York. It had been a difficult winter, and I needed a bit of buoyancy. At Bliss I could sink back in a sand-colored upholstered chair, gaze at the mural of the seashore on the walls, and laugh as I eased my feet into a basin of warm milk. I could luxuriate in the post-milk rubdown with sea salts and almond oil. Beauty can be sheer self-indulgent pleasure as well as downright fun, and it's best not to forget it.

"People are so quick to say beauty is shallow," says Ann Marie Gardner, beauty director of W magazine. "They're fearful. They say: 'It doesn't have substance.' What many don't realize is that it's fun to reinvent yourself, as long as you don't take it too seriously. Think of the tribesmen in New Guinea in paint and feathers. It's mystical. It's a transformation. That's what we're doing when we go to a salon. We are transforming ourselves."

Until she was a hundred years old, my grandmother Mollie Spier lived in a condominium in Hallandale, Florida, and had a "standing," a regular appointment, at the beauty salon down the street. Every Friday she would drive, then later be driven, for a shampoo, set, and manicure.

This past year, too frail to live on her own, she moved to a nursing home and away from her Friday appointment.

A month before she died, I went to visit her. Before I did, I called to ask if she wanted me to make an appointment for her at the salon.

"I could drive you, Grandma. We could take your nurse and wheelchair. Do you think you could handle it?"

"Of course," she replied, as if I'd asked the silliest question in the world. "What's the big deal? All I have to do is sit there and let them take care of me."

On a Friday afternoon I picked my grandmother up at the nursing home and drove her to the salon she hadn't visited in more than a year.

I wheeled her in and watched as she was greeted and fussed over by Luis, who washed and combed her fine pewter gray hair into swirls, then settled a fog of hair spray over her head.

When he was finished, Yolanda, the manicurist, appeared. "Mollie, what color would you like your nails?"

"What's new this year? I want something no one else has," she shot back, as if in impossibly fast company at the Miami Jewish Home for the Aged.

Afterward I drove my grandmother back to the nursing home. She admired her fire engine red nails every quarter mile. Glancing in the car mirror, she patted her cloud of curls and radiated happiness.

"Mollie," said the nurse behind the desk when I brought her back. "You look absolutely beautiful."

Discussion Questions

1. Write down your definition of beauty. Be specific in your definition about what beauty includes and what it excludes. Trade definitions with a classmate. How are your definitions similar? How do they differ?

2. List current "beauty" practices that can be fatal, dangerous, or unhealthy. Which ones have you engaged in? Which ones have you avoided? Why?

3. What do you think the consequences would be of everyone looking alike? Would this be a positive outcome? Why? Would this be negative? Why?

4. Note all of the cultural and historic examples of beauty mentioned in the article. Do you know the reasons behind these beauty practices? How/where could you learn more about these practices?

CHAPTER 5

APPEARANCE FOR GENDER AND SEXUAL IDENTITY

Andrew Reilly

After you have read this chapter, you will understand:

- The comparison of the cultural meaning of being a man or woman, and the link of gender norms to appearance
- How gender is socially and culturally determined and is a significant component in the study of appearance
- The diversity of human appearance that may be influenced by sexual orientation

Social Construction of Gender

How did you become a woman or a man? You were born as male or female, certainly, but there was more to shaping your femaleness or maleness than your XX or XY chromosomes. You learned how to become a woman or man. You were taught very early how girls do or do not behave and how boys do or do not behave. Girls are given dolls and boys are given toy trucks. What happens when a boy plays with a doll? He is told, "Boys don't do that."

The biological category into which you are born is your **sex**. Your sex is determined based on your primary sex characteristics—your reproductive organs. Your birth certificate, driver's license, marriage certificate, and death certificate all note your sex. Your secondary sex characteristics are related to your sex but not essential to reproduction: breast or pectoral development, body hair, musculature, bone structure, etc. These secondary sex characteristics help craft your gender. The psychological/social/cultural category of how you behave (which includes dress) is your **gender**. Foucault (1976/1998) argues that gender is socially constructed, meaning it is learned in, and governed by, social settings such as at home with the family, in school, with friends, and at work. How you become a woman or man is taught to you, and any diversions (e.g., a boy wearing a skirt) are quickly corrected. Thus, the concept of female and male is not inherent or biological but created. You learned to be a woman or man, and that included your dress.

Figure 5.1 Men commonly wore skirts in ancient civilizations, before a distinction was made about gender-appropriate clothing.

Early civilizations noted some differences between men's and women's appearance, however for the most part they dressed similarly. Drawings, frescoes, hieroglyphs, and statues have given us clues as to how people dressed. Generally, clothing was of a draped and/or wrapped nature. For example, in ancient Mesopotamia, the Sumerian men and women both wore skirts and cloaks (c. 3500–1000 B.C.) and Babylonian and Assyrian men and women both wore tunics (1000–600 B.C.). In Egypt, both men and women wore skirts, tunics, and robes (3000–300 B.C.). The men and women of the ancient Minoan civilization (2900–1150 B.C.) both wore loincloths, skirts, and tunics. The men and women of ancient Greek (800–300 B.C.) and Roman (500 B.C.– A.D. 400) civilizations wore a variety of draped and wrapped garments, with some designated specifically for each gender. But it was after the fall of Rome, during the early Middle Ages (900–1300), that we see significant differences between the genders in regard to their dress, with women wearing long gowns and men in tunics and hose. Since then the division between appropriate dress for men and women continued to grow and become fixed (see Figure 5.1).

One interesting difference between men's and women's clothing that has developed over the years is how pockets are designed and used. Whereas men seem to have an abundance of pockets in their clothing (e.g., pockets on shirts above their heart, pockets on shirtsleeves, pockets in shorts, cargo pants, jackets, etc.) to carry around their necessities, for women pockets have become scarce. One reason is that pockets interrupt the silhouette of the design, and as women's fashion became more body-conscious, pockets had to disappear to give a pleasing line to the female body (Burman, 2002). This is just one example of how differences in dress emerged—based on different forms of function—agonic or hedonic.

Agonic and Hedonic Power

Women and men obtain their social power differently. A woman's power rests in her appearance, a man's in his earning potential. Historically, women needed to look attractive to men in order to gain the attention of (and marry) men who could support them. And men needed to secure a career where they could earn enough money to attract beautiful women. The effect was circular; one was dependent on the other.

What was considered appropriately masculine and feminine has shifted over time and changed according to culture, status, and nationality. Today only a very secure man would wear tights, lace collars, glittering fabrics, and heeled slippers, but in 16th-century Europe, exactly that was prescribed for men of noble rank. Men's clothing lost its luster after the French Revolution in what has become known as the Great Masculine Renunciation when utility became a virtue and fashion a vice. Women, however, retained their right to aesthetic forms of expression.

Dress scholar Susan Kaiser (1997) refers to the differing forms of power as **agonic** versus **hedonic**, or "doing versus being." Agonic power is active and direct, whereas hedonic power is passive and indirect. Men's power is agonic because it is rooted in doing work, earning a living, and providing for a family. Women's power is hedonic because it is rooted in appearing attractive to others (though one could certainly argue that much work goes into looking attractive). This dichotomy isn't all-encompassing and doesn't apply to all men and women (Kaiser calls it artificial); there are many women who obtain their power from their careers (e.g., Hillary Clinton and Oprah Winfrey) and many men who obtain their power from their looks (e.g., model Marcus Schenkenberg) (see Figures 5.2a–c).

Figure 5.2 Hillary Clinton (a), Oprah Winfrey (b), and Marcus Schenkenberg (c) are examples of people whose power does not come from the typical sources of power for their gender.

The agonic/hedonic dichotomy began to break down when women started gaining economic independence. Beginning with World War II when women entered the workforce out of necessity and when some women remained after the war ended, women had started to earn their own living. As women entering the workplace increased with each decade; they no longer needed a man to support them. Their goals in a relationship could move beyond simply finding a man with a solid career. Now, good looks were required of men too, and this is when we start to see a change in men's aesthetics and grooming routines. Men weren't going to the gym simply because it was healthy, but because they needed to lose a few pounds or tone up. Women had known for many decades that their appearance was a commodity, but men are just learning that theirs is too. Mary Thompson (2000) explored men's sexualized appearance in fashion magazine advertising and found that men in various forms of undress have become just as prevalent as women. Equal opportunity doesn't discriminate.

It can be argued that today's expectations of dress for men and women are rooted in the Industrial Revolution. During this time, a significant portion of labor moved from the agricultural field to the building. Suits replaced overalls and became the standard for men's office attire. However, at this time, women weren't going to the office. Their duties included managing the home and family. So, whereas men needed to look serious and somber in their business dealings, women had more freedom to follow fashion because their activities were more socially oriented than business oriented. During the 19th century through the 1950s, men followed a restricted code of appearance, limited to angular design lines, neutral and subdued color palettes, bifurcated garments (e.g., pants) for the lower body, natural but not tight silhouettes, sturdy fabrics and shoes, and simple hair and facial grooming. This simple, restricted code helped them to focus on work and accomplishments rather than appearance. Thus, men dressed for the agonic role in society. Women, in contrast, had an elaborate dress code through the 1950s. They could wear some of what men wore, and a lot more. Their unlimited options for fabrics, colors, design lines, and silhouettes gave them a useful treasury for attending to their hedonic role, emphasizing pursuit of beauty and physical being. Their tight or flowing skirts, high heels, and nylons did not facilitate emphasis on physical activity, however. As previously mentioned, women were encouraged to spend their time and attention on clothes, hair, weight control, and makeup to render themselves beautiful for men (who would marry and support them).

Though many people do not realistically meet ideal expectations for their gender, they are expected to meet minimum standards. For example, women should not have facial hair or large feet and men should not have large breasts or wear skirts. Anyone who defies the

Figure 5.3 Women and men are expected to meet certain expectations regarding dress and their gender. When they do not, they are usually labeled as freaks.

minimum expectations is stigmatized. People who fail to meet the minimum expectations are viewed as freaks of nature and historically have been featured as oddities in circuses (e.g., the bearded lady or the she-man) (see Figure 5.3). Though today we are more sensitive to differences and don't necessarily put people with differences on display, many people are still stigmatized based on failure to reach the minimum expectations. Physical disabilities, extremely thin or overweight bodies, and hair loss are all conditions that can cause a person to be socially stigmatized.

Figure 5.4 Bare breasts were considered erotic by Europeans when they landed in Polynesia, but the Polynesian inhabitants viewed it as natural.

People—especially women—can also be stigmatized for dressing immodestly or too sexually. Modesty is defined as the covering of part of the body that if exposed in public would have a sexual connotation. In Muslim cultures hair is considered erotic and therefore must be covered for a woman to remain modest. In the antebellum period of the United States it was considered erotic for women to show their ankles (though, ironically, plunging necklines and vast décolleté were acceptable); a modest woman therefore kept them covered. In Polynesia it was acceptable for women to have bare breasts until missionaries arrived in the 18th and 19th centuries and "informed" them it was immodest; bare breasts, to the missionaries, were erotic (see Figure 5.4).

Changes in modesty and eroticism are explained by the theory of shifting erogenous zones (Laver, 1969). The theory is based on the principle that complete nudity is anti-erotic. The mind needs to fantasize about what is hidden, and therefore fashion serves to hide and reveal different body parts, which are fetishized during different eras. Once the body part becomes overexposed, new styles serve to cover it and reveal a new body part. One reason why the movie *Jaws* was so scary when it was first released is that the shark was rarely seen; a glimpse of a fin here, a shadow there. The mind is highly imaginative and sensitive to suggestion. In the same way, a partially clothed body is more erotic than a nude body—the possibility of what lies underneath is more interesting than the reality. In 2003 Britney Spears's bare midriff style gave way to long, tight sweaters. Though the sweaters concealed the body, the silhouette and the allure of what was underneath was erotic.

Susan O. Michelman further explores how the aesthetics of postmodernism are embracing modesty in "Reveal or Conceal? Examining the Meaning of Modesty in Postmodern America." Today, many women are confronted with fashions that are revealing. This becomes a point of contradiction for women who desire to remain covered (or modest) and look stylish (or immodest). Michelman reviews what is considered modest in today's world, and how it contradicts or aligns with fashion trends, religion, and American society.

Gender Bending

One of the clothing hallmarks of the male/female dichotomy is that women wear skirts/dresses; men don't. Though the reverse is acceptable—women in pants—and is a common sight today, it wasn't too long ago that such cross-dressing was seen by some as scandalous. Though there were notable exceptions (in the 1920s and 1930s actress Katharine Hepburn eschewed dresses and skirts for pants), it wasn't until World War II that sweeping changes took effect

Figure 5.5 It was acceptable for women to wear pants during WWII when they worked in manufacturing plants. However, when the war ended, it was expected for them to return to wearing skirts and dresses.

(see Figure 5.5). Women were working in manufacturing jobs that had previously been held by men who were now in combat on the battlefields. Women's dresses and skirts weren't conducive to working with heavy machinery. They needed clothing that was utilitarian, allowed for quick movement, and wasn't likely to get caught in gears. Women began wearing pants. Though after the war ended, women were expected to return to their former wardrobes (and many did), many more women continued to wear pants. Today, women in pants—or any variety of "men's" clothing—is ubiquitous.

Occasionally, a designer will produce a men's collection that includes a skirt, but rarely does that become a trend or fashionable. In 2002 retailer H&M offered skirts for men and in 2009 fashion shows for Yves Saint Laurent, Jean-Paul Gaultier, Alexander McQueen, and Marc Jacobs for Louis Vuitton all featured skirts for the male consumer. This style has yet to become trendy, save for a few cultural niches, such as among some gay subcultures, the über-trendy, or practioners of pagan religions.

When gender appearance roles are challenged, it creates problems. Society expects men and women to dress according to their sex. When people wear what is not expected of them they are often discriminated against, bullied, and treated differently. School systems are dealing with these issues as more and more students are challenging traditional gender appearances. When children and adolescents experiment with their clothing as they find their individual identities, sometimes they cross-dress. Some schools are banning cross-dressing and striving to uphold traditional gender-appearance norms, while others are trying to foster an atmosphere of tolerance and acceptance (Hoffman, 2009).

When women dress in men's clothing, it is considered a move upward. This is certainly the case in cultures where there is an obvious preference for men. In Afghanistan, dressing as another gender is a necessity to better one's life. In that country boys are valued over girls, and in order to get an education, hold a job, or walk freely in public, girls dress as boys and assume a male identity. Jenny Nordberg explores the issue of dressing girls as boys in "Afghan Boys Are Prized, So Girls Live the Part." Many parents are deciding to raise their daughter as a boy, at least until puberty, in order to give her an education and hope for a better economic future, and due to social pressure to have a son. The practice, Nordberg writes, has been practiced for centuries.

While some people prefer to dress either masculine or feminine, others wish to eliminate differences and blend them. The blending together of the two primary genders—male and female—is known as **androgyny**[1]. Despite rigid Westernized, social standards of what is acceptable for men to wear and women to wear, there have been instances where androgynous styling was fashionable. In the 1920s Chanel's garçonne style for women was an effortless look of tubular silhouettes, loose fit, and cropped hair, giving women a boyish appearance. In the 1960s the androgynous look for women was represented by the model Twiggy (Figure 5.6). In the early 1980s women began adopting a fair amount of androgyny in business dress in the United States and avidly appropriated the business suit and its corresponding masculine body with motivations similar to their male business counterparts (e.g., to achieve financial and career success; McCracken, 1985). With the current emphasis on skintight clothing in the 2010s, some men are shopping in women's departments that offer tighter fits for jeans and shirts than men's cuts do. Patrik Steorn discusses unisex clothing further in "Lifestyle and Politics of Fashion and Gender in 1960s Sweden: Unisex Fashion in Theory and Practice."

This discussion so far has looked at sex and gender as binary—either men or women. However, there exist other sex and gender categories. Recall from Chapter 4: Body Image that the body is a significant part of creating one's appearance and people strive to modify or change their bodies to align with their desires or identities. For the most part, people's bodies correspond with their gender identity, but for some this is not the case.

Figure 5.6 Twiggy's androgynous look was typical of the 1960s when there was social concern about equality and women's rights.

It is estimated that 1 in every 1,500–2,000 births in the United States are born **intersexed** (Intersex Society of America; formally called hermaphrodite, from the Greek legend of Hermaphroditus, who was both man and woman). In Western societies today, parents of an infant born with both sex organs typically decide to raise the child as male or female and have the extra reproductive organs surgically removed, thus conforming to the binary standards of appearance.

Another category that doesn't fit the male/female dichotomy is **transgender**, where a person dresses and behaves as the other gender. Many non-Western societies have a third gender category. Native Americans or First Nations people have Two-Spirit people, Samoans have the fa'afafine, Hawaiians have the mahu, Tongans have the fakaleiti, New Zealand Māori have the whakawhine, the Maale of Ethopia have the Ashtime, and the Mbo of Congo have the Mangaiko. Although their bodies correspond to one gender, they behave and dress as the other gender, adopting their clothing and some taking herbs and organic medicines that produce breasts or reduce testicles. Although they dress and may "pass" as the male or female gender, they remain a third gender.

Whereas the third gender is another form of identity for some societies, in the United States and many similarly Westernized countries, people who do not match the ideal male/female appearance expectations are stigmatized and categorized as "cross-dressers." These include transvestites, drag performers, and transsexuals.

Transvestites are typically heterosexual men who wear women's clothing. Their purpose is sexual and erotic. Drag queens (and their counterpart, drag kings) lampoon gender by creating an artificial, overstyled version of their opposite gender (see Figure 5.7). Their purpose is entertainment and political; they are not trying to "pass" as a member of the other gender. Faux drag queens and faux drag kings are people who lampoon their own gender in the same overdone, heightened style as drag queens and drag kings.

Transsexual people are born as one sex but feel they are the other. Hence their biological sex and their gender identity are at conflict with each other. Transsexual people wear

Figure 5.7 Drag queens lampoon expected gender roles in order to entertain and make a political point.

the clothing of the gender with which they identify and may have surgical and hormonal treatments to align their sex with their gender. Their purpose is to "pass" as the gender with which they identify, so they really should not be identified as cross-dressers because their identity and appearance are aligned.

Sexual Identity

The above paragraphs on cross-dressing address the issue of gender, not sexual orientation. Sexual orientation refers to the gender to whom a person is physically and romantically attracted. Thus a man physically and romantically attracted to a woman is straight or heterosexual. A woman attracted physically and romantically to another woman is gay or lesbian. And a person attracted to both genders is bisexual. These categories, however, are relatively recent social conventions. Foucault (1976/1998) argues that sexuality, like gender, is socially constructed, meaning that society created words and categories for people based on their sexual and romantic behaviors, and people are expected to fit into often-rigid definitions. Not only are people categorized as straight, gay, or bisexual, but also as prude, slut, or stud based on their sexual behaviors—as well as their appearance.

During the Edwardian era in England, gay men could be imprisoned and sentenced to hard labor for their same-sex attraction. So, in order for gay men to find other gay men, they used a code: they wore a green carnation in their lapel. Other gay men knew what it signified, and it kept gay men safe from those who did not know the significance of the flower.

The study of coded systems is known as semiotics; a symbol represents meaning. In the past (and still in some regions today) coded signs were used to remain safe yet covertly identify one's sexual orientation or sexual identity. In recent modern history, other items have been encoded to represent (covertly or not) an alternative sexual identity, including handkerchiefs worn in the back pocket, earrings worn in the right ear, baseball caps worn in reverse, pinkie rings, the pink triangle, and the rainbow flag. The inverted pink triangle was originally used by Nazi Germany when that government required all gay men to wear a *rosawinkle*, but the symbol was later adopted as a more affirming emblem. The rainbow flag was introduced to visually depict the diversity of sexual identities via its many colors. Coding can even occur in the form of pop culture prevalent among LGBTI (lesbian/gay/bisexual/transgender/intersex) people, such as ruby slippers (from *The Wizard of Oz*) or T-shirts with slogans from films popular among the lesbian, gay, and bisexual population (e.g., "But you are Blanch, you are," from *Whatever Happened to Baby Jane* or "This ain't my first time at the rodeo," from *Mommie Dearest*). Of course, other forms of appearance are more straightforward in relaying sexual identity, like T-shirts with slogans such as "I'm not gay but my boyfriend [girlfriend] is" and "Nobody knows I'm gay."

Lesbian, gay, and bisexual people have often challenged gender norms in their appearance, by dressing either androgynously or contrary to their expected gender norms. Two articles in this chapter explore the tension between personal identity and society. First, in the article "Gay, Lesbian, Bisexual, and Transgendered Persons" Andrew Reilly writes of the aesthetics used among the lesbian, gay, bisexual, and transgender populations to communicate (secretly or openly) their identity and establish community. Second, in "Queers and Mods: Social and Sartorial Interaction in London's Carnaby Street," Shaun Cole examines the influence of gay men on the Mod look of London in the 1960s and notes how language and images were coded in the advertising and catalogs of one particular retailer.

Summary

Expectations of sex, gender, and sexuality contribute to how and why people dress the way they do. Some people dress in a particular way because it is expected of their gender, while others dress to defy normative expectations or to align their outward appearance with their inward psyche. Sometimes, dressing as one gender is advantageous, and other times it is ostracizing. Clothing can be used to conceal the body for modesty or used to reveal body parts in order to beguile or attract—or empower the wearer. Sex, gender, and sexuality are inextricably linked, but when teased apart we can understand different motives to dress and adorn the body.

Suggested Readings

Burman, B. (2002). Pocketing the Difference: Gender and Pockets in Nineteenth-Century Britain. In *Gender & History* 14 (3): 447–469.

Cosbey, S. (2008). Something Borrowed: Masculine Style in Women's Fashion. In A. Reilly and S. Cosbey (Eds.) *The Men's Fashion Reader*, pp. 18–32. New York: Fairchild Books.

Femenias, B. (2003). *Gender and the Boundaries of Dress in Contemporary Peru*. Austin, TX: University of Texas.

Levi, J. L. (2007). Some Modest Proposals for Challenging Established Dress Code Jurisprudence. *Duke Journal of Law and Policy* 14: 234–256.

McNeil, P. (1999). "That Doubtful Gender": Macaroni Dress and Male Sexualities. *Fashion Theory* 3 (4): 411–448.

Schofield, K., and R. A. Schmidt. (2005). Fashion and Clothing: The Construction and Communication of Gay Identities. *International Journal of Retail & Distribution Management* 33 (4): 310–323.

Learning Activity 5.1: Male or Female?

Procedure

Students should pair up. Ideally, females should pair with a male. This may not always be possible, however. Each student should obtain 10 images from magazines, mail-order catalogs, or newspapers that depict items of clothing. To make the images slightly more ambiguous, cut off the head in the image. Try to pick some images that are more androgynous than others. Include some unisex clothing.

Show each image to your partner. Have your partner indicate if the item is typically worn by males or females. If the item is typically used by both males and females, have your partner indicate "both."

Discuss and compare your responses with those of your partner. What are the items of clothing that are worn only by females? What items of clothing are worn only by males? What items are worn by both males and females?

Learning Activity 5.2: Gender Roles through Time

Review current and historic magazines to identify exposed body parts (e.g., shoulders, arms, chest, thighs, calves, etc). For each category, note the year. Keep a list for women's images and a list for men's images. Do you notice any trends or eras when a specific body part was more prominent than others? Why do you think this was the case? Were there any gender differences?

Discussion Questions

1. As a class, discuss why certain items of clothing are restricted to females. Why are some items worn predominantly by males? Analyze how dress has a role in reinforcing gender stereotypes. How have some of these "rules" of dress and gender changed within the past 10 to 15 years? What social, economic, political, and ideological influences have affected gender and appearance issues? How might different cultures and their dress influence our typically "American" attitudes toward gender and appearance?

2. In this chapter Hillary Clinton, Oprah Winfrey, and Marcus Schenkenberg are mentioned as people whose social power does not originate from their expected sources of social power (agonic vs. hedonic). Who are some other women who gain their power agonically, or men who gain their power hedonically?

3. When women wear men's clothing it is considered a move upward, but when men wear women's clothing it is considered a move downward. Why is this?

References

Burman, B. (2002). Pocketing the Difference: Gender and Pockets in Nineteenth-Century Britain. *Gender & History* 14 (3): 447–469.

Intersex Society of North America (n.d.). Frequently Asked Questions. www.isna.org. Accessed September 13, 2010.

Foucault, M. (1976/1998). *The History of Sexuality, Vol. 1: The Will to Knowledge*. London: Penguin.

Hoffman, J. (2009, November 8). Can a Boy Wear a Skirt to School? *New York Times* http://www.nytimes.com/2009/11/08/fashion/08cross.html?pagewanted=all. Accessed February 20, 2012.

Kaiser, S. B. (1997). *The Social Psychology of Clothing: Symbolic Appearances in Context*. New York: Fairchild Publications, Inc.

Laver, J. (1969). *A Concise History of Costume and Fashion*. London: Thames & Hudson.

McCracken, G. (1985). The Trickle-Down Theory Rehabilitated. In M. R. Solomon [Ed.], *The Psychology of Fashion*, 39–54. Lexington, MA: Lexington Books.

McKinley, N. M. (2002). Feminist Perspectives and Objectified Body Consciousness. In T. F. Cash and T. Pruzinsky [Eds.], *Body Image: A Handbook of Theory, Research, and Clinical Practice*. New York: The Guilford Press, 55–62.

Thompson, M. J. (2000). Gender in magazine advertising: Skin sells best. *Clothing and Textiles Research Journal* 15 (3), 178–181.

Endnote

1. Androgyny should not be confused with unisexual, which lacks gender designations.

AFGHAN BOYS ARE PRIZED, SO GIRLS LIVE THE PART

Jenny Nordberg

KABUL, Afghanistan—Six-year-old Mehran Rafaat is like many girls her age. She likes to be the center of attention. She is often frustrated when things do not go her way. Like her three older sisters, she is eager to discover the world outside the family's apartment in their middle-class neighborhood of Kabul.

But when their mother, Azita Rafaat, a member of Parliament, dresses the children for school in the morning, there is one important difference. Mehran's sisters put on black dresses and head scarves, tied tightly over their ponytails. For Mehran, it's green pants, a white shirt and a necktie, then a pat from her mother over her spiky, short black hair. After that, her daughter is out the door—as an Afghan boy (Figure 5.8).

There are no statistics about how many Afghan girls masquerade as boys. But when asked, Afghans of several generations can often tell a story of a female relative, friend, neighbor or coworker who grew up disguised as a boy. To those who know, these children are often referred to as neither "daughter" nor "son" in conversation, but as "bacha posh," which literally means "dressed up as a boy" in Dari.

Through dozens of interviews conducted over several months, where many people wanted to remain anonymous or to use only first names for fear of exposing their families, it was possible to trace a practice that has remained mostly obscured to outsiders. Yet it cuts across class, education, ethnicity and geography, and has endured even through Afghanistan's many wars and governments.

Afghan families have many reasons for pretending their girls are boys, including economic need, social pressure to have sons, and in some cases, a superstition that doing so can lead to the birth of a real boy. Lacking a son, the parents decide to make one up, usually by cutting the hair of a daughter and dressing her in typical Afghan

Figure 5.8 In Afghanistan, girls aren't permitted to go to school, so many parents dress their daughters as sons. Here, Mehran Rafaat (left) is pictured with her sisters near their home in Badghis Province.

men's clothing. There are no specific legal or religious proscriptions against the practice. In most cases, a return to womanhood takes place when the child enters puberty. The parents almost always make that decision.

In a land where sons are more highly valued, since in the tribal culture usually only they can inherit the father's wealth and pass down a name, families without boys are the objects of pity and contempt. Even a made-up son increases the family's standing, at least for a few years. A bacha posh can also more easily receive an education, work outside the home, even escort her sisters in public, allowing freedoms that are unheard of for girls in a society that strictly segregates men and women.

But for some, the change can be disorienting as well as liberating, stranding the women in a limbo between the sexes. Shukria Siddiqui, raised as a boy but then abruptly plunged into an arranged marriage, struggled to adapt, tripping over the confining burqa and straining to talk to other women.

The practice may stretch back centuries. Nancy Dupree, an 83-year-old American who has spent most of her life as a historian working in Afghanistan, said she had not heard of the phenomenon, but recalled a photograph from the early 1900s belonging to the private collection of a member of the Afghan royal family.

It featured women dressed in men's clothing standing guard at King Habibullah's harem. The reason: the harem's women could not be protected by men, who might pose a threat to the women, but they could not be watched over by women either.

"Segregation calls for creativity," Mrs. Dupree said. "These people have the most amazing coping ability."

It is a commonly held belief among less educated Afghans that the mother can determine the sex of her unborn child, so she is blamed if she gives birth to a daughter. Several Afghan doctors and health care workers from around the country said that they had witnessed the despair of women when they gave birth to daughters, and that the pressure to produce a son fueled the practice.

"Yes, this is not normal for you," Mrs. Rafaat said in sometimes imperfect English, during one of many interviews over several weeks. "And I know it's very hard for you to believe why one mother is doing these things to their youngest daughter. But I want to say for you, that some things are happening in Afghanistan that are really not imaginable for you as a Western people."

Pressure to Have a Boy

From that fateful day she first became a mother—Feb. 7, 1999—Mrs. Rafaat knew she had failed, she said, but she was too exhausted to speak, shivering on the cold floor of the family's small house in Badghis Province.

She had just given birth—twice—to Mehran's older sisters, Benafsha and Beheshta. The first twin had been born after almost 72 hours of labor, one month prematurely. The girl weighed only 2.6 pounds and was not breathing at first. Her sister arrived 10 minutes later. She, too, was unconscious.

When her mother-in-law began to cry, Mrs. Rafaat knew it was not from fear whether her infant granddaughters would survive. The old woman was disappointed. "Why," she cried, according to Mrs. Rafaat, "are we getting more girls in the family?"

Mrs. Rafaat had grown up in Kabul, where she was a top student, speaking six languages and nurturing high-flying dreams of becoming a doctor. But once her father forced her to become the second wife of her first cousin, she had to submit to being an illiterate farmer's wife, in a rural house without running water and electricity, where the widowed mother-in-law ruled, and where she was expected to help care for the cows, sheep and chickens. She did not do well.

Conflicts with her mother-in-law began immediately, as the new Mrs. Rafaat insisted on better hygiene and more contact with the men in the house. She also asked her mother-in-law to stop beating her husband's first wife with her walking stick. When Mrs. Rafaat finally snapped the stick in protest, the older woman demanded that her son, Ezatullah, control his new wife.

He did so with a wooden stick or a metal wire. "On the body, on the face," she recalled. "I tried to stop him. I asked him to stop. Sometimes I didn't."

Soon, she was pregnant. The family treated her slightly better as she grew bigger. "They were hoping for a son this time," she explained. Ezatullah Rafaat's first wife had given birth to two daughters, one of whom had died as an infant, and she could no longer conceive. Azita Rafaat delivered two daughters, double the disappointment.

Mrs. Rafaat faced constant pressure to try again, and she did, through two more pregnancies, when she had two more daughters—Mehrangis, now 9, and finally Mehran, the 6-year-old.

Asked if she ever considered leaving her husband, she reacted with complete surprise.

"I thought of dying," she said. "But I never thought of divorce. If I had separated from my husband, I would have lost my children, and they would have had no rights. I am not one to quit."

Today, she is in a position of power, at least on paper. She is one of 68 women in Afghanistan's 249-member Parliament, representing Badghis Province. Her husband is unemployed and spends most of his time at home. "He is my house husband," she joked.

By persuading him to move away from her mother-in-law and by offering to contribute to the family income, she laid the groundwork for her political life. Three years into their marriage, after the fall of the Taliban in 2002, she began volunteering as a health worker for various nongovernmental organizations. Today she makes $2,000 a month as a member of Parliament.

As a politician, she works to improve women's rights and the rule of law. She ran for re-election on Sept. 18, and, based on a preliminary vote count, is optimistic about securing another term. But she could run only with her husband's explicit permission, and the second time around, he was not easily persuaded.

He wanted to try again for a son. It would be difficult to combine pregnancy and another child with her work, she said—and she knew she might have another girl in any case.

But the pressure to have a son extended beyond her husband. It was the only subject her constituents could talk about when they came to the house, she said.

"When you don't have a son in Afghanistan," she explained, "it's like a big missing in your life. Like you lost the most important point of your life. Everybody feels sad for you."

As a politician, she was also expected to be a good wife and a mother; instead she looked like a failed woman to her constituents. The gossip spread back to her province, and her husband was also questioned and embarrassed, she said.

In an effort to preserve her job and placate her husband, as well as fending off the threat of his getting a third wife, she proposed to her husband that they make their youngest daughter look like a son.

"People came into our home feeling pity for us that we don't have a son," she recalled reasoning. "And the girls—we can't send them outside. And if we changed Mehran to a boy we would get more space and freedom in society for her. And we can send her outside for shopping and to help the father."

No Hesitation

Together, they spoke to their youngest daughter, she said. They made it an alluring proposition: "Do you want to look like a boy and dress like a boy, and do more fun things like boys do, like bicycling, soccer and cricket? And would you like to be like your father?" Mehran did not hesitate to say yes.

That afternoon, her father took her to the barbershop, where her hair was cut short. They continued to the bazaar, where she got new clothing. Her first outfit was "something like a cowboy dress," Mrs. Rafaat said, meaning a pair of blue jeans and a red denim shirt with "superstar" printed on the back.

She even got a new name—originally called Manoush, her name was tweaked to the more boyish-sounding Mehran.

Mehran's return to school—in a pair of pants and without her pigtails—went by without much reaction by her fellow students. She still napped in the afternoons with the girls, and changed into her sleepwear in a separate room from the boys. Some of her classmates still called her Manoush, while others called her Mehran. But she would always introduce herself as a boy to newcomers.

Khatera Momand, the headmistress, with less than a year in her job, said she had always presumed Mehran was a boy, until she helped change her into sleeping clothes one afternoon. "It was quite a surprise for me," she said.

But once Mrs. Rafaat called the school and explained that the family had only daughters, Miss Momand understood perfectly. She used to have a girlfriend at the teacher's academy who dressed as a boy.

Today, the family's relatives and colleagues all know Mehran's real gender, but the appearance of a son before guests and acquaintances is just enough to keep the family functioning, Mrs. Rafaat said. At least for now.

Mr. Rafaat said he felt closer to Mehran than to his other children, and thought of her as a son. "I am very happy," he said. "When people now ask me, I say yes and they see that I have a son. So people are quiet, and I am quiet."

Economic Necessity

Mehran's case is not altogether rare.

Ten-year-old Miina goes to school for two hours each morning, in a dress and a head scarf, but returns about 9 a.m. to her home in one of Kabul's poorest neighborhoods to change into boys' clothing. She then goes to work as Abdul Mateen, a shop assistant in a small grocery store nearby.

Every day, she brings home the equivalent of about $1.30 to help support her Pashtun family of eight sisters, as well as their 40-year-old mother, Nasima.

Miina's father, an unemployed mason, is often away. When he does get temporary work, Nasima said, he spends most of his pay on drugs.

Miina's change is a practical necessity, her mother said, a way for the entire family to survive. The idea came from the shopkeeper, a friend of the family, Nasima said: "He advised us to do it, and said she can bring bread for your home."

She could never work in the store as a girl, just as her mother could not. Neither her husband nor the neighbors would look kindly on it. "It would be impossible," Nasima said. "It's our tradition that girls don't work like this."

Miina is very shy, but she admitted to a yearning to look like a girl. She still likes to borrow her sister's clothing when she is home. She is also nervous that she will be found out if one of her classmates recognizes her at the store. "Every day she complains," said her mother. "'I'm not comfortable around the boys in the store,' she says. 'I am a girl.'"

Her mother has tried to comfort her by explaining that it will be only for a few years. After all, there are others to take her place. "After Miina gets too old, the second younger sister will be a boy," her mother said, "and then the third."

Refusing to Go Back

For most such girls, boyhood has an inevitable end. After being raised as a boy, with whatever privileges or burdens it may entail, they switch back once they become teenagers. When their bodies begin to change and they approach marrying age, parents consider it too risky for them to be around boys anymore.

When Zahra, 15, opens the door to the family's second-floor apartment in an upscale neighborhood of Kabul, she is dressed in a black suit with boxy shoulders and wide-legged pants. Her face has soft features, but she does not smile, or look down, as most Afghan girls do.

She said she had been dressing and acting like a boy for as long as she could remember. If it were up to her, she would never go back. "Nothing in me feels like a girl," she said with a shrug.

Her mother, Laila, said she had tried to suggest a change toward a more feminine look several times, but Zahra has refused. "For always, I want to be a boy and a boy and a boy," she said with emphasis.

Zahra attends a girls' school in the mornings, wearing her suit and a head scarf. As soon as she is out on the steps after class, she tucks her scarf into her backpack, and continues her day as a young man. She plays football and cricket, and rides a bike. She used to practice tae kwon do, in a group of boys where only the teacher knew she was not one of them.

Most of the neighbors know of her change, but otherwise, she is taken for a young man wherever she goes, her mother said. Her father, a pilot in the Afghan military, was supportive. "It's a privilege for me, that she is in boys' clothing," he said. "It's a help for me, with the shopping. And she can go in and out of the house without a problem."

Both parents insisted it was Zahra's own choice to look like a boy. "I liked it, since we didn't have a boy," her mother said, but added, "Now, we don't really know."

Zahra, who plans on becoming a journalist, and possibly a politician after that, offered her own reasons for not wanting to be an Afghan woman. They are looked down upon and harassed, she said.

"People use bad words for girls," she said. "They scream at them on the streets. When I see that, I don't want to be a girl. When I am a boy, they don't speak to me like that."

Zahra said she had never run into any trouble when posing as a young man, although she was occasionally challenged about her gender. "I've been in fights with boys," she said. "If they tell me two bad words, I will tell them three. If they slap me once, I will slap them twice."

Time to "Change Back"

For Shukria Siddiqui, the masquerade went too far, for too long.

Today, she is 36, a married mother of three, and works as an anesthesiology nurse at a Kabul hospital. Short and heavily built, wearing medical scrubs, she took a break from attending to a patient who had just had surgery on a broken leg.

She remembered the day her aunt brought her a floor-length skirt and told her the time had come to "change back." The reason soon became clear: she was getting married. Her parents had picked out a husband whom she had never met.

At that time, Shukur, as she called herself, was a 20-year-old man, to herself and most people around her. She walked around with a knife in her back pocket. She wore jeans and a leather jacket.

She was speechless—she had never thought of getting married.

Mrs. Siddiqui had grown up as a boy companion to her older brother, in a family of seven girls and one boy. "I wanted to be like him and to be his friend," she said. "I wanted to look like him. We slept in the same bed. We prayed together. We had the same habits."

Her parents did not object, since their other children were girls, and it seemed like a good idea for the oldest son to have a brother. But Mrs. Siddiqui remained in her male disguise well beyond puberty, which came late.

She said she was already 16 when her body began to change. "But I really had nothing then either," she said, with a gesture toward her flat chest.

Like many other Afghan girls, she was surprised the first time she menstruated, and worried she might be ill. Her mother offered no explanation, since such topics were deemed inappropriate to discuss. Mrs. Siddiqui said she never had romantic fantasies about boys—or of girls, either.

Her appearance as a man approaching adulthood was not questioned, she said. But it frequently got others into trouble, like the time she escorted a girlfriend home who had fallen ill. Later, she learned that the friend had been beaten by her parents after word spread through the neighborhood that their daughter was seen holding hands with a boy.

"My Best Time"

Having grown up in Kabul in a middle-class family, her parents allowed her to be educated through college, where she attended nursing school. She took on her future and professional life with certainty and confidence, presuming she would never be constricted by any of the rules that applied to women in Afghanistan.

Her family, however, had made their decision: she was to marry the owner of a small construction company. She never considered going against them, or running away. "It was my family's desire, and we obey our families," she said. "It's our culture."

A forced marriage is difficult for anyone, but Mrs. Siddiqui was particularly ill equipped. She had never cooked a meal in her life, and she kept tripping over the burqa she was soon required to wear.

She had no idea how to act in the world of women. "I had to learn how to sit with women, how to talk, how to behave," she said. For years, she was unable to socialize with other women and uncomfortable even greeting them.

"When you change back, it's like you are born again, and you have to learn everything from the beginning," she explained. "You get a whole new life. Again."

Mrs. Siddiqui said she was lucky her husband turned out to be a good one. She had asked his permission to be interviewed and he agreed. He was understanding of her past, she said. He tolerated her cooking. Sometimes, he even encouraged her to wear trousers at home, she said. He knows it cheers her up.

In a brief period of marital trouble, he once attempted to beat her, but after she hit him back, it never happened again. She wants to look like a woman now, she said, and for her children to have a mother.

Still, not a day goes by when she does not think back to "my best time," as she called it. Asked if she wished she had been born a man, she silently nods.

But she also wishes her upbringing had been different. "For me, it would have been better to grow up as a girl," she said, "since I had to become a woman in the end."

Like Mother, Like a Son

It is a typically busy day in the Rafaat household. Azita Rafaat is in the bathroom, struggling to put her head scarf in place, preparing for a photographer who has arrived at the house to take her new campaign photos.

The children move restlessly between Tom and Jerry cartoons on the television and a computer game on their mother's laptop. Benafsha, 11, and Mehrangis, 9, wear identical pink tights and a ruffled skirt. They go first on the computer. Mehran, the 6-year-old, waits her turn, pointing and shooting a toy gun at each of the guests.

She wears a bandage over her right earlobe, where she tried to pierce herself with one of her mother's earrings a day earlier, wanting to look like her favorite Bollywood action hero: Salman Khan, a man who wears one gold earring.

Then Mehran decided she had waited long enough to play on the computer, stomping her feet and waving her arms, and finally slapping Benafsha in the face.

"He is very naughty," Mrs. Rafaat said in English with a sigh, of Mehran, mixing up the gender-specific pronoun, which does not exist in Dari. "My daughter adopted all the boys' traits very soon. You've seen her—the attitude, the talking—she has nothing of a girl in her."

The Rafaats have not yet made a decision when Mehran will be switched back to a girl, but Mrs. Rafaat said she hoped it need not happen for another five or six years.

"I will need to slowly, slowly start to tell her about what she is and that she needs to be careful as she grows up," she said. "I think about this every day—what's happening to Mehran."

Challenged about how it might affect her daughter, she abruptly revealed something from her own past: "Should I share something for you, honestly? For some years I also been a boy."

As the first child of her family, Mrs. Rafaat assisted her father in his small food shop, beginning when she was 10, for four years. She was tall and athletic and saw only potential when her parents presented the idea—she would be able to move around more freely.

She went to a girls' school in the mornings, but worked at the store on afternoons and evenings, running errands in pants and a baseball hat, she said.

Returning to wearing dresses and being confined was not so much difficult as irritating, and a little disappointing, she said. But over all, she is certain that the experience contributed to the resolve that brought her to Parliament. "I think it made me more energetic," she said. "It made me more strong." She also believed her time as a boy made it easier for her to relate to and communicate with men.

Mrs. Rafaat said she hoped the effects on Mehran's psyche and personality would be an advantage, rather than a limitation.

She noted that speaking out may draw criticism from others, but argued that it was important to reveal a practice most women in her country wished did not have to exist. "This is the reality of Afghanistan," she said.

As a woman and as a politician, she said it worried her that despite great efforts and investments from the outside world to help Afghan women, she has seen very little change, and an unwillingness to focus on what matters. "They think it's all about the burqa," she said. "I'm ready to wear two burqas if my government can provide security and a rule of law. That's O.K. with me. If that's the only freedom I have to give up, I'm ready."

Discussion Questions

1. How do you think gender relations will change for this generation once the girls (who were dressed as boys) grow into adulthood?
2. If you were a parent, under which circumstances would you dress your daughter as a boy?

5.2

REVEAL OR CONCEAL? EXAMINING THE MEANING OF MODESTY IN POSTMODERN AMERICA

Susan O. Michelman, University of Kentucky

This paper examines some of the contradictions and complexities associated with the meanings of modesty and immodesty of dress in contemporary American culture. American television, movies, music videos, and fashion have increasingly shown more and more skin (Thompson, 2000). Recent movies (such as *Charlie's Angels: Full Throttle*, starring Cameron Diaz, Drew Barrymore, and Lucy Liu; and *Gigli*, with Ben Affleck and the notorious Jennifer Lopez, who bared a lot at the Academy Awards ceremony several years ago in a revealing dress that challenged the boundaries of decorum) present contradictions to those who feel dress can be modest and still be fashionable. Some of the current reality television shows, including *Fear Factor*, *Survivor*, and *Dog Eat Dog*, create advertised excitement by using scantily clad women and men who perform acts of physical danger while the audience is taunted by the possibility that their very minimal attire will fall off while they are on camera.

Britney Spears, a leading pop icon to millions of young girls, has in four years gone from the cute girl next door to posing practically naked for the cover of *Rolling Stone* magazine. On the fashion runway, nudity is commonplace and a quick way for a designer to get a little extra attention in the press. Baring of breasts is not a new or recent phenomenon in fashion. For example, Rudi Gernreich designed a topless bathing suit in the 1960s. However, designers of American swimwear for women are testing new waters by revealing more of the body in mainstream pop culture. Immodesty is certainly more than just showing more and more skin. It can also be the actual act of being immodest, including the "attitude" or shock value of such behavior. It is also about how the behavior is read by the viewer and the corresponding response. A recent article in *The New York Times* illustrates how the bikini, an immodest clothing item, is now associated with aggressive behavior of some women in movies.

> . . . the bikini has undergone a transition from a symbol of languorous sexuality . . . to a symbol of tough, bloodletting, physical showmanship. In movies like "Charlie's Angels: Full Throttle," and television series like "Boarding House: North Shore" on the WB and "Surf Girls" on MTV, the tiny, triangle-topped bikini is the millennial equivalent of the power suit—the costume for women who ride 20-foot waves or smash foreheads of evildoers, thus proving they are just as combative as men. (Bellafante, 2003)

American consumers of pop culture are aware of the increasing immodesty that has become more and more commonplace and seemingly accepted and assimilated into mainstream American culture. One needs only to go to the local shopping mall to see how these fashions have

---

Original for this text.

filtered into all retail, from Nordstrom to the Gap. Abercrombie & Fitch has been censored for their use of nudity in their advertising campaign, and Victoria's Secret posts oversized ads in malls and on billboards of women in scanty underwear who dwarf the viewer with their well-endowed physical attributes.

Current Discourse on Modesty

In the midst of all this body-baring, there is an increasing backlash in American society advocating a return to a more conservative appearance. In *A Return to Modesty*, Shalit (1999) explores the broader topic of contemporary modesty for young women that speaks of innocence, mystery, sexual reticence, protection of hope, and vulnerability. She examines immodesty in dress as part of a larger issue that encompasses behaviors associated with the way one appears. The author agrees that talking about modesty or immodesty in dress is a complex issue, because revealing clothing does not always signify immodesty as exemplified in the dress of other cultures:

> In Western societies modesty in dress will manifest itself differently from that among the Andamanese, and within Western society different things will be immodest at different times. But that doesn't mean we can't establish what immodesty in dress is. When a culture becomes immodest, it is immodest with respect to the conventions that have gone before. (p. 67)

Shalit looks at the problems of appearance within the context of what she describes as the "normalization of pornography" (pp. 49–54). The contemporary debate volleys between conservative censorship and civil libertarians with, as she describes, ordinary men and women suffering the nonresolution of this conflict. The looseness of contemporary sexual mores for unmarried young adults is at the heart of Shalit's concerns, and she addresses women's immodest dress as an important component of the problem. In an effort to find a way back to a more modest approach

to sexuality, she turns to religious themes taken from her own Jewish background. She observes that, almost unanimously, religions view modesty as inextricably linked to spirituality and holiness.

In *Secret Keeper: The Delicate Power of Modesty*, Gresh (2002) appeals to teenage girls from a conservative Christian perspective to examine how immodesty in dress works against them to create a social environment that promotes sexual promiscuity. She uses the Gestalt Theory of visual design to explain how a plunging neckline or a short skirt creates a response of sexual arousal in men through the visual and psychological completion of a body-revealing appearance. In Gresh's view, this is not just fashion, it is a sin. Likewise, Pollard (2001), in *Christian Modesty and the Public Undressing of America*, evaluates the significance of the increasingly revealing bathing suit for women during the twentieth century and the acceptance of immodesty and, more importantly, a weakening of Christian morality. Pollard, as well as the other authors cited, is particularly concerned with the proliferation of barer images in the American media and the increasing acceptance of their existence by the majority of the American public.

The proliferation of websites on the topic of modesty is another way to view the current and increasing interest in this topic, primarily from religious groups such as conservative Jews and fundamental Christians, Mormons, and Muslims, as well as neo-conservative interest groups who feel that the degree of immodesty in American culture has gone too far.

Why has tension over this issue surfaced at this time in America? And why is a fundamental religious viewpoint now gaining rapid acceptability? In the current social environment, the interest in modesty is much more than a shift in fashion from immodest to modest or a predictable change in the continuous cycle of fashion that discards something old for something new and trendy. The increased interest in modesty is more than an attempt to renew or distance ourselves from our former immodest selves. Rather, I believe we are witnessing the ascendance and assertion of religious views on fashion and the body. Currently in America, the act of being modest and fashionable are not two mutually exclusive behaviors.

It is important to examine how and why religious groups are entering the fashion discourse, contesting the idea that modest dress is incompatible with being fashionable. The concerns of fundamental religions are being mainstreamed into the larger popular culture of fashion, particularly among the adolescent and postadolescent age group of young women who spend more on fashion than other age groups of women. Current changes in Americans' perception of religion create a social environment open to a re-examination of issues of modesty and immodesty.

Current Religious Trends in America and Modesty

A current Gallup survey discloses that roughly four out of ten Americans identify themselves as evangelical or born-again Christians (Tolson, 2003). Evangelical colleges across the United States are gaining broader acceptance and moving closer to the academic mainstream (Silverstein & Olsen, 2003). According to the Council for Christian Colleges and Universities, U.S. enrollment at its schools climbed 26.6 percent from 1997 to 2002. Although evangelical schools account for only 3.1 percent of students in U.S. four-year colleges, the schools' enrollment growth has outpaced that of public and other private institutions. Wolfe (2003) argues that religion in the United States is being transformed in radically new directions. Evangelicalism dominates the culture. For example, President Bush, whose conversion experience reportedly launched him onto the road of politics, is only one of many American political leaders who are self-proclaimed evangelicals. This identity permeates the language, concerns, and faith-based social initiatives in contemporary American society. Americans are highly influenced by this evangelical milieu in high places:

> . . . many characteristics of the evangelical style—its strongly personalist and therapeutic tendencies, its market-savvy approaches

to expanding the flock and even a certain theological fuzziness—have permeated other faith traditions in America, including Roman Catholicism and Judaism. Wolfe says, only half facetiously, "We are all evangelicals now." (Tolson, 2003)

The current evangelical following is differentiated from fundamentalism, a hypermoralistic, biblically literalist, and anti-intellectual viewpoint. Evangelicalism dominates the culture and is "personalist, therapeutic, entrepreneurial" (Tolson, 2003).

Evangelicals, like fundamentalists, are concerned with feminist trends toward gender equality, which they believe are symptomatic of a declining moral order (Ferrante, 1995). Evangelicals and other fundamentalist religious groups believe that female sexuality is dangerous if left unharnessed and uncontrolled (Fernea & Fernea, 1995). This belief leads to the religious practice of proscribing modest and proper dress for female members. Modest dress for women includes covering the body in an attempt to obliterate body curves and avoid exposure of too much skin through plunging necklines and short skirts or shorts. Muslim and Orthodox Jewish women practice covering their heads in public, as hair is interpreted as a sexual sign for these groups (Miller & Michelman, 1997).

Covering body curves appears to be somewhat less of an issue for Christian evangelical, Mennonite, and Orthodox Jewish women than for Islamic women. Thinness is the ideal body shape for Mennonite men and women. Their religious view defines thinness as an expression of self-denial and control. Sensory enjoyment such as eating is considered sinful; therefore, a properly dressed Mennonite woman is both modest and thin (Arthur, 1997).

In 1986, Concerned Women of America, a group of female religious advocates drawn from both the fundamentalist and evangelical movements, wrote of the "supernaturalism" inherent in a woman's beauty and its potential for good or evil in the workplace (Edwards, 1993). However, since the 1980s, fundamentalist and evangelical women have had to adapt to the new economic realities of entering corporate America. For example, at Bob Jones University in South Carolina, classes begin with prayer but also teach young women to be Christian, competitive, and fashionable:

> In a classroom where 20 female students sat recently, Bibles and notebooks stacked neatly before them, facing half a dozen headless dress forms draped in deft knockoffs of Todd Oldham and Donna Karan, Prof. Diane Hay of the home economics department was teaching one of her popular safe beauty classes. (Edwards, 1993)

For years, many evangelical and fundamentalist women were directed to find work at home or in low-wage jobs at Christian hospitals and schools. Since the 1980s, these women have successfully entered the more competitive business world and have learned how to dress fashionably to both fit in and move ahead. The trend in the 1980s set the stage for fundamentalist women's current interest in dressing in a more mainstream and also fashionable way to fit in and compete. Today, the evangelical trend encompasses a broad swath of society and is thus having an increasingly influential impact on consumer America—more specifically, the fashion industry.

The Modesty Discourse with Fashion

During the spring semester of 2002, while I was teaching a class titled "Dress, Gender, and Culture" to undergraduate students at the University of Massachusetts, I devoted a section of the course to the topic of modesty. I was frankly surprised at the high level of interest and discussion on this topic. I thought that these students, who had been raised on a steady diet of Madonna and more recently Britney Spears, would have some reluctance to engage in topics of modesty. Despite relentless marketing techniques pushing young women toward more provocative appearances, these students were anxious to discuss modesty and the general lack of it in American popular culture and fashion.

The Internet is a good place to examine grassroots interests in topics. When I first began exploring the topic of modesty in the late 1990s, there were a few websites devoted to modest dress. Today, there is a proliferation from varying perspectives, still largely religious in orientation but conveying the visual message that this is not just a fringe movement in American society. For example, the website www.modestprom.com gives directions to young women on how to "fill in" strapless prom gowns. From the perspective of the creator of this website, the dress can be transformed to give it "more glamour and personality." They state that "strapless gowns are so common, you just might be able to get a used one very inexpensively—then with the purchase of just a little material, you can transform it into a modest gown." Figures 5.9a–c show how a strapless neckline considered too revealing can be transformed to a more modest and yet fashionable presentation. In these illustrations, the point is well taken that the modest presentation is fashionable.

A group of young women in Kansas City, Missouri, generated enough interest in the modest prom dress issue to get the attention of a Nordstrom buyer, who was convinced to purchase a selection of more modest dresses. They now have a website (www.goodworks.net) and have generated 10,000 signatures on a petition they want to take to stores to show how important this issue is to them. They are hoping for 200,000 signatures. *Inside Edition*, an American television news show, aired a segment about these young women in contrast to a high school prom in Los Angeles where the dress was very revealing. This action indicates the growing interest and demand for more modest clothing and the impact its supporters can have on the retail market.

One of the great spokeswomen for the modesty movement is Danah Gresh (2002), a guest columnist on the Christian Broadcasting Network (www.cbn.com). In an article dated December 4, 2003, "The Fashion Battle: Is It One Worth Fighting?," you can watch and listen to her being interviewed on this topic. What you see is a very attractive and well-spoken young woman who

Figure 5.9 A strapless and body-baring prom gown (a) undergoes a makeover on www.modestprom.com (b and c).

a

b

c

advocates for purity and what she describes as "pure freedom," the title of her website. She appeals to the positive power of modesty for young women and argues that the end result of today's immodest fashion is sexual promiscuity:

> We believe that the temptation to fail sexually comes in different forms for girls and for boys. We also believe that they will one day enjoy God's gift of sex within the confines of marriage for different reasons. Whereas the girls are primarily emotionally driven, the guys are primarily driven by sight. Because of this dichotomy, it is vital that we educate them separately and emphasize different areas of temptation. (www.purefreedom.org)

This website is designed to appeal to young women. Gresh is using trendy and fashion-conscious marketing techniques to promote her message. She advertises that her first book, *And the Bride Wore White: Seven Secrets to Sexual Purity*, is the basis for a girls' retreat in over 2,000

churches in different countries, reaching over 60,000 teenage girls.

This consumer group of evangelical young women is gaining a larger voice in mainstream consumer culture; likewise, they are demanding a greater influence in the design and production of modest fashions.

Conclusion

A sociological trend of changes in American religion is having a profound impact on consumer culture, specifically fashion for young women. Religious values can lead fashion, as demonstrated in the increasing interest in more modest fashion and the movement against immodesty. Ironically, this backlash against the fashion industry and subsequently popular culture, which historically came from feminists, is not led by them at the current moment, but rather by evangelical young women who are opposing the rampant immodesty in consumer culture and, based on their religious beliefs, are saying no to bare fashion.

A review of the literature on modesty and anthropological research demonstrates that views on modesty vary historically and also with cultural beliefs. Despite highly media-hyped immodest style, often aimed directly at young women, an increasing number of modesty-seeking consumers, often linked by strong religious values, are influencing the consumption of fashion. Through a proliferation of websites and campaigns directed at retail, these young women, choosing to buy modest clothes, have created an assertive discourse with fashion.

References

Arthur, L. (1997). Clothing, control, and women's agency: The mitigation of patriarchal power. In M. L. Damhorst, K. Miller, & S. Michelman (Eds.), *The Meanings of Dress*. New York: Fairchild.

Bellafante, G. (2003). More itsy-bitsy teeny-weeny than ever. *The New York Times*. Accessed July 15, 2003, at www.nyt.com.

Edwards, L. (1993, May 30). Worldly lessons. *The New York Times*, C1, C9.

Fernea, E. W., & Fernea, R. A. (1995). Symbolizing roles: Behind the veil. In M. E. Roach-Higgins, J. B. Eicher, & K. K. P. Johnson (Eds.), *Dress and Identity*. New York: Fairchild.

Ferrante, J. (1995). *Sociology: A Global Perspective*. Belmont, CA: Wadsworth Publishing Co.

Gresh, D. (1999). *And the Bride Wore White: Seven Secrets to Sexual Purity*. Chicago: Moody Press.

Gresh, D. (2002). *Secret Keeper: The Delicate Power of Modesty*. Chicago: Moody Press.

Gresh, D. (2003, December 4). The fashion battle: Is it one worth fighting? Christian Broadcasting Network. Accessed January 15, 2004, at www.cbn.com.

Michelman, S. (2003). Reveal or conceal: American religious discourse with fashion. *Etnofoor*, XVI(2):76–87.

Miller, K., & Michelman, S. (1997). Dress and world religions. In M. L. Damhorst, K. Miller, & S. Michelman (Eds.), *The Meanings of Dress*. New York: Fairchild.

Pollard, J. (2001). *Christian Modesty and the Public Undressing of America*. San Antonio, TX: Vision Forum, Inc.

Shalit, W. (1999). *A Return to Modesty*. New York: Free Press.

Silverstein, S., & Olsen, A. (2003, December 14). Evangelical colleges gaining wider acceptance in academia. *Lexington Herald-Leader*, A23.

Thompson, M. (2000). Gender in magazine advertising: Skin sells best. *Clothing and Textiles Research Journal*, 18(3):178–181.

Tolson, J. (2003, December 8). The new old-time religion. *U.S. News and World Report*. Accessed February 16, 2004, at www.usnews.com.

Wolfe, A. (2003). *The Transformation of American Religion*. New York: Free Press.

Discussion Questions

1. How influential are conservative religious groups on mainstream fashion? Do you feel that the current political environment encourages more modesty?

2. When Janet Jackson bared her breast while performing at the Super Bowl in the 2004 halftime show, why do you feel there was such a strong public reaction?

5.3

LIFESTYLE AND POLITICS OF FASHION AND GENDER IN 1960S SWEDEN: UNISEX FASHION IN THEORY AND PRACTICE

Patrik Steorn, PhD
Centre for Fashion Studies, Stockholm University, Sweden

In Sweden unisex fashion was a topical issue for about a decade, from the mid-1960s to the mid-1970s. Various media reported on unisex fashion as a new and modern way of organizing everyday life in union with a reorganization of social categories on a structural level. General interest magazines with a left-wing orientation (i.e. *Vi/*

Original for this text.

We, published by Swedish Cooperative Union) as well as influential design journals (i.e. *Form*, published by Swedish Society for Industrial Design) reported regularly on fashion and included unisex fashion in feature photos, lifestyle reports, and published patterns of unisex clothes for home sewing, and they frequently discussed fashion, especially androgynous models, in their reports on Swedish design in the late 1960s. Unisex fashion as a phenomenon brought the political left as well as the art and design community toward the field of fashion as an arena for social and political change.

Unisex fashion was an international phenomenon in the late 1960s, and it seems to be one of these ideas that appear more or less simultaneously in the minds of people in different places. In France, Jacques Esterel designed skirts for men and pants for women, and Yves Saint Laurent became famous for pants for women and a unisex safari-suit. Pierre Cardin's "boy/girl" collection from 1968 (Figure 5.10) is often included as part of this phenomenon. However, French designer Ted Lapidus is considered to be the pioneer of unisex fashion, as his first haute couture shows in 1963 reportedly included "boy/girl" mixes. Austrian-American designer Rudi Gernreich did a collection called UNISEX in 1970 as part of a larger art project that included films and photos. (Lobenthal, 1990; Moffitt & Claxton, 1990; Bolton, 2002; Breward, Gilbert, & Lister, 2006)

This paper will study the unisex phenomenon with a focus on Sweden in the 1960s and 1970s and discuss how unisex garments can be related to gender theory and fashion theory, as well as their role as a symbol of opposition to traditional values, such as sex roles.

Figure 5.10 Designer Pierre Cardin's unisex fashions from 1968.

Unisex—Fashion, Gender, and Society

Women dressing in men's clothes, fashion design for men inspired by women's wear, or clothes designed for men and women alike—what is unisex fashion?

The terminology of unisex fashion is slightly confusing because it refers both to a technical term (to specific garments) as well as to a style. When unisex is used as a technical term within the production of ready-to-wear, it refers to a certain category of clothes, comparable to menswear, women's wear, and children's wear. However, I think it is important to make a difference between this tailor-related understanding of unisex on the one hand and on the other hand an understanding that implies the creation of fashions that disavow the social categories of masculinity and femininity, not only in cut but also in style. In the 1960s media, the term *unisex* included both the creation of new types of garments such as the jumpsuit or the monokini, which were not traditionally assigned to men or women, as well as making men's fashion in fabrics, colors, and patterns that had been considered to be typically feminine, and vice versa. For example, clothes for men were designed in soft fabrics like jersey, and in strong colors and floral patterns. Women dressed in denim and jeans and workers' overalls. Unisex fashion can, according to my perspective, be defined as a set of practices of design and of dressing up that oppose a traditional fashion industry's division between men and women in clothing, and which produce a social and aesthetic symbol of the individual's free choice of lifestyle beyond gender division that can also be used as a symbol of political activism for full gender equality.

Unisex as a general term refers to clothes that are not at all gender specific, whereas androgynous fashion combines feminine and masculine dress conventions in unpredictable ways. Cross-dressing refers to the practice of dressing like the opposite sex, while drag makes this into a performing art—on stage or in everyday life. All of these terms refer to designs and styles or practices that problematize the relation between fashion and gender.

Unisex fashion has been theorized by French sociologists Olivier Burgelin and Marie–Therese Basse as a symbolic end of what they called "vestimentary apartheid," the practice and rule of strict separation of dress that had been prevalent since the 19th century. They point to the women's liberation movement, the rise of youth culture, and the appearance of anti-fashion as the main reasons for unisex fashion of the 20th century (Burgelin & Basse, 1987, pp. 285, 296). Women's gradual appropriation of pants in general and jeans in particular is their main example, and they even argue that unisex fashion is all organized around jeans (Burgelin & Basse, 1987, p. 291). They omit to mention the types of garments that were explicitly designed as unisex fashion such as jumpsuits or safari jackets. American sociologist Mark Gottdiener (1995) interprets unisex fashion much the same way but also points out that unisex fashion did have differing implications for men and for women in relation to their respective commercial and professional arenas: for men it marked their entrance as a target group on the fashion market, while it signaled women's strengthened professional position in business and politics. Unisex dress is often interpreted as a consequence of changed social attitudes, which is an important contextualization of this phenomenon. Making unisex dress into vestimentary illustrations of the women's liberation movement, however, risks disregarding the creative energy that this idea also came to symbolize.

Sociologist Herbert Blumer, in the 1960s, challenged a traditional view that fashion was bizarre, frivolous, and irrational and in doing so particularly questioned fashion theorist Georg Simmel's idea that fashion arose as a form of class differentiation: "Fashion appears much more as a collective grouping for the proximate future than a channelled movement laid down by prestigious figures" (Blumer, 2007 [1969], p. 237). In his own empirical research he pointed out that the determination of fashion is a collective process of selection. According to Blumer the role of the designer is to translate themes from the arts, literature, political debates, happenings, and the media into dress design and to be oriented toward a certain clientele and to make clothes that this group would adopt.

Blumer's statement that fashion should be understood as a result of collective selection, not class, resonates in many of the comments on fashion in general and on unisex fashion in particular of the 1960s. Instead of simply confirming a bourgeois society order, fashion had the potential of shaping new social orders, based on the process and forming of collective taste. "Fashion is a very adept mechanism for enabling people to adjust in an orderly and unified way to a moving and changing world which is potentially full of anarchic possibilities" (Blumer, 2007 [1969], p. 245). Blumer's words on fashion as a creative driving force in forming a modern world articulate an ideological background of unisex fashion.

Gender was conceived as one of the social conventions that could be refashioned. During the 1960s and 1970s the theorizing of gender was launched and used by activists and scholars all over the Western world (Rosaldo & Lamphere, 1974). Recent scholars have noted that sex role theories imply that there is a natural body beyond the gendered masks of "male" and "female" constructions (Butler, 1999, pp. 9–11, 32–33; Connell, 1995, p. 21–17). Unisex fashion was about clothes that in themselves would appear so neutral that the wearer would stand out on their own terms. The clothes were supposed to be neutral so that the individual could be expressive in her/himself and be able to perform "man" or "woman" in his or her own way. New and unforeseen versions of sex roles and altered gender structures motivated the unisex vision, but what should these material garments look like, and how should they be worn?

Transgressing Genders—Performing Unisex

Whereas men's fashion had historically been dominated by suits in various and often subtle variations and fashionable detail, this period of the 1960s has been referred to as "the Peacock Revolution" (Frazier, 1968). Integrating traditional signs of femininity into men's dress signaled a new type of masculinity that was socially progressive—or just fashionable. Swedish designer Sighsten

Herrgård stressed the role of soft fabric in unisex fashion, and in the following quote he describes its role as more or less able to liberate all gendered bodies from any physical restraint and from a square, polished ideal:

> I like jersey, jersey, jersey . . . It is the material for our age. I design for today and tomorrow—not for yesterday nor for the space age. I want to make clothes void of gender thinking. Away with men's and women's buttoning, for example and away with age thinking—it is the environment, the mood and the way of life that decide which clothes we want to wear.[1]
>
> (Bort med ålderstänkandet, 1969)

The quote also exemplifies how the trope of unisex is established as part of a modern lifestyle through the distinction from allegedly old and stiff gender thinking. In the following quote Herrgård explains how unisex fashion was performed in everyday life (or at least in front of the journalist):

> London designer Sighsten Herrgard and his girlfriend, model Ann Jennifer, share almost everything—"pants, sweaters, shirts, belts. We don't worry about what belongs to whom; we just pick out what we want to wear that day."
>
> (The Genderation, 1968)

This narrative on the total freedom of wearing unisex fashion evokes a fashionable ideal that men and women could share, which marked this era in various areas.

In 1974 feminist psychologist and Professor Sandra Bem introduced the concept of "psychological androgyny" to describe men and women who combined traits from traditionally defined gender roles and she suggested that androgyny could be the solution to a traditional gender division. (Bem, 1974, pp. 155–162) According to platonic myth and spiritual tradition, androgyny is the origin of heterosexual attraction; all the while the idea of *conjuncto oppositorum*, uniting of opposites, has played an important role within alchemy, theosophy, kabbala, and other spiritual movements as a symbol of the complete individual: male and female in perfect union (McCleod, 1998). The androgynous appearance is thus based on the primordial existence of two separate sexes that complete each other, physically and spiritually.

From a 1990s queer perspective the American philosopher Judith Butler argues that the division between social and physical gender actually conserves and deepens the understanding of sex and gender according to a fundamental heteronormative structure (Butler, 1999 [1990], pp.162–166). The unisex ideal of indifference to sex roles thus generated fashion ideas in a paradoxical way: sex difference was denied at a theoretical level at the same time as it was emphasized in practice. Looking closer at images of people wearing unisex jumpsuits, it is clear that the tight cut and the soft materials accentuated the physical characteristics of the wearer's body instead of erasing them visually. The tight cut seems to reveal the "natural body within," suggesting that gender difference in fashion is artificial whereas physical gender difference is natural. Herrgård also articulates this side of unisex fashion:

> "Unisex clothes don't conceal the sexes," he said, cinching the wide black leather belt tighter around the black ribbed sweater which topped a pair of grey tweed trousers. "There is no doubt that even though we are the same size in trousers and in sweaters and though her shoulders are wider than mine, she is a woman and I am a man."
>
> (These Swedes put pants on everyone, 1969)

Social gender difference was questioned to a certain extent, but the division of male and female bodies was taken for granted and a heterosexual attraction between these body types was implied. Sighsten Herrgård and the female models that he was dating in the beginning of his career posed together in magazines all over the world. In his unisex jumpsuit they performed the perfect heterosexual couple—an androgynous union of male and female. At the same time he engaged in same-sex activities in between girlfriends or behind their backs. He could pass both as heterosexual and gay, the unisex jumpsuit being the perfect disguise—gender bending and heterosexual at the same time. Gay and bisexual men and women in the metropolitan areas used unisex fashion to work out social identities of their own during this period (Cole, 2000, p. 89; Lomas 2007, p. 88). Tight colorful clothing was frequently used among gay men to signal nonheterosexual interests in other men.

The emphasis on the adornment of the body accentuates the erotic and sensual potentials of the wearer's physique and the potential agency to subvert traditional sexual orders. However, this potential seems only to have been explored implicitly, in private. Rather than dissolving gender categories, unisex fashion during the 1960s seems to have strengthened the belief in men and women as natural categories.

Lifestyle or Politics— Cultural Meaning of Unisex

The intensive gender role debate in Sweden in the 1960s generated a political movement that questioned the male norm within all aspects of society. An institutionalized gender equality politics was established by the Swedish Social Democratic government, who appointed a mission for these issues, Delegationen för jämställdhet mellan män och kvinnor (The Delegation for Equality between Men and Women) in 1972. Simultaneously, designers, media, and consumers explored new ways of shaping, representing, and performing gender with the objective of changing the polarized gender positions of previous eras. The interest in making unisex clothes appeared both in the Swedish art world and in the fashion business.

In the University College of Arts, Crafts and Design (Konstfackskolan) in Stockholm a group of students, young artists whose art was grounded in the 1960s debate on gender roles, formed a collective that designed clothes with soft materials and strong colors and simple, often organic patterns (Eldvik, 1988, pp. 101–120; Hallström Bornold, 2003). The group was called Mah-Jong, signalling their sympathy with Maoist ideology (Figure 5.11).

They wanted to make art and fashion more political and social, "closer to the people." According to these thoughts, art should be something that could be used, an everyday object. Posters, happenings, and dress collections came out of their creative work. They wanted to create anti-fashion, in opposition to the established fashion world, aiming at empowerment and enabling of women, children, and the working class. Their objective was clothes that were primarily functional, clothes that did not necessarily flaunt social status, in opposition to the world of haute couture. The production was located in small-scale industry in a small Swedish town and the clothes were sold in a small boutique in central Stockholm. Mah-Jong clothes are legendary in Sweden today, part of the "political primary scene" of this era.

Designer Sighsten Herrgård's career as a designer started already at the age of 15, when he was announced "Dior of Bromma" (Bromma is an upper-class suburb of Stockholm) after winning a designer contest for girls. In the early

Figure 5.11 Family wearing Mah-Jong tights and tunics.

1960s he designed bath-clothes for Jantzen in London, and it was in 1968, when Herrgård was employed by House of Worth in London, that his career took off (Herrgård & Werkelid, 1989). A unisex jumpsuit made of jersey was designed for this old fashion house, which got immediate and worldwide coverage that made him and Swedish fashion known all over the world (Figure 5.12). The jersey jumpsuit, in graphic black or discreet beige, was designed to fit both women and men and was combined with accessories such as pendant necklaces and long scarves, sandals or high boots, and a belt in the waist, in Herrgård's unisex style. Among the clippings in his archive there are several advertisements where unisex fashions appear on models who figure in commercials for example for beer and detergent or in a feature report on buffet food serving (Sighsten Herrgård archive, Nordic Museum, Stockholm). The clothes form part of a change in social conventions, promoting a new, fashionable, and relaxed lifestyle.

There is a very interesting tension between the unisex ideas within the Mah-Jong group that aimed at political change and the unisex ideas held by the commercial designers such as Herrgård. Mah-Jong distributed their clothes themselves through one single shop and consequently did not reach a very large audience. The men's collection was produced in such modest numbers that

hardly anyone outside the family and friends of the group could buy it (Hallström Bornold, 2003, p. 139). Herrgård's unisex jumpsuit was launched and distributed all over the world, not only the Western world, but also during fashion weeks in Mexico City and in Tehran in 1970. (Herrgård & Werkelid, 1989, pp. 89–94, 114–129) The outreach was incomparable, the political intentions as well, and I suggest that there is a fundamental difference here—Herrgård wanted to change the individual's potential to express personality and identity through fashion while the Mah-Jong group wanted to use fashion as a tool in order to change the relation between individual and society at large. Both sides, however, imbued these designed garments with the cultural meaning of liberation, in the sense that individual behavior is the foundation of transforming both political and fashionable society.

References

Bem, S. (1974). The Measurement of Psychological Androgyny. *Journal of Consulting and Clinical Psychology*, 2.

Blumer, H. (2007). From class differentiation to collective selection. [1969] In Barnard, M (ed.), *Fashion Theory. A Reader*. New York: Routledge.

Bolton, A. (2002). *Men in skirts*. London: V&A.

Bort med ålderstänkandet. Unisexmode för oss alla. (1969, November 26). Hallands nyheter.

Breward, C., Gilbert, D., Lister, J. (ed.) (2006). *Swinging sixties: fashion in London and beyond 1955–1970*. London: V&A Publications.

Burgelin, O. & Basse, M-T. (1987). L'unisexe. Perspectives diachroniques. *Communications*, 46. Paris: Centre d'études transdisciplinaires.

Butler, J. (1999). *Gender Trouble. Feminism and the subversion of identity*. London & New York: Routledge.

Cole, S. (2000). *Don we now our gay apparel*. Oxford: Berg.

Connell, R. (1995). *Masculinities*. Berkeley: University of California Press.

Eldvik, B. (1988). Mah-Jong. In *Kläder. Fataburen*. Stockholm: Nordiska museet.

Frazier, G. (1968). The Peacock Revolution. *Esquire*, 10.

Gottdiener, M. (1995). *Postmodern Semiotics. Material Culture and the Forms of Postmodern Life*. Oxford & Cambridge: Blackwell.

Hallström Bornold, S. (2003). *Det är rätt att göra uppror: Mah-Jong 1966–1976*. Stockholm: Modernista.

Herrgård, S., Werkelid, C. O. (1988). *Sighsten*. Stockholm: Norstedts.

Figure 5.12 Swedish designer Sighsten Herrgård and his fiancée, Ann Jennifer, model the designer's unisex belted jacket with wide-legged double-knit trousers.

Lobenthal, J. (1990). *Radical rags. Fashions of the Sixties.* New York: Abbeville Press.

Lomas, C. (2007). Men don't wear velvet you know! Fashionable gay masculinity and the shopping experience London 1950—early 1970's. *Oral history, 1.*

MacLeod, C. (1998). *Embodying ambiguity: androgyny and aesthetics from Winckelmann to Keller.* Detroit: Wayne State University Press.

Moffitt, P., Claxton, W. (1990). *The Rudi Gernreich Book.* Cologne, Germany, & London: Taschen.

Rosaldo, M. Z. & Lamphere, L. (ed.) (1974). *Woman, culture, and society.* Stanford, Calif.: Stanford Univ. Press.

Sighsten Herrgård archive, Nordic Museum, Stockholm, Sweden.

The genderation. (1968, August 23). *Womens Wear Daily.*

These Swedes put pants on everyone. (1969, March 14). *Newsday.*

Endnote

1. (Author's translation) "Jag gillar jersey, jersey, jersey . . . det är materialet för vår tidsålder. Jag formger för idag och imorgon, inte för igår och rymdåldern. Jag vill göra kläder utan könstänkande. Bort med herr-och damknäppning, t.ex. Och bort med ålderstänkandet—det är miljön, humöret och levnadssättet som avgör vilka kläder vi vill ha på oss."

Discussion Questions

1. According to the author, what is the difference between unisex clothing and androgynous clothing? What are some current styles that fall to the unisex category and the androgynous category, respectively?

2. What were the philosophical ideals of unisex clothing? Did the clothing achieve these ideals? Why or why not?

5.4

GAY, LESBIAN, BISEXUAL, AND TRANSGENDERED PERSONS
Andrew Reilly

Reliable information about dress in the lesbian, gay, bisexual, or transgendered (LGBT) community has become available only recently. For many years negative attitudes held by much of the non-LGBT population resulted in beliefs and stereotypes that were often superficial and inaccurate. Research into the dress of members of the LGBT community is now providing a more detailed and nuanced view of the subject. When a person "comes out" or acknowledges an LGBT identity, it is often a mixed blessing; the relief of finally knowing oneself is often met with resistance from society and culture. Some people may hide their sexual orientation, whereas others proclaim it, often through dress. The process of coming out is usually continual, for sexual orientation is not necessarily visible to others, and dress provides a (coded) visual medium for expression of the self when words may be redundant or secrecy necessary.

Many scholars have presented models of coming out. While the models vary in the number of phases one goes through in the formation of a gay identity, they all do proffer a similar succession of steps. At first, one questions his or her sexual orientation, noting that something is "different" about oneself in comparing oneself to others. This is then followed by a series of stages in which the person adopts the label of "gay" on a trial basis and (possibly) informs a few people of the secret identity. This is followed by a permanent acceptance of the label and telling more people of the identity, followed by incorporating the sexual orientation within the greater scope of his or her sense of self. It is during the stages of acceptance and announcing one's gay identity that a person may adopt clothing that is associated with gay people.

Using dress to identify one's self as LGBT can be viewed as a form of community development. Social psychologists H. Tajfel and J. C. Turner's *social identity theory* posits that groups of people want to distance themselves from other groups in order to show superiority. When applied to the coming-out process, the theory explains the phenomenon of dressing different from the accepted norm of straight or heterosexual society; upon realizing their identity is different from the status quo, LGBT people strive to distance themselves from straight people to show their identity and freedom from cultural norms to which straight people are likely to adhere. However, in accord with many coming-out models, eventually dress passes into one of personal and not group identification.

Yet not all LGBT people will choose to identify their sexual orientation via dress. Depending on the social and cultural climate in which one lives and one's acceptance of one's sexual orientation, the dress of LGBT people varies along a continuum from assimilating within the dominant heterosexual society (i.e., to pass as heterosexual) to radically displaying their sexual orientation through aesthetic or cultural affectations.

Semiotics

The history of LGBT persons, in the industrialized world at least, has been one of oppression. Historically, LGBT persons have been persecuted and prosecuted for their same-sex attraction.

For example, in Edwardian England, "the love that dare not speak its name" was punishable by imprisonment and hard labor; under the Nazi regime in Europe, gay men were confined to con-

centration camps and identified by an inverted pink triangle (rosawinkle) attached to their clothing; in the United States, homosexual behavior was classified as a mental illness until 1973, when it was removed from the *Diagnostic and Statistical Manual of Mental Disorders*. Though these examples are of an extreme nature, they show the cultural conditions in which LGBT persons have likely been raised and live. Even today, LGBT people are likely to encounter discrimination from family, work, and landlords or are prohibited by law from adopting children, marrying, and serving in the military. Given this climate, many LGBT people chose to remain incognito, yet they have found avenues to communicate their identity to similar others through semiotics.

Semiotics are coded sign systems in which a sender and receiver both understand the message embedded within a seemingly innocuous artifact or gesture. Gay men in Edwardian England used a green carnation in their lapel or a red tie as a way to communicate their sexual identity to other men. In the 1980s, men communicated their gay identity by an earring in their right ear and later in both ears. Once this communication became public knowledge, the rhyme "left is right and right is wrong" was used by straight men to remember which ear was socially acceptable for jewelry. Additionally, wedding bands worn by same-sex couples were often on the right hand rather than the left hand, symbolic of one's identity but also implying a difference regarding one's attraction.

Other symbols were also used to self-identify as LGBT. The inverted triangle is a popular and easily recognized symbol. In the 1970s, the LGBT community in the United States and Germany began using the rosawinkle of Nazi Germany in order to remind people that oppression and discrimination of LGBT people still persisted. In the 1980s, lesbians began using the inverted black triangle to symbolize their own sexual orientation (the black triangle was used in Nazi Germany to identify people who were antisocial; although no hard evidence exists that demonstrates lesbians were routinely identified as such, it appears this is an instance where rumor and legend were the basis for the semiotic).

Though it is curious for LGBT people to use the inverted triangle, a symbol so steeped in their own violent history, one could argue that the philosophy behind it is a form of empowerment and that one should never forget the past. The rainbow flag was introduced as part of the annual Gay Pride Parade in San Francisco in 1978. Designed by Gilbert Baker, it is a flag of six rows of colors (originally designed with more colors but reduced for economical reasons). Though it was intended to represent all aspects of sexual orientation, a flag to represent bisexual people had also been designed by Michael Page. This flag contains three horizontal stripes: the top stripe is pink (symbolizing same-sex attraction), the bottom is blue (representing opposite-sex *attraction*), and in the middle is a blend of the two to create purple (representing attraction to both sexes). Other variations of the rainbow flag were developed to identify specific gay subcultures:

The leather subculture is identified by a flag, first used in 1989, of nine horizontal stripes alternating between blue and black with a white stripe in the middle, whereas the bear subculture is identified by a flag first used in the 1990s that contains seven stripes changing in color from brown to black and has a bear paw print in the upper left corner.

Other symbols, including the Greek letter lambda, the labrys (a double-bladed axe), or two male or female signs linked, are also used to identify one's sexual orientation. Some of these symbols are more subtle than the widely known flag and triangle, so they may appeal to LGBT people who cannot or do not want their sexual orientation known to the mass majority but still want a way of self-affirmation within the limits of their environment. Variations on these symbols abound, with subtle shifts in cultural meanings, but all of them demonstrate the willingness on the part of the wearer to communicate his or her sexual orientation to oneself or to others. Whether worn on T-shirts or tattooed to one's body, they no doubt speak to one's identity. Overall, whether subtle or overt, semiotics has played an important part in the history of LGBT people and their dress. In a society where everyone is assumed straight, visual codes have helped LGBT people socialize and form networks with other LGBT people while at the same time reinforcing awareness.

Aesthetics of Gay Men

To say that all gay men hold one specific aesthetic above all others would be incorrect; but it does appear that gay men gravitate to specific aesthetic styles. Gay men prefer to interact and date other gay men who are dressed in similar fashion to themselves. This implies that not only do gay men like what they see in the mirror but that they are attracted to their own aesthetic as well. Additionally, it means that in order to interact with a specific group of gay men, one must meet certain appearance expectations of that group. For example, in the novel by Armistead Maupin (and subsequent PBS miniseries) *Tales of the City*, which chronicles and captures the life of fictionalized people in 1970s San Francisco, gay character Michael explains to a friend why he is dressed in penny loafers: "It was best to dress like the people you wanted to pick you up" (p. 113). Research into this notion of dressing like those you want to meet has demonstrated that gay men have preferences for similar clothing and fragrance styles that are different from the preferences espoused by straight men. However, it should be noted not all gay men are attracted to their own image.

Just as in the straight community, often opposites attract. One of the earliest identifiable gay male subcultures was the leather subculture. Beginning in the 1960s, members of the leather subculture displayed their nonstereotypical appearance through a muscular physique and leather apparel, including jackets, chaps, caps, and harnesses. As a textile-like material, leather is tough and durable, a good analogy for men wanting to display strength in the face of adversity. Leathermen also developed a sexual code using a handkerchief hanging from the back pocket of their pants, with the color and location indicative of one's sexual interest. "Castro clones" of the 1970s created a style for gay men by using working-class dress—jeans, plaid shirts, boots, and mustaches—to create an overly emphasized masculine aesthetic. (The Castro District of San Francisco was, and still is, an LGBT neighborhood.) By the early 1980s, AIDS had become closely associated with gay men in general, and the wasting away of the body had become an outward signifier (if not entirely accurate) of one's HIV status. Though there had always been overweight gay men, it was during this time that they became more valued and recognized: this may have been a causative factor in the formation of the bear subculture, whose members rejoice in the eroticization of a natural physique, bulky and hirsute. However, these subcultures were not simply an imitation of straight men in order to pass as straight; rather, they were perfecting the male form (for other men) through what social scientist M. P. Levine has called "parody and emulation" or camp and irony. Members of the leather community sported a hanky in the back pocket of their pants indicating their sexual desires for other men; bears celebrated the ideal, natural, male form through bear contests; clones paid attention to achieving the flawless masculine form.

Even today, myriad other gay subcultures exist, such as ones that center on gym-sculpted bodies, uniforms, or Levi's jeans.

The body plays an important role in personal and cultural identity for many gay men. The shape of the body often allows for introduction or exclusion from subcultures, where identity and affiliation are equated to appearance. Gay men report being more interested in their appearance (which includes the shape of the body) than straight men and are more concerned with their weight; they are more fearful of being overweight and have lower ideal weights than straight men. Other research reported by body image researchers M. A. Morrison, T. G. Morrison, and C. Sager found "a small, but real, difference between heterosexual and gay men in terms of body satisfaction."

Lower body satisfaction among gay men may be a reason why gay men work out for appearance reasons, whereas straight men seem to be more likely to work out for health reasons. Unlike straight women who desire to lose weight, gay men may desire to lose weight while also gaining muscle mass. Workout regimes are often coupled with eating habits that can be dangerous when taken to the extreme. The result may be painful and often deadly behavior patterns, such as anorexia, bulimia, and chronic dieting. When research showed that, compared to straight men, gay men are more likely to develop an eating disorder, the belief that gay men are more appearance conscious than straight men was reinforced.

Researchers have looked for explanations of behavior related to appearance-related eating and workout regimens and have concluded that one explanation may be *internalized* homophobia, which is a form of self-hatred directed toward one's own sexual orientation. Studies showed that men with high internalized homophobia have lower body satisfaction than men with low internalized homophobia. Such men may engage in body building in order to look masculine. Research has also linked eating disorders with internalized homophobia. The resulting conclusion was that a negative view of one's body coupled with internalized homophobia can lead to eating disorders in attempts to *create* an idealized figure.

Another possible explanation for body dissatisfaction among gay men is exposure to media in which male models are routinely muscular and in various stages of undress. These images have increased in muscularity and stages of undress in the past few decades. Advertising for men's underwear typically had focused on the product alone, sans any model, or else the model was of average physique. However, Calvin Klein's explosive campaign in the early 1990s featuring actor/singer Mark Wahlberg changed the landscape and began the craze for ever more muscular models in advertising. Gay men may internalize these idealized images and strive to assimilate the bodies they see on television, in magazines, and in advertisements, resulting in increased body dissatisfaction.

However, it should be noted that this desire for a thin, toned body is not indicative of all gay men. Bears, a subculture of gay men whose body type is typically overweight, revere their excess poundage, and some gay men who are of average physique do not strive to achieve a hypermuscular body due to self-esteem, lack of interest, or general contentment with their body. Thus, cultural affiliation and personal psychology play a role in satisfaction with body shape.

Fragrance use is an important part of dress, in general, and gay and straight men differ on fragrance preferences and usage.

Fragrances are grouped by notes, such as floral, citrus, woody/green, or Oriental. When surveyed, gay men prefer floral and Oriental scents, while straight men prefer woody/green scents.

Floral scents are made from, or made to mimic, flowers, and Oriental scents are spicy and exotic, whereas woody/green scents are earthy and musky (e.g., patchouli). One possible explanation for this is that gay men may feel freer to cross gender boundaries.

Gay men may not be held to the same social expectations as are straight men and are thus permitted more freedom to express an identity that is not strictly traditionally masculine. Thus, it may not be that gay men prefer feminine scents due simply to their sexual orientation but that they feel more comfortable in admitting their preferences for scents typically considered feminine.

Additionally, the results of research revealed that gay men owned more bottles of fragrances than straight men (five compared to four) and that many gay men used fragrance on a daily basis, whereas straight men used cologne less frequently. This could possibly be due to a higher interest in self-presentation among gay men. Men who frequently use fragrances have been reported as being concerned with their body image and are more social, findings that align with research that reports gay men are more attuned to their personal aesthetic. Straight men may use fragrances less frequently because they view colognes as something reserved for special occasions, such as holidays and celebrations; thus, gay men may view every day as an opportunity to present themselves in the best way they know how.

It should be noted, however, that this research does not apply to all gay men. Fragrances have come in and out of fashion through history with the practice either embraced or shunned. For example, in the 1970s, men's fragrance was an important part of self-presentation for both gay and straight men. And in the early twenty-first century, *metrosexual* men (straight men who take an interest in personal aesthetics) embraced the use of fragrances.

Likewise, not all gay men are as enamored of fragrances as readers of the previous research would assume. Some gay subcultures, such as the leather and bear subcultures, shun the use of fragrances because their aesthetics are based on historic notions of manliness.

Aesthetics of Lesbians

Lesbian aesthetics have historically been divided into butch and femme styles. *Butch* styles are closely associated with the stereotype of lesbians (masculine), whereas *femme* styles are associated with the stereotype of straight women (feminine). Here, too, research leads to the following conclusions. For butch lesbians, the aesthetic was cultural as well as a way to identify other lesbians and to separate oneself from the dominant culture (as well as being related to class structure). In the 1950s, the aesthetic mode was split; butch lesbians (who were usually working class) wore leather jackets, pinky rings, and short hair combed back (Figure 5.13), whereas femme lesbians (who were middle-class women passing as straight) adopted makeup, dresses, skirts, and blouses. These looks were strictly enforced at this time, with a woman not adhering to the either/or dichotomy finding herself an outcast and called "kiki." It has been argued that this method was intended to protect the lesbian community from arrest; the popular thought at the time was that a woman who did not look either butch or femme was most likely an undercover officer who did not know the dress codes.

Figure 5.13 The butch aesthetic. In the United States in the 1950s this was characterized by leather jackets, pinky rings, and short hair combed back.

By the 1970s, the androgynous look—jeans, T-shirts or flannel shirts, boots, long hair—gained popularity, but over the next two decades, there was more inclusion of different ethnicities and cultures in the aesthetic, including a return to the butch/femme dichotomy.

While it has been argued that femme women wanted to pass as straight, some lesbian women find the aesthetic attractive and actively cultivate the look within themselves or seek it in others. Butch aesthetics encompassed a variety of masculine styles on a continuum from androgynous to hypermasculine. The butch aesthetic may be a function of acceptance of one's sexual orientation. Some researchers argue that all women, regardless of their sexual orientation, experience pressure to dress in a feminine manner and state that there is pressure to look "lesbian" after first coming out. The butch aesthetic is a way for lesbians to stand out from the dominant (feminine) female crowd by creating a radical departure from the expected appearance of women, with an intentional motive to display the self as sexually unavailable to men. However, after incorporating one's sexual orientation into one's complete identity, lesbians select a style more representative of their composite identity.

One particular style that tends to lend itself to controversy is the sadomasochist (S/M) style. Akin to the leather aesthetic of gay men, the S/M lesbian wears uniforms of leather or rubber garments with breasts barely covered or entirely revealed. For some women, this style is sexually exciting; S/M and leather tend to convey power and authority and may be used as a form of wish fulfillment for people who are marginalized or feel powerless in society. For others, it is a radical statement meant to provoke and question social dress codes: Why cannot a woman go shirtless as a man; what gives men the privilege and not women?

Popular thought argues that lesbians are free from the beauty constraints that straight women face because their bodies are not intended to please men and, therefore, they are happier with their bodies than straight women. Research has not yet answered this question conclusively. All that can be said is that the effects of gender may be more salient for some lesbians. Women who rate their appearance as feminine have lower body satisfaction when compared to women who rate their appearance as androgynous or masculine. Feminine women may be comparing themselves to the hyperfeminine image portrayed in the media, and androgynous or masculine women may not.

Interestingly, it has been noted that the butch aesthetic (which typically includes an overweight body) was originally intended to free women from the chains of heterosexual expectations of women. However, it evolved into rigid expectations of lesbian appearance, where even if lesbians are dissatisfied with their bodies, they learn not to voice their concerns. It is interesting to notice that this is similar to the socialization of men who are taught not to complain about their bodies because it is considered feminine to do so.

Gender Identity: Transsexual

A *transsexual* is a person who believes he or she was born as the incorrect sex. Physically, a transsexual may be a man who identifies as a woman or vice versa (Figure 5.14). Transsexuals seek to change their physical bodies to match gender identity and can accomplish this via dress, hormone treatment, cosmetic surgery, and/or sex-reassignment surgery. Transsexuals dress as the gender with which they identify, though this may result in issues with the body, such as body hair distribution and body proportion. The majority of transsexuals tend to be male-to-female (MTF). Often, transsexuals employ a creative bevy of methods to disguise features that are inherent to the sex into which they were born. For example, scarves are often used to cover Adam's apples of MTF transsexuals, while breasts are bound down with gauze among female-to-male (FTM) transsexuals. Hormone therapy or cosmetic surgery is used to transform the silhouette of the body, the shape of the face, and the sound of the voice. Sex-reassignment surgery (where the genitalia are transformed into that of the desired sex) is performed after the patient has undergone a series of psychological evaluations and has lived as the gender with which they identify for a period of time. Hormone and surgical practices help transsexuals confirm their identity and feel authentic, underscoring the notion that having the body that aligns with one's identity fosters feelings of validity. Additionally, the embodiment of gender via body changes is more rigorous for MTF than FTM and may include retraining the body to conform to societal standards of the new gender.

If MTF transsexuals see themselves as women, then it is easy to assume that they would have a body image poorer than that of men because women generally do have a poorer body image than men. However, postoperative MTF transsexuals have a body image similar to that of men, but they feel just as feminine as women. This does not mean that eating disorders relating to appearance are nonexistent. They do exist and there have been some reports of cases of

anorexia and bulimia. Though low, eating disorders in MTF transsexuals may be a way for them to meet the social expectation of a thin, female body.

Gender Identity: Drag

Drag is a term associated with gender performance, whether applied to a man dressing as a woman (drag queen) or a woman dressing as a man (drag king). However, the aesthetics, which revolve around the concept of camp and exaggeration of features, also allow for a woman to dress as a faux drag queen or a man as a faux drag king. Drag is usually associated with the LGBT community, though it is not exclusive to this community.

Drag performers are not trying to pass as another gender, as a transsexual desires to be accepted as a woman or a man. Rather, drag performers are the embodiment of robust gender. Literary theorist Susan Sontag defined *camp* as an esoteric sensibility of pretense and unnatural exaggeration/expression. With this definition, drag is camp, or campy, meaning that what is expressed via drag is not meant to be taken seriously but is meant to entertain, provoke, and perhaps question conventional wisdom. For drag queens and faux drag queens, a powdered face becomes the canvas on which to apply large, colorful lips; extreme eyebrows; and perhaps a mole or two. Hair, or more frequently wigs, is styled to enhance a large personality; padded breasts are added; unwanted hair is removed, and clothing is, if nothing else, at least glamorous.

For drag kings and faux drag kings, breasts are bound, padding is used to present a more masculine appearance, and faux facial hair is attached or mimicked with makeup. Drag performers may create unique personas, sometimes with creative names such as Syphilis Diller or Bertha Nation, or they may imitate celebrities who themselves were larger than life, such as Bette Davis or Joan Crawford.

Additionally, dress scholar J. Jacob has identified a subgroup within the drag community that is aesthetically different from traditional drag queens and termed them *radical drag queens*.

Figure 5.14 Chaz Bono underwent female-to-male gender transition surgery between 2008 and 2010 and has since been an advocate for the transgendered community.

Radical drag queens do not impersonate female identity as traditional drag queens but rather take it to a ridiculous extreme. Additionally, radical drag queens may eliminate the illusion of femaleness by revealing the male body and revealing the tricks of the trade that traditional drag queens use to create their persona (e.g., shape-enhancing garments).

Conclusion

While the popular notion is that gay men are effeminate and lesbians are masculine, the truth reveals a rich landscape of LGBT style and identity. Historically, LGBT people have created or found subcultures within the LGBT community where their interests are shared by others and, by virtue of necessity or identity, used dress and appearance as a means of identification. Some embrace the stereotype; some reject it. Some use dress for political purposes; some, in order to establish identity; others, for pure shock value.

Perhaps the best example of the notion of gay aesthetics is found in LGBT dolls. With an audience that is not necessarily children, the dolls have become favorites among the LGBT community. Billy is manufactured by Totem and was introduced in the 1990s as the first "out" gay doll. Billy and his friends come in a variety of clothing styles and uniforms. Whether dressed as a sailor, cowboy, delivery person, or in casual wear, underneath the clothing is a muscular physique. Likewise, Bobbie, produced by Dykedolls, comes in a variety of styles including Diesel Dyke, Rockabilly, and Southern California Skater, though all styles have the same physique. While these dolls are an adventure in camp, they are underscored by the popular notion of what gay people look like.

References and Further Reading

Atkins, D. *Looking Queer: Body Image and Identity in Lesbian, Bisexual, Gay and Transgender Communities.* New York: Haworth, 1998.

Faderman, L. *Odd Girls and Twilight Lovers: A History of Lesbian Life in Twentieth-Century America.* New York: Columbia University Press, 1991.

Hepp, U., and G, Milos. "Gender Identity Disorder and Eating Disorders," *International Journal of Eating Disorders* 32 (2002): 473–478.

Jacob, J. "Classifying Radical Drag Queen Appearances: The Importance of Shared Aesthetic Codes." In *ITAA Proceedings #60.* (Abstract obtained from http://www.itaaonline.org/downloads/P2OO3-Res-JacobJ-Classifying-Reso5i.pdf, 2003, accessed 19 July 2008.)

Levine, M. P. *Gay Macho: The Life and Death of the Homosexual Clone.* New York: New York University Press, 1998.

Morrison, M. A., T. G. Morrison, and C. Sager "Does Body Satisfaction Differ between Gay Men and Lesbian Women and Heterosexual Men and Women? A Meta-Analytic Review." *Body Image* i (1994): 127–138.

Pope, H. G., Jr., K. A. Phillips, and R. Olivardia. *The Adonis Complex: The Secret Crisis of Male Body Obsession.* New York: The Free Press, 2000.

Reilly, A., and N. A. Rudd. "Is Internalized Homonegativity Related to Body Image?" *Family and Consumer Sciences Research Journal* 35, no. i (2006): 58–73.

Rothblum, E. D. "Lesbians and Physical Appearance: Which Model Applies?" In *Psychological Perspectives on Lesbian and Gay Issues*, vol. i, edited by B. Greene and G. M. Herek, 84–97. Newberry Park, CA: Sage, 1994.

Rudd, N. A, "Appearance and Self-Presentation Research in Gay Consumer Cultures: Issues and Impact." *Journal of Homosexuality* 31, no. 1–2 (1996): 109–134.

Shrock, D., L. Reid, and E. M. Boyd. "Transsexuals Embodiment of Womanhood." *Gender & Society* 19, no. 3 (2005): 317–335.

Tajfel, H., and J. C. Turner. "An Integrative Theory of Intergroup Conflict." In *The Social Psychology of Intergroup Relations*, edited by E. G. Austin and S. Worchel, 33–47. Monterey, CA: Brooks-Cole, 1986.

Wolfradt, U., and K. Neumann. "Depersonalization, Self-Esteem and Body Image in Male-to-Female Transsexuals Compared to Male and Female Controls." *Archives of Sexual Behavior* 30, no. 3 (2001): 301–310.

Discussion Questions

1. Why is "dressing gay" or "dressing lesbian" necessary for some people?
2. Are there LGBT semiotic codes you know about that weren't included in this article? If so, what are they?
3. In what ways have LGBTI aesthetics influenced mainstream fashion?

QUEERS AND MODS: SOCIAL AND SARTORIAL INTERACTION IN LONDON'S CARNABY STREET

Shaun Cole

Menswear in Britain in the 1950s still to a great extent followed rules that had been established over the previous 150 years. Men's clothing had been developing into a form of camouflage, disguising differences in body shape and sexuality. On the whole men's clothing was conservative, particularly for those men not interested in fashion or those who could not afford to sustain an interest. There were, of course, exceptions: notably the young men influenced by the new generation of American stars of film and rock 'n' roll, "eccentrics" and flamboyant homosexuals. It was into this sombre and monochrome world, in November 1954, that physique photographer Basil 'Bill' Green introduced Vince Man's Shop and its European-influenced clothing, which was to lead the way in changes to come and was at the forefront of presenting an ostensibly queer look to fashionable heterosexual male consumers. With the subsequent opening three years later of former Vince's employee John Stephen's first Carnaby Street men's boutique, His Clothes, a previously "queer" look was disseminated to a broader straight male audience. This article examines how in the late 1950s and early 1960s members of the new youth subculture mod[1] wore the same clothes as gay men bought at Vince's and John Stephen's shops and created a fluid interchange of stylistic choices.

In the Beginning There Was Vince

Bill Green's first venture into clothing was producing swimming briefs "made from women's roll-ons from a well-known chain store" (Green on BBC, 1964). Such was their success that within six months he closed his photographic studio to concentrate on his mail-order business. By advertising his briefs in the very magazines, such as *Health and Strength*,[2] where he published his photographs, Green ensured increasing sales amongst the (gay and straight) bodybuilding community. Following a trip to France Green expanded his mail-order business by introducing the tight black jeans, shirts and sweaters favoured by French youth and "were unheard of in England [where] everyone still dreamed of imported Levi's" (Green cited in Cohn 1971, 64). Demand was such that on 1 November 1954 Green opened a shop at 5 Newburgh Street in London.[3] The choice of location was key: running parallel to Regent Street's main shopping and just a few streets away from Shaftesbury Avenue where Austin's and Cecil Gee were selling Italian influenced suits and American Ivy League college clothes. It was also close to Marshall Street baths, where Green's "muscle boys and butch trade" trained (Cohn 1971, 61), and on the fringes of Soho with its numerous gay clubs, bars and cafés,[4] which provided a receptive clientele for his clothes. Initially Vince's clothes were based on close-fitting European casual wear in sombre colours. Gradually Green introduced unusual fabrics, such as bed ticking, and vivid colour—reds, purples, and pinks—not normally used for men's clothes, but associated with gay men: "Pink shirt was definitely queer, colourful clothes were definitely queer" (Brighton Ourstory Project 1992, 52).[5]

John Stephen, who had worked as a sales assistant at Vince's after being poached from Moss Bros, initially based his influential and much-vaunted menswear shop, His Clothes, on Vince. By selling similar tight-fitting brightly coloured clothes and opening his shop on Carnaby Street just around the corner from Vince's he guaran-

---

Original for this text.

teed that he would attract the same customer base. As Robert Orbach noted, "the mods bought madras jackets and white jeans from Vince and had to pass John Stephen on the way" and so were drawn to the opportunity for greater choice (Orbach to Cole, 2011). Stephen's advantage over Green was that "I was the same age [as my customers] and into pop music, so I gave kids something they could wear to complement that" (Gorman 2006, 53). The success of His Clothes led Stephen to open a whole series of men's clothes shops in Carnaby Street, and precipitated an influx of new menswear shops, such as Lord John and Domino Male. By 1963 Stephen owned eighteen shops all over central London, His Clothes was worth £1 million, and the *Observer* named him the Million-Pound Mod. Peter Burton noted "as a queen designing and cutting clothes that were tighter and tighter" he was projecting a gay man's ideal of the sixties male body "on the straight boys as well" (Burton to Cole, 1997). Stephen himself became a style icon for mods, but in wearing his own designed clothes, sharply tailored suit, shirt, tie, and highly polished shoes (Reed 2010, 19), he was subliminally promoting a "gay male style" to an ostensibly straight but narcissistic image-obsessed group of young males, as Stephen was presented to the majority of his customers and the press as "straight" and thus could be described as "passing."

Vince's wasn't the only shop in London selling specifically to gay men. Others included Dale Kavanagh in Kinnerton Street, described by Christopher Gibbs as "Noel Coward-y—fancy bits of tailoring for people who wanted to startle the evening" (Gorman 2006, 32) and John Ingram's Sportique on Old Compton Street, which sold "fey clobber" (Loog Oldham cited in Gorman 2009, 67) such as narrow lapel madras cotton blazers, black polo-neck sweaters, and fly front voile shirts and was where shop assistant Richard Young "first came across gays, art, cinema, theatre and a much heavier sense of rock 'n' roll" (cited in Gorman 2009, 67).[6] Like Vince's, these shops were also introducing "queer" styles to adventurous and stylish young heterosexual men. Vince's, His Clothes, and Sportique were all cited in an article in *The Outfitter* trade jour-

nal in April 1963, where these boutiques were described as catering and appealing to "the Doubting Thomases, Kinky, fetishist, queer" (Wright 1963, 14).

Discourse Communities

In his discussion of gay fashions in Montreal, Ross Higgins utilises John Swales's "discourse community" model to study gay men as consumers of fashion in relation to the development of public gay communities. He employs this model because a discourse community uses "its genre for the expression of knowledge and attitudes particular to its social viewpoint" (Higgins 1998, 134). Higgins's argument is that fashion as a topic of conversation was a major constituent in the formation and development of a sense of collective gay identity. This model could similarly be applied to both the gay and mod worlds of 1960s London. The early mods, or modernists, operated as a discourse community "when a few teenagers emerged as utter clothes fanatics, obsessive to a degree that had been unknown before" (Cohn 2009b, 167) and began to be drawn to one another over their individual style. As the style of the individual "faces" evolved into the subculture of "mod" so consensus on clothing and styles formed a key part of the discourse among this subcultural community; as Justin de Villeneuve noted, "you became a modernist by wearing the right kind of clothes . . . it was a group thing, a way of life interpreted by clothes" (Gorman 2006, 37).

Overt gay men had been discussing their use of dress to announce their sexuality and sexual interests for decades. Within this specific "discourse community" discussion must have played a part to enable the members of the "community" to devise strategies and to follow (often female) fashions, for elements such as hair colour. Among covert gay communities too there was discussion of fashions and dress, particularly around the smaller signifiers, such as suede shoes or pinkie (little finger) rings, that were appropriate to signify homosexuality.[7] Covert homosexuals resented the presence of overt gay men as they drew unnecessary attention to a subculture that otherwise could pass through mainstream society and life relatively unnoticed or ignored. Cohen and Dyer (1980, 172–173) meanwhile recognise the importance of collective knowledge within gay communities as a means of communication and association. Among London's gay "community" of the 1960s this can also be related to the use of the underground language Polari, which despite its secret gay usage was "exposed" on the BBC radio programme Round the Horne. Two particular episodes, "Bona Drag" and "Carnaby Street Hunt," used Polari to discuss fashion and approximates clothing descriptors in Vince's catalogues.[8]

Selling Gay Style

Reactions to the clothes at both His Clothes and Vince's were mixed. In 1964 Green observed, "People said the stuff was so outrageous that it would only appeal and sell to the rather sort of eccentric Chelsea set or theatrical way-out types" (Green, 1964). Seven years later Green was more explicit, stating "everyone thought we only sold to Chelsea homosexuals" but "in actual fact, we catered to a very wide public . . . artists and theatricals, muscle boys, and celebrities of every kind" (Cohn 1971, 61).[9] I would argue that this description only serves to underline the gayness of Vince's clients—"theatricals" and "artists" were expressions frequently employed to euphemistically describe men who were, or were suspected of being, gay, and his list of celebrities included John Gielgud (who officially came out as gay in the 1990s but was well known in London circles to be gay). John Hardy, who worked as both a model and shop assistant at Vince's, confirms that a high percentage of Vince's clients were gay and the clothes appealed because "[we] were looking for something different to wear" and Vince's was "the first firm that made things that were really chic" (Hardy to Cole 1995). Mod Martin Stone recalled buying a red-and-white gingham shirt at Vince's after initially hesitating about entering the shop because of its reputation as a shop for gay men (Reed 2010, 11). Stephen's early customers recalled the impact: "We didn't realise

it then, but the John Stephen revolution was a very gay thing. Youth wanted this way of dressing for themselves because it was a way of rebelling. . . . It was self-consciously trendy and camp in the true sense of the word" (Gorman 2006, 55). The association of homosexuality with Stephen's and Green's shops may not, of course, have been unquestionably good for business in those pre-liberation days. While there were many homosexuals in London buying his clothes this was limited market, and Green was keen to expand. His clothes were advertised in trade press such as Men's Wear and by continuing to advertise in non-fashion magazines such as Films and Filming, Green ensured that Vince's had a wider audience. Stephen of course had the advantage of a new youth market.

As well as selling "camp" and outrageously coloured clothing, many of Vince's garments, particularly those for sale in the twice-yearly catalogues, were designed to show off the body (Figure 5.15).[10] The close-fitting white "Torso Shirt" (which first appeared in the 1961 catalogue but had been available earlier simply as "tailored T-shirt") was presented on muscular young men with the description "Thumbs up for this masculine modern T-shirt . . . with bicep-baring sleeves." A development of Vince's original tight black jeans, the "Corsair slacks," was described as "beautifully cut Bermuda style (and that means made for a close fit everywhere)," a barely euphemistic way of emphasising their crotch-hugging nature.[11] Names of swimwear—"Tangier," "Mallorca," "Capri" (1963), "Bondi beach" (1964)—and shirts—"Ibiza" and "Fire Island" (1967)—referenced gay holiday destinations, while swimming trunks called "Butch" and "Trade Wind" and a jacket called "Sun Cruiser" demonstrated a familiarity with underground gay slang Polari, that to the unsuspecting would have seemed perfectly innocent.[12] Many of the non-professional models' poses were drawn directly from physique photography; at least a quarter of the shots were devoted to muscular young men modeling brief swimwear.[13] The catalogue photographs and illustrations (that drew on the work of illustrators such as George Quaintance) confirm that for some gay men a masculine image held a certain appeal. When advertising His

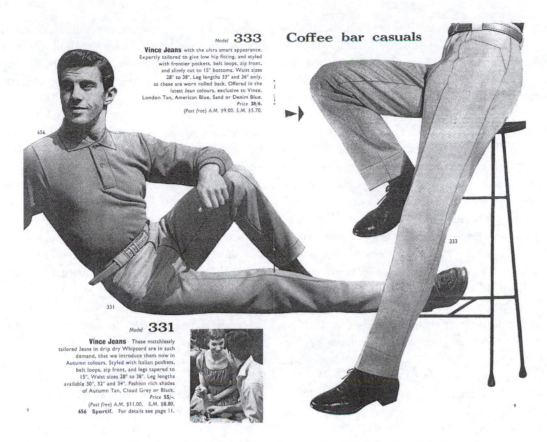

Figure 5.15 Many of the garments by Vince Man's Shop, particularly those for sale in its catalogs, were designed to show off the body.

Clothes, John Stephen initially employed similar illustrations of both muscular young men and fashionable figures wearing tight trousers, sweater shirts, and quaffed hair, that Jeremy Reed has argued were "recognisable to readers as a gay stereotype" (2010, 36).

In a clever appointment Green employed the bodybuilder (and later actor) John Hamill as a shop assistant. Dressed in a white Torso T-shirt and jeans (the new uniform of the sexy teenager, musician, and delinquent), he attracted customers who had previously bought Vince's photographs of Hamill and wanted to see his toned body "in the flesh" (Smith to Cole, 2011). John Stephen and his (gay) interior designer Myles Antony employed a similar technique in 1962 when they invited boxer Billy Walker to model for blow-up photographs for the Carnaby Street windows of His Clothes. While this reinforced a queer presentation of men's clothing, as Nik Cohn observed, Walker was "worshipped so much that not even pink denims could sully his manhood" (Cohn 2009a, 51). Antony's use of camp referencing in his interiors and window displays provided a further gay sensibility in Carnaby Street. As well as offering "gay" clothes to the customers, the surroundings of the shop projected a gay man's fantastical ideas to an unknowing but appreciative young, predominantly, though by no means exclusively heterosexual audience.[14]

Italian Style and Tight Trousers

The popularity of well-tailored fitted Italian-style suits, initially introduced in Britain by Cecil Gee in 1956, lay in their difference from the heavy structured double-breasted American-style suits that had been popular in the years after the Second World War. Using lighter fabrics and less heavy tailoring techniques, they offered a stylish alternative to the growing number of independent young teenage men with a disposable income and a desire to dress differently from their fathers. Tony Woodcock (well aware of his sexual orientation even as a teenager) remembered "the Italian look, with three buttons, that was very mod . . . My trousers were creased, my sleeves creased, everything" (Woodcock to Cole, 1993). Similarly heterosexual John Pearse wore "ridiculous short jackets with little belts on them, tight trousers and shoes which seemed to go on and on and extended into infinity" (Gorman 2006, 35). Some young men (both gay and straight) saw the slim-fitting European styles when visiting the continent during or after their National Service or in the new wave of French and Italian films. Willie Deasey from east London recalled, "The clothes the French guys wore were so well-cut . . . They had hipster trousers and round-toed shoes, beautiful shoes. They had well-cut suits made from lightweight fabrics" (Barnes 1991, 9). John Hardy observed that "if you look at some of the Italian cinema of the time, like . . . *Bitter Rice* . . . all the men wore jeans that were very tight" (Hardy to Cole, 1995). Similarly, Johnny Moke and his friends went "to all those foreign movies" such as *A Bout de Souffle* and "watched the way they smoked a cigarette, how they buttoned their shirts and jackets, which shoes they wore" (cited in Gorman 2006, 62–63).

The snug European-style clothes appealed particularly to young gay men who were aware of their bodies and the sexual allure of showing them off. Michael Brown was drawn to the body-conscious nature of Vince's clothes, which he initially saw in advertisements in *Health and Strength* magazine. In 1958 he bought a pair of "tight-fitting gold coloured trousers" from Vince's that were "quite thin to show everything." The crotch-hugging fit appealed to Brown because he "wanted to show off my packet" to "attract men's attention" and so he "wore them without underwear" for an even more revealing fit (Brown to Cole, 2011). After viewing Vince's catalogues Brown

agreed that his gold trousers were almost certainly "Vince jeans model 333" featured in the 1958/59 catalogue: "Expertly tailored to give low hip fitting . . . Offered in the latest Jean colours, exclusive to Vince. London Tan, American Blue, Sand or Denim Blue" (see Figure 5.15). Dick Lawson recalled in a similar vein, "I wore extremely tight, light-coloured trousers with no underwear, and you knew, on the tube that somebody was always going to be offended. And I was intending to offend them" (Reed 2010, 241). While there was a similarity in the gay and straight adoption of tight trousers in the period, Vince's customer James Gardiner believes that a difference lies in the way in which gay men are "conscious of their powers of sexual attractiveness in a way that straight men aren't" and subsequently "in the sixties the queens wore much tighter trousers" (Gardiner to Cole 1997). In Colin MacInnes's *Absolute Beginners*, the fashionable gay character, the Fabulous Hoplite, wears "a pair of skin-tight, rubber-glove thin, almost transparent cotton slacks, white nylon-stretch" (1992 [1959], 51) which were almost certainly based on Vince or John Stephen's garments. Contemporary newspaper reporters and commentators also noted the crotch-revealing nature of young (straight) men's trousers, with John Crosby noting in *Weekend Telegraph* "tight pants that fit on the hips like ski pants" (cited in Gorman 2006, 56) and Tom Wolfe noting the "boys in codpiece pants" (1999, 89).

Mods, Effeminacy, and Androgyny

Dick Hebdige described mods as "typical lower-class dand[ies]" who were "obsessed with the small details of dress . . . the angle of a shirt collar, measured as precisely as the vents in his custom-made jacket" (Hebdige 1987, 52). This overt fastidious concern with their appearance was not something that was encouraged in working- or lower-middle-class men, as it was seen as essentially feminine, and by association as "queer." As Barry Fantoni recalled in 1967 "it was considered somewhat unmanly to take a proper interest in clothes, and the gay young men who began to make a regular pilgrimage to Carnaby Street were at first the only ones to appreciate what they were being offered. In those days you still wondered if a man in a pink shirt wasn't queer" (Reed 2010, 224).

While mod was not a predominantly homosexual style, many of the clothes the mods were wearing *were* those that certain gay men were wearing. Richard Barnes recalled that when shopping on Carnaby Street "the only other person we saw was a tall, well-dressed young negro [*sic*] who bought a pair of the coloured denim hipster trousers. The negro [*sic*] was obviously homosexual and I realised that homosexuals had been buying that stuff for years. They were the only people with the nerve to wear it, but in the early sixties the climate of opinion was changing, the mods were wearing the more effeminate and colourful clothes of Carnaby Street" (Barnes 1991, 10). Ken Browne similarly recalled that there was "a definite gay influence involved with the early Mods. The London clubs would have a lot of gays in them wearing outrageous white suits with big high heels. Mods took that influence" (Rawlings 2000, 50). Even if all mods were not consciously copying gay styles, many were aware of the associations of the garments they were wearing. "Some of our clothes are a bit effeminate," Peter Sugar told *Town* magazine in 1962, "but they have to be. I mean you have to be a bit camp. I mean who cares" (cited in Rawlings 2000, 46).

Both Lloyd Johnson and Carlo Manzi recalled the reactions they received after buying and wearing pink shirts. Johnson and his friend both bought pink tab-collared shirts, but Johnson's friend exchanged his for a white version "because people were calling him a poof." Johnson, however, kept his and wore it despite the concerned looks he received whilst commuting (Reed 2010, 44). Manzi's pink shirt elicited a horrified reaction from his mother, who tore it up to make dusters because, she told Manzi "everyone will think you're a poof" and offered him money to buy a new shirt that wasn't pink (Hewitt 2000, 54). The previously "queer" styles of clothes mods were adopting were accompanied by makeup and elaborate hairstyles, that were, according to David May, styled in women's hairdressers (Hewitt 2009, 52). This led increasingly to reflections on how the "boys looked a bit like girls" (Peter Townshend

cited in Reed 2010, 76) and as Willie Dearsy recalled "as the boys got more feminine, so the girls got more masculine" (Barnes 1991, 16).[15]

Along with queer and Italian influences, mods' dress was also, Hebdige noted, influenced by the smartness of West Indian immigrants, and the perceived "underworld" of that community offered an escape to where the "values, norms and conventions of the 'straight' world were inverted" (Hebdige 1987; 53). What Hebdige fails to note, though the use of his term "straight" world does perhaps give us an indication, is the crossover between the gay underworld and the emergent mod world. In his autobiography, Peter Burton (1985, 30–31) makes comparisons between the mods' clubs (the Scene in Ham Yard) and the gay coffee bars (La Duce in D'Arblay Street[16]) of Soho, London. Both groups, he notes, were wearing the same clothes (bought at Vince and John Stephen), listening to the same music (soul, ska, bluebeat, and Motown) and taking the same drugs (speed, known as blues or doobs) and inevitably interaction was occurring between the two. Richard Barnes anxiously concedes that "mods were more interested in themselves and each other than in girls" and that "the boys *were* effeminate" but concludes that "they weren't homosexual." He plays down any homosexuality that occurred among mods, stating that "there may have been a homosexual element, though, but then there might also have been among rockers, and it wasn't particularly important" (1991, 15). Ken Browne recalled that he "never knew any gay mods" and that although "every single one [he] met was very heterosexual," he does not deny the existence of gay mods (Rawlings 2000, 50). But gay men *were* present in the subculture: David Scoular told Murray Healy, "I was interested in mods. I was a mod then, shirts, cravats—I had a scooter . . . there were big changes going on, and it wasn't just about being gay" (Healy 1996, 63–64).

The interest in appearance with the almost exclusively male constituency of the early mod subculture led Mark Feld (later to be the bisexual glam rock star Marc Bolan) to reflect "that mod was mentally a very homosexual thing, though not in any physical sense" (Cohn 1971, 80). Drawing from the relative androgyny of some mod fashion Kenneth Leech stated that "it was an implicitly homosexual, or, more accurately, bisexual phenomenon" (Leech 1973, 3), promoting the presupposition that feminine representational codes evidenced homosexuality. Despite negative assumptions and denials, mod potentially provided access to a homosexual identity, for as Jon Savage stated, "the mods assumed what had been an exclusively and outrageously homosexual style and used it as a key to cross into the 'private' space of the body and of self-discovery" (Savage 1990, 160). Thus the mods were attempting to challenge the hegemony of men's fashion and acceptable appearance by adopting feminine or queer attributes, and in "sharing elements with established gay subcultures, it was potentially transgressive, delinquent, deviant and a little bit queer" (Healy 1996, 35).

Conclusion

The flourishing of the Carnaby Street men's shops brought an essentially "queer" look to a heterosexual market. Adolescents who abandoned conventional stereotypes of masculinity and adopted "effeminate" colours and long hair prompted much discussion. In 1964 the *Sunday Times Magazine* reassured the public that "there is nothing essentially queer about boys who display an overt, gossipy, fascinated interest in what to wear with what. Their other hobby is girls" (cited in Chenoune 1993, 258). Yet the association of homosexuality was still evident. A 1965 French guide to London joked that His Clothes should be called "*Her Clothes*, because shirts tend to be pink and the salesman only too willing to try them on for you" (cited in Chenoune 1993, 258). While the early mods had elicited much comment for their adoption of an effeminate appearance, as the subculture became more widespread it became more masculine. Instead of spending time preening and parading for each other, later mods were paying more attention to dancing, taking drugs, chasing girls, and fighting. But for many of the original modernists "clothes were still the most important factor" (Paul Stagg cited in Rawlings 2000, 77) and they "stopped calling themselves mods and carried on as before as Stylists" (Barnes 1991,

128). But as the 1960s progressed many fashionable young men continued to introduce elements of androgyny into their clothing. By the late 1960s when John Stephen had cornered the London market for young mods and continued to build his youth fashion empire and a new set of men's boutiques were opening up, Bill Green remained true to his now older, original muscle boy and gay clientele, selling clothes that "make the sophisticated man both look and feel younger" (Bennett-England 1967, 42). In 1967 Vince's moved out of the Carnaby Street area and in 1969 Green closed his clothing business to open a restaurant named Aunties. But the attitude toward clothes and the style that Green had launched at Vince's and that had been successfully translated into a new youth style by John Stephen clearly had an influence firstly on mod subcultural style and later on mainstream men's fashion, bringing to a broad audience of male consumers clothes that had previously been worn by "no one but queers" (Cohn 1971, 62).

References

Barnes, Richard. 1991 (1979). *Mods!* London: Eel Pie.
BBC Radio 'Gear Street' part of 'South East Special' Series. Broadcast 22 August 1964.
Bennett-England, Rodney. 1967. *Dress Optional: The Revolution in Menswear.* London: Peter Owen.
Brighton Ourstory Project. 1992. *Daring Hearts: Lesbian and Gay Lives of 50s and 60s Brighton,* Brighton: Queenspark Books.
Burton, Peter. 1985. *Parallel Lives.* London: GMP.
Chenoune, Farid. 1993. *A History of Men's Dress.* Paris: Flammarion.
Cohn, Nik. 1971. *Today there are no Gentlemen. The changes in Englishmen's clothes since the War,* London: Weidenfeld and Nicholson.
Cohn, Nik. 2009a. Carnaby Street. In *The Sharper Word: A Mod Anthology,* ed. Paolo Hewitt. London: Helter Skelter.
Cohn, Nik. 2009b. Mods. In *The Sharper Word: A Mod Anthology,* ed. Paolo Hewitt. London: Helter Skelter.
Cole, Shaun. 2000. *Don We Now Our Gay Apparel: Gay Men's Dress in the Twentieth Century.* Oxford: Berg.
Gorman, Paul. 2006 *The Look: Adventures in Rock and Pop Fashion.* London: Adelita.
Healy, Murray. 1996. *Gay Skins: Class, Masculinity and Queer Appropriation.* London: Cassell.
Hebdige, Dick. 1987. *Subculture: the meaning of style* London: Routledge.
Hewitt, Paolo. 2000. *The Soul Stylists: Forty Years of Modernism.* Edinburgh: Mainstream Publishing.

Hewitt, Paolo ed. 2009. *The Sharper Word: A Mod Anthology*. London: Helter Skelter.

Higgins, Ross. 1998. Fashioning Gay Community in Montreal. In eds. Anne Brydon and Sandra Niessen *Consuming Fashion: Adorning the Transnational Body*. 129–161. Oxford and New York: Berg.

Leech, Kenneth. 1973. *Youthquake: The growth of a counter-culture through two decades*. London: Sheldon Press.

Rawlings, Terry. 2000. *Mod: A Very British Phenomenon* London: Omnibus.

Reed, Jeremy. 2010. *The King of Carnaby Street: The Life of John Stephen*. London: Haus Publishing.

Savage, Jon. 1990. Tainted Love: The influence of male homosexuality and sexual divergence on pop music and culture since the war. In *Consumption, identity and style: marketing, meanings and the packaging of pleasure*, ed. Alan Tomlinson. London: Routledge.

Wolfe, Tom. 1999 [1969]. *The Pump House Gang*. New York: Bantam.

Wright, Keith. 1963. The Way of the Boutiques. *The Outfitter* 27 April. 14–15.

Interviews with Author

Michael Brown, 2011
Peter Burton, 1997
James Gardiner, 1997
John Hardy, 1995
Robert Orbach, 2011
Rupert Smith, 2011
Colin Woodhead, 2004

Endnotes

1. For more detail on the particulars of mod style and the development of the subculture see Richard Barnes, 1979, *Mods!*, London: Eel Pie; Paolo Hewitt, 2000, *The Soul Stylists: Forty Years of Modernism*, Edinburgh: Mainstream Publishing; Paolo Hewitt, ed., 2009, *The Sharper Word: A Mod Anthology*, London: Helter Skelter; and Terry Rawlings, 2000, *Mod: A Very British Phenomenon*, London: Omnibus.

2. British physical culture, such as boxing and wrestling magazines of the 1950s, were ostensibly heterosexual, but the scenarios created by the illustrators and photographers had a homoerotic appeal and a wide homosexual audience. American and European magazines were far more aware of their homosexual readership and some, *Der Kries* for example, were in fact early gay magazines, which changed hands "under the counter."

3. Date drawn from "The Vince Saga"—Bill Green's personal account of his interests. I would like to thank Stephen Cartwright for allowing me access to this document.

4. For more on the development of Soho see Frank Mort, *Cultures of Consumption*, London: Routledge, 1996, pp.151–157 and for the development of the Soho gay scene see James Gardiner, *A Class Apart: The Private Pictures of Montague Glover*, London: Serpent's Tail, 1992, pp.17–19; Peter Burton, *Parallel Lives*, London: Gay Men's Press, 1985, pp.14–45; and Derek Jarman, *At Your Own Risk*, London: Hutchinson, 1992, pp.47–49.

5. See Cohn 1971 and Cole 2000 for more on the association of bright colour and tight-fitting clothing with homosexuality.

6. The gay dandy Bunny Roger also frequented Sportique buying shirts, socks, and silk Jacques Fath ties, making a link between the burgeoning dandified modernist faces and the earlier upper-class "subcultural" style of the New Edwardians. For more on this as a gay-inspired style see Cole 2000, 22–24.

7. See Cole 2000, 59–69.

8. Polari, or Parlare, was an underground slang associated with the gay community. It was probably derived from the language of 18th- and 19th-century theatre and show people as well as a version of Romany known as "parlyaree." The version known to gay men appears to have been passed on through the Merchant navy. It drew words not only from theatre slang and romance languages but also from Cockney rhyming slang, back slang, and Yiddish. In the 1960s Polari was popularised by the camp characters of Julian and Sandy in the radio programme *Round the Horne*, with stock phrases such as "how bona to vada your dolly eek" ("How nice to see your pretty face") and "oo, in 'e butch" ("Isn't he masculine").

9. Interestingly Green does not mention homosexuals as clients in his interview in Rodney Bennett England's 1967 book *Dress Optional*. This was the year of the partial decriminalisation of homosexuality in Britain and this and the rise of a gay liberation movement may account for the more forthright description with Cohn in 1971.

10. Peter Burton noted that Vince's catalogues "could almost be classified as an early gay magazine" (1985, 30) and as such they were acquired by gay men as much for the images as for the opportunity to purchase clothes (Smith to Cole, 2011). Courtney Reeds, near Leicester Square, also produced a catalogue in the late 1950s which Graham Hughes described as "close to being able to buy a porn book as you could get" (Reed 2010, 11–12).

11. John Stephen, like Green, had deliberately set out to create close-fitting flattering trousers, as he told the *Sunday Times*: "it seemed to me that too much material was being used in most men's clothes. Trousers had so

much room in the seat that they were quite shapeless. Shirt manufacturers had no idea about tapering to the waist, and swimwear lacked any style" (cited in Reed 2010, 3). Tailor Joe Marcus told his nephew that he had developed close-fitting hipster trousers for Moss Bros for financial reasons; lowering the waist and shortening the rise meant that less fabric was used in each pair of trousers and so more pairs could be made from each roll of fabric (Orbach to Cole, 2011).

12. In Polari "butch" meant masculine, "cruising" meant looking for sex, and "trade" referred to men who were sexually available though not necessarily homosexual.

13. The men Green used were never professional models because "they look too much like what they are" (Bennett-England 1967, 129) but instead his existing bodybuilding clients or acquaintances. The young out-of-work actor Sean Connery appeared in the Summer 1953 catalogue and in 1954 he persuaded the handsome young guardsman John Hardy to model for the summer catalogue.

14. This reflected the fact that the clothes were born of the mind of a gay designer and had a particular aesthetic that would not have been present had Stephen (or Antony) been straight. For more on the ideas of queer space see Peter McNeil, 2010, Crafting queer spaces: privacy and posturing, In eds. Alla Myzelev and John Potvin, *Fashion, interior design, and the contours of modern identity*, Farnham: Ashgate.

15. There is not scope in this article to explore this increased masculinisation of women's clothes and the way in which men's and women's clothing and appearance became increasingly similar as the 1960s progressed, but this would make an interesting exploration, particularly if it addressed associations with lesbian subcultures.

16. John Stephen and his gay friends frequented Le Duce and so mixed with gay and straight mods who were his customers (Reed 2010,118).

Discussion Questions

1. How did shop owners try to attract a specifically gay audience in London during this period?
2. Describe your understanding of mod style.
3. How could you tell a mod from a queer based on appearance in late 1950s–early 1960s London?

CHAPTER 6

RACE AND ETHNICITY

Andrew Reilly

After you have read this chapter, you will understand:

- That people have culturally constructed categories of race and ethnicity affecting social issues and problems regarding appearance
- The relationship of race and ethnicity—particularly as they affect issues of appearance—to gain an appreciation for the experience of those in the minority in American society
- The impact that issues of race and ethnicity have on consumer culture

Race

The term **race** refers to certain visible and distinctive characteristics that are determined by biology. Along with gender and age, race is one of the first things we notice about another person. Race is also a social construction, meaning that, like gender and sexuality, the concept of race is created artificially, based on physical markers, as a way of grouping people together based on what one particular culture defines as socially significant. In the United States there are six government-created categories of race (created for the census): White, Black or African American, American Indian or Alaskan Native, Asian, Hawaiian Native or Pacific Islander, and Other.[1]

The terms "black" and "white" are problematic in that not all cultures understand the terms the same way. In the United Kingdom, the term "black" is used to refer to all people who are not white. In South Africa, the government recognizes four racial categories: black, white, colored, and Indian; but during Apartheid (legalized racial segregation in South Africa, 1948–1994) a person was considered black if a pencil placed in his or her hair remained or fell out (hair texture was a sign of "whiteness" or "blackness"). If it fell out, the person was white, if it remained, the person was black. An African American visiting Tanzania is likely to be considered white by the native African black people (Newman, 1995). Even in the United States the divisions between white and black were not always understood; in the not too distant past, Italians and Greeks were considered not white, though they were not black either. Hence, racial categories vary among geographic regions as a way of identifying people, based on place of birth and on arbitrary physical characteristics.

In the United States, people of mixed races usually are identified by one race or the other. The United States adheres to the one-drop rule. This applies mostly to black or African American people, coming from a common antebellum law in the South that defined a person as black if he or she had a "single drop of black blood." For example, President Barack Obama has a white mother and African father; however he is typically referred to as the "first black president." Anthropologists call this a "hypodescent rule," meaning that racially mixed people are always assigned the status of the subordinate group, likely in order to keep the dominant race "pure." Hence, a person with seven out of eight great-grandparents who are white and only one who is black is still considered black.

Racial categories often lead to judgments about beauty and attractiveness (among other characteristics). Historically, dominant groups were considered more attractive than subordinate groups. This has resulted in subordinate groups attempting to change their body aesthetics—skin tone, hair, facial features, body shape—in order to fit in with the dominant version of beauty. However, with various racial groups increasing in population and more sensitivity given to multicultural heritages, many people are rejecting dominant-white standards of beauty and looking to their ancestors for guidance. In this chapter, the article "Why Michelle Obama's Hair Matters" elaborates on the significance of and tensions surrounding the hair of black women.

Nonetheless, cosmetic surgeons in the United States are experiencing an increase in the number of patients of different races who want to become more socially attractive. Changes to eyes, nose, lips, and skin color are becoming common among minority groups. According to the American Society of Plastic Surgeons, 24% of all cosmetic procedures in 2007 were done on Hispanic, Asian, and other nonwhite patients. However, a recent study reveals that the perception that the dominate group is more attractive may be changing. A study by Lewis (2010) finds that people perceive mixed-race faces to be more attractive than either black or white faces. Several theories are offered for this finding, including the observation of more mixed-racial celebrities as well as Darwinian theory that cross-breeding yields stronger, healthier, more attractive species.

Ethnicity

The term **ethnicity** refers to learned cultural heritage that is shared by a group of people. It typically includes a common national origin, ancestry, language, dietary habits, ideology, and style of dress. Ethnicity is different from race yet the term is frequently, and inappropriately, used interchangeably. For example, Chinese Americans are quite different ethnically from Chinese people born in China, although their racial background may be identical. Furthermore, people in China may identify by one of 56 officially recognized Chinese ethnicities, including the most populous, the Han. Similarly, India has over 600 officially recognized ethnicities, and Africa, with between 1,000 and 3,000, is the most ethnically diverse continent in the world. Thus, even the concept of grouping people together by country or continent does not truly recognize different individual, cultural groups.

Ethnicity plays a significant role in others' perceptions of a person's appearance. Sociologist Paul Starr (1982) found that, in the absence of distinctive skin color and other physical characteristics, ethnicity is judged by others on the basis of many imprecise attributes such as language, residence, and dress (clothing, accessories, and body markings). Dress is an important marker of identity, as social identity theory posits (Tajfel and Turner, 1986; also discussed in Chapter 2). According to this theory, people are first categorized into groups; an individual then identifies with one of the groups; groups then compare themselves to other groups and develop group distinctiveness, or note what makes their group different (sometimes better) than other groups. Often, this revolves around dress and adornment to show differences between ethnic groups and affiliation with an ethnic group. Mikiko Ashikari further examines the question of "us versus them" in the reading "Japanese Kind of Whiteness: Women's Face-Whitening Practice and the Contemporary Japanese Identity." In Japan, skin tone is defined as white or black, with good or bad connotations, respectively. The desire for Japanese men and women to have white skin is not a desire to look Caucasian, as many people assume, but lies instead in Japanese ethnic identity.

Veena Chattaraman also explores the issue of ethnicity and dress in "Cultural Markers in Dress: Decoding Meanings and Motivations of College Students." She discusses how ethnic and ethnic-inspired dress is used to celebrate one's ancestral past, culture, and show respect to one's heritage. Note some similarities in this paper and in Mikiko Ashikari's paper on Japanese skin color in identifying "us versus them."

Ethnic dress, sometimes called "folk costume," is the dress of a particular group of people indigenous to a particular area, though one need not have lived in that area to claim ethnic affiliation. Ethnic affiliation might come in the form of color, silhouette, pattern motif, pattern size, or use of a garment. Many ethnicities have unique garments that are immediately recognizable (see Figures 6.1a–c). The Japanese have the *kosode*, with its loose fit and square sleeves.

Figure 6.1 Ethnic groups have clothing styles unique to their heritage. The Japanese wear a kosode (a), the Tuareg wear scarves that turn their skin blue (b), and the Indians wear a sari wrapped around their bodies (c).

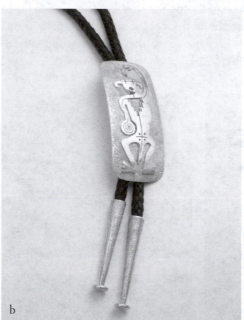

Figure 6.2 Like clothing, jewelry can also identify ethnic heritage, as seen in the different stylings of Navajo (a) and Hopi (b) jewelry.

The Scots have the woolen kilt, with each plaid design unique to a particular clan. The Tuareg of North Africa wear indigo-dyed cloaks, leaving their skin blue, giving them the epithet "the blue men." In India, the sari is ubiquitous. Made of one long strip of cloth, it is wrapped around and draped over the body, but the specific wrapping, draping, color, and embroidery vary by village or ethnic affiliation.

In addition to cloth garments, jewelry also designates ethnicity. For example, the Navajo, Zuni, and Hopi Native American tribes all wear jewelry, but the style of jewelry is different from each other (see Figures 6.2a and b). Navajo jewelry is made with stones, usually turquoise, in their natural shape. The stones are set in silver that outlines the stone's natural silhouette. In contrast, Zuni jewelry is made from stones that have been precisely cut and placed into mosaics outlined in silver. The Hopi, however, rarely use stones in their jewelry. Their jewelry tends to be polished silver with shapes and symbols carved into the smooth surface. Each of these differences in jewelry is immediately recognizable as being from its respective tribe.

In addition to cloth garments and accessories, altering the body is another way to display ethnic affiliation. Though tattoos in Polynesia are common, the style differs among tribes: traditional Hawaiian tattoos use straight lines and geometric motifs with no curves, traditional Samoan are geometric and linear and cover large portions of the body, traditional Tahitian tattoos are curved, and traditional Maori tattoos look like rope with curved ends (see Figure 6.3).

Ethnic Dress and Change

Although ethnic dress can remain unchanged for generations, that does not mean dress never changes. New technologies, new products, and new ideas that are introduced to a culture can be adapted to become "culturally authentic." Cultural authentication is the process whereby a foreign object (e.g., clothing) is incorporated into a culture and becomes authentic to that culture. There are four steps to cultural authentication (Eicher and Erekosima, 1980), though Arthur (1997) argues they need not occur in this specific order: selection (adopting an object); characterization (the new culture gives meaning to the object); incorporation (identifying the object to a social group); and transformation (physically altering the object to allow for cultural distinctiveness). Rachel Pannabecker uses this concept to examine how ribbons became culturally authenticated among Great Lakes Indians in the reading "Tastily Bound with Ribands: Ribbon-Bordered Dress of the Great Lakes Indians, 1735–1839."

Figure 6.3 Body art, such as tattoo, can be markers of ethnic identity, such as this Maori tattoo.

Ethnic dress is often used as a source of inspiration for a designer's collections. Ethnic dress was in vogue in the United States in the 1960s and 1970s when American society was taking a renewed interest in people's origins, news broadcasters were reporting on wars that were being waged in foreign countries, and new trading with countries (such as China) opened doors to new resources and aesthetics. Yves Saint Laurent presented many lines that were inspired by the everyday dress of people in Morocco, Africa, and Russia, and John Galliano took inspiration from Egyptian costume for one of his Dior Couture collections (see Figures 6.4a and b).

Yet, at times, the commoditization of ethnic dress as fashion is met with resistance. Some people find the co-opting of sacred or important markers of ethnic identity for a season or two by the fashion industry to be disingenuous. People argue that it degrades ethnicity into a mere costume party. Sunita Puri gives her opinion about fashion and ethnicity in the reading "'Ethnic Fashion' Obscures Cultural Identity." Other questions—such as the authenticity of ethnic garments used as fashion items—pose dilemmas, such as, who has the right to create ethnic

Figure 6.4 Fashion designers find inspiration in the unique attire of ethnic people and interpret it in their collections. YSL found inspiration from Russians (a) and Galliano for Dior found inspiration from the Egyptians (b).

fashions or who has the right to profit from ethnic fashions? Thomas Hylland Eriksen explores this issue of ethnic authenticity and fashion in his examination of the Norwegian *bunad* in the reading "Dress between the Sacred and the Commercial: The Case of the Norwegian Bunad."

Summary

This chapter focuses on the difference between race and ethnicity and how they are manifested through clothing and appearance. Race is a nebulous term whose purpose is to group people together based on very general appearance terms. Ethnicity, on the other hand, is a term that specifies a person's cultural heritage. Ethnic groups tend to have very specific forms of dress that do not change with the fashions. But then they are used as fashion and it can create conflict between established identity and temporary style.

Suggested Readings

Daly, M. C. (1999). "Ah, a Real Kalabari Woman?": Reflexivity and the Conceptualization of Appearance. *Fashion Theory* 3 (13): 343–362.

Forney, J. C. and N. J. Rabolt. (1986). Ethnic Identity: Its Relationship to Ethnic and Contemporary Dress. *Clothing and Textiles Research Journal* 4 (2): 1–8.

Holloman, L. (1990). Clothing Symbolism in African American Greek letter organizations. In B. Starke, L. Holloman, and B. Nordquist (Eds.), *African American Dress and Adornment: A Cultural Perspective*, 140–150. Dubuque, IA: Kendal Hunt Publishing Co.

Hooks, B. (1992). *Black Looks: Race and Representation*. Boston: South End Press.

Maynard, M. (2000). Grassroots Style. Reevaluating Australian Fashion and Aboriginal Art in the 70s and 80s. *Journal of Design History* 13 (2): 137–150.

Mercer, K. (1991). Black Hair/Style Politics. In *Out There: Marginalization and Contemporary Cultures*, 247–264. Cambridge: MIT Press.

Nag, D. (1991). Fashion, Gender, and the Bengali Middle Class. *Public Culture* 3 (2): 93–112.

Yu, H. L., C. Kim, J. Lee, and N. Hong. (2001). An Analysis of Modern Fashion Designs as Influenced by Asian Ethnic Dress. *International Journal of Consumer Studies* 25: 309–321. doi:10.1046/j.1470-6431.2001.00200.x

Women and Feminity in U.S. Popular Culture—Beauty and Race (2012). http://science.jrank.org/pages/11646/Women-Femininity-in-U-S-Popular-Culture-Beauty-Race.html.

Learning Activity 6.1: Ethnic Stereotypes and Their Consequences

Objective

This exercise is a challenging, in-class group activity that helps participants dissect a stereotype, consider the relationships of component parts of a multifaceted phenomenon, and understand consequences of labeling minority groups.

A stereotype is a classification or typing of a group of people that results in applying a set of generalized characteristics to them. Even though the stereotype usually does not completely fit any one individual, all members of the group are typed the same. In this in-class exercise, each student will be asked to verbalize a stereotype in society. Do not be afraid to "speak the unspeakable" and list highly controversial ideas. You are not saying that you hold this stereotype, but that these ideas are held by some people in the United States. We will examine the dangers of stereotypical thinking as we move through the exercise.

Procedure

Form groups of four to seven people. Think of a group of Americans (i.e., Native, Asian, African, or Hispanic) that is stereotyped in U.S. society. List the label given to the group. Next, work as a group to create a written list of characteristics commonly assigned to that group when stereotyped. When listing items, put a star next to those that relate to appearance. Next, identify those parts of the stereotype that are either negative or positive.

Ground Rules

Some essential ground rules for this exercise are:

1. It is OK to feel uncomfortable about writing down a stereotype; we can all learn valuable lessons from the discomfort.
2. It is OK to write socially and politically incorrect thoughts and words during this exercise. You will need to verbalize and understand the components of a stereotype that may seem ugly or even absurd. Laughing about the stereotypes is permissible; this can help to relieve tension about the stereotypes.

3.   It is important that no one gets angry at stereotypes that other groups construct; no one in class should be accused of actually holding the verbalized stereotypes. This is a learning exercise, not a statement of personal beliefs. An atmosphere of tolerance and openness is essential for learning.

Discussion Questions

When groups are through recording the stereotypes and noting positive and negative components, each group should:

1.   Read to the whole class the stereotype their group chose.
2.   Consider whether the appearance components of the stereotype help to trigger the labeling.
3.   Read what they consider to be negative about the stereotype and think about what consequences those negative components may have for the people to whom the stereotype is applied.
4.   Read what they consider to be positive about the stereotype and think what consequences those positive components may have for the people so labeled.
5.   Discuss whether any two or more individuals can have all the components of any of the stereotypes. Is it fair to apply the stereotype before knowing a person, even if the stereotype might fit somewhat?

References

Arthur, L. B. (1997). Cultural Authentication Refined: The Case of the Hawaiian Holokū. *Clothing and Textiles Research Journal* 15 (3): 129–139.

Eicher, J. B., and T. V. Erekosima. (1980). Distinguishing Non-Western from Western Dress: The Concept of Cultural Authentication [abstract]. *Proceedings of the 1980 Annual Meeting of the Association of College Professors of Textiles and Clothing*, 83–84.

Lewis, Michael B. (2010). Why Are Mixed-Race People Perceived as More Attractive? *Perception* 39 (1): 136. DOI: 10.1068/p6626.

Newman, D. (1995). *Sociology: Exploring the Adventure of Everyday Life*. Thousand Oaks, CA: Pine Forge Press.

Starr, P. (1982). *The Social Transformation of American Medicine*. New York: Basic Books.

Tajfel, H., and J. C. Turner. (1986). The Social Identity Theory of Inter-group Behavior. In S. Worchel and L. W. Austin (eds.), *Psychology of Intergroup Relations* (pp. 33–47). Chicago: Nelson-Hall.

Endnote

1. The U.S. government recognizes Hispanic/Latino as an ethnicity, not a race.

WHY MICHELLE OBAMA'S HAIR MATTERS

Jenee Desmond-Harris

When the First Lady attended a country-music event in July without a single strand of hair falling below her jawline, the blogosphere exploded with outbursts ranging from adoration to vitriol. Things settled down only when her deputy press secretary clarified that there had been no First Haircut. In the aftermath, a didactic post on MichelleObama Watch.com proclaimed that anyone "familiar with the amazing versatility of black hair" would have known that the new summer look was simply "pinned up" (see Figure 6.5).

Many Americans have dismissed this hair hubbub as simply more media-driven noise—like the chatter about Michelle Obama's sleeveless dresses, J. Crew cardigans, stocking-free legs or, for that matter, recent (shocking!) decision to wear shorts in the Arizona heat. But for African-American women like me, hair is something else altogether—singular in its capacity to command interest and carry cultural baggage. The obsession with Michelle's hair took hold long before Inaugural Ball gowns were imagined, private-school choices scrutinized or organic gardens harvested. It's not that she's done anything outrageous. The new updo wasn't really all that dramatic a departure from variations we've seen on her before (the "flip-out," the "flip-under," the long-ago abandoned "helmet"). Still, her hair is the catalyst for a conversation that begins with style but quickly transcends outward appearance and ultimately transcends Michelle herself—a symbol for African-American women's status in terms of beauty, acceptance and power.

The hair buzz heated up right after the Democratic National Convention. Websites dedicated to black hair posted and reposted a *Philadelphia Inquirer* article addressing what was presented as an urgent question: Were the silky strands that moved so gracefully with each tip of her head during her Denver speech straightened with chemicals or with heat alone? How exactly

Figure 6.5 Michelle Obama's hairstyles have very potent political and powerful connotations.

did she metamorphose what we know was once tightly coiled hair?

The choice many black women make to alter their hair's natural texture has undeniable historical and psychological underpinnings. It has been attributed to everything from a history of oppression and assimilation to media-influenced notions of beauty and simple personal aesthetics. But one thing is certain. For the many who wear straightened styles like Michelle's, the decision is deliberate, and the maintenance is significant.

A stylist hypothesized in the *Inquirer* article about the steps taken to attain her look, and a firestorm of online comments followed, including these two:

> Chemicals, hot comb, round brush and dryer . . . same effect, different methods. I could see it being a big deal or inspirational if she were natural and wore it in natural styles.

> Girl, ain't no braids, twists, afros, etc. getting into the White House just yet . . . LOL.

This could have been read as a lighthearted exchange about beauty and style. But it actually reflects a serious and clamorous debate. A growing community on sites like Nappturality.com urges black women to reject curl-relaxing methods, calling them "taking the easy road" and "conforming" to white aesthetics. Meanwhile, talk-show host Tyra Banks just announced via Twitter that she will abandon her weave and don "no fake hair at all!" for her show's season premiere. Mixed in with the supportive response to the former supermodel's decision was skepticism about whether she could be attractive with what she describes as her "out and free" look.

For black women, hair has classification power (witness the connection Don Imus made between hair and sexual promiscuity when he referred to the Rutgers women's basketball team as "nappy-headed hos"). Just as blond has implicit associations with sex appeal and smarts (or lack thereof), black-hair descriptors convey thick layers of meaning but are even more loaded. From long and straight to short and kinky—and, of course, good and bad—these terms become shorthand for desirability, worthiness and even worldview. (See pictures of Michelle Obama's fashion diplomacy.)

The notion of natural black hair as being subversive or threatening is not new. When the *New Yorker* set out last summer to satirize Michelle as a militant, country-hating black radical, it was no coincidence that the illustrator portrayed her with an Afro. The cartoon was calling attention to all the ridiculous pre-election fearmongering. But the stereotypes it drew from may be

one reason that 56% of respondents to a poll on NaturallyCurly.com say the U.S. is not ready for a "First Lady with kinky hair."

Some black women note that Michelle's choice to wear her hair straightened affirms unfair expectations about what looks professional. On Blacksnob.com a reader empathized with Michelle's playing it safe in the White House and outlined her own approach: "Whenever I start a new job I always wear my hair straight for the first three months until I get health care. Then gradually the curly-do comes out." Another echoed the practice: "I wait about four to six months before I put the [mousse] in and wear it curly . . . I have to pace myself because it usually turns into a big to-do in the office." (See the 50 best websites of 2009.)

The amount of money black women spend on hair will be explored in Chris Rock's upcoming comedic documentary Good Hair. "Their hair costs more than anything they wear," he said. Which helps explain the recent news out of Indiana University that black women often sacrifice workouts to maintain their hairstyles.

One might think having a black First Lady who is widely praised as sophisticated and stylish would represent a happy ending to the story of black female beauty and acceptance. Alas, our hair still simultaneously bonds and divides us. "There is no hair choice you can make that is simple," says Melissa Harris Lacewell, an associate professor of politics and African-American studies at Princeton. "Any choice carries tremendous personal and political valence."

Even though I'm biracial and should theoretically have half a share of hair angst, I've sacrificed endless Saturdays to the salon. It is unfathomable that I might ever leave my apartment with my hair in its truly natural state, unmoderated by heat or products. I once broke down at the airport when my gel was confiscated for exceeding the 3-oz. limit. (See 50 essential travel tips.)

I'm neither high maintenance nor superficial: I'm a black woman. My focus on hair feels like a birthright. It is my membership in an exclusive, historical club, with privileges, responsibilities, infighting and bylaws that are rewritten every decade.

Not once when I've seen an image of our First Lady has it been lost on me that she is also a member. I don't see just an easy, bouncy do. I see the fruits of a time-consuming effort to convey a carefully calculated image. In the next-day ponytail, I see a familiar defeat.

A black family at 1600 Pennsylvania Avenue signifies a shattered political barrier, but our reactions to Michelle are evidence that it takes more than an election to untangle some of the unique dilemmas black women face. Thanks to her, our issues are front and center. It feels a lot like when nonblack friends and colleagues ask those dreaded questions that force us to reflect and explain: whether we can comb through our hair, if we wash our braids or locks and the most complicated of all—why it all has to be such a big deal.

Discussion Questions

1. Why does Michelle Obama's hair matter?
2. Why are people more concerned about Michelle Obama's hair than Barack Obama's hair?
3. Research and compare the controversy over First Lady Hillary Clinton's hairstyles and Michelle Obama's hairstyles.

6.2

JAPANESE KIND OF WHITENESS: WOMEN'S FACE-WHITENING PRACTICE AND THE CONTEMPORARY JAPANESE IDENTITY

Mikiko Ashikari
University of Cambridge

Introduction

The face-whitening practice of Japanese women is a widely observed social phenomenon in present-day Japan. Japanese women make enormous efforts to make their complexions look lighter, staying in the shade when outside to avoid tanning, and using various face-whitening cosmetics. Furthermore, the majority of Japanese women wear foundation, which makes their faces look whiter than they really are, whenever they go to public places, both in the daytime and in the evening.[1]

Women's obsession for the white face became prominent in the 1990s, when face-whitening cosmetics became a big hit with Japanese women. As whitening cosmetics sold in Japan did not contain bleach, the desired result could only be achieved through continual long-term use. Women started to devote themselves to whitening their faces.

This social phenomenon, associated with a massive consumer industry with an annual turnover of some 160 billion yen, came to be called "the whitening boom" (*Nihon keizai shimbun*, 1998). In fact, Japanese women's face-whitening practice is not a recent invention. Some sorts of whitening cosmetics, both handmade organic products and commercial products, were continuously produced and sold before the whitening boom, even in the pre-modern period in Japan. But the market used to be rather small; dark-skinned Japanese women used them in the hope of whitening and beautifying their faces. Since the whitening boom, there has been an enormous

---

This paper is an updated and shortened version of "Cultivating Japanese Whiteness: the Whitening Cosmetics Boom and the Japanese Identity" published in *Journal of Material Culture* vol. 10 (1): 73–91. (2005).

increase in the use of whitening cosmetics nationwide. Now both fair- and dark-skinned women use whitening cosmetics in order to display what is referred to as the "Japanese skin."

Throughout the whitening boom, women's practice of face-whitening was transformed from a trivial, woman's matter to a public concern. Today the expression of the whitening boom has disappeared from the Japanese mass media. A strong preference for a white complexion has nevertheless survived and recent research shows that Japanese women's complexions have become whiter than those in the 1990s (*Asahi shimbun*, 2009).

Some studies of clothing in various societies have focused on body decoration as a means of communication (e.g., Abu-Lughod, 1986: 159–167; Barnes and Eicher, 1992; Eicher, 1995; Hendry, 1993: 70–97; Macleod, 1991). Barnes and Eicher point out that through body decoration, people communicate their gender and ethnicity (1992; 1995). In their introduction to the selection of studies in *Dress and Gender* (1992), Barnes and Eicher argue that clothing, in which they include the "direct modification of the body" (Ibid., 13), is a sensory system of nonverbal communication which includes and excludes (see also Eicher, 1995). The studies, which emphasize the function of body decoration as a means of communication, reveal the ironical position of the symbol in the study of body decoration.

These studies suggest that body decoration should not be understood simply as a static symbol to be read. They claim that body decoration serves at the same time as "a sign that the individual belongs to a certain group" (Barnes and Eicher, 1992, 1), and that it is only through this symbolic representation of meaning that body decoration can work as a vocabulary for communication. It is here that body decoration as a symbol reappears as central, but in a different context, because the theoretical issues that frame the ways in which we can "decode" the symbol have shifted. My study of women's white faces shows that what body decoration symbolizes in a community, and how, and in what context, it is used as a means of communication in everyday life, are not independent issues; on the contrary,

they heavily depend on and interact with each other (see Ashikari, 2003a). The power of a symbol cannot be attributed simply to its origin, but relies largely on how the symbol is remembered by the people in a particular society.

Japanese women's face-whitening after the whitening boom is no longer just a beauty issue; it is a matter of communicating Japaneseness (Figure 6.6). Hiroshi Wagatsuma, a Japanese anthropologist who studied in the U.S., was probably the first to conduct anthropological research on skin color in Japan. In his English article of 1967, he argued that a dichotomy observed in 1960s Japan, "white/beautiful versus black/ugly," should be attributed to Japanese aesthetic values. And the preference for whiteness should be rooted in the Japanese people's *own* history, rather than their Westernized ideas about race (Wagatsuma, 1967, 407). Indeed many of my own informants also insisted that their preference for white skin had nothing to do with any notion of "race," but was simply a matter of beauty. Nevertheless, as my fieldwork research progressed, it emerged that a notion of the "Japanese skin" existed among Japanese people. That is, my informants believed that the Japanese as a race share the same skin tone, and the notion of Japanese skin works as one medium to express and represent Japaneseness.

A lot of recent studies suggest that Japanese identity is largely based on a sense of racial identity (see Weiner, 1997; Siddle, 1997; Kondo, 1997; Yoshino, 1992 (1997); Oguma, 1995). In this paper, I argue that Japanese women's face-whitening practice is related to representation of Japanese-

Figure 6.6 To many in Japan, pale, white skin is an indicator of authenticity, not race.

ness (their ethnic and racial identity). First, I will explain what whiteness in skin means in Japan, and then will show how and why women's white face is able to represent Japaneseness.

Meanings of the White Skin in Japan

The skin tones of Japanese people are recognized and expressed as a dichotomy of "white" and "black" in Japan, and this dichotomy of skin tone is usually expressed with reference to many other dichotomies. This white/black dichotomy makes it possible for white skin to be a powerful medium that represents the Japanese identity. In Japan, the noun "color" (*iro*) indicates a "skin tone" when the word is used of persons. For example, "*Kobayashi-san wa iro ga shiroi* (literally, the color of Mr. Kobayashi is white)" means that "Mr. Kobayashi is a pale-skinned man." It never means "Mr. Kobayashi is a Caucasian." The only word that can be used to denote one's light skin is *shiro* (color of white), not light, pale, and fair in Japanese, and the word which denotes dark skin is *kuro* (black).

There is a linguistic problem here. Although the face color that Japanese women are pursuing actually does not look "white," the light complexion is called the "white" face. In 1994, I conducted a sociolinguistic survey concerning the cognitive perceptions of white skin and of dark skin among the Japanese people, which revealed that white skin represented multiple meanings (Ashikari, 1995). I collected 1868 nouns and adjectives, which were associated by 163 subjects with the image of white skin and of dark skin. These words fell into a variety of dichotomies, such as white/black: weak/strong, infirm/healthy, cute/wild, beautiful/ugly, womanly/manly, wimpy/brave, clean/dirty, sophisticated/vulgar, conservative/liberal, and so on. The survey suggested that white skin has different implications in different contexts, and white skin can have both positive and negative connotations in the everyday life of contemporary Japan. However, regardless of the multiple meanings of white skin, the expression "your color is white" is widely taken as praise, while "your color is black" is taken as an insult. Most Japanese people seemed to find it unacceptable that one should say, "your skin is dark," to someone's face.

My fieldwork was undertaken in Osaka and Kobe from 1996 to 1997. The subjects of my fieldwork consisted of so-called urban middle-class men and women. The topic of my research was quite sensitive, and therefore I did not ask my informants any direct questions about skin color. Instead I became involved in several groups, and then simply waited until topics relating to skintone, makeup styles, or appearance in general came up. The topic of skin tones quite often arose in everyday conversations. It was not hair color, or eye color, but skin tone which was one of people's main concerns when they spoke of appearance in Japan.

Throughout my fieldwork, I found several theories regarding skin tones. First, many informants, both men and women, insisted that white skin was the ideal only for *women*, and that dark skin was the ideal for men. But on many occasions, the dark skin of Japanese men, as well as of Japanese women, was spoken of negatively, as opposed to an "ideal" white skin.

One episode in an article about the birth of the Crown Prince (Okuno, 2001) provides the most prominent example of how the white skin can be a big issue in Japan. Recently, a doctor who dealt with the Empress's delivery in 1960 revealed that the very first thing the Emperor (who was Crown Prince at that time) asked him about the newborn Crown Prince was: "How about his (skin) color? Is he rather 'white'-skinned or rather 'black'-skinned?" (Okuno, 2001, 138). The doctor explains that he was surprised but soon replied that his color was rather white, adding that the baby took after the Empress. The Emperor had a relieved look on his face when he heard the doctor's answer. A court physician at that time explained that the Emperor was sensitive about his own dark skin because this used to be the target of jokes among his classmates when he was at elementary school. Another example came from one white-skinned male informant who said that a saleswoman in the menswear section of a department store is likely to tell him, "Your color is white. So this color tie will match your face." However, he realized that the saleswoman never tells a male customer with dark skin, "Your color is black. So . . ." Although people say that dark skin looks better than white skin on men, it is social etiquette to avoid calling a man "dark-skinned" to his face, whereas they *can* call him "white-skinned."

Secondly, in Japan, the distinction between naturally dark skin (*jiguro*) and tanned skin (*hiyake*) is significant. There is a whole range of expressions which describe suntanned skin (for both men and women) resulting from various leisure activities, such as *sukii-yake* (suntanned skin as a result of skiing), *tenisu-yake* (suntanned skin as a result of playing tennis), *gorufu-yake* (suntanned skin as a result of playing golf), *Hawai-yake* (suntanned skin as a result of holidays in Hawaii), and so on. All the words, which have become prevalent since the 1980s, emphasize that one's dark skin is the result of leisure activities, not of working outdoors, and also that one's dark skin is not hereditary dark skin.

It was also said by some of my informants that tanned skin looked healthy, while pale skin looked unhealthy and effeminate. As long as people know the person's dark skin is a *tanned* skin resulting from some leisure activity, talking about the dark skin in front of the person is acceptable.

However, it is difficult even for native Japanese to tell whether someone's dark skin is naturally dark, or the result of a suntan. Making any comments about someone's "tanned" skin involves a risk, because this dark skin might *not* be the result of any outdoor leisure activity. Dark skin can sometimes have positive connotations. Yet talking about someone's dark skin in front of them, whichever sex they are, is usually considered to be a social taboo in Japan.

There was another theory about skin tone among my informants, and this concerned the relationship between skin color and birthplace in Japan. The people from the northern part of Japan, which is overcast and snowy, have white skin, while those from the southern part, which is warmer and sunnier, have dark skin.[2] This theory happens to reveal that contemporary Japanese people see themselves as a distinct "racial" group. Women, but rarely men, casually chat about the skin tones of women in relation to their birthplaces. This is *not* a social taboo. Not a small number of informants, both men and women, originally from the northern part of Japan, admitted and brought it up in public that they had the impression that the people in Osaka and Tokyo looked much darker than those in their hometowns. In reality, every region has both white-skinned people and dark-skinned people. Even siblings often exhibit different skin shades, and such individual variations often seem more marked than regional differences. Then what is significant about this theory is that it emphasizes their belief that different skin tones among the Japanese are just due to the different weather in each region, and that *we Japanese* originally share a common Japanese skin color—which is white. According to this theory the Japanese, whether from the north or the south, constitute a unified race.

Although there may be no "Japanese race" in any scientific or biological sense, the Japanese tend to perceive themselves as a distinct "racial" group who share the same skin. The notion of the Japanese "white" skin works as a symbol of us/Japanese. Here the dichotomy of white and black is tied to another important dichotomy of "us and them." The recognizably dark skin of a Japanese person often throws a shadow over the person's membership of "us."

The expression "Japanese skin" often cropped up when my informants talked about their skin in contrast with the skin of other people outside Japan. My informants used the term "Japanese skin" as if there were a skin tone common to all Japanese. When they mentioned the Japanese skin, differences among individuals were not considered. The image of the Japanese skin is often idealized as a white skin that is soft, resilient, and slightly moist. Regardless of the Western social perception that regards Japanese, as well as other East Asians, as "yellow," very few informants perceived their skin as being yellow. To Japanese eyes, their skin has always been white. My informants admitted that some non-Japanese Asian women had smooth white skin. But they believed that the Japanese skin and that of other Asians were not the same and insisted that the Japanese skin has a whiteness that is "unique" and "peculiar" to the Japanese. The notion of the Japanese skin serves as one of the positive identifying features of the Japanese as a race. Once a Japanese knows that a person who in fact cannot be physically distinguished from a Japanese is a *non*-Japanese, the skin color of that non-Japanese person often comes to be perceived as darker or different. One woman in her thirties happened to find out that a friend of her friend was a Korean student. Then she said, "Uh ha, that's why her skin has a whiteness which cannot be found in *our* Japanese skin."

Japanese people's attitude toward the image of Caucasian skin is paradoxical. My informants, mainly women, insisted that Japanese skin was "superior" to Caucasian skin. Although many of my informants had had little personal contact with Westerners, they all made more or less identical negative comments about Caucasian women's skin, saying, for example, that it was "rough"; it "aged quickly"; and it had "too many spots." Nevertheless, in Japan many images of *haku-jin* women (literally, white people; Caucasians) are used in advertisements for various makeup products including whitening cosmetics. Most informants do not pay attention to the fact that those models are Caucasians. Caucasian models appear to be a transparent symbol of "world culture" and of "universal beauty" in the Japanese mass media. When my informants look at a beautiful young Caucasian model in an advertisement with a slogan such as "for making your skin beautiful and young," they can simply see "youth" and "beauty" in the model's face. They are looking at a beautiful woman in the advertisement, but not particularly at a beautiful *Caucasian* woman.

On the other hand, very few black models appear in adverts in the Japanese mass media. No matter how beautiful a black model looks, it seems to be almost impossible for the informants to see the model independently of her race. Russell, an anthropologist of dark skin, studies representations of blackness in Japanese popular culture: how the images of black people are portrayed in Japanese novels, cartoons, and advertisements. He argues that blackness is used in order to make the Japanese look whiter, and concludes: "the Japanese self emerges as white, near white, or aspiring to whiteness" (Russell,

1996, 12–13). The white skin appears as a symbol that enables the Japanese to feel they are part of world culture, the dominant population "us," but not "others," in the "universal" world.

In everyday conversations, both white skin and dark skin were talked about both positively and negatively. Sometimes the meanings of white skin even contradicted one another. The meanings of white skin in contemporary Japan are not unified but multiple, and these multiple meanings are always competing in real life. Some meanings became more important than others in certain contexts. For example, as I show, when informants talked about white skin as a feature of northern people, the idea of white skin as a sign of weakness or beauty was not much considered. Among many other meanings, the meaning of white skin as a symbol of Japaneseness, which is based on the powerful dichotomy of white/us and black/others, was dominant. When whiteness was understood in relation to the Japanese identity, other meanings were usually subjugated to the Japanese white skin as a symbol of "us," the Japanese. In this case, positive meanings of white skin were used to confirm the superiority of the Japanese people and its negative meanings were simply temporarily forgotten. This is why, although whiteness and blackness can be interpreted in many ways, members of contemporary Japanese society are able to share certain negative feelings surrounding black skin and the social taboo concerning the discussion of somebody's dark skin in public.

Japaneseness and Women's Beauty

Thus the white skin is related to the representation of Japanese racial identity. But none of my informants tried to protect their white face from tanning or presented the white face through the use of foundation in order to celebrate their Japanese identity. They did so because they just wanted and intended to look "pretty." One 25-year-old informant put it this way: "I like white skin simply because white skin looks prettier. And if you put on makeup, and your face looks white, you can wear any color of clothing. A dark face makes you look dull." Many female informants made similar comments and insisted that their preference for white skin derived from "traditional" and "domestic" aesthetic values or standards of beauty. In the midst of globalization, Japanese aesthetic values and standards of beauty cannot escape the influence of "universal" standards of beauty. Yet Japanese women, through the practice of whitening their faces, seem to be aiming at being beautiful *Japanese* women, rather than merely beautiful women.

There was a time when Western fashions had a more direct impact on the fashion in Japan. Around the late-1960s to the mid-70s, as soon as the fashion for tanned skin among Western women came in with images of women enjoying sunbathing on a beach in trendy places such as Nice, tanned skin in summer came to be considered highly desirable. Many Japanese women became keen on getting a tan in summer (Hirosawa, 1993, 120–127). Tanned skin is still very popular and much admired among European people, whereas today very few Japanese women want to get a tan in summer. On the contrary, most Japanese women devote themselves to avoiding tanning and try to keep their skin white by giving up most outdoor activities. The women often mentioned the harmful effects of tanning, such as the fact that it accelerated the aging of the skin or increased the number of lines and spots on the face, and described women who enjoyed tanning as "unthinking" women. By the late 1990s Japanese women no longer unreflectively followed the Western fashion.

The whitening boom that emerged in 1990s Japan was a new trend in women's fashions that was not seen in Western fashions. The trigger for this boom was a whitening cosmetic, named *Whitess essence* but developed under the misleading name *"whitening" essence*, which was produced by Shiseido, one of the biggest cosmetic companies in Japan. *Whitess essence* became a record-breaking best-seller as soon as it came onto the market in 1989. Two million packages of *Whitess essence* were sold in the first year, and twelve million in the following five years (Shiseido, 1995), despite the high price, i.e., ten thousand yen (about 110 dollars) for a 30g tube. Following Shiseido's big success, almost all do-

mestic cosmetics companies started to produce or reintroduce their own whitening cosmetics, and placed them on sale with large promotions. Since the mid-1990s, many major foreign cosmetics companies, such as Clinique, Yves Saint Laurent, Christian Dior, Chanel, and Helena Rubinstein, have developed their own whitening cosmetics particularly for Japanese customers, and started to sell them exclusively in Japan. Although most of my informants insisted that their preference for a white complexion was a "domestic" matter, the whitening products based on the Japanese idea of whitening faces, but produced by famous Western brand companies, sell as well as those produced by Japanese cosmetic companies. For advertisements, the Western companies always use Caucasian models, while Japanese companies usually use Japanese models. In the former case, the beautiful face of a Caucasian model, as well as that of a Japanese model, is used as an example of the white face that Japanese women should be able to achieve through the use of a particular whitening cosmetic. Many of my informants had had experiences of trying both Western and domestic whitening cosmetics. Some were keen on trying new products and others preferred to stick to the same one. But they rarely chose the product according to whether it was domestic or Western.

In 1984, Lakoff and Scherr, both of whom are non-Anglo-Saxons, "discovered" that the standard of female beauty in the U.S. was restrained by the idealized image of Anglo-Saxon women. Haiken (1997) shows, in her study of the history of cosmetic surgery in the U.S., that cosmetic surgery procedures for non-Anglo-Saxon Americans are often attempts on the part of the patient/ customer to become a part of a universal white population by making themselves look less Jewish, less Asian, and less African, and more like Anglo-Saxons (see also Kaw, 1993). Globalization seems to be spreading an image of universal beauty based on an idealized image of Anglo-Saxons; Western institutions, such as the Hollywood film industry and the European/American big brand companies, contribute to this history of celebrating whiteness. As the appearance of Caucasian beauties in the Japanese adverts for various cosmetics shows, the representation of the ideal image of Japanese women cannot be free from this standard, which is all-pervasive in contemporary Japanese society. On the other hand, globalization often sparks off localization. Many studies of beauty, or more particularly those of beauty contests, often point out that as worldwide beauty pageants, such as Miss Universe, spread the universal standard of beauty, more local beauty pageants in which the winner will be chosen according to the authentic looks of each society, and authentic female virtues and talents, have emerged (see Lavenda, 1996; Borland, 1996; McAllister, 1996). Major domestic cosmetics companies started to use Japanese models for their advertisements, instead of the Caucasian models that were very popular before the 1980s (see Mizuo, 1998, 263–282). Some Japanese models who emphasized their "oriental" looks (narrow eyes and straight dark hair) first attracted the attention of the Western media in Paris fashion collections and then became popular among young Japanese women (see also Kondo, 1997, 57–58; Tobin, 1992, 30–31).

Regardless of my informants' claims that their standards of beauty were strictly "domestic," recent rapid globalization has made it impossible to isolate the ideas of beauty in general and of ideal looks of Japanese people, and even of the Japanese identity per se. When my female informants talk of the superiority of the Japanese skin, two points are always emphasized. First, their admiration for white skin is based on intrinsic Japanese aesthetics, not on the influence of any concept of ideal beauty in the West. Secondly, the reason why the Japanese woman's skin is more beautiful than that of the Caucasian (or of any other non-Japanese) stems not only from the biological difference but also from their own "distinctive" and "diligent" skin-care practices. Their claims revealed that the ideal of Japanese beauty is constituted through a contest with images of Western women (or of any other non-Japanese people) and their relationship to "universal beauty" in the world. One informant, who has snow-white skin, said:

> I am keen on taking care of my skin, and go to a lot of trouble not to get a tan. This is because I want to keep my skin white

and blemish-free, definitely not because I admire *haku-jin* [the Caucasians]. *We* and such people are totally independent creatures. . . . But *we* think, there is little difference, well . . . actually no difference between the skin color of *haku-jin* and our own in terms of its whiteness. I have never thought that my skin tone is inferior to the *haku-jin's*. . . .

In reference to the ideal image of Western (or universal) beauty, and Western whiteness, the Japanese white skin and the ideal image of Japanese beauty are more closely linked and the meaning of the white skin as a symbol of Japaneseness has become more dominant.

Conclusion

Japanese women's quest for the ideal white face continues. An article in one of the most influential Japanese newspapers announced that research conducted by a major domestic cosmetic company shows that the average tone of Japanese women's facial skin color has become *10%* whiter over the last decade (*Asahi shimbun*, 2009). In addition to the established techniques of avoiding tanning and using whitening cosmetics, women keep trying new techniques, such as applying skin products using *collagen* and *hyaluronic acid*, ingesting drinks and supplements containing one or both of these two ingredients, or washing the face with a special soap made of green tea extract, and so on. All of my informants are clearly aware that no single method of whitening the skin has a particularly dramatic effect. As far as their motivation for face-whitening practice was concerned, women explained that they wanted to "protect" their white skin or that they wanted to recover their "innate" white skin tone.

None of them see the practice of face-whitening as an attempt to change their skin tone from dark or yellow to white. By presenting the white faces which all Japanese imagine that they originally have, the women want to present the ideal *Japanese* beauty. Through the nationwide phenomenon of face-whitening, the meaning of the white face as a symbol of Japaneseness has become a public and dominant one among the multiple meanings and the various interpretations of the white face. Exploring cutting-edge body techniques of face-whitening, what Japanese women are reproducing and presenting is a Japanese form of whiteness that is based on the Japanese identity as a race, and, therefore, very different from—and even "superior" to—Western whiteness.

References

Abu-Lughod, L. (1986). *Veiled Sentiments: Honor and Poetry in a Bedouin Society*, Berkeley: University of California Press.

Asahi shimbun (2009). *'bihaku-shiko kukkiri, 90 nendai yori 10% shiroku Shiseido chosa'* [Prominent preference for a white complexion, 10% whiter than in the 1990s by Shiseido research], 18 May.

Ashikari, M. (1995). Artificial light skin: as the sign of femininity and of national identity in contemporary Japan. (Unpublished MA thesis). University of California, Davis.

Ashikari, M. (2003a). The Memory of the Women's White Faces: Japaneseness and the Ideal Image of Women, *Japan Forum* 15 (1): 55–79.

Ashikari, M. (2003b). Urban middle-class Japanese women and their white faces: Gender, ideology and representation, *Ethos* 31 (1): 3–37.

Ashikari, M. (2005). Cultivating Japanese whiteness: The whitening cosmetics boom and the Japanese identity, *Journal of Material Culture* 10 (1): 73–91.

Barnes, R. and Eicher, J. B. (1992). Introduction, in R. Barnes and J. B. Eicher (eds.), *Dress and Gender: Making and Meaning in Cultural Contexts*, pp. 1–7. New York: Berg.

Borland, K. (1996). The India Bonita of Monimbo: The politics of ethnic identity in the new Nicaragua, in C. B. Cohen, R. Wilk, and B. Stoeltje (eds.), *Beauty Queen on the Global Stage: Gender, Contests, and Power*, pp. 75–88. London: Routledge.

Eicher, J. B. (1995). Introduction: Dress as Expression of Ethnic identity, in J. B. Eicher (ed.), *Dress and Ethnicity: Changes across Space and Time*, pp. 1–65. Oxford: BERG.

Haiken, E. (1997). *Venus Envy: A History of Cosmetic Surgery*. London: The John Hopkins University Press.

Hendry, J. (1993). *Wrapping Culture: Politeness, Presentation and Power in Japan and Other Societies*. Oxford: Clarendon Press.

Hirosawa, Ei (1993). *Kurokami to kesho no showa-shi* [The history of black hair and make-up in the Showa period]. Tokyo: Iwanami.

Kaw, E. (1993). Medicalization of racial futures: Asian American women and cosmetic Surgery. *Medical Anthropology Quarterly* 7 (1): 74–89.

Kondo, D. (1997). *About Face: Performing Race in Fashion and Theater*. New York: Routledge.

Lakoff, R. T. and Scherr, R. L. (1984). *Face Value*. Boston: Routledge and Kegan Paul.

Lavenda, R. H. (1996). "It's not a beauty pageant!" Hybrid ideology in Minnesota community queen pageants. In C. B. Cohen, R. Wilk, and B. Stoeltje (eds.), *Beauty Queen on the Global Stage: Gender, Contests, and Power*, pp. 31–46. London: Routledge.

Macleod, A. E. (1991). *Accommodating Protest: working women, the new veiling, and change in Cairo*. New York: Columbia University Press.

McAllister (1996). Authenticity and Guatemala's Maya queen. In C. B. Cohen, R. Wilk, and B. Stoeltje (eds.), *Beauty Queen on the Global Stage: Gender, Contests, and Power*. London: Routledge.

Mizuo, J. (1998). *Keshouhin no brando-shi* [the history of cosmetic brands]. Tokyo: Chuo-KoronSha.

Nihon keizai shimbun (1998). *Bihaku kesho hin ureyuki ko cho* [Whitening cosmetics are selling well], 4 August.

Oguma, E. (1995). *Tanitsu-minzoku shinwa no kigen: The Myth of the Homogeneous Nation*. Tokyo: Shinyou-sha.

Okuno, S. (2001). *Koutaishi Hironomiya no ubugoe wo rokuon-shita ishi* (The doctor who taped the first cry of Crown Prince Hironomiya), *Bungei-shunju*, 79.

Russell, J. G. (1996). Race and reflexivity: the black other in contemporary Japanese mass culture. In J. W. Treat (ed.), *Contemporary Japan and Popular Culture*, 17–40. Honolulu: University of Hawaii Press.

Shiseido (1995). *Shiseido Newsletter*. Tokyo: Shiseido.

Siddle, R (1997). The Ainu and the discourse of "race." In F. Dikotter (ed), *The Construction of Racial Identities in China and Japan*, pp. 136–157. London: Hurst & Company.

Tobin, J. (1992). Introduction: Domesticating the West. In J. Tobin (ed.), *Re-Made in Japan: Everyday Life and Consumer Taste in a Changing Society*, pp. 1–41. London: Yale University Press.

Wagatsuma, H. (1967). The Social Perception of Skin Color in Japan, *Daedalus* 96 (2):407–443.

Weiner, M. (1997). The invention of identity: Race and nation in pre-war Japan. In F. Dikotter (ed.), *The Construction of Racial Identities in China and Japan*, pp. 96–117. London: Hurst & Company.

Yoshino, K. (1992). *Cultural Nationalism in Contemporary Japan*. London: LSE.

Yoshino, K. (1997). The discourse on blood and racial identity in contemporary Japan. In F. Dikotter (ed), *The Construction of Racial Identities in China and Japan*, pp. 199–211. London: Hurst & Company.

Endnotes

1. Japanese people, both men and women, interpret women who present the same white face as "normal and right," and women who do not wear the everyday white makeup in public and fail to present the white face as not (see Ashikari, 2003b).
2. My informants usually excluded the Ainu (aboriginal people who live in small hamlets in Hokkaido) and Korean residents as well when they applied the white/the north—black/the south theory (see Ashikari, 2005).

Discussion Questions

1. Why do other cultures use skin tone as a marker of differences?
2. Compare how this article relates to "Skin Bleaching: The Complexion of Identity, Beauty, and Fashion" in Chapter 4 by Christopher A. D. Charles. What are the different motives for skin color change and processes by which skin color is changed?

6.3

CULTURAL MARKERS IN DRESS: DECODING MEANINGS AND MOTIVATIONS OF COLLEGE STUDENTS

Veena Chattaraman, Auburn University

The millennium began with talks about the changing ethnic and racial composition of the United States and how cultural diversity will increase over the coming decades. A decade into the millennium, and these predictions are revealed as facts. U.S. demographic evidence from cities, towns, and even rural areas documents that cultural pluralism is an all-pervasive phenomenon in the U.S. and is here to stay. Within this pluralist context, where racial and ethnic differences vary in their external visibility, due to color of skin, language, neighborhood, and other factors—dress serves as an important visibility factor in externalizing cultural pluralism. Beyond externalizing ethnicity, dress as visual communication also facilitates the construction and maintenance of cultural identities among diverse subgroups in the populations and becomes the critical locus for realizing the cultural self. The purpose of this paper is to decode the social meanings and motivations attached to the use of cultural markers in dress among college-aged multicultural students.

The paper employed a qualitative strategy of inquiry through an open-ended survey conducted among a convenience sample of 106 male and female students belonging to minority ethnic groups, who were enrolled at a large Midwestern university. A college campus provided the right setting for the research questions examined in this paper since it represents a truly diverse and pluralist environment, where self-expression in thought, dress, and appearance is encouraged, and where a diversity of clothing styles coexist. Four ethnic groups were represented in the sample: Asian or Asian American (55.7%); Black or African American (20.8%); Hispanic or Latino (5.7%); American Indian (1.9%); and Others, chiefly biracial (16%). The mean age in the

Original for this text.

sample was approximately 25 years and a majority of the participants were female (77.4%). A majority of the participants reported owning cultural dress (69.8%), of which 67% reported wearing cultural dress on casual occasions, 79% reported wearing cultural dress for ethnic celebrations and festivals, and 64.8% reported wearing cultural dress for non-ethnic special occasions. The open-ended data provided by the respondents addressed two questions: (1) what does wearing ethnic or ethnic-inspired items of dress mean to you? (2) when you use ethnic or ethnic-inspired items of dress, what emotions do you tend to feel? Participant responses were content-analyzed to identify underlying thematic meanings and motivations in the use of cultural dress.

Cultural Dress: Themes

Cultural Connection and Belonging

This was an important theme that repeatedly surfaced in participant responses while identifying the meanings ascribed to wearing cultural dress. The college students articulated that they used cultural dress to form, express, or sustain cultural connections and belonging to the culture, ancestry, or the ethnic group. Some students expressed using cultural dress for both the self and for communicating to others. The following statement articulates this theme:

"It shows that I have a sense of culture that I enjoy and am willing to share with others."

Others expressed using cultural dress to showcase cultural support:

"Belonging to my culture . . . showing support for Asian Awareness."

Some students used phrases such as "feel rooted" and "sense of nativeness" when discussing their relationship with cultural dress. A majority perceived that they could create a meaningful bond with their culture by wearing cultural dress: "It creates for me a strong sense of belonging and a closeness to my people and culture."

"It makes me feel as if I belong. I belong to a specific group that no one else does."

"Going back to my roots gives me that connection with my ethnicity which is not there in daily life."

"Culturally connected to my ancestors."

"I feel good, and comfortable. Especially when I go to certain events involving people from my ethnic group, I feel like that is where I belong."

Cultural Pride and Celebration

A closely related theme to the above and one that was equally mentioned by the multicultural participants was the demonstration of cultural pride through wearing cultural dress. Respondents emphasized pride in the accomplishments of the culture, their nationality, and respect for the struggle of their ancestors. The following quotes illustrate this theme:

"Adorning the cultural dress reminds me of my heritage and the pride of all the accomplishments made and the ancestors who made it possible. This gives me great PRIDE!"

"I respect my own country, pride."

"I feel very prideful, to think of what my ancestors went through so that I could live here in America. . . . I also, hold on to the past, and link it to the future. . . . I feel, proud, happy, strong."

Respondents also remarked on their feelings of pride or moderated pride in their cultural dress. One of the respondents interestingly noted that he/she did not feel too proud, rather grateful that his/her ethnicity "has decent traditional clothes." Others were more emphatic in their expression of pride in their dress:

"Proud and beautiful, truly like a Nubian queen—from earrings to a formal dress."

"I feel pride in the ethnic-dress of my country. . . . It gives me a sense of belonging to a rich heritage and tradition."

"My ethnic dress is the most beautiful in the world. . . . I used to feel that I became a special person. I try to behave very calm and elegant when I wear my ethnic costume."

Some respondents linked the sense of pride in cultural achievement to external celebration of the culture represented through cultural dress. For example, participants used phrases such as the following in discussing their emotions on wearing of cultural dress: "special, joyous, celebrated."

Identity, Expression, and Distinctiveness

Stryker and Serpe (1982) define identities as "reflexively applied cognitions in the form of answers to the question 'Who am I?'" (p. 206). This definition applies to personal or role identities. Ethnic identity, on the other hand, is a group identity, and has been defined as the shared identity of a group of people based on a common historical background, ancestry, and knowledge of identifying symbolic elements such as nationality, religious affiliation, and language (Forney & Rabolt, 1985–86). Respondents voiced that cultural dress serves to express both their personal identity and group identity. The following statement from a respondent well reflects both these dimensions of identity: "It means knowing WHO I am and WHO I represent."

"It means respecting my heritage and background. I do not usually wear ethnic dress, so when I do, it is a special occasion and I feel that I should remember where I came from because it is part of who I am."

"That identify with the traditions and customs of my culture."

"It's a representation of who I am."

Some respondents perceived that wearing cultural dress went beyond personal self-expression and expressed stories of the group's cultural history, and served to initiate cultural education. The following quotes illustrate these complex themes of identity and expression:

"It tells a story of all the goals accomplished and the trials and tribulations they had to go through for us."

"I feel that it is a good way to inspire others to learn about other cultures and ask questions."

Another important sub-theme that emerged in the context of identity is distinctiveness. Distinctiveness is defined as an individual's numeric (minority status) or social traits that are distinct in relation to the environment (McGuire, 1984). Being persistently different from the reference group's ethnicity makes the ethnic identity salient or important in a person's self-concept (McGuire & McGuire, 1981). Numerous respondents voiced the theme of distinctiveness either from a personal or a group perspective in using cultural dress to externalize differences from the mainstream. To some respondents, this externalization of ethnic difference was a way to reject assimilation into the mainstream culture and maintain and strengthen linkages with the ethnic culture. The following quotes from two respondents capture the deep personal and social struggles involved with their display of cultural distinctiveness through dress:

"It means to me that as an African, wearing clothing that can allow others to identify me as an African even if it is just one article of clothing sets me apart from other people. I feel complete and whole as an individual but I also become alienated from others and I become categorized and classified in negative ways. I have been discriminated against because my clothes made my ethnicity identifiable to others. Ethnic-inspired items are also a way of expressing my rejection of assimilation and maintaining my own unique ethnic identity."

"When I wear ethnic clothing/items I feel complete, whole, and satisfied. When I dress in clothes that are too mainstream and not ethnic, I feel distressed, dissatisfied, and uncomfortable. I am so used to standing out and being recognized because of my ethnic dress that when I wear mainstream clothing I feel like I am betraying my identity and myself. Also, when I do not wear ethnic dress I become alienated and feel unwelcome in my own ethnic community. After living in a non-ethnic relatively homogenous environment and having to make the difficult choice of assimilating or not I had to make a choice and I chose not to assimilate by wearing my ethnic dress. Living in an environment where I felt alienated caused me to have emotions such as feeling shame about my culture because it was not 'normal' and dressing in ethnic-inspired dress solidified my status in society as alien and not 'normal' and that I can never possibly be 'normal' because of my ethnic dress. I believe this has emotionally caused me to become a stronger person and has allowed me to make a clear definition of what my identity is."

Some respondents experienced feelings of enjoyment in being distinct for more personal and hedonic reasons. They enjoyed being able to "show off" their distinctiveness and the attention it brought them. The following quotes illustrate these perceptions:

"I like feeling unique and having a sense of heritage, while knowing I can be fashionable because I accept what I wear."

"I have some cute items that I picked up when I was in China and Hong Kong a couple of summers ago, and I think it's kind of cool to have something obviously from another country. They're kind of like souvenirs that I can show off."

"I love wearing them. It's fun and different from everyday jeans and T-shirts."

Other respondents experienced feelings of pride in the distinctiveness they achieved through cultural dress:

"I'm proud of being dressed differently than others."

"I feel that I am unique and it shows a side of me that I am very proud of."

There was also a small group of respondents who did not want to externalize their distinctiveness from the mainstream culture due to lack of attachment with cultural dress, discomfort, and self-consciousness:

"I am not really attached to our ethnic costume. When I wear the costume, I feel differently, but it is not because I am really proud of my culture or something. I like it and think it is pretty, nothing more than that."

"Distinctive. Uncomfortable for having to wear something that I never wear."

"More self-conscious."

Thus, distinctiveness revealed itself as a complex theme, laden with emotion, and reflecting both the positive and negative voices of respondents. Since cultural dress serves as a visible marker of ethnicity, the maintenance of a distinctive cultural identity lies at the heart of understanding multicultural college students' motivations to wear cultural dress.

Conclusion

This study suggests that a majority of multicultural college students own and wear cultural dress, and also associate deep, positive meanings and emotions with this act of dress. The qualitative strategy of enquiry employed in this study revealed three important themes reflecting the social meanings and motivations attached to the use of cultural markers in dress among college students. The first theme labeled "cultural connection and belonging" addressed the use of cultural dress to form, express, or sustain meaningful bonds with the culture, ancestry, and the ethnic group. The motivations behind this expression through dress were for both the "cultural self" of the individual, and for communicating the "cultural self" to others. This communication was perceived as a form of in-group support. The second theme labeled "cultural pride and celebration" addressed the use of cultural dress to demonstrate pride in the accomplishments of the culture and nationality and respect for the struggle of ancestors. This theme also addressed pride in the beauty and uniqueness of the cultural artifact of dress, which was recognized for its ability to transform the wearer. The third theme labeled "identity, expression, and distinctiveness" was a critical theme in understanding the deeper motivations underlying the use of cultural markers in dress. This theme addressed the use of cultural dress to express both personal and group identity. With respect to the latter, cultural dress was viewed as expression of the group's cultural history, and as a facilitator of cultural education. This theme also addressed the use of cultural dress as an externalization of ethnic difference. For some, this was a way to reject assimilation into the mainstream culture and maintain and strengthen linkages with the ethnic culture. For others, ethnic distinctiveness was either a source of enjoyment and pride, or a source of self-consciousness and discomfort.

In summary, social meanings and motivations attached with the use of cultural markers in dress are thematically similar and yet varied with respect to the undertones and perspectives that the respondent raised. Decoding these meanings and motivations is important in a multicultural society to better understand, communicate, and uphold cultural pluralism.

Discussion Questions

1.   Of the themes the author identifies, which one do you identify with, if you wear ethnic or ethnic-inspired clothing?
2.   What does the author mean when she writes "social meanings and motivations attached with the use of cultural markers in dress are thematically similar and yet varied"?

References

Forney, J. & Rabolt, N. (1985–86). Ethnic identity: Its relationship to ethnic and contemporary dress. *Clothing and Textiles Research Journal, 4*(2), 1–8.

McGuire, W. J., & McGuire, C. V. (1981). The spontaneous-self-construct as affected by personal distinctiveness. In M. D. Lynch, A. A. Norem-Hebeisen, & K. J. Gergen (Eds.), *Self-concept: Advances in theory and research* (pp. 147–171). Cambridge, MA: Ballinger.

McGuire, William (1984). Search for the self: Going beyond self-esteem and the reactive self. In R. A. Zucker, J. Aronoff, & A. T. Rabin (Eds.), *Personality and the Prediction of Behavior* (pp. 73–120). New York: Academic Press.

Stryker, S., & Serpe, R. T. (1982). Commitment, identity salience, and role behavior: Theory and research example. In W. Ickes and E. Knowles (Eds.), *Personality, Roles and Social Behavior* (pp. 199–218). New York: Springer-Verlag.

6.4

"TASTILY BOUND WITH RIBANDS": RIBBON-BORDERED DRESS OF THE GREAT LAKES INDIANS, 1735—1839

Rachel K. Pannabecker

Oliver Spencer was ten years old when he was captured by Shawnee and Mohawk Indians. The year was 1792 and Oliver was returning home from a July 4th celebration at Fort Washington near Cincinnati. While others in his party were left for dead, Oliver was marched north to the confluence of the Auglaize and Maumee Rivers, and subsequently taken into the home of Cooh-coo-cheeh, a Mohawk widow. His memoirs, published some 40 years after his eight-month captivity, contain an unusually rich description of the material life of Native Americans of the Great Lakes region. In particular, Spencer described the dress of the multitribal Indian community in what is now northwestern Ohio:

All the young and middle aged among the women are passionately fond of finery; the young belles, particularly, having the tops of their moccasins curiously wrought with beads, ribands, and porcupine quills; the borders of their leggins, and the bottoms and edges of their strouds *tastily bound with ribands*, edged with beads of various colours (Spencer, 1835, p. 84; emphasis added).[1]

Rachel K. Pannabecker. *Clothing and Textiles Research Journal,* 14 (4) pp. 267–275, copyright © 1996 by SAGE Publications. Reprinted by Permission of SAGE Publications.

The beads mentioned by Spencer are generally considered to be the marker for the ethnic dress of American Indians. Yet, the silk ribbon on their garments is overlooked evidence of contact with Europeans and the ensuing change in indigenous material culture (see Feather & Sibley, 1979). The continued use of ribbon on traditional items of dress and the adoption of ribbon-decorated garments by Indian nations of the prairies and plains are visual signals of the value of this dress tradition. (On ribbonwork in the twentieth century, see Abbass, 1979 and 1994; Coe, 1986; and photographs in Kelley, 1987.)

Unfortunately, research into the history of ribbon-bordered dress[2] has been inhibited by an overly pessimistic attitude toward the accessibility of historical evidence regarding European ribbon in the Americas. Alice Marriott, a former employee of the Indian Arts and Crafts Board and an ethnographic writer, exemplified this attitude when declaring that records on ribbon as trade goods were "hard to get" (Marriott, 1958, p. 49). However, through wide-ranging archival research I uncovered a variety of manuscript records and print materials for the Great Lakes region. These 18th- and early 19th-century writings, such as the description by Oliver Spencer, give life to the story of the adoption of silk ribbon by Native Americans of the Great Lakes and the spread of ribbon-bordered dress among them.

Silk Ribbon in the Great Lakes Region

Interaction between Native American men and women of the Great Lakes and European explorers, traders, and soldiers expanded during the 18th century. The exchange of animal pelts for European-produced articles became a particularly significant point of contact. New York City functioned as a major center for imports that reached Native Americans through trading posts in the Albany area. The 1752–1758 letter book . . . from Robert Sanders contained references to black, red, blue, and white ribbon as well as silver, paduasoy,[3] and flowered ribbon (Robert and John Sanders Papers,

Letter Book 1752–1758, pp. 92, 108, 148, 239). Merchants based in Montreal operated in the Great Lakes area from trading centers such as Detroit, Green Bay, and Michilimackinac (between Lakes Huron and Michigan). In the late 1770s, Michilimackinac trader David McCrae secured ribbon from Montreal firms such as William and John Kay. A 1777 invoice for McCrae's company recorded the purchase from the Kays of black, crimson, and pink ribbon as well as tinsel ribbon and ferreting[4] specifically for trimming leggings (W.D. Powell Collection, Invoice of Sundry Merchandises, pp. B75:198, 200). These selected documents reveal how imported silk ribbon was widely available to Great Lakes Indians through trade. Whereas the names of European purchasers were most prevalent in the records of major and regional trade headquarters, Native American names appeared as consumers of ribbon in many local trade accounts. For example, the 1786–1787 ledger kept by John Askin, a Detroit provisioner and merchant, included the sale of "Christian Ribbon" to a man named Key,ath,ta from an undesignated Woodlands tribe (John Askin Papers, Ledger 1786–87, p. Z-L4: 10).

Trade was not the sole method for transferring European-produced items to Native Americans. Material goods were exchanged in gift-giving, a traditional practice critical to the establishment of military and diplomatic alliances among American Indians (see Jacobs, 1950, for a comprehensive study on gift-giving and material goods). During the colonial period, rivalry between France and Britain resulted in a wide range of European-manufactured goods being presented during diplomatic negotiations with Native American nations. A 1749 memorandum admonished French government officials for sending wool braid instead of silk ribbon "necessary" for suspending the medals presented to Indian leaders (Archives des Colonies, Observations sur les envoyes, vol. 93, p. 426v). As part of the 1756 Treaty of Onondaga, the account book for the Northern Indian Department (British) listed gifts of "12 pieces Ribbons"[5] and "6 pieces flower'd Ribbond" (Johnson, 1922, vol. 2, p. 617). Diplomatic presents were requisitioned each year by the British commanders of outlying forts. In 1780, A. S. DePeyster of Detroit requested 250 pieces of "Ribband Sorted"; while Guy Johnson of Niagara requested 1,000 pieces of "Indian Ribband, Red, Blue, Yellow, Green Etc," and 500 pieces of figured ribbon in the same colors (Colonial Office, 1780, vol. 40, pp. 331, 333). In addition to lengths of ribbon, one document reported gifts of beribboned clothing. From November 1773 to May 1774, the British commandant of Detroit, Henry Basset, requisitioned several garments from trader James Sterling, including a "fine Aurora Stroud ornamented with Ribbon" to be presented to the Chippewa leader Mitiosaki (James Sterling Papers, Folder 1770–1797).

The presentation of ribbon as a diplomatic gift continued into the 19th century, and the United States government also adopted the practice. John Tipton, the U.S. Indian agent at Logansport, Indiana, recorded that between February 12 and March 31, 1828, he purchased eighteen yards of ribbon for presents for the people of the Miami and Potawatomi tribes (John Tipton Papers, Folder 51). Meanwhile, large amounts of ribbon continued to be distributed by the British Indian Department. An extract from a trader's estimate for presents supplied to Native Americans at Amherstburg, Ontario, for 1831 included 2,000 yards of ribbons (George R. Ironside Papers, R2:1831–1832). In summary, historical documents clearly indicate that European-produced ribbon was available to Great Lakes Indians through trade and as diplomatic gifts.

The Emergence of Ribbon-Bordered Dress

In the 17th and 18th centuries, the Iroquois confederation of five, then six, major tribes dominated the region south of Lake Ontario into the Adirondack and Allegheny Mountains. The Iroquois maintained extensive diplomatic and trade relations with the Dutch, then the French and English, and many primary records of these interactions are available. Thus, it is not surprising that the earliest account of ribbon on items of dress occurs among the Iroquois. Father Luc

François Nau, a Jesuit priest, proselytized among the Caughnawaga Iroquois (Mohawk) across the St. Lawrence River from Montreal. In 1735 Nau wrote to his superior saying, "Their mitasse, that is their Leggings, are adorned with ribbons and a variety of flowers embroidered with elk-hair dyed red or yellow" (Thwaites, 1959, vol. 68, p. 265). However, Nau gave no specific description of the types and colors of the ribbon or where the ribbon was attached to the leggings.

Reference to ribbon as borders on garments first appears in the writings of Peter Kalm, a botanist from Sweden. In 1748 and 1749 Kalm visited the Iroquoian tribes along the Mohawk and Hudson Rivers, around Albany, New York. He described the women as wearing "a short blue petticoat, which reaches to their knees and the brim of which is bordered with red or other ribbons" (Kalm, 1772, vol. 2, p. 116). Ribbon borders on the dress of Iroquoian men and women were confirmed by a Frenchman known only by his initials, JCB.[6] He traveled among the Iroquois of the eastern Great Lakes from 1751 to 1761. In his diary, JCB wrote:

> This skirt, which is called Machicôté, falls no longer than the knees and is often garnished or ornamented at the bottom with ribbons, porcupine quills, and small beads, like the moccasins, leggings, and breechcloths (JCB, 1978, p. 173; my translation).

These three documents on the Iroquois thus link ribbon to dress of both men and women: leggings, skirts, breechcloths, and moccasins (see Figure 6.7).

The geographic position of the tribes of the Iroquois confederation enabled them to pursue a role as a political and economic middleman between Europeans and other Native American nations residing further west. Yet European traders and their military protectors moved steadily inland in search of direct alliances to expand their influence over commerce and land. Simultaneously, some eastern Indians such as the Delaware (or Lenni Lenape) and Mohawk (an Iroquoian tribe) were displaced by European settlers and forced westward across the Allegheny Mountains. With continuous interaction among Indian tribes

Figure 6.7 The moccasin is made of deerskin with porcupine quill embroidery on the vamp and cuffs, and silk ribbon and glass beads edging the borders of the cuffs. A single row of European silk ribbon represents the simplest ribbon border used by Native Americans of the Great Lakes.

and the French and English, references to ribbon-bordered dress begin to appear in documents from the central and western Great Lakes areas.

James Smith was taken captive in 1755 in Franklin County, Pennsylvania, by Conestoga and Delaware Indians. The 18-year-old was taken west to the French Fort Duquesne, then to the Delaware-inhabited area of Kittanning, and finally to an Indian town on a branch of the Muskingum River (now in the state of Ohio). There Smith was adopted into a Caughnawaga family that had intermarried with Wyandots and Ottawas. As part of his adoption ceremony, Smith received:

> a new ruffled shirt, which I put on, also a pair of leggins done off with ribbons and beads, likewise a pair mockasons, and garters dressed with beads and red hair—also a tinsel laced cappo[7] (Smith, 1799/1907, p. 15).

Smith's captors and their neighbors in the Ohio region belonged to the Delaware tribe. John

Heckewelder belonged to the Moravian church (German-speaking Protestant), and his missionary work with the Delawares brought him into this same region in 1761. In his book on the manners and customs of American Indians, he described the burial of a highly respected Delaware woman, which occurred in 1762. About her garments Heckewelder wrote that "Her scarlet leggings were decorated with different coloured ribands sewed on, the outer edges being finished off with small beads also of various colours" (Heckewelder, 1876/1971, p. 271). Heckewelder's description is the earliest known document to indicate that the ribbon borders were sewn down to the garment base and that multiple ribbons of contrasting colors were being used.

Another Moravian, David Zeisberger, began mission activities among the Iroquois and then preceded Heckewelder in the mission to the Delaware people in the Ohio region. His manuscript completed in 1781 on the customs of the Iroquois and Delawares contained a description of their dress, including the mention of single and multiple rows of colored ribbons:

> If [the men] desire to go in state, they wear such hose with a silken stripe extending from top to bottom and bordered with white coral. . . . It is also customary for [the women] to sew red, yellow or black ribbon on their coats from top to bottom, being very fond of bright things (Zeisberger, 1910, p. 15).

Multiple rows of ribbon borders were also reported by Robert Hunter, Jr. This 20-year-old son of a London merchant was charged by his father to keep a diary during his trip to North America. The journal entry on his 1785 visit to Fort Niagara (United States) noted that:

> the young [Iroquois women] wear . . . a blanket over their shoulders, which is covered with spangles and different-colored silk-so many blue ribbons curiously sewed upon it half way down their back, and so many red ones to the rest of the blanket (Hunter, 1943, p. 111).

The emergence of multiple rows of ribbons on dress worn by Native Americans in the Lake

Erie region thus represents an expansion of the single ribbon used to border the garment edge.

As Europeans penetrated further inland, trading posts and forts were established on the upper Great Lakes, thus extending European influence and the distribution of European-produced goods. Alexander Henry, an English trader, was adopted and protected by a group of Chippewa Indians while hiding among them during Pontiac's uprising against the English in 1763. Henry reported that in 1764 he purchased at Michilimackinac "a pair of leggings, or pantaloons, of scarlet cloth, which, with the ribbon to garnish them fashionably, cost me fifteen pounds of beaver" (Henry, 1809, p. 156). The spread of ribbon-bordered dress to the northwest is further confirmed in the memoirs of Elizabeth Baird who recalled the 1819 wedding in Michilimackinac of an Ottawa woman (the stepdaughter of a French trader) with a Philadelphian. Baird related that ribbon-bordered garments were worn by the bride, her mother, and Mme. Laframboise and Mme. Schindler, two metis (part-Indian) traders (Baird, 1898, pp. 44–45).

The use of silk ribbon on Native American dress went beyond clothing intended for humans. A Scottish missionary to the Stockbridge Munsee of Wisconsin (a subgroup of the Delaware) wrote in 1838 that a Munsee from Canada visited him in order to give up a ceremonial doll. According to Rev. Cutting Marsh, the doll was:

> fantastically arrayed in Indian costume
> and nearly covered with silver broaches
> and trinkets; and whilst retained as an
> object of worship was kept wrapped up
> in some 20 envelopments of broadcloth
> trimmed with scarlet ribbon (Documents,
> 1900, p. 165).

The profusion of ribbon-decorated garments for this ceremonial doll was related to its ritual function. The Delaware people traditionally fed, danced, and dressed the ceremonial dolls with new clothing as part of a yearly rite relating to the health of the family.[8]

These historical references contain descriptions of ribbon-bordered dress from Montreal to Ohio to Wisconsin. Together they corroborate a century-long practice of using silk ribbon as a border on items of dress in the Great Lakes region. Yet these male authors only superficially noted the use of ribbon. Two referred specifically to sewing, but no one provided instructions about the application techniques, details of the ribbon (other than color), or information on how the ribbon was acquired.

Cut-and-Sewn Ribbonwork: an Innovation

One of the most intriguing aspects of the dress of Great Lakes Indians is the development of ribbonwork, ribbon strips of contrasting colors that are layered on a textile or leather foundation and which form designs based on the cutting, folding under, and sewing of the ribbon layers (see Figure 6.8).[9] Cut-and-sewn ribbonwork on garments and personal accessories is aligned with hems and edges as are the simple ribbon borders, and often both simple ribbon and ribbonwork borders appear on the same item of dress.

Ribbonwork is assumed to have begun sometime in the 18th century, yet no historical documents have been located that clarify the origin of this innovation.[10] The search for the origins of ribbonwork exemplifies the challenge of interpreting documentary and artifactual evidence. David Zeisberger's 1781 description of a Delaware woman's skirt appears to allude to the layering of ribbons required in ribbonwork:

> The dress which particularly distinguishes
> the woman is a petticoat or strowd, blue,
> red or black, made of a piece of cloth about
> 2 yards long, adorned with red, blue or
> yellow bands laid double and bound about
> the body (Zeisberger, 1910, p. 86).

Zeisberger wrote the original manuscript in German and his use of the term Band should more properly be translated as ribbon rather than band as in the English version. Furthermore, an examination of the German manuscript (Zeisberger, 1781) confirms that it is the "bands" that are laid double, and not the cloth as is typical in the wrapped skirt traditionally worn by Delaware

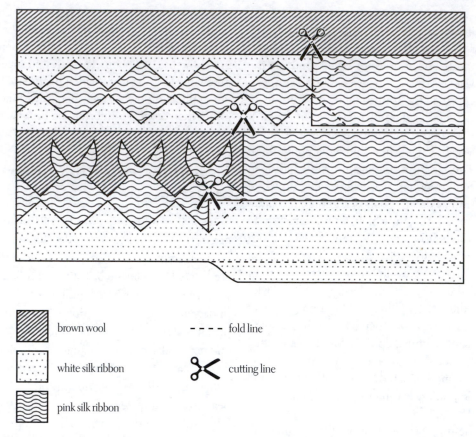

brown wool   ---- fold line

white silk ribbon   ✄ cutting line

pink silk ribbon

Figure 6.8 Top Strip: White silk ribbon is sewn to brown wool cloth. Pink silk ribbon is laid on top of the white ribbon and cut at regular intervals. Triangles of ribbon are folded under, and folded edges are sewn to the base ribbon to yield a sawtooth edge. The process is repeated along the other selvage. This band is a true example of the Developmental Style, considered to be the simplest and earliest form of ribbonwork (Abbass, 1980; 1994). Bottom Strip: Pink silk ribbon is laid on the brown wool and cut at varying intervals and angles. The raw edges are folded under and sewn to the base cloth to yield V-shapes. White silk ribbon is laid on top of the unworked portion of pink ribbon and cut at regular intervals. Triangles of white ribbon are folded under and then folded edges are sewn to base ribbon. Excess white ribbon is folded to the underside and sewn down as a binding. This band represents an elaboration of the Developmental Style.

women. Unfortunately, Zeisberger gave no specifics about the doubling process. A doubling process—or laying one ribbon on top of the other—is the prerequisite step for the cutting and folding necessary in the developmental ribbonwork style (explained in Figure 6.8). However, doubling could also mean that two ribbons were simply laid selvage to selvage. This multiple ribbon style frequently appeared on cloaks, breechcloths, and skirts worn by Great Lakes Indians or given as gifts to Europeans in the late 18th and early 19th centuries.[11]

Of the written records located, the earliest, most explicit description of ribbonwork was by an artist, George Winter (Winter's writings have been noted by Conn, 1980). Winter painted and kept journals of his visits to Potawatomi and Miami villages in central Indiana in 1837 and 1839. In the journals, Winter described leggings, mantles, and skirts on which multiple rows of one color or variously colored ribbons were used as borders. In addition, he wrote about the ribbons being "shaped into singular forms" and of petticoats "handsomely checkered by variously coloured ribbons etc." (Edmunds, 1993, p. 28; Winter 1948, pp. 110, 137). The cutting and sewing process of ribbonwork was noted in Winter's description of clothing worn by Mas-saw, a Potawatomi woman whom he referred to as a chieftess:

> . . .her petticoat was handsomely bordered by rows of ribbons of the primitive [primary] colors, an occasional row of a secondary color. These ribbons were about two inches wide, cut into points and vandykes-very neatly sewed. . . (Cooke & Ramadhyani, 1993, p. 77).

Finally, he directly referred to garments with both ribbonwork and simple ribbon borders that he saw in the home of Jean-Baptiste Brouillette (of Miami and French heritage):

> Two or three pairs of "leggings" with handsome borders, or "wings" decorated with the primitive coloured ribbons some sewed in diamond forms, others in straight lines (Cooke & Ramadhyani, 1993, p. 116; Winter, 1948, p. 173).

Similar diamond forms can be seen on the women's leggings. Winter's journal and paintings (which are reproduced in Cooke and Ramadhyani, 1993, and Winter, 1948) were preceded some thirty years by firmly dated items of dress with ribbonwork borders.[12] The foremost example is the wedding costume of Sophie Thérèse Rankin, of Menominee and French parentage, who in 1802 married Louis Grignon, a Green Bay trader. The garments show both simple ribbon and ribbonwork borders on the shawl, skirt, and leggings.[13] Other ribbonwork garments from the Great Lakes region were collected in the early years of the 19th century by Jasper Grant and Captain Malcolm.[14]

While the written record expands our knowledge of garments with ribbonwork borders, these documents have not provided evidence for the region or the date of origin of ribbonwork, its creators and the impulse for innovation, or clear evidence on style development. However, both artifacts and documents confirm that the Great Lakes region was a center of ribbonwork dress.

Interpreting Ribbon-Bordered Dress

Late 18th and early 19th-century evidence of ribbon-bordered dress was primarily recorded by Euro-American males, many of whom spent only a minimal amount of time among the Great Lakes tribes. Only Kalm was concerned with scientific methods of observation, and at least several writers were mostly concerned with the profitability of publishing an account of their frontier experiences. All were apparently oblivious to the process of culture change and wrote as if the garments they described were timeless. Yet despite these biases, there emerges a coherent core of information regarding the cultural context of ribbon-bordered dress among Native Americans of the Great Lakes.[15] This context can be summarized by an excerpt from the writings of John Heckewelder. Describing the late 18th-century Delaware residing in the Ohio region, Heckewelder wrote:

> The wealthy adorn themselves besides with ribands or gartering of various colours, beads and silver broaches. These ornaments are arranged by the women, who, as well as the men, know how to dress themselves in style (Heckewelder, 1876/1971, p. 203).

First, the ribbon was uniformly presented as ornamentation. This perception was expressed by the Euro-American writers through words such as "adorn," "decorate," "garnish," or "ornament"; Alexander Henry was the only one to equate ribbon ornamentation with "fashion" (Henry, 1809, p. 156). Some descriptions might lead to the interpretation that ribbon-bordered dress was the commonly worn style. But persons who lived among the Great Lakes Indian groups, such as Oliver Spencer, clearly differentiated ribbon-bordered dress as more ornamental than the garments worn for everyday (Spencer, 1835, pp. 84–85).

Second, silk ribbon was mentioned frequently in connection with other decorative media, which are also seen in articles of dress now in museums and private collections. Decorative materials listed in these early accounts were often indigenous to the region, such as porcupine quills or elk hair. Yet imported materials were also described, such as the ubiquitous glass beads, as well as silver in brooches, and tin in the shape of cones suspended along the hem edges. The mix of native and European decorative materials suggests that, in the 18th and early 19th centuries, Indian women of the Great Lakes used nontraditional media to expand their decorative capabilities rather than pursuing an immediate wholesale replacement of indigenous materials.

Third, ribbon-bordered garments were worn by both men and women, although they were made by women. Isaac Weld wrote of seeing ribbon-bordered dress on Indian men and women at Malden, the British fort on Lake Erie, in 1795–1797. Weld remarked that "The utmost ingenuity of the squaws is exerted in adorning the little aprons with beads, ribbands" (Weld, 1807, vol. 2, p. 233). The painter George Winter commented that the ribbon ornamentation "is the work of the squaws, and it displays much patience and ingenuity" (Winter, 1948, p. 96). Thus the imported silk ribbon was balanced by the retention of the indigenous pattern of apparel production and ornamentation.

Fourth, ribbon-bordered dress was seen as costly and thus equated with wealth. Jackson Kemper, an Episcopalian missionary who traveled to Green Bay in 1834, recorded that Mrs. Grignon, the Menominee trader from Green Bay whose wedding garments were mentioned previously, "has indian dresses that wld cost 80 or 100 dollars" (Kemper, 1898, p. 415). Winter's journal documenting his visit to the Potawatomis of central Indiana in 1837 noted:

> They wore red and black blankets, as their rich mantles are called, which are made of superfine broad cloth decorated with colored ribbons and silver ornaments are very costly. . . . Some of their dresses were estimated as being worth $200 (Cooke & Ramadhyani, 1993, p. 49; Edmunds, 1993, p. 28; Winter, 1948, p. 110).

The missionary Heckewelder wrote that ribbon borders and silver brooches on garments were "at the expense of their husbands or lovers" (Heckewelder, 1876/1971, p. 203).

Yet Oliver Spencer's comments suggest that the expense was in the labor to produce the ornamentation rather than the value of the ornamentation itself:

> The form of the dress is the same among the Indian women of all ranks and ages, varying only in its quality, and in the richness and variety with which it is adorned; its ornaments not being regulated by rank or station, but by the ability of the wearer (Spencer, 1835, p. 84).

The ribbonwork technique is particularly labor intensive because of the fine stitching involved in sewing the cut-and-folded edges of the ribbon. Furthermore, the layering and cutting of the ribbon represents an extravagant attitude toward the decorative material.

Finally, ribbon-bordered dress was uniformly perceived as representing an "Indian" style, not as a derivation or imitation of European dress. This generalization is further exemplified in an 1803 letter by Johan P. Kluge, of the Moravian Indian Mission on the White River in the Indiana Territory. Kluge wrote:

> . . . the heathen are so loath to put aside their heathenish mode of dress when they move to us. They never object to the request that they must not paint their faces, but they do not want to give up their silk-ribbon trimmings and beads and things with which they love to bedeck themselves. Shall we insist that they must put these things aside? (Gipson, 1938, p. 506).

Whether the ribbon-bordered garments were worn by Native Americans in the Great Lakes region or by the metis (the children of European and Indian parents) from Green Bay or central Indiana, ribbon-bordered dress signified an Indian aesthetic and style.[16]

Tastily Bound with Ribbons

The rise and spread of ribbon-bordered dress among the Indians of the Great Lakes is a story of culture contact and change. Through silk ribbon, Native Americans were bound together with Euro-Americans in relationships of trade and diplomacy. Yet ribbon-bordered dress incorporated the European-produced textile in a unique, non-European way, thus establishing a boundary between what was and what was not Indian. With the spread of ribbon-bordered dress across the Great Lakes region, American Indians were bound together in a regional expression of taste. The differences of language and dialect groups and kinship types, as well as past conflicts among these Woodlands tribes, were minimized and their commonalities reinforced in comparison to the culture of the Europeans. The common experience of contact with Europeans and the resulting changes in technologies and materials are symbolized in ribbon-bordered dress. Even with the disruption of the removal period of 1830 to the 1860s in which many Native American nations inhabiting the Great Lakes region were fragmented or forcibly displaced to west of the Mississippi River, ribbon-bordered dress remained a shared tradition that survived and expanded to prairie tribes.[17] For Great Lakes Indians of the 18th and early 19th centuries, ribbon-bordered dress signified a creative response to culture change, one that simultaneously established cultural boundaries while binding cultures together.

References

Abbass, D. K. (1979). Contemporary Oklahoma ribbonwork: Styles and economics (Doctoral dissertation, Southern Illinois University at Carbondale, 1979). Dissertation Abstracts International, 40, 3385A.

Abbass, D. K. (1980). American Indian ribbonwork: The visual characteristics. In G.P. Horse Capture (Ed.), *Native American ribbonwork* (pp. 31–43). Cody, WY: Buffalo Bill Historical Center.

Abbass, D. K. (1994). Ribbonwork. In Davis, M. (Ed.), *Native America in the twentieth century: An encyclopedia.* New York: Garland Press.

Archives des Colonies, Correspondence, C11A. Paris: Archives Nationales (microfilm in Public Archives of Canada, Manuscript Division MsG 1, Ottawa).

Art of the Great Lakes Indians (1973). Flint, MI: Flint Institute of Arts.

Askin, J. Papers. Detroit, MI: Detroit Public Library, Burton Historical Collection.

Baird, E. T. (1898). Reminiscences of early days on Mackinac Island. Collections of the State Historical Society of Wisconsin, 14, 17–64.

Brasser, T. J. (1976). "Bo'jou, Neejee!": Profiles of Canadian Indian art. Ottawa: National Museum of Man.

Brawer, C. C. (1983). *Many trails: Indians of the lower Hudson Valley.* Katonah, NY: The Katonah Gallery.

Coe, R. T. (1986). *Lost and found traditions: Native American art 1965–1985.* Seattle: University of Washington Press.

Colonial Office, Class 42: Canada, Original Correspondence. London: Public Records Office (microfilm in Public Archives of Canada, Manuscript Division MsG 11, Ottawa).

Conn, R. (1980). Native American cloth applique and ribbonwork: Their origins and diffusion in the Plains. In G. P. Horse Capture (Ed.), *Native American ribbonwork* (pp. 9–22). Cody, WY: Buffalo Bill Historical Center.

Cooke, S. E., & Ramadhyani, R. B. (Comps.) (1993). *Indians and a changing frontier: The art of George Winter.* Indianapolis, IN: Indiana Historical Society.

Documents relating to the Stockbridge Mission, 1825–48 (1900). Collections of the State Historical Society of Wisconsin, 25, 39–204.

Edmunds, R. D. (1993). George Winter: Mirror of acculturation. In S. E. Cooke & R. B. Ramadhyani (Comps.), *Indians and a changing frontier: The art of George Winter* (pp. 23–39). Indianapolis, IN: Indiana Historical Society.

Feather, B. L., & Sibley, L. R. (1979). Overlooked pages of North American clothing history. *Dress,* 63–73.

Feder, N. (1971). *American Indian art.* New York: Harry N. Abrams.

Gipson, L. H. (Ed.) (1938). *The Moravian Indian mission on White River.* Indianapolis: Indiana Historical Bureau.

Harrington, M. R. (1921). *Religion and ceremonies of the Lenape.* New York: Museum of the American Indian, Heye Foundation.

Hartman, S. (1988). *Indian clothing of the Great Lakes: 1740–1840.* Liberty, UT: Eagle's View.

Heckewelder, J. (1971). *History, manners, and customs of the Indian nations who once inhabited Pennsylvania and the neighbouring states* (rev. ed.). New York: Amo Press & the *New York Times.* (Originally published 1876).

Henry, A. (1809). *Travels and adventures in Canada and the Indian territories, between the years 1760 and 1776.* New York: I. Riley.

Hunter, R., Jr. (1943). *Quebec to Carolina in 1785–1786* (L.B. Wright & M. Tinling, Eds.). San Marino, CA: The Huntington Library.

Ironside, G. R. Papers. Detroit, MI: Detroit Public Library, Burton Historical Collection.

JCB (1978). *Voyage au Canada fait depuis l'an 1751 à 1761.* Paris: Aubier Montaigne.

Jacobs, W. R. (1950). *Diplomacy and Indian gifts: Anglo-French rivalry along the Ohio and Northwest frontiers, 1748–1776.* Stanford, CA: Stanford University Press.

Johnson, W. (1921–1925). *The papers of Sir William Johnson* (Vol. 1–4; J. Sullivan, Ed.). Albany: The University of the State of New York.

Kalm, P. (1772). *Travels into North America* (2nd ed., 2 vols.). London: T. Lowndes.

Kelley, H. (1987). *Scarlet ribbons: American Indian technique for today's quilters*. Paducah, KY: American Quilter's Society.

Kemper, J. (1898). Journal of an Episcopalian missionary's tour to Green Bay, 1834. Collections of the State Historical Society of Wisconsin, 14, 394–449.

Marriott, A. (1958). Ribbon applique work of North American Indians, part I. Bulletin of the Oklahoma Anthropological Society, 6, 49–59.

Montgomery, F. M. (1984). *Textiles in America, 1650–1870*. New York: W. W. Norton.

Pannabecker, R. K. (1986). Ribbonwork of the Great Lakes Indians: The material of acculturation (Doctoral dissertation, Ohio State University, 1986). Dissertation Abstracts International, 47, 961A–962A.

Pannabecker, R. K. (1988). The cultural authentication of ribbon: Use and test of a concept. *Clothing and Textiles Research Journal*, 7, 55–56.

Penney, D. W. (1992). *Art of the American Indian frontier*. Seattle: University of Washington Press.

Phillips, R. B. (1984). *Patterns of power: The Jasper Grant collection and Great Lakes Indian art of the early nineteenth century*. Kleinburg, Ontario: The McMichael Canadian Collection.

Phillips, R. B. (1987). Like a star I shine: Northern Woodlands artistic traditions. In *The spirit sings: Artistic traditions of Canada's first peoples* (pp. 51–92). Toronto: McClelland and Stewart.

Porter, G. R. (1831). *A treatise on the origin, progressive improvement, and present state of the silk manufacture*. London: Longman, Rees, Orme, Brown, and Green.

Powell, W. D. Collection. Toronto: Metro Toronto Library, Baldwin Room.

Roach, M. E., & Musa, K. E. (1980). *New perspectives on the history of western dress*. New York: NutriGuides.

Roach-Higgins, M. E., & Eicher, J. (1992). Dress and identity. *Clothing and Textiles Research Journal*, 10(4), 1–8.

Sanders, R., & Sanders, J. Papers. New York: New York Historical Society (microfilm in Public Archives of Canada, Manuscript Division MsG 18C6, Ottawa).

Shine, C. R. (1988). Scalping knives and silk stockings: Clothing the frontier, 1780–1795. *Dress*, 14, 39–47.

Simpson, J. A., and Weiner, E. S. C. (Eds.) (1989). The Oxford English Dictionary (2nd ed.). Oxford: Clarendon Press.

Smith, J. (1907). *An account of the remarkable occurrences in the life and travels of Col. James Smith*. Cincinnati: Robert Clarke. (Originally published 1799)

Speck, F. G. (1937). *Oklahoma Delaware ceremonies, feasts, and dances*. Philadelphia: The American Philosophical Society.

Spencer, O. (1835). *Indian captivity*. New York: B. Waugh and T. Mason.

Sterling, J. Papers. Detroit, MI: Detroit Public Library, Burton Historical Collection.

Thompson, J. (1977). *The North American Indian collection: A catalogue*. Berne: Historical Museum.

Thwaites, R. G. (Ed.) (1959). *The Jesuit relations and allied documents: Vol. 68 Lower Canada, Crees, Louisiana: 1720–1736*. New York: Pageant Book. (Originally published 1896–1901)

Tipton, J. Papers. Indianapolis: Indiana State Library, Indiana Division.

Torrence, G., & Hobbs, R. (1989). *Art of the Red Earth people: The Mesquakie of Iowa*. Seattle: University of Washington Press.

Weld, I. (1807). *Travels through the states of North America, and the provinces of Upper and Lower Canada, during the years 1795, 1796, and 1797* (4th ed., vols. 1–2). London: John Stockdale.

Winter, G. (1948). *The journals and Indian paintings of George Winter 1837–1839*. Indianapolis: Indiana Historical Society.

Zeisberger, D. (1781). Von den Indianern Gestalt und Lebensart. Records of the Moravian Mission Among the Indians of North America, Microfilm Reel 33, Box Number 2291–313. Bethlehem, PA: The Archives of the Moravian Church.

Zeisberger, D. (1910). *David Zeisberger's history of the Northern American Indians* (A. B. Hulbert & W. N. Schwarze, Eds.). Columbus, OH: F. J. Heer.

Endnotes

1. Original spellings are retained in all quoted material. Stroud or strowd was wool broadcloth, often red, which was manufactured in the Stroudwater region of England and used by Woodlands Indians as mantles, wrapped skirts, or leggings. See Montgomery (1984) and the Oxford English Dictionary (Simpson & Weiner, 1989) for information on terms for historical textiles. While Spencer's narrative has been accepted as an accurate description of life among Indians of the Ohio region, the book's illustrator did not enjoy the same first-hand experience, and apparently failed to read the details of Spencer's text before preparing the illustrations. Thus, the book depicted Indian men in Greek-style togas (already a conventional way to portray Native Americans) and the women in the puffed-sleeved gowns fashionable during the era when the book was published. See the Spencer illustration in Figure 4 in Shine (1988, p. 43).

2. For the artifacts under discussion I prefer the term dress because it retains the collective sense implied by the terms clothing and costume, but avoids their negative connotations (see Roach-Higgins & Eicher, 1992, p. 3). See also definition #2 of dress in Simpson and Weiner (1989, p. 1044). In this article, items of ribbon-bordered dress include mantles, wrapped skirts, breechcloths, leggings, moccasins, and the skirt of a ceremonial doll. Hoods, shirts, garter pendants, pouches, and cradle binders with ribbon borders are not specifically treated here but can be found in illustrations referred to in the footnotes.

3. Paduasoy or padusoy was a rich and heavy silk cloth or ribbon, and was generally corded and sometimes brocaded.

4. Tinsel or tinsell ribbon was a wool base interwoven with metallic threads. Ferret or ferreting was a general term for tape, ribbon, or binding, often of cotton but also of silk.

5. In 1831 a piece of ribbon was defined as measuring 36 yards (Porter, 1831, p. 231).

6. While the exact name of JCB remains unknown, he is sometimes referred to as J. C. Bonnefons (see p. 8 of the book's preface); but the published version of his manuscript is catalogued as J. C. Bonnefois in the Bibliothèque nationale de France, Paris.

7. Cappo is a corruption of capote, a hooded coat or cloak.

8. For other photographs of Delaware ceremonial dolls, see Brawer (1983, p. 111) and Harrington (1921, Plate VIII). For further information on the Delaware doll dance, see Harrington (1921) and Speck (1937).

9. The most inclusive typology of ribbonwork styles has been developed by Abbass (1980); see also Conn (1980).

10. Many scholars of Native American dress have not distinguished between simple ribbon borders and cut-and-sewn ribbonwork. Others have relied solely on dates provided by surviving examples of ribbonwork. Thus, estimates for the origin of ribbonwork have ranged from the early 18th century to the early years of the 19th century. See Pannabecker (1986, p. 105) for a complete overview of the secondary literature on ribbonwork.

11. See, for example, multiple rows of ribbons on items from Sir John Caldwell (Brasser, 1976, cover and p. 130; Phillips, 1987, p. 69), Captain Malcolm (Phillips, 1987, p. 73; Thompson, 1977, p. 121), and Sophie Thérèse Rankin (Conn, 1980, p. 20).

12. Many of Winter's watercolor paintings were executed 26 to 35 years after his field observations and working sketches. While it is generally accepted that Winter's depictions of Indian costumes and daily life are unique historical records (see Edmunds, 1993, p. 37), the ethnographic value of his journal must be considered more valuable than the paintings which could have been affected by the passage of time and artistic interpretation.

13. The ribbonwork on Rankin garments is illustrated in Figures 8 and 10 in Conn (1980, pp. 20–21). Hartman (1988, pp. 46–47) misreads and misrepresents my research and findings on the Rankin garments.

14. Grant was a British military commander stationed in Upper Canada at Fort George, in the Niagara region, and Fort Malden, at the western edge of Lake Erie. Color photographs of the Grant collection can be seen in Phillips (1984). The Malcolm collection lacks documentation, but he was also probably a British officer serving in Canada. See photographs of the Malcolm collection in Thompson (1977, p. 119) and Phillips (1987, p. 73). Later examples of simple ribbon borders and ribbonwork can be found in Art of the Great Lakes Indians (1973), Conn (1980), Penney (1992), and Torrence and Hobbs (1989). See also the ribbonwork skirts worn by Winnebago women in Roach and Musa (1980, p. 83, slide #2).

15. This core of evidence is particularly valuable since the majority of Euro-American writers of the period failed to record any substantive information on the dress of Native Americans. This omission can be attributed to a lack of interest on the part of many Euro-American males to material culture, to dress and adornment, or to women's work.

16. For a discussion on ribbonwork as culturally authentic, see Pannabecker (1988).

17. See ribbonwork by Osage women, for example in Feder (1971, colorplate 19).

Discussion Questions

1. What are the stages Pannabecker identifies that ribbon went through to become culturally authentic to the Great Lakes Indians?

2. What are other examples of styles or items adopted by one culture to become "culturally authentic"?

"ETHNIC FASHION" OBSCURES CULTURAL IDENTITY

Sunita Puri

I live a hyphenated existence. South Asian-American. Indian-American. Punjabi-American. Physically, I am also a patchwork of different cultures: I wear jeans and t-shirts, I braid my hair in Punjabi *kudiya* style, have a nose ring, and wear a *bindi*, a small colored dot worn in between the eyebrows by South-Asian women (Figure 6.9). Depending on who you talk to, though, I can be seen as an Indian trying to be "fashionably ethnic" in superficially "multicultural" American surroundings. While my extended family sympathizes with my efforts to reconcile my sense of belonging to both India and America, I do not meet with such understanding from those surrounding me who interpret my wearing *bindis* as a fashion statement rather than a statement of cultural belonging.

I recently had a conversation with an acquaintance who believed that I wear *bindis* because, in his words, "It's a, you know, convenient way to sort of like assert an identity. Like, you're making a statement, but it's not offensive or anything. It's actually fashionable." I was shocked, especially at his claim that many others agreed with him. I wear my *bindis* to demonstrate my adherence to and respect for my culture and religion and the large roles they occupy in my identity and everyday life—not to imitate a pop icon. My acquaintance then pulled out a picture of Destiny's Child, taken at a recent awards program. Not only were the women clad in outfits made from sari material, but they all sported matching, colorfully flashy *bindis*.

This is cultural imperialism at its worst. Pop icons like Madonna perpetuate a faulty understanding of Indian culture by selecting exotic images from India, such as the *bindi*, taking them completely out of cultural context and popularizing them in the West. What people like Madonna don't realize, however, is that appropriating the *bindi* in such a way has devastating effects on the symbol's meaning in South Asia. For example, while in Delhi over the summer, I was hard pressed to find plain red *bindis*, finding instead very flashy, so-called "export quality" *bindis*, replete with sparkles and a variety of colors. The *bindi* is no longer what it once was—a symbol of being Hindu and of having a symbolic union with God. Now, it is not only a fashionable item to wear, but is also mass-produced specifically for export to other countries. The Madonnas and Gwen Stefanis of the world—along with those who have blindly followed their example—have successfully changed the meaning of the *bindi* in South Asia, for the worse.

Figure 6.9 The *bindi* is a traditional mark among women of many Southeast Asian countries, however it has recently been controversially adopted as fashion.

Printed in *The Yale Herald*, Volume 31, Issue 4, February 2, 2001, http://www.yaleherald.com/archive/xxxi/2001.02.02/opinion/page12aethnic.html

And this new meaning obviously extends to South Asian Americans, among them young women such as myself who are labeled as consumers of teenybopper culture rather than as heirs to the cultural legacy represented in small part by *bindis*. My stomach turns when I see non-South Asians wearing *bindis* to proms, social events, or simply "as part of their outfits." Without realizing it, they are transforming the meaning of the *bindi* from an inherently sacred entity to an accessory whose popularity will undoubtedly fade, as all trends do. And the popularization of this trend may suggest to our peers that those of us who wear *bindis* to bridge our hyphenated existences do so only to assert cultural identity in an acceptable, Americanized way.

While I do not mean to imply that all Americans think this way, even knowing a handful that do is insulting, both to me personally and to South Asian culture. How am I, for example, supposed to react when I enter a bookstore and see *The Bindi Kit* lying on the shelf marked "International Books"? Am I supposed to be happy that *bindis* are now being sold along with body paint in kits that encourage girls to wear *bindis* as exotic belly button ring substitutes surrounded by colorful paint?

One could argue that the *bindi* phenomenon is a good thing because it could motivate interested Americans to examine diverse South Asian cultures and histories more closely. Even though this might be true, I resent the fact that a culture should be considered worthy of study or attention because of the fashion appeal of its symbols or traditions. Assigning new cultural meanings to symbols with very old traditions or deep personal significance is inappropriate and insensitive. It reduces the complexities of South Asian culture to mere physical items, rather than the continual process that culture is.

So please—don't wear *bindis*, and don't think of my homeland simply as the origin of yoga, incense, and exoticism if you are going to ignore the context and meanings of these cultural components as well as the reasons why we "ethnic folk" appreciate, treasure, and cling to them.

Puri wrote this article while an undergraduate at Yale University.

Discussion Questions

1. Do you believe it is acceptable to adopt ethnic styles for fashion purposes? Why or why not?
2. What are some other ethnic styles that have become fashions? Were there controversies over them?

6.6

DRESS BETWEEN THE SACRED AND THE COMMERCIAL: THE CASE OF THE NORWEGIAN BUNAD

Thomas Hylland Eriksen
University of Oslo

Clothes are sold and bought as commodities worldwide, but many forms of clothing are invested with cultural meanings that partly remove them from the logic of pure market economics. In the interstices between the logic of capitalism and concerted attempts to invest specific, culturally valued garments with a special, noncommoditized quality, struggles take place, symbolic meanings are contested, and attempts are made to copyright specific crafts, designs, and traditional forms of knowledge in the name of cultural tradition. Attempts to monopolize cultural symbols

Original for this text. This article is an abbreviated version of "Keeping the recipe: Norwegian folk costumes and cultural capital," *Focaal*, 44 (2004): 20–34.

and artefacts in order to commercialize them in a controlled way are widespread in this era of intensified globalization and increased mobility, as documented by Comaroff and Comaroff (2009), Harrison (1999), and many others. This article uses the example of the Norwegian folk dress, the *bunad*, to illustrate some of the issues and controversies at play when the commercial and the existential dimensions of cultural artefacts are intertwined.

The Bunad

There has been a certain scholarly attention to folk costumes, most of it concerned with their place in identity politics (see e.g., Eicher 1995). It has been shown, for example, that the kilt was never a popular garment in historical Scotland, but gained symbolic significance for political reasons after 1745 (Chapman 1992), and that certain folk costumes have been "frozen in time" while others have been adapted and modernized to fit changing circumstances (Lynch 1995), always with the political project of group cohesion and boundary maintenance as the underlying force.

The Norwegian bunad is a very popular kind of festive folk costume (Figure 6.10). Instead of seeing these symbolically laden garments primarily in the light of nation-building, as others have done, I shall analyze the bunad and controversies surrounding it in the context of cultural identity politics and commercialization.

The bunad is a kind of dress circumscribed with deep symbolic meaning. The term is a slightly archaic Norwegian dialect word, introduced into urban circles by the author and nationalist activist Hulda Garborg in her pamphlet Norsk klædebunad ("Norwegian garb") in 1903. Writing during a feverish phase of Norwegian nationalism (the country became independent from Sweden in 1905, and cultural nationalism was an enormously powerful force at the time), Garborg argued the need for a truly Norwegian and regionally diverse form of formal dress. She collected and systematized what she saw as intact and useful regional traditions, and designed some bunads herself. Interestingly, Garborg never denied the

Figure 6.10 The folk costume of Norway, the bunad, is a recent creation, but represents a traditional, ancient culture.

syncretist and partly invented character of the new, traditionalist folk costume. She nevertheless emphasized its role as a marker of rural, Norwegian identity. Very many Norwegian regions and even smaller valleys have their own bunads. Many have been designed long after Garborg; the Bergen bunad, for example, dates from 1956 but gives the impression of being a very traditional kind of dress.[1]

The bunad is an important, traditionalist symbol of modern Norwegianness. Most of these costumes are clearly related to regional and minority folk costumes from Central and Eastern Europe, and the German influence has been commented upon (Oxaal 2001). More important, the bunad confirms Norwegian identity as an essentially rural one, where personal integrity is connected to roots and regional origins. However, 18th- and 19th-century peasants would often wear European-style dress at formal occasions such as weddings, or they might wear a folk costume, which gradually went out of use. In other words, there is a clear element of modern invention (cf. Hobsbawm and Ranger, 1983), which nobody denies, in the currently widespread use of bunads. Fashions changed and were often inspired by the big European centers. The bunad, which has therefore often been reconstructed from historical sources, signifies adherence to roots and traditions. Indeed, the then prime minister of Norway, Mrs. Gro Harlem Brundtland, wore a bunad in what could be described as ostentatious display during the Winter Olympics at Lillehammer in 1994. Later in the same year, Norway would decide on whether to join the European Union. Mrs. Brundtland's dress must be read as a way of overcommunicating Norwegianness. She was the leader of a pro-EU government trying to persuade a skeptical population, and by wearing a bunad she seemed to try to convey the idea that there was no contradiction between being European and being a good Norwegian.

Although bunads have been a common sight on festive occasions, not least on Constitution Day (17 May), for generations, they have become increasingly common during the last few decades. Growing up in the 1970s in the coastal town Tønsberg, a place with weak connections to national romanticism, I used to see few bunads in town during the parades and public gatherings on 17 May. The town had for centuries been a prosperous center of trade, shipping, and whaling, and the fashions had always tended to be urban and European. Returning to my old hometown on that day in the mid-1990s, I was taken aback by the uniformity in dress during the public events. The regional bunad had been designed relatively recently, and bunads had not been common in this coastal region in the past.

Patrolling the Borders

The Bunad and Folk Costume Council (Bunad- og folkedraktsrådet) is a state-funded advisory body under the Ministry of Culture. The purpose of the Council is to offer advice and to stimulate an enhanced understanding of the traditional dress practices that are the foundation of today's bunads.

The Council has collected enormous amounts of knowledge about bunads, and states on its website that it has 55,000 different patterns of bunads and folk costumes in its database. The Council cannot legislate formally on patterns and designs, but its advice is taken very seriously. Often, a new or revised design is denied the term bunad, a garment which should have a strong historical element and a clear geographical provenance, but is instead called simply a regional costume (*drakt*), or—pejoratively—a "fantasy costume."

Interestingly, the current policies of the Bunad and Folk Costume Council are based on a stronger version of Romantic notions of cultural authenticity than were Garborg's views in 1903. Garborg emphasized that some degree of cultural continuity was desirable, and recommended that Norwegian bunads should be made from Norwegian fabrics such as wool, not from imported silk and linen. However, she also took a pragmatic stance on the issue of authenticity, admitting that the bunads needed to be modernized to suit the modern woman's taste. The Bunad and Folk Costume Council, on the contrary, states that "The main objective in our day and age is that the bunad should be as good a copy as possible of a local folk costume as it was used in a particular historical period."

More than 60 percent of Norwegian women owned a bunad at the turn of the millennium (Aagedal, 2002) along with a growing, but smaller number of men. In neighboring Sweden, the figure is six percent. These costumes are expensive garments with hand-embroidered details, ornamental silver jewellery and, often, accessories such as belts, sashes, ribbons, and bands. Some of the more popular ones cost as much as NOK 30,000 (€ 4,000). The total value of the one and a half million Norwegian bunads in existence is estimated at 30 billion kroner (€ 4 billion). In other words, the bunad business is economically significant, in addition to its strong connotations of political and cultural identity.

The economics of the bunad are deeply informed by cultural values and norms relating to tradition. Notably, there are strict informal rules regulating individual use of bunads. Some are considered more beautiful than others, but a person has no moral right to wear them unless she (it is usually a she) has documented kinship links with the place of origin. In contemporary society, many if not most individuals have two, three, or four options: they can legitimately wear a bunad designed in the place where they live, in the place where they grew up (which is often a different place, as urbanization has been considerable), or in one of their parents' places of origin. They cannot, however, legitimately wear a bunad from wherever they fancy. Of course, they could buy it, but their friends and relatives might react strongly. An expert says: "I am aware of people in the heart of Bunad Norway (Bunad-Norge) who are deeply offended. They have no time for West End ladies who claim Telemark ancestry when they buy the perhaps greatest status symbol of all bunads, namely the expensive and exclusive East Telemark bunad. They also dislike that people wear gold chains and earrings while they wear bunads."[2]

The purism within the Bunad and Folk Costume Council is also strong. The director of the Council comments, regarding the unhistorical, but often attractive "fantasy costumes": "Some companies use really aggressive marketing strategies to sell these fantasy costumes. They have nothing to do with old traditions. We just want to inform people that they have no business believing that they are wearing bunads if they buy this stuff."[3]

There are frequent conflicts over authenticity framed within the bunad discourse itself. In the valley of Numedal, competition between two alternative bunads actually led to the creation of two distinct factions in the 17 May parade of 2002. Family members fell out with each other, and local politicians groped for compromises. One of the alternatives, a simple folk costume, is woven in dark fabrics; the complex, reconstructed bunad sanctioned by the Bunad and Folk Costume Council is much more elaborate and colorful. The defenders of the simple costume argue that the new one, "overloaded with silver and embroideries," is inappropriate and inauthentic for a traditionally poor mountain valley; while the other faction see the simple bunad as sordid and joyless. Both factions claim that their bunad is the "real" one. The one sanctioned by the Council is the more expensive one. It is also an undisputed fact that embroideries and masses of fine silver jewellry have been added to bunads in modern times, as people were increasingly able to afford them. Interestingly, embroideries were widespread in 18th-century folk costumes, but went out of use following the availability of inexpensive (often imported) fabrics in the 19th century. Reconstructed bunads are therefore said, by their defenders, to be older than the 19th-century folk costumes, even if they can also be said to be more recent.

The Entrepreneur and the Bunad Police

The bunad industry sits, perhaps uncomfortably, but also profitably, in the crossroads between traditionalist identity politics and business. The largest actors in the field, such as the shop chain Husfliden, try to have it both ways; by guaranteeing the regional authenticity of the garments they sell, they are using culture as investment capital to justify exorbitant prices. Husfliden ("Home crafts"), which has outlets in many Norwegian towns, contributes in no small measure to defining what a certain bunad should look like and focusing the market on certain bunads and costumes at the expense of others. In one case, Husfliden organized courses for women wishing to save money by sewing their own bunads, but as a condition, the participants had to sign an agreement promising that they would only make bunads for themselves and for first-order blood relatives. Some talk about "the bunad police" (by analogy to Orwell's thought police), while a particular region in North-Western Norway, known for its heartbreaking local conflicts over authenticity issues, is spoken of as "the Yugoslavia of the bunad."

The bunad stirs up strong emotions. After the 17 May celebrations in 2001, Queen Sonja was criticized in public for wearing sunglasses along with her bunad; in the same year, Crown Princess Mette-Marit was reprimanded in the press for wearing a purely invented "fantasy costume" rather than an authentic bunad from her home region. Women are generally advised by the Bunad and Folk Costume Council not to wear makeup and earrings with their bunad. Moreover, although Husfliden has no formal connections with the Council, it tends to follow their norms, presumably for commercial reasons. It gives their enterprise credibility and trustworthiness. As its website states, "The simplest *and safest* way to find bunads and bunad equipment consists in visiting your local Husfliden shop" (emphasis mine).

Because of the wealth of detail, a proper bunad cannot be made industrially in its entirety. This partly accounts for its high market price. Moreover, the skills required to make a bunad are considered a cultural, local form of knowledge—a kind of inalienable possession. In the spring of 2002, a conflict erupted between the traditionalists and a young entrepreneur who wanted a slice of the market. This conflict inadvertently brought the implicit ideology underlying the bunad to the public eye.

What happened was this. A young Norwegian of Chinese origin, who originally worked as a cook, began to take interest in bunads. He took a bunad course, learning the basics of the craft. Before going into business, he changed his name from Aching to John Helge Dahl, realizing that he would have little credibility as a bunad salesman with a Chinese name. He then founded a company called Norske Bunader (Norwegian bunads), and subsequently contracted dozens of Chinese seamstresses in Shanghai to do the sewing and embroidery. The fabrics were sent from Norway, and the completed garments were returned at a much lower price than that of the Norwegian competition. He built the bunads from the garments himself. "To most people, it is the quality that counts," he says, "not who has done the embroidery."[4] Of course, he can offer bunads at a competitive price.

The Bunad and Folk Costume Council reacted very strongly against Mr. Dahl, as did Husfliden. At one point the latter threatened to sue him for plagiarism, but since bunad designs are not copyrighted, they were likely to lose a court case. Their argument was that the craft amounts to a locally embedded kind of knowledge which does not travel well, comparing it to dialects. Talking about mass production and industrialization of bunad production, they argue that the use of foreign labor leads to cultural flattening. The resulting products are said to have no *hau*, to use Marcel Mauss's (1990 [1925]) Polynesian term for the "soul" of an object.

A sociologist who defended the traditionalists said that this concerns "personal knowledge." Bunad embroidery, she added, was a kind of handwriting. "When anyone can take a pattern, send it abroad, and make a good profit from the product, people will ask: What is it that I am spending one or two months' salary on?" Responding to her own question, she said that this kind of garment would feel alienating, and that it would not satisfy people's emotional need to build their own history into the garment.[5]

Another argument concerns the low salaries in China, claiming that it is immoral to hire "underpaid women" to do this kind of work. Dahl's Shanghai seamstresses are paid about € 2 an hour, which he says is a good salary in China, but which is less than a tenth of a comparable Norwegian salary. Yet others have said, when pressed, that it may be acceptable to employ immigrant women living in Norway, who may have assimilated some local skill, but not to use foreign women living abroad.

The defenders of tradition and Norwegian craftsmanship also fear a development which could be described as a McDonaldization (Ritzer, 2004) of bunad production. Although the Dahl case was spectacular in that it simultaneously brought out both accusations of racism and controversy concerning criteria for authenticity, his business innovation was less original than it might seem. Several producers admit that they outsource parts of their production to the Baltic countries and elsewhere where wages are low, and even Husfliden has admitted that parts of their bunads are made industrially because of the extremely high cost of labor in Norway.

What Is at Stake?

Two separate bunad controversies have been presented:

- What makes a particular bunad or folk costume authentic in the eyes of the Bunad and Folk Costume Council and the business community, notably Husfliden? Age, continuity in use, or market value? (Aesthetic criteria are formally deemed irrelevant.)
- What kind of knowledge is required in order to make a bunad? Can it be acquired like any other technique, or is it necessarily locally rooted?

The bunad market seems to be about to be deregulated, and the cultural skills involved are slowly being commoditized like any other marketable skill. With a growing number of actors seeking to make a profit, several of them seeing possibilities in transnational production, the oligopoly held by a few powerful producers is being weakened. As a result, the cultural product (the bunad) may become just another commodity. As argued by Berkaak (1999) in connection with the 1994 Lillehammer Winter Olympics, commoditization has become the main way in which a Norwegian identity, which initially was defined politically, is promoted.

Secondly, bunad issues also reveal that culture is a potent political resource, as the example of Mrs. Brundtland indicates. The Dahl affair also brings up normative issues about the nature of Norwegianness and the place of immigrants. Actually, even migration within Norway has been seen as posing a problem to traditional identity, which should ideally be locally rooted. Commenting on the consequences of virilocal postmarital residence in the mountain valley of Valdres, one of Haugen's (1981) informants says, "Although they [the young housewives from outside] can naturally adapt to the new conditions, they will not be carriers of local culture." (Haugen 1981: 186).

Thirdly, both Husfliden and the Bunad and Folk Costume Council defend the view that the recipe belongs to the cultural group: they wish to keep the recipe secret while selling the food. However, the recipe is not merely the pattern, but it is rather the skill involved, which can apparently only be acquired in certain, partly implicit ways.

Fourthly and finally, both bunad controversies represent attempts to copyright culture. The authenticity issues are obvious, although they also have a strong economic element (some designs are more expensive than others). However, the stern messages from the Council, and the deep moral resentment expressed when someone wears a bunad she is not entitled to wear, create bounded entities; regions with a proud history. A South African anthropologist settled in Norway commented, after viewing a 17 May parade, that this reminded him more of a lineage-based tribal society than of a modern nation (Kramer, 1984). As shown above, however, the firm association between bunads and geographical provenance is a product of the 20th century. In the late 19th century, the Hardanger dress was an emblem of (anti-Danish and anti-Swedish) Norwegianness among nationalist women everywhere.

The above analysis indicates that there exists a shared discourse about folk costumes in Norway, but this is not to say that the "Norwegian people" exhibit one set of views. Disagreements, the examples have shown, are common and laden with emotion, which testifies both to the contested nature of Norwegianness and to the centrality of a Romantic symbol such as the bunad. It is therefore difficult to speak of "local perceptions" as opposed to "official views": The two are not mutually exclusive, do not refer to two distinct social groups, and the former is variable.

Conflict over the use of symbols is not new to anthropology. When A. P. Cohen (1985) argued that symbols fuse the practical and meaningful aspects of identity, he not only pointed out that important things are at stake when symbols fail to unify but he could also draw on an anthropological past of penetrating sociosymbolic analysis, stemming from Victor Turner's early work onwards. One of the aims of this article, however, has been to show that a symbolic or meaningful aspect of culture is in itself contested, as is its relationship to practical issues. Can I wear a fantasy costume if I think it is pretty? Can I buy a lavish Telemark bunad even if my ancestors came from Oppland? And—referring to the first point—can I be favorable to economic globalization and EU membership for Norway, and still wear my bunad with pride?

The bunad controversies, moreover, indicate that commercialization may "contaminate" the meaningful dimension of the symbol, in so far as the latter is conceived of as an inalienable possession, as something that you either have or don't have, and which you cannot give away, or pretend to have, without losing face (see Harvey, 2001: 402, for a Balinese parallel).

Questions of ownership to symbols of culture which are used in a political context are probably no less common than issues arising from commercial concerns. In the early 1990s, small, but very energetic, neo-Nazi groups nearly succeeded in discrediting the Swedish flag among ordinary Swedes; the flag acquired connotations of white supremacism, and since the emotional attachments of most Swedes to the flag were weaker than their moral values, the flag faded into the background of mainstream Swedishness for some years. Similarly, in the years following the Second World War, references to the Viking age and admiration for the Viking gods, chieftains, and so on were exceedingly problematic in an otherwise Viking-loving country like Norway. The reason was that the detested Quisling government had only a few years earlier used Viking symbolism extensively in its Nazi imagery. Also, commercial uses of culture may discredit it politically. In Hawaii, local identity politics uses few of the stereotypical Polynesian symbols used to market the archipelago to tourists.

There seem to be two general points to be made here.

1.   In order for culture to function as a strategic resource, its symbols must function in a dual way; they must simultaneously be meaningful (or sensory, to use Turner's term) and instrumental. To thousands of Norwegians (I have no statistics and dare not say millions), the bunad symbolizes not only their personal attachment to history but also a respect for (assumed) ancient craftsmanship. It represents the opposite, one might say, of ahistorical presentism and the standardized, mass-produced (and *hau*-less) goods of the shopping mall. To the Bunad and Folk Costume Council, the bunad represents nation-building; to Husfliden and others, it represents a way of making profits which is entirely contingent on the functioning of the meaningful dimension of the symbol.

2.   For culture to be turned into a form of property, a process of externalization and reification of symbols is necessary. The movement is one from the unmarked to the marked, from the implicit and embodied to the explicit. It is an instance, not of "all that is solid melts into air" but of a contrasting, less well-known observation by Marx, namely that "le mort saisit le vif" (Marx, 1968: 11) — the dead and frozen seizes that which is living. This process is likely to be accompanied by struggles for symbolic hegemony. Subsequently, cultural capital is converted and accumulated among users as well as by politicians and/or businessmen. Under certain circumstances, such as a massively neo-liberal economic regime, the inalienable possessions may then be converted to commodities.

The anxieties voiced by the traditionalists are related to all three dimensions: In a thoroughly neo-liberal situation (anyone can wear what she wants; anyone can design and make bunads anywhere in the world), nation-building (politics) suffers because regional roots are severed; economic interests suffer because prices go down; and the personal or emotional pole suffers since the garments lose their special quality.

Finally, we may ask: In what exactly does this "special quality" consist? What is the nature of the enormous personal resources invested into clothes? What is invested are (notions of) hundreds of years of accumulated, local skill which one is oneself somehow connected to as a legitimate wearer of a bunad: it is the *hau* of the local. It is the recipe, not the food. What is reaped from this investment is a handsome profit, an enhanced sense of community and visible boundaries to the outside world. Cultural property of this kind is intangible, it is legally oblique, and it is poised to lose against both the brisk efficiency of contemporary capitalism and against individualist ideology of choice. Marketing and selling bunads does not in itself challenge the distinction between commercialism and tradition, and the continued validity of the distinction becomes evident when the unspoken but essential connection between a cultural practice and a marketing strategy is severed. When the commodity character of the bunad is divorced from its cultural context, the magic spell is broken. Then, and only then, the bunad finally becomes just a garment.

References

Aagedal, Olaf. 2002. *Nasjonal symbolbruk i Skandinavia* (Use of national symbols in Scandinavia). Paper presented at the conference "Rasisme og ekstremtoleranse" (Racism and extreme tolerance) at Det norske diakonhjemmet, 2002.

Berkaak, Odd Are. 1999. In the heart of the volcano: The Olympic Games as mega drama. In Arne Martin Klausen, ed., *Olympic Games as performance and public event*, pp. 49–75. Oxford: Berghahn.

Chapman, Malcolm. 1992. *The Celts: The construction of a myth*. London: Macmillan.

Cohen, A. P. 1985. *The symbolic construction of identity*. London: Routledge.

Comaroff, John and Jean Comaroff. 2009. *Ethnicity, Inc.* Chicago: University of Chicago Press.

Eicher, Joanne B., ed. 1995. *Dress and ethnicity*. Oxford: Berg.

Harrison, Simon. 1999. Identity as a scarce resource. *Social Anthropology*, 7(3): 239–252.

Harvey, David. 2001. *Spaces of capital: Towards a critical geography*. Edinburgh: Edinburgh University Press.

Haugen, Inger. 1981. Ting og mening. Et analyseforslag. (Things and meaning. A proposed analysis) Oslo: Occasional Papers in Social Anthropology, no. 2.

Hobsbawm, Eric and Terence Ranger, eds. 1983. *The Invention of Tradition*. Cambridge: Cambridge University Press.

Kramer, Julian. 1984. Norsk identitet—et produkt av underutvikling og stammetilhørighet ("Norwegian identity—a product of underdevelopment and tribal belonging"), in Arne Martin Klausen, ed., *Den norske væremåten* ("The Norwegian way of being"), pp. 88–97. Oslo: Cappelen.

Lynch, Annette. 1995. Among American New Year's dress: the display of ethnicity. In Joanne B. Eicher, ed., *Dress and ethnicity*, pp. 255–268. Oxford. Berg.

Marx, Karl. 1968 [1863]. *Das Kapital*. MEW, Band 23. Berlin: Dietz.

Mauss, Marcel. 1990 [1923/24]. *The gift: the form and reason for exchange in archaic societies*. London: Routledge.

Oxaal, Astrid. 2001. *Drakt og nasjonal identitet 1760–1917: den sivile uniformen, folkedrakten og nasjonen* ("Dress and national identity 1760–1917: the civic uniform, the folk costume and the nation"). Doctoral thesis, University of Oslo.

Ritzer, George. 2004. *The McDonaldization of society: An investigation into the changing character of contemporary social life*, millennium edition. Newbury Park: Pine Forge Press.

Endnotes

1. Much of the information in this section is taken from websites devoted to bunads and folk costumes. www.husfliden.no has sections in English, nor does www.bunadraadet.no (The Bunad and Folk Costume Council).
2. Nina Granlund Sæter, former editor of the specialist magazine *Norsk Husflid*, to *Dagbladet* 16 May 2002.
3. Magny Karlberg to *Dagbladet* 16 May 2002.
4. John Helge Dahl to *Dagbladet* 16 May 2002.
5. Margunn Bjørnholt to *Dagbladet* 16 May 2002.

Discussion Questions

1.   Do you believe an item can only be ethnically accurate if it's produced by its own people?
2.   How does the *bunad* represent Norwegian identity?
3.   How can culture be copyrighted?

CHAPTER 7

DRESS AND RELIGION

Kimberly A. Miller-Spillman

After you have read this chapter, you will understand:

- Examples of dress in different religions
- How ideology in religion may be reflected through dress
- How morality and sexuality are reflected through religious dress
- Dress as a material artifact that mirrors change in religions

This chapter focuses on the meaning of dress within several religions. Specifically, the articles in this chapter will address issues of dress in the Orthodox sect of Judaism, Roman Catholicism, and among followers of Christianity, Islam, Buddhism, and Hinduism.

Membership in a religious group is not always associated with a particular style of dress. For example, in the United States, many Roman Catholics or Protestants wear the equivalent of work dress to worship at church. Other religious groups use dress to differentiate and set themselves apart from others in the larger society or surrounding world. The readings for this chapter have been chosen to illustrate how and why religious dress symbolizes the values and beliefs of religious organizations. Dress will be examined for its ability to promote social stability within religious organizations and resist the rapid style changes associated with the contemporary fashion process of secular society.

Ideology and Dress

To understand religious dress, the cultural context of a religious group must be considered. For example, each of the religions included in this chapter has dominant ideologies that guide decisions about dress. **Ideology** is a set of ideas that do not hold up under the rigors of scientific investigation and that support the interest of dominant groups (Ferrante, 1995). For instance, dress within Christianity is based in large part on the story of Adam and Eve in the Garden of

Eden; therefore, modesty should be a goal in dress. Judaism is based on the philosophy that individuals exist to glorify God; therefore, to be well-dressed is a religious duty—not one of personal preference. Islamic philosophy promotes the separation of the sexes, as do Mennonite beliefs. Women's bodies must be covered in public and their movements within society are highly restricted and carefully controlled by male family members. Buddhists in Bhutan wear garments to communicate a national identity while focusing on the inner soul. Hindu monks use body paint to communicate their identity, which includes rejecting material wealth.

What Is Religion?

Religion is a set of beliefs, symbols, and practices that is based on the idea of the sacred and unites believers in a socioreligious community (Marshall, 1994). **Sacred** refers to that which people define as extraordinary, inspiring a sense of awe and reverence. Contrasted to the sacred is the profane or that which is considered an ordinary element of everyday life. **Monotheism** is a belief in a single God (e.g., Islam, Judaism, and Christianity), whereas **polytheism** is a belief in many gods (e.g., Buddhism, Hinduism, Confucianism, Taoism, and Shintoism) (Marshall, 1994).

Monotheistic Religions

Islam is based on the principle of submission to Allah or God. Its holy texts are the Koran and the Hadith (or sayings of the Prophet). Islam pays special attention to the status and clothing of women (Marshall, 1994). Although there are no specific injunctions or rules in the Koran regarding veiling, women are believed to have sexual powers that may tempt males (Ribeiro, 1986). Therefore, many Islamic women veil their faces and cover their heads, hair, necks, and bodies to a greater or lesser extent. Some Islamic women do not veil at all and are indistinguishable in a group of Western women. The type and extent of veiling of women varies greatly from one Islamic nation and from one group to another, depending on the nature of their beliefs and the political context in which they live (see Figure 7.1.) For example, Sciolino (1997) examines the veiling practices of women in Iran in 1997 and stresses the importance of women's hair and social status. Veiling can also be associated with expressing nationalism and/or anti-Western sentiment associated with rejecting Western fashion. For example, under the Shah (king of Iran, 1941–1979), most Iranian women did not veil and wore Western dress. When Ayatollah Khomeini, an archconservative ruler who desired Iran to be a totally Islamic state, took power in 1978, women were mandated to veil. Currently, veiling is still in place but level of enforcement depends on location.

More recently, Aryn Baker reports in the article "Afghan Women and the Return of the Taliban" on the status of women in Afghanistan in 2010. Afghan women are suspicious of recent talk of negotiations between the Afghan government and the Taliban. Part of these negotiations includes encouraging moderate Taliban members to run for Parliament. Additionally, the United States plans to withdraw its military troops in Afghanistan for an eventual exit. Afghan women are aware that if America leaves Afghanistan, their rights may be sacrificed to the ultra-conservative Taliban regime. Afghan women hope for more government-protected rights such as the right to education and to work outside the home. Afghan women whose bodies are not fully covered by the burka risk beatings, stonings, or death by male family members who do not want the family name to be shamed by a daughter's or wife's behavior.

Women's hair is not the only concern among Islamists. In "Hair, Beards, and Power: Taking It on the Chin," men's hair, beards, and power are discussed among several religions. For example, controlling men's hair, especially young men's, is one way the military asserts authority the world around. In this reading, hairstyle is an issue when a young man wears an afro in an Islamic area. The young man argues his hairstyle is African and therefore not a threat to Islamic principles. The militia initially disagrees with him because of the afro's association with African Americans, which threatens Islamic states with Western ideas.

In France, a recent ban on full-face veils in public has caused anger and confusion. Steve Erlanger in the reading "France Enforces Ban on Full-Face Veils in Public" discusses the controversy about veiling among French citizens who happen to be Muslim. Should France prohibit an item of attire that many citizens consider to be a religious obligation? French officials say that they are now enforcing the ban in the name of the liberty and equality of women in a secular country. In an ironic twist, some Muslim women in France have begun to veil in protest of the ban. Zaretsky (2010) compares the current ban on veils in France to a similar effort in 1940 to ban Jews from many professions while revoking the citizenship of thousands of recently naturalized French Jews (see the suggested reading "Uncovering the French Ban on Veils"), indicating that we are regressing to a time when Nazi rule was affecting the lives of a religious group. On a similar note,

Figure 7.1 A 26-year-old California native and Muslim American dresses stylishly while remaining true to her faith.

in American culture, covering one's face suggests bank robbers, ski-mask rapists, and Ku Klux Klan members, groups that are peripheral to mainstream society; it can be argued that one is less suspicious if another has an openly visible face.

Judaism originated in prophesies about the God Yahweh. Jewish religious knowledge is founded in the Torah, the first five books of the Hebrew Bible (corresponding to the Christian Old Testament; Macionis, 1996). As with other religions, Jewish beliefs vary from liberal to highly conservative interpretations. "Conservative" Jews are actually less strict than Orthodox (although more so than Reformed). For instance, women who follow Orthodox tradition wear wigs in public from the time of their marriage. Covering their head with wigs ensures their modesty under Orthodox interpretation of Jewish law, while allowing them to visually fit into mainstream U.S. culture (Hayt, 1997). This desire of Jews to assimilate into U.S. culture was undoubtedly colored by the French government's decision in October 1940 to enforce the Nazi order that all Jews wear the Jewish star on their outer clothing. Given the history of Jewish persecution by Nazi Germany, it is little wonder why Jews want to blend in rather than stand out and be identified as Jews.

The adolescent fashion of wearing skullcaps with modern symbols has caused controversy among some parents and Jewish religious leaders. Kershaw (2000) examines the controversy over the skullcap—which historically symbolizes humility before God—and the recent commercialism of modern skullcaps with logos or symbols. Some Jewish leaders find this connection to commercialism problematic; others are delighted that teenage Jewish boys have made a connection to a traditional practice.

In a similar way, Kiryas Joel, a Hasidic (a member of a Jewish sect devoted to the strict observance of the ritual law) Jewish enclave in upstate New York (population 20,175), is causing controversy over its welcome sign, which reads "Welcome to Kiryas Joel. [We would appreciate it if you wear] . . . long skirts or pants, covered necklines, sleeves past the elbow . . . use appropriate language . . . maintain gender separation in all public areas." When some visitors complain that they are losing their First Amendment rights, Kiryas Joel residents are quick to point out that there are no consequences for not following the advice on the welcome sign. However, residents would appreciate the respect of visitors while in their community. (See the reading "Dress Properly, No Swearing, and Maintain Gender Separation: How Signs 'Welcome' Visitors to a Small U.S. Community.")

Christianity, which includes sects of Catholicism, Protestantism, and the Anabaptists (including the Amish and Mennonites), handed down a code of morals from early times, including strict rules about clothing. Early Christian teachings stress the link between the outward appearance of the body and the state of the person's soul (Ribeiro, 1986). Several articles in this chapter examine the strong influence of Christian religious beliefs on appearance. For example, Catherine Middleton arrived at Westminster Abbey on her wedding day dressed in a beautiful gown (see Figure 7.2) that communicated her respect for the historic church (see Box 7.1 "Dress Code") and the Royal family. In the reading "The Business Impact of the Royal Wedding," *Women's Wear Daily* analysts discuss the impact of Middleton's dress on the House of Alexander McQueen. The Duchess of Cambridge's choice of wedding dress has been described as modest with covered shoulders and arms and a slightly immodest V-shaped neckline. Middleton's dress surprised many who expected a more modern dress style with an edgy design. The classic style of Middleton's dress has been compared to Grace Kelly's iconic wedding dress of 1956. Some consider Middleton's dress to be quite elegant and classy for a young woman who wanted to show her willingness to become an adherent of Royal family traditions.

Figure 7.2 Catherine Middleton's wedding dress on April 29, 2011.

BOX 7.1
Dress Code

There is no specific dress code for the Abbey. For services we ask that you dress in a respectful manner, although we are aware that some people are on holiday—bear in mind that during the winter months it can become quite cold inside.

Westminster Abbey Dress Code. Retrieved from http://www.westminster-abbey.org/worship/daily-services/general-service-times.

Worship at the Abbey

Sundays
8.00am Holy Communion (BCP)
10.00am Choral Matins
11.15am Sung Eucharist
3.00pm Choral Evensong
5.45pm Organ Recital
6.30pm Evening Service

Weekdays
7.30am Matins (9.00am Saturday and Bank Holidays)
8.00am Holy Communion
12.30pm Holy Communion
5.00pm Choral Evensong (3.00 pm Saturday only, 5.00 pm June–September). Evening Prayer on Wednesdays

Everyone is welcome to all regular services. There is no charge to attend services and you do not need to reserve a seat in advance, although it is advisable to arrive early for some services. A collection is taken at Sunday services with the proceeds going to nominated organisations and charities.

Similar to the choice Kate Middleton made with a conservative wedding dress to signal her commitment to Royal family traditions, women who become nuns in the Catholic Church historically had to change their dress. Dress scholar Susan Michelman's article "From Habit to Fashion: Dress of Catholic Women Religious" examines how traditional habits or uniforms of nuns made their social identities more outwardly visible than their personal identities. When women take vows of religious life, they relinquish individuality in dress for social control of their bodies by the Church:

> Dress should reveal not just a humble state of mind, but show by its simplicity that the wearer spends little time on the adornment of the body, and is thus free to devote more—time and money—to the poor. This mixture of religious and personal morality is most evidenced in the habits of religious orders; their ample, loose robes of humble, often coarse fabrics, are both unprovocative and a protection against the temptations of the world. (Ribeiro, 1986)

From the time that nuns first wore religious attire as novices, they were instructed to view themselves not as individuals but as representatives of a group. Michelman uses Symbolic Interaction Theory to examine the personal and social conflicts that occurred when these women shed their habits but not their social roles in the 1960s. For another example of Roman Catholic dress, see the reading "Costume and the Play of Social Identities in an Andalusian Pilgrimage" in Chapter 9.

Polytheistic Religions

Two articles in this chapter illustrate dress related to polytheistic religions: Buddhism and Hinduism. **Buddhism** is an Indian religion that originated 2,500 years ago. *Buhdi* means "to awaken" and Buddha, the founder of the religion in 566 B.C., was enlightened (to receive spiritual or intellectual insight) at the age of 35. Buddhism is an old and complex religion that includes the concept of karma. Karma is the law that every action has an effect on the self and on others. Buddhism stresses mindfulness of one's actions and effects of those actions. Buddhism also stresses that material possessions do not bring happiness; happiness can only come from within. In the reading, "In Buddhist Bhutan, Happiness Counts," Vishal Arora explains how the Buddhist nation of Bhutan measures happiness. Bhutan's gross national happiness (GNH) is an index that measures quality of life rather than monetary wealth. Arora explains that "one tangible way of preserving culture is a national dress code in schools and government buildings." In Bhutan, men wear the *gho* and women wear the *kira* (see Figure 7.3). Given that Bhutan is a small nation between India and China, there is a need to assert a national identity through dress. That identity is rooted in the beliefs of Buddhism.

Hinduism, also an Indian religion, is unique from Christianity, Judaism, and Islam in that it does not have a founding member, nor is there one text or scripture that unites its members. Rather, Hinduism is a combination of South Asian and Western beliefs. Prominent themes in Hindu beliefs include (but are not restricted to) dharma (morals/ethics/duties), samsara (the continuing cycle of birth, life, death, and rebirth), and karma (action and subsequent reaction). In Hinduism, a Sadhu or holy man is a wandering monk whose lifestyle is characterized by abstinence from worldly pleasures in order to pursue the fourth and final stage of life. A Sadhu's life can include meditation, yoga, and body painting. In the reading "When a Holy Man's Skin

Figure 7.3 Bhutanese women in their *kira* and men wearing the *gho*, which is the national dress in Bhutan.

is the Canvas," we learn that American-born Thomas Kelly followed and photographed groups of Sadhus over three decades. After a morning bath, Sadhus paint their bodies as a form of identity and as an indication of which deity they follow (see Figure 7.10).

Dress and Religious Fundamentalism

Fundamentalism is a conservative religious doctrine that opposes intellectualism and worldly accommodation in favor of restoring traditional, otherworldly religion (Macionis, 1996). Fundamentalism is a more complex phenomenon than popular conceptions would lead people to believe. First, a fundamentalist cannot be stereotyped by gender, age, race, ethnicity, social class, or political ideology. Second, fundamentalists are characterized by a belief that a relationship with God, Allah, or some other supernatural force provides answers to personal and social problems (Ferrante, 1995). Third, fundamentalists do not differentiate between the sacred and the profane in their everyday lives. All areas of their lives, including work, family, and leisure, are governed by religious principles. For example, Edwards (1993) discusses how female students at Bob Jones University, a Christian fundamentalist school located in South Carolina, learn to dress in a "worldly" manner without denying their religious convictions. Similarly, residents of Kiryas Joel ask visitors to respect their Hasidic beliefs and dress accordingly (Figure 7.4).

Fourth, fundamentalists want to reverse the trend toward gender equality, which they believe is symptomatic of a declining moral order (Ferrante, 1995). Fundamentalists often believe the correct ordering of priorities in life requires subordinating women's rights to the concerns of the larger group and the well-being of the society, such as the "traditional" family.

Some of the articles in this chapter discuss dress and religious fundamentalism because it is often within these groups that dress practices widely diverge from the majority. Why is control of dress, particularly for women, frequently a component of fundamentalist beliefs? Fundamentalist religious groups have often emerged after a perceived threat or crisis—real or imagined. Any discussion of a particular fundamentalist group must include some reference to an adversary. Dress, then, can be linked to a way of expressing group solidarity as well as indicating opposition to the general culture.

Dress acts as a visible symbol for the precepts of fundamentalism, including the fact that religious principles govern all aspects of the fundamentalists' lives (including dress) and that women's roles are frequently more "traditional" with individual needs and beliefs relinquished to the greater good of the family and religious group. This leaves fundamentalists open to criticism by feminists regarding

Figure 7.4 Hasidic men follow a strict dress code of dark (black or navy) jackets and trousers and white shirts.

the oppression of women by the patriarchal nature of many fundamentalist groups. **Patriarchy** refers to cultural beliefs and values that give higher prestige to men than to women (Newman, 1995). Women's roles as wives, mothers, and supporters of the faith may be seen as important, but men are given priority or exclusive rights to govern and hold power in the group. Patriarchy has been regarded as a form of social organization and has been considered, particularly by feminists, as an undifferentiated theory to explain the whole of human history (Grimshaw, 1986):

> Patriarchy is itself the prevailing religion of the entire planet. . . All of the so-called religions legitimating patriarchy are mere sects subsumed under its vast umbrella/ canopy. . . All—from buddhism and hinduism to islam, judaism, christianity—to secular derivatives such as freudianism, marxism and maoism—are infrastructures of the edifice of patriarchy. (Daly, 1990)

Agency is a concept used by feminists to describe the resistance women use to combat patriarchy. Boynton-Arthur (1993) describes the agencies (i.e., the various forms of resistance) women in one Holdeman Mennonite community use in subverting the strict dress codes dictated by male ministers and deacons. Arthur describes the daily process of subtle changes in dress that give women an opportunity to express themselves creatively. Agency can also be found in the reading "Afghan Women and the Return of the Taliban" when women take seats in Parliament and work toward improving women's rights.

Dress, Religion, and Morality

Common themes can be identified among the articles included in this chapter. One theme is modesty and its relationship to morality in religious beliefs. Some Christians, Jews, and Muslims have rules about covering parts of the body that might be seen as having sexual connotations such as hair, neck, breasts, arms, and legs. Women are frequently targets of modesty rules, and certain religious groups feel that **morality** is maintained through the behavior of women, including their dress (see Chapter 8 for an article about dress that is too sexy for tween girls). Although not part of all religions, beliefs are held by some religions that regard female sexuality as dangerous if left unharnessed and uncontrolled (Fernea and Fernea, 1995). These beliefs lead to the religious practice of prescribing modest and proper dress for female members.

The result of modest dress is often physical restriction on women. In Afghanistan, wearing the burka can be dangerous, because it covers the head and face, and restricts vision of passing cars or carts in crowded areas. Peripheral vision was also restricted among Catholic nuns who wore full habit (see the reading "From Habit to Fashion"), preventing nuns from driving cars and moving freely through their daily activities serving the poor and sick.

For an Orthodox Jewish woman to be properly dressed, she must cover her hair after marriage (Hayt, 1997). This practice helps women to avoid expressing sexuality outside marriage. Holdeman Mennonite women must also cover their head and hair (Boynton-Arthur, 1993). The starched cap represents a Mennonite woman's humility to God and her resistance to worldly possessions. Submissiveness to her God, her community, and her husband is also symbolized by her head covering. Among Muslim women, the chador covers the entire body (with a slit for the eyes). (See Figure 7.5.)

Covering body curves appears to be somewhat less of an issue for Mennonite and Orthodox Jewish women than for Islamic women (Michelman, 2005). Compare Figures 7.5 and 7.6 and examine the differences in Mennonite (Christian) and Islamic dress for women. The evolution of silhouettes shown in Figure 7.6 indicates that an unmarried Mennonite woman can emphasize body curves more than an Orthodox woman.

There are also examples of demands for modest dress in secular society as well as among religious groups. Modest dress for teens and tweens is the subject of an article with an ecumenical focus written by Jayne O'Donnell. In the reading "Economic Downturn May Be Pulling Necklines Up: Struggling Retailers Widen Options for Teens, Tweens to Include More Modest Clothes," O'Donnell credits the economic downturn to a movement toward less-revealing clothing styles. In addition, customers who want to stretch their clothing dollar are less inclined to purchase extreme styles that will quickly become outdated. Many parents, regardless of religion, just want to find shorts that completely cover their daughter's rear end. In addition, an Evangelical tween (a girl who is 7–14 years old) group is petitioning retailers to offer more modest fashions; therefore the demand for modest tween clothing is not just coming from parents. Freedom of choice seems to be missing for those who don't want to participate in the fashionable trend of skimpy clothing.

Figure 7.5 A Muslim woman wearing a chador.

Religious Dress and Social Change

Although changes in dress occur with much less frequency among the religious than the general population, forces of social, economic, and political change do influence sacred dress, as discussed in this chapter. For example, Michelman's study demonstrates the identity struggle Catholic nuns experienced when moving from full

Figure 7.6 Dresses worn by Holdeman Mennonite women express both a religious affiliation and status (i.e., unmarried, married, and Orthodox) within the group.

Figure 7.7 Sciolino's 1997 article "The Chanel under the Chador" describes culturally elite women who wear Chanel suits (a) under a chador (b).

religious habit to secular dress after changes mandated by Vatican II in the 1960s. The first Vatican Council was held in 1870. The Second Vatican Council (also known as Vatican II) addressed relations between the Roman Catholic Church and the modern world. Her article "From Habit to Fashion" examines how difficult it was for nuns to make the transition from a well-recognized and revered social identity as a Catholic nun in full habit to non-uniform, secular dress. Sciolino's 1997 article "The Chanel under the Chador" provides an excellent example of the differences between sacred and secular dress. The differences are in sharp contrast. The irony of wearing a Chanel-style suit (secular dress) (see Figure 7.7a) under a chador (sacred dress) (see Figure 7.7b) would prove baffling to most non-Islamics.

Social class can also be expressed through religious dress. For example, at Bob Jones University, a Fundamentalist Christian college in South Carolina, students aspire to move among the cultural elite of American society (Edwards, 1993), which is an ambitious goal. Recognizing that dress can advance or hinder professional goals, "safe beauty classes" prepare women for entry into professional and well-paying positions. "Style" is described by church-sanctioned teachers as a woman's armor, while "fashion" is characterized as "letting oneself go"—a description that is a clear condemnation of the evils of worldliness.

Summary

This chapter covers examples of dress in different religions. In particular we focus on dress in the Orthodox sect of Judaism, Roman Catholic nuns, Islamic men and women, and adherents of Buddhism and Hinduism. Ideology reflects the beliefs of cultures that justify particular social arrangements (Marshall, 1994); these beliefs are reflected in religious dress. Several themes (i.e., morality, sexuality, patriarchy, and agency) were identified in this discussion of religious dress. Lastly, religious dress as a material artifact mirrors changes in religion that often coincide with changes in the greater society or culture. Dress within religious groups illustrates an apparent relationship between social stability and resistance to rapid style changes associated with fashion.

Suggested Readings

Kasson, E. G. (2010, June 6). [Clothes Culture] Wrapped in Style; Magazines and Websites Cater to Muslim American Women Who Want to Look Fashionable While Dressing Modestly and Staying True to Their Faith. *Los Angeles Times*. Retrieved on March 3, 2012 from www.101reasonshijab.com/in-the-news.html.

Kiracofe, C. (2010). Can Teachers Really Wear That to School? Religious Garb in Public Classrooms. *The Clearing House* 83: 80–83.

Sciolino, E. (1997, May 4). The Chanel Under the Chador. *New York Times Magazine*, 46–51.

Zaretsky, R. (2010, September 17). Uncovering the French Ban on Veils. *The Chronicle Review*, B4–B5.

Learning Activity 7.1: Religions' Rules for Dress

Objective

To learn about dress within a previously unfamiliar religion.

Interview

Interview someone who believes in a religious ideology with which you are unfamiliar. Consider religions (or faiths) of which you have little or no knowledge. Use the telephone directory in your area to determine whom you could interview. Depending on your background, you may want to consider some of the following:

- Amish
- Buddhist
- Catholic priest or nun
- Greek Orthodox priest
- Hindu
- Jewish rabbi (or layperson)
- Mennonite
- Mormon
- Muslim

Develop five or six questions about religion and dress for your interview. You may want to know about specific dress items you have seen in the media but did not understand. You may want to ask general questions about how dress is used during formal ceremonies (and by whom) compared to how a religious observer might dress on a daily basis. Other possible questions include: How is dress used in rituals of the faith? How does the dress of clergy (or religious leaders/teachers) compare to the dress of the worshipper?

After conducting the interview, share your information in small groups or during a class discussion. Or invite those interviewed to serve on a "religious panel" during class. Each speaker could be allowed 10 to 15 minutes to discuss dress within his or her own religion.

Learning Activity 7.2: Teachers and Religious Garb

Objective

To learn about rules that apply to teachers who want to wear religious dress to work.

Procedure

In the United States, the focus in schools is proper attire for students. But what about teachers who want to wear religious garb to school? Read the Suggested Reading "Can Teachers Really Wear That to School?" by Kiracofe (2010). After reading the article, have an online or a face-to-face discussion with your classmates about the article and its primary points.

References

Boynton-Arthur, L. (1993). Clothing, Control, and Women's Agency: The Mitigation of Patriarchal Power. In S. Fisher and K. Davis (Eds.), *Negotiating at the Margins*, 66–84. New Brunswick, NJ: Rutgers University Press.

Daly, M. (1990). *Gyn/ecology: The Metaethics of Radical Feminism*. Boston: Beacon Press.

Edwards, L. (1993, May 30). Worldly Lessons. *New York Times*, C1, C9.

Fernea, E. W., and R. A. Fernea. (1995). Symbolizing Roles: Behind the Veil. In M. E. Roach-Higgins, J. B. Eicher, and K. K. P. Johnson (Eds.), *Dress and Identity*. New York: Fairchild Books.

Ferrante, J. (1995). *Sociology: A Global Perspective*. Belmont, CA: Wadsworth Publishing Co.

Grimshaw, J. (1986). *Philosophy and Feminist Thinking*. Minneapolis: University of Minnesota Press.

Hayt, E. (1997, April 27). For Stylish Orthodox Women, Wigs That Aren't Wiggy. *New York Times*, 43, 48.

Kershaw, S. (2000, April 19). The Skullcap as Fashion Statement. *New York Times*, 1(Sec. B).

Macionis, J. J. (1996). *Society: The Basics* (3rd ed.). Upper Saddle River, NJ: Prentice Hall.

Marshall, G. (Ed.) (1994). *The Concise Oxford Dictionary of Sociology*. Oxford: Oxford University Press.

Michelman, S. O. (2005). Reveal or Conceal? In M. L. Damhorst, K. A. Miller-Spillman, & S. O. Michelman (Eds.), *The Meanings of Dress*, pp. 210–216. New York: Fairchild.

Newman, D. (1995). *Sociology: Exploring the Architecture of Everyday Life*. Thousand Oaks, CA: Pine Forge Press.

Ribeiro, A. (1986). *Dress and Morality*. London: Batsford Press.

Sciolino, E. (1997, May 4). The Chanel Under the Chador. *New York Times Magazine*, 46–51.

Zaretsky, R. (2010, September 17). Uncovering the French Ban on Veils. *The Chronicle Review*, B4–B5.

AFGHAN WOMEN AND THE RETURN OF THE TALIBAN

Aryn Baker

The Taliban pounded on the door just before midnight, demanding that Aisha, 18, be punished for running away from her husband's house. They dragged her to a mountain clearing near her village in the southern Afghan province of Uruzgan, ignoring her protests that her in-laws had been abusive, that she had no choice but to escape. Shivering in the cold air and blinded by the flashlights trained on her by her husband's family, she faced her spouse and accuser. Her in-laws treated her like a slave, Aisha pleaded. They beat her. If she hadn't run away, she would have died. Her judge, a local Taliban commander, was unmoved. Later, he would tell Aisha's uncle that she had to be made an example of lest other girls in the village try to do the same thing. The commander gave his verdict, and men moved in to deliver the punishment. Aisha's brother-in-law held her down while her husband pulled out a knife. First he sliced off her ears. Then he started on her nose. Aisha passed out from the pain but awoke soon after, choking on her own blood. The men had left her on the mountainside to die.

This didn't happen 10 years ago, when the Taliban ruled Afghanistan. It happened last year. Now hidden in a secret women's shelter in the relative safety of Kabul, where she was taken after receiving care from U.S. forces, Aisha recounts her tale in a monotone, her eyes flat and distant. She listens obsessively to the news on a small radio that she keeps by her side. Talk that the Afghan government is considering some kind of political accommodation with the Taliban is the only thing that elicits an emotional response. "They are the people that did this to me," she says, touching the jagged bridge of scarred flesh and bone that frames the gaping hole in an otherwise beautiful face. "How can we reconcile with them?"

That is exactly what the Afghan government plans to do. In June, President Hamid Karzai established a peace council tasked with exploring negotiations with Afghanistan's "upset brothers," as he calls the Taliban. A month later, Tom Malinowski, the Washington advocacy director for Human Rights Watch, a New York-based NGO, flew to Kabul seeking assurances that human rights would be protected in the course of negotiations. During their conversation, Karzai mused on the cost of the conflict in human lives and wondered aloud if he had any right to talk about human rights when so many were dying. "He essentially asked me," says Malinowski, "What is more important, protecting the right of a girl to go to school or saving her life?" How Karzai and his international allies answer that question will have far-reaching consequences. Aisha has no doubt. "The Taliban are not good people," she says. "If they come back, the situation will be worse for everyone." But for others, the rights of Afghan women are only one aspect of a complex situation. How that situation will eventually be ordered remains unclear.

As the war in Afghanistan enters its ninth year, the need for an exit strategy weighs on the minds of U.S. policymakers. The publication of some 90,000 documents on the war by the freedom-of-information activists at WikiLeaks—working with the *New York Times*, the *Guardian* in London and the German newsmagazine *Der Spiegel*—has intensified international debate. Though the documents mainly consist of low-level intelligence reports, taken together they reveal a war in which a shadowy insurgency shows determined resilience; where fighting that enemy often claims the lives of innocent civilians; and where supposed allies, like Pakistan's security services, are suspected of playing a deadly double game. Allegations of fraud and corruption in the Afghan government have exasperated Congress, as has evidence that the billions of dollars spent training and equipping the Afghan security forces have so far achieved little. In May, the U.S. death toll passed 1,000. As frustrations mount over a war that even top U.S. commanders think is not susceptible to a purely military solution, demands intensify for a political way out of the quagmire.

Such an outcome, it is assumed, would involve a reconciliation with the Taliban or, at the very least, some elements within its fold. But without safeguards, that would pose significant risks to the very women U.S. Secretary of State Hillary Clinton promised in May not to abandon. "We will stand with you always," she said to female members of Karzai's delegation in Washington. Afghan women are not convinced. They fear that in the quest for a quick peace, their progress may be sidelined. "Women's rights must not be the sacrifice by which peace is achieved," says Fawzia Koofi, the former Deputy Speaker of Afghanistan's parliament.

Yet that may be where negotiations are heading. In December, President Obama set a July 2011 deadline for the beginning of a drawdown of U.S. troops from Afghanistan. That has made Taliban leaders feel they have the upper hand. In negotiations, the Taliban will be advocating a version of an Afghan state in line with their own conservative views, particularly on the issue of women's rights, which they deem a Western concept that contravenes Islamic teaching. Already there is a growing acceptance that some concessions to the Taliban are inevitable if there is to be genuine reconciliation. "You have to be realistic," says a senior Western diplomat in Kabul, who spoke on the condition of anonymity. "We are not going to be sending troops and spending money forever. There will have to be a compromise, and sacrifices will have to be made." Which sounds understandable. But who, precisely, will be asked to make the sacrifice?

Stepping Out

When the U.S. and its allies went to war in Afghanistan in 2001 with the aim of removing the safe haven that the Taliban had provided for al-Qaeda, it was widely hoped that the women of the country would be liberated from a regime that denied them education and jobs, forced them indoors and violently punished them for infractions of a strict interpretation of Islamic law. Under the Taliban, who ruled Afghanistan from 1996 to 2001, women accused of adultery were stoned to death; those who flashed a bare ankle from under the shroud of a burqa were whipped. Koofi remembers being beaten on the street for forgetting to remove the polish from her nails after her wedding. "We were not even allowed to laugh out loud," she says.

It wasn't always so. Kabul 40 years ago was considered the playground of Central Asia, a city where girls wore jeans to the university and fashionable women went to parties sporting Chanel miniskirts. These days the streets of Kabul once again echo with the laughter of girls on their way to school, dressed in uniforms of black coats and white headscarves. Women have rejoined the workforce and can sign up for the police and the army. Article 83 of the constitution mandates that at least 25% of parliamentary seats go to female representatives.

During Taliban times, women's voices were banned from the radio, and TV was forbidden, but last month a female anchor interviewed a former Taliban leader on a national broadcast. Under the Taliban, Robina Muqimyar Jalalai, one of Afghanistan's first two female Olympic athletes, spent her girlhood locked behind the walls of her family compound. Now she is running for parliament and wants a sports ministry created, which she hopes to lead. "We have women boxers and women footballers," she says. "I go running in the stadium where the Taliban used to play football with women's heads." But Muqimyar says she will never take these changes for granted. "If the Taliban come back, I will lose everything that I have gained over the past nine years."

It would be easy to dismiss such fears as premature. The Taliban leadership has not yet shown any inclination to reconcile with Karzai's government. But a program to reintegrate into society so-called 10-dollar Talibs—low-level insurgents who fight for cash or over local grievances—is already in place. Koofi worries that such accommodations may be the first step down a slippery slope. Reintegrating low-level Taliban could mean that men like those who ordered and carried out Aisha's punishment would be eligible for the training and employment opportunities paid for by international donors—without having to account for their actions. "The government of Afghanistan needs to make it clear, not just by speaking but by action and policy, that women's rights will be guaranteed," says Koofi. "If they don't, if they continue giving political bribes to Taliban, we will lose everything."

Clinging to the Constitution

Both the U.S. administration and Karzai's government say such worries are overblown. Afghanistan's constitution, they insist—which promotes gender equality and provides for girls' education—is not up for negotiation. In Kabul on July 20, Clinton said that the red lines are clear. "Any reconciliation process . . . must require that anyone who wishes to rejoin society and the political system must lay down their weapons and end violence, renounce al-Qaeda and be committed to the constitution and laws of Afghanistan, which guarantee the rights of women."

Afghan women cling to such promises like a talisman. But ambiguities abound. Article 3 of the constitution, for example, holds that no law may contravene the principles of Shari'a, or Islamic law. What constitutes Shari'a, however, has never been defined, so a change in the political climate of the country could mean a radical reinterpretation of women's rights. Karzai has already invited Taliban to run for parliament. None have done so, but if they ever do, they may find some like-minded colleagues already there. Abdul Hadi Arghandiwal, the Minister of Economy and leader of the ideologically conservative Hizb-i-Islami faction, for example, holds that women and men shouldn't go to university together. Like the Taliban, he believes that women should not be allowed to leave the home unaccompanied by a male relative. "That is in accordance with Islam. And what we want for Afghanistan is Islamic rights, not Western rights," Arghandiwal says.

Traditional ways, however, do little for women. Aisha's family did nothing to protect her from the Taliban. That might have been out of fear, but more likely it was out of shame. A girl who runs away is automatically considered a prostitute in deeply traditional societies, and families that allow them back home would be subject to widespread ridicule. A few months after Aisha arrived at the shelter, her father tried to bring her home with promises that he would find her a new husband. Aisha refused to leave. In rural areas, a family that finds itself shamed by a daughter sometimes sells her into slavery, or worse, subjects her to a so-called honor killing—murder under the guise of saving the family's name.

Parliamentarian Sabrina Saqib fears that if the Taliban were welcomed back into the fold, those who oppress women would get a free ride. "I am worried that the day that the so-called moderate Taliban can sit in parliament, we will lose our rights," she says. "Because it is not just Taliban that are against women's rights; there are many men who are against them as well." Last summer, Saqib voted against a bill that authorized husbands in Shi'ite families to withhold money and food from wives who refuse to provide sex, limited inheritance and custody of children in the case of divorce and denied women freedom of movement without permission from their families. The law passed, and that 25% quota of women in parliament couldn't stop it. Saqib estimates that less than a dozen of the 68 female parliamentarians support women's rights. The rest—proxies for conservative men who boosted them into power—aren't interested.

Despite her frustrations with her parliamentary colleagues, Saqib is a firm supporter of the constitutional quota. "In a society dominated by culture and traditions," she says, "we need some time for women to prove that they can do things." If the constitution were revised as part of a negotiation with the Taliban, she says, the article mandating the parliamentary quota "would be the first to go." Arghandiwal, the Economy Minister, would love to see the back of it. "Throughout history, constitutions have changed, so we have to be flexible on this," he says. The quota for women, he claims, "makes them lazy."

Threats in the Night

For many women, debates over the constitution are an abstract irrelevance. What matters is that mounting insecurity is eroding the few gains they have made. Taliban night letters—chilling missives delivered under the cover of darkness—threaten women in the south of the country, a Taliban stronghold, who dare to work. "We warn you to leave your job as a teacher as soon as possible otherwise we will cut the heads off your children and shall set fire to your daughter," reads one. "We will kill you in such a harsh way that no woman has so far been killed in that manner," says another. Both letters, which were obtained by Human Rights Watch, are printed on paper bearing the crossed swords and Koran insignia of the Islamic Emirate of Afghanistan, the name of the former Taliban government. Elsewhere, girls' schools have been burned down and students have had acid thrown in their faces. In May, mounting violence in the west of the country prompted the religious council of Herat province to issue an edict forbidding women to leave their homes without a male relative. The northern province of Badakhshan quickly followed suit, and other councils are considering doing the same.

The edicts are usually justified as a means of protecting women from the insurgency, but Koofi, the member of parliament, says there is a better way of doing that: improved governance and security. That will not just protect women but also strengthen the Afghan government's hand in the course of negotiations. "We need to marginalize the Taliban by focusing on good governance," she says, fearing that a quick deal would bring only a temporary lull in the violence—enough to permit the international coalition a face-saving withdrawal but not much more than that. Afghanistan's women recognize that dialogue with the Taliban is essential to any long-term solution, but they don't want those talks to be hurried. They want a seat at the table, and they worry that Afghanistan's friends overseas are tiring of its dysfunctional ways. "I think it is possible to make things better if the international community supports good governance," says Koofi, "but they are too focused on an exit strategy. They want a quick solution."

For Afghanistan's women, an early withdrawal of international forces could be disastrous. An Afghan refugee who grew up in Canada, Mozhdah Jamalzadah recently returned home to launch an Oprah-style talk show, which has become wildly popular. Jamalzadah has been able to subtly introduce questions of women's rights into the program without provoking the ire of religious conservatives. "If I go into it directly," she says, "there will be a backlash. But if I talk about abuse, which is against the Koran, and then talk about divorce, which is permitted, I am educating both men and women, and hopefully no one notices." Jamalzadah says her audience is increasingly receptive to her message, but she knows that in a deeply traditional society, it will take time to percolate. If the government becomes any more conservative because of an accommodation with the Taliban, she says, "my program will be the first to go."

That would be Afghanistan's loss. Jamalzadah's TV show is an education for the whole nation, albeit sometimes in unexpected ways. On a recent episode, a male guest told a joke about a foreign human rights team in Afghanistan. In the cities, the team noticed that women walked six paces behind their husbands. But in rural Helmand, where the Taliban is strongest, they saw a woman six steps ahead. The foreigners rushed to congratulate the husband on his enlightenment—only to be told that he stuck his wife in front because they were walking through a minefield.

As the audience roared with laughter, Jamalzadah reflected that it may take about 10 to 15 years before Afghan women can truly walk alongside men. But once they do, she believes, all Afghans will benefit. "When we talk about women's rights," Jamalzadah says, "we are talking about things that are important to men as well—men who want to see Afghanistan move forward. If you sacrifice women to make peace, you are also sacrificing the men who support them and abandoning the country to the fundamentalists that caused all the problems in the first place."

Discussion Questions

1. Without legislation to protect the rights of Afghan women, how might they dress under an ultra-conservative government such as the Taliban? How might they dress under a liberal government?

2. If the legislature in Afghanistan is recruiting moderate Taliban members to run for Parliament, what effect will the possible election of Taliban members have on women's rights, including dress?

3. Thinking about the social movements such as the Slut Walks (see Chapter 3) that were organized after an assault of a young girl wearing a short skirt in Africa, what might be the reaction in Afghanistan to a similar demonstration by Afghan women?

7.2

HAIR, BEARDS, AND POWER: TAKING IT ON THE CHIN

The Economist

In free societies and tyrannies alike, the hair on, and around, a man's head always sends an ideological signal.

Shahryar, a fashion-conscious young socialite from Tehran, was immensely proud of his Jackson-5-style Afro. The *baseej*, Iran's thuggish militia, were less impressed. They arrested him and dragged him away to a local clerical court, on the grounds that his sprouting hairdo was a dangerous Western import. Shahryar argued that since his style was really African, it posed no threat to revolutionary principles. The *baseej* disagreed: it was African-*American* so it could pollute Iranian society with the mores of the country's greatest enemy.

The mullah in charge decided that although the fashion did indeed have American associations, it should be remembered that many black citizens of the United States had converted to Islam. In fact they represented the vanguard for *jihad* on the Western front—so in deference to them, Shahryar could hold onto his coif.

Long anxious to keep female hair under wraps, the rulers of the Islamic Republic have more recently become concerned about men's hairdos. For years the streets of Tehran have been filled with young men making exuberant experiments with quiffs and stiffly gelled manes. But in an attempt to get these undisciplined tresses under control, the Iranian authorities last month re-leased a list of approved haircuts for men: mostly neat variations on a short-back-and-sides. The Culture and Islamic Guidance ministry chose the "Veil and Chastity Day" festival to disclose this narrow range of options, explaining that they were intended to counter a "Western cultural invasion." Whether anyone will want a government-sanctioned style is another matter.

Of Mullahs and Mullets

Across the world, there are probably more arguments over women's hair or headgear than over the hair on men's heads. But whenever male hair is at issue, emotions run sky-high on both sides. For authoritarian regimes, controlling male appearance, and imposing absolute uniformity, seems to be a point of pride; and defying such controls soon becomes a matter of honour for dissidents.

The men of North Korea have been under orders to mind their hairstyles since 2005, when they were berated for their messy barnets by their leader, Kim Jong Il. A television campaign entitled

"Let's trim our hair in accordance with the socialist lifestyle" warned men that long hair could sap their brains. Draconian hair-regimes can be ghastly as well as ridiculous. At the height of the violence in Iraq, many barbers were murdered, accused of giving haircuts that were too Western or un-Islamic; this happened after Muqtada al-Sadr, a fiery Shia cleric, issued edicts telling men how their hair should be trimmed.

In many societies, beards and moustaches are even more ideologically charged than the question of what, if anything, sprouts from the top of male heads. Both in Muslim countries and in the Muslim diaspora, sporting a bushy beard—often with the upper lip shaven—has become a symbol of piety. Many of the sternest Islamic regimes give men absolutely no choice in the matter. In June Somalia's Islamic militants ordered men in Mogadishu to grow their beards and trim their moustaches. When the Taliban held power in Afghanistan, trimming one's whiskers was outlawed; luxuriant beards flourished everywhere. Secular regimes that govern mainly Muslim populations often ban or strongly discourage beards. But when Saparmurat Niyazov, the late despot of Turkmenistan, ordered young men to shave their goatees, it was not so much an anti-religious measure as a general crackdown on personal freedom of all kinds. It was in a similar spirit that Enver Hoxha, Albania's communist tyrant, outlawed beards (and almost every other show of individualism) in the 1970s.

One of the first changes decreed by the Islamists of Hamas after their victory over the secularists of Fatah in the 2006 Palestinian elections was that policemen were allowed to grow beards. But the theology of male hair can be controversial. Orthodox Christian priests generally sport beards in humble imitation of Jesus Christ; the most conservative say a priest's hair and beard should not be cut because his whole body has been sanctified by the rite of ordination. Christian theologians still argue over what Saint Paul meant when he told the people of Corinth that for men to have long hair was shameful, while for women, flowing tresses were something glorious (although they should keep them covered, perhaps to avoid tempting wayward angels). Samson, one of the heroes of the Hebrew scriptures, seems to exemplify a different understanding of the power of hair: his awesome strength abandoned him as soon as his locks were trimmed.

For Muslims, imitating the faith's founder is also given as a reason for growing beards. But there are many arguments over whether the practice is mandatory or just recommended. And the more beards are promoted in Islamic societies, the more unpopular they become in places that are wary of Islam—such as India, where a court opined last year that a Christian college was entitled to ban beards. To the dismay of Indian Muslims, the judge declared: "We do not want Talibans here."

In Iran men can choose whether to shave or not, but Afro-sporting youths avoid beards because they would carry a hint of conformity with authority. And as Anthony Synnott, a British-born sociologist, points out, the only constant in the history of hairstyles is that each generation of men likes to defy its fathers (and father figures). In the 1960s both skinheads and hirsute hippies were challenging the uniformity of a generation that had received its formative haircuts while in uniform. Once every possible length had been tried, the only way to impress the world was through colour: rainbow-hued Mohawks, stripes and wings.

But in free societies, anything—however outrageous it seems at first—becomes respectable after a while. (Think how the body-piercing favoured by punk-rockers lost its power to shock after young bankers started sporting discreet earrings with their pinstriped suits.) One of the rising stars in Japanese politics is 58-year-old Yoshimi Watanabe, whose "Your Party" has just won 11 seats in the upper house of the legislature. Among his trademarks is a faux-hawk or "antenna" hairstyle, reportedly modelled on David Beckham's appearance in 2002; voters apparently like it.

But Japan is no paradise for men in search of trichological freedom. The municipality of Isesaki has just told its male employees to shave their chins on grounds that "some citizens find bearded men unpleasant, so beards are banned." The announcement coincided with the start of the summer season, in which men are encouraged to cool down by doffing their jackets and ties and save on air-conditioning. A bearded, open-necked town clerk, it seems, just wouldn't look proper.

Discussion Questions

1. What are your reactions to an ideology that someone can control behavior by controlling hairstyles? Give examples from the reading to back up your answers.
2. With so much media attention about Muslim women veiling their hair to prevent sexual attacks by men, are you surprised to hear how men's hair is also controlled in countries around the world? Why or why not?
3. Many large corporations, such as the Disney Corporation, restrict the hairstyles of their employees by placing limits on men's hair length and color and facial hair, in addition to tattoos and piercings. Why might it be more acceptable for a business (e.g., Disney, Harrod's) to restrict hairstyles than religious groups or a government?

7.3

FRANCE ENFORCES BAN ON FULL-FACE VEILS IN PUBLIC

Steven Erlanger

Vénissieux, France—France on Monday formally banned the wearing of full veils in public places, becoming the first country in Europe to impose restrictions on a form of attire that some Muslims consider a religious obligation.

The ban, which came after a year of debate and months of preparation, is viewed by supporters as a necessary step to preserve French culture and to fight what they see as separatist tendencies among Muslims. But the ban set off protests in Paris and several other cities, and it has left many Muslims, including those in this heavily immigrant community near Lyon, worried about their rights as French citizens.

Karima, 31, who was born in France and asked to be referred to by only her first name, has worn the niqab since the age of 15 as a sign of her devotion to God. She says she feels as if France has betrayed her.

"It's as if I was married to a man who mistreated me, but I'm still in love with him," she said. "It's as if he had an identity crisis, and I would still stay with him after 31 years of marriage."

The police do not have the authority under the law to remove full veils, only to fine or require citizenship lessons for those who violate the new law. They also showed few signs of moving quickly to enforce the new rules for fear of causing unrest in big cities with Muslim communities.

"The law will be infinitely difficult to enforce, and will be infinitely rarely enforced," Manuel Roux, a union leader for local police chiefs, told France Inter radio.

Patrice Ribeiro, general secretary of Synergie Officiers, a police union, said the law was "a source of trouble more than anything else." In areas with large immigrant populations, he said in an interview, the law cannot be carried out strictly: "We'll create riots." He said the matter would need to be handled with the help of religious authorities.

The issue was set alight in April 2009 by André Gérin, then the Communist mayor of Vénissieux. Half of the town's 60,000 residents are non-French citizens or their French-born children, and the niqab has been a relatively normal sight here. Mr. Gérin said at the time that the full facial veil, which is known in France erroneously as the burqa, should be banned in the name of the liberty and equality of women in a secular country.

On Monday, in his office, Mr. Gérin said the burqa was "just the tip of the iceberg" of the spread of Muslim radicalism and separatism that threatened the French Republic.

The law does not mention Islam or women. It bans the covering of the face in any public place, including shops and the street, as a security measure. A clause says that anyone who forces a woman to cover her face can be imprisoned for up to a year and fined up to 30,000 euros, about $43,000.

But the law is "a point of departure," said Mr. Gérin, who retired as mayor but remains a member of the National Assembly. Speaking of young Muslim women who refuse to participate in school sports, or Muslim men who refuse to allow a male doctor to treat their wives or who allegedly compel their wives to wear the veil, Mr. Gérin called the law "a wake-up call," a means "to eradicate this minority of fundamentalists, 'the gurus' who instrumentalize Islam for political reasons."

Polls show that the law is broadly popular in France, and it passed the lower house of Parliament with only one vote opposed. But many Muslim women say it feels like an outrage. To them, it singles out and stigmatizes one gender of one religion.

Karima, who runs a business and uses public transportation, said she would lift the veil if required for an identity check, but added, "I won't remove it, I'll have to be buried in it."

Her husband supports her, she said, and she wants her daughter, 11, to respect Islam, too. She is thinking about buying a scooter so she can wear a helmet instead. But frankly, she said, the metro is much faster.

She cannot sleep with worry, she said. "From now on, I'll be treated like an illegal worker, an outlaw, a person wanted by the police, even though the only crime I've committed is to show myself as I am."

Nelly Moussaid, 28, a former national karate champion, has been wearing the niqab for two years "as a sign of faith." She lives in Marseille with her husband and their 4-month-old boy. While Marseille is a tolerant city with many immigrants and Muslims, she said, "those who keep wearing the niqab will go crazy," asking: "Will they manage to catch all of us, arrest us at every corner of every street?"

The mood in France is aggressive, she said. "Before, on the street, I got only stares. But now people look at us as if we had killed their mothers."

The Interior Ministry estimates that only about 2,000 women wear the niqab in France, while Mr. Gérin, who helped write a long parliamentary report on the issue, believes that the number is higher. But with an estimated six million Muslims in France, the action taken seems large compared with the problem, critics say, and they accuse President Nicolas Sarkozy and his center-right party of playing politics with a generalized and unjustified fear of Islam and immigrants.

Mr. Sarkozy has responded that Islam is not the problem, only radical Islam, which does not respect French values and separation of church and state.

Naima Bouteldja interviewed 32 women who wear the niqab for the Open Society Foundation, a nongovernmental organization. She found none who said they had been forced to wear the veil, and 10 said they started wearing the niqab as a response to the political controversy. Eight of the 32 were French converts to Islam; a third said they did not wear the niqab all the time.

"Some were angry, and some said that many 'niqabis' had already left France, and many of them talked about leaving France," she said. "Most of the women confront verbal abuse on a daily basis, with a lot of the abuse coming from Muslims." Her report, "Unveiling the Truth: Why 32 Muslim Women Wear the Full-Face Veil in France," was released Monday.

In Paris, a protest over the ban near the Cathedral of Notre-Dame, organized by a Muslim property developer, resulted in the arrest of two men and three women for an illegal gathering, the police said—not for the women's wearing of the full veil.

Discussion Questions

1. When you consider that a French town has a population of 60,000 and half of those residents are Muslims who may have lived there for decades and now have French-born children, who then can be called the "majority"?

2. This reading mentions that Muslims are viewed as having separatist tendencies, which reduces the ability to preserve the French culture. When the ban on full-face coverings is admittedly difficult and rarely enforced, in the end, what gains have been made by the legislating country?

3. Do you think this ban is within the right of the French government to legislate protection of its culture or do you think this is a divisive move that will only anger a certain segment of the French population? Explain your thoughts.

7.4

DRESS PROPERLY, NO SWEARING, AND MAINTAIN GENDER SEPARATION: HOW SIGNS "WELCOME" VISITORS TO A SMALL U.S. COMMUNITY

Daily Mail Reporter

As welcome signs go, it is one of the more unusual ones (Figure 7.8).

And for visitors to Kiryas Joel, a small Jewish community in Orange County, New York State, it has provoked quite a reaction. For the sign doesn't just greet visitors, but warns them to dress appropriately for their visit, amongst other things.

Written in both English and Spanish, the sign, posted by Congregation Yetev Lev at the entrances to the village, warns visitors to cover their legs and arms, maintain gender separation in public places and use appropriate language.

But it has left some who visit the Hasidic community unhappy.

Adia Parker, an Orange County resident, said: "They're telling us that we can't come into their community unless we dress a certain way."

Another said: 'I know it's a request, and it certainly was polite, but it puts me in an uncomfortable position. Why should it bother you what I'm wearing?'

But some are welcoming the decision of the community in response to a flood of visitors who used foul language and exposed their shoulders.

Taxi driver Tim Diltz said: "I think they have a right to do that. I mean, people do show up in inappropriate things and it offends them. So I can't argue with that."

David Ekstein, president of Congregation Yetev Lev, said the signs were meant to guide out-

Figure 7.8 Welcome sign for the village of Kiryas Joel in New York.

siders so they don't offend village residents, especially during the summer. No single incident or group of visitors with objectionable clothing triggered them, he said.

"If our standards of modesty are not what is practised in the surrounding communities, then it is even more incumbent to provide this polite reminder," Mr Ekstein added.

A village trustee pointed out the signs said nothing about consequences for violating these guidelines—because there are no consequences.

http://www.dailymail.co.uk/news/article-1308436/Kiryas-Joel-welcomes-make-sure-dress-appropriately.html.

"We're not threatening anyone," said Rabbi Jacob Freund. "Everybody is free to come in and be the same, like all other places in the United States."

"You're not going to be arrested. Whoever wants to come, I live here, I grew up here. Actually, people know what to do. This is for people that don't know," said Kahan, a Kiryas Joel resident.

The tradition in the villages of Satmar Hasidic Jews is modesty. Even on the hottest of days, most residents cover up from head to toe, with unmarried men and women kept apart at all times.

Women also cannot wear provocative clothes as men are not supposed to see anything that inspires inappropriate thoughts.

Discussion Questions

1. How would you feel if a town's welcome sign told you what you should wear while visiting there? What do you think about the lack of consequences for disregarding the welcome sign's instructions?

2. Given that modesty is the tradition in Kiryas Joel, and visitors from the outside may not be aware of this tradition, isn't it acceptable to post a sign telling visitors what to expect? Share your thoughts on this with others.

3. Kiryas Joel residents wear clothing that covers their entire bodies even during the heat of summer. How might the modest residents of Kiryas Joel be affected by the immodest dress of visitors?

7.5

THE BUSINESS IMPACT OF THE ROYAL WEDDING

Women's Wear Daily Reporter

Dressing Catherine Middleton for the royal wedding has catapulted the house of Alexander McQueen from niche designer business into household name, giving management the delicate task of balancing its exclusive reputation with the wider commercial potential now within its grasp.

That's how industry observers and retailers reacted to Friday's fashion coup, which also marked a dramatic trajectory for a label once synonymous with ragtag rebellion—and one whose future seemed tenuous a year ago in the wake of the suicide of its incendiary founder.

"It will have a phenomenal impact in terms of brand awareness. The brand is still a niche brand, and this exposure will definitely bring a wider clientele," said Ralph Toledano, the former Chloé executive who now operates a Paris-based consulting business, RT Management.

Still, Toledano said the feat of dressing Middleton, now known as the Duchess of Cambridge,

should not be trumpeted too loudly. "This assignment is an honor for the designer, a fantastic tribute to the legacy of Lee Alexander McQueen. I think it should be considered as that, and not become a marketing tool," he said.

Lucian James, creative director and founder of Paris-based strategic consultancy Agenda Inc., said the royal milestone transforms McQueen "into a true fashion house with guaranteed legacy, rather than a brand in transition centered around the original designer."

It also "tames the edginess of the brand, raising it to a new endorsement by A-list consumers," James said, highlighting that infamous McQueen story that, while working at Anderson & Sheppard in London, he incorporated an expletive into the lining of a jacket for the Prince of Wales.

"This moment tips the brand back to the focus on technique and on the Savile Row origins of Lee Alexander," he said. "Meanwhile, you have to wonder whether Sarah Burton has received any calls from Bernard Arnault."

John Guy, a retail and luxury goods analyst for The Royal Bank of Scotland, said, "Obviously, for the PPR group this is very positive," noting how "Other Brand" sales of which Alexander McQueen is a key sales contributor increased first-quarter sales year-over-year by more than 20 percent to 165 million euros, or $244 million at current exchange. (Also in PPR's "Other Brand" category are Balenciaga, Stella McCartney, Boucheron and Sergio Rossi.)

Given how well-received Middleton's wedding dress has been and how the Burberry Prorsum trench she wore for her first post-engagement appearance sold out, Guy said, "this bodes extremely well for the McQueen business."

While the Alexander McQueen business is significantly smaller than PPR's Gucci, it has been a strong performer sales-wise. Further growth for this more niche label would most likely stem from opening boutiques and concept shops rather than rolling out wholesale, Guy said.

But whether it was a casual enquiry about the dress or a friendly probe about what it might mean for sales, staff at the Alexander McQueen boutique on Bond Street in London were studiously tight-lipped on the subject of the wedding on Friday afternoon following the ceremony. Temporary staff with no history at the company were working at the store for the day to help maintain the silence. In addition, one enormous security guard was positioned at the entrance to the store to fend off giant groups of tourists posing for photos.

Betsy Pearce, a Paris-based legal adviser who represented McQueen in 2000 when he sold a majority stake in his London-based house to Gucci group, today PPR's luxury division, marveled at the transformation of McQueen, which went from something "feral" and "deeply antiauthority" through a slow "domestication" under the umbrella of a corporate behemoth to the brand's "coronation" last week before the eyes of the world.

"It's the quintessential rags-to-riches story," Pearce said. "My concern is that it's easy to take advantage of and cash in on it. With any brand, there's only so much time at the pinnacle."

Pearce noted the dressing coup is a tribute to Sarah Burton, and, "I have to imagine there's a mutual understanding of two young women thrown into a situation they didn't expect, with enormous media scrutiny."

In this instance, the media attention on the big day will pay off, many observers said.

"The amount of media impressions through TV, twitter and blogs will catapult the Alexander McQueen name to familiarity it never had," said Kim Vernon, president and CEO of Vernon Co. "Whether it translates to more perfume sales or made-to-order dresses, it is nothing but positive."

This could include more opportunities for licensing, said Robert Burke, president and chief executive officer of Robert Burke associates in New York. "This is a new chapter for his fragrance," Burke said. "The objective will be to maintain the high-fashion image and also be commercial."

Burke was alluding to the late designer's dismal foray into fragrance in 2003 and 2005 with the scents Kingdom and My Queen. When L'Oréal acquired YSL Beauté for 1.15 billion euros in 2008 from PPR, the fragrance brand was not part of the transaction and the McQueen license is now thought to be dormant.

Still, the fact that McQueen remains part of a large corporate group puts the company in a strong position to capitalize on the publicity windfall, according to Burke.

He also highlighted the already international reach of the McQueen franchise, unlike the "small, British designers" the royal family has favored in the past.

"One couldn't have scripted it better," Burke remarked, noting the hubbub around the wedding dress will surely dovetail with an exhibition dedicated to Alexander McQueen opening this week at New York's Metropolitan Museum of Art.

The events will also surely catapult the profile of Burton, the current creative director at McQueen, who is already on the radar of luxury titan Arnault as he hunts for a successor to John Galliano at Christian Dior and wields one of the biggest checkbooks in the industry.

Sources said Burton seems open to discussions about working for another big brand, but PPR would likely shore up more resources to keep her ensconced at McQueen. Burton has spent her entire career at the elbow of the acclaimed British designer, the son of a taxicab driver whose seminal and controversial highland rape collection of 1995 ignited his career, ultimately landing him, at age 27, as couturier at Givenchy, a role he kept for five years.

Armando Branchini, deputy chairman of Milan consultancy InterCorporate, characterized the bridal credit as an "assist" to the brand that would have a "very positive" influence on the business: "it won't increase its sales tenfold—and it would be a mistake to change its niche quality—but it will increase its allure and appeal."

The McQueen business has weathered some rocky years, and in 2004, then Gucci Group CEO Robert Polet set a 2007 break-even deadline, which the company met ahead of time. The founder's suicide also raised questions, given his renowned cutting skill, imagination and flair for showmanship.

"If there was any doubt about the future of the brand following Alexander McQueen's death, then that has been completely banished," said George Wallace, CEO of consultancy MHE Retail. Asked whether this was the moment to expand with brand extensions, he said: "the brand can now reach a wider audience, with fragrance and accessories lines. But they would need to be managed carefully."

Retailers said they expect an immediate bump to the business. And Saks Fifth Avenue could be first in line. Fortuitously, the company had already lined up Burton for a trunk show appearance Tuesday at its Fifth Avenue flagship. The private meet-and-greet will be her first official in-store appearance since McQueen's death. Per agreement with the house, Saks executives declined to comment Friday about the event and the retailer's plans for the business.

"This is a dream come true for a brand," said Jeffrey Kalinsky, executive Vice President of Nordstrom. "I do think the business will go through the roof."

Prior to the wedding, Nordstrom had already been exploring ways to build on the McQueen business, which has been "really strong" for ready-to-wear, as well as shoes and accessories, he said. "If you take a brand that is already successful and it gets that level of worldwide exposure, it will have a tremendous impact on the business," Kalinsky said.

"The wedding will have a big impact on the McQueen business," said Stephanie Solomon, Vice President of fashion direction at Bloomingdale's.

On Friday, Barbara Atkin, Vice President of fashion direction at Canada's Holt Renfrew, said the store was already receiving calls enquiring about Sarah Burton's collection for McQueen. "I do not believe that customers outside the fashion world were even aware of Sarah Burton prior to this wedding," Atkin said. She said McQueen has been performing "extremely well since Sarah has taken over the brand. We are repeating styles and seeing double-digit results exceeding our plans with this collection. We are opening more doors in our chain. We actually wrote the gown that [Middleton's sister] Pippa was wearing and we expect to get lots of enquiries on that stunning 'Pippa' gown."

Sarah Rutson, fashion director at Hong Kong-based Lane Crawford, said her McQueen business was on an upswing before the wedding. "However, for our market, I don't believe [the wedding] will have significant impact just because of the dress. The significant impact and success has always been its strong design regardless."

Averyl Oates, chief buying director at Harvey Nichols, said the wedding pumped up British pride. "This will have a spectacularly immediate impact on both the industry, and sales for the brand," Oates said. "Alexander McQueen has long proved itself a popular brand with our customers, but hopefully this will now extend its visibility across the world, and what better platform than to be adorning the future Queen of England."

"The brand is in much demand today and its desirability continues to grow," said Marigay McKee, fashion and beauty director at Harrods. "There is always a demand for exquisite couture and I'm sure the house has a great future. There is a new McQueen flagship going in store for spring 2012, which we are all tremendously excited about."

Caroline Burstein, creative director of Browns, director of Browns Bride in London, said Burton is now fully out of the shadows.

"I have always known that Sarah was the backbone of the McQueen brand. He brought what he brought to the brand, but it was Sarah who underpinned it. She has an amazing attention to detail, and always kept a balance at the brand—she wouldn't let it go too far," she said.

Burstein said when she launched Browns Bride in 2004, she brought in RTW pieces from McQueen. "There was always a sense of occa-sion about them. They were just beautiful," she said.

Burstein added that the royal wedding dress would give a bump to an already healthy brand. "The McQueen label stayed strong. His death did not affect sales at the label because the clothes are good. They are what women with style like to wear—and not just skinny women. They work on real women."

Discussion Questions

1. Several opinions have been expressed by those in the business world regarding how Catherine Middleton's wedding dress will affect business at the House of Alexander McQueen. From your reading of the article, what were the potential positive outcomes for the business and what were the potential negative outcomes?
2. Is the fact that Alexander McQueen is one of many holdings of a large French luxury company (PPR) an advantage or disadvantage at the time of the Royal wedding, and roughly one year after the original designer's suicide? Give reasons to back up your answers.
3. Right after the Royal wedding, an exhibit on Alexander McQueen opened at the Met in New York. Given the enormous name recognition as a result of one-third of the world's population watching the Royal wedding on television and the popular exhibit at the Met, what would be the best way for the House of McQueen to handle this success and windfall of name recognition?

7.6

FROM HABIT TO FASHION: DRESS OF CATHOLIC WOMEN RELIGIOUS

Susan O. Michelman
University of Massachusetts/Amherst

This article focuses on data with 26 Roman Catho-lic nuns, or as those in noncloistered orders prefer to be called, "women religious" who relinquished religious habits for secular dress. It examines dy-namics of personal identity announcements and social identity placements that are not congruous. Prior to the 1960s, women's religious orders were quite homogeneous both in exterior manifesta-tions such as their dress in the habit, and in the purpose and spirit that permeated them (Ebaugh, 1977). Their personal and social persona were one and the same. The life of a woman religious was highly prescribed and routinized. During the 1960s and 1970s, the majority of women in non-cloistered orders of the Roman Catholic Church, as part of larger reforms dictated by Vatican II in 1962, relinquished religious habits for secular fashions. Many had worn habits for a large por-tion of their lives, often between 20 and 35 years, dressing in them from the moment they arose in the morning until they retired in the evening. Their social identities were more outwardly vis-ible than their personal identities, as they had re-linquished individuality for social control of their bodies by the church. From the time that women

Original for this text.

first wore religious attire as novices, they were instructed to view themselves not as individuals, but as representatives of a group. Their habits symbolized their commitment and vows to the Church, which superseded their individual identities (Griffin, 1975). (See Figure 7.9.)

Prior to Vatican II, which occurred in 1962, for many women in noncloistered religious orders, the habit came to be viewed in a more negative than positive light. Their perception was that

Figure 7.9 Catholic nuns dressed in (a) modified habit and (b) full habit.

this dress communicated a social identity that inhibited their ability to express personal identities that would allow them to function more fully in secular environments. The habit clearly symbolized their total commitment to their order, but it was described by them as a social control in their ability to interact and communicate freely as individuals. As described by women in this study, the habit made them feel less than fully human.

Ebaugh (1977), in her research on religious orders, confirmed that personal identity issues were not addressed by the Church prior to Vatican II. She describes the indoctrination of women religious as demanding ideological totalism (Lifton, 1961). In her research, she discussed the mechanisms of social control that made totalism work. The symbolic gesture of exchanging secular dress for black religious garb was "the first symbolic gesture of 'putting off the world' and entering into a new life" (Ebaugh, 1977):

> The uniform was characterized by complete simplicity and modesty, being high-necked, long-sleeved, and ankle length. In addition to the uniform, feminine lingerie was exchanged for simple white cotton underwear, indicating that the postulant was exchanging her womanly enjoyments for austere dress that would now symbolize her as the spouse of Jesus Christ. In addition, henceforth the woman was no longer to be distinguished by dress from the other women in the institute with whom she would live.

Historically, the habit did not start as a symbol of religious life, rather, it was the widow's dress of the day. In the case of the Sisters of St. Joseph, it started with six women in France in the 17th century, who went out two by two to minister to the needs of the people (Aherne, 1983). They wore modest black dresses and veils, because women who were widows were allowed more personal freedom than those who were single or married. They could travel without male chaperones. These women were able to circumvent both church and state regulations. This early "habit" was a protection in a sense, and it allowed them to be free to do the work they wanted. Some of the

THE MEANINGS OF DRESS

women in this study felt that prior to Vatican II, the Church saw the habit as a protection against the "evils of the world." The voluminous layers of black serge and veiling covering their bodies, heads, and necks cloaked both femininity and sexuality. In the eyes of the women in this study, it also suppressed their personal identity. Ironically, whereas the "habit" had historically begun as a way of achieving autonomy, this type of dress had evolved into a way of suppressing personal identity, through the social control of their bodies. It is important to bear in mind that the women in this study did not leave religious orders after Vatican II; rather, they had remained as members and had negotiated their identity within the boundaries of the Church. They negotiated some social control issues with the Church symbolically by discarding the habit for secular dress.

The women in my study dressed in contemporary fashions that made them indiscernible from any other modestly dressed professional woman in American society. Some orders like their members to wear some visible indication of their affiliation as women religious, such as a ring or cross (Ebaugh, 1993), but many of the women in my study did not. The habit, for many women in noncloistered religious orders, came to be viewed by them prior to Vatican II in a more negative than positive light. Their perception was that dress inhibited their ability to have positive social interactions as people; rather, they were frequently stereotyped by the symbolic nature of the habit. The habit visually symbolized and promoted interactions with others that reinforced this belief.

Interviewer: If you were sitting there in a habit, I would feel differently. I would feel a little more inhibited, more cautious, more formal.
Respondent: Your experience is the other end of what I'm trying to describe to you about coming out of habit.
Interviewer: You are talking about it being an inhibition for you—an inhibition in social interaction?
Respondent: Yes it was—because immediately when people saw us, they didn't see us as the individual that you were. They saw you as the woman religious and they immediately raise you above the human level. We had privilege and prestige and we were considered to be in a holier state of life. That's not true. I've chosen another way to live but it is not a holier way—it's a different way.

At the present time, the work and lifestyles of women religious in active orders is highly liberated in contrast to the period prior to Vatican II. When the habit was relinquished, social control of the body by the Church decreased. For example, today, women exhibit a high degree of personal autonomy, many living alone or in small groups instead of orders, fully integrated into the noncelibate lay community (Ebaugh, 1993). Dress, in light of many social changes for women religious, has been critical in not only reflecting, but also helping them to construct social change, specifically by its role in symbolic interaction processes related to the formation and perpetuation of personal identity.

Emerging from the Habit: Fashion and Secular Clothing

After Vatican II, which was a period of emerging personal identity, the women experienced profound conflicts surrounding dress and its complex relationship with their vow of poverty. The essence of the vow of poverty of spirit is humility, which is facilitated by material poverty (Metz, 1968). The habit had come to be accepted as a visible symbol of humility, while fashion and cultural issues of women's appearance, such as makeup and hairstyle, were historically associated with worldliness and materialism (i.e., fashion). Yet, women religious found themselves visibly re-entering the secular world from the perspective of appearance. Because of their vow of poverty, there was little money for clothing. Most of their post-habit attire came as hand-me-downs, or from thrift shops or sales.

The following quote is from a woman religious who worked in a career in women's clothing sales for 13 years prior to entering religious training. She expresses ambivalence about her love of clothes:

> I maintained my ability over the years [while in habit] to be a very good shopper. I would go to Steigers [Department Store]—the girls [clerks] would really get to know me. Many of them I had known throughout the years and they would know when the bargains were coming in. I became a shopper for several other people, especially in the early days [of transition from habits]. Now I struggle tremendously. I have far too many clothes. I'm good for a while but I have to keep looking. Someone else might not see me as a person that has a lot of clothes.

The habit had obscured visible markers of womanhood such as the hair and figure. In my interviews, much discussion focused on the personal discomfort and even trauma of reemerging into secular society. Skills related to personal appearance had to be relearned. Hair was discussed frequently as the focus of anxiety. After years of deprivation from air and light under the habit, hair loss was common. In this interview segment, a woman religious discusses her personal viewpoint on hair.

Respondent: I saw older women buying wigs who had lost their hair because of the habit.
Interviewer: Was that because of rubbing?
Respondent: Yes, and also because they didn't get air. Even at night they wore caps.
Interviewer: Was this a permanent hair loss?
Respondent: Yes, for some. But for some it was O.K. [it grew back]. I color my hair. It's something I do for myself. In the 1960s we began to do a lot of more personalized and psychological study of ourselves. The spiritual was always part of it. How can you separate the spiritual and emotional? It's holistic.

The habit had given women religious surprising freedom from the tyranny of appearance experienced by women in North American cul-

ture. Women religious were confronted with issues of body weight that had previously been obscured under the folds of black serge. Some women interviewed went on diets. Their awareness of style and fashion became evident. Women made personal choices about makeup, jewelry, modesty issues (length of skirt, neckline), and even hair coloring. The move to secular dress had a dramatic impact on both women religious and society in general. "It revealed to the world in general the human being underneath the habit. But more important, it revealed the nun to herself: It was an experience in recognition" (Griffin, 1975).

Women emerged from habit during the turbulent period of the Civil Rights Movement, the Vietnam War, and the Women's Movement. Whether in habit or not, women religious are known for their involvement in social causes. Several women in the study referred to themselves as feminists, noting that historically they were role models for women who chose lives of dedication rather than marriage and family. Women religious also acknowledged their identities as single, professional women, and their continuing conflicts with the patriarchal structure of the Vatican. They have been active participants in social activism and the dual labor market of the parish, where they have frequently, despite achieving higher education than priests, been denied positions of authority and participation in aspects of the liturgy.

Their emergence from habit to secular fashion not only reflected gender controversy within the Church but also helped women construct new identities as educated and professional women religious, rather than cloistered icons of the Church. Two women in my study referred to identities of women prior to Vatican II as "women of service" or more derogatorily, "handmaids of the Church." In a symbolic feminist action after Vatican II that coincided with elimination of the habit, many women religious dropped the male component of their chosen names and reassumed the female. The names of male saints who possessed desirable virtues were assigned to the women by their Mother Superior before the women took their final vows:

There was something else going on . . . we were changing our clothes and we were also changing our names. It didn't happen like Friday and Saturday, but it happened that we just kind of rebelled against having men's names—Sister Mary Peter, Sister Mary John, Sister Mary Bartholomew. Many women religious were moving out of their dress identity and they were changing their names back. All that was happening at the same time.

Discarding the habit was perceived by the women in this study as a positive step toward allowing them to work and interact as human beings while interpersonal distance lessened. In a positive sense, the Church, prior to Vatican II, had viewed the habit as a protection against the evils of the world, yet that caused many women religious to perceive themselves as isolated and inhibited from mingling with the people. The women's bodies were restrained and controlled by the Church within the confines of the habit. Women religious in this study perceived secular dress as essential in allowing them normal, daily, human interactions, which greatly enhanced their ability to provide social service within the community. They symbolically reclaimed their bodies as they discarded the habit:

> From 1983 to 1987, I was in Kentucky in Appalachia. I could never have gone down there in the habit what I did in my [secular] clothes. It would have been an absolute impossibility. My freedom would have been restricted. I was living in a county where there were only 30 Catholic families. I didn't go in as a Sister, I went in as a person named Mary.

Theoretical Issues

Symbolic interaction theory asserts "that the self is established, maintained, and altered in and through communication" (Stone, 1962). Stone widened the perspective of symbolic interaction studies to include appearance as a dimension of communication, usually the precursor to verbal transactions. Furthermore, Stone asserted that appearance is a critical factor in the "formulation of the conception of self" (Stone, 1962). Appearance establishes identity by indicating to others what the individual projects as his or her "program" (i.e., one's social roles of gender, age, occupation). In turn, these are "reviewed" by others, thereby validating or challenging the self (Stone, 1962):

> It [identity] is not a substitute word for "self." Instead, when one has identity, he is situated—that is, cast in the shape of a social object by the acknowledgment of his participation or membership in social relations. One's identity is established when others place him as a social object by assigning him the same words of identity that he appropriates for himself or announces. It is in the coincidence of placements and announcements that identity becomes a meaning of the self and often such placements and announcements are aroused by apparent symbols such as uniforms. The policeman's uniform, for example, is an announcement of his identity as policeman and validated by others' placements of him as policeman.

Stone (1962) describes identity as being established by two processes, apposition and opposition, a bringing together and setting apart. "To situate the person as a social object is to bring him together with other objects so situated, and, at the same time to set him apart from still other objects. Identity, to Stone, is intrinsically associated with all the joinings and departures of social life. To have an identity is to join with some and depart from others, to enter and leave social relations at once."

In contrast to Stone, Goffman (1963) defines personal identity as "the assumption that the individual can be differentiated from all others." From an interactionist perspective, this was a real dilemma for some women religious in habit. Their dress clearly symbolized their total affiliation to their work in the order, but was described by them as "restricting" in their ability to interact and communicate freely. The consequences of these symbolic limitations led to a paradox described by the women as causing them to "feel less than fully human."

Fred Davis (1992) addressed the concept of ambivalence and appearance more directly than other symbolic interactionists who preceded him. He argued that personal identity announcements and social identity placements might not be congruous. For example, a person might dress as a police officer for a costume party and be incorrectly identified as someone who is actually responsible for law enforcement. Davis maintaining that dress serves as "a kind of visual metaphor for identity . . . registering the culturally anchored ambivalence that resonates with and among identities," suggesting that personal and social identity incongruity occurs regularly because dress is often an ambivalent form of communication. Davis is broadly interested in dress and its symbolic relationship to identity, but more specifically, he discusses his theories within the framework of fashion. Davis defines fashion by distinguishing it from style, custom, conventional or acceptable dress, or prevalent modes by stressing the importance of the element of change (1992). While the term "dress" communicates elements of stability, use of the term "fashion" implies the added element of social change (Roach-Higgins & Eicher, 1993).

A symbolic interaction perspective emphasizes social process and meaning(s) and is relevant for explaining how and why these women negotiated their visual and verbal awareness of their appearance (Kaiser, Nagasawa & Hutton, 1995). When the women emerged as visible females from the self-described "androgyny"[1] of how they felt in the habit, identity conflicts surfaced. Davis (1992) described how dress serves as "a kind of visual metaphor for identity . . . registering the culturally anchored ambivalences that resonate with and among identities." Ambivalence is acknowledged by Davis to be natural and integral to human experience and can be exhibited in symbolic issues of appearance.

The dialectic of the women's physical bodies, symbolized by their dress, to the social body of the Roman Catholic Church, is a critical one in understanding the power of dress in both reflecting and constructing social change for women religious. For example, both Marx (1967) and Durkheim and Mauss (1963) argued for the dialectic between the "natural" and "social" body. Other social scientists have viewed the body as the *tabula rasa* for socialization. Van Gennep (1960), Mauss (1973), Bordieu (1977), and Douglas (1966, 1970) have argued this dialectic to demonstrate the social construction of the body.

Conclusion

This study of women religious provides a model for examining how changes in enduring modes of dress such as habits can be examined not only in relation to the more predominantly held view of changing social roles but also from the perspective of personal identity. The relationship between dress and social change must be carefully examined, as with women religious, by examining their relationship to social roles, issues of social and personal identities, and their mediation through the symbol of dress.

Davis (1992) uses the term "fault lines" to describe "culturally induced strains concerning who and what we are" that find expression in dress. Vatican II certainly created an enormous quake for women religious, but the forces of change within orders ultimately came from the women themselves in the form of human agency. Women religious were poised and ready to address issues of roles, identities, and social change.

References

Aherne, M. C. (1983). *Joyous service: The history of the sisters of Saint Joseph of Springfield.* Holyoke, MA: Sisters of Saint Joseph.

Bordieu, P. (1977). *Outline of a theory of practice.* (R. Nice, trans.) Cambridge, England: Cambridge University Press.

Davis, F. (1992). *Fashion, culture and identity.* Chicago, IL: University of Chicago Press.

Douglas, M. (1970). *Nature symbols.* New York: Vintage Books.

Douglas, M. (1966). *Purity and Danger: An Analysis of Pollution and Taboo.* Washington: Frederick Praeger.

Durkheim E., & Mauss, M. (1963). *Primitive Classification* (R. Needham, trans.). London: Cohen & West.

Ebaugh, H. (1977). *Out of the cloister: A study of organizational dilemmas.* Austin: University of Texas Press.

Ebaugh, H. (1993). *Women in the vanishing cloister.* New Brunswick, NJ: Rutgers University Press.

Goffman, E. (1963). *Stigma: Notes on the management of a spoiled identity.* Englewood Cliffs, NJ: Prentice Hall.

Griffin, M. (1975). *Unbelling the cat: The courage to choose.* Boston: Little, Brown.

Heilbrun, C. (1964). *Toward a recognition of androgyny.* New York: Alfred A. Knopf, Inc.

Kaiser, S. Nagasawa, R. & Hutton, S. (1995). Construction of an SI theory of fashion: Part 1, ambivalence and change. *Clothing and Textiles Research Journal* 13 (3), 172–183.

Lifton, J. (1961). *Thought Reform and the Psychology of Totalism.* New York: Norton.

Marx, K. (1967). *Capital: A Critique of Political Economy*, 3 vols. New York: International Publishers.

Mauss, M. (1973). Techniques of the Body. (B. Brewster, trans.) *Economy and society 2 (1)*, pp. 70–88.

Metz, J. (1968). *Poverty of spirit.* New York: Paulist Press.

Roach-Higgins, M., & Eicher, J. (1993). Dress and identity. *ITAA special publication #5.*

Stone, G. (1962). Appearance the self. In A. Rose (Ed.), *Human behavior and social processes: An interactionist approach*, pp. 86–118. New York: Houghton, Mifflin, Co.

Van Gennep, A. (1960). *The Rites of Passage* (M. B. Vizedom & G. L. Caffee, trans.). Chicago: University of Chicago Press.

Endnote

1. Some women in the study used this word to elaborate on how they felt when wearing a habit. This is not my choice of words. The term "androgyny" is derived from the Greek word "andro" (male) and "gyn" (female). Heilbrun (1964) uses this term to define a condition in which the characteristics of the sexes and the human impulses expressed by men and women are not rigidly assigned. Therefore, the term may be more closely associated with perceptions of identity than solely with characteristics associated with physical appearance.

Discussion Questions

1. Uniforms (such as a nun's habit) make the wearer easy to identify but can also create barriers that make accessibility to the person wearing the uniform difficult. Can you think of other examples of a uniform dress that creates the same effect?

2. Describe the origin of the nun's habit and what freedoms and/or restrictions were placed on the wearer at the time of its origination.

7.7

IN BUDDHIST BHUTAN, HAPPINESS COUNTS

Vishal Arora

Thimphu, Bhutan—The Buddhist kingdom of Bhutan is the only nation that puts happiness at the core of public policy. But its thrust on a "gross national happiness" (GNH) index is not just a warm-and-fuzzy inheritance from Buddhism; it is integral to the nation's cultural and political security.

Bhutan's fourth king, Jigme Singye Wangchuck, coined the phrase GNH in 1972 on the belief that people's happiness did not depend on the nation's economic wealth, said Tshoki Zangmo, information officer at the Center for Bhutan Studies.

It was, Zangmo said, "a notion of wholeness that is embedded in Bhutan's authentic Buddhist culture." Ever since, all manner of government policies have centered on GNH in this land-locked Himalayan country—about half the size of Indiana—sandwiched between India to the south and China to the north.

In 2006, the king abdicated the throne in favor of his son, Jigme Khesar Namgyal Wangchuck, who in his first address as monarch said his main responsibility would be focusing on GNH.

Two years later, when Bhutan held its first democratic elections after centuries of absolute monarchy rule, GNH was the main agenda of the ruling, royalist Bhutan Peace and Prosperity Party.

GNH indicators—as opposed to more traditional measures like a nation's gross domestic product based on economic activity—recognize nine components of happiness: psychological well-being, ecology, health, education, culture, living standards, time use, community vitality, and good governance.

It's all tracked twice a year through a survey of 1,300 people conducted by Zangmo's agency.

Many of the GNH indicators find their roots in Buddhism. Psychological well-being, for example, includes measures of meditation, prayer, nonviolence, and reincarnation. The country's GNH secretary, Karma Tshiteem, said Buddhism is key to people's happiness.

"Happiness is about one's outlook on life, and Buddhist values help people appreciate and focus on what they have rather than what they do not," he said. "Values such as compassion and respect foster greater social interaction." In addition, belief in karma—"a force that unifies past and future through the present"—also figures into GNH, Tshiteem said. Buddhism also had a "tremendous influence" in creating Bhutan's unique culture and traditions, which he said are "the most important source of our identity." The Western notion of separation of church and state is, well, foreign to Bhutan. Here, the government and clergy operate from Buddhist monasteries, such as Home and Culture Minister Minjur Dorji's office in the palatial, whitewashed Tashichho Dzong monastery in the nation's capital.

Bhutan is perhaps the only country where culture is part of the interior ministry's portfolio. Dorji said preservation of culture is crucial for the nation's security, and Bhutanese culture, in turn, "is rooted in Buddhism." One tangible way of preserving culture is a national dress code in schools and government buildings. Men wear the gho, a knee-length robe tied at the waist by a cloth belt, and women wear the kira, an ankle-length dress clipped at one shoulder and tied at the waist (see Figure 7.3 on page 270).

Bhutan also mandates use of the national language, Dzongkha, and has strict architectural standards throughout the country.

Government officials say it's not just about looking nice in public, but fostering a physical sense of identity to distinguish Bhutan from its larger neighbors.

"Bhutan is a tiny nation between two giants, India and China, and therefore it has to have a distinct culture to reinforce its identity as an independent nation. Otherwise, how is Bhutan different from India?" Dorji said.

Such distinctions are deeply embedded in Bhutanese DNA. The Indian state of Sikkim, on Bhutan's western border, was once a separate Buddhist kingdom ruled by descendants of an Indian Buddhist saint who, according to tradition, brought Tantric Buddhism to Bhutan and Tibet in the 8th century.

Sikkim was gradually outnumbered by Nepalese Hindus and merged with India after a referendum in 1975. And Tibet, on Bhutan's eastern border, was incorporated into China in 1950.

Neither is it simply a matter of history. "Our little country, once blissfully isolated in a remote corner of the Himalayas . . . is now buffeted by powerful forces," Prime Minister Jigmi Thinley said at a recent workshop on GNH.

"Though some have brought benefit . . . some of them threaten not only our profound heritage but even our lives and land." Dorji, the culture minister, said Bhutanese leaders plan to integrate GNH, and its Buddhist underpinnings, into school curriculum, in part to help maintain the country's religious demography of three-quarter Buddhists and one-quarter Hindus.

"It's a small country with less than 700,000 people, so why do you need more religions?" he said, alluding to a few churches that operate underground, fearing persecution. Indeed, Bhutan's cultural and religious coexistence is fragile, and Bhutan has little patience for threats to that delicate balance. In the 1980s and the early 1990s, about 100,000 people from southern Bhutan—mainly Hindus of Nepalese origin or Christian converts—fled to Nepal after Bhutanese security personnel crushed a rebellion against the government's "one nation, one people" campaign to strengthen Bhutan's identity. "Unlike India, where tensions between Hindus, Muslims and Christians are commonplace," Dorji said, "Bhutan is not resilient."

Discussion Questions

1. This article about Bhutan is similar to the Erlanger article about the French ban on full-face veils. Bhutan is struggling to maintain its religious demography of three-fourths Buddhists and one-fourth Hindus by creating school curriculum underpinned by Buddhism tenets and crushing a Hindu rebellion. Is this maintaining of a cultural heritage a valid reason for causing non-Buddhists to flee Bhutan?

2. Should countries who harshly maintain their uniqueness be considered right for that effort? Or should countries find other ways to maintain their cultural heritage while welcoming newcomers with different ideas?

3. Given that the country of Bhutan (population of 700,000) is nestled between two giants (India and China), does having a national dress code make sense, so that Bhutan is not absorbed into its larger neighbors' countries? Explain your answer.

7.8
___

WHEN A HOLY MAN'S SKIN IS THE CANVAS

Stan Sesser

Figure 7.10 Mahant Bhagwan Das, renowned Sadhu. The large red area on his head represents "the seed of creation."

Sadhus, the holy men of northern India and Nepal, have long beards, matted hair and rail-thin bodies, frequently brightly painted and garbed in a loincloth—if that. (See Figure 7.10.) Now a photo exhibit at the Rubin Museum of Art in New York, together with a book by the same photographer, looks at their painted bodies as canvases representing inner visions and higher states of consciousness.

The exhibit, which opened Friday, is one of the rare occasions when an art museum has displayed body paintings, in this case via the photos of American-born Thomas Kelly, taken over three decades. The photographer, who is based in Kathmandu, Nepal, attached himself to groups of Sadhus and traveled with them. When they asked why he was there, he says, "I'd answer that I'm on a mission to document the history of a people that is unknown to most of us."

Still, there were risks. Many Sadhus angrily wave away photographers, and Mr. Kelly said that spontaneous photography of Sadhus can be dangerous: "You can easily be trampled or attacked." The Sadhus' acceptance of Mr. Kelly, who speaks both Hindi and Nepalese, required slow and careful cultivation. His Spanish-language book, "Sadhus," published in Chile in 2003, will be on sale at the exhibit.

There are anywhere from 8 to 15 million Sadhus, who have abandoned their worldly possessions and follow such Hindu gods as Shiva and Vishnu. Texts almost 5,000 years old refer to these holy men.

The Sadhus bathe every morning, washing off the body art. Then they paint it back on. Followers of Shiva, whose aspects include both destroyer and preserver, use ash from funeral pyres, symbolic of the naked self. Followers of Vishnu, a god of many avatars (who fights evil and protects moral law), use colors, once from natural ground roots but today mostly synthetic powders. Sometimes the Sadhus write on their bodies in devanagari, the Indian alphabet used to write such languages as Sanskrit and Hindi.

Sadhus always paint themselves. "Body art is a form of identity, defining who they are and which deity they are devoted to," says Becky Bloom, who curated the exhibit at the Rubin Museum, which is devoted to the art of the Himalayas. (It ran until May 30, 2011.)

Discussion Questions

1. Hindu monks paint their bodies every day to express who they are and to which deity they are devoted. Would you agree that people around the world practice a similar ritual when they shower and dress each morning? Discuss your answer in small groups.

2. Wandering as a monk is a unique lifestyle. Would you ever consider this way of life? Why or why not?

3. If most Westerners worship worldly possessions, how is that communicated each morning as they dress for the day?

7.9

ECONOMIC DOWNTURN MAY BE PULLING NECKLINES UP: STRUGGLING RETAILERS WIDEN OPTIONS FOR TEENS; TWEENS TO INCLUDE MORE MODEST CLOTHES

Jayne O'Donnell

Modesty in young women's clothing is getting a boost from the dismal economy.

When consumer spending was in overdrive, retailers could sell to the masses and ignore the more muted voices asking for, say, a decent supply of sleeved shirts or prom dresses that show more fabric than skin.

Now, however, it's the rare retailer who's willing to take the chance of turning off any possible customer. Luxury-store clerks can no longer afford to look down at scruffy shoppers, and store owners of every sort are recognizing the one-size-fits-all approach to retail buying no longer works.

Whether it's more of a fiscal or moral shift, understated girls' clothing may indeed be making a comeback.

Even flashy Chanel designer Karl Lagerfeld declared "bling is over" and noted the economy is prompting a "new modesty," in an interview with the *International Herald Tribune* this year.

Retail consultant Ken Nisch says the trend is more moderation than modesty, but the effect may be the same.

"It's not because of a moral revival but about sensibility," says Nisch, chairman of retail brand and design firm JGA. "What's provocative has often been ultra trendy, and it just doesn't make sense to buy things you can't wear for a lot of occasions anymore."

The evidence is found everywhere, from the baggy and shapeless "boyfriend" jeans that are replacing skin-tight ones for many young women to the basic fashions seen all over New York these days, says Meredith Barnett, CEO of retail boutique website StoreAdore.com.

"People want to be more comfortable and more covered," says Barnett. "You're not seeing nearly as much risk taking."

The trend is forcing a shift in the way retailers do business. Just as teen retailers have come to target the gothic girl, the diva and the street-wear aficionado, they now must recognize that skin is simply not always in. For every girl who embraces strapless tops and micro-mini dresses, there might be one who is trying to abide by either a school or moral dress code. Modest fashion typically calls for covered shoulders, thighs and cleavage but is hardly the definition of frumpy that the term often calls to mind.

"For those groups who want to be a little more reserved, [stores] must understand what their needs are and offer them what they want," says retail strategist Cari Bunch of consulting firm Kurt Salmon Associates. "It's essential for survival."

When he explained the chain's new local approach to investors last month, Macy's CEO Terry Lundgren cited the chain's ability to offer clothing to working women in Pittsburgh and St. Louis seeking "covered sleeves and more traditional silhouettes."

Too Provocative

Finding a bit more coverage in their clothing may be a goal of many adult women, but finding fashion that wouldn't be considered "sexy" can be an obsession for mothers of tween and teenage girls. When consumer insights firm BIGresearch polled 5,000 consumers last fall, 64% of those 18 and older agreed or strongly agreed with the statement, "Fashions for young people have gotten too provocative."

Brenda Sharman, who became national founder of the teen girl group Pure Fashion in 2006, already knew public sentiment was starting to lean in favor of her modesty mission. However, she didn't think there would be much concern about low necklines and high hemlines in a time of staggering economic pressure and spiraling unemployment. But now, she believes the economy has become a boon.

"Fashion's in our court right now," says Sharman, a former model.

Pure Fashion has about 700 members who work as models at spring teen fashion shows, which attract about 11,000 people. The group has affiliates in 10 countries, and is signing new groups on its website, PureFashion.com.

Pure Fashion was an offshoot of a Catholic missionary organization, but Sharman believes its message resonates from Muslims to Orthodox Jews to parents who simply believe it shouldn't be hard to find shorts that completely cover the rear end.

"Girls need to understand: What they wear sends a message," Sharman says.

Evangelical tween group Secret Keeper Girl was founded in 2004 by author Dannah Gresh, partly in response to a 2003 *Time* magazine report that $1.6 million was spent the year before on thong underwear for girls ages 7 to 12. The group is circulating a petition it plans to send to the Council of Fashion Designers of America and the Apparel & Footwear Manufacturers Association urging them to consider modesty in their designs.

Gresh is hoping to have 50,000 signatures by fall. She says 5,000 have come in on their website, SecretKeeperGirl.com. When they do, Gresh plans to organize a day of shopping at the few stores they think offer appropriate fashion choices for pre-teen girls, including Old Navy, Gap Kids and Children's Place.

Gresh, who also started teen group Pure Freedom, which hosts fashion events in up to 80 cities annually, says the parents of her members are relieved the movement is getting traction.

"When clothes get skimpier and skimpier, moms get angrier and angrier," says Gresh, who's written several books including *And the Bride Wore White*. "But it's harder to appeal [to retailers] when it's become the norm and you're just one mom trying to hold the line."

Many parents agree.

Joe Cummings of Universal City, Texas, links self-esteem issues about appearance in young women to influences including suggestive apparel stores, Hannah Montana and the Bratz doll line. "It is no wonder that this might be the most difficult period in recent history to be a teenage girl in school, or a parent of one," says Cummings, who has a 12-year-old daughter.

Jenny Carpenter of Washington has applauded moves by apparel makers such as Shade and Layers to offer more modest choices, but she remains appalled by the marketing many retailers use to pitch their products.

"Why are retailers using sex to sell to young women?" asks Carpenter, who has four sons. "My boys will one day be men, and I want them to respect women for who they are—mind, body and soul—instead of drooling after them because of the amount of skin they're showing."

Retailers Respond

Ella Gunderson unwittingly amped up the modesty movement when she complained to Nordstrom in 2004.

"Dear Nordstrom, I am an 11-year-old girl who has tried shopping at your store for clothes (in particular jeans), but all of them ride way under my hips and the next size up is too big and falls down," she wrote, according to an excerpt on PureFashion.com.

Gunderson's story made national news, and Nordstrom responded with higher cut jeans—and more—when it realized hers was hardly a lone cry. "Around that time, a fair amount of people were looking for modest options," says Nordstrom spokeswoman Brooke White.

That prompted the company to add a "modest" category on its website. Although the designation was later dropped because there weren't enough people using "modest" as a search term, White says the chain did make sure to keep modest selections, which are available depending on demand in different regions of the country.

Macy's new "localization" strategy tailors apparel and other products by store and will include all Macy's by June. Spokesman Jim Sluzewski says, "In those stores where a more modest apparel assortment is expected by the customer, that's what we're working to deliver."

Modest or not, young people tend to prefer specialty stores over department stores, and that trend was evident during recent "mall missions" conducted by Pure Fashion. During these trips, groups of girls who are 14 to 18 years old fanned out across shopping areas to rate retailers on their apparel and atmosphere. They awarded Pure Fashion seals of approval to those that passed muster on at least seven out of 10 areas on their checklist, which includes appropriate apparel, mannequins and music.

American Eagle, Anthropologie and Banana Republic got the Washington, D.C., group's highest ratings, while Delia's, J. Crew and Ann Taylor all got the Pure Fashion thumbs up elsewhere.

"J. Crew is my favorite store," says Ashley Nowak, a 14-year-old Pure Fashion member from Alpharetta, Ga. "Almost all of the other stores today have booty shorts and tube tops, that are not only revealing, but also set an inaccurate image of what beauty is supposed to look like."

Elsa Rose Hoffmann, who leads Pure Fashion in the D.C. area, says most stores were "very receptive" during a recent outing in Georgetown: Store managers would ask, "What can we do to improve?"

No Lack of Material

Preparing to address a group of teen girls at a Pure Fashion camp last year, Sharman had props ready to convince them just how far into the gutter fashion—and our culture—have gone.

There was an 8-inch-long skirt from Abercrombie & Fitch, one of the store's shopping bags with a near-naked man on it and a "Bling Bling Barbie," who looked suspiciously like a prostitute. Sharman also showed a camisole that's now sold as a top but was considered lingerie at the time

Sharman modeled it in the 1990s, when she says bras and underwear "were more full coverage."

Sharman didn't have to go any farther than her local mall to collect her examples. A floor-to-ceiling photo graphic of a young man with his pants unzipped has greeted many visitors to Abercrombie & Fitch stores. The home page for the chain's lingerie line, Gilly Hicks, has seven men with bare behinds posing with a young model in a bra and underwear. American Apparel's website home page recently featured a topless model wearing see-through leggings.

Still, the stores' sales suggest sex does often sell. Although Abercrombie's sales have plunged with the economy—February's sales dropped a record 30% from Februrary 2008—it's widely attributed to the chain's resistance to discounting, not a conservative backlash. And along with sister store Hollister, Abercrombie remains one of the stores teens most often list as favorites.

American Apparel, which sells basic cotton tees and other casual wear, had a 9% sales increase in February and is often cited as one of the retail success stories of the downturn. Abercrombie & Fitch declined to comment. American Apparel says its ads are all done in-house and feature employees.

"Sometimes that means our ads are more controversial than other companies' but they are, at least, always sincere and genuine," says company spokesman Ryan Holiday, who says provocative ads are at the "core of many fashion brands." While she's pleased by the response her cause is getting, Sharman suspects some of retail's embrace of modesty may cycle back out of fashion again in a few years.

"Fashion has been so sexy for the past seven to 10 years, they wanted to do something different to keep sales going," she says.

Still, all her members really want are options. Hoffmann says most stores these days are acceptable for girls who "know how to shop" with an eye toward modesty.

"Everybody's seeing their bottom lines shrinking, so they want to sell to those who wear modest clothing, as well as those who want to wear it in a more risqué manner," says Hoffmann. "And that's fine with us."

Discussion Questions

1. Looking for styles that can be worn for most occasions is one way to save on your clothing budget. Would you agree that the economic downturn in 2009 may have prompted sales of more modest clothing? Why or why not?

2. In order for retail stores to survive during an economic downturn, they must have dress for teens who want skimpy dress and dress for more modest teens. Do you think there is a category between risk-taking skimpy and frumpy? Brainstorm ideas with classmates to generate alternatives..

3. If you were the parent of a girl between 7 and 12 years of age, would you limit her purchase of thong underwear? Most consumers want options. With skimpy clothing always at the forefront of fashion, how can a retailer advertise a modest clothing line for young girls without it sounding old-fashioned or outdated?

CHAPTER 8

DRESSING FOR LIFE AND DEATH

Patricia Hunt-Hurst

After you have read this chapter, you will understand:

- The many ways in which dress and appearance are an important part of life and death
- How relationships and culture impact dress and appearance
- How conformity and similarity in appearance can be positive experiences

In this chapter we will look at childhood, adolescence, and adulthood and how appearance and dress needs change through life. This chapter interweaves the influence that culture and relationships have on dress throughout life and death. Most of us learn about our cultures from our families or others close to us (Eicher, Evenson, and Lutz, 2000; Storm, 1987). Our families and friends impact how we dress and how we feel about our appearance (see Figure 8.1). Sometimes we are unaware of how we are influenced by significant people in our lives; other times we recognize clearly the opinions of others and purposely try to dress as they wish, carefully copy the dress of others, or deliberately dress the opposite of what is expected. Dress is a very important part of relationships and cultures, as you will learn from the readings in this chapter.

Throughout our lives there will be people who are significant to us: coworkers, sisters, brothers, friends, spouses, boyfriends, girlfriends, parents, and others. These significant others have an important role in how our personalities and behaviors develop, as well as how we see ourselves. According to Kaiser (1997, p. 166), "We see ourselves, in part,

Figure 8.1 Young children learn about dress and appearance expectations from their parents and other close relationships.

through the eyes and impressions of others." She calls this kind of view "reflected appraisals," and these views of ourselves influence our dress and appearance. In the first months of life, babies are not aware of how people perceive them. Young children may begin to notice the attention they are given when they dress up in a costume or for a special occasion. They may also begin to have preferences about what they wear and make those preferences known. Perception and understanding of dress and how we feel about it begins in childhood.

Childhood

Dress and appearance are pertinent components in child development. Involvement with dress progresses at each major developmental stage: infancy, toddler, early childhood, and middle childhood. In this section we will examine some of the major features of a child's developmental changes and how children respond to culture and relationships as they develop an awareness of clothing choices. Parents have more of a role in our clothing choices in childhood than they do in the adolescence years; the choices made for us may be based on cultural norms, parental requirements, or developmental needs. Let's take a look at some specific examples.

Infants and Toddlers

Infants have a small range of movements, yet they are constantly moving when awake. Consequently, their clothing should not be too binding, so as to allow small motor movements in exploring the surrounding environment and developing skills such as reaching and grasping. During the infant months, sensory skills and memory structures develop. Clothing and blankets are part of the infant's tactile and visible environment. Textures and colors may be interesting and stimulating to infants as they touch the fabric of their "onesies" and feel the softness of the cotton material, or they might be attracted to the red and green animals hanging from a mobile over their heads.

Gender is learned through socialization and is expressed through dress as well. Infants and toddlers obviously do not make independent choices about apparel, so purchase agents such as parents play a dominant role in "investing" gender in the child through the selection of gender-specific apparel (Stone, 1962). In the 21st century, parents may decide that in the early months of infancy it is important to dress baby girls in pink and boys in blue to help identify their gender. In the 19th-century, middle- and upper-class parents in the United States and Great Britain dressed both boys and girls similarly. In early photographs, only the type of haircut or the location of the part in the hair identifies whether the young child is male or female (Severa, 1995). Today we understand the practice of girls wearing pants, and young infant boys may have a christening gown or two, yet today parents don't typically put boys in dresses (see Figure 8.2).

Some parents may reject the idea of dressing their infant in colors that denote their gender. These parents might pick out green and yellow outfits instead of blue or pink. Many parents consider clothing brands and the expense of the items important to the family concept of being well or fashionably dressed. In other words, they might shun hand-me-downs or inexpensive clothing because they can afford expensive designer clothing and want to make sure their baby is appropriately dressed for the family's social and economic status. It is not unusual for parents to reflect their ideals in how they dress their infants. One or both parents may choose to express environmental values and prefer to dress their infant in clothing made from organic cotton or decide to use cloth diapers over disposable ones. The article "A Cheeky New Business: Lexington Mom Starts Cloth Diaper Company" describes a young woman who debated during her pregnancy whether or not to use cloth diapers, and used disposable diapers for the first six weeks. She changed her mind once she experienced the cost and the amount of trash created by disposable diapers. She devised a business plan not only to develop the diapers but also to teach consumers about them.

Large motor coordination progresses as the toddler learns to crawl and walk. The fit of clothing (i.e., loose but not too bulky) should not impede these activities and thus becomes more vital at this stage (Ryan, 1966; Stone and Sternweis, 1994). The transition from diapers to training pants usually begins during the toddler stage; this is an important step toward building a feeling of independence in the child. Verbal skills also emerge during the toddler years. The child often learns names of colors, garment pieces, and recognizable figures in prints and embroidery, making clothing one of many tools in the process of learning how to talk. The toddler also recognizes people and objects and begins to develop a sense of ownership of clothing items (Allen and Marotz, 1999). Garanimals clothing provides young children with mix-and-match separates that help them learn to dress themselves. The website for the brand says, "Garanimals was born in 1972 out of the idea that there is a positive

Latham & Bott   LONGTON, STAFF.

Figure 8.2 It is often difficult to tell a little boy from a little girl in late-nineteenth-century photographs. Sometimes the hairstyle is the only clue.

connection between how children dress and how they feel about themselves" (www.garanimals .com/about.htm). Thus, clothing helps children learn the skill of dressing.

The toddler frequently mimics dress of others and begins to learn meanings of dress through adults' often-bemused responses to seeing their son or daughter prancing around the house in a pair of high heels or Dad's baseball cap (Cahill, 1989). Engaging in dressing activities can be fun, and the gaudier and frillier the dress, the more fun it can be for many toddlers (Ryan, 1966). Toddlers also learn that cute or new garments and clothing patterned with well-known cartoon characters and logos can generate positive responses from adults and some not-so-positive responses, as you will learn in a reading in Chapter 12, "'What Disney Says': Young Girls, Dress, and the Disney Princesses." In this article a teacher discusses her dismay at the interest that young girls have in dressing like a princess and being part of a "corporate conception of princess." This article provides a different perspective about wearing costumes during childhood and developing self-image.

Children start developing role-taking skills at an early age (Schickedanz et al., 1998). It is not unusual for children to **play with dress** to help them "put on a role" and experiment with identities, whether it be the identity of a fireman, a cowboy, a mother, or a princess (Stone, 1962). During early childhood, a garment similar to that of an admired parent, adult, or older sibling may make the child feel grown-up and similar to the admired person. Play with dress also helps the child learn gender roles (see Chapter 5 for more information about gender roles and dress). Cahill (1989) described how preschool children through age three seem quite comfortable playing with opposite gender roles. Play with clothing and makeup may be encouraged more among girls who are being socialized in order to develop greater interest in dress and the hedonic aspects of appearance. But around age four, boys in particular start to become increasingly sensitive to teasing and criticism from peers if they stray from the restricted code of male clothing. Some parents are disturbed to see cross-dressing in their children and may make every effort to stop the behavior. However, there is no evidence that cross-dressing during childhood necessarily leads to transvestism or homosexuality in adult life. In the reading "Parent Power: Raising Kate—One Mom's Fight for Her Child's Identity," Connie Matthiessen explores the decision an American couple made to let their son, Ben, dress as a girl and become Kate. The article gives information about transgender children and the recommendations that therapists give to parents. Clothing and hairstyle changes are just one of the factors involved in the social transitioning from one gender to another. Refer to Chapter 5 for more discussion about appearance and gender identity.

Middle Childhood

By middle childhood, children have learned codes for gender appropriateness of dress (Kaiser, 1989), often more rigidly than is apparent from the way the child actually dresses (Allen and Marotz, 1999). Again, the general societal norm in the Western world is that boys dress like boys and girls dress like girls. Yet there are examples from other cultures in which boys are more prized, so parents dress daughters as if they are boys. A reading in Chapter 5 tells about this custom in Afghanistan, where some families may dress one of their daughters as a boy.

During middle childhood, play with dress and enjoyment of fantasy through Halloween and other costumes continues. Play with dress facilitates creative activity and encourages practice at taking on the role of other people (Shickedanz et al., 1998; Stone, 1962). Children may play at roles they might take on in adult life (anticipatory socialization) and may engage in play at fantasy roles (fantastic socialization) by means of clothing choices (Stone, 1962). Kim Miller-Spillman (2005) found that adults have many memories of costumes they wore during childhood. The multitude of memories of dress that adults could recall clearly highlights the importance of dress in childhood. Adults remembered dressing up for holidays, religious events, parties, and visits to beloved grandparents. Dress clearly marks special events and helps to make the events special. Memories of school and everyday dress as well as of costumes and play dress indicate that dress is a pervasive part of the childhood experience. There are items of dress that children wore throughout the 20th century that continue to be available for children in the 21st century. Mary Jane shoes are one example of an item of dress that has been around for a long time; the shoes remain a classic style of footwear. Thompson and Michelman's article "The Mary Jane Shoe: A Return to Innocence" gives us some historical background on the shoe as well as its evolution into becoming a fashionable shoe in women's wear, a status it retains today.

Physical skills increase during early childhood as muscular coordination advances. Fit, flexibility of materials, and comfort continue to be crucial for the child and his or her clothing. Durability and safety (e.g., flame-retardant fabrics, no removable or swallowable buttons, etc.) of clothing and materials are important purchasing criteria. Fine motor skill coordination also develops during early childhood; children master many dressing skills in this period, giving them a sense of independence (Allen and Marotz, 1999). Therefore, clothing, dolls, and toys with large buttons, zippers, laces, and other fasteners can help children practice dressing skills (see Figure 8.3).

The link of appearance to social rewards is established early in life. The intriguing subculture of beauty pageants and child beauty queens in the United States is a controversial topic; child development specialists and others are concerned about the amount of emphasis given to appearance and the sexual provocativeness of some of the outfits worn in the pageants. With very young children, it is typically a parent behind the interest in this type of appearance competition. Are eyebrow waxing, fake nails, and fake tans necessary for these small children acting out the adult fantasy of Miss America?

During middle childhood, dressing for games also becomes common. Gregory Stone (1962) defined "game dress" as uniforms and team emblems that help the child identify and take on roles of self and other players in a game. Taking on the role of multiple others in a game is a complex cognitive task; game activity helps the child develop skills of thinking about perspectives of multiple others. The child may like wearing clothing that represents those sports off the field (e.g., soccer shirt) or that associates the wearer with well-known sports figures (e.g., Air Jordan shoes). Parents support these interests by purchasing clothing and encouraging sports participation. Culture also plays a role in encouraging athletic involvement for growth and development. It also fosters in the child a sense of belonging to a group, which is manifested in the uniform.

Figure 8.3 Dolls like this, with large buttons, zippers, laces, and other fasteners, can help children practice dressing skills.

Throughout childhood, parents and guardians are continually dressing their children to conform to socioeconomic, gender, religious, and other role expectations. In addition, conformity in appearance becomes increasingly important to the child as she or he ages (Schickedanz et al., 1998). Conformity fosters a feeling of belonging; similarity helps a child feel socially comfortable. Reference groups provide ideas about how to behave and think; they give members a feeling of interconnectedness. Dress marks membership in a group and may encode ideals and values of the group. A child may like uniforms, especially if the uniform links the child to a desired group such as a sports team or other youth organizations such as the Boy Scouts. The child may even like school uniforms if the child likes school (Figure 8.4). Also, dressing like friends in school and in the neighborhood becomes increasingly important, and by middle childhood, fitting in with neighborhood friends and at school is highly valued (Ryan, 1966).

Children can also learn some cultural stereotypes, many triggered by appearance stigmas such as obesity, physical unattractiveness, and old age (Brylinsky and Moore, 1994). Middle childhood is an important time for parents to be aware that peer groups and media may introduce negative and limiting stereotypes; parents need to talk openly with children about these stereotypes and their dangers. Sometimes, on the other hand, clothing aids in the removal of

Figure 8.4 School uniforms help children identify with each other on a more equal basis in an educational setting. These are schoolchildren in red-and-white uniforms in Beijing, China.

stereotypes. Watson, Blanco, Hunt-Hurst, and Medvedev (2010) found through interviews with parents and caregivers of children with severe to profound intellectual disabilities that dressing their children in colorful T-shirts of favorite sports teams or motorcycle brands (e.g., Harley-Davidson) brought positive rather than negative attention to the child's disabilities. In fact, even though the parents preferred clothing that was age appropriate and somewhat fashionable, they wanted clothing to also work effectively for the disability.

Adolescence

The ages of 11 to 14 years for girls and 12 to 15 years for boys are typically regarded as early adolescence. Dramatic changes occur in the body during adolescence. Primary and secondary sex characteristics develop, further increasing body awareness. Boys and girls reach sexual maturity, and concern about sexual attractiveness and defining sexuality also increases. Because of their growing interest in looking like an adult, both boys and girls start to prefer styles that, to them, do not look too childish. Increasing conflicts between adolescents and parents are common as the offspring, who seemed to have been children "just yesterday," attempt to experiment with adult appearances. Girls in particular receive cultural encouragement through media images, fashion trends, and certain peer groups to dress in a sexually provocative manner, often despite the objections of parents.

Today, more so than in the past, children are much more engaged in making clothing decisions, and the fashion industry knows this. A new target market for apparel manufacturers, retailers, and advertisers has emerged in recent years: the "tweens," defined as boys and girls from 7 to 14 years old (Brock, Ulrich, and Connell, 2010). Lately, the marketing of sexually provocative clothing to tween girls has become an issue followed in the media. Brock, Ulrich, and Connell (2010) interviewed mothers and their daughters in a study to find out what issues and concerns mothers and daughters had in regard to apparel. They found that fit, modesty, and price were concerns for the sample interviewed. The researchers found that "sexual innuendo of available apparel" (Brock, Ulrich, and Connell, 2010, p. 107) was a concern in the modesty realm, a view that goes back to the media's interest in this topic. Mary Beth Sammons in her article "Is Tween Fashion Too Sexy?" reports on the sexy clothing available to tweens, to the chagrin of their parents, who continue to have a voice in what their children wear, even in adolescence.

Of course, individual differences abound. Some mothers register concern that their daughters do not spend much time on their appearance and do not use makeup as soon as other teens do. Many early adolescents begin to pursue new looks in a dynamic search for self-identity (Kaiser and Damhorst, 1995) as they reach middle school. Sometimes, to the parents' dismay, their children make very obvious changes in appearance, while other young teens conform to the norm of what is popular at their schools. This adjustment might include dyeing the hair bright pink or orange, getting a lip or nose piercing, or not giving attention to their appearance at all.

Later Adolescence

The ages of 15 or 16 to 20 years are known as later adolescence. Body satisfaction among girls tends to increase slightly in later adolescence, probably resulting from greater satisfaction with the body as it more fully matures and develops (Damhorst, Littrell, and Littrell, 1987). As boys mature, they may become more involved in bodybuilding to develop upper body muscles for a culturally ideal male physique. Emphasis on priming the body for various sport activities may also occur. Deaths among adolescent boys who were starving themselves and exercising excessively to reach weight goals for wrestling raise questions about the pressures put on young men who are training for sports (Naughton, 1998). Other adolescent boys are under increasing pressure to build muscle mass and spend time on their appearance. The use of supplements and steroids to take shortcuts to bodybuilding has increased. Boys report endless teasing and physical harassment if they are smaller or fatter than other boys. Becoming "buff" is seen as a ticket to having girls and other boys give positive attention. Hall (2005) contends that men's bodies are now becoming as objectified as boys' bodies, and increasingly girls are often encouraged by coaches, family members, and peers to endanger personal health and safety through extremes of weight management and drug abuse for the sake of sports achievements. During adolescence, socialization to body norms occurs as much or more through peer interactions as it does through parents. As we age, some relationships seem to become less important, while others (like friends) take on more value.

Adolescence is a time of testing, and one obvious way to test boundaries and also learn about oneself is through dress and appearance. Some dress practices create controversy, as with the case of boys who wear oversized and sagging pants. Even though the cartoon (Figure 8.5) makes us giggle, the apparel is no laughing matter; parents, politicians, and civic leaders have taken a stand against sagging pants. In "Put This on a Billboard: Droopy Pants Can Kill," Clyde Haberman reports on the actions that a New York State senator is taking to get young men to pull up their sagging pants. Recently, a town in Georgia started fining young men and women if their pants or skirts are more than three inches below the top of the hips and expose the skin or

Figure 8.5 This cartoon pokes fun at the baggy pants trend.

undergarments. The fine is $25 for first offenders, and it increases for multiple offenses. Over-sized pants and shirts often cause alarm for teachers who identify these apparel items as cues to gang behavior. However, it is important to note that one or two clothing items do not mean a young person is in a gang (Struyk, 2006). Another aspect of the sagging pants that cannot be overlooked is the trickle-up effect it has made into fashion. In 2011, the lead singer for Green Day (a punk-rock band), Billie Joe Armstrong, was kicked off a Southwest Airlines flight because his pants were too low, showing his underwear. So does this reaction tell us that even though the style has moved into mainstream fashion, it is still not regarded as socially appropriate—no matter who you are?

Another form of dress in this category is tattoos. For years North Americans linked these skin embellishments to soldiers, sailors, bikers, and others who don't want to conform. However, in the late 20th century young people began to get tattoos as an aspect of self-expression. As rock stars, movie stars, and other celebrities began to show off their own tattoos, more and more Americans, young and old, began getting tattoos to celebrate an important event, reveal a hobby, or just participate in a growing fashion phenomenon. Today it is not unusual to see someone's tattoos; more people are deciding to get them in places that used to be generally taboo: on the hands, neck, and face. The stigma of tattoos has declined significantly in recent years; television shows about tattoo artists like Miami Ink provide information on the safety of getting a tattoo and the artistry involved in their design and application. Tattoos have a long history in other cultures. For example, tattooing was a rite of passage for Amazigh girls (Morocco). When they reached puberty, their mothers, aunts, or family friends tattooed their face and wrists. Today, the Amazigh follow Islamic belief and no longer tattoo; however, with the decline of tattooing, women have reassigned the symbolism to designs now embroidered on their veils (Becker, 2006).

Adulthood

Adulthood typically begins at age 17 and ends at death. It is a time full of major life events, both personal (marriage, divorce, children, home) and occupational. Important experiences related to family formation, occupations, definition of sexuality, and realization of life goals occur (Levinson, 1986). Clothing and appearance mirror these events and experiences.

Careers are an important aspect of adulthood. Whether white collar or blue collar, most jobs require a uniform or a dress code that individuals must follow to engage successfully at their jobs. Some teens and young adults find it challenging to follow the norms established for job or career apparel. Yet endless studies have shown that how an employee dresses makes an impact not only on the close family and friend relationships but also on work relationships. Chapter 10, Dress in the Workplace, examines dress for the workplace and provides some important advice for dressing for interviews.

Many people marry during adulthood. The wedding day involves a ritual celebration that symbolically marks passage from being single to the relationship of marriage. The marriage ceremony and its costumes for the bride, groom, and attendants require extensive planning and preparation. Reality TV programs like *Say Yes to the Dress* illustrate the positive and negative dynamics that occur when a bride is in the process of selecting a wedding dress and the entire family is present. The bride often wants to please her mother, yet wants to make the best decision for herself. Wedding customs vary around the world. Brides in the United States traditionally wear white dresses. In the 19th century it was not unusual for a bride to wear a color other than white, particularly with middle-class women who might wear their best dress rather than spend the money on having a white dress made for the wedding. Today brides are choosing colors other than white, crème, or champagne to express individual preferences rather than following tradition. Colorful dresses and accessories with symbolic meanings remain a part of the wedding traditions of many other cultures. Figure 8.6 shows traditional fabrics, dress, and jewelry worn for weddings in India.

The marital relationship has a substantial impact on how one feels about the self and appearance. The **similarity-attraction theory** indicates that we are attracted to others we believe are like us. Thus, we associate with those who are similar because we share common interests and may even dress in a similar style (e.g., preppy, hip, grunge, Goth). In regard to spouses and partners, similarity-attraction reflects the degree of physical attractiveness and how alike the two are (Kaiser, 1997). In an article in the *Daily Mail*, Fiona Macrae (2011) reported that a group of British scientists studied whether it is true that individuals pair up with those who have the same level of attractiveness. The researchers took photos of more than 100 male-female couples. Some had been together for just a few months, others for several years. The individual men and women were then rated on their looks. The analysis revealed that having an attractive husband or boyfriend was not a guarantee to a relationship succeeding. However, if the woman was more attractive than the man, the relationships lasted a shorter amount of time.

Pregnancy indicates the beginning of a major life change that requires a change in dress. For centuries women have been faced with the challenge of how to dress for pregnancy. During the 15th century it was fashionable for wealthy women to look pregnant even when they were not. "The ideal," according to Susan Kaiser (1997, p. 111) "was shaped by the need in Europe to replenish the population following war and the plague." However, for most of the centuries up until the late-19th century, women made modifications to existing clothing, altering dresses to accommodate their changing bodies. In the late 19th century women wore loose-fitting dresses like the Mother Hubbard or tea-gowns. At the turn of the century, Lane Bryant supplied maternity wear to her New York clients, and the first advertisements for ready-to-wear maternity dresses appeared (Severa, 1995; Farrell-Beck and Parsons, 2007; Tortora and Eubank, 2010). In the 1930s a stylish dress of the period might be designed in a wrap style to accommodate changes in the body (Farrell-Beck and Parsons, 2007). By the mid-20th century maternity clothes were limited to two-piece styles including loose-fitting tunics over narrow skirts with a stretch panel over the stomach area or loose-fitting dresses, often designed with a fitted yoke through the shoulders with fullness arranged in pleats and gathers below the yoke. Even Jacqueline Kennedy wore an unfitted Givenchy coat while pregnant on the campaign trail with her husband in 1960. There

Figure 8.6 A couple from India wearing traditional wedding attire.

just were not many choices until the 1990s when designers began to design maternity clothes that looked more like fashionable styles. At the same time celebrities were leading the way in showing off their growing abdomens rather than keeping them hidden behind lots of loose-fitting tops and dresses. Today, designers like Liz Lange create a variety of styles for pregnant women: suits, dresses, and casual wear that are stylish and formfitting, yet provide stretch where it is most needed as the body changes.

Research has found that married couples have a strong impact on how each partner feels about his or her own looks. Ogle, Tyner, and Schofield-Tomschin (2011) studied married couples' reactions to the changes the wife experienced in her body after pregnancy and the desire by both for the wife to return to a pre-pregnant body and self. The study found that the wives used their husbands' feedback as a means of reassurance as they worked (through diet and exercise) to reclaim their pre-pregnancy bodies. Thus the husbands served as a mirror to the wives' understanding of their post-pregnant bodies and the reclaiming of their pre-pregnant shapes and sizes. Another study of married couples established that, among older couples, each spouse had a strong impact on how the other felt about his or her own attractiveness. In a study of 94 married couples aged 60 and older who lived in Florida, Oh (1999) found that a good predictor of a man's or woman's body satisfaction was what he or she believed his or her spouse thought about his or her attractiveness. But the best predictor of the older men's and women's body satisfaction was what the spouse actually thought. Even when a person is not totally aware of what the other thinks, the way in which one spouse acts nonverbally and verbally toward the other spouse over time has a profound influence on feelings of attractiveness and body satisfaction.

Aging of the body begins during this time of life. Great variety occurs among individuals as to when they will start noticing changes in hair, skin, and weight. With a double standard still in force in society (that as men age they develop an attractive "patina," while aging women become less attractive), many women feel that their worth as females deteriorates with the aging of the body. North America, in particular, has a culture obsessed with youthfulness. Signs of aging do not fit with cultural ideals for attractiveness. Victoria Secunda (1984) suggested that the United States is so obsessed with the physical self that Americans feel that as aging deteriorates the body, the self also degrades and "depreciates." The fear of physical obsolescence associated with aging leads increasing numbers of men and women during middle age to resort to body modifications that restore youthfulness or delay the appearance of aging. Most middle-aged individuals want to look younger and increasingly feel that it is acceptable to try to look younger (Harris, 1994). Many adopt hair, skin, and cosmetic surgery treatments to delay signs of aging.

By middle age, individuals have lived and dressed themselves through decades of fashion changes. It seems intuitively logical that many would have defined and settled into a preferred personal style by this age. However, many middle-aged consumers still want to look current and do not reject all fashion changes. Boomers are considered smart consumers who are willing to spend more to get what they want if they can find clothing that appeals to them. Some retailers have made positive strides to focus on "baby boomer" consumers in styling and sizing to provide fashionable clothing (A Battle of the Ages, Fall 2010).

Dressing for Death

Death is a normal part of life, coming at the end of adulthood. In past centuries it was very important to express grief over the death of a family member or friend through clothing in a sartorial reflection of feelings. In the Western world, dressing to mourn those we have lost through death includes wearing black garments. Early in the 20th century a person might have been considered rude if he or she attended a funeral in a color other than black. For some ancient civilizations, the dark color was worn in a particular accessory. For example, ancient Greek women donned a dark-colored veil for mourning, whereas the ancient Romans wore a dark toga pulled up over the head. In early Europe violet cloaks and mantles were worn in some countries, while pleated white garments were preferred in others. Noblemen in Europe might also signify their grief by attaching a long veil to their hats. It is well documented through paintings that Catherine de Medici, Queen of France, wore black after the death of her husband during the 16th century, as did Queen Victoria of England during the 19th century after the death of her husband, Prince Albert. As time progressed, the wearing of black became the great signifier for all classes in 19th-century Europe and America, and etiquette books provided advice on how much black to wear (multiple garments) and for how long (Davenport, 1976; Payne, Winakor, and Farrell-Beck, 1992; Severa, 1995). Today we continue to wear black to funerals. However, some families prefer that a funeral be regarded as a celebration of the person's life and encourage family and friends to wear bright colors in honor of the life rather than black as a traditional symbol of sorrow.

In other parts of the world there is a very long tradition of dressing for death. In the West African country of Ghana, the Asante people wear clothing made of adinkra cloth to communicate grief. Adinkra is large pieces of cotton fabric dyed black, red, russet, or dark brown and stamped with motifs that have symbolic meanings. The symbols are carved out of cassava gourds, dipped in black dye, and stamped or pressed onto the cloth (Figure 8.7). The symbols present both visual and verbal messages that represent proverbs, parables, historical events, and Asante sayings. Some of the symbols are purely Asante in origin, while others are recognizable: moon, star, crocodile, turtle, bird, and others. The cloth may be stamped with a single symbol or with a combination of several symbols. Family members and friends wear clothing

Figure 8.7 Asante family wearing adinkra cloth for a funeral service. Adinkra means "farewell" and the cloth represents honor and respect shown to the departed family member.

made from adinkra cloth in two main styles: men wear a toga-like garment; women, a skirt and blouse. Adinkra cloth in different colors is worn at specific times during funerals and the mourning period, which can last up to a year. Today, Ghanaians still wear the traditional colors for mourning, yet they wear other colors (royal blue, yellow, and turquoise) for special occasions, thus allowing a very long tradition to extend its meaning and use (Fortune, 1997; Salm and Falola, 2002). In another example from Africa, a type of fabric designates a respect for the deceased. There is a tradition in northwest Tanzania for family members to wear cloth known as "kanga" around their necks for a few weeks after the death of a family member. The wearing of the cloth symbolizes mourning and "mediates relations between the living and the dead" (Weiss, 1996, p. 140).

Dressing for death traditions also exists in America. Jenna Kuttruff, in "Dressing the Deceased in Nineteenth Century America," provides us with information about how families dressed their relatives for death. She differentiates between dress for death as sleep and dress for death as a journey. The practices she found in the 19th century reflect the importance that families continue to put on dressing for death.

It is also tradition in Ghana to adorn the deceased in special jewelry that supposedly protects the deceased "in their journey to the land of the ancestors" (Salm and Falola, 2002, p. 91). Jewelry was also important in mourners' expression of grief in Europe and America. In the 18th century it was common to give out finger rings to those attending funerals. Patricia Warner (1986, p. 57) notes "they combined the function of souvenir of the dead person and lugubrious reminder that every one of us must die sooner or later." Hair from a deceased family member was used for jewelry as early as the 17th century and had huge popularity throughout the 19th century. Hair was woven or braided into intricate designs and formed into bracelets, chokers, and earrings. Queen Victoria in the 19th century started wearing jet (a form of petrified wood, a hard coal polished like a stone) jewelry in mourning for a cousin. Jet was worn in brooches and beads. Similar traditions remain in the 21st century. Wearing the engagement or wedding ring of a deceased parent or keeping a favorite pin or necklace from a grandmother and wearing it on special occasions are a few examples of how Americans show respect for or honor deceased loved ones.

Summary

In this chapter we have examined dress from the beginning of life until death. Throughout life we use other people as mirrors to tell us who we are in the complex process of understanding ourselves. Our relationships with significant others such as family members are reflected in dress, and significant others have impact upon our feelings about our appearance and the choices we make regarding dress. Dress may also reflect our culture(s) and the reference group(s) (e.g., friends, sports teams) to which we belong.

Dress and appearance are critical components of child and adolescent development. Conformity to peers begins to become important by early childhood and increases in importance through early adolescence. Dress plays an important role in helping the individual feel a sense of belonging and acceptance and helps in searching for self-identity. During adulthood a variety of life experiences occur, and individuals experience these in varied order. However, general trends in life stages create dress needs and consumer wants at each stage.

This chapter also examines some cultural traditions in dressing the deceased in the southern United States and how death impacts the dress of those left behind. Traditions in wearing certain types of cloth, colors, and jewelry remain important in cultures around the world.

Suggested Readings

Becker, C. (2006). Amazigh Textiles and Dress in Morocco: Metaphors of Motherhood. *African Arts* 39 (3) 42–55.

Brock, M. K., P. V. Ulrich, and L. J. Connell. (2010). Exploring the Apparel Needs and Preferences of Tween Girls and Their Mothers. *Clothing and Textiles Research Journal* 28 (2): 95–111.

Cahill, S. E. (1989). Fashioning Males and Females: Appearance Management and the Social Reproduction of Gender. *Symbolic Interaction* 12: 281–298.

Fortune, L. F. (1997). *Adinkra, The Cloth That Speaks*. Washington, D.C.: National Museum of African Art, Smithsonian Institution.

Learning Activity 8.1: Memories of Childhood and Adolescent Dress

Objective

Analyze examples from your own childhood or adolescence to understand how stages of human physical and mental development influence feelings about and use of dress.

Procedure

In small groups, recall and share memories from childhood or early adolescence. Try to think of memories that involve some aspect of dress (e.g., wearing a favorite costume, a hated suit, or shoes on the wrong feet; trying on Mom's or Dad's clothes; ruining a favorite piece of clothing). If you cannot remember any incidents with dress, try to recall an event for which you remember what a sibling, cousin, or friend was wearing at the time.

Then identify the stage of development you or the person you remember were in at that point. Was it infancy, toddler years, early childhood, middle childhood, or early adolescence? Remembering the approximate age at which the event took place will help you identify the stage of development.

Finally, examine how the examples of dress in each memory illustrate concepts and principles of development. Review the chapter introduction to see if concepts such as motor coordination, family economics, play, formal operations, etc., help to explain what happened in the memory. Work with your group to identify concepts involved. Then share an example with the whole class.

Note: Adapted from a class exercise by Hazel A. Lutz.

References

Fall (2010). A Battle of the Ages: Will Gen Xers, Millenials, or Boomers Shape Economic Recovery? *Cotton Incorporated Lifestyle Monitor* retrieved at http://lifestylemonitor.cottoninc.com/LSM-Issue-Fall-2010/Retail-Economic-Recovery/.

Allen, K. E., and L. R. Marotz. (1999). *Developmental Profiles* (3rd ed.). Albany, NY: Delmar Publishers.

Becker, C. (2006). Amazigh Textiles and Dress in Morocco: Metaphors of Motherhood. *African Arts* 39 (3): 42–55.

Brock, M. K., P. V. Ulrich, and L. J. Connell. (2010). Exploring the Apparel Needs and Preferences of Tween Girls and Their Mothers. *Clothing and Textiles Research Journal* 28 (2): 95–111.

Brylinsky, J., and J. Moore. (1994). The Identification of Body Build Stereotypes in Young Children. *Journal of Research in Personality* 28: 170–181.

Cahill, S. E. (1989). Fashioning Males and Females: Appearance Management and the Social Reproduction of Gender. *Symbolic Interaction* 12: 281–298.

Damhorst, M. L., J. M. Littrell, and M. A. Littrell. (1987). Age Differences in Adolescent Body Satisfaction. *Journal of Psychology* 121: 553–562.

Davenport, M. (1976). *The Book of Costume*. New York: Crown Publishers, Inc.

Eicher, J. B., S. L. Evenson, and H. A. Lutz. (2000). *The Visible Self: Global Perspectives on Dress, Culture, and Society*. New York: Fairchild Publications.

Farrell-Beck, J., and J. Parsons. (2007). *Twentieth Century Dress in the United States*. New York: Fairchild Publications.

Fortune, L. F. (1997). *Adinkra, the Cloth That Speaks*. Washington, D.C.: National Museum of African Art, Smithsonian Institution.

Hall, S. S. (2005). The Bully in the Mirror. In M. L. Damhorst, K. A. Miller-Spillman, and S. O. Michelman (Eds.), *The Meanings of Dress* (2nd ed.), pp. 274–283. New York: Fairchild Publications.

Harris, M. B. (1994). Growing Old Gracefully: Age Concealment and Gender. *Journal of Gerontology* 49 (4): 149–158.

Higham, W. (2010, March 17). "Opinion: Old is the New Young." Brandweek.Com. Retrieved from www.adweek.com/news/advertising-branding/opinion-old-new-young-107177.

Kaiser, S. B. 1989. Clothing and the Social Organization of Gender Perception: A Developmental Approach. *Clothing and Textiles Research Journal* 7 (2): 46–56.

Kaiser, S. B. (1997). *The Social Psychology of Clothing: Symbolic Appearances in Context* (2nd ed.). New York: Fairchild Publications.

Kaiser, S. B., and M. L. Damhorst. (1995). Youth and Media Culture: Research and Policy Issues. In *Invest in Youth: Build the Future*, 153–169. Alexandria, VA: American Association of Family and Consumer Sciences.

Levinson, D. J. (1986). A Conception of Adult Development. *American Psychologist* 41:3–13.

MacRae, F. (2011, January 3). Downside of Dating a Beauty: If a Woman's More Attractive Than Her Man, the Relationship May Be Doomed. *Mail Online* retrieved at www.dailymail.co.uk/femail/article-1361658/Downside-d/index.html.

Miller-Spillman, K. A. (2005). Playing Dress-Up: Childhood Memories of Dress. In M. L. Damhorst, K. A. Miller-Spillman, and S. O. Michelman (Eds.), *The Meanings of Dress* (2nd ed.), 274–283. New York: Fairchild Publications.

Naughton, J. (1998, March 18). The Weighting Game: High Schools Taking Action for Wrestlers. *The Des Moines Register*, 1S, 5S.

Oh, K. Y. (1999). Body Image and Appearance Management Among Older Married Dyads: Factors Influencing Body Image in the Aging Process. Unpublished doctoral dissertation, Iowa State University, Ames.

Ogle, J. P., K. E. Tyner, and S. Schofield-Tomschin. (2011). Jointly Navigating the Reclamation of the 'Woman I Used to Be': Negotiating Concerns about the Postpartum Body within the Marital Dyad. *Clothing and Textiles Research Journal* 29 (1): 35–51.

Payne, B., G. Winakor, and J. Farrell-Beck. (1992). *The History of Costume: From Ancient Mesopotamia through the Twentieth Century* (2nd ed.). New York: Harper Collins.

Ryan, M. S. (1966). *Clothing: A Study in Human Behavior*. New York: Holt, Rinehart and Winston.

Salm, S. J., and T. Falola. (2002). *Culture and Customs of Ghana*. Westport, CT: Greenwood Press.

Schickedanz, J. A., D I. Schickedanz, P. D. Forsyth, and G. A. Forsyth. (1998). *Understanding Children and Adolescents* (3rd ed.). Boston: Allyn & Bacon.

Secunda, V. (1984). *By Youth Possessed: The Denial of Age in America*. Indianapolis, IN: Bobbs-Merrill.

Severa, J. L. (1995). *Dressed for the Photographer: Ordinary Americans and Fashion, 1840–1900*. Kent, Ohio: The Kent University Press.

Stone, G. (1962). Appearance and the Self. In A. Rose (Ed.), *Human Behavior and Social Processes*, 86–118. Boston: Houghton Mifflin.

Stone, J., and L. Sternweis. (1994, September). *Consumer Choices: Selecting Clothes for Toddlers, Ages 1 to 3*. University Extension Bulletin Pm-1105. Ames: Iowa State University, Cooperative Extension Service.

Storm, P. (1987). *Functions of Dress: Tools of Culture and the Individual*. Englewood Cliffs, NJ: Prentice-Hall, Inc.

Struyk, R. (2006, September/October). Gangs in Our Schools: Identifying Gang Indicators in Our School Population. *The Clearing House* 80 (1): 11–13.

Tortora, P., and K. Eubank. (2010). *Survey of Historic Costume*. New York: Fairchild Books.

Warner, P. C. (1986). Mourning and Memorial Jewelry of the Victorian Age. *Dress* 12: 55–60.

Watson, A. F., J. Blanco, P. Hunt-Hurst, and K. Medvedev. (2010, June). Caregivers' Perceptions of Clothing for People with Severe and Profound Intellectual Disabilities. *Perceptual and Motor Skills* 110 (3): 961–964.

Weiss, B. (1996). Dressing at Death: Clothing, Time, and Memory in Buhaya, Tanzania. In H. Hendrickson (Ed.), *Clothing and Difference: Embodied Identities in Colonial and Post-Colonial Africa*, pp. 133–154. Durham, NC: Duke University Press.

A CHEEKY NEW BUSINESS: LEXINGTON MOM STARTS CLOTH DIAPER COMPANY

Laura Soldato

Annette Manlief was not sold on using cloth diapers for her baby at first.

"I knew people who used them, but when a friend mentioned it to me in my eighth month of pregnancy, I thought, 'Oh I am not doing this,'" she said.

But soon after her friend's suggestion, Manlief and her husband researched cloth diapers and realized they had evolved quite a bit. "We thought about the plastic covers, the pins, and all that," Manlief said. "But I read so many reviews and looked at cost comparisons, and we decided to register for some.

"I kept the diapers in the closet until my baby was 6 weeks old. I thought I'll just send them back," she said. "I kept thinking about the cleaning, the maintenance of them. I was so scared." But then Manlief noticed how much garbage was created by disposable diapers. She also realized how expensive diapers were.

"I saw how much waste we generated, an extra garbage bag a week," she said. "I saw how much money we were shelling out. I knew I had to legitimately try" cloth diapers. From then on, she was hooked.

The dilemma isn't new. Like Manlief, many new moms and dads debate the choice of cloth versus disposable diapers. Lexington mom Mika Pryor hated the thought of her baby's diapers filling a landfill.

"I am concerned with what we pass on to our kids—it is what they are going to have to deal with," Pryor said. "If we use all these disposable diapers and put them into landfills, our babies are going to have to deal with the environmental issues."

Pryor, who has used cloth diapers since her 10-month-old daughter was born, recently started her cloth and bamboo diaper line, Groovy Cheeks. She trademarked a design, worked with a retailer to have the diapers made, and ordered her first shipment. She sells the diapers online at Groovycheeks.com out of her Lexington home and at The Cottage in Lexington Green. The diapers are $17.50 to $22.50 each, and Pryor sells a wet bag for storing soiled Groovy Cheeks diapers when you're away from home for $7.50. A starter pack includes 16 cloth diapers, a wet bag and free shipping for $275. A similar kit made with bamboo diapers sells for $350.

Pryor's diapers are the "all-in-one type." They have an insert to absorb moisture, and a cover with snaps that adjusts to a baby's size. Unlike some cloth diapers, her design does not have adjustable elastic because she noticed that caused a lot of leaking with her daughter.

Pryor chose to sell her own line to help raise awareness about cloth diapers.

"The new cloth diapers are cute and colorful. When I would go out with my baby, people would see the cloth diapers and say, 'Wow, those are pretty cool. Those aren't the plastic pants and safety pins.' I thought I could raise awareness and do something I enjoy by selling them," Pryor said.

As Pryor and Manlief explained, many people's notion of cloth diapers is old-fashioned. In the past, those who used cloth diapers often sent them out to be laundered or had to mix a solution in a diaper pail to disinfect them. This is not true anymore, said Cerise Bouchard, owner of Mother Nurture, a Lexington store that specializes in natural parenting items. "Washing the diapers is really simple," Bouchard said of the new cloth ones. "You don't have to mix a solution today," and you can wash the diapers at home, she said.

Bouchard sells many types of cloth diapers at Mother Nurture and explained that they look very similar to disposables. "Cloth diapers used

Republished with permission of MCCLATCHY COMPANY, from *The Lexington Herald Leader*, Laura Soldato, November 29, 2011; permission conveyed through Copyright Clearance Center, Inc.

to be giant, bed-sheet size," she said. "Cloth diapers today look like disposables. Someone finally decided you can shape them and put snaps on them." Cloth diapers are a money saver, too, said Bouchard. "There is more of an investment up-front," she said. "But then you have all the diapers you will ever need for all the kids you'll ever have."

Bouchard sells two types of cloth diapering systems. The first includes two sizes of pre-folds and their covers. They cost $500 to $600. The newer design, the all-in-one type, is about $600 for 24, or $900 for 36. "I like to recommend 36, especially for newborns, but you definitely can do 24 and just wash them more frequently," she said.

Lexington mom Angie Elser has used cloth diapers with her two daughters. She said saving money played into her decision to use cloth diapers. "I compared how much we would have spent on disposables versus what we've spent on cloth. I estimated we have saved over $2,500. And that's conservative," Elser said. Her calculations are based on estimating that disposables would have cost her $2,700 per child, or $5,400. Her initial investment was $190 on pre-fold diapers and covers. Then she spent $460 on accessories—diaper bags, diaper pail, liners, etc.—and more diapers for

an initial investment of about $650. Since then, she has bought more diapers (the all-in-ones and some newborn sizes for her second child), bringing her total to $980. She calculated that washing the diapers during the past four-plus years has cost about $500, for a total of about $1,480. That comes to a much bigger savings than her conservative estimate.

While money was a factor for Elser, she said the facts that cloth was better on her babies' skin and the diapers were environmentally friendly were key in choosing cloth diapers. "It ended up being one of those decisions where the more research I did, the more of a no-brainer it seemed," Elser said. "You're keeping trash and human waste out of landfills, saving money, and it's better for the baby."

Megan Wilson is hosting a cloth diapering class for the Fayette County Cooperative Extension Service on Dec. 8. Wilson works for Everything Birth, a company that specializes in selling cloth diapers. "Cloth diapers have really evolved in the past 10 or so years to where they are just as easy as disposable," she said. "They are better on [the] baby, better on the wallet and better on the environment."

Discussion Question

1.   What are the pros and cons of using cloth diapers? Would you use them? Why or why not?

8.2

PARENT POWER: RAISING KATE—ONE MOM'S FIGHT FOR HER CHILD'S IDENTITY

Connie Matthiessen

It all started at a family wedding in Colorado. Ellen James* took her 4-year-old son, Ben, to the bathroom. It was crowded, so they shared a stall. Watching his mother going to the bathroom, he began to loudly pepper her with questions about her unfamiliar anatomy. "He seemed shocked," James recalls. "He had two brothers, and I guess

he assumed everyone had a penis, the same way everyone has a nose, or an elbow."

At the time, her son's response made her laugh. Later, she realized it marked a turning point. Ben had never shown any interest in his older brother's toys, and he'd always been drawn to girls' clothes. To simulate long hair, he wore towels or arm chair covers on his head. When he was 3, he was a princess for Halloween.

Until the trip to Colorado, Ellen James and her husband suspected their son might be gay. But this was different. "After that, he started talking about being a girl," she says. "He began to make it clear who he was, and who he was didn't match his anatomy."

Living in a conservative Midwest town, James and her husband didn't know anyone with gender identity issues. The family is solidly middle class: Ellen James practices family law, her husband manages a manufacturing company. All three of their children were baptized in the Catholic Church, where James attended Sunday services. The prospect of raising a child who felt like he was born into the wrong body pushed them to the edges of their understanding. "It was a whole new reality—and not something we were prepared for," James says.

Born in the Wrong Body

After the Colorado trip, Ben began drawing pictures of himself in boy's clothing, but then added thought bubbles above his head to show what he felt to be his actual self: a long-haired girl in a bathing suit. He asked his family to call him Kate. And at night, he prayed for God to "make his outsides match his insides," as he put it.

Ellen James and her husband began reading everything they could find on gender identity and transgender children. One high-profile expert's research warned that allowing children to dress in the clothing of the opposite sex and to identify themselves as the opposite gender—even in play—could create a self-fulfilling prophesy. In response, James and her husband tried to keep the door open for Ben to embrace a male identity if that was what he decided: James kept Ben's hair in a boyish buzz cut and persuaded him to paint his room teal instead of pink.

But such expert opinions conflicted with other research James read—and ultimately with her instincts as a parent. James says her child never

wavered. Whenever she checked in and asked him what he liked about being a boy, the answer was always the same: "Nothing."

Ultimately, Ellen James and her husband consulted a therapist who specialized in transgender issues; they took Ben to see the therapist as well. The more they learned, says James, the more convinced they became that they should allow Ben to live as a girl named Kate, if that was what he wanted.

There's no solid data on the number of transgender people in the world, but recent analysis of U.S. census data by UCLA's Williams Institute estimates that there are 700,000 transgender people in the U.S. (3 percent of the U.S. population). What is known is that transgender people face more risks and more obstacles no matter where they live. Transgender young people in particular are at high risk for suicide (one-third of all transgender youth have attempted suicide, according to one estimate), drug use, HIV and STD infection, depression, and homelessness.

Recent research by San Francisco State University's Family Acceptance Project suggests that parental attitudes can change those odds. Researchers found that transgender youth who are accepted and supported by their families are less likely to engage in risky behavior and demonstrate a high degree of optimism about their futures. In contrast, transgender and gay youth who are rejected by their parents are eight times more likely to attempt suicide, six times more likely to be depressed, and three times more likely to use illegal drugs and to be at high risk for HIV and sexually transmitted diseases, than youth whose families accept them.

In the end, Ellen James says she and her husband took the advice of one expert who suggested that they follow their child's lead. "The counselor said Kate would tell us what she needed and when," James says. "As adults, that's excruciating. You want to know what to expect, what the next step will be. But it's been true: She's let us know every step of the way."

Difficult Transition

In first grade, their child was Ben at school and Kate fulltime at home. The following year, Kate asked her mother when she could, "go to school as myself." Ellen James wanted to move slowly—"At that point we were still second-guessing ourselves," she says—and she suggested that third grade would be a good time to make the transition. "Katie threw herself face down on the couch," James recalls. "That seemed like forever to her."

Deciding that his mother wasn't moving fast enough, Ben outed himself. He told close friends at school that he was a girl; he also told the school counselor.

As the school year wore on, James realized that living a double life was taking a toll on her child. At home, Kate was exuberant, spirited, and happy; at school, Ben was withdrawn, quiet, and shy.

So Ellen James met with school officials and told them Ben wanted to start third grade as a girl. She was apprehensive about how officials at the Catholic school would respond, and was pleased that their initial reaction was positive. "At first, everyone seemed to be on board," James recalls.

When word got out to the archdiocese, however, the school changed its tune. Over Easter break school officials informed Ellen James that if it was "Kate" who showed up after summer break, she would no longer be welcome at school. James said that from this point on, the principal, teachers, and other parents stopped speaking to her. After the break, her child's social life also took a turn for the worse. Teachers no longer called on the student whose name was still Ben on the roster. On the playground, kids taunted Ben, and told him he was headed for hell. "My father says you're committing one of the Seven Deadly Sins," one kid said.

"It was tough on Kate, because these were kids she thought were her friends," Ellen James says. "It bothered her that they were fine until the adults got involved: That was when the remarks got vicious."

As a lifelong Catholic, Ellen James felt equally devastated. "I felt my whole world come crashing in," she says. "Everything I'd been raised to believe—lessons about tolerance and acceptance—seemed like a joke."

New School, New Child

Now, two years later, Kate attends a public school where she's thriving, according to her mother. School administrators and teachers know Kate's situation, and they've been supportive from the start. Kate has friends and is invited to play dates and slumber parties. (Kate's close friends at school know about her identity, but many other kids at her school do not.)

"Your goal as a parent is for your child to be healthy and happy, and she is now," Ellen James says.

But James' relief is tinged with apprehension. There have been problems: Last year, for example, a friend turned on Kate when she learned that Kate had been born a boy. The girls are in different classrooms this year, and so far everything has been peaceful. Still, Ellen James knows there are rough patches ahead, particularly in middle and high school, when kids can be intolerant—especially about sexuality and gender issues.

Kate and her parents will also face a choice about whether or not to start hormone therapy. The treatment, which originated in the Netherlands and has been used in the U.S. for just a decade, initially forestalls puberty; later, around age 16, the child can take estrogen or testosterone to develop appropriate physical characteristics. (Once a transgender young person reaches adulthood, he or she can elect to have a surgical sex change.)

For now, Ellen James is too busy to worry about the future. Along with three kids and a legal practice, she's regional director for Parents, Families and Friends of Lesbians and Gays (PFLAG). James gives speeches regularly to civic groups, school counselors, and other organizations, telling her family's story. "I feel like I'm educating the world around Kate," she says.

Ellen James knows many people don't agree with the choice she and her husband have made to let Ben become Kate. "People act as if a little redirection would fix it, as if she were a bratty kid in a candy store," James says. One teacher even suggested that James was indulging her child's behavior because she really wanted a daughter.

"But this isn't a whim we came up with when we were bored one day," Ellen James says. "This transition has been going on for years." Ultimately, James is convinced that there wasn't an alternative ending to her child's identity story. "It isn't a choice," James says. "It's who she is."

*Ellen James uses a pseudonym to protect her family's privacy.

Discussion Questions

1.   Do you agree with the parents' decision? Why or why not?
2.   What are the pros and cons for each decision the parents could have made regarding Kate?

8.3

THE MARY JANE SHOE: A RETURN TO INNOCENCE

Mary Thompson, Professor Emeritus, Brigham Young University
Susan O. Michelman, Associate Professor, University of Kentucky

Introduction

Mary Jane shoes were worn by one of the most influential dolls ever sold in the United States—the Shirley Temple doll. Shirley Temple, a child icon of movies, captivated everyone's attention with her curly locks, sweet smile, and those shoes. She wore the Mary Jane shoes in her very first film at 6, *Bright Eyes*, in 1934 and continued wearing them for the rest of her childhood film career (Figure 8.8). America was captivated by her innocence and her shoes were an important part of that trademark image.

Since the period of Shirley Temple's popularity, Mary Jane shoes[1] have continued to remain in fashion classics, leading to questions about their origin; who wore them, when, and how have they evolved? This paper analyzes how this shoe symbolizes a time and state of innocence still desired by many women and reflects the relationship of the shoe to gender identity, past and present.

Historically, the prototype of this style was worn by both men and women. This historic, androgynous shoe style contrasts sharply with the contemporary popularity of the high-heeled Mary Jane, which communicates sexuality, but with a child-like, little-girl allure. The original design worn by both genders further contrasts with the context in which they are currently worn by fash-

Figure 8.8 Mary Jane shoes were an important part of Shirley Temple's cute and innocent image.

Original for this text.

ion-conscious women. It is the simplicity of styling and the complexity of meanings associated with Mary Janes that has given these shoes so much enticement and appeal, sustaining them since their first appearance in the history of fashion. For shoe styles "communicate not only our emotions but our hopes, dreams and what is important to us at the time" (Lawlor, 1996, p. 63).

The name for these shoes first came through R. F. Outcault's "Buster Brown" comic strips. During the early 1900s Buster and his dog, Tige, increased in fame as they became the emblem for a shoe company, a textile firm, and others. Boys' Buster Brown-like suits were always paired with black shoes, spawning the name "Buster Browns." Shoes similar to those popularized by Buster Brown, but worn by girls, trace their name to Buster Brown's sister in the comic strip, Mary Jane. Buster Browns and Mary Janes originally "[signaled] a child's transition from baby to little girl or boy" (O'Keefe, 1996, p. 234). However, in current years they have been popularly adapted for various age groups and styles.

The definition of Mary Janes goes beyond their etymological history, particularly because the shoes are reinvented each fashion season, never appearing to be out of fashion. While the traditional criteria of Mary Janes consists of a flat, single strap, blunt toed shoe, this definition too is not all-encompassing because Mary Janes have hundreds of variations, from the traditional T-strap made of shiny black, red, white, or brown patent leather, to Calvin Klein's 1996 Mary Jane set on high, with a chunky heel and a thin strap (O'Keefe, 1996, p. 234), to slip-ons and mules with a T-strap. Thus, this shoe has been around for centuries to evolve into the shoe it is today.

To gain information about contemporary perceptions of Mary Janes, we distributed a survey of 245 females (number = 213) and males (number = 32), with a median age of 21 on three separate college campuses. This age group is fashion-conscious and its members are consumers of current styles. Questions were asked about Mary Jane shoes, varying from their knowledge of that type of footwear to symbolic associations about those who wore Mary Janes. Results of the survey will be discussed in relation to issues of

identity ambivalence and ambiguity as well as the values associated with the shoe. The data sheds light on the contemporary meaning of Mary Janes particularly with college-age students. In order to understand contemporary interpretations of the shoe, understanding some of the history of this shoe will be presented.

History of Mary Janes

The oldest shoe on record belongs to the Egyptians and is documented as early as 3500 B.C. (O'Keefe, 1996, p. 22). The Egyptians made "imprints of their feet in wet sand, molded braided papyrus into soles the same size, and attached rawhide thongs to keep them on the foot" (O'Keefe, 1996, p.22). From this time forward, every civilization has crafted their own designs to fit their individual needs. Fashion, adapting to a specific culture and time, appears to work in cycles, and so, shoes "never come back exactly as they were. Instead, they . . . are influenced by the way of life and the technical developments of the period into which they are re-introduced" (Wilson, 1970, p. XV). This holds true for Mary Janes, which were merely a reintroduction of the shoe to a new generation.

Even as early as A.D. 34 the Romans were wearing a shoe resembling Mary Janes made of thick black leather and heavily decorated with hole-punched patterns (Wilson, 1970, p. 36). Another group, the Normans in 1066–1154, also had a similar shoe, which was worn by the commoners (Wilson, 1970, p. 64). But, the most striking resemblance to the current Mary Janes was a shoe style worn by the Tudors in 1485–1558 (Wilson, 1970, p. 108). This shoe is the exact replica of the current Mary Jane and was known as the "bar shoe" and is described as having "very square toes fashionable for both men and women [that] are fastened by a button with high-cut or low vamps and a strong sole. They are plain, black, worn by the peasant classes; slashed with colored satin puffs, worn with varying toe-widths by the upper classes" (Wilson 1970, p. 108). In 1558–1603 the Elizabethan Tudors also had their own variation of this "bar shoe," which included a rough form of a buckle fastening, which was also worn by the country people (Wilson, 1970, p. 118).

Bar shoes have been documented at much earlier times than most would have imagined. However, as recorded in the History of Clothing website (http://histoclo.hispeed.com, 2001) "it was not at that time considered a child's style" (p.3). These shoes do not seem to have been adapted into children's fashion until the 17th century (Young, 1938, p. 23). Interestingly enough, when "bar shoes," or Mary Janes, were worn by children, they were not only worn by little girls, but also little boys. Girls' and boys' dress was not differentiated until they were at least five years old (Paoletti , J. & C. Kregloh, 1989).

As the Renaissance ended, it became very popular for little boys, even infants, to wear feminine-type dresses accompanied by what would appear to be a pair of Mary Jane shoes, as demonstrated in artistic renderings. "The extreme types of costumes continue to be the vogue for children so long as it was the accepted fashion for adults. In the first few years of life, boys were dressed in the long skirts of their sisters and the same style of shoes" (Young, 1938, p. 22–23). It is not difficult to see these shoes being depicted, worn, and redefined in almost every century.

A number of figures in advertising and entertainment have provided additional help in popularizing Mary Janes for generations. The Morton Salt Girl (1848) wears her Mary Janes with her dress in the rain, and has adorned our salt containers for decades. In the original book by Lewis Carroll (1865), *Alice's Adventures in Wonderland*, Alice is depicted in the drawings as wearing black Mary Janes. The little girl's creator, Carroll, "dressed Alice in flat, ankle-strap shoes with rather square toes" (Ewing, 1977, p. 97) (Figure 8.9).

Another character whose footwear is attributed as the forerunner to the current Mary Janes is Little Lord Fauntleroy, from the 1800s, who wore the popular "bar shoes" with his suits. Christopher Robin, of A. A. Milne's short books, written and drawn in 1925, was another popular boy who wore these shoes.

Figure 8.9 In his 1865 book *Alice's Adventures in Wonderland* Lewis Carroll depicted his main character wearing Mary Jane shoes.

But it was R. F. Outcault, creator of the popular comic strip "Buster Brown," around the turn of the 20th century, that made the shoe a household name (Figure 8.10).

Buster Brown was clothed in a smock-like suit, which hung below the waist and showed his bloomer pants, and was frequently accompanied by a large bow at the neck. The suit was worn with long over-the-knee stockings or three-quarter-length socks. His bar shoes, as described in this paper, completed the image. By contemporary standards, the image of Buster Brown appears rather feminine. However, as Gathorne-Hardy discusses, during the Victorian and Edwardian periods "petticoat discipline" was a broad term applied to the dressing of boys in feminine clothing in order to humiliate them so much that they were careful not to engage in any activity that might draw attention to themselves, making boys easier to control in public (Gathorne-Hardy, 1972).

In the 1960s, concurrent with the second wave of the women's movement, Mary Janes were made popular by the British designer Mary Quant, who redefined the shoe's symbolic quality. She flaunted Twiggy "in an art smock and black [Mary Janes]" giving innocence its sexy edge (O'Keefe, 1996, p. 235). "Now, Mary Janes in every variation—brown sueded, triple-strapped,

THE CLOWNS TOOK TO HIM.

THE PELICAN SCARED HIM.

HE WAS ALMOST FOOLED.

THE CLOWN SHOOK HANDS WITH HIM.

HE MADE A RESOLUTION

HE RODE THE PONY.

Figure 8.10 The popular comic strip "Buster Brown" helped to popularize Mary Jane shoes for both girls and boys in the 1920s.

Doc Martens-soled—are turning up everywhere: at Prada, Manolo Blahnik, Gucci, John Fluevog, Na Na, Michael Perry, J. Crew. And they are becoming fast sellers" (Szabo, 1994, p. 82).

Currently a popular style, they are versatile and comfortable, and can be paired with anything from a baby doll dress to jeans, leggings or leotards to tutus. The question, then, is why these shoes are so popular with many women, particularly in contrast to high heels. Furthermore, research done on the history of shoes has shown that most shoes "are relatively less expensive now and [women] can discard them for a new fashion without a pang of conscience" (Wilson, 1970, p. 313).

What significance does the increasingly frequent ebb and flow of fashion have on the way we perceive and wear Mary Janes? While previous articles and studies have examined the sexual symbolism of women's shoes (Kaiser, Schutz, and Chandler, 1987), this paper examines the ambivalent and ambiguous nature of Mary Janes that invites multiple interpretations and explains why this is relevant in a postmodern context.

Theoretical Perspective

Symbolic interaction theory provides a helpful framework for examining the meaning of the current popularity of Mary Janes. Furthermore, the shoe's current association with both a feminine and childlike innocence, while simultaneously being "sexy," invites interpretation on a symbolic level, for "fashion communicates in nonverbal ways meanings and values that are produced and exchanged" (Barnard, 2002, p. 48). As a style originally and historically worn by men, the shoe's current popularity with women is both ambivalent and ambiguous. These terms seem similar, but while ambiguity refers to multiple meanings, ambivalence suggests the presence of contradictory and oscillating subjective states (Davis, 1992). Ambivalence is acknowledged by Davis (p. 25) to be natural and integral to human experience and can be exhibited in symbolic issues of appearance. By definition, ambivalence entails being pulled in conflicting directions, or experiencing contradictory yearnings or emotions. Drawing on the notion of ambivalence, Davis focuses on basic polarities in identities, such as masculine versus feminine, or old versus young, that lead to a state of tension (p. 175).

While Davis (1992) is broadly interested in dress and its symbolic relationship to identity, more specifically, he discusses his theories within the framework of fashion. Davis stresses the element of change within fashion, distinguishing it from style, custom, conventional, and acceptable dress (p. 14). While the term "dress" communicates elements of stability, the use of the term "fashion" implies an added element of social change (Roach-Higgins and Eicher, 1992). Whatever adjustments are made according to the latest trends, "a consumer" will still "hold strong, favorable and unique associations about a brand in memory," because of a product's ability to acquire a certain "personality" (Solomon and Rabolt, 2003, p. 253). Wilson (1970) states that "the present time period takes ideas from the past and refashions them for the age in which we live" (p. 278).

Molloy (1977), in his well-known book *Dress for Success*, highlights one current social alteration; he states, "the best shoe for a businesswoman is the plain pump in a dark color, with closed toe and heel. The heel should be about an inch and a half. The colors that test best for office wear are blue, black, deep brown, and gray. All multicolored or lightly colored shoes flunk. Boots should not be worn to work" (p. 25). In the 1970s there was a trend toward proscriptive dress for women in the workplace with sexy shoes reserved for eveningwear.

In the contemporary context, the Mary Janes, in contrast, are symbolic of shoes inviting multiple interpretations for the viewer. In the 26 years since John Molloy wrote his proscriptive dress for women at work, the current popularity of Mary Jane's communicates, in part, an identity choice that has not always been historically available to women. Brownmiller (1984) explains some of these contradictions from a feminist perspective:

A feminine shoe imposes a new problem of grace and self-consciousness on what would otherwise be a simple act of locomotion, and in this artful handicap lies its subjugation and supposed charm . . . Sensible shoes announce an unfeminine sensibility, a value system that places physical comfort above the critical mission of creating a sex difference where one does not exist in nature (Brownmiller, 1984, p. 186–187).

Mary Jane shoes serve as a bridge between these two identities. They can be both practical and comfortable, or incredibly feminine because of the shoe's "product personality."

Data

A questionnaire was distributed to 245 students at three universities. The population of students consisted of 213 females and 32 males. Median age was 21 for females and 22 for males. Questions were geared to eliciting respondents' knowledge about Mary Janes, as well as more general information concerning their personal views on the history of the shoe, who would wear Mary Janes and under what circumstances, as well as the social meanings and values, if any, that the shoe conveys. Specifically, the questionnaire asked the students if Mary Janes would be considered a classic and associated with an "age of innocence." Students were also questioned about whether or not males would wear this type of shoe and under what circumstances.

The majority of respondents could describe the traditional Mary Jane shoe; in fact 84% could describe their first pair of this type of shoe. However, females could remember more than males what their first pair of shoes looked like. For 65% of females their first pair of Mary Janes were black with a strap and buckle, while only 14% of males could identify the shoe. Twice as many women than men indicated they would wear a pair of Mary Jane shoes.

Students were asked if young boys would ever wear Mary Jane shoes. Both women and men answered that young boys would wear this shoe. However, with only a 16% difference between the yes and no answers, respondents were about equally divided on this question. When questioned if men today would wear Mary Janes,

two-thirds of the respondents indicated that they did not think men would wear the shoe. But of the female and male respondents who said men would wear Mary Jane's, 65% answered that young professional men would wear them while 39% of these same respondents answered yes to trendy, fashion-conscious, and funky men wearing the shoe. However, no male respondents predicted homosexuals and transvestites as wearing Mary Janes, while 17% of females saw men in this category wearing them.

The questionnaire asked students to identify words associated with the Mary Jane shoe. Five categories were developed by the researchers from the students' responses based on similarity of words. In Category I, which included the words "fun, casual, and comfortable," males used these words more often than females. In Category II, the words "dressy, church shoe, and dress shoe" were included and both females and males responded the same, while in Category V, with the words "black, buckle, shiny leather, and patent leather," females used these words slightly more often than men. In Category III, with the words "stylish, money, status, trendy, and classy," and in Category IV, with the words "wholesome, cute, youth, dainty, childlike, and innocent" females used these words twice as often as males. Category IV suggests that women use value words associated with Mary Janes for the qualities of innocence and youth 50% more than males. This was an open-ended question and the graph shows the results discussed in percentages (Figure 8.11).

Both sexes agree that values of society are represented in the clothing people wear with no significant differences between female and male responses. Overwhelmingly, 96% of respondents felt that values could be represented in one's clothing, including shoes.

When participants were asked specifically what values they associated with Mary Janes or the Buster Brown shoe, females and males were equally divided (Figure 8.12). Females answered that values were indicated by Mary Jane shoes more often than males. In Category I in Figure 8.12, using the value words "long wearing, belonging, conservative, religious, school girl, and Catholic uniform," male response was slightly

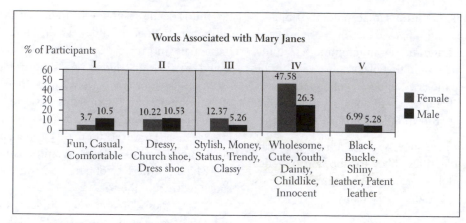

Figure 8.11 Words associated with Mary Jane shoes.

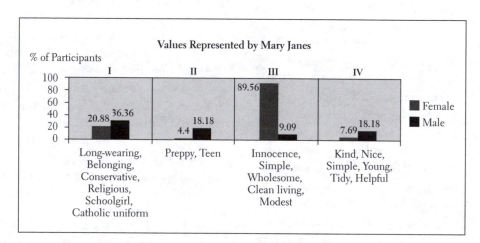

Figure 8.12 Values associated with Mary Jane shoes.

higher than female that the shoes represented these values (number = 20.8 for females and number = 36.4 for males). In Category II, with the words "preppie and teen" and Category IV, with the words "kind, nice, simple, young, tidy, and helpful," males used these value words more than females; males used approximately the same percentage for both categories. Only in Category III were the words "innocence, simple, wholesome, clean living, and modest" used by females more than males, in a 3:1 ratio. It would appear from this survey that the shoe represents traditional values. The value words in percentages given to Mary Janes by females and males is shown in Figure 8.12.

In response to the question regarding whether the Mary Jane or Buster Brown shoe is associated with an "age of innocence," 82% of the respondents felt that this was a true statement. The majority of respondents or 84% answered that the Mary Jane or Buster Brown shoe is a classic piece of clothing, while only 16% did not.

Discussion

Why are Mary Jane shoes an enduring fashion? Perhaps it is because of their ability to evolve. Mary Janes were worn not only by children in the 20th century, but are now worn by just about everyone: women, men, children, celebrities, and models. This could be attributed to the ability of Mary Janes to lend themselves to an individual style and their ability to "reflect changing lifestyles" (Benstock and Ferriss, 2001, p. 35). A perfect example is Courtney Love, who prides herself in having established the "kinder-whore" fashion (Figure 8.13). Love "used this kiddy-based fashion to send an entirely different message. By reusing these little-girl images, she and other celebrities have turned them into an ironic symbol of postfeminist empowerment" (O'Keefe, 1996, p. 237). They convey an image of sexual control and competence despite conflicting aspects of their appearance. While a "feminist" appearance might allude to discarding feminine stereotypes, the "postfeminist" appearance exploits feminine appearances for power and control. There are numerous examples of women in popular culture that convey this image to their advantage. Mary Jane shoes draw on the historic imagery of Shir-

Figure 8.13 Singer Courtney Love wears Mary Jane shoes ironically as a symbol of postfeminist empowerment.

ley Temple, Alice in Wonderland, and children's dress from more "innocent" times. By incorporating such an item of clothing in a postfeminist appearance the wearer indicates that she is "in control" and can seemingly make choices about her identity.

The popularity of Mary Janes could be attributed to their unique way of making a woman feel like a little girl and allowing little girls to feel like grown-ups. The ambivalent meaning attached to this item of clothing allows for use and interpretation depending on the age and gender of the wearer as well as their social and cultural setting. In the course of Western history concepts of childhood have been reflected in the accessories that children have worn. Style reflects expectations for children's behavior (Rubinstein, 2000, p. 4). This type of antifashion subculture promoted by Courtney Love has taken Mary Janes into their transformed, postmodern styling.

However, even in the midst of American popular culture where body-baring is pervasive, there is also an increasing backlash advocating a return to a more conservative appearance (Michelman, 2003). In A Return to Modesty, Shalit (2000) explores the broader topic of contemporary modesty for young women that speaks of innocence, mystery, sexual reticence, and protection of hope and vulnerability. Shalit looks at immodesty in dress as part of a larger issue that encompasses behaviors that are associated with the way one appears. It is the rising popularity of this viewpoint in a politically conservative America that creates ambivalence and anxiety around dress, even for stars like Britney Spears and Courtney Love, who are frequently photographed in varying stages of undress. At the minimum, wearing Mary Janes, particularly in the context of a fashion statement, nonverbally communicates the wearer's awareness of a conservative public opinion about a more modest and conservative appearance. This creates both tension and interest about their appearance.

In anxious and conservative times there is a preference for solid values in all areas of one's life. If the swing to conservative values is pronounced, any marked originality or informality in dress may indicate political and/or social radicalism. The person whose clothes become more conservative then may simply be responding to the spirit of the times, or s(he) may be expressing a change in his/her own outlook or both (Lurie, 1981, p. 159).

One can say "it's progressive, it's authentic, it has an historical edge" (Davis, 1992, p. 176). It would seem that Mary Janes have continued to be successful because all people can fit them into their wardrobe. Any segment of society, from infants to punk rockers, alternative dressers to the high fashion elite, the average stay-at-home mothers to members of the gay community, can adapt this look to the image they are trying to achieve and still maintain some sort of storybook innocence.

This innocence inherent in Mary Janes holds even when they are tweaked to achieve a certain image. One designer, Isaac Mizrahi, remembers wearing Mary Janes as an infant, with suspender shorts and a jacket and white knee socks. The shoes figured prominently in his first shoe collection, which included two high-heeled versions as well as a traditional flat. "I adore that there's this incredible innocence about them," he explains. "There are so few innocent things around that suddenly it's a big surprise" (Szabo, 1994, p. 82).

One of the most quintessential reasons for the popularity of Mary Janes is because it represents values associated with days past, a time not so harried and stressed, where ideas, beliefs, and values were well-defined, not blurred or deconstructed as in the current postmodern society. The shoe represents innocence of old, an "innocence [that] was considered childhood's most distinguishing characteristic" (Rubinstein, 2000, p. 134). The Mary Janes are refreshing and yet nostalgic. Thinking of the pouty-faced, dimple-cheeked Shirley Temple reminds us of the "good old days" when girls were submissive, meek, and never domineering. Perhaps that is why it has become so popular to pair these shoes with anything extreme. Women today espouse the ambivalence of being "in fashion" while still maintaining their innocence and femininity.

Women may like the way that Mary Janes allow them to feel like a little girl again. "Mary Janes are the quickest way to telegraph a feeling best understood by young women: 'I enjoy being a girl'" (Szabo, 1994, p. 82). "Style reflects expectations for children's behavior" (Rubinstein, 2000, p. 4). Possibly women that wear Mary Janes feel compelled to wear them, because they are trying to send a message to the world. "Could it be that adults in Mary Janes are all sending the same message? With an emphatic stamp of their Mary-Janed feet, they seem to be saying: Life's my party, and I'll wear pretty shoes every day if I want to" (Szabo, 1994, p. 82).

As supported by the data in the study, Mary Janes in a nonverbal way create attributes often associated with the young: children, childlike, innocent/innocence, religious, straight, gentle, carefree. These same nonverbal cues seem to have the same effect on the adult women who wear these shoes that are associated with children. Perhaps they want to be treated more like a child, and have less expected of them. However, this creates an interesting paradox when one considers the fact that more women are currently dressing their babies like miniature adults, while they themselves are wearing Mary Janes to feel like little girls again. Children are no longer being dressed in just sleepers anymore. It has become a status symbol to have children that are "dressed to the nines." Perhaps those mothers are clothing their children in hand-me-downs, topping the outfit off with a pair of Mary Janes.

Mary Janes are popular among all types of women because of their ability to adapt to specific needs. "The basic theme of avoiding sexy shoes, especially open-toed sandals, on the part of working women in the management realm has been pervasive in the advice of wardrobe consultants. This advice has been supported by some research indicating that sandals are perceived to be sexually attractive . . . a close-toed shoe such as a pump is considered . . . more appropriate for a woman striving to climb the corporate ladder" (Kaiser, Schutz and Chandler, 1987, p. 17). Mary Janes seem to have a mystical power about them which allows the shoe to be nonoffensive to men and to the work force, while still allowing women to feel incredibly feminine and pretty.

Past history reveals that it was not always fashionable for women to show their shoes at all.

"Prior to the 20th century, the female foot was a forbidden delight to the male eye; it was hidden beneath layers of inner and outer skirts . . . Once the foot and leg were fully exposed in the 20th century, shoes began to provide sexual interest" (Kaiser, Schutz and Chandler, 1987, p. 15).

Mary Janes have enjoyed popularity and staying power through the centuries. It would appear that they do represent a form of innocence to the wearer and to others who perceive the storybook image. Mary Janes have been recorded for centuries and have been worn by all people: male, female, young, old, rich, and poor. They are a universal symbol of innocence and youth in a postmodern society that appears to not be losing any momentum.

References

Barnard, M. (2002). *Fashion as Communication*. London: Routledge.

Benstock, S. and S. Ferriss (2001). *Footnotes: On shoes*. New Brunswick, NJ: Rutgers University Press.

Brownmiller, S. (1984). *Femininity*. New York: Linden Press.

Davis, F. (1992). *Fashion, culture, and identity*. Chicago: The University of Chicago Press.

Ewing, E. (1977). *History of children's costume*. New York: Charles Scribner's Sons.

Gathorne-Hardy, J. (1972). *The rise and fall of the British nanny*. London: Hodder and Stoughton.

History of Clothing website (October 2003). http://histoclo.hispeed.com.

Lawlor, L. (1996). *Where will this shoe take you? A walk through the history of footwear*. New York: Walker and Company.

Lurie, A. (1981). *The language of clothes*. New York: Vintage Books.

Kaiser, S. B., H. G. Schutz, and J. L. Chandler. (1987). Cultural codes and sex role ideology: A study of shoes, *American Journal of Semiotics*, 5 (1), 13–34.

Michelman, S. (2003). Reveal or conceal? American religious discourse with fashion. *Etnofoor*, XVI (2), 76–87.

Molloy, J. T. (1977). *Dress for success*. Chicago: Follet Publishing Company.

O'Keefe, L. (1996). *Shoes: A celebration of pumps, sandals, slippers and more*. New York: Workman Publishing.

Paoletti, J. and C. Kregloh. (1989). The children's department. In C. Kidwell & V. Steele (Eds.), *Men and women: Dressing the part*. Washington: Smithsonian Press.

Roach-Higgins, M. and J. Eicher. (1992). The definition and classification of dress: Implications for analysis of gender roles. In R. Barnes and J. Eicher (Eds.), *Dress and gender: Making and meaning* (pp. 8–28). Oxford: Berg.

Rubinstein, R. (2000). *Society's child: identity, clothing, and style*. Boulder, CO: Westview Press.

Shalit, W. (1999). A Return to Modesty: Discovering the lost virtue. New York, NY: Free Press.

Solomon, M. R., and N. J. Rabolt. (2003). *Consumer behavior in fashion*. New Jersey: Prentice Hall.

Szabo, J. (March 1994) What ever happened to Mary Jane? *Harpers Bazaar*, pp. 82.

Wilson, E. (1970). *A history of shoe fashions*. New York: Pitman Publishing.

Young, A. (January 2004). http://atdpweb.soe.berkeley.edu/quest/Mind&Body?Portrayl.html.

Young, F. E. (1938). *Clothing the Child*. New York: McGraw-Hill Book Company.

Endnote

1. This type of shoe is described as a Mary Jane for girls and a Buster Brown shoe for boys. Although the styling has historically been similar for both boys and girls, for simplicity's sake, the shoes will be referred to in this paper as Mary Janes.

Discussion Questions

1. Did you or someone you know wear Mary Janes when they were young? What about now?
2. Do you or someone you know have a version of Mary Janes in their closet?
3. Why has this style become classic?
4. Can you think of other styles of clothing, accessories, or shoes that you or a family member wore as a child that are still fashionable and offered in adult versions?
5. Is there something in boys and menswear that has a similar history to Mary Janes? What is it? Why has it survived?

IS TWEEN FASHION TOO SEXY?

M. B. Sammons

A recent shopping trip to her local mall turned into a jaw-dropping experience for Roxann Reid-Severance. As the Chicago-area mother of two girls, ages 10 and 7, shopped with her oldest daughter for a dress for the tween to wear to a family wedding, she says she discovered rack after rack of low-cut, sequined sheaths.

"I was blown away by how provocative the dresses were," Reid-Severance tells ParentDish. "It was a nightmare. There has to be a balance between fashion fun and good taste. These dresses were skinny straps, lower cut and the fabric had as many sequins as I would have worn on New Year's Eve. It's not age appropriate."

Many moms are agreeing with Reid-Severance, finding themselves on shopping excursions with their young daughters that take them through a Material Girl jungle of animal-patterned, lace, leather and faux-fur tween fashions. "Hookers on parade" is how one mom describes the dresses she saw on display during a recent mall visit.

"It's almost as if the fashion world is trying to make preteens look like they are going to the high school prom," Reid-Severance says.

Billions of dollars are on the line in the fashion industry, which targets the 8-to-12 set known as tweens, according to ABC News.

But it's a line increasingly blurred between cute and hot, adorable and sexual. In addition to spending $30 billion of their own money, American tweens hold sway over another $150 billion spent by their parents each year, ABC reports.

"You go into a juniors department, you have a rack of clothing that is appropriate for an 11-year-old next to a rack of clothing that isn't," Alex Morris, who recently reported on tweens and fashion for *New York* magazine, tells ABC. "It's certainly blurring the lines. . . . It's making it harder for parents to set boundaries."

New research released by the American Psychological Association earlier this year found that sexual imagery aimed at younger girls is harmful to them and increases the likelihood they will "experience body dissatisfaction, depression and lower self-esteem," Morris tells ABC.

Compounding the issue is the fact that tween girls look to celebrity idols, such as 17-year-old Miley Cyrus, who often dresses in daringly sexual outfits, ABC reports. Other teen stars have dressed the sexy part, too: Britney Spears went from a bubblegum pop image morphed to provocateur. Ashley Tisdale left "High School Musical" to "Crank It Up." And former Nickelodeon star Amanda Bynes is now on the cover of *Maxim*, Morris tells ABC.

"The easiest way for a celebrity to transition from being a child star to an adult star is the pathway through their sexuality," Morris tells ABC. "Children are attracted to this kind of look; it's what they see Miley Cyrus wearing, Demi Lovato wearing, Lindsay Lohan wearing."

It's also what "Gossip Girl" actress Taylor Momsen is wearing on the pink carpet as the face of Material Girl, the recently unveiled clothing line created by Madonna and her 14-year-old daughter, Lourdes, according to ABC.

"I think the reality of the tween fashion market is that the clothes are just more grown-up," Michelle Madhok, founder and editor-in-chief of SheFinds.com and MomFinds.com, tells ParentDish. "Whereas a few years ago parents were up in arms about clothes being too revealing (belly shirts, short shorts), the clothes we're seeing now don't show as much skin, but the silhouettes and prints are what you'd normally expect to see an adult wear. No more smiley faces and peace signs, that's for sure."

Critics, such as Washington, D.C.-area mom Michele Woodward, tell ParentDish these clothes might work for 20-somethings, but are too racy for girls in their tweens and young teens.

"My daughter and I have had the discussion about what's appropriate just this week, in fact," Woodward, mother to Grace, 14, tells ParentDish.

"The new hot trend at her school is wearing tights under a plaid shirt. A shirt which doesn't come down and cover her butt, tunic style, but a short shirt. Nothing is left to the imagination. As we talked about this trend, my daughter leveled her gaze at me and said, 'Mom, if you dress like a ho, you get treated like a ho.' Precisely."

Discussion Questions

1. Visit websites of retailers that target the tween market. Look at the clothing offered; does this particular retailer offer provocative clothing to tweens? What does this mean?
2. Would you interfere if your 11- or 12-year-old sister wanted to wear something too sexy for her age? Why? Why not?

8.5

PUT THIS ON A BILLBOARD: DROOPY PANTS CAN KILL

Clyde Haberman

Hector Quinones didn't amount to much in life, but he managed in death to make a powerful fashion statement. The statement boiled down to this: Don't be a jerk like me.

Not nearly enough people seem to be taking his lesson to heart.

Back in December, Mr. Quinones killed three men in an apartment on the Upper West Side, a bloodbath described by the police as drug-related. Mr. Quinones was intent on shooting more people, they said, only he was forced to flee. He ran to the fire escape. But the low-slung pants he was wearing fell down, the police said. He tripped over them, took a tumble and landed with a thud in the building's backyard.

There you had it: death by trousers.

Could there be a better argument for hitching up one's pants? And yet countless young men continue to parade about the streets in their own boxer rebellion, wearing trousers so low that their shorts—and sometimes more than that—are on display.

"I was on a subway train, and there was this young man," State Senator Eric Adams of Brooklyn said. "His behind was showing, literally. He had underwear, but even the underwear was sagging. All the passengers were looking at each other in disgust, but nobody was saying anything."

For Mr. Adams, that silence was deafening. Now he is speaking up. He began a campaign this week to do something about the saggy-bottom boys and the adults who have "a high tolerance for antisocial behavior," whether out of indifference or fear.

Under his sponsorship, messages intended principally for young black men went up on several billboards in Brooklyn (Figure 8.14). Raised trousers mean raised respect, they said. The senator also posted a video on his Web site. To doleful background music, it shows a series of offensive

Figure 8.14 A billboard in Brooklyn that is part of a campaign sponsored by State Senator Eric Adams, who hopes parents will take action.

racial stereotypes over the years: minstrel performers, Aunt Jemima, watermelon-loving Negroes—and, the new addition to this sorry lineup, sagging pants on African-American men.

They're all of a piece, Mr. Adams says in the video. But what's insidious about the latest degradation is that it is totally self-inflicted. "Let us not be the ones who make our communities seem foolish," he says. (He himself is impeccably dressed in the video in a gray suit, green tie and white pocket square.)

Actually, the senator said in an interview, his target audience is adults more than youngsters. Grown-ups are supposed to act like grown-ups.

"The children aren't doing anything different, because children always push the envelope," he said. "We have abdicated our responsibility of telling them when they've gone too far. Even if they don't follow our advice, the adult is supposed to say, 'This is not acceptable.'"

"Our communities have turned almost into minstrel shows," he added.

Eye-rolling over what children do has, of course, only been going on for thousands of years. But the droopy pants look that has men shuffling along as if they were Attica inmates has hung around for a surprisingly, and distressingly, long time.

It has prevailed over constitutionally flawed efforts by various municipalities to enact legal bans. It has defied no less than Barack Obama. "Brothers should pull up their pants," Mr. Obama said in an appearance on MTV just before his election as president. "You are walking by your mother, your grandmother, your underwear is showing. What's wrong with that? Come on."

The problem, Mr. Adams said, is an absence of presidential follow-up. Messages require repetition to sink in.

Some people have asked him if he doesn't have better things to do and bigger problems to address. "I tell them no," said Mr. Adams, a former police captain.

"In my 22 years of policing, there was a common denominator," he said. "The first indicator that your child is having problems is the dress code. Prior to the sagging pants, it was the shoestrings out of sneakers. All this is born out of prison. We took the shoestrings and the belts from prisoners."

"This is probably not a perfect science," he added, "but if you start looking at how your child is dressing, it is an indicator of who his friends are and what group he's associated with. It's all in the clothing."

Nothing is guaranteed with the senator's campaign. Should it not do the trick, how about Hector Quinones as a backup? Posters could show him after the fall, with a tag line on the order of, "Sagging pants kill."

The message isn't particularly subtle or even tasteful. But it just might work.

Discussion Questions

1. What is your opinion about teenagers wearing oversized pants?
2. Do you think the senator is correct? Or are adults making a big fuss over nothing? Explain your position.

DRESSING THE DECEASED IN NINETEENTH-CENTURY AMERICA

Jenna Tedrick Kuttruff

Just as birth signifies the beginning of life, death signifies the end of life. The decisions reached on how to dress the deceased for the "hereafter" are important ones and are shaped at several different levels. These decisions are influenced by history, culture, and individuals (Hintlian, 2001); however, the time period in which decisions are made transcends both cultural and individual influences. Culture is a participatory and shared social activity and various cultural, subcultural, and multicultural influences come into play in dressing the deceased. The blending of cultural practices may take place in today's global society. In American society the individuals involved in decision making related to dressing the deceased frequently include the individual who has died (prior to their death), their close loved ones and family members, and members of a professional funerary industry (Hintlian, 2001).

As in life, the dress of the dead can communicate socio-personal information about the deceased and socio-economic information about the deceased and the family of the deceased. Age and gender are two types of information most often reflected in the dress of the deceased. Additionally, information regarding religious beliefs, group membership, occupational category, and social and economic status can be communicated.

In nineteenth-century America, the preoccupation with death is evident in the elaborate mourning ritual of the Victorian Era as well as the mourning clothing and jewelry worn after the loss of a loved one. However, an important question often remains unanswered: How were the deceased dressed for eternity? How can we learn about the way people in the past dressed the deceased? As in the study of any historical subject the two primary sources of information are written documents and material culture or physical artifacts, which generally provide bits of information that can be used to piece together historical and cultural patterns. Unfortunately, few detailed written accounts of burial dress remain and most garments that were buried deteriorated long ago.

Death was a part of everyday life in the nineteenth century due to high child mortality rates, difficult childbirths, disease, epidemics, limited medical care, and the Civil War. Burying the dead was a far more intimate experience than it is today with our fully developed and elaborate funerary industry. The transition from life to death commonly occurred within the household as death most often occurred in the home, and family members usually washed and dressed the body and laid it in the coffin. A wake was held in the home of the deceased, while family members sat with the body and friends came to pay their respects. The burial would take place in a family cemetery, church cemetery, or in larger cities public cemeteries. The experience was literally very close to home.

Written references to burial dress are sometimes included in diaries, but most often these descriptions are very brief and lack detail. One such example in a diary from Louisiana was written by Kate Stone during the Civil War (Anderson, 1972). She describes her brother Walter's death as follows, "I see him lying cold and still, dressed in black, in his plain black coffin" (p. 187). Another of Kate's brothers' burial dress was mentioned in a letter by a friend who was with him when he died, "We dressed Coley in a nice suit of clothes furnished by a young friend of his, . . . Everything of the best kind was prepared for his funeral . . ." (p. 261)

Original for this text.

Death Metaphors

In the nineteenth century death metaphors, some of which we still use today, were used poetically as a means to avoid direct reference to death. Many are found in literature. Because death pervaded nineteenth-century culture, metaphors were a way of coping and expressing ideas and beliefs related to death (Aldridge, 2009). The two types of metaphors most prevalent in this period are those that refer to death as sleep and those that refer to death as a journey. Examples of such metaphors include:

Death as Sleep	Death as Journey
Sleeps the long sleep	Passed on
Is sleeping the final sleep	Passed to a better home
Gone to his last sleep	Passed within the pearly gates
Gone to a well-earned rest	Crossed the river
Called to heavenly rest	Crossed over
Laid to rest	Gone home
Rests in peace till we meet again	Gone to Heaven
Called to the eternal sleep	Gone to his heavenly home
	Gone beyond the horizon
	Gone to meet the beyond

Postmortem Photography

Photographing the dead before burial was a common practice in the second half of the century when memorial postmortem photographs became a part of the extensive paraphernalia of the mourning process. Postmortem photography was one of the most popular genres of photography in the nineteenth century (Burns, 1999, 2002; Ruby, 1995) but is largely unheard of today. These photographs provide dress historians insights into the way people were dressed in death. The majority of postmortem photographs from this period depict two types of burial dress and positioning of the body within specific surroundings that relate directly to the two prevalent death metaphors presented above. Most often the surrounding of a deceased individual in a photograph portrayed death as sleep, as they include beds, couches, pillows, textiles, and coffins or caskets that are lined and padded to look like beds. The individual is depicted lying or seated with closed eyes, another indication of sleep. People in the nineteenth century were sometimes buried in nightgowns and shrouds (burial-specific garments that resemble long nightgowns). They were also wrapped in winding sheets, either a household sheet or a large, flat textile made specifically for burial purposes. However, the clothing of the deceased in postmortem photographs relates more often to death as a journey than to death as sleep. The majority of evidence from this period indicates that individuals were buried in clothing that they either wore or would have worn in life. Sometimes new garments were purchased, but often a person's better clothing from everyday life was chosen for burial. These garments would be more appropriately worn for a special journey than for sleep.

A recent study of postmortem photographs taken between 1840 and 1900 revealed that "deceased individuals were most often photographed and buried in their Sunday's finest or nicest items of day dress" (Aldridge, 2008, p. 94). These photographs were compared to period photographs of the living and were interpreted as having "given the impression of a respectable final portrait of the deceased individual" (Aldridge, 2008, p. 94). While many of the surroundings and the pose of the individual in the photographs are supportive of the death as sleep metaphor, the dress of the deceased most often supported that of death as a journey. Shrouds and nightgowns provided alternative choices to day dress styles but postmortem dress reflected changes in fashionable dress styles during the period.

Dress categories were defined by age and gender (Aldridge, 2008). Infants were not differentiated by gender but by age; infants too young to walk were buried in long white gowns while infants who were old enough to walk were dressed in shorter gowns. Younger children wore styles reserved only for children while older male and female children dressed in styles that resembled adult styles for their gender. Within the adult male and female categories, it was sometimes evident that younger adults wore more current fashions while older adults wore more outdated styles. Occupations of deceased males were also reflected in dress, such as a soldier wearing a military uniform, a clergyman wearing ecclesiastic dress, a businessman in a business suit, and a laborer in work clothes. Eighty percent of the 89 individuals in this study were dressed in day dress and only twenty percent wore shrouds or night dress. Formal evening clothing was not seen on the deceased.

Surviving Burial Garments

The occasional preservation of burial garments, such as those recovered from nineteenth century cast-iron coffin burials, provide intimate and detailed information that can be used to help answer questions on how the deceased were dressed. Generally speaking, it is against our cultural norm to disturb the dead once they are buried. Only under special circumstances are burial remains disinterred and it is even less common for these remains to become the subject of scientific and historical analysis.

Archaeological evidence from nineteenth-century burials recovered in the eastern United States supports the evidence obtained from postmortem photographs of the deceased. Dress is often one of the first things mentioned when an individual recovered from a coffin or casket is described. Examples of the preserved burial dress of infants, children, and adult males are described in Haglund and Sorg (1997). An infant girl from the 1860s was buried in a white muslin frock with a rosebud in her hand. A child was dressed in a white robe (probably a shroud) with a large yellow rose pinned on the breast. A boy of five from the late 1800s wore a smock (shroud?), undershirt, pants, socks, and shoes. A 20- to 30-year-old male was described as wearing a cotton shirt with a separate collar, a bow tie, cotton trousers, and a long-sleeved, cotton shroud. A 31-year-old male who died in 1870 wore a black wool, quilted frock coat, matching trousers, a white cotton vest, and white shirt with a detachable collar, black silk bow tie, socks, but no shoes. A 50- to 60-year-old male wore a ready-made black wool frock coat and trousers whose manufacturer was in business between 1860 and 1874; he also wore a pair of shoes. A male of approximately 50 years of age who was thought to have been buried in the 1860s wore a narrow bow tie, shirt, black wool frock coat and trousers, and shoes.

Schmid (2005, 2007) investigated the remains of a 15-year-old boy who died in 1852 and was buried wearing a shirt, vest, pants, drawers, and socks. Owsley et al. (2006) described the dress of a 35-year-old man buried in 1862; he wore a black single-breasted frock coat, trousers, vest, necktie, shirt, and tall boots. Based on fragmentary textile evidence in the coffin of a 19-year-old woman who died in 1859, she is believed to have been buried in a white nightgown, chemise, petticoat, and possibly a winding sheet (Kuttruff and Rabalais, 1991). In the 1864 burial of an adult male the only evidence of clothing that survived was extremely fragmentary and indicated that he wore a red-and-white cotton pique waistcoat that had elaborate porcelain and gold button studs down the front and a metal buckle in the back (Kuttruff, 2001).

Four complete examples of burial dress from the 1850s in the American South (Kuttruff, 2010) were preserved because the individuals were buried in sealed cast-iron coffins. Researchers were given the opportunity to study the contents of the burials, including their dress, before the human remains were reburied in the cemetery. This archaeological evidence provides additional information on burial dress to complement that found in postmortem photographs or verbal descriptions from the period.

The dress of an adult woman and her young son both represent the death as sleep metaphor. The woman was buried in 1857 in one of her nightgowns (Hintlian, 2001). Underneath the nightgown she wore a pair of stockings that had been mended, a towel pinned around her as a diaper, her chemise, a petticoat, and a tortoise-shell comb in her hair. The diaper and petticoat both had her name on them as a laundry mark. One of her husband's handkerchiefs was tied around her head as a jaw cloth to prevent her mouth from falling open as she lay in her home in her coffin before she was buried. Her young son, who died late in 1846 when he was 9 years old, was buried in a shroud made specifically for burial (Brantley, 1998). This shroud was styled like a long nightgown and the sleeves were tied with silk ribbons around his wrists. Under his shroud he wore his underdrawers, an undershirt, socks, a dress shirt, and a necktie made out of a man's handkerchief cut on the diagonal, folded, and tied in a knot. He also had a handkerchief tied around his head as a jaw cloth (Figure 8.15). Flowers and herbs were present in his burial. Both of them wore symbols of their Catholic faith, which included a scapular, rosary, cross, and religious medals. Neither wore shoes, which might be deemed essential if one were dressing for a journey, but not for sleep.

The two other burials were those of an adult woman and a young girl who were dressed in fashionable dress of the period; both were buried in 1852. The woman wore a black silk dress with a full skirt and pagoda sleeves (Welker, 1999). With it she wore beautifully embroidered undersleeves and a chemisette that filled the neckline of her dress. (See Figure 8.16.) Underneath she wore a diaper, a chemise, two petticoats, new stockings, and a new pair of black cloth shoes. An embroidered kerchief was pinned under her chin as a jaw cloth. She wore a carved tortoise-shell comb in the chignon of her long black hair, an engraved gold wedding band, and a gold locket that contained a hair weaving. The young

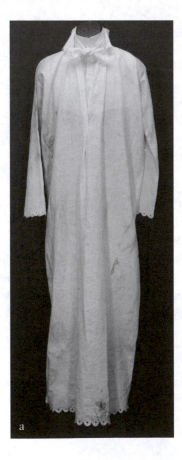

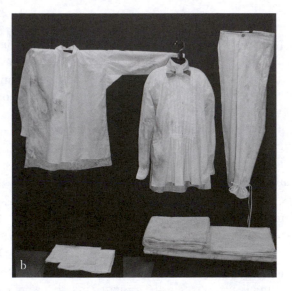

Figure 8.15 Burial garments worn by a young boy who died circa 1847. a) His linen shroud with cut-out decorations along the edges of the collar, sleeves, and hem. It is placed over a replication shirt and handkerchief tie. b) His dress shirt with tie made from half of a man's handkerchief, his underdrawers with ankle ties, men's handkerchiefs used as a jaw cloth and face cloth, and a household blanket that was placed under his body in the coffin.

THE MEANINGS OF DRESS

girl wore a white cotton checked-dimity dress with embroidery on the standing collar and cuffs (Manhein, Listi, & Kuttruff, 2011). It had a full cartridge pleated skirt with two horizontal growth tucks. One of the tucks had been released before burial. Her undergarments consisted of a diaper, pantalettes, a chemise, a camisole, and a pair of new stockings. Her black leather shoes were decorated with gold embossed roses, cherubs, and cornucopia. She also wore a cross and religious

Figure 8.16 Burial garments worn by a 28-year-old woman in 1852. Shown in the photograph are her embroidered kerchief that was pinned under her chin to serve as a jaw cloth, her embroidered undersleeves, replications of her black silk dress, chemisette and undersleeves, her cotton chemise, her black cloth ankle-high shoes, and her cotton knit stockings with the manufacturer's stamp still visible.

medal around her neck and floral remains were scattered over her in her coffin. These fashionably dressed individuals, whose ensembles were complete with new stockings and shoes, more aptly portray the death as a journey metaphor than that of death as sleep.

Even though there are only limited numbers of examples of extant burial dress that have been studied, the findings support those based on postmortem photographs of the same period. The infants and young children were dressed in white and were accompanied with floral remains. The majority of the adults were dressed in day dress with only one adult male dressed in a shroud and two adult females buried in nightgowns.

Nineteenth-Century Burial Dress

During the nineteenth century the customs of the living and the dead blended together (Aldridge, 2008). High mortality rates made death a part of everyday life and the life of the individual was reflected in death with the transition from life to death often taking place in the home. Following the Civil War there was an elaboration of death paraphernalia, mourning rituals, and a professional funerary industry in America. Burial dress reflected changes in fashionable dress that took place throughout the century. The most common type of dress for burial was fashionable day dress with an alternate choice of shrouds or night dress. Both were worn with appropriate undergarments of the period, although such women's items as hoop petticoats and corsets do not appear to have been worn.

The dress of the deceased reflected not only the time period, age, and gender but also economics, religion, ethnicity, and culture. Personal choice of the deceased and/or their family members played a role in burial dress, but are often more difficult to identify and interpret from an historical perspective. The same factors that influenced dress worn by an individual in life also influenced dress worn by an individual in death. This is true today just as it was in nineteenth-century America.

References

Aldridge, R. J. (2008). *Dress in the United States of America as Depicted in Postmortem Photographs, 1840–1900.* Unpublished master's thesis, School of Human Ecology, Louisiana State University, Baton Rouge.

Aldridge, R. J. (2009, July). Postmortem Dress and Nineteenth Century Death Metaphors. Paper presented at the Save Our Cemetery Symposium, New Orleans, LA.

Anderson, J. Q. (1972). *Brokenburn: The Journal of Kate Stone 1861–1868.* Louisiana State University Press, Baton Rouge.

Brantley, E. (1998). *Burial Dress of an 1850s Male: A Material Culture Study from South Louisiana.* Unpublished master's thesis, School of Human Ecology, Louisiana State University, Baton Rouge.

Burns, S. (1999). *Sleeping Beauty: Memorial Photography in America.* Korea: Twelvetrees Press.

Burns, S. (2002). *Sleeping Beauty II: Grief, Bereavement and the Family in Memorial Photography. American and European Traditions.* New York: Burns Archive Press.

Habenstein, R.W., & Lamers, W. M. (1955). *The History of American Funeral Directing.* Milwaukee, IL: Bulfin Printers, Inc.

Haglund, William. D., & Sorg, M. H. (Eds). (1997). *Forensic Taphonomy: The Postmortem Fate of Human Remains.* Boca Raton: CRC Press.

Hintlian, P. (2001). *Clemence's Clothes: The Mortuary Material Culture of an 1857 Burial.* Unpublished master's thesis, Department of Geography and Anthropology, Louisiana State University, Baton Rouge.

Kuttruff, J. T. (2001, January). Col. Derussy's Coffin Lining and Burial Waistcoat. Paper presented at the Society for Historical Archaeology Conference, Long Beach, CA.

Kuttruff, J. T. (2010, January). Dead Clothes: Mid-Nineteenth Century Burial Dress in Louisiana. Paper presented in the symposium, *Mortuary and Cemetery Studies,* Society for Historical Archaeology, Amelia Island, FL.

Kuttruff, J. T., & Rabalais, P. P. (1991, June). Recreating the Burial Attire of Alice Taylor. Paper presented at the Costume Society of America, Region VI Symposium and Annual Meeting, Jackson, MS.

Manhein, M. H., Listi, G. A., & Kuttruff, J. T. (2011). Analysis of a Historic Child's Burial from St. Joseph Cemetery, Thibodaux, Louisiana. *Louisiana Archaeology.*

Owsley, D. W., Bruwelheide, K. S., Carmell, Sr., L. W., Burgess, L. E., Foote, S. J., Chang, S. M., & Fielder, N. (2006). The Man in the Iron Coffin: An Interdisciplinary Effort to Name the Past. *Historical Archaeology,* 40(3):89–108.

Ruby, J. (1995). *Secure the Shadow: Death and Photography in America.* Cambridge, MA: The MIT Press.

Schmid, R. E. (2005). Coffins Reveal Clues to Past, Scientists Examine 1800s Remains. Associated Press. Retrieved from http://www.ecu.edu/cs-admin/news/inthenews/archives/2005/08/080505anthropologycoffin.cfm.

Schmid, R. E. (2007). Mystery Boy in Iron Coffin Identified. Retrieved from http://www.redorbit.com/news/science/1071988/mystery_boy_in_iron_coffin_identified/index.html.

Welker, D. L. (1999). *An 1852 Female Burial Gown from South Louisiana.* Unpublished master's thesis, School of Human Ecology, Louisiana State University, Baton Rouge.

Discussion Question

1. What do you think about 19th-century death practices? Do you think we should continue some of the customs? Why? Why not?

CHAPTER 9

FASHION, STATUS, AND INEQUALITY IN DRESS

Patricia Hunt-Hurst

After you have read this chapter you will understand:

- That fashion, status, and inequality are interrelated
- The relationship between fashion and status
- Inequality in dress is documented by historic and cultural examples

The three words used in the title of this chapter—fashion, status, and inequality—all require human interaction in order to occur. People have to be involved for each to exist. As discussed in previous chapters, fashion is a social process; individuals must accept and reject styles of clothing and accessories for fashion to occur. "Status," as defined by Kaiser, "involves a person's position in a social hierarchy" (1997, p. 414). *Webster's Dictionary* defines "inequality" as "the condition of being unequal or uneven" or "social disparity." These definitions give us a framework to examine in this chapter the interconnectedness of fashion, status, and inequality as expressed through dress.

Fashion and Status

There must be people willing to start new fashions and be the first to adopt new styles. Likewise, there must be people who are fashion followers, like to wear something new and different, yet are not comfortable in being the first to wear it. Dress (clothing, accessories, hairstyles) may be in fashion—the prevailing style that a majority of people are wearing. Or dress may be a national costume or identity. Sometimes dress may be fashionable, particularly if elements change and come to be considered the prevailing mode of dress for many people. Dress, in either context, can be an obvious indicator of status and inequality. In the past fashionable dress was one of the most obvious indicators of a person's status, styles changed slowly, and the time that it took for mass manufacturers to reproduce a style took longer. Today, as a result of technology, a new style can appear on the runway, be quickly copied at different price points, and then be made almost simultaneously available to a range of consumers. This process is explained in Chapter 2 and is known as the Trickle-Across Theory.

College campuses were not always regarded as bastions of fashion, yet as the reading "The Campus as Runway" informs us, there is a lot of fashion going on across the United States on college campuses. You can probably think of particular styles worn on your campus that highlight an across the board, or across the majors (e.g., art, fashion, history, sociology, pre-med, engineering) look at your college or university. Or like some of those featured in the reading, many fashion-forward students want individual looks that define them rather than looks that are "mirrored" by others on campus. However, the process of fashion insists that the look is copied and that the student innovators have already moved on to different fashion looks to keep them separate from the group—and a new look is started to keep the fashion process moving.

The concept of fashion relies on people wanting to dress like other people, or more precisely to emulate others through dress (e.g., clothing, shoes, accessories, and hairstyle). The upper class in centuries past reflected its social and economic status by the luxuriousness of the silk fabric worn, the specific type of fur, or the amount of hand-made lace on a garment. In the late 19th century, the bustled silhouette of an upper-class woman's dress with a long train symbolized her husband's wealth and status by the very fact that she was dressed to impress rather than for function or practicality (Figure 9.1). As the middle class copied the upper-class silhouette with less expensive fabrics and trim, inequality began as soon as the upper class changed its dress in reaction to the fact that the lower classes were dressing like the upper class. Then the process of copying occurs again and fashion continues.

Another symbol of wealth and status that existed as far back as the 19th century is the wearing of couture clothing. Couture clothing is admired for its innovativeness, its use of expensive materials, and its rarity. In today's market, if someone admires high-style clothing presented in couture yet cannot afford the Chanel suit or Givenchy dress, they can find a similar style at a fraction of the cost. Fast fashion, as it is known, "has been embraced by consumers as a luxury alternative" (Bye, 2010, p. 166). Fast fashion is temporary and consumers know that something new will almost daily be available. Other luxury items like leather handbags are also sought out by consumers that cannot easily afford the price of a Louis Vuitton or Prada handbag. Counterfeits of these items have been produced since the 1980s and continue to exist in the marketplace. A counterfeit handbag is "an identical copy of the authentic product, including packaging, trademarks, and labeling" (Yurchisin and Johnson, 2010, p. 134). A counterfeit item is different from a knock-off. The industry defines a knock-off as "a line-for-line copy that sells under a different brand name" (Yurchisin and Johnson, 2010, p. 134). The U.S. fashion industry does not endorse the production or use of counterfeits whereas knock-offs are a recognized part of the industry.

Figure 9.1 In the 19th century, luxurious fabrics and garment details signified elevated social and economic status of the wearer.

We know that fashion is a global industry and the names of designers like Chanel, Alexander McQueen, Marc Jacobs, and others are well known around the world. Yet fashion can also be regional, country, and place specific. The reading "Asante *Hightimers* and the Fashionable Display of Women's Wealth in Contemporary Ghana" gives us insight about the value of fashionable dress for Asante women in Ghana. With prestigious cloth and "fanciful" styles, women who are wealthy market-traders in the West African country (Gott, 2009, p. 161) reveal their social and financial status.

Status and Dress

Status is a person's position in a social hierarchy (Workman and Freeburg, 2009). We do not often think of gangs in terms of status, yet one aspect of gang behavior is involvement in criminal activities, a pursuit that enhances their status within the gang community (Struyk, 2006). A young man's or woman's clothing often identifies membership in a gang: oversized pants and shirts, sleeveless basketball jerseys, and other items more subtle in their symbolism. For example, wearing the jerseys of professional sports teams that happen to have the same colors as the gang colors, wearing caps that indicate a particular brand because the letters of the company represent the initials of the gang (e.g., Louis Vuitton caps represent the Vice Lords' initials in reverse), and wearing web belts with the gang insignia worn on the inside while at school and turned over after school to reveal the gang letters and symbols are several gang clothing markers. Thus, clothing is both an obvious way to proclaim gang membership to outsiders and a hidden way to keep membership secret.

In some parts of the world female status begins when a girl reaches puberty. In Kenya, Tanzania, and Madagascar girls are given special cloths to denote womanhood. These cloths are given to women throughout their lives as gifts. In Madagascar the cloth is called Lamba Hoany or "proverb cloth." These cloths are primarily worn as a skirt, shawl, or sling to carry a baby on the back (Green, 2003, p. 31). The reading "Female Tradition in a New Context: The Case of the *Khanga*" explores the evolution of messages on a similar cloth in Tanzania. Like the Lamba Hoany, the khanga originally included community sayings and proverbs, however, over time and in particular during the development of the socialist government of Julius Nyerere, the cloth began to include political messages and represent a form of national dress for women in Tanzania. The *Oxford English Dictionary* defines socialism as "a theory or system of social organization based on state or collective ownership and regulation of the means of production, distribution, and exchange for the common benefit of all members of society" (www.oed.com/). This reading provides another example of the power of dress to express status (with a focus in this case as dress relates to a particular political system).

Inequality and Dress

Status disparities result from the unequal distribution of money, power, and prestige among social classes (Workman and Freeburg, 2009, p. 133). An inequality in fashion appears when an individual cannot afford a particular brand of clothing and thus is ostracized or ridiculed because of it. This kind of inequality can be onerous for anyone. Some schools have counterbalanced this situation by requiring that all students wear school uniforms. This regulation attempts to unify everyone's dress and de-emphasize differences. Discrimination toward people because of their status or inequality can result in the adoption of dress to decrease the discrimination and/or proudly represent it. Raul J. Vásquez-López and José Blanco F., in the chapter reading "Dressing the *Jíbaros*: Puerto Rican Peasants' Clothing through Time and Space," examine the clothing worn by the *jíbaroto* to express Puerto Rican national identity. The costume of the *jibaro* had humble origins as the daily dress of peasants immortalized in literature and paintings. Over time the dress of the *jibaros* became the national costume of Puerto Rico, rather than the specific dress of peasants. Another reading, "Costume and the Play of Social Identities in an Andalusian Pilgrimage," describes the different costumes worn by participants in a religious pilgrimage to a church in Spain, *La Romeria del Rocio*. Authors Murphy and González-Faraco explain the disparate social identities expressed by the costume since "Rocio attracts people from all segments of Spanish society, from the Queen of Spain and members of the Spanish jet-set to beggars and pickpockets." The authors explain how by the 1980s the costumes no longer expressed class membership, but evolved to represent symbols of the festival surrounding the pilgrimage and of the Andalusian region. Both of these readings give evidence about how the meanings of an outfit can change from a dress representative of a social and economic class, sometimes disadvantaged, sometimes not, to become a costume associated with a region or a nation.

An example of dress-related inequality that occurred during the 18th and 19th centuries is revealed by the dress of slaves in the United States. Scholars writing about slave clothing give us some perspective on the inequality. Slaves were issued one set of clothing twice a year. For men, this clothing typically included a pair of pantaloons, a shirt, and a jacket of some sort, often called a "roundabout." Women were given a skirt, bodice, sometimes a petticoat, and a piece of fabric large enough to wrap around the head like a turban or kerchief. If shoes were issued, they were made of rough and coarse cowhide and known as "brogans." Slaves who worked in the plantation house as butlers, maids, cooks, and nannies were often better dressed than field laborers. House slaves were in close proximity to and worked side by side with the plantation mistress and her children. This closeness required them to be better dressed in their role as representatives of the plantation family and thus within a system of inequality—an element of status for the house slaves (Hunt-Hurst, 1999; Warner and Parker, 1990).

Another type of inequality in dress comes from gender inequality. Men in Western Europe around the fall of the Roman Empire (A.D. 476) continued to wear the Roman tunic with elements of barbarian dress. Tortora and Eubank (2010) explain that barbarian "means those tribes from northern Europe who were not citizens of the Roman empire" (p. 99). The barbarian touch included a type of trouser, known as "breeches" or "braies." However, the trousers were not always visible under the long tunic. About mid-14th century, styles for men changed to short skirts, "always a part of peasant dress, returned to fashion for men of all classes" (Tortora and Eubank, 2010, p. 151). In the 15th century, tunics continued to shorten and hose became visible. By the early 16th century in northern Europe, a separate breeches were available for men to wear, including knee-length or shorter versions. From this point on in menswear, the breeches, later known as "knee breeches," became a signifier of status. Men of the laboring classes wore trousers, longer than knee breeches, while men of the upper and middle class wore knee breeches. The knee breeches and silk stockings worn with them signified a man's class standing and were an obvious sign he was not a laborer. As the 18th century ended, styles were changing: knee breeches had lengthened for riding, and young boys were already wearing ankle-length trousers. By 1794 some fashionable young men were wearing long, tight-fitting, ankle-length trousers known as "pantaloons." Men retained knee breeches for formal occasions, and by 1807 most men were wearing long pants for day and evening wear. The inequality perpetuated by knee breeches was therefore no longer present by length, only by fit and construction. From this point on most men would wear long trousers that varied in fullness and shape as fashion dictated (Payne, Winakor, and Farrell-Beck, 1992; Tortora and Eubank, 2010).

In the 16th century fashion began to separate men's and women's dress. Prior to this time, men and women both wore long gowns with only minor gender differences. Some separation had happened before in the fit of the gown or style of sleeves, but the lines were more clearly drawn when men's tunics shortened and their breeches were exposed. As the centuries progressed, it was obvious that men (or males) wore pants of some sort, while women wore full-length skirts or gowns. It would be unusual to see a woman wearing pants. However, during the 1850s a group of dress reformers tried to start the practice of women wearing pants. Women donned pants underneath shortened dresses and received much ridicule as a result. Since these daring women were more interested in finding support for women's rights than in dress reform, they eventually gave up the bifurcated gear and went back to wearing skirts. However, the pants-like costume was adopted in a shorter version for swimwear and in the late 19th century became essential for women who desired to ride bicycles. With this acceptance for sportswear, the bifurcated garment slowly was accepted for women, first in sports and then later as leisure wear. Unlike skirts for men (Figure 9.2), pants for women did catch on through a slow process of promotion in fashion magazines and the movies. So inequality in dress can be rectified even today, at least by gender.

Figure 9.2 Skirts for men were not so unusual in the 16th century, however, the skirt has not made it into mainstream fashion for men in the 21st century.

But there are times when a group wants to distinguish itself in dress to represent an inequality. Subcultures often outwardly express inequality by dressing differently or creating a unique slant to prevailing styles that within the group may also represent status. A subculture includes groups that belong to or are a part of a larger culture, but differ in substantial ways from mainstream and hegemonic groups in the culture. The subculture sets itself apart and creates a relationship of contrast to and sometimes rebellion toward the mainstream. Ted Polhemus (1994) called these groups "style tribes" and indicated that style tribes reflected not only the outward connectedness of the group through how they looked and dressed, but also the values and norms of the specific group. He noted that the deviant subculture group gives a sense of community and common purpose to its members, who frequently feel that mainstream society lacks values and characteristics that members desire as a part of their lives. Some of the most notable style tribes in the past centuries include beatniks, mods, hippies, punks, Goths, and emos. Among style tribes there is a shared awareness of group conformity that causes the members to act and dress in a way that is different from the outside world, yet develops a sense of cohesiveness among the group members (Kaiser, 1997). Many of these groups have a place in fashion history because their particular styles of dress have trickled into mainstream fashion.

Members of subcultures may choose to look different from the mainstream majority for a variety of reasons. Groups that express religious identity and difference were discussed in Chapter 7. Some groups express political resistance against the dominant society and gain power through visible resistance (Majors and Billson, 1992). A difference in styles can give subcultures an alternative approach to **status attainment** by affording a sort of power through controlling the gaze of others. In other words, the unusualness of how someone dresses in a subculture draws attention to them (Hebdige, 1997). Those in the mainstream tend to notice those who look different. The unusual appearance also distinguishes the individual as authentic and hip with the subculture (Majors and Billson, 1992).

Dress and fashion history provides us with some examples of how inequality has been represented by clothing. Holly Alford (2004, p. 225), in *The Zoot Suit: Its History and Influence*, states, "Throughout the twentieth century, African-American men had been discriminated against and stereotyped, but relied on one thing that set them apart from others, and that is the clothing they chose to wear" (p. 225). The zoot suit was popular in the late 1930s and 1940s in the United States. It is one example of a style of clothing worn by young men (both Mexican American and African American) who were socially and culturally disadvantaged, who were letting people know who they were through their clothing. The zoot suit was an exaggerated form of the sack suit. It had an extra-long jacket with wide shoulders worn with pegged-topped trousers (Figure 9.3). Alford (2004, p. 226) tells us that the zoot suit was "a total look" with V-knot tie, extra-long watch chain, tight collar, and wide-brimmed hat. Some men continued to wear the zoot suit in the 1940s even after the American War Production Board issued regulations applied to length of jackets, trouser inseams, cuffs, and pleats in trousers. The regulations were an attempt to control materials and focus attention on needs of the military. As the zoot suiters continued to wear their distinctive garb, which did not meet Production Board regulations, the suit gained notoriety. In fact, a riot broke out in Los Angeles in 1943 between mostly white servicemen and Mexican-American youth because the servicemen considered the wearing of the zoot suit unpatriotic. Tortora and Eubank (2010, p. 482) point out that the zoot suiters were already "alienated and disaffected as a result of social upheavals related to World War II." Thus, the zoot suit was a symbol of inequality and alienation.

The Teddy Boys of post–World War II England highlighted social and economic inequality in dress by taking a fashionable style and making it their own. The Teddy Boys came from working-class backgrounds and lived in the "bleakest and most blitzed parts of London" (Cross, 2008, p. 219); they offer a clear example of a subcultural group that utilized prevailing styles of menswear originated by the elite tailors of Savile Row in London and transformed the style into their own. The Teds, as they were known, took the Savile Row single-breasted, long, fitted suit jacket, often with collar and cuff trimmed in velvet, and the narrow trousers and brocade vest and added their own touches, including the American elements of Western shoelace necktie and zoot suit styling (longer jacket and drainpipe trousers) along with brightly colored socks worn with crepe-soled shoes with pointed toes (Cross, 2008; Walker, 1988;

Figure 9.3 The zoot suit is an example of inequality and alienation expressed through dress.

Wilson, 2003). According to Cross (2008) the Teddy Boys made a "direct challenge to the authority of adult society, particularly the authority of what the Teds refused to accept as their social superiors" through their clothing styles (p. 219). Cross continues, "The Teds were the first teenage subculture in Britain to construct new identities for themselves in order to compensate for socioeconomic marginalization." The Teddy Boy style caught on and spread around the country (De Marly, 1989). At the time the Teddy Boys were creating their "look," rationing of clothes and fabric was still in force in mid-1950s Great Britain, so the Teddy Boys were making a "defiant statement" not only in their dress but also in the practice of snubbing their nose at the government policy (Cross, 2008, p. 218). The Teds, like the young African American and Mexican American men in the United States in the 1940s, were socially and economically disadvantaged; their clothing reflected the inequality they lived with in the British class system. Yet their dress gave them a way to be recognized rather than disappearing in the midst of other disadvantaged youth.

Hippies are another example of a subcultural group from the past that adopted dress totally opposite from that of their elders and peers. Originating in the Haight Ashbury section of San Francisco and grabbing the attention of newspapers and magazines in 1966–1967, the Hippies were anti-fashion: long hair, beards, baggy and mismatched clothing, blue jeans, love beads, ethnic clothing, and long skirts and dresses. The looks of the hippies fit into the *zeitgeist* of the late 1960s and early 1970s, so soon their styles filtered into mainstream fashion as de-

signers gained inspiration from the freedom of dress expressed by the hippie style (Figure 9.4) (Tortora and Eubank, 2010). This is not an example of inequality in the same way that the zoot suiters and Teds' dress was because the young people who adopted the hippie way of life were not necessarily from working-class families in America. They were more interested in being totally separate from the existing population, so they created their own level of inequality by being different. Can you think of other subculture groups or style tribes in existence today that express themselves through their dress?

The inverse of inequality is equality. One example occurred when China (prior to 1976) required all of its citizens to wear blue Maoist uniforms. These made everyone look alike, no matter the person's age or gender. Fashion began to reappear in China after the death of Mao Zedong in 1976. China moved from "a sluggish . . . Communist system" into a "socialist-capitalist" economy that "promoted trade and growth" (Steele, 1983; Kunz and Garner, 2007, p. 265). Today it is almost impossible to open a *Women's Wear Daily* and not find an article about some aspect of fashion in China. A lot has changed for the nation in 35 years in respect to dress. This change

Figure 9.4 The hippie style included: long hair (males and females), ethnic styles in clothing and accessories, and an overall comfort and freedom in dress.

can be observed in an article in the September 2011 issue of *Vogue*: "Made in China: the Explosive Rise of a Style Superpower" by Jonathan Van Meter. The article includes photographs of models in designer dresses standing among some of China's most famous sights (e.g., the Great Wall). Van Meter (2011, p. 649) states, "The Chinese are currently the second-largest consumers of fashion and luxury goods, representing more than a quarter of all sales worldwide." The story of China's rise in the fashion world is a far cry from the days when the official intention was that everyone be equal. China went from equality in dress to inequality in dress.

Summary

By examining the interconnectedness of fashion, status, and inequality, particularly in regard to dress, we gain a better understanding of the issues and the outcomes. The articles presented in this chapter provide examples of disparities in dress and explore the results. Inequality in dress has existed for many centuries; interestingly, in the 20th century many subcultures dressed differently from the mainstream on purpose. In other examples, dress worn by working-class citizens became items of national dress in Puerto Rico and Spain.

Suggested Readings

Alford, H. (2004, June). The Zoot Suit: Its History and Influence. *Fashion Theory* 8(2): 225–236.
Bolton, A. (2003). *Bravehearts: Men in Skirts*. London: Harry N. Abrams, Inc.
Cross, R. J. (2008). The Teddy Boy as Scapegoat. In A. Reilly and S. Cosbey (Eds.), *Men's Fashion Reader*, pp. 214–230. New York: Fairchild Books.
Green, R. L. (2003) LambaHoany: Proverb Cloths from Madagascar. *African Arts* 36(2): 30–43.
Polhemus, T. (1994). *Streetstyle: From Sidewalk to Catwalk*. New York: Thames and Hudson.

Learning Activity 9.1: Fashion Messages

Procedure

This activity aims to help you understand the messages of fashion, status, and inequality that dress expresses. It asks you to think-write-pair-share. First, think about items of dress that men, women, and children wear today that reflect status and inequality. Take about 30 seconds to 1 minute. Second, write down your responses. Third, pair up with someone in class to tell and explain your responses to each other for 3 to 5 minutes. Next, your instructor will appoint someone in the class to be note taker while the rest of the class shares their items of dress and gives brief reasons why they made these selections. At the end of the discussion, the note taker shares the commonalities between the items selected as well as the differences. As a class, discuss the commonalities, differences, and why they exist.

References

Alford, H. (2004, June). The Zoot Suit: Its History and Influence. *Fashion Theory* 8(2): 225–236.
Bolton, A. (2003). *Bravehearts: Men in Skirts*. London: Harry N. Abrams.
Bye. E. (2010). *Fashion Design*. New York: Berg.

Cross, R. J. (2008). The Teddy Boy as Scapegoat. In A. Reilly and S. Cosbey (Eds.), *Men's Fashion Reader*, 214–230. New York: Fairchild Books.
De Marly, D. (1989). *Fashion for Men: An Illustrated History*. New York: Holmes and Meier.

Gott, S. (2009). Asante *Hightimers* and The Fashionable Display of Women's Wealth in Contemporary Ghana. *Fashion Theory* 13 (2): 141–176.

Green, R. L. (2003). LambaHoany: Proverb Cloths from Madagascar. *African Arts* 36 (2): 30–43.

Hebdige, D. (1997). Posing . . . Threats, Striking . . . Poses: Youth, Surveillance and Display. In K. Gelder and S. Thornton (Eds.), *The Subcultures Reader*, 393–405. London: Routledge.

Hunt-Hurst, P. (1999, Winter). "Round Homespun Coat & Pantaloons of the Same": Slave Clothing as Reflected in Fugitive Slave Advertisements in Antebellum Georgia. *The Georgia Historical Quarterly* 83 (4): 727–740.

Kaiser, S. B. (1997). *The Social Psychology of Clothing: Symbolic Appearances in Context* (2nd ed.). New York: Fairchild Publications.

Kunz, G. I., and M. B. Garner. (2007). *Going Global: The Textile and Apparel Industry*. New York: Fairchild Books.

Majors, R., and J. M. Billson. (1992). *Cool Pose: Dilemmas of Black Manhood in America*. New York: Lexington Books.

Oxford English Dictionary, 2nd ed., s.v. "Socialism," http://dictionary.oed.com/ (accessed August 20, 2011).

Payne, B., Winakor, G., and J. Farrell-Beck. (1992). *The History of Costume* (2nd ed.). New York: HarperCollins.

Polhemus, T. (1994). *Streetstyle: From Sidewalk to Catwalk*. New York: Thames and Hudson.

Steele, V. 1983. Fashion in China. *Dress* 9:8–15.

Struyk, R. (2006, September/October). Gangs in Our Schools: Identifying Gang Indicators in Our School Population. *The Clearing House*, 80 (1): 11–13.

Tortora, P. G., and K. Eubank. (2010). *Survey of Historic Costume* (5th ed.). New York: Fairchild Books.

Van Meter, J. (2011, September). "Go East!" *Vogue*, 644–665.

Walker, R. (1988). *Savile Row: An Illustrated History*. New York: Rizzoli.

Warner, P. C., and D. Parker. (1990). Slave Clothing and Textiles in North Carolina: 1775–1835. In B. M. Starke, L. O. Holloman, and B. K. Nordquist (Eds.). *African American Dress and Adornment: A Cultural Perspective*, 82–92. Dubuque, Iowa: Kendall/Hunt.

Wilson, E. (2003). *Adorned in Dreams: Fashion and Modernity*. New Brunswick, NJ: Rutgers University Press.

Workman, J. E., and B. W. Freeburg. (2009). *Dress and Society*. New York: Fairchild Books.

Yurchisin, J. and K. K. P. Johnson. (2010). *Fashion and the Consumer*. New York: Berg.

THE CAMPUS AS RUNWAY

Ruth La Ferla

Julia Flynn was darting to her classes at Columbia University last week in a Marc by Marc Jacobs daisy-patterned dress and high-heeled Chloé boots, her polished turnout accessorized with a Starbucks venti latte. "I'm really loving the whole Chanel, Valentino and McQueen shows," she said. "They completely inspired me." She had gleaned her information that very morning from Style.com.

Ms. Flynn, 24 and a sophomore, is one in a small but self-aware and increasingly vocal contingent of college women who dress to impress. The campus is their runway, a place to show off a style sense that is derived in part from their friends but more often attained through a click of a mouse, a gesture that affords them instant access to the once arcane universe of fashion shows and to the style blogs and shopping sites so many imbibe with their morning brew.

If at one time college women subscribed to a regionally prescribed uniform—twin sets and loafers in the East, frayed jeans and ponchos farther west—now, thanks to the democratizing influence of the Web, trends are disseminated at warp speed, traversing regional borders and, paradoxically, encouraging a more individualized approach to dress.

Whether students' tastes run to an urbanely preppie composite of mannish shirts, slim skirts and blazers, flowered dresses and Ferragamo flats, or to a cutting-edge pastiche of long loose-fitting sweaters, calf-length skirts and platform booties, their absorption with fashion points to a sea change, suggesting that the style bar has been raised, reaching a level of sophistication all but unknown a mere decade ago.

"The stereotype used to be that college students live in sweat pants and don't care about fashion," said Zephyr Basine, the editor of Collegefashion.net, a blog written by college women. "But today that isn't so." If at one time coeds signaled their cool by a kind of willful dishevelment, arriving for 8 a.m. classes in trench coats tossed over pajamas, today that sort of carelessness marks them as out of touch.

"People now put more thought into what they're wearing," said Amy Levin, 24, a recent graduate of Indiana University and editor of Collegefashionista.com, an influential blog. "Getting ready for class is important. Students want to up their game. That means looking a little more serious, not just throwing on a graphic T-shirt and jeans."

Many of those students might relate to Diarra White, 18, a freshman at Columbia University. "I'm not a sweats-and-T-shirt kind of person," said Ms. White, who was decked out for class last Wednesday in a cropped leather jacket, white cotton dress and the camel-colored knee-high boots that she alternates on other days with high-heeled pumps. "Even at the library, I'll see people in heels. There's a lot of energy in that."

"Besides," she added saucily, "you never know who you're going to see in the library."

Today Ms. White and her cohort routinely trawl fashion Web sites like the Sartorialist, Fashion Toast, the Cut and Style Stalker; they scour cheap and chic outposts like Topshop and Forever 21 for approximations of coveted labels like J. Crew and Tory Burch, and for the chunky oversize sweaters, generous scarves, platform pumps and high-heeled loafers that made a splash on fall runways. Then they fill in wardrobe gaps with treasures picked up at vintage fashion boutiques.

They shop well in advance of the school year, some stepping up their purchasing throughout the term.

Spending by these inveterate bargain hunters typically adds up to a few hundred dollars each year or, in rarer instances, $1,000 or more.

"I used to shop constantly," said Elisabeth Dickson, 22, who graduated in May from Oberlin College in Ohio. At one time, Ms. Dickson confided, she spent hours on the Internet, scouring the Style Stalker, Fashion Toast, Man Repeller and Style Bubble sites, and making the occasional detour to J. Crew or Topshop "when I was in the market for something edgier or a little bit upscale."

"There was a point in my sophomore year," she said, "when I would read fashion blogs religiously in the morning. I bookmarked them and used them for inspiration, or just out-and-out thievery."

Planning to create a blog of her own, she found herself jotting elaborate descriptions of her daily ensembles. An entry marked October 14, 2009 described a vintage blue and white sweater with gold buttons and shoulder pads over navy-blue tights and a white H & M tunic and vintage lace-up cream booties.

"Most people may not have been as obsessed," she acknowledged, "but the point is that we cared."

For Ms. Dickson and others, the Internet acts as a primary resource. "Students can watch fashion shows live on the runway," said Ms. Basine of Collegefashion.net. "They can see what people are wearing on the other side of the globe. Trends now are dispersed faster than ever. They're not going to stay in one isolated area for long."

Trends are on Julie Soffen's radar for sure, as attested by her creamy, quilted chain bag and the faux Burberry scarf that was looped luxuriantly around her neck. Ms. Soffen, 21, who was visiting a friend at Princeton University last week, had put rigorous thought into her turnout, which she may alternate on other days with, she said, "Ralph Lauren head to toe."

"Some of us," she added, "like to make an effort when we dress."

Some of her contemporaries, slouching around campus that day in floppy shirts, tattered jeans or track pants incongruously paired with pricey accessories, had clearly not gotten that brief. Ms. Soffen tossed an acidic glance in their direction. "They think that if they rock it with a $3,000 purse, that makes it work," she said. "But it doesn't."

Chelsea Cawood, 22, a senior at the University of Oklahoma, logs on to the Web when she plans to shop, expertly combing sites like ShopNastyGal.com, as well as the Urban Outfitters online store. Her online sprees have whetted an appetite for mismatched patterns and textures, leopard prints, oversize knits, fake fur vests and platform heels. All told, they contribute to an aesthetic mash-up that Ms. Cawood defines as "a little boho and downtown L.A., mixed with a bit of Eurotrash."

Her influences are by no means confined to the Web. Like many of her peers across the country, she takes her style cues from movies, recent and vintage, favoring hits like "Pretty in Pink" and "Almost Famous."

Tamara Belopopsky, 21, a senior at the State University of New York at Purchase, finds Fellini films more inspiring. "La Dolce Vita," which she has seen more than once, prompted her to seek out horn-rimmed glasses like those worn on screen by Marcello Mastroianni. She shops at discount outlets like T. J. Maxx and in a string of local consignment shops, rarely laying out more than $200 to $300 on her wardrobe during the school year. Her intention is to pull off a look she defines as "a bit androgynous and completely individual"—in short, one she will not see mirrored on her friends.

Does she compete with those friends to score style points? Not so much, Ms. Belopopsky said. But her friend Jamie Pasquarella, 20, a senior at SUNY, who was clad in a camel-tone cape bought at Macy's, a Vera Wang shirt and Michael Kors boots, was less certain. "People here get angry if someone is trying to cop their style," she said.

The reason, she indicated, ought to be obvious. "Around here we are trying to define ourselves by the way we look."

1. This chapter explores fashion, status, and inequality. Is status and inequality also reflected in this reading? If so, how?
2. Think about your own college campus—are there people in your classes that are seen as fashion leaders, wearing new looks? Are they copied? Why or why not?

9.2

ASANTE *HIGHTIMERS* AND THE FASHIONABLE DISPLAY OF WOMEN'S WEALTH IN CONTEMPORARY GHANA

Suzanne Gott

In southern Ghana's Ashanti Region, there is a certain category of woman that the Asante people commonly call *preman* (pl. *premanfoo*), using a word that is the local version of the English *play-man* or *playboy*. Despite this word's seemingly male cast, *preman* is a term applied primarily to women, particularly wealthy market traders. A *preman*, people say, is a "very expensive" type of woman, a *high-timer*, who always wants to be seen at every social occasion dressed "gorgeously" in the latest, most fashionable, and "fanciful" styles (Figure 9.5).[1]

This article explores the relationship between the flamboyantly fashionable behavior of the *preman* and the long-established Asante cultural practice of *poatwa*,[2] a term meaning "challenge" that references both visual and verbal assertions of superior status (Christaller 1933: 397). In the past, *poatwa* displays of costly textiles and golden regalia provided a major means of proclaiming the wealth and power of the Asante state's ruling elite.[3] In the Ashanti Region over the course of the twentieth century, fashionable dress developed into a particularly female mode of high-status display that provided visible proof of a woman's success in accumulating the prestigious textiles that became an increasingly important form of female wealth. The most extreme form of such displays are the extravagant, highly visible, and sometimes scandalous fashions of the Asante *preman*, which I argue may be best understood as a distinctively female mode of contemporary Asante *poatwa* behavior.

Figure 9.5 Cries of "*Qye preman!*" ("She is a *preman!*") for this Asante woman attending a Kumasi funeral wearing a particularly fanciful and costly *kaba* ensemble, 1990.

This study, based on research in Ghana during 1990, 1999, 2003, and 2005, examines the intersection of cultural ideals, historical developments, and gendered socioeconomic realities that have fueled Asante women's strong interest in cloth acquisition and fashionable display.

Hightimers and Asante Competitive Display

Within Ghana's Ashanti Region, funerals are at the center of Asante social life. On Fridays and Saturdays, the days dedicated to the observance of customary funeral rites, the streets of the capital Kumasi and towns and villages throughout the Ashanti Region are filled with throngs of women and men dressed in mourning ensembles of red, black, and brown textiles. Men abandon their everyday clothing of shirts and trousers for Akan men's customary dress, a stately eight- to ten-yard toga-like wrapped ensemble. Women, depending on their relationship to the deceased and bereaved family members, dress in either wrapped *dansinkran* or sewn *kaba* ensembles (Figure 9.6).

Asante funerals constitute what might be termed *totalizing events* that touch on almost every dimension of social life.[4] Funeral observances bring together great numbers of extended family, friends, and colleagues from throughout Ghana, and sometimes from abroad, to honor and attest to the social standing of the deceased and their matrilineage. In addition to being occasions for honoring the deceased, funerals in the Ashanti Region are important, high-visibility social occasions. Kumasi funerals, especially the widely attended commemorative funeral rites (*ayie*) held on Saturday afternoons following burial, are considered to be fashion showcases where one will see prestigious textiles sewn into the latest, most fashionable *kaba* ensemble styles (Figure 9.7).

It is at these large Kumasi funerals where one finds the greatest concentration of Asante *hightimers*, or *premanfoo*, dressed in the latest

Figure 9.6 Mrs. Elizabeth Longdon, a Kumasi dressmaker (fourth from left), with members of her workshop and other sympathizers with a bereaved colleague (center, wearing white head-cloth) at the commemorative funeral rites for her father, 1990.

Figure 9.7 Emelia Damptey (left) and Evelyn Damptey dressed in the latest styles to attend a Kumasi funeral, 1990.

fashions of the costliest funeral *cloth* (see Figures 9.5 and 9.8). Such high-visibility status-seeking behavior is, in fact, considered to be the hallmark of the Asante *preman*:

> If you are a *preman*, more properly a *preman baa* ("*preman* woman") everything you wear is "high cost": superior dressing, superior shoes, superior *cloth*. Food, drinks, everything is costly . . . [they like] to live ostentatiously, to show off. *Premanfoo* have to show themselves. At any celebration— funerals, festivals—they will be there. They have to show themselves off.[5]

It is said that *premanfoo* will even attend grand funerals of perfect strangers in order to have the largest possible audience for assertions of wealth and social prominence by means of their costly and flamboyant styles of fashionable dress.

From the late-seventeenth-century beginnings of the Asante state until British colonial rule in the early twentieth century, public expressions of wealth and superior status were restricted according to a regulated ranking system based on political power and authority. On public occasions, members of this ruling elite dressed in ensembles of costly textiles and displayed golden regalia as a means of proclaiming the political power and wealth of the Asante state (Bowdich 1966[1819]; Garrard 1989; Kyerematen 1964; Ross 1977, 1998, 2002). The political monopoly on such displays was maintained by strict sumptuary controls (Arhin 1990: 531–33).

"Wealth, like power," Arhin observes, was also closely controlled (1990: 525). Asante officials maintained a rigorous system of death duties and inheritance taxes that effectively transferred most subjects' accumulated wealth to the Asante state, thus preventing the transfer of accumulated individual and familial wealth to future generations. However, those individuals who accumulated substantial wealth during their lifetime were honored for the magnificence of this monetary contribution to the state by the bestowal of the rank of *obirempon* (pl., *abirempon*), a term derived from the pairing of the word *obarima* ("valiant man") with *pon* ("great, powerful"). An individual's attainment of this exalted rank was publically proclaimed and

Figure 9.8 An Asante *preman*, scandalously dressed in a flamboyant funeral ensemble of imported black and gold wax-print cloth, 1990.

celebrated by a ceremonial procession of royal proportions in which they were honored as magnanimous benefactors of the state (Wilks 1979).[6]

Given the inextricable linkage between gold, wealth, and power in Asante, great quantities of gold ornaments figured prominently in these regal, status-asserting performances. One such *obirempon* display was witnessed in 1817 by William Hutchison, Acting British Consulin Kumasi. The main preparation for this *obirempon* procession, he found, consisted of fashioning "their gold into various articles of dress for show." Hutchison described the variety of gold regalia that this important court official, Gyaasewahene Opoku Frefre, had commissioned for this once-in-a-lifetime ceremonial exhibition of his riches:

> Apokoo . . . shewed [*sic*] me his varieties, weighing upwards of 800 bendas [£7,200 currency] of the finest gold; among the articles, was a girdle two inches broad. Gold chains for the neck, arms, legs, &c. ornaments for the ancles of all descriptions, consisting of manacles, with keys, bells,

chairs, and padlocks. For his numerous family of wives, children, and captains, were armlets and various ornaments . . . New umbrellas made in fantastical shapes, gold swords and figures of animals, birds, beasts, and fishes of the same metal (Bowdich 1966 [1819]: 395).

While all known accounts of *obirempon* displays have been those of wealthy men, Akyeampong has observed that "scattered historical evidence stretching back to the seventeenth century" reveals a similar, yet often overlooked "ethic of accumulation" among Gold Coast women.

Such evidence, he argues, indicates that there "were 'big women' [female *abirempon*], just as there were 'big men'" (2000: 223–5).[7] In eighteenth- and nineteenth-century Asante, the influential moneyed elite known as *asikafoo* (from *sika*, "gold") included wealthy female entrepreneurs who, like their male counterparts, engaged in conspicuous displays of wealth, including generous gifts to the community and Asante state (Wilks 1975: 693–95).

Among the coastal Akan, the accumulation of wealth and sumptuary display had gradually become freed from the customary system of state regulation. Nineteenth-century accounts of life in the trading port of Elmina describe the manner in which women of this independent coastal elite orchestrated eye-catching public performances showcasing their wealth and superior status:

> If a woman wore gold ornaments, so did her "maids"; thus one might see a wealthy woman going through the streets of Elmina followed by ten of her slave women, all finely dressed and wearing gold ornaments. A woman of high status might spend hours dressing her female slaves and arranging their hair (Jones 1995: 106).

Away from the more fluid social milieu of the coast, Asante authorities were able to maintain state controls of wealth and high-status display for a significantly longer period of time. However, by the late nineteenth and early twentieth centuries, state regulatory powers had become seriously eroded, first as a result of internal instability, and then, by the imposition of British colonial rule (Arhin 1990: 525–28; McCaskie 1983: 39).

The weakening of state power permitted, for the first time, the development of an independent Asante entrepreneurial elite. Yet, although this new business class was now free of the customary system of state-regulated wealth accumulation, death duties, and sumptuary display, it soon became evident that "they were still enmeshed—as their descendants are—in the received (if modified) cultural imagery of behaving like a 'big man,' an *obirempon*" (McCaskie 1986: 8). Such behavior, Arhin observes, continues to flourish in contemporary Asante:

> Much of the well-known present-day Asante competitive acquisition, *poatwa*, of the biggest buildings, the latest and largest car models and extremely expensive funeral rites is calculated self-assertion: it is a message that one may not be an indigenous ruler but one is in certain material respects equal to or even above such a ruler (1990: 533).[8]

Over the course of the twentieth century, increasing numbers of the Asante population have found ways of engaging in the once strictly regulated practice of *poatwa*, or competitive sumptuary display. Asante funeral rites have served as particularly popular high-visibility display frames for such status-seeking behavior, with the staging of prestigious funerals greatly facilitated by the development of rental businesses specializing in funerary display goods and regalia (De Witte 2003; Gott 2003). The social prominence accorded such high-status displays, both genuine and spurious, demonstrates the continuing salience of the Asante *obirempon* ethos.

During the twentieth century, with the development of women's sewn clothing styles, fashionable dress embodying Asante customary values and aesthetic sensibilities emerged as a new, ever-changing resource for women's *poatwa* displays. Within this dynamic Asante fashion system, the costly, flamboyantly fashionable dress of the "hightiming" *premanfoo*, who "have to show themselves" at all high-visibility social events, especially Asante funerals, may be best understood as a contemporary, and distinctively female, mode of Asante *obirempon* display.

The Importance of Dressing Well in Asante

Within contemporary Ghana, the Asante are characterized as being especially concerned with dressing well as a means of gaining social prestige. Residents of Kumasi, the Ashanti Region's capital city, often contrast dress behavior in their city with that of Accra, the nation's coastal capital. In Accra, they say, people are free to dress as they choose, but in Kumasi, people "gossip too much," with that gossip frequently focusing on the quality of an individual's dress.

Although it is Ghana's second largest city, Kumasi is, in the words of one local woman, more "like a big village," with an ongoing sense of social accountability maintained by regular face-to-face interaction. Kumasi residents move in interconnecting social networks of kinship, marriage, church membership, occupation, residence, and personal ties, such as those developed during school days. Both Asante and non-Asante report strong social pressure to dress well and often beyond their means, with particular scrutiny directed toward the dress behavior of women.

In Kumasi, women dress with an awareness that their clothing and appearance are subject to critical appraisal on trips to town and the market, while attending church events and funerals, and at important life transition points. All women, except for the most elderly, are considered to take great pride in their fashionable dress and sense of style.

The popular term for fashion or fashionable dressing is *life* (*laif* in Twi-English), from *highlife*, a name coined in early-twentieth-century Ghana for the cosmopolitan lifestyle and dance-orchestra music of the mission-educated urban elite. "*O pe laif*" ("she likes *life*") is a commonly used compliment for a woman who dresses fashionably. The opposite of such a positive evaluation, explained long-time Kumasi resident and cultural studies teacher Mr. M. H. Frempong, is "*o ye atetekwaa*," a pejorative assessment that most Kumasi women endeavor to avoid:

> The Ashanti coined this word, *tete*, meaning ancient dressing all the time. In the olden days, this was an old-fashioned way of dressing, of not putting on fine clothes . . . Other women look down on such a woman, saying, "*O ye atetekwaa*." This means the woman doesn't like to dress well all the time. This is a terrible thing to call somebody, they will be very much angered . . . If you visit friends in faded cloth, they will say out of your hearing, "*O ye atetekwaa*." The Gas [a coastal people] will never do that, but the Ashantis will do that—they want to be dressing beautifully all the time. If you don't do what they do, they say "*atetekwaa*."

A related term, he continued, is *pepee*, used to describe a person who doesn't dress well because of extreme frugality or "miserliness,"—a quality conventionally attributed to men, rather than women:

> A woman could never be *pepee*. Because for a woman, if she has the means, she will buy things to go out and better appear neatly [well-dressed]. She will never be *pepee* if she has the means, even if she is not married.[9]

The Special Significance of African-print Cloth

Within Ghana's Ashanti Region, women of different economic levels, educational backgrounds, ethnic identities, and religious beliefs all participate in a unified system of value in respect to ensemble fabric and style.

Women's ensemble fabrics are grouped into two basic categories: *ntoma* ("cloth")[10] and *material*. *Ntoma*, as well as the English word *cloth*,[11] serve as umbrella terms for the first category, which is comprised of three highly valued textiles. Two of these prestigious textiles are products of local industry: hand-woven *kente*, a silk, rayon, or cotton strip-cloth textile historically associated with Akan rulership (Ross 1998); and *adinkra*, a cotton cloth stamped with symbolic designs, which is customarily associated with Asante funerals (Mato 1986). The third highly esteemed textile is the distinctive factory-produced fabric known as *African-print cloth*, initially developed by late-nineteenth-century Europe manufacturers for the lucrative western and central African textile markets, with African manufacture beginning in the 1950s (Addae 1963[1956]; Bickford 1997; Littrell 1977; Nielsen 1974, 1979; Pedler 1974; Picton 1999; Rabine 2002; Spencer 1983; Steiner 1985). The borrowed English word *material*, the term for the second category of ensemble fabrics, is used in referring to factory-made fabrics other than African-print cloth.

West African peoples first gained access to European textiles in the late fourteenth century, when Europe's interest in the West African market was spurred by European economic expansion and an ever-increasing demand for West African gold. Initially, European products were brought into West Africa by means of Muslim controlled trans-Saharan caravan routes. By the late fourteenth or early fifteenth centuries, Muslim merchants established trading settlements on the northern border of southern Ghana's forest zone (Posnansky 1987: 14–18; Wilks 1962). In the late fifteenth century, European merchant ships succeeded in gaining direct access to the area by establishing trading forts along the West African coast, including the region that came to be known as the Gold Coast (i.e., modern Ghana).

From their earliest contact, European merchants endeavored to discern and meet local consumer preferences, first by insinuating themselves into the established indigenous trade in highly esteemed north and West African textiles, and later by importing colorful East Indian cottons and Javanese batiks (Alpern 1995: 6–8, 10; Sundström 1974: 156–57). European manufacturers also modified their own textile products in order to appeal to African tastes and standards of quality. An early example of such efforts took place during a 1720–50 trade war between dealers in British Manchester cloth and those importing cottons from the East Indies. By the end of this thirty-year period, Manchester's coarse, dull-colored linen cloth had been significantly modified to suit West African consumers' preference for the lighter weight, brightly colored East Indian cottons (Nielsen 1979: 469). The eventual preeminence of European manufactured cloth in the nineteenth-century African market was, in fact, only accomplished by the "large-scale imitation" of East Indian textiles by Europe's expanding cotton industry (Sundström 1974: 157).

The great popularity of the Javanese batiks, which were introduced into West Africa in the mid-nineteenth century, also prompted European textile producers to use recently developed technology to manufacture wax-print imitations of Javanese batiks for the African market (Nielsen 1979: 470–76; Pedler 1974: 242). To further ensure the commercial success of this new "African-print," European manufacturers also developed designs based on indigenous textiles, investigated the color and pattern preferences of different West African peoples, and employed a variety of marketing strategies, all aimed at furthering their efforts to meet local tastes (Addae 1963[1956]: 27; Cordwell 1979; Nielsen 1974: 25, 38; Steiner 1985: 97–106).

The designs of the African-print cloth produced for Gold Coast markets were given names, in a manner similar to the named designs of indigenous *kente* and *adinkra* textiles, in order to meet Akan standards of cultural and aesthetic value (Warren and Andrews 1977: 14).[12] For the Asante, all highly valued forms of material culture must possess a name (McLeod 1976). Within Ghana, it is the endowment of African print designs with culturally meaningful names, often by *cloth* traders of the Ashanti Region (Boelman and van Holthoon 1973: 239), that distinguishes African-print cloth from all other manufactured textiles.

The names given to African-print designs may reference important events in Asante political history, as in the *cloth* named *Bonsu* ("Whale"), named for the early-nineteenth-century Asantehene Osei Tutu Kwame, who earned the title "Bonsu" after becoming the first Asante king to successfully lead a southern military campaign all the way to the sea (Buah 1998: 95). African-print names may have religious meanings, such as the *cloth* called *Yesu Mogya* ("The Blood of Jesus"), while other African prints are named after common elements of everyday life, as in the *cloth* designs *Aya* ("Fern") and *Kwadusa* ("Bunch of Bananas").[13] New African-print designs have also been given the names of popular *highlife* songs (van der Geest and Asante-Darko 1982: 28–29).

The strong interrelationship between Akan verbal art and visual culture, which Cole and Ross have termed the "verbal-visual nexus" (1977: 9–12), finds expression in the particular value accorded those visual forms that are associated with "some more-or-less fixed verbal expression" (McLeod 1976: 88–89). The Akan refer to such verbal expressions as *ebe*—a speech genre conventionally translated as "proverb"—that includes not only proverbs but "moral-embedded extended metaphors, illustrative anecdotes, and parables" (Yankah 1989: 88–89). *Ebe* or *ebebuo* ("speaking" *ebe*), Yankah observes, may be expressed aurally in speech, song, or tonal drumming, and visually in sculptural form, textile design, dance gesture, or demeanor (1989: 98).

THE MEANINGS OF DRESS

Asante *ebe* provide a major source of textile names, such as the popular African-print design *Akwadaa bo nwa* (Figure 9.9), which is an abridged version of the saying *Akwadaa bo nwa na ommo akyekyedee* ("A child can break the shell of a snail, but cannot break that of a tortoise," i.e., only attempt what is appropriate to your level of ability). Other *ebe*-derived names, such as the funerary African-print designs *Nsuo afa borodee hono* ("The stream carries away plantain peels," i.e., death carries people away) and *Owuo atwedee* ("The ladder of death," everybody climbs it) visually express philosophical commentaries on the transience of life and inevitability of death.

Marriage and motherhood are ever-popular subjects. The African-print *Nsubura* ("Wells"), whose concentric circular designs are likened to small natural wells, signifies the "stillness," or stability, and depth of an ideal marital relationship. On a more cautionary note, the *cloth* named *Barima nye sumye* ("Man is not a pillow," i.e., "you cannot rely on a man for security"), stresses the need for female self-reliance and financial autonomy, even within marriage. Asante maternal ideals of nurturance and protection find expression in African-print cloth with the well-known image *Akokobaatan ne ne maa* ("Mother hen and her chicks").[14]

While a sophisticated knowledge of named African-print designs remains strongest among *cloth* traders and older women, the fact that African-print cloths are generally known to possess names continues to endow these factory-produced textiles with a cultural and economic value recognized by women of all ages and from all walks of life. As Juliana Osei, a young schoolteacher in her twenties, explained: "If you put on *cloth* with no name, it is not good *cloth*. It is important to show people that you have put on good *cloth*."[15]

The Relationship between Fabric and Ensemble

Distinctions of value between *ntoma*, or *cloth*, and *material* are also expressed in local conventions regarding the matching of fabric to ensemble style. Only *kente*, *adinkra*, and African-print cloth are used for women's prestigious *dansinkran* and *kaba* ensembles, while those fabrics called *material* are relegated to that category of Western-style ensemble called *ataadee* ("dress" or "skirt and top"). A woman's selection from among these three categories depends on the occasion and on her stage of life.[16]

Ataadee, the umbrella term for sewn dresses, skirts, and blouses, is the usual attire of girls and younger women. However, as a woman matures, three-piece *kaba* ensembles of African-print cloth become an increasingly important part of her wardrobe. Women who have reached their fifties rarely wear *ataadee* ensembles in public because only *dansinkran* or *kaba* ensembles are considered appropriate to the "respectability," or dignity, of an older woman.

Asante women's customary two-piece *dansinkran* ensemble, consisting of a wrapped lower

Figure 9.9 A Kumasi trader wearing the African-print design *Akwadaa bo nwa na ommo akyekyedee* ("A child can break the shell of a snail, but cannot break that of a tortoise"), 1990.

and upper cloth, is named for the distinctive As-ante *dansinkran* hairstyle.[17] The *dansinkran* hair-style and wrapped ensemble, which is worn by queen mothers, elderly women, and chief mourn-ers at Asante funerals, is regarded as an especially beautiful expression of time-honored Asante cus-tom (*ammamere*) and cultural pride (Figure 9.10).

The *kaba*, a syncretic three-piece ensemble, consists of a sewn blouse (*kaba*), a wrapped or sewn skirt (*abosoo* or *slit*), and an unsewn cloth (*akatasoo*, or *second cloth*) that can be worn as a second wrapper, or folded and tied into stylish headgear (Figure 9.11). The term *kaba*—a local adaptation of the English word "cover"—prob-ably originated within the pidgin trade languages of Africa's western coast.[18] During the nineteenth century, *kaba* was the name given to three very different regional styles that incorporated ele-ments of European dress: Ghana's three-piece *kaba* ensemble; the *kaba sloht* dress of Sierra Le-one (Wass and Broderick 1979); and the smocked *kaba* dress style of Cameroon.[19]

The Ghanaian *kaba* ensemble was cre-ated by the addition of a European-inspired, sewn blouse to the one- or two-piece wrapped ensem-ble that was commonly worn by women in many West African societies. This syncretic ensemble first developed in coastal towns, which had trade relationships with European merchants dating to the late fifteenth century, and in those commu-nities strongly influenced by nineteenth-century European missionary activity. However, the *kaba* did not become an established style in the Asante interior until the early twentieth century, after the imposition of British colonial rule in 1896 pro-vided access to European missionaries and immi-grants from the coast (Gott 2005).

Over the course of the nineteenth century, European-style clothing increasingly became the preferred attire of Ghana's mission-educated elite, while the *kaba* came to be regarded as the dress of women who had no formal schooling (Figure 9.12). However, during the decades preceding Ghana's 1957 independence from Great Britain,

Figure 9.10 An Asante queen mother sitting in state, with the *dansinkran* hairstyle and two-piece wrapped *dansinkran* ensemble, 1990.

Figure 9.11 Mrs. Mary Owusu-Ansah, dressed in a *kaba* ensemble of African-print cloth, 1990.

Figure 9.12 Abetifi seminary: the housemaster, catechist Ofori, with his family, 1896–1912.

the *kaba* ensemble gained new popularity among educated women as a symbol of national pride. On the eve of Ghanaian independence, Beauchamp noted the widespread use of European-produced African wax-prints in Ghana "for making up into

the noble national costume" (Beauchamp 1957: 209), and film footage of the 1957 Independence Ball, broadcast annually on government sponsored television, shows women stylishly attired in *kaba* ensembles worn as evening dress, with the *second cloth*, or *akatasoo*, folded and draped around their shoulders as an elegant matching stole.[20]

In present-day Ghana, fashionable *kaba* ensembles of African-print cloth are worn either daily or for special occasions by women from all walks of life. This practice is especially apparent within the Ashanti Region, where African-print *kaba* ensembles have a particularly strong association with female maturity and women's wealth.

African-print Cloth as Women's Wealth

In Asante, the accumulation and wearing of prestigious African-print cloth is considered emblematic of respectable female maturity and financial well-being. The particular significance of *cloth* accumulation and display for the women of contemporary Asante is based in textiles' historical value as a widely circulated commodity and currency form throughout western and central Africa (Johnson 1980; Martin 1986). In Ghana's Ashanti Region, textiles have also been regarded as a distinctively female form of wealth since at least the mid-eighteenth century (Mikell 1989: 16).

Momentous social and economic changes followed the 1896 imposition of British colonial rule, some of which proved particularly detrimental to the financial security and well-being of Asante women. Women responded to these challenges with new strategies for financial autonomy in which textiles, with their historic status as female wealth, proved to be an important resource.

During the early decades of the twentieth century, Ghanaian agriculture, under colonial influence, made a major shift from customary food crop production to a cocoa-based cash-crop agricultural economy largely controlled by male farmers. As a result, a wife's work on her husband's land ceased to produce crops that would feed their family, because labor on a husband's cocoa farm only yielded monetary profits. Rural wives therefore became dependent on a husband's willingness to contribute a portion of his cocoa profits to the subsistence needs of his wife, or wives, and their children (Allman 2001: 139–40; Roberts 1987: 54).

The concerted efforts of Christian missionaries and colonial institutions to replace Asante's matrilineal kinship system with the Western nuclear model simultaneously succeeded in weakening matrilineal loyalty and "the moral imperative of blood kinship" that customarily ensured support from a woman's brothers and other matrilineal kin. During the course of the twentieth century, Asante women became increasingly dependent on what is generally considered to be the more tenuous marital bond and on financial support contingent on a husband's "continued loyalty and prosperity" (Clark 1999b: 71–72).

Then, in the early 1960s, a sudden drop in the value of cocoa on the international market initiated a chronic state of economic crises that has substantially reduced the real income of most Ghanaians. In subsequent decades, the substantial decline in Ghanaians' real incomes brought about "a dramatic shift in the balance of contributions between husband and wife" that made it even more difficult for wives to obtain the food money and children's school fees customarily expected of husbands and fathers (Clark 1999b: 67, 73–76). The steadily deteriorating economy has led Asante women to regard financial self-reliance as a fundamental requirement for female maturity and motherhood, by providing a mother with the capacity to feed and educate her children if her husband is unable to fulfill his customary paternal obligations (Dinan 1983: 351–2; Manuh 1993: 179).

Good-quality African-print cloth, an asset that only increases in value, provides Asante women with a ready source of cash when funds are needed to pay for children's school fees or to weather times of financial crisis. One such crisis can be the death of a husband.

Within the Asante matrilineal inheritance system, a husband's death may result in members of his extended matrilineage not only laying claim to the husband's property but to jointly acquired marital assets as well.[21] However, on such occasions the widow's cloth and clothing usually remain untouched because of textiles' customary status as relatively sacrosanct forms of female wealth. Conversely, in the event of a wife's death, strong social sanctions will usually prevent her husband from acquiring the wife's clothing and textiles in order to sell them, or present them to another wife or girlfriend. The relatively inviolable wealth embodied in a woman's cloth and clothing thus provides Asante wives with a valuable means of safeguarding financial assets, as well as a strategic means of securing an inheritance for their children.

In the Ashanti Region, women of widely differing financial means are united by their strong interest in acquiring and accumulating good-quality African-print cloth. This distinctive textile has been at the center of Asante women's *cloth* accumulation strategies since the early twentieth century, a period marked by a substantial increase in the importation and sale of African-print cloth.[22] At that time, women also began moving into the previously male-dominated market trade in such prestigious imported goods, which men were abandoning in favor of more lucrative cocoa farming and wage work. Increasing numbers of women began trading in imported cloth, liquor, and tobacco (Clark 1994: 316–18). Soon, cloth trading came to be regarded as not only a distinctly female enterprise, but a profession with the potential for achieving the status of a wealthy woman.

During the 1990s, assessments of female prosperity were, in fact, frequently expressed in terms of the number of African-print cloths a woman owned, as in Mrs. Selina Aggrey's description of her wealthy landlady:

> She is rich! She has a large wardrobe filled with *cloth* . . . She has so much that you would think she is selling it . . . Any new *cloth* that comes, she wants to be the first person to buy it.[23]

This landlady's daughter, she added, was "just like her," with a substantial bank account that was equaled by the cash value of the daughter's own stockpile of over 150 pieces of high-quality African-print cloth.

THE MEANINGS OF DRESS

Women's *Cloth* Wealth and the Asante Display Imperative

Given the long-established nature of Asante culture's emphasis on high-status display, it is not surprising that women are expected to demonstrate their capacity to acquire and accumulate good-quality African-print cloth. A woman's dress receives particular scrutiny after she reaches adulthood, marries, and bears children. It is generally said that a woman who fails to wear a sufficient number of good-quality African-print ensembles or who wears only the cheaper grades of African-print cloth will be "laughed at," or ridiculed.

Kaba ensembles of African-print cloth are endowed with particular significance because of their capacity to communicate unequivocally their economic worth (Boelman and van Holthoon 1973: 247; Gott 1994: 59–67). When Kumasi women comment on an African-print *kaba* ensemble they see worn at a social event or by a woman they pass on the street, their evaluation characteristically begins with an astute appraisal of the ensemble's monetary value. Such assessments are facilitated by two important characteristics of African-print ensembles, one being the standard six-yard unit in which African-print cloth is sold and worn. The second characteristic is the well-established ranking system, based on quality and price, for different kinds of African-print cloth.[24]

Most women keep well informed as to the current market value of the varieties of African-print cloth. The simple statement, *"eye Holland"* ("it is *Holland*," i.e., a Dutch wax-print), is an appreciative evaluation of the highest order because imported Dutch wax-print *cloth* has long been regarded as the most prestigious African-print cloth in Ghana, with the required six yards costing 400,000 to 500,000 cedis (US$48 to US$60 in 2003, in an economy where the average annual income is equivalent to US$350). A woman who wears only cheaper grades of locally produced African-print cloth, costing 60,000 to 70,000 cedis (US$7 to US$8 in 2003), is subject to ridicule, and for this reason, all but the very poorest women

endeavor to have at least one ensemble of Dutch wax-print *cloth*. Women are considered to spend a significant percentage of their income on *cloth* and clothing. In the words of one Kumasi woman, "after chop [food] money, the dressing is next."[25]

Husbands are expected to provide gifts of *cloth* and clothing, or the money to purchase these items, particularly upon marriage and childbirth, and as a customary gift at Christmas. Married men, who may have more than one wife in this polygynous society, report feeling considerable pressure to provide their wives with African-print cloth, citing such demands as a common source of marital stress for financially strapped husbands. Yet, as one sympathetic husband observed, Asante women, especially those living within the urban sophistication of Kumasi, feel keenly aware of social imperatives to dress well and perhaps above their means. A good husband, he explained, must try to help his wife acquire good-quality African-print cloth.[26]

However, most Asante women find men's gifts insufficient in meeting social demands for dressing fashionably and well. Women instead rely more heavily on their own financial initiative for acquiring a respectable quantity of good-quality African-print cloth. During adolescence, girls also begin receiving assistance in this endeavor by occasional gifts of *cloth* from their mother or other family members.[27] And, although younger, unmarried women generally wear *ataadee* ("dress") ensembles of less prestigious *material*, they work to acquire African-print cloth to wear after marriage, and particularly after giving birth.

In the Ashanti Region, a woman's attainment of motherhood has long been an occasion for distinctive personal display. In the past, new mothers would paint their bodies with *hyere* (a local white clay) in order to express their "victory" and "joy" in successfully giving birth (Figure 9.13).[28] In present-day Asante, new mothers wear fashionable *kaba* ensembles of white (*fufuo*) African-print cloth (i.e., white with indigo patterning) to convey their victory and success (Figure 9.14).[29] A new mother is, in fact, expected to wear a substantial number of new *kaba* ensembles of good-quality wax-print *cloth*, particularly following the birth of her first child.

Figure 9.13 An Asante mother, "dressed in her best attire, with shoulders, breasts, and arms smeared over with white clay," holding her newborn infant during the "outdooring" rites customarily held eight days following childbirth.

Figure 9.14 A new mother dressed in "victory white" attending the postnatal clinic at Kumasi Central Hospital, 1990.

One friend in her mid-twenties described how she began buying and saving wax-print *cloth* during her adolescence in order to fulfill the African-print cloth display imperative that accompanies marriage and motherhood. "If you are a young woman who gives birth and are not rich enough to buy *cloth*," Julie explained, "then people will laugh at you, saying that you are not of an age to give birth."[30] In 1990, Mrs. Bea Asare, a new mother, described the social consequences of failing to meet social demands for wearing a sufficient quantity of new *kaba* ensembles of higher quality African-print cloth:

> When a woman is pregnant, she will find every avenue to get *cloth* so people won't talk against her . . . Especially in Kumasi when you give birth, they will start counting the *Holland* [Dutch wax-print *cloth*] you wear, because they know that *Holland* is the most expensive *cloth*. If you don't

wear many, they will say, "Oh, when she brought forth, she only put on two *Holland* cloths!"[31]

Fashion as Status-seeking Display

Fashion, with its changeability and aesthetic appeal, has become an important component in women's display of African-print cloth. Within Asante, the desire to appear fashionably attired in prestigious *cloth* is generally regarded as a distinctly female characteristic. In the words of an oft-repeated phrase, "while a man will be content to wear the same shirt and trousers for two years, a woman will always be wanting the newest *cloth* and the newest styles."

Fashionable new styles develop and spread rapidly throughout Kumasi's bustling urban environment in a grassroots fashion system that is facilitated by individuals commissioning most of their clothing from local seamstresses or tailors. Male tailors, considered to excel in sewing Western-styled garments because of training in sewing men's tailored styles, are often sought after by younger women desiring dresses or skirt and top (*ataadee*) ensembles. However, female seamstresses are considered to possess greater expertise in designing and sewing the *kaba* ensembles that become an increasingly important part of a woman's wardrobe as she matures, marries, and bears children. As a friend, Mrs. Angelina Bilson, explained:

> While a young woman may spend all her money sewing new dress styles with a tailor, no mature woman is going to spend her money sewing dresses of *material*. If she has the money, she will buy *cloth* and take it to her seamstress to sew *kaba*.[32]

Women distinguish between two categories of *kaba* ensembles: *simple* styles and *fanciful*, or *complicated*, styles. Simple styles are said to be more modest and "ladylike." Most women tend to have their better quality, imported wax-print *cloth* sewn in simple *kaba* styles that will remain in fashion for two or three years (Figure 9.15). Fanciful, or complicated, styles are more distinctive and intricate (Figure 9.16). Most women only use less expensive local wax-print or imitation wax-print *cloth* for these relatively short-lived styles. However, the Asante *hightimer*, or *preman*, is noted for wearing fanciful *kaba* styles of costly, imported wax-print *cloth*.

The fanciful styles favored by *premanfoo* are distinctive in several important ways. First, fanciful styles are more expensive to sew, both in terms of the higher labor costs of such intricate styles and because of the large quantity of expensive decorative materials that are often used, such as yards of satin ribbon, or gold braid and thread. Fanciful *kaba* styles are also emblematic of the wearer's wealth not only due to the expense in sewing a particular style, but because of the extravagance of sewing valuable *cloth* into

Figure 9.15 Mrs. Nora Kyei dressed in a three-piece *kaba* ensemble sewn into a simple style, 1990.

Figure 9.16 A Kumasi woman attending a funeral dressed in a *kaba* ensemble sewn into a complicated, or fanciful style, 1990.

a distinctive, fanciful style that will remain stylish for only a short period of time, compared to the lasting stylishness of simpler fashions. Finally, the fanciful *kaba* styles associated with *premanfoo* may be described as "extraordinary" because of more provocative and revealing features, such as a low-cut neckline or short *slit* skirt. In Ghana, excessive exposure of the female body is considered improper and is said to be the behavior of "prostitutes," of women who want to attract the attention and patronage of men.

Yet despite such negative associations, the fanciful styles associated with the *preman* may, in fact, become popular fashions worn by numerous women at important social events in Kumasi, albeit in a somewhat modified form (see Figure 9.17; compare with Figure 9.5). In the 1990s, Abidjan, capital of neighboring Côte d'Ivoire, was reputed to be the source of many of the more fanciful, flamboyant styles favored by the *preman*. Wealthy Asante market women on business trips to Abidjan might commission new *kaba* styles there, and upon returning home, these new styles would be seen and reproduced, often with certain modifications, by Kumasi seamstresses.

Certain popular fashions, such as the low-cut *show-your-shoulders* neckline and the stiffened *big sleeve* of the 1990s, have served to accentuate the physical "greatness" or "majesty" (*kesee*) that is the Asante ideal. The term *kesee*, often appearing in Akan proverbs referring to all-powerful entities, such as *Onyame ye kesee* ("God is great," i.e., all-powerful), or in proverbial allusions to individuals of high position, such as *Aboa kesee na ne nwoma so* ("A large animal's skin is also large"), expresses Asante conceptual linkages between social and physical greatness.

In terms of the Asante *preman*, Madame Akua Abrafi, a Kumasi trader, describes *premanfoo* as women who "make everything *kesee* . . . they make everything about their appearance higher than others . . . big sleeves, big earrings."[33] During the 1990s, when fashionable *kaba* blouses featured an enlarged *big sleeve* stiffened with interfacing, the *kaba* styles favored by *premanfoo* exhibited the most extreme versions of the *big sleeve*, resulting in *"kesee" kaba* styles that served not only as a means of augmenting the physical presence of the *preman*, but of asserting the superior social standing of the *preman*, as well.

An additional, associated meaning of *kesee* is "stoutness," or "fatness" (as it is often spoken of in English), a term used in describing the ideal body shape for the mature Asante woman. Greeting a woman with the complimentary statement *"woaye kese paa"* ("you have grown nicely fat") is a way of telling a woman that she is "looking very attractive." A plump, rounded appearance is considered visible evidence of a woman's inner state, indicating wealth, a good marriage, and a contented, peaceful state of mind. Because of the importance accorded plumpness as a visible sign of a woman's personal well-being and success, some Kumasi women have reportedly taken steroids in order to retain water and achieve the appearance of "fatness."[34] *Kaba* styles revealing such ideal plumpness, such as the *show-your-shoulders kaba* blouse style, are understandably popular (Figure 9.18).

Figure 9.17 A new mother dressed in a modest version of a fanciful and revealing *preman* style, 1990.

Figure 9.18 Mrs. Gladys Prempeh (right) with her close friend, wearing the popular *show-your-shoulders* neckline, 1990.

Fashionable Display and the Controversial *Preman*

For those women committed to Asante custom and cultural values, who find *cloth* accumulation a valuable strategy for financial security, the wearing of costly, prestigious dress is regarded as emblematic of the hard work and determination of an ideal Asante woman. Such a sentiment was expressed by one prosperous market trader in 1990: "Dressing is expensive! You can't pay 25,000 cedis for a shoe [roughly US$72 at the time] unless you work hard. So when people see you wearing this expensive shoe, they will say, 'that woman works hard!'"[35]

However, not all women in the Ashanti Region participate wholeheartedly in this local display system with its emphasis on expensive dress, especially those Asante and non-Asante civil servants and teachers whose education, as well as limited incomes, often place them at odds with Asante customary status-seeking behaviors. These women tend to regard all contemporary *poatwa*

displays, especially the extravagant dress and behavior of the *preman*, as highly visible instances of the "wastefulness" and "backwardness" of Asante excess and ostentation. For such women, the display imperative associated with the Ashanti Region's fashion system is an unnecessary burden, not a status-seeking opportunity.

In fact, pejorative comments concerning *preman* dress and behavior reflect an ongoing critical commentary within Asante society concerning the illusory nature of elite prestige displays. Thus, although the "gorgeous dress" of a *preman* may elicit an admiring appraisal that the wearer is "a very rich woman," her costly dress may also evoke the wry observation that *premanfoo* are only able to dress so beautifully by borrowing or "hiring" [renting] the clothing of other women. Such skepticism concerning the substantiality of conspicuously displayed wealth is not new in Asante culture, being articulated by such popular proverbs as "Empty barrels make the most noise" (*Ankore a hwee nnim no na ekasa dodo*), and the proverb "You say you have become fat, but you are full of water" (*Wose waye kese, nso woahye nsuo*).

Such criticisms of *premanfoo* have implications beyond questions of dress as an element of *poatwa* displays of wealth. Many women are also highly critical of the deviance of *preman* behaviors from the social expectations for a modest Asante woman. For one well-educated Kumasi woman, the *preman* constitutes a particularly scandalous type of person, known "by the way she dresses and the way she moves around." She characterized *premanfoo* as being:

> . . . those women who want these fanciful styles [and who] move about spending a lot of money on drinks and so forth, having fun by themselves. They like moving with men, [they] can't stay at one place, you meet them at any funeral, any social gathering.[36]

She also described the fanciful styles she associated with the *preman* as being "extraordinary" (i.e., highly visible and even scandalous), with low-cut, revealing necklines and *slit* skirts cut scandalously high. The wearing of such revealing styles causes some women and men to say that *premanfoo* behave "like prostitutes" by dressing in a provocative manner in order to attract male attention and financial favors.[37]

The concept of the flamboyantly wealthy *preman* as being "like a prostitute" has some illuminating parallels in early-twentieth-century Ghana. At that time, when colonialism and the new cocoa-based agricultural economy placed married women at a distinct disadvantage, Allman found that Asante women who chose to remain unmarried in order to pursue their own financial autonomy were frequently accused of being prostitutes. Their efforts to remain independent from male control and authority caused great unease among many local chiefs, who actually imprisoned women until they consented to marry (Allman 2001: 130–33). During the early colonial period, Ghanaian women who migrated into towns in order to pursue wealth and autonomy outside the confines of marriage and patriarchal village life were criticized for their acquisitiveness and promiscuity, as in the 1930s *highlife* song quoted by Akyeampong, "Wo pe tam wo npe ba" ("You like *cloth* but you don't want children") (Akyeampong 2000: 228).

In contemporary Asante, the independence of *premanfoo* from the control of husbands, as well as male and female elders, is a major factor in *preman* impropriety. Although Asante is a matrilineal society, in which inheritance passes through the maternal line, senior men have customarily exercised significant control over the women of their matrilineage. The twentieth-century introduction of Christianity, with its emphasis on the Euro-American model of a nuclear family under the authority of the husband and father, has provided a new, even more restrictive ideology that inhibits female autonomy. Mrs. Mary Owusu-Ansah, a retired civil servant, expressed the association of *preman* dress with social marginality:

> When they call a woman a *preman*, it means she has been a hooligan before. It is not good. They are those women who do not respect themselves, married women who are free to be approached by men with their dressing . . . If you are a married woman, you can't dress like that . . . Some women, as soon as you see them, you know that they are not under anyone, a husband or family member. The average woman can't go out in such a manner. A woman who respects her husband can't go out that way. If girls come from good homes, they don't dress in such a manner . . . *Preman* people are always the people who wear gorgeous things everywhere. They will go to a funeral not wearing funeral costume . . . They won't abide by what others say.

However, when questioned further, Mrs. Owusu-Ansah made a marked distinction between the propriety required of married women, daughters, or nieces, and the greater latitude acceptable for an unmarried, financially independent woman. When asked if an unmarried woman could be a *preman*, she responded:

> Yes, a woman can if she is not married, is well-to-do and controls herself. If she is a wealthy woman who can do what she likes. If she's the breadwinner of her family; if she is wealthy, sometimes has her own

THE MEANINGS OF DRESS

building. She is an all-around woman. You see her with necklaces, bangles, high heels, gorgeously dressed. She can talk as she likes.[38]

Conclusion

Asante *premanfoo* flaunt their wealth and independence by wearing fanciful *kaba* styles of prestigious African wax-print cloth. Such fashionable, high-visibility displays of *cloth* wealth and superior status constitute a distinctly female mode of Asante *poatwa* display, which is based in the special status of African-print cloth and clothing as a major form of female wealth. Yet, the revealing styles favored by the flamboyant *preman* also represent a freedom from customary restraints on female behavior and sexuality that has provoked the notoriety associated with the Asante *preman*.

Most women do not engage in such extreme displays of financial well-being and autonomy. However, virtually all women living in Ghana's Ashanti Region actively pursue the accumulation and fashionable display of good-quality African-print cloth. Some, such as the Asante *premanfoo*, are enthusiastic participants in this endeavor. Other women may, in fact, voice displeasure at the social pressure to acquire and wear expensive *cloth*, as in the following conversation in 1990 among three schoolteachers—Angelina, Bea, and Nora.[39] Bea, an Asante woman who had recently returned from teaching near the coastal capital of Accra, complained that:

> In Accra, people don't care what you put on, but when you come to Kumasi, people are very particular about dressing . . . Illiteracy is the reason. For people in the Ashanti Region, education came late. In Accra, people don't care, but in Kumasi there is a special *cloth* and everyone would want it, and even styles, everyone would want to sew that style with even one in that particular *cloth*.

Yet, even within the context of this sometimes heated discussion about the burdensome pressures for women to dress fashionably and well, Bea concluded by drawing attention to the particularly fashionable character of her friend and fellow schoolteacher Angelina, exclaiming *"Angie pe laif paa!"* ("Angie likes *life*, i.e., dressing fashionably, very much!"); and Bea commented on the special interest in fashionable dress that she observed in her own four-year-old daughter, Amma Seiwaa, who regularly expressed special admiration for Angelina's stylishness:

> Amma Seiwaa is always talking about money and dressing . . . Angie is her idol. Amma Seiwaa used to come to school and when we came back home, all she would talk about is Angie and her dressing, saying *"Angie pe laif!"* . . . When we are going out, every person Amma Seiwaa sees, she will comment on their dressing—their hairdo, shoes, dresses.

"She's like Abigail [Nora's six-year-old daughter]!" Angelina interjected, as Bea continued:

> I tell Amma Seiwaa, "You like dressing too much," but my husband says, "She's just like you. *O pe laif na nso wo pe laif*" ("She likes fashionable dress because you also like fashion") . . . When going to church on Sunday, Amma Seiwaa will select her own dress on Saturday . . . I'm embarrassed, she's too young. But my mother says I was like that, too.

Thus, in a discussion critical of the dress display imperatives for women in the Ashanti Region and of the extravagant, flamboyant fashions of the Asante *preman*, these three schoolteachers also admitted their own special interests in dressing well, as well as their daughters' precocious preoccupation with *life*—the fashionable stylishness considered to be a fundamental feature of contemporary Asante womanhood.

Epilogue

During the late 1980s and early 1990s, women invested significant percentages of their income in costly Dutch wax-print textiles and more affordable West African factory prints. By the late

1990s, Ghana's worsening economy began limiting women's acquisition of African-print cloth; although money or *cloth* sent by family members living abroad provided one means of continuing to dress well. By 2007, new, cheaper versions of African-print cloth manufactured in China had become increasingly popular, enabling women to continue wearing fashionable African-print *kaba* ensembles. At the same time, world fashions, especially imported second-hand clothing, have become increasingly popular not only with Ghanaian men and youth, but with a growing percentage of middle-aged women who now largely reserve their African-print ensembles for church, funerals, and special occasions.

References

Addae, Gloria. 1963[1956]. "The Retailing of Imported Textiles in the Accra Market." Ibadan, Nigeria: Nigerian Institute of Social and Economic Research.

Akyeampong, Emmanuel. 2000. "'Wo pe tam won pe ba' ('You like cloth but you don't want children'): Urbanization, Individualism, and Gender Relations in Colonial Ghana, c. 1900–39." In David M. Anderson and Richard Rathbone (eds) *Africa's Urban Past*, pp. 222–34. Oxford: James Currey.

Allman, Jean. 2001. "Rounding Up Spinsters: Gender Chaos and Unmarried Women in Colonial Asante." In Dorothy L. Hodgson and Sheryl A. McCurdy (eds) *"Wicked" Women and the Reconfiguration of Gender in Africa*, pp. 130–48. Portsmouth, NH: Heinemann.

Alpern, Stanley. 1995. "What the Africans Got for Their Slaves: A Master List of European Trade Goods." *History in Africa* 22: 5–43.

Arhin, Kwame. 1990. "Trade, Accumulation, and the State in Asante in the Nineteenth Century." *Africa* 60(4): 524–37.

Arhin, Kwame. 1994. "The Economic Implications of Transformations in Akan Funeral Rites." *Africa* 64(3): 307–22.

Beauchamp, P. C. 1957. "A Gay Garb for Ghana." *West Africa* March 2, 41(2081): 209.

Bickford, Kathleen E. 1997. *Everyday Patterns: Factory-printed Cloth of Africa*. Kansas City, MO: University of Missouri-Kansas City.

Boelman, V. J. and F. L. van Holthoon. 1973. "African Dress in Ghana." *Kroniek Van Afrika* (Leiden) 3: 236–58.

Bowdich, T. Edward. 1966[1819]. *Mission from Cape Coast to Ashantee*. London: Frank Cass & Co.

Buah, F. K. 1998. *A History of Ghana*. London: MacMillan Education.

Christaller, J. G. 1933. *Dictionary of the Asante and Fante Language called Tshi (Twi)*, 2nd ed., revised and enlarged. Basel: Basel Evangelical Missionary Society.

Clark, Gracia. 1994. *Onions Are My Husband: Survival and Accumulation by West African Market Women*. Chicago, IL: University of Chicago Press.

Clark, Gracia. 1999a. "Mothering, Work, and Gender in Urban Asante Ideology and Practice." *American Anthropologist* 101(4): 717–29.

Clark, Gracia. 1999b. "Negotiating Asante Family Survival in Kumasi, Ghana." *Africa* 69(1): 66–86.

Cole, Herbert M. and Doran H. Ross. 1977. *The Arts of Ghana*. Museum of Cultural History. Los Angeles, CA: University of California.

Collins, E. J. 1976. "Ghanaian Highlife." *African Arts* 10(1): 62–68, 100.

Cordwell, Justine M. 1979. "Appendix: The Use of Printed Batiks by Africans." In Justine M. Cordwell and Ronald A. Schwartz (eds.) *The Fabrics of Culture*, pp. 495–96. The Hague: Mouton.

De Marees, Pieter. 1987[1602]. *Description and Historical Account of the Gold Kingdom of Guinea*. Trans. and edited by Albert van Dantzig and Adam Jones. The British Academy. London: Oxford University Press.

De Witte, Marleen. 2001. *Long Live the Dead! Changing Funeral Celebrations in Asante, Ghana*. Amsterdam: Aksant Academic Publishers.

De Witte, Marleen. 2003. "Money and Death: Funeral Business in Asante, Ghana." *Africa* 73(4): 531–59.

Dinan, Carmel. 1983. "Sugar Daddies and Gold-Diggers: The Whitecollar Single Women in Accra." In Christine Oppong (ed.) *Female and Male in West Africa*, pp. 344–66. London: George Allen and Unwin.

Domowitz, Susan. 1992. "Wearing Proverbs: Anyi Names for Printed Factory Cloth." *African Arts* 25(3): 82–87, 104.

Garrard, Timothy F. 1989. *Gold of Africa: Jewellery and Ornaments from Ghana, Côte d'Ivoire, Mali, and Senegal*. Barbier-Mueller Museum. Munich: Prestel-Verlag.

Gott, Suzanne. 1994. "In Celebration of the Female: Dress, Aesthetics, Performance, and Identity in Contemporary Asante." PhD dissertation, Indiana University, Bloomington.

Gott, Suzanne. 2003. "Golden Emblems of Maternal Benevolence: Transformations of Form and Meaning in Akan Regalia." *African Arts* 36(1): 66–81, 93–96.

Gott, Suzanne. 2005. "The Dynamics of Stylistic Innovation and Cultural Continuity in Ghanaian Women's Fashions." In Ilsemargret Luttman (ed.) *Mode in Afrika*, pp. 61–70, 79. Hamburg: Museum für Völkerkunde.

Hagan, George P. 1970. "A Note on Akan Colour Symbolism." *Research Review* (Ghana, University College Legon: Institute of African Studies) 7(1): 8–14.

Johnson, Marion. 1980. "Cloth as Money: The Cloth Strip Currencies of Africa." In Dale Idiens and K. G. Ponting (eds) *Textiles of Africa*, pp. 193–202. Bath: Pasold Research Fund.

Jones, Adam. 1995. "Female Slave-owners on the Gold Coast: Just a Matter of Money?" In Stephan Palmié (ed.) *Slave Cultures and the Cultures of Slavery*, pp. 100–11. Knoxville, TN: University of Tennessee Press.

Kyerematen, A. A. Y. 1964. *Panoply of Ghana: Ornamental Art in Ghanaian Tradition and Culture.* New York: Praeger.

LeBlanc, Marie Nathalie. 2000. "Versioning Womanhood and Muslimhood: 'Fashion' and the Life Course in Contemporary Bouaké, Côte d'Ivoire." *Africa* 70(3): 442–81.

Littrell, Mary A. 1977. "Ghanaian Wax Print Textiles: Viewpoints of Designers, Distributors, Sellers, and Consumers." PhD dissertation, Purdue University, West Lafayette, Indiana.

Loyer, Godefroy. 1935[1714]. "Relation du voyage du Royaume d'Issyny." In Paul Roussier (ed.) *L'Etablissment d'Issiny 1687–1702*, pp. 109–235. Publications du Comité d'Études Historiques et Scientifiques de l'Afrique Occidentale Française, Série A, No. 3. Paris: Librairie Larose.

Manuh, Takyiwaa. 1993. "Women, the State and Society Under the PNDC." In W. Gyimah-Boadi (ed.) *Ghana under PNDC Rule*, pp. 176–95. Chippenham: Council for the Development of Social Science Research in Africa.

Manuh, Takyiwaa. 1995. "Changes in Marriage and Funeral Exchanges among the Asante: A Case Study from Kona, Afigya-Kwabre." In Jane Guyer (ed.) *Money Matters: Instability, Values, and Social Payments in the Modern History of West African Communities*, pp. 188–201. London: James Currey.

Manuh, Takyiwaa. 1998. "Diasporas, Unities, and the Marketplace: Tracing Changes in Ghanaian Fashion." *Journal of African Studies* 16(1):13–19.

Martin, Phyllis M. 1986. "Power, Cloth, and Currency on the Loango Coast." *African Economic History* 15: 1–12.

Mato, Daniel. 1986. "Clothed in Symbol—The Art of Adinkra Among the Akan of Ghana." PhD dissertation, Indiana University, Bloomington.

McCaskie, T. C. 1983. "Accumulation, Wealth and Belief in Asante History, I. To the Close of the Nineteenth Century." *Africa* 53(1): 23–42.

McCaskie, T. C. 1986. "Accumulation: Wealth and Belief in Asante History: II The Twentieth Century." *Africa* 56(1): 3–23.

McLeod, M. D. 1976. "Verbal Elements in West African Art." *Quaderni Poro* 1: 85–102.

Mikell, Gwendolyn. 1989. *Cocoa and Chaos in Ghana.* New York: Paragon House.

Nielsen, Ruth T. 1974. "The History and Development of Wax-printed Textiles Intended for West Africa and Zaire." MA thesis, Michigan State University, East Lansing.

Nielsen, Ruth T. 1979. "The History and Development of Wax-printed Textiles Intended for West Africa and Zaire." In Justine M. Cordwell and Ronald A. Schwartz (eds) *The Fabrics of Culture*, pp. 467–98. The Hague: Mouton.

Pedler, Frederick. 1974. *The Lion and the Unicorn in Africa: A History of the Origins of the United Africa Company, 1787–1931.* London: Heinemann.

Picton, John. 1999. *The Art of African Textiles: Technology, Tradition, and Lurex.* London: Lund Humphries.

Posnansky, Merrick. 1987. "Prelude to Akan Civilization." *The Golden Stool: Studies of the Asante Center and Periphery, Anthropological Papers of the American Museum of Natural History* 65(1): 14–22.

Rabine, Leslie W. 2002. *The Global Circulation of African Fashion.* Oxford: Berg.

Rattray, Robert S. 1927. *Religion and Art in Ashanti.* Oxford: Clarendon Press.

Roberts, Penelope A. 1987. "The State and the Regulation of Marriage: Sefwi Wiawso (Ghana), 1900–40." In Haleh Afshar (ed.) *Women, State, and Ideology: Studies from Africa and Asia*, pp. 48–69. Binghamton, NY: State University of New York Press.

Ross, Doran H. 1977. "The Iconography of Asante Sword Ornaments." *African Arts* 9(1): 16–25, 90–91.

Ross, Doran H. 1998. *Wrapped in Pride: Ghanaian Kente and African American Identity.* UCLA Fowler Museum of Cultural History Textile Series, No. 2. Los Angeles, CA: UCLA Fowler Museum of Cultural History.

Ross, Doran H. 2002. *Akan Gold from the Glassell Collection.* Houston, TX: Museum of Fine Arts.

Spencer, Anne M. 1983. *In Praise of Heroes: Contemporary African Commemorative Cloth.* Newark, NJ: Newark Museum.

Steiner, Christopher B. 1985. "Another Image of Africa: Toward an Ethnohistory of European Cloth Marketed in West Africa, 1873–1960." *Ethnohistory* 32(2): 91–110.

Sundström, Lars. 1974. *The Exchange Economy of Pre-colonial Tropical Africa.* New York: St Martin's Press.

van der Geest, Sjaak and Nimrod K. Asante-Darko. 1982. "The Political Meaning of Highlife Songs in Ghana." *African Studies Review* 25(1): 27–35.

Warren, Dennis M. and J. Kweku Andrews. 1977. "An Ethno-scientific Approach to Akan Arts and Aesthetics." *Working Papers in the Traditional Arts*, No. 3: 1–42.

Wass, Betty M. 1979. "Yoruba Dress in Five Generations of a Lagos Family." In Justine M. Cordwell and Ronald A. Schwartz (eds) *The Fabrics of Culture*, pp. 331–48. The Hague: Mouton.

Wass, Betty M. and S. Modupe Broderick. 1979. "The Kaba Sloht." *African Arts* 12(3): 62–5, 96.

Wilks, Ivor. 1962. "A Medieval Trade-Route from the Niger to the Gulf of Guinea." *Journal of African History* 3(2): 337–41.

Wilks, Ivor. 1975. *Asante in the Nineteenth Century: The Structure and Evolution of a Political Order.* Cambridge: Cambridge University Press.

Wilks, Ivor. 1979. "The Golden Stool and the Elephant Tail: An Essay on Wealth in Asante." *Research in Economic Anthropology* 2: 1–36.

Yankah, Kwesi. 1989. *The Proverb in the Context of Akan Rhetoric: A Theory of Proverb Praxis.* New York: Peter Lang.

Endnotes

1. Use of the term *hightimer* for those engaged in an extravagant, elite lifestyle, is conceptually linked to *highlife*, the name given to the elite cosmopolitan lifestyle and syncretic Ghanaian-European dance-orchestra music that developed among Ghana's early-twentieth-century educated urban elite (Collins 1976: 62–63).

2. The Asante constitute the largest subgroup of the linguistically and culturally related Akan peoples of southern Ghana. Their language is Asante Twi, the most widely spoken dialect of the Akan language.

3. See the following selected works on Asante leadership regalia: Cole and Ross (1977), Garrard (1989), Kyerematen (1964), and Ross (1977, 1998, 2002).

4. Similar characterizations of Asante funerals are made by Arhin (1994: 307) and by Manuh (1995: 188).

5. Interview with Mr. M. H. Frempong, Kumasi, June 1990.

6. This practice had historical precedents among the Akan peoples living on the coast. A 1602 account by Dutch merchant Pieter de Marees describes and illustrates a "triumphal ceremony" held to celebrate a man's rise to the status of "Brenipono," or "Nobleman" (1987[1602]: 167). French prefect Fr. Godefroy Loyer's 1714 account of his visit to a different coastal region records one male trader's prayer for "Brembi," or *obirempon* status (1935[1714]: 213), indicating that similar ennoblement ceremonies may have taken place among various coastal peoples.

7. In present-day Asante, the honorific title of *obirempon* ("valiant, powerful man") has a female corollary in the term *obaa barima* ("valiant, manly woman"), which is used for market women who achieve "the level of financial success and economic independence considered essential for men" (Clark 1999a: 722).

8. In Asante, the assumption of "royal" prerogatives by members of the moneyed, rather than royal, elite remains a point of contention that continues to the present day, as in the restrictions concerning the wearing of *ahenemma mpaboa* ("royal children's sandals") by nonroyals at ceremonial and ritual gatherings.

9. Interview with Mr. M. H. Frempong, Kumasi, May 1990.

10. For the Fante, a coastal Akan people, the term for cloth is *ntama*.

11. In this article, the word *cloth* will be italicized when referring to African-print cloth, in keeping with the Asante linguistic convention of using the term *ntoma*, or the English *cloth*, to distinguish African-print cloth from other factory-produced textiles.

12. The Akan practice of assigning names to textile designs has been well documented in respect to the three most valued forms of cloth: locally produced hand-woven *kente* and hand-stamped *adinkra*, as well as imported and, more recently, local factory-produced African-print cloth (Boelman and van Holthoon 1973; Bowdich 1966[1819]; Domowitz 1992; Gott 1994; Mato 1986; Rattray 1927; Ross 1998; Warren and Andrews 1977).

13. The deeper levels of meaning that may be associated with seemingly mundane names is exemplified by the *cloth* Aya ("Fern"), an African-print whose fern-like designs and name are reminiscent of an earlier *adinkra* pattern. In Rattray's discussion of the *adinkra* design Aya, he observed that in addition to "fern," the Asante word *aya* "also means 'I am not afraid of you,' 'I am independent of you,' and the wearer may imply this" by wearing this design (1927: 265). Certain women also find deeper meaning in the *cloth* name Kwadusa, as a metaphorical allusion to matrilineal unity and support.

14. See Gott (1994: 71–106) for an extended discussion of African-print cloth naming practices and Gott (2003) for a discussion of the particular salience of maternal imagery in matrilineal Asante.

15. Interview with Juliana Osei, Kumasi, January 1990.

16. See LeBlanc (2000) for a study of the relationship between dress and Muslim women's life course in Bouaké, Côte d'Ivoire.

17. Asante women's *dansinkran* hairstyle consists of closely cropped and darkened hair, with a shaved, recessed hairline outlined with a mixture of soot and shea butter in order to create a high, clearly delineated forehead.

18. Personal communication, Dr. Kofi Agyekum, Department of Linguistics, University of Ghana, Legon, July 1999.

19. Personal communication, Dr. Virginia DeLancey, African Studies Program, Northwestern University, Evanston, Illinois, September 1995.

20. Personal communication, Mrs. Angelina Bilson, Kumasi, March 1990. See Wass (1979), and LeBlanc (2000), for investigations into the impact of historical change and political identity on dress in Lagos, Nigeria, and in Bouaké, Côte d'Ivoire.

21. In 1985, the national government passed the Intestate Succession Law to ensure that the widow and a man's children receive a portion of his estate. In actual practice, however, the law has had limited effect on customary inheritance practices (De Witte 2001: 173–79).

22. See Boelman and van Holthoon (1973) for more information.

23. Interview with Mrs. Selina Aggrey, Kumasi, June 1990.

24. *African-print cloth* is an umbrella term for three closely related fabrics — *African wax-prints*, *Java prints*, and *fancy prints* — all with designs created to suit consumers' tastes in different regions of western and central Africa: *African wax-prints* are machine-made batiks manufactured in a process that imitates the Javanese handmade batik method. Designs are applied in hot wax or resin to both sides of plain cotton cloth using mechanized rollers. This printing process has been carefully developed to create the imperfections that are distinctive to handmade batiks, such as crackling of the wax or drip spots of wax.

   The fabric is then dyed indigo, leaving a blue pattern on a white background after the wax or resin is removed. Additional colors may then be added by hand blocking or by a special printing run. *Java prints* are high-grade imitations of wax-prints produced by direct roller printing, preceded and/or followed by special dyeing or chemical processing. *Fancy prints* are lower quality wax-print imitations produced by direct roller printing with no additional dyeing or chemical procedures (Bickford 1997; Nielsen 1974, 1979; Picton 1999).

25. Interview with Mrs. Bea Asare, Kumasi, July 1990.

26. Interview with Mr. Maxwell Gyamfi, Kumasi, March 1990.

27. See Manuh concerning the increasingly important role of Ghanaian emigrants' financial contributions and gifts of European-manufactured African-print cloth in keeping "close family members well clothed and able to maintain a semblance of well-being" (1998: 14).

28. See Rattray's documentation of Asante body-painting practices for new mothers (1927: 62) and Hagan's discussion of Akan color symbolism for *fufuo* ("white") (1970: 11–13).

29. Women often compare childbirth with "going off to battle," and describe labor as a perilous event in which the woman or baby may not survive — a fear borne out by the continuing threat of maternal and infant mortality in West Africa. A new mother therefore wears white to signify her victory over death, as well as her joy and success in giving birth.

30. Interview with Juliana Osei, Kumasi, June 1990.

31. Interview with Mrs. Bea Asare, Kumasi, July 1990.

32. Interview with Mrs. Angelina Bilson, Kumasi, September 1990.

33. Interview with Madame Akua Abrafi, Kumasi, September 1990.

34. Personal communication, Dr. John Bilson, Kumasi, July 1990.

35. Interview with Mrs. Gladys Prempeh, Kumasi, November 1990. At that time, 300 to 350 cedis (US$0.85 to US$1) was considered to be the average worker's daily income.

36. Anonymous interview, Kumasi, June 1990.

37. Certain cultural factors, however, complicate assigning the label of prostitute to all women seeking financial favors from men: As Dinan observes, there is a long-established sense of reciprocity associated with customary courtship and marriage, in which men are expected to provide gifts and maintenance in exchange for sexual access (1983: 353). Akyeampong also notes that, given "the traditional context of gender relations among the peoples of southern Ghana, it is not surprising that sexuality became a key resource in women's endeavor to acquire wealth in towns" (2000: 228).

38. Interview with Mrs. Mary Owusu-Ansah, Kumasi, September 1990.

39. Interview with Mrs. Angelina Bilson, Mrs. Bea Asare, and Mrs. Nora Boakye, Kumasi, July 1990.

Discussion Questions

1. How has Asante status been shown historically? By men? By women?
2. Why does fabric play such an important role in the indication of status? Can you think of examples in your own family of status represented by fabric? Specific garment(s)?

FEMALE TRADITION IN A NEW CONTEXT: THE CASE OF THE *KHANGA*

Katalin Medvedev and Lioba Moshi

All ideologies strive for sartorial expressiveness (Eicher et al.,1995; Baker, 1997; Parkins, 2002); socialist ideology is no exception. Dress was a political issue under socialism primarily because of its potential class implications. As a result, socialist leaders all over the former socialist bloc often personally implicated themselves in the official sartorial discourse. They would go to extreme lengths to inform their subjects about their personal views on issues of dress. They prescribed modesty requirements for their subjects as well as provided them with personal and concrete directives on what they deemed "proper socialist attire." Socialist visionaries, such as Julius Nyerere, Mao Zedong, and Fidel Castro to name a few, tried to set an example with their own sartorial presentation.

Socialist dress had to become a tool of projecting the social and economic values of egalitarianism and serve primarily utilitarian purposes. People's sartorial presentation was also meant to testify to the self-reliance, productivity, and successes of the socialist economy. Furthermore, socialist fashion was expected to be visually distinct and markedly different from Western (bourgeois) fashion (Medvedev, 2008, 2009).

In addition, the official socialist sartorial discourse initiated by the aforementioned statesmen had to ensure that it visually conveyed the basic principles of socialism and superiority of socialist morality, which, at least on paper, included gender equality.

The *Khanga*, the Garment of the Female Masses

The *khanga* originated from the coastal areas of East Africa (Hanby and Bygott, 1984). It is a rectangle of pure cotton cloth with a border all around it, usually printed in bold designs and bright colors (Figure 9.19). A *khanga* is as long as one's outstretched arm and wide enough to cover one from neck to knee, or from breast to toe (Hanby and Bygott, 1984). The *khanga*'s earliest form comes from sewing together 6 kerchief squares that had been brought to Africa by Portuguese traders from the Far East (Green, 2005). The designs at that time included a border and a pattern of white spots on a dark background that had the likeness of the local guinea fowl, hence the name *khanga*, which means guinea hen in Swahili (Figure 9.20).

The *khangas* are a symbol of womanhood. After a girl reaches puberty she begins to receive gifts of *khangas* from her family. *Khangas* change hands several times in wedding rituals as well. For example, the mother of the bride gets several *khangas* from her family and friends, during the send-off party of the bride, to thank her for raising her daughter. These gifts are also meant to remind a mother that even though she will miss her daughter, she will not be alone to cope with her loss because her loved ones will continue to be part of her life. The bride's aunt, who traditionally gives away the bride, is also supposed to get a pair of *khangas* from the bridegroom's family as a way of formally establishing and materially solidifying the relationship with the bridegroom's family. These *khangas* are displayed for the wedding assembly and closely examined by the bride's wedding party. The quality and estimated value of these *khangas* provide a way to evaluate the wealth and dedication of the bridegroom's family to the bride and her extended family.

An extended version of this article appeared in the *Paideussis Journal for Interdisciplinary and Cross-Cultural Studies*, edited by Linda Arthur and Andrew Reilly. Reprinted by permission of the authors.

Figure 9.19 Detail of a *khanga* depicting Nyerere. He is referred to as Maliwu, the teacher.

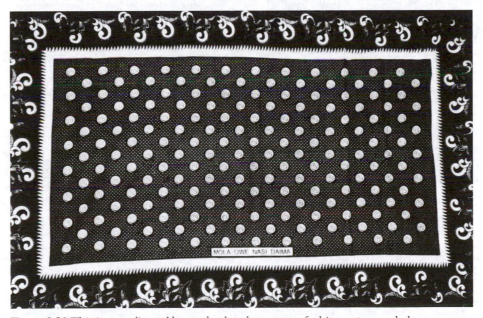

Figure 9.20 This is an ordinary *khanga* that has the pattern of white spots on a dark background. The white spots are supposed to create a likeness to the local guinea fowl. In this *khanga* the background is dark blue and the white spots are accentuated by black circles around them.

After the marriage has been consummated, customarily, the new bride gives a set of *khangas* to her new husband as a sign of belonging, affection and intimacy. In Tanzania *khangas* are always sold in pairs. The young wife will wear one of the set at home as an easily removable wrapper for the upper torso, while her husband will wear the other on his lower torso. However, the man will never be seen in his *khanga* in public, only in the presence of his wife, mostly in the bedroom, which underscores the intimate meaning it carries for the newlyweds. Later, the husband is expected to buy his wife a pair of *khangas* every time he receives a salary. Thus, how many *khangas* a woman possesses indicates her husband's wealth and demonstrates his appreciation for her at the same time.

What Are the Reasons for the Politicization of the *Khanga*?

The colonial project in many parts of Africa was intimately linked to textiles, so much so that researchers even coined a term, "cotton imperialism," to describe this relationship (Perani and Wolf, 1999). Under cotton imperialism, the goal was the exclusive control of African (and Indian) cotton production. Another aim was to create a market for British finished products made from African (or Indian) raw material. For the same reason, it is logical that textiles played and continue to play a very important role in post-colonial Africa, where the production and control of textiles has been a way to assert economic self-reliance and has become a means and symbol of taking charge of the national economy.

In fact, one of the first instances of women's politicization in East Africa in the 1940s took place through their involvement in the so-called *khanga* boycott. During the boycott, coastal women, who were the primary wearers of *khangas*, attempted to put an end to Indian merchants' monopoly of the sale of *khangas* (Mirza and Strobel, 1989). Because these foreign merchants were charging local sellers too much for the privilege of importing and selling *khangas*, East African women began to devise ways to cut out these middle men and order their supply directly from the producers. However, because of the practice of the *purdah*, which is the cultural and religious constrictions of Muslim women and the resulting limitations on their physical mobility, women, after a while, were unable to continue to bring in the shipments from the ports themselves and the boycott ended. Despite the defeat, the boycott made the *khanga* a politically charged dress item already prior to socialism.

How Did the *Khanga* Change under Socialism?

Women's socialist sartorial makeover in Tanzania was not as radical as men's. Most women continued to wear *khangas* that had already been popular before Nyerere's ascendance to power. Nyerere's social changes did not affect this dress for a number of reasons. First, the *khanga* had already been embraced by the people before independence. However, as socialist dress, it had to convey new messages. Before independence, written words on the *khanga* expressed social messages or what was going on in the community, together with proverbial and traditional wisdom (Green, 2005). Under socialism, the *khanga* became an important means of communicating political messages (Figure 9.21).

So, *khanga* texts often served as literal political billboards, commissioned by parties and used in political rallies as means of identification of party affiliations. At political rallies women were either wearing such *khangas* or threw a *khanga* with a political inscription over their shoulders. The *khanga* has also been used to mobilize people to support public health campaigns as well as creating awareness about particular development projects (Hanby and Bygott, 1984). *Khangas*, thus, were used as a utilitarian, low-cost way of campaigning and convenient means of communicating political content to the masses.

The second reason for Nyerere's support of the *khanga* was that it was the closest any female dress type could come to national dress in the

Figure 9.21 This is a part of a typical *khanga* that was used as a political billboard. The background is light blue; the other colors are yellow, dark blue, black and white. The little images are self-explanatory. They stand for the achievements of the new socialist Tanzanian state, such as its defense, industry, energy production, technical expertise, high-quality produce, telecommunication, transportation, agriculture, information service, as well as its medical system.

ethnically diverse Tanzania (there are 129 ethnic groups in Tanzania), so the *khanga* was used as an important "nationalist tool of empowerment and self-expression." The khanga was also more modern than "bark clothes" or animal skins that women used to wear in the past (Ivaska, 2004).

The third reason for Nyerere's approval of the *khanga* may have been that over time it became *the* garment of the female masses because it was utilitarian, multifunctional, versatile and affordable. *Khangas* were made of relatively cheap cotton fabrics and could be re-draped for all types of work—especially agricultural—and social functions. For example, the *khanga* was used as a protective layer over other clothes or to cradle a baby against one's back while working around the house or in the fields (Green, 2005). In addition, *khangas* were not only imported, but often produced by local manufacturers, which was another important consideration why Nyerere supported it.

The *khanga* was the symbol of Tanzania's educational success as well. Women's education

especially was minimal in Tanzania before independence. Therefore, the proverbial, commemorative, and educational messages *khangas* displayed proved that the new, socialist Tanzania was literate and cared about mass education. In fact, when Tanzania gained its independence in 1961, 80 percent of its population was illiterate, but in 1985, at Nyerere's resignation, in marked contrast, 85 percent of adults could read and write, making Tanzania's literacy rate the highest on the continent (Smith, 1986).

The *khanga* remained the visual icon of proper African womanhood under socialism. Other types of female garments, because of their Western and urban associations, seemed to have sparked Nyerere's ideological ire throughout his presidency. For example, on Nov. 1, 1968, *Time* magazine published a short report on Tanzania, titled *Battle of the Minis*, stating that, in the streets of Dar es Salaam, "an angry screaming mob halted buses and dragged off African girls wearing tight dresses and mini-skirts." The report described the phenomenon as a "cultural revolution, African style." What the anonymous reporter refers to is that President Julius Nyerere has decreed that Tanzania shall copy Mao Tse Tung's Great Proletarian Cultural Revolution, which included the rejection of all things foreign. The "Operation Vijana" to prohibit mini-skirts, wigs, skin-lightening creams and other cosmetics that the journalist refers to was carried out by the TANU Youth League's mostly male members (Ivaska, 2004; Ross, 2008). Although many Tanzanian women, especially university students and young female urban professionals, fought back and staged loud protests, demanding a woman's right to choose what to wear, Nyerere and his followers remained unconvinced and unyielding in their verdict: the "un-African" mini-skirt had to go because it symbolized Western decadence, the "cultural enslavement of the African," and was "antithetical to Tanzania's national culture" (Ivaska, 2004:104). In sum, Nyerere likely left the traditional *khanga* alone, because he might have viewed it as a convenient means of political propaganda, a symbol of educational progress and also a means of reinforcing traditional and new socialist morality and values.

Conclusion

Under socialism, in Tanzania, just like in any other part of the socialist bloc, dress had a metaphorical role. It was an ideologically charged and highly politicized medium. It was a symbol of ideological unity, economic independence and self-sufficiency, as well as national and cultural cohesion. Because of these multiple functions, its control by the highest political leadership seemed to be imperative and had to be absolute.

At first, the Tanzanian socialist subjects subscribed to Nyerere's sartorial policies because they could discern the symbolic role dress played in his nation-building efforts and in combating the legacy of colonialism. They embraced the policies also because the prescribed dress was familiar, non-Western, affordable and easily accessible. At the same time, especially young, educated, urban socialist women were not willing to give up their

rights to a modern sartorial identity (Ivaska, 2004; Ross, 2008).

The control of sartorial self-expression was key in building socialism. This study in a Tanzanian context supports previous research findings on socialist dress practices in Eastern Europe, and has argued that dress was one of the most important areas where socialism as a world system became constructed, embodied and articulated. At the same time, sartorial representation was also the area where socialist uniformity became first challenged, revealing the internal contradictions of socialist ideology and social policy.

References

Baker, P. L. (1997), Politics of dress: The dress reform laws of 1920/30s Iran, in: Lindisfarne-Tapper, N. and Ingham, B. (eds.), *Languages of dress in the Middle East*. Richmond, UK:Curzon, 178–191.

Eicher, J. B., Roach-Higgins, M. E., and Johnson, K. K. P. (eds.). (1995), *Dress and identity*. New York: Fairchild.

Green, R. L. (2005), Kanga, in: Steele, V. (ed.), *Encyclopedia of clothing and fashion*, 2. New York: Charles Scribner's Sons, 297–298.

Hanby, J., and Bygott, D. (1984), *Kangas: 101 uses*. Nairobi, Kenya: Ines May Publicity.

Ivaska, A. M. (2004), Anti-mini militants meet modern misses: Urban style, gender, and the politics of "national culture" in the 1960s Dar es Salaam, Tanzania, in: Allman, J. (ed.), *Fashioning Africa: Power and politics of dress*. Bloomington, IN: Indiana University Press, 104–121.

Medvedev, K. (2008), Ripping up the uniform approach: Hungarian women piece together a new communist fashion, in: Blaszczyk, R. L. (ed.), *Producing fashion: Commerce, culture and consumer.*, Philadelphia: University of Pennsylvania Press, 250–272.

Medvedev, K. (2009), Divat es Bunozes az 50-es es 60-as Evekben Magyarorszagon. [Crime and Fashion in Hungary in the 1950s and 1960s], in: Simonovics, I., and Valuch, T. (eds.), *Kirakat: Divat a szocializmusban.* [Shopwindow: Fashion under socialism]. Budapest, Hungary: Argumentum, 126–143.

Mirza, S., and Strobel, M. (eds.). (1989), *Three Swahili women: Life histories from Mombasa, Kenya*. Bloomington, IN: Indiana University Press.

Parkins, W. (ed). (2002), *Fashioning the body politic*. New York: Berg.

Perani, J., and Wolf, N. (1999), Cloth, dress and art patronage in Africa. Oxford: Berg.

Ross, R. (2008), *Clothing: A global history*. Cambridge, UK: Polity Press.

Smith, W. E. (1986, March 3), A reporter at large: Transition. *New Yorker*, 72–83.

Discussion Questions

1. How did the *khanga* originate?
2. *Khangas* are given as gifts to girls and women during what life events? When is a man presented a *khanga*, and how does the *khanga* denote wealth?
3. How did *khangas'* design change under socialism? Reread the definition of socialism provided in the chapter. Do you agree that the changes made in the *khanga* represented socialism? Why or why not?

9.4

DRESSING THE JÍBAROS: PUERTO RICAN PEASANTS' CLOTHING THROUGH TIME AND SPACE

José F. Blanco and Raúl J. Vázquez-López

The jíbaro is arguably one of the two most important symbols of Puerto Rican national identity. The term refers to the nineteenth-century, mountain-dwelling Puerto Rican white peasant of Spanish descent. Jíbaros were farmers; men worked in coffee and later sugarcane plantations while women—besides doing agricultural work—tended to the family and did laundry for pay. The image and dress of the jíbaro has undergone changes since the term first appeared in print on June 17, 1814 in *El Diario Económico* (Pedreira as cited in Babín, 1963, p. 61). It quickly secured an important place in Puerto Rican cultural and political production and has been ascribed a variety of meanings over the last two centuries. Literature professor Carmen L. Torres-Robles (1999) states: "for many critics and Puerto Ricans in general, the image of the jíbaro represents the essence of Puerto Rican nationality" (our translation of Torres-Robles, 1999, p. 241).

The jíbaro, it can be argued, became the locus of Puerto Rican identity as a response to sociopolitical and economic uncertainties on the island during the turn of the twentieth century. Historian Lillian Guerra (1998) presents an account of the appropriation of the image of the jíbaro as resistance against hegemony and American colonialism. Guerra—referring to Puerto Ricans living in New York—explains: "By invoking the jíbaro as the symbolic habitus of the Puerto Rican soul, Puerto

Rican migrants and their descendants actively and consciously locate the roots of their identity in the history of the island" (Guerra, 1998, p. 5). The jíbaro provides a point of reference to many Puerto Ricans who do not fully identify themselves with native Taino culture, African culture, or even the cultures of the two powers that have colonized the island: Spain and the United States. It is through the jíbaro that many see the history of the island as a constant movement from one region to the other in search of progress and a better life. Identifying oneself as a jíbaro is a claim to a connection with a group of people that has struggled to find a place within the history of an island facing social, political, and economic challenges that spun in part from the fact that Puerto Rico has never been an independent nation. The term jíbaro, though, has a variety of connotations. It may be used pejoratively in reference to a person who—allegedly similarly to the peasants—lacks proper education and social manners, or, as previously discussed, it can be appropriated as an honorary title as one claims a connection to the struggling working peasant class and their association with agricultural productivity and the land. It is in this second use that many see the essence of Puerto Rican identity, in a state of romantic freedom connected to nature.

Original for this text.

Coquí or the Jíbaro out of Context

The jíbaro, however, is not the only symbol of Puerto Rican national identity. Its role as central locus of this identity is equally shared by the coquí. The coquí, or *Eleuterodactilus coquis*, is a small brown frog that makes the distinctive sound "co-ki." Puerto Ricans are often taught that the coquí is unable to survive outside of Puerto Rico.[1] The idea of the coquí not being able to survive outside of Puerto Rico is parallel to the image of the Puerto Rican jíbaro struggling to survive the Puerto Rican diaspora of the 1950s.[2] Puerto Rican literature often portrays the jíbaro as a struggling individual when placed outside of his context as in the collection of vignettes *Spiks* by Pedro Juan Soto and implied in the poem *Boricua en la luna* by Antonio Corretjer. Doris Troutman Penn presents a diasporic coquí, named Pepe Coquí, in *La canción verde* (The Green Song). In this short novel Pepe Coquí travels by plane to New York (where he even gets the key to the city) only to find out that he can only live in Puerto Rico. The coquí becomes then the zoomorphic representation of Puerto Ricaness, and, as in the case of the jíbaro, "the coquí forms part of an iconography of puertorriqueñidad . . . a symbol of cultural pride and nostalgia" (Goldman, 2004, p. 378). Furthermore, tourists visiting Puerto Rico can purchase souvenirs of the tiny tree frog dressed as a jíbaro. When recognizing fellow Puerto Ricans outside the island—and occasionally inside the island—it is not uncommon to hear the phrase "yo soy de aquí como el coquí" (I'm from here, like the coquí).

Dressing the Jíbaro in Puerto Rican Literature

The first Puerto Rican authors to employ the term "jíbaro" were Antonio Vidarte with his 1844 poetry book *Aguinaldo puertorriqueño* (Puerto Rican Carol), and Miguel Alonso with his 1880 collection of vignettes *El gíbaro*. According to Antonio Pedreira (1970) there are two cycles of cultural production related to the jíbaro. In the first cycle

of the nineteenth and early twentieth centuries the jíbaro emerges as the locus of Puerto Rican identity. The end of the nineteenth century marks a period of transition in Puerto Rico as the former Spanish colony is ceded to the United States as a result of the Spanish-American War of 1898. The jíbaro of this period was romanticized and "traditionalized" in Puerto Rican cultural production in part because of the dominant romantic zeitgeist of the nineteenth century. This appropriation can be traced to Puerto Rican intellectual elites. As Mary Cannizzo suggests (1955, p. 472), "since the nineteenth century, Puerto Rican writers have focused their creative interest on local and national manners and customs," the jíbaro being the subject of most of these writings. The focus on the peasant in the literary production of this period is neither accidental nor exclusive to Puerto Rican cultural production. Peasant life, after all, plays an integral part in the literature of the period internationally. The nineteenth century is the time of *costumbrismo*[3] and naturalism. In 1894 Manuel Zeno Gandía published the quintessential naturalistic novel *La charca* (The Pond), one in a series of four novels titled *Crónica de un pueblo enfermo* (Chronicle of a Diseased People). The naturalistic style of the work bluntly portrays the tragic life of the peasants and their dire conditions and total marginalization. It shows jíbaros as a group without cohesion, unable to act, and merely at the mercy of nature and an established social structure (Beauchamp, 1976, pp. 50–51). The jíbaros of *La charca* are described as physically drained, skinny, and emaciated, with a languid appearance. The author makes it clear that their pain—a result of social injustice and abuse—is reflected on their faces and their bare feet, hardened by contact with the ground. Far from following dress practices of those in Puerto Rico's urban areas, the jíbaros wore functional clothing to pick coffee beans. Women are described as wearing loose skirts with baskets attached to their waists and loose peasant-style blouses. (See Figure 9.22.) Men wore simple trousers and worked shirtless or wore sleeveless shirts and straw hats known as *pavas*. (See Figure 9.23.) These elements of jíbaro dress are essentially descendants of European peasant clothing. The jíbaro wardrobe shows very little influence from native pre-Columbian cultures such as the Tainos or from material creations of African slaves and their descendants.

The jíbaros dressed up for special occasions such as a dance. In *La charca* Zeno Gandía describes women wearing linen dresses in yellow or red with colorful ribbons, flowers, or hairpins in their loose or braided hair. Men wore white shirts, working pants, starched white jackets, wide-brimmed straw hats, and carried machetes in their hands, which the author indicates was used for labor, as support, and as a weapon—all in one. An extraordinary luxury for the peasants was the use of any type of shoes; wearing them required an effort on their part due to the damaged conditions of their feet as a result of constantly walking barefoot. The author explains that they would carry their shoes to the dance and put them on upon arrival, not only to be comfortable during their walk but also as a way to protect the shoes from additional wear and tear, as they were considered a special commodity.

A second cycle in literary production related to the jíbaro extended from the 1930s to the early 1950s. The early cycle had shown the effects of American colonization and the struggle of the *hacendados* (land owners) trying to maintain coffee plantations competitive against the American-controlled sugar plantations. The second cycle emphasizes Puerto Rico's move toward industrialization and away from agriculture and in turn the burden on peasants struggling with the decision of staying in the countryside or emigrating to the city—first San Juan, then New York City—unprepared for either environment. Important literary creations of the period portraying jíbaros include *Terrazo* (1947) by Abelardo Díaz Alfaro, a collection of short stories, some dramatic and others comedic, describing the life of peasants in the mountain and sugarcane plantations; and René Marqués' *La carreta* (1951), a play about a peasant family dealing with the consequences of moving first to the capital San Juan and then to New York City. The most striking image of the jíbaro portrayed during this cycle, however, is in the 1937 song *Lamento borincano* (A Puerto Rican Peasant's Lament, also known *as El jibarito*), by Rafael Hernández. The lyrics capture "[the] island's socioeconomic plight during the Great Depres-

Figure 9.22 Wife and child of a jíbaro tobacco worker near Cidra, Puerto Rico. January 1938.

Figure 9.23 Old jíbaro, patriarch of a clan of twenty-one tobacco hill farmers, Puerto Rico. January 1938.

sion, the dismal conditions of the poverty-stricken jíbaro" (Acosta & Santiago, 2006, pp. 57–58). The song narrates the tale of a young peasant riding his mare to the city market, hopeful that he could sell his scant agricultural produce in order to support his family and buy a dress for his mother. The jíbarito returns home empty-handed, overwhelmed by sadness and hopelessness, lamenting his fate, and wondering what the future would bring to the country.

The most important change in jíbaro wardrobe during this cycle is the wearing of shoes on a daily basis, an indication of adapting to urban life and the abandonment of traditions. As the jíbaro peasants face further discrimination and challenges in the urban landscape due to their lack of preparation for the new environment, their clothing becomes a clear visual marker of their status as peasants, an image interpreted by the urbanites as reflecting a lack of education and manners. Dress functions as an indicator of the perceived and actual inequality of the jíbaro. These "urban" peasants learn quickly that in order to fit into their new landscape and avoid being labeled as "others," they must change their wardrobe and adapt their appearance to match the clothing styles of those in the city.

The Image of the Jíbaro as a Political and Cultural Commodity

It is during this second cycle of literary production that the jíbaro emerges as a political image in the logo of the Partido Popular Democrático de Puerto Rico (Democratic Popular Party of Puerto Rico). Founded by Luis Muñoz Marín in 1938, the party supports Puerto Rico's current political status as a commonwealth—some will argue, a colony—of the United States. The logo, designed in 1938 by Antonio I. Colorado, reads "Pan, Tierra y Libertad" (bread, land, and liberty) and includes the red silhouette of a jíbaro, wearing the pava, against a white background.[4] Although somewhat modernized, the logo is still in use. In the 1940s, Luis Muñoz Marín used a political campaign photo with a superimposed image of a jíbaro. The populist leader made the countryside his stomping ground and was in direct contact with poor peasants, emphasizing his connection with them. The image of the disadvantaged, impoverished jíbaro became—in the hands of politicians—a tool to denounce class inequality in Puerto Rico. The clothing of the jíbaro, by extension, acquires a new meaning in the political arena, becoming a symbol of inequality.

There are also canonic representations of the jíbaro in visual arts. *El velorio* (The Wake) (1893) by Francisco Oller is an oil-on-canvas painting depicting the wake of a child or *baquiné*. The scene shows the interior of a jíbaro mountain house where children and adults attending the wake join in dance, song, and prayer. The child's corpse rests on top of a table covered with white linens and wears a crown made out of flowers. Men are depicted barefoot, wearing long pants and long-sleeve shirts. Women are painted wearing solid-color long dresses cinched at the waistline with full skirts and blouses with short sleeves and low necklines. The 1905 painting *El pan nuestro* (Our Bread), by Ramón Frade, depicts an old jíbaro man on a mountain trail carrying a plantain cluster. The iconic character wears mid-calf mustard-color trousers, a white collarless long-sleeve shirt, and a wide-brim straw hat. Like any other typical jíbaro depiction, the painting would not be complete without the traditional machete tied around the waist. These quintessential paintings have become the most widely accepted visual images of jíbaro dress. It can be assumed that the pieces do depict some basic elements of jíbaro clothing observed firsthand by the artists, just as the literary canon probably contains descriptions based on the authors' observation of primary sources.

Jíbaros depicted in these two paintings or described in literature, however, have little in common with the modern costumes used in folkloric performances where men wear bright white ensembles with colorful sashes and handkerchiefs around their necks and women use low-cut peasant blouses and full flounced skirts in bright solid colors or prints with lace embellishments. This cleaned-up, colorful version—partially inspired by both European peasant and fashionable dress—romanticizes jíbaros and ignores the poverty conditions that dominated their lives. As a matter of fact, jíbaros never had a characteristic form of dress and did not imitate Spanish dress. As in many similar cases in Latin America and around the world, a romanticized version of the peasantry has been frozen in time and adopted as a national symbol. In the case of dress traditions, this version of the peasants' appearance has been turned into the national costume of several countries. This adoption of appearance often ignores the lower status of the population that purportedly originated this dress and pays little attention to the inequalities of which they were or are still victims. Dress practices that were born out of a struggle for survival and a necessity for hard labor are cleaned up, embellished with some elegant detailing and brighter colors, and proudly claimed as authentic national dress. The Puerto Rican government actually created Law No. 21 in 1983 defining parameters for representative dress of Puerto Rico. The law provides guidelines for materials, silhouette, construction, color, embellishments, and accessories of female dress. There are no penalties for not constructing a garment accurately except that it shall not be considered representative.

Rebecca Earle explains: "In Europe, national dress, and 'national culture' more broadly, often derived from a romanticized vision of a folk culture rooted in the land and exemplified by the peasantry" (2007, p. 64). In nineteenth-century Spanish America, according to Earle, national dress played a part in the process of nation formation. The elites did not trust indigenous and mixed-race populations but considered peasant culture acceptable. They regarded peasant dress as the basis for national dress as it held connections to white European groups even though indigenous dress was widely seen as the clear marker of regional variations (Earle, 2007, p. 68).

Mattel's 1997 Puerto Rican Barbie also features the approved national dress. The doll is a light-skinned mulatta with long, dark, and wavy hair and brown eyes. She wears a white cotton dress with lace ruffles and a pink ribbon. Her features and dress were criticized for the lack of representation of Puerto Ricans as a mixed race, including the pale and tattered historic jíbaras. The box describes the dress in the doll's voice, asking: "Like the special white dress I am wearing? It is very typical of a dress I might wear to a festival or a party." The elaborate costume was never worn by a peasant in any visual record and it resembles more a Spanish colonial dress than any other style ever worn in Puerto Rico. It includes lace—a very expensive material that only wealthy women could purchase during the first part of the century—and accessories such as white high heels, earrings, and a ring, none of which would have been worn by the impoverished white peasants.

As discussed earlier, most traditional costumes in Latin America are creolized variations of Spanish dress and are a product of fantasy and aesthetic synthesis. Thus the dress that should reflect the misfortunes and pain of the working rural classes is transformed into a symbol of national pride, ignoring the historic disadvantaged conditions of the groups that purportedly originated it. The romantic nationalism of the nineteenth century idealized peasant life as genuine and invented a timeless context where unchanging "traditional" dress was said to come from, making it "authentic." Already in 1953, after a competition to select a representative Puerto Rican "regional dress," the cultural critic Nilita Vientós Gastón denounced the existence of any such costume and argued that any creation could only be a product of fantasy. Through time, however, this dress has come to be known and accepted not only as authentic but also as unchanging. The connection with the dress of jíbaro peasants is rarely questioned and the "national costume" has contributed to the elaboration of a national myth that ignores the political and economic struggles of peasants in Puerto Rico. Negrón-Muntaner adds: "The main irony of this identification, particularly for future generations, is that the elites fashioned national identity as a simulacrum—technically dead but symbolically alive, like a doll" (2004, p. 219).

The Cyber-jíbaro: Another Cycle, Another Migration

Digital manifestations of the jíbaro abound on the World Wide Web. Zeno Gandía, Frade, Laguerre, and other authors and painters worked toward a representation of the jíbaro on the page, the canvas, and the stage, but they did this from the point of view of an observant; they did not consider themselves jíbaros. They wrote or painted the Other. The latest representations of the jíbaro—those in cyberspace—differ in one significant element: the cyber-jíbaros are individuals who choose to represent themselves through the image of the jíbaro regardless of their respective agendas. These cyber-jíbaros construct a postmodern identity from a pastiche of possibilities using elements of dress—whether jíbaro or not—to create said identity.

Orlando Vázquez, for instance, hosts and writes the website *Don Jíbaro*, whose purpose, Vázquez explains, is to celebrate "the humble Puerto Rican campesino [sic], the one that makes mistakes but seeks resiliently to bounce back without missing a beat. He learns from his errors and will not allow history to repeat itself on him." He further explains that Don Jíbaro Barbanegra is his nom de plume, adopted to conceal his civil identity, presumably not his physical identity, as the website has multiple pictures of Vázquez, sometimes of him as a twenty-something-year-old musician, and other times posing as Neo, the lead character played by Keanu Reeves in the blockbuster movie franchise *The Matrix* or, thanks to digital manipulation, flanked by iconic figures such as Alfred E. Neuman (the kid from *MAD* magazine).

Throughout the website Vázquez usually sports a *guayabera* and occasionally a Panama hat, clothing items associated with a landowner, the historic antagonist of the jíbaro. As it was told by the costumbrista writers, the relationship between landowners and jíbaros was similar to feudalism; peasants were allowed to live on the *hacendados*' land in exchange for labor. Eventually, with the distancing powers of time, many Puerto Ricans—including people who could perhaps be considered jíbaros—adopted the guayabera. The guayabera, the official Cuban national costume since 1935, is one of the most important symbols of cultural heritage among Cuban expatriates around the world. Once more, a piece of clothing not related historically or socially to the jíbaro is appropriated to create a recognizable image. Don Jíbaro, writing from exile, maintains a physical appearance somewhat associated with the traditional jíbaro, but uninformed readers of his website might assume that Don Jíbaro looks and acts like an "actual" jíbaro.

Another example of a cyber-jíbaro is that of Genoveva Baños, the character name of an actress for hire at www.lajibara.com. She wears a costume associated with the jíbara—a full skirt made out of a vivid flower print, a flounced bright red or white top, a purple bead necklace, gold bracelets, a flower in her hair, and occasionally, a red-hair wig—but it differs from the guidelines stipulated by Law 21 of 1983, which calls for white fabric and little embellishment. Her cyber-identity is built using imagery popularly acknowledged and accepted as jíbaro. Like Vázquez she appropriates an image that does not correspond to her reality outside from her acting. For Don Jíbaro and Genoveva Baños the jíbaro solidifies a connection with Puerto Rico and their own national selves. Both individuals adopt visual elements closely related to the jíbaro; yet at the same time they both distance themselves from the jíbaro characters of the Puerto Rican literary canon. Unlike Silvina, the tragic heroine of *La charca*, Genoveva is in charge of her time, space, and business.

The cyber-jíbaros are urban and/or write from exile and they do not handle the tools of the farm, but they can handle the tools of the Web. Their wardrobe is postmodern and may include elements of the original jíbaro wardrobe (a straw hat) but also may appropriate symbols of other cultures (Cuban guayabera), objects from completely unrelated worlds (the *Matrix* coat), or as with Genoveva alterations of a sanctioned traditional dress.

Conclusion

Jíbaro culture remains intrinsic to Puerto Rican identity. Jíbaro traditions are continued in a number of ways. The image of the jíbaro is a malleable commodity responding to the cultural, social, and political context in which it is framed. Jíbaro dress has been used in different ways throughout history to communicate changing ideas of identity and ethnicity. The meaning and material culture of jíbaro dress, therefore, has been reinvented and appropriated in different ways, as needed, by singular groups including intellectuals, politicians, and diaspora emigrants. The social reality of the deprived jíbaros can be embraced or ignored while appropriating jíbaro dress. At any rate, jíbaro identity seems to be a process, not an essential characteristic. Stuart Hall (1994) believes that cultural identity is a matter of "becoming," not "being." The cultural identity of the jíbaro is an example of what Hall argues is a cultural product in constant transformation, an identity that belongs to the future as much as to the past, transcending place, time, history, and culture. Material culture objects associated to ethnic identity—such as "traditional" or "national" dress—can be traditions that are invented or re-invented by those belonging or claiming to belong to an ethnic group—even in the case of Puerto Rico, where a traditional dress (at least for women) is sanctioned by law. Michael Fischer (1986), among others, sees ethnicity as reinvented and reinterpreted in each generation by each individual and not simply passed from one generation to another. Jíbaro dress, although regarded as traditional and authentic by many or even by law, is susceptible to forces that have changed—and will continue changing—not just its form but also its meaning.

References

Acosta-Belé, E. & Santiago C. E. (2006). *Puerto Ricans in the United States: A contemporary portrait.* Boulder, CO: Lynne Rienner Publishers.

Babín, M. T. (1963). Prologue to R. Marqués *La carreta.* Río Piedras, Puerto Rico: Editorial Cultural.

Beauchamp, J. J. (1976). *Imagen del puertorriqueño en la novela:* En Alejandro Tapiay Rivera, Manuel Zeno Gandía y Enrique A. Laguerre. San Juan, Puerto Rico: Editorial Universitaria.

Brameld, T. (1959). *The remaking of a culture: Life and education in Puerto Rico.* New York: Harper & Brothers.

Cannizzo, M. (1955). The article of manners and customs in Puerto Rico. *Hispania*, 38(4), 472–475.

Coquigrams Inc. (2007). La jíbara. Retrieved March 20, 2010, from http://www.lajibara.com

Earle, R. (2007). Nationalism and national dress in Spanish America. In M. Roces & L. Edwards (Eds.), *The politics of dress in Asia and the Americas* (pp. 63–81). Brighton, Australia: Sussex.

Fischer, M. M. J. (1986). Ethnicity and the post-modern arts of memory. In J. Clifford & G. E. Marcus (Eds.), *Writing culture: The poetics and politics of ethnography* (pp. 194–233). Berkeley: University of California Press.

Goldman, D. E. (2004). Virtual islands: The reterritorialization of Puerto Rican spatiality in cyberspace. *Hispanic Review*, 72(3), 375–400.

González, J. L. (1987). *El país de cuatro pisos y otros ensayos.* Río Piedras, Puerto Rico: Ediciones Huracán.

Guerra, L. (1998). *Popular expression and national identity in Puerto Rico: The struggle for self, community, and nation.* Gainesville, FL: Univ. Press of Florida.

Hall, S. (1994). Cultural identity and diaspora. In P. Williams & L. Chrisman (Eds.), *Colonial discourse and post-colonial theory: A reader* (pp. 392–401). London: Harvester Wheatsheaf.

Negrón-Muntaner, F. (2004). *Boricua pop: Puerto Ricans and the Latinization of American culture.* New York: New York Univ. Press.

Pedreira, A. S. (1970). La actualidad del jíbaro. In L. F. Negrón García & C. López Baralt (Eds.), *Obras de Antonio S. Pedreira* (pp. 652–703). San Juan, Puerto Rico: Instituto de Cultura Puertorriqueña.

Rak, J. (2005). The digital queer: Weblogs and Internet identity. *Biography*, 28(1), 166–182.

Silén, J. A. (1971). *We, the Puerto Rican people: A story of oppression and resistance* (C. Belfrage, Trans). New York: Monthly Review Press.

Torres-Robles, C. L. (1999). La mitificación y desmitificación del jíbaro como símbolo de la identidad nacional puertorriqueña. *Bilingual Review*, 24(3), 241–253.

Vázquez, O. (2001). Don Jíbaro's Jibaros.com. Retrieved March 20, 2010, from http://www.jibaros.com

Vientós Gastón, N. (1962). El traje típico puertorriqueño. *Indice cultural* (Vol. 1). Río Piedras, Puerto Rico: Ediciones de la Universidad de Puerto Rico.

Whalen, C. T. & V. Vázquez-Hernández (Eds.). (2005). *The Puerto Rican diaspora: Historical perspectives.* Philadelphia: Temple University Press.

Endnotes

1. Ironically, the frog was able not only to survive, but also to proliferate on some Hawaiian Islands where it has no romantic meaning and is considered a nuisance. It is believed that the coquí was accidentally transported to Hawaii from Puerto Rico on plants and soil and there are concerted efforts to eradicate the species.

2. The Puerto Rican diaspora refers to the mass migration of Puerto Ricans to the United States. It is popularly associated with migration to New York but as Carmen Teresa Whalen and Víctor Vázquez-Hernández (2005) point out, the Puerto Rican diaspora reached as far as Hawaii and included the cities of Boston, Chicago, and Philadelphia, among others. This mass migration was facilitated by the colonial relationship between the United States and Puerto Rico and it was, at times, sponsored by the U.S. government.

3. *Costumbrismo* refers to a nineteenth-century literary tradition in which artists paid close attention to the costumes and manners of a region and/or social group, often from a Hispanic country. It is closely related to realism and tends toward a faithful representation of the folkloric without interpretation.

4. "Historia del Partido Popular Democrático," Partido Popular Democrático, accessed February 16, 2011, http://ppdpr.net/info/. It should also be mentioned that The Partido Popular Democrático de Puerto Rico is also known as the PPD and as "La pava," in direct reference to its logo.

Discussion Questions

1. What does the term *jíbaro* mean?
2. What aspects of their dress would represent inequality?
3. How did their dress evolve into a national costume for Puerto Rico? Can you think of other items of dress that have made similar transitions? Are there examples in dress and fashion history?

9.5

COSTUME AND THE PLAY OF SOCIAL IDENTITIES IN AN ANDALUSIAN PILGRIMAGE

Michael D. Murphy and J. Carlos González-Faraco

In this paper we discuss the symbolic role of attire in one of Spain's most brilliant pilgrimages, *La Romeria del Rocio*, which venerates a statue of the Virgin Mary known as *Nuestra Señora del Rocío*, "Our Lady of the Dew." Our "ethnographic present" is 1986, a pivotal year in the extraordinary expansion during the 20th century of this spectacular devotion to the Virgin Mary. This Virgin's basilica is located some 35 miles from Seville by car in a village of the Andalusian municipality of Almonte. Both the shrine village and the entire pilgrimage ritual complex are known as *El Rocío*.

The spirited commentary surrounding this Catholic devotion is shaped by the competing claims of proponents of different ideologies, members of different communities, and champions of different social classes. Both the conduct of the pilgrimage and discourse about it have unfolded in the context of the display of specific social identities. One potent source of cultural contention in Rocío's pilgrimage concerns the donning of two class-coded costumes by some *rocieros* (Rocío pilgrims and devotees) during the events enacted in her honor. Although explicitly concerned with class, the conflicting understandings of these costumes cannot be divorced from considerations of community and ideology. While once reliable indicators of class membership, by the 1980s these costumes were so no longer; the resulting misreading of dress by some observers was used by the people of Almonte to discount the efforts of outsiders to interpret the social meaning of their rituals. We first discuss three specific sources of dissension surrounding Rocío. Then, after presenting some ethnographic background about the town of Almonte and its pilgrimage, we describe how during the 1980s different readings of two modes of pilgrim dress, the *traje corto* (the "short suit") and the *camisa caqui* (the "khaki shirt"), summoned up contradictory interpretations of the significance of El Rocío for social class, regional identity, and local community

This is a shortened and revised version of a paper by Murphy (1994) originally published in *Anthropological Quarterly*. Reprinted by permission of *Anthropological Quarterly*.

Figure 9.24 The *traje corto* or "short suit" (a) and the *camisa caqui* or "khaki shirt" (b) were two modes of costumes donned by Rocío pilgrims and devotees.

(Figure 9.24). Finally, we consider how the contested social significance of dress in El Rocío was used by Almonteños in their efforts to retain control over the expanding interest in their patroness.

Identities and Dissension in Pilgrimage

The issues of cultural contradiction and contention are of particular relevance to the monumental pilgrimage to Rocío, which by the 1980s attracted over a million people to her spring rituals. Perched at the edge of the great marshlands of the Guadalquivir River of southern Spain, Rocío's sanctuary convenes a diverse assemblage of devotees, merrymakers, tourists, and spectators from throughout Andalusia and beyond. The pilgrimage receives such massive coverage on TV and radio as well as in newspapers, magazines, and websites that for many Spaniards El Rocío has become a national media rite.

There are at least three vectors of social distinction informing discussions about Rocío's huge pilgrimage. The first is based on ideological differences that implicate both politics and religion and divide Rocío's complex following.

While Perry and Echeverria (1988) have demonstrated that devotion to the Virgin Mary has often been manipulated by authoritarian conservatives, Zimdars-Swartz (1991) has argued convincingly that the far right has not yet succeeded in monopolizing Marian enthusiasm. Many moderate and leftist Andalusians refuse to concede Rocío devotion to the right and, in fact, they actively seek to frame the pilgrimage in such a manner as to deflect its associations with the landed elite, ecclesiastical authorities, and Spain's authoritarian political heritage. The second source of debate about Rocío's pilgrimage lies in the competing claims and divergent interests of three social constituencies: the people of Almonte, the much larger number of devotees and spectators from beyond Almonte who attend the festivities, and the enormous audiences whose opinions about Rocío are based entirely on media depictions of the event. The Virgin of the Dew is simultaneously the symbol of a community (Almonte) and of the larger region (Andalusia) of which it is a part, with resulting tensions between different categories of devotees based on locality. A third significant source of contention concerns the class membership of the socially diverse participants in the pilgrimage. Rocío attracts people from all segments of Spanish society, from the Queen of Spain and members of the Spanish jet-set to beggars and pickpockets. Despite the frequently invoked assertion that at El Rocío all such distinctions are set aside, members and allies of the different social classes interested in the pilgrimage have elaborated alternative understandings about the significance of class and community for Rocío devotions and festivities.

Almonte and El Rocío

The shrine housing the statue of Rocío is located in a remote part of the municipality of Almonte. Each year, shortly before Pentecost Sunday, upwards of a million Andalusians converge on Rocío's basilica to participate in her pilgrimage. Although the vast majority spend only a day or so at the sacred village, arriving by car or bus, the preferred manner of participation is to travel by foot, horse, or cart over one of the venerable pilgrimage routes that connect the sacred village to the provincial capitals of Lower Andalusia, namely, Huelva, Sevilla, and Cadiz. Tens of thousands of Andalusians embark upon the pilgrim road in the company of dozens of affiliated lay brotherhoods (*hermandades filiales*). Based in communities scattered throughout Andalusia and beyond, these brotherhoods constitute both the organizational backbone of the devotion and the primary mechanism of communication between Spanish ecclesiastical authorities and Rocío's lay devotees. Almonte's brotherhood (known as the *Hermandad Matriz*, or Principal Brotherhood) exercises both ritual primacy in and administrative control over the pilgrimage by virtue of the fact that the statue resides in Almonte where she serves as that community's official patroness.

As is the case with many Andalusian communities, Almonte has long been politically polarized along class lines. For centuries the town had been dominated by a few landowning families and their allies in the relatively small middle classes. Throughout much of the 20th century the largest segment of the population consisted of *jornaleros* (landless agricultural day workers) and

petty landowners whose tiny, dispersed plots were inadequate to support a family. The progressively inequitable distribution of wealth within the community led to the formation of class antagonism and the political polarization of the landed and the landless into hostile camps.

Class polarization inspired both the Second Republic (1931–1936), which threatened sweeping reforms hostile to the large landowners, and the right-wing military rebellion that initiated the Civil War (1936–1939). During the four decades of the Franco regime, the landed elite of Almonte controlled the municipal government and dominated the town's labor market, effectively suppressing any effort on the part of agricultural workers to improve their economic and political positions.

Yet even before Franco's demise in 1975, the local economy began to diversify and Almonte emerged as one of the most prosperous rural communities in the region. By the 1980s, only a minority of Almonte's active population pursued traditional agricultural occupations. Many former *jornaleros* had found employment in the construction, service, and tourism industries. The rather rapid economic transformation of Almonte quickly eroded the economic basis of the traditional political power of the great landowning families.

Faced also with the loss of political power, the conservative elites of the town focused their energies on administering Almonte's Hermandad Matriz. The left conceded the direction of the brotherhood to the right because of its necessary, and to them distasteful, working relationship with the ecclesiastical hierarchy of the Catholic Church. Although, like many other brotherhoods in Andalusia, the *Hermandad Matriz* has on occasion come into conflict with priest and bishop, the members of its board of governors are invariably practicing Catholics who do not hesitate to proclaim their allegiance to the Church and its values.

The political skills of the officials of the *Hermandad Matriz* were put to the test many times in the 20th century as Rocío's pilgrimage experienced prodigious growth. After four decades of attracting approximately 30,000 participants to Rocío's annual pilgrimage, the construction

THE MEANINGS OF DRESS

of a road between Almonte and the village of El Rocío in 1958 produced an immediate doubling of the size of the pilgrimage. In rapid succession the number of pilgrims doubled again by 1964 (100,000), tripled once more by 1974 (300,000), and doubled yet again by 1979 (700,000). In 1984 an estimated 1.5 million people attended the spring rituals honoring the Virgin of the Dew.

The pilgrimage is renowned as much for its festive brilliance as it is for its vivid religious ritual. Both during the journey to Rocío's shrine and at the sacred village itself, *rocieros* sing, dance, eat, and drink, effectively mixing Marian devotion with carefree revelry. Rocío's romería epitomizes Andalusian style and cultural distinctiveness, so that participation in the pilgrimage is as much about asserting Andalusian identity as it is about devotion to the Virgin Mary. Clearly, one of the factors contributing to the spectacular growth of the pilgrimage in the last half of the 20th century is that the Virgin of the Dew and her colorful pilgrimage came to be embraced as key symbols of a resurgent Andalusian regional identity.

Traje Corto: Regionalism, Class, and Festive Attire

An attractive feature of the pilgrimage for many Andalusians is its glorification of selected aspects of the region's agrarian traditions. The horse is an especially important element in the pilgrimage, serving not just as a nostalgic means of transport but also as a symbol of full, privileged participation in the event. Riding a horse to Rocío's shrine and having a mount during the festivities at the shrine's village sets one apart from more pedestrian participants. The horse is part of the authentic, traditional Rocío of the protagonist that increasingly is contrasted with the modern Rocío of the tourist and the spectator who arrive in cars and buses.

To walk to Rocío, particularly in fulfillment of a vow made to the Virgin, is another authentic mode of participation in the pilgrimage. Indeed, it is the clearest way to underscore one's religious motives for making the journey to El Rocío. But having arrived at the Virgin's crowded village, the alternatives of riding and walking are quite literally those of treading and being trod upon. The status implications of riding above the throng are not lost on those on foot, who must be prepared to dodge rambunctious horses.

Reinforcing the equestrian theme of the pilgrimage, many pilgrims, including quite a few who do not have horses at the event, wear costumes that are instantly recognizable both as quintessentially Andalusian and as the festive riding attire of the privileged rural gentry of the region, the *señoritos*. The male costume, known as the *traje corto*, includes striped pants, a short jacket, suspenders, a wide-brimmed cordoba hat, riding boots, and leather chaps. In the mid-1980s, the average price for a set of this clothing in Almonte ranged from $650 to $1,000. The chaps alone could cost as little as $200 or as much as $2,500.

Many women attending the pilgrimage dress in the female complement of the *traje corto*, the *traje de faralaes* (ruffled dress) or the *traje de gitana* (gypsy dress). This costume, which admits of some variation and undergoes periodic stylistic changes, consists of a full, flowing dress characterized by ruffles and polka dots. The dress is frequently complemented by a shawl with long fringes. Invariably, this outfit is worn with bracelets, long looped earrings, and flowers in the hair. Conservatively estimated, the cost of the average costume worn by Almonteñas in the mid-1980s was $500.

Both their origins as elite attire and their considerable expense contributed to the strong continuing identification of these outfits with the *señoritos*. Nevertheless, these costumes also emerged as unmistakable symbols of Andalusia, the region, not just of the most privileged participants in events like El Rocío. Indeed, these styles of dress have been introduced in other Andalusian festivities in which they were entirely unknown until relatively recently, becoming a kind of trans-Andalusian costume overlaying, or even replacing, sub-regional traditions of festive attire. In short, these costumes may now be read to denote membership in a regional community and/or membership in a particular social class.

The uneasy juxtaposition of the class and regional resonances of the *traje corto* was revealed during what must in retrospect be regarded as the pivotal pilgrimage of 1986. In that year, for the first time in the pilgrimage's history, all eight provinces of Andalusia were officially represented by filial brotherhoods. In order to commemorate an occasion which was interpreted by many commentators as confirming Rocío's status as the region's most popular Virgin, Almonte's Principal Brotherhood invited the president of the regional government to become a member of their brotherhood, an honor not lightly extended to those not born in the community. When the president received his honor, however, he was not dressed in the *traje corto*, but in rather ordinary casual attire, a fact that did not go unnoticed by traditionalists. The president's choice of clothing for the ceremony was widely interpreted as the desire of a socialist politician to avoid wearing the garb of the region's landed elite. The socialist mayor of Almonte at the time also pointedly refrained from wearing the *traje corto* when participating in Rocío events in which others of a more conservative bent were traditionally dressed.

Despite the fact that the elitist connotations of these clothes repulse some—like the president of the regional government and the mayor of Almonte—for ideological reasons, a wider range of people can afford to "dress up" for the pilgrimage (that is, wear the attire of a higher social class), and choose to do so, than was the case in the recent past. Many who now wear the clothing associated with *señoritos* are themselves members of a much more modest social class. The dramatically increased prosperity enjoyed by many Almonteños and other Andalusians at the end of the 20th century made it possible for them to purchase rather expensive festive attire. Although the symbolic blurring of class boundaries made possible by the economic and political transformation of Andalusia toward the end of the last century undoubtedly played a part in the decision of some working-class and lower middle-class *rocieros* to adopt the *traje corto*, the successful redefinition of elite attire as regional costume has also contributed to its more extensive use. Both the wearer of the costume and observers of it are perfectly free to emphasize whichever of its social referents—class or region—they choose.

Camisa Caqui: Community, Class, and Ritual Attire

While the pilgrimage to Rocío became a focus for those who wish to promote and strengthen Andalusian regional identity, the Virgin simultaneously remained the beloved patroness of the small Andalusian town of Almonte. Moreover, despite Almonte's increasing social complexity, its townsmen had come to represent Andalusia's rural working classes for many outside observers who often seek to place them in dramatic opposition to *traje corto*-clad *señoritos*.

Although the town's most important religious organization was clearly understood to be a bastion of the politically conservative minority of the town, most Almonteños, however grudgingly, recognize the important role the *Hermandad Matriz* plays in dictating policy to the many Rocío brotherhoods scattered throughout Andalusia and beyond. The Principal Brotherhood organizes Rocío rituals with a firm hand aimed at maintaining the town's primacy in the huge pilgrimage. Indeed, retaining control over the pilgrimage in the face of its enormous growth in the last half-century unites Almonteños of all social classes and many opposing political ideologies. They aggressively resist any attempt to expropriate an event in which they are monumentally outnumbered by more socially powerful outsiders—outsiders who they believe would seize control of their symbol of corporate identity, given the chance.

Almonteño resistance to outsiders has taken many forms, but certainly the most notorious is the unique style of their participation in the premier ritual of the pilgrimage: a raucous and grueling procession of the statue of Rocío through the streets of her sacred village. Accounts from the late nineteenth and early twentieth centuries indicate clearly that the procession, although very enthusiastic even then, was conducted well within clerical standards of ritual orderliness. However, as the number of affiliated brotherhoods increased and the overall scale of the pilgrimage grew spectacularly in the 20th century, the procession became increasingly tumultuous, disorderly and even violent. This controversial development is clearly related to the Almonteño insistence that no outsider so much as touch Rocío's float without their permission; only Almonteños and those they invite may help carry the statue and they are prepared to fight outsiders who dare to try. As the float zig-zags erratically along its processional route, Almonteños fiercely struggle to retain physical control over Rocío during the procession, and this is but the most visible element of an Almonteño strategy that has so far insured their primacy in the burgeoning pilgrimage.

In the mid-1980s many commentators identified Rocío's procession as a singularly working-class rite embedded in a more socially heterogeneous ritual complex. Indeed, that early in the century it was enacted almost exclusively by Almonte's *jornaleros* is clear from Manuel Siurot's description of the procession first published in 1918:

> There is nothing in the world comparable to this truly tragic procession . . . They are not men, they are wild beasts. The Virgin moves on their shoulders like the foam on the crest of a tumultuous wave. They are uncivilized, they are sons of work, they cannot offer gifts of intelligence, gifts of imagination, or delicate offerings. If they do not possess these things, how can they offer them? But they do have blood and physical force, and they offer up all of their blood and all of their force. They give what they have. Poor things! (Siurot 1918: 28–29; authors' translation)

For much of the first half of this century, working-class Almonteños came to the procession dressed not in special festive clothing but in their oldest work clothes simply because of the likelihood that they would be torn during the raucous ritual. An examination of old photographs reveals that the drab work shirts worn by the working-class participants in the procession contrasted sharply with the fancier dress of the middle- and upper-class pilgrims who watched the ritual from the sidelines.

But by mid-century members of Almonte's dominant social classes began to "dress down," shedding the *traje corto*, to join in the ritual parading of the Virgin through her village. By the time that the pilgrimage really began to boom in the late 1950s, virtually all segments of the town's population were involved in what previously had been the exclusive domain of the working class. In a reversal of a well-established pattern in Spain, the upper and middle classes did not retreat from this ritual when it turned tumultuous; they joined in and helped make it even rowdier. All social classes came to be fully represented in the procession, from the richest of Almonte's citizens to the poorest.

Despite the new social heterogeneity of the procession, its image as a working-class ritual was reinforced by the adoption of a de facto uniform for the ritual. Some men began to wear the sturdy shirts that they were allowed to keep after being mustered out of military service. Eventually other Almonteños adopted the use of khaki, olive drab, and ocher-colored shirts. Known collectively as *la camisa caqui* ("the khaki shirt"), these plain blouses, so reminiscent of the old *jornalero* work shirt, came to symbolize the fierce determination of Almonteños to protect their ritual preeminence. In the 1980s and 1990s, when outsiders regarded the Almonteños as having gone too far in their pursuit of ritual dominance, their khaki shirts were often invoked in stinging condemnation of their alleged working-class brutishness. Increasingly, the traditional condescension of the sort expressed by Siurot in an earlier era gave ground to the growing irritation of those *rocieros* from other communities who felt that Almonteños had overreached themselves.

The Contested Significance of Dress in El Rocío in the 1980s

During the 1980s media critiques of Rocío's famous procession frequently included statements about social class in which the two costumes we have just described figured prominently, despite the fact that these once reliable markers of social class had ceased being so. Many Almonteños of that era wore the *traje corto* during the first phase of the pilgrimage and then changed into the khaki shirt in preparation for the procession. Indeed, in some families the changing of the costumes clearly assumed a ceremonious air. The donning of the processional shirt characteristically took place late in the afternoon or early in the evening of the day before the procession. Typically the shirt was neatly pressed and folded and it was put on with a solemn air marking a dramatic shift in mood. The time had come to assume the processional garb, to put aside the fun, and to begin preparations for the climactic ritual of the year.

In the hours before the procession began, young, khaki-clad Almonteños proudly strolled around the village for all to see. Some outsiders made the often painful mistake of thinking that the Almonteños adopted the use of these shirts so that they could identify each other during the procession, thus knowing who to permit participation and who to prevent access to the Virgin's float. Those outsiders who wore the khaki shirt in order to pass themselves off as Almonteños generally fooled no one during the 1980s. Most Almonteños recognized each other at that time and even those who did not could clearly distinguish the confidence and skill with which Almonteños got under the float from the hesitancy and awkwardness of most inexperienced outsiders.

By the 1990s teenage girls and young women from Almonte began to adopt the *camisa caqui*, although their own participation in the procession was limited. Certainly, then, the display of the khaki shirt served not to help Almonteños identify each other, but rather to communicate proudly to outsiders that the wearer was one of a select few: an Almonteño during El Rocío. Moreover, from the local perspective it was the status "Almonteño" that was being underscored by this emblem, not "member of the working class." Many people of the middle and landed classes of the town did not hesitate to wear the khaki shirt, not even those who make it clear in other contexts that they had little or no sympathy for workers. The khaki shirt served both to articulate and to stimulate Almonteño community solidarity at just that social moment when it was most decisively put to the test.

The khaki shirt had decidedly different symbolic connotations for Almonteños than it had for outsiders. For Almonteños of different ages, social classes, and political inclinations, putting on the khaki shirt signaled the temporary suspension of those social distinctions that are so important to the quotidian flow of social life in this community.

Outsiders, however, typically depicted the khaki-clad Almonteños as working-class men engaged in a fierce ritual of rebellion against the *traje corto*-clad *señoritos* who appeared to dominate the rest of the pilgrimage. Yet, the men of the middle classes and even some of the largest land owners were invariably to be found among the ranks of those struggling to carry the Virgin. While it is true that the majority of the men participating in the ritual were of the working classes, their presence was not disproportionate to their representation in the total population. A stronger case could be made for characterizing the procession as working-class if men of that social stratum attempted to exclude or constrain the participation of men of higher social position. Certainly, this sort of exclusion occurs in other ritual contexts in other Andalusian communities. Rather than denoting the symbolic reversal of the social order, Rocío's procession was perhaps the single occasion, apart from the democratic elections revived in the wake of Franco's long dictatorship, in which all the men of Almonte stood on equal footing with one another.

Conclusion

Michael Sallnow advises that when "people converge in pilgrimage, meanings collide" (1991: 137). Such is certainly the case with the conflicting readings that various participants and observers made of the significance of dress in Rocío. Outsiders who took the traditional class/costume code at face value failed to appreciate that in the 1980s Almonteños, most neither *señoritos* nor *jornaleros*, effortlessly dressed up and dressed down during the different phases of the pilgrimage. Moreover, the same symbolically charged accouterment, the khaki shirt, simultaneously communicated the temporary washing away of social distinction to some participants and the heightening of just those distinctions to some observers.

We have sought here not only to document the different readings of the *traje corto* (Andalusian costume versus elite attire) and the *camisa caqui* (Almonteño marker versus working-class emblem) in the mid-1980s, but also to show how the naive resort to the apparently simple class coding of these costumes constituted clear evidence to Almonteños that outsiders, of whatever ideological persuasion, failed to comprehend the true significance (that is, the range of locally acceptable meanings) of these symbols. Outnumbered at the event and allowed only very limited access to the controls of media presentations, the Almonteños took heart from the ubiquitous errors of those who would authoritatively explain their most complex pilgrimage. Ironically, the very lack of consensus about the meaning of the pilgrimage's costumes, particularly in their representation of social identities, was capitalized upon as yet another resource in the Almonteño struggle to resist the appropriation by outsiders of the most important symbol of their social identity, the statue known as Rocío.

References

Murphy, M. D. (1994) Class, Community, and Costume in an Andalusian Pilgrimage. *Anthropological Quarterly*, 67 (2), 49–61.

Perry, N. & Echevarria, L. (1988) *Under the heel of Mary.* London: Routledge.

Sallnow, M. J. (1991) Pilgrimage and cultural fracture in the Andes. In *Contesting the sacred: The anthropology of Christian pilgrimage* (pp. 136–153), ed. by J. Eade & M. J. Sallnow. London: Routledge.

Siurot, M. (1918) *La Romería del Rocío.* Huelva (Spain): n.p.

Zimdar-Swartz, S. L. (1991) *Encountering Mary: From LaSalette to Medjugorje.* Princeton: Princeton University Press.

Discussion Question

1. This reading reveals that even in religious activities where it would seem that all people are equal, there was a difference in dress of the pilgrims based on their social and economic status. What were these specific items of dress and how did they evolve over time into a regional costume for the Andalusian region of Spain?

CHAPTER 10

DRESS IN THE WORKPLACE

Patricia Hunt-Hurst

After you have read this chapter, you will understand:

- How dress facilitates or hinders human interaction in the workplace
- Why dress helps individuals acquire, learn, and perform job roles
- How dress affects and reflects specific jobs in business, sports, and the military
- How to present one's self in a professional setting to the best advantage

As you sit in your college classes, you may notice the very different ways that your professors dress for work: one professor might always wear suits and heels; another always wears blue jeans, a plaid shirt, and cowboy boots; another wears a suit and tie; still another wears clothing that reflects his African heritage. Academia is often regarded as a career for which appropriate dress is not clearly defined. Professors may choose to reflect their individuality through their dress rather than to follow a strict professional dress code (Figure 10.1). On the same college campus you will find employees who must follow a prescribed dress code of a uniform (campus police, for example). Therefore, college campuses are a good place to start the examination of dress in the workplace.

Working takes up a large portion of adult life. Spending 40 to 60 hours a week at work, in addition to commuting time and getting ready for work (including dressing), makes our time devoted to work-related activities substantial. Work dress becomes one of the most frequently used parts of the wardrobe and, for many individuals, the part of the wardrobe on which they spend the most money. Because work provides money for family and self-support, work tends to be highly valued by most individuals. In addition, many people prepare for careers through long years of education, training, and building a professional reputation and accomplishments. For many adults, work roles define much of one's self-identity.

This chapter describes how dress affects work. Dress is a powerful communicator, especially when people interact at work. Clothing researchers have attempted to unravel the role that dress plays in the work environment, but more research is needed to fully understand

Figure 10.1 College professors dress in a range of outfits for work. Some days may require a suit while other days it is acceptable to wear blue jeans.

the phenomenon. For instance, researchers have examined body type (Thurston, Lennon, and Clayton, 1990), the wearing of masculine dress (Johnson, Crutsinger, and Workman, 1994), and the ideal business image (Kimle and Damhorst, 1997) on a woman's success in the workplace. The readings for this chapter address both men's and women's dress at work to demonstrate the importance of appropriateness of dress in the workplace.

Knowing how to dress for work has been a concern for a long time (see Figure 10.2). Dress historians Sara Marcketti and Jane Farrell-Beck (2008–2009) found that during the 20th century American women received an excess of advice about how to dress correctly for the workplace from 1900 to 1970. Their article "Look Like a Lady; Act Like a Man; Work Like a Dog: Dressing for Business Success" explores the advice women received about how to dress for work. Their study focuses on the late 20th century, when women's participation in the labor force and the number of higher-paying jobs for women increased. As more women earned managerial positions, they "faced a challenge in the 1970s of finding clothing that was attractive and appropriate for their new middle-management positions" (p. 57). In the 1970s women were encouraged to wear a masculine, tailored "skirted two-piece suit in a dark color" or a conservative, yet "interesting" dress. Marcketti and Farrell-Beck found that the introduction of pantsuits for women created further confusion as some employers in the 1970s did not consider pants an acceptable alternative for skirts or dresses for the corporate workplace. In the 1980s some relaxation of this strict expectation of dress for women occurred as a wider variety of clothing styles (e.g., knit suits, silk dresses, blouses, and skirts) gained acceptance for work. Yet, Marcketti and Farrell-Beck found that "dress for success" literature continued to place "emphasis on dressing conservatively early in one's career" and "the gray flannel business suit remained the benchmark for women entering lower-level management positions and for interview attire" (p. 61). In the late 20th and early 21st centuries, women had greater involvement in all levels of corporate management and with that came greater opportunities for "individual dressing" as well as the use of "professional image coaches" to assist in clothing selection. While suits remained a foundation of business apparel for women, there was more flexibility in color and style. However, as Barbara Burgess-Wilkerson and Jane Boyd Thomas reveal in "Lessons from *Ugly Betty*: Business Attire as a Conformity Strategy," today's college students do not always understand the value of dressing for success. However, authors from a variety of disciplines write books and articles that give men and women advice about how to dress for success in the workplace. Many of these publications are updated to give each new generation a dose of the invaluable commentary.

Many companies have a formal dress-code policy, meaning that a suit and tie are required for men, suit and skirt or pants for women. Some companies have a business-casual dress code or require employees to wear a specific outfit that represents the overall branding of the organization. Examples of this strategy include Target's red shirt and khaki pant, Best Buy's blue shirt, and Walmart's blue vest. This kind of dress has become especially important to promote company cohesiveness and identity (it makes it easy to find a sales associate if customers know how they dress). Other companies may not have specific dress regulations but may instead encourage employees to show good taste. Good taste typically means no skimpy tops, short-short skirts or shorts, and no flip-flops. Appearance is important, and this is directly tied to clothing as well as other aspects of dress in the workplace.

Many years ago, some employers prohibited women from wearing pants to work for white-collar jobs and for teaching. It took the women's movement of the 1970s for this option to happen, and then, as dress historian Patricia A. Cunningham (2003) notes, even after the 1970s it remained "a struggle" (p. 221) since many male employers were not receptive to the change. Fortunately, most compa-

Figure 10.2 Jackets are often regarded as a symbol of authority. The bow tie blouse, earrings, and simple hairstyle also add to a professional look in the office.

nies revised these dress codes in the late 20th century to correspond to contemporary ideas of appropriate dress for the workplace. An article in the *Los Angeles Times* reported that the Walt Disney Company changed its dress-code policy to indicate that female employees at Disney theme parks around the world no longer have to wear pantyhose when wearing skirts/dresses, unless the costume requires it. In recent years, objections to dress codes have developed when employees are asked to remove religious apparel or jewelry. For example, in the United Kingdom a Muslim teaching assistant refused to remove her veil in the classroom, and a British Airways employee was fired for wearing a visible cross. A more recent controversy has emerged about piercings and tattoos: these body modifications are considered to be in "bad taste" by some employers, so an employee might be required to remove piercings and cover tattoos during the work day. In another example, the style of what a person wears may come into question. For example, television often depicts female attorneys, police detectives, and hospital administrators in low-cut, revealing tops, tight-fitting skirts and pants, and 4-inch heels. Is this appropriate for most workplaces today—or has television influenced us to think it is? See the reading "Too Sexy for My Bosses: Why Lawsuits Based on Looks Discrimination—Even Good Ones—Are a Bad Idea" for a discussion about "appearance discrimination" in the workplace, and employees' lawsuits to challenge this practice.

Another form of discrimination—racism—continues into the modern workplace. Skin color can exclude a person from a position or make it difficult to advance in the corporate hierarchy although this is illegal in the United States and in violation of laws enforced by the Equal Employment Opportunity Commission. Edwards, in "How Black Can You Be?," describes how dress can increase the comfort factor for whites—one of the main challenges blacks have to face when working in an executive position. Edwards reminds black professionals that others in the office (often white coworkers) may wonder if minority executives value black culture more than corporate culture. All professionals must assume responsibility for the work culture they have chosen to inhabit. There are many behaviors (e.g., sexual harassment) and dress items (e.g., dirty T-shirts) that are not acceptable to employers. Darlene Gavron Stevens in the reading "Casino Gives Workers Look They Can, Must Live With" tells us about appearance standards mandated for beverage servers at Harrah's Casino. As noted earlier, it is not unusual for employers to establish dress codes applied to specific types of clothing to wear on the job (e.g., red shirt and khaki pants). Harrah's is taking it a step further by focusing on a standard of appearance.

In the late 1990s, the topic of casual dress received attention from corporations and clothing scholars. The casual-dress trend was interesting from several perspectives. One explanation is that following the turbulent late 1980s and early 1990s, when downsizing was prevalent in business, employers wanted to give employees a perk, especially one that did not cost money. So casual dress days (and casual Fridays) became a cost-effective way to raise morale among apprehensive employees. Another possible reason for the development of casual-dress policies was to minimize distinctions between employees, no matter the person's rank, salary, or position in the corporation. Some college campuses and corporations instituted a "casual" Friday during which staff could dress down and wear blue jeans or khakis to work rather than dress slacks and suits. Over the years of this practice in business, industry, and academia, some employees took casual dress to an extreme, and employers got tired of employees showing up for work looking as though they had just woken up. Adomaitis and Johnson (2005) studied how flight attendants perceived their work performance in casual and formal uniforms. They found that the type of uniform influenced the behavior and attitudes of the flight attendants "as well as his or her perceptions concerning abilities to perform their job." In other words, flight attendants stated that the formal uniform "enhanced their abilities" whereas the casual uniform resulted in a more relaxed attitude on their part, and rude and disrespectful behavior from their passengers (p. 99). This study shows that appropriate dress in the workplace matters. There seems to be a turnaround in thinking about the idea to "dress for success," also known as dress for advancement. In other words, companies are rethinking "casual Friday" policies and creating more stringent dress codes that reflect corporate dress and a move away from unprofessional dress or "anything goes" attitudes. Recent articles in the *New York Times* and the *Wall Street Journal* echo this, reporting that the pendulum appears to be swinging back toward more formal dress in the workplace. The movement away from casual Fridays has to do with the informal, unprofessional manner that some employees were communicating through their dress. Today "dress for success" is linked to the desire to get ahead. Women are particularly encouraged to dress better than their peers to present a professional image, even on casual Fridays.

Dress for a Job Interview

People often make judgments about others in just a few seconds. The term "person perception" refers to the way we learn and think about others and their characteristics, intentions, and inner states (Taguiri and Petrullo, 1958). Forming an initial impression is the first step in person perception (Figure 10.3). A job interview is one situation in which a first impression can determine one's future earning capacity; appropriate dress for an interview is therefore crucial. Magazines and professional journals provide up-to-date information on how to dress appropriately in the workplace and for job interviews. Not surprisingly, clothing researchers have studied the effect of dress during a job interview (Damhorst and Pinaire Reed, 1986; Damhorst and Fiore, 1999; Johnson and Roach-Higgins, 1987; Rucker, Taber, and Harrison, 1981). More recently, researchers have surveyed potential employees about their beliefs and attitudes regarding clothing for the corporate workplace (Blalock, 2006; Peluchette, Karl, and Rust, 2006). Some of this research reveals that college students are very aware that how they dress for job interviews is important and that specific requirements may differ from one type of job to another. For example, if you are interviewing for a job with a company that specializes in apparel for surfing and other water sports, they may expect you to show up for your interview in something more casual than a typical suit. However, researchers indicate that if in doubt,

Figure 10.3 Career coaches often recommend that we dress conservatively on job interviews.

one should dress conservatively for a job interview; it is better to overdress than underdress. Today most college career center websites continue to provide guidance on appropriate dress for interviews and work. It would not be surprising in the second decade of the 21st century to learn that a conservative suit continues to remain the basis of professional dress. Dressing appropriately for interviews is even more important in today's economy than in the past. Numerous websites give advice on how to dress for job interviews; college career center websites are an excellent place to start.

Dress and Human Interaction at Work

Why is the discussion about appropriate dress in the workplace important? Dress at work provides visual cues to a person's role and guides an understanding of the value of being appropriately dressed for the workplace. In Chapter 1, we learned that roles are positions that people occupy in a group or society. Workplace roles typically give structure and guidance to clothing on the job; many roles require a specific type of dress. For example, a farmer needs overalls, a lawyer needs a business suit, and a judge needs a robe. To a large extent, one who looks the part through appropriate dress can be confident that others will assume he or she legitimately holds the claimed position. The reading "Up the Career Ladder, Lipstick in Hand" tells about a Harvard University study that found that how much or little makeup females wear can significantly impact how other people viewed them in regards to competency. In this study participants judged women wearing makeup as more competent than those without makeup, indicating that for women makeup can be as important as how they are dressed in the workplace.

Because dress is such a powerful communicator, appropriate clothing in the workplace conveys the idea that individuals understand their work roles and perform them effectively; dress also cues workers into the roles of other employees in the workplace. However, in some corporations a relaxed dress code is practiced by the CEO of the company as well as the designer, the logistics manager, and the shop foreman. In fact, some clothing companies may expect only that the employees wear a T-shirt or sweatshirt that bears the company logo, and the rest (a pair of khakis, jeans, or shorts) depends on the employee. So what is appropriate for one company is often not okay for another. Therefore, it is important for job seekers to learn about an employer's dress codes. This information is often available via a company's website or human resource office.

Roles within a society can be either achieved or ascribed. Achieved roles are those that we work to earn. College degrees, work skills, even marriages are roles that people must strive to attain. A wedding band and an academic robe are examples of achieved roles expressed through dress. An ascribed role is a position that people acquire through no fault or virtue of their own. Age, gender, skin color, and birth order are examples of ascribed roles. These roles have an immense impact on individuals because they are so visible and, with the exception of gender, they can rarely be changed. Age, gender, and skin color are difficult to hide in ev-

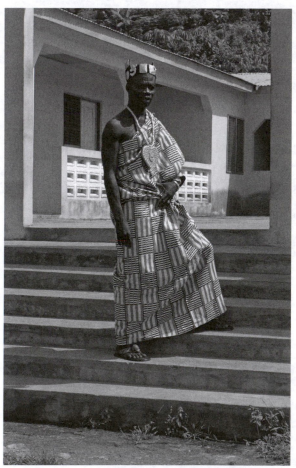

eryday interactions with others, and therefore their impact is very great. Both achieved and ascribed roles are expressed through dress at work. A good example about how ascribed and achieved roles may merge and are reflected in one's dress comes from Ghana, West Africa. A young lawyer (achieved role) in Ghana may be chief of his traditional Asante village (ascribed role), which is inherited through the male lineage of his family. As a lawyer, he wears a suit and tie to work each day; however, on the weekends or for traditional Asante ceremonies, he wears the traditional kente wrap that signifies his ascribed role as a village chief (Figure 10.4).

Because ascribed roles can rarely be changed, using dress to offset stereotypes becomes a useful tool in the workplace. Age, gender, and skin color—in certain situations—may be perceived by some as a negative (e.g., female firefighter or young-looking college professor or neurosurgeon). Presenting one's self appropriately through dress can often help to offset negative stereotypes. For example, one might be perceived as too young to do a job if one's dress is not appropriate. A youthful appearance may be read as too inexperienced, too naive, or too avant-garde to be trusted to do a good job. The reverse is also

Figure 10.4 In some countries ascribed roles may be expressed by wearing traditional dress and fabrics.

true. An older appearance may be read as too old-fashioned, too conservative, or possessing a skill set that is too outdated. Dressing "older" or "younger" might help to overcome these misperceptions.

Gender becomes an issue in the workplace when a professional woman is pregnant. It can be difficult to convince bosses and colleagues that her work will not suffer or that she doesn't secretly plan to quit her job soon after the baby is born. Although many women are now postponing pregnancy until careers are well established, negative perceptions about pregnant women in the workplace still persist. Maternity career apparel is one way to visually and subconsciously combat those stereotypes (Belleau, Miller, Elliot, and Church, 1990). Apparel companies are providing many more options for styles of professional dress for pregnant women than in previous years and at a variety of price points. Therefore, an expectant mother can continue to dress professionally for her job throughout her pregnancy. Other issues may arise after the baby is born based on company policies. Expectations that a woman will be back to her pre-pregnancy size just 12 weeks after giving birth, even if nursing, is causing stress for some employees. As industries become more service-oriented and image-conscious, more and more employers may require that employees meet these kinds of specific appearance standards (see "Casino Gives Workers Look They Can, Must Live With").

Dress and Status at Work

If roles are special tasks that a person performs in a society, status or prestige is the social stratification with which groups and individuals are ranked and organized by legal, political, and cultural criteria (Marshall, 1994, p. 510). In addition, a status hierarchy reflects the value society places on certain roles or groups of roles (Storm, 1987). The presence (or absence) of a status symbol is one way the perceptions regarding status are formed. A Rolex watch, for example, is a major status symbol in U.S. culture. If a doctor or lawyer wears a Rolex watch, others may assume that he or she has not only the financial means to purchase such an item but also the skills required to achieve occupational success in his or her field. This is readily evident by men and women in the United States military, where dress codes are strict. Men and women in the U.S. Army wear the same type of uniform with a universal digital pattern, no matter their rank. However, it is the insignia on the uniforms that denotes a person's rank (and status) within the army; these emblems are visual cues, well understood by men and women of the military. Thus, a military uniform is a very good example of how dress at work functions to visually express status distinctions in the workplace (Figure 10.5).

Social class is a concept that is related to and greatly defined by one's occupation. Although social class distinctions are blurry, in the United States individuals are generally divided into three classes: upper, middle, and lower. Social class is a complex issue involving a person's social background, education, occupation, and income. When social class and dress become a concern in the workplace, it is typically because an individual does not adopt dress appropriate to the position. For example, a woman who is promoted to management but continues to wear dress similar to what a secretary wears in her firm may hit the "glass ceiling," preventing further promotion or even causing demotion (cf. Form and Stone, 1957).

The terms "white-collar dress" and "blue-collar dress" refer to types of occupations. These terms imply the social classes historically associated with white-collar and blue-collar occupations. Management and labor jobs have typically reflected their status in dress: a man's white shirt worn with a suit for a management role, but a denim shirt or uniform worn by a laborer. Some presidential candidates have borrowed the traditional symbolism of blue-collar and white-collar dress. These candidates have worn a blue shirt while campaigning in parts of the

Figure 10.5 Badges, pins, and stripes identify a military person's rank while in uniform.

country that have organized labor unions. The message of the blue shirt is "I may be running for president, but I know what it means to physically work hard." Wearing a blue shirt is meant to establish connections with constituents and gain voter support. Wearers of white-collar dress are perceived as professional. Awareness of different environments and expected dress is often half the battle when dressing for work. One way to ensure appropriate work dress is to observe others at work and adopt their dress codes.

Dress and Specific Occupations

Whereas it might be difficult to describe the dress of a mother in U.S. society (a role that has undergone significant changes), most people have a clear picture of what a police officer should wear. A police uniform is an example of role-related dress, that is, dress that has become inextricably tied to a particular occupation. Police uniforms communicate ideas such as power and authority. Research confirms that clothing such as uniforms can legitimize and convey power (Bickman, 1974). In order for police officers to successfully do their job, they must be perceived as legitimate and authoritative. Another example would be the robes that judges wear in the U.S. judicial system. The black robe signifies a judge's authority over the court proceedings and reflects his or her position of respect. The appropriate clothing symbols help make this perception possible.

As jobs become more specialized, clothing for specific needs becomes important. With the advancement of technology, some workers are required to wear clothing that protects the product (e.g., sensitive computer equipment, electronics) from the worker (e.g., hair, lint, tobacco smoke). There are many other types of jobs that require a uniform. In some cases, the uniforms are required to provide protection against injury and illness. This includes protective clothing for agricultural workers, bullet-proof vests for police officers, and cooling vests for firefighters. Researchers continuously work to develop gear for athletes to better protect them from injury while the athletes engage in physically demanding and dangerous sports. Many new products protect while reducing the weight of previous gear. For example, new chest protectors, wrist, and shin guards designed for baseball players provide greater protection with less weight than previous bulky pads made of plastic and foam. These new products are one-third the size of the old and offer greater resistance to injury (See "Swinging for the Fences with Evoshield" in Chapter 13).

Summary

Dress in the workplace is important because most working people spend 40 to 60 hours a week at their jobs. That is a lot of time and a lot of human interaction to consider. Appropriate dress can make the different in receiving a job offer, appearing effective in a job role, and receiving a promotion. Understanding how dress can facilitate or hinder human interaction in the workplace can help employees make favorable impressions at work. Most important, dress is a powerful communicator—especially in the workplace.

Suggested Readings

Adomaitis, A.D., and K. K. P. Johnson. (2005). Causal Versus Formal Uniforms: Flight Attendants' Self-Perceptions and Perceived Appraisals by Others. *Clothing and Textiles Research Journal* 23(2): 88–101.

Cunningham, P. A. (2003). *Politics, Health, and Art: Reforming Women's Fashion, 1850–1920.* London: The Kent State University Press.

Kimle, P. A., and M. L. Damhorst. (1997). A Grounded Theory Model of the Ideal Business Image for Women. *Symbolic Interaction* 20:45–68.

Learning Activity 10.1: Visit a Career Center Website

Procedure

To gain information from your college/university website about dressing for a job interview, visit its career center website. What do's or don'ts does the website provide? Were you surprised by any of this information? Do you agree with the advice? Why or why not?

Learning Activity 10.2: Interview a Professional

Objectives

- To observe and interview a professional about his or her work dress, including casual dress policies and personal preferences.
- To form an opinion about dress in the workplace based on an interview with a professional in a field of personal interest.

Procedure

Choose a profession that's interesting to you. Talk to a professional in that field for a minimum of 20 minutes about his or her dress for work. Ask the person if you can meet him or her at work, so you can see that person in a professional setting. Ask as many of the following questions as time allows.

1. Does your company have a dress code? Formal or informal? If so, what are some specifics?
2. What do you wear to work on most days? Do you vary your dress according to activities you have planned for that day?
3. How much time and energy do you spend on dress for work?
4. Does your company allow casual dress? If so, why? If not, why not?
5. Is casual dress allowed every day or just on certain days of the week or month?
6. How do you feel about the company's casual-dress policy? Do you like it? Why or why not?
7. How do you prefer to dress at work?
8. Have you seen a difference in your performance when dressed in formal dress versus casual dress?

Discussion Questions

1. What did you learn about dress at work that surprised you?
2. Are you still interested in this profession after completing this assignment? If so, why? If not, why not?
3. How do you want to dress when you begin your career?

Writing Activity

1. Write two or three paragraphs about your thoughts on casual dress in business.
2. Do you think that casual dress was a fad that has passed? Or do you think that casual dress will be a part of business dress in the future?
3. What effect (if any) do you think that dress that emphasizes status distinctions will have on the effectiveness of teamwork? Explain the reasons behind your position.

References

Adomaitis, A.D., and K. K. P. Johnson. (2005). Causal Versus Formal Uniforms: Flight Attendants' Self-Perceptions and Perceived Appraisals by Others. *Clothing and Textiles Research Journal* 23(2): 88–101.

Belleau, B. D., L. A. Miller, P. Elliot, and G. E. Church. (1990). Apparel Preferences of Pregnant Employed Women. *Journal of Consumer Studies and Home Economics* 14:291–301.

Bickman, L. (1974). The Social Power of a Uniform. *Journal of Applied Social Psychology* 4:47–61.

Blalock, E. C. (2006). African American College Students' Perceptions of Professional Dress. Unpublished master's thesis, University of Georgia, Athens, Georgia.

Cunningham, P. A. (2003). *Politics, Health, and Art: Reforming Women's Fashion, 1850–1920*. London: The Kent State University Press.

Damhorst, M. L., and A. M. Fiore. (1990). Women's Job Interview Dress: How Personnel Interviewers See It. In M. L. Damhorst, K. A. Miller, and S. O. Michelman (Eds.), *The Meanings of Dress*, 92–97. New York: Fairchild Publications.

Damhorst, M. L., and J. A. Pinaire Reed. (1986). Clothing Color Value and Facial Expression: Effects on Evaluations of Female Job Applicants. *Social Behavior and Personality* 14:89–98.

Form, W. H., and G. P. Stone. (1957). *The Social Significance of Clothing in Occupational*

Life (Technical Bulletin 262). East Lansing: Michigan State University, Agricultural Experiment Station.

Johnson, K., C. Crutsinger, and J. Workman. (1994). Can Professional Women Appear Too Masculine? The Case of the Necktie. *Clothing and Textiles Research Journal* 12:27–31.

Johnson, K., and M. E. Roach-Higgins. (1987). Dress and Physical Attractiveness of Women in Job Interviews. *Clothing and Textiles Research Journal* 5:1–8.

Kimle, P. A., and M. L. Damhorst. (1997). A Grounded Theory Model of the Ideal Business Image for Women. *Symbolic Interaction* 20(1): 45–68.

Marshall, G. (Ed.). (1994). *The Concise Oxford Dictionary of Sociology*. Oxford: Oxford University Press.

Marcketti, S. B., and J. Farrell-Beck. (2008–2009). "Look Like a Lady; Act Like a Man; Work Like a Dog": Dressing for Business Success. *Dress* 35:49–67.

Peluchette, J. V., K. Karl, and K. Rust. (2006). Dressing to Impress: Beliefs and Attitudes Regarding Workplace Attire. *Journal of Business and Psychology* 21 (1): 45–63.

Rucker, M., D. Taber, and A. Harrison. (1981). The Effect of Clothing Variation on First Impressions of Female Job Applicants: What to Wear When. *Social Behavior and Personality* 9:53–64.

Storm, P. (1987). *Functions of Dress: Tool of Culture and the Individual*. Englewood Cliffs, NJ: Prentice Hall.

Taguiri, R., and L. Petrullo. (1958). *Person Perception and Interpersonal Behavior*. Stanford, CA: Stanford University Press.

Thurston, J., Lennon, S., and R. Clayton. (1990). Influence of Age, Body Type, Fashion and Garment Type on Women's Professional Image. *Home Economics Research Journal* 19:139–150.

"LOOK LIKE A LADY, ACT LIKE A MAN, WORK LIKE A DOG": DRESSING FOR BUSINESS SUCCESS

Sara B. Marcketti and Jane Farrell-Beck

This pithy advice to working women from *Fortune* in 1990[1] may seem a bit uncouth to the twenty-first century reader, but it captures the expectations from this time all too well. Throughout the twentieth century, and especially from the 1970s onward, working women in the United States received a plethora of advice in magazines, books, and newspapers on the ways to dress appropriately in the workplace. Advice about business dress reflected expected career paths. Women were encouraged to follow such advice to communicate their professional aspirations and (presumably) earn success within the workplace. The advice does not appear in a vacuum, however, as the sartorial prescriptions reflected prevailing societal norms. The goal of this research was to consider the ways in which the types of advice supplied by the "dress for success" literature were informed by women's involvement in previously male-dominated management positions within the workforce. Using information disseminated by image consultants in books and magazines, feminist theories, and statistical data concerning women in the workforce, we have analyzed changes in the women's dress for success literature.

Women have long worked for pay, both inside and outside of the home—often however, in what Wendy Gamber calls "feminine pursuits" of the sex-segregated occupations of food preparation, the needle trades, and childcare.[2] While women's work in the creation of consumer goods and services is vitally important,[3] from the 1970s through the 2000s, U.S. women's workforce participation surpassed that of men's. It is through examination of the ways women navigated their new roles with the assistance of dress that we may better understand the societal norms and expectations of a period. The increase in women's opportunities for and attainment of leadership positions in business and management and their use of dress

to signal these roles from the 1970s to 2000s casts light on the communicative meaning of clothing.[4] During these decades, the "correct" professional apparel signaled the social status of the wearer (education, scholastic achievement, and position) as well as legitimizing and even normalizing a woman's role within a particular organization.[5] Clothing, particularly business dress, had the power to influence the perception of an individual's performance, credibility, intelligence, motivation, and personality, even serving as a powerful symbol of the values and beliefs of an organization.[6]

Advice literature, while not a sure guide to actual dress practices, illuminates expectations within specific social groups at particular times. Combined with other primary evidence, advice literature can reveal prevalent ideals of dress, and a comparison of writings through time suggests how ideals have shifted. A few scholars have delved into clothing advice for various groups. In the nineteenth-century United States, ideals of female domesticity collided with some women's search for better health and wider opportunities for useful work. Writers debated which goals were legitimate and how to achieve them.[7] Health reform movements generated a surfeit of advice alluded to briefly by Rabun and Drake and much more fully explored by Cunningham.[8] Children's apparel was also subject to copious advice, including healthful attire for girls and suitably boyish garments for their brothers.[9] Schorman revealed the detailed coaching given to late-nineteenth-century men on choosing high-quality, manly business attire.[10] During the 1920s, proscriptions and prescriptions for professional apparel covered

"Look Like a Lady, Act Like a Man, Work Like a Dog: Dressing for Business Success," by Sara B. Marcketti and Jane Farrell-Beck appeared in the journal *DRESS*, vol. 35, 2008–2009, pp. 49–69. Reprinted with permission.

topics such as appropriateness, functionality, and the avoidance of extremes in appearances.[11]

One problem with advice columns and books, revealed by Wehrle and Paoletti, was plagiarism among writers, so that verbatim instructions appeared among a variety of titles from supposedly independent authors.[12] Researchers thus have had to decide if it is one opinion voiced multiple times, or converging but distinct opinions. In the litigious late twentieth century, plagiarism without penalty is not so easy to commit, and the personalities who write the books and articles are well-known individuals, reducing the likelihood that several writers are working from one script. Knowing something about the authors' credentials and general views helps to evaluate the applicability of their advice. For example, the conservative social views of Edward Bok, editor of *Ladies' Home Journal*, colors the preference for home sewing over ready-made apparel expressed in his magazine's pages.[13] Other sources point to a broad acceptance of ready-mades among American women.

Less problematical in recent advice books, compared to earlier writings, is the divergence of recommended ideals from accepted fashion. Authors now spell out the distinctions between business-worthy styles and short-lived fashions. News articles report on what business people are currently wearing, allowing readers to make their choices in context.

In order to track the changes in the dress for success literature, we analyzed information disseminated by image consultants and writers and published in books such as John Molloy's *The Women's Dress for Success Book*, Janet Wallach's *Looks That Work*, and Emily Cho's *Looking Terrific*. Periodical articles from *U.S. News and World Report, Time, Working Woman, Glamour, Redbook Magazine, Mademoiselle*, and newspaper articles from *The New York Times* and *The Wall Street Journal* were examined. A systematic analysis of the *Readers' Guide to Periodical Literature* and our University's Expanded Academic ASAP database facilitated the search for sources. United States (U.S.) Department of Labor and U.S. Census data established the number and types of management occupations women engaged in from the 1970s to

the 1990s. Because this paper concentrates on the 1970s through the 2000s, we made a less comprehensive search of older advice, but did seek out fashion and women's magazines and occasional book chapters that mentioned business-worthy attire. Our purpose was to provide a point of reference for the abundant advice proffered over the past forty years.

Supporting Roles in Business

Women participated in the white-collar workforce even before the twentieth century, but became particularly active starting in World War I through World War II. Writers supplied advice about women's business dress and general wardrobes throughout the twentieth century. Women holding office jobs in the early 1900s were expected to adopt severely plain apparel, reserving frilly touches for after-hours and private time, and dressing at a level appropriate with their "station" in the hierarchy.[14] Writers described proper business dress in very general terms: neat, comfortable, durable, and—the Progressive watchword—"efficient." Hairstyles and grooming were to be tidy and easily maintained.[15]

The proliferation of academic high schools, vocational schools, and colleges with programs in typing, shorthand, and stenography prepared women for female-dominated careers.[16] Office work for women, usually limited to secretarial and bookkeeping functions in the 1910s, called for the staple tailored wool skirt and washable shirtwaist blouse. Not all writers found this uniform becoming, and suggested tailor-made wool dresses or suits with unfussy blouses.[17] The growth of department stores and popular press coverage of ready-to-wear apparel encouraged participation in consumption. Magazine columnists recommended better quality clothes that would fit well and stand up to daily wear, discouraging overly fashionable details that would quickly become outmoded. Working women were urged to maintain a dignified appearance, neither provocative nor too severe, and to treat their work seriously, not as a mere bridge between school and marriage.[18]

By 1920, American women workers numbered 8,346,796.[19] They had substantially taken over the functions of the business office, where opportunities increased in the 1920s, as business bureaucratized. Contemporary observers also thought suffrage had given women added economic clout, although some disparaged them with the new expression "working girls." Books dealt in verbal generalities, but periodicals used illustrations and showed how current fashion could be selected for the office, meeting the magazines' goal of promoting the clothes of their advertisers. Avoid being a slave of fashion, urged Lillian Eichler. She recommended shunning gaudy or alluring styles and designs that were too new to be acceptable. No woman bent on a career should look like a stenographer. Tweed or jersey suits remained staples. A dress-plus-coat ensemble worked well in chilly weather; a sleeved dress sufficed for summer. Dressy dresses had no place in the office.[20]

During the 1920s, writers emphasized budgeting for a business wardrobe with an extended life. Margaret Matlack set forth three-year budget plans for different salaries, from $1800 to $4000 per year, and suggested balancing conservative dresses for several seasons' wear with modish styles for short-term use.[21] *Vogue* recommended clothes that would stand up to a day's wear and that were current in style, not the end-of-season finds with an abbreviated fashion life.[22] In general, 1920s advice became more specific and accommodated broad changes in fashion, such as the prevalence of dresses compared to the ever-present tailored separates of the early 1900s. The importance of appearance to success was definitively stated in *Independent Woman: A National Magazine for Business and Professional Women*: "Part of the business woman's stock in trade is a smart, trim appearance, and so long as she is in business she must adopt higher clothes standards as her earnings increase."[23]

Tempting as it is to characterize the 1930s as a uniformly grim time in American economic life, the picture for women was more mixed. Of the 13 million unemployed Americans at the depth of the Depression, 400,000 were women. However, women were able to reenter the work force more quickly than men were because their white-collar work contracted less than men's jobs in manufacturing.[24] The expansion of the federal government, beginning in 1933, created jobs for many women. In 1935, 1,964,000 women were office workers.[25] Yet, less than 20 percent of the nation's adult women worked outside of the home.[26] Women in the private sector suffered reduced wages. Surprisingly, women still managed to buy clothes to the tune of about $20 per month. Those rare holders of executive secretary posts earned $3500 to $6000 annually, giving them more discretionary dollars for clothes.[27] The introduction of manufactured fibers, such as rayon and acetate, provided cheaper alternatives to cotton and silk dresses.

Advice to businesswomen (or "girls") varied only slightly from the previous period. Dresses were deemed more economical for office wear, although suits were offered as an alternative. Color coordination became a popular topic. In light of the increasingly close-fitting fashions, one advisor noted the need for a good girdle, corset, or corselet.[28] Advice about having a repair kit in the office for grooming purposes suggests a more modern approach to cosmetics compared to the 1910s and 1920s, when makeup was slowly becoming acceptable.

In a world just recovering from the Depression and quickly engulfed in war, civilian matters such as wardrobe advice became a low priority. The female labor force grew by 6.5 million in the early 1940s, a rise of 46 percent.[29] However, substantial numbers of new jobs were in factory work, where typical attire included coveralls, slacks, smocks, hair confiners, and sturdy shoes. Young women working alongside men in engineering departments were described as wearing "street clothes," with no details given.[30] *Mademoiselle* periodically presented seasonal clothing budgets for young women at different salary levels. The columnist promoted coordination of pieces, for economy and—after the United States entered the war—conservation. An adaptable suit and dresses with or without jackets in dark colors with bright accents offered economy.[31]

Once the war ended, many women in heavy industry lost their jobs to returning veterans. However, some displaced workers returned to the labor force by 1947. Increasing numbers of married women entered the labor force and the number of married working mothers increased by 400 percent between 1940 and 1960.[32] Bea Danville's advice to "career girls" tended toward dark colors, carefully edited, and a mixture of dresses, a suit, and separates.[33] Clothing advice of the 1950s and early 1960s leaned heavily on "typing" of personalities and figures, with a view to personal expression and improvement rather than advancement into the executive suite.

Women's Employment

The decades from the 1960s to 2000 brought notable changes in women's labor-force activities, including increased participation and growth in higher paying occupations. In 1960, about 38% of women aged 16 and older were in the labor force; by 1980, over half of U.S. women worked; and in the 2000s, working women accounted for nearly 60% of the female population (see Table 10.1).[34] As women's labor-force participation increased, so did their employment in higher paying occupations. According to the U.S. Bureau of the Census, women's roles in managerial, professional, and related occupations grew from 33% in 1960 to levels nearly equal to men in 2000 (see Table 10.2).[35] Despite these improvements, women's earnings relative to men, while increasing, were still not equal. In 1979, among full-time workers, women's earnings were approximately 62 percent of men's; by 2006, the ratio had grown to about 81 percent.[36] Much empirical work was devoted to explaining differences in earnings between the sexes, examining discriminatory practices, gender-segregated employment patterns, and the predominant role of women in child and home care.[37]

The increased movement of women into the labor force and into higher paying occupations went hand in hand with the pursuit of higher education. In 1970, just over one tenth of women in the labor force had completed four or more years of college; by 2006, one-third of women held at least a bachelor's degree (see Table 10.3). Further, women made great strides in advanced education. By 1980, women earned more than two-fifths of all master's degrees in the U.S. and approximately one-fourth of all law, medical, and doctorate degrees. Because women's potential earnings increased with education, women realized high returns on their investment.[38]

Institutional and social changes were also associated with rising labor-force participation. Opportunities afforded working women were buttressed by state and federal legislation. Laws such as the Equal Pay Act (1963, extended to management jobs, 1972), the Civil Rights Act (1964), affirmative action (1965), Title IX (1972), and the Higher Education Act (amended 1975) all helped reduce discrimination against women in education and labor force. Individual states also prohibited sex discrimination in employment.[39]

TABLE 10.1

Number and Percent of Working Women in the Labor Force, 1955–2005 (Number In Thousands)

Year	Number of Women Employed	Percent of Female Population Employed
1955	20,548	35.7
1960	23,272	37.8
1965	26,232	39.3
1970	31,543	46.3
1975	37,475	46.3
1980	45,487	51.5
1985	51,050	54.5
1990	56,829	57.5
1995	60,944	58.9
2000	66,303	59.9
2005	69,288	59.3

Source: Women in the Labor Force: A Databook (Washington, DC: U.S. Department of Labor and U.S. Bureau of Labor Statistics, 1981, 2007).

TABLE 10.2

Occupations of the Women's Participation in the Workforce (Female as Percent of Total)

Occupation	1970	1980	1990	2000
A. Managerial and Professional	33.9	42.6	46.3	49

A. Managerial and Professional includes executive administrators and managers and professional specialties such as architects, engineers, teachers, lawyers, etc. The inclusion of teachers in this category could mean a fair number of women in relatively low-paying jobs.

Source: Statistical Abstract of the United States (Washington, DC: U.S. Department of Commerce, 2001).

TABLE 10.3

Female Labor-Force Participation Rates by Educational Attainment, 1970–2000

Year	Percent of Women in the Labor Force with Only a High School Degree	Percent of Women in the Labor Force with 4 or More Years of College*
1970	44.3	11.2
1975	45.5	14.1
1980	45.4	18.7
1985	44.4	22.0
1990	42.4	24.5
1995	34.1	26.9
2000	31.6	30.1
2005	28.2	33.3

*Note: Beginning in 1992, data on educational attainment are annual averages and are based on the "highest diploma or degree received" rather than the "number of years of school completed." Therefore, the 1970 to 1990 data refers to women who attended four or more years of college, whereas the 1995 to 2005 statistical data refer to women with college degrees.

Source: Women in the Laborforce: A Databook (Washington, DC: U.S. Department of Labor and U.S. Bureau of Labor Statistics, 2007).

Entry-Level Management

Women entered the U.S. work world in force in the late 1960s due to economic need, labor demands, changes in legislation, and ongoing modifications in societal norms, such as increases in white-collar openings, a drop in the birth rate, inflationary trends, and the increased number of single, divorced, or widowed women.[40] Women's workforce involvement was also influenced by "second wave" feminism that pushed beyond the early quest for political rights to fight for greater equality. Although the revolution in societal sex roles was taking place in the 1960s, women's progress in the job market, as measured by their earn-

ings and employment opportunities, was limited. Women's participation in work increased, from 35% in 1955 to 38% in 1960, yet they entered roles in the traditional female sector, particularly clerical work and teaching and health services.[41]

While the Equal Pay Act, the *Presidential Report on American Women*, the *Feminine Mystique*, and the creation of the National Organization of Women (NOW) contributed to a growing sense of gender consciousness, these changes in women's involvement in work called forth a less single-minded flood of advice on dressing for business success. Some were guides to elegant style, advice for the woman who wanted to look slimmer, taller, or more confident, or primers on personal style imitating Hollywood glamour. Edith Head's *How to Dress for Success* tome included advice for finding and keeping a job—and a man.[42]

Middle Management

While legislation such as the Higher Education Act supported women's entry into certain male-dominated fields, women continued to flood traditionally female-held jobs such as secretaries, nurses, bank tellers, primary-school teachers, and librarians. To remedy the lack of inclusion in male-dominated fields such as business, the sciences, and engineering, several government agencies and private organizations sought to promote women through legal action and educational programs and pamphlets for employers.[43] These steps increased women's attainment of higher-level middle management positions in finance, marketing, personnel and labor relations, and properties and real estate. In 1960, women composed less than 6 percent of the executive, administrative, and managerial occupational group in the U.S. Census. By 1970, that percentage rose to 18.5%, in 1980 to 30.5%, and in 1990 to 40.6% of the total (see Table 10.4). The proportional gains women made in the managerial category from the 1960s to early 1980s were larger than in any other major occupational group.[44]

In their newly found roles, women faced enormous challenges in proving their worth as well as outperforming their predecessors in the stereotypical responsibilities of homemakers, wives, and secretaries. Women faced the very real challenge in the 1970s of finding clothing that was attractive *and* appropriate for their new middle management positions. During the 1970s, there was no dress protocol for women managers and business directors, as there was for men throughout the nineteenth and twentieth centuries. Former teachers and insurance underwriters (John Molloy), booking agents for modeling agencies (Emily Cho), and fashion merchandisers (Janet Wallach) sought to fill this gap. Numerous authors penned books and articles describing in detail looks that would afford women success in the workplace. The prescriptive "dress for success" movement was born.

John T. Molloy, probably the best-known dress for success author, promoted the "Success Suit": a conservative, skirted two-piece suit in a dark color and natural fabric worn with a modest high-necked blouse, plain pumps, and an attaché case. Advocates of this look urged women to adopt the "uniform" as a way of taking a "firm and dramatic step toward professional equity with men." The stated purpose of the success suit was not to imitate men, but rather to provide "a simple set of rules" to advance women professionally and socially.[45]

The tailored business look starkly contrasted with the wrap dresses popularized during the time. Suit designer for Arthur Richards, Suzie Cracker, encouraged women to eschew sexy dresses so that male bosses would not confuse their middle level managers with their "lovers or secretaries," and writer Polly Bergen urged women to "dress for business, not monkey business."[46] John

TABLE 10.4

Occupations of the Women's Participation in the Workforce (Female as Percent of Total)

Occupation	1970	1980	1990	2000	1970–2000
Executive administrative and managerial workers	18.5	30.5	40.6	45.3	+144%
Financial managers	19.4	31.4	45.9	52.7	+172%
Marketing, advertising, and public relations	7.9	17.6	30.6	37.6	+375%
Personnel and labor relations	21.2	36	57.6	61.8	+192%
Properties and real estate	32.1	41.1	46.0	50.9	+59%
Accountants and auditors	24.6	38.8	51.5	56.7	+130%

Source: *Statistical Abstracts of the United States* (Washington, DC: U.S. Department of Commerce, 1985, 1992, 2006).

Molloy echoed this sentiment in the introduction to his *Women's Dress for Success* book, in which he wrote, "Women dress for failure because they make [these] mistakes, they let the fashion industry influence their choice of business clothes and they often still view themselves as sex objects."[47] Molloy urged women to show their business goals by dressing for the job they wanted, stressing the importance of clothing in establishing and legitimizing leadership.

The uniform look promoted by Molloy and others changed the clothing industry. Of the top ten suit producers for men in the 1970s, seven added women's lines. Women affirmed their "big spender" stereotype, accounting for over 15% of total sales for Brooks Brothers (who added women's clothing in 1976) and helping to move over $3.5 million of Joseph-Picone women's suits.[48] As pointed out by Susan Faludi, "the uniform" could liberate women from fashion-victim status because suits were not as subject to the wild swings in fashion as dresses, and they could be worn with varying blouses and accessories, thus saving time and money necessary for shopping the latest business trends.[49]

Indeed, not all women customers, fashion designers, or writers liked the uniform look for women. Caroline Bird, the feminist author of *The Two Paycheck Marriage*, charged suit makers with "making a fast buck off of the insecurities of women" believing suits "pushed women back to being an object."[50] Some feminists questioned the rationale that looking similar to a man through dressing for success would bring about equal treatment. Journalist Ellen Goodman stated,

> When the "male" standard is regarded as the "higher" one, the one with the most tangible rewards, it is easier for women to reach "up" than to convince men of the virtues of simultaneously reaching "down." It has proved simpler—though not simple, God knows—for women to begin traveling traditional (male) routes than to change those routes. It is simpler to dress for success than to change the definition of success . . .[51]

Debating the actual correlation between dressing for success with women's professional advancements, writer Michael Korda refused "to believe that women are being kept off the boards of corporations because they don't know what to wear."[52] Indeed, while the prescriptions for dressing for success were heavily illustrated and clear, the apparel industry proffered a huge variety of often-contradictory advice. While Molloy and others were promoting the male-inspired business suit, *Vogue* editor-in-chief Grace Mirabella and *Harper's Bazaar* Fashion Editor Elsa Klensch insisted a woman did not need tailored jackets to have authority, but "gets her own way by using feminine wiles."[53] Writer Emily Cho suggested women managers "dress distinctively and look interesting," foregoing suits and ascots for flattering dresses.[54] The "stratified homogeneity" of dress suggested by some in the 1970s (wrap dresses recommended by fashion editors and suits suggested by some consultants) hinted at women's discrepant roles. The introduction of pantsuits further inflamed the dilemma of what to wear, as the very act of wearing them proved controversial.[55]

While *Glamour* magazine introduced the now-common pie chart to help women visualize their daily activities and plan purchases to cover all slices of their lives, the writers do not really explain which styles might help the wearer attain the executive suite.[56] Rather, writers and consultants consistently mentioned dressing to impress with attractive and appropriate dress, hair, and makeup styles and dressing for the role women wanted. Perhaps some of the ambiguity and contradictions in the advice literature came from the lack of role models in upper-level positions. Further complicating the discussion, women were consistently warned that too much emphasis on clothing and not enough on business and leadership development might lead a woman solely to the dressing room and not to the executive-level boardroom, a persistent theme in twentieth-century appearance management.[57]

Attacking the Glass Ceiling

Women's participation in the U.S. labor force equaled male levels by 1980. However, women remained in the distinct minority in the highest-levels of executive positions. According to a 1984 estimate, 49,000 men and only 1,000 women held top policy-making jobs in major corporations. Further, only 367 women, compared with 15,500 men, held board positions in the top 1,300 public companies in the United States, and among the 6,543 directorships in the Fortune 500, a mere 2.8 percent were occupied by women.[58] In the federal government, only 6.2 percent of employed women were at or above the level of upper-middle management; men, however, were four times more likely to reach those levels, with nearly 28 percent of all federally employed males located in the highest categories.[59]

Faced with this dramatic imbalance, the Federal Glass Ceiling Commission assessed the barriers hindering the advancement of women.[60] Numerous scholarly and popular studies investigated the many factors (e.g., education; gender-role stereotypes; lack of mentors and training programs; discrimination; access to power) that contributed to or inhibited the success of women in upper-echelon careers.[61] Some authors noted the difficulties of successfully combining work and family, little support from senior executives, increased competition, and male *and* female resentment as obstacles hindering women's advancements in the business world.[62] One study published in the *Journal of Applied Psychology* and reported in periodicals such as *Science Digest*, *Working Woman*, and *Nation's Business* went so far as to say beauty was a hindrance in women achieving an office in the executive suite.[63]

All explanations seemed controversial to one group or the other as to why women had made so many inroads in middle management but had not broken into the highest levels of management. In an article adapted from the book *Breaking the Glass Ceiling: Can Women Reach the Top of America's Largest Corporations?*, women were advised to do the near impossible: "take risks, but be consistently outstanding," "be tough, but don't be macho," "take responsibility, but follow others' [even subordinates] advice." Without outrage or anger, the authors stated, "be ambitious, but don't expect equal treatment"—advice that was surely not inspiring or encouraging to emerging professionals.[64]

There was an increased realization in the 1980s that geographic location, specific industry, company policy, job responsibility, and personal tastes were necessary factors (overlooked in the 1970s) when "dressing for success." The work of Evans and Thornton suggest that feminist discourse in the 1980s shifted from an emphasis on being controlled by fashion—a perspective dominant in the 1970s—to an emphasis on choosing to control fashion.[65] Feminist writer Betty Friedan lamented, "I think it is too bad that dressing for success had become a symbol of trying to copy men. We're at a halfway point, exchanging the rigidity of one role for the rigidity of another. It really isn't liberation yet."[66] One may see the beginning of this shifting perspective in women's shying away from the "tailored boredom" of mannish suits, bowties, pumps, and attaché cases—uniform of the 1970s—into a greater diversity of knit suits, silk dresses, blouses, and skirts in the 1980s.

There remained, however, emphasis on dressing conservatively early in one's career. The gray flannel business suit remained the benchmark for women entering lower-level management positions and for interview attire. Yet, the "dress for success" literature, and society as a whole, deemed softer silhouettes, lighter and brighter colors, and versatility dressing with simple pieces such as dresses, blazers, and cardigans appropriate for middle and upper management positions.[67] In a *Glamour* special report on "clothes and clout," women in diverse business settings from the corporate world to creative ad firms stressed their desire to "liven up business suits without divesting it of authority, looking feminine without looking frilly and shopping wisely given high prices and limited time."[68]

In books such as Janet Wallach's *Working Wardrobe: Affordable Clothes That Work for You!* and Gerrie Pinckney and Marge Swenson's *New Images for Women*, working women were urged to consider their personalities when choosing business attire, a persistent theme from the 1920s through the 1960s.[69] Through quiz questions such as "Your favorite acting role would be: a) Faye Dunaway in *Network*, b) Joan Collins in *Dynasty*, c) Lauren Bacall in *Woman of the Year*, d) Sally Field in *Absence of Malice*, e) Jane Fonda in *Julia*, or f) Diane Keaton in *Annie Hall*," Wallach's book profiled women as either corporate, communicator, or creative types. These profiles dictated the silhouette, fabric, and color selections Wallach found appropriate to the personality types. Designers and brands such as Kasper, Chaus, and Evan Picone served as resources for corporate women; Ellen Tracy, Bill Blass, and Liz Claiborne best suited communicators; and Calvin Klein, OMO Norma Kamali, and Oscar de la Renta best fit creative types.

Writers often used Wallach's synopsis of clothing specifications based upon personality types and individual characteristics in the 1980s. Pinckney, Swenson, and Carole Jackson of the company *Color Me Beautiful* divided all women into four types: winter (dark hair and skin), summer (pinkish skin), spring (peach skin and golden hair), and autumn (beige skin and dark hair). Figure analysis, professional aspirations, income, and lifestyle needs provided less esoteric subdivisions.[70] Advice concerning accessories and fine points of grooming skin, hands, makeup, and hair were new topics for authors and image consultants.

In the 1980s, specialty stores, including La Cabine in New York and Jack Henry in Kansas City, and department stores such as San Francisco's I. Magnin and Boston's Filene's, created special sections devoted to career clothes. The increasing complexity and variety of available goods, as well as competing role demands and specializations, increased the need for personal shoppers and consultants in the 1980s. As women were promoted to 60-plus-hour workweeks, personal shoppers (of the expensive consulting breed and the inexpensive department-store and specialty-shop variety) advised professionals what to wear, selected everything from earrings to pumps, and personally delivered purchased wardrobes.[71] Retailers such as Dayton Hudson Corp., Lord & Taylor, and Bloomingdale's heavily advertised their "personal shoppers" and "wardrobe consultants" to boost sales and win customers' loyalty.[72] Employers such as General Electric, Merrill Lynch, and Price Waterhouse and graduate schools of business such as Harvard, Columbia, and the University of Tennessee hired image consultants to teach women how to select and coordinate clothes for work.[73]

These speakers expounded on overall elements of style including the importance of separates to mix and match, quality goods over quantity of goods, the necessity of proper fit and proportion, and the importance of clothing to take the woman from day to night. As researchers and authors discussed the possibility of career and motherhood, and working women campaigned for such a combination, sartorial consultants stressed versatility and comfort in clothing selections.[74]

When women joined the ranks of middle and upper management in the 1980s, jewelers witnessed an increase in purchases made by women for themselves. High-priced jewelry designers reacted to this shift in purchasing behavior by offering their goods in department stores such as Bloomingdale's and Macy's. Leading jewelry stores such as Tiffany & Co., Cartier, and Black, Starr & Frost expanded their lines to include "quietly handsome pieces" more fitting with the executive polished look than pieces encrusted with stones suitable for the CEO's wife.[75]

Corporate Leadership versus Self-Employment

By the 1990s, while corporations struggled to improve competitiveness, flexibility, and even prospects for their survival, many firms restructured their management styles to incorporate new models of leadership. Leadership styles that emphasized persuasion over power and cooperation over competition provided fodder for discussions concerning the supposed "feminization of management." Women rising in corporate ranks were encouraged by the popular press to capitalize on their supposed natural talents of nurturing and effective communication skills.

Literature trumpeted lead stories such as "Women smash business myths," "Vive la difference: Female characteristics as applied to business," "Ways women lead," and "The female advantage," but men continued to hold the lion's share of upper management.[76] In 1993, the *Wall Street Journal* reported that women would not reach parity with men in terms of upper-level management positions until 2023. According to Robin Ely,

Until women receive adequate representation at the top levels of the organization, sex role stereotypes will persist, largely to the detriment of women, as the basis for women's *own* sense of how they differ from men and as the basis for their *own* sense of their individual and collective value to their organizations.[77]

While legislation in the early 1990s made it a federal crime to discriminate in hiring or compensation because of gender, by the late 1990s, women earned just 76 cents for each dollar earned by a man with the same job title.[78] This wage gap was heatedly debated among professionals and was often explained in part by the greater career interruptions experienced by women. Several authors in the 1990s noted that since biology would not change, the corporate world's handling of maternity leave and compensation would need substantial alteration. This was particularly significant because from 1975 to 2000, the labor force participation rate of mothers with children under the age of 18 rose from 47 to 73 percent.[79] To meet the needs of this growing demographic, the catalog company Mothers Work (renamed Destination Maternity Corporation) offered value-priced to high-end career maternity apparel in luxury stores Pea in the Pod and value-priced Motherhood Maternity. The growth of the company from $31 million in 1993 to $602 million in 2006 attested to the working woman's need to look professional, even when pregnant.[80]

When corporations made insufficient changes in handling maternity leave and child-care problems, the career paths of many women shifted. The 1990s and early 2000s brought a dramatic increase in the sheer number and success of women entrepreneurs. In 1992, female-owned businesses employed more of the U.S. population than Fortune 500 companies did. While debates continued throughout the 1990s as to the relevance of affirmative-action programs and related laws to reduce employment discrimination against women, women founded their own businesses in record numbers. By 1996, women owned an estimated one-third of all U.S. businesses. The number of such businesses grew twice as fast as

all firms between 1997 and 2002, jumping 14 percent to 6.2 million, according to the Center for Women's Business Research. By 2008, America's 10.6 million women-owned businesses employed 19.1 million people and contributed $2.46 trillion to the national economy.[81]

Telecommuting, flextime, and self-employment created complications in characterizing women's employment and resultant flexibility in advice literature. Women who glorified (or simply wore) power suits and polished "images" in the previous decades had increased opportunities to shift their dressing for success to dressing for their own needs.[82] Feminists held contrasting views on the importance of dress for success. In the *Lipstick Proviso*, Karen Lehrman wrote, women have the prerogative, indeed the right, to embrace their femininity and dress and act according to their own whims and desires, if that meant wearing "slinky dresses and heels or baggy overalls and combat boots."[83] In contrast, feminist authors Susan Faludi and Norma Wolfe argued that the ever-changing rules of the dress for success movement represented a ploy by advertising executives to make women feel inferior and then foist expensive clothes upon them to improve their status.[84] The contradictory nature of these opinions is in part explained by Elizabeth Wilson's argument that the relationship between women and fashionable dress is often viewed as either stifling or creating the self.[85]

Without a doubt, women's increased involvement in all facets of the business world in the 1990s and 2000s inspired greater confidence in individual dressing while also leaving the door open to professional image coaches. With so many workers situated behind computers in the 1990s, many companies including Ford, IBM, AT&T, Dow Jones, and Internet start-up firms relaxed their dress codes. In 1998, 60 percent of U.S. companies had some degree of business casual.[86] Retail firms such as Brooks Brothers, Eddie Bauer, Dockers, and Banana Republic tried to meet the needs of executives by offering on-site boutiques at business locations, providing fashion consultants and "800" numbers through which individuals could consult with "casual counselors." As men were deciding if business casual meant a less formal shirt and no tie or blue jeans and T-shirts, many female executives were also trading in their expensive business suits for more casual and inexpensive clothing that could move from the executive offices to the grocery store to a late-night dinner entertaining clients. Some sources even recommended dressing for each particular day's activities, with an emergency change of clothes in the office closet for quick upgrades.[87] Sharon Stone epitomized the casual confusion so evident in the 1990s when she appeared at the 1996 Oscars wearing a Valentino ready-to-wear skirt, an Armani dress worn as a coat, and an androgynous black Gap turtleneck. This signified the great ambiguity between casual, work, and formal dress.

Apart from the paradigmatic shift from business professionalism to corporate casual, many women, particularly successful baby boomers, found a general lack of desirable clothing choices in retail outlets. Growing competition from other types of products led to a 40 percent increase in personal consumption from 1989 to 1995 but a 12 percent *decrease* in purchases of women's apparel. Personal care services and products boomed in the 1990s. Facial treatment goods like anti-wrinkle creams and mud masks grew 5 percent over a five-year period in the early 1990s; sale of bath products grew nearly 30 percent in the same period; and fitness club and gym memberships rose 108 percent between 1987 and 1995. Women also spent their money on gardening, leisure trips, and stock market investments. Couture designers had to change their product lines to meet the changing needs of corporate women in the 1990s. Anne Klein closed its top lines in April 1996, concentrating on its lower-priced, more casual collections. Businesswomen also found other venues in which to shop in the 1990s. Discount stores, such as Target, Ross, and Wal-Mart, increased their share of the women's clothing market to 21 percent in 1996, as women found new freedom in finding and wearing "bargains" with pride.[88] First Lady Michelle Obama embodies this mix-and-match philosophy as she regularly pairs garments from lower priced retailers J. Crew and H & M with pricier designer items from Jimmy Choo and Narciso Rodriguez.[89]

While advice literature continued to recognize suits as the cornerstones of corporate apparel for women, the establishment of business dress set the stage for industry-specific norms. At least one book dealt with the levels of dressing for an interview, early years on the job, and advanced executive status, with increased color, pattern, and flexibility at each succeeding level. In the financial world, the power-dress code for women in finance included colorful dresses, feminine-fitting suits, bold handbags, and tall boots with skirts. Even pantyhose, a mainstay of the 1970s dress for success looks, became optional in the most conservative fields.[90] In spite of these freedoms of expression, in 2008, one business-etiquette consultant advised women to wear lighter-colored suits the higher she climbed on the corporate ladder "to be less intimidating,"[91] advice presumably never offered to black-suited businessmen.

Despite great gains made by women in managerial and executive positions, the advice literature continued to stress the "shifting style rules" for women in power. Business-casual dressing remained a minefield, particularly for women, who could lose hard-won authority by looking too amiable. Further, with the varied norms in business casual, switching companies could mean great expenditure of money and time in acquiring a new business-casual wardrobe.[92]

While types of career dressing advice, such as the necessity of wearing pantyhose, were specific to women, advice in the 2000s also reflected economic up- and downturns. During a time of great prosperity and low unemployment rates, a 2007 article heralded "entitled" young lawyers wearing Ugg boots and clingy t-shirts. In 2009, the same writer stressed the return of power dressing even among mailroom clerks as fear of unemployment signaled the heightened need of at least looking important.[93] Common themes of advice in the 2000s continued from previous decades of the investment in good quality, classically styled clothes. Depending on the mood of the moment, these books and articles included everything from wool suits to pantsuits with fine knit tops and loafers, or skirts with knit twin sets.[94] Putting into action feminist theory that parity was not based solely on gender, but also racial and class hierarchies that contributed to oppression, the non-profit charity "Dress for Success" provided women of limited means with interview suits as well as grooming advice to enhance their chances of business success.[95]

Conclusions

During the twentieth century, a few notable differences appeared in advice literature. The core of a businesswoman's wardrobe shifted from dresses to suits between the 1940s and the 2000s. In part, this may reflect a closer correspondence between women's wear and menswear, as women have assumed many of the roles once exclusive to men. Perhaps, too, it represents a shift in the composition of ready-to-wear: fewer "tailored" dresses are produced, compared to festive, seasonal, and informal dresses in the dressmaker tradition rather than the tailor's mode.

Budgeting, a staple of advice for businesswomen in the early twentieth century, largely disappeared from the advice literature since the 1970s. Instead of specific prices or budget tallies, writers give tips for assessing quality in apparel, allocating limited money to important garments, and shopping with savvy. Perhaps greater inflation, particularly in the 1970s through early 1980s, dissuaded authors from committing to price points for anything. Sources of apparel have widened over the last 35 to 40 years to include specialty stores, chic discounters, and conventional department stores. Particularly since the mid-1990s, the Internet has opened almost limitless options, including resale via eBay and other specialty websites. "Shopping in your closet" has become a cliché of advice literature, to dissuade women from making duplicative purchases or falling for a nifty garment that does not work with what they already own.

Much prescriptive advice on how to dress for success, and the nature of success, has changed from 1900 to the present. The shift from manufacturing to services as primary business types and the movement of women from behind desks as secretaries and shop girls to managers and executives contributed to the variety of the dress for success

literature. Industries and businesses unimagined in 1960 became powerful in the 2000s. Business travel put new stresses on wardrobes. Mannish apparel that sought to legitimize women's roles within an organization in the 1970s was replaced with feminine skirts and blouses that signaled new freedoms of expression in the 2000s. Yet, many of the underlying principles of the 1970s to 2000s career dressing advice remained the same: Have clear goals, wear business suits to interviews, know what colors and fabrics are best suited for your complexion and career path, and always recognize that clothing is a billboard for the self and should be chosen with care. Despite women's increased responsibilities, visibility, and confidence in upper management corporate positions, the emphasis remains on dressing "careful[ly] and correct[ly]."[96] Women continue to walk the line between femininity and masculinity, balance dedication to the organization and care of family, and navigate the rules of matching their clothes to their skills, education, position, and ambition. *Fortune* magazine's advice to the 21st century worker might well read, "Look like a professional, act like a professional, and work like a dog."

References

Andre, Mary Lou. *Ready to Wear: An Expert's Guide to Choosing and Using Your Wardrobe.* New York: A Perigee Book/Berkley Publishing Group, 2004.

Baker, Laura Nelson. *Wanted: Women in War Industry: The Complete Guide to a War Factory Job.* New York: E. P. Dutton & Company, Inc., 1943.

Bird, Caroline. *The Two-Paycheck Marriage: How Women at Work Are Changing Life in America: An In-Depth Report on the Great Revolution of Our Times.* New York: Rawson, Wade Publishers 1979.

Blackwelder, Julia. *Now Hiring.* College Station, Texas: Texas A & M University Press, 1997.

Catalyst. *The Double Bind Dilemma for Women in Leadership: Damned if You Do, Doomed if You Don't.* New York: Catalyst, 2007.

Cho, Emily, and Linda Grover. *Looking Terrific.* New York: G. P. Putnam's Sons, 1978.

Cunningham, Patricia A. *Reforming Women's Fashion, 1850–1920.* Kent, Ohio: Kent State University Press, 2003.

Danville, Bea. *Dress Well on $1 a Day.* New York: Wilfred Funk, Inc., 1956.

Dariaux, Genevieve Antoine. *Elegance.* Garden City, New York: Doubleday & Company, Inc., 1964.

Eichler, Lillian. *Book of Etiquette, Volume II*. Garden City, New York: Nelson Doubleday, Inc., 1923.

Faludi, Susan. *Backlash: The Undeclared War Against American Women*. New York: Three Rivers Press, 2006.

Fiedorek, Mary B., and Diana Lewis Jewell. *Executive Style: Looking It . . . Living It*. Piscataway, New Jersey: New Century Publishers, Inc., 1983.

Giles, Nell. *Punch In, Susie: A Woman's War Factory Diary*. New York: Harper & Brothers Publishers, 1943.

Head, Edith and Joe Hyams. *How to Dress for Success* New York: Random House, 1967.

Hemingway, Patricia Drake. *The Well-Dressed Woman: A Complete Guide to Creating the Right Look for Yourself and Your Career*. New York: David McKay Company, Inc., 1977.

Hoerle, H. C., and F. B. Saltzburg. *The Girl and the Job*. New York: Henry Holt and Company, 1919.

Gross, Kim Johnson, Jeff Stone, and Kristina Zimbalist. *Dress Smart Women: Wardrobes That Win in the New Workplace*. New York: Warner Books, 2002.

Molloy, John T. *The Women's Dress for Success Book*. New York: Warner Books, 1977.

Norwood, Mandi. *Michelle Style: Celebrating the First Lady of Fashion*. New York: William Morrow, 2009.

Picken, Mary Brooks. *Harmony in Dress*. Scranton, PA: Women's Institute of Domestic Arts and Sciences, 1926.

Pinckney, Gerrie, and Marge Swenson. *New Images for Women*. Virginia: Reston Publishing Company, Inc., 1981.

Schorman, Rob. *Selling Style: Clothing and Social Change at the Turn of the Century*. Philadelphia: University of Pennsylvania Press, 2003.

U.S. Bureau of the Census, *Fourteenth Census of the United States Taken in the Year 1920: Volume IV, Population* (Washington, D. C.: Government Printing Office, 1923).

U.S. Department of Labor, *Report on the Glass Ceiling Initiative*. (Washington, D. C., Government Printing Office, 1991).

U.S. Department of Labor and U.S. Bureau of Labor Statistics, *Women in the Labor Force: A Databook*. (Washington, D. C., Government Printing Office, 2007).

Wallach, Janet. *Working Wardrobe: Affordable Clothes That Work for You!* New York: Warner Books, 1981.

Wolf, Naomi. *The Beauty Myth*. New York: William Morrow and Company, Inc., 1991.

Endnotes

1. Jaclyn Fierman, "Why Women Still Don't Hit the Top," *Fortune*, July 30, 1990, 40–48.
2. Wendy Gamber, "A gendered enterprise: Placing nineteenth-century businesswomen in history," *Business History Review* 72 (1998): 205. See also Elizabeth Wayland Barber, *Women's Work: The First 20,000 Years* (New York: W. W. Norton & Co., 1994).
3. Kathy Peiss, "Vital Industry and Women's Ventures: Conceptualizing Gender in Twentieth Century Business History," *The Business History Review* 72 (1998): 218–241; Joan Scott, "Conceptualizing Gender in American Business History," *The Business History Review* 72 (1998): 242–249.
4. Sandra M. Forsythe, "Dressing for Success: The Myth and the Reality," *Journal of Home Economics* 85 (1993): 49–54; Anat Rafaeli and Michale G. Pratt, "Tailored Meanings: On the Meaning and Impact of Organizational Dress," *Academy of Management Review* 18 (1993): 32–55.
5. Jennifer P. Ogle and Mary Lynn Damhorst, "Dress for Success in the Popular Press," in *Appearance and Power*, ed. Kim P. Johnson and Sharon P. Lennon, 79–101 (New York, Berg, 1999).
6. Mary Lipitsky and Cynthia M. Smith, "Impact of Clothing on Impressions of Personal Characteristics and Writing Ability," *Home Economics Research Journal* 9 (1981): 327–335; Dorothy U. Behling and E. A. Williams, "Influence of Dress on Perceptions of Intelligence and Expectations of Scholastic Achievement," *Clothing and Textiles Research Journal* 9 (1991): 1–7; Sandra M. Forsythe, Mary F. Drake, and Charles A. Cox, "Dress as an Influence on the Perceptions of Management Characteristics in Women," *Home Economics Research Journal* 13 (1985): 112–121; Mary Ellen Roach-Higgins and Joanne Eicher, "Dress and identity," *Clothing and Textiles Research Journal* 10 (1992): 1–8; Fred Davis, *Fashion, Culture and Identity* (Chicago: University of Chicago Press, 1992); Michael R. Solomon and S. P. Douglas, "Diversity in Product Symbolism: The Case of Female Executive Clothing," *Psychology and Marketing* (1987): 184–212.
7. Sally Helvenston, "Popular Advice for the Well-Dressed Woman in the 19th Century," *Dress* 5 (1980): 31–46.
8. Josette H. Rabun and Mary Frances Drake, "Warmth in Clothing: A Victorian Perspective," *Dress* 9 (1983): 24–31; Patricia A. Cunningham, *Reforming Women's Fashion, 1850–1920* (Kent, OH: Kent State University Press, 2003).
9. Christina Bates, "How to Dress the Children? Prescription and Practice in Late-Nineteenth-Century North America," *Dress* 24 (1997): 43–54; Jo B. Paoletti, "Clothes Make the Boy, 1860–1910," *Dress* 9 (1983): 16–20.
10. Rob Schorman, *Selling Style: Clothing and Social Change at the Turn of the Century* (Philadelphia: University of Pennsylvania Press, 2003).

11. Ann Kellogg, "Advice on Dress and Appearance to Business Women in the 1920s from Selected Business Periodicals" (master's thesis, Michigan State University, 1995).

12. Louise Wehrle and Jo Paoletti, "What Do We Wear to the Wedding Now That the Funeral Is Over? A Look at Advice and Etiquette Literature, and Practice during the Years 1880–1910 in America," *Dress* 16 (1990): 81–88.

13. Schorman, *Selling Style*.

14. Schorman, *Selling Style*, 1–2, 69.

15. Alyson Rhodes-Murphy, "The "Art and Science of Dress" for 'Well-dressed' Women as Directed by Etiquette and Advice Literature, 1870–1920" (master's thesis, Iowa State University, 1999), 232–233.

16. Julia Blackwelder, *Now Hiring* (College Station, TX: Texas A & M University Press, 1997).

17. Caroline Trowbridge Radnor-Lewis, "Her Wardrobe: The Business Woman's Outfit," *Good Housekeeping Magazine*, November 1911, 633–636; "The Clothes of a Business Woman," *Good Housekeeping*, October 1915, 527.

18. H.C. Hoerle and F. B. Saltzburg, *The Girl and the Job* (New York: Henry Holt and Company, 1919), 248.

19. U. S. Bureau of the Census, *Fourteenth Census of the United States Taken in the Year 1920: Volume IV, Population* (Washington: Government Printing Office, 1923), 964.

20. Lillian Eichler, *Book of Etiquette, Volume II* (Garden City, New York: Nelson Doubleday, Inc., 1923), 178–184; "A Guide to Chic for the Business Woman," *Vogue*, September 15, 1924, 98–99, 134.

21. Margaret Matlack, "Budgeting the Successful Business Woman's Clothes," *Ladies' Home Journal*, April 1926, 93, 97–98, 103.

22. Virginia Dibble, a former fashion editor of *Woman's Home Companion*, encouraged women to adopt becoming colors for at least two seasons, preferably two years if money was limited. Virginia Dribble, "The Dress Critic: What Is Your Goal," *Independent Woman*, May 1927, 23, 43. "A Guide to Chic for the Business Woman," *Vogue*, November 15, 1926, 70–71, 142.

23. "You—As Others Now See You," *Independent Woman*, May 1927, 13.

24. David M. Kennedy, *Freedom from Fear: The American People in Depression and War, 1929–1945* (New York: Oxford University Press, 1999): 164.

25. "Women in Business: I," *Fortune*, July 1935, 55.

26. Gaye Tuchman, "The Impact of Mass Media Stereotypes upon the Full Employment of Women," in *Women in the U. S. Labor Force*, ed. Anne Foote Cahn (New York: Praeger Publishers, 1979).

27. "Women in Business: II," *Fortune*, August 1935, 55, 85.

28. Julia Coburn, "If at First You Don't Succeed, Change the Way You Dress," *Ladies' Home Journal*, November 1934, 32–35, 88.

29. Blackwelder, *Now Hiring*, 123.

30. Laura Nelson Baker, *Wanted: Women in War Industry: The Complete Guide to a War Factory Job* (New York: E. P. Dutton & Company, Inc., 1943), 89–98; Nell Giles, *Punch In, Susie: A Woman's War Factory Diary* (New York: Harper & Brothers Publishers, 1943), 86.

31. Marian Van, "If Wishes Were Wardrobes, I'd Abolish Budgets," *Mademoiselle*, May 1939, 72–73, 117; "Budgeting Your Wardrobe on the Basis of a $25-a-Week Salary," *Mademoiselle*, May 1942, 129, 133.

32. Blackwelder, *Now Hiring*, 143; Ruth Rosen, *The World Split Open* (New York: Viking, 2000).

33. Bea Danville, *Dress Well on $1 a Day* (New York: Wilfred Funk, Inc., 1956), 48–52.

34. *Women in the Labor Force: A Databook* (Washington, D. C.: U.S. Department of Labor and U.S. Bureau of Labor Statistics, 1981, 2007).

35. *Statistical Abstracts of the United States* (Washington, D. C.: U.S. Census Bureau of Labor Statistics, 2001).

36. *Women in the Labor Force: A Databook*.

37. See for example Paula England, *Comparable Worth: Theories and Evidence* (New York: Aldine De Gruyter, 1992) and Catalyst, *The Double Bind Dilemma for Women in Leadership: Damned if You Do, Doomed if You Don't* (New York: Catalyst, 2007).

38. Blackwelder, *Now Hiring*; Dayle A. Mandelson, "General Patterns of Employment/Unemployment," in *Women and Work: A Handbook*, ed. Paula J. Dubeck and Kathryn Borman (New York: Garland Publishing, Inc. 1996).

39. Prior to 1964, only two states (Hawaii and Wisconsin) prohibited sex discrimination in employment. By 1975, just six states had no law regarding either sexual discrimination. U.S. Department of Labor, *State Labor Laws in Transition: From Protection to Equal Status for Women*, Pamphlet 15 (Washington, D. C.: Government Printing Office, 1976).

40. "For Women: More Jobs, But Low Pay," *U.S. News and World Report*, October 8, 1973, 41–42.

41. Nancy S. Barrett, "Women in the Job Market: Occupations, Earnings, and Career Opportunities," in *The Subtle Revolution: Women at Work* ed. Ralph E. Smith (Washington, D. C.: The Urban Institute, 1979).

42. Genevieve Antoine Dariaux, *Elegance* (Garden City, New York: Doubleday & Company, Inc., 1964); Joan O'Sullivan, *How to Be Well-Dressed* (Garden City, New York: Doubleday & Company, Inc., 1963); Michael Drury, *How to Develop Poise and Self-Confidence* (Garden City, New York: Doubleday & Company, Inc., 1963); Edith Head and Joe Hyams, *How to Dress for Success* (New York: Random House, 1967).

43. "The Drive to Open Up More Careers for Women," *U.S. News and World Report*, January 14, 1974, 69–70; Margaret Higginson, "How Women Can Get Ahead in a 'Man's World,'" *U.S. News and World Report*, March 29, 1976, 46–48.

44. Robert L. Dipboye, "Problems and Progress of Women in Management," in *Working Women: Past, Present, and Future*, ed. Karen Shallcross Kozaria, Michael H. Moskow, and Lucretia Dewey Tanner (Washington, D. C.: Industrial Research Association, 1987).

45. John T. Molloy, *The Women's Dress for Success Book* (New York: Warner Books, 1977), 32.

46. Susan Cheever Cowley, "Dress for the Trip to the Top," *Newsweek*, September 26, 1977, 76–77.

47. Molloy, *The Women's Dress for Success Book*, 16.

48. Designer Giorgio Armani offered less heavily structured suits for women executives beginning in 1975, complementing his success with unstructured menswear. Teri Agins, *The End of Fashion* (New York: William Morrow and Company, Inc., 1999), 135; Carol Curtis, "Tailoring the Corporate Woman," *Forbes*, February 16, 1981, 47–48.

49. Susan Faludi, *Backlash: The Undeclared War Against American Women* 15th anniversary edition of original printing (New York: Three Rivers Press, 2006); Naomi Wolf, *The Beauty Myth* (New York: Doubleday, 1991).

50. This seems to be a regular complaint against the fashion industry. In 1991, Naomi Wolf maintained that the changing ideals of appearance management were tools of "the power structure . . . to undermine women's advancement." Naomi Wolf, *The Beauty Myth* (New York: William Morrow and Company, Inc., 1991): 20; Caroline Bird, *The Two-Paycheck Marriage, How Women at Work Are Changing Life in America: An In-Depth Report on the Great Revolution of Our Times* (New York: Rawson, Wade Publishers 1979).

51. Quoted in Betty Friedan, *The Second Stage* (New York: Summit Books, 1981), 33.

52. Susan Cheever Cowley, "Dress for the Trip to the Top," *Newsweek*, September 1977, 76–77.

53. Cowley, "Dress for the Trip to the Top," 77.

54. Diane Weathers, "The Power of Dressing for Success," *Black Enterprise*, August 1978, 30–32.

55. Jane Farrell-Beck and Jean Parsons, *20th Century Dress in the United States* (New York: Fairchild Books, 2007).

56. Barbara Coffey and the Editors of *Glamour*, *Glamour's Success Book: Executive Dressing on the Job, at Home, in Your Community, EVERYWHERE* (New York: Simon and Schuster, 1979).

57. This is a common argument and complaint, even if appearance management has shown to increase perceptions of one's self and others. Deborah Scott-Denney, "Success Dressing: In Our Eagerness to Show That We Deserve Every Rung on the Corporate Ladder, We've Created an Entire Generation of Fashion Clones," *Glamour*, December 1980, 208; Eleanor Kelley, Susan Jones, Dora Ann Hatch, and Rogene Nelsen, "How to Help Your Students Be Successful at Job Hunting," *Journal of Home Economics* 68, (November 1976): 32–35; "How Women Can Get Ahead in a Man's World," *U.S. News and World Report*, March 29, 1976, 46–48; "Glamour's First Financial Makeover: How to Get More from Your Job, Salary, Life," *Glamour*, January 1978, 120–121, 165–166.

58. *Business Week*, "You've Come a Long Way Baby—But, Not as Far as You Thought," October 1, 1984,126–131.

59. United States Federal Glass Ceiling Commission, "A Solid Investment: Making Full Use of the Nation's Human Capital" (Washington, D. C.: U.S. Government Printing Office, 1995).

60. In 1991, the U.S. Department of Labor defined glass ceiling as "those artificial barriers based on attitudinal or organizational bias that prevent qualified individuals from advancing upward in their organization into management-level positions." U.S. Department of Labor, *Report on the Glass Ceiling Initiative* (Washington, D. C.: U.S. Government Printing Office, 1991). In describing her move as editor of *Working Woman* to editor of *Family Circle*, Gay Bryant stated, "Women have reached a certain point—I call it the glass ceiling. They're in the top of middle management and they've stopped and are getting stuck. There isn't enough room for women at the top." Nora Frenkiel, "The Up-and-Comers: Bryant Takes Aim at the Settlers-In." *Adweek, Special Report: Magazine World 1984*, March 1984, 8.

61. Georgia Dullea, "On Ladder to the Top, a Mentor is Key Step," *New York Times*, January 26, 1981; William Hoffer, "Businesswomen: Equal but Different," *Nation's Business*, August 1987, 46; Kato Keeton, "Characteristics of Successful Women Managers and Professionals in Local Government: A National Survey," *Women in Management Review* 11 (1996): 27–34; Tom Lester, "A Woman's Place . . . in Management," *Management Today*, April 1993, 46–51; "Women in Management: The Spare Sex," *The Economist*, March 29, 1992, 17–20.

62. Vincent Bozzi, "Assertiveness Breeds Contempt," *Psychology Today*, September 1987, 15; Susan Fraker, "Why Women Aren't Getting to the Top," *Fortune*, April 16, 1984, 40; Katarzyna Morena, "Generational Warfare (Friction between Women in Corporations)," *Forbes*, March 22, 1999, 62.

63. Elizabeth Horton, "No Beauties in the Executive Suite," *Science Digest*, October 1985, 24.

64. One remedy to increase women's assumption of advanced leadership roles was the sharp increase in graduate school enrollment. Gay Bryant, "The Working Woman Report: Succeeding in Business in the 80s" (New York: Simon & Schuster, 1980); Ann M. Morrison, Randall P. White, and Ellen Van Velsor, "Executive Women: Substance Plus Style: To Be Successful in Upper Management, Women Must Constantly Monitor Their Behavior, Making Sure They Are Neither Too Masculine nor Too Feminine," *Psychology Today*, August 1987, 18–27.

65. Caroline Evans and Minna Thornton, *Women and Fashion* (London: Quartet Books, 1989).

66. Janet Wooldridge, "Dressing for the Top," *New York Times Magazine*, July 26, 1981, 50.

67. "Dressing on the Job," *Essence*, March 1982, 108–111; "Getting the Facts on Success Dressing," *Essence*, September 1983, 77–80; "Clothes Strategies," *Glamour*, December 1986, 134; "Clothes Strategy," *Glamour*, January 1986, 86.

68. "A *Glamour* Special Report Clothes and Clout," *Glamour*, October 1982, 240–247.

69. Gerrie Pickney and Marge Swenson, *New Images for Women* (Virginia: Reston Publishing Company, Inc., 1981); Janet Wallach, *Working Wardrobe: Affordable Clothes That Work for You!* (New York: Warner Books, 1981).

70. Wallach, *Working Wardrobe*; Carole Jackson, *Color Me Beautiful* (New York: Ballantine Books, 1987).

71. Joanne Lipman, "Personal Advisers Save Shoppers Money, but Beware of Their Expensive Tastes," *Wall Street Journal*, April 1, 1985, 1; Elaine Louie, "Personal Shoppers Join the Support Network," *Working Woman*, 1985, 123–128; Michael R. Solomon, "The Wardrobe Consultant, Exploring the Role of a New Retail Partner," *Journal of Retailing* 63 (1987): 111–128.

72. Sales through personal shoppers at Dayton Hudson grew from $3 million in 1985 to $15 million in 1988. Teri Agins, "Retailers Turning to 'Personal Shoppers' to Boost Sales, Win Customers' Loyalty," *Wall Street Journal*, December 23, 1998, 1.

73. Carrie Tuhy, "A Working Woman's Guide to Successful Dressing," *Money*, April 1982, 144–146, 148.

74. "Clothes Strategy," *Glamour*, January 1986, 86; "Dressing on the Job," *Essence*, March 1982, 111; "Winner's Guide to Job-Smart Dressing," *Glamour*, March 1986, 302; Jani Wooldridge, "Dressing for the Top," *New York Times Magazine*, July 26, 1981, 49–50.

75. Susan Caminiti, "Jewelers Woo the Working Woman," *Fortune*, June 8, 1987, 71–72.

76. This refers to the upper echelon of management positions. Jackie Castro, "Get set: Here they come!" *Time*, 1990, 50–53; Cynthia Griffin, "Vive la Difference! Female Characteristics as Applied to Business," *Entrepreneur*, November 1999, 52; Sally Helgesen, *The Female Advantage* (New York: Broadway Business, 1995); Chris Lee, "The Feminization of Management," *Training* 31 (1994): 25–32; Richard Miniter, "Women's Successes Smash Business Myths," *Insight on the News*, February 21, 1994, 20–24; Judy B. Rosener, "Ways Women Lead," *Harvard Business Review* 68 (1990): 119–125; Lawrence Van Gelder, "Welcome to the Club, Finally," *New York Times*, July 11, 1999, B9.

77. As quoted in Nancy A. Nichols, "Whatever Happened to Rosie the Riveter," *Harvard Business Review* 71 (1993): 54–60.

78. "Gender Pay Gap," *The Kiplinger Letter*, April 17, 2003, 3.

79. *Women in the Labor Force: A Databook* (Washington, D. C.: U.S. Department of Labor and U.S. Bureau of Labor Statistics, 2005).

80. Cherie Serota and Jody Kozlow Gardner, *Pregnancy Chic: The Fashion Survival Guide* (New York: Villard Books/Random House, 1998); "Expecting in Style," *Business Week*, September 24, 1990, 154; Destination Maternity, *Who we are*, http://www.motherswork.com (accessed February 3, 2009).

81. Marilyn M. Helms, "Women and Entrepreneurship: The Appealing Alternative," *Business Perspectives*, July 1997, 16–20; Paula Mergenhagen, "Her Own Boss," *American Demographics*, December 1996, 36–42; Rhonda Reynolds, "The Personal Touch: Cultural Differences Between the Sexes Is a Plus for Entrepreneurs," *Black Enterprise*, July 1995, 42; The Office of Women's Business Ownership, Small Business Administration, Accessed February 5, 2009, from http://www.sba.gov/aboutsba/sbaprograms/onlinewbc/aboutus/index.html.

82. Jennifer Steinhauer and Constance C. R. White, "Women's New Relationship with Fashion," *New York Times*, August 5, 1996, A1, D9; Constance C. R. White and Jennifer Steinhauer, "Fashion Relearns Its Darwin: Be Adaptable or Be Extinct," *New York Times*, August 6, 1996, A1, D5.

83. Karen Lehrman, *The Lipstick Proviso: Women, Sex, and Power in the Real World* (New York: Doubleday, 1997), 30.

84. Susan Faludi, *Backlash*; Naomi Wolf, *The Beauty Myth*.

85. Elizabeth Wilson, *Adorned in Dreams: Fashion and Modernity*, revised edition, (New York: I. B. Tauris, 2003).

86. Abby Ellin, "Going to Work to Sell Business Casual," *New York Times*, November 5, 2000, B6; Jane Farrell-Beck and Jean Parsons, *20th Century Dress in the United States*.

87. Henry Alford, "Fear of Fridays. Are the New Relaxed Office Dress Codes Making Women's Lives Easier or Harder?," *Vogue*, 1996, 136, 138; Peggy Post and Peter Post, *Emily Post's The Etiquette Advantage in Business*, second edition (New York: Harper Collins Publishers, 2005).

88. Bette Sack, "Old Gold: Advertisers Are Discovering That Again Boomers Spend Money Too," *Mpls. St. Paul*, March 2003, 38–39; Jennifer Steinhauer, and Constance C. R. White, "Women's New Relationship with Fashion," *New York Times*, August 5, 1996, A1, D9.

89. Mandi Norwood, *Michelle Style: Celebrating the First Lady of Fashion* (New York: William Morrow, 2009).

90. Kim Johnson Gross, Jeff Stone and Kristina Zimbalist, *Dress Smart Women: Wardrobes that Win in the New Workplace* (New York: Warner Books, 2002); Hymowitz, Carol, "Female Executives Use Fashion to Send a Business Message," *Wall Street Journal*, September 16, 2003; Christina Binkley, "General Counsel: Fashion Fuels a Friendship," *Wall Street Journal*, July 31, 2008; Juju Chang, "Workplace Protocol: Is Pantyhose Over?" *ABC News*, June 9, 2008.

91. Christina Binkley, "Want to Be CEO? You Have to Dress the Part," *Wall Street Journal*, January 10, 2008, D1, D8.

92. Christina Binkley, "Business Casual: All Business, Never Casual," *Wall Street Journal*, April 17, 2008, D1, D8; Christina Binkley, "Does this Book Make Me Look Chic?," *Wall Street Journal*, March 20, 2008, D1, D8.

93. Christina Binkley, "Inside a Bastion of Old-School Power Attire," *Wall Street Journal*, February 5, 2009, D8. See also Michele Meyer, "All Hail Shoulder Pads," *USA Weekend*, June 5–7, 2009, 13, in which Jane Buckingham, president of trend forecasting for The Intelligence Group, stated, "When people are losing jobs, they want a look that says, 'I'm strong and in charge, not defeated,'" and hairstylist Ted Gibson commented, "You want to stand out and look like you can get the job done."

94. Mary Lou Andre, *Ready to Wear: An Expert's Guide to Choosing and Using Your Wardrobe* (New York: A Perigee Book/Berkley Publishing Group, 2004).

95. Joyce Walder, "Looking Sharp, Landing Jobs," *New York Times*, December 28, 1997, 1, 27.

96. Christina Binkley, "Wall Street Women: Dress Code of Silence," *Wall Street Journal*, March 22, 2007, http://www.cmra.com/press-2007.php (accessed June 6, 2009).

Discussion Questions

1. Have dress for success recommendations for women changed much from the 1920–1990s? If so, how? If not, why not?

2. What is the glass ceiling?

10.2

LESSONS FROM *UGLY BETTY*: BUSINESS ATTIRE AS A CONFORMITY STRATEGY

Barbara Burgess–Wilkerson and Jane Boyd Thomas
Winthrop University

In today's marketplace, a premium is placed on corporate image and business attire. The rationale is that appearance reflects on the employer (Andres & Baird, 2005). We tell students that first impressions, made within the first 60 seconds of meeting, are critical to their future success. As professors of management and marketing, we are routinely engaged in preparing students for professional occupations inclusive of an awareness

Barbara Burgess-Wilgerson & Jane Boyd Thomas. Business Communication Quarterly pp. 365–368, © 2009 by SAGE Publications. Reprinted by Permission of SAGE Publications.

that business attire is often reflective of a willingness to conform to workplace norms.

We have known for quite some time that appearance can be indicative of conformity (Tseelon & Kaiser, 1992). Countless stories and lawsuits reveal lost career opportunities because employees failed to "look the part." This reality is exemplified in the sitcom *Ugly Betty*, which provides weekly challenges encouraging us to consider the value of conformity as reflected by our appearance. Betty is an aspiring editor of a major fashion magazine. Raised in a blue-collar, working-class family, Betty does not conform to contemporary notions of style. Clothes in her world have a practical application that should not overshadow the individual's inner beauty. Betty functions with the utmost integrity in a world of competition and greed as her counterparts claw their way up the corporate ladder. Interestingly, they, unlike Betty, remain under the radar as their fashionable sense of style provides a veneer of honesty, fair play, and an unquestionable willingness to conform to the company dress code. Betty, on the other hand, is singled out, the target of ridicule and disparaging jokes not because of her incompetence but for her outlandish wardrobe, a combination of early Salvation Army and Kmart. Her appearance, offensive to the fashion elite, overshadows her kind disposition. As her altruistic personality competes with a signature candy-apple red, patent-leather belt, she is at times the victim of mistrust and resentment. Salt-of-the-earth Betty would be the next senior VP were it not for a terrible sense of style; nonetheless, she is a highly capable team player. Despite the outstanding results reaped by the magazine for which she works, she remains relegated to the bottom. We wonder why Betty doesn't just buy a Chanel suit, a matching pair of Prada shoes, and a Gucci bag to help her gain that well-deserved promotion to fashion editor. However, in Betty's mind, one's character should speak louder than one's outward appearance. Good luck, Betty!

The lesson from *Ugly Betty* can serve as a tool to stress the importance of conformity through business attire. Students in business communications and consumer behavior classes ($N = 100$) were asked to watch an episode of *Ugly Betty*. Afterward, a class discussion was held to determine the extent to which students felt that dress can be an expression of conformity and the extent to which one should dress to conform to workplace norms.

The classroom discussion on the topic was lively and provided insight into how today's college students view attire as indicative of conformity. The majority of the students felt that conforming to the company dress code would be beneficial to Betty. Comments included, "Although she would be more successful, her dress should have nothing to do with her ability" and "Conformity is not a bad word." The students understand the value of conformity; however, a theme that emerged was a desire for individuality. A female marketing major commented as follows: "We are interested in individualism. We customize our Nikes because we feel the need to show our individuality even when we are conforming to workplace norms . . . Maybe wear a pin or a fashionable pair of shoes with an outfit." A 20-year-old marketing major commented on the generational differences: "The 40-year-old is about rules and everyone looking the same. I want to be an individual." These thoughts are supported by the findings of Guy and Banim (2000), who surmise that, for women, clothing is an extension of self and assists in expressing who they are. Tseelon and Kaiser (1992) argue that a woman's identity is realized through clothing and that garment selections are made to fit a certain role. Another female marketing major offered this personal account that further illustrates the complexity of conforming and the generational differences regarding acceptable professional attire:

> I was called into the manager's office for dressing too casually. The manager explained the expected code of dress for the office. I argued that I did not interact with clients or others outside the business and felt more comfortable in my clothes. I did not want to spend my salary on new clothes. Furthermore, nothing was written about what I should and should not wear.

This notion of individuality is consistent with descriptions of Generation Y (1977–1998) as "self-inventive, individualistic, not intimidated by authority and willing to re-write the rules" (Kogen, 2001; Thielfoldt & Scheef, 2004). In a phone interview, Paula Harvey, president and CEO of K & P Consulting and 2005 Human Resources Professional of the Year, confirms the notion of individuality and argues that Generation Y has carried on the notion of individualism, which was started by Generation X. In her opinion, "Generation Y is breaking down the door that was opened by Generation X." She believes that employers are attempting to redefine dress as a talent recruitment and retention strategy (P. Harvey. Personal communication, March 12, 2009).

Conclusion

Business students should understand the relevance of professional attire as an indication of conformity. Of equal importance is the recognition that some companies have loosened their dress codes to a more flexible policy to recruit young talent. *Ugly Betty* could serve as a teaching tool to initiate the dialogue on conformity in a light-hearted, yet thoughtful manner. A follow-up to this lesson

might be to have students research by industry those companies that require strict adherence to a company dress code and those industries, such as the information technology field, that allow for more flexibility. While it appears that companies are moving toward a more liberal dress code, students are well-advised to err on the side of tastefully conservative business attire.

References

Andrews, P., & Baird, J. (2005) *Communication for business and the professions.* Long Grove: Waveland Press.

Guy, A., & Banim, M. (2000) Personal collections: Women's clothing use and identity. *Journal of Gender Studies. 9*, 313–317.

Kogan, M. (2001) Bridging the gap. *Government Executive. 33*(12), 16.

Thielfoldt, D., & Scheef, D. (2004, August) Generation X and the new millennials: What you need to know about mentoring the new generations. *Law Practice Today.* Retrieved March 13, 2009, from http://www.abstract.org/lpm/lpt/articles/mgt08044.html.

Tseelon, E., & Kaiser, S. B. (1992) A dialog with feminist film theory: Multiple readings of gaze. *Studies in Symbolic Interaction. 13*, 199–137.

Discussion Questions

1.   What does having a "sense of style" mean to you?
2.   Should the fashion industry have different rules in regards to professional dress? Why or why not?

10.3

HOW BLACK CAN YOU BE?

Audrey Edwards

Affirmative action. Equal opportunity. Multiculturalism. Diversity. Sensitivity training. Workforce 2000. A whole new language has sprung up in the last 30 years attempting to account for a new phenomenon in the corporate workplace: the entrance of African-Americans (Figure 10.6). Of course we've been in other American workplaces since the very beginning: in the fields and the big house, the kitchens and factories, civil-service

posts and self-employed enterprises. But it's only been within this civil-rights generation that we've landed in any great numbers in what's been called the corporate arena, that bastion of Europower and privilege where companies and nations are run—and fortunes made—by a group still largely

---

Reprinted by permission of the author.

White and male. The fact that so many African-Americans now sit at the head of the table in corporate boardrooms is the surest sign of just how much things have changed. We have Kenneth I. Chenault running American Express; Lloyd Ward heading Maytag; Ann M. Fudge ruling at Maxwell House; Mark Whitaker the editor at *Newsweek*; Sylvia Rhone calling the shots at Elektra Records.

The list goes on, at big and small companies. The phenomenon, however, has also given rise to a sticky new question: Can you run White and remain Black? Can you succeed in White, corporate, private-sector America, a culture that at times seems the very antithesis of Black culture, without selling out your own culture?

The questions speak to the "dual consciousness" W.E.B. Du Bois first observed at the beginning of the last century, a conflict still stirring in the souls of Black folks. We're a people in perpetual unrest because we still feel forced to choose: between identifying Black or American; acting Black or White; siding Black or female; thinking Black or corporate, as if the two must be separate. We are the only people known to say things like "I'm a manager who happens to be Black," or "I'm a woman first and Black second."

The trouble with this is that whenever we try to deny, make incidental or compartmentalize the defining feature of our race in the workplace (or any other place, for that matter), we tend to be less effective.

The most successful corporate Blacks don't consciously decide to be Black. They just never forget they are Black. Race is one of the things that defines them, but not a thing that limits them. There is no dual, schizoid war raging in their souls, for they are clear about who and what they are. And while they don't necessarily lead with their Blackness in the workplace, the acknowledgment of its reality is a part of what gives them their power.

It's one thing, though, to embrace a Black identity; it can be quite another to express that identity at work—to literally wear our ethnicity on our sleeve, in how we dress, speak or (perhaps most significant for us as Black women) wear our hair. The issue here usually gets down to what makes Whites comfortable.

Figure 10.6 Black male executive.

Sharon Davis (not her real name), a television news reporter in the local market of a major city, let her hair go natural a few years ago and now wears it in twists. But she knows her bosses are more comfortable with female broadcasters having straight hair. So when she's on the air, she puts on what she calls "my hat"—a straighthaired wig—to cover the twists.

Is Davis a sellout or just strategic? "Wearing a wig works for me," she says without apology.

"It's cheaper and easier than always getting my hair done and saves my hair from the damage of relaxers. To me the wig just goes along with the makeup and other props you use for TV." Davis is not only clear about *why* she wears a wig on air but also clear on why she *should*, given the folks she works with. "As long as they [Whites] have a problem with your just being here," she says wearily, "why should you give them something else to have a problem with?"

Like other Black veterans in the corporate culture, Davis knows how much race still fuels the work environment. As Blacks in the White-run workplace, we still too often have to prove ourselves, if not legitimize our very presence.

Whether in the boardroom or the newsroom, we can be made to feel we must alter, contort or even deny who we are in order to make it. As a successful news reporter for more than 20 years, Davis is clearly making it, and at this point in her career feels she no longer has to prove herself. Or at least no longer has to contort, damage or deny her hair to prove she can do her job.

Dress Pumps and Dreadlocks

Hair, like skin color, has always been a defining feature of Black culture. It is the striking thing that sets us apart from other cultures. It shouldn't be surprising, then, that in the workplace where our hair can be kinky, curly, permed, locked, twisted, braided, cornrowed, relaxed, weaved or wigged, it is the one thing most likely to make Whites least comfortable. "For Black women, one of the issues around corporate image has to do with the difference in hairstyles," says psychologist Ronald Brown, Ph.D., president of Banks Brown, a management-consulting firm in San Francisco. "For instance, when a woman wears dreadlocks in a corporate environment, the core message others receive is that you are probably more involved with your own culture than the corporate culture. There may be the sense that you're rejecting the very culture that's made the rest of us successful."

But what really makes Whites uncomfortable, argues Davis, is that "they just don't know what we do with our hair, and they think they should know, which is why they never ask. I really think they feel that not knowing might somehow make them racist. And it's the more astute, liberal-minded ones who feel this way. Conservative Whites don't think their ignorance makes them racist, so they will come right on out and ask about our hair."

Yet deeper than any discomfort Whites may have about hair is their great distress when they can't categorize, label or identify at all, contends another televison reporter, Lloyd Gite, of Fox News in Houston. "Nothing trips up White folks more than not being able to tell who you are when they look at you," says Gite, 48, a light-skinned Black man who shaved his head a few years ago. Gite says that before his head was shaven, people mistook him for anything from Puerto Rican to Chinese to Greek when they saw him on TV. There has been much more comfort with his shaved head, the look Michael Jordan made distinctly Black. The television news business, says Gite, basically wants its Black men to look Black, and its Black women to look a little closer to White culture. It is a function of the culture itself: Who sets the policy at the top—someone fair-minded? Or someone closed and rigid? What are the rules? What product is the culture producing?

How much in the way of conformity is necessary to get the product out? In the culture of television news, where the image is as important as the message, there is more pressure to adhere to a certain look. Blacks who make it in such "show" businesses come in understanding that and are willing to play by those rules. "I learned very early in my career not to do anything to change my look without letting them [her White bosses] know," says Davis.

New Battlefield, Same Old Struggle

If the culture in one industry rewards "sticking to a look," other industries, technology, for one, reward innovation and improvisation. There's more room for mavericks and Lone Rangers in Silicon Valley's Wild West tech culture. There's room for Zandra Conway, who works at Hewlett-Packard's Atlanta office as a technology-solutions specialist. In the old days, Conway, 43, would have been called a militant or an activist. These days, with her locked twists, colorful head wraps, Black posters, calendars and photos displayed in her office cubicle and her in-your-face ethnic pride, she is in the corporate workplace to *represent*.

"Embracing who you are is what gives you power and strength," she says.

It was natural, then, that Conway would help start an Atlanta chapter of Hewlett-Packard's

Black Employees Forum when she arrived in the city from San Jose, California, three years ago. It makes sense that she invites Black experts like diversity trainer Roosevelt Thomas and business author Dennis Kimbro to come in to speak to both Black and White employees. It's a given that she makes sure there is a Black History Month program at the company every year and ongoing professional and educational workshops. "White males are still trying to understand things like diversity, quotas and affirmative action," she explains. "Once they sit down and talk—and they see we can talk—it helps break down stereotypes. We have to be the key in sensitizing Whites to our presence. If we don't, they will just ignore it and keep going. They should know about the wonderful things we've done in our history and know why we're proud of our heritage." But it hasn't always been easy getting other company Blacks involved. "That's one of the struggles," Conway says. "Some don't want their White coworkers to know they're going to a Black Forum program. They're afraid there'll be backlash. And there has been some. But nobody's ever said anything to me." Conway's up-front activist style has proven to be a natural fit at Hewlett-Packard, which is why she's been there 19 years. Like every other cutting-edge company, Hewlett-Packard wants to make profits and stay ahead of the competition.

But it also knows that the companies most likely to have the winning edge in the future will have to have all sorts of people and points of view contributing to the bottom line. As Conway points out, Hewlett-Packard is aware that the American workforce will be increasingly made up of people of color in this new century. "They know they need to make sure they can retain African-American employees," she says. "So they look to me when it comes to diversity issues. They understand that diversity has got to be an important part of the corporate aim."

And Conway understands, indeed relishes, her role as corporate conscience. What makes all the difference is that the company she works for supports that role. Zandra Conway is successful expressing her full, Black self because she works in a corporate environment that values her full, Black self. But even at such politically correct

companies, it can take a minute for the policies mandated by headquarters to filter down to the troops. "This is the South, and there's still some Jim Crow mentality," Conway says of the Black resistance to diversity she encounters. That resistance, that Jim Crow mentality, is expressed every time Blacks think they shouldn't talk too much or too long to other Blacks at work or join Black employee groups (don't want Whites to think you're not a "team player"). It's expressed every time they refuse to hang socially with Whites, be it during or after work (don't want them to think you're not going to be their friend!); or feel they have to make a point to high-five the brothers in the mail room (don't want them to think you ain't down); or wish that sister from accounting would stop trying to talk to them (doesn't she know you're a department head and can't socialize with the clerks?).

It's expressed every time Blacks in the corporate workplace think or act along separate, conflicted and segregated racial lines on the job. It should go without saying that just about the worst thing you can do as a Black person in the workplace is act as if race is incidental to who you are. Whites may appear to be more comfortable with such self- and race-denial on your part, but they never really respect it and don't really trust it either. A corporate player who thinks of herself as a manager who "happens to be Black," or as a company woman but not a race woman, or as a smart and talented young sister who will always be rewarded on merit and not ever tripped up by race, comes across as naive. And naïveté makes you vulnerable.

So does not forming alliances across the board—with Whites, Blacks and others—since such alliances can benefit you. "When you segregate and leave yourself out of forming friendships with people, it's very limiting, professionally and personally," says Jerri DeVard, vice president of customer acquisition and new business development at Citibank in New York City.

"Why would you want to do that? If you perceive there is going to be some negative impact on claiming and expressing who you are as a Black person, then there will be. The thing is to just be yourself. I wear who I am on my sleeve. I don't happen to be Black. I am."

Yet DeVard, the epitome of corporate chic, with her soothing but authoritative voice and friendly style, does not make the Whites she works with uncomfortable. The Black-American art and African sculpture that adorn her office, the Black causes she gets her company to support and the personal time she takes to make sure younger Blacks coming up avoid the "land mines" still littering the corporate landscape all say she is a race woman. Her vice-president's title says she is an officer at one of the largest banks in the world. The fact that she manages to integrate both into one smooth-running Black corporate whole is perhaps the truest measure of her success—and her power.

Black as You Wanna Be?

Like DeVard, many high-profile corporate Blacks are quite comfortable being who they are.

They've learned not only how to be themselves but also to express an authentic ethnic self and make it work for them. Take Mae Watts Brown, 47, sales manager for radio station WAIT in Chicago, who will occasionally lapse into Black colloquialisms to lighten things up. "The biggest challenge Blacks have in the corporation is in how we speak," she contends, recalling a White female coworker at another job who took a "huge account" from her after she'd made it profitable. Brown said the colleague would refer to her as "Mae Ax Brown."

"Now, I've never said *ax* for *ask*," Brown says, still miffed by the memory, "but that was her way of trying to put me down as a Black person." Brown eventually sued over the stolen account and they settled. Interestingly, though, she now uses Black slang herself in one-on-one interactions with Whites when she wants to ease up. "I might say something like 'Girl, please!' or 'I know that's right!' It's my way of cutting Whites some slack. Plus, it makes me more comfortable."

This is the ultimate challenge: to find what makes us comfortable in the workplace without making Whites uncomfortable working with us.

Now sometimes this is a no-win proposition. Some work environments, no matter what we do, are just hostile, even dangerous to Black emotional health. Think Texaco or Denny's before both were exposed and sued. In such arenas the best move may be simply to split. For the most part, however, the workplace is not particularly dangerous, even when it's not being especially welcoming. What it really is, says psychologist Ron Brown, is artificial. We spend much of our waking lives interacting with people who have nothing to do with our lives after work. We may do work that has no intrinsic meaning to us beyond a paycheck. We may have to act nice when we don't feel like it or cooperate when we'd rather tell you where to go. The thing is, this is true for everybody in the workplace.

This is the nature of work.

Like Mae Brown, we have to learn to cut everybody some slack. "Black women don't realize they enter the corporate workplace with what's viewed as very confident styles," says Brown. "What's normal in African-American culture— dressing in vibrant colors, gesturing to make a point, speaking in voices that tend to be deeper, louder, with more power and resonance—comes across as confident. That can be very startling to Whites who are used to thinking of Black people as being disadvantaged. They aren't used to seeing self-possessed Black women who may be just one of a few [Blacks] in a sea of many [Whites]. And if that woman dresses well, speaks well and seems to fit in very well, some Whites are subtly intimidated." Much of the time Black women at work are just "coping," Brown says, but that's not the perception.

As a result, there are times we may, indeed, have to tone it down. Not deny who we are, but soften who we are if it is keeping us from being heard or understood. This may mean anything from not wearing a kente-cloth suit if the corporate look is button-down Brooks Brothers to refraining from doing a gooseneck or rolling your eyes the next time a coworker gets on your nerves. It is ultimately up to you to figure out what will work and not work in the corporate culture you've chosen to do business in, just as you must, in the first place, choose a work environment that's likely to be compatible with who you are. "Part of our self-care involves choosing a workplace in which we're comfortable," says Linda Anderson,

Ph.D., a New York City psychotherapist and corporate coach. "The ideal corporate environment acknowledges our differences without making the mistake of either exaggerating or minimizing those differences. On the other hand, we've become savvy enough to understand that if we choose to work in corporate America, the cultural workplace can't be what affirms us."

Affirmation is more likely to come in afterwork activities through Black professional organizations or outreach programs involving the company you work for and the community you live in. And for many, the corporate work experience is just the temporary means to a larger end: attaining the skills needed for entrepreneurship or for working in a Black-owned business. Finding a comfortable corporate fit isn't really all that difficult, when you think about it.

"This is not hard at all, compared with our foremothers picking cotton," says Zandra Conway.

We at least now have the freedom to choose the line of work we do. And if the ancestors could figure out how to make it when there was no choice, how can we do any less in an era that certainly has more, if not always equal, opportunity?

Discussion Questions

1. What do you think about the idea that those who deny their race are less effective in the workplace?
2. What is "the nature of work" that Edwards refers to in her article? Does this idea apply only to African Americans? Why or why not?

10.4

TOO SEXY FOR MY BOSSES: WHY LAWSUITS BASED ON LOOKS DISCRIMINATION—EVEN GOOD ONES—ARE A BAD IDEA

Richard Thompson Ford

Debrahlee Lorenzana made news this week with the unusual civil rights claim that her employer, Citigroup, has discriminated against her because she is a hottie. "At five-foot-six and 125 pounds . . . she is J-Lo curves meets Jessica Simpson rack meets Audrey Hepburn elegance—a head turning beauty," drools the *Village Voice*. According to her lawsuit, Lorenzana is so smoking hot that her co-workers couldn't concentrate on their jobs. Her bosses eventually demanded that she revamp—or, rather, de-vamp—her wardrobe: They banned tight pants, pencil skirts, high heels, and clingy turtlenecks. When Lorenzana pointed out that other women in her office wore more revealing clothes than she did, Lorenzana says her bosses replied, in essence: "Yeah, but they aren't as hot as you are." And when Lorenzana came to work, still looking just as jaw-droppingly sexy as ever,

Citibank fired her. Believe it or not, Lorenzana is not the first person to claim in court that she's too sexy for her job. In 2005 librarian Desiree Goodwin sued Harvard University for discrimination, complaining that she was denied promotions because she was "seen merely as a pretty girl who wore sexy outfits, low cut blouses, and tight pants."

Don't hate me because I'm beautiful isn't the best line to inspire public sympathy, much less to begin your complaint for employment discrimination. But Lorenzana might have stronger arguments than her crippling gorgeousness:

For instance, she claims her supervisors refused to enroll her in the training sessions she needed to do her job; handed off clients she had cultivated to men, then dinged her for not bringing in enough business; and fabricated incidents of tardiness as an excuse to put her on probation. This sounds like straightforward sex discrimination and harassment. In other words, if these more straightforward claims are true, the whole sexy wardrobe issues are a pointless—if headline-grabbing—distraction.

But is it illegal to fire someone just for being too sexy? Should it be? Federal civil rights law prohibits sex discrimination, and some courts have interpreted that law to forbid dress codes that are "demeaning" to women or impose "unequal burdens" in terms of time and money for men and women. Most cases challenging employer dress codes as sex discrimination have involved requirements that women wear makeup or revealing outfits—these women lost their jobs not for being too sexy but, arguably, for not being sexy enough. But for the most part, workplace dress codes are legal, even when they impose different requirements for men and women. For instance, in *Jespersen v. Harrah's Operating Co.*, a bartender at a Reno, Nev., casino sued when her employer adopted a new dress code that required her to style her hair and wear makeup. Jespersen complained that she found wearing makeup "degrading." But the 9th Circuit Court of Appeals found that Harrah's grooming code was equally burdensome for men and affirmed the dismissal of her lawsuit.

A handful of jurisdictions prohibit "appearance discrimination." Almost all of those laws are limited to things like unequal treatment for height, weight, and immutable physical characteristics. Yet high-profile cases like *Jespersen* have led some legal commentators—such as my Stanford colleague Deborah Rhode—to insist that dress codes that clash with the personal values or self-image of employees violate their civil rights unless that dress code is objectively job-related. And if that's true, shouldn't we be just as concerned with protecting the rights of the hotties as the notties? Debralee Lorenzana's complaint may look like the opposite of Darlene Jespersen's, but in a sense they're the same. In reaction to Citibank's demand that she wear looser-fitting clothes, Lorenzana complained: "Where I'm from . . . women dress up—like put on makeup and do their nails—to go to the supermarket." Jespersen said hair and makeup had nothing to do with her job and complained that she found getting dolled up demeaning. Both women objected that the dress codes clashed with their own personal self-image. If Jespersen should have a right *not* to wear makeup because she finds it degrading, shouldn't Lorenzana have a right not to wear baggy clothes if she finds them bland and stifling?

The strongest arguments against appearance discrimination focus on its effect on women. Existing laws against sex discrimination can and should prohibit policies that are sexually demeaning (hence the entire Hooter's business model might violate federal law, but that's another article) or impose discriminatory burdens. But beyond that, it's hard to know where civil rights based on appearance would end. Hundreds of American businesses have strict dress codes, especially for employees who interact with the public. For instance, according to the *Los Angeles Times*, the Ritz Carlton hotel chain forbids "beards and goatees, 'mutton chop' sideburns, dreadlocks, big hair . . . earrings larger than a quarter, more than two rings on each hand, skirt lengths higher than 2 inches above the top of the knee and long fingernails." Lots of people really like their goatees, dreads, and door-knocker earrings, but must every workplace permit them? Thousands of employers insist that employees wear understated suits and ties, skirts and nylons, polished shoes, conservative haircuts. None of these norms of dress and grooming are directly related to objective job performance—but should they be outlawed? Many employers try to cultivate a workplace culture and image—whether staid and professional like Citibank or glitzy and glamorous like Harrah's—by establishing standards of grooming and dress.

In the end, dress and grooming codes are just another job requirement—no different from rules about how employees should greet and interact with customers—and they should be evaluated as such. And explicit requirements may be better for many employees than the alternatives. In many workplaces no one tells you what to wear, but inappropriate attire is taken as a symptom of more serious flaws: poor judgment, vulgar taste, or bad upbringing. A dress code or a boss who offers explicit wardrobe guidance can be an egalitarian counterweight to the subtle class biases that inappropriate clothing choices would otherwise trigger.

It's a sign of how informal we've become as a society that people think the imposition of an office dress code is a civil rights violation. Perhaps a generation used to being evaluated on the ideas in their essays but not on grammar or exposition can be forgiven for thinking that expectations about style and appearance are not only superficial but outdated. But surely the triumph of Apple over Microsoft has put to rest the idea that the CPU is always more important than the interface. It's tempting to think of civil rights against "appearance discrimination" as a victory of liberty and equality over oppressive conformism. Opposing judgments based on appearance suggests a refined sensibility, attuned to deeper and higher concerns, and it also fits nicely with the increasing informality of modern culture—the era of "business casual" and the barefoot wedding.

But proposals to ban appearance discrimination reflect a patrician sensibility of their own: a conviction that supposedly objective merits, raw intelligence, and technical mastery—the values of the professor, the bohemian intellectual and the high-tech startup—should always trump "superficial" social virtues such as decorum and good taste. There's a troubling immodesty about the perfectionist quest to blind us all to appearances—a quest that would dismiss as bias so much of what many people consider a sign of professionalism, respect, and good form.

Discussion Questions

1. Can someone be too sexy for his or her job? Why? Or why not? Who defines sexy?
2. If you were asked to advise Debrahlee Lorenzana about how to professionalize her dress, what would you say; what recommendations would you make?

10.5

UP THE CAREER LADDER, LIPSTICK IN HAND

Catherine Saint Louis

Want more respect, trust and affection from your co-workers? Wearing makeup—but not gobs of Gaga-conspicuous makeup—apparently can help. It increases people's perceptions of a woman's likability, her competence and (provided she does not overdo it) her trustworthiness, according to a new study, which also confirmed what is obvious: that cosmetics boost a woman's attractiveness.

It has long been known that symmetrical faces are considered more comely, and that people assume that handsome folks are intelligent and good. There is also some evidence that women feel more confident when wearing makeup, a kind of placebo effect, said Nancy Etcoff, the study's lead author and an assistant clinical professor of psychology at Harvard University (yes, scholars there study eyeshadow as well as stem cells). But no research, till now, has given makeup credit for people inferring that a woman was capable, reliable and amiable.

The study was paid for by Procter & Gamble, which sells CoverGirl and Dolce & Gabbana makeup, but researchers like Professor Etcoff and others from Boston University and the Dana-Farber Cancer Institute were responsible for its design and execution.

The study's 25 female subjects, aged 20 to 50 and white, African-American and Hispanic, were photographed barefaced and in three looks that researchers called natural, professional and glamorous. They were not allowed to look in a mirror, lest their feelings about the way they looked affect observers' impressions.

One hundred forty-nine adults (including 61 men) judged the pictures for 250 milliseconds each, enough time to make a snap judgment. Then 119 different adults (including 30 men) were given unlimited time to look at the same faces.

The participants judged women made up in varying intensities of luminance contrast (fancy words for how much eyes and lips stand out compared with skin) as more competent than barefaced women, whether they had a quick glance or a longer inspection.

"I'm a little surprised that the relationship held for even the glamour look," said Richard Russell, an assistant professor of psychology at Gettysburg College in Gettysburg, Pa. "If I call to mind a heavily competent woman like, say, Hillary Clinton, I don't think of a lot of makeup. Then again, she's often onstage so for all I know she is wearing a lot."

However, the glamour look wasn't all roses.

"If you wear a glam look, you should know you look very attractive" at quick glance, said Professor Etcoff, the author of "Survival of the Prettiest" (Doubleday, 1999), which argued that the pursuit of beauty is a biological as well as a cultural imperative. But over time, "there may be a lowering of trust, so if you are in a situation where you need to be a trusted source, perhaps you should choose a different look."

Just as boardroom attire differs from what you would wear to a nightclub, so makeup can be chosen strategically depending on the agenda.

"There are times when you want to give a powerful 'I'm in charge here' kind of impression, and women shouldn't be afraid to do that," by, say, using a deeper lip color that could look shiny, increasing luminosity, said Sarah Vickery, another author of the study and a Procter & Gamble scientist. "Other times you want to give off a more balanced, more collaborative appeal."

In that case, she suggested, opt for lip tones that are light to moderate in color saturation, providing contrast to facial skin, but not being too glossy.

But some women did not view the study's findings as progress.

"I don't wear makeup, nor do I wish to spend 20 minutes applying it," said Deborah Rhode, a law professor at Stanford University who wrote "The Beauty Bias" (Oxford University Press, 2010), which details how appearance unjustly affects some workers. "The quality of my teaching shouldn't depend on the color of my lipstick or whether I've got mascara on."

She is no "beauty basher," she said. "I'm against our preoccupation, and how judgments about attractiveness spill over into judgments about competence and job performance. We like individuals in the job market to be judged on the basis of competence, not cosmetics."

But Professor Etcoff argued that there has been a cultural shift in ideas about self adornment, including makeup. "Twenty or 30 years ago, if you got dressed up, it was simply to please men, or it was something you were doing because society demands it," she said. "Women and feminists today see this [as] their own choice, and it may be an effective tool."

Dr. Vickery, whose Ph.D. is in chemistry, added that cosmetics "can significantly change how people see you, how smart people think you are on first impression, or how warm and approachable, and that look is completely within a woman's control, when there are so many things you cannot control."

Bobbi Brown, the founder of her namesake cosmetics line, suggested that focusing on others' perceptions misses the point of what makes makeup powerful.

"We are able to transform ourselves, not only how we are perceived, but how *we* feel," she said.

Ms. Brown also said that the wrong color on a subject may have caused some testers to conclude that women with high-contrasting makeup were more "untrustworthy." "People will have a bad reaction if it's not the right color, not the right texture, or if the makeup is not enhancing your natural beauty," she said.

Daniel Hamermesh, an economics professor at the University of Texas at Austin, said the conclusion that makeup makes women look more likable—or more socially cooperative—made sense to him because "we conflate looks and a willingness to take care of yourself with a willingness to take care of people."

Professor Hamermesh, the author of "Beauty Pays" (Princeton University Press, 2011), which lays out the leg-up the beautiful get, said he wished that good-looking people were not treated differently, but said he was a realist.

"Like any other thing that society rewards, people will take advantage of it," he said of makeup's benefits. "I'm an economist, so I say, why not? But I wish society didn't reward this. I think we'd be a fairer world if beauty were not rewarded, but it is."

Discussion Questions

1. What do you think about wearing or not wearing makeup on the job? Does it really reflect how well a person does her job?
2. Should a person be discriminated against because she doesn't wear makeup?

10.6

CASINO GIVES WORKERS LOOK THEY CAN, MUST LIVE WITH

Darlene Gavron Stevens

Laura Moore thought she already had all that it took to be a good cocktail waitress at Harrah's Casino in Joliet.

But beginning this month, long-wearing lipstick and buttery hair highlights will be as vital to Moore's job as remembering customer orders and showing up to work on time. Every workday, she will have to look just as she does in a photograph taken after she was given a makeover by the company's image consultants.

"I was appalled," said Moore, a seven-year Harrah's veteran. "What if I don't want to keep my highlights up? I have to get it approved? I don't even know how they can do this legally. It seems like we are jogging back 50 years."

Mandatory makeovers, "personal best" photos and unprecedented new appearance standards are part of the Las Vegas-based company's Beverage Department Image Transformation Initiative, a program officials say is needed as an antidote to the anything-goes attitude of the '90s.

It goes so far as to say a woman who gives birth is expected to fit into her old uniform by the time the baby is 12 weeks old.

"In some ways, it's like being in the military," said spokesman Gary Thompson of Harrah's Entertainment, which hopes the policy will unify its 21 casinos and distinguish the brand. "There's a certain standard you have to meet before you come to work."

The move is drawing double-takes from workplace activists who last decade cheered the downfall of rigid weight requirements and mandatory makeup for flight attendants, five-inch heels and skimpy outfits for Atlantic City cocktail waitresses.

Harrah's action also comes at a time when more employers are relaxing dress codes. Even

Walt Disney World, which since 1957 has been known for stringent standards, recently began allowing men to wear mustaches and beards after it became more difficult to recruit workers.

Although it may seem like a throwback, Harrah's contends that the carefully constructed policy is legal, in part because it applies equally to women and men.

The policy appears to be legal, unless it discriminates on the basis of age or religion, according to legal experts interviewed Friday. Companies are permitted to set fairly strict standards of appearance for employees, the legal experts say. They can ban jewelry, require men to wear suits, mandate a certain hair length and even discriminate based on weight, to a degree.

"They have broad latitude in prescribing how you look and appear on the job," said Bill Gould, a law professor at Stanford University and former chairman of the National Labor Relations Board.

If an employer wants to create an atmosphere through employee appearance, it is perfectly within the employer's right, said Sheribel Rothenberg, an employment attorney in Chicago. "Basically, employers can ask a lot," she said.

Harrah's prefers to view the program as a perk for its 1,400 beverage servers. Thompson estimates that it costs $3,000 per person for all the personal, professional attention given by its hand-picked team of makeup, hair and image consultants, plus new uniforms.

And Harrah's is betting that workers will be lining up to take advantage of the new program, which spells out grooming "requirements" with the detail of a women's magazine.

For female servers, hair "must be teased, curled or styled every day you work. Hair must be worn down at all times, no exceptions."

Men cannot wear ponytails, and hair must not extend below the top of their shirt collars.

Workers may get a new hairstyle—but only if it is approved and a new photo is taken. Generally speaking, extreme changes will be frowned on, Thompson said.

Women must wear face powder, blush and mascara, and "lip color must be worn at all times." Men are not allowed to wear makeup.

As for the new uniforms, a seam can't be touched for a year—unless the alteration is for medical reasons or "positive body enhancements," which the company says is self-explanatory.

Even women returning from maternity leave are expected to zip into their old, form-fitting costumes within 12 weeks, nursing or not. But the company will "work with" employees who need help trimming post-baby fat, Thompson said.

"If someone was a size 8 and they come back (from leave) a size 12, that's not acceptable," said Charlotte Rogers, food and beverage manager of the Lake Tahoe Harrah's. "They should be coming back as a size 8, but we can help them along."

Workers are expected to look like their "personal best" photo every day or risk being disciplined for insubordination, according to the policy. Updated photos will be taken each year to account for "subtle body changes," it states.

Corporate managers, Thompson said, are not undergoing the makeovers.

"Seems like someone is pushing the envelope," said Paul Paz of the National Waiters Association. "They're going to have a heck of a time finding someone to work there."

It is one thing to have standards, noted Anne Ladky, executive director of Women Employed, "but to require a certain look for a year sounds fundamentally intrusive."

Harrah's says it is simply attempting to raise the bar for dress codes by giving workers—men and women, equally—the tools to look and feel better.

Joliet is the 12th property in 75 days to be introduced to the program, said Reimi Marden, the Las Vegas consultant and coach hired by Harrah's. Her pitch has spread like glitter to the Bellagio, Desert Inn and other image-minded hotels.

Marden oversaw last week's training and makeover sessions for about 150 Joliet beverage workers, and she helped hire local hair and makeup artists who carried out the makeovers.

"This is a gift for you guys, an opportunity for you to do and be your personal best," a perky Marden told the generally subdued gathering of Harrah's servers, some of whom wore ponytails and hair clips—styles strictly banned under the new policy.

"What is it our players connect to?" Marden asked before plowing through grooming tips such as the importance of tongue brushing and why men should wear socks that cover the calves. "Our image, from the inside out."

While some Harrah's have embraced the dress code or gone along ("We wanted to bring some class back," said Lake Tahoe server Barbara Campbell, 43), others said it was a waste of time.

"I'm OK with myself," said Tracey Drewniany, a Harrah's Joliet server for a year. "It doesn't make me feel better to put lipstick on. If you don't have self-esteem it doesn't matter how much lipstick you put on."

Moore, who is seven months' pregnant, worries about being able to keep up her approved image in the final weeks of her pregnancy.

"If it wasn't mandatory, it might be nice," said Moore of the make-overs. "A lot of people were insulted."

Some employees, she added, left an information meeting in tears.

Over the years, a sensitivity to gender issues in the workplace—and fear of lawsuits—has prompted many employers to allow workers more leeway in what they wear to work.

"This controversy disappeared off the road as dress codes loosened up and as women in general were less willing to take jobs that have costumes," said Ladky of Women Employed.

Companies also may be less inclined to require revealing outfits because "more employers understand now that they have a responsibility to maintain a workplace free of sexual harassment," she added.

Employers have every right to establish a dress code and portray a certain image to customers, but federal law requires that men and women be treated equally, said Reginald Welch, a spokesman for the Equal Employment Opportunity Commission.

"Of course it sounds odd," he said of the Harrah's initiative. "Our question would be, is it easier for men to meet the standards than the women?"

Thompson said Harrah's policy is not discriminatory.

"It's not a case of forcing them to look like models," he said. The company wants the employees to be "clean and well-groomed."

"We are trying to say, 'This is the way you look now. We expect you to maintain [that look],'" he said. "We will work with you on it, but we expect you to maintain these standards."

In the past, employees have waged some successful battles against rigid dress codes. A 1992 lawsuit by a Sands Casino waitress who thought it was unfair that male servers got to wear pants and low shoes while women had to wear scanty clothes and 5-inch heels was settled after the Atlantic City casino agreed to give female servers the option of wearing slacks and lower shoes.

Hyatt Hotels Corp. in 1998 cracked down on local hotel policies that prohibited cornrow hairstyles after several women filed complaints with the EEOC.

In 1991, Continental Airlines dropped a policy that required makeup on flight attendants after a former employee charged she was fired for complaining about the standard. That same year, American Airlines settled a 17-year-old legal fight by agreeing to relax its weight standards for flight attendants by taking into account the worker's age as well as height.

So far, there have been no reported complaints at Harrah's in Lake Tahoe, which gave the staff makeovers in February, said Rogers, the food and beverage manager.

Rogers said she has not had to discipline anyone for not looking like the photos in a Rolodex on her desk.

"We had some who liked that 'oatmeal' look," she said, referring to employees who didn't wear makeup before the new policy. "Now, they don't look like they just rolled out of bed."

Discussion Questions

1. Do you think that an employer, such as Harrah's, should be allowed to make its employees live up to a picture taken after a makeover for one year? Why or why not?

2. Is it legal to tell an employee how he or she must look when on the job? When is it illegal?

3. Other large corporations have dress policies similar to the one described in this article. For instance, Walt Disney has a booklet devoted to appropriate dress styles, hairstyles, etc., for their employees. What about an individual's personal rights?

10.7

HEALTH TO PAY: PRESSURES PUSH JOCKEYS TO EXTREMES FOR WEIGHT LOSS

Maryjean Wall

As a 9-year-old boy, Randy Romero rode races where the jockeys were really light. Sometimes the "jockey" was no more than a few strips of plastic substituting for a rider on a horse.

A horse can run a hole through the wind when you take the weight off its back. And there's nothing like plastic flapping in the breeze to scare a horse into running fast. Romero grew up in the bayou country of Southwest Louisiana observing strange ways for racing horses "light."

The boys he rode against were also light. But Romero was not. He starved himself to 70 pounds. Later he learned to "flip" his meals by sticking a finger down his throat, forcing himself to vomit. At 16 he started taking the diuretic Lasix. Now he says those habits have ruined his health.

At 44, Romero has become an outspoken advocate of raising the minimum weights to benefit jockeys (Figure 10.7). Although he's been retired four years from riding, Romero has raised a timely topic among jockeys.

The world's top money-winning jockey, Chris McCarron, said when he retired last month that he is "absolutely" behind a growing momentum to see jockeys riding at least a few pounds heavier than the average 111 to 113. McCarron also said that jockeys need to understand the damage they inflict on their bodies by using extreme weight-loss techniques. Romero, in fact, has blamed his need for a liver and kidney transplant on his lifelong battle with weight.

On closer reflection, however, he says his kidney and liver problems probably did not result from radical weight-loss techniques but from other hazards he encountered during his jockey career.

He now says his diseased liver might have resulted from a blood transfusion received after severe burns he suffered in a weight-loss "box" years ago at Oaklawn Park.

He says his failing kidneys might have resulted from the large number of anti-inflammatory medications he says he had to take after 22 surgeries.

Nonetheless Romero and retired jockey Shane Sellers have seized on Romero's illness to seek a forum for the weight-loss plight of jockeys. McCarron, who plans to keep up his leadership in The Jockey's Guild even in retirement, said from California that Romero's plea should not be taken lightly. According to McCarron, traditionally low riding weights and radical weight-loss methods are for many riders a very real problem.

Evaluating Scale of Weights

Romero estimates that "out of 10 riders, two do not reduce at all." California-based Kent Desormeaux, who won the Kentucky Derby with Real Quiet and then with Fusaichi Pegasus, said that "98 percent of us have to reduce."

Republished with permission of MCCLATCHY COMPANY, from *The Lexington Herald Leader*, Maryjean Wall, July 7, 2002.

Figure 10.7 Jockeys must weigh in prior to racing. Some jockeys adopt dangerous habits to make the weight standard.

Their estimates, while unscientific, are validated by the empirical findings of a study conducted in Australia and published in March.

Australian scientists discovered what professional jockeys already knew too well. Their conclusion was that "the majority" are forced to practice at least one radical technique to meet the sport's weight requirements. The study was published in a journal called "Sport Nutrition and Exercise Metabolism."

Significant to racing authorities was the scientists' conclusion that dehydration resulting from these rapid weight-loss techniques "increases the risk of accident and injury to both horse and jockey."

Yet racing authorities have paid little attention to this danger through the years. Jockeys continue to ride at weights that have not changed radically since the late 19th century, when The Jockey Club's Scale of Weights was devised. The scale represents the weights to be assigned to horses according to the time of year, the sex of the animal, its age and the distance of the race.

The Scale of Weights has been raised by about 20 pounds in some categories through the years, according to racing steward Pete Pederson, in California. Still, he said, "some of it's antiquated."

The Jockey Club no longer controls the Scale of Weights, which now falls under the jurisdiction of individual racing commissions. The jockey's dilemma remains the same, however.

Either he meets his horses' weight assignments or he soon finds himself out of work.

That's not a problem for Pat Day, who maintains an average weight of about 103 pounds. He's naturally light and does not have to reduce.

That gives Day an edge even beyond his extraordinary talent. Other jockeys say that Day probably rides with more strength than a rider who spends hours in the sauna, sweating his strength away.

All the same, Day does not think that clearing the way for jockeys to ride at heavier weights will solve the big problems.

"It's a short-term answer to a long-term problem," said Day, the third-winningest rider in history. Raise the window of opportunity, according to Day, and you'll see the same scenario only with larger people trying to make the weight.

Carl Nafzger, who trained Kentucky Derby winner Unbridled, said higher weights won't hurt horses—as long as the spread between highest and lowest weights in a race is not too great.

The heavily-weighted horse is forced to race harder. That's how breakdowns can occur, according to Nafzger.

But Hall of Fame trainer D. Wayne Lukas sees the weight-loss cycle only continuing if jockey weights go higher. Like Day, he sees heavier people trying to become riders if that window opens.

Yet for the safety of horses, Lukas said, it's "most important" to have them ridden by the lightest possible people.

"We race year-round," Lukas said, "which means more stress on the horses. Speed and weight are the detrimental things to a horse's longevity."

Doing Whatever It Takes

Many concur that weight is detrimental to a horse's speed. That's why jockeys have to keep their weight low however they can. No one wants the jockey checking in at a couple of pounds overweight.

Before the Civil War, when many jockeys were slaves, their owners reportedly kept the small boys from eating too much to keep them from getting too big.

Reducing has taken some creative twists since then. Readers of Laura Hillenbrand's *Seabiscuit* will recall Eddie Arcaro's comment: "Some riders will all but saw their legs off to get within the limit."

The book mentioned a few other old-time methods, including swallowing a pill containing the egg of a tapeworm. Then there were the bottles of "bowel scourer" that surely must have been fairly potent, if not effective—a few of them spontaneously exploded in the jockeys' room in Tijuana.

Chick Lang, a former jockeys' agent and former general manager of Pimlico Racecourse, can recall riders donning rubber sweat suits and burying themselves up to their necks in horse manure piles, to induce more heat.

"In the meantime, the racing secretaries (who assign weights, according to the Scale of Weights) sit back and eat a double hamburger," opined jockey Craig Perret. Perret made that comment tongue-in-cheek.

He said it wasn't intended as criticism. He's not even actively campaigning for adjusting the Scale of Weights. But every day he rides, he has to reduce. He fears that someday he will suffer consequences to his health.

Reducing strategies cover every ground from flipping to swallowing diuretics to taking diet pills and sweating in the sauna. "We don't have two months to reduce," Perret said. "We play with minutes. We've got hours to take it off." Perret says he loses one to one and a half pounds daily, but on rare days he might have to lose up to five pounds.

Flipping is perhaps the most controversial practice, one that jockeys and racetrack managements are not keen to discuss. Some observers have even compared flipping to bulimia.

"I see it every day," said Pederson, the steward in California. "I see top riders coming out of the [sauna] or flipping. These are really bad things that should be addressed."

Dr. David Richardson, a surgeon in Louisville who has owned racehorses and is familiar with the racetrack lifestyle, said he does not believe the majority of jockeys are suffering severe problems as a result of reducing. But he also said that flipping has side effects, including irritation of the stomach or esophagus.

Veteran jockeys also tell how their teeth enamel becomes eroded after years of flipping.

Some even lose their teeth. Romero said his body got so accustomed to years of flipping that when he retired from riding, his body needed another "one and a half years to quit flipping." It's racing's dirty secret. Yet racetrack managements accommodate the practice of flipping by providing jockeys with a special "heaving bowl." The porcelain bowl is larger than a toilet but smaller than a washtub. It can be found in any jockeys' locker room among the toilet stalls.

Fifteen years ago, UPI reporter Pohla Smith began a provocative series on jockeys and weight with an observation about the widespread practice of flipping.

"At the core of horse racing lies a self-imposed misery," Smith wrote, "that racing's owners and trainers do not want to see, fans are largely unaware of, and most jockeys cannot escape.

"It is represented by a sound better suited to back alleys and washrooms than to a sport known for its riches, beauty and power. It is the sound of someone vomiting."

Sweating Away the Weight

The other popular weight-loss strategy, more suited to polite conversation, is the sauna that jockeys still call the "hot box." The term is a holdover from days when the box was a one-man contraption that enclosed the jockey up to his neck. A multitude of light bulbs inside the box generated the heat that made the jockey sweat. The sweating removed fluids and reduced the rider's weight.

Romero suffered severe burns in such a box years ago. He'd rubbed himself down with alcohol and oil before tightening the hatch on the hot box. Then his arm hit a lighted bulb. "The combustion blew me out of there," he said.

Three of his 22 surgeries resulted from that incident. Romero said that 10 years after the burn incident, he got a $1.8 million settlement that comes to him in installments.

The modern-day hot box is actually a system of three rooms: a dry heat room, a steam room and a "cooling down" room that is still warm, but cooler than the other rooms.

Temperatures in the dry heat and steam rooms might be between 150 and 160 degrees. Desormeaux, at Hollywood Park, said the hot box routine is "very difficult." Sometimes he sits in the steam room for 30 minutes. Sometimes he incorporates calisthenics into his sweating regimen.

Safer Alternatives

Raising weights likely will be discussed in Kentucky, in the opinion of Bernie Hettel, the Executive Director of the Kentucky Racing Commission. He says it might be time to reexamine the Scale of Weights, as some states already have.

But as talk heats up, Lukas and Day both wonder why more jockeys can't follow Laffit Pincay's lead.

Pincay, 55, the winningest jockey ever, has fought weight throughout his career. Lukas often told the story of how he flew cross-country with Pincay—and watched him eat only a single peanut the entire way, after slicing it into tiny bits.

Then Pincay found relief. He'd refined what he'd learned from nutritionists until he formulated a diet that allowed him some fruit, oil and salt.

At 52 he became the winningest rider ever in 1999 passing Bill Shoemaker's 8,830 wins.

At the same time, Pincay told how he felt far better than he had before his new diet. Using this regimen, he maintains a weight of 115 pounds.

In Lukas's view, the weight question always has and will revolve around one premise: "If you want to be a rider," Lukas said, "you're going to have to make sacrifices. Laffit Pincay," he said, "is living proof it can be done."

Discussion Questions

1. Do you agree that raising weight limits will only increase the number of people using extreme weight-loss techniques to "make weight"? Why or why not?
2. Did you know about the extreme measures that jockeys use to make their weight limit? How does it compare to wrestling? To bodybuilding? To runway modeling?
3. List the ways that jockeys reduce their weight before a race. What are some of the consequences of these methods?

CHAPTER 11

DRESS AND MEDIA

Patricia Hunt–Hurst

After you have read this chapter, you will understand:

- The fashion industry's use of technology changes as media opportunities change
- How magazines retouch photographs to create a perfect image
- How media images impact body image
- How media is responding to the aging of the population

Fashion is at our fingertips. With the simple press of a button, we can click on an icon and journey into our favorite fashion magazine, television show, blog, or website. These venues treat us to our favorite designer's latest runway show, a critique of red carpet dresses, an article about how to lose 10 pounds, and how to dress appropriately for a job interview. This information and its accompanying images are often infused with views of flawless human bodies and faces. The fashion media can be helpful in the information it dispenses, but the information can also create anxiety. This chapter discusses the multifaceted aspect of dress and the media: the good, the bad, and the ugly.

Fashion media, whether it be magazine, television, a website, Facebook, Twitter, or a blog, gives us the latest fashion information. Social media sites expand viewership to beyond Lincoln Center and the Paris runways. A student can sit in a dorm and watch live streams of Marc Jacobs's runway show. Some designers utilize the live streaming option as a selling tool, giving shoppers 24 hours to preorder items straight from the runway. Retailers have taken social media to a new level by listening to what customers are saying about products they want. In one example, American retailer The Loft posted photos of a new pair of pants on a skinny model. Customers responded with negative comments like "Sure, they look great, if you're 5'10" and a stick like the model in the photo." The retailer quickly reacted with new photos, this time of employees from sizes 2 to 12 wearing the same pair of pants. After this change, The Loft received positive comments about the pants and the realistic models. This is an example of how the fashion industry is utilizing technology changes in the media.

Figure 11.1 Models show us the latest runway styles and represent the contemporary image of beauty.

Figure 11.2 Early-20th-century fashions presented a curving figure: large bust, tiny waist, and curving hips.

The tall, thin models that walk the runway, adorn fashion magazine pages, and decorate retailers' websites are not what most women look like. (See Figure 11.1.) Cultural ideals of beauty and appearance are constant throughout media and have been for as long as practices of adornment have been recorded. Fashion publications have been around since the 18th century when Paris and London printed journals to disseminate the latest fashions in men's and women's clothing, accessories, and hairstyles. These early publications included drawings and color illustrations of dresses, hats, carriages, and much more. The use of illustrations continued into the 20th century when magazines' drawings and illustrations documented the newest styles and promoted the ideal figure for the time. For example, the Gibson Girl personified the ideal woman of the early 20th century with her large bust, tiny waist, and rounded hips, supposedly perfected by the "S" corset (Figure 11.2). The Flapper epitomized the flat-chested, straight figure of the 1924 to 1928 period, while bust, waist, and hips in a slender form prevailed in the 1930s. The ideal figure of the 1940s included broad shoulders with the noticeable curves of the breasts, waist, and hips; these curves were further accentuated in the 1950s with a noticeably smaller waist. This ideal was replaced in the late 1960s by a thin, androgynous figure made famous by Twiggy. Non-European models appeared for the first time in the 1960s, including the first African American model in a major fashion publication. All these changes in cultural ideals were reflections of changes in society as a whole during each period. A 2009 exhibition called "The Model as Muse" at the Metropolitan Museum of Art in New York showcased these ideals and more through fashion's famous faces from the 1950s to the present, supporting the notion that the models from each period represented the ideals of beauty for that particular time. Today fashion magazines continue to promote the ideal cultural image. Currently, thinness continues to be the image filling the pages, indicating that it is valued. Yet, actresses like Christina Hendricks, Sophia Vergara, and Jennifer Lopez provide an alternative to thinness as a beauty image (Figure 11.3). Some retailers are responding. Talbot's is showing curvy models in its catalogs and recently hired Ashley Falcon as style advisor for Talbot's Woman and Woman Petite fashions. Ashley Falcon is known for her curvy, full figure and for the style advice she gives plus-size girls and women through her *Marie Claire* columns. This is a move in the right direction for designers and retailers. It will be interesting to see if other retailers, magazines, and advertisers take notice and refocus to include the vast majority of women and their needs.

Making Them Perfect

Images of actresses, singers, and other entertainers, whether male or female, appear flawless and blemish-free in magazines. Research

Figure 11.3 Actresses like Christina Hendricks provide an alternative to thinness as a beauty image.

has found that media images impact how girls, boys, men, and women feel about their own bodies, particularly if they don't match the idealized standard: muscular build, thin body, small hips and breasts, long blonde, straight hair, and flawless skin. Along with the ideal body, celebrities and models are depicted with perfect, blemish-free faces and bodies. In reality, these images are retouched digitally. Two readings in this chapter explain how the media retouches photographs. "I Don't Want to Be Perfect!" illustrates how a photograph of actress Aisha Tyler was retouched to make her picture perfect. In another article, famous 1960s fashion model Twiggy, now in her late 50s, appears in an airbrushed skin-care advertisement in which she looks 30 years younger. The article also includes an untouched photograph of how she really looks at age 59. Simpson states in "The Two Faces of Twiggy at 59: How Airbrushing in Olay Ad Hides Truth of the Skin She's In" that the real Twiggy looks good for her age, but does have the typical signs of aging (e.g., wrinkles around the eyes and sagging jowls). Do these idealized cultural images of men and women in the 21st century matter?

All people are adversely affected by these fake images (Bordo, 2004), and young girls are especially vulnerable. To show that models and actresses are perfect and flawless is deceptive and encourages women and girls to believe that something is wrong with them because they have wrinkles, blemishes, and cellulite.

Outside of the United States, the public in some instances is beginning to protest the retouching of images and even believe that it is the media's social responsibility to notify its readers of the retouched photos. A protest organization in the United Kingdom has started a campaign called "Real Women" with the goal of encouraging companies to include realistic images of women in advertisements. The group is working toward a warning system or symbol that notifies the reader (and/or viewer) about whether an image has been digitally modified and to what degree. The article "Australia Pushes New Body Image Standard" discusses a voluntary program that, among other things, encourages companies not to use retouched images or, if they do, to notify readers (and/or viewers) that an image has been retouched. These are small steps in the movement away from the falseness of retouched bodies and faces.

Research: Objectification and Impact

One long-standing cliché in the advertising industry is "Sex sells." This belief is a matter of concern in regard to how men and women are represented in magazines. Research has indicated that since the 1960s fashion advertising has become more sexually overt in that women are shown nude or partially nude to help sell products. Thompson studied the sexual portrayal of both male and female models in advertising from 1964 to 1994 in two magazines: *Vogue* and *GQ*. Not surprisingly, she found that there was an increase in sexually overt images of women between 1964 and 1994. However, the first sexually explicit imagery involving men's bodies appeared in 1984. The overall number of images was higher in the women's category than for the men's, yet men were also objectified after 1984.

Jung and Lee (2009) conducted a cross-cultural study of women's fashion and beauty magazines in the United States and Korea. One component of their research included an examination of women as sex objects in advertisements. The researchers wanted to find out if there were differences or similarities between how female models were portrayed in advertisements in the United States and Korea. The authors of the study indicated that:

> When objectification occurs, the female body is seen as a decorative object that is used as part of the scene for the advertised products/services. Sexual objectification often occurs when the focus is on isolated body parts, such as a bare stomach, cleavage, or buttocks, and it is not unusual that isolated body parts are being used in ads as part of or in comparison to product features such as shape, weight, and texture (2009, p. 277).

Jung and Lee also found that female models were mostly represented as sexual objects in both the U.S. and Korean magazines, with more in the Korean than in the U.S. fashion and beauty publications. In addition, they found that more models were shown in partial or full nudity in advertisements in the U.S. magazines, and more faces were hidden, indicating greater frequency of female objectification in the U.S. magazines. They also found that the traditional Korean concept of female attractiveness that concentrates on the face rather than on the body was maintained. In addition, Jung and Lee found a standardized ideal of beauty based on the Western concept of thinness and noted that the Korean traditional concept of female beauty that included mild plumpness with a round face was replaced by models who followed the U.S. standard of thin bodies and prominent facial features. Another finding in this study was the fact that magazines from both countries were primarily using Caucasian models, thus moving toward a Western standard of beauty rather than a focus on the unique and differing features of women's bodies and faces.

Over the years researchers have studied the effects of media on self-esteem, body image, and how satisfied or unsatisfied girls and women are with their bodies. This research focused on the impact that advertisements and photographs of thin models in magazines and on television have on young women (Ju and Johnson, 2010; Jung, 2006; Jung and Lee, 2009; Kim and Lennon, 2007). The **Social Comparison Theory** often serves as a theoretical framework for analysis of the impact of media. This theory, developed by social psychologist Leon Festinger, indicates that humans compare themselves with others, particularly in regard to appearance. He considered this a basic need "for purposes of self-evaluation" (Kaiser, 1997, p. 171). Comparing ourselves to celebrities, models, and others in the media is not unusual; it is how this comparison affects us that makes it a controversial topic. Kim and Lennon (2007) found that there is a connection between looking at ideal images in fashion or beauty magazines and dissatisfaction with one's appearance, as well as with a propensity to develop eating disorders. Jung (2006) studied the impact of media on mood and body image. She found that advertisements in fashion magazines may negatively affect the mood of research participants rather than their perception of body image. Jung found that exposure to media images in magazines decreased "a positive mood and elevated depression and anxiety" (p. 341). These findings confirm the alienation that people can feel if their bodies and other aspects of their appearance (hair color and texture) do not match cultural standards.

Adolescents are also surrounded by media images of thin and perfect bodies and tend to be more susceptible to believing that those impossible norms are attainable. Recent research found that greater involvement with visual media such as TV and fashion magazines correlates with greater body dissatisfaction and desire to achieve thinness norms.

There is hope, however. Ogle and Thornburg (2003) analyzed *Girl Zone*, an online teen magazine that takes a socially responsible approach to encourage girls to accept and have healthy attitudes and practices toward their bodies. For example, *Girl Zone* advises girls with comments about being overweight to move their body more, to walk or ride their bikes to school, and to make healthy food choices. Ogle and Thornburg note the increase of positive body-related articles in magazines such as *Seventeen*. In addition, not all teenagers are helplessly sucked into accepting the impossible standards presented in media, particularly as they move into later adolescence. Lisa Duke (2002) studied African American and European-American girls' assessments of their favorite teen magazines. She found that the African American girls were often critical of the lack of representation of real girls like themselves in the magazines (see Figure 11.4).

Even though they often liked the articles in mainstream teen magazines, they wanted to see more representation of girls who weren't so thin, so perfectly and unrealistically made up, and so white. The white girls in the study did not tend to notice the limited representation of diversity and were less critical consumers of the magazines.

Men and boys are likewise not immune to cultural ideals. If boys are too thin or overweight, they are often teased, a problem that starts as early as elementary school. Due to the influence of the media, men are paying more attention to their appearance

Figure 11.4 Fashion publications often provide us with homogenous images of beauty rather than the real diversity of beautiful faces.

Figure 11.5 Many young men also give attention to their body image by working out and exercising daily.

(Rohlinger, 2002) (Figure 11.5). Today doctors and medical media warn about the dangers of steroids, bodybuilding, and weight loss, a combination that many boys and men use to change their appearance and better fit the ideal body image. Jones (2001) found that boys, like girls, make social comparisons of themselves to media celebrities and models. A study on body image among adolescents found that there has been an increase in male body image concerns due to changes in media portrayal of men. In addition, children are not immune to ideal images of thinness as attractive. Researchers are finding that girls as young as *four years old* express concern about their weight and mimic dieting behaviors and restrict their food intake (Smolek and Levine, 1994). Many girls in middle childhood talk about their need to diet, indicating that socialization to weight control is learned at an early age. The reading "Do Thin Models Warp Girls' Body Image?" discusses the current standard of even thinner models on the runway, how this perception is affecting girls, links to eating disorders, and what some fashion professionals are doing to move away from extreme thinness.

Global Views

The discussion of flawless images also reveals the fact that most models and celebrities do not represent Western society as a whole. By 2025, one-fifth of the U.S. population will be age 65 and older. It is well known that baby boomers spend more money on consumer goods than Generation X or Y, so this demographic fact indicates that the fashion industry and fashion publications should already be preparing for these changes (Underhill, 2009). In the article "How Does *Vogue* Negotiate Age?: Fashion, the Body, and the Older Woman," Julia Twigg studies issues of UK *Vogue* to discover how the very popular fashion publication addresses the aging of the world's population. Magazines may tell readers how to look good at age 40, 50, 60, and beyond, but they rarely use models who actually look these ages. Instead, they use models who look younger and show no visible signs of aging other than perhaps silver hair. This deception also appears in the use of African American models photographed with straight hair and light skin. Tracey Owens Patton (2006) contends that these features relate to the European-American standards of beauty and compel African American women to evaluate their looks based on these standards rather than to take an "Afro-centric" point of view (p. 46). Patton encourages a new attitude for all women, challenging them to disregard these standards and instead honor the uniqueness of human faces and body types.

Supporting Patton's argument is the relationship between an advertising image and a consumer's attraction to the image (Solomon et al., 1992; Hornik, 1980). Research findings in a cross-cultural study by Bjerke and Polegato revealed that women in five different European cities had differing images of what they considered healthy and beautiful. They showed women in five European cities (London, Hamburg, Paris, Madrid, and Milan) a black-and-white photograph of two different women's faces: a woman with (A) light hair and eye color, and (B) dark hair and eye color. The researchers asked, "If you want to look more healthy (or beautiful), which of these women would you prefer to look like?" Respondents could answer A, B, or neither. They were also asked to respond to eye and hair color. The findings revealed that there were differences in preference for one over the other, indicating that images of health and beauty are not the same across the five cultures. Woman B, however, was most preferred across the five cultures; therefore, Woman B can be "considered more cross-culturally acceptable" as an ideal image of beauty and health (Bjerke and Polegato, 2006, p. 874). This finding has implications for advertisers and others in the fashion industry to value multicultural and multi-ethnic features instead of cookie-cutter, blemish-free, tall, thin, and young models.

Summary

This chapter explores the topic of dress and the media, particularly the negative impacts that images in the media can create in the minds of consumers. Articles relate industry methods to disguise flaws and create perfect images of celebrities and models in advertisements, fashion layouts, and articles, as well as discuss the results of fashion's fascination with thinness. Although some magazines, advertisers, and retailers use models that represent different ethnicities, ages, and body sizes to model clothing and other products, this is not a major trend in the fashion industry.

Suggested Readings

Duke, L. (2002). Get Real!: Cultural Relevance and Resistance to the Mediated Feminine Ideal. *Psychology & Marketing* 19 (2): 211–233.

Ogle, J. P. and E. Thornburg. (2003). An Alternative Voice amid Teen 'Zines: An Analysis of Body-Related Content in *Girl Zone. Journal of Family and Consumer Sciences* 95 (1): 47–56.

Patton, T. O. (2006). Hey Girl, Am I More Than My Hair?: African American Women and Their Struggles with Beauty, Body Image, and Hair. *Feminist Formations* 18 (2): 24–51.

Thompson, M. J. (2000). Gender in Magazine Advertising: Skin Sells Best. *Clothing and Textiles Research Journal* 18 (3): 178–181.

Learning Activity 11.1: Fashion Ad Assessment

Review recent issues of your favorite fashion magazines and count how many advertisements you see that represent only 1) faces, 2) bodies with no head, 3) heads and bodies, and 4) nudity or partial nudity. This exercise can also be done with a menswear magazine. What did you find? Share with the class.

Learning Activity 11.2: Beauty Debate

Create a team of students who can debate in support of a homogenized standard of beauty in the United States or globally. Also create a team with the opposite position. Think about your arguments for and against, research your position, and have a debate in class.

Learning Activity 11.3: 1950s Beauty Ideals

If you can find a copy at your college library of a *Vogue, Essence, Ebony, Harper's Bazaar,* or other fashion publication from the 1950s, try this activity. Examine body types, faces, hair, and body size in the 1950s. What do you find in comparison to one of these magazines today? Are you finding differences? Similarities? What do you think are the reasons for the differences and similarities? Write up your findings; include photos of the images to back up your findings and analysis.

References

A Battle of the Ages: Will Gen Xers, Millennials, or Boomers Shape Economic Recovery? Lifestyle Monitor Cotton Incorporated. Retrieved March 23, 2011, from http://life stylemonitor.Cottoninc.com/LSM-Issue-Fall -2010/Retail-Economic-Recovery/.

Bjerke, R., and R. Polegato. (2006, October). How Well Do Advertising Images of Health and Beauty Travel across Cultures? A Self-Concept Perspective. *Psychology & Marketing* 23 (10): 865–884.

Bordo, S. (2004). *Unbearable Weight: Feminism, Western Culture, and the Body.* Berkeley: University of California Press.

Duke, L. (2002). Get Real!: Cultural Relevance and Resistance to the Mediated Feminine Ideal. *Psychology & Marketing* 19 (2): 211–233.

Hornick, J. (1980). Quantitative Analysis of Visual Perception of Printed Advertisements. *Journal of Advertising Research* 20:41–48.

Horyn, C. (2009, May 5). Perhaps More Than Just Pretty Faces. *The New York Times.* Retrieved August 25, 2010, from http://www.ny times.com/2009/05/06/arts/design/obmode. html?_v=1&scp=1&sq=perhaps.

Jones, D. (2001). Social Comparison and Body Image: Attractiveness Comparison to Models and Peers among Adolescent Girls and Boys. *Sex Roles* 45 (9/10): 645–663.

Ju, H. W., and K. K. P. Johnson. (2010). Fashion Advertisements and Young Women: Determining Visual Attention Using Eye Tracking. *Clothing and Textiles Research Journal* 28 (3): 159–173.

Jung, J. (2006). Media Influence: Pre- and Post-Exposure of College Women to Media Images and the Effect of Mood and Body Image. *Clothing and Textiles Research Journal* 24 (4): 335–344.

Jung, J., and Y. J. Lee. (2009). Cross-Cultural Examination of Women's Fashion and Beauty Magazine Advertisements in the United States and South Korea. *Clothing and Textiles Research Journal* 27 (4): 274–286.

Kaiser, S. B. (1997). *The Social Psychology of Clothing: Symbolic Appearances in Context* (2nd ed.). New York: Fairchild Publications.

Kim, J. H., and S. J. Lennon. (2007). Mass Media and Self-Esteem, Body Image, and Eating Disorder Tendencies. *Clothing and Textiles Research Journal* 25 (1): 3–23.

Ogle, J. P., and E. Thornburg. (2003). An Alternative Voice amid Teen 'Zines: An Analysis of Body-Related Content in *Girl Zone. Journal of Family and Consumer Sciences* 95 (1): 47–56.

Patton, T. O. (2006). Hey Girl, Am I More Than My Hair?: African American Women and Their Struggles with Beauty, Body Image, and Hair. *Feminist Formations* 18 (2): 24–51.

Rohlinger, D. (2002). Eroticizing Men: Cultural Influences on Advertising and Male Objectification. *Sex Roles* 46 (3/4): 61–74.

Smolek, L., and Levine, M. (1994). Toward an empirical basis for primary prevention of eating problems with elementary school children. *Eating Disorder: The Journal of Treatment and Prevention,* 2 (4): 293–307.

Solomon, M. R., R. D. Ashmore, and L. C. Longo. (1992). The Beauty Match-Up Hypothesis: Congruence between Types of Beauty and Product Images in Advertising. *Journal of Advertising* 21:23–34.

Underhill, P. (2009). *Why We Buy: The Science of Shopping.* New York: Simon and Schuster.

I DON'T WANT TO BE PERFECT!

Aisha Tyler

I once did a photo shoot for a big magazine that shall remain nameless. Even though I'm usually teeth-chatteringly nervous before photo shoots, in this case I was pretty excited because I'd been working out regularly, eating right (the occasional glass or three of champagne notwithstanding) and getting lots of rest (ever since I read that getting plenty of sleep can help you lose weight, I'd been lolling in bed like a hungover college freshman). I walked in there thinking, *bring on the bathing suits! Bring on the hot pants (despite the fact that they're tragically outdated)! I'm ready for anything!*

The shoot went fine. (Of course, there's no way to look slinky when you're folded up like a yogi in a modern wire chair—you can only look pained. That's why models look so vacant. They've gone to their mental "happy place" to escape the fact that the sculpture they're perched on is jammed dangerously far up their hoo-ha.) But as I was getting ready to leave, the photographer handed me a batch of Polaroids and said a handful of the most soul-crushingest words I have ever heard: "Don't worry—we'll retouch them." I smiled wanly. Gee, thanks for the monster karate chop to my self-esteem. What could be so terrible about the real me that the photos would only be acceptable after digital manipulation?

The sundae I ate that night was as big as a toddler. (No matter what anyone says, ice cream makes you feel better. That's just the way it is.)

Now, I know what you're thinking: Good Lord, sister. Cry me a river. It must really suck to be you. But believe me, actresses are riddled with the same anguish and self-doubt as every other woman. We all wish our butts were rounder, our tummies flatter and that our second toe wasn't longer than our first (on the upside, I can pick up quarters with my feet). Actresses may look "perfect" in fashion magazines, where they've been pulled, pushed, pinned, posed, perfectly lit—and

are sucking in their stomachs so hard they're in danger of denting their spleens—but the truth is, they obsess over their imperfections just like everyone else. *Unlike* everyone else, though, when they get a huge zit or an unholy lip rash, some sweaty paparazzo is waiting in the bushes to snap a nice humiliating close-up.

There's nothing like seeing a photo of yourself in a tabloid, dressed in your "time of the month" sweats, to make you *pray* for a little retouching. So when *Glamour* asked if I'd be willing to engage in an experiment to show how extreme the retouching process can be, I agreed warily, worried it would make me feel just as self-conscious and crappy as that earlier shoot. Even though I knew what I was getting into, I was still floored when I got the "before" pictures from the retoucher (Figure 11.6).

They were *covered* in notes. Covered. I knew they were going overboard for the sake of this story, but it looked like some macabre all-you-can-cut shopping list written by a crazed plastic surgeon. Then I pulled out the "after" photo. A mad computer scientist, high on beaker juice, had doctored it up, and voila! Presenting: Robot Aisha.

Is Robot Aisha "prettier"? She's a bit thinner, I suppose, and she certainly has "flawless" skin. But it's a bit creepy to look at a picture of yourself and wonder what happened to your freckles and that mole you've had since you were a baby, or why your boobs look as if someone blew them up like inner tubes. Robot Aisha is glowing, but not from within. Glow has been meticulously applied through a software program. Robot Aisha looks as if she'd be sweet at first, lure you close, and then shoot you with a ray gun that popped out of her left breast. Between you and me, Robot

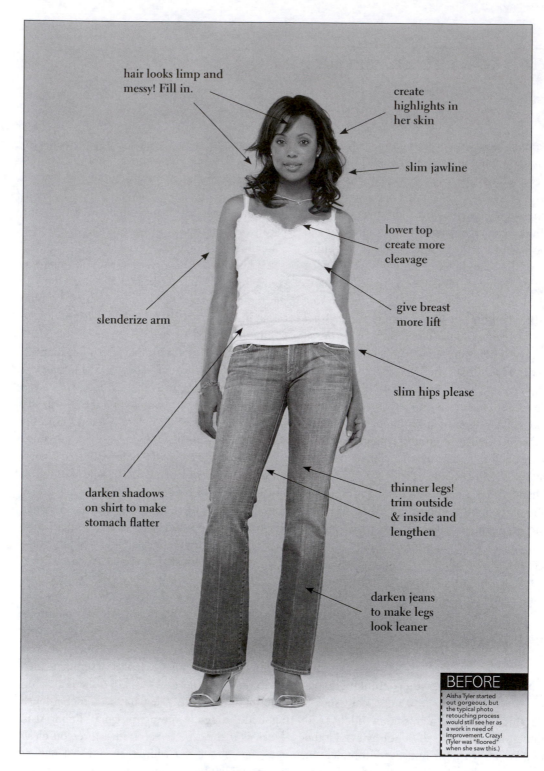

Figure 11.6 Aisha Tyler's magazine shoot.

Aisha is a little scary. If I saw her on the street, I'd look behind her to see whether the clone army had arrived to take over the city.

To me, beauty is the whole of a person, her flaws and imperfections, the way her smile is a little crooked (mine is) or her chin comes to a point when she grins (mine does) or the way one of her ears is just a little higher than the other one (it used to bother me but now I think it makes my head look jaunty!). And I *love* my freckles! How could something as sweet and personal as freckles be a *flaw*? It made me wonder: How skinny is skinny enough? How flawless should skin be? First you remove a freckle, then you even out skin tone, and next thing you know the person's got no pores and her face looks like a department store mannequin's.

Trying to achieve perfection means you miss out on someone's sweet, crooked smile, the way her eyes crinkle when she laughs and, yes, those few extra pounds she gained in Miami on vacation with her boyfriend, drinking, having oodles of sex and eating Cuban food. Would we like to lose those pounds? Of course. Are we willing to give up ropa vieja and mojitos? Are you *kidding* me?

The "after" photo did get rid of those last five pounds I've been trying to lose since, I dunno, preschool. But it's a hollow victory, because I didn't earn it. And honestly, I'd like to earn it, but not at the expense of a full and fun life. I suppose I could spend every free minute I have in the gym, living on wheatgrass and water vapor, but that would pretty much suck, wouldn't it? I want to be able to order dessert when I go out to dinner, have an extra glass of wine on Friday nights and sleep in when I should be working out. And I want to wake up on Mondays and vow that *this* is the week I start going to the gym every day. Life should be like that: naughty, delicious and full of promising Monday mornings.

Otherwise, what's the point?

So the next time you see some model or actress with perfect skin, thighs like reeds and eyes like shimmering pools giving you the voodoo stare from a makeup ad or a monster billboard, remember: It's all a big load of digital crap. You, too, could easily look like that if you had a squad of mad geeks fussing over you with retouching software. Remind yourself that she looks *nothing* like that in real life. Oh, and if you see Robot Aisha on the street, run for your life. The digital invasion has begun.

Discussion Question

1. How could American culture change to be more accepting of the natural blemishes, crooked teeth, and body shapes that people are born with?

11.2

THE TWO FACES OF TWIGGY AT 59: HOW AIRBRUSHING IN OLAY AD HIDES TRUTH OF THE SKIN SHE'S IN

Richard Simpson

It recently emerged that Twiggy was again to be the face of anti-ageing cream Olay, 25 years after she first won the job to become the fresh new face of one of the biggest beauty brands. Yet pictured in a natural state a few weeks shy of her 60th birthday, Twiggy, who is often referred to as the origi-

nal supermodel, showed she does in fact age just like the rest of us.

Originally published in the *Daily Mail*. Reprinted by permission of Solo Syndication.

Figure 11.7 Twiggy isn't the only victim of youthful retouching. Actress Diane Keaton, 66, (a) appears "Age Perfect" in this ad for L'Oréal (b).

Out on a grocery shop to her local London Marks and Spencers, a brand she also promotes, she appeared to be the age of, well, a woman of 59. Twiggy in her Olay ad looks a far cry from her more natural appearance on a trip to the supermarket. With slight jowls and only hairline wrinkles around her eyes and mouth, Twiggy does indeed look good for her age. However she bares very little resemblance to pictures, apparently of her, recently distributed to advertise Olay, whose catchphrase is "Love the skin you're in."

Airbrushing expert Michelle Facey of Facey Media said the amount of work done to wizard away the signs of aging in the advert picture was "a sham" and "totally misleading to the customer." (See Figure 11.7.) She said: "I think they have really gone overboard. It's a sham. I did not realize she looked so different in real life. She always seems so youthful. What I can see from the picture is that she has plenty of age spots all over face neck and decolletage. I would say she has had lip filler too. I am shocked by how much airbrushing has been done. She looks like a woman in her late 20s or 30s. This has to be the worst airbrushing I have ever seen in terms of making someone look younger—it's completely unnatural and untrue. In my opinion, it's totally misleading to the customer."

Almost a quarter of a century after she first became the face of Olay, Twiggy has been chosen to star in its latest advertising campaign. She has signed up for a 12-month stint as the face of Olay Definity the brand's anti-ageing range. Twiggy first promoted the Olay range back in 1985, when it was known as Oil of Ulay.

She became one of the most recognized faces of the sixties after modeling boss Nigel Davies spotted her as a 16-year-old schoolgirl called Lesley Hornby. Her waif look, which gave her new name, was an immediate hit with the British public and within weeks she became the "Face of 1966." A year later pictures of Twiggy, complete with gamine haircut, long eyelashes and Mary Quant clothes, were adorning billboards in New York. Her enduring appeal has seen her take a central role in the highly successful Marks & Spencer advertising campaign.

Sarah Clark, spokesman for Olay Definity, would not say how much the new deal was worth, but said: "We were thrilled to welcome Twiggy back to the brand. She is a true beauty icon who continues to be an inspiration to millions of women across the UK."

The stunning new pictures of Twiggy were taken by Karan Kapoor, the 1980s Bollywood actor turned photographer. In the past Twiggy has spoken of her desire to maintain a natural look as she gets older. "I'm grateful for my lines of wisdom," she said. "Of course, there are days when I think: 'Oh my gawd, I look a bit tired.' But I can pull it together if I have to."

Discussion Questions

1. Do you think it's OK for magazines to retouch wrinkles, sags, and other signs of aging? Why or why not? Why do magazines find this necessary?

2. What aspects of American society make this approach to picturing women (or men) acceptable?

11.3

AUSTRALIA PUSHES NEW BODY IMAGE STANDARD

Patty Huntington

Sydney—Three days after Australia got its first female prime minister, the federal government unveiled what it's claiming is the first body image initiative in the world.

On Sunday, Youth Minister Kate Ellis unveiled a voluntary code of conduct and a "body image friendly" logo that will be awarded to compliant magazines, modelling agencies and fashion labels and retailers. The code was developed in consultation with the government's Body Image Advisory Group, which includes former model and "Australia's Next Top Model" host Sarah Murdoch, wife of Rupert Murdoch's son Lachlan. A war chest of $500,000 Australian dollars, or $437,448, has been earmarked for promotion and education, in partnership with The Butterfly Foundation, an eating disorder group.

Recommendations include disclosing and avoiding the digital enhancement of images; banning ultra-thin female models or overly muscular male ones, in addition to models under the age of 16 to advertise adult clothes; employing a greater diversity of ethnicities and model body sizes; eschewing editorial and advertising content that promotes negative body image through rapid weight loss and cosmetic surgery, and, for retailers, carrying a wider variety of clothing sizes that better reflects the demands of the community.

Australian Fashion Week and upscale department store chain David Jones won't have is-sues with the model age recommendation: in 2008, following several underage model controversies, they banned under-16 and under-18 models, respectively, from their runways. Sydney-based retailer Belinda Seper, who was a model before launching her 10-unit designer fashion chain, applauded the initiative. "It's voluntary and I think it's fantastic; there's awareness that there's an issue and that there's a link, a step has been taken—yes, there are thin girls but they are thinner than ever before," said Seper.

When it comes to the recommendation of stocking a wider variety of sizes in her boutiques, however, like several other retailers, Seper harbors doubts that larger sizes would in fact sell. Just 10 percent of her merchandise is a size 16 (size 14 in the U.S.). Seper's biggest seller in the Belinda stores is a size 10, or size 8 U.S. In her youth-skewed Corner Shop boutiques, it's a size 6, or size 4 U.S.

"Am I supposed to carry things up to a size 20 or 24 [18 or 22 in the U.S.]?" she asked. "I will skew my buying towards the sizes that sell. I'm not a department store. Fashion is for, generally speaking, women who are in good physical shape, who choose to take care of themselves."

© 2010 Condé Nast Publications. Reprinted with permission.

Discussion Question

1. Do you think a group of concerned parents/people could create a similar advisory group in the United States?

DO THIN MODELS WARP GIRLS' BODY IMAGE?

Nanci Hellmich

When Frederique van der Wal, a former Victoria's Secret model, attended designers' shows during New York's Fashion Week this month, she was "shocked" by the waiflike models who paraded down the catwalk. They seemed even skinnier than in previous years.

"This unnatural thinness is a terrible message to send out. The people watching the fashion shows are young, impressionable women," says van der Wal, host of *Cover Shot* on TLC.

Psychologists and eating-disorder experts are worried about the same thing. They say the fashion industry has gone too far in pushing a dangerously thin image that women, and even very young girls, may try to emulate (Figure 11.8).

"We know seeing super-thin models can play a role in causing anorexia," says Nada Stotland, professor of psychiatry at Rush Medical College in Chicago and vice president of the American Psychiatric Association. Because many models and actresses are so thin, it makes anorexics think their emaciated bodies are normal, she says. "But these people look scary. They don't look normal."

The widespread concern that model thinness has progressed from willowy to wasted has reached a threshold as evidenced by the recent actions of fashion show organizers.

The Madrid fashion show, which ended Saturday, banned overly thin models, saying it wanted to project beauty and health. Organizers said models had to be within a healthy weight range.

That means a 5-foot-9 woman would need to weigh at least 125 pounds.

Officials in India, Britain and Milan also have expressed concerns, but some experts say consumers in the USA will have to demand models with fuller figures for it to happen here.

"The promotion of the thin, sexy ideal in our culture has created a situation where the ma-

Figure 11.8 Many experts feel that excessively thin models promote an unrealistic image of the female body.

jority of girls and women don't like their bodies," says body-image researcher Sarah Murnen, professor of psychology at Kenyon College in Gambier, Ohio. "And body dissatisfaction can lead girls to participate in very unhealthy behaviors to try to control weight."

Experts call these behaviors disordered eating, a broad term used to describe a range of eating problems, from frequent dieting to anorexia

From USA TODAY, a division of Gannett Co., Inc. Reprinted with Permission.

nervosa (which is self-starvation, low weight and fear of being fat) to bulimia nervosa (the binge-and-purge disorder).

Girls today, even very young ones, are being bombarded with the message that they need to be super-skinny to be sexy, says psychologist Sharon Lamb, co-author of *Packaging Girlhood: Rescuing Our Daughters from Marketers' Schemes*.

It used to be that women would only occasionally see rail-thin models, such as Twiggy, the '60s fashion icon. "But now they see them every day. It's the norm," Lamb says, from ads, catalogs and magazines to popular TV shows such as *America's Next Top Model* and *Project Runway*. "They are seeing skinny models over and over again."

On top of that, gaunt images of celebrities such as Nicole Richie and Kate Bosworth are plastered on magazine covers, she says.

What worries Lamb most is that these images are filtering down to girls as young as 9 and 10. Some really sexy clothes are available in children's size 6X, says Lamb, a psychology professor at Saint Michael's College in Colchester, Vt. "Girls are being taught very young that thin and sexy is the way they want to be when they grow up, so they'd better start working on that now," she says.

Lamb believes it's fine for girls to want to feel sexy and pretty when they are teenagers, but that shouldn't be their primary focus. "If they are spending all their time choosing the right wardrobe, trying to dance like an MTV backup girl and applying lip gloss, it robs them of other options."

Some girls don't want to participate in sports because they're afraid they'll bulk up. Some won't try to play an instrument such as a trombone because it doesn't fit their image of what a "girly girl" should do, she says.

It Begins in Youth

There's no question younger girls are getting this message, says Murnen, who has studied this for 15 years. "We have done studies of grade-school girls, and even in grade 1, girls think the culture is telling them that they should model themselves after celebrities who are svelte, beautiful and sexy."

Some girls can reject that image, but it's a small percentage: 18% in Murnen's research. Those girls were shown to have the highest body esteem. Murnen and her colleagues reviewed 21 studies that looked at the media's effect on more than 6,000 girls, ages 10 and older, and found those who were exposed to the most fashion magazines were more likely to suffer from poor body images.

Societies throughout the ages have had different ideals for female beauty, says Katie Ford, chief executive officer of Ford Models, whose megastar models include Christie Brinkley and Rachel Hunter. "You can look as far back as Greek statues and paintings and see that. It's part of women's fantasy nature," Ford says. "The question is: When does that become destructive?"

She doesn't buy into the idea that fashion models are creating a cult of thinness in the USA. "The biggest problem in America is obesity. Both obesity and anorexia stem from numerous issues, and it would be impossible to attribute either to entertainment, be it film, TV or magazines."

Anatomy of a Runway Model

This year's fashion shows in New York featured a mix of figure types, some of them a little more womanly and some thin, says Ford, whose agency had about 20 models in shows of top designers, including Ralph Lauren, Bill Blass, Marc Jacobs and Donna Karan. "Our models who did very well this season were not super-skinny. However, there were some on the runway who were very thin."

Cindi Leive, editor in chief of *Glamour* magazine, says some models were teens who hadn't developed their curves yet, which is one reason they appeared so thin. "You do see the occasional model on the runway looking like she should go from the fashion show to the hospital. You hear stories of girls who come to model and are collapsing because they haven't eaten in days. Any responsible model booker will tell you they turn away girls who get too thin."

Runway models have to have a certain look, says Kelly Cutrone, owner of People's Revolution, a company that produces fashion shows around the world. Her company produced 16 fashion shows in New York, including one for designer Marc Bouwer.

The runway models this year were no thinner than years before, she says. "I didn't see any difference in the girls at all. When they bend over, are you going to see the rib cage? Yes, they are thin naturally."

Women shouldn't be comparing themselves with these girls, she says. "These girls are anomalies of nature. They are freaks of nature. They are not average. They are naturally thin and have incredibly long legs compared to the rest of their body. Their eyes are wide set apart. Their cheekbones are high."

Most runway models are 14 to 19, with an average age of 16 or 17, she says. Some are older. Many are 5-foot-10 or 5-foot-11. They average 120 to 124 pounds. They wear a size 2 or 4. "If we get a girl who is bigger than a 4, she is not going to fit the clothes," Cutrone says. "Clothes look better on thin people. The fabric hangs better."

Stephanie Schur, designer of her own line, Michon Schur, had her first official runway show in New York a few weeks ago. When she was casting models, she looked for women who had "a nice glow, a healthy look."

She encountered a few models who looked unhealthy. "They tend to be extremely pale, have thin hair and don't have that glow."

But many of today's runway models look pretty much alike, Schur says. "They are all pretty girls, but no one really stands out. For runway it's about highlighting the clothes. It's finding the girls that make your clothes look best."

Schur says she doesn't believe many young girls today are going to try to imitate what they see on the fashion runways. She says they are more likely to look to actresses for their ideal body image.

It's not surprising that women want to be slender and beautiful, because as a society "we know more about women who look good than we know about women who do good," says Audrey Brashich, a former teen model and author of *All Made Up: A Girl's Guide to Seeing Through Celebrity Hype and Celebrating Real Beauty*.

For several years, Brashich worked for *Sassy* and *YM* magazines and read thousands of letters from girls and teens who wanted to become a famous model, actress or singer.

And no wonder, she says. "As a culture, we are on a first-name basis with women like Paris Hilton or Nicole Richie," she says. "The most celebrated, recognizable women today are famous primarily for being thin and pretty, while women who are actually changing the world remain comparatively invisible. Most of us have a harder time naming women of other accomplishments." The idolizing of models, stars and other celebrities is not going to change "until pop culture changes the women it celebrates and focuses on."

Women Come in All Sizes

Glamour's Leive believes the media have a powerful influence on women's body images and a responsibility to represent women of all sizes. "We do not run photos of anybody in the magazine who we believe to be at an unhealthy weight. We frequently feature women of all different sizes. We all know that you can look fabulous in clothes without being a size 2."

Ford believes the trend next year will be to move toward more womanly figures. Model van der Wal agrees and says she's trying to include women of varying figure types in *Cover Shot*. "Women come in lots of different sizes and shapes, and we should encourage and celebrate that."

Cutrone says models will become heavier if that's what consumers demand. "If people decide thin is out, the fashion industry won't have thin models anymore. Have you spent time with fashion people? They are ruthless. They want money.

"And the one thing they know is people want clothes to cover their bodies," Cutrone says. "Unfortunately, most people aren't comfortable with their bodies."

Discussion Questions

1. Why is thinness regarded as beautiful? The author states, "The widespread concern that model thinness has progressed from willowy to wasted has reached a threshold as evidenced by the recent actions of fashion show organizers." Will thinness continue into the future? If not, what do you think the next ideal image will be?
2. What could fashion magazines or designers do to counterbalance the thinness craze?

HOW DOES *VOGUE* NEGOTIATE AGE?: FASHION, THE BODY, AND THE OLDER WOMAN

Julia Twigg

Introduction

Fashion and age do not fit easily, or happily, together. There is a discordant quality in the mix. Fashion is assumed to be all about youth and beauty—so far removed from the world of age. And yet many older women are elegantly and smartly dressed. And many have relatively high spending power. From the perspective of a high-end magazine like *Vogue* this presents a conundrum: how to address a growing sector of the market without compromising its status as the premier organ of the fashion world. From the perspective of student of culture, or old age, however, the tensions between fashion and age and the responses of *Vogue* to them offer an opportunity to explore the changing ways in which ageing is experienced, understood and imagined in modern culture. Age and ageing, it has been suggested, are in the process of being reconfigured under the impact of demographic and social change. The nature of identity in later years may be changing, becoming more fluid, more open to negotiation. In this, cultural products such as clothing potentially have a role to play. An analysis of the responses of a magazine like *Vogue* offers us a means of evaluating these processes.

It also offers a means of extending the remit of fashion studies, which has been slow to engage with questions of age. Though there is a copious literature on clothing and identity, this has largely addressed younger age groups and radical, transgressive styles (Rolley 1993, Khan 1993, Pol-hemus 1994, Evans 1997, Holliday 2001). Older people rarely if ever feature in mainstream books on fashion; and what literature there is on clothing and age is sparse (Fairhurst 1998, Gulette 1999, Gibson 2000).

Ageing, the Body and Dress

The article forms part of a UK-based empirical study funded by ESRC*, exploring the nature of embodiment in later years, using the arena of dress as a means to interrogate the complex interrelationships between bodily and the cultural factors in the constitution of age. Clothes mediate between the body and the social world (Entwistle 2000). They are the vestimentary envelope that contains and presents the body; and they thus play an important part in the presentation and negotiation of identities, including aged identities (Twigg 2007, 2009).

"Age," "ageing," and "older people" are all culturally contingent terms and, as we shall see, their definitions are fluid and changing. "Age" and "ageing" do not necessarily imply old age; they need to be understood as processes as much as categories, operating throughout the life course. For magazines like *Vogue*, however, ageing sets in early, starting at the point at which youth begins to fade, often regarded as the late twenties. The primary focus of this article, however, is late middle years and beyond, broadly understood as fifties onwards.

*Based on qualitative interviews with older women (55 and over), interviews in the world media and retail, and content analysis of women's magazines, the study addresses the ways in which older women negotiate changes in the appearance and social identity through dress; the tensions between age resistance and age denial; and the role of consumption culture and the fashion system in re-configuring the experience of age. © Julia Twigg 2010, "How Does *Vogue* Negotiate Age?: Fashion, the Body, and the Older Woman," *Fashion Theory*, Volume 14, Issue 4, pp. 471–490. Berg Publishers, an imprint of Bloomsbury Publishing Plc.

Women's Magazines and the Constitution of Identities

We are familiar with the role of women's magazines in the constitution of gendered—and classed—identities through extensive work that has explored such processes, particularly in relation to younger women. Though feminists of the second wave like Friedan and Tuchman presented magazines as key sites in the generation of oppressive and distorting versions of femininity (Gough-Yates 2003), later writers such as Winship (1987) and Hermes (1995) offer more nuanced accounts, unpacking the complex, polysemic messages within magazines, and the interactive processes whereby their content is made meaningful through the practices and perceptions of readers. Gough-Yates (2003) focusing on the phenomenon of the New Women magazines of the '80s and '90s, explored how new markets of potential readers were discursively constituted by media professionals through a focus on identity constitution and lifestyles, particularly in relation to the imagined category of the "new middle class." More recently McRobbie (2008) has returned to her earlier work on girls' magazines and the intersecting themes of gender and class, to attack current work within cultural studies for its complicity with postfeminist values. There is, thus, a large body of work that explores the role of magazines in the constitution of gendered—and classed—identities.

As yet, however, these perceptions have not been extended to age; we have not seen a corresponding discussion of the potential role of women's magazines in the constitution of aged identities. Partly this arises from systematic biases within cultural studies, which focuses heavily in the youthful and transgressive, reflecting the values of its subject matter in its own analyses. Partly it arises from a more general reluctance in sociology and social theory to incorporate age within the debate on intersectionality: other categories of difference or identity formation have been more readily acknowledged (Brewer 1993, Maynard 1994, Anthias 2000, Krekula 2007). In many ways, we are at the same point in relation to age as we were in the seventies in relation to gender, when it was so obvious a category, so naturalised in biologi-

cal difference, that we could not see its centrality. The significance of age and age ordering has been similarly obscured. We need to unpack those categories, to acknowledge their significance, but also to recognise their socially constructed and negotiated character. This article is a contribution to that intellectual and political process.

Vogue

Vogue UK has a dual character as the premier British fashion magazine (together with the trade paper *Draper's Record*), and a lifestyle magazine aimed at well-off women. One of a stable of glossy journals produced by Condé Nast, it is part of an international publishing empire, with editions in 15 countries. Each is distinctive, and reflects local commercial and visual culture, though in recent decades they have together become carriers of a globalised style that supports international branding (Moeran 2004, David 2006, Kopnina 2007). *Vogue* is notable for an almost perfect match between editorial and advertising, with the high production values of its fashion spreads reflected in the adverts for major perfume and garment houses. Its high advertising revenue means it is one of the most profitable women's magazines. The current UK circulation is around 220,000, with an attributed readership of 1.2 million. Its target readership is described as "concentrated in the ABC1 20–44 demographic group. A high proportion are in some kind of job or profession and are in the higher income groups (BRAD 2008)." In terms of age, the profile is biased towards those in twenties and thirties, with a clear falling-off from the mid fifties.

15–24	23–34	35–44	45–54	55–64	65+
215	124	92	88	52	39

A hundred represents the population profile, with values above and below representing greater and lesser uptake.

What issues does age pose for *Vogue*? The magazine, like other media outlets, is increasingly aware of changing demographics that mean that older people constitute a growing proportion of the population. Alexandra Shulman, the editor of UK *Vogue*, noted in 2008 how "fifty percent of women are over 40." Many of these women have high disposable incomes and a personal history of consumption. In 2006 men and women over 45 spent £12.2 billion on clothing, an increase of 21 percent over 2001 (Mintel 2006). The Grey Pound represents a potentially profitable segment of the market, one of interest to advertisers (Key Note 2006). Mintel notes however that this group are often "frustrated shoppers," failing to find their desires or interests reflected in the market. *Vogue* thus has a clear institutional interest in addressing these groups. But there is also a more personal reason that make the subject relevant to the magazine, in the form of the lives of the journalists who work on *Vogue*, who need to be recognised as independent actors within this system of cultural production. Though most of the stylists and fashion editors in magazines like *Vogue* are young, senior journalists and editors are not. Alexandra Shulman, the editor of UK *Vogue*, is in her early fifties, and Anna Wintour of US *Vogue* is in her early sixties. At a personal level they face the dilemmas of growing older while still retaining an active interest in dress and fashion. The fact that *Vogue* has, as we shall see, featured age-themed issues and debates under Shulman's editorship reflects this.

The difficulty for *Vogue*, however, comes from the nature of fashion itself, which is profoundly youth oriented. The high-fashion scene is dominated by youth. Styles are designed for, and shown on, very young models, often with prepubescent bodies of extreme thinness; and this trend has grown over the last two decades. Most designers openly admit they design for young beautiful women, and they have little or no interest in other categories. Age is simply not fashionable or sexy. *Vogue*, if it is to succeed, needs to reflect this fashion *zeitgeist*.

Youth and beauty have, of course, always been linked, but the nature of late modern consumption culture gives a new twist to the story. The dominance of the visual in modern culture means we are surrounded by images, particularly from advertising, that celebrate bodily perfectionism, and from which all signs of imperfection are erased. We are familiar with the malign effects of this on younger women in relation to widespread levels of bodily dissatisfaction and anxiety, underlying conditions such as anorexia (Wolf 1990, Bordo 1993, MacSween 1993). But it has an impact on older women also, supporting the widespread culture of fear of ageing; for this new visual culture of perfectionism rests on an erasure of age. We are simply not accustomed to seeing older faces, except in certain defined settings (for example in advertising, largely confined to food [Zang et al. 2006]). These settings do not include fashion. Ageing has thus become a disruption in the visual field, a form of spoilt identity (Gullette 1997, 1999, Woodward 1991, 1999). To include such images in *Vogue* would be discordant, potentially undermining its status as a high-fashion publication.

Vogue UK 1990–2009

The article is based on a content analysis of UK *Vogue* from 1990–2009. All covers and content pages were scrutinised and material relevant to age followed up; and from 2005 onwards, whole issues reviewed. A large part of the content of *Vogue*, as with other glossy magazines, is advertising. This is important both for its profitability and appeal. In this article, however, I will confine my analysis to the editorial pages. Fashion adverts almost never address older women in an overt way. They may do so covertly, but they can rarely be definitively identified as doing so. This is in contrast to the skincare adverts, which constantly and clearly address ageing. Work by Coupland (2003) and others (Williamson 1982, Reventos 1998, Kang 1997) has explored the discursive strategies adopted in cosmetic adverts and accompanying beauty pages; and other work in cultural gerontology has addressed questions of facial appearance and its relationship to cultures of ageing (Furman 1997, 1999, Gilleard 2002, Hurd 2000). Though these questions are relevant to the central themes of this article, my primary focus here is on fashion and dress. In other work I plan to analyse fashion as it is featured in magazines aimed at older women, where the overall remit of the publication means that adverts and editorial copy are addressed to this age group: there the task is to see how fashion is integrated into magazines aimed at older women. Here, however, the task is to understand how ageing is integrated into a magazine centred on fashion.

Up until 2007, age was only intermittently featured in *Vogue*, and was wholly absent from its covers. The pattern was broken in July 2007 with an issue that addressed "Ageless Style." This was followed in 2008 and 2009 (again July) with more extensively themed issues on the same subject. The 2007 cover featured eight models integrated into unity through being dressed in white. None showed any visible signs of age, though close scrutiny of one slightly blank face might suggest cosmetic enhancement. Inside, however, their ages are revealed as 19–53 (the cosmetically enhanced Marie Helvin). The reader's experience of the cover is one of lightness (white with touches of red), glamour and youth. There are no visible signs of age. The sell lines include: "Vogue celebrates Ageless Style"; "working the trends: from seventeen to seventy"; and "forever young: insider beauty tricks." The 2008 cover depicts a single image, the actress Uma Thurman, described in the sell line as "facing forty with glamour." (She is in her late thirties.) There are no visible signs of age on her face or hands, which are air brushed to perfection. There is, however, a slightly sombre quality to the cover with predominate colours of grey, black and gold. The sell lines include: "Ageless style: the best pieces at any age" and "How to grow old fashionably." The latter, though it echoes the phrase "growing old gracefully," is notable for its direct reference to growing old, something rare in magazine culture.

Vogue had on occasion addressed age in earlier issues, though not on the cover. Notably in 1998 it was the topic of a Vogue Debate. There were four such, which took the form of round-table discussions by eight or so invited guests. The subjects were: ultra-slim models; appropriate dress for professional women; the absence of black models; and ageing. Each carried a sense that it was a topic where *Vogue* was under fire: for promoting malign versions of the female body that supported the culture of anorexia; for failing to acknowledge the changes in women's lives resulting from entry into work where ultra-fashionable, frivolous or overtly sexual dress was inappropriate; for endorsing implicit racism through its promo-

tion of an exclusively white model of beauty; and for excluding older women from view. The model and work debates were mentioned on the cover: the ageing one was not. The panel for the ageing debate were: the deputy editor of *Vogue* (42), the beauty director (age not given), a novelist (Fay Weldon, 66), a director of a model agency (54), a property administrator (66), a retailing director (48), a designer (Edina Ronay, age not given), and a private GP (50). The discussion mostly turned around appearance rather than dress, with particular attention paid to cosmetic surgery and HRT. The tone was largely upbeat, with a characteristic magaziney emphasis on feeling good, the importance of positive thinking and inner beauty. This last note was somewhat punctured, however, by the intervention of the beauty editor: "I have to say that it's an irony to listen to us all sitting around saying it's great to be older, when I know that the phones are ringing in the beauty department with women our age asking 'Where can I get botox injections?'" (p. 266) The discussion was interspersed by full-page commissioned images of four older women, each named, and wearing *Vogue* styled fashions. As we shall see, this is unusual, the predominant treatment of age being small multiple images. The discussion ended with an editorial note that explained that unlike the other three debates, this one produced "no clear conclusions," and it was described as "not an easy topic."

Inside the 2007 issue there is a brief editorial by Shulman defining her approach: "When I first thought about putting together an 'ageless style' issue of *Vogue* I was obsessed with what I didn't want it to be: something that told you what to wear at what age. The whole point of style and fashion is that it should be ageless . . . we have concentrated on what you can wear at *any* age, whether you are in your teens or your seventies" (p. 12). In the 2008 special issue Shulman wrote more directly on the experience of becoming fifty. The tone of the article is unanxious and balanced. She states that she is unwilling to get involved in battles that she is going to lose: "you can't win a battle against time." She notes how it is easier to face age if one has been nice looking but never beautiful: "For those whose identities are completely bound up in their good looks, the diminution is terrifying" (p. 143). Her work means that she is steeped in fashion, but on a personal level, though she enjoys clothes, she keeps them slightly at arm's length. In relation to age she comments "there is no doubt that the question of what you *can* wear becomes more charged and complex as you age . . . The fear of dressing inappropriately lurks like some ghastly spectre around the wardrobe: the insecurity about whether you are heading into a mutton-alert territory hovers determinedly." She concludes the article on a note confirming continuity of identity and pleasure in dress:

> At some point we all think that we lose the person that we were when younger and become somebody old. But we don't, and our clothes, and the pleasures we take in them, should reflect that (p. 185).

How Does *Vogue* Negotiate Age?

Three strategies characterise *Vogue's* response: localisation, dilution and personalisation. Localisation refers to the strategy whereby older women are confined to certain parts of the magazine. Typically, and most strongly, they feature in the beauty pages where anti-ageing strategies are a central concern. As noted earlier, these are not the main focus of my analysis, but they form an important background to it. In terms of covers, as we have seen age only really features in text, not images: *Vogue* avoids compromising the visual appeal of this key sales feature. Beyond this, questions of age are confined to the features pages. They rarely if ever are included in the fashion spreads that form the heart of *Vogue* and are its most prestigious part. These pages are dedicated to the mainstream of fashion. One exception did occur in 2005 with a fashion spread featuring a glamorous Charlotte Rampling as the heroine of a noir film, but it was shot in such low light that her features (and signs of age) were almost wholly disguised. Older women are thus localised in the features and beauty sections and largely absent from the mainstream, core fashion.

Dilution strategies are pursued through a number of classic techniques. The first of these, widely used across the magazine sector, is the De-cades approach in which fashions are illustrated on women in their twenties, thirties, forties. . . . Until recently such decades tended to stop at the forties, with fifties being a daring extension. The "endpoint" of fashionability is however in the process of being pushed later, and the 2005 feature in *Vogue* included—exceptionally—a woman in her seventies. The article illustrated key trends, showing how these could be worn by all ages; the woman in her seventies featured "white." She did, however, look somewhat different from the earlier decades—more distinctly old. By the time the format was repeated in 2008, *Vogue* managed to illustrate a woman in her seventies who, presumably through cosmetic surgery and airbrushing, was fully integrated with other images, being almost wholly devoid of the appearance of age.

Another classic dilution technique is that of Generations. The July 2007 issue featured Jane Birkin accompanied by her glamorous daughter in her twenties. It is strategy often used by advertisers who want to show their clothes as relevant and sellable to all ages without compromising their fashionability, and so illustrate them in family groups. Calvin Klein and Ralph Lauren pioneered such lifestyle advertising, featuring elite WASP pseudo-families. Dilution can also be achieved by features that show stylish women of all ages, typically illustrated by small pictures. These contrast with the full-page fashion spreads. Here the images of older women are diluted by small images and a predominance of younger women. Such pages enable the magazine to reach out to and relate to older readers by showing something of their lives, but without defining the magazine as aimed at this group. Another dilution strategy rests on showing style icons (July 2007) or famous designers such as Mary Quant (July 2008). This enables the feature to include pictures of these in their heyday as well as now. *Vogue* has an incomparable archive of past images that it deploys with great skill to make up spreads that address current visual interests. Older women can be integrated into this as part of the wider engagement with the history of style.

The third strategy is that of personalisation. In every case where an older woman is featured in *Vogue*, she is a named individual. These are always real women, not models, with real lives, though with the proviso that these are *Vogue* lives and, as a result, far from the lived reality of most people, even most readers.

This account of the treatment of age and ageing should not lead us to think, however, that these are central themes for UK *Vogue*. They are not. They are marginal and sporadic. We noted how the three age-themed issues were published in July, a dead period for fashion magazines (though Alexandra Shulman confirmed in a research interview that the issues had put on readership). Otherwise features on older women are infrequent, and older women only appear occasionally. But this was not always so. During the 1950s, the older women had a regular slot in *Vogue* in the guise of Mrs. Exeter.

Mrs. Exeter

Mrs. Exeter was a character developed by *Vogue* in the late 1940s to represent the older woman (Halls 2000). In 1949 she was described as "approaching sixty" (March 1949). She appeared twice on the cover of *Vogue* (1948 and 1951), including in a glamorous shot by Cecil Beaton, and was a regular and successful feature through the 1950s. Initially represented by drawings, including by the artist John Ward, she developed a distinctive photographic image in the 1950s. By the end of the decade, however, Halls notes that she was getting steadily younger; and she eventually disappeared in the mid-sixties, killed off by the rise of youth fashion. The styles of the sixties were particularly youth oriented, with very short skirts and a body ideal that valorised the prepubescent teenager. A quotation from Margot Smyly, the model most closely associated with the character of Mrs. Exeter in the UK, conveys the pressures of the time, as fashion became more youth oriented, as well as the anger and pique of an older women cast aside. Describing the 1960s she says: "It was a terrible time, a nasty, catty, horrible decade with a lot of ill feeling. Nothing blossomed" (November 1982, p. 154).

One of the things that is striking about Mrs. Exeter from the perspective of today is how old she is, and how unrepentantly so: *Vogue* writes in 1949, "Approaching 60, Mrs. Exeter does not look

a day younger, a fact she accepts with perfect good humour and reasonableness." This is in marked contrast to the dominant discourse today, where the aim is to look ten years younger. It is true that the cover images in forties and fifties do cheat slightly, showing her with grey hair but a smooth face, but at least she does feature clearly as an older woman and on the cover. This is in contrast to today when even the age themed issues of 2007 and 2008 show much younger women, and erase all signs of age. One area where *Vogue* always refused to compromise, however, was weight. Halls notes that *Vogue* never addressed the problem of middle aged spread: Mrs. Exeter was always shown as extremely slim. Today, of course, slimness is a prominent anti-ageing strategy.

The phenomenon of Mrs. Exeter is an interesting one; and we can ask why, despite remaining something of a memory in *Vogue's* collective consciousness (she features from time to time in articles), she has not been—and indeed could not be—revived. Part of the reason is that she is so much a figure of her times, the 1950s, and she remains confined by that period. Her identity is heavily inflected with class and gender. With her elegant, restrained clothes, she epitomises the bourgeois lady of the period. Always referred to by her married name, she remains encased within her marriage. It is inconceivable that she could have a job. She thus represents a way of life that has ceased to exist for the majority of middle- and upper-middle-class women who are the main audience for the magazine.

There are, however, other reasons why she is beyond revival, and these relate to the changed ways in which age is experienced, understood and imagined today. Though Mrs. Exeter was a minor figure in *Vogue* in the 1950s, she was a regular one, and to that degree occupied an acknowledged position within the magazine. As we noted, she appeared on two covers, featured as a distinctively older woman with white hair. This is in contrast to today when age is featured on the cover only through text, not image. Though she is more defined—and confined—by her age than would be the case today, she is oddly also more visible. She has a clear presence within the structure of the magazine, reflecting her secure place in the age structure of society. She has a distinctive slot in the age hierarchy, as she does in the gender and class ones, reflecting an era when identities were more fixed culturally in terms of social categorisations and structures.

The Changing Cultural Location of Age

Since that period, however, a series of social and cultural shifts have reconstituted the meaning and experience of age. Theorised under the broad terminology of the condition of postmodernity (or late or second modernity), these changes present a set of interconnected processes that together impact on the situation of age. The first concerns the disembedding of the normative life course, with the growth of longer and recurring periods of education and training; the decline of single, life-long employment; portfolio careers; more fluid family forms; and less fixed sexual and marital mores. This has its impact on the definition and experience of old age (Gilleard and Higgs 2006). In the early part of the twentieth century, retirement marked the point of entry into old age, as it still does in government statistics where older people are defined as those over pensionable age (60/65). But with greater fluidity in careers, early retirement, and more women in the labour force in part-time occupations, retirement is not the fixed point it once was. Moreover the lives of those in their sixties, particularly those in good health and with adequate income, are not greatly different from those in their fifties. As a result a new social space has emerged, that of the Third Age, marked by leisure, pleasure, self realisation and consumption. Indeed some theorists (Öberg and Tornstam 1999, 2001) argue that later life has been reconceptualised in terms of an extended plateau of late middle years, only disrupted by the onset of serious illness, marking the shift into the Fourth Age. In relation to magazines and retailing, what this means is that there is a large category of people who do not perceive themselves as old and see no reason why they should be treated as such. As Biggs and colleagues (2007) found, they identify with younger-age cohorts and expect to remain integrated with them, not be treated as a separate or different category.

The second major change since the 1950s and the era of Mrs. Exeter concerns the shift in locus of identity from production to consumption. The declining salience of class in people's lives has meant that consumption has come to be an increasingly important marker of identity. Indeed, as Giddens (1991) and others argue, under conditions of post- or high modernity, identities themselves become more fluid and open, less embedded in social structures such as class or the normative life cycle. As a result they are more the product of choice and self creation, though at the same time more fragile and unstable. In this context, cultural goods become an increasingly important means whereby individuals construct "narratives of the self," anchor identities, as well as display aspects of Bourdieu's Distinction (1984). Lifestyle thus becomes an increasingly important marker of the self. These changes are reflected in the magazine sector in the shift from segmentation based broadly on class, as in the 1950s, to more complex forms based on lifestyle. Gough-Yates (2003) has analysed the changes that occurred from the 1960s, accelerating in the nineties, with the rise of lifestyle segmentation. Women's magazines, of course, still retain very strong class and age segmentation, but the dominant presentation is in terms of lifestyle, appealing to all with a particular attitude or lifestyle. This is part of the meaning of UK *Vogue*'s recurring tag line of Ageless Style—presenting an approach that transcends age categorisation and seeks to appeal on the basis simply of attitude and style of life; what this says is that fashionability does not have to be confined by age structures. But ageless style does not represent the whole truth for *Vogue*. However much the magazine promotes the ideal of lifestyle, the reality of marketing is that segmentation is closely based on traditional categorisations like age, class and gender. *Vogue* cannot allow itself to appear in any way to be a magazine aimed at older women; to do so would undermine its core appeal. It would, furthermore, fly in the face of all the values of fashion and the fashion world which, as we have seen, are wholly centred on youth, and rigorously exclude age from view.

The third interrelated development is the rise of consumption culture. Consumption is sometimes presented as performing an integrative function in modern culture, acting to incorporate individuals into a common culture of lifestyle; and to this degree it potentially offers older people a means whereby they can remain part of the mainstream, counteracting the cultural exclusion traditionally associated with old age. Those currently in their fifties and sixties—sometimes loosely termed baby boomers—are often presented as a pioneer generation (Gilleard and Higgs 2000, Jones et al. 2008)—the cohort that grew up with youth culture in the sixties and matured with the consumption boom of the eighties and nineties. They are accustomed to consumption, and see no reason to give it up. In relation to clothes this means refusing to adopt the frumpy age-related styles of previous generations. Age ordering in dress, it is asserted, has gone. Older women can wear the same clothes and shop in the same fashion-conscious stores as the rest of the population. Or that, at least, is what the ideology suggests. The reality is less clear, and norms of age-appropriate dress are still operative. We saw how Shulman, despite espousing the ideology of ageless style, still referred to the anxieties and dangers of being inappropriately dressed, and in terms of the old cultural trope of mutton dressed as lamb. Dreams of integration through consumption are also predicated in capacity to spend, and though *Vogue's* target readership will always be well off, many—indeed most—older women are not.

The extension of fashionability to older women, however, comes at a price: consumption culture presents new demands as well as new pleasures; new threats of exclusion as well as integration. Magazines, particularly ones like *Vogue*, present clothes as a source of pleasure, in which putting together distinctive looks is regarded as a creative act, an opportunity to express one's individuality. But as Clarke and Miller (2002) demonstrate, clothes can be as much a source of anxiety as joy, as individuals try to measure up to cultural norms of which they feel they have limited grasp. The truth is that most people want to be acceptable, to fit in and to meet current appearance norms. That, rather than standing out, is the dominant impulse. With regard to age, this means avoiding clothes that are deemed "unsuit-able," usually by virtue of being too young, too showy, too blatantly sexy. In a culture like the 1950s where age norms for older women were relatively clear, and where age ordering in dress was stronger, dressing appropriately was easier, even if more limiting. But in the more transitional or fluid culture of today, where such norms are believed to be no longer relevant, individuals are forced to puzzle it out for themselves. Articles about ageing and dress are replete with expressions of uncertainty and anxiety; and advice from journalists typically veers between caution and boldness: advising on the need to be "careful" and to avoid "inappropriate" looks, at the same time as containing injunctions that "there are no rules now." The possibility of giving up, and of opting out, is also less available today. In cultures and periods where older women are wholly out of the orbit of fashion, it is possible to retire from the demands of appearance, to embrace invisibility, but as culture extends new opportunities to older women, it also imposes new demands. The influx of cheap mass clothing in the 1990s has driven forward the further democratisation of fashion, extending the market for fashion to new social groups, among which are children and the middle aged. As a result, the life world and bodies of older women (and children) have—for better or worse—been increasingly colonised by the ideal of fashionability.

Vogue's response also needs to be understood in relation to the culture of anti-ageing. Bordo (1993) and other critics (Wolf 1990) have commented on the ways in which women in modern cultures spend more and more of their time disciplining their bodies according to the beauty ideal; and these tendencies have been extended to older women through the culture and industry of anti-ageing. Fear of ageing, or of displaying the visible marks of age, has become a major cultural preoccupation of western societies, supporting a multi-billion-pound industry (Gilliard and Higgs 2000). This is largely located in the beauty sector, but dress also plays a part, as the popularity of magazine features and makeover shows demonstrates (McRobbie 2004, Smyczynska 2008). Successful ageing within consumption culture is increasingly presented in terms of ageing without showing the visible signs of doing so. We noted how in 2008 *Vogue* chose as an image in a decades spread to represent the seventies, a women whose appearance was almost indistinguishable from that of a fashionable woman in her fifties. *Vogue* consistently features older women who look decades younger than their age, and achieving that state is valorised as the ideal. Here the aim is not to move graciously on to the next stage of life like Mrs. Exeter, but to look ten years younger and to remain actively integrated into the world of appearance and consumption.

Conclusion

Vogue is an aspirational magazine that floats on dreams of aesthetic perfection and youthful beauty. As such it has a symbiotic relationship with consumption culture. It is unsurprising therefore that it should face tensions in engaging with the issue of ageing. Age and ageing are problematic subjects within the world of *Vogue*—disruptive of its visual field. How it negotiates these tensions is therefore a subject of interest both to students of fashion studies and cultural gerontology.

From the perspective of fashion studies, *Vogue* is always a key source, embodying the current vision of the fashion world and its reception in the broader culture. Fashion studies has, however, neglected older people. Reflecting the values of the fashion world, it has remained preoccupied with the youthful and transgressive; remarkably little work has been undertaken that addresses older people or the processes of ageing. Beyond forty there is silence. And yet, as we noted, a growing proportion of the population—over half—is now over forty. They too wear clothes, select garments, express their identities, buy and discard fashions; and their choices and behaviours merit analysis. Fashion studies needs to encompass this group. A focus on age is also significant for fashion studies because of changes within the wider culture. We noted how consumption culture is being extended to older age groups as the current cohort of baby boomers ages. The nature of later years is in the process of shifting, as the new social space of the Third Age opens out. Here consumption offers the promise of new forms of social integration,

ones that link older people to the mainstream through shared lifestyle. The growth of mass markets of cheap fashionable clothing means that more and more people—including the middle aged and old—are brought within its orbit. Fashion studies need to be able to reflect this shift in the nature and remit of fashionability. Embracing the topic of age would also assist fashion studies to move beyond its current core, to encompass a larger analytic territory in which clothing and dress are more broadly conceived, in Entwistle's terms, as "situated body practice" (2000).

But *Vogue* is also a significant source from the perspective of the student of age. The body is a key dimension in ageing, but until recently social gerontology has fought shy of it, fearing to endorse falsely reductionist accounts in which age is seen as solely the product of bodily decline. More recently however there has been a recognition of the need to recapture the subject, to acknowledge the ways in which the body plays a part in the social and cultural constitution of age. Clothes are part of this, lying as they do on the interface between the self and society. They are central to how we present our bodies to the world. How fashion and the fashion system treats age is therefore instructive for the wider understanding of the processes of age.

Vogue also allows us to explore the role of consumption culture in the changing cultural location of older women. We saw how the responses of *Vogue* in the 1950s differed from now. Then older women were differently positioned in the magazine, reflecting their different position in culture, more separate, more contained within age structures—as they were within class and gender ones. Mrs. Exeter is more limited by her age—and yet in a certain way also more openly acknowledged. Today the cultural position of older women has changed. As we saw, *Vogue* promotes an ideal of Ageless Style in which seamless integration is the goal, and in which older women—if they choose and if they pursue the ideal of fashionability—can remain part of the mainstream. And yet, as we also noted, this integration was based on an effacement of age. The covers that featured Ageless Style showed no signs of age at all. *Vogue* repeatedly features, and sets up as the ideal, women who look decades younger than their chronological age. The new cultural ideal of successful ageing is indeed to age without showing the visual signs of doing so.

Lastly *Vogue* is also potentially significant as a source of images of how to age that are current within contemporary culture. We noted the role of magazines in the cultural constitution of identities, particularly in relation to gender, class and youth, but they can play a part in relation to age also, assisting older women to negotiate changing aspects of their identities. *Vogue*, of course, is not aimed at older women; and the vast majority of them will never see a copy. But it does contribute to the general culture, particularly visual culture that is increasingly significant under conditions of late or second modernity. As such, it has things to say about how age is imagined, negotiated and, to some degrees, experienced in modern culture.

References

Aronson, A. 2000. "Reading women's' magazines." *Media History* 6 (2): 111–13.

Anthias, F. 2001. "The concept of 'social division' and theorising social stratification: looking at ethnicity and class." *Sociology* 35 (4): 835–54.

Biggs, S., Phillipson, C., Leach, R., and Money, A-M. 2007. "The mature imagination and consumption strategies: age and generation in the development of a United Kingdom baby boomer identity." *International Journal of Ageing and Later Life* 2 (2):13–30.

Borelli, L.O. 1997. "Dressing up and talking about it: fashion writing in *Vogue* from 1968 to 1993." *Fashion Theory* 1 (3): 247–60.

Bordo. S. 1993. *Unbearable Weight: Feminism, Western Culture and the Body*. Berkeley: University of California Press.

Bourdieu, P. 1984. *Distinction: A Social Critique of the Judgement of Taste*. London: Routledge.

BRAD. 2008. *British Rate and Data*. (October): 559. London: Emap Media.

Breward, C. 2000. "Cultures, identities, histories: fashioning a cultural approach to dress." In N. White and I. Griffiths (eds) *The Fashion Business: Theory, Practice, Image*, pp 23–36. Oxford: Berg.

Brewer, R. M. 1993. "Theorizing race, class and gender: the new scholarship of Black feminist intellectuals and Black women's labor." In S. M. James and A.P.A Busia (eds). *Theorizing Black Feminisms: The Visionary Pragmatism of Black Women*, pp 13–30. London: Routledge.

Clarke, A. and Miller, D. 2002. "Fashion and anxiety," *Fashion Theory* 6 (2): 191–214.

Coupland, J. 2003. "Ageist ideology and discourses of control in skincare product marketing," pp 127–50. In J. Coupland and R. Gwyn (eds) *Discourse, the Body and Identity*, London: Palgrave.

Crane, D. 2000. *Fashion and Its Social Agendas: Class, Gender and Identity in Clothing*. Chicago: University of Chicago Press.

David, A. M. 2006. "*Vogue's* new world: American fashionability and the politics of style," *Fashion Theory*, 10 (1/2): 13–38.

Entwistle, J. 2000. *The Fashioned Body: Fashion, Dress and Modern Social Theory*. Cambridge: Polity.

Evans, C. 1997. "Street style, subculture and subversion." *Costume* 31: 105–10.

Fairhurst, E. 1998. "'Growing old gracefully' as opposed to 'mutton dressed as lamb': the social construction of recognising older women." In S. Nettleton and J. Watson (eds) *The Body in Everyday Life*, pp 258–75. London: Routledge.

Featherstone, M. and Hepworth, M. 1991. "The mask of ageing and the postmodern life course" In M. Featherstone, M. Hepworth and B. S. Turner (eds) *The Body: Social Process and Cultural Theory*, pp 371–87. London: Sage.

Furman, F. K. 1997. *Facing the Mirror: Older Women and Beauty Shop Culture*. New York: Routledge.

Furman, F. K. 1999. "There are no old Venuses: Older women's responses to their aging bodies" In M. U. Walker (ed) (1999) *Mother Time: Women, Aging and Ethics*, pp 7–22. Boulder: Rowman & Littlefield.

Gibson, P. C. 2000. "'No one expects me anywhere': invisible women, ageing and the fashion industry." In S. Bruzzi and P. C. Gibson (eds) *Fashion Cultures: Theories, Explorations and Analysis*, pp 79–90. London: Routledge.

Giddens, A. 1991. *Modernity and Self Identity*. Cambridge: Polity.

Gilleard, C. 2002. "Women, ageing and body talk." In L. Andersson (ed) *Cultural Gerontology*, pp 139–60. Westport, Conn: Auburn House.

Gilleard, C. and Higgs, P. 2000. *Cultures of Ageing: Self, Citizen and the Body*. London: Prentice Hall.

Gough-Yates, A. 2003. *Understanding Women's Magazines: Publishing, Markets and Readership*. London: Routledge.

Gullette, M. M. 1997. *Declining to Decline: Cultural Combat and the Politics of Midlife*. Charlottesville: University Press of Virginia.

Gullette, M. M. 1999. "The other end of the fashion cycle: practising loss, learning decline." In K. Woodward (ed) *Figuring Age: Women, Bodies, Generations*, pp 34–58. Bloomington: Indiana University Press.

Halls, Z. 2000. "Mrs Exeter—the rise and fall of the older woman," *Costume* 34: 105–12.

Hermes, J. 1995. *Reading Women's Magazines: An Analysis of Everyday Media Use*. Cambridge: Polity.

Higgs, P. 2006. "Departing the margins: social class and later life in second modernity." *Journal of Sociology* 42 (3): 219–41.

Holliday, R. 2001. "Fashioning the queer self." In J. Entwistle and E. Wilson (eds) *Body Dressing*, pp 215–32. Oxford: Berg.

Hurd, L. C. 2000. "Older women's body image and embodied experience: an exploration." *Journal of Women and Aging* 12 (3/4): 77–97.

Jobling, P. 1999. *Fashion Spreads: Word and Image in Fashion Photography Since 1980*. Oxford: Berg.

Jones, I. R., Hyde, M., Victor, C. E., Wiggins, R. D., Gilleard, C., and Higgs, P. 2008. *Ageing in Consumer Society: From Passive to Active Consumption in Britain*. Bristol: Policy Press.

Kang, M. E. 1997. "The portrayal of women's images in magazine advertisements: Goffman's gender analysis revisited." *Sex Roles* 37 (11–12): 979–96.

Khan, N. 1993. "Asian women's dress: from burqah to bloggs." In J. Ash and E. Wilson (eds) *Chic Thrills*, pp 61–74. Berkeley: University of California Press.

Key Note 2006. *Market Assessment: Grey Consumer*. London: Key Note.

Kopina, H. 2007. "The world according to Vogue: the role of culture in international fashion magazines." *Dialectical Anthropology* 31: 363–81.

Krekula, C. 2007. "The intersection of age and gender: reworking gender theory and social gerontology." *Current Sociology* 55: 155–71.

MacSween, M. 1993. *Anorexic Bodies: A Feminist and Sociological Perspective on Anorexia Nervosa*. London: Routledge.

McRobbie, A. 2004. "Notes on 'What not to wear' and post feminist symbolic violence." In L. Adkins, and B. Skeggs (eds) *Feminism After Bourdieu*, pp 99–109. Oxford: Blackwell.

McRobbie, A. 2008. "Young women and consumer culture," *Cultural Studies*. 22 (5): 531–50.

Maynard, M. 1994. "'Race', gender and the concept of 'difference' in feminist thought." In H. Afshar and M. Maynard (eds) *The Dynamics of 'Race' and Gender: Some Feminist Intervention*, pp 9–25. London: Taylor and Francis.

Mintel 2004. *Women's Magazines—Market Intelligence—October*. London: Mintel.

Mintel 2006. *Fashion for the Over 45s—UK—November*. London: Mintel.

Moeran, B. 2004. "Women's fashion magazines: people, things and values," In C. Werner and D. Bell (eds) *Values and Valuables: from the Sacred to the Symbolic*, pp 257–81. Walnut Creek: Altamira.

Öberg, P. and Tornstam, L. 1999. "Body images among men and women of different ages," *Ageing & Society* 19 (5): 629–44.

Öberg, P. and Tornstam, L. 2001. "Youthfulness and fitness—identity ideals for all ages?" *Journal of Ageing and Identity* 6 (1): 15–29.

Phillipson, C. 1998. *Reconstructing Old Age: New Agendas in Social Theory and Practice*. London: Sage.

Polhemus, T. 1994. *Streetstyle: From Sidewalk to Catwalk*. London: Thames & Hudson.

Reventos, D. M. 1998. "Decoding cosmetics and fashion advertisements in contemporary women's magazines." *Cuadernos de Filologica Inglesa* 7 (1): 27–39.

Rolley, K. 1993. "Love, desire and the pursuit of the whole: dress and the lesbian couple." In J. Ash and E. Wilson (eds) *Chic Thrills*, pp 30–39. Berkeley: University of California Press.

Smyczynska, K. 2008. "Escaping Grannydom: fashion and identity in Trinny and Susannah's makeover shows." Paper presented to Xth conference of Cultural Gerontology, Lleida, Spain 2008.

Twigg, J. 2007. "Clothing, age and the body: a critical review." *Ageing & Society* 27 (2): 285–305.

Twigg, J. 2009. "Clothing, identity and the embodiment of age." In J. Powell and T. Gilbert (eds) *Aging and Identity: A Postmodern Dialogue*. New York: Nova Science Publishers.

Williamson, J. 1982. *Decoding Advertisements: Ideology and Meaning in Advertising*. London: Marion Boyars.

Winship, J. 1987. *Inside Women's Magazines*. London: Pandora.

Wolf, N. 1990. *The Beauty Myth*. London: Vintage.

Woodward, K. 1991. *Aging and Its Discontents: Freud and Other Fictions*. Bloomington: Indiana University Press.

Woodward, K. (ed.) 1999. *Figuring Age: Women, Bodies, Generations*. Bloomington: Indiana.

Woodward, K. 2006. "Performing age, performing gender." *NWSA Journal* 18 (1) Spring: 162–89.

Zhang, Y. B., Harwood, J., Williams, A., Ylanne-McEwan, V., Wadleigh, P. M. and Thimm, C. 2006. "The portrayal of older adults in advertising: a cross national review." *Journal of Language and Social Psychology* 25 (3): 264–82.

Discussion Questions

1. Have you noticed silver-haired models gracing the pages of your favorite fashion magazines? What about printed copies of apparel catalogs? Online shopping websites?

2. Are there any women who fit the baby boomer or gray market generations in your family? Have you ever wondered how they feel about seeing models their age? Or not seeing models who are their age? Is this really an issue today? Why or why not?

CHAPTER 12

FASHION AND FANTASY

Kimberly A. Miller–Spillman

After you have read this chapter, you will understand:

- How fantasy and fashion are interrelated
- Public, private, and secret levels of fantasy and dress
- How fantasy occurs in almost every aspect of fashion (i.e., shopping behavior, runway shows, popular culture, advertising, and fashion design)
- How escapist fantasies and fantasy bodies can help individuals temporarily escape challenges of everyday life

Fantasy can be found in many aspects of fashion. Actually, it is sometimes difficult to separate fashion from fantasy or vice versa. Fashion and fantasy includes but is not limited to advertisements, shopping, designer runway shows, gender identity, the body, costuming, fashion design, and historic and futuristic reenactments. Is fantasy a tangible commodity we purchase—or is it an idea that cannot be bought? Merriam-Webster's dictionary defines **fantasy** as follows: (n.) the free play of creative imagination and (v.) to indulge in reverie: create or develop imaginative and often fantastic views or ideas. For our purposes, fantasy is both the product (an apparel design) and the process (daydreaming/images in the mind).

The Public, Private, and Secret Self Model

To assist in this discussion of fantasy dress, we will use the public, private, and secret self model as an organizational tool in this chapter (see Table 12.1). Fashion and fantasy will be explored on three levels as indicated by the shaded cells in the table: a) a public level (cell #3), b) a private level (cell #6), and c) a secret level (cell #9). **The public, private, and secret self (PPSS) model** was developed by dress scholar Joanne Eicher (1981), who built on sociologist Gregory Stone's (1965) ideas of appearance and the self. Later, Eicher and the author collaborated on an expanded version (Eicher and Miller, 1994) of her original model. Still later, historic reenactor's experiences were added to the model (Miller-Spillman, 2008).

TABLE 12.1

The Public, Private, and Secret Self Model (Miller-Spillman, 2008) Based on Previous Collaboration with Joanne Eicher (Eicher & Miller-Spillman, 1994)

	Reality Dress	Fun/Leisure Dress	Fantasy Dress

Public Self	Gender
	Uniforms
	Businesswear
	Reenactors' love
	   of history
	(1)
		Office parties
		Dating
		Sports events
		Reenactors' public
		   performances
		(2)
			Fashion as a collective fantasy
			Halloween costuming
			Living history first-person
			   interpretations
			Festivals
			(3)

Private Self	Housework Gardening Novelty items (4)	Home Exercise Reenactors' interests shared with family and friends (5)	Childhood memories Sensual lingerie Drag shows (6)
Secret Self	Tight Underwear (7)	Some tattoos Novelty underwear (8)	Sexual fantasies Assume another persona Reenactors' magic moments (9)

Sources: Miller-Spillman, K. A. (2008). Male Civil War reenactors' dress and magic moments. In A. Reilly & S. Cosbey (Eds.), *The Men's Fashion Reader* (pp. 445–463). New York: Fairchild.

Eicher, J. B. & Miller-Spillman, K. A. (1994). Dress and the Public, Private, and Secret Self: Revisiting a Model. *ITAA Proceedings*, Proceedings of the International Textiles & Apparel Association, Inc., 145.

The PPSS model connects types of dress (reality, fun/leisure, fantasy) with parts of the self (public, private, and secret). The public part of the self (row 1) is the part we let everyone see. The private part of the self (row 2) is the part we let family members and friends see, and the secret part of the self (row 3) is the part we let no one or only close intimates see. Reality dress (column 1) is the dress that is seen weekdays at work between 9:00 a.m. and 5:00 p.m., for running errands and attending religious observances. Fun/leisure dress (column 2) is the dress worn when relaxing after 5:00 p.m. on work days and on weekends with family and friends. Fantasy dress (column 3) is dress that helps us articulate and express our fantasies and secret desires. In this chapter we will focus on the highlighted column labeled fantasy dress.

Public Level

On a **public level**, fashion is a multibillion-dollar business that very deliberately offers fantasies to consumers via dress. Fashion is a public expression that everyone can see and a collective fantasy on a societal level. This collective fantasy called fashion is a creative outlet; it allows consumers to have fun in a culturally sanctioned way. How can fashion students use this collective fantasy called fashion to create a profitable career? One way is to help consumers connect their fantasies to products. One example is the Ralph Lauren polo look of traditional polo-style clothing and weathered leather and denim. Very few people actually play polo, but you can still live the fantasy of being a wealthy person who plays polo for leisure while your investments make money by purchasing Ralph Lauren clothing (see Figure 12.1). Public examples of fantasy and dress often consume the majority of information in the research literature because they are the easiest to observe and study. This does not mean that private and secret fantasies are less important. They are just harder to observe than public fantasies.

Figure 12.1 Live the fantasy of Ralph Lauren Polo even if you don't play polo or live off of the interest from your inheritance.

Private Level

Secondly is the **private level**. Private fantasies can include memories of playing dress-up as a child, or, as an adult, dressing in Victoria's Secret (VS) lingerie for personal fantasies. Most people would agree that VS is a successful business, and part of that success comes from its ability to tap into a culture-wide fantasy for Americans in a socially acceptable manner (see Figure 12.2). The same can be said of the Halloween costume market for children, a successful business that is socially acceptable.

Not all examples of public or private fantasies are easy to distinguish. For the purposes of this chapter I will categorize examples of public fantasy if the dress is worn in public and everyone can see it, such as costumes worn in parades, for festivals, or other events that take place between 9:00 a.m. and 5:00 p.m. Examples of private fantasy will be those where dress is worn in limited venues or after 5:00 p.m. For example, shopping in

Figure 12.2 Victoria's Secret lingerie can be a part of personal fantasies.

a store is a public activity and takes place during business hours. When you enter a Victoria's Secret store in the mall you are participating in a public fantasy. Conversely, once you take the Victoria's Secret items home to wear or give to an intimate, the dress items are then considered dress for a private fantasy. Likewise, venues that are reserved for a select group pare down a public event to a private one. Examples include couture shows—which may be covered by the media but attended by a select group—and costuming at conference hotels or in remote locations suitable for the event in which only those with a specific interest will attend.

Secret Level

Lastly, the **secret level** of fashion and fantasy is usually held close and not easily revealed. If no one knows the secret or only an intimate knows, this makes a fantasy difficult to document. However, it is safe to say that some individuals have sexual fantasies that involve dress. One example would be heterosexual male cross-dressers. Often these are married men who would not want their secret known. Another example are "magic moments" for historic reenactors who feel as though they have stepped back in time to experience the actual moment in history they are reenacting (see Figure 12.3). This level of fantasy fuels historic dress purchases in order to make the fantasy successful.

A photo essay by Colleen Moriarty that appeared in the October 2005 issue of *Marie Claire* (see suggested reading) illustrates dress and the public, private, and secret parts of the self (see Table 12.1). In "Can You Guess My Body Secret?" Moriarty illustrates how five women use dress to hide body features. This photo essay captures these women both dressed and undressed, demonstrating that what you see in the dressed body is not necessarily the same as what you would see in the undressed body. Photos of the dressed women represent dress for the public

Figure 12.3 Having historically correct clothing can lead to a "magic moment" among reenactors.

self: dress for work at a hospital, in sales, as a dog walker, and as a musician. Turn the page and you see these same women photographed decorously in the nude revealing the private self (naked with husband/boyfriend) and the secret self (their body secret—toned abs, lots of curves, or small breasts supported by a miracle bra to look larger). If you have ever been advised to play up your strong features or camouflage your weak ones you will relate well to this article. This type of advice was once standard for young women in home economics courses and can now be found in self-help books written by image consultants.

To illustrate the different forms fantasy can take, consider this scenario. A woman has a secret fantasy to be a rock 'n' roll star. Although this fantasy is not likely to come true, she can at least "dress out" her fantasy on weekends or choose rock-star dress for Halloween. Unless she tells others of the fantasy of being a rock star (making the fantasy public), only she knows her secret desire (secret fantasy). Others may view her rock 'n' roll dress only as an indulgence into "fashion" (public level) rather than associating her dress with a fantasy (secret level). In addition to wearing dress to express the fantasy, she enjoys shopping for and assembling the pieces for her rock 'n' roll appearance. She can also own the clothing for this fantasy and never wear it, experiencing pleasure from simply having it (Eicher, 1981).

Consequently, fantasy in fashion can be found almost everywhere; whether it appears in consumers' fantasies, popular culture, gender socialization, or couture runway shows, fantasy in fashion offers individuals an outlet for fun and play. Fashion also offers society a collective mechanism to facilitate change. **Collective selection** is a term that Herbert Blumer (1969) devised to describe the collective experience of following fashion. When viewed in this way, fantasy in fashion can help individuals relax, escape the responsibilities of everyday life, and prepare for future societal changes.

Theory, Research, and PPSS Model

Stone (1965) identified two types of socialization through dress: anticipatory and fantastic socialization. **Anticipatory socialization** through dress is described by Stone as dressing for a job or a position one could realistically hold in the future. **Fantastic socialization** through dress is described as dressing in roles that could not be realistically played in the future, such as Wonder Woman or Superman. Both types of socialization through dress are essential for the social development of children and adults. According to Stone, all individuals benefit when they dress in roles to prepare for the future and use their imagination to dress as an unrealistic character. Our dress choices may receive positive feedback from others (e.g., a smile) or we may receive negative feedback (e.g., someone scoffing at our outfit).

Researchers have used the public, private, and secret self model with two groups of adolescents. Michelman, Eicher, and Michelman (1991) studied adolescent psychiatric patients and Eicher, Baizerman, and Michelman (1991) studied adolescents in a general high school population (see Figures 12.4a and b). Among the adolescent psychiatric patients studied, all three levels of dress for the public, private, and secret self were expressed (Michelman, Eicher, and Michelman, 1991). By comparison, Eicher, Baizerman, and Michelman (1991) found only expressions of the public self through dress among a general high school population. The high school students studied, unlike the psychiatric patients, did not understand dress related to any self other than the public self and were confused and embarrassed by questions regarding a private or secret self.

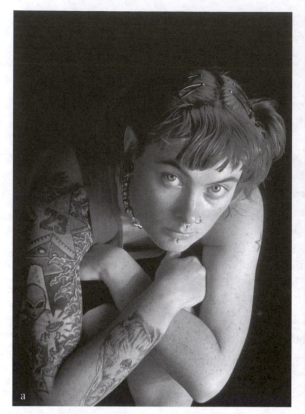

Figure 12.4 Teens' appearances can reflect the possible levels of the self that can be identified and dressed. Alternative teen appearance with tattoos and piercings may indicate all levels of the self (a) and mainstream teen appearance reveals the public self (b).

These differences among adolescents were found in studies with small samples, but it does raise questions about possible differences among adolescents regarding dress and the public, private, and secret self model. One question: is this a real difference or is there a shortcoming in the research methods? It also raises questions about how age may affect dressing different parts of the self. Perhaps dressing different levels of the self (private and secret) is a development issue. It could be that the high school adolescents have not had enough life experiences to distinguish between dressing different parts of the self, compared to adolescents in a psychiatric setting.

Eicher's ideas about dress and the public, private, and secret self have been applied cross-culturally in one study about the design effects of garments between 1890 and 1927. Kim and DeLong (1992) found that Sino-Japanism (a renewed enthusiasm for Far Eastern, mostly Chinese and Japanese, art and culture) dress elements were adopted in Western fashionable dress for both public and private situations. In the earlier periods studied, the adoption of Sino-Japanism in Western dress was found in dress for the **private self**, such as a negligee, dressing jacket, or bathrobe. Later, the adoption of Sino-Japanism in Western dress was found in dress for the **public self**, such as a frock (dress) or a wrap (outergarment). The researchers also noted the cultural authentication (see Chapter 1) of Asian dress elements into Western dress, such as an asymmetrical closure and a Mandarin-style collar. Morgado's article about the kimono worn as a Halloween costume (see Chapter 3) is an example of Americans adopting Asian garments for a private party.

Public Fantasy: Fashion and Consumers

Retailing and Marketing

When consumers enter a store, there are many possibilities for creating a personal "look." The shopping experience can be one of creatively imagining oneself in all sorts of dress styles for many different roles, e.g., employee, jogger, religious observer, etc. "Show royal blue, sell navy blue" was once a slogan used by retailers to indicate how to market and sell clothing successfully. In other words, display royal blue clothing in a store window to attract customers into the store, but once the customer is in the store, he or she will probably forgo the royal blue clothing for the more practical navy blue.

A theory that helps to explain the reasoning behind this slogan comes from sociologist George Herbert Mead (1934), recognized as the father of symbolic interaction theory. Mead identified parts of the self as the "I" and "me." The "I" is the impulsive and unpredictable part of the self that engages in impulsive actions or behaviors (such as impulse buying). Coexisting with the "I" is the "me" or the social conscience part of the self that considers what is socially acceptable. The "I" part of the self is attracted to royal blue pants as a vibrant, bright, and, for some, daring wardrobe choice. Once in the store, the "me" part of the self emerges as a voice in your head that asks, "But where would I wear this?" or "What would my friends think of me in this color?" therefore causing the individual to reconsider and purchase the more practical navy blue pants.

Apparel shopping satisfaction can have two values, hedonic or utilitarian. **Hedonic shopping** includes consumers' shopping mood and satisfaction, while **utilitarian shopping** can be described as more practical and goal oriented. Hedonic values include increased arousal, heightened involvement, perceived freedom, fantasy fulfillment, and escapism. Hedonic shopping in conjunction with gender differences in apparel shopping was investigated to develop successful marketing strategies in the competitive Korean market (Chang, Burns, and Francis, 2004). Researchers found that for the male and female Korean undergraduate students studied, females place greater value on hedonic shopping than men. Men may possess greater utilitarian constructs for apparel shopping satisfaction rather than hedonic constructs.

Scholars Fiore and Ogle (2000) examined the connection between a consumer's fantasy life and attachments to fashion items and/or fragrances. One outcome of this research is to help merchandising students understand the importance of their role in helping customers connect their fantasies to products in the store. For instance, visual merchandisers create store displays that draw customers to products which fulfill a fantasy, or a desire of what could be. For example, "masquerade or period costumes as well as vintage clothing provide pleasure by allowing the wearer to take on the aura of a different person, place, and/or time" (p. 40). Store displays and catalog ads (e.g., J. Peterman) are two environments that draw customers to products that fulfill or create a fantasy. Referring to the previous example of wanting to be a rock 'n' roll star, a window display with rock 'n' roll attire and equipment (i.e., guitars, amplifiers, microphones, etc.) would appeal to this woman's secret fantasy and draw her into the store for further exploration.

Marketers often use fantasy in advertising campaigns. Lyons (2005) analyzed a Maidenform advertising campaign between 1949 and 1970. The slogan: "I dreamed I . . . in my Maidenform bra" featured a glamorous young model doing anything imaginable (see Figure 12.5). She was influencing juries, on safari, or working as an editor conspicuously wearing a Maidenform bra. The ads appeared to connect with women's discontent in the 1950s and were interpreted as a classic example of wish fulfillment psychology (Lyons, 2005). The ads struck a

Figure 12.5 Through this popular ad campaign between 1949 and 1970 American women could picture themselves doing anything imaginable, all in their Maidenform bra.

psychological chord with women who capably managed homes and finances during World War II. Following the war, many women took on more traditional roles of housewife and mother. The Maidenform bra ads fed women's secret fantasies for independence, power, and influence. An unexpected result of the campaign was the large number of customers' photos sent to Maidenform of themselves in scenes of "I dreamed I . . . in my Maidenform bra." An interesting twist is that a bra is considered a private item of dress; however, this ad turns the bra into a very visible, public item.

Designers and Inspiration

Designers need inspiration from a variety of sources in order to create fresh and new designs. For example, inspiration can come from a Shaker costume collection when holding and closely examining a tissue-thin scarf spun from silk worms that were fed, and whose silk was harvested and woven, by Shakers in the mid-19th century. One history of costume student was inspired by such a visit to a Shaker collection and created several contemporary designs for a class project (Myser, 2009) (see Figures 12.6a–c). Other times, inspiration for design comes from dreaming up ideas just for fun. When we allow ourselves to brainstorm the most far-fetched and ludicrous ideas, those ideas often lead to workable design solutions or onetime exercises in excess such as Lady Gaga's "meat" dress worn to an awards show.

a

b

c

Figure 12.6 Student designs for contemporary garments inspired by Shaker clothing in a collection at Shaker Village at Pleasant Hill near Harrodsburg, KY (a–c).

Since designers work with fashion figures, there is a certain amount of fantasy incorporated into their job. Given that many women do not have the ideal figure shape (Danielson, 1989), fashion figures or *croqui* represent models on the runway rather than actual customers. In view of the fact that these idealized figures reflect our fantasies or desires rather than reality, the element of fantasy is at work as a designer creates the next apparel line.

In one of this chapter's readings, Kate Carter describes fantasy alliances among European fashion designers in "Fantasy Fashion Collaborations." Carter begins with examples of collaborations that have been short lived, such as select celebrity and fashion house partnerships. But Carter quickly moves to what she describes as a real match between John Paul Gaultier (he designed Madonna's pointy concert corset) and La Perla (a high-end lingerie company). Can you think of other fantasy matchups in Europe? In the United States? Or international collaborations?

Inspiration to create new designs can also come from movies, plays, concerts, nature walks, museum exhibits, or current events. The movie *Avatar* is one example of inspiration for designers. *Avatar* was a visual feast for the eyes and inspired Anthropologie's textile designer, Alexandra Becket, to create otherworldly shapes for clothing and home furnishings. In the reading "Fantasy Fashion: *Avatar*'s Look Is Influencing Designers—Whether They're Aware of It or Not," Pike suggests that *Avatar* has designers asking about the zeitgeist of "What else is out there?" In addition, the fantastic images in the movie have inspired at least one jewelry designer to create a sea horse pin encrusted in gems by taking on the color scheme of the movie and reinterpreting the accessory item. (See Figure 12.9 on page 488.)

Halloween and Identity

Halloween, especially for children, is a public fantasy. American children look forward to dressing in costume and collecting candy each year at Halloween. Child development scholar Jeanne Iorio shares her experience in dressing her daughter for Halloween in the reading "'What Disney Says': Young Girls, Dress, and the Disney Princesses." Iorio uses the popularity of princess merchandise to pose questions regarding society's expectations of girls. Iorio also questions the effect large corporations have on a girl's view of her own individual identity. In other words, will girls be passive consumers and buy what all their friends are buying or will girls become critical thinkers and creators of their own identity by purchasing items counter to their friends' choices? And lastly, who will help girls navigate these choices that affect their identities? The peer group? Large corporations? Parents?

The connection between girls' princess dresses and theory helps to explain the larger implications beyond the attitude "What's the big deal if a little girl wants to dress up as a princess?" In her article, Iorio challenges the Disney Corporation to forgo the easy sell and instead promote individuality rather than conformity through princess costuming. Iorio uses examples of stark window displays in the Disney Store she visits. It is almost as though Disney knows the princess dresses will sell, therefore no effort in the displays is necessary. Consider how you feel about this issue. Can a young girl feel accepted by her peers while also creating her own individual identity through dress? This is most likely a case of personal agency (a concept used by feminists to describe the resistance women use to combat patriarchy) that develops as one grows up, similar to private and secret dress discussed earlier among adolescents.

Dressing in costume to attend an event not only occurs among children in Halloween costumes but is practiced by adults as well. Consider the following examples: Harry Potter fans who dress as their favorite book character to see the latest movie or buy the latest book; midnight screenings of the cult favorite *Rocky Horror Picture Show* attended by fans with newspapers, umbrellas, and water guns (props appearing in the film); and lastly, the Royal wedding of Prince William and Catherine Middleton in 2011, which inspired some U.S. party guests to dress as members of the wedding party. Many Americans are fascinated by European royalty and fantasize about being an English royal or a royal descendant.

Runway Shows and Fantasy

Alexander McQueen was known for his dramatic and fantastic runway shows, such as his October 2006 show in an uncharacteristic environment—the *Cirque d'Hiver* (a show staged in the round runs counter to the typical designer show, which has a straight runway). This show included unusual set designs, a chamber orchestra, and exquisite clothing (Horyn, 2006). McQueen created a fantasy through clothing, environment, and music that was unique among runway shows. This uniqueness made his shows irresistible to customers who wanted an exclusive experience. Two examples of McQueen's fantastic shows include his Spring 2010 collection with controversial Armadillo shoes (see Figure 12.7a) inspired by Charles Darwin's *Origin of the Species* and his 1998 collection with Marie Antoinette-style designs (see Figure 12.7b) (Rawi and Abraham, 2010). McQueen's runway shows were covered in the public media; however, his ability to create a private fantasy among those who could attend made him a success.

Figure 12.7 Fantasy on the runway. Alexander McQueen's Spring 2010 collection including Armadillo shoes (a) and Alexander McQueen's 1998 collection with Marie Antoinette-style designs (b).

Ames (2008) points out that runway couture shows often feature a **showpiece item** that produces feelings of nostalgic and escapist fantasy; these showpieces are also usually unwearable and nonsaleable. Ames states that the purpose of the runway showpiece is to be noticed, not to sell—to create an image of the design house as confident and bold (p. 104). As such, couture is considered a creative laboratory for the development of fantastic items; not necessarily for the sale of their showpiece items. However, if the showpiece is successful it will generate sales for the designer's ready-to-wear line. This is a good example of how fantasy (runway showpieces) can indirectly fuel sales (ready-to-wear).

Next are examples of fashion and fantasy on a private level.

Private Fantasy: Consumption to Create a Fantasy

Costuming and Identity

Since clothing enhances one's imagination, then costuming is an ideal pastime for those looking to experience a fantasy. There are several opportunities to dress in costume in American culture, such as Halloween, reenactments, science fiction conventions, and theater productions. While there are costuming opportunities, most would hesitate to publically announce they love to costume. So, there may be real or perceived stigma with those who openly embrace costuming on a regular basis. However, the experiential benefits of costuming may outweigh the risks.

Costume is one way that reenactors of earlier times embrace their fantasies and communicate their level of historical authenticity. Members in the Society of Creative Anachronism (SCA) often provide the characters (jousters, blacksmiths, etc.) for medieval festivals. Decker (2010) used ethnographic methods (participant observation) to query SCA members to determine how a large membership with many diverse interpretations of authenticity could continue to survive. Wearing tennis shoes to an event (often referred to as a "rendezvous") because one has forgotten their period boots (p. 283) or having to wear Birkenstocks because it is one's first year in reenacting (p. 290) and there hasn't been time to invest in all of the necessary clothing items creates a confusing picture for those attending the event (often called spectators).

What causes one person to embrace costuming while others actively avoid anything that involves costume? Since many people associate a person's dress with their personality, perhaps personality differences could help explain the difference. Johnson, Francis, and Burns (2007) researched this intriguing possibility using the Five Factor Model of Personality (McCrae and John, 1992) and a questionnaire about appearance. The five factors are neuroticism, extraversion, openness to experience, agreeableness, and conscientiousness. Of particular interest here is **openness to experience**, which includes fantasy, aesthetics, feelings, actions, ideas, and values. Persons who score high on openness to experience are curious, have broad interests, and are creative, original, imaginative, untraditional, artistic, perceptive, and insightful. The results of this study indicate that openness to experience had a significant negative relationship with appearance, meaning that if an individual is open to experiences, he or she is not overly concerned with appearances but is more experientially oriented. This leads us to believe that those who enjoy the experience of being in costume are less concerned with public appearances and more focused on their experiences.

A **consumer consumption fantasy** is described by marketing researchers Belk and Costa (1998) as one way that consumers participate in fantasy through shopping. These researchers use the example of mountain men reenactors purchasing items needed for a successful reenactment or production of their fantasy as historic mountain men. These men must purchase items such as tents, cooking equipment, buckskin pants, boots, shirts, and guns. Through their online and event purchases they are building a fantasy.

Figure 12.8 Re-creating the *Star Wars* Stormtrooper armor can lead to a new identity and a sense of community with others with the same interest.

A similar case is described in the reading "Much More Than Plastic: Reflections on Building *Star Wars* Stormtrooper Armor." Anthropologist Eirik Saethre shares his personal journey in the reading and illustrates how costuming is a marker of identity. The process of building *Star Wars* Stormtrooper armor (see Figure 12.8) facilitates building a new identity as someone who knows specialized information and signals membership in a community. In contrast to wanting to be an action figure, Saethre was intrigued by the level of detail required in achieving screen accuracy in his Stormtrooper armor. The author compares his transformation from his initial satisfaction to purchase a kit from a website to starting from scratch to achieve Centurion Standards of screen accuracy to a "rite of passage."

Feeling membership with a group has motivated a select group of North American and Japanese individuals to participate in anime and manga (hardcore) costuming. Theresa Winge's article "Costuming the Imagination: Origins of Anime and Manga Cosplay" delves into the social benefits for those who attend costume conventions where anime and manga costuming are featured. Since this type of costuming involves two cultures (Japanese and North American), Winge explored the origins of **cosplay** (combination of "costume" and "play"). Cosplay merges fantasy with reality into carnivalesque environments where people are not themselves but instead are transformed into robots, part-robot-part-man, and Lolitas. Cosplayers who are considered geeks or social outcasts in everyday life get a chance at the spotlight and interact with others with similar interests at cosplay venues.

Another example of using fantasy to counter social frustration comes from dress scholar John Jacob. Jacob combines personal experience and theory to express dissatisfaction with the limitations society places on his gender expressions. In the reading "A Drag Experience: Locating Fantasy in the Construction of Alternative Gendered Appearances," Jacob eloquently describes how his ability to create through fantasy and dress is inhibited by the either-or approach to gender in American culture. Sociologist Michael S. Kimmel (2000) explains this occurrence through the lens of U.S. culture's definition of masculinity.

> The first rule, maybe the most important rule of all masculinity, is no sissy stuff. What makes a man a man is that he is relentlessly repudiating the feminine. These stereotypes [of how a man should be] are what keep [men] acting really traditionally masculine. . . . This becomes a kind of negative rule book. And so as a result, homophobia becomes a real straitjacket pushing individuals toward a very traditional definition of masculinity (www.pbs.org/wgbh/pages/frontline/shows/assault/etc/script.html).

Jacob uses his drag experience to create an alternative identity that challenges traditional heterosexual gender roles. By questioning the reality of gender differences, Jacob suggests that we are all participating in a collective fantasy of appearing as ideal men and women in our everyday dress. Citing gender theorists, Jacob uses a philosophical approach to explain his personal experiences. The fantasy expressed during drag liberates Jacob to imagine a place in society that currently exists only in limited venues (similar to cosplayers who get a chance at the spotlight at conventions). (See Figure 12.12 on page 510.)

Secret Fantasy: Assuming Another Persona

Costuming for Fantasy

Individuals experience fantasy in a variety of ways: through reading, daydreaming, watching movies, and searching for information on the Internet. Some individuals want an actual experience in which they "become" a character in a book, movie, or online game. Examples can include people with long-held interests in topics such as science fiction or history. A *Star Trek* enthusiast is one example of someone who has watched all the TV shows but now wants to actually portray a *Star Trek* character. He or she decides to attend a Costume Convention (or Costume Con) to participate in a costume contest of his or her favorite *Star Trek* character. There are also many historic examples such as The Jane Austen Society (individuals who reenact the time period of Jane Austen books), Civil War Reenactments (American Civil War period), the previously mentioned Society of Creative Anachronism (Medieval), Buckskinners or Fur Traders (Daniel Boone era), and dance organizations such as English country dancers, Morris dancers, and Scottish country dancers. People in these groups want to experience another time and place by making or buying period-correct costumes/accessories, attending events in costume, and meeting others with similar interests. (For more information, see Miller-Spillman, 2008.) These individuals also share a desire for an escapist fantasy: a way to temporarily escape day-to-day problems or boredom. Two dress researchers have examined dress for those who reenact earlier times (Miller, 1997 and 1998; Strauss, 2002 and 2003). In addition, there are many fantasy sports/music camps now available to those who want that type of experience.

Miller-Spillman (2008) examined male Civil War reenactors' dress and their experience of magic moments or time travel during reenactments. Magic moments are times when reenactors feel as though they are actually participating in an historical event. They are no longer reenacting but are experiencing time travel to the actual moment in history. Wearing historically accurate clothing as well as being surrounded by others in accurate historic dress can set the stage for a magic moment to occur.

Researchers in the field of psychology have identified a fantasy-prone personality (Wilson and Barber, 1983). **Fantasy proneness** has been studied in relation to childhood memories and imaginings (Rhue and Lynn, 1989), hypnosis (Green and Lynn, 2011), excessive daydreaming (Schupak and Rosenthal, 2008), creative experiences (Merckelback, Horselenberg, and Muris, 2001), and extreme celebrity worship (Maltby et al., 2006). One researcher found evidence connecting fantasy proneness to dress and the public, private, and secret self model (Miller, 1998). Miller found in a sample of historic and futurist reenactors that female respondents were more fantasy prone than male respondents.

Shopping for a fantasy self is described in the suggested reading "Dressing for Your Dream Life." Nigella Lawson reveals that her mundane, day-to-day wardrobe is quite uniform and ignores several "selves" that clamor for a wardrobe all their own (pp. 165–166). Many people would agree that reality has a way of making one's day-to-day dress boring. Everyday dress has to be professional (i.e., for employees) and practical (i.e., washing clothes daily is not practical). But what about those impractical parts of the self that never get a wardrobe of their own? In her article, Lawson describes her hippie, boho self that dresses in floaty Indian things; a rock chic self, complete with leather trousers and biker jacket; and the dainty, little-girl cutesiness of pretty dresses with puffed sleeves. The habit of dressing every day can limit the imagination, leaving other parts of the self screaming for attention.

Recall that earlier in this chapter the issue of young girls dressing in princess dresses without inhibition was discussed; this is an interesting contrast to Lawson, who feels trapped in a uniform look as an adult. Even the fact that Lawson is a successful TV cooking-show host who can afford any dress she desires doesn't necessarily mean that she feels free to indulge that desire beyond the purchase of the items. Eicher (1981), in her original framework of dressing the public, private, and secret self, notes that we often find pleasure in garments we own but never wear. This suggests that there may be a part (or parts) of the self that is pleased just knowing the item is in our closet. This unworn item reminds us that we could be that other person if we wanted it badly enough.

Fantasizing about having a body different than the one we were born with can be supported by our clothing choices. The desire to fantasize about a different body can be triggered in several ways. For instance, a teenager who reads magazines realizes he or she doesn't look like the models featured. This perceived physical limitation because of comparing oneself to airbrushed models can cause a person to fantasize about having the "ideal" body. Another way a person can fantasize about a different body is because of an actual physical condition or illness. For example, one study respondent gave this example: "I had eczema as a child and could not wear the frilly sundresses or shorts that other young girls wore" (Miller-Spillman, 2005, p. 278).

Lastly, one could feel constrained by society's limited gender expectations. For example, many transgendered individuals feel as though society expects people to fit into very small categories of either male or female with no mixing of the two in appearance (see Box 12.1).

Since most everyone has access to the Internet, the creation of a character or avatar as a representation of the self is a commonly understood concept. Merriam-Webster's online dictionary defines *avatar* as an electronic image that represents and is manipulated by a computer user (as in a computer game). Creating a body double to virtually try on clothing and hairstyles is another example. There is a lot of freedom of expression offered through computer representations of oneself. Images can range from realistic to fantastic.

In Rivera's reading "Video Game Attire," World of Warcraft online players experience a "make-believe" environment and choose one or several avatars with which to represent themselves in the game. Each avatar choice offers the player specific skills for the game, and as a player's skill level increases, so do their choices for sought-after attire for their avatars. Rivera compares this playing for attire to fashion interest outside of the game or in real life. Since most of the players in this game are male, the players can openly vie for better gear without the stigma

---

BOX 12.1

Illustration of Gender Expectations of Dress in American Society

DRESS IN AMERICAN CULTURE:
Creates Difficulty Experiencing Fantasies Across Gender Lines
Represented on a Gender Continuum

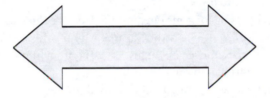

MALES
-pants only
-no dresses
-no makeup
-no colored nail polish
-can wear earrings
-can wear pastel colors
-no large prints in bright colors

FEMALES
-pants or skirts
-dresses allowed
-makeup expected
-colored nail polish allowed
-earrings allowed
-no restriction on colors worn
-large prints in bright colors allowed

• Dress of males and females are represented as opposites above on the continuum and in day-to-day appearances.

• Female dress overlaps male dress more than male dress overlaps female dress.

• Behaviors can overlap, i.e., women are allowed to be ambitious, direct, and tough; men are allowed to be loving, nurturing, and helpful. However, male dress cannot overlap female dress without problems.

of being considered feminine or gay, a likely consequence for men who express interest in fashion outside of the game. In addition, players are free to choose the gender of their avatars and do not feel compelled to choose an avatar that represents their true gender. Online games offer men the opportunity to openly express interest in fashion without stigma and the opportunity to choose female avatars.

Summary

Fashion and fantasy appear to go hand in hand. Fashion is a serious multibillion-dollar business and it provides a fun outlet that can support individuals' fantasies. Given the part that fantasy and dress may play to a larger or smaller degree in a person's life, this area is relevant to fashion adherents worldwide. Several theoretical approaches can be used to study fantasy in dress. Examples include anthropological concepts of rite of passage in the Stormtrooper armor, carnivalesque in cosplay, dressing parts of the self in hiding body secrets, wish-fulfillment psychology in advertisements, gender socialization in girls' Halloween costumes, collective selection theory in which fashion (and by association fantasy) offers society a mechanism to tolerate change, personality traits such as openness to experience and fantasy-prone personality, and consumer consumption fantasies among historic reenactors.

Suggested Readings

Groom, A. (2011). PowerPlay and Performance in Harajuku. New Voices (vol. 4), *A Journal of Emerging Scholars of Japanese Studies in Australia and New Zealand*, 188–214. Retrieved from http://www.jpf.org.au/newvoices.

Guy, A. and M. Banim. (2000). Personal Collections: Women's Clothing Use and Identity. *Journal of Gender Studies* 9 (3): 313–327.

Lawson, N. (2006). Dressing for Your Dream Life. *Harper's Bazaar*, 165–166.

Massimo, R. 2010 (2010, July 3). Lady Gaga: A Mix of Music, Visual Fantasy. Boston: *The Providence Journal*. Retrieved on August 15, 2011, from http://artsblog.projo.com/2010/07/lady-gaga-takes-a-trip-in-boston-sh.html.

Moriarty, C. (2005, October). "Can You Guess My Body Secret?" *Marie Claire*, 122–128.

Nelson, A. (2000). The Pink Dragon Is Female. *Psychology of Women Quarterly*, 24: 137–144.

Stanton, C. (1997). Being the Elephant: The American Civil War Reenacted. Unpublished master's thesis, Vermont College of Norwich University.

Learning Activity 12.1: The Business of Design

Topics

Design process and changes in the way designers do business.

Sources

1. *Unzipped*, 1995, video about Isaac Mizrahi.
2. Teri Agins, 1999, What Happened to Fashion? Excerpt from *The End of Fashion*, pp. 1–16.

Procedures

After watching *Unzipped* and reading "What Happened to Fashion?" answer the questions below and discuss your answers in small groups.

1. A movie about a woman stranded in the Alaskan tundra with perfect hair and makeup was the fantasy that inspired Isaac Mizrahi's designs for his 1994 collection. What have you learned about Isaac Mizrahi's creative process? Where did he get his training?
2. What parts of the job does Mizrahi enjoy? Which parts does he dislike?
3. How would a film documentary about Calvin Klein or Ralph Lauren differ from *Unzipped*? How would it be similar?
4. Why do you think Chanel discontinued financing Isaac Mizrahi in 1998?
5. Do you think Mizrahi was successful from 2002 to 2008 with his Target venture? Why or why not?
6. If you believe that Mizrahi's Target venture was successful between 2002 and 2008, what aspects of the "cultural moment" in the late '90s with Chanel differ from that of the early-to-late 2000s when Mizrahi was at Target? (Use the article in "The End of Fashion" for information about the 1990s.)
7. Did Mizrahi's combined Target and couture ventures between 2002 and 2008 have more in common with Oprah Winfrey and Martha Stewart than Ralph Lauren and Calvin Klein? Why or why not?
8. In 2009, Mizrahi designed for Liz Claiborne as the creative director and head designer. Why do you think this venture lasted only one year?
9. Is Mizrahi's design work too fantastic to be profitable? Do you think Mizrahi deserves credit for trying multiple avenues for his design work? What is your opinion of Mizrahi's career?

References

Ames, A. (2008). Fashion Design for a Projected Future. *Clothing and Textiles Research Journal* 26 (2): 103–118.

Belk, R. W., and J. A. Costa. (1998). The Mountain Man Myth: A Contemporary Consuming Fantasy. *Journal of Consumer Research* 25(3): 218–240.

Blumer, H. (1969). Fashion: From Class Differentiation to Collective Selection. *Sociology Quarterly* 10: 275–291.

Chang, E., L.D. Burns, and S. K. Francis. (2004). Gender Differences in the Dimensional Structure of Apparel Shopping Satisfaction among Korean Consumers: The Role of Hedonic Shopping Value. *Clothing and Textiles Research Journal* 22 (4): 185–199.

Danielson, D. R. (1989). The Changing Figure Ideal in Fashion Illustration. *Clothing and Textiles Research Journal* 8 (1): 35–48.

Decker, S. K. (2010). Being Period: An Examination of Bridging Discourse in a Historical Reenactment Group. *Journal of Contemporary Ethnography* 39 (3): 273–296.

Eicher, J. B. (1981). Influences of Changing Resources on Clothing, Textiles, and the Quality of Life: Dressing for Reality, Fun, and Fantasy. *Combined Proceedings, Eastern, Central, and Western Regional Meetings of Association of College Professors of Textiles and Clothing*, 36–41.

Eicher, J. B., S. Baizerman, and J. Michelman. (1991). Adolescent Dress: Part 2. A Qualitative Study of Suburban High School Students. *Adolescence* 26:679–686.

Eicher, J. B., and K. A. Miller. (1994). Dress and the Public, Private, and Secret Self: Revisiting a Model. *ITAA Proceedings*, Proceedings of the International Textile & Apparel Association, Inc., 145.

Fiore, A. M., and J. P. Ogle. (2000). Facilitating Students' Integration of Textiles and Clothing Subject Matter, Part One: Dimensions of a Model and a Taxonomy. *Clothing and Textiles Research Journal* 18 (1): 31–45.

Green, J. P., and S. J. Lynn. (2011). Hypnotic Responsiveness: Expectancy, Attitudes, Fantasy Proneness, Absorption, and Gender. *International Journal of Clinical and Experimental Hypnosis* 59:103–121.

Horyn, C. (2006, October 9). Two Madmen in Paris, Maybe Just a Little Bit Lost. *New York Times*. Retrieved March 3, 2012 from http://query.nytimes.com/gst/fullpage.html?res=9907E1DE1330F93AA35753C1A9609C8B63.

Johnson, T. W., S. K. Francis, and L. D. Burns. (2007). Appearance Management Behavior and the Five Factor Model of Personality. *Clothing and Textiles Research Journal* 25 (3): 230–243.

Kim, H. J., and M. R. DeLong. (1992). Sino-Japanism in Western Women's Fashionable Dress in Harper's Bazaar, 1890–1927. *Clothing and Textiles Research Journal* 11 (1): 24–30.

Kimmel, M. S. (2000). Assault on Gay America. Frontline transcript of PBS video with Forrest Sawyer. www.pbs.org/wgbh/pages/frontline/shows/assault/etc/script.html.

Lyons, N. N. (2005). Interpretive Reading of Two Maidenform Bra Advertising Campaigns. *Clothing and Textiles Research Journal* 23 (4): 322–332.

Maltby, J., L. Day, L. E. McCutcheon, J. Houran, and D. Ashe. (2006). Extreme Celebrity Worship, Fantasy Proneness and Dissociation: Developing the Measurement and Understanding of Celebrity Worship within a Clinical Personality Context. *Personality and Individual Differences* 40:273–283.

McCrae, R. R., and O. P. John. (1992). An Introduction to the Five Factor Model and Its Applications. *Journal of Personality* 60(2): 175–215.

Mead, G. H. (1934). *Mind, Self and Society: From the Standpoint of a Social Behaviorist.* Chicago: University of Chicago.

Merckelback, H., R. Horselenberg, and P. Muris. (2001). The Creative Experiences Questionnaire: A Brief Self-Report Measure of Fantasy Proneness. *Personality and Individual Differences* 31:987–995.

Michelman, J. D., J. B. Eicher, and S. O. Michelman. (1991). Adolescent Dress: Part 1. Dress and Body Markings of Psychiatric Outpatients and Onpatients. *Adolescence* 26:375–385.

Miller, K. A. (1997). Dress: Private and Secret Self-Expression. *Clothing and Textiles Research Journal* 15 (4): 223–234.

Miller, K. A. (1998). Gender Comparisons Within Reenactment Costume: Theoretical Interpretations. *Family and Consumer Sciences Research Journal* 27 (1): 35–61.

Miller-Spillman, K. A. (2005). Playing Dress-Up: Childhood Memories of Dress. In M. L.

Damhorst, K. A. Miller-Spillman, and S. O. Michelman (Eds.), *The Meanings of Dress* (2nd ed.), 274–283. New York: Fairchild Books.

Miller-Spillman, K. A. (2008). Male Civil War Reenactors' Dress and Magic Moments. In A. Reilly and S. Cosbey (Eds.), *The Men's Fashion Reader*, 455–473. New York: Fairchild Books.

Myser, A. (2009). Shaker Inspired Apparel Line. Unpublished class project in History of Costume at University of Kentucky.

Rawi, M., and T. Abraham. (2010, February 25). A Life in Fashion: How Alexander McQueen Became "the Most Influential Designer of His Generation." Retrieved on August 15, 2011, from www.dailymail.co.uk/femail/article-1250252/Alexander-McQueen-A-life-fashion.html.

Rhue, J. W., and S. J. Lynn. (1989). Fantasy Proneness, Hypnotizability, and Absorption—A re-examination. *International Journal of Clinical and Experimental Hypnosis* 37:100–106.

Schupak, C., and J. Rosenthal. (2008). Excessive Daydreaming: A Case History and Discussion of Mind Wandering and High Fantasy Proneness. *Consciousness and Cognition* 18 (1): 290–292.

Stone, G. P. (1965). Appearance and the Self. In M. E. Roach and J. B. Eicher (Eds.), *Dress, Adornment and the Social Order*, 216–245. New York: John Wiley.

Strauss, M. D. (2002). Pattern Categorization of Male U.S. Civil War Reenactor Images. *Clothing and Textiles Research Journal* 20 (2): 99–109.

Strauss, M. D. (2003). Identity Construction among Confederate Civil War Reenactors: A Study of Dress, Stage Props, and Discourse. *Clothing and Textiles Research Journal* 21 (4): 149–161.

Wilson, S. C., and T. X. Barber. (1983). The fantasy-prone personality: Implications for Understanding Imagery, Hypnosis, and Psychological Phenomena. In A. A. Sheikh (Ed.), *Imagery: Current Theory, Research, and Application*, 340–390. New York: Wiley.

FANTASY FASHION COLLABORATIONS

Kate Carter

What makes a good collaboration? Not long ago it seemed that every celebrity and their chihuahua was designing a collection for a fashion house. And when we say "celebrity," naturally we mean "Z-list offspring of someone who was famous back in the '80s." Indeed, it was only at the beginning of this year that Fashion Statement (FS) was pondering some of the more ill-fated meetings of fashion minds. And when we say "minds," we mean "pay cheques."

But recently, all has been quiet on the collaboration front. And a good thing too, you might say—particularly if you work in H&M and had to shift the forklift truckloads of unwanted Madonna-designed, er . . . *product* into the bargain bin. Perhaps fashion houses realised that celebrity might mean column inches but it doesn't always mean sales, particularly if said celebrity is hardly someone whose style your average shopper has any desire to emulate. Or perhaps they just ran out of celebrities.

However, FS was delighted to hear the news earlier this week that Jean-Paul Gaultier has teamed up with La Perla to create an exclusive collection. It is not, FS hastens to add, that we dress in Gaultier to the office, or that our underwear drawer is stocked by anyone other than Marks & Spencer, but it's rather refreshing to read of a match-up that actually IS a match. Who better than the creator of the pointy corset to design underwear for a top brand? It's a marriage made in lingerie heaven.

So could this be the beginning of a golden era of collaborations? We hope so. Wouldn't it be great if brands had a good old think about what designers would actually FIT into their look and their ethos (and vice versa)? FS would like to suggest a few of these collaborations that we'd really, really like to see. How about Anya Hindmarch for Marks & Spencers? Gorgeous bags, high street prices, great quality. Or how about making the lovely Holly Fulton art deco pieces affordable with a range for Tatty Devine? We also love the idea of River Island and Cavalli. Prada and Cos. Finally, John Lewis—home of many a nice print—would be a top match-up with Marni.

Of course, if any of these happen, Fashion Statement will be claiming royalties.

Discussion Questions

1. Brainstorm as many fantasy fashion collaborations as you can. Include the most mundane collaborations to the most whimsical. Share your ideas with others in small groups and let the process build on individual ideas into group ideas. Share your best ideas with the class.
2. Since fashion design is a very competitive business, most designers are very secretive and independent. How can these characteristics be overcome to allow for collaboration? Is independence a trait that should not be compromised? Or do design ideas improve with collaboration?
3. Reflect on your own creative process. Consider projects that you completed alone as well as those you completed with a group. What were the strengths and weaknesses of each?

FANTASY FASHION: *AVATAR*'S LOOK IS INFLUENCING DESIGNERS—WHETHER THEY'RE AWARE OF IT OR NOT

Laurie Pike

After watching *Avatar* at the Cinerama Dome in January, Alexandra Becket returned to her studio in the Fairfax District and began to sketch. The textile designer, whose prints are used for Anthropologie clothes and Pottery Barn home furnishings, riffed on images in the 3-D film. "Trumpet-shaped mushroom plants, glowing night foliage, floating jellyfish—these are my latest shapes and forms to reinterpret," says Becket. The movie was also evocative for jeweler Martin Katz, who recognized the underwater inspiration behind its creatures and colors (Figure 12.9). "The visuals in the movie look like the sort of life you see on a coral reef," says Katz. For his Beverly Hills boutique he plans to reprise his gem-encrusted pieces depicting a sea horse, an octopus, and a fish.

Now that *Avatar* has become the top-grossing film of all time, Pandora's kaleidoscopic palette, Thomas Kinkade-like lighting, and organic curviness are positioning the movie to replace *Project Runway* as the fashion industry's latest pop culture touchstone. "Any designer or artist who sees it will be inspired either directly or subliminally," says Tarina Tarantino, whose eponymous line of accessories is known for its candy colors. "My fall story for our collection has an otherworldly theme. It feels even more appropriate after seeing this film. I think there is a general feeling in the air of 'What else is out there?'"

Although *Avatar* won't have the instantaneous trendsetting impact of *Flashdance*'s ripped sweatshirts or *Clueless*'s plaid miniskirts, it could bring butterfly prints and jungle motifs to shops this year, stemming the tide of dark minimalism

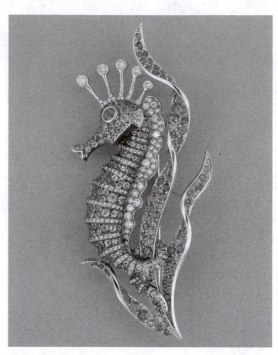

Figure 12.9 A sea horse pin that was inspired by the movie *Avatar*.

that was building before the film's release. Subconsciously, *Avatar* will enhance the public's visual sophistication, says dress designer Juan Carlos Obando. "By bringing the fantasy genre to the masses, the movie will help train people's eye to appreciate visuals with a narrative behind it," he says. "And the more they are able to understand the visual of a garment, the more they are able to value it."

Reprinted by permission of Emmis Publishing.

Discussion Questions

1. What types of activities influence your imagination?
2. Describe other movies, TV shows, or concerts that have had a similar effect on fashion. Watch the movie *Unzipped*, the documentary film about Isaac Mizrahi's 1994 collection. (See related Learning Activity on p. 484.)
3. List all of the ways you can think of how/where designers can get inspiration for future designs.

"WHAT DISNEY SAYS": YOUNG GIRLS, DRESS, AND THE DISNEY PRINCESSES

Jeanne Marie Iorio
University of Hawai`i—West Oahu

With a wave of the wand ($10.99 at Target, tiara included) they were all elevated to royal status and set loose on the world as an imperial cabal, and have since busied themselves achieving global domination. Today, there is no little girl in the wired, industrial world who does not seek to display her allegiance to the pink- and purple-clad Disney dynasty.

Ehrenreich, 2007

Recently I was visiting a preschool to observe one of my early childhood teaching students. During the visit, two four-year-old girls began a conversation with me. It moved quickly from "Who are you?" to "Would you like to play with us?" I agreed and inquired about what they were playing. The response was one word, "Princesses." I then asked, "What is a princess?" Without hesitation, the same girl replied, "What Disney says."

As I reflected on the conversation over the next few days, I was disturbed by how these young children were creating what it means to be a girl in terms of a large corporation. This is not surprising as the marketing strategy for the Disney Princesses is targeted at girls as young as two years old (Strauss, 2004). In 2006, there were over 25,000 different princess-related merchandise, including clothing, available for purchasing, moving profits into the billions (Orenstein, 2006) (Figure 12.10).

After my experience with the preschoolers, I spent time online viewing Gymboree, a children's clothing site, looking at Halloween costumes for my daughter (at the time, she was about to turn one year old). The first costume I saw was a pumpkin princess, right next to a peacock princess. The trend initiated by Disney has moved beyond one corporation and is part of the young girl's clothing culture as being a pumpkin is left behind for the pumpkin princess. Observing the princess phenomenon in another company besides Disney brought up questions for me, as an early childhood educator and mother—How do the "princess" clothes of a specific marketing

Figure 12.10 Princess-related merchandise is a billion-dollar industry.

strategy determine how girls are constructed in society? How do these corporate constructions of "princess" influence girls in constructing their identity? It is with these questions in mind and an understanding that one of the foundational purposes of dress is to define identity (Reilly & Cosbey [Eds.], 2008) that I began my own journey exploring the presence of princess and its marketing impact on retail.

For six months, I visited several stores and their websites including (but not limited to) The Disney Store, Gymboree, The Gap, and Old Navy—all large clothing stores for young girls.

Original for this text.

I also collected various catalogs delivered to my home with a targeted audience of children. Observing both the clothing and marketing offered views on my questions as well as the space for other questions and observations to emerge.

Framing my exploration are ideas of philosopher Michel Foucault (1972, 1995), in particular surveillance, technologies of power, and ethics. From this perspective, "princess" clothing and marketing function as a means to impose homogeneity and conformity on what it means to be a girl in our current society. Further, Foucault's ideas imply as larger corporations perpetuate a discourse like "princess," children police themselves, ostracizing those who may not follow the "princess" ideals and terms or wear the clothing. I also consider how gender identities develop for young children in the presence of corporate marketing strategies. Construction of identity is dependent on the relationship between self and society (Reilly & Cosbey [Eds.], 2008), creating identity through experiences and navigation through the discourse presented and utilized (MacNaughton, 2000; MacNaugton & Hughes, 2001). Identities are "multiple and complex, and even changing" (Greishaber & Cannella, 2001, p. 13) and "are always historically produced through a range of discursive practices" (Weedon, 1997, p. 146). Further, as children come to understand and discuss gender, experiences along with culture and context contribute to their perceptions of gender (Iorio & Visweswariah, 2011; Wohlwend, 2007; Lind, 2005; Ochsner, 2000; Dyson, 1993: Heath, 1983; Yelland, 1998).

The Emergence of the Disney Princesses

Although the various princesses of Disney movies existed individually, in the year 2000, the princesses were joined together under the collective The Disney Princesses (Cinderella, Sleeping Beauty, Ariel, Belle, Snow White, Jasmine, Mulan, Pocahontas, and Tiana [added in 2009]). This marketing scheme, born from Andy Mooney, Chairman of Disney Consumer Products Worldwide, while attending a Disney on Ice performance in Phoe-

nix, Arizona, was a response to the children in attendance donning their own homemade princess costumes (Orenstein, 2011). To Mooney, the creation of a princess line was a huge branding prospect constructed with an ambiguous conception of princess. "Princess," Mooney admitted, "[has a] meaning [that is] so broadly constructed that it actually has no meaning" (Orenstein, 2011, p. 13). This princess frame allowed for those characters to become part of the princess line without actually being princesses as well as expanding the possibilities of product.

Disney released the first princess items without any market testing, profiting over $300 million within the first year of sales (Orenstein, 2011). Targeted at children two to six years old, The Disney Princesses offer over 25,000 pieces to choose from. By 2009, the revenue reached $4 billion (https://www.disneyconsumerproducts.com/Home/display.jsp?contentId=dcp_home_ourfranchises_disney_princess_us&forPrint=false&language=en&preview=false&imageShow=0&pressRoom=US&translationOf=null&region=0). "We simply gave girls what they wanted," Mooney said of the line's success, "although I don't think any of us grasped how much they wanted this" (Orenstein, 2011, p. 14).

Under the guise of presenting family-friendly entertainment, Disney markets their products to their consumers—children—and misses the chance to empower children by choosing first to make a profit; "behind the vocabulary of family fun and wholesome entertainment is the opportunity for teaching children that critical thinking and civic action in society are far less important to them than the role of passive consumers" (Giroux, 1999, p. 158). Targeting the young girl through programming and products, young girls are sold on The Disney Princesses (Kilbourne, 1999), framing childhood so it is harmonious with consumerism (Smoodin, 1994). Mooney's statement about giving girls what they want creates a facade of Disney as benign in their marketing choices and as responsive to their customer. The all-powerful Disney situates young girls as falsely empowered to have these "choices," and without knowing, young girls take on the passive consumer role. Inspiring critical thought or active democratic citizens is not a goal because thinkers and activists might question the choices of the company and lessen the profits.

Searching for Princesses

My journey into The Disney Princesses marketing scheme began by visiting The Disney Store in October 2010, focusing first on the Halloween costumes. The front windows were simply decorated with three headless mannequins each dressed in a princess costume—one Sleeping Beauty, one Belle (from *Beauty and the Beast*), and one Cinderella—and nothing else. The choices inside the store continued along the Princess line with other characters taking on princess themes—for example, Tinkerbell had a crown even though she is not a princess. Not only were costumes available, but an entire line of clothes depicting princesses and their storylines were present: skirts with rosebuds on the hem to pay homage to Belle, T-shirts with face pictures of princesses, and dresses with dropped waists and tulle skirts illustrating a princess across the bodice.

Although not deemed Disney-related costumes, other stores illustrated the strong influence of the Disney Princess marketing scheme on their own merchandise. On the Gymboree (children's clothing chain) website, girls' costumes included a Peacock Princess and Pumpkin Princess, both also available in the store. Target (large big-box chain store) featured a whole row of princess costumes and accessories (which are always present no matter what time of year) as well as The Disney Princesses and other princess costumes in the Halloween section of the store. Further, in the regular clothes department, infant and toddler T-shirts included a princess T-shirt for costume wear and licensed wear depicting The Disney Princesses. Costume Express catalog included the whole line of Disney Princess costumes (including infant sizes), a butterfly princess, kimono princess, pink kimono princess, Princess Wildflower (Native American princess), tower princess, pumpkin princess, and candy corn princess.

Continuing through the months after Halloween, I continued to visit stores, websites, and peruse catalogs. Princess seemed to be an ever-present theme. Gymboree had an entire line of everyday clothes focused on princesses entitled Castle Princess. The colors of the clothes included lavender, mint green, and white with the word *princess* written in script on several pieces including shoes, bibs, and onesies. One onesie claimed "kiss me" on the front with a frog wearing a crown, reminiscent of the frog prince story, while another onesie was flanked with a tutu and matching tulle sleeves.

Tutus seemed to be part of many stores lines of clothes. Gymboree has its own tutu shop with a plethora of choices including sparkle, striped, and ruffled-hem tutus. Leggings are also trimmed in tulle for a tutu-like feel for those girls wanting to wear pants. Even lines of clothing with non-related princess themes included a tutu skirt. For example, the Greek Isle Style line included a two-tiered blue sparkle tutu while the Burst of Spring line included a tutu resembling a strawberry. Upon a visit to The Gap (family clothing chain), tulle skirts punctuated one wall in a rainbow of colors. Old Navy (family clothing chain) had its own tutu bathing suit for the days princesses wanted to hit the water.

Other stores continued a princess theme. For example, the store at the local zoo displayed a Jungle Princess shirt. Carters (children's clothing store) added princess shirts to their line, heralding from the wall when I walked into their store. In a Land of Nod (children's furniture, toy, gear, and clothing chain) catalog, categories are presented as ways to label children. The princess category is described as "Hear ye! Hear ye! The Princess approaches. In preparation, we, her loyal subjects, have polished her crown, dispatched all local dragons, and assembled a collection of the girliest gifts from lands near and far." The child dressed in this section is wearing a tutu advertising offerings including a petal pusher tutu. For further ideas beyond the paper catalog, an actual website is offered—www.landofnod.com/princess.

Interestingly enough, as my search for princesses ended, I experienced a little déjà vu. I walked back into The Disney Store in March 2011 to witness another window of just princesses. Three headless mannequins back again—

Sleeping Beauty, Belle, and Cinderella—this time in princess nightgowns, fancy enough to wear at the ball, complete with drapes of chiffon, sparkles, and ribbons. Inside the store, I saw an organic shirt proclaiming, "Once a princess, always a princess," cotton princess dresses with mesh and ruffle tutu-like skirts, and princess swimsuits. The beginning and end of my short-term observation was punctuated with a plethora of princess as imagined by corporate decision-makers.

Clothing and Identity: Looking through the Theory Lens

The Disney Princesses have created a discourse, which manifests itself throughout the retail market. This discourse is steeped in capitalism, consumerism, and materialism, offering "an artifact of culture" (Apple & Christian-Smith, 1991; Aronowitz & Giroux, 1991) reflective of both the historical and present perspective on the society (Foucault, 1972). The ease of success in the marketplace (Orenstein, 2011) and development of a discourse positions The Disney Princesses in a place of power over people and sculpting society (Foucault, 1972). As young girls choose to wear a princess product, they are perpetuating the discourse and continuing to give power to a corporate conception of princess. This is evident as the children engage in playing princess and define princess as "what Disney says." Through this princess discourse, Disney has found a way to state what is normal and acceptable (Foucault, 1995; Gallagher, 1999). Other retailers continue to perpetuate this as normal when they also place princess items in their stores. As young girls dress in princess-themed items, there is an acceptance of corporations as systems of power, making decisions about what someone should wear. Disney's perpetuation of children's innocence through The Disney Princesses is an imposition on young girls' identities of what is right. At the same time, this choice aligns with the societal ideas of children as innocent (Grieshaber & Cannella, 2001) and continues to set a societal dichotomy of right

and wrong in terms of childhood identity. If society believes young girls as innocent is the right identity and Disney supports this belief, adults and peers engage in surveillance, judging those that do not follow the norm (Foucault, 1995) or, in this case, choose not to wear princess clothes.

Disney knows that its princess products sell. Consider the very simple window dressing schemes I observed on two occasions over a short period of time. Just three mannequins, headless, wearing princess products, placed all alone in the window. Essentially, the discourse speaks for itself. Here is how you speak princess, wear our products. The choice for these windows is like a public slap in the face reiterating Mooney's statement that the products are just giving girls what they want as well as implying to the consumer, "Why think? We have already given you the means to express being a princess." There is no need for imagination. Disney is kind enough to present the mannequins as headless so children can easily imagine themselves dressed in the presented garb. In considering other retailers' version of princesses, The Land of Nod offers an actual script for parents and children to consider when becoming a princess. If a young girl can be The Land of Nod princess, then The Land of Nod princess clothing is critical and ensures a sale for the company.

And how does all of this impact young girls' identities? Identities are formed through interactions with others (Grieshaber & Cannella [Eds.], 2001; MacNaughton, 2000, MacNaughton & Hughes, 2001). When young children interact with corporations' conceptions of princess, then the identity emerges as a mixture of the child and the corporation. Whether it is a Disney or Gymboree princess, a system based in profit is having some influence on how identity is shaped. What should be noted is that a variety of companies do carry princess-related products that may or may not emulate the Disney definition of princess. Could the differential frames of princess be a resistance to Disney's corporate definition of princess? Could Gymboree, The Gap, and The Land of Nod become sources of resistance for young girls? Or could their presence offer young girls a myriad of ways to consider princess? With several means of defining princess, young girls could be interacting with different perspectives as they shape their identities. But should princesses be the only way a young girl can consider her identity?

Even with possible resistance in mind, it should be noted that the presentations of princess are still through a capitalist and consumer lens. The choice for retailers to add princess to their clothing lines is probably not steeped in offering young girls different experiences to influence their identities. Rather, the purpose is to make money. The awareness of this purpose delineates a whole other question—Should retailers with the purpose of making money be an influence on young girls' identities? MacNaughton discusses how the interactions between children and other people can "protect or transform their identities" (MacNaughton, 2000, p. 28). Essentially, moneymaking corporations are providing the defining ideas of princess to young girls based in consumerism. Navigating the princess products alone, a young girl's interaction could delineate an identity based on consumption. For example, a girl chooses to purchase more princess products in order to ensure her own identity as a girl. Yet, it should be noted, the very presence of the corporate princess could be a site of critique. The active interaction between a child and an adult discussing the limitations and purposes of marketing like The Disney Princesses could empower a young girl to consider other marketing strategies with a critical lens. These types of experiences influence identity development in a completely different manner.

Young girls can define self as princess but at the same time can be defining self through consumption (as previously suggested in their allegiance to corporate-defined princesses). Engaging in the "Princess" culture could function as a symbol of success and social class. For example, a child clothed in The Disney Princesses could be symbolic of a family with enough money to afford the clothes as well as imply the ability to purchase the related entertainment like going to the movies, owning the DVD, or vacationing at Disney World. In this facet, The Disney Princesses influence family identity and possible social transformation of the family able to afford fun and leisure activity (Tricarico, 2008).

Throughout this discussion, I consider my own observations in terms of theory, exploring a postmodern perspective on identity. Yet, it is important to note how my interpretations are based on how I assume young girls are influenced by the corporate idea of princess. Children's voices are definitely missing from the conversation. Research about young girls' developing identities in conjunction with princess clothing which includes interviews with children is imperative to further understanding the impact of princess. This discussion should be a first step in many exploring the influence of marketing practices on young girls' identities.

And Her Identity Lived Happily Ever After?

The presence of princesses is part of the current young girl's environment. Walking into Nordstroms (department store), my daughter sees The Disney Princesses on a T-shirt. At sixteen months old, her reaction is to point and then move on to something else, but what happens when she wants to stay and look? Should a corporation's conception of princess be one of the experiences my daughter interacts with in order to form her own identity? She may not have a choice, as princesses in some form seem to be everywhere, from the zoo store to the department store. The choice may begin with me. Much like Orenstein (2011) suggests, my part is not about restricting my daughter's access to the world, but about empowering her so she "can thrive within it" (p. 191). As her mother, I am positioned to offer her many experiences to influence her identity development. So yes, she will see princess clothing, but I will be available to listen to her viewpoint, share my perspective, and interact with her beyond her initial "princess" experience.

Consider the experience with the preschoolers I share at the beginning of this essay. How might I have responded to these two young girls upon their statement of how Disney defines princess? My response could have included questions about why Disney gets to decide what a princess is or if there are other ways to consider a princess besides Disney's suggestion. I might have asked about who benefits each time they buy another piece of The Disney Princesses clothing or how they treat friends that do not follow the Disney Princess ideal in both clothing and defining princess. Maybe Disney has given us a way to help young girls begin to develop their critical thinking processes and civil action abilities as part of their identities or at least to begin to see all the possibilities a young girl may have—regardless of how she dresses.

References

Apple, M. & Christian-Smith, L. K. (1991). *The politics of the textbook*. New York: Routledge.

Aronowitz, S. & Giroux, H. A. (1991). *Postmodern education: Politics, culture, and social criticism*. Minneapolis: University of Minnesota Press.

Dyson, A. (1993). *Social worlds of children learning to write in an urban primary school*. New York: Teachers College Press.

Enhrenreich, B. (2007). The bonfire of the Disney Princess. *The Nation*, December 24. Retrieved from http://www.thenation.com/article/bonfire-disney-princesses.

Foucault, M. (1972). *The archeology of knowledge*. New York: Pantheon.

Foucault, M. (1995). *Discipline and punish: The birth of the prison*. New York: Vintage.

Gallagher, S. (1999). An exchange of gazes. In J. Kincheloe, S. Steinberg, & L. Villaverde (Eds.), *Rethinking intelligence* (pp. 69–84). New York: Routledge.

Giroux, H. (1999). *The mouse that roared: Disney and the end of innocence*. New York: Rowman & Littlefield.

Grieshaber, S. & Cannella, G. (2001). *Embracing identities in early childhood education: Diversity and possibilities*. New York: Teachers College Press.

Heath, S. B. (1983). *Ways with words: Language, life, and work in communities and classrooms*. New York: Cambridge University Press.

Iorio, J. & Visweswariah, H. (2011). Do daddies wear lipstick? And other child-teacher conversations exploring constructions of gender. In T. Jacobson (Ed.), *Gender in early childhood*. St. Paul, MN: Red Leaf Press.

Kilbourne, J. (1999). *Deadly persuasion*. New York: Free Press.

Lind, U. (2005). Identity and power, "meaning," gender and age: Children's creative work as a signifying practice. *Contemporary Issues in Early Childhood* 6(3): 256–68.

MacNaughton, G. (2000). *Rethinking gender in early childhood education*. Thousand Oakes: Paul Chapman Publishing, Ltd.

MacNaughton, G. & Hughes, P. (2001). Fractured or manufactured: Gendered identities and culture in the early years. In S. Grieshaber & G. Cannella (Eds.), *Embracing identities in early childhood education: Diversity and possibilities* (pp. 114–132). New York: Teachers College Press.

Ochsner, M. (2000). Gendered make-up. *Contemporary Issues in Early Childhood* 6(2): 209–13.

Orenstein, P. (2006, July 24). What's Wrong with Cinderella? *New York Times*. Retrieved from www.NYTimes.com.

Orenstein, P. (2011). *Cinderella ate my daughter: Dispatches from the front lines of the new girlie-girl culture*. New York: Harper.

Reilly, A. & Cosbey, S. (Eds.) (2008). *Men's fashion reader*. New York: Fairchild Books.

Smoodin, E. (1994). *Disney discourse: Producing the magic kingdom*. New York: Routledge.

Strauss, G. (2004, March 2). Princesses Rule the Hearts of Little Girls. *USA Today*. Retrieved from www.USAToday.com.

Tricarico, D. (2008). Dressing up Italian Americans for the youth spectacle: What difference does a guido perform? In A. Reilly & S. Cosbey (Eds.), *Men's fashion reader* (pp. 265–278). New York: Fairchild.

Weedon, C. (1997). *Feminist practice and poststructuralist theory*. Oxford: Basil Blackwell.

Wolhwend, K. (2007). Friendship meeting or blocking circle? Identities in the laminated spaced of playground conflict. *Contemporary Issues in Early Childhood* 8 (1): 73–88.

Yelland, N. (Ed.) (1998). *Gender in early childhood*. New York: Routledge.

Discussion Questions

1. How might a parent help his or her daughter to reject the role of a passive consumer and gravitate toward critical thinking and active democratic citizenship?

2. Explain the meaning of the phrase "Corporate princess could be a site of critique between parent and child."

3. How does Stone's (1965) ubiquitous mother and investiture through child's dress fit with Iorio's reading?

4. How can the "girlie-girl" look be contested while wearing a princess costume?

MUCH MORE THAN PLASTIC: REFLECTIONS ON BUILDING *STAR WARS* STORMTROOPER ARMOR

Eirik Saethre
University of Hawai`i at Mānoa

For many *Star Wars* aficionados, collecting memorabilia is an important part of fandom. Not content with purchasing commonly available merchandise, some fans choose to transform themselves into characters from the movies through dress. While a number of costuming organizations exist, the 501st Legion: Vader's First is the largest, with over 5,000 members and garrisons in 40 countries. To qualify for entry, individuals must accurately replicate "villain" costumes, such as Stormtroopers, Bounty Hunters, Sith Lords, AT-AT Drivers, Biker Scouts, Sandtroopers, Clonetroopers, and others. Appearing in costume at conventions and events, members "troop" with their garrison, often posing for photos. (See Figure 12.8 on page 480.) Although troopers are assigned a designation number when they enter the 501st, the goal of the 501st is to encourage costume ownership, not role play. While other researchers have examined the mythic and religious undercurrents in *Star Wars* and its fandom (Geraghty, 2005; Jindra, 1994), I wish to explore the ways in which costuming has become an important marker of identity.

Several months ago, I began the process of obtaining my own costume in the hopes of joining the ranks of the 501st. Like many others, I chose the classic white Stormtrooper attire from the initial movie trilogy (Episodes IV–VI). However, I quickly discovered that joining the 501st was far more complex than I had at first thought. To achieve the "screen accuracy" required for entry, members were required to learn important costume details and meticulously assemble their armor to meet specific guidelines. Sometimes lasting months, this process was taken very seriously. During a heated debate on the First Imperial Stormtrooper Division forum, one poster commented, "It's just plastic." Summing up the fervor of many members, the reply was, "It's much more than plastic to me, my friend." As work on my own suit progressed, I realized that this statement was very true.

Plastic armor gains importance because it is a meaningful tool through which identity is articulated. Clothing can be a powerful symbol that creates and reinforces membership in social communities (McCracken, 1990). Examples include white wedding dresses or red *isicholo* hats act to signify a woman's status in American or Zulu society. In the realm of science fiction and fantasy, clothing and other merchandise can also signal membership in a fan community (Stevens, 2010). Dressing like anime characters, *Star Trek* captains, or *Star Wars* villains reflects social identities. Before I began to build my Stormtrooper armor, I assumed that costuming was simply one way in which fandom was commodified and communicated. In other words, fans of the *Star Wars* films bought costumes to express their admiration of the films. While this is certainly the case, I discovered that the situation was more complex. Costuming was not just an expression of a preexisting identity; acquiring and building Stormtrooper armor engendered new ways of perceiving the films as well as other fans. While the costume was the focal point for members of the 501st, the process of assembling white plastic armor was itself transformative.

The Quest for Screen Accuracy

One of the first film franchises to capitalize on merchandising, *Star Wars* spawned a plethora of products. Growing up in the 1970s, *Star Wars*,

---

Original for this text.

and its merchandise, was an integral part of my childhood. Although I only saw each film a few times in theaters, every day after school I reenacted scenes and made up new ones using my action figures. My Christmas memories include unwrapping presents containing miniature versions of X-Wing Fighters and Luke Skywalker. Thirty years later, I remember the movies fondly but have not watched them in years. I have never attended a science fiction convention and although many adults continue to collect action figures, I am not one of them. Nevertheless, my interest in *Star Wars* was reawakened when I viewed a video of shiny white Stormtroopers marching in a parade. I was enthralled. The Stormtroopers were part of the 501st Legion, whose website states, "Some fans are content to collect action figures . . . other fans want to *be* action figures." Deciding that I was in the latter category, I began a quest to acquire my own Stormtrooper armor.

After searching the Internet for "Stormtrooper costume," one suit appeared repeatedly: Rubies Supreme Edition Stormtrooper Costume. Sold on sites such as eBay and Amazon, the suits ranged in price from $700 to $1,200. The costume was easily obtainable, preassembled, and licensed by Lucasfilm Limited. I thought that I had found my armor. However, I soon learned that it was not acceptable for membership into the 501st. Message board postings, such as on TheForce.net, repeatedly disparaged the Rubies armor: "To the average person who knows nothing about *Star Wars* costuming, they'd think it was awesome. To costumers/people in the 501st: It was atrocious." Another poster commented, "The thing is—those of us who have spent lots of time studying the movie costumes can spot the inaccuracies a mile away. However, the more casual fan or costumer may well miss these things and snap these 'replicas' right up." I was certainly one of the "casual" fans. Reading posts about the armor, I was struck by the many details that I had not previously considered. Describing the inaccuracies in the Rubies helmet, one poster noted, "A one-piece cast it has no assembly extras . . . mic tips rubber strips. The mouth frown is way too steep and indented too much on either side of the nose ridge. The bubble lenses are too large and

mounted outside of the helmet instead of inside like the correct way." I realized that if I were to join the 501st, I would need to learn a great deal more about armor than I had at first thought.

Over the next several weeks, I spent hours combing through websites, message boards, and blogs. One phrase that appeared repeatedly was "screen accuracy." To gain entry into the 501st, prospective members were expected to meticulously emulate the attire worn in the films. Strict costuming guidelines were laid out on the 501st website. The helmet requirements are as follows:

- Traps (trapezoids on dome of helmet) and tears (area beneath the corners of eye lenses) are gray.
- Rear traps and tears have vertical black lines.
- Lenses are a flat green sufficiently dark enough to obscure the costumer's eyes.
- The gray "ear" bars have three of four bumps, with a black outline. The bumps may or may not be painted.
- Frown is painted gray and does not leave the teeth area. Eight total teeth on the frown are cut out.
- Tube stripes are medium blue, numbering between 9 and 15 per side with the curve bends extending backwards.
- Vocoder (vertically ribbed chin detail) is painted black.
- Aerators (cylinders on either side of the vocoder) are black.
- Tears, traps, and tube stripes may be hand painted, decals, or decals that replicate hand painting.

This extensive and detailed list was not provided by Lucasfilm Limited or the original makers of the Stormtrooper armor; it was devised by fans methodically studying the films. As I gained a greater knowledge of screen accuracy, I began to see the errors in the Rubies suit. What had at first seemed to be an ideal costume now looked flawed.

I discovered that the best method of ensuring screen accuracy and acceptance into the 501st was to build the armor myself. While a few troopers sculpt their own armor, most assemble a kit of precast plastic parts. When choosing one of the approximately seven kits currently on the market, factors such as material, cost, size, and degree of screen accuracy are carefully considered. All kits are made from either Acrylonitrile Butadiene Styrene (ABS) or High Impact Polystyrene (HIPS). Although HIPS is generally cheaper than ABS and easier to trim, it is also less durable and requires painting to achieve a glossy finish. As each kit is produced in a single size, another important concern is fit. While some kits are designed for taller troopers, others are better suited for shorter individuals. Finally, troopers must decide whether they want armor with some components made from casts of an actual suit worn in the movies (TE-derived) or those created by enthusiasts (fan sculpts). Although both are considered acceptable for entry into the 501st, debates continue to rage concerning which is the most "screen accurate." Supporters of TE-derived armor assert that it is the most precise because its ancestry can be traced to a screen-used suit. Opponents counter by noting that the original suit was based on later designs and incomplete, requiring manufacturers to substitute some parts and modify others. Consequently, it is up to each individual to decide which kit is "the best."

After conducting a great deal of research and weighing my many options, I finally chose a kit. However, kits are not easily obtainable, in part because they are unlicensed. As Stormtroopers are registered trademarks of Lucasfilm Limited, anyone producing and selling unauthorized armor is vulnerable to legal action. To avoid provoking a lawsuit, kit manufacturers are careful to disguise their identities and refrain from advertising their products. While a number of vendors sell licensed Rubies armor online, it is not possible to order any of the seven kits through a website.[1] Even message boards dedicated to discussing the kits are circumspect. When referring to manufacturers, initials are used. In addition, prices are never publically revealed. One of the most comprehensive sources of information, the First Imperial Stormtrooper Detachment website, prohibits threads asking "where do I buy armor." However, anyone conducting careful research will eventually locate or receive the e-mail addresses of armor producers. My own investigations unearthed the address that I needed and only after contacting the manufacturer did I learn the price.

After waiting five months for my armor to be cast, I received a box containing thirty pieces of white plastic. There was no packing slip; there were no instructions. To assemble the armor correctly, I would once again have to rely on the Internet, 501st members, and my own research abilities. The first decision that I had to make was which type of Stormtrooper suit I would be constructing. In each of the original three movies, Stormtrooper armor displayed slight, but important, variations. For instance, in *A New Hope* (ANH) two separate helmet styles were used, which are now labeled stunt and hero. The former was the generic helmet with nine "teeth" in the frown, while the latter—worn by Luke Skywalker and Han Solo—possessed a smaller frown of only seven "teeth." ANH Stormtroopers wore trapezoidal-shaped hand plates, while those in the *Empire Strikes Back* (ESB) and *Return of the Jedi* (ROTJ) were clam shaped. Whereas the butt and kidney plates were separated in *ANH*, they were joined in *ROTJ*. For acceptance into the 501st, my armor would need to be tailored specifically to one of four standards: *ANH* Stunt, *ANH* Hero, *ESB*, or *ROTJ*. Like most, I chose an *ANH* Stunt configuration.

Before I began trimming, fitting, and gluing my suit together, I was faced with one final decision. While the 501st possesses strict entry requirements, prospective members often hope to exceed these guidelines. Building armor with the highest degree of screen accuracy is a goal for many. Consequently, the 501st offers two additional levels of membership: Expert Infantryman and Centurion. For entry into the former, helmets must meet the following additional requirements:

- Ears should have three screws used per side, one above and below the ear bar and one at the base of the helmet.
- Ear bars should have four bumps only, not three.
- Correct "hovi mic" aerator tips.

The Centurion level necessitates an even greater awareness of screen accuracy, meeting previous guidelines as well as:

- Ear bars should have only one or two bumps painted in black.
- Neck trim should be of an s-type profile rather than a u-type profile.
- Tears/traps should be hand painted or use decals that emulate hand painting.
- FX, MRCE and ANHv2 helmets are not allowed.

Wanting to achieve the maximum level of accuracy, I decided to build my kit to Centurion standards. Not long after I made this resolution, I was struck by how much the process of locating, purchasing, and constructing armor had altered my initial goal. When I first began, I would have been content to own a Rubies suit. I did not know or care about screen accuracy. However, that had changed. The act of costuming had exerted a profound influence on my own perceptions and identity.

Constructing Armor, Constructing Identity

When I initially decided to join the 501st, I assumed that it would be akin to purchasing a very large action figure. But Stormtrooper armor, I discovered, was not simply a commodity that people bought to express their fandom. While membership is ostensibly linked to merchandise, successfully locating a manufacturer and correctly assembling armor entails possessing detailed and specialized knowledge. Although informed by the *Star Wars* movies, these standards are established and reinforced through consensus. Unlike buying an action figure, building armor requires initiation into a community. Consequently, I believe that assembling Stormtrooper armor can be best understood as a rite of passage, a ritual marking a transition from one social status to another. Rituals embody "standards of perfection," invoking common symbols and conventions that bind groups together (Luhrmann, 1989, 38). Realizing

the importance of symbols in maintaining social relations, Durkheim (2008) asserted that ritual was a primary tool to construct and preserve social worlds. Consequently, anthropologists contend that the symbolic construction of community occurs through ritual and other important social acts (Cohen 1985). One of these acts is the creation of clothing. Hendrickson (1995) and Zorn (2004) examine how the process of weaving expresses identity while imbuing objects with signification. Through the adoption of clothing styles and the physical act of making personal adornment, notions of who we are can be created and conveyed (Hanson 2004, Stone 1962).

For members of the 501st, screen accuracy was the primary symbolic tool through which identity was constructed and maintained. Much more than a requirement for acceptance into the legion, screen accuracy was the nexus around which knowledge, meaning, and identity was structured. Members not only strove to obtain Expert Infantryman and Centurion rankings, they hoped to exceed them. The "most screen accurate" kit was constantly debated on the First Imperial Stormtrooper Division forum. Debate occurred because the criteria for screen accuracy were open to a degree of interpretation and revision. There was no single inflexible catalogue of screen accuracy. Even the original films were not completely "accurate": different helmet styles were used in the same scene, hand plates did not match, and parts were switched. A running joke on the forum is that mismatched components and scuffed armor are, in fact, screen accurate. Consequently, I believe that screen accuracy is simultaneously a standard, a socially negotiated construct, and a symbol of difference. Acting as a focal point for community membership, screen accuracy is a powerful expression of belonging. It is through the act of belonging that identity is created and reinforced.

In constructing a kit, prospective members also construct a boundary between themselves and the "average person" or "casual fan," who are portrayed as knowing little or nothing about screen accuracy. Membership is contingent upon replacing mundane notions of Stormtroopers with detailed knowledge of suit design. Details that might appear tedious to outsiders become extremely meaningful to troopers. To illustrate this point, consider the helmet requirements that I enumerated above. No doubt many readers found these lists confusing and perhaps even monotonous. This was certainly my initial reaction. But as my interest in, and knowledge of, armor increased, I commenced the transition from mundane novice to experienced trooper. I began reading the lists of requirements with great interest and understanding. The shift in status from "casual fan" to "trooper" is only completed once a suit is successfully finished and membership in the 501st is achieved.

Identity is tied to knowledge, which is learned and demonstrated, in part, through the acquisition and use of a specialized language. Anthropologists have documented the important role that innovative speech plays in socially constructing communities, including British witches (Luhrmann 1989), fundamentalist Baptists (Harding 1987), and doctors (Good and Good 1993). Examining the creation of medical identity, Good and Good (1993, 97–98) note, "Learning the language of medicine consists not of learning new words for the commonsense world, but the construction of a new world altogether." A similar shift occurs when constructing Stormtrooper armor. I now comfortably discuss the clarity of "pulls" (the process of initially forming plastic), post questions concerning "returns" (a technique of bending plastic to make it appear thicker), and am familiar with a host of acronyms including: ANH, ESB, ROTJ, HIPS, ABS, EIB, FISD, MRCE, AP, TE2, TM, and FX. Appearing confusing or nonsensical to the casual observer, this language is immediately intelligible to 501st members and seamlessly incorporated into their conversations. But acronyms and terminologies are not simply jargon that is learned and repeated. Novel modes of expression engender novel techniques of viewing the world. After reading several posts about "returns," I acquired a new term and a new object of focus when examining movie stills of Stormtroopers. My perceptions were altered as a result of attaining the unique descriptive language of screen accuracy. In adopting a new language, a new way of seeing,

and new symbols, the process of building armor also bestows a new identity.

While a complete screen-accurate costume is ostensibly the goal, it is actually the process of obtaining and assembling a kit that matters most. After Museum Replicas displayed a prototype of its new line of licensed Stormtrooper armor, members of the 501st were quick to criticize its inaccuracies. However, some expressed relief that despite the release of this new fully assembled suit, achieving screen accuracy still required building armor from a kit. One poster wrote:

> I must admit, I'm actually a bit **relieved** to see this suit **NOT** meet the standard of 501st members! :) The integrity of this hobby lies in the effort we all put into the endless research, discovery and building. The fun and reward comes from recognizing the subtlety of movie-accurate details and achieving an overall better understanding and respect for the prop/costume making process as an art! . . .

In reply, another commented:

> I agree 100%. I just spent 3 months working on my build and worked on every detail. If they put out an accurate suit that someone with money could buy and join the 501st in the same weekend, I would not be happy at all. Each one of our builds has our personality, blood and sweat all over them and I wouldn't have it any other way.

A costume is not simply a commodity; it is a social product. For members of the 501st, Stormtrooper armor is a tangible representation of months of research, hard work, and conversations with others. While wearing costumes expresses identity, so does making them. Similar to weaving a traditional textile, the value of armor is firmly embedded in the process and experience of its creation. Consequently, I believe that a set of screen-accurate armor—like many other handcrafted costumes—embodies specialized knowledge, identity, and community. It is "much more than plastic."

References

Cohen, A. P. (1985). *Symbolic Construction of Community*. New York: Routledge.

Durkheim, E. (2008). *The Elementary Forms of Religious Life* (C. Cosman, Trans.). Oxford: Oxford University Press.

Geraghty, L. (2005). Creating and Comparing Myth in Twentieth-Century Science Fiction: Star Trek and Star Wars. *Literature Film Quarterly*, 33(3), 191–200.

Good, B., & Good, M.-J. D. (1993). "Learning Medicine": The Constructing of Medical Knowledge at Harvard Medical School. In S. Lindenbaum & M. Lock (Eds.), *Knowledge, Power, and Practice: The Anthropology of Medicine and Everyday Life* (pp. 81–107). Berkeley: University of California Press.

Harding, S. (1987). Convicted by the Holy Spirit: The Rhetoric of Fundamental Baptist Conversion. *American Ethnologist*, 14(1), 167–181.

Hansen, K. T. (2004). The World in Dress: Anthropological Perspectives on Clothing, Fashion, and Culture. *Annual Review of Anthropology*, 33, 369–392.

Hendrickson, C. (1995). *Weaving Identities: Construction of Dress and Self in a Highland Guatemala Town*. Austin: University of Texas Press.

Jindra, M. (1994). Star Trek Fandom as a Religious Phenomenon. *Sociology of Religion*, 55(1), 27–51.

Luhrmann, T. (1989). *Persuasions of the Witch's Craft: Ritual Magic in Contemporary England*. Cambridge, Mass.: Harvard University Press.

McCracken, G. D. (1990). *Culture and Consumption: New Approaches to the Symbolic Character of Consumer Goods and Activities*. Bloomington: Indiana University Press.

Stevens, C. S. (2010). You Are What You Buy: Postmodern Consumption and Fandom of Japanese Popular Culture. *Japanese Studies*, 30(2), 199–214.

Stone, G. P. (1962). Appearance and the Self. In A. Rose (Ed.), *Human Behavior and Social Processes: An Interactionist Approach* (pp. 86–118). Boston: Houghton Mifflin.

Zorn, E. (2004). *Weaving a Future: Tourism, Cloth, and Culture on an Andean Island*. Iowa City: University of Iowa Press.

Endnote

1. Used armor is sold on the First Imperial Stormtrooper Division website and occasionally on eBay.

Discussion Questions

1. What theories did the author use to explain his experience? Describe each theory and how it was used in the reading.

2. Give other examples of rites of passage that are connected to dress.

3. Can you relate to Saethre's experience? Have you ever started a project only to watch your expectations rise with each level of learning?

12.5

COSTUMING THE IMAGINATION: ORIGINS OF ANIME AND MANGA COSPLAY

Theresa Winge
Michigan State University

All over the world, cosplay fans gather at conventions and parties to share their appreciation of and affection for anime and manga (McCarthy 1993; Napier 2001; Poitras 2001). These fans, who also refer to themselves as *otaku*,[1] wear detailed makeup and elaborate costumes modeled after their favorite anime, manga, and related video game characters (Poitras 2001; Richie 2003). Cosplayers spend immeasurable monies and hours constructing or purchasing costumes, learning signature poses and dialogue, and performing at conventions and parties, as they transform themselves from "real world" identities into chosen (fictional) characters. This is the essence of cosplay, or kosupure (Aoayama and Cahill 2003; Richie 2003).

The term *cosplay* combines costume and play (or role-play). Cosplay also refers to the activities, such as masquerades, karaoke, and posing for pictures with other otaku, that are associated with dressing and acting like anime, manga, and video game characters (Macias and Machiyama 2004; Poitras 2001). While the term *cosplay* encompasses various types of costumed role-playing, such as science fiction, fantasy, horror, mythology, fetish, and so forth, this chapter focuses only on Japanese and North American cosplay related to anime, manga, and video games.

My objective here is to provide the reader with an understanding of anime and manga cosplay, cosplayers, and their social structures. First, I explore the origin stories of cosplay to establish contributions from both Japan and North America. Next, I discuss the distinguishing characteristics of Japanese and North American cosplay to determine the similarities and differences between the two cultural settings. I contextualize four cosplay elements: (I) anime and manga cosplayers, (2) social settings, (3) character and role-playing, and (4) dress,[2] which includes clothing or costumes, makeup, wigs or hairstyles, jewelry, and accessories. Last, I offer an introduction to the anime and manga cosplay social structures (i.e., interactions, environments, and experiences) in order to provide the reader with an awareness of the complexities and dynamics of the cosplay world.

Origin Stories of Cosplay

The few sources that discuss the origins of cosplay are primarily found on Web sites, online publications, and weblogs. Constructed and maintained by anime and manga fans, these sources communicate information about anime and manga (most with a personal bias). Therefore, it is not surprising that the specific origins of anime and manga cosplay are highly debated topics among anime and manga *otaku* (Hlozek 2004). One side speculates that cosplay began in North America, during the 1960s, when people dressed as and role-played their favorite science fiction and fantasy characters, such as Spock from *Star Trek* and Robin from *Batman* (Bruno 2002a). This type of costumed role-playing (not yet called cosplay) spanned a variety of genres and may have inspired Japanese anime and manga fans to dress as their favorite characters. On the other side of the debate are those who speculate that cosplay was imported from Japan, coming to North America with the formations of anime and manga fan clubs (Bruno 2002a; Ledoux and Ranney 1997).

The origin story that appears to have the most evidence to support it actually blends the Japanese and North American contributions. In 1984 Takahashi Nobuyuki (known in the United States as "Nov Takahashi"), founder of and writer for Studio Hard, an anime publishing company, attended World-Con, a science fiction convention, in Los Angeles (Bruno 2002a; Hlozek 2004). He was impressed with the costumed science fiction and fantasy fans whom he saw, especially those competing in the masquerade (Bruno 2002a). Consequently, when he returned to Japan and wrote about his experiences at the convention, he focused on the costumed fans and the masquerade. Moreover, Takahashi encouraged his Japanese readers to incorporate costumes into their anime and manga conventions (Bruno 2002a).

Takahashi was unable to use the word *masquerade* because this word translated into Japanese means "an aristocratic costume party," which is drastically different from the costume competitions seen at conventions (Bruno 2002a). Instead, he created the phrase *costume play*, which was eventually shortened to *kosupure*, or *cosplay* (Bruno 2002a). As a result, Takahashi added two new words to the subculture and pop culture lexicon: *cosplay* and *cosplayer*.

In 1980, at the San Diego, California, Comic-Con, several fans dressed as anime and manga characters in the masquerade (Ledoux and Ranney 1997). It was not long before anime and manga *otaku* were donning cosplay dress to attend Japanese conventions (Bruno 2002a). During the 1980s, there was a growing demand for Japanese anime (and manga) imports (Drazen 2003), and an increasing number of otaku attended North

American science fiction and fantasy conventions (Hlozek 2004; Poitras 2001). As a result, these types of North American conventions began to include anime- and manga-focused activities, such as panels, guest speakers, anime video rooms, and masquerades (i.e., organized costumed performances). In time, *otaku* organized conventions expressly for fans of anime, manga, and related media. Overall, North American and Japanese cosplay have many commonalities, such as a dedicated fan base and the use of costumes. They also have distinguishing characteristics, such as variations within masquerade competitions, appropriate locations for wearing cosplay dress, and cosplay markets.

Context of Cosplay

The context of anime and manga cosplay is a combination of the presence of basic components and related interactions between those components. The four basic components are anime and manga cosplayer, social settings, (fictional) character and role-playing, and dress (e.g., hair, costume, makeup, and accessories, including weapons). Furthermore, these components facilitate complex interactions between people (e.g., cosplayers, spectators, masquerade judges, etc.), environments (e.g., personal, private, public, and virtual), and fantasy (e.g., imagination, fictional characters, etc.). The following four sections are an overview of the basic components and complex interactions that create the context of cosplay.

Anime and Manga Cosplayer

Anime and manga cosplayers may be any age, gender, and ethnicity. They have varied educational backgrounds, occupations, disposable incomes, and resources. Essentially, an anime or manga cosplayer can be almost anyone who expresses his or her fandom and passion for a character by dressing and acting similarly to that character. Since the exact cosplay demographics are currently unknown, this is an area in need of further research.

A cosplayer researches and studies an already existing anime or manga character with a keen eye for detail, in order to create a cosplay character. The interpretation usually takes shape by reading or watching the chosen character within its given medium (i.e., manga, anime, or video game). The level of research and study is ultimately guided by the cosplayer's objectives (e.g., masquerade participation, socializing, etc.).

Cosplayers exist at various places along a cosplay continuum, which is based on their level of commitment. At one end are cosplayers content with dressing (e.g., wig, makeup, and costume) as their chosen character and attending conventions and events for socializing and having fun. At the other end are those cosplayers obsessed with a given character, re-creating that character with meticulous attention to detail and performing as that character as often as time and money allow. Between these extremes, there are cosplayers who research, study, and practice their characters and participate in cosplay events, such as masquerade and karaoke. Regardless of his or her place on the cosplay continuum, each cosplayer has an extraordinary level of dedication and commitment to the depiction of a chosen character, based on individual objectives that may include, but are not limited to, the following criteria: humor, accurate depiction, and casual participation.

Social Settings

Cosplay is primarily a social activity associated with various activities and conventions, where cosplayers gather to share their passions for anime and manga characters (Aoyama and Cahill 2003). The cosplay social settings may include, but are not limited to, the following: masquerades (i.e., character-based costume or performance competitions), photograph sessions, themed parties, karaoke, club meetings, and conventions. While the social settings for cosplay may vary greatly, conventions are often the primary space where large numbers of cosplayers gather, socialize, and perform.

Conventions are held at all times of the year, around the world, for fans of science fiction, fantasy, horror, anime, manga, and the like to share their interests and passions with like-minded individuals (Poitras 2001). The dedicated cosplayer may attend conventions on the average of one a month. As a result, many science fiction and fantasy conventions include a variety of activities, such as discussion panels, skits, film screenings, and masquerades specifically aimed at anime and manga *otaku*.

The convention activity that attracts the most interest from *otaku*, especially cosplayers, is the masquerade. Cosplayers compete in masquerades by posing or acting in skits relevant to their characters. At science fiction and fantasy conventions, anime and manga cosplayers compete against various genres of cosplayers. Despite slight variations between each masquerade, participants are generally judged on three main criteria: accuracy of the costume's appearance to the actual character; construction and details of the cosplay dress; and entertainment value of the skit and/or accuracy to the character.

Spectators play an important role in the social settings of cosplay. In fact, it could be argued that cosplay events, especially the masquerade, would be pointless if it were not for the spectators, even if they are composed of friends and other cosplayers. Spectators use applause, verbal cues, and laughter to encourage cosplayers to perform and interact.

Furthermore, the cosplay social settings exist beyond the stage of a masquerade. Cosplayers interact with each other, often role-playing their chosen characters while participating in hallway conversations, karaoke parties, and online chat rooms. These social settings take any shape or form desired by cosplayers. Often the settings extend beyond tangible spaces, into virtual spaces, such as Web sites, weblogs, and online journals (Poitras 2001). Cosplayers utilize Web sites to register and plan activities for conventions, as well as to promote and communicate about their fandom for anime and manga cosplay. They also use weblogs and online journals to confide in others, express opinions, and argue about the finer details of cosplay. Additionally, traditional print media, such as the magazines *Animerica* and *Newtype*, feature several pages per issue of cosplay photographs from recent conventions.

Character and Role-playing

An *otaku* chooses an anime, manga, or video game character to cosplay based on personal cri-

teria. A resourceful cosplayer has few limitations in character choice, beyond his or her imagination. The pool of characters to choose from is vast, including characters from anime feature movies and serials, manga single image and series, and related video games. Some cosplay characters are featured in all three media, such as Dragon Ball Z and Fist of the North Star. In fact, there are so many characters to choose from that they have been informally classified into subgenres.

Among these subgenre are mecha, cyborg, furry, and Lolita (Figures 12.11a and b). Mechas (short for "mechanicals") are giant robot characters, often piloted or operated by humans (Napier 2001). Some examples of mecha characters are Gundam Wing Zero (Gundam Wing television series, 1995–96) and EVA units (Neon Genesis Evangelion television series, 1995–96). Cyborgs are part machine and part human, such as Major Kusanagi Motoko (Ghost in the Shell, 1995) and the Knight Sabers (Bubblegum Crisis, 1987–91). Furries are characters that have "fur," and the cosplay costumes for them are usually created from faux fur. Some examples are Totoro, a giant, gray catlike creature (My Neighbor Totoro, 1988) and Ryo-ohki (an alternate romanization of Ryôôki), a cute, furry cabbit (cat-rabbit) (Tenchi muyô yôôki series, 2000, known by the alternate romanization Tenchi Muyô Ryo-ohki in the United States). A Lolita character attempts to convey a kawaii image, which is young, childlike, and cute (Aoyama and Cahill 2003; Schodt 1996). The character may don a baby-doll dress trimmed with layers of lace, kneesocks, and sometimes carry a stuffed animal or a parasol. A common anime reference for the Lolita character is the *Wonder Kids' Lolita Anime* I: *Yuki no kurenai keshô* and *Shôjo bara kei* (1984); however, this character has an earlier reference in Vladimir Nabokov's *Lolita* (1955). Both of these references for the Lolita character define and emphasize its sexualized imagery; however, not all Lolita cosplayers intend to communicate that image.

Certain anime and manga characters are more popular than others, which results in trends within cosplay. The popularity of anime and manga characters is most evident by the numerous observations of cosplayers dressed as the same

Figure 12.11 Gothic Lolita (a) and Rainbow Brite Lolita (b) costumes designed and constructed by Erin Hamburg, 2005, Cedar Falls, Iowa.

character at a convention. For example, in the September 2003 issue of *Newtype*, there is a photograph of multiple depictions of Inuyasha (i.e., a half dog-demon and half human male, with silver or black hair and dog ears, wearing a red kimono-style garment with a sword) at the Anime Expo convention in Anaheim, California. Another example is the frequent sightings of Lolita characters at anime and manga conventions. The Lolita genre is so popular that there are numerous Web sites, costume shops, and publications dedicated to it.

An additional cosplay character type is known as "crossplay" (Hlozek 2004). Crossplay is where a cosplayer employs gender reversal (i.e., a female who dresses as a male character or vice versa). Depending on the cosplayer's objectives, the crossplay may portray the opposite gender with accuracy or it may have humorous intentions within its display (e.g., dress, role-playing, etc.). For example, at CONvergence 2004 (a science fiction and fantasy convention held in Bloomington, Minnesota) there were several males dressed

as each of the Sailor Moon Scouts (teenage heroines who assist Sailor Moon in her endeavors to save the world from evil), and a young woman was dressed as Tuxedo Mask (the young hero who often assists Sailor Moon and the Scouts in their quest). In this example, crossplay was utilized for humorous effect and social levity. These Scouts had deep voices and visible chest and leg hair, along with five o'clock shadows, and this Tuxedo Mask had a high-pitched voice and curvaceous silhouette. Moreover, the group was continuously making gender-related puns and jokes aimed at further identifying and establishing their gender role reversals.

Crossplay among cosplayers is not unusual, considering the many gender reversals, confusions, and ambiguities within anime and manga. For example, Oscar Francois de Jarjayes, from the *Rose of Versailles* (1972–74), was raised as a male; however, she is actually a female. The story centers on Oscar's ambiguity and duality. Another example is the Three Lights from *Sailor Moon*. In the manga, the Three Lights females pose as human males in a rock band, but in the anime they transform from male pop stars into female sailor *senshi*-Sailor Starlights.

The cosplayer relies on dress and role-playing to display a given character. Cosplay role-playing is the ability to dress, walk, talk, and act similarly to the chosen anime or manga character in order to portray a character in a desired fashion. Role-playing is an essential skill for a cosplayer, regardless if he or she is accurate to a character, creating a parody, or just having fun. Role-playing a character is greatly aided by cosplay dress.

Dress

Cosplay dress includes all body modifications and supplements, such as hair, makeup, costume, and accessories, including wands, staffs, and swords. This dress is often referred to as a "costume"; however, cosplay dress goes well beyond a simple costume. Cosplay dress may be the most important tool the cosplayer has to nonverbally communicate his or her chosen character and character traits. This dress functions as character identification and provides a basis for role-playing and interactions with other cosplayers. Cosplay dress also enables cosplayers to move from their actual identities to their chosen cosplay characters, and sometimes back again.

For example, "Sailor Bubba," a bearded male cosplayer (and crossplayer) dressed as Sailor Moon (i.e., manga and anime teenage, female heroine with magical powers), speaks with a deep voice, walks with a gait natural to a 6-foot-tall, 250-pound man, and has dark black chest hair poking out of the top of his schoolgirl uniform. Still, anime and manga cosplayers recognize the dress and accept his change in personality (and gender) when a man in a tuxedo and top hat, the costume for Tuxedo Mask, enters the room. Suddenly it is a cosplay version of Sailor Moon and Tuxedo Mask having a conversation about saving the world (with not-so-subtle references to a room party as the scene for the next battle with a villain called "Mr. Jagermeister").[3]

Each cosplayer determines the accuracy of his or her cosplay dress and character-portrayal.

For some cosplayers the costume must be an exact replica of that worn by an anime character, which is no easy feat, given the unrealistic aspects of animated costumes. These cosplayers take extreme care to get every physical detail correct, such as adding padding for muscles, dyeing hair to bright, unnatural colors, and wearing platform shoes. They often spend significant amounts of money and time to create the perfect replica of their character's dress (Aoyama and Cahill 2003). Still other cosplayers are content with the bare minimum of dress that communicates their chosen character.

Typically, cosplay dress is either self-created or purchased, or a combination of the two. Wigs, cosmetics, and jewelry are often purchased because these items are difficult to make or may be less expensive than construction from raw materials. The constructed portions of cosplay dress usually include the clothing, but may also include foam swords and (faux) gem-encrusted wands. Some portions of cosplay dress that usually are a combination of purchased and constructed often need to be modified, such as shoes and accessories.

Japanese and North American Cosplay

A distinguishing characteristic between Japanese and North American cosplay is the way in which cosplayers perform in competition. In North America, during masquerades cosplayers wear their dress onstage and perform skits, often humorous but not necessarily an exact mime of their chosen character. In Japan, cosplayers also wear their dress on stage during competitions; however, they usually give only a static display, such as striking their character's signature pose or reciting the motto of their chosen character (Bruno 2002b).

Another distinguishing characteristic is where cosplay dress is worn. In North America, cosplayers wear their dress in nearly any setting (Bruno 2002b). For example, fully costumed/dressed cosplayers may leave a convention and eat at a nearby restaurant. In Japan, cosplayers are not welcome in certain areas beyond the convention, and some conventions request that cosplayers not wear their dress outside the convention (Bruno

2002b). Both Japanese and North American cosplayers gather with friends for cosplay at conventions and private events.

Since Japanese culture values community above the individual, cosplayers exist as a subculture, outside the acceptable norms of the dominant culture, where acts of discrimination have occurred by the dominant culture (Aoyama and Cahill 2003; Richie 2003). As a result, Japanese cosplayers have a negative reputation as individualists within some areas of Japanese culture (Bruno 2002b; Richie 2003). In Japan, unlike North America, there are areas, such as the Akihabara and Harajuku districts in Tokyo, strictly designated for cosplay costume shops, cafes, and restaurants (Prideaux 2001). Although Japanese cosplayers may venture into areas not designated for cosplayers, such activity is discouraged because of the negative reputation of cosplayers, and to protect young female cosplayers from unwanted attention (Richie 2003).

A final distinguishing characteristic between Japanese and North American cosplay is the available goods and markets for cosplayers. In Japan, there are districts where anime and manga cosplayers are the target market for consumable goods, such as cosplay costumes, accessories, and publications. North American anime and manga conventions feature dealers who sell a limited selection of cosplay items (e.g., magazines, DVDs, action figures, etc.). Within science fiction and fantasy conventions, anime and manga cosplayers compete with other fandoms, such as *Star Trek* and *Star Wars* fans, for a portion of the market. Outside the convention setting, anime and manga cosplayers must resort to catalogs and online shops for cosplay items, such as wigs, costumes, and makeup.

During the latter portions of the twentieth century, Japan and North America exchanged pop and subcultural ideas (Napier 2001; Poitras 2001). This is evident in Hollywood movies influenced by Japanese anime (e.g., *The Matrix* was influenced by *Ghost in the Shell*). An example of how Japanese anime and manga story lines have been influenced by North American subcultural activities is the *Record of Lodoss War* stories, which were influenced by *Dungeons and Dragons* role-playing games (Poitras 2001). This Japanese and North American exchange has extended to anime and manga and is apparent within the sources of inspiration for anime and manga cosplay.

Social Structures of Cosplay

Cosplay is a highly social activity that occurs in specific environments, such as anime and manga conventions, karaoke events, and club meetings (Aoyama and Cahill 2003). Therefore it provides significant social benefits for cosplayers, who are often labeled "geeks" (i.e., socially and culturally inferior individuals) by the dominant culture. As a result, the anime and manga cosplay subculture provides cosplayers with "social structures" (Merton 1968). This social structure is composed of social interactions, environments, and experiences.

Most of the social interactions take place via the cosplay character(s). The character provides a (protective) identity for the cosplayer, which may allow for more confident and open interactions. Moreover, cosplay dress and environment(s) permit the cosplayer to role-play the character he or she is dressed as and engage in such social activities within a "safe" and "supportive" social structure. In this way the cosplay social structure is established, developed, and maintained.

The environments and spaces created for and by cosplay provide cosplayers with a variety of spaces for social interactions. Some of these environments include, but are not limited to, the following: an intimate space (dress), a private space (solitary rehearsals and research), a public space (interactions with other cosplayers, both in person and virtual), and a performance space (ranging from small parties to masquerades). Cosplay merges fantasy and reality into "carnivalesque" environments and spaces, where individuals have permission to be someone or something other than themselves (Bakhtin 1968; Napier 2001; Richie 2003). It is here that cosplay characters, distinctive from their anime and manga origins, emerge and interact with other cosplay characters. This further suggests the malleable identities of the cosplayers created in these environments where people are "not themselves" but instead are fictional anime and manga characters.

Cosplay social interactions and environments provide cosplayers with unique and significant experiences. These experiences include making new friends to claiming a moment in the limelight. Moreover, cosplay experiences appear to have real benefits for the cosplayers, because of the continued participation and growing interest in cosplay and related activities. The variety of cosplay experiences contributes to the social structure of cosplay.

In summary, cosplay inspired by anime, manga, and related video games expands not only the anime and manga art form but also the interactions of two global cultures—Japan and North America. The interactions begin with origin stories of cosplay and continue as cosplayers share fandom from both Japan and North America (via surfing the Internet and attending conventions). The impact of these interactions is visually evident at conventions where the context of cosplay, which includes social settings, cosplayers, characters and role-playing, and dress, is on display. Moreover, these interactions contribute to, build on, and develop into the social structures of cosplay, providing cosplayers with unique interactions, environments, and experiences.

References

Aoyama, T., and J. Cahill. 2003. *Cosplay Girls: Japani Live Animation Heroines*. Tokyo: DH.

Bakhtin, M. 1968. *Rabelais and His World*. Trans. H. Iswolsky. Cambridge, MA: MIT.

Bruno, M. 2002a. "Cosplay: The Illegitimate Child of SF Masquerades." *Glitz and Glitter Newsletter*, Millennium Costume Guild. October. http://millenniumcg.tripod.com/glitzglitter/1002articles.html (accessed March 20, 2005).

Bruno, M. 2002b. "Costuming a World Apart: Cosplay in America and Japan." *Glitz and Glitter Newsletter*, Millennium Costume Guild. October. http://millenniumcg.tripod.com/glitzgliaed1002articles.html (accessed March 20, 2005).

Drazen, P. 2003. *Anime Explosion! The What? Why? & Wow! of Japanese Animation*. Berkeley, CA: Stone Bridge.

Eicher, J. B. 2000. "Dress," in Routledge *International Encyclopedia of Women: Global Women's Issues and Knowledge*, ed. C. Kramarae and D. Spender. London: Routledge.

Hlozek, R. 2004. Cosplay: The New Main Attraction. May. http://www.jivemgazine.com/article.php?pid=1953 (accessed March 20, 2005).

Ledoux, T., and D. Ranney. 1997. *The Complete Anime Guide*, 2nd ed. Issaquah, WA: Tiger Mountain.

Macias, P., and T. Machiyama. 2004. *Cruising the Anime City: An Otaku Guide to Neo Tokyo*. Berkeley, CA: Stone Bridge.

McCarthy, H. 1993. *Anime! A Beginner's Guide to Japanese Animation*. London: Titan Books.

Merton, R. K. 1968. *Social Theory and Social Structure*. New York: Free Press.

Napier, S. 2001. *Anime from Akira to Princess Mononoke: Experiencing Contemporary Japanese Animation*. New York: Palgrave.

Poitras, G. 2001. *Anime Essentials: Eveything a Fan Needs to Know*. Berkeley, CA: Stone Bridge.

Prideaux, E. 2001. "Japanese Trend Sees Teens Dress in Costume." CNews. Associated Press (Tokyo), February 7.

Richie, D. 2003. *Image Factory: Fads and Fashions in Japan*. London: Reaktion Books.

Schodt, F. L. 1996. *Dreamland Japan: Writings on Modern Manga*. Berkeley, CA: Stone Bridge.

Endnotes

1. In North America, *otaku* refers to an anime and manga (hardcore) fan or enthusiast. However, in Japan, *otaku* is an honorific and is used to address a good friend or the like (Shodt 1996).
2. In this chapter, I utilize J. B. Eicher's (2000) definition of dress—any body modification or supplement, which includes makeup, wigs, shoes, clothing, jewelry, and piercings—when I refer to as cosplay dress.
3. *Jagermeister* is an herbal (anise) liqueur that is popular in North America.

Discussion Questions

1. How do the divisions of environments Winge offers compare to the public, private, and secret self model? Compare Winge's divisions to the PPSS model in Table 12.1.
2. What are the cultural similarities and differences in cosplay between Japan and North America?
3. Winge notes the benefits for geeks who costume at cosplay conventions. Can you think of other benefits?

A DRAG EXPERIENCE: LOCATING FANTASY IN THE CONSTRUCTION OF ALTERNATIVE GENDERED APPEARANCES

John Jacob

The purpose of this essay is to share a personal account of how fantasy operates in the construction of alternative identity creation and expression using dress. I define alternative gender identity as one that does not conform, and in some ways challenges traditional heterosexually defined gender roles for men and women respectively. The specific alternative gender identity that I will discuss is the one that I have created in response to the contradiction of gay male experience in a heterosexual male-dominated society.

Gay Male Appearances and Identity: Contradictions of a *Third Category*

Appearance is a creation, which involves dress, the intentional changes to the physical body including such things as clothing, hairstyles, shaving, makeup, jewelry, etc. I understand both appearance and identity as personal creations. I therefore recognized several options in creating gay male identity and appearances that might aim to express or hide it. One might try blending in with mainstream gendered appearances and cultivate a *straight-looking/straight-acting* gay male appearance, on the one side of the heterosexual male/heterosexual female dichotomy. Or, one might choose, on the other extreme, to dress like a woman and acknowledge the connection that many people make between gay identity and femininity. But there are many ways in which gay male identity makes room for gendered appearances that are not decisively related to the ideals of heterosexual male or heterosexual female appearance.

Scholars have noticed that society creates rather strict rules for male and female appearances, respectively, and sometimes casts gay men

as a *third category* that is not really male (Bergling, 2001; Jacob & Cerny, 2004). Yet society has an overriding tendency to categorize gay men as feminine, and thereby ignore the biological facts of primary and secondary sex characteristics, and individual personalities. Remarkably also, society tends to ignore the variation in levels of masculinity/femininity apparent in heterosexual men and women. It seems that such variation is much more an issue when the person is perceived to be gay. These circumstances show that gender rules may appear arbitrary; but gender rules serve to maintain social order. This social order that prescribes acceptable appearances and behavior for men and women reflects a very specific version of reality. It is therefore useful to consider reality.

Gender Fantasy and Reality: Truth Claims and Physical Evidence

Many traditions question the concept of *reality*, which people often think of as the opposite of fantasy. When people perceive reality, it often involves two sources of information: 1) sensory information gathered from what one can see, hear, touch, and smell; and, 2) definitions of phenomena that are based on social learning and consensus. Therefore, it is not just what people perceive, but *how* they perceive that defines reality. Societies aim for people to perceive reality in ways that will preserve their power structures, authority, and class distinctions (Berger and Luckmann, 1967). Thus effort goes into teaching boys how to be boys, and girls how to be girls (Cahill, 1989). Many of the apparent differences between

---

Original for this text.

THE MEANINGS OF DRESS

males and females, therefore, involve social effort as much as they do biology.

The word *sex* refers to biological distinctions between male and female, and *gender* refers to socially created and learned differences between male and female (Unger & Crawford, 1993). Following Mulvey (1975), in seeing gender differences, I have suggested that the individual acquires a *cultural lens* through which one perceives gendered bodies, which Mulvey called *the gaze*. This cultural lens is composed by the assumptions and expectations people learn growing up. For example, in the United States, gender assumptions and expectations deem it acceptable for women to wear dresses, but usually not men. Men lose social credibility and are often the brunt of humor and ridicule when they wear dresses. This occurs because the male body is laden with social expectations for appearance that establish it as something distinct from the female body and feminine appearances (Butler, 1994). These social expectations that define acceptable male appearances compose a mental picture of the "ideal man," which people use as a point of comparison in determining a person's gender, and to some extent, sexual orientation also (Butler, 1994).

Yet this ideal image of how a man is supposed to appear is a fantastic image that people keep in their heads (Butler, 1994). It is part of the cultural lens they use to perceive and identify others (Jacob & Cerny 2004). When one sees a man that does not look like a man is *supposed to*, his identity comes into question. These questions emerge: Is this really a man, or is he gay? Either way, mainstream male identity is uncertain. Many suggest that U.S. society perceives and treats gay men as though they are *not really* men (Bergling, 2001).

Thus it takes more than physical evidence provided at birth to *create* a man. Sexual orientation, which has implications for identity, and behavior, is also important. Mainstream male identity is disqualified by non-heterosexual orientation. This disqualification lays bare the fantasy necessary to perceive gender, and create gendered identities, even though these identities are often treated like biological facts, pertaining to an absolute reality (Butler, 1990; 1994).

Although sexual orientation can refer to identity, it also refers to sexual behavior, which usually occurs in private. Imagining a person's sexual behavior, whether one's own, or that of another, is therefore a fundamental part of identity in the U.S. Fantasy is everywhere in such identity transactions. Sexual desire involves fantasy, and imagining another's sexual behavior also involves fantasy. Yet when a person's appearance disrupts the fantasies that people take for granted, people usually question the person's authenticity, as if it was the person that was not real. It is much less likely that they will question the gender system that stipulates unrealistic limitations. Nonetheless, the gender contradiction of *a man in a dress* bears further consideration.

The questions and identity threats that arise at seeing a man in a dress are revealing. Societies often impose rules upon the body, aiming to limit its appearances and behavior into conformity with the version of reality that it prefers. Such versions of reality are stories people use to make sense of their lives and experience of the world. When people buy into a story about gender to make sense of experience, it operates at the level of belief, and sometimes takes on the power of myth (Butler 1990; 1994). When experience shows one something that does not fit with one's beliefs, one can adjust one's beliefs, or find ways to discount or dismiss the information that contradicts. Unfortunately, with regard to men who challenge gender rules, it is a person that may be discounted, dismissed, or worse. In such unfortunate cases, some people reveal that their fantasy is more important than valuing their own ability to perceive, and others' human experience.

An Account of Gay Appearance and Identity in the Gender Fantasy Context

My experience of gay identity and doing drag occur against this backdrop of a gender fantasy, which suggests how men and women, respectively, are supposed to appear, behave, and express sexuality. For the purposes of this essay, doing drag is a process that results in male appearances that intentionally do not conform to mainstream gender expectations. (See Figures 12.12a and b.) Yet this doing drag can occur without necessarily trying to look like a *real* woman. It has never been my intention in doing drag to look like a real woman. It was at first my intention to use drag as a form of rebellion against the strict gender rules for men that I perceived from society. This was very important to me after I first came out at age 28.

However, when I became a student of feminist theory and gender studies in graduate school, I learned that much of gender was artificial, instead of natural, and that its artificiality involved people's engagements with fantasy (Butler 1990; 1994). It was then that I became motivated to do drag in ways that *disrupted* the mainstream gender fantasy, to create appearances that were neither completely male nor completely female, so that

people would have to stop, look, and question. I would put on a dress and makeup without shaving my face. My five o'clock shadow would make it clear that I was a man in a dress. Other times, I would shave my face and wear a dress, makeup, and a wig. But I have a lot of body hair and did not shave the hair on my chest, legs, and arms. Women in the U.S. usually do not have such a heavy covering of body hair as I, whether they are that way naturally, or use hair removal techniques to make their bodies appear smooth.

Other times, I might choose to wear only a dress and high heels, but no makeup or wig. (See Figure 12.12b.) In my experience, this is the appearance that people find most disturbing when I have appeared that way in public, usually at nightclubs. I suppose this appearance is most disturbing because it is the most ambiguous. There are not enough visual cues to encourage the viewer to perceive me either more on the side of masculine,

Figure 12.12 Images of the author for his job as a university professor (a), and in drag to express an alternative gender identity (b).

or more on the side of feminine. They also cannot tell if I am a heterosexual cross-dresser, or a gay man doing drag. People seem more comfortable when ambiguity is minimized, especially when it comes to gender and sexual orientation.

Yet, it is precisely in this grey area between male and female that I feel the most potential to create myself. It offers opportunity to turn the third category that society lumps together with female into something else, which is hard to categorize. In this way, I am able to express creativity while I exercise personal freedom and control over my body, appearance, and identity, instead of doing *exactly* what society proposes. However, there are many ways in which I do conform to society's gender expectations. I wear pants and a shirt to work every day. I wear men's shoes to work. I usually keep my hair short. I sometimes wear a short beard.

On a day-to-day basis, I currently bleach and color my hair, which is not traditionally masculine behavior. I choose vibrantly colored shirts, socks, and accessories, which creates a visual emphasis that men usually avoid since appearance is traditionally the domain of women (Kaiser, Lennon and Damhorst, 1991). I sometimes wear women's pants, belts, and other accessories to work to create a gender-blended appearance. Yet I do not think most people realize that I sometimes wear women's pants, which I have chosen because they often possess much more design interest than men's pants. (See Figure 12.12a.)

Gaining this freedom and control over my appearance and the body it covers is very personal. At the same time, it is very political. Creating alternatives to the strict, heterosexual male/female dichotomy challenges the authenticity and *natural* correctness of that gender order on which society and systems of privilege and oppression are founded. I have shared some examples from my everyday life appearance, where I manipulate and create my appearance to communicate an alternative identity and gain freedom for my appearance and the identity that it helps express. It is now that I shall delve more deeply into the concept of drag, which for me means wearing a dress, or other ensembles, that are designed exclusively for women's use.

Some Purposes of Drag

Drag is a term that originated from a time in history when skirts *dragged* on the floor (Baker, 1968). It is a term that refers to men intentionally dressing in women's clothing and accessories, and often using women's wigs, cosmetics, and fragrance. The purposes of drag vary in nightclub settings, from encouraging humor to creating a convincing illusion of womanhood (Jacob & Cerny, 2004; Jacob, 1999). Yet the personal intentions associated with doing drag may be much more varied. It is also worth noting here that not all men who do drag are gay and that many men choose to do drag only in private (Bullough & Bullough, 1993). Some men report having a *feminine side* that drag allows them to express (Jacob & Cerny, 2004). Others, whether gay or straight, report enjoying the sensuality of women's clothing and underwear, which often feel very differently against the body than men's clothing and underwear do (Bullough & Bullough, 1993). Yet others report that doing drag opens opportunities for creative expression that ordinary men's appearances do not provide (Jacob & Cerny, 2004). While I do not perceive that I have a feminine side that requires drag to gain expression, I do enjoy the visual, tactile, and kinetic sensuality of women's clothing, and the creative opportunities that doing drag makes possible. For me this creativity is all about constructing and transforming images that rest temporarily on my body, and using the digital camera to record these creative explorations. After photographing myself in the wig, makeup and dress, for example, it is a source of fascination to examine the person the camera has captured. I find myself wondering in what ways this temporary creature is just like the *me* whom I present in everyday life. I also wonder in what ways the drag image is merely a creative exercise that satisfies my desire for experimentation, exploration, and novelty, which I presume most people satisfy (to more or less extents) through involvement with fashion.

But ultimately, dress is an activity, which occurs on the body, while it tells a story about its wearer, and the connection between the body, the mind, and the self. Although I do not wish to appear like a real woman when I do drag, I think the inclination to do drag is facilitated by gay identity. There is less status to lose in doing drag if one is openly gay. If one is out, then there is less to hide in everyday life. Being out creates an opening in social relations for appearances that those most publically invested in mainstream heterosexual identities and appearances cannot gain. While some may fear discrimination and status loss at expressing appearance alternatives to heterosexual male identity, I find it liberating to imagine a place for myself in society, which I have created and negotiated with others. In this place, I have more freedom to create appearances. Here I also gain the power to face the sometimes negative feedback coming from others. Some people are disturbed by my courage and ability to express myself as I choose. Others are upset by the challenges that alternatively gendered appearances pose to the version of reality that they hold so dear. Indeed, some people become frightened when the versions of reality that they take for granted are called into question. It may be from this position of fear that most public violence against cross-dressed men occurs.

I have offered discussion explaining why doing drag challenges and in some ways dismantles mainstream, heterosexually coded male gendered appearances. It is within the context of this social critique of heterosexual society and its gender code that my doing drag emerges. I have discussed the fantasy necessary to create an appearance that communicates identity, and how mainstream society's male appearance ideals represent a heterosexual fantasy script for how men are supposed to appear and behave. I will now explain more directly the connection between fantasy and my drag appearances and experience.

My Engagement with Drag: Fantasy, Belief, and Creation

People of varied cultural backgrounds perceive their religious belief systems, complete with deities, as matters of fact. Yet these are myth-driven systems that rely on individuals' fantastic engagement with deities to make their religious experience real. I contend that in the religious experi-

ence, what is real and what is fantasy may be a moot point. It is, with all experience, that the divide between fantasy and reality is hard to precisely locate. I therefore do not discount the personal and collective value of religious belief systems, but merely wish to notice the mental activity that makes religion powerful—belief in products of the imagination and fantasy. What makes religion powerful is the same thing that makes social order possible, that is, shared belief and fantastic imaginings. Language, for example, would be impossible without shared belief and imagination. Moreover, it is from imagination and fantasy that creation takes place. Many religions esteem creation and appreciate it as an activity that occurs in concert with the divine. Furthermore, one can perceive drag appearances as works of art, creative expressions that exceed the purposes and limits of everyday dress, to the extent that these creative expressions serve purposes similar to those of art: a) to help people recognize their shared experiences of life; b) to suggest new ways of seeing; c) to surprise; and, d) to inspire awe, wonder, and contemplation (Jacob, 1999).

I wish to make this point in summarizing this discussion of fantasy, belief, and creation: Realities not only emerge from people's engagements with fantasy; these realities also indicate a rather narrow range of possibilities extracted from the infinite realm of creation. This narrowing of possibility obviously occurs for the sake of simplicity and order. However, in achieving simplicity and order, power relations also emerge, where specific ways of seeing, knowing and being in the world gain privilege over others. These systems of privilege become so ingrained that people take privilege structures for granted as the *natural* order of things, sometimes as if a divine creator had established these arrangements. Meanwhile, creation is an active process among humans, by which those things which either improve living conditions, or possibly elevate awareness of the human condition and the divine, also come into being.

There are many indigenous cultures in which homosexuality and transgendered people are perceived as natural creative expressions of the divine, with places of importance in religious rituals and society (Thompson, 1988). For me, doing drag is but one of many ways in which I undertake creation. It marks my engagement with the divine, where I notice religious traditions that value alternative gender expressions, while seeing beauty and value in the diversity of creation. There is a spiritual aspect to doing drag, where it allows me to connect with creation and the state of creativity from which every knowable thing comes. Imagination is necessary to create anything. This is also true for creating a drag appearance.

For the sake of understanding, now, I therefore explain how the drag appearances that I create operate at the level of fantasy. The Merriam-Webster online dictionary defines fantasy as the "free play of the creative imagination." Creative imagination involves not only sensing something that is not immediately present, it also involves creation, by which things come into being. My drag appearance is almost always a new creation that calls into being a temporary existence that had not occurred to me previously, and may not occur again. Although I might appear in drag similarly from one time to the next, what I try to accomplish visually and what I see when I apprehend my drag image, each time, is almost always different. But when I do drag, it always involves the engagement of fantasy—my creative imagination, by which I aim to create a place for myself where my mind, body, and identity are not confined to the fantasies that society and other people might try to impose. Thus drag represents, for me, the ultimate fantasy of self-determination

and the perfect freedom to be me, and change, without worrying about what a man or a woman is supposed to be.

References

Baker, R. (1968). *Drag: A history of female impersonation on the stage*. London: MacDonald and Company.

Berger, P.L. & Luckmann, T. (1967) *The social construction of reality: A treatise in the sociology of knowledge*. London: Allen Lane.

Bergling, T. (2001). *Sissyphobia: Gay men and effeminate behavior*. Binghamton, NY: Southern Tier Editions.

Bullough, V. & Bullough, B. (1993). *Crossdressing sex and gender*. Philadelphia: University of Pennsylvania Press.

Butler, J. (1990). *Gender trouble: Feminism and the subversion of identity*. New York: Routlege.

Butler, J. (1994). *Bodies that matter: On the discursive limits of sex*. New York: Routledge.

Cahill, S. (1989). Fashioning males and females: Appearance management and the social reproduction of gender. *Symbolic Interaction 12*(2), 281–298.

Jacob, J. (1999). *The Haus of Frau: Radical drag queens disrupting the visual fiction of gendered appearances* (Dissertation). Retrieved from Electronic Theses and Dissertations at Virginia Tech. (Accession Order No. etd-051799-115007).

Jacob, J. & Cerny, C. (2004). Radical drag appearances: The embodiment of male femininity and social critique. *Clothing and Textiles Research Journal 22*(3), 122–134.

Kaiser, S. B., Lennon, S. J., & Damhorst, M. L. (1991). Forum: Gendered appearances in twentieth-century popular media. *Dress 18*, 49–67.

Mulvey, L. (1975). Visual pleasure and narrative cinema. *Screen, 16*(3), 6–18.

Thompson, M. (1988). *Gay spirit: Myth and meaning*. New York: St. Martin's Griffin Press.

Unger, R.K., & Crawford, M. (1993) Commentary: Sex and gender: The troubled relationship between terms and concepts. *Psychological Science 4*(2), 122–124.

Discussion Questions

1. Why do you think that the appearance that Jacob describes as a dress and high heels with no makeup or wig is the most disturbing to others?
2. Explain how Jacob's drag experience is both personal and political.
3. What do you think about Jacob's proposal that gender is a collective fantasy in which all individuals participate?
4. How might cosplayers (see reading by Winge) and individuals like Jacob safely expand their venues for personal expression?

VIDEO GAME ATTIRE

Keoni Rivera
University of Hawai`i, Manoa

Introduction

The start of the twenty-first century parallels the start of the digital era, heralding the beginning of a cultural ethos that would recognize the valuable social implications of digital technology. Over a decade later, the world is saturated in it to the point that almost every person on Earth is touched, either directly or indirectly, by one type of digital technology or another, and the Internet is at the forefront of this phenomenon. This essay focuses on the psychology behind the creation of the in-game avatar for the mass multiplayer online role-playing video game World of Warcraft (WoW), but more specifically, it will examine in-game attire and the unique social dynamics that thrive within the virtual environment. It especially covers men and their in-game relationship with fashion. The nature of WoW encourages men to more freely develop and explore interests in clothing to a degree that they would perhaps avoid pursuing in their real lives for fear of embarrassment or ridicule. These elements will be tethered to the notion of the second identity, a product of the Internet, and its subsequent socially emancipating effects.

The Internet has become a tool that allows for astonishing and unprecedented events to take place, and this is largely ascribed to its ability to instantaneously connect people who are thousands of miles apart so that they may, for example, express their love for one another face-to-face through technology like the modern-day webcam. The ability to bridge the gap between people who are at the opposite ends of town—or at opposite ends of the globe—is an astounding attribute that has proven to be a truly powerful force. The Internet carries the potential to topple entire government regimes, as seen in Egypt, Tunisia, and Libya, while at the same time providing mundane conveniences like electronically managing one's bank account or shopping for holiday gifts from the comfort of one's living room. The Internet's propensity to bring people and ideas together, to spread breaking news thousands of miles in the blink of an eye, and to provide everyday conveniences contains ramifications that are continually being uncovered and understood today.

While the Internet's capability to connect people is indubitably one of its more attractive qualities, its anonymous nature is another. It entirely rends the mind from the body: on the Internet, one may uninhibitedly express oneself with a much more subdued fear of backlash. An online identity is as interchangeable as clothing—it is entirely abstract, impossible to trace back to one's real-life identity, and conveniently amorphous. Thus, the backlash that one may experience online is not as personal because it is not one's "real" identity, or rather, one's "real life" identity. The power of anonymity allows for change on a whim, with a few keystrokes, and the possibilities are in no way finite. This essentially provides endless opportunity for one to adopt multiple identities that can push social boundaries and express interests that the fixed paradigm of reality's society may suppress or exclude in some way.

In essence, the Internet immerses one into an unprecedented environment that is dependent on the disconnect between a person's real life identity—an identity composed of both the mind and the human body—and a person's cyberspace identity, which includes just the mind. Within this disconnect lies the ability to create an identity that is neither encumbered nor inhibited by fear,

---

Original for this text.

specifically the fear of ridicule or embarrassment, that is often succumbed to outside of the Internet. For example, a male may choose to freely discuss and express keen interests in haute couture, or citizens of a severely oppressed nation may use the Internet to organize a resistance and push for government reform.

According to the *New York Times*, as of June 2010, the Internet has had 1.97 billion users tap into its resource (Bilton, 2011). With people spending so much time in cyberspace, the video game industry has capitalized on this phenomenon quite successfully with a genre of gaming called the mass multiplayer online role-playing game, or MMORPG. The genre allows people from all corners of the globe to play the same game simultaneously—a person in London is able to play WoW, in real time, with someone else in Honolulu. This dynamic introduces components to the online identity that effectively expands its concept. One of most significant is the online avatar. The online avatar is not a revolutionary idea established out of the MMORPG genre itself, but it is the variation within WoW that is notable. The avatar plays a very important role in the gaming genre and thrives off the Internet's anonymous nature. It introduces the notion of a more complete identity that I call the "second identity," because it takes the online identity, which was hitherto constructed around online text, interests, and ideas, and transfers these particles into a more physical representation that, in turn, would reflect them. It is a much less abstract dynamic and a much more corporeal one.

The phrase "second identity" is partially self-defined: one's second identity is entirely mutually exclusive from one's real life identity. Second identity is very similar to the online identity, except it is made corporeal by the in-game avatar. It is partially in this virtual physicality that an online identity becomes an entire "second identity." The in-game avatar expands the notion of the online identity by, firstly, ascribing the identity to an avatar and, secondly, ascribing the identity to an avatar that is exceptionally customizable. The second identity is made complete by the environment of the game, which, in many ways, reflects real life environments—the verisimilitude of the WoW world that continues to exist, function, and grow while players are offline, allowing players to easily assume an identity in-game. The key difference between the two forms of identity is that the latter has potential to be less affected by social fear of ridicule. This is connected to the Internet's inherent anonymous nature that remains ubiquitous in WoW's virtual universe.

The Determination of Avatar Gender in World of Warcraft

To fully understand the psychology behind the creation of the avatar, a further explanation of the nature of second identity is necessary, as it is important to understand that the dichotomy between one's identity in the real world and one's identity in the gaming world varies from one MMORPG to the next. This variation is rooted partly in the demographics of a particular MMORPG game that specifically concerns the ratio of men and women who play the game. For example, in the case of World of Warcraft (WoW), a 2007 census done by the Daedulus Project discovered that an overwhelming 84% of players were male. This dynamic allows for the dichotomy between a player's real life identity and a player's in-game identity to be exceedingly more mutually exclusive than, say, if 50% of players were male (Yee, 2009). How can the ratio between male and female players determine the severity of this dichotomy? In the case that an MMORPG is overwhelmingly male-dominated, which is the case for most, the male player may feel less inclined to represent himself with a male avatar than he would were the female demographic more corresponding. This is because the conscious connection between the avatar's gender and player's gender becomes less solid when the demographics are overwhelmingly male. The unbalanced demographic creates an assumption that all players are male, and, thus, players feel that a true representation of themselves in terms of gender is not needed. In the case that the gender demographics were 50/50, the assumption is less affecting and one is more likely to feel obligated in some ways to represent themselves true to his or her actual gender. Furthermore, as a result of the general assumption that all players are male, the social aspect of an overwhelmingly male MMORPG eliminates gender as a factor in terms of in-game credibility, and all are respected solely in terms of how well they play the game.

The gender demographic is not a lone factor in one's gender preference when it comes to the avatar. Other determinants include: a player's gender out-of-game, personal tastes, sexual orientation, and so on. It is important to understand that while the male-female demographic does have its influences, its full effect can only affect WoW players who are (1) experienced in that they have come to understand that the game is generally overwhelmingly male, or (2) new players who have come to understand this concept elsewhere. The ratio of male and female players in a particular MMORPG game has the potential to create an environment where male players more comfortably represent themselves with female avatars because of the underlying assumption that everyone is male supplemented by the subsequent absence of male-female social dynamics, as has happened in World of Warcraft. While the video game industry is indeed heavily male-dominated, this phenomenon is in no way universal. For example, in the MMORPG Maplestory, the male-female demographic is more evenly balanced than that of World of Warcraft. As a result, the rift between a player's real life identity and a player's in-game identity is not as wide, and, thus, there is a truer representation and heavier correlation between player and avatar gender identity.

The Next Step: Forming the Second Identity

Within World of Warcraft, a player creates a second identity that goes far beyond the gender of their avatar. The game itself provides a wide range of customizability that starts at the character creation menu. The player first chooses between two factions, the Horde and the Alliance. Within each, there contains six mutually exclusive races that are, by premise of the game, pinned in a perpetual conflict against other races of the opposing faction. It is elements like this that further feed a second identity; the game is forming who a gamer will be, what a gamer will do and the morals a gamer will hold in terms of who is a friend and who is an enemy.

Customizability stretches beyond race and into a category called class. The term *class* refers to a set of abilities, strengths, and weaknesses that a character will inherit once assigned to a particular class. Furthermore, each class's attributes are mutually exclusive between one another. Class is unlike race in that all classes are available to both factions, Horde or Alliance. Classes include the magic-based abilities: the warlock, mage, priest, and druid; stealth-based abilities: the rogue; strength-based abilities: warrior; and an amalgamation of both magic and strength abilities: the paladin.

To make these notions clearer, a magic-based character relies entirely on magic to defend itself. The abilities it uses, along with the attire it will eventually wear, are entirely different than, for example, a strength-based character, like the warrior, who is far more gifted with close combat weaponry and relies on the might of his sword to defeat enemies. The magic-based character will don lighter items such as staves, cloaks, and robes because it is not anatomically suited in terms of strength to wear heavy armor like the strength-based characters who, quite pragmatically, use equipment that is far more protective and cumbersome—for example, heavy chest and body armors and helmets. The logic behind this variation in attire is the notion that the warrior will be involved in up-close and personal combat with his sword, and the warlock or mage will fight from a distance, casting long-range spells as well as forming magical barriers or buffers that will enhance the power of their fortifications and offensive abilities. It is also important to understand that each class is entirely different. For example, there are four magic-based classes: the warlock, mage, priest, and druid, but they are by no means similar to one another. The warlock is in many ways an apple, and the mage is in many ways an orange, despite both being heavily dependent on magic—essentially, the abilities that are unique to each magic-based class is what matters. After a player chooses their loyalty and class, they may then customize their avatar's facial features and hairstyle. Everything considered, a player can choose from varying combinations in terms of the avatar's anatomy, skills, and aesthetics to create an identity that they consider good enough to assume in-game.

Premise and Attire in World of Warcraft

The MMORPG exploits the green world of cyberspace and subsequently introduces players to an industry that has been dominantly thought of to be feminine and for women—the fashion industry. In literary terms, the green world describes an environment that is atypical to real life in that it may be free from socio-cultural predeterminations. For example, the stereotype that the fashion industry is an interest held solely by women and feminine or gay men may not hold to be as valid in a green world because those socio-cultural predeterminations may not persist as strongly there. The MMORPG is in some sense a green zone all its own. It is a world that is unlike that of real life in which cultural norms have been rebuilt and reestablished. While real-world norms are reflected to some extent in WoW, it is generally not as severe and more accepting, and this could be in part attributed to the nature of the general gamer who tends to be relatively liberal. Important components that hold the green world of WoW together include: second identity, anonymity, and game demographics. Second identity and its anonymous nature provide players an opportunity to emancipate themselves from everyday societal constrictions and taboos. A player can express themselves in ways that are stereotyped and discouraged in real life: a male player may express his identity through a female avatar and the same may be said with a female player and a male avatar. While not all players choose to seize the opportunity to actively emancipate themselves, most do not realize that they unknowingly participate in a brand of cultural emancipation. The connotation of video game culture as being primarily a male-dominated activity, coupled with the heavy dedication required to play WoW in particular—which in turn reinforces its "maleness"—shroud the fact that all who play WoW are essentially heavily and devoutly in-tune to fashion.

The premise of World of Warcraft is to methodically obtain better gear (clothing) and improve abilities until one's avatar has obtained the best that there is available. To acquire clothing or gear sets, a player must dedicate a tremendous amount time, often hundreds of hours. The individual pieces of gear—generally involving a helmet, chest piece, shoulder pads, pants, shoes, and cape—each have a ranking ascribed to them that gamers refer to as a gear score. The gear score is a general indication of how experienced a player is or how much a player's avatar is utilized. (A player may have more than one avatar: there is the main avatar and then there are the alternate avatars, or the alts, so the gear score is not always a true reflection of a player's experience, but it is definitely that of an avatar's.) A leveling system monitors avatars' worthiness of advanced gear by awarding them valuable experience points for completing quests, killing creatures, and various other undertakings. When the avatar reaches the experience point quota for any particular level, it is promoted to the next level and the process is repeated until the avatar reaches the level cap or the last level. In WoW, there are 85 levels.

As an avatar rises to the next level, gear and skills appropriate to that level become available; the caveat, however, is that one must continue to complete tasks to obtain higher leveled gear. The efficiency of the player notwithstanding (an efficient player who works solely toward leveling their avatar without deviation), reaching the last level will involve hundreds of hours of gameplay. It is important to understand that the aspects of the game that players most look forward to become available only once they reach the last level. This is the point when the best—and also the most time-consuming—features of the game are unlocked. The content that opens up at level 85 is referred to as the end-game content, and it is largely composed of an activity called raiding. Keep in mind that this is done in the attempt to obtain the latest in WoW fashion.

Raids are exceedingly difficult, team-based, tactical, and require a player who is keenly familiar with the game in all respects. On top of achieving the level cap, 85, all raiders must meet five general requirements to participate: (1) a player must understand the general concepts of the raid (what to do in certain situations) and the opponents that will be fought in terms of their unique battle strategies; (2) a player must understand their avatar's abilities (when to use which moves in particular situations); (3) they must effectively implement those abilities in battle (for example, a warlock that specializes in cursing must be exceedingly precise in the way that each curse is applied and then reapplied once it expires); (4) they must be a team player; and (5) the player's avatar must be equipped with suitable raiding gear. Being a team player is the easiest requirement to meet because, unlike the other four, it generally does not require out-of-game research. This means that to understand the concepts of the raid and to exhaust one's avatar for all that it is inherently worth is a talent that is oftentimes learned in gaming forums, YouTube, and the like. The game is stringently particular when it comes to raids. It requires one to use their avatar in an exceedingly scrupulous manner that is drastically different from the way one would play with the same avatar in all other aspects of the game. The raiding process is in some ways a measure of gaming knowledge, and one will be invited to a successful raid party on the condition that they meet all of the requirements. With this information in mind, essentially the hundreds of hours and the varying components all feed into the player's ultimate goal to obtain the game's latest fashions. As a result, WoW players essentially become fashionistas in the sense that they are acutely aware of what is presently the best gear set in the game and are passionately dedicated and perpetually struggling and operating to obtain statistically and aesthetically enhanced armor for their avatar. The ultimate goal in WoW is to become the ultimate fashionista. When one exhausts the game of all it has to offer, one also becomes the master of the game's fashion.

The art of distinguishing between what is good clothing and what is bad clothing is an integral function of the MMORPG that has transformed WoW players to be unconsciously dedicated to fashion. This notion of good and bad fashion in relation to the game resides at the center of the genre. It is the driving force that is extensively built upon and around and, in effect, produces a game that is cohesive, functional, enjoyable, successful, and revolutionary in terms of how it has, in some ways, broken the stigma that fashion is feminine and for the feminine.

Attractive Gear

What makes gear aesthetically attractive is partially answered by the theme a player wants his or her avatar to convey: strength, power, and intimidation; risqué beauty and seduction; grim and death; oneness with nature, etc. In this sense, the notion of attractive gear is in many ways relative, but in a general sense, attractive gear is a set of gear that is, in one way or another, conducive to a particular theme.

The building blocks to the creation of a theme start off at the login screen of the game. As discussed earlier, WoW contains a wide variety of features that allow for a grand scale of customizability. For example, a player first chooses between the Horde and the Alliance and the avatar's gender, race, and class. As the avatar levels and grows, it is exposed to thousands of different types of gear that it may wear throughout the course of the game. It is up to the player to reduce the number to around nine pieces—head, shoulders, back, wrists, gloves, body, legs, shoes, and a weapon—that is aesthetically as well as statistically adequate to the player.

The theme a player adopts, like the nature of fashion, is constantly changing. Developers continually expand and add new gaming content (e.g., races, gears, raids, etc.). A player grows with the game, especially in the fashion sense, because there is always new gear to obtain and themes to convey. For example, attire that had formerly been subtle and demure may be replaced with regalia that is ostentatiously risqué; a player is constantly mixing and matching gear to get both the best statistical and aesthetic values. This is especially true when new content is introduced.

Statistical value is so much an essential component of quality gear that it, many times, enhances the aesthetic value of a particular item. As such, statistical value is a vital component in deciding the direction a player will take in terms of what gear an avatar will don. For example, the best gear is organized into an ever-expanding tier list by developers, with the larger-number tiers holding outfits with more statistical value but not necessarily aesthetic value. It can be argued that the Tier 11 set is not as aesthetically valuable as the Tier 10 gear. But when a player measures the statistics involved, the Tier 11 gear holds superior, and this, in some ways, enhances the aesthetic value of the attire. It adds no small influence to the player's final decision. Another dynamic is the idea that the Tier 10 gear set is old and outdated; the Tier 11 set is novel and new, and these forces tend to reduce the aesthetic value of the lower tiers as well. Thus, it is an imperative element in determining avatar fashion.

Fashion is a phenomenon that is very important in WoW's gaming dynamic and is a form of expression that male players can explore and experiment with deeply. A male player from the Hawai`i-based guild "Da Kine" states in an online forum interview:

> It is an environment where I can express myself the way I want. I never thought of it as being through fashion, but when I think about it, that's what it is, essentially. I have my Tier 10 [warlock] raiding gear, and I also have my sexy Santa Suit (see Figure 12.13) for when I'm feeling a bit facetious.

While this player chooses to be anonymous, he is a prime example of how the dynamics that

Figure 12.13 Santa Suit Gear is one example of how an avatar can be dressed in the video game World of Warcraft.

have been discussed come together: the notions of second identity, green world, and the concepts that solidify these notions, like the game's demographics. Another member of the guild Da Kine, whose in-game name is Leonidas, expresses a potent virtual fashion sense that has helped regulate his avatar's overall look:

> My main [avatar] for the past two years has been an undead male warlock. (I am male [in real life]). Most gear looks [absolutely] terrible on the undead [race] and [warlocks] usually get stuck in dresses [aka warlock robes]. I have found some gear I really like though. Some reflect the demonic nature of a warlock [with dark colors], other pieces I like have some kind of glow or aura about it. I have an old hood that creates a dark spinning aura, which I love [to use] on my warlock. I also have the awesome helm that [summons] demon wings. The key for this [alternate character] seems to be that it fits the class more than the race—possibly because very little seems to suit the race particularly well.
>
> Another favorite [of my alternate characters] is my Blood Elf female [Dark Knight]. I find I enjoy putting interesting gear on this [alt], and the fact that they can wear such a variety of armor and weapon types has led me to use an old warehouse guild bank as a closet for various gear sets and such. I'm particularly fond of a blood-red set that works particularly well color-wise. [It] has a sexy look and is pretty badass.

Leonidas demonstrates a form of expression that is quite permissible through the environment of World of Warcraft—the open flirtation and in-depth experimentation with both male and female fashion. In real life, this form of expression would generally be labeled as feminine or homosexual, and perhaps discourage interest. Leonidas is male in real life and openly tells that he enjoys playing on his female avatar in part because of the different fashions that become available, to the degree that he has become a connoisseur of sorts, storing clothing items in an in-game warehouse. This open pursuit and exploration of women's fashion would perhaps be suppressed were it not for the freeing dynamics that go into the construction of World of Warcraft. Second identity has allowed players to comfortably express themselves in ways that are, at times, stereotyped in real life. This is brought to an ultimate fruition by the substantial parallels of the video game to real life.

Conclusion

World of Warcraft is substantially important in the notion that it has, through the power of the Internet, generated a space where males can freely express themselves through fashion, without an entirely suppressing fear of ridicule. This MMORPG has dramatically broken through the stigma that fashion is for women and continues, even now, to thrive, expand, and develop this unique green world where inhibitions that thrive in the everyday tend to dwindle. The game has widened the scope on the idea of personal expression—particularly expression through clothing—

to a gender that has been culturally designed to be unreceptive to it. WoW is, in some ways, the foot-in-the-door in terms of a more invested and open male acclimation to fashion in the same way that it is to females in the real world. The genre is, in this way, revolutionary for both the gaming universe and real life, as it heralds the beginning of a socio-cultural emancipation that communicates tolerance and acceptance for those whose interests may deviate from the cultural norm.

References

Bilton, Nick. "2010 Online, by the Numbers—NYTimes.com." Technology—Bits Blog—NYTimes.com. *New York Times*, 14 Jan. 2011. Web. 22 Sept. 2011. <http://bits.blogs.nytimes.com/2011/01/14/2010-online-the-numbers/>.

Kirina's Winter Wardrobe. Digital image. Kirina's Closet. Wordpress.com. Web. 22 Sept. 2011. <http://wowrpc.waddellconsulting.com/?page_id=85>.

Yee, Nick. "WoW Gender-Bending." *The Daedalus Project: The Psychology of MMORPGS*, Web. 9 March 2009. <http://www.nickyee.com/daedalus/archives/001369.php>.

Discussion Questions

1. Clothing/gear is a visible badge of skills acquired in the online game Rivera describes. How does this compare to Boy Scout badges, badges signifying rank in the military, or in sports?
2. After reading this article, describe how you would explain why male online game players might choose a female avatar.
3. If clothing/gear equal abilities in the game (and clearly they do), explain how this might be similar or different to fashion.

CHAPTER 13

DRESS AND TECHNOLOGY

Kimberly A. Miller-Spillman

After you have read this chapter, you will understand:

- Where research on apparel technology is performed
- The variety of innovation within the apparel industry
- How technology, status, and time intersect
- Consumer preferences for apparel technology
- How tradition and technology are related to culture

In this chapter we observe the many effects that technology has on dress and fashion. For example, prior to the 1850s the method of obtaining clothing was to visit a seamstress or tailor and to sew by hand at home to mend and keep clothes up-to-date. However, the invention of the sewing machine changed the social custom of visiting a seamstress or tailor to going to a store for readymade clothing. Later, women could purchase a home sewing machine and paper patterns (available in the 1860s) to create their own clothing at home. The invention of the sewing machine also made mass production of apparel possible and created a new social class of factory workers. At the conclusion of this chapter you will have the opportunity to reflect on the changes brought about by the Industrial Revolution in the late 1800s and early 1900s and compare those changes to the current state of the apparel industry.

Technology and fashion both change rapidly, replacing the old with the new. For instance, the invention of the cage crinoline in the 1850s offered women a lightweight alternative to expand skirt widths without layers of heavy, starched petticoats (Tortora and Eubank, 2010). The weight of the petticoats had become a health and safety concern for women as they moved through daily tasks. In this case, innovation in women's support garments allowed women healthier and safer lives.

During any given era, there are consumers who will embrace new technology and those who reject it. Technophobes come in all ages but, in general, older consumers tend to stick with familiar processes while younger consumers embrace new technology (see Figure 13.1).

Figure 13.1 Generation Z use technology in all aspects of their lives.

A consumer's adaptation of technology is influenced by their generational cohort. "Generation Z" refers to people born between the early to mid-1990s through 2010 (also known as the Internet Generation). They were born after the World Wide Web became increasingly available, and are the first generation to be born completely in an era of postmodernism and globalism. Generation Z has grown up with mobile technology, thus creating a consumer who expects technology to continue making life easier, faster, and convenient. (See also "The Campus as Runway" in Chapter 9 for a description of how Gen Zers use the Internet to get dressed in the morning.)

Research in the Apparel Industry

Innovation is the development of something new, whether a thought or idea, a practice, or a tool or implement. Technological advances in apparel can be found in a variety of places according to the reading "Haute Technology: A New Wave of Designers Is Experimenting with Electronic Textiles, Reactive Fashion and Wearable Computers for a Generation That Grew Up Wired." **University faculty** is one group that conducts research on apparel technology by obtaining funding from the government, corporations, and the military. **Entrepreneurs** who have a hot idea for the latest in wearable electronics merge nanotechnology with apparel. The **United States Military** is one of the largest producers and consumers of apparel and has a vested interest in researching wearable technology to assist soldiers in the field. **Large consumer appliance companies** in Europe are also interested in nanotechnology and purchase fashion and technology patents because they are invested in the future of consumer electronics. Lastly, **Canadian designers** who are less interested in military and consumer electronics applications focus on the beauty and novelty of the garment. Canada, according to Graham, is a culture that invests in the arts by providing grants to apparel designers.

Variety of Innovations in the Apparel Industry

Nanotechnology is the science of making electronics as tiny as possible. When nanotechnology companies partner with apparel companies, it results in the development of **wearable electronics**. Everything you can imagine—and probably a few things that you can't—has been tried or is in the process of being tested (Warren, 2001). From clothes that "talk" to washers, telling the washer how the garment should be cleaned, to a Global Positioning System woven into a jacket collar to track a wandering child or an Alzheimer's patient, wearable electronics can do amazing things. There's clothing that adjusts to your changes in size, clothes that change color to match another garment in your closet, children's sleepwear that sounds an alarm if a baby stops breathing, gym-suit fabrics that absorb odors and can be worn three or four times without offending other exercisers, and fiber-optic wedding dresses or disco trousers that sparkle.

Other innovations in the apparel industry can be found in clothing for specific needs, a segment of the apparel industry that accommodates consumers outside of the mainstream (Watkins, 1995a). Clothing for specific needs includes astronauts, firefighters, disabled individuals, and older adults. Any specialized occupation, such as football players, motocross riders, hockey players, people in the microchip manufacturing industry, and underwater divers, could fit under the broad umbrella of clothing for specific needs. For example, "smart" spacesuits can monitor an astronaut's physical condition. This sophisticated and expensive technology is slowly trickling down to consumers who are willing to pay $200 for a T-shirt (or running bra) that monitors heart rate, body temperature, respiration, and number of calories burned and can warn the wearer of a potential heart attack or heat stroke.

A new technology that can make textiles germ-free was developed by a researcher at the University of Georgia (see reading "New UGA Technology Makes Textiles Germ-Free"). This inexpensive technology can be applied to medical linens and clothing, face masks, athletic socks, and diapers. Given that many "new" technologies are initially expensive and are not available at the price points the public can afford, it will be interesting to see how rapidly this technology will become available.

New technologies target Generation Z consumers, which include having clothing that changes color from day to night, trousers that multitask by bearing keyboards and iPod or GPS systems built directly into their designs at the fiber level (see the reading "Haute Technology"). Instead of having pockets sized for electronic devices in your clothing, your wardrobe will actually be your BlackBerry. Of course, the challenge is to manufacture these garments in quantities so that they are affordable. Companies can be encouraged to develop these designs if there is enough consumer demand.

Another innovation was developed by a former consumer economics student at the University of Georgia. Justin Niefer used his marketing skills to become an entrepreneur (see the reading "Swinging for the Fences with Evoshield"). Niefer is cofounder of the company Evoshield, which produces a lightweight, malleable substance that hardens to fit the wearer's body and disperses impact. The primary application for the product is in sports, namely baseball and football. A YouTube video features Niefer demonstrating the product's effectiveness (www.youtube.com/watch?v=KUjSylfDcgw).

Innovations in digital technology are revolutionizing the process and delivery of design, as discussed in the reading "Prints for the Cyberage." Designers are happy to no longer be limited by screen printing. Digital printing has given designers the ability to produce a fabric pattern that will follow the shape of the body, thus looking less "flat" and more natural. Screen prints restrict the complexity of prints as well as the amount of colors that can be produced on a garment. (You may want to count the number of colors on your favorite T-shirt.) There is much more flexibility with digital printing and designers are thrilled to have more choices. (See Figure 13.2.) In some ways the difference between

Figure 13.2 This digital print from Alexander McQueen's Spring 2010 RTW collection follows body contours.

screen printing and digital printing can be compared to a box of eight crayons versus a box of 120 crayons.

Other designers are excited by innovations in electronics added to dress. The Galaxy Dress (www.youtube.com/watch?v=rX9FOGFxN9A) was the commissioned centerpiece of the "Fast Forward: Inventing the Future" exhibit at the Museum of Science and Industry in Chicago in 2009. The Galaxy Dress is one example of the many developments in clothing technology (see the reading "Excuse Me, but My Dress Is Ringing: Technology Gives Fabrics Greater Function as the Daily Demands of Everyday Life Are Met in Style"). Turkish designer and two-time winner of the British Designer of the Year award Hussein Chalayan is a staunch supporter of technology in fashion and has created dresses that glow with built-in LEDs or emit spectacular red lasers. For Chalayan, the future of technology and dress is already here.

Still other designers prefer to experiment with eco-friendly methods to create clothing. Designer Suzanne Lee discusses how a person can grow his or her own clothes at www.ted.com/talks/suzanne_lee_grow_your_own_clothes.html. Still others show how clothes can be differently applied (discussed in the reading "The Shirt You Spray On: For Clothes That Fit like Second Skin, Try Instant Fabric in Can"). See a demonstration at www.youtube.com/watch?v=ScvdFeh1aOw. The concept that clothing is nondiscursive (McCraken, 1988)—or fixed for several hours at a time—may be obsolete by 2020 if these technologies continue to improve and become cheaper.

Technology, Status, and Time

Technology and fashion have a lot in common. Both thrive on the status of being the latest "it" item. Therefore, the friend with the latest technology for his or her iPhone holds a certain status among friends. The same phenomenon occurs in fashion when one member of a group shows up wearing the latest fashion. Technology as well as fashion depends on time to achieve status. For example, timing was critical for Target customers to purchase a Missoni item in 2011. Customers employed the technology of the Internet to purchase a reasonably priced Missoni outfit that was fashionable. Target customers were so excited by the Missoni sale that they shut down the retailer's website from an overwhelming number of orders. Even Fashion Week in New York is employing technology by sending invitations and handling check-ins through a computer system (Smith, 2010). Early adopters, who want tomorrow's fashions today, are using technology to radically change the way fashion is distributed and marketed.

In the reading "It Costs More to Save: Eco-Elitism Comes with a Price Tag. That Dress Made of Leaves and Flowers Will Be Dead by Morning," Reddy discusses how the well-heeled express their environmental concerns without giving up the lifestyle to which they are accustomed. If you have noticed the difference in pricing between, say, organic bananas and regular bananas, you have an idea that eco-friendliness can be costly. Ironically, as Reddy points out, the era of the eco status symbol coincides with a worldwide financial crisis.

Consumer Preferences for Apparel Technology

Given enough consumer demand, more innovative technologies will reach the mass consumer. For example, one technology is already available—however, not widespread—scanners take 10 seconds to collect thousands of body measurements to produce a garment that fits an individual precisely (see Figure 13.3). The individual steps into a cylinder, fully clothed, for 10 seconds and a computer spits out her exact measurements. With the measurements, a company can produce a perfect-fitting pair of jeans for between $160 and $180. If women complain that finding well-fitting jeans are hard to find, why are they not demanding this technology at an affordable price? Consumer acceptance is one reason and price is another. Perhaps the average-size woman is not comfortable knowing that all of her body measurements can be seen by store employees, nor does she want to invest $160 on a pair of jeans.

The next step in this technology would allow the customer to select fabric, color, and style details such as pant leg fullness and pocket style from an array of options. Not only would the garment be customized to fit precisely, but also the consumer would take part in designing the style of garments she or he wants. This process is called **co-design** (Fiore, Lee, and Kunz, 2004; Lee et al., 2002; Lee et al., 2011). Apparel industry experts often refer to custom-fit garments ordered through a mass retailer or producer as "**made-to-measure**" (Gellers, 1998). Garments ordered through a mass retailer or producer for which the consumer has made personal style design choices are referred to as **mass customized** (Pine, 1993).

Figure 13.3 Computerized body scanners can take a customer's precise body measurements.

Made-to-measure and mass-customized apparel is already available (Coia, 2003; Lee and Chen, 1999), but advances in computerized imaging and production systems probably will make customized apparel more readily accessible and less expensive sometime around the year 2020.

Only a small minority of consumers (about 9%) had purchased apparel through the Internet by early 1999 (Yoh et al., 2003). But more than one-third of shoppers had purchased apparel via the Internet by 2001 (Pastore, 2001), and apparel is now one of the top five most purchased product categories ("Online Spending," 2003). Why shouldn't we believe that these modes of shopping will play a more substantial role in how consumers shop by 2020?

Mass customization of fit is beginning to attract more customers; Lands' End has found that four of its top-selling products are in the customized-fit category (Coia, 2003). And the chances are good that a variety of modes of shopping will continue to be used through the next 10 years. Made-to-measure apparel will require extensive development of computer systems and new retail systems. The eventual changes in the fashion system that could result from widespread use of made-to-measure and mass-customized ordering are almost too immense to comprehend, but certainly intriguing. Increased variety and diversity in appearances and more uniqueness in what can be purchased could certainly emerge. The fashion system will become increasingly complex during the 21st century and consumers will determine which technologies are implemented and which are not.

Technology, Tradition, and Culture

Tradition in all fields has a habit of slowing things down. The terms *Western* and *non-Western* are often used interchangeably with *industrial* and *non-industrial* and create boundaries between cultures that embrace technology and those that do not. Cultures are often described by their level of technology. Think of the Egyptian pyramids and the roads and bridges engineered by the ancient Romans. In the apparel industry, one can create a technology continuum with a back-strap loom on one end and computer-operated industrial looms on the opposite end (see Figure 1.2 in Chapter 1 to view these looms side-by-side). What one gains in speed and standardization with computer-operated looms, one loses in creativity and variation of hand-made items.

Is tradition gender-specific? Women in most developing countries are considered more traditional than men. Women are often the last to give up their traditional dress and their cultural traditions because women are more likely than men to stay at home with children while men are more likely to seek employment away from the home. In fact, "women's work" often invokes images of slow, repetitive, low-tech labor that takes place in the home while women tend children. "Men's work" invokes images that are fast paced and include high production. Although not all developing countries divide labor between the private sphere (female) and the public sphere (male), many do (Barnes and Eicher, 1992).

Tradition is naturally resistant to innovation, and technological change is not always embraced with open arms. However, preserving traditions is valuable to cultural richness and to maintaining the history of a culture. In the reading "Kente as an Indigenous Ghanaian Textile," author Fianu describes the traditions of producing Kente cloth. Fianu outlines the process, including the sources of raw materials, equipment needed, and the weaving process (Figure 13.4).

On the other end of the technology continuum is a computerized loom used in most industrialized countries. This loom requires human intervention only when there is a problem (i.e., a thread has broken). The computerized loom needs to be programmed and maintained by a human, but the actual work of producing the cloth is done by the machine.

The apparel industry itself is resistant to change. Susan Watkins provides two examples, heat sealing and molding, as possible alternatives for the American apparel industry (Watkins, 1995b). Some of these processes have been around since the 1950s and were perfected after initial endeavors. These processes, which are practiced in European apparel industries, are time-efficient and economical. However, adopting these processes would mean changing the way clothing is designed, produced, and marketed in the United States. The American apparel industry evidently is not ready for these changes.

More recently, clothing researchers Armstrong and LeHew have considered the impact of the apparel industry on the environment and recommend a new **dominant social paradigm** for the apparel industry (see the reading "Shifting the Dominant Social Paradigm in the Apparel Industry: Acknowledging the Pink Elephant"). A paradigm is defined as an assembly of practices and protocols characterizing a discipline or field (Kuhn, 1996). Beginning with the Industrial Revolution the apparel industry's paradigm has dictated the exploitation of the earth's resources, which is now taking its toll on the environment. This mind-set of the apparel industry, to produce new fashions quickly while ignoring the earth's limits, is now being called into question by eco-conscious consumers. How can the apparel industry re-create itself so that it

Figure 13.4 Kente cloth woven in Bonwire, Ghana.

will be profitable and eco-friendly? Tradition has prevented the industry from changing and consumers are just now realizing that the costs of their consumer goods include costs to the earth. Armstrong and LeHew admit that changing the apparel industry will be difficult—but it can be done.

In her article, Susan Hack considers the likely disappearance of several tribes in Ethiopia once a dam is completed and begins operation in July 2013 (see the reading "Twilight of the Tribes: Ethiopia's Omo River Valley"). The dam is being built by the Ethiopian government, in which the tribes have no voice or representation. The introduction of the dam will change the traditions of this very old culture (believed to be the location of Adam and Eve, from whom every living human is descended), where tribes live in the desert of the Omo River Valley. In the article, Hack takes a hard look at the realities of tourism, voyeurism, and tribal cultures. You may want to compare this reading to Wade Davis's reading in Chapter 1 ("On Native Ground") about the disappearance of cultures.

Is technology a good thing? Governments often think that providing water to a desert area is the answer to problems, but they may not have considered the loss of cultural traditions once the area is no longer a desert. Similarly the Canadian government provided permanent housing to the Inuit and changed their nomadic lifestyle forever. But isn't it better for people to have water than to live in a desert? Isn't it better for people living in subzero temperatures to have permanent housing than to live as nomads? Perhaps, but one must remember that for centuries people have survived in the desert and in the Arctic creating incredible cultural traditions that may not survive modern technology. In many cases, the history of human resourcefulness and resilience is lost forever when new technology is introduced. Dress has been made in these harsh environments (see suggested reading by Issenman, 1997) for centuries in ways that have not depleted the earth's resources. As eco-fashionable dress becomes more acceptable, it might be wise to have these disappearing cultural traditions to examine.

Summary

Technology and dress is a wide-ranging topic with many avenues for innovation. Many groups and individuals are currently involved in the research and development of new technologies in dress. Many innovations are in the works that join nanotechnology and clothing to create wearable electronics. Time and status are important elements of both technology and fashion. Consumers may not be uniformly receptive of new technology and may reject technology or take time to adopt new technologies. However, new technology connected to dress will undoubtedly appeal to those who can afford it and eventually trickle down to the mass consumer. Both technology and traditions to create dress are uniquely tied to culture. Interventions into cultural groups with new technology should be considered carefully before moving forward.

Suggested Readings

Conley, K. (2002, December 9). Pointe Counterpointe. *The New Yorker*, 69–70, 72–73, 76, 79.

Hatcher, M. (2002, October 8). Fiber-Optic Dress Goes Down the Aisle. Accessed October 8, 2002, at optics.org/articles/news/8/10/11/1.

Issenman, B. K. (1997). *Sinews of Survival: The Living Legacy of Inuit Clothing*. Vancouver: University of British Columbia Press.

Latour, A. (2000, September 3). Full Wired Jacket. *Lexington Herald-Leader*, E1.

Parker, G. (2004, February 14). Woman Endures Surgeries to Lengthen Limbs. Netscape News. Accessed March 12, 2004, at search.netscape.com.

Rush, George. (2010, September). Trying (Hard) to Be a Good Man in Africa. *CondéNast Traveler*, 162–173, 208, 210.

Sagario, D. (2001, October 15). Now I Lay Thee Down: Device Helps Shape Skull. *The Des Moines Register*, 1E–2E.

Wells, Rachel. (2010, May 9). All Hail the New Prints of Fashion. *The Age* (Sunday), Melbourne, Australia. Retrieved from www.theage.com.au/lifestyle/fashion/all-hail-the-new-prints-of-fashion-20100509-ul5p.html.

Learning Activity 13.1: Dress and Technology

Objective

To find the most current information on wearable electronics.

Procedure

Do an online search to find out what is currently available in technology and dress. Use the following terms or a combination of terms to search for current information. You should prepare a report on your findings to share with the class. This can also be done in groups.

CuteCircuit	Nanotechnology and clothing
DuPont and smart garments	Philips NV
Fiber-optics and dress	Smart fabrics
ICD+ Smart garments	Technology and clothing
Levi-Strauss	Textronics
Luminex	Wearable electronics
M-Dress	

References

Barnes, R., and J. B. Eicher (Eds.). (1992). *Dress and Gender: Making and Meaning*. Oxford: Berg Press.

Coia, A. (2003). Channeling E-Tail Resources. *Apparel* 44 (12): 18–20.

Fiore, A. M., S. Lee, and G. Kunz. (2004). Individual Differences, Motivations, and Willingness to Use a Mass Customization Option for Fashion Products. *European Journal of Marketing* 38 (7): 835–849.

Gellers, S. (1998, July 8). Made-to-Measure: Raising the Stakes for Better Clothing. *Daily News Record* 9:16.

Kuhn, Thomas S. (1996). *The Structure of Scientific Revolutions* (3rd ed.). Chicago: University of Chicago Press.

Lee, S., and J. C. Chen. (1999, December). Mass Customization Methodology for Apparel Manufacturing with a Future. *Journal of Industrial Technology* 16 (1). Accessed August 5, 2002, at www.nait.org.

Lee, H. H., M. L. Damhorst, J. R. Campbell, S. Loker, and J. L. Parsons. (2011). Consumer Satisfaction with a Mass Customized Internet Apparel Shopping Site. *International Journal of Consumer Studies* 35 (3): 316–329.

Lee, S., G. Kunz, A. M. Fiore, and J. R. Campbell. (2002). Acceptance of Mass Customization of Apparel: Merchandising Issues Associated with Preference for Product, Process, and Place. *Clothing and Textiles Research Journal* 20 (3): 138–146.

McCraken, G. 1988. *Culture and Consumption*. Bloomington: Indiana University Press.

Online Spending Keeps Growing in Q3. (2003, October 1). Accessed November 1, 2003, at www.bizrate.com/content/press/release_rel_147.html.

Pastore, M. (2001, January 16). Consumer Continues Online Purchases. Accessed September 13, 2004, at www.clickz.com/stats/markets/retailing/article.php/560781.

Pine, B. J., II. (1993). *Mass Customization: The New Frontier in Business Competition*. Boston: Harvard Business School Press.

Smith, R. A. (2010, August 19). Sequins, Fur and Bar Codes: New York Fashion Week Tries to Ditch Clipboard Culture for Electronic Efficiency. *Wall Street Journal*, D1.

Tortora, P. G., and K. Eubank. (2010). *Survey of Historic Costume: A History of Western Dress* (5th ed.). New York: Fairchild Books.

Warren, S. (2001, October 10). Ready-to-Wear Watchdogs: "Smart" Garments Keep Track of Vital Signs, Hide Odor. *Wall Street Journal*, B1, B3.

Watkins, S. M. (1995a). *Clothing: The Portable Environment* (2nd ed.). Ames: Iowa State University Press.

Watkins, S. M. (1995b). Stitchless Sewing for the Apparel of the Future. In M. E. Roach-Higgins, J. B. Eicher, and K. K. P. Johnson (Eds.), *Dress and Identity*, pp. 270–274. New York: Fairchild Books.

Yoh, E., M. L. Damhorst, S. Sapp, and R. Laczniak. (2003). Consumer Adoption of the Internet: The Case of Apparel Shopping. *Psychology and Marketing* 20 (12): 1095–1118.

HAUTE TECHNOLOGY: A NEW WAVE OF DESIGNERS IS EXPERIMENTING WITH ELECTRONIC TEXTILES, REACTIVE FASHION AND WEARABLE COMPUTERS FOR A GENERATION THAT GREW UP WIRED

David Graham

Not too long ago all a dress had to do was look good.

And if it was comfortable—even better.

But those days may be numbered, particularly if a new generation of technologically inclined fashion designers has its way.

As they struggle to blend the hard elements of technology with the soft and intimate nature of fashion, the common wardrobe may start performing in ways that had previously been considered science fiction. A shirt will have multiple personalities—changing colours from day to night, for example. Trousers will multitask with keyboards, iPods or GPS systems built directly into their design, perhaps right into the very fibres.

Clothing will no longer accommodate technology with handy little pockets. Your wardrobe will *be* your BlackBerry.

Far beyond the possibility of clunky wearable computers are electronic textiles, reactive fashion and soft computation.

Ying Gao creates "modulatable" garments that change depending on the wearer's environment. Pleats open and close. Floral embellishments mutate according to light conditions, for example, or as people approach the wearer. It serves no real purpose—unless you believe fashion and beauty are purpose enough.

Gao, a fashion designer and professor at the University of Quebec at Montreal, was just awarded a $10,000 grant from the City of Montreal.

Gao says her interest in fusing technology and fashion began when she recognized that the once highly conceptual world of haute couture seemed to be losing its creative edge, that because it was not embracing technology, it was no longer modern. It lost its reputation for innovation, she says.

Also in Montreal, Joanna Berzowska is researching yarns woven with strands of silver or stainless steel that are able to conduct electricity. She's even dipped into electronic inks that are incorporated into traditional textile manufacturing techniques such as spinning, weaving, knitting and embroidery to create mutable, beautiful clothes that change colours.

This is the future, says Berzowska, who acknowledges there are some kinks to work out. Berzowska, an assistant professor of computation arts at Concordia University, founded XS Labs in Montreal to carry out her design work.

Some wearable technology seems too uncomfortable to be wearable or too fragile to endure the rigours of everyday life.

"What if you get caught in the rain?" she asks. The technology has to be wearable like a cashmere sweater or a pair of Spandex pants.

Around the world, fashion and textile designers with a flair for technology are taking various paths. In the United States, research into wearable technology is funded largely by the military, an industry that embraces fabrics, for example, that inform soldiers when they've been shot. Now they are developing materials that step in and heal the wound. A jacket sleeve may stiffen to become a splint following an injury.

By contrast, European research into the fusion of technology and fashion is supported by giant consumer appliance companies such as Philips and Nokia.

"Philips has already taken out patents on much of this new technology," Berzowska says. "They appreciate it's the wave of the future in consumer electronics."

In Canada, however, a growing design culture enamoured with the possibilities of haute technology is less fascinated by military or baldly commercial applications. Here, the guiding principle for wearable technology designers is that, first, it must be beautiful and novel.

". . . What is often forgotten in current research is the intimacy of textiles, their close proximity to the body, and their potential for personal expression and playful experimentation," Berzowska has written in a German textile magazine.

Still, funding for such research is abundant here.

"In Canada this is a culture-backed industry," Berzowska says. Assistance comes from sources including the Canada Council for the Arts and even Canadian Heritage. There is a broad relevance to this research in science, design and culture.

She is also convinced the fruit of her research may help Canada's struggling textiles industry by providing innovative products and value-added design.

Canadians are more likely to follow the creative path taken by Turkish designer Hussein Chalayan, known as a strident supporter of technology's role in fashion. Chalayan, who lives in London and shows in Paris, has been named British designer of the year twice. He has a reputation for mounting highly conceptual fashion shows that employ tricks of technology to make a point—zippers that move, fabric that folds and unfolds and hemlines that rise and fall—electronically.

"It's very designer-based here," Berzowska says. "Designers accept that pleasure and beauty are functions."

"The other thing we have to remember is that a whole generation has grown up with personal technology. These technologies are a core part of their identity. This is a natural thing for them to explore."

Another challenge will surface once designers attempt to manufacture their garments in quantities large enough to turn a profit.

"It has to be made affordable," she says.

Berzowska has approached Gap and Banana Republic, but she says they were concerned that even the inclusion of simple technologies would interrupt the efficiency in their streamlined factories.

"Right now, it's a novelty," Berzowska says. "It's always seen in the context of an experiment."

But she has seen the future and warns we should be prepared. Some day soon, a dress will no longer be just a dress.

Discussion Questions

1. Can you envision wearing clothes that contain the technology in iPhones or BlackBerrys, etc.? Why or why not?
2. Does joining the hardware of technology with the soft wear of fashion sound like science fiction to you, or does it sound more like a normal evolution that is inevitable? Explain your answer.
3. Do you believe that the haute couture industry needs to be updated with the latest technology in order to be relevant to today's consumers? Or, do you believe that the lack of technology is what gives haute couture its uniqueness? Explain your answer.

13.2

NEW UGA TECHNOLOGY MAKES TEXTILES GERM-FREE

UGA News Service

A university researcher has invented a new technology that can inexpensively render medical linens and clothing, face masks, paper towels—and yes, even diapers, intimate apparel and

Retrieved from: http://www.redandblack. com/2011/07/05/new-uga-technology-makes-textiles-germ-free/

athletic wear, including smelly socks—permanently germ-free.

The simple and inexpensive antimicrobial technology works on natural and synthetic materials. The technology can be applied during the manufacturing process or at home, and it doesn't come out in the wash. Unlike other antimicrobial technologies, repeated applications are unnecessary to maintain effectiveness.

"The spread of pathogens on textiles and plastics is a growing concern, especially in health care facilities and hotels, which are ideal environments for the proliferation and spread of very harmful microorganisms, but also in the home," said Jason Locklin, the inventor, who is an assistant professor of chemistry in the Franklin College of Arts and Sciences and on the Faculty of Engineering.

The antimicrobial treatment invented by Locklin, which is available for licensing from the University of Georgia Research Foundation, Inc., effectively kills a wide spectrum of bacteria, yeasts and molds that can cause disease, break down fabrics, create stains and produce odors.

According to the Centers for Disease Control and Prevention, approximately one of every 20 hospitalized patients will contract a health-care-associated infection. Lab coats, scrub suits, uniforms, gowns, gloves and linens are known to harbor the microbes that cause patient infections.

Consumers' concern about harmful microbes has spurred the market for clothing, undergarments, footwear and home textiles with antimicrobial products. But to be practical, both commercial and consumer antimicrobial products must be inexpensive and lasting.

"Similar technologies are limited by cost of materials, use of noxious chemicals in the application or loss of effectiveness after a few washings,"

said Gennaro Gama, UGARF senior technology manager. "Locklin's technology uses ingeniously simple, inexpensive and scalable chemistry."

Gama said the technology is simple to apply in the manufacturing of fibers, fabrics, filters and plastics. It also can bestow antimicrobial properties on finished products, such as athletic wear and shoes, and textiles for the bedroom, bathroom and kitchen.

"The advantage of UGARF's technology over competing methods," said Gama, "is that the permanent antimicrobial can be applied to a product at any point of the manufacture-sale-use continuum. In contrast, competing technologies require blending of the antimicrobial in the manufacturing process."

"In addition," said Gama, "if for some reason the antimicrobial layer is removed from an article—through abrasion, for example—it can be reapplied by simple spraying."

Other markets for the antimicrobial technology include military apparel and gear, food packaging, plastic furniture, pool toys, medical and dental instrumentation, bandages and plastic items.

Locklin said the antimicrobial was tested against many of the pathogens common in health-care settings, including staph, strep, E. coli, pseudomonas and acetinobacter. After just a single application, no bacterial growth was observed on the textile samples added to the culture—even after 24 hours at 37 degrees Celsius.

Moreover, in testing, the treatment remained fully active after multiple hot-water laundry cycles, demonstrating the antibacterial does not leach out from the textiles even under harsh conditions. "Leaching could hinder the applicability of this technology in certain industrial segments, such as food packaging, toys, IV bags and tubing, for example," said Gama.

Discussion Questions

1. Would you buy a germ-free T-shirt if it were close in price to the T-shirts you buy today that is not germ-free? Why or why not? Or do you think that germ-free technology has more application in the hospital and hospitality industries than in the consumer sector? Explain your answer.
2. If germ-free clothes were affordable, would the feel of the fabric next to the body (i.e., comfortable and soft or scratchy and coarse) outweigh the benefits of it being germ-free?
3. Would you be concerned that this product, like others, might lead to the development of stronger and more resistant bacteria strains?

SWINGING FOR THE FENCES WITH EVOSHIELD

Denise Horton

Justin Niefer (BSFCS '05, Consumer Economics) wasn't sure where his future lay. Having completed his eligibility with the University of Georgia's baseball team, he spent the summer of 2005 in Crestwood, Ill., with the Windy City Thunderbolts, a member of the Frontier League, but realized that professional baseball lacked the camaraderie he found most appealing about sports.

Niefer returned to Athens and to his final semester of classes in consumer economics believing he'd likely join a large financial planning firm upon graduation. But fate intervened in the form of a part-time job helping kids with their batting skills.

Company owner "Stan Kanavage had called coach [David] Perno, asking if he knew of any former players with a marketing background who could also give baseball lessons," Niefer recalls. "So I spoke with Stan, and we agreed I'd receive internship credit for helping market his business, All Sports Training, and offer lessons."

Just a few months later, Kanavage announced that he was starting an additional business, one focused on developing sports-protection gear made of a new lightweight and malleable substance that hardens to fit the wearer's body and disperses impact (Figures 13.5a and b). Kanavage invited Niefer and Stan Payne, another All Sports employee, to join David Hudson and himself in establishing this new company.

"The people you're around every day bring value that money can't buy," Kanavage says of his decision to include Niefer and Payne in the venture. "I told them: 'You guys are my friends and family. I'll pay you what I can: but sweat equity will be expected.'"

For Niefer, the new product, originally dubbed All Sports Armour, offered the opportunity to be in on the ground floor of a commercial phenomenon that may someday be as well known as Gatorade. "For a 23-year-old, this was pretty

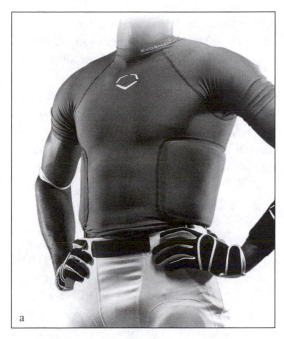

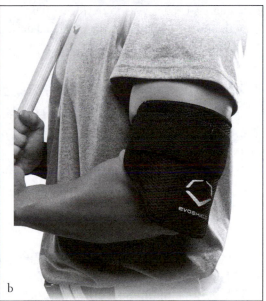

Figure 13.5 Protective athletic equipment by Evoshield is lightweight and flexible (a and b).

Reprinted by permission of the author.

exciting," he recalls, "especially when I saw what the material could do. Instead of foam and plastic and bulky padding, this is only a quarter-inch thin." And it works like a charm, he adds. "We have a YouTube video showing someone hitting me in the ribs with a bat, and it clearly doesn't hurt. After classes, I'd buy poster board and start drawing different designs. I'd cut them out, see how they would fit and then work on them some more."

From January 2006 until spring 2008, Niefer continued to teach baseball lessons in addition to getting the new company off the ground. Because money was so tight, he also lived cheaply, managing to find a house that rented for a mere $150 per month in exchange for Niefer painting the interior and resurfacing the wood floors.

During that time, the business began to grow. By the end of 2006, chest and back protectors were being produced, and its product line now also includes wrist guards, a shin/foot guard, and an elbow guard, among others. In 2007 Niefer proposed a new name for the company—Evoshield—which his colleagues embraced.

"The 'Evo' stands for how the material evolves from a soft material into a hard shell, but it also stands for our vision of evolving the world of sports and the way athletes are protected during competition," he says.

A Bulldog from Buffalo

Niefer spent his childhood in Buffalo, N.Y., with an Old World influence. "My mom is from Poland, so we grew up with an Eastern European family dynamic where everything was earned," he says. "My athletic endeavors were important, but my parents taught us that sports were an opportunity to be a good leader as well as a team player. They also could facilitate higher learning."

From ages 6 to 16, Niefer participated both in hockey and baseball. While the baseball season for kids growing up in the Northeast is short, he could play hockey nearly year-round as he participated on travel teams. And because he stood out in both sports, as Niefer entered his junior year of high school recruiting letters began to arrive. His father told him the time had come to choose which sport he would pursue in college. The choice was easy. "Hockey had become a job for me," Niefer recalls. "But I *loved* baseball. When I told my dad I was choosing baseball, he said, 'Be the best you can at it.'"

During his senior year of high school, his dad, an electrical engineer, landed a new job that resulted in his parents moving to Cumming, Ga., while Niefer headed off on a baseball scholarship to the University of Cincinnati. There he became captain of the school's team and was named to the All-Conference USA Team.

"Even with a scholarship, I still worked in the library re-shelving books and as a valet," Niefer says. "So I started thinking that if I transferred to Georgia I would have the HOPE Scholarship and not have to worry about out-of-state tuition. Besides, I'd also be closer to my parents."

After three years, he did transfer, though an administrative snag resulted in his not being able to enroll in fall 2003 as he had intended. "I spent that fall working at a local gas station," Niefer says, "and that was when I began to realize my entrepreneurial nature. I established a keg refrigerator—which was popular with the college students—and opened up a little memorabilia section."

In January, he enrolled as a business major and "redshirt senior" on the baseball team. But "in the business school I was in an auditorium with 150 other students," he says. "When I transferred to consumer economics I was looking for something more intimate, but I also got a variety of knowledge in housing, economics and consumer-buying behavior—a cornucopia of real-life applications. It was an environment that allowed me to find out what I was good at."

In spring 2005, Niefer suited up for the Diamond Dawgs and quickly established himself as a hitting threat, moving into the top 10 in the nation during the first 20 or so games. But a freak accident during fielding practice in Louisville, Ky., virtually ended his college baseball career.

"We were warming up for our game, in the snow, at the old Louisville fairgrounds," he recalls. "A coach hit me a deep fly ball. I put out my hand to stop myself and caught it on the old metal lettering they still had on the fence. It ripped a hole in my hand that resulted in nerve damage."

The injury limited Niefer's throwing ability for the rest of the season, and while he did serve as designated hitter, his statistics dropped. But "I consider it a blessing," he says. "If that hadn't happened, I might be playing in the minor leagues and this [he motions around his Evoshield office] might not have happened."

Evoshield Prospers

In 2007, Niefer traveled to spring training in Florida and experienced notable success when the first seven Major League Baseball teams he met with placed orders for the rib, wrist, and ankle protectors. Back home, the Georgia baseball team began wearing Evoshield products and word soon filtered to UGA quarterback Mathew Stafford and his football teammates.

"What we heard was that the players felt faster and more protected in Evoshield gear," Niefer says. Independent testing has in fact shown that Evoshield disperses energy rather than absorbing it, which is what occurs with traditional foam and plastic gear.

Despite their growing success, the Evoshield founders were still juggling two businesses. "We were working on Evoshield from 9 to 4 and then giving baseball lessons from 4 to 10 p.m. It was especially tough for Stan Payne, who is married and has kids," Niefer recalls. "By the end of 2007, we began to realize that we needed to commit to either the new business or All Sports Training; we couldn't keep doing both."

The decision to pursue Evoshield full-time came after what Stan Kanavage calls divine intervention: "Two gentlemen came to see me and said, 'Our church has voted to buy your building,'" a purchase that meant there would no longer be a location to teach baseball and other sporting lessons. Thus for the past 2½ years the founders have dedicated all of their energies to growing their Evoshield business. And through word of mouth and grassroots marketing, interest in the products has indeed continued to grow. Last year, Niefer set up a booth at the College World Series in Omaha, Neb., and saw sales of Evoshield wristbands and other items rise dramatically as player and fans alike sought him out.

A particular boon was when 2009 Rookie of the Year and former UGA standout Gordon Beckham became the first professional athlete to endorse Evoshield—free of charge. Beckham was shown on the cover of Baseball Express, a publication of a leading equipment company, tagging third base, with his glove hand raised high in the air and the Evoshield logo prominently displayed.

A Team Culture

While the company has expanded to include 12 different products and lists 80 college and professional teams among its customers, it still operates like a start-up business. Housed in borrowed offices on the outskirts of Athens, three of Evoshield's most recent hires share space with inventory, such as the foil packages that hold the malleable material. When large orders arrive, everyone joins in packaging the products for shipment.

But things may soon change. Evoshield has hired Bob Pickney, a UGA business-school graduate who also holds an MBA from Harvard, to move the company to new levels. Niefer, now 29 and product-development manager at Evoshield, welcomes the skills Pickney brings and his commitment to maintaining the company's team-like culture.

"We've had a lot of investment offers, but they also want to change our culture. Bob liked our tight-knit group, and he'll allow us to continue focusing on what we're each good at. I think he'll provide us the infrastructure to support our growth."

Kanavage speaks with pride about the accomplishments of Niefer and Payne in growing Evoshield from an idea into a business that was listed as the second-fastest-growing business in the Bulldog 100, a program sponsored by the UGA Alumni Association that rated companies by their compounded annual revenue-growth rates during the past three years.

"They've worked diligently, developing ideas, selling, and showing. They've done everything that needed to be done." Kanavage says, "Whatever Justin does, he does with passion, and he's been very passionate about what we do and how we do it. He's matured into someone who could today start and run his own company."

Discussion Questions

1. How many YouTube videos can you find featuring Evoshield products? How have the founders of Evoshield used YouTube as a marketing tool? Do you think it has been effective?
2. Sports, such as baseball and football, want lightweight protection that does not slow the athlete down, either mentally or physically. Explain how the differences between traditional padding and Evoshield can affect an athlete mentally as well as physically.
3. Can you envision applications other than sports for this product? Explain.

13.4

PRINTS FOR THE CYBERAGE

Suzy Menkes

London—Torrents of color, turbulent whorls of pattern, violent clashes—the effects that appear on summer dresses often look more like a wild weather chart than the more familiar prints charming.

Printed matter has undergone a digital revolution, as the new millennium has witnessed a dramatic change in the way that a pattern is developed to follow the shape of the body and to overlay actual images with virtual versions.

The cauldron of cyberspace wizardry has bubbled up in London, where, as Erdem Moralioglu, the recent winner of the British Fashion Council/Vogue Designer Fashion Fund award, says: "I don't know anywhere else where I could study prints in a printing studio, like when I started at the Royal College of Art."

"I've always been able to do all my prints digitally," adds the designer, who is known as Erdem. "It's about tricking the eye, whether it is done by digital technique or by human hand. I didn't really learn the techniques. It is much more about trial and error. My prints are quite organic—I might find a piece of old wallpaper, Photoshop the print and add watercolor."

The result for the summer collection was florals that seemed to grow like a patchy herbaceous border, some faded away by computer, others "cut-and-pasted" by handwork, creating a magical, but modern, effect.

Overlays of print creating striking collages was the summer focus of Peter Pilotto. For the

Antwerp-trained design duo behind the label, most of the work is digital.

"Every season we work differently," says Mr. Pilotto, whose co-designer is Christopher de Vos. "But we always do illustrations of the collage on the figure, because the pattern needs to connect with the body."

For the summer collection, Mr. Pilotto's starting point was seeing fireworks exploding over the Venice Lido. That was then enhanced by asking a photographer to capture "linear light reflections" on the Thames in London. The duo then reworked the colors, but kept to the original story line.

"It is so easy to use crazy effects—and I don't like it when the computer does it for you," says Mr. Pilotto, adding that he might have up to 100 trials for one finished print.

The way that the late Alexander McQueen embraced technology led to an explosion of print, whether it was the 3-D Art Nouveau patterns in his last men's collection or the writhing snakes and super-enhanced nature effects on sculpted dresses.

Another producer of vivid and original prints, including effects of blown glass and giant jewelry, is Mary Katrantzou, a designer of Greek origin and a graduate of Central Saint Martin's College of Art and Design in London.

"My training is as a textile designer and in traditional screen printing, but because of the nature of what I was doing with trompe l'oeil, digital collages give greater plasticity," the designer says. "With a screen print 10 or 15 color separations need great expertise. With digital, there is no limitation—you can print a photographical version of anything."

Susannah Handley, a former teacher at the Royal College of Art in London, and now a Paris-based fabrics consultant for Louis Vuitton, saw the global impact of the new digital age in the mid-1990s.

She describes the difference between traditional and digitally printed textiles as akin to painting versus photography. Her heart remains with "the picturesque romance of copper rollers, silk screens, and the luxury of eye-mixed liquid color." But she admits that it is "as antiquated as grinding up lapis lazuli to make paint."

"Directly from computer to cloth is how many patterns are realized these days—it is a more clinical, faster method with the advantage that an instant result can be achieved," Ms. Handley says, referring to the computer's arsenal of "hundreds of options and thousands of color tones."

When still at the college, the fabric specialist realized that while a digital sketchbook was a great tool for ideas, it eliminated the physical connection with color and cloth. She says that is why the luxury universe still sees digital designs as inferior and as belonging to the mass market, compared to historic screen printing.

Does anyone really care about the method behind the special effects?

A discriminating customer can apparently tell the difference, as screen-printed pigments saturate the cloth and the image penetrates both sides, while digital "sits on the surface." Yet the ink-jet printers are integral to materials sourced in a country like Turkey—and even the famous Italian fabric manufacturers of Lake Como are now using both methods.

For young designers, the power of digital is that it requires only a desk, a chair, a computer and a creative mind. And if the price of a complex and originally patterned designer dress is lowered by new technology—so much the better for the consumer.

Although Ms. Handley regrets the passing of "some kind of magic hanging over the long-stained print tables," who can be sure that Photoshop will beat out traditional pigments?

"The question for the future is how to understand and accept the new textile balance," Ms. Handley says. "Painting was declared dead the day photography was invented in 1839—but we know now that it was not."

Discussion Questions

1. To determine the difference between digital prints on fabric and screen-printed fabrics, use the Internet to find images of both. Place the images side-by-side and e-mail to your instructor in PowerPoint format so that examples can be presented in class. Discuss the differences between these two types of technology at the consumer level. Do consumers really care how their fabrics are printed?

2. Why is digital printing such a revelation in fashion design? Research the screen-printing process and list its pros and cons. Repeat with the digital printing process. What are the advantages and disadvantages of both processes, such as cost and environmental issues? Why are designers so enamored of the digital printing process?

3. From your research on digital printing, can you determine if this process is currently used in high-end (expensive) products only, or has it trickled down to mass fashion? How much more will a customer have to pay for a digitally printed garment than a screen-printed one?

EXCUSE ME, BUT MY DRESS IS RINGING: TECHNOLOGY GIVES FABRICS GREATER FUNCTION AS THE DAILY DEMANDS OF EVERYDAY LIFE ARE MET IN STYLE

The Toronto Star

The '60s TV sitcom *Get Smart* brought us the shoe phone, but now a dress phone?

It's the M-Dress—a silk garment that doubles as a mobile phone. Produced by UK firm CuteCircuit, the M-Dress works with a standard SIM card. When the dress rings, you raise your hand to your head to answer the call.

This futuristic fusion of fashion and technology is becoming more common as clothing designers are increasingly incorporating electronics into their garments (Figure 13.6).

Jane McCann, director of Smart Clothes and Wearable Technology at the University of Wales, says the clothing and electronics industries are collaborating in an unprecedented way—what she describes as "a new industrial revolution."

McCann predicts that, in the next 10 years, clothes will have all kinds of functionality. "A garment might have devices on it to help you find your way somewhere, or to tell you how fit you are. It could tell you where someone is to help you meet them, or tell you what's on at a museum or club," she told CNN.

She notes the sports and fitness industries have led the way in wearable technology, producing shoes with built-in pedometers and active wear with iPod controls.

"Wearable technology is coming through into useful everyday clothing more than it is on the catwalk. The catwalk still treats wearable tech as flashing earrings or sensational things," McCann says.

While high fashion may be slow to adopt practical technology, designers have been quick to embrace technology in order to create dazzling new styles. Hussein Chalayan, twice selected as British Designer of the Year, has used his shows to experiment with dresses that glow with built-in LEDs or emit spectacular red lasers.

Others, like Angel Chang, have produced beautiful designs using thermochromic inks that change colour when you touch or breathe on them, while Montreal's XS Labs has used a shape-memory alloy called Nitinol to produce extraordinary dresses that change shape while you wear them.

As well as functionality, McCann believes mass customization will emerge as a major trend in clothing. "You can already go into a sizing booth and get measurements of your size and shape."

Figure 13.6 Embedded sensors in CuteCircuit's "Hug Shirt" enable people to send and receive the sensation of an actual hug through their mobile phones.

Reprinted with permission, Torstar Syndication Services.

Perhaps you could store that information on a card and that could be used to customize clothing.

"In theory, if you've got technology that's cutting out garments one at a time it could produce clothes informed by your own size requirements," she says.

But mass customization could extend beyond getting the perfect fit—you might also be able to customize the technology in your clothes.

Says McCann: "You might want built-in controls for an MP3 player, but I might like heartbeat monitoring. I'd like mine to have a digital print of the (album) sleeve, but my friend wants a picture of her boyfriend on the back. Some of that could happen in the next 10 years."

Discussion Questions

1. Would you want your phone embedded in your clothing? Why or why not?
2. This reading mentions a new industrial revolution in clothing and electronics; another reading in this chapter ("Prints for the Cyberage") is demostrating how much easier digital printing is than screen printing. Do you think these new developments will pave the way for the current apparel industry to move toward a new Dominant Social Paradigm (as discussed in the Armstrong and LeHew reading)?
3. What is mass customization? Does the mass consumer want mass customization? It is predicted that around 2020 some mass-customization features will be available. Search the Internet to find the mass-customization capabilities nearest your university. What is available and how far away is it? How much does it cost?

13.6

THE SHIRT YOU SPRAY ON: FOR CLOTHES THAT FIT LIKE A SECOND SKIN, TRY INSTANT FABRIC IN A CAN

Tamara Cohen

Rummaging through a drawer, grabbing a T-shirt and slipping it over your head would certainly be simpler. But some of us are willing to put a little more effort into our wardrobes.

The result? A shirt that fits so snugly it looks as if it has been sprayed on to the body. Actually, it has.

Thanks to a liquid mixture made of cotton fibers, we could soon be spraying ourselves into everything from T-shirts, dresses and trousers to swimwear and hats (Figure 13.7).

Fabrican—literally fabric in an aerosol can—is the brainchild of Spanish designer Dr. Manel Torres, who has spent ten years working on his invention.

In a video demonstrating how it works, he sprays a blue and white T-shirt on to a model in just under 15 minutes.

Drying as soon as it hits his skin, the garment can be taken off, washed and re-worn.

Dr. Torres teamed up with Paul Luckham, Professor of Particle Technology at Imperial College London, to create Fabrican, which consists of cotton fibers, polymers (the plastics which hold them together) and solvents which keep it in liquid form.

Originally published by the *Daily Mail*. Reprinted by permission of Solo Syndication.

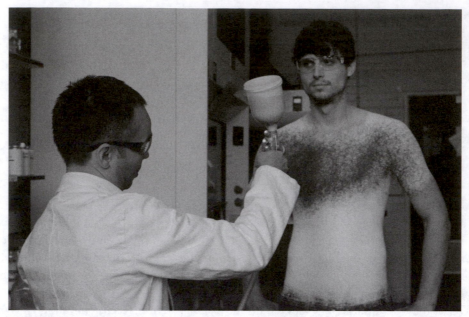

Figure 13.7 Designer Dr. Manel Torres sprays Fabrican onto a model.

When you get bored with your creation it can be dissolved and the material used again to make something new or repair old designs.

Dr. Torres said the idea was to be able to create clothes instantly and cheaply, all of which would be a perfect fit.

The Power of Fabrican

Dr. Torres has also suggested other areas where his flexible adhesive invention could be used:

- **Medical:** wound-healing products, dressings and patches.
- **Automotive:** instant nonwoven fabric for interiors, stain-resistant upholstery.
- **Hygiene:** household/hospital wipes, nappies and towels.

"I really wanted to make a futuristic, seamless, quick and comfortable material," he said.

"To show science and technology can help fashion designers, I ended up returning to the principles of the earliest textiles such as felt, which were also produced by taking fibers and finding a way of binding them together without having to weave or stitch."

Fabrican is still a couple of years from hitting the shelves.

Dr. Torres is working on ways to create more forgiving shapes as not everyone likes their clothes clinging to every curve. He is also trying to minimize the distinct whiff of solvent about the garments.

And although some spray-on designs will be on show at London Fashion Week, the instant fabric could end up being used for everything from bandages to furniture upholstery.

Discussion Questions

1. Would you wear a spray-on T-shirt? Why or why not?
2. What would be your biggest concern when purchasing a spray to make a T-shirt? Would the design possibilities outweigh the cost? Would sensitive skin react adversely to the spray?
3. Would your body type/size influence your decision to buy a spray-on T-shirt? Would the spray hitting your body initially turn you off? Why or why not?

IT COSTS MORE TO SAVE: ECO-ELITISM COMES WITH A PRICE TAG. THAT DRESS MADE OF LEAVES AND FLOWERS WILL BE DEAD BY MORNING

Sameer Reddy

Between Brad Pitt's new biodegradable body wash for Kiehl's and recent green issues of glossy magazines like *Vanity Fair*, it's easy to forget that eco-consciousness hasn't always had upscale cachet. When I was growing up in the 1980s, it consisted mainly of hippie-dippie products like Birkenstocks and hemp T-shirts, along with annoying tasks like recycling. Now that saving the earth has become trendy, entrepreneurs have begun to brand green products across all price points—including the highest ones. For the carbon-footprint-erasing jet set, this translates into a new breed of luxury products that allow them to indulge in the kind of excess to which they've become accustomed, while still feeling virtuous about their impact on the planet. The age of the eco status symbol is upon us, even at a time of worldwide financial crisis.

The automobile provides one of the most obvious applications for green technology, but until recently it didn't get much more exciting than Toyota's electric hybrid, Prius, which isn't exactly competing with Mercedes for clientele (except perhaps in some Hollywood garages). Luxury consumers with more-traditional tastes can take heart, as some of their favorite gas guzzlers are being retooled to meet SULEV (super ultralow emission vehicle) standards. Lexus's 2008 LS 600h L features a 438-horsepower V-8 engine that delivers V-12 power, with an additional high-output, electric-drive motor. Packed with the same over-the-top options as its gas-only sibling, the LS 460—including a reclining rear seat with a massage function and an automatic parking-guidance system—it comes at a much steeper base price: $104,900, compared with the LS 460's $62,900.

BMW is looking past electricity to hydrogen as an energy source, with the advent of the Hydrogen 7, a modified version of its top-of-the-line 760Li sedan. The V12 engine can run on either liquid hydrogen or gasoline, and spokesmen have been quoted as saying it could be sold at a "manageable premium" over the standard $125,000 for the 760Li (the Hydrogen 7 has not yet been released). For wealthy auto enthusiasts, the sticker shock isn't an impediment. If anything, it's the opposite—the extreme price tag makes these cars seem even more appealing as a way to stand out while making a progressive statement.

For those who wear their planetary concern on their sleeves, the fantastical creations from Franz Gräbe Flower Couture (see Figure 13.8) are the ultimate expression of conviction in both sustainable, and conspicuous, consumption. The series of outfits recently unveiled during the Auditions show at Sanlam South Africa Fashion Week were constructed exclusively from natural materials like twigs, leaves, flowers and reeds, accessorized with more than $775,000 worth of avant-garde gold jewelry. No chance that these frocks will sit unworn for years in your closet; within hours the blossoms begin to wilt, and by the following day your dress is literally dead. As they say, in fashion, what's in one day is out the next.

Diamonds have a much longer shelf life, but many also come with a controversial pedigree that involves being mined in a war zone and sold in order to finance nongovernmental military action (see reading "Diamonds Aren't Forever" in Chapter 14). Additionally, the industrial processes used to mine gold include destructive large-scale machines and toxic chemicals like mercury. A

Figure 13.8 Flower Couture by Designer Franz Gräbe.

unused jewelry." Maybe Grandma's ugly engagement ring isn't so useless after all.

For those who have acquired all the trappings of an environmentally elite life—a tricked-out sedan, grass skirt and recycled gold earrings—there's one more major purchase yet to make: a home. A minimum of $1 million will buy a manor in Florida's Sky real-estate development. Set in the state's northwest foothills, the project promises to redefine the planned-community paradigm around environmentally sound initiatives. With its own recycling center, composting yard, extensive organic gardens and orchards, and a farmers market, Sky aims to encourage a local food cycle. Homes will incorporate solar technology, and amenities will include equestrian stables, hiking trails, a wildlife sanctuary, electric community transportation and natural spring-fed pools. In an era marked by unease about the repercussions of our ecologically unsound decisions, Sky will allow its residents to lead the good life in more ways than one.

Fortunately for the lovers and purveyors of old-fashioned luxury standbys—like 30-carat canary yellow diamonds and Lamborghinis—the market for ecofriendly luxury is still in its nascent stage. Its cost premiums require buyers to appreciate the idea of sustainability in order to accept higher prices. But in the coming years, especially if economic hard times improve, the market will likely boom as luxury consumers express their concern the way they know best: with their credit cards. There's nothing like a fat bank account to make it easy being green.

company called GreenKarat offers a solution by manufacturing its pieces with recycled precious metals and either recycled or lab-created stones. The company states "there is enough gold above ground (already mined) to satisfy all demands of the jewelry industry for the next 50 years. Much of it sits in bank vaults and in the form of old and

Discussion Questions

1. How much are you willing to spend to be eco-friendly? How often, if ever, do you buy eco-friendly products (food, clothes, or accessories)?
2. Do you think eco-elitism is a positive way to encourage the wealthy to care about the environment? Or do you think this is just another status symbol (or fad) that will be adopted by those who want to appear "above others"? Explain your answer.
3. What is your reaction to the Florida development planned community around environmentally sound initiatives? How long do you predict it will be before this type of community becomes mainstream?

KENTE AS AN INDIGENOUS GHANAIAN TEXTILE

Docea A. G. Fianu

Production Process

Sources of Raw Material

Raffia was originally used for Kente weaving. This was replaced by cotton yams locally hand spun and dyed with dyes prepared from the bark of the "Indigofera" tree. Early cloths were, however, in plain white. Dutch silk was later used for Kente weaving because of its lustre, and it was regarded as prestigious. Silk cloths in bright colours were bought, unravelled and then rewoven in traditional designs that were suited to Ashanti taste (Sjarief, 1970). Unravelled European linen, wool and rayon were also used. Today, dyed skeins of cotton, rayon, and cotton/polyester blends are imported from either Europe, India, Cote d'Ivoire or Burkina Faso for Kente weaving. One Mr. B.A. Mensah established a factory in Tema, Ghana, where he produces dyed yams for sale. A packet of yams costs about ¢60,000 (cedis).

Equipment for Weaving Kente

The equipment for weaving are made by a specialist or by the weaver himself. These include a wooden loom called "Kofi Nsadua" (Friday-born loom). (See Figure 13.4 on page 526.) The loom is so named because it is traditionally believed to be masculine, first built on Friday. The accessories and other parts that go with the loom are the heddles, pulleys, spools, shuttles, bobbins, sword stick, skier, bobbin winders and holder.

The Weaving Process

Many apprentices study in Bonwire. Apprenticeship takes two to three years. Young trainees receive miniature looms with which to study. When a weaver decides on a design, he prepares the warp threads. A simple design is carried in his head.

However, for a complex design with much variety and combination of colour schemes, he prepares a sample showing the colour combination with the exact number and order of threads in each colour (Rattray, 1969). Kente cloth is manufactured in strips of three and one-half to four inches (9 to 10 cm) wide on narrow looms. A Kente design, however, determines the width of the strip.

The typical traditional loom with a very low stool was called "Noah" (no explanation could be given for this name). An improved traditional loom is named "The Boke Loom." It has a slightly high stool and a Reader (Twisoo) on which warp yams are rolled instead of outstretched warp yams.

Besides the narrow looms, broad looms that make cloths which are 32 inches (81 cm) wide and 144 inches (366 cm) long are now used to produce traditional Kente. After weaving, the strips are sewn together lengthwise by hand. Currently, many weavers join the strips with a sewing machine using the zigzag stitch to produce a toga-like wrap for men and women (Adler and Barnard, 1995). A completed cloth appears like a patchwork (see Figure 3.5a on page 91).

The size of a male's cloth is made up of 23 strips of Kente and the length of each strip is 144 inches (366 cm). A female's completed cloth consists of 10 strips for the "Ntama" (Skirt), 9 strips for the cover cloth and 7 strips for the "Kaba" (blouse). It is not uncommon to find Kente cloth with 9 strips for the "Ntama," 8 and 6 strips for the "Kaba" and cover cloth respectively. The length of the strips for females' cloth, however, is 72 inches (183 cm) each. When broadlooms are used, a strip of 432 inches (1,098 cm) long

Excerpted from *Ghana's Kente & Adinkra: History and Socio-Cultural Significance in a Contemporary Global Economy*. Accra, Ghana: Black Mask Ltd., 2007. Reprinted by permission of the author.

for a male's cloth is produced, which is cut into three, lengthwise. These are sewn together to give a cloth which is 96 inches wide and 144 inches (366 cm) long. A female's cloth is produced on the broad loom by weaving a strip of 216 inches (549 cm) long, and it is cut into three, lengthwise, and sewn together to make a cloth of 72 inches (183 cm) long and 96 inches (244 cm) wide.

It is the colour combination of the warp and the variation of the strips that give a cloth its name. The weft enhances the warp threads' beauty but may not be considered when naming the cloth. In occasional cases, however, both the weft and warp designs may be used to name a cloth. Similar patterns made of silk or cotton are given different names. Kente designs, traditionally, indicate the clan, social status and the sex of the wearer.

References

Adler, P. & Barnard, N. (1995). *The African Majesty: The Textile Art of the Ashanti and Ewe*. Thames and Hudson Ltd. London.

Rattray, R. S. (1969). *Religion and Art in Ashanti*. Oxford University Press, pp. 220–268.

Sjarief, H. (1969). *Kente Cloth of Ghana*. African Arts. Merton D. Simpson Inc., pp. 26–29.

Discussion Questions

1. Describe a loom used to produce Kente cloth. Look for images and videos on the Internet to share with your classmates via Blackboard or other instruction platform.
2. In which village and country did Kente cloth originate? Is Kente cloth still being produced there? Is weaving Kente cloth a gendered activity? Do both men and women wear Kente cloth?
3. For your own clothing selections, do you prefer textiles/apparel items that are handmade (or custom made) to those that are mass produced? Describe the differences between these two methods of production and the resulting fabrics.

13.9

SHIFTING THE DOMINANT SOCIAL PARADIGM IN THE APPAREL INDUSTRY: ACKNOWLEDGING THE PINK ELEPHANT

Cosette M. Armstrong, Oklahoma State University
Melody L. A. LeHew, Kansas State University

Fashion . . . suggests a passing trend or fad—something transient, superficial and often rather wasteful. It represents the opposite of longevity and, as such, would appear to be an impediment to sustainability.

Walker 2006:71

It is reasonable to conclude that the apparel industry is a guilty culprit in the current ecological crisis. Since the Industrial Revolution, the industry's impact has grown unceasingly, and there are now social, environmental, and economic consequences that must be addressed. Industrialization has been characterized by an endless hunger for growth and expansion that the ecosystem cannot accommodate. Central to this system is an accounting approach in which costs of environmental goods and services are never expressed in the economic bottom line; meanwhile, natural capital and assets continuously evaporate. No business could survive using this model. Thus, industrialization has ignored the natural scale and limits of our natural world in the name of progress (Schumacher 1973). A key component of this denial of limits is the problematic pink elephant of consumerism that is becoming increasingly difficult to ignore when attempting to define a new

Original for this text.

mind-set for the apparel industry: a sustainable one. In this paper, the authors explore what a new mind-set for the industry might look like.

A fundamental driver of consumerism and this subsequent denial of limits are essential to the concept of fashion where newness becomes an end in itself, and resource limits are best ignored. Products that rely heavily on the concept of fashion, like apparel, are at odds with sustainability, which raises a unique set of challenges for designers and product developers. Their decisions are *the* chief instigators of environmental and social impacts because choices made early in the design process, such as materials selection and production method, significantly influence the impact of a product's life cycle. Products are encoded for a specific purpose, resulting in a domino effect throughout the remainder of the product development process (see Armstrong and LeHew 2011 for more details).

But, fashion is an important aspect of modern culture and may, therefore, be a powerful conduit for the transition to environmentally friendly and socially responsible production and consumption (Walker 2006: 74–75). If designers are perceptive and open to the principles of sustainability, the concept of fashion may be used to attract attention, energy, and imagination around sustainable solutions. Fields such as engineering and industrial design have recently demonstrated a shift in practice that may serve as a basis for a new paradigm for the apparel industry.

A paradigm is defined as an assembly of practices and protocols characterizing a discipline or field (Kuhn 1996). A paradigm shift occurs as knowledge evolves; old procedures and rules are replaced as a new paradigm makes them flawed. Such an event in a scientific community (where the concept originated) can be abrupt as new knowledge replaces old.

A shift within a *social* paradigm, on the other hand, may occur in stages over time as the diverse values and beliefs of members of the social system evolve. Here, dominant ways of thinking may remain even after a new paradigm has indicated a more enlightened way of going about things. Thus, a dominant social paradigm (DSP) is a chief indicator of social behavior, and therefore, plays a primary role in maintaining or changing unsustainable practices (Dunlap and Van Liere 1984). A DSP is essentially a belief system that characterizes a community (Shafer 2006), and the practice and protocols in the current apparel industry community are shaped by the DSP of the twentieth century.

Characteristics of the DSP that currently perpetuate unsustainability in the Western world include (1) unlimited growth in free markets, (2) a liberal regulatory environment, (3) an emphasis on individualism and private ownership, and (4) an overreliance on technology as a solution to environmental problems (Shafer 2006: 124–126). At present, the apparel industry too heavily relies on technology to solve its environmental problems, focusing on efficiency and new technology, rather than addressing the pink elephant (consumerism). The authors argue in this paper that if the apparel industry is going to make a meaningful shift toward a more sustainable DSP, a more sustainable *pattern* of practice, acknowledging the pink elephant is a prerequisite. The authors explore a number of emerging sustainable approaches from other fields to propose a new DSP for the apparel industry.

Industrial Ecology

Industrial ecology (IE) is a supply chain organization that supports sustainable design and product development, using the principles of sustainable development. Embodying the Golden Rule, sustainable development is defined as meeting the needs of the present without prohibiting future generations from meeting their own needs (World Commission on Environment and Development 1987). Sustainable development emphasizes the environmental health, social equity, and economic viability of industrial systems. This approach is based on the idea that industry, economy, and technology should work in concert with nature. Just as nature regenerates itself infinitely and uses solar energy as its only input, IE addresses how natural resources are consumed and given new life in a system where disposal of waste is not an option (Graedel and Allenby 1995).

IE pays special attention to material and energy use, the preservation of local landscapes and biodiversity, and cooperation and communication throughout the supply chain. First, material use is minimal; form matches function precisely. Any waste generated in production is given new life when used to create new products (e.g., Climatex carpet, Kenaf International paper, Lafarge cement). Thus, products are often designed with remanufacturing and reuse in mind, avoiding the extraction of new materials. To reduce contamination, toxic materials are used only when and where they are necessary and are not stored or transported long distances. Further, all energy used for production, preferably solar, results in some type of material transformation. Finally, the products that result from IE are more reflective of the real costs to the environment (Graedel and Allenby 1995). Table 13.1 compares IE to the apparel industry.

On the positive side, the apparel industry has integrated its supply chain, formed strategic partnerships, and advanced its technological sophistication (Keiser and Garner 2008), aligning itself in many ways to IE. But, challenges remain for the apparel industry. These are the key components required for a paradigm shift: the development of partnerships *outside* the apparel supply chain, a more cooperative than competitive approach in the market, and a more realistic costing strategy that acknowledges the real costs of products to the environment and people.

Sustainable Approaches

Sustainable design (SD) and sustainable product development (SPD) approaches fall along a continuum, from approaches that permit the consumer to maintain traditional consumption habits (the pink elephant) to approaches that require significant changes to the consumer culture. Four levels of intervention occupy the continuum between these two polar positions (Vezzoli and Manzini 2007).

The *first and lowest level* of intervention, called end-of-pipe strategies, addresses only the consequences of traditional consumption by adjusting the materials and energy levels used to create products. Common considerations at this level are things like ease of maintenance and repairs, upgrading, component recovery for remanufacturing or reuse, materials recycling, and ease of sorting and collection in the disposal stage. Considerations may also be made to ensure that packaging, instructions, and overall appearance of

TABLE 13.1

Comparing the Apparel Supply Chain to Industrial Ecology

	Apparel Supply Chain	Industrial Ecology
Scope	Global	Local
Scale	Large	Large
Supply chain relationships	Integrated, cooperative, but not completely reliant	Integrated, cooperative, collaborative, reliant
Relationships outside specific industry	Limited	Strategic partnerships within and without
Environment	Highly competitive	Highly cooperative
Basis of competition	Speed of delivery; product innovation; manufacturing expertise; technology; resources	Efficiency, productivity, product innovation
Tools	Technology	Technology
Customer	Well-defined niches; specialized consumer preference	Narrow niches that *complement* current market assortment
Costing	Market price	Ecological value

the product encourage efficient and environmentally friendly use.

The *second level* makes similar substitutions to increase efficiency in the production systems, but is encompassed by a life cycle assessment (LCA). LCA is an analysis of a product's life cycle and its environmental impact. Thus, impacts are reduced across the product's life cycle. This framework replaces some product elements with environmentally conscious ones that are still common enough to remain socially acceptable to consumers.

The *third level* of intervention begins to address consumer culture (the pink elephant). Instead of producing traditional products, this system designs new ways for consumers to achieve satisfaction that may or may not include a tangible product.

Lastly, *the fourth level*, and by far the most challenging, is one in which new qualitative criteria for sustainable lifestyles are created. At this level, *designers lead consumers* into a more sustainable pattern of consumption. Here, design is heavily reliant on the designer's ability to perceive human needs that are more social than material in nature. It is fair to assume that these latter two levels of intervention are distinct in the high degree to which the pink elephant is acknowledged and navigated. These intervention levels are noted in the following discussion of sustainable approaches.

Design for Environment and Design for X

Design for environment (DfE) is an approach that seeks sustainability while retaining competitiveness. Design for X (DfX) refers to specific design strategies such as design for disassembly. In this case, each design strategy has its own set of methods and measurements, but both rely on technology (Guidice, La Rosa, and Risitano 2006).

Cradle to Cradle

The most widely recognized set of principles for sustainable product design is McDonough and Braungart's (2004) *Cradle to Cradle* (C2C) procedure, which aligns with the principles of DfE and IE. C2C is the antithesis to the current cradle-to-grave production model and has three primary tenets: celebrate diversity, use solar income, and waste equals food.

The waste equals food tenet has attracted attention in the industry, inspiring an increase of materials analyses to determine the biological (biodegradable) or technical (recyclable) food value of products at the end of their life cycle. The C2C protocol was recently used to create a production model for sustainable apparel in the industry. The model, called Cradle to Cradle Apparel Design (C2CAD), includes consideration for consumer preferences, materials analysis, collaboration in the supply chain, and an analysis of the environmental impacts of the production process. However, the model does not address the first or second principle of C2C with any confidence. When Gam (2007) attempted to implement the model in a manufacturer of children's knitwear in Korea, the manufacturer could not comply with the tenets outlined in the model. Collaboration in the supply chain, knowledge and expertise for analysis of materials selection, and considerations for energy use were absent.

Product Service Systems

Products and services have always been linked. But recently, product service systems (PSS) have received renewed attention as a possible channel to increase consumer satisfaction while dematerializing the traditional production-consumption system. In developed countries, an increase in consumption of material goods is equated with an increase in quality of life, though no relationship has ever been documented. PSS seeks to replace product ownership with utility. When material consumption is substituted by services, this increases the likelihood of using fewer material resources and energy, giving way to fewer products and less waste (Maxwell and Van der Vorst 2003). Businesses may compensate for lost revenue from material goods by selling unique services that support their products. PSS is a direct and long-term approach with customers, the creation of collaborative networks with various stakeholders, and low capital intensity. Admittedly, this approach requires a dramatic shift in traditional consumption habits.

Emotionally Durable Design, Slow Design, and Design Activism

Design strategies situated at the highest level on the intervention continuum most often emphasize the exceptional delivery of human needs, basic needs that transcend social and cultural norms. These approaches to design have the potential to yield the most sustainable products because they incorporate consumer behavior into the product strategy. Importantly, these strategies more successfully acknowledge and navigate around the pink elephant.

The *emotionally durable* product-consumer relationship can be created through designing for attachment, creating a symbiotic relationship of mutual need and caring through product attributes that stimulate things like memory development and pleasure. In this approach, lifelong partnerships (consumer-to-product, consumer-to-manufacturer) are subsequently formed that make it easy to nurture a product's life through repair, upgrades, and service.

Slow design implies that the design is no longer controlled by time, which eliminates the need for constant updates and production to compete in the marketplace. Slow design has been used interchangeably with design for well-being. Here, the designer focuses on well-being (social and environmental) early in the design process instead of only individual well-being (economic). Thus, the well-being of individuals is less dependent on acquisition and more reliant on sustainable development to create products that embody deeper meaning for the consumer.

Design activism is a powerful force for change in which designers are inspired by issues personal to them and the world. These products may be designed for humanitarian aid (natural disasters, postwar), services to the poor or excluded (homeless, disabled, elderly), or human rights (fair trade, ethical trade).

Tools for Sustainable Approaches

A variety of conceptual and scientific tools have evolved to support strategic decision-making during sustainable design and sustainable product development processes. However, the most common scientific tool used to support SD and SPD approaches is the previously mentioned Life Cycle Assessment. In an LCA, products and the production processes used to create them are systematically summed up in an environmental impact equation, typically categorized across the product life cycle stages. The five life cycle stages are material, design, distribution, use, and disposal. The LCA is an important decision-making tool, as it offers a precise way to compare the impact of different product life cycle stages to each other as well as to make product comparisons. There are generally three types of LCAs: inventory analyses (resource use impacts), impact analyses (description and assessment impacts), and improvement analyses (discovery of opportunities to reduce environmental burdens) (Lowe, Warren, and Moran 1997: 52). Conducting an LCA requires ample time and money and only addresses the environmental impact of the product, but does not account for social and economic impacts on the environment.

To There from Here: A New Dominant Social Paradigm for the Apparel Industry

When we compare apparel design and product development processes to sustainable approaches we find some commonalities (Table 13.2): both originate from similar disciplines; both rely on multidisciplinary collaboration and concurrent and iterative activities; both rely on sophisticated technology; and both are beholden to basic responsibilities such as market research, preproduction tasks, production, marketing, distribution, and retailing. But, there are considerable disagreements between the two approaches that merit exploration for a new dominant social paradigm in the apparel industry.

First, the most important difference is that of costing. Apparel products are sold at market price rather than based on their ecological value, whereas sustainable product development products reflect the real costs of the impacts of resource use. This is why sustainable products typically

TABLE 13.2

Comparison of Apparel Design and Product Development Processes to Sustainable Approaches

Method	Apparel Design & Product Development	Sustainable Design & Product Development
Origins	Industrial design, engineering & architecture	Industrial design, engineering, architecture, environmental & agriculture
Authored by	Academicians; tested in industry	Collaboration of academic & industry
Purpose	Education	Solve environmental issues in industry
Process	Collaborative, sequential, nonlinear, concurrent, iterative	Collaborative, nonlinear, concurrent, iterative
Team	Multidisciplinary; design, product development, merchandising, marketing, production, manufacturing related to apparel	Multidisciplinary; design, product development, marketing, production, manufacturing, pollution prevention, environmental risk, occupational health & safety, waste management, ecological conservation & other stakeholders
Tools	Technology	Technology; scientific & conceptual tools
Common activities	Market & consumer research, design, costing, sample making, line development, line presentation, preproduction preparation & technical development, sourcing, production, quality assurance, marketing, packaging, distribution	Marketing & consumer research, defining the problem, evaluating solutions quantitatively & qualitatively, backcasting, risk analysis, prototype development, prototype modeling of product system, communication of environmental qualities to market
Guiding information	Trend, market & consumer research	LCA & analysis; model nature's system; checklists; the Golden Rule
Costing	Market price	Ecological value
Product	New line/collection or products; ever-changing, disposable, beholden to concept of fashion	Single product, revised product, product-service system; reflective of art, science, culture, nature, place; form fits function

cost more than traditionally made products. Developing a metric for ecological costing has been problematic and even if we could accurately cost natural resources, we would likely discover we could not afford them. Market mechanisms of the global economy such as quotas, tariffs, and subsidies further complicate this effort. These systems are implemented to protect developing countries from the rigors of the free market; however, these manipulations often drive down prices, ignoring the real cost of the ensuing impacts on people and the planet.

This picture gets muddier when structures designed to offer economic assistance to developing countries from firms like the International Monetary Fund and the World Bank are considered. In this case, loans are made to developing countries to stimulate struggling economies on a short-term basis and stabilize the economic system. But, these firms have a tendency to impose unrealistic terms, which can prompt countries to overproduce to stay current on these loans (Weisbrot 2009). In sum, these market mechanisms complicate global trade because they impact how products are valued, inflating values for exportation from developing countries and deflating them for consumption in developed countries (Schor 2005). Economies around the globe, particularly those reliant on apparel and textile business, have collapsed under these conditions.

There are some cases of changing costing policies. A number of product developers are beginning to shift their costing policies to better reflect real costs of production, rather than the price retailers are willing to pay for goods. This suggests that these strategies may inspire changes for sustainability throughout the apparel supply chain (Interfaith Center on Corporate Responsibility 2010). Nevertheless, this predicament is not easily solved, but being aware of the standards, regulations, and monetary policies that drive the machine is a beginning. A new dominant social paradigm for the industry would undoubtedly reflect the real costs of doing apparel business in social and environmental terms.

Second, the cooperative nature of product development expands in the context of sustainable product development and industrial ecology. Sustainable product development relies heavily on partnerships with many stakeholders *outside* the apparel field, such as environmental expertise. This type of cooperation provides efficiency and risk reduction. Further, consultation with stakeholders is central to decision making. As the apparel industry is already increasingly integrated, it is well poised to begin reaching beyond the context of its own vacuum. A new dominant social paradigm for the apparel industry would include an expansion of infrastructure designed to foster collaboration and cooperation. Partnerships may reflect greater inclusion of outside organizations that offer sustainability-related savvy, such as assisting firms with materials analyses or environmental impact assessments. Additionally, the diminishing availability of virgin materials will drive the need to form partnerships with unrelated industries to source waste that may be used for materials or with companies that may process or redesign second-hand apparel. To foster such symbiotic arrangements, the development of collaborative and cooperative skills among apparel industry professionals cannot be underestimated.

Third, it is clear that sustainable design and product development approaches utilize a variety of conceptual and scientific tools to better balance market demands with ecosystem health, a prospect virtually untouched by apparel firms. A new dominant social paradigm for the industry would embrace continuous research and exploration related to the impact of its products. Though the apparel industry has begun to dabble with these tools, future industry professionals must also have the competence to utilize and administer such tools. Most recently, a pilot of the Eco Index was launched through a collaboration of two outdoor organizations and the Zero Waste Alliance that seems like a promising step toward the development of tools to analyze apparel and textile products. But, the use of these tools admittedly commands greater knowledge of the natural sciences. In the new dominant social paradigm, apparel industry professionals would understand the mechanics of sustainability science and be able to administer a variety of impact analyses.

Finally, the apparel industry must come to grips with its own belief system. A new dominant social paradigm would scrutinize the following industry tendencies: the purpose and consequences of economies of scale, a relentless competitive environment, and the use of the concept of fashion that may degrade rather than enhance quality of life. In a new dominant social paradigm, the practice of creating products that are only responsive to the market, rather than to the ecosystem's limits, would seem simplistic and wasteful. Recently, several common industry concepts were described as increasingly dysfunctional in light of sustainability, such as: Growth is good, progress equals material progress, and consumers as a profit-making resource. These components characterize the pink elephant that has contributed to a growing conflict of interest between producers and consumers. Some propose a needs, rather than wants, approach to marketing, such as well-being marketing (Varey 2010). Whatever the case, a new DSP for the industry would focus on creating apparel products that are more efficient in material use, production, and consumer utility while also delivering the fundamental human needs of consumers, needs that are inherently more social than material. Apparel industry professionals would hold competences such as perceiving human needs and ecosystem limits, working cooperatively *with* the market rather than trying to dominate it, and understanding local culture and tradition. In the new dominant social paradigm, practice in the industry would encompass the Golden Rule, better supporting sustainable development.

Conclusion

Though the apparel industry is a substantial source of livelihood for many people worldwide, it is also a principal culprit in the ecological crisis. Social, environmental, and economic consequences in the industry pose a threat to sustainability on an unimaginable scale, and some argue that the apparel industry has been tardy in its response. Nevertheless, it is fair to suggest that the future will require a new *pattern* of thinking and action, *a new dominant social paradigm*, far beyond the one that created the industrial world. Solutions or adaptations must work in step with the ecological realities of today, acknowledging the pink elephant of growth, consumption, and limitless accumulation.

References

Armstrong, Cosette M. and Melody L.A. LeHew. 2011. Sustainable apparel product development: In search of a new dominant social paradigm for the field using sustainable approaches. *Fashion Practice*, 3 (1): 29–62.

Dunlap, Riley E., and Kent D. Van Liere. 1984. Commitment to the Dominant Social Paradigm and Concern for Environmental Quality. *Social Science Quarterly*, 65:1013–1028.

Gam, Hae Jin. 2007. Development and Implementation of a Sustainable Apparel Design and Production Model. Ph.D. dissertation, Oklahoma State University, United States—Oklahoma. Accessed April 25, 2009, from Dissertations & Theses: Full Text database. (Publication No.AAT 3259611).

Graedel, Thomas E. and Braden Richard, Allenby. 1995. *Industrial Ecology*. Englewood, NJ: Prentice Hall.

Guidice, Fabio, Guido La Rosa, and Antonio Risitano. 2006. *Product Design for the Environment: A Life Cycle Approach*. Boca Raton, FL: Taylor & Francis Group.

Interfaith Center on Corporate Responsibility (ICCR). 2010. Best Current Practices in Purchasing: The Apparel Industry. http://www.asyousow.org/publications/Apparel_Report.pdf, accessed July 16, 2010.

Keiser, Sandra J. and Myrna B. Garner. 2008. *Beyond Design*. New York: Fairchild Publications, Inc.

Kuhn, Thomas S. (1996). *The Structure of Scientific Revolutions* (3rd ed.). Chicago, IL: University of Chicago Press.

Lowe, E. A., John L. Warren, and Stephen R. Moran. 1997. *Discovering Industrial Ecology*. Columbus, OH: Battelle Press.

Maxwell, Dorothy and Rita Van der Vorst. 2003. Developing Sustainable Products and Services. *Journal of Cleaner Production*, 11:883–895.

McDonough, William and Michael Braungart. 2004. *Cradle to Cradle*. New York: North Point Press.

Schor, Juliet B. 2005. Prices and Quantities: Unsustainable Consumption and the Global Economy. *Ecological Economics*, 55:309–320.

Schumacher, E.F. 1973. *Small Is Beautiful*. New York: Harper & Row, Publishers, Inc.

Shafer, William Eugene. 2006. Social Paradigms and Attitudes toward Environmental Accountability. *Journal of Business Ethics*, 65:121–147.

Varey, Richard J. 2010. Marketing Means and Ends for a Sustainable Society: A Welfare Agenda for Transformative Change. *Journal of Macromarketing*, 30 (2): 112–126.

Vezzoli, Carlo A. and Ezio Manzini. 2007. *Design for Environmental Sustainability*. New York, NY: Springer.

Walker, Stuart. 2006. *Sustainable by Design: Explorations in Theory and Practice*. London, UK: Earthscan.

Weisbrot, Mark. 2009, October 13. A New Role for the IMF? *Tikkun Magazine*. http://www.tikkun.org/article.php/20091013105540620, accessed June 19, 2010.

World Commission on Environment and Development (WCED). 1987. *Our Common Future*. Oxford: Oxford University Press.

Discussion Questions

1. Do you agree that the current dominant social paradigm (DSP) shaping apparel design, production, and consumption is at odds with a sustainable future? Discuss your view.

2. Several sustainable design and sustainable product development models were presented in the article. In your opinion, which model holds the greatest promise for firms in an apparel industry operating within a new ecologically minded dominant social paradigm? Discuss the reasons for your choice.

3. Describe the "pink elephant" presented in this article and its relevance to the fashion industry. Why might apparel designers, apparel marketers, and even apparel educators be reluctant to acknowledge the "pink elephant"?

4.   Two readings in this chapter ("Excuse Me" and "Haute Technology") have mentioned aspects of a new industrial revolution in the apparel industry. Do you think that widespread use of these technologies could place enough pressure on the apparel industry to invest in a new dominant social paradigm? Why or why not?

13.10

TWILIGHT OF THE TRIBES: ETHIOPIA'S OMO RIVER VALLEY
Susan Hack

To travel to Ethiopia's remote Omo River Valley is to wade into a morass of moral ambiguities. You will be on a safari where people—not wildlife—are the attraction. You will observe traditions that seem exotic, and at times shocking. You will feel like an intruder and a human ATM. You will witness ancient cultures about to disappear, in part because of your presence. Susan Hack reports on the ultimate trophy trip—and culture clash.

We're traveling by boat on the southern reaches of the Omo River, motoring up a swift current from our camp toward Mago National Park. A large crocodile swimming across our bow submerges in a swirling eddy. Startled baboons dash up a riverbank, stirring dust at the feet of ancient fig trees whose exposed, handlike roots hold the land in place and the water at bay. Although the 472-mile-long Omo was first mapped from its highland source near Addis Ababa to its mouth on Lake Turkana in 1896, this part of Ethiopia is still so undeveloped that a GPS device shows no details, just the snaking line of our route through a land with few roads and no bridges, the size of New Hampshire.

A few miles from the park boundary, we spot a family striding along a bluff, carrying their household possessions toward a dry-season settlement. Long-limbed women wearing nothing but hide skirts balance sleeping mats and butter gourds on their heads. Men with vintage rifles slung over their shoulders take up the front and rear, while small boys run ahead wielding bows and arrows. These are Kwegu people, our guide tells us, one of sixteen ethnic groups living on the

banks of the Lower Omo as it flows down from the Shewan Mountains toward the harsh semi-desert of the Ethiopia-Kenya border.

Farther upriver, we wave to Nyangatom men, tall Nilotic warriors guarding a west bank path where their cattle come down to drink. Ahead lies Lebuk, an east bank outpost of the Karo tribe where locals have tipped us off to an evening courtship dance; at sunset, we find a circle of youths painted in white clay and yellow ocher singing about cattle raiding while leaping and strutting their stuff in front of the village girls.

For the next six days, I am on a human safari. I have not come to see wildlife (dry and pestilent, the terrain supports abundant birdlife and not much else) but to photograph some of the most extraordinary tribes in Africa as they go about their daily life. Essentially, I am a voyeur, a gawker, and already my trip's eleven-thousand-dollar price tag and the business of intruding on people who have little control over the forces of tourism have me feeling a bit uneasy. Some of my encounters will prove so troubling that I will, at points, wish I had never come to this place, whose extremes seem to pitch between a wild, primordial version of It's a Small World and a twenty-first-century *Heart of Darkness*.

In 1980, UNESCO declared the Lower Omo Valley a World Heritage Site in recognition of its uniqueness: Nowhere else on the planet do so many genetically and linguistically diverse people

---

Hack, Susan. (2012, January). *Twilight of the Tribes. Condé Nast Traveler*, pp. 118–133, 152, 154. Reprinted by permission of Condé Nast Publications.

live as traditionally and in such a small space. It has been a crossroads for humans migrating in many directions over many millennia. Improbably in an era of cloud-based businesses and Internet revolutions, 200,000 Omo pastoralists, cultivators, and hunters still pursue preindustrial lifestyles in a region that until now has been judged by outsiders too scrubby and remote for exploitation. Possessing few items from the modern world besides plastic jerry cans for carrying water, the men, women, and children here ritually adorn themselves to express status and tribal identity, sculpting their hair with animal fat and clay, scarifying limbs and torsos, wearing jewelry of beads, bone, and metal, and painting their entire bodies with white minerals, black charcoal, and red and yellow ocher. The unlikely survival of these customs and of still-authentic rituals such as bull jumping and gladiatorial stick fighting attracts a few hardy missionaries, anthropologists, and, increasingly, photographers and curious travelers like me.

The significance of the Omo tribes is more profound than their visual appeal. Amid layers of cracked mud and volcanic tuff along the Lower Omo's banks, paleontologists have discovered precious remnants of our shared heritage: the oldest known remains of anatomically modern humans, folks who might not look out of place in Times Square, who hunted and gathered here an astonishing 195,000 years ago. DNA analysis suggests that every person now living is related to a single woman from the Omo Valley, some of whose descendants left the Horn of Africa during a period of climate change and migrated across the Bab el Mandeb strait to Arabia and beyond somewhere between 60,000 and 120,000 years ago. Her relatives who remained behind branched into fourteen genetically distinct founder populations from which all African ethnic groups descend. If Ethiopia is humanity's womb, the Omo River is its umbilical cord.

Abruptly, after so many millennia, the old river world may be entering its twilight. In a gorge three hundred miles upstream from where we are photographing the young people of Lebuk sweating in their beads and animal skins, construction is under way on the colossal Gibe III dam, the second-largest hydroelectric project in Africa—

designed by Italian engineers, partly funded by Chinese banks, and scheduled to begin generating 1,870 megawatts of electricity in July 2013. With 83 million citizens, Ethiopia is Africa's second most populous country, and one of its poorest. Planners of the dam say that the output, the equivalent of that of two nuclear plants, will make Ethiopia electricity sufficient, with enough power left over to sell to neighboring states. Crews are paving roads connecting major towns like Jinka and Omorate. According to Survival International, an NGO working in the region, Ethiopia is contracting corporations in India, Israel, Malaysia, and elsewhere to run giant farms that will be irrigated with Omo water. As a result, fragile cultures that are crucial to the study of art, anthropology, and genetics may soon be displaced and disappear before we fully appreciate that they were here in the first place. There's another conundrum: Foreign travelers—thirty thousand last year, according to the government—are arriving to see the tribes before development overturns their way of life. But by taking pictures of the tribes, I am actually hastening that change.

Foreigners began trickling into the Omo River Valley just prior to the 1936–1941 Italian occupation, after historian Carlo Conti Rossini described Ethiopia as a "Museum of Peoples," a still-repeated reference to its eighty-three ethnic groups. But those early visitors were mostly military officers and anthropologists. Organized tourism didn't really take off until the 1990s, after the country abandoned socialism (introduced by Ethiopian soldiers who overthrew Emperor Haile Selassie in 1974) and Addis-based tour operators began marketing expeditions on which foreigners could meet tribes who are in effect distant relatives with colorful customs living in the homeland of our earliest ancestors. Starting from Addis, it takes three bone-jarring days in a four-by-four over unpaved tracks to reach a handful of southern towns with basic hotels and weekly markets. Tribal people reliably show up in traditional garb after walking long distances to barter animals and bush honey for coffee husks and chewing tobacco.

The "highlight" of the Omo market circuit is usually a six-hour round-trip from Jinka for a chaotic half-hour stop at a village deep within Mago National Park. Here, travelers photograph women of the Mursi tribe, famous for their pierced lower lips holding clay plates up to seven inches in diameter. In exchange for permission to be photographed, the Mursi demand from each tourist five *birr*, about thirty cents in the Ethiopian currency. To attract the lens, the women riff on their culture, for example by wearing old puberty belts on their heads. The resulting scrum is full of antagonism, as foreigners compete with one another over camera angles, and the Mursi vie for attention from these human ATMs.

To travel to the Omo as responsibly as possible, I join a weeklong photo expedition organized by Steve Turner, a second-generation safari guide from Kenya and the head of Origins, a Nairobi company with a reputation for respectful dealings with local people. Its clients, who have to be willing to put up with physical hardship and ethical challenges to spend time amid indigenous cultures, include environmental activists, photojournalists, European royalty, business tycoons, and philanthropists; the Omo sub-tribe includes retired schoolteachers, a cofounder of Starbucks, and several well-known fashion designers.

"If you are inconvenienced by spartan accommodations or intense human contact or are apprehensive in unfamiliar situations, then I'm sorry but this expedition is not for you," Steve emails me before it's too late to back out. Lumale Camp, our base, receives fewer than sixty guests a year. Although my Omo trip seems terribly short given the cost and logistics of getting here, few visitors choose to stay longer in a river environment prone to tsetse flies and hot, dusty ninety-five-plus-degree days with no air-conditioning, Wi-Fi, swift medical evacuation, or flush toilets.

I charter a Cessna from Nairobi to the northeastern end of Lake Turkana and am driven three hours across the desert to the Ethiopian border town of Omorate for my rendezvous with two other travel companions. Charlotte Rush Bailey is a retired marketing and communications executive from Connecticut with a side career in fine arts photography, and Gul Chotrani, an economist from Singapore, is packing the latest

Leica M9 and S2 models, along with a satellite phone and a chronometer with an emergency transponder. Accompanied by Steve, the gregarious son of a former British Colonial Police officer, we set off in a cobbled-together Toyota Land Cruiser to meet the boat that will take us the final leg to camp.

Any illusions we have about being among the only outsiders to reach tribes in a pristine environment evaporate before we even reach the river. Leaving Omorate, we drive past a labor barracks and newly planted seedlings on the edge of a vast Italian-managed palm oil facility. Transiting the Murelle hunting concession, we see the work camp and helicopter pad of a Chinese company prospecting for oil amid ant chimneys, camel thorn acacias, and herds of tiang antelope.

The six-tent Lumale Camp, on a bend in the river, proves more comfortable than I expected. There are high-thread-count sheets on the mattress inside my private tent. In the morning, Karo camp staff lay a carpet of green leaves and bring fire-heated river water for my bucket shower.

Lumale Camp is managed by Lale Biwa, a locally respected translator and Karo community leader who also serves as our translator and guide during the trip. Except for a visit to a Hamar market, we will ditch the car that brought us from Omorate and use the river as our highway, voyaging by day aboard the Omo's only motorized boat, a hand-built replica of an Azores whaler. The plan is to visit three Karo villages and locate temporary dry season settlements of the Mursi, Kwegu, and Nyangatom peoples, some of whom, Lale claims, have not seen a foreigner in more than three years.

I awake to the dawn howls of colobus monkeys clambering in the fig tree above my tent. After breakfast in camp we climb into the boat and slalom upriver between floating logs—many of which turn out to be crocodiles—past fish eagles and goliath herons hunting along the riverbanks. Our first glimpse of Dus, the Karo capital, is thin silhouettes of villagers drawn to the bluff edge by the noise of the boat engine. Carrying daypacks and digital cameras, we climb out of the boat and hike a goat path to a collection of conical huts, stilted granaries, and animal corrals on the far side of sorghum fields. To the north, rising over acacia plain and myrrh studded hills, I see blue mountains marking the start of Ethiopia's highlands, where the Omo originates with rainfall tumbling down gorges and scouring mineral silt that turns the river the color of milk chocolate as it winds south. Vultures lurk on the ground near the ceremony house where Karo tribal elders receive tributes of sorghum beer and discuss important business. Dus lacks electricity and running water, and wild scavengers know that the settlement offers a reliable source of food: human excrement.

With fewer than two thousand people spread among a handful of villages on the Omo's east bank, the Karo are one of the smallest ethnic groups in Ethiopia, indeed in all of Africa. Rain is infrequent and irregular, and the Karo depend for survival on the river's annual flood, as did the ancient Egyptians living along the Nile. Between September and October, the Omo spills its banks and recedes, leaving behind a new layer of silt. The Karo plant sorghum, maize, and beans; keep goats and cattle; and cleave to rituals they believe ward off bad luck.

A bare-breasted young woman wearing trade bead necklaces and a supple goatskin skirt offers us shade from the midday heat by inviting us to rest on a cowhide inside her house of sticks, leaves, and long grasses. Her name is Gilty, meaning "the dark of midnight, when something can't be seen," according to Lale Biwa. She is the treasurer of the Dus Women's Association, formed two years ago when Steve donated two thousand dollars to enable village women to buy foodstuffs in bulk—grain, coffee, tobacco—to create a market for Dus that would remove the need to walk three days to Dimeka, the nearest trading town. Gilty admits that most of the cash was actually spent hiring a truck to transport cases of novelties—bottled beer, Fanta, and Pepsi—a mistake, in retrospect, since Dus has no means of refrigeration.

Gilty offers us hollow gourds filled with *buno*, a scalding traditional drink of boiled coffee husks that tastes of wood smoke, tannin, and animal fat. When I ask what she thinks about the dam, she shrugs. "We've heard about it, but we don't know what will happen," she says. "The government claims they consulted the Karo, but most of the people can't read," Lale Biwa interjects, "and we don't have television or even a representative in parliament, so what can she really know about it?" I've read that the government has promised to release a ten-day artificial flood each year from a ninety-four-mile-long reservoir behind the dam to replicate the Omo's cycle. But it's unclear, according to the environmental group International Rivers, whether this volume will be sufficient for farmers downstream, whether the Omo's level will drop, and whether nutrients that had fertilized the land near the river will sink to the bottom of the reservoir. Whatever trepidation Gilty feels about the future is a mystery she keeps to herself. I put down my notebook, and catch myself staring at the rows of ritual scars on Gilty's stomach, her hammered-metal armbands, and the scar on her forehead made by a wildcat that was stalking her baby goats and which she surprised in the night.

According to oral tradition, the Karo settled on the banks of the Omo after following a red bull there almost two centuries ago. A devastating disease—possibly sleeping sickness—is reported to have diminished the population at the end of the nineteenth century. Surrounded by larger tribes, they developed a complex social hierarchy to prevent intermarriage and to keep their bloodlines pure. Before wedding a Karo woman, a young Karo man must complete a bull-jumping ritual. Leaping naked across the backs of lined-up cattle four times without falling is the easy part. The difficulty lies in the preparation. A man cannot jump until all of his older brothers have married, and bull jumping will not be staged for an individual: Cohorts in the same age group must prepare simultaneously. Each candidate must grow enough sorghum to make beer for a party hosting every female of his clan, and he must also provide beer for all the tribal elders. With all the requirements, it can be as many as seven years between rituals. In times of drought, there is not enough sorghum, the main food staple, to spare for beer, and since polygamy is permitted, there can be a shortage of women. Just nineteen candidates participated at the last Karo bull jumping, in 2010. "I'm actually thinking about whether I will ever become a bull jumper," says Gudree, a student I meet later on the riverbank, with a sigh, adding that he is considering marrying outside the tribe. He is on summer holiday from the Department of Natural Resources at Dilla University, dressed in a T-shirt, sweatpants, and sneakers. "It's very difficult. I'll have to come live in the bush and wear kudu skins, and making beer for everyone is very expensive. Plus I'm the youngest of three brothers, and I have to wait for them to jump first."

Like other Omo tribes, the Karo require each safari client to pay a small sum of *birr* to every individual they choose to photograph, in addition to a general fee paid to the village elders for the privilege of visiting; like the beer tribute, demanding money from outsiders is a ritual, another way for the community to share resources. So when the sun lowers, offering a soft, sideways, tangerine light, my travel companions and I stand under an acacia, holding wads of five-*birr* notes, surveying a crowd of old men, women, adolescents, and small children who've turned their entire bodies into abstract canvases of spirals, polka dots, and handprints of white, yellow, and red paint. Patterns mimic guinea fowl feathers, zebra stripes, and leopard spots. In the Karo's eyes I read pride, hope, curiosity, and, in some cases, utter boredom. It feels as awkward as a high school dance—and as mercenary as a model agency cattle call.

To help break the ice, Steve and Lale have previously drilled Charlotte, Gul, and me on Karo language greetings. "*Hoe-poe!*" I say cheerily, offering a handshake to an elderly woman with a silver ring in her chin. I've been told that the ritual reply is *Hoe-poe-na*, to which I should respond *Sali*, and then she *Sali-na*. The lady cuts right to the chase. "Photo," she says, in English, spitting a brown stream of chewed tobacco next to my sandals, "five *birr*!" To be equitable, I try to photograph everyone who asks and then search for interesting faces.

It's impossible, in this situation, to get to know people slowly or to hang back, observe, and then wander around taking pictures incognito. Each camera click requires negotiation and sometimes confrontation, as when a mother demands not just five *birr* for herself but two *birr* for the infant riding on her back as she grinds sorghum on a millstone. I don't know what's more troubling, the discrepancy between the two *birr* (the equivalent

of twelve cents) and the five-figure cost of my safari, or the fact that I corrupt her culture and her child by placing the *birr* in the baby's fingers. Our presence in the village is an entertainment for the children, who follow us incessantly. They respond to Charlotte's grandmotherly warmth, but I can hear the frustrated Gul bellowing, "Kids, kids, you're ruining my picture!" The village rock star is a charismatic old man with two ostrich feathers in his mud skullcap and ivory piercing his chin. He's carrying a carved wooden headrest, a hide-sheathed knife, and a walking stick, and he puts his chest out and his chin up, the Karo Mick Jagger.

Near dusk, I ask a heavily pregnant woman with a yellow- and red-beaded goatskin covering her belly if I can take her portrait, but she is hesitant. It emerges that while she is newly married, she and her husband have not observed the protocols required before intercourse. The baby, Lale explains, will be considered *mingi*, or cursed. The custom, still practiced, is for tribal elders to take the infant from the parents as soon as it's born and kill it so its bad blood won't pollute the tribe and cause misfortune. Twins and toddlers whose upper teeth erupt before their lower are also considered *mingi* and face the same fate. Babies born to unwed girls who get pregnant after having sex with their boyfriends are *mingi* too.

The Ethiopian government, as part of a campaign to eliminate harmful traditional practices, has begun requiring its health clinic in Dus to register all Karo pregnancies and births, Lale tells me. But the system is not perfect. It remains easy to deny a newborn food until it starves, telling the government worker it died naturally—or, in the old manner, to slip into the bush, stuff its mouth with dirt, and leave it for the hyenas, or just fling it into the river.

As Lale relays this information, I'm horrified and paralyzed. What seemed to me a benign request has turned into a moral crisis. I want to ask this woman what she intends to do with her baby. Hand it over to the government? There's a private orphanage for rescued *mingi* kids in a distant town called Jinka. Can she take the baby there? Should I follow up the case? Is it even any of my business? This is the dispiriting, ambivalent outcome: I respect her privacy, ask no questions. I take her picture, pay her the five *birr*, and wish her good luck.

That night, over red wine and barbecued steaks, we have the first of many discussions about the ethics of Omo travel and our personal motives for this trip. Steve tells us that he has wealthy clients who have been to the Omo as many as ten times, drawn back by the desire to help. One American, John Rowe, a photographer and philanthropist, joined with Lale Labuko, from the Karo tribe, to found the Omo Child Foundation, which oversees the shelter in Jinka where more than thirty *mingi* children now live.

Charlotte, Gul, and I all admit that we traveled to the Omo with a "soon it will be too late" mind-set; we share a desire to witness cultures before imposed change and pressure to assimilate render them unrecognizable. But the experience has been a reality check, offering insights not mentioned in the safari brochure into the lives of people whose customs we find exotic.

We have been hoping to photograph a bull-jumping among the Hamar, whose men, unlike the Karo, perform the ritual individually. Part of the frisson for outsiders is the custom of women begging to be whipped by the *maza*—men who have already completed the jump. A woman's scars are proof of her courage and ability to bear pain—qualities important to a man seeking a wife—and a kind of life insurance. If ever the woman finds herself in difficult circumstances, she can count on the bull jumper for material support and protection. The next day at the Hamar village of Arba, there are no bull jumpers, but there is a public beating. As we walk around taking photographs of Hamar women in their iron neck and leg rings and thickly ochered tresses, a drunk man named Arko staggers from his thatched house, shouting and lashing his young wife Koto with a switch. Her brother Ama and his friends pull them apart, and Koto sinks to the ground, stunned, her back against the tire of our vehicle. Koto has old welts from prior bull-jumping rituals, and the men have rallied to rescue her from violence they consider unjust. The dust settles, some elders drag Arko off to cool down, and Ama poses for us, jauntily wearing a pair of Charlotte's reading glasses to break the tension.

Violence extends well beyond ritualized beatings. The lack of roads—which keeps out global goods, HIV-infected truckers, and, happily for us at Lumale Camp, other tourists—has also kept out widespread schooling and medical care. But it has not kept out guns. During many of our village visits, we observe that the only piece of modern technology widespread among the tribes is the automatic weapon. The end of the Mengistu reign in the 1990s and ongoing conflict in Sudan and Somalia have created trade in surplus Russian Kalashnikovs and European G-3 rifles. Guns are used to hunt, to protect cattle, and to settle scores. Battles are so commonplace that in Kareme'ngima, a Nyangatom village, I photograph children wearing jewelry made out of empty shell casings.

On the drive to the weekly market in Dimeka, three hours by car from camp, we pass bullet traders from the Konso tribe marching cattle bartered for ammunition. In Dimeka, where Hamar women sit on blankets beside small piles of sorghum, and men trade surplus goats for cows and vice versa, an alarming thought becomes inescapable: The market rate for a bullet is fifteen *birr*, the price of three photographs. Some of the faces I capture are haunting—the light-eyed Hamar mother with butter and ocher-matted ringlets, who would be beautiful no matter what she was wearing; the young Karo men painted in yellow and white diatomite for courtship dancing; the Nyangatom warrior whose Nilotic skull and carved cheekbones look like the bust of Pharaoh Akhenaten in Cairo's Egyptian Museum. But it seems entirely possible that some of the *birr* I pay for my Omo portfolio could in turn purchase bullets that spill human blood.

On our last night in camp, I ask Lale if it's been difficult for him to help us visit tribes who are sometimes considered his community's enemies. "It's complicated," he says with a sigh, and goes on to tell us a chilling story. When he was a toddler, a party of Nyangatom cattle raiders waded across the Omo during the dry season and attacked his family. Lale's mother put him on her back and ran into the forest along a baboon trail, intending to hide in a tree. Lale's oldest brother, a boy of seventeen, refused to flee. "He was proud, but he didn't have a gun, and the Nyangatom killed him," Lale tells us. "I remember seeing a body covered in yellow paint."

Lale's uncle eventually killed two Nyangatom to exact revenge for his brother. Two years ago, Lale's best friend was murdered by the relative of a slain Nyangatom man, and weeks before our visit, another of the fragile cease-fires negotiated by the government broke down. Lale relates these facts with equanimity. One of the first Karo to be formally educated, he spent six years at a missionary school and came home from university fluent in Amharic, English, and several Omo languages spoken by his schoolmates. Because he holds no grudges—and brings tourist income—he is liked and respected up and down the river.

The government says that the controversial Gibe III dam will make the Omo region less susceptible to conflict over increasingly scarce arable and grazing lands by permitting controlled flooding even in poor rain years—which in theory will irrigate South Omo farms and replenish grazing land. However, conservation and human rights groups, as well as UNESCO, question Ethiopia's agenda and environmental-impact studies. They say the Christian-dominated, Amharic-speaking government wants to divert water from the Omo to irrigate several areas, which combined are larger than Rhode Island and are earmarked for industrial sugarcane and cotton plantations. These critics say the government intends to do so without consulting the tribes, which it considers primitive, about whether they want to be relocated or become industrialized farm laborers. They also condemn the lack of consultation with the rural communities downstream, including the 300,000 Kenyans who depend on the lake, which the nutrient-rich Omo feeds, for both fishing and water for their livestock. Prime Minister Meles Zenawi has lashed out at dam opponents, claiming that "even though [South Omo] is known as backward in terms of civilization, it will become an example of rapid development." Zenawi has also said that those opposed to the dam, many from the West,

"want the pastoralists and their lifestyle to remain as a tourist attraction forever" and "a case study of ancient living for scientists and researchers."

As important as it is for the government to exercise wise leadership, it should, in an ideal world, be up to the people of the Omo Valley to determine whether their children go to university, marry whom they want, and never have to worry about their brother being gunned down or their child bringing a curse on the village. Currently, only minorities with populations of between 10,000 and 100,000 qualify for direct representation in Ethiopia's parliament, and the Mursi, Karo, Kwegu, and other small Omo tribes remain largely voiceless about their future, including the issue of how and whether their homes should remain a tourist attraction. I try to imagine myself on the other end of the lens barrel, how I would feel if I lost the power to decide what was right and wrong for my family, how much grace I might summon if random strangers turned up at my door offering money to photograph me in my bathrobe making coffee, or how hurt I would feel if I were a little Karo girl and some tourist blew me off because my face paint seemed inadequate.

Meanwhile, change is drifting down from the north. The television signal arrived two years ago enabling the Omo peoples to watch the World Cup taking place in South Africa. Cell phone towers are under construction. In Dimeka, highland traders offer tribespeople radios, batteries, bras, and Barack Obama and Michael Jordan T-shirts.

Lale Biwa, one of the few university educated members of his tribe, who wears beaded bracelets, khaki pants, a canvas sun hat, and a striped polo shirt, tells me he's convinced that "in twenty years, everything will be finished—the bull jumping, the *mingi*, all the rules." He's talking about the beliefs that make up his culture, not external aesthetics that could remain as a tourist asset. For good and bad, the world as he knows it is receding. He's already in a nostalgic mode—and one of the first of his tribe to carry a digital camera.

Discussion Questions

1. How will the new technology of the dam affect the tribes in the Omo River Valley? Find the likely positives and negatives of the dam to the tribes' culture in the reading. What is the one item of modern technology that is widespread among the tribes?

2. List items worn by the Omo tribe as clothing, body decorations, and accessories. Which items can be found in the natural environment? Which items have been imported by tourists/ outsiders? Do you think the imported items somehow detract from the natural or authentic looks of the locals? Why or why not?

3. In small groups, pick out descriptions of dress (body enclosures and modifications) to conjure up a mental image of what these tribes' people look like. For example, lip and earlobe disks and raised scars are mentioned in the article. Although the level of technology to create these body modifications is low, these are now in use in the United States and other Western cultures. Given these written descriptions of appearance, can you speculate why "several well-known fashion designers" were on the trip? What kind of designs could result from such a trip? What kind of designs would be sold at retail?

CHAPTER 14

ETHICS IN FASHION

Andrew Reilly, Kimberly A. Miller–Spillman, and Patricia Hunt–Hurst

After you have read this chapter, you will understand:

- The complex relationships between ethics and the fashion industry
- Some specific types of ethical dilemmas in the fashion industry
- How consumer demand for unique products can lead to unethical practices

Introduction

Life is full of ethical dilemmas, and the fashion industry has its share of controversy around ethics. All one has to do is read or watch the news to find examples of ethical issues in the fashion field. For instance, John Galliano was fired from his job as head of the fashion house Dior and fined for anti-Semitic statements and behavior in a Paris bar in February 2011. Fashion designers often take on the status of celebrities and their behavior is watched carefully. Would you say that Galliano was a victim of freedom of speech? Do we hold celebrities to higher standards than regular people? Or did Galliano get what he deserved? Often ethical issues are not black and white; there is not always one "right" answer.

Ethics is the study of right and wrong. The origins of ethics date back to Greek philosophers Socrates (496–399 B.C.) and his student Aristotle (384–322 B.C.). Both argued that self-knowledge through questioning what was right and wrong was necessary to achieve enlightenment and fulfillment. There are no clear lines between what is right and wrong, and topics related to ethical issues are usually controversial and vary from culture to culture.

A civilization decides what is criminal based on its code of morality. As we have seen in prior chapters, morality varies from culture to culture. Examples from the fashion industry include co-opting ethnic costumes and using objectified images in advertising and promotions. In Westernized countries, it is acceptable for a woman to show her face, hair, and body shape in public; in Islamic countries, that might be illegal. The legal issue depends on who is in charge of the government. As recently as 2011 the government of Saudi Arabia has considered passing a law that would require women with "sexy eyes" to keep them covered in public (see reading in Chapter 3). What is legal is not always considered ethical.

Knockoffs, Copies, and Counterfeits

In the fashion industry gray-market, knockoff, and counterfeit merchandise is a significant problem. For example, in 2009, United States customs officers seized $260 million dollars in goods; counterfeit footwear was the leading commodity (U.S. Customs and Border Protection). Gray-market merchandise is a legitimate, genuine product but is not sold by an authorized representative. Rather, manufacturers that are hired to make the goods produce greater quantities than the contract specifies in order to sell them on the side, which is not only a violation of the contract but illegal as well. Sometimes this deceptive practice is known as third-shift manufacturing.

Unlike gray-market goods—which are authentic—knockoffs are variations of authentic goods. Knockoff items use another item as inspiration and are considered imitations but not the real thing (such as Target creating an affordable version of a Dior couture gown). The creation of knockoffs is illegal in Europe, where fashion designs are protected for 25 years, but the practice is currently legal in the United States. However, legislation is currently being considered in the United States to protect fashion designs from imitation for three years; the government reasons that this time period is adequate time for a fashion's life span. In Europe, and if passed in the United States, not all designs would be protected, only those considered unique enough to require registration. Supporters of legislation outlawing knockoffs argue that it will protect their intellectual property and creativity; opponents argue that it will cripple the fashion industry because much of fashion is about copying and imitation of others.

Counterfeit merchandise—copies of items, intended to defraud the consumer—is another problem (see Figure 14.1). Counterfeit goods are illegal because they violate trademarks and intellectual property laws. Many consumers do not see purchasing counterfeit products as unethical (Ha

Figure 14.1 Counterfeit merchandise is a big problem in the fashion industry.

and Lennon, 2006; Ang et al. 2001), perhaps due to the fact that the effects are not immediately visible: counterfeit items are usually produced in sweatshops, deny the owner of the authentic good profit, and have been linked to terrorism. The counterfeit industry accounts for 7% of world trade and thousands of jobs lost (Yurchisin and Johnson, 2010). The counterfeit industry has also been linked to terrorist organizations and organized crime (Ha and Lennon, 2006; Gelther, 2004). Such organizations often use slave labor or sweatshops to manufacture the merchandise. Brian Hilton and colleagues provide a good overview of these issues and more in their paper "The Ethics of Counterfeiting in the Fashion Industry: Quality, Credence, and Profit Issues."

Sweatshops

Sweatshops—work environments that endanger the physical and mental welfare of employees, underpay their employees, or use slave labor—are banned in many Westernized countries, but there still exist questionable practices that work under the radar. A 2006 report called "Conduct Unbecoming" (authored by the union Unite Here!) documents how the U.S. Department of Defense, the largest consumer of U.S.-made apparel, contracted with manufacturers whose businesses can be described as sweatshops. Workers earned less than the legal minimum wage and reported pay cuts and paycheck irregularities, little to no benefits, forced overtime, and unsafe work conditions that violated OSHA (Occupational Safety and Health Administration) standards. A situation like this is not uncommon in the fashion industry where many goods are produced in countries or areas with different labor laws.

In many developing countries or territories, such as China, Saipan, and Bangladesh, sweatshops are not illegal and are the means by which inexpensive products are manufactured. Workers earn literally pennies an hour; for example, in Bangladesh over 80% of people earn less than $2 per day (World Bank, 2004). Additionally, workers must work long days in unsavory conditions such as rooms with poor ventilation and abuse. While it is technically not illegal for U.S.-based companies to contract with sweatshops in foreign countries, it is not necessarily ethical. Nike, Martha Stewart, and Kathie Lee Gifford were all "outed" for contracting with foreign sweatshops. Many consumers are demanding that companies take responsibility for their actions and contract only with manufacturers that pay their employees a fair wage and treat them with dignity. The result is that company representatives visit their contractors to verify that working conditions are safe and sound. However, as *BusinessWeek* reported in 2006, manufacturers are adept at hiding infractions and abuses, as discussed in the reading "Secrets, Lies, and Sweatshops."

Many U.S. consumers purchase apparel produced in the United States believing that it was made under ethically sound conditions. However, sometimes they can be misled. The "Made in . . ." label reports a country where the consumer believes the garment was manufactured, but the question of when a garment becomes a garment remains. A shirt can be made from cotton grown in one country that is made into yarns in another country, woven into fabric in another, designed in another, cut in another, sewn in another, and finished in another. At what point does the shirt become a "shirt"? Advocates for transparency in manufacturing are calling for labels that detail each step of the process. Until then, consumers who wish to purchase ethically traded products should purchase from fair-trade associations and companies that guarantee a fair wage and work condition to their employees. The country of origin label may be misleading in another way. For example, sweatshops are not uncommon on the island of Saipan (in the Pacific Ocean), but because the island is a commonwealth of the United States, garments manufactured there are labeled "Made in the U.S.A." Consumers trying to make ethical choices are frustrated by these types of issues.

Blood Diamonds

Blood diamonds are another ethically questionable area in fashion (see Figure 14.2). Sometimes called conflict diamonds or war diamonds, blood diamonds come from war-torn areas (usually in developing nations) where the sale of such gems helps support an armed conflict. Typically, the diamonds are mined and sold by insurgents or the party attempting to overthrow the current regime, and slaves are used to mine the diamonds. The sale of conflict diamonds from Angola was first banned by the United Nations in 1998; since then diamonds from Liberia, Sierra Leone, Côte d'Ivoire, and the Republic of Congo have been banned (the ban on diamonds from Liberia and the Republic of Congo has since been lifted).

Figure 14.2 Diamonds from war-torn countries are used to continue the insurgency and therefore have been banned in many countries around the world.

Many consumers were unaware of the background of their diamond purchases. While efforts such as international bans are made to curtail the sale of blood diamonds, many are still on the market via smuggling through other countries or the black market. Consumers wanting to ensure that their diamond purchases are not from conflict areas should buy only those that come with a Kimberley Process Certification, which is a guarantee from the World Diamond Congress that the diamond is from a legitimate mine. The negative publicity surrounding blood diamonds—including a Hollywood blockbuster movie (*Blood Diamond*, 2006)—have helped to raise awareness of the controversy, but there are still many problems in the diamond industry, as Vivienne Walt highlights in her article "Diamonds Aren't Forever." Walt discusses the wages of diamond miners, smuggling, and the underground diamond trade, which make it increasingly difficult for consumers to know if their diamonds are bloody or not.

Animal Products

The use of animals in fashion is an ethical issue due to the treatment of animals, which is frequently cruel and painful. Birds and other animals have a long history of use in fashion. In fact, The Metropolitan Museum of Art devoted an entire exhibition to the use of skins, furs, feathers, and animal prints in its 2004 exhibition "Wild: Fashion Untamed." Curator Andrew Bolton, in the book for this exhibition, states, "The history of fashion's appropriation of animal skins, prints, and symbolism is also a history of society's changing attitudes and ambivalences toward human-animal relations" (2004, p. 11).

In the late 19th and early 20th centuries, bird feathers and other parts (body and head) were extensively used in millinery to decorate women's hats. During this period hats were an essential accessory worn to complete a woman's daily outfit. Amy D. Scarborough (2009) found that at the end of the 19th century the Audubon Society and women's groups ignited efforts to stop the decline of birds related to millinery practices. They promoted their social-responsibility agenda through public lectures on the killing of birds for fashion, held fashion shows offering hat designs with no birds or feathers, and used other tactics to persuade fashionable women to stop accessorizing with birds. Scarborough found that although fashion magazines showed hats with birds and feathers in their pages, some also provided discourse on the fact that the use of birds and feathers in millinery was adversely affecting bird populations. In fact, one fashion magazine in particular, *Harper's Bazaar*[1], "changed the type of bird and plumage trimmings presented that reflected change in American bird protection legislation" (Scarborough, 2009, p. 107). This historic example shows us that combined efforts toward social responsibility can work to the betterment of the use of birds and animals in the fashion industry. Elizabeth Nevile explores current issues of feather accessories in today's fashion world in the reading "Feather Hair Extensions: Fashion without Compassion." This reading provides fashion-conscious consumers with information to consider before they take part in the trend.

Animal fur and skins have always been used in clothing; the earliest examples of apparel are animal hides. The pelts and skins were necessary for warmth and protection from the elements. Throughout human history, animals have continued to be used for warmth and protection—but also for accessorizing and showing status and wealth. It is only in the last century that the use of animals has been questioned as being unethical.

The issue is not necessarily the product itself but how the animal is treated. The picture is not pretty. Animals are either hunted in the wilderness or raised specifically for their fur or skins in unsanitary and cramped cages. They are clubbed, suffocated, poisoned, skinned alive, and boiled alive or otherwise mutilated in efforts to retrieve their hides. Many consumers empathize with the animal and object to the treatment. However, there appears to be less empathy for the non-cuddly type of animal. Snakes, lizards, silkworms, and cows garner less outrage than baby mink, seals, and exotic animals like tigers and leopards. (See Figure 14.3.)

Animal activists argue that alternatives to animal products exist. Synthetic furs offer similar warmth, tactile, and visual qualities as the genuine article. Artificial silk is available, but for people who want the real deal there is wild silk—where the moth is allowed to break through before the cocoon is used for fabric production. However, others argue that the alternatives don't provide the same degree of aesthetics or exclusivity as the original.

The controversy has resulted in marketing campaigns and niche producers that promote "ethical fur" or "ethical leather" or "ethical skins." Hunters and farmers support the humane treatment of animals while in their care and provide good nutrition, housing, and veterinary care for the livestock. They also advocate the hunting of animals to help balance wilderness ecology rather than as a commercial response to the fashion industry.

Consumers who want to avoid fur products or purchase products that have been made with animals raised and killed in humane

Figure 14.3 Products made from animal hides or skins are controversial due to the way animals are treated during harvesting.

conditions do not necessarily find it easy to make informed decisions. Often, fur is deliberately mislabeled. The Humane Society reports that fur from dogs is commonly labeled as other types of fur or not labeled at all. The Truth in Fur Labeling Act helps consumers make informed decisions when they are considering purchasing fur products. The law requires that fur items must be labeled with country of origin and type of fur, but an undercover investigation by the Humane Society reports some high-end retailers are ignoring this law. One city, West Hollywood, California, passed a law in 2011 that bans the sale of fur clothing within city limits—a first in the United States.

Advertising with Idealized Models

Marketing and advertising are other areas where ethical situations are likely to be encountered. As has been discussed in previous chapters, most advertising for fashion goods uses models whose bodies are unrealistically thin or muscular. Models are valued exactly for that—their unusual ability to look "perfect"—but many critics argue that consumers feel pressured to look like the models they see. They argue that the thin or muscular ideal is internalized and results in unhealthy behaviors such as restrictive eating or excessive exercise. It is estimated by the National Eating Disorders Association that 10 million women and 1 million men live with an eating or appearance disorder in the United States. At least one company—Dove—realizes that their consumers do not look like stick-thin models, and in a keen advertising campaign are using "real" women as models (Figure 14.4). Proponents of this campaign hail the authenticity and "realness." Several Chapter 11 readings provided information on how magazines retouch photographs to remove signs of aging in famous faces and how some communities around the world respond to this issue.

Figure 14.4 Advertising campaign by Dove that uses "real" women as models.

Circumcision

In the discussion of body image, people undergo sundry practices to alter their bodies. For the most part, body changes are left until an individual reaches puberty or adulthood. Rarely does a child undergo a body modification (at least in the West) with one exception—circumcision. Circumcision is the act of removing the foreskin from the penis (for a boy) or removing the clitoris (for a girl), usually in their youth, hence requiring parents' permission. Circumcision has been practiced for millennia, is found in numerous societies, and is supported by fashionable, cultural, religious, and health platforms. The issue of female circumcision has ignited outrage around the globe, as it is viewed as barbaric and unnecessary; however, male circumcision, while it does have its detractors, does not ignite the same frenzy. Hellsten (2004) reviews the motivations and ponders the ethical dilemmas surrounding this global practice in "Rationalizing Circumcision: From Tradition to Fashion, from Public Health to Individual Freedom—Critical Notes on Cultural Persistence of the Practice of Genital Mutilation."

Required Dress and Diversity Courses

Dress and culture is a common course offered for diversity requirements through merchandising and apparel programs across the United States. Since dress is seen first (including skin color, hairstyle, and facial features) when encountering another person, it is important to teach students not to judge an individual by appearance. But, is it ethical to encourage students to become more pluralistic through required courses? Or should students be allowed to choose whether or not to take courses on cultural diversity? Many universities have required general education courses that students must take. Do these courses work? Are students getting the information from these classes that were intended by faculty and administrators who created them? Lastly, should faculty be in the position of trying to change students' perceptions of other cultures? There is evidence that one type of required course, a multicultural course, has the opposite effect on some students than was intended. Brown (2004) reported that some students complete a multicultural, stand-alone course with previous stereotypes increased rather than softened or eliminated. Brown recommends that the method—how and in what sequence the information is presented—is as important as the message when it comes to diversity courses. See the reading "Are Required Cross-Cultural Courses Producing Pluralistic Students?" for research on Dress and Culture students.

Summary

Discussed in this chapter are several ethical issues found in the fashion industry. The media has brought many of these issues to light, however, because within the fashion industry often these issues are not taken seriously. But given the breadth of fashion globally and the tremendous demand for unique and fashionable objects, ethical issues in fashion are not small considerations. Hopefully the reader is now aware of the many ways in which consumer demands can lead to unethical practices primarily because of the money involved. In the future, we hope that before buying a counterfeit item or an item made from an animal you will reflect on what you have read in this chapter.

Suggested Readings

Dolin, E. J. (2001). *Fur, Fortune, and Empire: The Epic History of the Fur Trade in America*. New York: W. W. Norton.

Kanfer, S. (1994). *The Last Empire: DeBeers, Diamonds, and the World*. London: Coronet Books.

Ross, R. J. S. (2004). *Slaves to Fashion: Poverty and Abuse in the New Sweatshops*. Lansing, Michigan: University of Michigan Press.

Vaughn, H. (2001). *Sleeping with the Enemy: Coco Chanel's Secret War*. New York: Knopf.

Learning Activity 14.1: Animal Fashion

In a small group, generate a list of all animals that have been used for clothing and/or fashion. Which animals get the most sympathy? Which animals aren't widely used anymore? Why?

Learning Activity 14.2: Real or Fake?

Instructor, bring in a faux fur jacket and a real fur jacket (either from a private collection or from a college costume collection). Analyze the differences in color, texture, and hand. Discuss why people might prefer one jacket to the other.

References

Ang, S. H., P. S. Cheng, E. A. C. Lim, and S. K. Tambyah. (2001). Spot the Difference: Consumer Responses Towards Counterfeits. *Journal of Consumer Marketing* 18 (3): 219–235.

Bolton, A. (2004). *Wild Fashion Untamed*. New Haven: Yale University Press.

Brown, E. L. (2004, September/October). What Precipitates Change in Cultural Diversity Awareness during a Multicultural Course: The Message or the Method? *Journal of Teacher Education* 55 (4): 325–340.

"Conduct Unbecoming: Sweatshops and the U.S. Military Uniform Industry." (2006). New York: Unite Here!

John Galliano Convicted for Anti-Semitic Rant. Aljazeera. Retrieved on November 10, 2011, from www.aljazeera.com/news/europe/2011/09/201198124129538913.html.

Geltner, P. (2004, May 26). Counterfeit Goods Fueling Terror Groups. *The Columbus Dispatch*, A11.

Ha, S., and S. J. Lennon. (2006). Purchase Intent for Fashion Counterfeit Products: Ethical Ideologies, Ethical Judgments, and Perceived Risks. *Clothing and Textiles Research Journal* 24 (4): 297–315. DOI: 10.1177/0887302X0623068.

The Humane Society. (n.d.). Fur in Fashion. www.humanesociety.org/issues/fur_fashion/. Accessed October 13, 2010.

Kandel, J. (2011, November 8). West Hollywood Approves First Fur Ban in United States. Retrieved from http://news.yahoo.com/west-hollywood-approves-first-fur-ban-u-181344531.html. Accessed November 10, 2012.

Scarborough, A. D. (2009). Fashion Media's Role in the Debate on Millinery and Bird Protection in the United States in the Late Nineteenth and Early Twentieth Centuries. Unpublished doctoral dissertation, Oregon State University.

"Secrets, Lies, and Sweatshops." (2006, November 27). *BusinessWeek*. http://www.businessweek.com/magazine/content/06_48/b4011001.htm.

U.S. Customs and Border Protection. (2009). CBP, ICE Release Annual Report on Counterfeit Seized Goods. http://www.cbp.gov/xp/cgov/newsroom/news_releases/archives/2009_news_releases/dec_2009/12032009_2.xml. Accessed February 20, 2012.

World Bank (2004) *World Development Indicators Online*. http://www.worldbank.org/data. Accessed February 20, 2012.

Yurchisin, J., and K. K. P. Johnson. (2010). *Fashion and the Consumer*. New York: Berg.

Endnote

1. Prior to November 1929 the spelling of the magazine was *Harper's Bazaar*.

THE ETHICS OF COUNTERFEITING IN THE FASHION INDUSTRY: QUALITY, CREDENCE, AND PROFIT ISSUES

Brian Hilton, Chong Ju Choi, and Stephen Chen

Introduction

In this paper we examine the ethical issues involved in counterfeiting in the fashion industry. We argue that the problem partly lies in the industry itself. Copying of designs is endemic and condoned, which raises several ethical dilemmas in passing judgment on the practice of counterfeiting. As illustrated by several recent reports in the press, the problems are extensive, growing and global. For example, according to the European Commission, customs seized almost 85 million counterfeit or pirated articles at the EU's external border in 2002 and 50 million in the first half of 2003 (European Commission, 2003) while the U.S. customs made over 6,500 seizures in 2003 worth over $94 billion (International Anti-Counterfeiting Coalition, 2004a). Worldwide the International Chamber of Commerce estimates that 7 percent of world trade is in counterfeit goods and that the counterfeit market is worth $350 billion (George W. Abbott and Lee S. Sporn, Trademark Counterfeiting 1.03 [A] [2] quoted in International AntiCounterfeiting Coalition report, 2004b).

In some countries, such as the United States, such problems are compounded because their legal system only protects functionality and not design or style. In other countries there is not even this level of protection (Belhumeur, 2000). There is either no formal legal protection for design or functionality or what little protection there is is incapable of being enforced, either through incompetence or corruption.

This ensures that it is very difficult in practice, if not in theory, to enforce any rights that exist. It is always possible to find a country where one can manufacture blatant copies or counterfeits with no fear of falling foul of the law.

As industries have globalized their distribution and production operations, counterfeiting has become easier and easier to sustain and is a problem affecting a whole range of industries worldwide. No entirely reliable figures exist for such a clandestine trade but the best estimates available place it at some 3–6% of world trade, with sectoral estimates quoted as follows: watches (5%), medicine (6%), perfumes (5%), aircraft parts (10%), toys (12%), music (33%), video (50%), software (43%) (OECD, 1998). In its annual "Special 301" review, the office of the U.S. Trade Representative (USTR) identified more than 30 countries as centers for counterfeiting and piracy and estimated that American industries lose $200 billion–$250 billion a year to counterfeiting (*The Economist*, 2003).

The industry we will focus on in this paper is high-end clothing and accessories that derive a significant proportion of their market value from brands and reputations of designers such as Dior, Versace, Chanel, etc. This is one of the most highly publicized sectors where counterfeiting is rife. According to the International Anti-Counterfeiting Coalition about 18% of the $98 million of counterfeit products seized by U.S. Customs in 2002 were made up of fashion-related items: apparel, sunglasses, watches, handbags and headwear.[1] It should also be noted that the figures are probably an understatement of the problem as many cases do not reach the public domain and action is not taken in many cases.

There have been a few cases of successful prosecution, such as Tommy Hilfiger's suit against Goody's Family Clothing Inc. for $11 million[2] and the case of the U.K. counterfeiter ordered to pay back more than £354,000 after police discovered more than 100,000 labels and packaging for 52 different designer brands, including Nike,

Reprinted with permission from *Springer Science+Business Media: Journal of Business Ethics*.

Adidas and Armani, in a raid.[3] However, in most cases offenders are rarely prosecuted and in some cases they openly sell fake goods. For instance, boutiques that sell fake designer goods at a fraction of the normal retail price are now available in many cities worldwide. In most cases the damages awarded against counterfeiters are relatively minor and in many cases authorities may decline to prosecute offenders, placing the onus on copyright owners to take action.[4] Other cases are settled outside the legal system and do not enter the public domain. For example, where the counterfeiting involves a "legitimate" producer, fashion houses simply stop using them rather than take them to court.

As in other innovation businesses (Fassin, 2000) ethical issues can arise in fashion at different stages of the innovation process such as disputes over intellectual property rights, confidentiality of information, marketing and finance. One of the authors has been active in fraud investigation in the fashion industry and has informally interviewed a number of colleagues in the industry. What follows is an analysis of the ethical issues that surfaced in the course of this work. We start by explaining the concept of credence goods and discussing the role of credence in the fashion industry. We then analyze the ethical issues in a number of different types of counterfeiting encountered in the fashion industry. We conclude with some observations on the general ethical implications of intellectual property rights.

Concept of Credence Goods

A key concept in our paper is the idea of "credence goods" (Ekelund et al., 1995; Emons, 1997). These are goods whose quality is difficult to assess before or after purchase and use. Many luxury products fall in this category. Technically unsophisticated consumers cannot be certain of their quality even after purchase. Their value is dependent on the credence given to them by others, e.g., the designer's or distributor's reputation and their use by a particular set of consumers, the fashionable. Advertisers use such reputations or standing

with a sub-class of consumers as a powerful part of their advertising strategy. The opulent, successful consumer, who is admired for her wealth, power, or celebrity status, endorses a product by using it and so doing implies it has utility to them and, by inference, others aspiring to their lifestyle.

Credence goods can be viewed as lying at one end of a spectrum determined by whether quality can be assessed before or after purchase or never. This spectrum starts with what we call "search goods" and passes through what we will call "experience goods," before ending with "credence goods." "Search goods" have an intrinsic worth objectively assessable prior to purchase. An example would be lettuce, where staleness and blemishes are difficult to hide from potential purchasers. "Experience goods" are those where experience of use after purchase reveals quality with a fair degree of certainty. A bed or toy would be good examples. The quality of "credence goods" is uncertain both before and after purchase.

Common examples of credence goods would be some medical services, consulting advice or the luxury goods already mentioned. In all these examples there are cases when even after purchase one does not know whether a promised result has been effected or not, e.g., if the diet or treatment will in the end affect the prognosis; whether the consultancy advice received or another factor produced a performance improvement; whether the goods purchased have had the desired social impact.

For "search goods" perceived and actual quality are the same by definition so counterfeiting is difficult. For "experience goods," in the short run, quality as known by the purchaser, and subsequent user, can diverge from quality as perceived by an external observer. In the longer run it will not. Eventually bad experience in use will have an impact on the reputation of the supplier or producer. However, for credence goods their value can only be inferred from the credence given them by others. In the case of professional services such as medicine where there is a real danger to the life of a consumer as a consequence of bad practice, the matter is handled by professional bodies that give credence to their registered practitioners who are able to convince their peers that they are competent. Such social protection is seen as unnecessary in the fashion industry. Credence goods offer counterfeiters considerable opportunities to exploit trusting consumers. Between these extremes there is a vast range of products. Buyers may attribute various degrees of credence to the quality of these products but they can never do so with absolute certainty.

The Nature of the Fashion Industry

The whole fashion industry relies heavily on credence. Obviously for goods where the distinguishing features involve a high degree of technical sophistication or intricacy, the quality is actual as well as perceived. However, in the fashion industry, designs are often simple and much of the value lies in the perception of the buyer. In the case of haute couture much of the value for the buyer lies in the belief that he or she is purchasing something novel and exclusive. Top designers limit the impact of copying and counterfeiting by changing designs from season to season and by limiting production and distribution. This has the added value in their field that it confirms their reputation as leading highly creative designers as demonstrated by their capacity to continually re-invent themselves in a manner that others are totally unable to emulate. The costs of this strategy are huge but are sustained by a very small number of very rich buyers.

Who is buying and from whom is what gives a product its credibility. In the absence of a means to assess quality directly people use "surrogate" indicators of quality. In the fashion industry such an indicator would be the choices made by those regarded by the public as fashionable, such as movie stars or other celebrities. They demonstrate to their admirers what fashion is through their choices in design. However, they too are maybe unsure of what is good taste and so they turn to a few key designers who their "set" admires or trusts. It is the latter who ultimately determine the fashion. Another key factor is a designer's reputation with his peers, the fashion writers and his endorsement, directly or indirectly, by the fashionable. For ex-

ample, Chanel experienced an explosive increase in sales when Karl Lagerfeld became their house designer, reaching $400 million a decade after he joined.[5] By changing designers Chanel showed that an image allowed to grow old and become a little tired could be revitalized and successfully re-launched to attract a new generation of clientele. In other cases a firm such as Disney, with a well-known brand name and characters such as Mickey Mouse, may license the use of the brand or image in a fashion item. The public perception of what quality entails is, therefore, shaped very much by these image-makers.

Three distinct segments may be identified in the market for fashion items according to their intrinsic and perceived quality. At the top end of the quality spectrum, both actual quality and perceived quality are high. The quality of the design, quality of the materials and quality of the tailoring are all immediately obvious. At the other end of the quality spectrum are cheap, shoddy, badly presented clothes, or what the clothing industry labels with the Yiddish word *schmutter*. Here both perceived and actual quality are low and such goods behave more like "search goods." The items that cause most problems are those of medium quality that are not of obvious high intrinsic quality but have a high perceived value.

Here the representational features associated with the product will then be crucial to potential buyers' assessment of their worth, e.g., the position and status of the outlet where they are purchased, the label, the logo affixed to them, etc.

Ethical Bases for Intellectual Property

There are many ethical bases according to which such intellectual property issues can be analyzed. However, Sama and Shoaf (2002) have shown how intellectual property rights dilemmas can be usefully analyzed from four theoretical perspectives:

- Utilitarianism or ends-based reasoning, which aims to produce the greatest good for the greatest number of people;

- Distributive justice or an equity-based reasoning aims to provide beneficiaries an equitable (not necessarily equal) distribution of costs and benefits;
- The Moral Rights of Man perspective, which bases decisions on universal laws that assume basic human rights;
- Ethical Relativism that uses a "comparison-based" reasoning based on what others are doing in similar circumstances.

The first two of these are derived from theories of the nature of justice while the latter two are more general ethical principles. Utilitarian reasoning (Bentham, 1948; Mill, 1998; Strasser, 1991) is a cost/benefits approach to ethical decision-making emphasizing outcomes or teleological arguments. According to this approach the most ethical decision is one that results in the greatest good for the greatest number of people and has been the dominant approach in economics and public policy for over 200 years.

The utilitarian argument has been the most commonly used argument for intellectual property protection. It is argued that intellectual property needs to be protected in order to provide sufficient incentive to develop new technology and creative products. Without adequate intellectual property protection, potential inventors and creators of new products might decide not to develop new technology for fear of not obtaining adequate returns from investments of time and resources. So it is argued one would have a less creatively productive world with lower levels of welfare. Hence the primary ethical basis for judgment is the economic good of society. For example, patents originated from the fourteenth century practice of issuing "letters patent" or official documents from the sovereign publicly conferring certain rights and privileges. These were believed to have originated in Italy and granted the holder protection from any competition they might encounter from other artisans or apprentices they might train up in the new technology brought into the country. The aim was to encourage foreign technology transfer and innovation and so benefit the local economy.

In contrast, distributive justice is a deontological approach that aims for solutions whereby beneficiaries of the decision receive an equitable (not necessarily equal) distribution of costs and benefits (Kelly, 2001; Rawls, 1971). For example, according to this approach if a consumer pays more for a service or good, he or she might expect better delivery of the service or good; or if an individual makes a greater contribution to a project, he or she should expect a greater reward. Intellectual property rights could be defended in this approach on the basis that it is only fair that inventors and creators of original works should receive proper compensation for their creative efforts.

The moral rights approach to ethics harks back to the philosophy of Kant (Bowie, 1999; Kant, 1963, 1990, 1994) and is predicated on a belief that there are certain basic human rights that need to be respected at all costs. This idea of moral rights in intellectual property dates back to the Republican revolution in France in the late 18th century and the subsequent movement throughout Europe that asserted the "Rights of Man." This rejected the assertion of royal prerogative and asserted instead the rights of citizens to enjoy the fruits of their creative labor, including intellectual and artistic works. Thus, in these countries, protecting the moral rights of the author is regarded as paramount.

Like moral rights reasoning, ethical relativism is rules-based. However, this perspective rejects the notion of the universal laws and bases decisions on what others are doing under similar circumstances (Sims and Keon, 1999; Wyld and Jones, 1997) or "moral approval from oneself or others" (Jones and Ryan, 1997). According to this approach, intellectual property rights, like other rights, should be based on precedents or what others have done in similar cases. For example, copyright protection can be justified on the basis that historically this has been accepted practice and is the accepted practice in most countries.

As Resnick (2003) has noted, intellectual property is particularly prone to ethical disputes because there are many different types of intellectual property to which rights can be attached, and there is a variety of different values according to which claims can be assessed. It is, therefore, necessary to distinguish carefully between different types of counterfeiting and different bases for ethical claims. Accordingly we distinguish below between four different types of counterfeit products:

- vanity fakes or low intrinsic, low perceived value products,
- overruns or copies made from leftover material,
- condoned copies made by other designers or fashion houses, and
- copies made by the fashion houses themselves, and analyze each according to the four ethical bases described by Sama and Shoaf (2002).

Vanity Counterfeits

Vanity counterfeits of low intrinsic and low perceived quality are usually not an immediate problem to the suppliers of the original as they tend to be very evidently not the real thing. However, such a flood of poor quality imitations can be very damaging to a brand in the longer term as it becomes difficult to disassociate the genuine product from the mass of cheap copies produced to look like it.

While both moral rights and utilitarian arguments have generally been used to defend the rights of designers, as outlined above, it should be noted that arguments could also be made on both grounds to justify counterfeiting. While designers may assert their moral right to benefit from their work, an equal moral argument might be made in favor of counterfeiters. Given that many operate in countries where they face economic hardship, some might consider it a basic human right to make a living whatever way one can in order to survive. The question then becomes which moral right takes precedence—that of the designer or the counterfeiter. Similarly, although designers might argue that counterfeiting deprives them of their legitimate economic rights to benefit from their work and will harm society in the long term, it could be argued equally on utility grounds that counterfeiters are merely serving a market of consumers that would otherwise not be able to afford the legitimate product. In such circumstances, it could be argued that the welfare of society as a whole may be increased by relaxing copyright restrictions and that counterfeiters perform a social service. If it pleases a lowly paid worker in a poorly developed country to flaunt a fake of a designer product to which he or she aspires but cannot afford, where is the harm, given that in such cases there is complicity between the buyer and the seller? The buyer knows he or she is buying a fake, so it is also not clear who is harmed by this deception. The only ones who are being deceived are the less knowledgeable who see the buyer wearing the fake and assume that the buyer has purchased an original item. Do the rights of the less knowledgeable public not to be deceived outweigh the rights of the buyer to knowingly purchase a fake for whatever reason? Given that counterfeiting is accepted in many countries and for certain products, the practice could also be justified on relativistic grounds. The music and software industries are facing just such a problem worldwide.

Overruns

The least offensive counterfeit is one of a high quality product whose provenance may be suspect but which has all the other attributes of an original designer labeled item. This product may have been made to the original design specification by a legitimate producer who, in order to gain additional profit, has run-off a few extra garments to the original pattern from the often very expensive material supplied by the original designer or fashion house. It has all the hallmarks of the original product and only lacks the proper authorization of its creator. Such goods can sell with ease in local markets especially when that local market has been swollen by both local and international tourism. Often such sales local to the source of production end up competing with the genuine article. That this practice is commonplace was confirmed in interviews conducted by one of the authors with counterfeit investigators and buyers in the industry.

In many cases the out-workers see such profit from overruns as a right. As Steidlmeier

(1993) has described, the perspectives of developing countries toward intellectual property claims are often quite different from those in well-developed countries, especially when it involves exploitation of local resources. Some of the differences can be attributed to different value systems. However, an examination of the profit figures points to other reasons.

There are numerous reports that the use of "sweatshops" is still common practice in the clothing industry (e.g., Bonacich et al., 2000; Smithsonian Institution, 1997; Ross, 1997; Varley, 1998), particularly in developing countries. (According to the pressure group Sweatshopwatch, a sweatshop is defined as a workplace where workers are subject to extreme exploitation, including the absence of a living wage or benefits, poor working conditions, such as health and safety hazards, and arbitrary discipline.) Several studies have shown that the workers who produce these items make barely enough to survive. For example, according to a U.S. Commerce Department report, the base wage for garment workers in Honduras is $0.43 per hour, or $3.47 per day. After deducting costs for transportation to and from work, breakfast and lunch costs $2.59, that leaves only $0.80 a day for families' other basic needs.[6] Similarly according to independent labor rights organizations in Hong Kong, the minimum wage rate is $0.21/hour in Shanghai and $0.26/hour in Guangzhou compared to an estimated living wage of about $0.87/hour.[7] Researchers have also found that it is not unusual for garment workers to be paid below the legal minimum wage.

While clothing workers are earning barely enough to survive, retailers and fashion houses are reaping handsome profits. For example, it is estimated that the price breakdown of a pair of jeans produced in Eastern Europe and sold in Western Europe is as follows: value-added tax (17.5%), brand name company (25%), retailer (50%), transport, import duties (11%) and production costs (13%, of which worker wages constitute approximately 1%) while the approximate cost of producing a pair of trousers made in Madagascar for retail in France at approximately U.S. $23.57 is as follows: fabric ($3.50), accessories ($1), transport ($0.17), production ($2), of which the workers wages earn $0.49.[8]

Comparing the large profit margins earned by designers and retailers in the clothing industry with the low wages earned by the clothing workers, the rights of workers to a small share of the profit from leftover materials might seem strong on equity grounds. As in the previous case of vanity counterfeits, counterfeiting could also be defended on utility and relativistic grounds.

Condoned Copies

As already indicated, creating new fashion is in itself a means of protecting reputation in design.

By continuously creating new designs the truly creative can always upstage less capable individuals. Faced with a flow of high quality creativity the latter cannot aspire to be much more than copyists or clever counterfeiters. This is understood and condoned to some extent by the industry itself. The bulk of the revenues in the industry are earned in high street stores. Their buyers go to the fashion shows to capture ideas. They then commission others to produce simplified versions of the designs they see there and like in high volumes. Some producers simply make cheap copies from the pictures of "haute couture" that appear in fashion magazines. People such as Victor Costa and Jack Mulqueen have created businesses grossing over two hundred million dollars by producing products similar to the original creations of others.

In one sense it could be argued that the mass-produced fashion goods industry is about copying or, less contentiously, simplifying current designs to make available products in high volume at low prices. Copying is thus endemic and could be said to be a core activity of the industry. This copying is accepted not only because the fashion houses benefit from the publicity, but also because the copying legitimates their designs as ones that are desirable and worth copying. In the absence of other indicators of desirability, copying is an indicator of worth. To coin an aphorism, "imitation is the best form of flattery," and in accepting this one must also accept that within this boundary of "legitimacy" one will find an inevitable optimal amount of "true" fraud (Darby and Karni, 1973).

The ethical issue then arises in deciding when copying is considered unacceptable. As before, based on utility reasoning it could be argued that copying is justified since it serves a larger market that would not otherwise be able to afford such items. However, since copying is commonplace in the industry and condoned to some extent by designers themselves, the defense of counterfeiting on relativistic grounds becomes even stronger. On distributive equity grounds it could even be argued that copyists deserve some compensation as they are providing valuable publicity for the brand. Weighed against these various arguments the moral rights of the designer seem less significant.

Self Copies

The issues become even less clear when the copying is perpetrated by the fashion houses themselves. Firms in the fashion industry, like those of other luxury goods, face a paradox of how to profit from exclusivity. Luxury goods have different economic characteristics from others such as a lower price elasticity of demand. Price increases reduce demand less than in other industries and in some cases higher prices can actually generate more demand since scarcity plays a key role in determining value and image.

This usually means limiting production. However, this may then mean that the firm has insufficient volume of sales to recover their costs of production. This tempts many firms to increase production beyond the bounds set by perceived exclusivity. The problem is that increased production may then impact negatively on the exclusivity of the product.

Gucci is a classic case. During the 1980s Gucci expanded output rapidly. Its products became widely available in an uncontrolled way to too many stores and outlets. The overall image of the brand for exclusivity suffered. It was also tarnished by a huge increase in the volume of poor quality counterfeits that then reached the market. This led to decreased sales for the original product. It even led to some losses on some of the company's own products. Gucci's strategy in the 1990s has been to withdraw its products from thousands of points of sale. It has then systematically set out to re-create its air of exclusivity. Another way out of this marketing conundrum is for the designer or producer, e.g., Giorgio Armani, Gucci, Lacoste, etc., to use a designer label and or logo. The idea is to attach his name, or symbol, or logo, to the good quality, "prêt a porter," high-volume products that modern machinery makes it possible to produce profitably. Top fashion houses in effect use haute couture as a marketing tool to boost the profits that they mainly earn from ready-to-wear clothes. For example, Resener (1990) writes that "Lanvin was gambling that an attention grabbing haute-couture line would also boost sales of the women's ready to wear line—the real money maker in any French fashion firm."

Some designers even go as far as franchising their name to others. Clearly the buyer of the designer labeled item understands this and accepts she is not buying haute couture. However, she might have some expectation of an exclusivity that may not be there if the designer produces in high street volumes. Similar ethical arguments (greater utility, equity and relativism) apply as in the previous case except now the counterfeiter is the fashion house itself and the potentially damaged party is the buyer of the good. The problem of copying can be compounded further if the designer creates a market for "seconds," "factory rejects," or "re-labeling" to sell at even large volumes at a discounted price. The designer's leverage over his market then becomes even more tenuous. Such a marketing strategy gives credence to poorer quality counterfeits as they can claim to be "legitimate" factory rejects. Similar issues arise when there is a robust "second hand" market in out-of-fashion items sold on by their original purchasers through model agencies. Some fashion houses attempt to resolve this ethical dilemma by re-labeling products to allow surreptitious discounting of stock that has not moved fast enough. Then they hope they cannot be accused of cheating their high-paying customers who buy the original brand. However, given the high markup for the original, the value of the brand name would need to be considerable in comparison to the intrinsic value of the item, otherwise the issue of whether the buyer is being cheated arises again.

The Problem of High Quality Counterfeits

So far we have considered only the problems of counterfeits that are lower in quality than the original. However, with the advent of new technologies a different set of ethical issues arises with products that are of higher intrinsic quality than the original. Given the ease with which copies can be made with new technology, one now finds imitations reaching the market before the originals. The less scrupulous do not even wait until the fashion shows to release their product. This adds a new dimension to the debate about the ethics of counterfeiting. On utility grounds it could even be argued that the copyists are the ones who are the true innovators in all but name and it is the designers holding back progress. Drawing an ethical distinction between counterfeiters and entrepreneurs, who are simply exploiting a market opportunity, becomes more difficult. As Hannafey (2003) notes, many entrepreneurs approve of actions that maximize their personal financial reward even if that comes at the expense of others. When the other is a large multinational fashion house that is making substantial profits, some entrepreneurs may consider it perfectly legitimate to earn money through counterfeiting especially when they are providing a high quality product at a low price.

Discussion and Conclusions

Here we have concentrated on the high-end fashion clothing and accessories industry. However, many similar issues also arise in other industries where fashion is a significant factor. For example, the practice of discounting "second-hand" goods is also well known in the automobile industry. Most manufacturers keep up sales volumes by leasing cars at a huge discount to hire companies, who after using them for a while, return them to the manufacturer with exceedingly low mileages on the clock. The manufacturer then sells the now "second hand" vehicle at a discount to their dealer network for sale as used vehicles. Hire companies will even do this on their own account if the manufacturers will sell to them at a large enough discount. It is also a well-accepted practice that competitors attempt to match the features brought out in a new model, even to the extent of employing industrial espionage in the automobile and other industries.

The practice of condoning or encouraging others to copy designs is also commonplace in the computing industry where benefits of cloning include the reduction of competition and the creation of industry standards that can lead to increased profits (Conner and Rumelt, 1991). For example Digital deliberately gave its main competitors such as IBM direct access to its very fast Alpha chip.[9] This ensured that IBM did not compete by developing a product with similar features. If such a product were developed and introduced into the market it is likely that neither party would be able to recover its sunk development costs before the next generation of chips came on the market.

Our examination of counterfeiting in the clothing industry illustrates the difficulties that can exist in making ethical judgments about cases of intellectual property rights. Cases that seem quite clear-cut on legal grounds often have underlying contextual factors that need to be considered before making ethical judgments, for example norms in the industry itself and disparities in cultural values and economic resources between countries. We believe many similar issues arise in other knowledge-intensive industries such as biotechnology and art. Recent highly publicized cases such as the patenting of the human genome (Flowers, 1998; Sagoff, 1998) have highlighted the difficulty in balancing the rights of the innovator with rights of the public or the world in general to enjoy the fruits of that technological innovation. One could argue that all citizens of the world are entitled to enjoy a great work of art or wear a fashionable item of clothing regardless of their income. There is also a wider issue about what we mean when we talk about the "good of society." Should this only apply to societies in well-developed countries? Those in less-well-developed countries may have different claims when considering benefits from such knowledge.

On the other hand the industry for high-end fashion goods does have some characteristics that make it atypical compared with other industries. The first is that high-end fashion goods are luxury or aspirational goods (at least the authentic goods are) and most of the value arises from the look rather than the functionality of the item and raw materials used. The second is that production of the good and copying of designs are relatively easy. Thirdly, copying of designs is endemic and to some extent condoned in the industry. Lastly, demand for the goods is subject to credence and social-network effects.

These factors contribute to practices in the industry that are probably quite unusual.

Clearly we have not attempted to resolve all the above questions in our paper. However, we hope to have stimulated thinking and encouraged further research in this area of business ethics that will surely grow in importance.

Acknowledgments

This paper benefited greatly from discussions between Chong Ju Choi and Thomas C. Schelling and between the authors and participants in the research seminars at the Australian National University in Canberra.

References

Belhumeur, J.: 2000, *International Law of Fashion* (Canova Editrice, Trevise, Italy).

Bentham, J.: 1948, *An Introduction to the Principles of Morals and Legislation* (Clarendon, Oxford).

Bonacich, E., R. Appelbaum and K.-S. Chin: 2000, *Behind the Label: Inequality in the Los Angeles Apparel Industry* (University of California Press, Berkeley, CA).

Bowie, N. E.: 1999, *Business Ethics: A Kantian Perspective* (Blackwell, Oxford).

Conner, K. R. and R. P. Rumelt: 1991, 'Software Piracy: An Analysis of Protection Strategies', *Management Science* 37(2), 125–140.

Darby, M. R. and E. Karni: 1973, 'Free Competition and the Optimal Amount of Fraud', *The Journal of Law and Economics* 16, 67–88.

Department of Labor Bureau of International Labor Affairs: 2001, Findings on the Worst Forms of Child Labor.

Ekelund, R. B., G. Franklin, F. G. Mixon and W. Ressler: 1995, 'Advertising and Information: An Empirical Study of Search, Experience and Credence Goods', *Journal of Economic Studies* 22(2), 33–44.

Emons, W.: 1997, 'Credence Goods and Fraudulent Experts', *The Rand Journal of Economics* 28(1), 107–120.

European Commission: 2003, 'Customs: Counterfeiters and Pirates are Increasingly Turning to Mass-produced Goods', Press release, Brussels, 24 November 2003.

Fassin, Y.: 2000, 'Innovation and Ethics: Ethical Considerations in the Innovation Business', *Journal of Business Ethics* 27(1/2), 193–203.

Flowers, E. B.: 1998, 'The Ethics of Patenting the Human Genome', *Journal of Business Ethics* 17, 1737–1745.

Hannafey, F. T.: 2003, 'Entrepreneurship and Ethics: A Literature Review', *Journal of Business Ethics* 46(2), 99–110.

International AntiCounterfeiting Coalition: 2004a, FY2003 Top IPR Commodities Seized (available at http://www.iacc.org/teampublish/uploads/Commodities.pdf).

International AntiCounterfeiting Coalition: 2004b, Facts on Fakes (available at http://www.iacc.org/teampublish/uploads/factsupdated.pdf).

Jones, T. M. and L. V. Ryan: 1997, 'The Link Between Ethical Judgment and Action in Organizations: A Moral Approbation Approach', *Organization Science* 8(6), 663–680.

Kant, I.: 1963, *Lectures on Ethics* (Harper, New York).

Kant, I.: 1990, *Foundation of the Metaphysics of Morals*, 2nd Edition. Translated by L. W. Beck (Macmillan, NewYork).

Kant, I.: 1994, *Metaphysical Principles of Virtue in Ethical Philosophy*. Translated by J. W. Ellington (Hackett Publishing, Indianapolis).

Kelly, E. (ed.): 2001, *Justice as Fairness: A Restatement* (Belknap Press, Cambridge, MA).

Mill, J. S.: 1998, in R. Crisp (ed.), *Utilitarianism* (Oxford University Press, Oxford).

OECD: 1998, The Economic Impact of Counterfeiting.

Rawls, J.: 1971, *A Theory of Justice* (Harvard University Press, Cambridge, MA).

Resener, M.: 1990, 'Haute Couture's Financial Makeover', *Institutional Investor* (March), 80–85.

Resnick, D. B.: 2003, 'A Pluralistic Account of Intellectual Property', *Journal of Business Ethics* 46(4), 319–335.

Ross, A.: 1997, *No Sweat: Fashion, Free Trade, and the Rights of Garment Workers* (Verso Books, New York).

Sagoff, M.: 1998, 'Patented Genes: An Ethical Appraisal', *Issues in Science and Technology* 14(3), 37–42.

Sama, L. M. and V. Shoaf: 2002, 'Ethics on the Web: Applying Moral Decision Making to the New Media', *Journal of Business Ethics* 36, 93–103.

Sims, R. L. and T. L. Keon: 1999, 'Determinants of Ethical Decision Making: The Relationship of the Perceived Organisational Environment', *Journal of Business Ethics* 19(4 (part 1)), 393–401.

Smithsonian Institution: 1997, Between a Rock and Hard Place: A History of American Sweatshops 1820–Present (available at http://americanhistory.si.edu/sweatshops).

Steidlmeier, P.: 1993, 'The Moral Legitimacy of Intellectual Property Claims: American Business and Developing Country Perspectives', *Journal of Business Ethics* 12(2), 157–164.

Strasser, M.: 1991, *The Moral Philosophy of John Stuart Mill: Toward Modifications of Contemporary Utilitarianism* (Longwood Academic, Wakefield, NH).

The Economist: 2003, 'Imitating Property is Theft', May 15.

Varley, P.: 1998, The Sweatshop Quandary: Corporate Responsibility on the Global Frontier (Investor Responsibility Research Center, Washington, DC).

Wyld, D. C. and C. A. Jones: 1997, 'The Importance of Context: The Ethical Work Climate Construct and Models of Ethical Decision Making—An Agenda for Research', *Journal of Business Ethics* 16(4), 465–472.

Endnotes

1. Available at http://publish.iacc.org
2. 'Hilfiger Settles Counterfeiting Suit against Retailer', *New York Times* (Late Edition, East Coast). New York, NY, June 28, 2003, p. C.4.
3. 'Anti-Counterfeiting Group: Convicted Counterfeiter Ordered to Pay Back Unlawful Earnings or Face Eight Years in Prison', M2 Presswire. Coventry: December 6, 2002, p. 1.
4. 'Minnesota Stores Openly Sell Designer Knock-offs; Prosecution Unlikely', Knight Ridder Tribune Business News. Washington, D.C.: July 24, 2002, p. 1.
5. *Hello Magazine*, 15 March 2004.
6. 'Wal-Mart Sweatshops in Honduras', November 17, 1998, National Labor Committee.
7. 'Behind the Label: Made in China', March 1998, Charles Kernaghan/National Labor Committee.
8. SOMO Bulletin on Issues in Garments and Textiles, Number 1, May 2003 (available at http://www.cleanclothes.org).
9. Gorman, R. and Lynch, D. 'Digital and IBM Sign Network Systems Management Agreement', Digital Press Release, 7 September. 1993, p. 2.

Discussion Questions

1. What are three reasons people choose to purchase counterfeit products?
2. Should there be penalties for people who purchase counterfeit products? If so, what types—fines, jail, community service?

14.2

SECRETS, LIES, AND SWEATSHOPS

Dexter Roberts and Pete Engard

American importers have long answered criticism of conditions at their Chinese suppliers with labor rules and inspections. But many factories have just gotten better at concealing abuses.

Tang Yinghong was caught in an impossible squeeze. For years, his employer, Ningbo Beifa Group, had prospered as a top supplier of pens, mechanical pencils, and highlighters to Wal-Mart Stores (WMT) and other major retailers. But late last year, Tang learned that auditors from Wal-Mart, Beifa's biggest customer, were about to inspect labor conditions at the factory in the Chinese coastal city of Ningbo where he worked as an administrator. Wal-Mart had already on three occasions caught Beifa paying its 3,000 workers less than China's minimum wage and violating overtime rules, Tang says. Under the U.S. chain's labor rules, a fourth offense would end the relationship.

Help arrived suddenly in the form of an unexpected phone call from a man calling himself Lai Mingwei. The caller said he was with Shanghai Corporate Responsibility Management & Consulting Co., and for a $5,000 fee, he'd take care of Tang's Wal-Mart problem. "He promised us he could definitely get us a pass for the audit," Tang says.

Lai provided advice on how to create fake but authentic-looking records and suggested that Beifa hustle any workers with grievances out of the factory on the day of the audit, Tang recounts. The consultant also coached Beifa managers on what questions they could expect from Wal-Mart's inspectors, says Tang. After following much of Lai's advice, the Beifa factory in Ningbo passed the audit earlier this year, Tang says, even though the company didn't change any of its practices.

For more than a decade, major American retailers and name brands have answered accusations that they exploit "sweatshop" labor with elaborate codes of conduct and on-site monitoring. But in China many factories have just gotten better at concealing abuses. Internal industry documents reviewed by *BusinessWeek* reveal that numerous Chinese factories keep double sets of books to fool auditors and distribute scripts for employees to recite if they are questioned. And a new breed of Chinese consultant has sprung up to assist companies like Beifa in evading audits. "Tutoring and helping factories deal with audits has become an industry in China," says Tang, 34, who recently left Beifa of his own volition to start a Web site for workers.

A lawyer for Beifa, Zhou Jie, confirms that the company employed the Shanghai consulting firm but denies any dishonesty related to wages, hours, or outside monitoring. Past audits had "disclosed some problems, and we took necessary measures correspondingly," he explains in a letter responding to questions. The lawyer adds that Beifa has "become the target of accusations" by former employees "whose unreasonable demands have not been satisfied." Reached by cell phone, a man identifying himself as Lai says that the Shanghai consulting firm helps suppliers pass audits, but he declines to comment on his work for Beifa.

Wal-Mart spokeswoman Amy Wyatt says the giant retailer will investigate the allegations about Beifa brought to its attention by *BusinessWeek*. Wal-Mart has stepped up factory inspections, she adds, but it acknowledges that some suppliers are trying to undermine monitoring: "We recognize there is a problem. There are always improvements that need to be made, but we are confident that new procedures are improving conditions."

Chinese Export manufacturing is rife with tales of deception. The largest single source of American imports, China's factories this year are expected to ship goods to the U.S. worth $280 billion. American companies continually demand lower prices from their Chinese suppliers, allowing American consumers to enjoy inexpensive clothes, sneakers, and electronics. But factory managers in China complain in interviews that U.S. price pressure creates a powerful incentive to cheat on labor standards that American companies promote as a badge of responsible capitalism. These standards generally incorporate the official minimum wage, which is set by local or provincial governments and ranges from $45 to $101 a month. American companies also typically say they hew to the government-mandated workweek of 40 to 44 hours, beyond which higher overtime pay is required. These figures can be misleading, however, as the Beijing government has had only limited success in pushing local authorities to enforce Chinese labor laws. That's another reason abuses persist and factory oversight frequently fails.

Some American companies now concede that the cheating is far more pervasive than they had imagined. "We've come to realize that, while monitoring is crucial to measuring the performance of our suppliers, it doesn't per se lead to sustainable improvements," says Hannah Jones, Nike Inc.'s (NKE) vice-president for corporate responsibility. "We still have the same core problems."

This raises disturbing questions. Guarantees by multi-nationals that offshore suppliers are meeting widely accepted codes of conduct have been important to maintaining political support in the U.S. for growing trade ties with China, especially in the wake of protests by unions and anti-globalization activists. "For many retailers, audits are a way of covering themselves," says Auret van Heerden, chief executive of the Fair Labor Assn., a coalition of 20 apparel and sporting goods makers and retailers, including Nike, Adidas Group, Eddie Bauer, and Nordstrom (JWN). But can corporations successfully impose Western labor standards on a nation that lacks real unions and a meaningful rule of law?

Historically associated with sweatshop abuses but now trying to reform its suppliers, Nike says that one factory it caught falsifying records several years ago is the Zhi Qiao Garments Co. The dingy concrete-walled facility set near mango groves and rice paddies in the steamy southern city of Panyu employs 600 workers, most in their early 20s. They wear blue smocks and lean over stitching machines and large steam-blasting irons. Today the factory complies with labor-law requirements, Nike says, but Zhi Qiao's general manager, Peter Wang, says it's not easy. "Before, we all played the cat-and-mouse game," but that has ended, he claims. "Any improvement you make costs more money." Providing for overtime wages is his biggest challenge, he says. By law, he is supposed to provide time-and-a-half pay after eight hours on weekdays and between double and triple pay for Saturdays, Sundays, and holidays. "The price [Nike pays] never increases one penny," Wang complains, "but compliance with labor codes definitely raises costs."

A Nike spokesman says in a written statement that the company, based in Beaverton, Ore., "believes wages are best set by the local marketplace in which a contract factory competes for its workforce." One way Nike and several other companies are seeking to improve labor conditions is teaching their suppliers more efficient production methods that reduce the need for overtime.

The problems in China aren't limited to garment factories, where labor activists have documented sweatshop conditions since the early 1990s. Widespread violations of Chinese labor laws are also surfacing in factories supplying everything from furniture and household appliances to electronics and computers. Hewlett-Packard (HPQ), Dell (DELL), and other companies that rely heavily on contractors in China to supply notebook PCs, digital cameras, and handheld devices have formed an industry alliance to combat the abuses.

A compliance manager for a major multinational company who has overseen many factory audits says that the percentage of Chinese suppliers caught submitting false payroll records has risen from 46% to 75% in the past four years. This manager, who requested anonymity, estimates that only 20% of Chinese suppliers comply with wage rules, while just 5% obey hour limitations.

A recent visit by the compliance manager to a toy manufacturer in Shenzhen illustrated the crude ways that some suppliers conceal mistreatment. The manager recalls smelling strong paint fumes in the poorly ventilated and aging factory building. Young women employees were hunched over die-injection molds, using spray guns to paint storybook figurines. The compliance manager discovered a second workshop behind a locked door that a factory official initially refused to open but eventually did. In the back room, a young woman, who appeared to be under the legal working age of 16, tried to hide behind her co-workers on the production line, the visiting compliance manager says. The Chinese factory official admitted he was violating various work rules.

The situation in China is hard to keep in perspective. For all the shortcomings in factory conditions and oversight, even some critics say that workers' circumstances are improving overall. However compromised, pressure from multinationals has curbed some of the most egregious abuses by outside suppliers. Factories owned directly by such corporations as Motorola Inc. (**MOT**) and General Electric Co. (**GE**) generally haven't been accused of mistreating their employees. And a booming economy and tightening labor supply in China have emboldened workers in some areas to demand better wages, frequently with success. Even so, many Chinese laborers, especially migrants from poor rural regions, still seek to work as many hours as possible, regardless of whether they are properly paid.

In this shifting, often murky environment, labor auditing has mushroomed into a multi-million-dollar industry. Internal corporate investigators and such global auditing agencies as Cal

Safety Compliance, SGS of Switzerland, and Bureau Veritas of France operate a convoluted and uncoordinated oversight system. They follow varying corporate codes of conduct, resulting in some big Chinese factories having to post seven or eight different sets of rules. Some factories receive almost daily visits from inspection teams demanding payroll and production records, facility tours, and interviews with managers and workers. "McDonald's (MCD), Walt Disney (DIS), and Wal-Mart are doing thousands of audits a year that are not harmonized," says van Heerden of Fair Labor. Among factory managers, "audit fatigue sets in," he says.

Some companies that thought they were making dramatic progress are discovering otherwise. A study commissioned by Nike last year covered 569 factories it uses in China and around the world that employ more than 300,000 workers. It found labor-code violations in every single one. Some factories "hide their work practices by maintaining two or even three sets of books," by coaching workers to "mislead auditors about their work hours, and by sending portions of production to unauthorized contractors where we have no oversight," the Nike study found.

The Fair Labor Assn. released its own study last November based on unannounced audits of 88 of its members' supplier factories in 18 countries. It found an average of 18 violations per factory, including excessive hours, underpayment of wages, health and safety problems, and worker harassment. The actual violation rate is probably higher, the FLA said, because "factory personnel have become sophisticated in concealing noncompliance related to wages. They often hide original documents and show monitors falsified books."

While recently auditing an apparel manufacturer in Dongguan that supplies American importers, the corporate compliance manager says he discussed wage levels with the factory's Hong Kong-based owner. The 2,000 employees who operate sewing and stitching machines in the multistory complex often put in overtime but earn an average of only $125 a month, an amount the owner grudgingly acknowledged to the compliance manager doesn't meet Chinese overtime-pay requirements or corporate labor codes. "These goals are a fantasy," the owner said. "Maybe in two or three decades we can meet them."

Pinning down what Chinese production workers are paid can be tricky. Based on Chinese government figures, the average manufacturing wage in China is 64 cents an hour, according to the U.S. Bureau of Labor Statistics and demographer Judith Banister of Javelin Investments, a consulting firm in Beijing. That rate assumes a 40-hour week. In fact, 60- to 100-hour weeks are common in China, meaning that the real manufacturing wage is far less. Based on his own calculations from plant inspections, the veteran compliance manager estimates that employees at garment, electronics, and other export factories typically work more than 80 hours a week and make only 42 cents an hour.

BusinessWeek reviewed summaries of 28 recent industry audits of Chinese factories serving U.S. customers. A few factories supplying Black & Decker (BDK), Williams-Sonoma, and other well-known brands turned up clean, the summaries show. But these facilities were the exceptions.

At most of the factories, auditors discovered records apparently meant to falsify payrolls and time sheets. One typical report concerns Zhongshan Tat Shing Toys Factory, which employs 650 people in the southern city of Zhongshan. The factory's main customers are Wal-Mart and Target (TGT). When an American-sponsored inspection team showed up this spring, factory managers produced time sheets showing each worker put in eight hours a day, Monday through Friday, and was paid double the local minimum wage of 43 cents per hour for eight hours on Saturday, according to an audit report.

But when auditors interviewed workers in one section, some said that they were paid less than the minimum wage and that most of them were obliged to work an extra three to five hours a day, without overtime pay, the report shows. Most toiled an entire month without a day off. Workers told auditors that the factory had a different set of records showing actual overtime hours, the report says. Factory officials claimed that some of the papers had been destroyed by fire.

Wal-Mart's Wyatt doesn't dispute the discrepancies but stresses that the company is getting more aggressive overall in its monitoring. Wal-Mart says it does more audits than any other company—13,600 reviews of 7,200 factories last year alone—and permanently banned 141 factories in 2005 as a result of serious infractions, such as using child labor (Figure 14.5). In a written statement, Target doesn't respond to the allegations but says that it "takes very seriously" the fair treatment of factory workers. It adds that it "is committed to taking corrective action—up to and including termination of the relationship for vendors" that violate local labor law or Target's code of conduct. The Zhongshan factory didn't respond to repeated requests for comment.

An audit late last year of Young Sun Lighting Co., a maker of lamps for Home Depot (HD), Sears (SHLD), and other retailers, highlighted similar inconsistencies. Every employee was on the job five days a week from 8 a.m. to 5:30 p.m., with a lunch break and no overtime hours, according to interviews with managers, as well as time sheets

and payroll records provided by the 300-worker factory in Dongguan, an industrial city in Guangdong Province. But other records auditors found at the site and elsewhere—backed up by auditor interviews with workers—revealed that laborers worked an extra three to five hours a day with only one or two days a month off during peak production periods. Workers said they received overtime pay, but the "auditor strongly felt that these workers were coached," the audit report states.

Young Sun denies ever violating the rules set by its Western customers. In written answers to questions, the lighting manufacturer says that it doesn't coach employees on how to respond to auditors and that "at present, there are no" workers who are putting in three to five extra hours a day and getting only one or two days off each month. Young Sun says that it follows all local Chinese overtime rules.

Home Depot doesn't contest the inconsistencies in the audit reports about Young Sun and three other factories in China. "There is no perfect factory, I can guarantee you," a company

Figure 14.5 A young textile worker in a factory in Delhi, India.

spokeswoman says. Instead of cutting off wayward suppliers, Home Depot says that it works with factories on corrective actions. If the retailer becomes aware of severe offenses, such as the use of child labor, it terminates the supplier. A Sears spokesman declined to comment.

Coaching of workers and midlevel managers to mislead auditors is widespread, the auditing reports and *BusinessWeek* interviews show. A document obtained last year during an inspection at one Chinese fabric export factory in the southern city of Guangzhou instructed administrators to take these actions when faced with a surprise audit: "First notify underage trainees, underage full-time workers, and workers without identification to leave the manufacturing workshop through the back door. Order them not to loiter near the dormitory area. Secondly, immediately order the receptionist to gather all relevant documents and papers." Other pointers include instructing all workers to put on necessary protective equipment such as earplugs and face masks.

Some U.S. retailers say this evidence isn't representative and that their auditing efforts are working. *BusinessWeek* asked J.C. Penney Co. (JCP) about audit reports included among those the magazine reviewed that appear to show falsification of records to hide overtime and pay violations at two factories serving the large retailer. Penney spokeswoman Darcie M. Brossart says the company immediately investigated the factories, and its "auditors observed no evidence of any legal compliance issues." In any case, the two factories are too small to be seen as typical, Penney executives argue. The chain has been consolidating its China supply base and says that 80% of its imports now come from factories with several thousand workers apiece, which are managed by large Hong Kong trading companies that employ their own auditors. Quality inspectors for Penney and other buyers are at their supplier sites constantly, so overtime violations are hard to hide, Brossart says.

Chinese factory officials say, however, that just because infractions are difficult to discern doesn't mean they're not occurring. "It's a challenge for us to meet these codes of conduct," says Ron Chang, the Taiwanese general manager of Nike supplier Shoetown Footwear Co., which employs 15,000 workers in Qingyuan, Guangdong. Given the fierce competition in China for foreign production work, "we can't ask Nike to increase our price," he says, so "how can we afford to pay the higher salary?" By reducing profit margins from 30% to 5% over the past 18 years, Shoetown has managed to stay in business and obey Nike's rules, he says.

But squeezing margins doesn't solve the larger social issue. Chang says he regularly loses skilled employees to rival factories that break the rules because many workers are eager to put in longer hours than he offers, regardless of whether they get paid overtime rates.

Ultimately, the economics of global outsourcing may trump any system of oversight that Western companies attempt. And these harsh economic realities could make it exceedingly difficult to achieve both the low prices and the humane working conditions that U.S. consumers have been promised.

Discussion Questions

1. How can the average consumer be sure that he or she is purchasing goods manufactured ethically?
2. Many times working in sweatshop conditions is preferable to living on the street, engaging in prostitution, or going hungry. What would you do if you had the authority to close down a sweatshop but your action meant that 100 people would be out of work?

DIAMONDS AREN'T FOREVER

Vivienne Walt

A new Hollywood movie is raising tough questions about Africa's bloody diamond trade. *Fortune's* Vivienne Walt reports from the pits.

Sahr Amara is stooped low, knee-deep in a muddy river, in the fifth hour of his workday. As he has each day for the past week, the 18-year-old will earn a stipend of only 7 cents, enough to buy himself a bowl of porridge to see him through the day.

Yet he returns every morning to dig in the wilting heat on the edge of Koidu, a town in eastern Sierra Leone, hunting for the one thing he says could transform his life: a diamond. Since he is the oldest of six children—three others have died of diseases—much of his family's future rests on his prospects.

"If I find a big diamond, I can afford to go to school, I can learn, and then I can help my family and even my village," he says. So far the plan has proved elusive; he has found no gems during his first week of work. "It's not easy," he says. "I think it depends on God."

Whether or not divine intervention leads Amara to a big find, his tale is anchored in a much more earthly economy: the $60-billion-a-year diamond industry, which has built its growth on dreams of love rather than of raw survival.

Koidu, whose diamonds have been mined since the 1930s, is thousands of miles away—and a galaxy removed—from the glittering displays in jewelry stores in New York, Tokyo and London. It is set in a country where the average man earns $220 a year and dies at 39. In the dwellings along Koidu's dirt tracks, residents eat dinner by candlelight not because it is romantic but because there is no electricity in town, just as there are no telephone lines and little indoor plumbing.

In short, it is hard to imagine a starker contrast between Amara's world and that of the people who might one day wear whatever diamond he finds, and they live in deep ignorance of each other. When asked what diamonds are used for, Amara draws a blank. "I only know they are valuable," he says.

Hollywood Weighs In

But after 130 years of diamond mining in Africa, that ignorance is unraveling fast as the two worlds collide over the image of diamonds. The conflict, which has rocked the industry in recent years, may reach fever pitch this month with the release of the movie "Blood Diamond." Set in wartime Sierra Leone during the late 1990s, the film depicts a South African diamond smuggler, played by Leonardo DiCaprio, trying to recover a rare pink stone from a local fisherman whom rebels have forced to dig in the diamond pits.

The story line—a mixture of villainy and heroism—is classic Hollywood. But its roots are fact: In the 1990s rebels in Sierra Leone and Liberia financed their carnage from diamonds plucked out of the rivers and traded for arms. During a decade of war about 50,000 people were killed, and thousands had their hands hacked off by rebels.

Months before it opened, the movie had garnered media attention, aided by a marketing blitz by Warner Bros. (owned by Time Warner, parent of *Fortune's* publisher) and a $15 million counterattack by the World Diamond Council, an organization founded by more than 50 producers and dealers to end illegal diamond trading.

"We have been engaged in a massive educational campaign," says Eli Izakhoff, chairman and

CEO of the council, which is heavily financed by De Beers, the company that sources about 40 percent of the world's diamonds, all of them from Africa. "This movie gives the industry a great story to tell." The council's message: More than 99 percent of diamonds are now from conflict-free sources, and millions of Africans have schooling and health care thanks to diamond revenues.

The movie is indeed a period piece: The civil wars in Sierra Leone and Liberia ended a few years ago. But the war over perceptions is just warming up. Many in the industry fear that as the end credits roll, moviegoers might glance down at their diamond rings and wonder under what circumstances the gems were dug. Unlike oil prospecting or coal mining—essentials for modern life—those questions could roil an industry whose lifeblood is ephemeral.

Controversy Affects Value

"Diamonds are essentially worth nothing," says Mordechai Rapaport, whose Rapaport Group price list is the industry standard. It's all about what they signify, he explains: In the case of a wedding ring, it's the guy, not the one-carat diamond. By that logic, he adds, "when a guy gives a woman a diamond and someone was killed for it, it is not worth anything."

Diamond producers and dealers did not need Hollywood to reach that conclusion. As war raged in the past decade, they realized that so-called blood diamonds carried a risk to their business that was far out of proportion to the tiny number of stones. Even during the bloodiest years no more than 15 percent of the world's diamonds were controlled by rebels in Sierra Leone, Liberia, Angola and the Democratic Republic of Congo.

The vast majority of diamonds, then and now, come from deep-level mines run by well-ordered international corporations, including Koidu Holdings, Sierra Leone's newest such operation, which opened in 2003 and exports $2.5 million in diamonds a month.

And although UN investigators recently found that rebels in the Ivory Coast had smuggled millions of dollars' worth of diamonds onto the world market through Ghana, blood diamonds account for only 0.2 percent of today's global supply.

But the industry's problem is far trickier than percentages. Consumers cannot be sure which diamonds are blood diamonds. And therein lies the potential for a boycott, especially since synthetic diamonds now look close to the real thing. "Diamonds are a luxury, so we depend completely on the consumer's faith," says Rory More O'Ferrall, director of external affairs for De Beers. "Anything that affects the integrity of that we need to address."

Tackling the problem took an unlikely alliance: Industry executives joined forces in 2003 with governments and the UN to end the trade of conflict diamonds. The resulting Kimberley Process Certification Scheme is a rare experiment by a major industry to monitor its own abuses. The 71 member countries agree to trade only among themselves. They inspect one another's facilities, then issue certificates declaring their diamonds conflict-free.

In theory, rigorous paperwork tries to trace all diamonds from mines to consumers. Transgressors are ousted: The Republic of Congo was banned in 2004, and Venezuela was threatened with suspension last month after reporting zero diamond exports for 2005.

But the system is hardly flawless, even in the U.S. In September the U.S. Government Accountability Office found that Customs and Treasury officials were only haphazardly enforcing the system, leaving companies to monitor themselves. Last year about 300,000 more carats were exported from than imported to the U.S.—which produces no commercial diamonds itself. Representatives from all 71 countries met last month in Botswana to try to tighten loopholes and squeeze out nonmembers. "There are fewer and fewer countries left that nonmembers can trade with," says Sue Saarnio, the U.S. State Department's representative to the November conference.

The Underground
Diamond Trade

A far grimmer assessment of the Kimberley Process can be found in the back alleys of Koidu. As the clammy heat eases off in the late afternoon, dozens of men converge on the neighborhood dubbed by the locals "Open Yei," Creole for "keep your eyes open," a reference to its thriving unlicensed diamond trading.

The action is the area's major entertainment, drawing a crowd of curious men and children. In a dirt clearing between the small wooden storefronts, Abdollai Koroma runs his business from a chair under a shade tree, clutching a yellow calculator and a jeweler's loupe in a weathered pouch. During just one hour eight men arrive with their wares wrapped in scraps of paper stuffed in their pockets. Koroma takes each stone and swirls it in his mouth before examining it briefly under the loupe. "This is 1.20 carats," he says after spitting out a glittering stone the size of a shirt button.

Koroma, who started trading diamonds at age 17, taps on his calculator, peels off a wad of banknotes, and makes his biggest purchase of the day: 200,000 leones, about $66. The previous day the neighborhood trade was equally brisk, as men gathered to sell diamonds to Komba Fillefaboa, a 47-year-old trader who began digging when he was 12. Fillefaboa says he buys dozens of stones on an average afternoon.

"We buy piece by piece and then gather them into a parcel to sell to dealers," he says. Once the parcel of diamonds is sold to a licensed dealer, illegally mined diamonds are easily mixed in.

Fillefaboa says he has no problem finding buyers, despite Sierra Leone's strict licensing laws, which ban illegal diamond dealing. Licenses are regarded as too costly and laws too cumbersome. "We are all illegal here," boasts the neighborhood's chief, Sahr Sam. "If the monitors come, we scatter."

Smuggling

In reality, government monitors rarely come to Open Yei. There are only 200 for the entire country, sharing ten motorcycles donated by the U.S. Agency for International Development. "At every level people say to us, 'If you harass us, we will just smuggle the diamonds,'" says Dan Joe Hadji, a senior monitoring officer in Koidu. "So we allow people to move around and hope and pray that they find religion"—by obeying the law.

Diamond producers and dealers frequently tout Sierra Leone as a Kimberley Process success story, since its official exports soared from near zero in 1999 to about $142 million last year, suggesting that smuggling has plummeted. Not necessarily so: The official statistics cannot be proved, says Jan Ketelaar, mine manager of Koidu Holdings and a former diamond advisor to Sierra Leone's President.

Worse, this year's exports are likely to drop about 10 percent, suggesting that bigger diamonds are being smuggled illegally, says a Western ambassador in Freetown who sits on a high-level diamond committee of diplomats and aid organizations but asked not to be identified. Director of Mines Alimany Wurie admits smuggling is widespread—perhaps as much as one-third of all Sierra Leone's diamonds.

Enforcement is nearly impossible. The frontier with Liberia, whose diamonds are banned from world trade, is just 30 miles from Koidu and riddled with old smuggling routes. Only three of the 36 border crossings into Guinea are guarded, says Hadji, and even those are left unmanned for a few days each month when border officials walk to town to collect their pay.

Yet the rampant smuggling, though illegal, does not kill. And with peace restored in West Africa, it is tempting to think of blood diamonds as little more than a dramatic movie plot. Those who have witnessed Africa's bloodletting up close say it's a mistake to relegate the issue to history, because history could repeat itself.

In any future conflict in the region, diamonds would be one of the surest ways with which to buy weapons. "Diamonds were very much the fuel for the war but not the root cause, and those root causes are still very much with us," says the Western ambassador. "Corruption, unemployment, poverty—I could well imagine another blood-diamond scenario here."

Fair Trade

Faced with that stark possibility, diamond companies have begun trying to tackle the crippling poverty at the bottom of the industry, where, according to Global Witness, a British organization that has done extensive research on blood diamonds, about one million Africans earn pennies a day in the backbreaking and increasingly fruitless search for alluvial stones.

Flying low over Koidu in a twin-propeller plane shows how daunting that task is. Hundreds of men can be seen bent low in the rivers around Koidu. "They are working in absolutely horrific conditions in the hopes of striking it rich, but the majority never do," says Susie Sanders, a Global Witness researcher.

Little of the region's innate mineral wealth has filtered down to residents. "A billion dollars' worth of diamonds have come out of Sierra Leone in the last several years, and there is no electricity or water wells," says Rapaport, who toured the villages around Koidu last summer with his father, Martin, chairman of the Rapaport Group.

Shaken by the chasm between the diggers and the diamond buyers, the Rapaports are trying to start a Fair Trade association of producers along the lines of Starbucks, which buys coffee beans for a premium price from some growers, then sells them for more money to socially conscious coffee drinkers. Rapaport is predicting that the current controversy over diamonds will jolt consumers into asking retailers probing questions about the gems' origins.

If so, they are unlikely to find much information: Two years ago a survey of 40 major American retailers by Amnesty International and Global Witness found that almost none had policies in place against blood diamonds.

Rapaport believes consumers would happily pay a little extra to ensure they are buying African diamonds mined for decent wages under humane conditions. "Our idea," he says, "is that Tiffany is going to wake up one morning and see that Cartier is selling fair-trade jewelry and say, 'Oh, my God, we need to do that.' They will change not from an ethical point of view but from greed."

In Koidu a U.S.-funded program trains diggers in how to grade and value the diamonds they find as a way of avoiding being fleeced by local traders. Last year De Beers and two activist organizations founded the Diamond Development Initiative, an international organization to train diggers in safety and economic issues, and ultimately to try to persuade many to grow crops instead. De Beers has begun a similar pilot training project in Tanzania, which it says it will replicate elsewhere in Africa if it is successful.

But for 18-year-old Sahr Amara all those projects seem abstract. His parents grow crops in a village about 20 miles from Koidu and cannot afford to buy his schoolbooks or pay his yearly tuition of 35,000 leones ($11.66). "I would like to find a diamond so I can go back to school," Amara says. "If I stay digging at this site for a long time and find nothing, maybe I will leave and try to find a job somewhere." That would leave Africa's 999,999 other diamond diggers still searching for a dream.

Discussion Questions

1. How can people be made aware of the consequences of purchasing blood diamonds?
2. Do you think that the film *Blood Diamond* had an effect on people's attitudes toward these conflict gems?

FEATHER HAIR EXTENSIONS: FASHION WITHOUT COMPASSION

Elizabeth Neville

Feather "hair extensions" are roosting upon manes across the nation (Figure 14.6). A trend popularized by celebrities such as Miley Cyrus, adding plumage to one's coiffure is now such a coveted fashion statement that one Internet company even sells feather extensions for dogs. But, where do these lovely feathers come from? Before feathering your own locks (or your dog's), please consider the thousands of innocent lives which are taken to produce these plumes.

If you know fly fishing paraphernalia, and thought that these silky bits in people's hair seemed strangely familiar . . . well, you're on to something. The feathers used for hair extensions are the same ones used by fly fishermen as lures, and feather-craving fashionistas everywhere are now snatching them up at hundreds of dollars above the market price.

According to an article on Bloomberg Businessweek, "A package of the most popular fly tying hackle for hair extensions, a black and white striped feather called grizzly saddle, would normally retail anywhere from $40 to $60. It sold for $480 on eBay last month after 31 bids." At the most, these feather hair extensions can be worn for three months.

So, why pay so much for these feathers? Well, the roosters in question have been specifically bred to produce unnaturally long and strikingly beautiful saddle feathers (the ones on the bird's backside), which are considered more desirable for fly fishing—and now, for fashion.

Naturally, this price inflation has become a major annoyance to fly fishermen, but whether for bait or coiffure accessorizing, to take the lives of sentient beings for such fleeting and trivial purposes is troubling in itself.

Whiting Farms in western Colorado is the world's largest producer of fly tying feathers. There, the roosters are given only a year to live while their saddle feathers grow as long as possible. (Research varies, but when they aren't killed for their plumage, roosters can naturally live to be 10–15 years old).

Once the feathers are deemed satisfactory, the rooster is slaughtered, and his feathers plucked. His lifeless body is then thrown out for compost; Thomas Whiting, the company founder (via the Orange County Register), claims that "they aren't good for anything else." The Whiting Farms website boasts that "over 125,000 total birds [were] harvested in 2000."

Figure 14.6 Feather hair extensions have attracted concern from animal activist groups.

According to the Orange County Register article, Whiting Farms now ships out 65,000 bird hides per week as it tries to meet the aggressive demands of salon owners and stylists, as well as its classic fly fishing clientele. Needless to say, that is quite a haunting increase in rooster death . . . all for a faddish, temporary hair accessory, produced in a manner that screams disconnect.

As "supply" (here, meaning animal slaughter) levels respond to demand, it is within our collective power as consumers to dictate what is worth buying. Do you want to feed your money and image into this bloody phenomenon? Fashion trends come and go, but compassion is always cool.

Discussion Questions

1. Why do you think the campaigns against wearing fur have not been as successful as the early 20th century campaign to end the use of bird feathers?
2. Do you think the campaign against using furs and feathers is important? Why or why not?

14.5

RATIONALIZING CIRCUMCISION: FROM TRADITION TO FASHION, FROM PUBLIC HEALTH TO INDIVIDUAL FREEDOM—CRITICAL NOTES ON CULTURAL PERSISTENCE OF THE PRACTICE OF GENITAL MUTILATION

S.K. Hellsten

Despite global and local attempts to end genital mutilations, in their various forms, whether of males or females, the practice has persisted throughout human history in most parts of the world. Today both male and female genital mutilation are particularly common in poor, developing countries with wide traditional communities, but these practices have also been maintained in many modern Western multicultural societies. This is particularly the case with male circumcision, which in many parts of the Western world is still practiced almost routinely, as the articles by Hutson, Short, and Viens on the justification of male circumcision in this journal show.[1, 2, 3]

Short and Hutson focus more on scientific, medical, and public health aspects while Viens discusses the issue of religious freedom and identity. More precisely, Hutson analyzes whether the public health argument holds water in justifying male circumcision as a routine operation in relation to its health related consequences (whether these are negative or positive). Short's commentary on Hutson defends male circumcision on the basis of medical evidence that the procedure (on males) has been scientifically proven to improve both male and female reproductive health. Short goes as far as suggesting that we might have some kind of duty to develop better procedures to make the operation the "kindest cut of all." Viens, on the other hand, argues for the justification of male circumcision on the basis of individual freedom. Rather than speaking for the right of an individual to make his or her own autonomous choices, however, Viens draws his arguments from the parents' right to decide what is best for their children as well as from the parents' religious freedom to choose the (religious) identity of, and for, their children.

J Med Ethics 2004;30:248–53. Reprinted with permission.
© 2004 Journal of Medical Ethics.

While Hutson is the most hesitant of these three authors to defend the general benefits of the operation, none of these articles directly argues against male genital mutilation. While Viens is most sensitive to religious freedom and cultural identity, none of the authors discuss in detail the different cultural, social, and economic contexts of these values and practices across the globe. Instead, all the above mentioned authors keep their discussion almost exclusively within the framework of Western medicine and a pluralist society. While, albeit briefly, supporting other cultures' rights to maintain their religious identities, Viens is even willing to offer Western assistance in developing less painful and medically safer practices for the operation on children elsewhere in the world. In this symposium, and against the background of the articles by these three authors, I have taken it as my task to set this discussion on the justification of male circumcision within a wider, global context. I want to discuss how we find a range of rationalizations to support various types of genital mutilation and to evaluate whether these rationalizations have anything to do with a critical and reflective moral justification of these practices.

I shall pay attention to the following issues. Firstly, I find it disturbing that even within the Western medical community, there is evidently still a wide consensus on such an intrusive and violent procedure as male circumcision, albeit that this consensus is evidently based on very different "moral" justifications, which vary from public health, to scientific proof, to religion and to a diversity of Western values. More worrying is the fact that there appears to be a general agreement that this violent procedure (as a therapeutic and non-therapeutic one) can (and according to Viens, even should) be carried out on infants and/ or very small children. In addition, male genital mutilation (MGM) should not be considered in isolation from the issue of female genital mutilation (FGM). In this symposium only Viens recognizes the existence of "female genital cutting." He, however, regards it as part of the same tradition which encourages MGM—that is, a tradition based on religious freedom/cultural identity— without making any attempt to distinguish the different nature of the medical and moral reasons put forward in favour of FGM.

Secondly, I find that both the medical and the value based arguments presented by these three authors lack either plausible evidence or logical consistency. Instead of discussing each article separately, however, I shall describe a wider global framework that provides false reasons in defense of genital mutilation, rather than providing any truly plausible moral justification for this practice.

Religious Freedom, Pain, and Children's Rights

Throughout history human beings have mutilated and harmed their bodies (and minds) in the name of culture, tradition, religion, and concepts of beauty, health, normality, or social status. One of the most persistent forms of these physical violations is mutilation of human genitalia. This practice has been related to: taboos about human sexuality; children's initiation to adulthood, maturity, and reproductive age; aesthetic values; the demands set by various religions; and to hygienic, individual, and public health medical beliefs. (See the articles by Hutson, Short and Viens in this journal, and also those by Aldeeb Abu-Salieh, Bigelow, and by an anonymous author in *Echo*.)[1-7] All in all, mutilation of human sexual organs reflects our fears about human biological needs—and even deeper fears about human sexual needs—as well as fears to do with the maintenance of established social hierarchies in a society.

In this symposium we are discussing the most common form of genital mutilation, male circumcision. In its mildest form, this means the cutting of the foreskin of the penis. (For more detailed explanations see the articles by Hutson, Short, and Viens.)[1, 2, 3] It is important to note, however, that the same term, "circumcision," is also used in relation to women's genital mutilation, where it refers to the cutting of the tip or the whole of the clitoris. There are, however, various other, more radical and more harmful mutilations of human genitalia, which can be relatively minor or extremely serious. Female genital mutilation, for example, includes a wide range of ritual and nonmedical operations undertaken on women's genital organs, which include their total or partial removal and amputation or incisions in the interior of the vagina. According to the World Health Organization (WHO) female genital mutilation can be classified into three major types: type I or clitoridectomy—removal of the tip of the clitoris; type II—cutting of the clitoris and all or part of the labia minora; and type III or infibulation or pharaonic circumcision, in which the clitoris is cut together with part or the whole of the labia minora and incisions are made on the labia majora. When this latter operation is performed, the edges of the wound are often tied up again leaving a small opening through which body liquids such as urine or menstrual blood can flow. The resulting mass of scar tissue, which covers the urethra and the upper part of the vagina, completely closes the vulva. If the opening is wide enough, sexual intercourse may occur after a gradual dilatation, which can take days, weeks or even months. When the opening is too small to allow sexual intercourse, it must be widened with a razor or knife on the wedding night. Given the severity of cuts and stitches occurring during initial and repeated interventions, infibulation is the most harmful form of genital mutilation, both to reproductive health and to health in general. Other practices which prevail in certain countries of Central, Southern, and South Africa consist in pulling the labia and introducing substances and minerals into the vagina to dry it and to increase men's sexual pleasure (Anonymous,[6] p 5). Male genital mutilation can vary from body piercing through a range of various other modifications to amputation, and castration. While the moral justification for any type of genital mutilation has been challenged from time to time, its continuation for both men and women has been rationalized over and over again via various medical, legal, moral, and cultural arguments. The campaigns against MGM have not been as vigorous as those against FGM since FGM is in general considered to be a more violent and socially suppressive practice than MGM. In addition FGM has more serious and damaging physical, as well as psychological or social, implications. On the other hand, the operation itself has no medical justification, whereas a medical justification is still put forward for MGM, as the articles by Hutson, Short, and Viens show. Thus, male circumcision has been easier to accept as a minor harm that can be justified, or at least tolerated, if not sometimes encouraged (see Short's paper in this journal) as a part of a particular religious or cultural tradition or as a measure promoting individual or public health.

In general, the arguments against MGM or FGM claim that both practices violate the physical integrity of children and cause avoidable pain. In the worst cases they can lead to irreversible physical or psychological harm, as noted by Hutson in his contribution to this symposium. It appears, however, that while neither Hutson, Viens, nor Short recommend male circumcision as a public health measure, in individual cases they all accept male circumcision either on medical or on religious grounds, as long as it does not cause pain. Thus, they recommend better pain management measures and more refined procedures to perform the operation.

This is particularly true of Viens's argument, which defends the practice in the name of religious freedom but denies the fact that the operation is—or should be—painful. This position appears to be contradictory, since as a religious or cultural practice, the endurance of pain is often an essential part of the ritual, showing the readiness of individuals to transit from childhood to adulthood, from boy to man, in the case of MGM, and from girl to woman in the case of FGM. The other problem with Viens's argument for religious freedom in relation to male circumcision is that it supports male circumcision being carried out on infants and small children at the request of their parents, rather than waiting for the children to be "old" enough to give their "informed consent" and to understand the real significance of the ritual and "the need to tolerate pain."

From a human rights perspective both male and female genital mutilation, *particularly* when performed on infants or defenseless small children, and for nontherapeutic reasons, can be clearly condemned as a violation of children's rights whether or not they cause direct pain. Parents' rights cannot override children's rights. If we allow parents to decide what is best for their children on the basis of the children's religious or cultural identity, we would have no justification for stopping them cutting off their children's ears, fingers, or noses if their religious and cultural beliefs demanded this. Also, if we allow parents' rights to override children's rights, we could not then forbid them from making any other physical and spiritual sacrifices (such as cannibalism or human sacrifice as extreme examples), particularly if we follow Viens's recommendation and manage to develop techniques that minimize or abolish pain.

Tradition of Genital Mutilation and Gender

This article focuses on male circumcision, but I do not want to disregard the importance of mentioning female genital mutilation in the same context. Some advocates of women's rights who emphasise FGM as a sign of gender based violence which springs from the patriarchal oppression of women tend to be reluctant to allow any comparison between male and female genital mutilation and may disagree with my comparisons.[8] In this article, however, parallels between FGM and MGM are drawn only in respect of the implications of performing any potentially harmful nontherapeutic, nonconsensual procedure that in the end is, in one way or another, a social issue rather than a medical one. My purpose is not to diminish the ethical, social, and medical dangers involved in FGM, but to widen the scope of the discussion in this symposium. Focusing merely on male circumcision—and leaving it almost exclusively within a medical context—may make us forget that what we are discussing here is a historical tendency to look for rationalizations that allow us to practice genital mutilation in one form or another, across geographical, cultural, and religious boundaries.

I believe that examining the traditions of genital mutilation from the point of view of both sexes may reveal more clearly the irrationality involved in the justifications that are made for continuing the practice of mutilating human genitals.

Thus, while there is a need to pay special attention to the elements of social and political oppression involved in FGM, it is also important to note that throughout time men, as well as women, have learned to accept that there are good reasons for the mutilations of human genitalia. Usually these reasons raise false hopes that undergoing the operation somehow improves people's lives—and the lives of their children—whether this be in the context of social status or of a medical condition, while the true reasons for the practice may lie elsewhere.

Autonomy vs. Cultural Rights—Untangling the Dichotomies of Cultural Traditions

When the justification of genital mutilation is discussed, the disputes are usually tangled around issues about the universality and relativity of our value systems, and can often centre on the conflict between the different rights that might be involved. In most cases, the debates for and against genital mutilation are set within the framework of collective cultural rights vs. individual rights. The arguments against the practice of genital mutilation tend to appeal to the promotion of individual autonomy and universal human rights to various freedoms, while those who defend the practice draw support for their claims from demands to respect a person's particular cultural identity and/to protect the rights of minorities (minority cultures) as for instance is argued by Viens.[3] (See also Mills[9, 10] and in connection with genital mutilation my own paper of 1999.)[11]

In fact, Viens's argument further complicates this debate between individualism and collectivism by supporting male circumcision not only via an appeal to (religious) freedom and identity as such, but also by defending parents' rights to decide what is the best for their children. He supports MGM further by going on to defend our autonomy to decide what our concept of the good life and well being is, while simultaneously refuting children's rights as not being real "rights" of autonomous and fully rational persons. This sets "autonomous," "adult" rights against children's rights. While children's rights tend to create a problem for the defense of autonomy and informed consent in general, Viens's view presents a rather contradictory rationalization for male genital mutilation by championing parents' "cultural identity" against their children's physical integrity. There is always a danger in combining cultural and religious identity. The issue of religion and religious identity in the context of culture is in itself very complex: different cultures have different influences on the interpretations of religious norms, practices, and identities. Whether we talk about Islam, Christianity, Hinduism or any other world religion, each is followed very differently, depending on the original culture and the historical changes that have affected it: Islam and Christianity, for example, are practiced very differently in Saudi Arabia, in Uganda, and in the UK.

On the other hand, Viens's argument provides a good example of how the dichotomy between individualism and collectivism presents a rather black-and-white picture of the cultural history of our world: individualism is tied inseparably to universalism and the universal promotion of human rights, while collectivist lifestyles are related directly to relativism, which allows social suppression. This polarization of the positions simply overlooks the fact that individualistic values and lifestyles can also fall into relativist reasoning that rejects any interference with individuals' "autonomous" choices. This position clearly disregards the fact that most of our choices are made in a social context and may often be influenced by social pressures, or even by some refined forms of social coercion.

Also, an individualist culture, in the name of tolerance and freedom, may justify extremely violent and irrational practices, and "autonomous" parents can ask for their children to be physically mutilated in the name of their preferred collective identity. Collectivist value systems and cultural traditions, for their part, rely on a universal demand for the protection of religious and/or cultural rights and identities.[12, 13]

Reconsidering descriptive and prescriptive senses of value systems can help us overcome normative cultural dichotomies and to avoid culturally biased discussions about genital mutilation and other harmful practices. In order to curb injurious practices we need to acknowledge that what makes some of these harmful customs so persistent is the tendency to see them as essential, integral, and identifying parts of particular cultures or belief systems. If, however, we recognized openly that the same or similar practices tend to appear universally—that is, the same or similar practices exist in one form or another in most parts of the world but with different rationalizations—we could see more easily the smokescreen that tends to blur moral argumentation around these practices. The best way to curtail any harmful and violent custom is to find a way to raise resistance to it within the communities themselves, by revealing the irrationality and dishonesty of the reasons put forward to maintain such customs as genital mutilation, and so their irrelevance to any cultural identity.

Men and Circumcision in the "Wild" West

Arguing about conflicting rights and cultural identities may lead us astray, if we do not invalidate some of the central fallacies that persist as part of the rationalization process of genital mutilation. Firstly, if we are to have a serious "moral debate" on the persistent existence of genital mutilation, we need to recognize the various rationalizations used to defend it throughout human history, not merely in any particular time or age. Secondly, we need to further evaluate these rationalizations to see how they are successfully shaped to fit their local traditions and social environments. In most cases, these rationalizations are full of inconsistencies and act as a mere smokescreen to cover up the actual social, political, or economic reasons that are behind the preservation of genital mutilation in any given cultural context. Thirdly, recognizing the complexity of the cultural and ethical issues involved in the justification process of genital mutilation may help us to find new ways to get rid of the false reasons for the practice and better ways to combat this violent practice worldwide.

Since the practice of genital mutilation has existed in almost all known civilisations at some time or another in various forms, we cannot say genital mutilation is a tradition that is unique to a particular culture or religion as such; and therefore we cannot say that defending the practice means defending the right of that culture to exist and defending the rights of its members to maintain their cultural identities. Since genital mutilation has appeared in a number of cultures and is related to various belief systems, it is not important whether these cultures or belief systems themselves are (more) individualist or (more) collectivist in their value structure: what is important is to pay more attention to the differences in the types of rationalization put forward to support them within different types of cultural frameworks. In most cases it appears that whether the practice withers away or remains an integral part of that culture's identity depends on the strength of the rationalizations and the availability of education in that culture.

Since genital mutilation is not alien to individualist cultures, we can look at the medical rationalization of male circumcision in the Western individualist tradition. Within Western medical history cutting off or extracting the male foreskin has been believed to cure insanity, masturbation, epilepsy, cancer of the penis, and even cancer of the cervix of the future wives of the circumcised boys as well as sexually transmitted diseases and particularly *phimosis* (either as a disease or as a cause of other diseases such as cancer). Even today the relation between male circumcision and HIV/AIDS is still extensively studied and debated, as the articles by Hutson, Short, and Viens show.[1,2,3] In particular, the claim that male circumcision is able in fact to prevent HIV/AIDS can have negative consequences, especially in parts of the world where medical hygiene is poor and/or relevant health education is not readily available.

The claim that being circumcised helps to prevent HIV/AIDS may in fact lead to triple jeopardy in the fight against AIDS. Firstly, where there is a lack of medical facilities for the operation the knives and other utensils used for the procedure might actually fuel the spread of AIDS. This further complicates Viens's argument for religious freedom, because he also recommends that the operation be carried out in modern medical facilities with more advanced pain management. If this requirement is set in a global context, a logical, but nevertheless contradictory, consequence would be that (male or female) circumcision should be allowed in the name of religion only in those parts of the world where hygiene and advanced medical treatments and technology are readily available. From the point of view of religious freedom this is a rather restrictive requirement.

Secondly, the fact that people believe they are somehow protected against HIV by being circumcised may cause them to be somewhat careless or dismissive about the need for other protection, to have promiscuous sex, and in general to feel they are now immune to the virus. Thirdly, the fact that male circumcision is seen to be medically related to the prevention of HIV/AIDS may lead onto a slippery slope that ultimately leads to it being culturally required that FGM is practiced for the same purpose. This would be even more counterproductive, since there is medical evidence that women are more vulnerable to the virus to start with. Whatever medical indication there might be that male circumcision actually prevents the spread of HIV/AIDS, the effect of this in stopping the spread of the virus would be undermined if, as a result, more women were infected because of unsafe, and maybe also forced, sex.

All this shows that while opinions about the diseases that male circumcision is to be used to prevent or to cure have changed throughout time, male circumcision as such has persistently maintained its place as a medically justifiable practice in Western countries, and is gaining further justification, as the papers by Hutson, Short, and Viens show. In addition, male circumcision has also had a longstanding religious rationalization in the Western cultural context within Judaism, Islam, and even Christianity, as explicated by Viens; it has medical rationalization to the level of being almost routinely practiced in the United States and in Australia, as discussed by Hutson and Short; and in most cases it has an individual justification which is based on alleged medical conditions, as noted by Short. The medicalization of this operation in the West has given the practice a stronger "rational" justification in a modern society than even traditional and religious demands can provide.[14–17]

Whether the rationalizations of genital mutilation are cultural, aesthetic, religious, hygienic, medical, or scientific, the truth behind the practice of genital mutilation might still be a very different story. Even a medical rationalization may cover up other more hidden purposes. If we compare the persistent continuation of male circumcision in the United States with the same phenomenon in Europe we find rather interesting results. The studies by Fletcher,[14] and Fleiss[18] show how in the United States, where the routine circumcision of newborn males has been common until rather recently, because of the widespread diffusion of the scientific myths about its benefits, the medical data with counter results were deliberately ignored or misinterpreted in order to maintain the practice. For instance, the latest reports from European medical research on the issue were neglected in order to maintain the practice in the USA even when it was already rapidly disappearing in Europe, as also noted by Hutson.[1] Behind the disguise of alleged medical benefits we can find more gruesome reasons for the maintenance of the practice. In a modern, American, market oriented society male circumcision became a form of commercial exploitation of children when physicians, in cooperation with transnational biotechnology corporations, looked for the sales of marketable and economically profitable products made from harvested human foreskins that could further be used in the pharmaceutical industry (Fletcher,[14] pp 259–71); (Sorrells,[15] pp 331–7).[17]

Male Circumcision in Africa and Beyond

The practice of genital mutilation plays a central role in social hierarchies and personal relationships (not only between the different genders, but also between men themselves and between women themselves). Whether the rationalization for male circumcision is a religious, cultural, medical or hygienic one, those men who remain uncircumcised in the societies in which the practice is common are made to feel somehow abnormal and/or not equal to those who have undergone the operation. Just to take a few local examples: in East Africa, for instance, men of the Masai tribe see uncircumcised men as adolescent, spineless, and timid cowards who do not have full male qualifications (whether we talk about the uncircumcised men of their own community, or those of other tribes or races). Within the Cameroonian Nso tribe the three main rationalizations for male circumcision have been firstly, the belief that circumcision prepares the penis, puts it in a state of readiness for coitus and procreation, secondly that it tests the courage and endurance of a boy at the threshold of adulthood, and thirdly, but rather in contradiction of the first claim, it is thought to tame and moderate the sexual instinct thereby helping a man to act more responsibly.[19]

The Tanzanian Chagga tribe, for its part, circumcises young boys in different age groups (thus the age for circumcision may vary from 4 to 18). In cases where the circumcision is postponed for a long time, for one reason or another, by the parents and relatives, many of the boys seek a way to go through the operation on their own, endurance of pain being a central element of the ritual. Before having the operation done to them they feel socially and physically immature. With the modern Chagga, many of whom are now Catholics by religion, the rationalization for circumcision is nowadays hygienic rather than traditional. The Islamic Chagga, for their part, can appeal to the demands of their religion for circumcision. In reality, however, the practice is clearly based on peer pressure and the community's social expectations. Uncircumcised men in many African communities are seen as undeveloped or "child like" and are thought to be inclined to poor sexual or reproductive performance.

Social pressures are also typical in the societies in which the rationalization is more purely based on religious demands. It may seem inconsistent to require genital mutilation on a religious basis since this is perfecting the work of God by cutting off, modifying or redesigning any part of a human body which has been created by God. The human ability to find the needed false reasons, however, is boundless; in the case of genital mutilation the attempt to reduce sexual pleasure and to maintain chastity is seen not only as an improvement of God's work, but also as showing obedience to whatever is believed and interpreted to be God's will in any given culture. In traditional Judaism, for instance, male circumcision is a means to moderate the sexual pleasure of men and their attraction to women.

Similar views, to do with reducing the sexual pleasure rather than fully suppressing it, have been presented in Islam. In Islam the argument linking pleasure to circumcision, however, is used more frequently in the case of female genital mutilation. In most religions (as for Jews and Muslims) circumcision is also a mark that distinguishes the believer from the non-believer. The fact that circumcision has, throughout history, been practiced also within traditional belief systems—for example, by Australian Aborigines, the Mayas of Borneo, various Native American tribes, the ancient Aztecs and Mayas, etc—is not taken as undermining the claim that this practice is seen as a sign that distinguishes a believer from a non-believer in such world religions as Islam or Judaism.[4, 5, 20–23] In general then when the justification of genital mutilation is based on traditional or religious grounds, whether in Arab, Eastern, Western or Southern cultures, the emphasis has been on God's will as well as the purity of body and mind.

All in all, the inconsistencies between sexual performance and religious identity in relation to genital mutilation do not seem to reduce the power of the false reasons put forward to support the practice. In some cultures circumcision is justified as a means to control men's and women's sexual desires, while in others it is used for precisely the opposite purpose, that is to prove the sexual virility and endurance of men. In yet other cultures it is used to enforce traditional and natural cultural identity and social order, and in others it is used to mark religious affiliation and God's will.

Female Genital Mutilation and Gender Equality

Female genital mutilation, for its part, is usually seen as part of traditional and collectivist cultures with patriarchal social structures. It is not, however, fully alien to the more individualist Western cultural tradition. Female genital mutilation used to be practiced in Western civilizations as a cure for various medical conditions while the actual social reasons for its maintenance may have lain elsewhere in Western history. Clitoridectomy was, for instance, used both in Europe and in America for hygienic reasons, as a medical cure for masturbation, and for mental disorders such as hysteria. Since in the West both male and female circumcision were practiced by qualified doctors for allegedly legitimate medical indications, they were not considered to be the same brutal and intervening mutilations of the human body as they were seen to be elsewhere in so called "more primitive" societies. This shows that science can be a double edged sword that readily lends itself as an alibi for strongly held preferences and cultural biases. In particular, the medicalized nature of the Western culture itself can give legitimization to even violent and unnecessary physical interventions on the human body in the name of science, progress, normality, and health while the actual reasons for such interventions may remain hidden.[11]

Today, female genital mutilation, now called traditional circumcision, no longer exists openly in the Western cultural mainstream, but it persists in the developing world. With the relatively recent emphasis on pluralist values, tolerance, and respect for personal autonomy, however, practices of genital mutilations have recurred in the West. Body piercing and other rather extremist forms of sexual (pleasure seeking) subcultural practices have introduced new, less openly condemned, forms of genital mutilation. These contemporary forms of genital mutilation are taken to be more acceptable since they are thought to have come about as a result of one's autonomous choice and free will. Thus, the main ethical battle against genital mutilation in Western culture still focuses more on preventing the traditional forms of FGM, which also is practiced (though mostly in secret) within various immigrant communities in multicultural Western societies. Here again, we can note that the culture itself introduces the same practice (in different forms) over and over again, succeeding always in finding a culturally fitting justification for it, while being simultaneously more than ready to reject the same or similar custom in other cultures.[8, 24]

While, however, many traditional communities where FGM is practiced remain clearly more patriarchal and use female genital mutilation to control women's sexual behavior, economic factors should not be ignored. Those performing the operation earn a good income out of it and thus, the practice provides livelihoods for many. Also, circumcised girls guarantee better bride prices and higher social status for their families. This may help us to understand why not only men, but also women themselves, while victims of the practice of FGM, are often its strongest proponents. It is true that the more traditional types of female genital mutilation clearly have more devastating medical consequences for their victims, particularly in poor environments and in unhygienic conditions. In addition, they are usually performed on vulnerable and defenseless children. Thus, evidently there is an urgent need to find ways to curtail the practice. Additionally, as noted, female genital mutilation tends to persist in societies that have a more traditional, more patriarchal social structure; thus its maintenance is more directly related to the low social status of women. Female genital mutilation in traditional environments is said to be harder to combat, since its persistent maintenance is usually based on women's lack of education and decision making power in their communities. Thus, the abolition of FGM is not merely in the hands of its direct victims. It is also in the hands of the society as a whole, and particularly in the hands of those in social and political or religious power. Power relations between the sexes, however, are difficult to change and thus, the practice persists and is justified in a manner that makes women themselves adopt it as a part of their cultural identity and of their social pride through history. In Africa, for instance, the history of female genital mutilation dates back to 4000 years B.C. Even today in Africa FGM is still practiced in at least 27 countries and every year two million girls at least are exposed to sexual mutilation. These mutilations constitute one aspect of a series of traditional practices harmful to women's health and welfare—that is, forced marriages and early pregnancies, force feeding, tattooing, scarification, and nutritional taboos. Also, although some people consider the practice of FGM to be recommended by Islam, Christianity, and traditional religions, there are nonbelievers who practice this as well. These practices are also found in Egypt, as well as in the majority of Arab Muslim countries of the Middle and Near East, as well as in Islamic societies in the Far East.[6, 8, 25] Finally, it should not be overlooked that women are also involved in the maintenance of male genital mutilation. In the case of MGM, setting aside religious or traditional rationalizations or social pressures from the community, women (those who themselves have not undergone any genital mutilation, as in the U.S.—for example) may prefer circumcised men as sexual partners, either because their performance in sexual intercourse lasts longer or because they consider a circumcised penis to be more hygienic and/or more aesthetic than an uncircumcised one.

Conclusion

Human sexuality and the attempts to control it, particularly to reduce or add sexual pleasure, have been, in one way or another, a part of all known cultures and civilizations. While sometimes this fact is acknowledged openly as the main purpose for genital mutilation, in most cases other rationalizations are put forward for the practice. These false reasons have varied from religious and cultural demands to a number of medical "explanations," depending on the wider cultural tradition within which the practice has appeared. These different rationalizations for the maintenance of the practices in various cultures show that no matter what the cultural differences are in beliefs and lifestyles, genital mutilation is a universal sign of human civilization—or maybe the lack of it. All societies have found the arguments that best fit their local cultural traditions and environments in order to introduce or maintain genital mutilation in its various forms. In the Western, rather individualist tradition, these rationalizations are based on benefit to the individual and/or autonomy; in the Southern and Eastern cultures their support is drawn more directly from social values and ties, or from the need to protect one's unique cultural identity against Western cultural imperialism. Thus, in this regard one cultural tradition cannot be said to be better than another. Rather, with further education and knowledge the cultural smokescreen around the real reasons for the maintenance of the practice can be overcome in all societies no matter what their cultural background.

Endnotes

1. Hutson JM. Circumcision: a surgeon's perspective. *J Med Ethics* 2004; 30:238–40.
2. Short R. Male circumcision: a scientific perspective. *J Med Ethics* 2004; 30:241.
3. Viens A. Value judgment, harm, and religious liberty. *J Med Ethics* 2004; 30:241–7.
4. Aldeeb Abu-Salieh SA. Muslims' genitalia in the hands of the clergy: religious arguments about male and female circumcision. In: Denniston GC, Mansfield Hodges F, Fayre Milos M, eds. *Male and female circumcision: medical, legal, and ethical considerations in pediatric practice.* New York: Kluwer Academic/ Plenum, 1999: 131–71.
5. Bigelow JD. Evangelical Christianity and its relation to infant male circumcision. In: Denniston GC, Mansfield Hodges, Fayre Milos M, eds. *Male and female circumcision: medical, legal, and ethical considerations in pediatric practice.* New York: Kluwer Academic/Plenum, 1999:173–7.
6. Anon. Female genital mutilation. *Echo. Bilingual Quarterly of the Association of African Women for Research and Development.* 2001 Oct 6:2.
7. Anon. Female genital mutilation. *WHO Chronicle* 1986;40:31–6.
8. Toubia N. Female genital mutilation. In: Peters J, Wolper A, eds. *Women 's rights, human rights.* London: Routledge, 1995:2–7.
9. Mill JS. *On liberty.* New York: Prometheus Books, 1986.
10. Mill JS. *Utilitarianism.* New York: Prometheus Books, 1997.
11. Hellsten SK. Pluralism in multicultural liberal democracy and the justification of female circumcision. *J Appl Philos* 1999;16:69–83.
12. Hellsten SK. Multicultural issues in maternal fetal medicine. In: Dickenson DL, ed. *Ethical issues in maternal fetal medicine.* Cambridge: Cambridge University Press, 2002:39–60.
13. Kukathas C. Are there any cultural rights? *Polit Theory* 1992;20:105–39.
14. Fletcher CR. Circumcision in America in 1998: attitudes, beliefs, and charges of American physicians. In: Denniston GC, Mansfield Hodges F, Fayre Milos M, eds. *Male and female circumcision:medical, legal, and ethical considerations in pediatric practice.* New York: Kluwer Academic/Plenum, 1999:159–271 at 259–71.
15. Sorrells ML. The history of circumcision in the United States: a physician's perspective. In: Denniston GC, Mansfield Hodges F, Fayre Milos M, eds. *Male and female circumcision: medical, legal, and ethical considerations in pediatric practice.* New York:Kluwer Academic/Plenum, 1999:331–7.
16. Whitfield HN. Publication on circumcision in the medical literature: the role of an editor. In: Denniston GC, Mansfield Hodges F, Fayre Milos M, eds. *Male and female circumcision: medical, legal, and ethical considerations in pediatric practice.* New York:Kluwer Academic/Plenum, 1999:403–7 at 403–6.
17. Denniston GC. Tyranny of the victims: an analysis of circumcision advocacy. In: Denniston GC, Mansfield Hodges F, Fayre Milos M, eds. *Male and female circumcision: medical, legal, and ethical considerations in pediatric practice.* New York: Kluwer Academic/Plenum, 1999:221–239.
18. Fleiss PM. An analysis of bias regarding circumcision in American medical literature. In: Denniston GC, Mansfield Hodges F, Fayre Milos M, eds. Male and female circumcision: medical, legal, and ethical considerations in pediatric practice. New York: Kluwer Academic/Plenum, 1999:379–401.
19. Tangwa GB. Circumcision: an African point of view. In: Denniston GC, Mansfield Hodges F, Fayre Milos M, eds. *Male and female circumcision: medical, legal, and ethical considerations in pediatric practice.* New York: Kluwer Academic/Plenum, 1999:183–93 at 186.
20. Baker JP. Unifying language: religious and cultural considerations. In: Denniston GC. Mansfield Hodges F. Fayre Milos M. eds. *Male and female circumcision: medical, legal, and ethical considerations in pediatric practice.* New York: Kluwer Academic/Plenum, 1999: 195–9.
21. Goodman J. Jewish perspective on circumcision. In: Denniston GC, Mansfield Hodges F, Fayre Milos M, eds. *Male and female circumcision: medical, legal, and ethical considerations in pediatric practice.* New York:Kluwer Academic/Plenum,1999: 179–81.
22. Trachtenberg M. Psychoanalysis of circumcision. In: Denniston GC, Mansfield Hodges F, Fayre Milos M, eds. *Male and female circumcision: medical, legal, and ethical considerations in pediatric practice.* New York: Kluwer Academic/Plenum, 1999:209–13.

23. Toubia N. Evolutionary cultural ethics and circumcision of children. In: *Male and Female Circumcision: Medical, Legal, and Ethical Considerations in Pediatric Practice*, In: Denniston GC, Mansfield Hodges F, Fayre Milos M, eds. *Male and female circumcision: medical, legal, and ethical considerations in pediatric practice*. New York: Kluwer Academic/Plenum, 1999:1–7.

24. Benhabib S. Cultural complexity, moral interdependence, and the global dialogical community. In: Nussbaum M, ed. *Women, culture and development*. Oxford: Clarendon Press, 1995:235–55.

25. UNICEF research report: *The girl child in Tanzania*. Dar es Salaam: UNICEF 1995.

Discussion Questions

1. Why is female circumcision considered more barbaric than male circumcision?

2. What are some reasons for circumcision? How do these reasons reflect religious, social, and cultural motivations?

14.6

ARE REQUIRED CROSS-CULTURAL COURSES PRODUCING PLURALISTIC STUDENTS?

Kimberly A. Miller-Spillman, PhD; Susan O. Michelman, PhD; and Nicole Huffman, MS
University of Kentucky

Many Family and Consumer Science (FCS) units offer service courses to the university. Family Studies typically offers courses such as Human Sexuality, which fulfills a Social Sciences requirement. Nutrition and Food Science typically offers courses such as Human Nutrition and Wellness, which meets a Natural Sciences requirement. Merchandising departments typically offer a Dress and Culture course, which meets a cross-cultural or diversity requirement. Texts such as *The Meanings of Dress, The Visible Self, Social Psychology of Clothing* and others are often used in these general university courses exposing students from many majors to a diversity of human appearances and multiple cultural meanings of appearance.

Because FCS faculty are teaching these courses and, in many cases, publishing the texts, there is substantial responsibility to demonstrate course effectiveness. In the case of cross-cultural requirements, the concern is, How effective are these courses in promoting diversity among students? Once students leave cross-cultural courses, are they less ethnocentric? Do students become more pluralistic? When FCS faculty can objectively demonstrate the effectiveness of these service courses, they will move from the perception of competent service provider to essential to the university's mission. Given the history of teaching excellence among FCS, service courses provide faculty an opportunity to demonstrate course effectiveness. For example, in the field of clothing and textiles a recent focused issue of *Clothing and Textiles Research Journal* (2005) was published on the scholarship of teaching and learning, and an article on student surveys of teaching effectiveness was recently published in *Journal of Family and Consumer Sciences* (Stewart, Goodson, Miertschin & Faulkenberry, 2007). Clearly, FCS educators are good teachers who are looking for ways to improve. As such, FCS educators are poised to elevate their contributions to the university community.

Most universities offer several course options that meet a diversity or cross-cultural requirement with the assumption that a required course will affect change, an assumption that needs to be tested. Examples include courses in anthropology, sociology, geography, psychology, Hispanic

---

Original for this text.

Studies, Women's Studies, etc. At our university, 72 courses were listed in the bulletin from which students choose to fulfill their cross-cultural requirement. Approximately 36 of those courses are offered in a given semester. Our university bulletin states that upon completion of the cross-cultural requirement, students will be able to:

1. describe some of the major developments in at least one non-Western culture; and
2. demonstrate an understanding of the impact of cultural differences on social interactions.

These learning objectives offer a starting point for measuring the effect of cross-cultural courses.

To begin this process, a Dress and Culture course was chosen for the study. Dress and Culture courses often have wide appeal among nonmajors because some find the course material to be more visual than their other coursework, enhancing their learning experience. A common perception that FCS courses are an "easy A" often attracts large numbers of nonmajors to Dress and Culture courses. However, with the recent trend in increased enrollment of merchandising majors nationwide (our department majors have increased 92% since 2001), service courses are often viewed as a drain on the department's resources. Time spent on evaluation of service courses is often a luxury few departments can afford. One strategy is to manage course enrollments so that merchandising majors are given registration priority. Even though the majority of Dress and Culture students may be merchandising majors, merchandising faculty still bear a responsibility to address the issue of course effectiveness.

The objective of this study was to begin the process of determining the effectiveness of required cross-cultural courses in reducing student ethnocentrism. Three methods were tested in the current study: 1) student ranking of course assignments; 2) students' self-reported level of ethnocentrism/pluralism; and 3) survey of prior multicultural experiences. Data collected were both quantitative and qualitative.

Conceptual Framework

A helpful framework on multicultural education comes from the discipline of teacher education. Brown's (2004, 1998) research focused on teacher education and examines how an individual's social and ethnic background impacts his/her ability to be either receptive or nonreceptive to multicultural experiences. Brown's framework is particularly relevant to our study, as research has shown that 95% of future public school classroom teachers trained at universities will be Caucasian, middle-class, female, and monocultured (Haberman, 1989; Hodgkinson, 1992). National university programs in FCS are dominated by female, largely Caucasian students, as indicated by statistics of attendance in university programs and subsequent similar membership in American Association of Family and Consumer Sciences (AAFCS). Although many FCS units offer cross-cultural courses to a broad audience of women and men within the university, they frequently remain a required course within most FCS curriculums. Furthermore, all students, not just teacher educators, will be forced to make the shift from a monocultural perspective to a multicultural one.

Brown's models are helpful in examining the perceptions of students and the relationship between the students' largely monocultural backgrounds and their approach to required multicultural courses. In the field of teacher education, multiple studies have shown that teachers who are sensitive to the diversity of cultures that students bring to the classroom can address the social and academic needs of the "minority majority" and can advocate equal access to educational opportunity for all students (Brown, 1998, p. 82). Brown acknowledges that although most teacher education programs contain multicultural education, less is understood about the connection between the cognitive and affective domains of the students being taught. In Brown's attempt to more effectively understand this relationship, she has developed a model (Brown, 1998, p. 83) that explains the process of transforming monocultural perceptions into a multicultural perspective (see Figure 14.7).

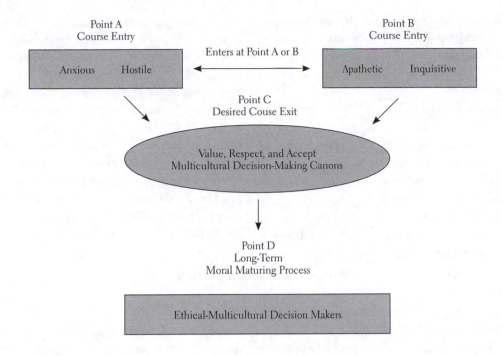

Point A
Course Entry

Enters at Point A or B

Point B
Course Entry

Anxious   Hostile

Apathetic   Inquisitive

Point C
Desired Couse Exit

Value, Respect, and Accept
Multicultural Decision-Making Canons

Point D
Long-Term
Moral Maturing Process

Ethical-Multicultural Decision Makers

Figure 14.7 Process of Transforming Monocultured Perceptions to Multicultural Worldview.

According to Brown's model, students who enter a cultural diversity course with limited cross-cultural experience (Point B, 14.7) will be "apathetic" or "inquisitive" about other cultures. In contrast, those who have had negative encounters or whose reference groups hold negative beliefs about the value of other cultures (Point A, Figure 14.7) will enter a cross-cultural experience in an anxious or hostile state.

Brown's model allows education students to examine five aspects of multiculturalism: (1) their beliefs and perceptions about themselves as individuals and members of a cultural group; (2) their attitudes and perceptions relating to the culture, ethnicity, and socioeconomic status of groups that differ from themselves; (3) how their worldview influences their behavior toward divergent culture; (4) the effect of their attitudes and behaviors on the students they will encounter during their teaching careers; and (5) the strategies that promote and reinforce ethical and equitable multicultural decision-making (Brown, 1998, p. 82). Brown (1998) advocates four phases in the

process to develop ethical-multicultural decision making that are employed in classroom teaching: Phase one is self-examination, phase two is cross-cultural inquiry, phase three is ethical reflection, and phase four is multicultural classroom strategies. Since many FCS graduates will be employed in some aspect of the service economy, they will also benefit from a multicultural worldview.

Brown (2004), Banks (1995), Sleeter (1995b), and Irvine (1992) have found that many students in teacher education enter and exit stand-alone diversity courses unchanged, often reinforcing their stereotypical perceptions of self and others in the process. The research of Banks (1995) and Irvine (1992) attribute the failure to resentment and/or resistance to multicultural doctrine, instruction application and interaction (Brown, 2004). Research (Allport, 1979) has proposed that prejudices established in childhood use selective perception and group support strategies to resist changing beliefs about self and others. Brown's model illustrates how value judgments may be processed in the classroom (2004, p. 326). As a follow-up to her earlier work, Brown developed a framework for examining ways students process value judgments in classroom settings based on their prior experience and learning (see Figure 14.8).

Brown found in her study that although the message and previous experience do have an influence on increasing student cultural diversity awareness, the gains are more substantial when coupled with appropriate teaching methods. Brown found that "focusing the initial eight classes on reducing student resistance and providing students with opportunities for self-examination is the most effective method of course introduction" (2004, p. 336). Banks (1997), Brown (1999), and others have found that incoming student attitudes and behaviors can be modified and changed with appropriate instructional methods.

For the purposes of the present study, student resistance is a part of our collective teaching experience in Dress and Culture courses. Student resistance in Dress and Culture courses was often identified as resentment that the "easy A" expectation of nonmajors wasn't met. We also assumed that students are typically steeped in popular culture and therefore very open to multiculturalism,

needing some structured guidance to jump start or facilitate the process. Since we did not recognize student resistance to multiculturalism, we did not employ teaching methods to reduce student resistance. Instead we began with self-reported measures allowing students to rate themselves and explain in their own words their prior multicultural experience and any perceived movement from ethnocentrism to pluralism as a result of the course. This approach gives us a baseline of data in a Dress and Culture course from which we can improve course effectiveness helping students become more pluralistic and less ethnocentric.

Method

Setting

A mid-sized, Southern land grant university was selected for the study because of its nationally recognized FCS programs and status as the only AAFCS accredited program in the state. The sophomore-level, 3-credit-hour course is offered Fall, Spring, Winter Intersession, and Summer Semesters and is a required course for merchandising majors and as a university cross-cultural elective for non-merchandising majors. Course

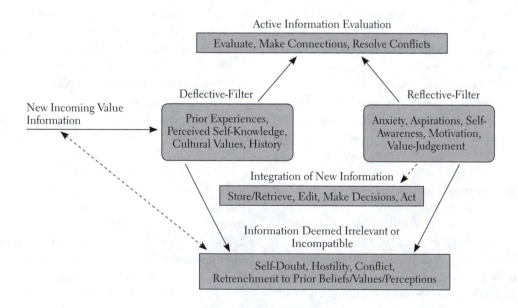

Figure 14.8 Processing Value Judgments. Dotted lines indicate potential to recycle information.

emphasis is on diversity of personal appearances worldwide and supporting cultural values. The course goal stated on the first page of the syllabus is: Students develop critical thinking skills related to culture instead of learning the specifics of any one particular culture's dress. The long-term objective of this requirement is to start students on a personal journey preparing for world citizenship (Peace Corps, 2002).

Within the course is a major project (i.e., Culture Sharing Project) which pairs a non-Western student with a Western student for three one-hour meetings. Written reports are handed in following each meeting and a summary paper of the students' experience completes the project. (For a more detailed description of the Culture Sharing Project, see Miller-Spillman, Jackson & Huffman, 2006). The course project runs concurrent with course materials, which stress the value of a multicultural view. Course materials include: textbook, lectures, group discussions on Blackboard (an Internet teaching platform), twice-weekly quizzes covering reading assignments, videos, etc.

Participants

Seventy-two students were enrolled in Dress and Culture during the Fall 2005 semester and participated in the study. Fifty-five of these students were merchandising majors and 17 were nonmajors. The majority of students were Caucasian females.

Instruments

Quantitative and qualitative measures were used in the study: 1) evaluation of course assignments (quantitative); 2) self-evaluation of ethnocentrism/pluralism (quantitative and qualitative); and 3) a survey of prior multicultural experience (quantitative and qualitative).

The purpose of the Course Assignment Evaluation was to gather student feedback on each assignment's helpfulness in learning course material. At the end of the semester, students were asked to rate each item (i.e., video, guest speaker, assignments, etc.) for its helpfulness in learning course material on a scale of: 1=not helpful, 3=neutral, 5=very helpful. Mean scores were cal-culated and assignments were ranked from highest to lowest. Space for written comments was provided for each course assignment.

A second measure was distributed the last week of class and asked students to indicate their level of ethnocentrism/pluralism at the **beginning** of the class on a continuum where: 1=Ethnocentrism (My culture is right) and 5=Pluralism (Acceptance of differences). Positions 2, 3, and 4 were marked on the continuum but not labeled. Similarly students were asked to mark on a second scale where they were at the **end** of the class.

A third measure was a survey of students' multicultural experience prior to enrolling in the course. Since students are required to interact with someone from a culture different than their own as part of the course project, we wanted to know how much experience students were bringing with them to the task. In other words, do students with considerable multicultural experience previous to the course benefit from the Culture Sharing Project as much as students without prior multicultural experience? Qualitative and quantitative data regarding students' prior multicultural experience were collected. Qualitative data were organized by category after multiple readings following the grounded theory approach (Strauss & Corbin, 1990). In addition, two administrative questions were added to the survey, they were: 1) Why do upperclassmen wait to take the 200-level course in their junior or senior year? and 2) Why do non-merchandising majors chose Dress and Culture over other options?

Procedure

An evaluation of course assignments was scheduled the last week of the semester to avoid falling on the same day as university course evaluations. Course Assignment Evaluation forms were distributed to students in the last 15 minutes of the class. Students were asked not to write their name on the form and to provide honest, constructive feedback. The instructor explained that the assignments ranking lowest would be replaced in subsequent semesters. Students left the forms on the instructor's desk as they exited the class.

The last two items on the Course Assignment Evaluation form were questions regarding students' self-evaluation of their level of ethnocentrism/pluralism at the beginning and at the end of the course. Students were asked to provide reasons why the scales were different (change) or why the scales were the same (no change).

At midterm of the semester, students were given a three-point bonus opportunity on Blackboard. Students were given one week to complete the survey. By midterm, students would have had two meetings (out of a total of three) with their culture sharing partner. The instructions to the survey were:

> The purpose of this survey is to determine how useful the Cultural Sharing Project is in meeting a need for multicultural interaction at [your university]. Please answer each question honestly and fully. You will receive 3 bonus points for completing the survey regardless of your answers. Names will not be attached to your answers.

Students were asked the following questions:

1.   Multiple choice. Prior to this class, have you had similar experiences to the Culture Sharing Project (i.e., interactions with others that included one person from a Western culture and one person from a non-Western culture)? A. Yes. B. No. If yes, please go to question #2. If no, please go to question #3.
2.   Essay. If you answered yes to question #1, describe your multicultural interactions with others. For example, did you join an organization with members from many cultures, have you interacted with a student in your major who is from another culture, have you attended events similar to International Night and interacted with others, is your dorm floor/neighborhood multicultural, etc. Please give as much detail as you can.
3.   Essay. If you answered no to question #1, explain why you haven't had multicultural interaction. Possible roadblocks might include: living off campus, lack of time, assumed it would be awkward/uncomfort-able, didn't see the value for the time spent, thought it was a good idea but couldn't figure out how to make it happen, etc. Please give as much detail as you can.
4.   Essay. *To Juniors and Seniors:* Why did you wait to take this course until now since it is a 200-level (sophomore-level) course?
5.   Essay. *To non-merchandising majors:* Given that there are other options available for cross-cultural credit, what is it about dress that is of particular interest to you?

Results

The results of the course assignments evaluation indicated that the Culture Sharing Project (CSP) ranked fifth (mean score of 3.68) out of eleven assignments (mean scores of assignments received a high score of 4.36 and a low score of 2.76). (See Table 14.1.)

The results of the ethnocentrism/pluralism measure indicated that, on average, students begin the class at a 3.59 on the scale of 1=Ethnocentrism and 5=Pluralism and end the class at a 4.25. Therefore, students, on average, perceived that they had moved 0.66 points on the scale in the direction toward pluralism. Students were also asked to explain any change (or lack of change) between the two scales. Comments included: "I have always been accepting of all people" (example of lack of change) and "I understand more about different cultures" (example of change).

Survey results indicate that students possess a wide range of multicultural experiences prior to enrolling in the Dress and Culture course. From 72 enrolled students, 64 responses to the survey were received, an 88.8% response rate.

To the first question, i.e., have you had prior multicultural experience, 45.3% of the respondents (29 students) answered "yes" and 54.7% of the respondents (35 students) answered "no." Researchers felt encouraged by this initial result given that the class was almost evenly split between the two choices.

Student descriptions of the type of prior experience were placed in the following categories in descending order: a) work/job, b) mutual friends, c) culture is a long-held interest, d) high school experiences, e) dorm/apartment/living arrangements, f) family, g) university classes/other university classes, h) exchange student/refugee family/church host families, i) travel, j) university organizations/clubs, k) university sports teams and events, l) prior interactions but have learned more through Culture Sharing Project. The total number of responses to question #2 was 29. See Table 14.2.

This student describes his/her long-held interest in culture:

I personally love meeting different people out[side] of my own culture, it opens my eyes to what else is out there that everyone else is missing. The neatest thing about being DIFFERENT is learning. I have interacted with many non-Western people before, I have met a lot of them at my high school . . . whose parents got shipped here to work and also at U of X and in my various classes. I also used to live next to an international dorm so I would often see a lot of foreign students walking around. Also,

TABLE 14.1

Student Rankings of Course Assignments for Fall Semester, 2005, on a Scale of Where 1 = Not Helpful in Learning Course Material and 5 = Very Helpful in Learning Course Material (n = 72)

Rank	Assignment	Mean Score
1	Video: Palm Beach: Money, Power & Privilege	4.36
2	Video: Slim Hopes	4.23
3	Video: Paris Is Burning	4.00
4	Video: Transgender Revolution	3.87
5	Culture Sharing Project	3.68
6	Video: Mauritius	3.52
7	Video: Jewish Religious Dress	3.38
8	Video: Hispanic Culture	3.28
9	Potluck with ESL Students	2.84 (tie)
9	Group Discussion Assignments on Bb	2.84 (tie)
10	Video: Civil War Reenactors	2.76

For more information on videos, please contact first author.

TABLE 14.2

Categories of Where and/or How Multicultural Interaction Has Occurred in Descending Order by Number of Student Responses. Total Responses: 29

Category	# of Responses
(1) Work/job	10
(2) Mutual friends	9
(3) Culture is a long-held interest (tie)	8
(4) High school experiences (tie)	8
(5) Dorm/apartment/living arrangements (tie)	8
(6) Family	6
(7) U of X classes/other university classes	5
(8) Exchange student/refugee family/church host families (tie)	4
(9) Travel (tie)	4
(10) U of X organizations/clubs (tie)	3
(11) U of X sports teams and events (tie)	3
(12) Prior interactions but have learned more through CSP	1

I wanted to state that I am Hispanic and I often travel to Puerto Rico with my family to visit many relatives there and when I do, I tend to get a huge culture shock and how different things are done there compared to here. I am very excited about the Culture Sharing Project and it has helped two individuals learn things they never knew about the other culture and more importantly become friends! Thank you.

This student has interacted with others from another culture at work:

I am a server at [a chain restaurant] and the whole kitchen line is Mexican. . . . I experience the language and some of their culture daily. I also worked as a leasing agent . . . and we had several residents from India, China, etc.

This student describes church assignments, travel, and work as a means of meeting others from another culture:

My church did assignments with people who are from different backgrounds. One of these assignments included going to a Muslim church and learning about their beliefs and actions. I have also traveled . . . to visit Spain, Portugal, and Morocco. When I traveled to Morocco it was quite the culture shock because we had to cover our legs and wear long sleeve shirts. I am also an RA (resident assistant in a university dormitory) on campus and deal with international people on a daily basis; [one of my co-workers at the dorm is] a student from India.

The indication from the above student is that one can hardly avoid interacting with others from cultures different than one's own. If one attends a church that is active, has the resources to travel, and works at a campus job one would be hard-pressed to miss such encounters

These students were exposed to diversity through their family:

With my dad's job . . . he works with a lot of people from India. When I was little we gave one of his co-worker's families some

of our old winter clothes, because they weren't prepared for what winter was like in America. Also, we would constantly have these families over for dinner. One Indian couple with a toddler came to dinner and brought us a cordless phone as a thank you gift. I thought it was odd, but nice.

When I was about 8 years old my parents met a married couple who [had] just arrived in the US from Russia . . . We had them over to our house often. . . . When the woman walked into a Winn Dixie for the first time she was absolutely stunned at the wide variety and selections consumers were able to choose from. A few years later my parents befriended another family [at] our church . . . from Bosnia.

Data describing reasons why students had not had prior multicultural experiences were organized in a similar manner: a) not personally relevant—didn't take the initiative, b) lack of opportunity (hometown/school lacked diversity), c) live off campus, d) regret not having opportunity, e) wearing blinders but [Dress and Culture] class has helped, f) awkward/language barrier/assumed nothing in common, g) shy/introvert, h) have only associated with others like myself, i) thought it would be fun, but did not find the time or means before this class. The total number of responses to question #3 was 39. See Table 14.3.

This student describes why s/he did not have prior multicultural experience:

My lack of multicultural interaction started in my hometown. It wasn't a very diverse place [named place] and we had very few minorities. These minorities were heavily stereotyped (i.e., Indian doctors, Mexican restaurant workers) and most people at my high school were Caucasian. At U of X, there is more diversity, but I don't actively seek friends who are from different backgrounds. It's not that I mind interacting with people from other cultures, it's just that I don't actively seek their friendship. Most of my classes have been primarily Caucasian, as have my living arrangements.

TABLE 14.3

Categories of Reasons Why Multicultural Interaction Has Not Occurred in Descending Order by Number of Student Responses. Total Responses: 39

Category	# of Responses
(1) Not personally relevant—didn't take the initiative	9
(2) Lack of opportunity (hometown/school lacked diversity)	7
(3) Live off campus (tie)	5
(4) Regret not having opportunity (tie)	5
(5) Wearing blinders but Dress and Culture has helped	4
(6) Awkward/language barrier/assumed nothing in common	4
(7) Shy/introvert	2
(8) Like seeks like	2
(9) Thought it would be fun, but . . .	1

These students' responses indicate critical self-reflection:

> I think a number of factors have played into the fact that I have never had an experience with a non-Western individual. I think that lack of opportunity to meet an individual that was non-Western was the main cause. I also think that people get stuck in a routine, and it is hard to venture outside of their social circle. I feel that laziness is a contributing factor to my lack of experience with a non-Westerner. Also, I have lived off campus so I missed out on the whole dorm experience, and meeting new people.

> I never had the chance to interact with other students or people from a non-Western culture. I do regret this decision because I believe that when you meet with someone from a different culture, you learn so much. When I did live on campus I always hung around my friends from high school or other people that I met through the dorms. The people that I hung out with were all the same ethnicity as me and we never made the effort to go outside of our "box." Another reason is that when I did have time to meet people, I would already be with my friends, taking my mind off of the idea of meeting others. When I think about it, I do think that it would be an awk-

ward situation [to meet others] and did not want to put the effort into it. All you need is someone to open you up to the experience and make you realize that it is worth it. I am very glad for this project and it has prompted me to open up more to people I normally would not meet.

Another student describes her background as insular, i.e., all white, upper-class Chicago suburb, all white high school, all white sorority at U of X, and then ends her essay this way:

> But I did not avoid [multicultural] interaction because I felt uncomfortable. I am open to it and have been open to it. I just never really found it important, useful, or that I had time for it.

This student describes herself as open to multicultural interaction but simultaneously admits that it is not relevant.

While reading and organizing the data, it became evident that the gap between students who had multicultural experience compared to those who did not was quite large, much larger than the simple yes/no responses to question #1 would have led us to believe. For example, one student who had prior experience wrote: "I enjoy immersing myself in other cultures, and regularly find myself trying to learn new things about what life is like in the Middle East and other countries." On the contrary, this quote, from a student who did not have prior experience, illustrates the other end of the continuum: "A culture sharing project never crossed my mind prior to this course. I was not exposed to non-Westerners before I came to this [university]. At this [university], I never associated with non-Westerners because I was never put in a situation where I needed to get to know them." This response is an example of Allport's (1979) use of group support strategies to resist changing beliefs about self and others.

The first of two administrative questions provided information about why students wait until their junior/senior year to enroll in Dress and Culture. Total number of responses to this question were 45. Results of why juniors and seniors waited to take a 200-level class indicate the reality of limited resources for service courses. For example, one student noted, "it was always full because of the incoming freshman and this class's ability to fill the cross-cultural USP requirement." Another student pointed out that waiting later may have been a benefit:

> Honestly, I kept putting it off. I concentrated on my major courses and got them out of the way before I finished my USP credit. Now that I am taking it though, I feel like it has been a good idea to put if off because I am getting more from it and taking it more seriously than I would have as a freshmen or sophomore. So, in a round about way, it has been a positive thing. I enjoy the class and look forward to attending.

This student represents transfer students coming into the merchandising major:

> Actually I just changed majors from chemical engineering to merchandising and I didn't have the requirements until this semester to take the course. So I didn't actually wait it was just a matter of circumstance. Plus people said Dr. X's tests were hard and detailed and I needed to be prepared.

Therefore, responses to this question ranged from "I've wanted this class since freshman year" (commitment) to "it never fit my schedule until now" (convenience).

The second administrative question addressed why non-merchandising majors chose Dress and Culture over other options. Total number of responses to this question were ten. Here are some examples of responses:

> I think the flexibility and the openness of the class is very attractive. It is interesting to be able to talk and learn about sensitive topics that are often skipped over in other courses, but people really want to know about [these issues]. It's nice to feel comfortable talking about American cultural ideals and compare ourselves to other societies.

> I do not need this course for cross-cultural credit because I've taken anthropology. However, I have studied this topic in high school and found it very interesting. I decided to take something that I would enjoy as an elective. That is why I am in this class. I love learning about traditions and other cultural aspects different from mine. I think people get too caught up in their own culture that they forget to see [people from other cultures].

> There was no real reason for taking this specific class other than my friends had taken it in the past and said it was pretty good. They also talked about the unit on body modification and being the proud owner of several different tattoos. I felt it would be an interesting class.

Overall, responses to this question range from personal interest (tattoos, studied dress in high school) to enjoy learning about other cultures and taking more cross-cultural courses than required.

Discussion and Conclusions

The results of the Course Assignment Evaluation indicate that students perceive the Culture Sharing Project (CSP) slightly above the midpoint of the scale (3.68) where 1=not helpful in learning course material and 5=very helpful in learning course material. Results indicated that the project is meeting the needs of students with past multicultural experiences (gave them an opportunity to go into more depth) as well as students with no previous multicultural experience.

On closer examination of the data, the four assignments with scores higher than the CSP were videos with high entertainment value manipulated by the instructor for educational purposes (i.e., through handouts with evenly spaced questions, and follow-up questions and discussions). The assignments that scored below the CSP were primarily instructional (with the exception of a potluck meal). Therefore, the CSP ranked highest among instructional assignments for its helpfulness in learning course material. This is notable as most major course projects which require a substantial amount of time and effort (arranging 3 meetings with a partner, writing reports, and compiling a notebook) would not be expected to be rated higher than videos (passive, just come to class and watch). The indication is that the project is a major factor in meeting student needs.

A second class assignment that required multicultural interaction was the potluck meal with students enrolled in English as a Second Language (ESL) courses. The potluck ranked 10th out of 11 assignments (and tied with group discussion assignments on Blackboard) with an average score of 2.84. The potluck included food, music, and a festive atmosphere and was planned during class time (convenient for Dress and Culture students). However, students ranked the Culture Sharing Project higher than the potluck. This could be interpreted to mean that students valued the more demanding CSP more than the potluck, where interaction may have felt somewhat contrived and superficial compared to the more meaningful and longer sustained interaction through the Culture Sharing Project.

One question arises when comparing students' self-evaluation scores to their actual behavior during the potluck with English as a Second Language (ESL) students. Although students rated themselves overall as moving 0.66 on the

scale toward pluralism, their behavior during the potluck was reticent. Dress and culture students hesitated to welcome ESL students into the room and were awkward when finally approaching one of our guests. The question is, would Dress and Culture students been even more hesitant to welcome ESL students to the potluck with a score of less than 0.66 on the pluralistic measure? Was the observed behavior actually an improvement over how it would have been had there been less movement toward pluralism? Or was the problem just the lack of an effective ice-breaker to get the potluck started?

Results of the ethnocentric/pluralistic measure indicated that students believed they had become less ethnocentric and more pluralistic as a result of the class. The average change in scores for the class was 0.66 points on a scale where 1=ethnocentrism (My culture is right) and 5=pluralism (Acceptance of differences). This difference was discovered by comparing the average score from the beginning of the semester (3.59) to the average score at the end of the semester (4.25). This indicates a collective self-perceived migration of 15.5% toward pluralism over the duration of the course.

The survey results indicate that students enrolled in Dress and Culture during the Fall 2005 came from a variety of past multicultural experiences, ranging from those who recognized the opportunity for multicultural interaction in many aspects of life (work, church, travel) to those who did not recognize opportunities and did not believe they were responsible for initiating such experiences on their own. The survey provided instructors with insight into the thoughts and opinions of our students. The opinions of a minority who remained committed to their ethnocentric values despite the fact that by midterm students had attended 8 lectures, viewed 4 videos and had 2 meetings with their CSP partners, all of which promoted pluralism, were particularly informative.

Although the ranking of the CSP as 5th among 11 assignments and the ethnocentric/pluralistic scales indicating students moved 15.5% toward pluralism, the survey yielded a more comprehensive picture of the makeup of the class.

Despite the positive student rankings on the CSP project and on the ethno/plural measure indicating movement toward a multicultural worldview, we discovered strong resistance among a small minority of students. This is an indication that a variety of measures provide a fuller picture of what is going on in a given class.

Brown's models are helpful in examining the perceptions of students in this study and the relationship between the students' largely mono-cultural backgrounds and their approach to a multicultural course on Dress and Culture. According to Brown's model, students who enter a cultural diversity course with limited cross-cultural experience will be "apathetic" or "inquisitive" about other cultures. This would represent the majority of people in our study. In contrast, those who have had negative encounters or whose reference groups hold negative beliefs about the value of other cultures will enter in an anxious or hostile state. This would be the minority of our study, but nonetheless, a critical component when considering pedagogical strategies. In our study, although the average student moved toward pluralism from the beginning of the class to the end, there was a certain small percentage that remained resistant to embracing cultural diversity.

The beginning of Dress and Culture includes several videos, slide lectures, and guided course discussions that, in an unstructured way, allow students to conduct self-examinations of American culture. Brown's model recommends 8 initial classes focused on reducing student resistance and providing students with opportunities for self-examination. In future Dress and Culture courses it is suggested that instructors use Brown's more structured methods to reduce student resistance prior to beginning the Culture Sharing Project. The project has been adapted in a course titled: International Trade in Textiles and Apparel by LeHew and Meyer (2005, p. 294–295), indicating its flexibility and broad application among merchandising courses.

Future research could include less subjective ways of reporting changes from the beginning of the class to the end of the class by using a pre-test, post-test method in addition to, or replacing, the ethno/plural measure. For example, Brown (2004) includes a Cultural Diversity Awareness Inventory (CDAI) on the first and last days of class to objectively measure student changes in cultural diversity awareness. The CDAI was developed by Henry (1995) and used by others (Banks, 1997; Grant & Gomez, 1996; and Sleeter, 1995a) and has been shown to be a reliable and valid measure. Also, written reports from the Culture Sharing Project could be compared between students with prior multicultural experience and students without. A study of learning styles (i.e., cognitive, theoretical, etc.) and how different learning styles impact learning in Dress and Culture courses would also be beneficial. Comparing Dress and Culture courses to other FCS cross-cultural courses and to other cross-cultural courses university-wide would indicate where multicultural learning is thriving and where it is not.

Are specific university objectives being met by this Dress and Culture course? The objectives of cross-cultural courses at our university include that students will be able to: 1) describe some of the major developments in at least one non-Western culture; and 2) demonstrate an understanding of the impact of cultural differences on social interactions. Major developments in several non-Western cultures are covered throughout the semester in our Dress and Culture course. One example would be the video of Mauritius (1999). This video gives an account of the island's long history of occupation by other nations. In addition, instructors perform an Internet search once a year to report to the class more current information about Mauritius both socially and economically.

After completion of the CSP project, students have first-hand experience of the impact of cultural differences on social interactions. Securing a partner, arranging meetings that work for both partners' schedules, and working through clarification of questions are just a few examples of how this understanding would be gained through the project.

Finally, are cross-cultural courses producing pluralistic students? It would appear as though they do, however, we cannot be sure until we have reliable and consistent measures performed with a large number of students at a variety of geographic locations.

References

Allport, G. (1979). *The nature of prejudice* (25th ed.). Reading, MA: Addison-Wesley.

Banks, J. (1995). Multicultural education: Historical development, dimensions, and practice. In J. A. Banks & C. A. McGee Banks (Eds.), *Handbook of research on multicultural education* (pp. 3–24). New York: Simon & Schuster.

Banks, J. A. (1997). *Teaching strategies for ethnic studies* (6th ed.). Needham Heights, MA: Allyn & Bacon.

Brown, E. L. (1998). The relevance of self-concept and instructional design in transforming Caucasian preservice teachers' monocultured world-views to multicultural perceptions and behaviors (Doctoral dissertation, The University of Akron, 1998) *Dissertation Abstracts International*, 59(7), A2450.

Brown, E. L. (2004 Sept./Oct.). What precipitates change in cultural diversity awareness during a multicultural course: The message or the method? *Journal of Teacher Education*, 55(4), 325–340.

Grant, C. A., & Gomez, M. L. (1996). Journeying toward multicultural and social reconstructionist teaching and teacher education. In C. Grant & M. Gomez (Eds.), *Making schooling multicultural: Campus and classroom* (pp. 4–16). Englewood Cliffs, NJ: Prentice Hall.

Haberman, M. (1989). More minority teachers. *Phi Delta Kappan*, 70(10), 771–776.

Henry, G. B. (1995). Determining the reliability and validity of the cultural diversity awareness inventory (CDAI) (Multicultural Education) (Doctoral dissertation, Texas A&M University, 1995). *Dissertation Abstracts International*, 56(9), A3483.

Hodgkinson, H. L. (1992). *A demographic look at tomorrow*. Washington, DC: Institute for Educational Leadership. (ERIC Document Reproduction Service No. ED359087).

Irvine, J. I. (1992). Making teacher education culturally responsive. In M. E. Dilworth (Ed.), *Diversity in Teacher Education* (pp. 779–792). San Francisco: Jossey-Bass.

LeHew, M. L. A., & Meyer, D. J. C. (2005). Preparing global citizens for leadership in the textile and apparel industry. *Clothing and Textiles Research Journal*, 23(4), 290–297.

Miller-Spillman, K. A., Jackson, V. P. & Huffman, N. (2006). Cross-cultural learning in a university-wide course. *Journal of Family and Consumer Science*, 98(3), 62–67.

Peace Corps. (2002). *Building bridges: A Peace Corps classroom guide to cross-cultural understanding*. Washington, DC: Peace Corps Paul D. Coverdell Worldwise Schools.

Sleeter, C. E. (1995a). Reflections on my use of multicultural and critical pedagogy when students are white. In C. E. Sleeter & P. L. McLaren (Eds.), *Multicultural education, critical pedagogy, and the politics of difference* (pp. 415–437). Albany: State University of New York Press.

Sleeter, C. E. (1995b). White preservice students and multicultural education course work. In J. M. Larkin & C. E. Sleeter (Eds.), *Developing multicultural teacher education curriculum* (pp. 17–30). Albany: State University of New York.

Stewart, B. L.; Goodson, C. E.; Miertschin, S. L. & Faulkenberry, L. M. (2007). Student surveys of teaching effectiveness: One measure for FCS evaluation. *Journal of Family and Consumer Sciences*, 99(4), 36–41.

Strauss, A., & Corbin, J. (1990). *Basics of qualitative research: Grounded theory procedures and techniques*. Newbury Park, CA: Sage.

Discussion Questions

1. Do you have required diversity or cross-cultural courses at your university? If there are several options, why did you choose this course (assuming it fulfills this requirement)?

2. Do you think that required diversity courses are helpful? Explain your answer.

3. Many students reported lives prior to college that included only white people of their same social class (i.e., in high school). Once at the university, those students replicated their high school experience, citing that they just didn't have the opportunity to meet people of different cultures/backgrounds. Brainstorm (in small groups) all the ways that you can think of how a person could encounter other cultures on your college campus and beyond campus.

CREDITS

Chapter 1
1.1 © Purestock/Alamy
1.2a © Ulana Switucha/Alamy
1.2b © Tips Images/Tips Italia Srl a socio unico/Alamy
1.3 © Dundee Photographics/Alamy
1.4a © 2010 Artists Rights Society (ARS),
   New York/ADAGP, Paris
1.4b Courtesy of Tracy Jennings
1.5 © Everyday Images/Alamy
1.6a Courtesy of Cassidy Herrington
1.6b Courtesy of Cassidy Herrington
1.7 © Yury Kuzmin/iStockphoto
1.8a Courtesy of Tracy Jennings
1.8b Courtesy of Tracy Jennings

Chapter 2
2.1 Illustration by Tronvig Group
2.2 A) Grant Cornett/CN Digital Studio B) Karineh
   Gurjan-Angelo/CN Digital Studio C) Aimee
   Barychko/CN Digital Studio
2.3 OFF/AFP/Getty Images
2.4 © Mary Kent/Alamy
2.5 Emma Innocenti/Getty Images
2.6 Illustration by Tronvig Group
2.7 Courtesy of WWD/Yukie Kasuga

Chapter 3
3.1 Illustration by Tronvig Group
3.1 Illustration by Tronvig Group
3.2 © Keystone Pictures USA/Alamy
3.3 © Corbis RF/Alamy
3.4 Courtesy of WWD/John Aquino
3.5a © Seattle Art Museum/Corbis
3.5b © Christine Osborne Pictures/Alamy
3.5c © Corbis
3.6 Image provided by Marcia Morgado
3.7 Image provided by Marcia Morgado
3.8 Image provided by Marcia Morgado
3.9 Image provided by Marcia Morgado
3.10 Image provided by Marcia Morgado
3.11a Frank Herholdt/Getty Images
3.11b Stuart McClymont/Getty Images
3.12 © Danny Shanahan/The New Yorker Collection/
   www.cartoonbank.com
3.13 Sharon Smith/Getty Images
3.14a Frank Herholdt/Getty Images
3.14b Dale Durfee/Getty Images
3.14c DKAR Images/Getty Images
3.14d Comstock/Getty Images
3.15 © Robert Mankoff/The New Yorker Collection/
   www.cartoonbank.com
3.16 DAJ/Getty Images

3.17 Nano Calvo/Getty Images
3.18 © Richard Wareham/Demotix/Demotix/Corbis

Chapter 4
4.1 altrendo images/Getty Images
4.2 © Ben Molyneux People/Alamy
4.3 Image Courtesy of The Advertising Archives
4.4a Randy Plett/Getty Images
4.4b Grant Faint/Getty Images
4.4c © Blend Images/Alamy
4.5 © The Art Gallery Collection/Alamy
4.6 Photo by Larry White
4.7 © celebrity/Alamy
4.9 WireImage/Getty Images
4.10 Bloomberg via Getty Images
4.11 Kevin Nixon/Metal Hammer magazine via
   Getty Images
4.12 Copyright © The Granger Collection, New York/
   The Granger Collection

Chapter 5
5.1 Copyright © The Granger Collection, New York/
   The Granger Collection
5.2a Courtesy of WWD/Steve Eichner
5.2b ASSOCIATED PRESS
5.2c WireImage/Getty Images
5.3 © Bettmann/CORBIS
5.4 Alinari via Getty Images
5.5 © Bettmann/CORBIS
5.6 Popperfoto/Getty Images
5.7 Courtesy of WWD/Steve Eichner
5.8 © Adam Ferguson/VII
5.9a–c www.modestprom.com
5.10 © Jack Burlot/Apis/Sygma/Corbis
5.11 Ewa Rudling © 1969 Condé Nast Publications
5.12 Copyright Bettmann/Corbis/AP Images
5.13 © Katherine Welles/Shutterstock
5.14 © ZUMA Wire Service/Alamy

Chapter 6
6.1a © Corbis Cusp/Alamy
6.1b Panoramic Images/Getty Images
6.1c © Gianni Muratore/Alamy
6.2a Grant Faint/Getty Images
6.2b © George H.H. Huey/Alamy
6.3 © Maurice Crooks/Alamy
6.4a Gamma-Rapho via Getty Images
6.4b © Stephane Cardinale/People Avenue/Corbis
6.5 FilmMagic/Getty Images
6.6 © Franck Guiziou/Hemis/Corbis
6.7 Copyright © The Granger Collection, New York/
   The Granger Collection

6.8 Illustration by Tronvig Group
6.9 © Fly Fernandez/Corbis
6.10 © Bo Zaunders/CORBIS

Chapter 7
7.1 Photo by Christina House
7.2 © Trinity Mirror/Mirrorpix/Alamy
7.3 © LMR Media/Alamy
7.4 © Robert Holmes/CORBIS
7.5 © Hunter/Corbis
7.6 Illustration by Mary Lou Carter
7.7a Courtesy of Fairchild Publications
7.7b AP Photo/CP, Mohammad Sayyad
7.8 Courtesy of Sasha Chavkin/The New York World
7.9a ELVIS BARUKCIC/AFP/Getty Images
7.9b Franco Origlia/Getty Images
7.10 © Lindsay Hebberd/CORBIS

Chapter 8
8.1 © Dinodia Photos/Alamy
8.2 © Antiques & Collectables/Alamy
8.3 © Doug Steley A/Alamy
8.4 © maggiegowan.co.uk/Alamy
8.5 ZITS © 2011 ZITS PARTNERSHIP,
    KING FEATURES SYNDICATE
8.6 Courtesy Megha Gupta
8.7 © blickwinkel/Alamy
8.8 © Bettmann/CORBIS
8.9 © FromOldBooks.org/Alamy
8.10 © Old Paper Studios/Alamy
8.11 Illustration by Tronvig Group
8.12 Illustration by Tronvig Group
8.13 © AF archive/Alamy
8.14 © Richard Levine/Alamy
8.15a Courtesy of JT Kutruff
8.15b Courtesy of JT Kutruff
8.16 Courtesy of JT Kutruff

Chapter 9
9.1 iStockphoto © Ivan Burmistrov
9.2 Courtesy of WWD/Giovanni Giannoni
9.3 © Everett Collection Inc/Alamy
9.4 © INTERFOTO/Alamy
9.5 Courtesy of Suzanne Gott
9.6 Courtesy of Suzanne Gott
9.7 Courtesy of Suzanne Gott
9.8 Courtesy of Suzanne Gott
9.9 Courtesy of Suzanne Gott
9.10 Courtesy of Suzanne Gott
9.11 Courtesy of Suzanne Gott
9.12 Basel Mission Archives/Basel Mission Holdings
9.13 © Pitt Rivers Museum, University of
    Oxford/1998.312.452.1
9.14 Courtesy of Suzanne Gott
9.15 Courtesy of Suzanne Gott
9.16 Courtesy of Suzanne Gott
9.17 Courtesy of Suzanne Gott
9.18 Courtesy of Suzanne Gott
9.19 Courtesy of Katalin Medvedev and Lioba Moshi
9.20 Courtesy of Katalin Medvedev and Lioba Moshi
9.21 Courtesy of Katalin Medvedev and Lioba Moshi
9.22 Photograph by Edwin Rosskam for the Farm Security
    Administration–Office of War Information Photograph
    Collection. Library of Congress.
9.23 Photograph by Edwin Rosskam for the Farm Security
    Administration–Office of War Information Photograph
    Collection. Library of Congress.
9.24a Courtesy of Michael D. Murphy and J. Carlos
    Gonzalez-Faraco
9.24b Courtesy of Michael D. Murphy and J. Carlos
    Gonzalez-Faraco

Chapter 10
10.1 © Stockbroker/Alamy
10.2 © Bill Bachmann/Alamy
10.3 © Business Office Career/Alamy
10.4 © Greenshoots Communications/Alamy
10.5 © Tim Graham/Alamy
10.6 © Blend Images/Alamy
10.7 Courtesy of Lexington Herald-Leader

Chapter 11
11.1 Courtesy of WWD/George Chinsee
11.2 © Victoria and Albert Museum, London
11.3 Courtesy of WWD/ Donato Sardella
11.4 © Gino Santa Maria/ Veer images
11.5 © Asia Images Group Pte Ltd/Alamy
11.6 Copyright © Condé Nast Publications Inc./
    Andrew Macpherson
11.7a © ZUMA Press, Inc./Alamy
11.7b Image Courtesy of The Advertising Archives
11.8 Courtesy of WWD/Giovanni Giannoni

Chapter 12
12.1 Image Courtesy of The Advertising Archives
12.2 Courtesy of WWD
12.3 © MICHAEL REYNOLDS/epa/Corbis
12.4a © Picade LLC/Alamy
12.4b © Laura Doss/Corbis
12.5 Image Courtesy of The Advertising Archives
12.6a Courtesy of Amanda Myser
12.6b Courtesy of Amanda Myser
12.6c Courtesy of Amanda Myser
12.7a Courtesy of WWD/Giovanni Giannoni
12.7b Courtesy of WWD/Giovanni Giannoni
12.8 © Daniel Lewis/Alamy
12.9 Courtesy of Martin Katz Ltd
12.10 © VStock/Alamy
12.11a Courtesy of Theresa Winge
12.11b Courtesy of Theresa Winge
12.12a Courtesy of John Jacob
12.12b Courtesy of John Jacob
12.13 Picture of Kirina (World of Warcraft) from
    Kirina's Closet 2009–2012

Chapter 13
13.1 © Terry Vine/Blend Images/Corbis
13.2 Courtesy of WWD/Giovanni Giannoni
13.3 Courtesy of Unique Solutions Design Ltd.
13.4 Courtesy of Kimberly Spillman
13.5a Courtesy of EvoShield
13.5b Courtesy of Evoshield
13.6 The Hug Shirt by Cute Circuit. Courtesy of
    Cute Circuit
13.7 Caroline Prew/Imperial College London
13.8 Franz Gräbe Flower Couture. Courtesy of
    Franz Gräbe

Chapter 14
14.1 Courtesy of WWD/John Aquino
14.2 © Tomislav Zivkovic/Alamy
14.3 Courtesy of WWD/Kyle Ericksen
14.4 Image Courtesy of The Advertising Archives
14.5 © paul prescott/Alamy
14.6 © ZUMA Wire Service/Alamy
14.7 Illustration by Tronvig Group. Original source
    by Brown, 1998.
14.8 Illustration by Tronvig Group. Original source
    by Brown, 2004, p. 326.

INDEX

Chattaraman, Veena, 225, 241–245
Chen, Stephen, 569
Childhood and dress
  appearance stigmas, 307
  beauty pageants, 307
  burial dress for, 337, 338, 382
  cloth diapers for infants, 123, 304–305, 318–319
  conformity and, 307, 309
  costumes and, 304
  cross-dressing by, 184, 189–194, 306, 319–322
  dressing skills, 305, 306, 307
  fantasy play, 306
  games and sports, 307
  gender and, 304, 306, 319–322, 490
  Halloween costume, 478
  infant and toddler stage, 304–306
  innocence and, 322, 329, 330, 492
  intellectually-disabled children, 308
  Mary Jane shoes, 306, 322–331
  memories of dress in, 306, 316, 330, 471
  negative stereotypes and, 307–308
  peer groups and, 307
  preferences, 304
  role play with dress, 305–306, 490, 493
  school uniforms, 82, 307, 308, 343
  special occasion dress in, 304
  tanning behaviors of, 132
  See also Boys; Girls; Tweens
Children
  School uniforms, 82, 307, 308, 343
Children, circumcision of, 567, 591–593
China, 224
  fashion in, 347–348
  footbinding in, 172
  Maoist uniforms in, 347
  Norwegian bunads made in, 261
  plastic surgery in, 175
  sweatshop labor in, 578–583
Choi, Chong Ju, 569
Christianity, 265–266, 268
  African women and, 368
  female modesty and, 196, 197–198
  men's hair in, 282
  See also Catholic nuns; specific sect
Circumcision of men, 589–598
  See also Genital mutilation
Civil War reenactments, 472, 482
Class. See Social class
Classic fashions, 44, 45
Clinton, Hillary, 120, 278, 279, 432
Cloth diapers. See Diapers, for infants
Clothing materials, 83
  See also Textiles
Coded systems, 186
  See also Semiotic principles
Co-design, 525
Codes of dress. See Dress codes
Cofán culture, in Ecuador, 20
Cogals, 73
Cohen, Tamara, 539–540
Cole, Shaun, 187, 214–220
Collective selection theory, 9, 48, 202, 473
Collectivism, 4
College education, women and, 409, 410
College professors, dress of, 395, 396
College students, 85–86
  conformity and, 82
  cultural diversity courses and, 5, 567, 599–610
  cultural markers in dress and, 241–245
  dress for job interviews and, 399
  fashion and, 342, 350–351

Mary Jane shoes and, 323, 327–328
  modesty and, 197
  prison study and, 2
Color choices
  for children, and gender, 304
  cultural context and, 84
  for funeral rituals, 313–315
  in Kente cloth, 93
  for wedding dress, 311
Colorism, skin bleaching and, 154–155, 156, 157
Committee for the Promotion of Virtue and Prevention of Vice (Saudi Arabia), 114–115
Communication, in dress. See Nonverbal communication in dress
Conformity, in dress, 49, 82
  children and, 307, 309
  style tribes and, 345
  women's business attire and, 422–424
Consumer, fashion and, 47, 59, 60
  eco-consciousness, 524, 526–527
  public fantasy and, 475–479, 480
  technology and, 61, 521–522, 524–525
  See also Shopping
Consumer appliance companies, 522
Consumer-product relationship, 548
Consumer Reports (magazine), 57
Consumption culture
  aging and, 463–464, 465
  girls and, 493
  sustainability and, 544–545
Context, dressing out of, 88–89
Conway, Zandra, 426–427, 428
Cooley, C. H., 7
Coquí frog, in Puerto Rico, 380
Corporate casual. See Business casual
Cosmetic surgery, 132, 224, 238, 313, 460
  See also Plastic surgery
Cosplay (costume play), 73–74
  in anime and manga, 481, 500–507
  character and role playing in, 503–505
  context of, 502–505
  origin stories of, 501–502
  social setting for, 502–503, 506–507
Costuming, and identity, 478, 479–481, 499
  See also Cosplay; Halloween costumes; Princess costume
Counterculture, 75, 77
  See also Subcultures, dress of
Counterfeit goods, 569–577
  condoned copies, 574–575
  credence goods concept, 570–571
  fashion industry and, 571
  high-quality, 576
  intellectual property and, 571–573
  knock-offs and copies, 342, 562–563
  overruns, 573–574
  self copies, 575
  vanity counterfeits, 573
Country-of-origin label, 126, 563
Couture shows, 479
  See also Haute couture
Cradle to Cradle Apparel Design, 547
Creativity, 124–126
  in drag performance, 511, 512–513
Credence goods concept, 570–571
Cross, R. J., 346–347
Cross-cultural college courses, 599–610
Cross-cultural misunderstanding, 11–12
Cross-dressing, 183, 184, 201
  by children, 184, 189–194, 306, 319–322

by drag performers, 120, 185
  by heterosexual men, 472
Crossplay, 504–505
CSP. See Cultural Sharing Project
Cuba
  Castro and, 120–121
  guayabera shirt in, 384
Cultural authentication, 5, 227, 474
Cultural complexity, 3–4
Cultural diversity courses, 567, 599–610
Cultural heritage, ethnicity and, 224
Cultural identity, 243, 385
  in Bhutan, 296
  circumcision and, 592–593, 594
  ethnic fashion and, 227, 256–257
  in Puerto Rico, 379–380, 384–385
Cultural lens, gender and, 509
Cultural markers in dress
  college students and, 241–245
  ethnicity and, 224–225
  identity and distinctiveness, 243–244
  pride and celebration, 242–243
Cultural rules, 27
Cultural sensitivity, 6
Cultural Sharing Project (CSP), 603, 604, 606, 608–610
Cultural stereotypes, 307
Cultural system, fashion and, 45–47
Cultural tightness, 4
Culture, 3–6, 17–21
  body space difference and, 11
  defined, 3
  dressing the deceased and, 335
  globalization and, 17
  importance of, 5–6
  indigenous peoples and, 18, 19–21
  jogging alone and, 11–12
  language and, 18
  material, 5
  semiotic principles and, 27
  standards of beauty and, 135–136
  technology, tradition and, 525–527
Custom-fit garments, 525, 538–539
Cutrone, Kelly, 455–456

Dahl, John Helge, 261, 262
The Daily Beast, 114, 115
Davis, Fred, 294, 326
Davis, Wade, 6, 17–21, 527
Death, dressing for, 313–314, 335–339
  death metaphors, 336
  postmortem photography, 336–337
  See also Funeral dress
Death's head image, 28
Delaware Indians, 248, 249–250, 251
DeLong, Marilyn, 130
Dembrow, Jenny, 161–162
Design, elements of, 82
Design activism, 548
Designers, 47
  counterfeiting and, 571, 573
  digital printing and, 523
  ethnic dress and, 227, 228
  image and, 58
  inspiration and, 476–478, 488
  Parisian, 46, 55–56
  research by, 522
  skirts for men and, 184
  wearable electronics and, 524
  See also specific designers
Design for environment (DfE), 547
Design for X (DfX), 547
Desmond-Harris, Jenee, 231–233
DeVard, Jerri, 427–428
Diamond smuggling, 564, 584–587
Diana, Princess of Wales, 137–138
Diapers, for infants, 123, 304–305, 318–319
Dickson, Elisabeth, 351